NEW GOSPEL PARALLELS

PUBLISHED VOLUMES

NEW GOSPEL PARALLELS

Volume One, The Synoptic Gospels

designed and edited by

ROBERT W. FUNK

Fortress Press
Philadelphia

Biblical Quotations are from the Revised Standard Version of the Bible, copyright 1946, 1952, ©
1971, 1973 by the Division of Christian Education of the National Council of Churches of Christ in
the U.S.A. and are used by permission.

Parallels from the Oxyrhynchus Papyrus 840, Papyrus Egerton 2, Oxyrhynchus Papyrus 1224,
Papyrus Cairensis 10 735, Gospel of the Nazoreans, Gospel of the Ebionites, Gospel of the
Hebrews, Gospel of the Egyptians, Gospel of Peter, Protevangelium of James, Infancy Gospel of
Thomas, and Acts of Pilate are reprinted from *New Testament Apocrypha: Volume One: Gospels and
Related Writings,* by Edgar Hennecke; edited by Wilhelm Schneemelcher; English translation
edited by R. McL. Wilson. Copyright © 1959 J. C. B. Mohr (Paul Siebeck), Tübingen; English
Translation © 1963 Lutterworth Press. Reprinted and used by permission of The Westminster
Press, Philadelphia, PA.

Parallels from the Apocryphon of James are from *The Other Gospels: Non-Canonical Gospel Texts,*
edited by Ron Cameron. Copyright © 1982 Ron Cameron. Reprinted and used by permission of The
Westminster Press, Philadelphia, PA.

Parallels from the Gospel of Thomas are reprinted from *The Nag Hammadi Library in English,*
edited by James M. Robinson; translated by Thomas O. Lambdin. Copyright © 1977 by E. J. Brill.
Reprinted and used by permission of Harper and Row, Publishers.

Parallels from Oxyrhynchus Papyrus 1, Oxyrhynchus Papyrus 655, and Oxyrhynchus Papyrus 654,
which are Greek fragments of the Gospel of Thomas, are taken from Joseph A. Fitzmyer, *Essays on
the Semitic Background of the New Testament,* Chico, CA: Scholars Press, 1974, and are used by
permission of the author and Scholars Press.

Parallels from the Didache, I Clement, and II Clement are reprinted from *The Apostolic Fathers,*
volume 2, translated by Kirsopp Lake; The Loeb Classical Library; Cambridge, MA: Harvard
University Press, 1912.

Library of Congress Cataloging in Publication Data

Bible. N.T. Gospels. English. Revised Standard.
1985.
New Gospel parallels.

(Foundations and facets. New Testament)
Includes index.
1. Bible. N.T. Gospels—Harmonies, English
I. Funk, Robert Walter, 1926- . II. Title.
III. Series.
BS2560.F84 1985   226'.1   84-48727
ISBN 0-8006-2104-2

TYPESET ON AN IBYCUS SYSTEM AT POLEBRIDGE PRESS

1418E85   Printed in the United States of America   1–2104

Contents

Photographs, Charts, and Illustrations

Foundations and Facets: New Testament is designed to serve two related functions.

Much of the more creative biblical scholarship on the contemporary scene is devoted to facets of biblical texts: to units of the text smaller than canonical books, or to aspects of the New Testament that cut across or exceed canonical limits. An intensive treatment of the aphorisms of Jesus, for example, need not require a full treatment of Matthew, any more than a generic study of the great narrative parables of Jesus demands a complete study of Luke. *Facets* in this sense refers to any textual unit or groups of such units that does not coincide with canonical books. Such units may be as short as an aphorism or as extensive as source Q, as limited as the birth and childhood stories or as diffuse as hymns in the New Testament. On the other hand, tracking the various strands of the gospel tradition from the time of Jesus down into the second century can better be pursued independently of specific biblical books, just as the destiny of the Pauline tradition transcends the limits of individual letters. In this second sense, *Facets* refers to strands of early Christian tradition that are woven through and go beyond particular books.

In yet another sense, facets indicates features of biblical books themselves, such as the literary method of Luke, the use of irony in the Fourth Gospel, or the formal structure of the gospel as literary genre. There may be good reason to isolate one or more for special and extended consideration.

As it turns out, these creative and innovative impulses in current scholarship are linked to emerging new methods in biblical criticism or to the reconception of old ones. Accordingly, a second function of *Foundations and Facets* is to accommodate the creation or revision of the correlative foundational instruments and tools. Such foundational works, properly conceived, will form the basis for the next phase of biblical scholarship.

The pioneering work of the form critics more than a half century ago rested on comparative evidence then newly acquired. Recent efforts to interpret the same oral forms—parables, pronouncement stories, miracle tales, and the like—have led to revised and expanded collections of comparative data. *Foundations and Facets* will be open to these primary materials, so that every student of the New Testament will be able to examine the comparative evidence firsthand.

Similarly, new methods allied with literary criticism, the study of folklore, and linguistics bring with them newly conceived grammars and lexica. Grammars include a poetics of biblical narrative, a handbook of hellenistic rhetoric, and a systematic hermeneutics. Other alliances with the social and psychological sciences are producing correlative new methodologies, vii which will themselves eventually require precise formulation. To be sure, older methodologies are being revised and refurbished as well. The cultural and religious milieu of the New Testament, together with its sociological and economic substratum, remain ingredient to an understanding of early Christianity and the literature it produced.

The new series thus addresses both the foundations and facets of the biblical canon, seeking to harness mature as well as creative and innovative impulses impinging upon it.

The complete scope of *Foundations and Facets* has yet to be determined. It is the plan of the series to adapt itself, as nearly as possible, to the unfolding requirements of sound biblical scholarship. The series may thus eventually embrace works the exact dimensions of which are presently unknown, and it may well omit projected works for which suitable authors do not appear.

The expansion of biblical instruction into secular contexts, such as the public university, presents biblical scholarship with a fresh and serious challenge: in addition to exposition for the reader trained in the fundamental disciplines of biblical science, exegetes must now make the text intelligible for persons generally rather than technically literate. It is the intention of the authors and editors of *Foundations and Facets* to meet this challenge: they aspire to a mode of biblical scholarship that will illumine the text for the general reader, while simultaneously serving the most stringent requirements of the advanced student. If the series succeeds in achieving this goal, it will have attained a new level of scholarly integrity.

Polebridge Press
Riverbend 1985

Robert W. Funk, editor

The *New Gospel Parallels* was conceived in conjunction with the formal narrative analysis of the gospels. As I worked on a poetics of narrative, it became increasingly clear to me that the synopses and harmonies I had known and used were created in another time and place, largely for purposes of textual, source, and form criticism. These forms of criticism are by no means behind us, yet there are new and pressing needs a gospel parallels must also serve. The urge to create a new study instrument oriented to the gospels as narratives grew stronger as I worked. Eventually I heeded the call. *New Gospel Parallels* is the result.

The resolve to bring *New Gospel Parallels* into existence owes in no small measure to encouragement received from my colleagues on the *Foundations and Facets* board and Norman Hjelm at Fortress Press. These good colleagues immediately perceived the virtues of the project. They also alerted me to potential pitfalls.

The origins of the project lie, however, in the undergraduate classroom at the University of Montana. I have endeavored to teach formal narrative grammar to several generations of students. Some of those students—the ones who make an instructor's efforts seem worthwhile—have not only learned narrative grammar, they began to press across frontiers into new territory. Janet Hanson and David Carter turned in analyses of Mark to which I still occasionally refer. Jim Knudtson took up with the Gospel of Peter and charted its intricacies on scrolls large enough to fill the classroom. Brian Cook submitted an analysis of the Infancy Gospel of Thomas that exceeds anything in print. Mr. Cook and Mr. Knudtson have stayed on with me to assist in bringing this enormous project to conclusion. To these and other, unnamed students I am grateful for eagerness and discerning criticism.

Robert Tannehill has made it his special concern to advise me on thematic parallels in Luke and Acts. His own literary analysis of Luke-Acts is to appear eventually in this same series. Meanwhile, he was kind enough to provide me with hundreds of observations that I was able to turn to good account in preparing the materials especially for Luke.

William G. Doty also read the first pages with an eagle eye. Both his general and his specific comments have proved useful. I am especially indebted to him for reminding me that this book is to be used also by, or especially by, undergraduates.

Charlene Matejovsky created the software that enabled me to collect parallels out of the corpus by computer. It is difficult to overestimate how much time and headache this saved me. She is also responsible for the typographical design of the page, which many reviewers believe to be simply superb. Stephanie Funk has labored over page makeup, using the state-of-the-art equipment and software created by David Packard. The entire project was of course done on an Ibycus System.

At Fortress Press, Phyllis Carson as usual has identified flaws in composition and design and made creative suggestions for improvement. John Hollar has assisted particularly with graphics.

Special thanks goes to Ron Cameron, first, for his fine translation of the *Apocryphon of James,* which appeared in his *The Other Gospels* (Philadelphia: The Westminster Press, 1982), and, second, for his subsequent corrections and emendations to the translation which he made accessible to the editor.

The final word is reserved for Fred Francis. As it turned out, Fred worked through the first pages when he was deathly ill from radiation treatments and was on the point of death. He did not live to see revised pages. But his notations were insightful and incisive: I am pleased to be able to acknowledge his help in this project, as in many others. Above all, I am honored to claim him as friend and colleague.

Accordingly, this volume is dedicated to the memory of Fred O. Francis (1934–1984).

Robert W. Funk
Riverbend on the Blackfoot
January 1985

GOSPEL NARRATIVES:
VERTICAL AND HORIZONTAL DIMENSIONS

1.   The gospel narratives, like other narratives, have both left-to-right or horizontal dimensions and vertical or paradigmatic dimensions.

Specific narrative segments or stories, like the cleansing of the temple, because they are narrated more than once (usually by different authors), can be compared and contrasted with each other, apart from the narrative setting in which each occurs. Vertical relationship means the material connection between and among different accounts of the same event. There are thus at least three accounts of the baptism of Jesus that are materially related to each other because they refer to the same event. And there are four accounts of the cleansing of the temple in the gospels:

Cleansing of Temple

Matt 21:12–13

⇧ ⇩

Mark 11:15–19

⇧ ⇩

Luke 19:45–48

⇧ ⇩

John 2:13–25

It is helpful, indeed essential, to study these four accounts in relation to each other, without reference to narrative context.

The cleansing of the temple nevertheless also occurs in particular narrative sequences in the several gospels, and it is also to be studied in relation to these sequences. This is the horizontal or left-to-right dimension.

The horizontal dimension of narrative may be illustrated by brief sketches of the sequence of narrative segments in Matthew, Mark, and John in which that story is embedded:

Matthew

1. Entry into Jerusalem (21:1–11) ⇨ 2. Cleansing of the Temple (21:12–13) ⇨ 3. Children Praise Jesus (and return to Bethany) (21:14–17) ⇨ 4. (Return to city next morning) Jesus Curses a Fig Tree (21:18–22)

Mark

1. Entry into Jerusalem (and return to Bethany) (11:1–11) ⇨ 2. Cursing of Fig Tree (11:12–14) ⇨ 3. Cleansing of Temple (departure from city) (11:15–19) ⇨ 4. (Return to city next morning) Lesson of Fig Tree (11:20–25)

John

1. Miracle at Cana (2:1–11) ⇨ 2. Sojourn in Capernaum (2:12) ⇨ 3. (Journey to Jerusalem) Cleansing of Temple (2:13–25) ⇨ 4. Jesus and Nicodemus (3:1–21)

A cursory examination of the sequence of narrative segments listed above reveals that the cleansing of the temple takes place in John almost at the beginning of the public ministry, while in Matthew and Mark it occurs at the outset of the passion week, just prior to the crucifixion. There is a further minor discrepancy: in Mark, Jesus enters Jerusalem on Palm Sunday, looks around in the temple, and then returns to Bethany for the night; the next day he returns to Jerusalem and cleanses the temple. In Matthew, Jesus enters the temple and drives out the vendors on the first day of that week.

In addition to these differences in sequence, the three (four) accounts of the cleansing of the temple differ in detail when compared vertically with each other. In Mark, for example, Jesus will not let anyone carry anything through the temple; this detail is omitted in the other accounts. In John, the forecast of Jesus' resurrection is linked to the destruction of the temple in this narrative; this prediction occurs elsewhere in the Synoptics.

The vertical dimensions of narrative are called paradigmatic (or associative) in terminology derived from Ferdinand de Saussure, a Swiss linguist, whose work has become very influential. The horizontal dimensions of narrative are termed syntagmatic.[1] This technical terminology will be employed in the discussion to follow.

The horizontal or left-to-right dimension of the gospel narratives is presented in standard editions of the New Testament. Gospel harmonies or parallels were created to provide the vertical or paradigmatic dimension. In Gospel harmonies the paradigmatic has engulfed or obscured the syntagmatic dimension.

The design and layout of materials in the *New Gospel Parallels* is intended to keep both the vertical (paradigmatic) and horizontal (syntagmatic) dimensions of the gospel narratives steadily in view, without sacrificing one to the other. That is an exceedingly complex task, and it must be achieved without creating an unduly complicated page.

SYNOPSES AND HARMONIES

2.   In recent gospel synopses, the emphasis has been on the paradigmatic or vertical dimensions of the gospel materials, as a consequence of the influence of form criticism and in reaction against older study instruments which sought to "harmonize" the fourfold canonical tradition. On the other hand, harmonies, as they are called, endeavor to weave all the elements of the tradition into a single chronological strand, into one composite order or sequence. Harmonies are therefore predominantly syntagmatic.[2]

---

1. Cf. syntax, "ordering together" (of words, phrases, clauses, sentences).
2. David Dungan, "Theory of Synopsis Construction," *Biblica* 61 (1980) 305–29, gives definitions of the "harmony" and the

We may consider, first, the more recent synopses and then return, subsequently, to the older harmonies.

Synopses were originally created for the microscopic comparison of words and phrases in parallel texts; a synopsis of this type is oriented primarily to source criticism. Synopses were later fabricated also for the close comparison of oral pericopes; this kind of synopsis came into being under the aegis of form criticism. Redaction criticism eventually made use of synopses as well, although special synopses seem not to have been created for that specific purpose.

The first kind of synopsis is concerned with the synoptic problem, that is, with the problem of the relationships among written sources; the second type was interested as much or more in the oral prehistory of the materials. More recent versions of synopses, such as Huck-Greeven and its English language counterparts, attempt to combine the two interests with increasingly dubious results.

The two types of synopses betray differing judgments about the character of the gospel materials.

The synopsis oriented to source criticism was concerned to determine which of the gospels was chronologically prior and was employed as a source by the other two synoptic writers. Once the two-source hypothesis (and its variations) became established, the consensus formed around Mark as the original written gospel. Matthew and Luke were taken to be dependent on Mark and another source, now lost, called Q (which stands for the German word *Quelle*, meaning source). John dropped out of the picture as a contender for highest historical honors, and consequently dropped out of many synopses as well. The function of the source-critical synopsis then became to show how Matthew and Luke edited Mark in the process of creating their own gospels: the columnar treatment, which has once served primarily to demonstrate the priority of Mark, was converted, under redaction criticism, to the second purpose, now taken to be the more interesting question.

After the flowering of source criticism and the consensus that consigned the priority to Mark, but before the advent of redaction criticism, form criticism took the field. Karl Ludwig Schmidt, Martin Dibelius, and Rudolf Bultmann demonstrated how the written sources of the canonical gospels were preceded by a significant period of oral creativity and transmission of the Jesus tradition. If one breaks the written gospels apart at their editorial seams, clearly demarcated oral units separate themselves from the editorial dross utilized by the canonical authors to weave the pieces together into weak narratives. These oral units may be classified according to form and compared with other units of like form, in the same gospel and in other gospels. A properly designed synopsis can assist with this process of paradigmatic comparison. The cohesive editorial material is of course discarded or given a relatively low value quotient by the form critics.

The form-critical use of synopses took the oral segments to be relatively stable and reliable in relation to the rest of the material; it placed little or no value on the narrative sequences in each of the gospels.

The older interest of synopses in source criticism perpetuated a certain interest in sequence, particularly in Mark, although here, too, the synopsis was obviously more concerned with vertical comparison of words and phrases than with order or chronology.

The gospel harmony, on the other hand, lacks a genuine interest in the differences revealed by paradigmatic study; its concern is to smooth the versions out and work them up into one sequence. The resulting sequence, of course, was entirely arbitrary: there were as many sequences as there were harmony editors, and none of them was congruent with the sequence presented by one of the evangelists.

When the harmony was generally discredited, interest in sequence collapsed. That is to be regretted, although it is not to be regretted that the harmonizing strategy was abandoned. Nevertheless, sequence is an important feature of narrative and cannot be ignored in any serious study of narrative, gospel or other. The paradigmatic study of the gospels was subsequently challenged as well, but without decisive results. A renewed interest in biblical narrative, especially on the part of literary critics, has nevertheless served to infringe the domination of source, form, and redaction criticism, and thus of the paradigmatic. This new interest and its impact suggest that gospel criticism is going through a transitional stage. It is probably correct to say that the balance between the paradigmatic and the syntagmatic is being restored.

The restoration of balance between the paradigmatic and the syntagmatic signals a new phase of gospel criticism. The paradigmatic study of the gospel materials will no longer be motivated primarily by the interests of form criticism, with its more or less overriding concern to establish the oral history of the units of material. Instead, associative comparison will range over a much broader spectrum of material—miracle stories, pronouncement stories, *chreia*, parables, aphorisms drawn from all over the hellenistic world. The new aim will be to learn as much as possible about how these particular linguistic vehicles, rather than some other types of discourse, came to be employed as building blocks of the gospels.

The syntagmatic study of the gospels will not be concerned to recover or reconstruct the historical chain of events lying behind the gospels—which are, in any case, simply beyond reach, given our present sources—but will take an interest in the gospel narratives in and of themselves. Narrative is a form of discourse having its own grammar; as such, narrative is a linguistic screen through which the story of Jesus must pass. By

"synopsis" (310) which are adopted here. Dungan's analysis of the issues connected with synopsis construction and his constructive proposals are worth careful study. However, his views suffer from a narrow orientation to the synoptic problem and the question of gospel priority. These questions need not be permitted to tyrannize the design of a study instrument.

examining that screen closely, we may learn why the first raconteurs elected to narrate the things they did, in the way they did. We will certainly learn something of the rules to which they had to subscribe in narrating anything at all. We will do this, in this first instance, because the gospel narratives are, in fact, all we have; we may wish to make as much of them as possible.

The combination of paradigmatic and syntagmatic research in their new forms will open up new horizons in understanding the gospel narratives. The *New Gospel Parallels* is designed to make such study possible. It is also designed to make many other uses possible, some or many of which cannot be forecast.

PRIMARY FEATURES

3. The canonical gospels, along with many of the apocryphal gospels, are predominantly narrative in form. The *New Gospel Parallels* will therefore present each gospel in its own narrative integrity. To maintain this integrity three things are required:

1. Each gospel must be taken in turn as the primary text;
2. The narrative sequence of the primary text is to be strictly observed;
3. Each gospel is to be divided into segments in accordance with its own narrative markers, and utilized in such narrative segments wherever narrative units are being compared.

These requirements call for further explication.

3.1 In order to avoid the artificial chronology of the harmonies and the arbitrary sequences of the synopses, the *New Gospel Parallels* will present each of the gospels, in turn, as the primary text, in its own narrative integrity. The *New Gospel Parallels* will thus have as many parts as there are primary texts. Each part will consist of a different gospel as primary term, in relation to which the comparative materials are identified and collected onto the page or folio.

The entire work will consist of two divisions: (a) narrative gospels; (b) sayings gospels. The primary narrative texts, of course, are Matthew, Mark, Luke, and John. The principal sayings gospel is the Gospel of Thomas; its counterpart is the hypothetical source Q. The two divisions are of unequal length. As a consequence, volume 1 of the *New Gospel Parallels* will contain only Matthew, Mark, and Luke.

By following this more elaborate design, *New Gospel Parallels* will avoid the impression left by both harmonies and synopses, in spite of themselves, that the three (or four) gospels constitute a single narrative. It will not be necessary to look back several pages to see where the last pericope taken from the primary gospel occurs, nor will there ever be any doubt about what comes next in the primary text: what precedes and what follows will never be more than one page away. Moreover, since only

one gospel at a time will function as the primary text, parallels may be selected to go with that specific gospel; in current synopses, where the gospels are conflated, parallels relative to all the gospels are to be found on the same page. By featuring one gospel at a time, it has also been possible to include a full range of parallels—from the Gospel of Thomas, from the apocryphal gospels, and from other parts of the New Testament, such as Acts.

In addition to these features, special collections of materials, such as all the traditions relating to John the Baptist and the commissioning and instruction of the twelve (seventy), will be assembled in appendices to facilitate comparison and study.

These features have been made possible by redesigning the traditional synopsis or harmony page. If one sacrifices the word-for-word, or phrase-by-phrase, juxtaposition of the text in opposing columns, it is possible to get much more text on the page. Yet verbal correspondences may be readily indicated by carrying the bold type of the primary gospel over into other columns. This is a much more satisfactory procedure than the curious distribution of words or phrases along the column, in an effort to match them up, yet without being able to do so where the words or phrases in question vary in order. In addition, it is possible to make several distinctions on the page by the use of varying fonts and flags; these distinctions will allow the reader to tell at a glance what is primary text, what is parallel at various levels, and what constitutes the notes.

3.2 The sequence of narrative units in the primary text is to be strictly observed. The sequence of the segments in the primary gospel is perspicuously presented in each case by printing that text in bold type and locating it always in the lefthand column on the page. This arrangement will enable the reader to follow the primary text, forwards or backwards, without difficulty, without lengthy gap, without confusion.

Each narrative segment is assigned a number in the *New Gospel Parallels*. The numbers are sequential from the beginning to the end of each gospel, and are combined in each case with an identifying letter:

M = Matthew
K = Mark
L = Luke
J = John

Segments are thus numbered M1, M2, M3, K1, K2, etc.

Sequences in each gospel are identified in running feet: S1:K2–4, Introduction, Mark 1:2–13, means that the first sequence in Mark consists of segments K2–4, and that this sequence has the label "Introduction," and corresponds to Mark 1:2–13. The head on the same page identifies K2 as Mark 1:2–8 and labels this segment, "Appearance of John the Baptist."

The sequence of segments in a narrative is hierarchical. A narrative consists of segments joined into shorter sequences, which are joined, in turn, into longer sequences, and these are combined into still longer sequences, the last of which will be coterminus with the narrative itself.

In the Gospel of Luke, for example, the births and child-hoods of John and Jesus are presented in five narrative sequences (L2–6), consisting of sixteen narrative segments:

S1:L2   Introduction to the Birth of John and Jesus   1:5–56

    L2.1   The Prediction of John's Birth   1:5–25
      L2.1a Introduction   1:5–7
      L2.1b Zechariah's Vision   1:8–23
      L2.1c Conception of John   1:24–25
    L2.2   The Annunciation to Mary   1:26–38
    L2.3   Mary's Visit to Elizabeth   1:39–56

S2:L3   Birth and Childhood of John   1:57–80

    L3   The Birth and Childhood of John   1:57–80

S3:L4–6   Birth and Childhood of Jesus   2:1–52

    L4   The Birth of Jesus   2:1–21
    L4.1   The Birth of Jesus   2:1–7
    L4.2   The Shepherds   2:8–20
      L4.2a The Annuciation to the Shepherds   2:8–14
      L4.2b The Visit of the Shepherds   2:15–20
    L4.3   The Circumcision of Jesus   2:21

    L5   The Presentation of Jesus in Jerusalem   2:22–40
    L5.1   The Presentation of Jesus   2:22–24
    L5.2   Simeon Blesses Jesus   2:25–35
    L5.3   Anna the Prophetess   2:36–38
    L5.4   Return to Nazareth   2:39–40

    L6   Jesus Visits Jerusalem at Twelve   2:41–52
    L6.1   Jesus' Parents Take Him to Jerusalem   2:41–45
    L6.2   Jesus among the Teachers in the Temple   2:46–52

As the outline indicates, there are three sequences in this narrative stretch: S1, S2, and S3. S3 consists of three sub-segments: L4, L5, and L6. Among these, L4 has three sub-subsegments: L4.1, L4.2, and L4.3. Again, L4.2 has two sub-sub-subsegments: L4.2a and L4.2b. This hierarchy is indicated, for the most part, on each page of the *New Gospel Parallels* by the running heads and feet (the segment and sequence labels at the top and bottom of each page). It is also presented in the analytic tables that appear at the front of each gospel in the *New Gospel Parallels*.

The hierarchical grouping of narrative segments is carried out, wherever possible, on the basis of markers in the narrative itself. For example, S3 in Mark, the Second Galilean sequence, contains five segments, K13–17. K14, however, consists of three subsegments:

K14.1   Teaching beside the Sea   2:13
K14.2   Call of Levi   2:14
K14.3   Eating with Tax Collectors
        and Sinners   2:15–17

These three brief segments could have been numbered separately, but they are linked together by the narrator in such a way that they constitute a subsequence within the larger sequence, S3. They are therefore given a single number, K14, and the units are given subordinate numbers.

The fifth sequence in Mark, furthermore, consists solely of K21 (Mark 4:1–34), which has nine subparts. The reason is that the subparts of the entire sequence, Teaching in Parables, are linked closely together by the narrator; he sets them off unequivocally from what precedes and what follows (note 4:1–2, 10–12, 33–34 for the narrative framework). Moreover, the material enclosed by these narrative markers is largely instructional in nature (i.e., it is not narrative in the strict sense). One number for the sequence as a whole (K21), with subordinate numbers for the subparts, is thus entirely appropriate. The numbering of Luke 6:20–49 (sermon on the plain) and Matt 5:1–7:29 (sermon on the mount) was handled in a similar fashion for comparable reasons.

The numbering of narrative segments, which involves interpreting their hierarchical structure, is not entirely unambiguous. The two brief stories of the call of the pairs of disciples (Mark 1:16–18, 19–20//Matt 4:18–20, 21–22) are closely tied together, principally because one repeats the other almost verbatim. They are often printed as one pericope in harmonies and synopses. Yet Mark 1:16–18 and 1:19–20 and Matt 4:18–20 and 4:21–22 are clearly two narrative segments, differentiated by formal markers. Because the narrator does not mark them off by other means as an immediately larger narrative sequence, the editor has elected to number them separately (K6, 7//M9, 10). The close verbal identity of the two segments has nevertheless prompted the editor to print them on the same page.

3.3   It was not possible, until recently, to segment narratives on the basis of a narrative grammar. Editors divided the gospel texts into units for a variety of reasons, often inconsistent within a single synopsis or harmony, and sometimes for no apparent reason at all. The emergence of a grammar of narrative discourse makes it possible to segment narratives on the basis of formal properties.

The study of narrative discourse for its grammar or structural properties is relatively new. Yet the discipline is far enough advanced to warrant the identification of certain formal criteria for segmenting narrative texts. The results of the narrative analysis of particular texts, such as the gospels, are subject, of course, to modification and correction as narrative grammar is advanced and refined. The segmentation of the gospels as evidenced in the *New Gospel Parallels* is as certain as the current state of narrative grammar: both represent a firm beginning, yet both will undoubtedly be corrected and improved.[3]

THE DESIGN OF THE PAGE

4.   The page of the *New Gospel Parallels* is divided into three vertical columns, and divided again horizontally to produce six columns, three above and three below (in the case of folios, the six columns are full page depth and run across two pages). For descriptive purposes it will be helpful to number the columns: the top three columns, from left to right, are columns one, two, and three; the bottom three columns on the page, again numbered from left to right, are four, five, and six.

4.1   The primary text is always presented in bold type in the (upper) lefthand column of each page or folio. Narrative segments are numbered consecutively.

4.2   Parallels are presented in columns two through six and always in canonical order, followed by the Gospel of Thomas and Other (parallels). Since the primary text appears in column one, column assignment will vary. When Matthew is the primary text, the order is canonical, followed by Thomas and Other. When Mark is the primary text, however, Matthew will appear in column two, Luke in column three, John in four, Thomas in five, and Other in six. Luke as the primary text will be followed by Matthew, Mark, John, Thomas, and Other. The order is thus constant, except that the primary text is taken from its position and placed on the (upper) left.

4.3   Primary parallels are printed in regular type (contrast the bold face of the primary text). Primary parallels are those in which verbatim agreement is high or substantial or in which there is substantial concurrence in narrative content and function, but not necessarily in diction.

Verbal agreements between the primary text and the parallel texts are indicated by bold type. Such agreements in words or phrases are readily identified by allowing the eye to scan columns two through six for bold type. Verbal agreements are based solely on the English text.

4.4   Secondary parallels are also printed in regular type, with bold to mark verbal agreements with the primary text.

Secondary parallels belong to two classes.

The first class or type is the parallel that serves the same narrative function, but lacks substantial verbal agreement or

agreement in narrative content (see §4.3 above). This type is flagged by means of a single dagger (†).

An example of a secondary parallel of type (1) is Luke 5:4–11 (L17.2) in relation to Mark 1:16–20 (K6, 7) and Matt 4:18–22 (M9, 10). Luke's account of the miraculous catch of fish bears little or no verbal resemblance to the call stories in Mark and Matthew, and yet, in Luke's narrative sequence, it functions as a call story and replaces the double stories in Mark and Matthew.

A secondary parallel of type (2) is one in which there is substantial agreement in diction or narrative content or both, but where the parallel segment serves a distinctive narrative function. This type of secondary parallel is flagged by means of a double dagger (‡).

John 21:1–14 (J39) is a secondary parallel of type (2) in relation to Luke 5:4–11 (L17.2): there appears to be substantial agreement in narrative content, although the two narrative segments clearly fulfill different functions in John and Luke.

Secondary parallels are distinguished solely by the single and double daggers which appear in the segment head. In all other respects have the same appearance as primary parallels.

4.5   There are a few doublets in the gospel tradition. Doublets are units of narrative or discourse material that appear to duplicate another segment of material. These are flagged by means of a bullet (•). Doublets are often duplications of aphorisms or groups of aphorisms and are therefore not narrative segments in the strict sense.

4.6   Additional parallels, which may be termed tertiary parallels, are segments of material that illuminate the primary text in some particular way or ways, but which cannot be classified as either primary or secondary parallels. They are often drawn from apocryphal gospels and elsewhere in the New Testament. Tertiary parallels are printed in italic, with verbal agreements again in bold.

The possibilities of tertiary parallels are virtually unlimited. The number printed on the page is often determined by available space.

4.7   As a rule, parallels are printed by narrative segment and not in fragments. However, when fragments of narrative units are being compared, rather than whole narrative units, the fragment alone is printed and the verse or verses in the primary text to which the fragment is related is indicated by an arrow (⇨). Fragmentary parallels may be of any type.

4.8   Notes to the primary text consist of textual notes and references to the Hebrew bible.

Textual notes are related to the primary text by means of a superscript letter. The notes are printed in reduced type in column one.

Passages drawn from the Old Testament indicate a quotation or allusion in the primary text, or they provide the relevant

---

3.   The justification for the segmentation and sequencing utilized in the *New Gospel Parallels* is provided by Robert W. Funk in *The Poetics of Biblical Narrative* (Fortress Press, forthcoming).

background for a remark or point. The verse or verses in the primary text to which the passages are related is always indicated by an arrow (⇨).

4.9 References to the three special collections of related materials in the appendices are designated by a degree mark (°).

4.10 The reader should be aware of two modifications in the layout of pages that were introduced to conserve space. Occasionally, the parallels and notes in column one are run over into column two (rarely columns three and four). Note, for example, M1 and M7.1–5. More frequently, very short independent segments are doubled up on a single page in order to save space; printing only one segment to the page would have increased the size of the work another thirty percent. M12.3/M12.4 and M40.4/M40.5 are examples.

New Testament

Matt	Matthew
Mark	Mark
Luke	Luke
John	John
Acts	Acts
Rom	Romans
1 Cor	1 Corinthians
Gal	Galatians
Phil	Philippians
1 Thess	1 Thessalonians
1 Tim	1 Timothy
Jas	James
1 Pet	1 Peter
Rev	Revelation

Old Testament and Apocrypha

Gen	Genesis
Exod	Exodus
Lev	Leviticus
Num	Numbers
Deut	Deuteronomy
Josh	Joshua
Judg	Judges
1 Sam	1 Samuel
2 Sam	2 Samuel
1 Kgs	1 Kings
2 Kgs	2 Kings
Isa	Isaiah
Jer	Jeremiah
Ezek	Ezekiel
Hos	Hosea
Joel	Joel
Jonah	Jonah
Mic	Micah
Hab	Habakkuk
Zech	Zechariah
Mal	Malachi
Ps	Psalms
Job	Job
Prov	Proverbs
Esth	Esther
Dan	Daniel
2 Chr	2 Chronicles
1 Macc	1 Maccabees
Sir	Sirach
Tob	Tobit

Extracanonical Books and Fragments

AcPil   Acts of Pilate

AcPil is an elaborate account of Jesus' trial before Pontius Pilate, his crucifixion and burial, accounts of the empty tomb, and a discussion of his resurrection by a council of Jewish elders. It is an example of early Christian apologetic in narrative form.

The original AcPil was probably written in Greek sometime during II/III CE. The prologue to AcPil claims that it was written by Nicodemus in Hebrew shortly after Jesus' death. AcPil was eventually incorporated into the Gospel of Nicodemus. It is preserved in several medieval Greek manuscripts. (Cameron: 163–65)

ApocJa   Apocryphon of James

ApocJa is a Coptic translation of a Greek original containing a dialogue of Jesus with Peter and James. ApocJa was found among the codices of the Nag Hammadi Library in Egypt in 1945.

ApocJa lacks a narrative framework; like GThom and Q, it consists entirely of sayings, parables, prophecies, and rules governing the Christian community attributed to Jesus. It is the risen Jesus who speaks. The whole is embedded in a letter purportedly written in Hebrew by James.

ApocJa was probably composed during the course of II CE. (Koester 2: 224–25; Cameron: 55–57)

DialSav   Dialogue of the Savior

DialSav is a fragmentary and composite document containing dialogues of Jesus with three of his disciples, Judas, Matthew, and Miriam. It was found at Nag Hammadi, Egypt, in 1945.

The earlier portions of the dialogue may be dated to the second half of I CE, while the final form of DialSav is probably to be dated to the second half of II CE.

DialSav is closely related to GThom and the Gospel of John. (Koester 2: 154–55; Cameron: 38–39)

Fayyum Fragment

Fayyum Fragment is a fragment of III CE containing an excerpt from an unknown gospel. The text is too fragmentary to warrant definitive conclusions. (Hennecke 1: 115–16)

Freer (Logion)

The Freer logion is a variant reading in codex W acquired by Charles L. Freer of Detroit in 1906 and now lodged in the Freer Museum of the Smithsonian Institution in Washington, D.C. (late IV or early V CE). The variant in question is an insertion in the Gospel of Mark at 16:4 (cited there in full).

GEbi   Gospel of the Ebionites

A Jewish-Christian gospel preserved only in quotations by Ephiphanius (IV CE). The original title is unknown. The Ebionites were Greek-speaking Jewish Christians who flourished II–III CE. Their gospel, erroneously called the Hebrew Gospel by Epiphanius, probably dates to mid-II CE. (Koester 2: 202–3; Cameron: 103–4)

GEgy Gospel of the Egyptians

GEgy consists of sayings of Jesus. The few fragments extant are preserved in Greek by Clement of Alexandria (end of II CE). The gospel appears to be oriented to sexual asceticism, to judge by the few remaining fragments. GEgy arose in the period 50–150 CE. (Koester 2: 229–30; Cameron: 49–51)

GHeb Gospel of the Hebrews

GHeb contains traditions of Jesus' pre-existence and coming into the world, his baptism and temptation, a few of his sayings, and an account of his resurrected appearance to James, his brother (1 Cor 15:7). The provenance of GHeb is probably Egypt. It was composed sometime between mid-I CE and mid-II CE. GHeb has been lost except for quotations and allusions preserved by the Church Fathers. (Koester 2: 223–24; Cameron: 83–85)

GNaz Gospel of the Nazoreans

GNaz is an expanded version of the Gospel of Matthew. It is preserved in quotations and allusions in the Church Fathers and in marginal notations found in a number of medieval manuscripts. These marginal notations appear to go back to a single "Zion Gospel" edition composed prior to 500 CE. GNaz is evidently a translation into Aramaic or Syriac of Greek Matthew, with additions.

GNaz is first quoted by Hegesippus ca. 180 CE. Its provenance is probably western Syria. (Koester 2: 201–2; Cameron: 97–98)

GPet Gospel of Peter

GPet is preserved only as a fragment discovered in upper Egypt in 1886–1887; the language is Greek and the fragment dates to the VIII or IX CE. However, two Greek papyrus fragments from Oxyrhynchus, dating to late II or early III CE, may also belong to GPet.

GPet contains a passion narrative, an epiphany story, an account of the empty tomb, and the beginning of a resurrection story.

In its original form, GPet may have arisen in the second half of I CE. (Koester 2: 162–63; Cameron: 76–78)

GThom Gospel of Thomas

GThom is a sayings gospel: it consists of wisdom sayings, parables, proverbs, and prophecies attributed to Jesus. It has virtually no narrative content.

GThom is extant in complete form only in a Coptic translation found among the fifty-two tractates that make up the Coptic Gnostic Library discovered at Nag Hammadi, Egypt, in 1945. Three fragments of the original Greek version of GThom were discovered at Oxyrhynchus in Egypt around the turn of the century (POxy 1, 654, 655: see these entries).

GThom is widely regarded as an independent witness to the sayings of Jesus, comparable in form to so-called Q, a sayings collection believed to function as one of two sources utilized by Matthew and Luke in creating their gospels.

GThom can probably be dated to the second half of I CE. (Koester 2: 150–54; Cameron: 23–25)

InThom Infancy Gospel of Thomas

InThom is a narrative of the miraculous works of the young magician-hero, Jesus, prior to his twelfth birthday. InThom continues the *divine man* tradition of the ancient world: itinerant miracle workers accredited by their amazing deeds.

InThom is preserved in a Syriac manuscript of the VI CE and in Greek manuscripts of XIV–XVI CE. The gospel is based on oral sources and the Gospel of Luke. In its original form it may be as old as II CE. (Cameron: 122–24)

PCairo Papyrus Cairensis 10 735

PCairo is allegedly a fragment of a non-canonical gospel containing the story of Jesus' birth and flight to Egypt. The fragment is dated to VI or VII CE. Further identification has not been possible. (Hennecke 1: 114–15)

PEger2 Papyrus Egerton 2

A fragment of an unknown gospel dated to the beginning of II CE. Contains: healing of a leper, controversy over payment of taxes, miracle of Jesus on the Jordan, plus two segments closely related to the Gospel of John. (Koester 2: 181–83)

PJas Protevangelium of James

PJas is an infancy gospel containing an account of the birth and dedication of Mary and the birth of Jesus. The title *Protevangelium* indicates that the events recorded precede those narrated in the canonical gospels. PJas is dated in the period mid-II CE to early III CE. (Cameron: 107–9)

POxy 1 Oxyrhynchus Papyrus 1

POxy 1 is a fragment from a papyrus codex dated ca. 200 CE. It is written on both sides (recto and verso) and contains sayings 26, 27, 28, 29, 30 with the end of 77, 31, 32, 33 of the Coptic Gospel of Thomas.

POxy 1 is obviously from a different copy of Greek GThom than either POxy 654 or 655.

POxy 654 Oxyrhynchus Papyrus 654

POxy 654 is a fragment of forty-two lines of sayings of Jesus appearing on the back of a survey-list of various pieces of land. The fragment is dated to III CE. It contains the prologue and the first five sayings of the Gospel of Thomas in Greek.

POxy 654 is from a different copy of Greek GThom than either POxy 1 or 655.

POxy 655 Oxyrhynchus Papyrus 655

POxy 655 is made up of eight small scraps of a papyrus scroll dated not later than 250 CE. It contains five sayings of Jesus, which correspond to Coptic GThom 36, 37, 38, 39, 40.

POxy 655 is from a different copy of Greek GThom than either POxy 1 or 654.

POxy 840   Papyrus Oxyrhynchus 840

POxy 840 is a single leaf of a Greek parchment codex that can be dated to IV CE. It contains: the conclusion of a discourse between Jesus and his disciples and a controversy story involving Jesus and a Pharasaic chief priest in the temple court. (Cameron: 53)

POxy 1224   Oxyrhynchus Papyrus 1224

POxy 1224 is the remains of a papyrus codex containing fragments of an unknown gospel. The fragments can be dated to the beginning of IV CE.

SecMk   The Secret Gospel of Mark

SecMk is a fragment of an early edition of the Gospel of Mark containing a story of the raising of a young man from the dead, a rite of initiation, and an encounter of Jesus with three women in Jericho. These stories are presently embedded in a letter of Clement of Alexandria (II CE), the copy of which dates to XVIII CE. SecMk, however, may go back in its original form to early II CE. (Cameron: 67–69)

Church Fathers and Jewish Authors

Barn   Barnabas

1 Clem   1 Clement, a letter from Clement of Rome to the church at Corinth, ca. 95 CE

2 Clem   2 Clement, a sermon attributed to Clement of Rome, dating ca. 150 CE

Clement (of Alexandria)   II/III CE
Stromateis
Excerpta ex Theodoto

Did   Didache, a compendium of teachings or catechetical work attributed to the twelve apostles; early II CE

Epiphanius (of Salemis)   IV CE
Haer   Haereses

Eusebius (of Caesaria)   III/IV CE
Theophania

Ign   Ignatius (bishop of Antioch in Syria)   early II CE
Smyr   Smyrnaeans, a letter to the church at Smyrna

Irenaeus (of Lyons)   II CE
Adv. Haer.   Adversus Haereses

Josephus   I CE
Against Apion

Jerome (of Jerusalem)   IV/V CE
Adversus Pelagianos
Commentary on Matthew
Commentary on Isaiah
De viris inlustribus

Justin (Martyr)   II CE
Apology
Dialogue

Origen (of Alexandria and Caesaria)   III CE
Commentary on Matthew
Commentary on John

Philo (of Alexandria)   I CE
On the Life of Moses

Zion Gospel, an edition of Matthew dating from about 500 CE reflected in a group of thirty-six medieval manuscripts of the text of Matthew (Cameron: 97)

Sigla

†   A single dagger denotes a secondary parallel that serves the narrative function but lacks substantial agreement.

‡   A double dagger indicates a secondary parallel that exhibits substantial verbal agreement but serves a distinctive narrative function.

°   A degree mark indicates that parallel material has been collected in a special appendix.

•   A bullet denotes a doublet (material repeated within the same gospel); see Introduction §4.5.

{ }   Braces indicate words the editors of a text take to be erroneous or superfluous.

< >   Angular brackets denote an editorial correction of a scribal error or omission.

[ ]   Square brackets indicate a gap in the manuscript. If letters or words appear within brackets, they have been supplied or restored by the editors.

Modern Authors

Cameron   *The Other Gospels: Non-Canonical Gospel Texts.* Edited by Ron Cameron. Philadelphia: Westminster Press, 1982.

Hennecke   Edgar Hennecke, *New Testament Apocrypha.* Edited by Wilhelm Schneemelcher. English translation edited by R. McL. Wilson. Vol. 1: *Gospels and Related Writings.* Philadelphia: The Westminster Press, 1963.

Koester   Helmut Koester, *Introduction to the New Testament.* Vol. 1: *History, Culture, and Religion of the Hellenistic Age;* Vol. 2: *History and Literature of Early Christianity.* Foundations and Facets. Philadelphia: Fortress Press, 1982.

Textual Notes

The evidence cited in the textual notes is based on the third edition of *The Greek New Testament,* edited by Aland, Black, Martini, Metzger, and Wikgren (1975), and on Bruce Metzger's *A Textual Commentary on the Greek New Testament* (corrected edition, 1975). For the most part, the notes follow items cited in the *Revised Standard Version: An Ecumenical Edition (Common Bible)* (New York: Collins, 1973).

Witnesses are cited in the customary categories, with papyri coming first, followed by the uncials and then the minuscules. The ancient versions are also cited where appropriate. The evidence is normally abbreviated; for full citations the reader is referred to the UBS *Greek New Testament* or to Nestle-Aland, *Novum Testamentum Graece.*

The Papyri

Number	Content	Location	Date
$\mathfrak{P}^1$	gospels	Philadelphia	III
$\mathfrak{P}^{25}$	gospels	Berlin	late IV
$\mathfrak{P}^{37}$	gospels	Ann Arbor	III/IV
$\mathfrak{P}^{45}$	gospels, acts	Dublin & Vienna	III
$\mathfrak{P}^{75}$	gospels	Geneva	early III

The Letter Uncials

Designation/Name	Content	Location	Date
ℵ, Sinaiticus	NT	London	IV
A, Alexandrinus	NT	London	V
B, Vaticanus	gospels, acts, epistles	Rome	IV
C, Ephraemi Rescriptus	NT	Paris	V
D, Bezae Cantabrigiensis	gospels, acts	Cambridge	V/VI
K	gospels	Paris	IX
L, Regius	gospels	Paris	VIII
N, Purpureus Petropolitanus	gospels	Leningrad etc.	V
P, Porphyrianus	gospels	Wöltenbättel	VI
T, Borgianus	gospels	Rome	V
W, Freerianus	gospels	Washington, D.C.	V
X	gospels	Munich	X
Γ	gospels	Leningrad & Oxford	X
Δ	gospels	St. Gall	IX
Θ, Koridethi	gospels	Tiflis	IX
Ξ, Zacynthius	gospels	London	VIII
Π	gospels	Leningrad	IX
Ψ	gospels, acts, epistles	Athos	VIII/IX

The Numbered Uncials

073	VI
084	VI
090	VI
0106	VII
0107	VII
0119	VII
0138	IX
0148	VIII
0170	V/VI
0196	IX
0250	VIII

The Greek Minuscules

28	XI		
33	IX		
157	XII		
304	XII		
565	IX		
700	XI		
892	IX		
1009	XIII		
1010	XII		
1195		1123	
1216	XI		
1230		1124	
1241	XII		
2148		1337	
2174	XIV		

The Ancient Versions

arm	Armenian version
cop	Coptic version
cop^{bo}	Bohairic dialect
cop^{sa}	Sahidic dialect
eth	Ethiopic version
geo	Georgian version
goth	Gothic version
it	Itala or Old Latin version
it^d	Bezae Cantabrigiensis V
it^k	Bobiensis IV/V
syr	Syriac version
syr^c	Curetonian Syriac version
syr^s	Sinaitic Syriac version
vg	Vulgate version

Other Abbreviations and Symbols

f^1	"Family 1": manuscripts 1, 118, 131, 209
f^{13}	"Family 13": manuscripts 13, 69, 124, 174, 230 (174 and 230 not used in Mark), 346, 543, 788, 826, 828, 983, 1689
*	The reading of the original hand of a manuscript
c	The corrector of a manuscript
c,2,3	The successive correctors of a manuscript
a,b,c	The successive correctors of a manuscript in ℵ D
mg	Textual evidence found in the margin of a manuscript
gr	The Greek text of a bilingual manuscript
supp	A portion of a manuscript supplied by a later hand to fill in a blank in the original
( )	Means that the witness reads something trivially different but in general conforms to what is cited; or, the reading of the witness is uncertain
pc	*pauci:* a few (other witnesses)
al	*alii:* other (witnesses; more than *pc*)
pm	*permulti:* a great many (witnesses)
LXX	The Septuagint or Greek translation of the Hebrew Old Testament

MATTHEW

S1:M1–4	BIRTH AND CHILDHOOD OF JESUS	1:1–2:23

M1	GENEALOGY OF JESUS CHRIST	1:1–17
	Luke 3:23–38	

M2	BIRTH OF JESUS	1:18–25
Isa 7:14	Luke 2:1–7	
	PJas 14:1–2	

M3	VISIT OF THE MAGI	2:1–12
M3.1	INTRODUCTION	2:1–6
M3.2	SUMMONS OF HEROD	2:7–9a
M3.3	VISIT TO THE CHRIST CHILD	2:9b–12

2 Sam 5:2	Luke 2:8–14
Mic 5:2	Luke 2:15–20
Ps 72:10–11	PJas 21:1–4
Isa 60:6	GNaz 28
John 7:40–44	

M4	FLIGHT AND MASSACRE	2:13–23
M4.1	FLIGHT INTO EGYPT	2:13–15
M4.2	MASSACRE OF THE BABIES	2:16–18
M4.3	RETURN TO NAZARETH	2:19–23

Hos 11:1	Luke 2:39–40
Jer 31:15	PCairo 1–2
Judg 13:5	GNaz 1
	PJas 22:1–2

S2:M5–7	INTRODUCTION TO THE PUBLIC MINISTRY	3:1–4:11

M5	APPEARANCE OF JOHN THE BAPTIST	3:1–12
Matt 7:19	Mark 1:2–8	Luke 3:1–20
Isa 40:3	Mark 1:15	Acts 19:1–7
2 Kgs 1:8		GEbi 2
John 1:19–28		GEbi 3
John 8:39		Acts 1:5
		Acts 11:16
		Acts 13:24–25
		ApocJa 9:24–10:6

M6	BAPTISM OF JESUS	3:13–17
Ps 2:7	Mark 1:9–11	Luke 3:21–22
Isa 42:1	Mark 9:7	Luke 9:34–35
Isa 44:2		GEbi 4
John 1:29–34		GNaz 2
		GHeb 2

M7	TEMPTATIONS OF JESUS	4:1–11
M7.1	INTRODUCTION	4:1–2
M7.2	FIRST TEMPTATION	4:3–4
M7.3	SECOND TEMPTATION	4:5–7
M7.4	THIRD TEMPTATION	4:8–10
M7.5	CONCLUSION	4:11

Exod 34:28	Mark 1:12–13	Luke 4:1–13
Deut 9:9		GNaz 3
Deut 8:3		GHeb 3
Ps 91:11–12		
Deut 6:16		
Deut 6:13		
John 1:51		

S3:M8–11	FIRST GALILEAN	4:12–25

M8	BEGINNING OF THE PUBLIC MINISTRY	4:12–17
Matt 14:3	Mark 1:14–15	Luke 4:14–15
Isa 9:1–2	Mark 6:17	Luke 4:16–30
John 1:43		Luke 3:19–20, 23a
John 4:1–3		
John 4:43		

M9	CALL OF PETER AND ANDREW	4:18–20
M10	CALL OF JAMES AND JOHN	4:21–22
John 1:35–42	Mark 1:16–18	Luke 5:1–3
John 1:43–51	Mark 1:19–20	Luke 5:4–11
		GEbi 1

M11	PREACHING AND HEALING IN GALILEE	4:23–25
Matt 9:35	Mark 1:35–39	Luke 4:42–44

S4: M12	SERMON ON THE MOUNT	5:1–7:29

M12	SERMON ON THE MOUNT	5:1–7:29
M12.1	INTRODUCTION	5:1–2
John 6:3	Mark 3:13	Luke 6:12–16
		Luke 6:17–29
		Luke 6:20a

M12.2	BEATITUDES	5:3–12
Isa 61:2	GThom 54	Luke 6:20–26
Ps 37:11	GThom 69b	1 Pet 4:15–16
Ps 24:3–4	GThom 69a	
	GThom 68	

M12.3	SALT AND LIGHT	5:13–16
	Mark 9:50	Luke 14:34–35
	Mark 4:21	Luke 8:16
	POxy1 7	Luke 11:33
	GThom 32	
	GThom 33	

M12.4	ON THE LAW AND THE PROPHETS	**5:17–20**
		Luke 16:17
		GEbi 6

M12.5a	ON MURDER	**5:21–26**
Exod 20:13	Mark 11:25	Luke 12:57–59
Deut 5:17		GNaz 4

M12.5b	ON ADULTERY	**5:27–30**
Matt 18:8–9	Mark 9:43–48	
Exod 20:14		
Deut 5:18		

M12.5c	ON DIVORCE	**5:31–32**
Matt 19:3–9	Mark 10:2–12	Luke 16:18
Deut 24:1–4		

M12.5d	ON SWEARING	**5:33–37**
Matt 23:16–22		
Lev 19:12		
Isa 66:1		
Ps 48:2		

M12.5e	ON RETALIATION	**5:38–42**
Exod 21:23–25	GThom 95	Luke 6:27–36
Lev 24:19–20		Did 1:2–5
Deut 19:21		

M12.5f	ON NEIGHBOR AND ENEMIES	**5:43–48**
Lev 19:17–18		Luke 6:27–36
Deut 18:13		Did 1:2–5
		POxy1224 2
		2 Clem 13:4

M12.6a	INTRODUCTION	**6:1**

M12.6b	ALMSGIVING	**6:2–4**
	POxy654 6	
	GThom 6	
	GThom 14	
	GThom 62	

M12.6c	PRAYER	**6:5–15**
Matt 6:32	Mark 11:25	Luke 11:1–4
Matt 18:35	POxy654 6	Did 8:2–3
Isa 26:20	GThom 6	GNaz 5

M12.6d	FASTING	**6:16–18**
	POxy1 2	Did 8:1
	POxy654 6	
	GThom 6	
	GThom 14	

M12.7a	ON TREASURES	**6:19–21**
	GThom 76	Luke 12:33–34

M12.7b	THE SOUND EYE	**6:22–23**
	Mark 4:21–23	Luke 11:33–36
	GThom 24	DialSav 125:18–126:1

M12.7c	ON SERVING TWO MASTERS	**6:24**
	GThom 47	Luke 16:10–13

M12.7d	ON ANXIETY	**6:25–34**
	POxy655 1	Luke 12:22–34
	GThom 36	

M12.7e	ON JUDGING	**7:1–5**
	Mark 4:24–25	Luke 6:37–42
	POxy1 1	1 Clem 13:2
	GThom 26	GNaz 6

M12.7f	ON PROFANING THE HOLY	**7:6**
	GThom 93	Did 9:5

M12.7g	GOD ANSWERS PRAYER	**7:7–11**
Matt 21:22	Mark 11:24	Luke 11:9–13
	POxy654 2	
	GThom 2	
	GThom 92	
	GThom 94	

M12.7h	THE GOLDEN RULE	**7:12**
Tob 4:15	POxy654 6	Luke 6:31
Sir 31:15	GThom 6	Did 1:2

M12.8a	THE NARROW GATE	**7:13–14**
		Luke 13:22–30

M12.8b	FALSE PROPHETS	**7:15–20**
Matt 12:33–37	Mark 13:22	Luke 6:43–45
Matt 3:10	GThom 45	Luke 3:9

M12.8c	FALSE PROFESSIONS	**7:21–23**
Ps 6:8	Mark 9:38–40	Luke 6:46–49
		Luke 13:22–30
		GNaz 6
		2 Clem 4:2
		2 Clem 4:5

M12.8d	HEARERS AND DOERS OF THE WORD	**7:24–27**
		Luke 6:46–49

M12.9	CONCLUSION	**7:28–29**

Matt 7:28–29	Mark 1:21–22	Luke 4:32
Matt 13:54	Mark 11:18	InThom 19:2c
Matt 22:33		
John 7:46		

S5:M13–16	SECOND GALILEAN	**8:1–17**

M13	HEALING OF A LEPER	**8:1–4**

	Mark 1:40–45	Luke 5:12–16
		PEger2 2

M14	HEALING OF THE CENTURION'S SERVANT	**8:5–13**

Matt 13:42		Luke 7:1–10
Matt 13:50		Luke 13:28–30
Matt 22:13		
Matt 24:51		
Matt 25:30		
John 4:45–54		

M15	HEALING OF PETER'S MOTHER-IN-LAW	**8:14–15**

	Mark 1:29–31	Luke 4:38–39

M16	SUMMARY: HEALING AND EXORCISMS	**8:16–17**

Isa 53:4	Mark 1:32–34	Luke 4:40–41

S6:M17–19	ACROSS THE SEA	**8:18–34**

M17	FOLLOWERS AND FOLLOWING	**8:18–22**

	Mark 4:35	Luke 9:57–62
	GThom 86	Luke 8:22

M18	STILLING OF THE STORM	**8:23–27**

Matt 6:30	Mark 4:35–41	Luke 8:22–25
Matt 14:31		
Matt 16:8		
Ps 65:5–8		

M19	GADARENE DEMONIACS	**8:28–34**

M19.1	HEALING OF THE DEMONIACS	**8:28–33**
M19.2	TOWNSPEOPLE BEG JESUS TO LEAVE	**8:34**

John 2:4	Mark 5:1–14a	Luke 8:26–34
	Mark 1:24	Luke 8:35–39
	Mark 5:14b–20	

S7:M20–25	JESUS RETURNS TO HIS OWN CITY	**9:1–34**

M20	HEALING OF THE PARALYTIC	**9:1–8**

John 5:1–9a	Mark 2:1–12	Luke 5:17–26

M21	IN THE COMPANY OF TAX COLLECTORS	**9:9–13**
M21.1	CALL OF MATTHEW	**9:9**

	Mark 2:14	Luke 5:27–28

M21.2	EATING WITH TAX COLLECTORS AND SINNERS	**9:10–13**

Matt 12:7	Mark 2:15–17	Luke 5:29–32
Hos 6:6		Luke 15:1–2
		POxy1224 1
		Justin, *Apology* 1.15.8

M22	QUESTION OF FASTING	**9:14–17**

	Mark 2:18–22	Luke 5:33–39
	GThom 27	Luke 7:33–34
	GThom 104	Luke 18:12
	GThom 47	Did 8:1

M23	TWO HEALING STORIES	**9:18–26**

M23.1	RULER'S DAUGHTER: INTRODUCTION	**9:18–19**
M23.2	WOMAN WITH THE INTERNAL HEMORRHAGE	**9:20–22**
M23.3	RULER'S DAUGHTER: CONCLUSION	**9:23–26**

	Mark 5:21–24a	Luke 8:40–42a
	Mark 5:24b–34	Luke 8:42b–48
	Mark 10:52	Luke 7:50
	Mark 5:35–43	Luke 17:19
		Luke 18:42
		Luke 8:49–56

M24	HEALING OF TWO BLIND MEN	**9:27–31**

Matt 20:29–34	Mark 10:46–52	Luke 18:35–43
John 9:1–7		

M25	DUMB DEMONIAC	**9:32–34**

Matt 12:22–24	Mark 3:22	Luke 11:14–15

S8: M26–28	THE MISSION CHARGE	**9:35–11:1**

M26	INTRODUCTION	**9:35–38**

Matt 4:23	Mark 1:39	Luke 8:1
Matt 14:14	Mark 6:6b	Luke 10:2
Matt 15:32	Mark 6:34	
Num 27:16–17	GThom 73	
1 Kgs 22:17		
Zech 10:2		
John 4:35		

M27	COMMISSIONING OF THE TWELVE	**10:1–4**

John 1:42	Mark 3:13–19	Luke 6:12–16
	Mark 6:7	Luke 9:1
		Acts 1:12–14
		GEbi 1

M28	THE CHARGE	10:5–42

M28.1	INSTRUCTIONS	10:5–15
Matt 15:24	Mark 6:7–13	Luke 9:1–6
Matt 4:17	Mark 1:15	Luke 10:1–16
		Luke 22:35–36
		1 Cor 9:14
		1 Tim 5:18
		Did 13:1

M28.2	FATE OF THE DISCIPLES	10:16–23
Matt 24:9–14	Mark 13:9–13	Luke 21:12–19
Mic 7:6	POxy655 2	Luke 10:3
John 16:2	GThom 39	Luke 12:11–12
John 14:26		Rom 16:19
John 15:18		2 Clem 5:2–4
		GNaz 7

M28.3	SERVANT AND MASTER	10:24–25
Matt 9:34	Mark 3:22	Luke 6:40
Matt 12:24		Luke 11:15
John 13:16		
John 15:20		

M28.4	HAVE NO FEAR	10:26–33
	Mark 4:21–23	Luke 12:1–12
	Mark 8:38	Luke 8:16–17
	POxy654 5	Luke 21:18
	GThom 5	Luke 9:26
	GThom 6	2 Clem 5:2–4
	POxy1 8	2 Clem 3:2
	GThom 33	

M28.5	THE WAY OF THE CROSS	10:34–39
Matt 16:24–25	Mark 8:34–35	Luke 12:49–53
Mic 7:5–6	GThom 16	Luke 14:25–27
John 12:25	GThom 55	Luke 9:23–24
	GThom 101	Luke 17:33

M28.6	REWARDS	10:40–42
Matt 18:5	Mark 9:37	Luke 9:48
John 12:44–45	Mark 9:41	Luke 10:16
John 13:20		

M28.7	CONCLUSION	11:1
Matt 7:28		
Matt 13:53		
Matt 19:1		
Matt 26:1		

S9:M29–35	THIRD GALILEAN	11:1–12:21

M29	INTRODUCTION	11:1
Matt 7:28		
Matt 13:53		
Matt 19:1		
Matt 26:1		

M30	JESUS AND JOHN THE BAPTIST	11:2–19

M30.1	JOHN QUERIES JESUS	11:2–6
Isa 35:5–6		Luke 7:18–23
John 1:15		Luke 4:18–19

M30.2	JESUS PRAISES JOHN	11:7–15
Matt 13:9	Mark 1:2	Luke 7:24–30
Matt 13:43b	Mark 9:13	Luke 16:16
Mal 3:1a	Mark 4:23	GNaz 8
Mal 4:5	GThom 78	Rev 13:9
John 1:21	GThom 46	

M30.3	CHILDREN IN THE MARKETPLACE	11:16–19
		Luke 7:31–35

M31	JESUS UPBRAIDS CHORAZIN AND BETHSAIDA	11:20–24
Matt 10:15		Luke 10:13–15
Isa 14:13–15		Luke 10:12
		GNaz 27

M32	COMPENDIUM OF SAYINGS	11:25–30
Sir 51:23–27	GThom 90	Luke 10:21–22
Jer 6:16	POxy654 3	GNaz 9
John 3:35	GThom 4	GHeb 4
John 7:29	POxy654 1	DialSav 141:3–11a
	GThom 2	

M33	PLUCKING GRAIN ON THE SABBATH	12:1–8
Matt 9:13	Mark 2:23–28	Luke 6:1–5
Deut 23:25	GThom 27	GEbi 6
Exod 20:10		InThom 2:1–5
Deut 5:14		
1 Sam 21:1–6		
Lev 24:5–9		
Num 28:9–10		
Hos 6:6		

M34	HEALING OF THE MAN WITH THE WITHERED HAND	12:9–14
	Mark 3:1–6	Luke 6:6–11
		Luke 13:15–16
		Luke 14:3–5
		GNaz 10
		InThom 2:1–5

M35	NARRATIVE SUMMARY	**12:15–21**
Isa 42:1–4	Mark 3:7–12	Luke 6:17–19
		Luke 4:41

S10:M36–39	FOURTH GALILEAN	**12:22–50**

M36	BY WHOSE POWER?	**12:22–37**
Matt 9:32–34	Mark 3:20–22	Luke 11:14–23
Matt 10:25	Mark 3:23–30	Luke 12:10
Matt 7:16–20	Mark 9:40	Luke 6:43–45
Matt 15:18	GThom 35	Luke 9:50
John 7:20	GThom 44	POxy1224 2
John 8:48	GThom 45	
John 8:52	GThom 21	
John 10:20		

M37	DEMAND FOR A SIGN	**12:38–42**
Matt 16:1–4	Mark 8:11–13	Luke 11:29–32
Jonah 1:17		Luke 11:16
Jonah 3:5		GNaz 11
John 2:18		
John 6:30		

M38	RETURN OF THE EVIL SPIRIT	**12:43–45**
		Luke 11:24–26

M39	TRUE RELATIVES	**12:46–50**
John 15:14	Mark 3:31–35	Luke 8:19–21
	GThom 99	GEbi 5
		2 Clem 9:11

S11:M40–41	TEACHING IN PARABLES	**13:1–52**

M40	PARABLES FROM THE BOAT	**13:1–35**

M40.1	INTRODUCTION	**13:1–2**
	Mark 4:1	Luke 8:4
		Luke 5:1–3

M40.2	PARABLE OF THE SOWER	**13:3–9**
	Mark 4:2–9	Luke 8:4–8
	GThom 9	InThom 12:1–2
		ApocJa 12:20–31

M40.3	WHY JESUS SPEAKS IN PARABLES	**13:10–17**
Matt 25:29	Mark 4:10–12	Luke 8:9–10
Isa 6:9–10	Mark 4:25	Luke 8:18
John 12:40	GThom 41	Luke 19:26
	GThom 38	Luke 10:23–24
		Acts 28:25–28
		ApocJa 7:1–10

M40.4	INTERPRETATION OF THE SOWER	**13:18–23**
	Mark 4:13–20	Luke 8:11–15
		ApocJa 8:10–27

M40.5	PARABLE OF THE WHEAT AND TARES	**13:24–30**
	Mark 4:26–29	
	GThom 57	

M40.6	PARABLE OF THE MUSTARD SEED	**13:31–32**
Dan 4:20–22	Mark 4:30–32	Luke 13:18–19
	GThom 20	

M40.7	PARABLE OF THE LEAVEN	**13:33**
	GThom 96	Luke 13:20–21

M40.8	SUMMARY: PARABLES FULFIL SCRIPTURE	**13:34–35**
Ps 78:2–3	Mark 4:33–34	

M41	PARABLES IN THE HOUSE	**13:36–52**

M41.1	INTERPRETATION OF THE WHEAT AND TARES	**13:36–43**
Matt 24:31		
Matt 8:12		
Matt 13:50		
Matt 22:13		
Matt 24:51		
Matt 25:30		
Dan 12:3		

M41.2	PARABLE OF THE HIDDEN TREASURE	**13:44**
	GThom 109	

M41.3	PARABLE OF THE PRICELESS PEARL	**13:45–46**
	GThom 76	

M41.4	PARABLE OF THE FISHNET	**13:47–50**
Matt 13:40–42	GThom 8	
Matt 8:12		
Matt 22:13		
Matt 24:51		
Matt 25:30		

M41.5	CONCLUSION: THE DISCIPLE AS SCRIBE	**13:51–52**

S12:M42–49	FIFTH GALILEAN	**13:53–15:20**

M42	REJECTION AT NAZARETH	**13:53–58**
Matt 7:28–29	Mark 6:1–6	Luke 4:16–30
Matt 22:23	POxy1 6	
John 4:44	GThom 31	
John 7:15		
John 6:41–45		
John 6:61		

M43	HEROD BEHEADS JOHN	**14:1–12**
Matt 16:14	Mark 6:14–29	Luke 9:7–9
John 1:19–21, 25	Mark 8:28	Luke 9:19
		Luke 3:19–20

M44	NARRATIVE TRANSITION	**14:13–14**
Matt 4:12	Mark 6:30–34	Luke 9:10–11
Matt 9:36		

M45	JESUS FEEDS THE FIVE THOUSAND	**14:15–21**
Matt 15:32–39	Mark 6:35–44	Luke 9:12–17
2 Kgs 4:42–44	Mark 8:1–10	Luke 22:19
John 6:1–15	Mark 14:22	Luke 24:30
		Acts 27:35

M46	NARRATIVE TRANSITION	**14:22–23**
Matt 15:39	Mark 6:45–46	
John 6:15	Mark 8:10	

M47	JESUS WALKS ON THE WATER	**14:24–33**
John 6:16–21	Mark 6:47–52	Luke 24:37

M48	HEALINGS AT GENNESARET	**14:34–36**
Matt 4:23–25	Mark 6:53–56	Luke 4:40–41
Matt 8:16–17	Mark 1:32–34	Luke 6:17–19
	Mark 3:7–12	

M49	LAWS OF PURITY	**15:1–20**

M49.1	EATING WITH DEFILED HANDS	**15:1–9**
Exod 20:12	Mark 7:1–13	POxy840 2
Exod 21:17		GNaz 12
Lev 20:9		PEger2 3
Deut 5:16		
Isa 29:13		

M49.2	DEFILEMENT	**15:10–20**
Matt 12:34	Mark 7:14–23	Luke 6:39
	GThom 14	
	GThom 40	
	GThom 34	

S13:M50–54	TYRE AND SIDON	**15:21–16:12**

M50	JESUS HEALS A CANAANITE WOMAN'S DAUGHTER	**15:21–28**
Matt 10:6	Mark 7:24–30	

M51	JESUS HEALS MANY IN THE HILLS	**15:29–31**
	Mark 7:31–37	

M52	JESUS FEEDS THE FOUR THOUSAND	**15:32–39**
Matt 14:15–21	Mark 8:1–10	Luke 9:12–17
Matt 9:36	Mark 6:35–44	Luke 22:19
2 Kgs 4:42–44	Mark 14:22	Luke 24:30
John 6:1–15		Acts 27:35

M53	JESUS REFUSES TO GIVE A SIGN	**16:1–4**
Matt 12:38–42	Mark 8:11–13	Luke 11:29–32
John 6:30	GThom 91	Luke 12:54–56
		Luke 11:16
		GNaz 13

M54	THE LEAVEN OF THE PHARISEES AND SADDUCEES	**16:5–12**
Matt 14:5–21	Mark 8:14–21	Luke 12:1
Matt 15:32–39		

S14:M55–57	AT CAESAREA PHILIPPI	**16:13–28**

M55	PETER'S CONFESSION	**16:13–20**
Matt 18:18	Mark 8:27–30	Luke 9:18–22
John 1:49	GThom 13	GNaz 14
John 6:68–69		
John 20:22–23		

M56	JESUS PREDICTS HIS DEATH AND RESURRECTION	**16:21–23**
Matt 17:22–23	Mark 8:31–33	Luke 9:18–22
Matt 20:17–19	Mark 9:30–32	Luke 9:43b–45
	Mark 10:32–34	Luke 18:31–34
		ApocJa 5:31–6:11

M57	THE WAY OF THE CROSS	**16:24–28**
Matt 10:38–39	Mark 8:34–9:1	Luke 9:23–27
John 12:25	GThom 55	Luke 14:27
	GThom 101	Luke 17:33

S15:M58–61	ON THE MOUNTAIN	**17:1–27**

M58	JESUS IS TRANSFIGURED	**17:1–13**

M58.1	JESUS IS TRANSFIGURED	**17:1–8**
Matt 3:16–17	Mark 9:2–8	Luke 9:28–36
Ps 2:7	Mark 1:10–11	Luke 3:22
Isa 42:1		

M58.2	ELIJAH MUST COME FIRST	**17:9–13**
Mal 4:5–6	Mark 9:9–13	
1 Kgs 19:1–3, 9–10	GThom 51	

M59	JESUS EXORICISES A DEMON	**17:14–20**

M59.1	HEALING OF A BOY	**17:14–18**
M59.2	EXPLANATION OF DISCIPLES' FAILURE	**17:19–20**

Matt 21:21	Mark 9:14–27	Luke 9:37–43a
Matt 18:19	Mark 9:28–29	Luke 17:6
	Mark 11:22–23	
	GThom 48	
	GThom 106	

M60	JESUS PREDICTS HIS PASSION AGAIN	**17:22–23**

Matt 16:21–23	Mark 9:30–32	Luke 9:43b–45
Matt 20:17–19	Mark 8:31–33	Luke 9:18–22
	Mark 10:32–34	Luke 18:31–34

M61	DOES JESUS PAY THE TEMPLE TAX?	**17:24–27**

Exod 30:13

S16:M62–63	JESUS TEACHES THE DISCIPLES	**18:1–35**

M62	THE LITTLE ONES	**18:1–14**

M62.1	THE LITTLE ONES	**18:1–10**

Matt 5:29–30	Mark 9:33–37	Luke 9:46–50
Matt 23:12	Mark 9:42–50	Luke 18:15–17
Matt 10:40	Mark 10:13–16	Luke 10:16
John 3:3–5	GThom 12	Luke 17:1–4
	GThom 22	

M62.2	THE PARABLE OF THE LOST SHEEP	**18:12–14**

	GThom 107	Luke 15:3–7

M63	DISCIPLINE AND FORGIVENESS	**18:15–35**

M63.1	DISCIPLINE AND FORGIVENESS	**18:15–22**

Matt 16:19	POxy1 5	Luke 17:1–4
Deut 19:15	GThom 30	GNaz 15
John 20:23	GThom 77	

M63.2	PARABLE OF THE UNFORGIVING SERVANT	**18:23–35**

Matt 6:14–15

S17:M64–70	JOURNEY TO JERUSALEM	**19:1–20:34**

M64	DEPARTURE FROM GALILEE	**19:1–2**

Mark 10:1

M65	QUESTIONS OF MARRIAGE AND DIVORCE	**19:3–12**

M65.1	LAW OF DIVORCE	**19:3–9**

Matt 5:31–32	Mark 10:2–9	Luke 16:18
Gen 1:27	Mark 10:10–12	1 Cor 7:10–11
Gen 2:24		
Deut 24:1		

M65.2	CELIBACY	**19:10–12**

GThom 22	2 Clem 12:1–6	
	GEgy 1–6	

M66	JESUS BLESSES THE CHILDREN	**19:13–15**

	Mark 10:13–16	Luke 18:15–17
	GThom 22	

M67	ON RICHES	**19:16–20:16**

M67.1	RICH YOUNG MAN	**19:16–22**

Matt 20:16	Mark 10:17–22	Luke 18:18–25
Deut 5:16–20		GNaz 16
Lev 19:18		

M67.2	DANGER OF RICHES	**19:23–30**

	Mark 10:23–31	Luke 18:18–25
	GThom 25	Luke 22:26–30
	POxy654 4	Luke 22:28–30
	GThom 4	Luke 13:30
	GThom 81	GNaz 16
		ApocJa 4:22–37

M67.3	PARABLE OF THE LABORERS IN THE VINEYARD	**20:1–16**

Matt 19:30	Mark 10:31	Luke 13:30
	POxy654 4	
	GThom 4	

M68	THIRD PREDICTION OF THE PASSION	**20:17–29**

Matt 16:21–23	Mark 10:32–34	Luke 18:31–34
Matt 17:22–23	Mark 8:31–33	Luke 9:18–22
	Mark 9:30–32	Luke 9:43b–45

M69	THE MOTHER OF THE SONS OF ZEBEDEE	**20:20–28**

M69.1	REQUEST FOR POSITIONS OF HONOR	**20:20–23**
M69.2	THE TEN DISCIPLES ARE INDIGNANT	**20:24–28**

Matt 23:11–12	Mark 10:35–40	Luke 22:24–27
Matt 18:1–4	Mark 10:41–45	Luke 9:46–50
	Mark 9:33–37	

M70	JESUS HEALS TWO BLIND MEN	**20:29–34**

Matt 9:27–31	Mark 10:46–52	Luke 18:35–43

S18:M71–76	IN JERUSALEM	**21:1–22:46**

M71	ENTRY INTO JERUSALEM	**21:1–11**

M71.1	TWO SENT FOR COLT	**21:1–6**
M71.2	TRIUMPHAL ENTRY	**21:7–9**
M71.3	RECOGNIZED AS PROPHET	**21:10–11**

Zech 9:9	Mark 11:1–3	Luke 19:28–32
Ps 118:26	Mark 11:4–6	Luke 19:33–34
John 12:12–19	Mark 11:7–10	Luke 19:35–40
	Mark 11:11	

M72	IN THE TEMPLE	**21:12–17**

M72.1	CLEANSING OF THE TEMPLE	**21:12–13**
M72.2	CHILDREN PRAISE JESUS	**21:14–17**

Isa 56:7	Mark 11:15–19	Luke 19:45–48
Jer 7:11		
Ps 8:1–2		
John 2:13–22		

M73	JESUS CURSES A FIG TREE	**21:18–22**

Matt 17:19–20	Mark 11:12–14	Luke 13:6–9
Matt 18:19	Mark 11:20–25	Luke 17:5–6
John 14:13–14	GThom 48	InThom 3:1–3
John 15:7	GThom 106	InThom 4:1–2
John 16:23		

M74	CONTROVERSIES	**21:23–26**

M74.1	QUESTION OF JESUS' AUTHORITY	**21:23–27**

John 2:18	Mark 11:27–33	Luke 20:1–8
		POxy840 2

M74.2	PARABLE OF THE TWO SONS	**21:28–32**

		Luke 7:29–30

M74.3	PARABLE OF THE WICKED TENANTS	**21:33–46**

Isa 5:1–2	Mark 12:1–12	Luke 20:9–19
Ps 118:22–23	GThom 65	
	GThom 66	

M75	PARABLE OF THE ROYAL MARRIAGE FEAST	**22:1–14**

Matt 8:12	GThom 64	Luke 14:15–24
Matt 13:42	GThom 23	
Matt 13:50		
Matt 24:51		
Matt 25:30		

M76	QUESTIONS ADDRESSED TO JESUS	**22:15–46**

M76.1	IS IT LAWFUL TO PAY TAXES?	**22:15–22**

John 3:2	Mark 12:13–17	Luke 20:20–26
	GThom 100	PEger2 3
		Rom 13:7

M76.2	WHOSE WIFE WILL SHE BE?	**22:23–33**

Matt 7:28–29	Mark 12:18–27	Luke 20:27–40
Matt 13:54		1 Cor 15:12
Gen 38:3		
Deut 25:5–6		
Exod 3:6		

M76.3	WHICH IS THE GREATEST COMMANDMENT?	**22:34–40**

Deut 6:5	Mark 12:28–34	Luke 10:25–29
Lev 19:18	GThom 25	Rom 13:8–10
		Gal 5:13–15
		Did 1:2
		Barn 19:5

M76.4	WHOSE SON IS THE CHRIST?	**22:41–46**

2 Sam 7:12–16	Mark 12:35–37	Luke 20:41–44
Mic 5:2	Mark 12:34	Luke 20:40
Ps 89:3–4		1 Cor 15:20–28
Ps 110:1		
John 7:40–44		

S19:M77–79	DISOURSE ON JUDGMENT	**23:1–25:46**

M77	JUDGMENT ON ISRAEL	**23:1–39**

M77.1	DENUNCIATION OF THE SCRIBES AND PHARISEES	**23:1–12**

Matt 18:1–5	Mark 12:38–40	Luke 20:45–47
Matt 20:24–28	Mark 9:33–37	Luke 9:46–50
Num 15:37–39	Mark 10:41–45	Luke 22:24–30
		Luke 14:11
		Luke 18:14

M77.2	SEVEN WOES AGAINST SCRIBES AND PHARISEES	**23:13–36**

Matt 3:7	POxy655 2	Luke 11:37–44
Gen 4:8	GThom 39	Luke 11:45–54
2 Chr 24:20–21	GThom 102	Luke 3:7
Zech 1:1	GThom 89	POxy840 2
		GNaz 17
		PJas 24:1–4

M77.3	LAMENTATION OVER JERUSALEM	**23:37–39**

Isa 31:5		Luke 13:34–35
Ps 118:26		

M78	APOCALYPTIC DISCOURSE	**24:1–51**

M78.1	JESUS PREDICTS THE DESTRUCTION OF THE TEMPLE	**24:1–2**

	Mark 13:1–2	Luke 21:5–6

M78.2	SIGNS OF THE END	**24:3–14**

Matt 10:22	Mark 13:3–13	Luke 21:5–19
Matt 24:23–26	Mark 13:21–23	Luke 17:23
Matt 10:18		
John 15:18–21		

M78.3	TRIBULATION BEFORE THE END	**24:15–28**

Matt 24:5	Mark 13:14–23	Luke 21:20–24
Dan 9:27	GThom 79	Luke 17:31
Dan 11:31	GThom 113	
Dan 12:11		
1 Macc 1:54		
Dan 12:1		
Deut 13:1–3		

M78.4	Coming of the Son of Man	24:29–36
Matt 26:64	Mark 13:24–32	Luke 21:25–33
Matt 16:28	Mark 9:1	Luke 9:27
Isa 13:10		Rev 1:7
Isa 34:4		1 Thess 4:15–16
Dan 7:13–14		
Deut 30:3–4		

M78.5	The Need for Watchfulness	24:37–51
Matt 8:12	Mark 13:33–37	Luke 21:34–36
Matt 13:42	GThom 21	Luke 17:26–36
Matt 13:50	GThom 103	Luke 12:39–40
Matt 22:13		Luke 12:42–46
Matt 25:30		1 Thess 5:2
Gen 7:6–10		Rev 16:15
		GNaz 18

M79	Parables of the End	25:1–46

M79.1	The Wise and Foolish Maidens	25:1–13
	Mark 13:35–37	Luke 12:35–36
		Luke 13:25
		Did 16:1

M79.2	Parable of the Talents	25:14–30
Matt 13:10–12	Mark 4:24–25	Luke 19:11–27
Matt 8:12	GThom 41	Luke 8:18
Matt 13:42		Luke 13:28
Matt 13:50		GNaz 18
Matt 22:13		
Matt 24:51		

M79.3	Last Judgment	25:31–46
Dan 12:2		Justin, *Dialogue* 76.5
John 5:28–29		

S20:M80–87	The Passion Narrative	26:1–27:66

M80	Introduction	26:1–16

M80.1	Introduction to the Passion	26:1–2
M80.2	Leaders Plot against Jesus	26:3–5
Matt 21:45	Mark 14:1–2	Luke 22:1–2
John 11:45–53	Mark 11:18	Luke 19:47–48
John 11:54	Mark 12:12	Luke 20:19
John 11:55–57		

M80.3	A Woman Anoints Jesus	26:6–13
John 12:1–8	Mark 14:3–9	Luke 7:36–50

M80.4	Judas Makes a Deal	26:14–16
Zech 11:12	Mark 14:10–11	Luke 22:3–6

M81	The Passover Meal	26:17–29
M81.1	Preparations	26:17–19
M81.2	Jesus Foretells His Betrayal	26:20–25
M81.3	The Last Supper	26:26–29
Exod 24:8	Mark 14:12–16	Luke 22:7–13
Jer 31:31	Mark 14:17–21	Luke 22:14–23
Zech 9:1	Mark 14:22–25	1 Cor 11:23–25
John 13:21–30		Did 9:1–5
John 6:48–58		Justin, *Apology* 1.66.3
		GEbi 7

M82	Events in Gethsemane	26:30–56

M82.1	Jesus Predicts Peter's Denial	26:30–35
Zech 13:7	Mark 14:26–31	Luke 22:31–34
John 13:36–38		Luke 22:39
John 18:1		Fayyum Fragment
John 16:32		
John 11:16		

M82.2	The Prayers of Jesus	26:36–46
M82.2a	Introduction	26:36
M82.2b	Jesus Takes Three	26:37–38
M82.2c	First Prayer	26:39
M82.2d	The Three Sleep	26:40–41
M82.2e	Second Prayer	26:42
M82.2f	The Three Sleep	26:43
M82.2g	Third Prayer	26:44
M82.2h	The Hour Has Come	26:45–46
John 18:1	Mark 14:32	Luke 22:39
John 12:27	Mark 14:33–34	Luke 22:40–42
John 18:11	Mark 14:35–36	Luke 22:45–46
John 14:31	Mark 14:37–38	
	Mark 14:39	
	Mark 14:40	
	Mark 14:41–42	

M82.3	The Arrest	26:47–56
John 18:1–12	Mark 14:43–52	Luke 22:47–54a
John 18:20		

M83	Before the Council; Peter's Denial	26:57–75
M83.1	Introduction	26:57–58
M83.2	Trial before the Council	26:59–68
Matt 24:30	Mark 14:53–54	Luke 22:54b–62
Ps 110:1	Mark 14:55–65	Luke 22:63–65
Dan 7:13–14	Mark 13:26	Luke 22:66–71
Lev 24:16	GThom 71	Luke 21:27
John 18:13–14		GPet 3.9
John 18:19–24		
John 2:19		

M83.3	PETER'S DENIAL	**26:69–75**
M83.3a	FIRST DENIAL	**26:69–70**
M8c.3b	SECOND DENIAL	**26:71–72**
M8c.3c	THIRD DENIAL	**26:73–75**

John 18:15–18	Mark 14:66–72	Luke 22:54b–62
John 18:25–27		GNaz 19

M84	BEFORE PILATE	**27:1–26**

M84.1	INTRODUCTION	**27:1–2**
John 18:28	Mark 15:1	Luke 23:1

M84.2	JUDAS REPENTS	**27:3–10**
Zech 11:12–13		Acts 1:15–20

M84.3	PILATE INTERROGATES JESUS	**27:11–14**
M84.4	PILATE CONDEMNS JESUS	**27:15–26**

John 18:29–19:16	Mark 15:2–5	Luke 23:1–7
		Luke 23:13–25
		AcPil 2:1
		AcPil 3:2
		AcPil 4:4–5
		AcPil 9:4–5
		GNaz 20
		GPet 1.1–2

M85	THE CRUCIFIXION	**27:27–56**

M85.1	THE MOCKING	**27:27–31**
John 19:1–3	Mark 15:16–20	GPet 2.5b–3.9
		AcPil 10:1a

M85.2	SIMON OF CYRENE	**27:32**
	Mark 15:21	Luke 23:26–32

M85.3	THE CRUCIFIXION	**27:33–44**
Ps 69:21	Mark 15:22–32	Luke 23:33–43
Ps 22:18	GThom 71	GPet 4.10–14
Ps 22:7		AcPil 10:1b–2
Ps 22:8		
John 19:17–24		
John 2:19		

M85.4	THE DEATH	**27:45–56**
Ps 22:1	Mark 15:33–41	Luke 23:44–49
Ps 69:21		Luke 23:36
Ps 38:11		Luke 8:1–3
John 19:25–37		Luke 23:55
		GPet 5.15–20
		AcPil 11:1–3a
		GNaz 21
		GNaz 36

M86	THE BURIAL	**27:57–61**
Josh 10:18	Mark 15:42–47	Luke 23:50–56
Josh 10:27		GPet 2.3–5a
Deut 21:22–23		GPet 6.21–24
John 19:38–42		AcPil 11:3b

M87	THE GUARD AT THE TOMB	**27:62–66**
		GPet 8.28–9.34
		GNaz 22

S21:M88	THE RESURRECTION	**28:1–20**

M88	THE RESURRECTION	**28:1–20**
M88.1	TWO WOMEN DISCOVER THE EMPTY TOMB	**28:1–8**
M88.2	JESUS MEETS THE TWO WOMEN	**28:9–10**
M88.3	THE GUARD IS BRIBED	**28:11–15**

John 20:1–18	Mark 16:1–8	Luke 24:1–12
		GPet 9.35–13.57
		AcPil 13:1–3

M88.4 JESUS COMMISSIONS THE DISCIPLES IN GALILEE **28:16–20**

	GPet 14.58–60
	AcPil 14:1

MATT

MARK

LUKE

Matt 1:1–17 (§M1)

[1] The book of the genealogy of Jesus Christ, the son of David, the son of Abraham.

[2] Abraham was the father of Isaac, and Isaac the father of Jacob, and Jacob the father of Judah and his brothers, [3] and Judah the father of Perez and Zerah by Tamar, and Perez the father of Hezron, and Hezron the father of Ram,[a] [4] and Ram the father of Amminadab, and Amminadab the father of Nahshon, and Nahshon the father of Salmon, [5] and Salmon the father of Boaz by Rahab, and Boaz the father of Obed by Ruth, and Obed the father of Jesse, [6] and Jesse the father of David the king.

And David was the father of Solomon by the wife of Uriah, [7] and Solomon the father of Rehoboam, and Rehoboam the father of Abijah, and Abijah the father of Asa,[b] [8] and Asa[b] the father of Jehoshaphat, and Jehoshaphat the father of Joram, and Joram the father of Uzziah, [9] and Uzziah the father of Jotham, and Jotham the father of Ahaz, and Ahaz the father of Hezekiah, [10] and Hezekiah the father of Manasseh, and Manasseh the father of Amos,[c] and Amos[c] the father of Josiah, [11] and Josiah the father of Jechoniah and his brothers, at the time of the deportation to Babylon.

[12] And after the deportation to Babylon: Jechoniah was the father of Shealtiel, and Shealtiel[d] the father of Zerubbabel, [13] and Zerubbabel the father of Abiud, and Abiud the father of Eliakim, and Eliakim the father of Azor, [14] and Azor the father of Zadok, and Zadok the father of Achim, and Achim the father of Eliud, [15] and Eliud the father of Eleazar, and Eleazar the father of Matthan, and Matthan the father of Jacob, [16] and Jacob the father of Joseph the husband of Mary, of whom Jesus was born, who is called Christ.[e]

[17] So all the generations from Abraham to David were fourteen generations, and from David to the deportation to Babylon fourteen generations, and from the deportation to Babylon to the Christ fourteen generations.

[a] Greek: *Aram*

[b] Greek: *Asaph*

[c] *Amos:* ℵ B C Δ Θ Π* *f*¹ 33 *al; Amon:* L W *f*¹³ *pm*

[d] Greek: *Salathiel*

[e] Text: 𝔓¹ ℵ B C K L P W Δ Π *f*¹ 28 33 *al; Joseph, to whom being betrothed the virgin Mary bore Jesus, who is called Christ:* Θ *f*¹³ it (in part); *Joseph, to whom was betrothed Mary the virgin, begot Jesus, who is called the Christ:* syr^c.

Luke 3:23–38 (§L9)

[23] Jesus, when he began his ministry, was about thirty years of age, being the son (as was supposed) **of Joseph,** the son of Heli, [24] the son of Matthat, the son of Levi, the son of Melchi, the son of Jannai, the son of Joseph, [25] the son of Mattathias, the son of Amos, the son of Nahum, the son of Esli, the son of Naggai, [26] the son of Maath, the son of Mattathias, the son of Semein, the son of Josech, the son of Joda, [27] the son of Joanan, the son of Rhesa, the son **of Zerubbabel,** the son of **Shealtiel,** the son of Neri, [28] the son of Melchi, the son of Addi, the son of Cosam, the son of Elmadam, the son of Er, [29] the son of Joshua, the son of Eliezer, the son of Jorim, the son of Matthat, the son of Levi, [30] the son of Simeon, the son of Judah, the son of Joseph, the son of Jonam, the son of Eliakim, [31] the son of Melea, the son of Menna, the son of Mattatha, the son of Nathan, the son **of David,** [32] the son **of Jesse,** the son **of Obed,** the son **of Boaz,** the son of Sala, the son **of Nahshon,** [33] the son **of Amminadab,** the son of Admin, the son of Arni, the son **of Hezron,** the son **of Perez,** the son **of Judah,** [34] the son **of Jacob,** the son **of Isaac, the son of Abraham,** the son of Terah, the son of Nahor, [35] the son of Serug, the son of Reu, the son of Peleg, the son of Eber, the son of Shelah, [36] the son of Cainan, the son of Arphaxad, the son of Shem, the son of Noah, the son of Lamech, [37] the son of Methuselah, the son of Enoch, the son of Jared, the son of Mahaleleel, the son of Cainan, [38] the son of Enos, the son of Seth, the son of Adam, the son of God.

⇨ Matt 1:2–6
Cf. 1 Chr 2:1–15

⇨ Matt 1:3–6
Cf. Ruth 4:18–22

⇨ Matt 1:7–12
Cf. 1 Chr 3:10–19

JOHN

THOMAS

OTHER

MATT

MARK

LUKE

Matt 1:18–25 (§M2)

[18] Now the birth of Jesus Christ[a] took place in this way. When his mother Mary had been betrothed to Joseph, before they came together she was found to be with child of the Holy Spirit; [19] and her husband Joseph, being a just man and unwilling to put her to shame, resolved to divorce her quietly. [20] But as he considered this, behold, an angel of the Lord appeared to him in a dream, saying, "Joseph, son of David, do not fear to take Mary your wife, for that which is conceived in her is of the Holy Spirit; [21] she will bear a son, and you shall call his name Jesus, for he will save his people from their sins." [22] All this took place to fulfil what the Lord had spoken by the prophet: [23] "Behold, a virgin shall conceive and bear a son, and his name shall be called Emmanuel" (which means, God with us). [24] When Joseph woke from sleep, he did as the angel of the Lord commanded him; he took his wife, [25] but knew her not until she had borne a son;[b] and he called his name Jesus.

[a] Text: 𝔓1 ℵ C K L P Δ Θ Π *f*1 *f*13 28 33 *pm; Christ* it (in part) vg syr[c] syr[s]

[b] Text: ℵ B *f*1 *f*13 33 it (in part) *pc; her firstborn son* (from Luke 2:7) C D* K W Δ Π

Isa 7:14 ⇨ Matt 1:23
[14] Therefore the Lord himself will give you a sign. Behold, a young woman **shall conceive and bear a son, and he shall** call **his name Immanuel.**

⇨ Matt 1:23
Cf. Isa 8:8, 10 (LXX)

† Luke 2:1–7 (§L4.1)

[1] In those days a decree went out from Caesar Augustus that all the world should be enrolled. [2] This was the first enrollment, when Quirinius was governor of Syria. [3] And all went to be enrolled, each to his own city. [4] And **Joseph** also went up from Galilee, from the city of Nazareth, to Judea, to the city of David, which is called Bethlehem, because he was of the house and lineage **of David,** [5] to be enrolled with **Mary,** his **betrothed,** who was **with child.** [6] And while they were there, the time came for her to be delivered. [7] And she gave birth to her first-born **son** and wrapped him in swaddling cloths, and laid him in a manger, because there was no place for them in the inn.

JOHN

THOMAS

OTHER

PJas 14:1–2

[1] *And* **Joseph** *feared greatly and parted from her, pondering what he should do with her. And* **Joseph** *said: "If I conceal her sin, I shall be found opposing the law of the Lord. If I expose her to the children of Israel, I fear lest that which is in her may have sprung from the angels and I should be found delivering up innocent blood to the judgment of death. What then shall I do with her? I will* **put her away** *secretly." And the night came upon him.* [2] *And behold, an angel of the Lord appeared to him in a dream, saying:* **"Do not fear because of this child. For that which is** *in* **her is of the Holy Spirit. She shall bear a son, and you shall call his name Jesus; for he shall save his people from their sins."** *And* **Joseph** *arose from sleep and glorified the God of Israel who had bestowed his grace upon him, and he watched over her.*

63 BCE	Pompey enters Jerusalem temple
63–40	Hyrcanus high priest, later ethnarch
40–38	Antigonus high priest and king
38–4	Herod the Great

	JUDEA		GALILEE
4 BCE–6 CE	Archelaus	4 BCE–39 CE	Antipas tetrarch
6–41 CE	Prefects:		
6–9	Coponius		
9–12	Ambibulus		
12–15	Annius Rufus		
15–26	Valerius Gratus		
26–36	Pontius Pilatus		
36–37	Marcellus	39–41	Agrippa I

	PALESTINE
41–44	Agrippa I king
44–66	Procurators:
44–46	Fadus
46–48	Tiberius Alexander
48–52	Cumanus
53–58	Felix
58–62	Festus
62–64	Albinus
64–66	Gessius Florus
66–70(73)	Jewish War

Source: Koester 1: 392

MATT	MARK	LUKE

MATT

INTRODUCTION

Matt 2:1–6 (§M3.1)

[1] Now when Jesus was born in Bethlehem of Judea in the days of Herod the king, behold, wise men from the East came to Jerusalem, saying, [2] "Where is he who has been born king of the Jews? For we have seen his star in the East, and have come to worship him." [3] When Herod the king heard this, he was troubled, and all Jerusalem with him; [4] and assembling all the chief priests and scribes of the people, he inquired of them where the Christ was to be born. [5] They told him, "In Bethlehem of Judea; for so it is written by the prophet:

[6] 'And you, O Bethlehem, in the land of Judah,

are by no means least among the rulers of Judah;

for from you shall come a ruler

who will govern my people Israel.'"

SUMMONS OF HEROD

Matt 2:7–9a (§M3.2)

[7] Then Herod summoned the wise men secretly and ascertained from them what time the star appeared; [8] and he sent them to Bethlehem, saying, "Go and search diligently for the child, and when you have found him bring me word, that I too may come and worship him." [9] When they had heard the king they went their way; . . .

VISIT TO THE CHRIST CHILD

Matt 2:9b–12 (§M3.3)

. . . and lo, the star which they had seen in the East went before them, till it came to rest over the place where the child was. [10] When they saw the star, they rejoiced exceedingly with great joy; [11] and going into the house they saw the child with Mary his mother, and they fell down and worshiped him. Then, opening their treasures, they offered him gifts, gold and frankincense and myrrh. [12] And being warned in a dream not to return to Herod, they departed to their own country by another way.

2 Sam 5:2 ⇨ Matt 2:6

[2] "In times past, when Saul was king over us, it was you that led out and brought in Israel; and the Lord said to you, 'You shall be shepherd of my people over Israel.'"

⇨ Matt 2:6
Cf. 2 Sam 7:12–13; Ps 89:3–4

MARK

Mic 5:2 ⇨ Matt 2:6

[2] But you, **O Bethlehem** Ephrathah,
　who are little to be among the clans **of Judah,**
from you shall come forth for me
　one who is to be **ruler** in **Israel**,
whose origin is from of old,
　from ancient days.

Ps 72:10–11 ⇨ Matt 2:11

[10] May the kings of Tarshish and of the isles
　render him tribute,
may the kings of Sheba and Seba
　bring gifts! [11] My all kings fall **down** before **him**,
　all nations serve **him!**

Isa 60:6 ⇨ Matt 2:11

[6] A multitude of camels shall cover you,
　the young camels of Midian and Ephah;
all those from Sheba shall come.
They shall bring **gold and frankincense**,
　and shall proclaim the praise of the Lord.

LUKE

† Luke 2:8–14 (§L4.2a)

[8] And in that region there were shepherds out in the field, keeping watch over their flock by night. [9] And an angel of the Lord appeared to them, and the glory of the Lord shone around them, and they were filled with fear. [10] And the angel said to them, "Be not afraid; for behold, I bring you good news of a great joy which will come to all the people; [11] for to you is **born** this day in the city of David a Savior, who is Christ the Lord. [12] And this will be a sign for you: you will find a babe wrapped in swaddling cloths and lying in a manger." [13] And suddenly there was with the angel a multitude of the heavenly host praising God and saying,

[14] "Glory to God in the highest,

and on earth peace among men with whom he is pleased!"

† Luke 2:15–20 (§L4.2b)

[15] When the angels went away from them into heaven, the shepherds said to one another, "Let us go over to **Bethlehem** and see this thing that has happened, which the Lord has made known to us." [16] And **they** went with haste, and found **Mary**, and Joseph, and the babe lying in a manger. [17] And when **they** saw it they made known the saying which had been told them concerning this **child**; [18] and all who heard it wondered at what the shepherds told them. [19] But Mary kept all these things, pondering them in her heart. [20] And the shepherds returned, glorifying and praising God for all they had heard and seen, as it had been told them.

JOHN	THOMAS	OTHER

John 7:40–44

[40] When they heard these words, some of the people said, "This is really *the prophet*." [41] Others said, "This is *the Christ*." But some said, "Is *the Christ* to come from Galilee? [42] Has not the scripture said that *the Christ* is descended from David, and comes from *Bethlehem*, the village where David was?" [43] So there was a division among the people over him. [44] Some of them wanted to arrest him, but no one laid hands on him.

PJas 21:1–4

[1] And behold, Joseph prepared to go forth to Judaea. And there took place a great tumult in Bethlehem of Judaea. For there came wise men saying: "Where is the [new-born] king of the Jews? For we have seen his star in the east and have come to worship him." [2] When Herod heard this he was troubled and sent officers [to the wise men], and sent for them and they told him about the star. [3] And behold, they saw stars [a star] in the east, and they [it] went before them, until they came to the cave. And it stood over the head of the child [the cave]. And the wise men saw the young child with Mary his mother, and they took out of their bag gifts, gold, and frankincense and myrrh. [4] And being warned by the angel that they should not go into Judaea, they went to their own country by another way.

GNaz 28

(28) For thus the Gospel which is entitled "According to the Hebrews" reports:

When Joseph looked out with his eyes, he saw a crowd of pilgrims who were coming in company to the cave, and he said: I will arise and go out to meet them. And when Joseph went out, he said to Simon: It seems to me as if those coming were soothsayers, for lo, every moment they look up to heaven and confer one with another. But they seem also to be strangers, for their appearance differs from ours; for their dress is very rich and their complexion quite dark; they have caps on their heads and their garments seem to me to be silky, and they have breeches on their legs. And lo, they have halted and are looking at me, and lo, they have again set themselves in motion and are coming here.

From these words it is clear that not merely three men, but a crowd of pilgrims came to the Lord, even if according to some the formemost leaders of this crowd were named with definite names Melchus, Caspar, and Phadizarda. (Sedulius Scotus, *Commentary on Matthew*, cited by Bischoff in *Sacris Erudiri* 6, 1954 p. 203f.)

MATT   MARK   LUKE

FLIGHT INTO EGYPT

Matt 2:13–15 (§M4.1)

[13] Now when they had departed, behold, an angel of the Lord appeared to Joseph in a dream and said, "Rise, take the child and his mother, and flee to Egypt, and remain there till I tell you; for Herod is about to search for the child, to destroy him." [14] And he rose and took the child and his mother by night, and departed to Egypt, [15] and remained there until the death of Herod. This was to fulfil what the Lord had spoken by the prophet, "Out of Egypt have I called my son."

MASSACRE OF THE BABIES

Matt 2:16–18 (§M4.2)

[16] Then Herod, when he saw that he had been tricked by the wise men, was in a furious rage, and he sent and killed all the male children in Bethlehem and in all that region who were two years old or under, according to the time which he had ascertained from the wise men. [17] Then was fulfilled what was spoken by the prophet Jeremiah:

[18] "A voice was heard in Ramah,
wailing and loud lamentation,
Rachel weeping for her children;
she refused to be consoled,
because they were no more."

RETURN TO NAZARETH

Matt 2:19–23 (§M4.3)

[19] But when Herod died, behold, an angel of the Lord appeared in a dream to Joseph in Egypt, saying, [20] "Rise, take the child and his mother, and go to the land of Israel, for those who sought the child's life are dead." [21] And he rose and took the child and his mother, and went to the land of Israel. [22] But when he heard that Archelaus reigned over Judea in place of his father Herod, he was afraid to go there, and being warned in a dream he withdrew to the district of Galilee. [23] And he went and dwelt in a city called Nazareth, that what was spoken by the prophets might be fulfilled, "He shall be called a Nazarene."

Hos 11:1 ⇨ Matt 2:15
[1] When Israel was a child, I loved him,
   and **out of Egypt I called my son.**

Jer 31:15 ⇨ Matt 2:18
[15] Thus says the Lord:
"**A voice** is **heard in Ramah,**
   lamentation and bitter weeping.
Rachel is **weeping for her children;**
   she refuses to be comforted for her children,
   because they are not."

Judg 13:5 ⇨ Matt 2:23
[5] "for lo, you shall conceive and bear a son. No razor shall come upon his head, for the boy **shall be a** Nazirite to God from birth; and **he shall** begin to deliver Israel from the hand of the Philistines."

† Luke 2:39–40 (§L5.4)

[39] And **when they had** performed everything according to the law **of the Lord,** they returned into **Galilee,** to their own **city, Nazareth.** [40] And **the child** grew and became strong, filled with wisdom; and the favor of God was upon him.

JOHN	THOMAS	OTHER
		PCairo 1–2 ⇨ Matt 2:13

OTHER

PCairo 1–2 ⇨ Matt 2:13

(1) The angel of the Lord spake: Jo[seph, arise,] take Mary, thy w[ife and] flee to Egypt [. .] [. .] [. .] every gift and if [. . .] his friends . . .[. . .] of the king . . .[. . .] [. . .]

(2) [. . .] should interpret to thee. The [archistrategus however] said to the virgin: Behold, [Elisabeth, thy relat]ive has also con[ceived, and it is the s]ixth month for her who [was called barren. In] the sixth, that is [in the month Thoth, did his mother] conceive John. [But it behoved] the archistra[tegus to an]nounce [beforehand John, the] servant who go[es before his Lord's] coming . . .

GNaz 1 ⇨ Matt 2:15, 23

(1) To these (citations in which Matthew follows not the Septuagint but the Hebrew original text) belong the two: "Out of Egypt have I called my son" and "For he shall be called a Nazaraean." (Jerome, *De viris inlustribus* 3)

PJas 22:1–2 ⇨ Matt 2:16

[1] *But when* **Herod** *perceived that he had been tricked by the wise men he was angry and sent his murderers and commanded them to kill all the children who were two years old and under.* [2] *When Mary heard that the children were to be killed, she was afraid and took the child and wrapped him in swaddling clothes and laid him in an ox-manger.*

MATT

Matt 3:1–12 (§M5) °

[1] In those days came John the Baptist, preaching in the wilderness of Judea, [2] "Repent, for the kingdom of heaven is at hand." [3] For this is he who was spoken of by the prophet Isaiah when he said,

"The voice of one crying in the wilderness:

Prepare the way of the Lord,
make his paths straight."

[4] Now John wore a garment of camel's hair, and a leather girdle around his waist; and his food was locusts and wild honey. [5] Then went out to him Jerusalem and all Judea and all the region about the Jordan, [6] and they were baptized by him in the river Jordan, confessing their sins.

[7] But when he saw many of the Pharisees and Sadducees coming for baptism, he said to them, "You brood of vipers! Who warned you to flee from the wrath to come? [8] Bear fruit that befits repentance, [9] and do not presume to say to yourselves, 'We have Abraham as our father'; for I tell you, God is able from these stones to raise up children to Abraham. [10] Even now the axe is laid to the root of the trees; every tree therefore that does not bear good fruit is cut down and thrown into the fire."

[11] "I baptize you with water for repentance, but he who is coming after me is mightier than I, whose sandals I am not worthy to carry; he will baptize you with the Holy Spirit and with fire. [12] His winnowing fork is in his hand, and he will clear his threshing floor and gather his wheat into the granary, but the chaff he will burn with unquenchable fire."

°Appendix 1 ⇨ §M5

Matt 7:19 ⇨ Matt 3:10
[19] Every tree that does not bear good fruit is cut down and thrown into the fire.

Isa 40:3 ⇨ Matt 3:3
[3] A **voice** cries:
"**In the wilderness prepare the way of the Lord,**
make **straight** in the desert a highway for our God.

2 Kgs 1:8 ⇨ Matt 3:4
[8] They answered him, "He **wore a garment of** hair-cloth, with **a girdle of leather** about **his** loins." And he said, "It is Elijah the Tishbite."

MARK

Mark 1:2–8 (§K2)

[2] As it is written in **Isaiah the prophet,**
"Behold, I send my messenger before thy face,
who shall **prepare** thy **way;**
[3] the voice of one crying in the wilderness:
Prepare the way of the Lord,
make his paths straight—"

[4] John the baptizer appeared **in the wilderness, preaching** a baptism of **repentance** for the forgiveness of **sins.** [5] And there went out to him all the country of **Judea,** and all the people of **Jerusalem;** and **they were baptized by** him in the river Jordan, confessing their sins. [6] Now John was clothed in **camel's hair, and had a leather girdle around his waist,** and ate **locusts and wild honey.** [7] And he preached, saying, "**After me comes he who is mightier than I,** the thong of **whose sandals I am not worthy to** stoop down and untie. [8] I have baptized **you with water;** but **he will baptize you with the Holy Spirit."**

Mark 1:15 ⇨ Matt 3:2
[15] and saying, "The time is fulfilled, and **the kingdom** of God **is at hand; repent,** and believe in the gospel."

LUKE

Luke 3:1–20 (§L7)

[1] In the fifteenth year of the reign of Tiberius Caesar, Pontius Pilate being governor of Judea, and Herod being tetrarch of Galilee, and his brother Philip tetrarch of the region of Ituraea and Trachonitis, and Lysanias tetrarch of Abilene, [2] in the high-priesthood of Annas and Caiaphas, the word of God **came** to **John** the son of Zechariah **in the wilderness;** [3] and he went into **all the region about the Jordan,** preaching a baptism of **repentance** for the forgiveness of **sins.** [4] As it is written in the book of the words of **Isaiah the prophet,**

"**The voice of one crying in the wilderness:
Prepare the way of the Lord,
make his paths straight.**
[5] Every valley shall be filled,
and every mountain and hill shall be brought low,
and the crooked shall be made straight,
and the rough ways shall be made smooth;
[6] and all flesh shall see the salvation of God."

[7] **He said** therefore to the multitudes that came out to be baptized by him, "**You brood of vipers! Who warned you to flee from the wrath to come?** [8] Bear **fruits that befit repentance,** and do not begin to **say to yourselves, 'We have Abraham as our father'; for I tell you, God is able from these stones to raise up children to Abraham.** [9] Even now the axe is laid to the root of the trees; every tree therefore that **does not bear good fruit is cut down and thrown into the fire."**

[10] And the multitudes asked him, "What then shall we do?" [11] And he answered them, "He who has two coats, let him share with him who has none; and he who has food, let him do likewise." [12] Tax collectors also came to be baptized, and said to him, "Teacher, what shall we do?" [13] And he said to them, "Collect no more than is appointed you." [14] Soldiers also asked him, "And we, what shall we do?" And he said to them, "Rob no one by violence or by false accusation, and be content with your wages."

[15] As the people were in expectation, and all men questioned in their hearts concerning John, whether perhaps he were the Christ, [16] John answered them all, "**I baptize you with water; but he who is mightier than I is coming,** the thong of **whose sandals I am not worthy to untie; he will baptize you with the Holy Spirit and with fire.** [17] His winnowing fork is in his hand, to clear his threshing floor, and to gather the wheat into his granary, but the chaff he will burn with unquenchable fire."**

[18] So, with many other exhortations, he preached good news to the people. [19] But Herod the tetrarch, who had been reproved by him for Herodias, his brother's wife, and for all the evil things that Herod had done, [20] added this to them all, that he shut up John in prison.

| JOHN | THOMAS | OTHER |

JOHN

† John 1:19–28 (§J2.1)

¹⁹And this is the testimony of **John,** when the Jews sent priests and Levites from Jerusalem to ask him, "Who are you?" ²⁰He confessed, he did not deny, but confessed, "I am not the Christ." ²¹And they asked him, "What then? Are you Elijah?" He said, "I am not." "Are you the prophet?" And he answered, "No." ²²They said to him then, "Who are you? Let us have an answer for those who sent us. What do you say about yourself?" ²³He said, "I am **the voice of one crying in the wilderness, 'Make straight the way of the Lord,' as the prophet Isaiah said."**

²⁴Now they had been sent from the Pharisees. ²⁵They asked him, "Then why are you baptizing, if you are neither the Christ, nor Elijah, nor the prophet?" ²⁶John answered them, **"I baptize with water;** but among you stands one whom you do not know, ²⁷even **he who** comes **after me,** the thong of **whose** sandal **I am not worthy to** untie." ²⁸This took place in Bethany beyond **the Jordan,** where **John** was baptizing.

John 8:39 ⇨ Matt 3:9

³⁹They answered him, **"Abraham is our father."** Jesus said to them, "If **you** were Abraham's **children,** you would do what **Abraham** did . . ."

OTHER

GEbi 2 ⇨ Matt 3:1–6

(2) And:

*It came to pass that **John** was baptizing; and there went out to him **Pharisees** and were baptized, and all **Jerusalem.** And **John** had a garment of camel's hair and a leathern girdle about his loins, and **his food,** as it saith, was wild honey, the taste of which was that of manna, as a cake dipped in oil.*

*Thus they were resolved to pervert the word of truth into a lie and to put a cake in the place of **locusts.** (Epiphanius, Haer. 30.13.4f.)*

GEbi 3 ⇨ Matt 3:1–6

(3) And the beginning of their Gospel runs:

*It came to pass in the days of Herod the king of **Judaea,** <when Caiaphas was high priest,> that there came <one>, **John** <by name,> and **baptized** with the baptism of repentance in the river **Jordan.** It was said of him that he was of the lineage of Aaron the priest, a son of Zacharias and Elisabeth; and all went out to him. (Epiphanius, Haer. 30.13.6)*

ApocJa 9:24–10:6 ⇨ Matt 3:7–10

"O you (pl.) wretched! O you unfortunates! O you dissemblers of the truth! O you falsifiers of knowledge! O you sinners against the spirit! Do you even now dare to listen, when it behooved you to speak from the beginning? Do you even now dare to sleep, when it behooved you to be awake from the beginning, in order that the Kingdom of Heaven might receive you? In truth I say to you, it is easier for a holy one to sink into defilement, and for a man of light to sink into darkness, than for you to reign—or (even) not to (reign)!"

Acts 19:1–7 ⇨ Matt 3:11–12

*¹While Apollos was at Corinth, Paul passed through the upper country and came to Ephesus. There he found some disciples. ²And he said to them, "Did you receive **the Holy Spirit** when you believed?" And they said, "No, we have never even heard that there is a **Holy Spirit.**" ³And he said, "Into what then were you **baptized**?" They said, "Into John's baptism." ⁴And Paul said, "John baptized **with the** baptism of **repentance,** telling the people to believe in the one who was to come **after him,** that is, Jesus." ⁵On hearing this, they were baptized in the name of the Lord Jesus. ⁶And when Paul had laid his hands upon them, **the Holy Spirit** came on them; and they spoke with tongues and prophesied. ⁷There were about twelve of them in all.*

Acts 1:5 ⇨ Matt 3:11

*⁵"for John baptized **with water,** but before many days **you** shall be baptized **with the Holy Spirit.**"*

Acts 11:16 ⇨ Matt 3:11

*¹⁶"And I remembered the word of the Lord, how he said, 'John baptized **with water,** but you shall be baptized **with the Holy Spirit.**'"*

Acts 13:24–25 ⇨ Matt 3:11

*²⁴"Before his coming John had preached a baptism of **repentance** to all the people of Israel. ²⁵And as John was finishing his course, he said, 'What do you suppose that I am? I am not he. No, **but after me one is coming, the sandals of whose feet I am not worthy to untie.**'"*

MATT

MARK

LUKE

Matt 3:13-17 (§M6) °

13 Then Jesus came from Galilee to the Jordan to John, to be baptized by him. 14 John would have prevented him, saying, "I need to be baptized by you, and do you come to me?" 15 But Jesus answered him, "Let it be so now; for thus it is fitting for us to fulfil all righteousness." Then he consented. 16 And when Jesus was baptized, he went up immediately from the water, and behold, the heavens were opened a and he saw the Spirit of God descending like a dove, and alighting on him; 17 and lo, a voice from heaven, saying, "This is my beloved Son, b with whom I am well pleased."

a Add, *to him:* א b C D supp K L P W Δ *f*1 *f*13 28 33 *pm* it (in part) *al*; text: א* B *al*

b Or: *my Son, my* (or *the*) *Beloved*

°Appendix 1 ⇨ §M6

Ps 2:7 ⇨ Matt 3:17
7 I will tell of the decree of the Lord: He said to me,
 "You are **my son,**
 today I have begotten you."

Isa 42:1 ⇨ Matt 3:17
1 Behold **my** servant, **whom I** uphold,
 my chosen, in **whom** my soul delights;
I have put my **Spirit** upon **him,**
 he will bring forth justice to the nations.

Isa 44:2 ⇨ Matt 3:17
2 "Thus says the Lord who made you,
 who formed you from the womb and will help
 you:
Fear not, O Jacob **my** servant,
 Jeshurun whom **I** have chosen."

Mark 1:9-11 (§K3)

9 In those days **Jesus came from** Nazareth **of Galilee** and was **baptized by John** in **the Jordan.** 10 And when he came **up** out of **the water,** immediately he saw **the heavens opened** and the **Spirit descending** upon **him like a dove;** 11 and **a voice** came from heaven, "Thou art **my beloved Son; with** thee **I am well pleased."**

Mark 9:7 ⇨ Matt 3:16-17
7 *And a cloud overshadowed them, and a voice came out of the cloud, "This is my beloved Son; listen to him."*

Luke 3:21-22 (§L8)

21 Now when all the people were baptized, **and when Jesus** also had been **baptized** and was praying, the heaven was **opened,** 22 and the Holy **Spirit descended** upon **him** in bodily form, as **a dove, and a voice** came **from heaven,** "Thou art **my beloved Son; with** thee **I** am well pleased."

Luke 9:34-35 ⇨ Matt 3:17
34 *As he said this, a cloud came and overshadowed them; and they were afraid as they entered the cloud.* 35 *And a voice came out of the cloud, saying, "This is my Son, my Chosen; listen to him!"*

OTHER

GEbi 4
(4) And after much has been recorded it proceeds: When the people were baptized, Jesus also came and was baptized by John. And as he came up from the water, the heavens were opened and he saw the Holy Spirit in the form of a dove that descended and entered into him. And a voice (sounded) from heaven that said: Thou art my beloved Son, in thee I am well pleased. And again: I have this day begotten thee. And immediately a great light shone round about the place. When John saw this, it saith, he saith unto him: Who art thou, Lord? And again a voice from heaven (rang out) to him: This is my beloved Son in whom I am well pleased. And then, it saith, John fell down before him and said: I beseech thee, Lord, baptize thou me. But he prevented him and said: Suffer it; for thus it is fitting that everything should be fulfilled. (Epiphanius, Haer. 30.13.7f.)

GNaz 2
(2) Behold, the mother of the Lord and his brethren said to him: John the Baptist baptizes unto the remission of sins, let us go and be baptized by him. But he said to them: Wherein have I sinned that I should go and be baptized by him? Unless what I have said is ignorance (a sin of ignorance). (Jerome, Adversus Pelagianos 3.2)

GHeb 2
(2) According to the Gospel written in the Hebrew speech, which the Nazaraeans read, the whole fount of the Holy Spirit shall descend upon him . . . Further in the Gospel which we have just mentioned we find the following written:
And it came to pass when the Lord was come up out of the water, the whole fount of the Holy Spirit descended upon him and rested on him and said to him: My Son, in all the prophets was I waiting for thee that thou shouldest come and I might rest in thee. For thou art my rest; thou art my first-begotten Son that reignest for ever. (Jerome, Commentary on Isaiah 4 [on Isa 11:2])

JOHN

THOMAS

† John 1:29-34 (§J2.2)

29 The next day he saw **Jesus** coming toward him, and said, "Behold, the Lamb of God, who takes away the sin of the world! 30 This is he of whom I said, 'After me comes a man who ranks before me, for he was before me.' 31 I myself did not know him; but for this I came baptizing with water, that he might be revealed to Israel." 32 And John bore witness, "I **saw the Spirit** descend as **a dove** from heaven, and it remained **on him.** 33 I myself did not know him; but he who sent me to baptize with water said to me, 'He on whom you see **the Spirit** descend and remain, this is he who baptizes with **the** Holy **Spirit.'** 34 And I have seen and have borne witness that this is the **Son** of God."

MATT

INTRODUCTION

Matt 4:1-2 (§M7.1)

¹ Then Jesus was led up by the Spirit into the wilderness to be tempted by the devil. ² And he fasted forty days and forty nights, and afterward he was hungry.

FIRST TEMPTATION

Matt 4:3-4 (§M7.2)

³ And the tempter came and said to him, "If you are the Son of God, command these stones to become loaves of bread." ⁴ But he answered, "It is written,

'Man shall not live by bread alone,
but by every word that proceeds from the mouth of God.'"

SECOND TEMPTATION

Matt 4:5-7 (§M7.3)

⁵ Then the devil took him to the holy city, and set him on the pinnacle of the temple, ⁶ and said to him, "If you are the Son of God, throw yourself down; for it is written,

'He will give his angels charge of you,'
and

'On their hands they will bear you up,
lest you strike your foot against a stone.'"

⁷ Jesus said to him, "Again it is written, 'You shall not tempt the Lord your God.'"

THIRD TEMPTATION

Matt 4:8-10 (§M7.4)

⁸ Again, the devil took him to a very high mountain, and showed him all the kingdoms of the world and the glory of them; ⁹ and he said to him, "All these I will give you, if you will fall down and worship me." ¹⁰ Then Jesus said to him, "Begone,ᵃ Satan! for it is written,

'You shall worship the Lord your God
and him only shall you serve.'"

CONCLUSION

Matt 4:11 (§M7.5)

¹¹ Then the devil left him, and behold, angels came and ministered to him.

ᵃ Text: א B C* K P W △ ƒ¹ ƒ¹³ al; Get behind me: (from Matt 16:23) C² D L 28 33 al

JOHN

John 1:51 ⇨ Matt 4:11

⁵¹ And he said to him, "Truly, truly, I say to you, you will see heaven opened, and the **angels of God ascending** and descending upon the **Son of man**."

MARK

Mark 1:12-13 (§K4)

¹² **The Spirit** immediately drove him out **into the wilderness**. ¹³ And he was in the wilderness **forty days, tempted by** Satan; and he was with the wild beasts; and the **angels ministered to him**.

Exod 34:28 ⇨ Matt 4:2

²⁸ **And he** was there with the Lord **forty days and forty nights;** he neither ate bread nor drank water. And he wrote upon the tables the words of the covenant, the ten commandments.

Deut 9:9 ⇨ Matt 4:2

⁹ "When I went up the mountain to receive the tables of stone, the tables of the covenant which the Lord made with you, I remained on the mountain **forty days and forty nights**; I neither ate bread nor drank water."

Deut 8:3 ⇨ Matt 4:4

³ "And he humbled you and let you hunger and fed you with manna, which you did not know, nor did your fathers know; that he might make you know that **man** does **not live by bread alone, but** that man lives **by** everything **that proceeds** out of **the mouth of** the Lord."

Ps 91:11-12 ⇨ Matt 4:6

¹¹ For **he will give his angels charge of you** to guard you in all your ways,
¹² **On their hands they will bear you up,** lest you **dash your foot against a stone.**

Deut 6:16 ⇨ Matt 4:7

¹⁶ "You shall not put **the Lord your God** to the test, as you tested him at Massah."

Deut 6:13 ⇨ Matt 4:10

¹³ "You shall fear **the Lord your God; you** shall **serve** him, and swear by his name."

THOMAS

LUKE

Luke 4:1-13 (§L10)

¹ And **Jesus,** full of **the** Holy **Spirit,** returned from the Jordan, and was **led by the Spirit** ² for **forty days in the wilderness, tempted by the devil.** And he ate nothing in those days; and when they were ended, **he was hungry.** ³ The devil **said to him, "If you are the Son of God, command** this stone **to become bread."** ⁴ And Jesus **answered** him, **"It is written, 'Man shall not live by bread alone.'"** ⁵ And **the devil took him** up, and **showed him all the kingdoms of the world** in a moment of time, ⁶ and said to him, "To you **I will give** all this authority and their glory; for it has been delivered to me, and I give it to whom I will. ⁷ If you, then, will **worship me,** it shall all be yours." ⁸ And **Jesus** answered him, **"It is written,**

'You shall worship the Lord your God,
and him only shall you serve.'"

⁹ And he **took him to** Jerusalem, **and set him on the pinnacle of the temple, and said to him, "If you are the Son of God, throw yourself down** from here; ¹⁰ **for it is written,**

'He will give his angels charge of you,' to guard you,'

¹¹ **and**

'On their hands they will bear you up,
lest you strike your foot against a stone.'"

¹² And **Jesus** answered him, "It is said, '**You shall not tempt the Lord your God.'"** ¹³ And when **the devil** had ended every temptation, he departed from **him** until an opportune time.

OTHER

GNaz 3 ⇨ Matt 4:5

(3) The Jewish Gospel has not "into the holy city" but "to Jerusalem." (Variant to Matthew 4:5 in the "Zion Gospel" Edition)

GHeb 3 ⇨ Matt 4:8

(3) And if any accept the Gospel of the Hebrews—here the Savior says:

*Even so did my mother, the Holy Spirit, take me by one of my hairs and carry me away on to the great **mountain** Tabor. (Origen, Commentary on John 2.12.87 [on John 1:3])*

MATT

Matt 4:12–17 (§M8) °
[12] Now when he heard that John had been arrested, he withdrew into Galilee; [13] and leaving Nazareth he went and dwelt in Capernaum by the sea, in the territory of Zebulun and Naphtali, [14] that what was spoken by the prophet Isaiah might be fulfilled:
[15] "The land of Zebulun and the land of Naphtali,
toward the sea, across the Jordan,
Galilee of the Gentiles—
[16] the people who sat in darkness
have seen a great light,
and for those who sat in the region and shadow of death
light has dawned."
[17] From that time Jesus began to preach, saying, "Repent, for[a] the kingdom of heaven is at hand."

[a] Text: ℵ B C D K L P W Δ *f*[1] *f*[13] 28 33 *pm*; omit, *Repent, for:* it[k] syr[c] syr[s] *al*

° Appendix 3 ⇨ §M8

Matt 14:3 ⇨ Matt 4:12
[3] For Herod **had** seized **John** and bound him and put him in prison, for the sake of Herodias, his brother Philip's wife; . . .

Isa 9:1–2 ⇨ Matt 4:15–16
[1] But there will be no gloom for her that was in anguish. In the former time he brought into contempt **the land of Zebulun and the land of Naphtali,** but in the latter time he will make glorious the way of **the sea,** the land beyond **the Jordan, Galilee of the** nations.
[2] **The people who** walked **in the darkness have seen a great light;**
those **who** dwelt **in** a land of deep darkness, on them **has light** shined.

JOHN

John 1:43 ⇨ Matt 4:12–13
[43] The next day Jesus decided to go to **Galilee.** And he found Philip and said to him, "Follow me."

John 4:1–3 ⇨ Matt 4:12–13
[1] Now when the Lord knew that the Pharisees had **heard that** Jesus was making and baptizing more disciples than **John** [2] (although Jesus himself did not baptize, but only his disciples), [3] he left Judea and departed again to **Galilee.**

John 4:43 ⇨ Matt 4:12–13
[43] After the two days he departed to **Galilee.**

MARK

Mark 1:14–15 (§K5)
[14] Now after **John** was **arrested Jesus** came **into Galilee,** preaching the gospel of God, [15] and saying, "The time is fulfilled, and **the kingdom of** God **is at hand; repent,** and believe in the gospel."

Mark 6:17 ⇨ Matt 4:12
[17] For Herod **had** sent and seized **John and** bound him in prison for the sake of Herodias, his brother Philip's wife; because he had married her.

THOMAS

LUKE

† **Luke 4:14–15 (§L11)**
[14] And Jesus returned in the power of the Spirit **into Galilee,** and a report concerning him went out through all the surrounding country. [15] And he taught in their synagogues, being glorified by all.

† **Luke 4:16–30 (§L12)**
[16] And **he** came to **Nazareth,** where he had been brought up; and he went to the synagogue, as his custom was, on the sabbath day. And he stood up to read; [17] and there was given to him the book of **the prophet Isaiah.** He opened the book and found the place where it was written,
[18] "The Spirit of the Lord is upon me,
because he has anointed me to preach good news to the poor.
He has sent me to proclaim release to the captives
and recovering of sight to the blind,
to set at liberty those who are oppressed,
[19] to proclaim the acceptable year of the Lord."
[20] And he closed the book, and gave it back to the attendant, and sat down; and the eyes of all in the synagogue were fixed on him. [21] And he began to say to them, "Today this scripture has been **fulfilled** in your hearing." [22] And all spoke well of him, and wondered at the gracious words which proceeded out of his mouth; and they said, "Is not this Joseph's son?" [23] And he said to them, "Doubtless you will quote to me this proverb, 'Physician, heal yourself; what we have heard you did at **Capernaum,** do here also in your own country.'" [24] And he said, "Truly, I say to you, no prophet is acceptable in his own country. [25] But in truth, I tell you, there were many widows in Israel in the days of Elijah, when the heaven was shut up three years and six months, when there came a great famine over all the land; [26] and Elijah was sent to none of them but only to Zarephath, in the land of Sidon, to a woman who was a widow. [27] And there were many lepers in Israel in the time of the prophet Elisha; and none of them was cleansed, but only Naaman the Syrian." [28] When they heard this, all in the synagogue were filled with wrath. [29] And they rose up and put him out of the city, and led him to the brow of the hill on which their city was built, that they might throw him down headlong. [30] But passing through the midst of them he went away.

† **Luke 3:19–20, 23a**
[19] But Herod the tetrarch, who had been reproved by him for Herodias, his brother's wife, and for all the evil things that Herod **had** done, [20] added this to them all, that he shut up **John** in prison. . . . [23] **Jesus,** when he **began** his ministry, was about thirty years of age, . . .

OTHER

MATT

Matt 4:18–20 (§M9) °
18 As he walked by the Sea of Galilee, he saw two brothers, Simon who is called Peter and Andrew his brother, casting a net into the sea; for they were fishermen. **19** And he said to them, "Follow me, and I will make you fishers of men." **20** Immediately they left their nets and followed him.

Matt 4:21–22 (§M10) °
21 And going on from there he saw two other brothers, James the son of Zebedee and John his brother, in the boat with Zebedee their father, mending their nets, and he called them. **22** Immediately they left the boat and their father, and followed him.

° Appendix 2 ⇨ §§M9 and M10

JOHN

† John 1:35–42 (§J3.1)
35 The next day again John was standing with two of his disciples; **36** and he looked at Jesus **as he walked**, and said, "Behold, the Lamb of God!" **37** The two disciples heard him say this, and they followed Jesus. **38** Jesus turned, and saw them following, **and said to them,** "What do you seek?" And they said to him, "Rabbi" (which means Teacher), "where are you staying?" **39** **He said to them,** "Come and see." They came and saw where he was staying; and they stayed with him that day, for it was about the tenth hour. **40** One of the two who heard John speak, and followed him, was **Andrew, Simon** Peter's brother. **41** He first found **his brother Simon,** and said to him, "We have found the Messiah" (which means Christ). **42** He brought him to Jesus. Jesus looked at him, **and said,** "So you are **Simon** the son of John? You shall be called Cephas" (which means Peter).

† John 1:43–51 (§J3.2)
43 The next day Jesus decided to go to **Galilee. And** he found Philip **and said to** him, "**Follow me.**" **44** Now Philip was from Bethsaida, the city of **Andrew and Peter**. **45** Philip found Nathanael, and said to him, "We have found him of whom Moses in the law and also the prophets wrote, Jesus of Nazareth, the son of Joseph." **46** Nathanael said to him, "Can anything good come out of Nazareth?" Philip said to him, "Come and see." **47** Jesus **saw** Nathanael coming to him, and said of him, "Behold, an Israelite indeed, in whom is no guile!" **48** Nathanael said to him, "How do you know me?" Jesus answered him, "Before Philip called you, when you were under the fig tree, I saw you." **49** Nathanael answered him, "Rabbi, you are the Son of God! You are the King of Israel!" **50** Jesus answered him, "Because I said to you, I saw you under the fig tree, do you believe? You shall see greater things than these." **51** And he said to him, "Truly, truly, I say to you, you will see heaven opened, and the angels of God ascending and descending upon the Son of man."

MARK

Mark 1:16–18 (§K6) ⇨ §M9
16 And passing along **by the Sea of Galilee, he saw Simon and Andrew** the **brother** of Simon **casting a net in the sea; for they were fishermen.** **17** And Jesus **said to them,** "**Follow me and I will make you** become **fishers of men.**" **18** And **immediately they left their nets and followed him.**

Mark 1:19–20 (§K7) ⇨ §M10
19 And going on a little farther, **he saw James the son of Zebedee** and John **his brother,** who were **in** their **boat mending** the **nets**. **20** And **immediately he called them;** and **they left their father** Zebedee in **the boat** with the hired servants, **and followed him.**

THOMAS

LUKE

† Luke 5:1–3 (§L17.1)
1 While the people pressed upon him to hear the word of God, **he** was standing **by the** lake **of Gennesaret.** **2** And **he saw two** boats by the lake; but the **fishermen** had gone out of them and were washing **their nets.** **3** Getting into one of the boats, which was Simon's, he asked him to put out a little from the land. And he sat down and taught the people from the boat.

† Luke 5:4–11 (§L17.2)
4 And when he had ceased speaking, **he said to** Simon, "Put out into the deep and let down your nets for a catch." **5** And Simon answered, "Master, we toiled all night and took nothing! But at your word I will let down the nets." **6** And when they had done this, they enclosed a great shoal of fish; and as their nets were breaking, **7** they beckoned to their partners in the other boat to come and help them. And they came and filled both the boats, so that they began to sink. **8** But when Simon Peter saw it, he fell down at Jesus' knees, saying, "Depart from me, for I am a sinful man, O Lord." **9** For he was astonished, and all that were with him, at the catch of fish which they had taken; **10** and so also were **James** and **John,** sons of **Zebedee,** who were partners with Simon. And Jesus said to Simon, "Do not be afraid; henceforth you will be catching men." **11** And when they had brought their boats to land, **they left** everything **and followed him.**

OTHER

GEbi 1
(1) In the Gospel that is in general use amongst them, which is called according to Matthew, which however is not whole (and) complete but forged and mutilated—they call it the Hebrew Gospel—it is reported:
There appeared a certain man named Jesus of about thirty years of age, who chose us. And when he came to Capernaum, he entered into the house of Simon whose surname was Peter, and opened his mouth and said: As I passed along the Lake of Tiberias, I chose John and James the sons of Zebedee, and Simon and Andrew and Thaddaeus and Simon the Zealot and Judas Iscariot, and thee, Matthew, I called as thou didst sit at the receipt of custom, and thou didst follow me. You therefore I will to be twelve apostles for a testimony unto Israel.
(Epiphanius, Haer. 30.13.2f.)

MATT	MARK	LUKE

Matt 4:23–25 (§M11) °

²³ And he went about all Galilee teaching in their synagogues and preaching the gospel of the kingdom and healing every disease and every infirmity among the people. ²⁴ So his fame spread throughout all Syria, and they brought him all the sick, those afflicted with various diseases and pains, demoniacs, epileptics, and paralytics, and he healed them. ²⁵ And great crowds followed him from Galilee and the Decapolis and Jerusalem and Judea and from beyond the Jordan.

°Appendix 3 ⇨ §M11

Matt 9:35 ⇨ Matt 4:23

³⁵ And Jesus *went about all the cities and villages, teaching in their synagogues and preaching the gospel of the kingdom, and healing every disease and every infirmity.*

Mark 1:35–39 (§K11)

³⁵ And in the morning, a great while before day, **he** rose and **went out** to a lonely place, and there he prayed. ³⁶ And Simon and those who were with him pursued him, ³⁷ and they found him and said to him, "Every one is searching for you." ³⁸ And he said to them, "Let us go on to the next towns, that I may preach there also; for that is why I came out." ³⁹ **And he went** throughout **all Galilee, preaching in their synagogues** and casting out demons.

Luke 4:42–44 (§L16)

⁴² And when it was day he departed and **went** into a lonely place. And **the people** sought **him** and came to him, and would have kept him from leaving them; ⁴³ but he said to them, "I must preach the good news of the kingdom of God to the other cities also; for I was sent for this purpose." ⁴⁴ **And he** was **preaching in** the **synagogues** of Judea.

JOHN	THOMAS	OTHER

MATT	MARK	LUKE

Matt 5:1-2 (§12.1)
¹Seeing the crowds, he went up on the mountain, and when he sat down his disciples came to him. ²And he opened his mouth and taught them, saying: . . .

Mark 3:13
¹³And he went up on the mountain, and called to him those whom he desired; and they came to him.

Luke 6:12-16 (§L23)
¹²In these days **he went** out to **the mountain** to pray; and all night he continued in prayer to God. ¹³And when it was day, **he** called **his disciples,** and chose from them twelve, whom he named apostles; ¹⁴Simon, whom he named Peter, and Andrew his brother, and James and John, and Philip, and Bartholomew, ¹⁵and Matthew, and Thomas, and James the son of Alphaeus, and Simon who was called the Zealot, ¹⁶and Judas the son of James, and Judas Iscariot, who became a traitor.

Luke 6:17-19 (§L24)
¹⁷And **he** came **down** with them and stood on a level place, with a great crowd of **his disciples** and a great multitude of people from all Judea and Jerusalem and the seacoast of Tyre and Sidon, who **came to** hear **him** and to be healed of their diseases; ¹⁸and those who were troubled with unclean spirits were cured. ¹⁹And all the crowd sought to touch him, for power came forth from him and healed them all.

Luke 6:20a ⇨ Matt 5:2
²⁰**And he** lifted up **his** eyes on his disciples, **and** said: . . .

JOHN	THOMAS	OTHER

John 6:3
³Jesus went up on the mountain, and there sat down with his disciples.

MATT	MARK	LUKE

MATT

Matt 5:3–12 (§M12.2)
[3] "Blessed are the poor in spirit, for theirs is the kingdom of heaven.

[4] "Blessed are those who mourn, for they shall be comforted.

[5] "Blessed are the meek, for they shall inherit the earth.

[6] "Blessed are those who hunger and thirst for righteousness, for they shall be satisfied.

[7] "Blessed are the merciful, for they shall obtain mercy.

[8] "Blessed are the pure in heart, for they shall see God.

[9] "Blessed are the peacemakers, for they shall be called sons of God.

[10] "Blessed are those who are persecuted for righteousness' sake, for theirs is the kingdom of heaven.

[11] "Blessed are you when men revile you and persecute you and utter all kinds of evil against you falsely[a] on my account. [12] Rejoice and be glad, for your reward is great in heaven, for so men persecuted the prophets who were before you."

[a] Text: ℵ B C K W Δ Θ Π 0196 *f*[1] *f*[13] *pm* it (in part) vg syr[c] *al;* omit *falsely:* D it (in part) syr[s] *al*

Isa 61:2 ⇨ Matt 5:4
[2] to proclaim the year of the Lord's favor,
   and the day of vengeance of our God;
   to comfort all **who mourn;** . . .

Ps 37:11 ⇨ Matt 5:5
[11] But **the meek shall** possess **the** land,
   and delight themselves in abundant prosperity.

Ps 24:3–4 ⇨ Matt 5:8
[3] Who shall ascend the hill of the Lord?
   And who shall stand in his holy place?
[4] He who has clean hands and a **pure heart,**
   who does not lift up his soul to what is false,
   and does not swear deceitfully.

LUKE

Luke 6:20–26 (§L25.1)
[20] And he lifted up his eyes on his disciples, and said:

"**Blessed are** you **poor, for** yours **is the kingdom of** God.

[21] "**Blessed are** you that **hunger** now, **for** you **shall be satisfied.**

"**Blessed are** you that weep now, **for** you **shall** laugh.

[22] "**Blessed are you when men** hate **you,** and when they exclude you and **revile you,** and cast out your name as **evil, on account** of the Son of man! [23] **Rejoice** in that day, and leap for joy, for behold, **your reward is great in heaven; for so** their fathers did to **the prophets.**

[24] "But woe to you that are rich, for you have received your consolation.

[25] "Woe to you that are full now, **for you shall hunger.**

"Woe to you that laugh now, **for you shall mourn** and weep.

[26] "Woe to **you, when** all **men** speak well of **you, for** so their fathers did to the false **prophets."**

JOHN	THOMAS	OTHER

THOMAS

GThom 54 ⇨ Matt 5:3
(54) Jesus said, "**Blessed are the poor, for** yours **is the Kingdom of Heaven."**

GThom 69b ⇨ Matt 5:6
"**Blessed are** the hungry, **for** the belly of him who desires will **be filled."**

GThom 69a ⇨ Matt 5:10
(69) Jesus said, "**Blessed are** they **who** have been **persecuted** within themselves. It is they who have truly come to know the Father."

GThom 68 ⇨ Matt 5:11
(68) Jesus said, "**Blessed are you when you** are hated **and** persecuted. Wherever **you** have been persecuted they will find no Place."

OTHER

1 Pet 4:15–16 ⇨ Matt 5:11–12
[15] But let none of **you** suffer as a murderer, or a thief, or a wrongdoer, or a mischief-maker; [16] yet if one suffers as a Christian, let him not be ashamed, but under that name let him glorify God.

MATT

Matt 5:13–16 (§M12.3)

[13] "You are the salt of the earth; but if salt has lost its taste, how shall its saltness be restored? It is no longer good for anything except to be thrown out and trodden under foot by men.

[14] "You are the light of the world. A city set on a hill cannot be hid. [15] Nor do men light a lamp and put it under a bushel, but on a stand, and it gives light to all in the house. [16] Let your light so shine before men, that they may see your good works and give glory to your Father who is in heaven."

Matt 5:17–20 (§M12.4)

[17] "Think not that I have come to abolish the law and the prophets; I have come not to abolish them but to fulfil them. [18] For truly, I say to you, till heaven and earth pass away, not an iota, not a dot, will pass from the law until all is accomplished. [19] Whoever then relaxes one of the least of these commandments and teaches men so, shall be called least in the kingdom of heaven; but he who does them and teaches them shall be called great in the kingdom of heaven. [20] For I tell you, unless your righteousness exceeds that of the scribes and Pharisees, you will never enter the kingdom of heaven."

MARK

Mark 9:50 ⇨ Matt 5:13

[50] "Salt is good; but if the salt has lost its saltness, how will you season it? Have salt in yourselves, and be at peace with one another."

Mark 4:21 ⇨ Matt 5:15

[21] And he said to them, "Is a lamp brought in to be put under a bushel, or under a bed, and not on a stand?"

LUKE

Luke 14:34–35 ⇨ Matt 5:13

[34] "Salt is good; but if salt has lost its taste, how shall its saltness be restored? [35] It is fit neither for the land nor for the dunghill; men throw it away. He who has ears to hear, let him hear."

Luke 8:16 ⇨ Matt 5:15

[16] "No one after lighting a lamp covers it with a vessel, or puts it under a bed, but puts it on a stand, that those who enter may see the light."

Luke 11:33 ⇨ Matt 5:15

[33] "No one after lighting a lamp puts it in a cellar or under a bushel, but on a stand, that those who enter may see the light."

Luke 16:17 ⇨ Matt 5:17–18

[17] "But it is easier for heaven and earth to pass away, than for one dot of the law to become void."

JOHN

THOMAS

POxy1 7 ⇨ Matt 5:14b

(7) Jesus says, "A city built upon the top of a high mountain and made fast can neither fall nor be hidden."

GThom 32 ⇨ Matt 5:14b

(32) Jesus said, "A city being built on a high mountain and fortified cannot fall, nor can it be hidden."

GThom 33 ⇨ Matt 5:15

(33) Jesus said, "Preach from your housetops that which you will hear in your ear [(and) in the other ear]. For no one lights a lamp and puts it under a bushel, nor does he put it in a hidden place, but rather he sets it on a lampstand so that everyone who enters and leaves will see its light."

OTHER

GEbi 6 ⇨ Matt 5:17–18

(6) They say that he (Christ) was not begotten of God the Father, but created as one of the archangels. . . . that he rules over the angels and all the creatures of the Almighty, and that he came and declared, as their Gospel, which is called (according to Matthew? according to the Hebrews?), *reports:*

I am come to do away with sacrifices, and if ye cease not from sacrificing, the wrath of God will not cease from you. (Epiphanius, *Haer.* 30.16.4f.)

MATT

Matt 5:21–26 (§M12.5a)
[21] "You have heard that it was said to the men of old, 'You shall not kill; and whoever kills shall be liable to judgment.' [22] But I say to you that every one who is angry with his brother shall be liable to judgment; whoever insults his brother[a] shall be liable to the council, and whoever says, 'You fool!'[b] shall be liable to the hell[c] of fire. [23] So if you are offering your gift at the altar, and there remember that your brother has something against you, [24] leave your gift there before the altar and go; first be reconciled to your brother, and then come and offer your gift. [25] Make friends quickly with your accuser, while you are going with him to court, lest your accuser hand you over to the judge, and the judge to the guard, and you be put in prison; [26] truly, I say to you, you will never get out till you have paid the last penny."

Matt 5:27–30 (§M12.5b)
[27] "You have heard that it was said, 'You shall not commit adultery.' [28] But I say to you that every one who looks at a woman lustfully has already committed adultery with her in his heart. [29] If your right eye causes you to sin, pluck it out and throw it away; it is better that you lose one of your members than that your whole body be thrown into hell. [30] And if your right hand causes you to sin, cut it off and throw it away; it is better that you lose one of your members than that your whole body go into hell."

[a] Text: 𝔓[67] ℵ* B 2174 vg eth GNaz *al;* add *without cause:* ℵ[c] D K L W Δ Θ Π *f*[1] *f*[13] 28 33 *pm*

[b] Greek: *says Raca to* (an obscure term of abuse)

[c] Greek: *Gehenna*

●**Matt 18:8–9** ⇨ Matt 5:29–30
[8] "And if your hand or your foot causes you to sin, cut it off and throw it away; it is better for you to enter life maimed or lame than with two hands or two feet to be thrown into eternal fire. [9] And if your eye causes you to sin, pluck it out and throw it away; it is better for you to enter life with one eye than with two eyes to be thrown into the hell of fire."

Exod 20:13 ⇨ Matt 5:21
[13] "You shall not kill."

MARK

Mark 11:25 ⇨ Matt 5:23–24
[25] "And whenever **you** stand praying, forgive, if **you** have anything **against** any one; so that **your** Father also who is in heaven may forgive **you** your trespasses."

Mark 9:43–48 ⇨ Matt 5:29–30
[43] "And if **your hand causes you to sin, cut it off; it is better** for **you** to enter life maimed **than** with two hands to **go** to **hell**, to the unquenchable fire. [45] And if your foot causes you to sin, cut it off; it is better for you to enter life lame than with two feet to be thrown into hell. [47] And **if your eye causes you to sin, pluck it out; it is better** for **you** to enter the kingdom of God with **one eye than** with two eyes to **be thrown into hell,** [48] where their worm does not die, and the fire is not quenched."

Deut 5:17 ⇨ Matt 5:21
[17] "'You shall not kill.'"

Exod 20:14 ⇨ Matt 5:27
[14] "You shall not commit adultery."

Deut 5:18 ⇨ Matt 5:27
[18] "'Neither **shall you commit adultery.'"**

LUKE

Luke 12:57–59 ⇨ Matt 5:25–26
[57] "And why do you not judge for yourselves what is right? [58] As **you** go **with** your accuser before the magistrate, **make an effort to settle with** him on the way, **lest** he drag **you** to the **judge, and the judge** hand you over **to the officer, and** the officer **put you in prison.** [59] I tell **you, you will never get out till you have paid the** very last copper."

JOHN

THOMAS

OTHER

GNaz 4 ⇨ Matt 5:22
(4) The phrase "without a cause" is lacking in some witnesses and in the Jewish Gospel. (Variant to Matthew 5:22 in the "Zion Gospel" Edition)

MATT

MARK

LUKE

Matt 5:31–32 (§M12.5c)

[31] "It was also said, 'Whoever divorces his wife, let him give her a certificate of divorce.' [32] But I say to you that every one who divorces his wife, except on the ground of unchastity, makes her an adulteress; and whoever marries a divorced woman commits adultery."

● **Matt 19:3–9 (§M65.1)**

[3] And Pharisees came up to him and tested him by asking, "Is it lawful to divorce one's wife for any cause?" [4] He answered, "Have you not read that he who made them from the beginning made them male and female, [5] and said, 'For this reason a man shall leave his father and mother and be joined to **his wife**, and the two shall become one flesh'? [6] So they are no longer two but one flesh. What therefore God has joined together, let not man put asunder." [7] They said to him, "Why then did Moses command one to **give a certificate of divorce**, and to put her away?" [8] He **said** to them, "For your hardness of heart Moses allowed you to divorce your wives, but from the beginning it was not so. [9] And **I say to you**: whoever **divorces his wife, except** for **unchastity**, and **marries** another, **commits adultery**."

Deut 24:1–4 ⇨ Matt 5:31

[1] "When a man takes a **wife** and marries her, if then she finds no favor in his eyes because he has found some indecency in her, and he writes **her a bill of divorce** and puts it in her hand and sends her out of his house, and she departs out of his house, [2] and if she goes and becomes another man's wife, [3] and the latter husband dislikes her and writes **her a bill of divorce** and puts it in her hand and sends her out of his house, or if the latter husband dies, who took her to be **his wife**, [4] then her former husband, who sent her away, may not take her again to be **his wife**, after she has been defiled; for that is an abomination before the Lord, and you shall not bring guilt upon the land which the Lord your God gives you for an inheritance."

Mark 10:2–12 (§K51)

[2] And Pharisees came up and in order to test him asked, "Is it lawful for a man to divorce his wife?" [3] He answered them, "What did Moses command you?" [4] They said, "Moses allowed a man to write **a certificate of divorce**, and to put her away." [5] But Jesus **said** to them, "For your hardness of heart he wrote you this commandment. [6] But from the beginning of creation, 'God made them male and female.' [7] 'For this reason a man shall leave his father and mother and be joined to **his wife**, [8] and the two shall become one flesh.' So they are no longer two but one flesh. [9] What therefore God has joined together, let not man put asunder."

[10] And in the house the disciples asked him again about this matter. [11] And he said **to** them, "**Whoever divorces his wife** and **marries** another, **commits adultery** against her; [12] and if she divorces her husband and **marries** another, she **commits adultery**."

Luke 16:18 (§L68.2)

[18] "**Every one who divorces his wife** and **marries** another **commits adultery**, and he who **marries a woman divorced** from her husband **commits adultery**."

JOHN

THOMAS

OTHER

MATT | MARK | LUKE

Matt 5:33–37 (§M12.5d)

[33] "Again you have heard that it was said to the men of old, 'You shall not swear falsely, but shall perform to the Lord what you have sworn.' [34] But I say to you, Do not swear at all, either by heaven, for it is the throne of God, [35] or by the earth, for it is his footstool, or by Jerusalem, for it is the city of the great King. [36] And do not swear by your head, for you cannot make one hair white or black. [37] Let what you say be simply 'Yes' or 'No'; anything more than this comes from evil."[a]

Matt 5:38–42 (§M12.5e)

[38] "You have heard that it was said, 'An eye for an eye and a tooth for a tooth.' [39] But I say to you, do not resist one who is evil. But if any one strikes you on the right cheek, turn to him the other also; [40] and if any one would sue you and take your coat, let him have your cloak as well; [41] and if any one forces you to go one mile, go with him two miles. [42] Give to him who begs from you, and do not refuse him who would borrow from you."

[a] Greek: *the evil one*

Matt 23:16–22 ⇨ §M125.d

[16] *"Woe to you, blind guides, who say, 'If any one swears by the temple, it is nothing; but if any one swears by the gold of the temple, he is bound by his oath.' [17] You blind fools! For which is greater, the gold or the temple that has made the gold sacred? [18] And you say, 'If any one swears by the altar, it is nothing; but if any one swears by the gift that is on the altar, he is bound by his oath.' [19] You blind men! For which is greater, the gift or the altar that makes the gift sacred? [20] So he who swears by the altar, swears by it and by everything on it; [21] and he who swears by the temple, swears by it and by him who dwells in it; [22] and he who swears by heaven, swears by the throne of God and by him who sits upon it."*

Lev 19:12 ⇨ Matt 5:33
[12] And **you shall not swear** by my name **falsely**, and so profane the name of your God: I am **the Lord**.

Isa 66:1 ⇨ Matt 5:34–35
[1] Thus says the Lord:
"**Heaven is** my **throne**
   and the **earth is** my footstool;
what is the house which you would build for me,
   and what is the place of my rest?"

JOHN

Ps 48:2 ⇨ Matt 5:35
[2] beautiful in elevation,
   is the joy of all **the earth**,
Mount Zion, in the far north,
   the city of the great King.

Exod 21:23–25 ⇨ Matt 5:38
[23] "If any harm follows, then you shall give life for life, [24] **eye for eye, tooth for tooth**, hand for hand, foot for foot, [25] burn for burn, wound for wound, stripe for stripe."

Lev 24:19–20 ⇨ Matt 5:38
[19] "When a man causes a disfigurement in his neighbor, as he has done it shall be done to him, [20] fracture for fracture, **eye for eye, tooth for tooth**; as he has disfigured a man, he shall be disfigured."

Deut 19:21 ⇨ Matt 5:38
[21] "Your eye shall not pity; it shall be life for life, **eye for eye, tooth for tooth**, hand for hand, foot for foot."

THOMAS

GThom 95 ⇨ Matt 5:42
(95) *[Jesus said], "If you have money, do not lend it at interest, but give [it] to one from whom you will not get it back."*

Luke 6:27–36 (§L25.2) ⇨ §M12.5e

[27] "But I say to you that hear, Love your enemies, do good to those who hate you, [28] bless those who curse you, pray for those who abuse you. [29] To him who **strikes you on the cheek,** offer **the other also**; and from him who takes away **your coat** do not withhold even **your shirt**. [30] **Give to** every one **who begs from you; and** of him who takes away your goods **do not** ask them again. [31] And as you wish that men would do to you, do so to them.

[32] "If you love those who love you, what credit is that to you? For even sinners love those who love them. [33] And if you do good to those who do good to you, what credit is that to you? For even sinners do the same. [34] And if you lend to those from whom you hope to receive, what credit is that to you? Even sinners lend to sinners, to receive as much again. [35] But love your enemies, and do good, and lend, expecting nothing in return; and your reward will be great, and you will be sons of the Most High; for he is kind to the ungrateful and the selfish. [36] Be merciful, even as your Father is merciful."

OTHER

Did 1:2–5 ⇨ §M12.5e
[2] *The Way of Life is this: "First, thou shalt love the God who made thee, secondly, thy neighbour as thyself; and whatsoever thou wouldst not have done to thyself, do not thou to another."*

[3] *Now, the teaching of these words is this: "Bless those that curse you, and pray for your enemies, and fast for those that persecute you. For what credit is it to you if you love those that love you? Do not even the heathen do the same?" But, for your part, "love those that hate you," and you will have no enemy.* [4] *"Abstain from carnal" and bodily "lusts." "If any man smite thee on the right cheek turn to him the other cheek also," and thou wilt be perfect. "If any man impress thee to go with him one mile, go with him two. If any man take thy coat, give him thy shirt also. If any man will take from thee what is thine, refuse it not"—not even if thou canst.* [5] *Give to everyone that asks thee, and do not refuse, for the Father's will is that we give to all from the gifts we have received. Blessed is he that gives according to the mandate; for he is innocent. Woe to him who receives; for if any man receive alms under pressure of need he is innocent; but he who receives it without need shall be tried as to why he took and for what, and being in prison he shall be examined as to his deeds, and "he shall not come out thence until he pay the last farthing."*

MATT   MARK   LUKE

Matt 5:43–48 (§M12.5f)

⁴³"You have heard that it was said, 'You shall love your neighbor and hate your enemy.' ⁴⁴But I say to you, Love your enemies and pray for those who persecute you, ⁴⁵so that you may be sons of your Father who is in heaven; for he makes his sun rise on the evil and on the good, and sends rain on the just and on the unjust. ⁴⁶For if you love those who love you, what reward have you? Do not even the tax collectors do the same? ⁴⁷And if you salute only your brethren, what more are you doing than others? Do not even the Gentiles do the same? ⁴⁸You, therefore, must be perfect, as your heavenly Father is perfect."

Lev 19:17–18 ⇨ Matt 5:43

¹⁷"You shall not hate your brother in your heart, but you shall reason with your neighbor, lest you bear sin because of him. ¹⁸You shall not take vengeance or bear any grudge against the sons of your own people, but you shall love your neighbor as yourself: I am the Lord."

Deut 18:13 ⇨ Matt 5:48

¹³"You shall be blameless before the Lord your God."

JOHN   THOMAS

Luke 6:27–36 (§L25.2)

²⁷"But I say to you that hear, **Love your enemies**, do good to those who hate you, ²⁸bless those who curse you, **pray for those who** abuse you. ²⁹To him who strikes you on the cheek, offer the other also; and from him who takes away your coat do not withhold even your shirt. ³⁰Give to every one who begs from you; and of him who takes away your goods do not ask them again. ³¹And as you wish that men would do to you, do so to them.

³²"**If you love those who love you, what** credit is that to **you**? For even sinners love those who love them. ³³And if you do good to those who do good to you, what credit is that to you? For even sinners **do the same**. ³⁴And if you lend to those from whom you hope to receive, what credit is that to you? Even sinners lend to sinners, to receive as much again. ³⁵But **love your enemies**, and do good, and lend, expecting nothing in return; and your reward will be great, and you will be sons of the Most High; for he is kind to the ungrateful and the selfish. ³⁶**Be** merciful, even **as your Father is** merciful."

OTHER

Did 1:2–5

²*The Way of Life is this: "First, thou shalt **love the God who** made thee, secondly, thy neighbour as thyself; and whatsoever thou wouldst not have done to thyself, do not thou to another."*

³*Now, the teaching of these words is this: "Bless those that curse you, **and pray for your enemies**, and fast for those that persecute you. For what credit is it to you if you love those that love you? Do not even the heathen do the same?" But, for your part, "love those that hate you," and you will have no enemy.* ⁴*"Abstain from carnal" and bodily "lusts." "If any man smite thee on the right cheek turn to him the other cheek also," and thou wilt be perfect. "If any man impress thee to go with him one mile, go with him two. If any man take thy coat, give him thy shirt also. If any man will take from thee what is thine, refuse it not"—not even if thou canst.* ⁵*Give to everyone that asks thee, and do not refuse, for the Father's will is that we give to all from the gifts we have received. Blessed is he that gives according to the mandate; for he is innocent. Woe to him who receives; for if any man receive alms under pressure of need he is innocent; but he who receives it without need shall be tried as to why he took and for what, and being in prison he shall be examined as to his deeds, and "he shall not come out thence until he pay the last farthing."*

2 Clem 13:4 ⇨ Matt 5:43–44, 46

⁴*For when they hear from us that God says: "It is no credit to you, if ye **love them that love you**, but it is a credit to you, if ye love your enemies, and those that hate you";—when they hear this they wonder at this extraordinary goodness; but when they see that we not only do not **love those that hate us**, but not even those who **love us**, they laugh us to scorn, and the name is blasphemed.*

POxy1224 2 ⇨ Matt 5:44

*(2) And **pray for your enemies**. For he who is not [against you] is for you. [He who today] is far-off—tomorrow will be [near to you]....*

MATT	MARK	LUKE

Matt 6:1 (§M12.6a)

¹ "Beware of practicing your piety before men in order to be seen by them; for then you will have no reward from your Father who is in heaven."

Matt 6:2–4 (§M12.6b)

² "Thus, when you give alms, sound no trumpet before you, as the hypocrites do in the synagogues and in the streets, that they may be praised by men. Truly, I say to you, they have received their reward. ³ But when you give alms, do not let your left hand know what your right hand is doing, ⁴ so that your alms may be in secret; and your Father who sees in secret will reward you."

JOHN	THOMAS	OTHER

POxy654 6 ⇨ §M12.6b

(6) [His disciples] ask him [and s]ay, "How [shall we] fast, [and how shall] we [pray] and how [shall we **give alms,** *a]nd what shall [we] observe [when we sup?"] Jesus says, "[Do not lie and what] you [hate]* **do not** *do. [For all things will be full of (?)] truth bef[ore heaven. For there is nothing] hidden [which will not be (made) known. Ha]ppy is [he who does* **not** *do these things. For all] will be mani[fest before the* **Father who]** *is [in heaven]."*

GThom 6 ⇨ §M12.6b

(6) His disciples questioned Him and said to Him, "Do You want us to fast? How shall we pray? Shall we **give alms?** *What diet shall we observe?"*

Jesus said, "Do not tell lies, and do not do what you hate, for all things are plain in the sight of Heaven. For nothing hidden will not become manifest, and nothing covered will remain without being uncovered."

GThom 14 ⇨ §M12.6b

(14) Jesus said to them, "If you fast, you will give rise to sin for yourselves; and if you pray, you will be condemned; and if **you give alms,** *you will do harm to your spirits. When you go into any land and walk about in the districts, if they receive you, eat what they will set before you, and heal the sick among them. For what goes into your mouth will not defile you, but that which issues from your mouth—it is that which will defile you."*

GThom 62 ⇨ Matt 6:3

(62) Jesus said, "It is to those [who are worthy of My] mysteries that I tell My mysteries. **Do not let your left hand know what your right hand is doing."**

MATT

Matt 6:5–15 (§M12.6c)

⁵"And when you pray, you must not be like the hypocrites; for they love to stand and pray in the synagogues and at the street corners, that they may be seen by men. Truly, I say to you, they have received their reward. ⁶But when you pray, go into your room and shut the door and pray to your Father who is in secret; and your Father who sees in secret will reward you.

⁷"And in praying do not heap up empty phrases as the Gentiles do; for they think that they will be heard for their many words. ⁸Do not be like them, for your Father knows what you need before you ask him. ⁹Pray then like this:

Our Father who art in heaven,
Hallowed be thy name.
¹⁰Thy kingdom come,
Thy will be done,
   On earth as it is in heaven.
¹¹Give us this day our daily bread;ᵃ
¹²And forgive us our debts,
   As we also have forgiven our debtors;
¹³And lead us not into temptation,
   But deliver us from evil.ᵇ
¹⁴For if you forgive men their trespasses, your heavenly Father also will forgive you; ¹⁵but if you do not forgive men their trespasses, neither will your Father forgive your trespasses."

ᵃ Or: *our bread for the morrow*

ᵇ Greek: *the evil one*
Text: ℵ B D 0170 *f*¹ it (in part) *al;* add: *For Thine is the kingdom and the power and the glory forever. Amen.* K L W Δ Θ Π *f*¹³ 28 33 *pm;* other witnesses have variations of the addition

Matt 6:32 ⇨ Matt 6:8
³²"*For the Gentiles seek all these things; and your heavenly Father knows that you need them all.*"

Matt 18:35 ⇨ Matt 6:14
³⁵"*So also my heavenly Father will do to every one of you, if you do not forgive your brother from your heart.*"

Isa 26:20 ⇨ Matt 6:6
²⁰Come, my people, enter **your** chambers,
   and shut your doors behind you;
hide yourselves for a little while
   until the wrath is past.

JOHN

MARK

Mark 11:25 ⇨ Matt 6:12, 14–15
²⁵"And whenever **you stand** praying, **forgive**, if you have anything against any one; so that **your Father** also who is in heaven may **forgive you your trespasses.**"

THOMAS

POxy654 6
(6) [His disciples] ask him [and s]ay, "How [shall we] fast, [and how shall] we [pray] and how [shall we give alms, a]nd what shall [we] observe [when we sup?"] Jesus says, "[Do not lie and what] you [hate] do not do. [For all things will be full of (?)] truth bef[ore heaven. For there is nothing] hidden [which will not be (made) known. Ha]ppy is [he who does not do these things. For all] will be mani[fest before the Father who] is [in heaven]."

GThom 6
(6) His disciples questioned Him and said to Him, "Do You want us to fast? How shall we pray? Shall we give alms? What diet shall we observe?"
Jesus said, "Do not tell lies, and do not do what you hate, for all things are plain in the sight of Heaven. For nothing hidden will not become manifest, and nothing covered will remain without being uncovered."

LUKE

Luke 11:1–4 (§50.1) ⇨ Matt 6:9–15
¹He was praying in a certain place, and when he ceased, one of his disciples said to him, "Lord teach us to pray, as John taught his disciples." ²And he said to them, "When you **pray,** say:

"**Father, hallowed be thy name. Thy kingdom come.** ³**Give us** each **day** our **daily bread;** ⁴**and forgive us** our sins, for **we** ourselves **forgive** every one who is indebted to us; **and lead us not into temptation.**"

OTHER

Did 8:2–3
²And do **not** pray as **the hypocrites,** but as the Lord commanded in his Gospel, **pray** thus: "**Our Father, who art in Heaven,** hallowed be thy Name, thy **Kingdom come, thy will be done, as in Heaven** so also upon **earth; give us** to-day **our daily bread, and forgive us our** debt as we forgive **our debtors, and lead us not into** trial, **but deliver us from** the **Evil** One, for thine is the power and the glory for ever." ³Pray thus three times a day.

GNaz 5 ⇨ Matt 6:11
(5) In the so-called Gospel according to the Hebrews instead of "essential to existence" I found "mahar," which means "of tomorrow," so that the sense is:
***Our bread** of tomorrow—that is, of the future—give us this day.* (Jerome, *Commentary on Matthew* 1 [on Matthew 6:11])

MATT	MARK	LUKE

Matt 6:16–18 (§M12.6d)

16 "And when you fast, do not look dismal, like the hypocrites, for they disfigure their faces that their fasting may be seen by men. Truly, I say to you, they have received their reward. 17 But when you fast, anoint your head and wash your face, 18 that your fasting may not be seen by men but by your Father who is in secret; and your Father who sees in secret will reward you."

JOHN	THOMAS	OTHER

POxy1 2

(2) Jesus says: "If you do not fast (to) the world, you will not find the kingdom of God; and if you do not make the sabbath a (real) sabbath, you will not see the Father."

POxy654 6

(6) [His disciples] ask him [and s]ay, "How [shall we] fast, [and how shall] we [pray] and how [shall we give alms, a]nd what shall [we] observe [when we sup?"] Jesus says, "[Do not lie and what] you [hate] do not do. [For all things will be full of (?)] truth bef[ore heaven. For there is nothing] hidden [which will not be (made) known. Ha]ppy is [he who does not do these things. For all] will be mani[fest before the Father who] is [in heaven]."

GThom 6

(6) His disciples questioned Him and said to Him, "Do You want us to fast? How shall we pray? Shall we give alms? What diet shall we observe?"

Jesus said, "Do not tell lies, and do not do what you hate, for all things are plain in the sight of Heaven. For nothing hidden will not become manifest, and nothing covered will remain without being uncovered."

GThom 14

(14) Jesus said to them, "If you fast, you will give rise to sin for yourselves; and if you pray, you will be condemned; and if you give alms, you will do harm to your spirits. When you go into any land and walk about in the districts, if they receive you, eat what they will set before you, and heal the sick among them. For what goes into your mouth will not defile you, but that which issues from your mouth—it is that which will defile you."

Did 8:1

1 Let not your fasts be with the hypocrites, for they fast on Mondays and Thursdays, but do you fast on Wednesdays and Fridays.

MATT	MARK	LUKE

Matt 6:19–21 (§M12.7a)

[19] "Do not lay up for yourselves treasures on earth, where moth and rust consume and where thieves break in and steal, [20] but lay up for yourselves treasures in heaven, where neither moth nor rust[a] consumes and where thieves do not break in and steal. [21] For where your treasure is, there will your heart be also."

Matt 6:22–23 (§M12.7b)

[22] "The eye is the lamp of the body. So, if your eye is sound, your whole body will be full of light; [23] but if your eye is not sound, your whole body will be full of darkness. If then the light in you is darkness, how great is the darkness!"

[a] Or: *worm*

Mark 4:21–23 (§K21.3) ⇨ §M12.7b

[21] *And he said to them, "Is a **lamp** brought in to be put under a bushel, or under a bed, and not on a stand? [22] For there is nothing hid, except to be made manifest; nor is anything secret, except to come to **light**. [23] If any man has ears to hear, let him hear."*

Luke 12:33–34 ⇨ §M12.7a

[33] "Sell your possessions, and give alms; provide **yourselves** with purses that do not grow old, with a treasure in the heavens that does not fail, **where** no thief approaches and no **moth** destroys. [34] **For where your treasure is, there will your heart be also."**

Luke 11:33–36 (§L51.5) ⇨ §M12.7b

[33] "No one after lighting a lamp puts it in a cellar or under a bushel, but on a stand, that those who enter may see **the light**. [34] Your **eye is the lamp of your body; when your eye is sound, your whole body is full of light;** but when it **is not sound, your body** is **full of darkness.** [35] Therefore be careful lest **the light in you** be **darkness.** [36] If then **your whole body** is **full of light**, having no part dark, it will be wholly bright, as when a lamp with its rays gives you **light."**

JOHN	THOMAS	OTHER

GThom 76 ⇨ §M12.7a

*(76) Jesus said, "The Kingdom of the Father is like a merchant who had a consignment of merchandise and who discovered a pearl. That merchant was shrewd. He sold the merchandise and bought the pearl alone for himself. You too, seek his unfailing and enduring treasure where no **moth** comes near to devour and no worm destroys."*

GThom 24 ⇨ §M12.7b

(24) His disciples said to Him, "Show us the place where You are, since it is necessary for us to seek it."

*He said to them, "Whoever has ears, let him hear. There is **light** within a man of **light**, and he (or: it) lights up the whole world. If he (or: it) does not shine, he (or: it) is **darkness**."*

DialSav 125:18–126:1 ⇨M12.7b

*The Savior said, "**The lamp [of the] body is the mind;** as long as [20] you (sing.) are upright [of heart]—which is [...]—then your (pl.) bodies are [lights]. As long as your mind is [darkness], your **light** which **you** wait for [will not be]."*

Matt 6:24
Matt 6:25–34

ON SERVING TWO MASTERS
ON ANXIETY

M12.7c
M12.7d

MATT	MARK	LUKE

Matt 6:24 (§M12.7c)

²⁴"No one can serve two masters; for either he will hate the one and love the other, or he will be devoted to one and despise the other. You cannot serve God and mammon."ᵃ

Matt 6:25–34 (M12.7d)

²⁵"Therefore I tell you, do not be anxious about your life, what you shall eat or what you shall drink,ᵇ nor about your body, what you shall put on. Is not life more than food, and the body more than clothing? ²⁶Look at the birds of the air: they neither sow nor reap nor gather into barns, and yet your heavenly Father feeds them. Are you not of more value than they? ²⁷And which of you by being anxious can add one cubit to his span of life?ᶜ ²⁸And why are you anxious about clothing? Consider the lilies of the field, how they grow; they neither toil nor spin; ²⁹yet I tell you, even Solomon in all his glory was not arrayed like one of these. ³⁰But if God so clothes the grass of the field, which today is alive and tomorrow is thrown into the oven, will he not much more clothe you, O men of little faith? ³¹Therefore do not be anxious, saying, 'What shall we eat?' or 'What shall we drink?' or 'What shall we wear?' ³²For the Gentiles seek all these things; and your heavenly Father knows that you need them all. ³³But seek first his kingdom and his righteousness, and all these things shall be yours as well.

³⁴"Therefore do not be anxious about tomorrow, for tomorrow will be anxious for itself. Let the day's own trouble be sufficient for the day."

ᵃ *Mammon is a Semitic word for money or riches*

ᵇ Text: B W *f*¹³ 33 1230 it (in part) *al; omit or what you shall drink:* ℵ *f*¹ 892 it (in part) vg syr (in part) *al*

ᶜ Or: *to his stature*

JOHN

THOMAS

GThom 47 ⇨ §M12.7c

(47) Jesus said, "It is impossible for a man to mount two horses or to stretch two bows. And it is impossible for a servant to serve two masters; otherwise, he will honor the one and treat the other contemptuously. No man drinks old wine and immediately desires to drink new wine. And new wine is not put into old wineskins, lest they burst; nor is old wine put into a new wineskin, lest it spoil it. An old patch is not sewn onto a new garment, because a tear would result."

POxy655 1 ⇨ §M12.7d

(1a) [Jesus says, **"Be not** solicitous f]rom morning un[til evening, nor] from eve[ning until mo]rning either [for y]our [sustenance], **what** [you will] **eat,** [**or**] for [your] clo[thing], **what** you [will] **put on.** [You] **are** worth [far] **more than** [the lili]es whi[ch **g]row** but do not s[pi]n, a[nd] have n[o] clo[th]ing. And you, what do [you lack?] Who **of you can add to his** stature? He will [g]ive **you** your **clothing."**

(1b) His disciples say to him, "When will you be revealed to us and when shall we see you?" He says, "When you take off your clothes and are not ashamed, [and take your tunics and put them under your feet like little children and tread upon them, then you will become sons of the Living One and you will not fear]."

GThom 36 ⇨ §M12.7d

(36) Jesus said, **"Do not be** concerned from morning until evening and from evening until morning **about what you will** wear."

Luke 16:10–13 (§L67.2) ⇨ §M12.7c

¹⁰"He who is faithful in a very little is faithful also in much; and he who is dishonest in a very little is dishonest also in much. ¹¹If then you Consider the lilies of the field, how they grow; they neither toil nor spin; ¹²And if you have not been faithful in that which is another's, who will give you that which is your own? ¹³No servant **can serve two masters; for either he will hate the one and love the other, or he will be devoted to the one and despise the other. You cannot serve God and mammon."**

Luke 12:22–34 (§L55) ⇨ §M12.7d

²²And he said to his disciples, **"Therefore I tell you, do not be anxious about your life, what you shall eat, nor about your body, what you shall put on. ²³For life is more than food, and the body more than clothing. ²⁴Consider** the ravens: **they neither sow nor reap, they** have **neither** storehouse **nor** barn, **and yet** God **feeds them.** Of how much **more value are you than the birds! ²⁵And which of you by being anxious can add a cubit to his span of life? ²⁶If then you** are not able to do as small a thing as that, **why are you anxious about the** rest? ²⁷**Consider the lilies, how they grow; they neither toil nor spin; yet I tell you, even Solomon in all his glory was not arrayed like one of these. ²⁸But if God so clothes the grass** which is alive in **the field today and tomorrow is thrown into the oven,** how **much more will** he **clothe you, O men of little faith! ²⁹And do not seek what** you are to **eat and what** you are to **drink,** nor **be** of **anxious** mind. ³⁰**For** all the **nations of the world seek these things; and your Father knows that you need them. ³¹**Instead, **seek his kingdom, and these things shall be yours as well.**

³²"Fear not, little flock, for it is **your** Father's good pleasure to give **you** the kingdom. ³³Sell your possessions, and give alms; provide yourselves with purses that **do not** grow old, with a treasure in the heavens that does not fail, where no thief approaches and no moth destroys. ³⁴**For** where your treasure is, there will your heart be also."

OTHER

38 **Matt 5:1–7:29**

SERMON ON THE MOUNT

M12

Matt 5:1–7:29

SERMON ON THE MOUNT

S4: M12

M12.7e
M12.7f

ON JUDGING
ON PROFANING THE HOLY

Matt 7:1–5
Matt 7:6

MATT

Matt 7:1–5 (§M12.7e)
[1] "Judge not, that you be not judged. [2] For with the judgment you pronounce you will be judged, and the measure you give will be the measure you get. [3] Why do you see the speck that is in your brother's eye, but do not notice the log that is in your own eye? [4] Or how can you say to your brother, 'Let me take the speck out of your eye,' when there is the log in your own eye? [5] You hypocrite, first take the log out of your own eye, and then you will see clearly to take the speck out of your brother's eye."

Matt 7:6 (§M12.7f)
[6] "Do not give dogs what is holy; and do not throw your pearls before swine, lest they trample them under foot and turn to attack you."

MARK

Mark 4:24–25 ⇨ Matt 7:2
[24] And he said to them, "Take heed what you hear; the measure you give will be the measure you get, and still more will be given you. [25] For to him who has will more be given; and from him who has not, even what he has will be taken away."

LUKE

Luke 6:37–42 (§L25.3) ⇨ §M12.7e
[37] "Judge not, and you will not be judged; condemn not, and you will not be condemned; forgive, and you will be forgiven; [38] give, and it will be given to you; good measure, pressed down, shaken together, running over, will be put into your lap. For the measure you give will be the measure you get back."

[39] He also told them a parable: "Can a blind man lead a blind man? Will they not both fall into a pit? [40] A disciple is not above his teacher, but every one when he is fully taught will be like his teacher. [41] Why do you see the speck that is in your brother's eye, but do not notice the log that is in your own eye? [42] Or how can you say to your brother, 'Brother, let me take out the speck that is in your eye,' when you yourself do not see the log that is in your own eye? You hypocrite, first take the log out of your own eye, and then you will see clearly to take out the speck that is in your brother's eye."

JOHN

THOMAS

POxy1 1 ⇨ Matt 7:3–5
(1) [Jesus says, "You see the splinter in your brother's eye, but the beam in your own eye you do not see. Hypocrite, cast the beam out of your eye,] and then you will see in order to cast out the splinter which (is) in your brother's eye."

GThom 26 ⇨ Matt 7:3–5
(26) Jesus said, "You see the mote in your brother's eye, but you do not see the beam in your own eye. When you cast the beam out of your own eye, then you will see clearly to cast the mote from your brother's eye."

GThom 93 ⇨ §M12.7f
(93) <Jesus said,> "Do not give what is holy to dogs, lest they throw them on the dung-heap. Do not throw the pearls to swine, lest they grind it [to bits]."

OTHER

1 Clem 13:2 ⇨ Matt 7:1–2
[2] For he spoke thus: "Be merciful, that ye may obtain mercy. Forgive, that ye may be forgiven. As ye do, so shall it be given unto you. As ye judge, so shall ye be judged. As ye are kind, so shall kindness be shewn you. With what measure ye mete, it shall be measured to you."

GNaz 6 ⇨ Matt 7:5
(6) The Jewish Gospel reads here as follows:
If ye be in my bosom and do not the will of my Father in heaven, I will cast you out of my bosom. (Variant to Matthew 7:5—or better to Matthew 7:21–23—in the "Zion Gospel" Edition)

Did 9:5 ⇨ §M12.7f
[5] But let none eat or drink of your Eucharist except those who have been baptised in the Lord's Name. For concerning this also did the Lord say, "Give not that which is holy to the dogs."

M12
S4: M12

SERMON ON THE MOUNT
SERMON ON THE MOUNT

Matt 5:1–7:29
Matt 5:1–7:29

39

Matt 7:7–11
Matt 7:12

GOD ANSWERS PRAYER
THE GOLDEN RULE

M12.7g
M12.7h

MATT

Matt 7:7–11 (§M12.7g)
[7]"Ask, and it will be given you; seek, and you will find; knock, and it will be opened to you. [8]For every one who asks receives, and he who seeks finds, and to him who knocks it will be opened. [9]Or what man of you, if his son asks him for bread, will give him a stone? [10]Or if he asks for a fish, will give him a serpent? [11]If you then, who are evil, know how to give good gifts to your children, how much more will your Father who is in heaven give good things to those who ask him!"

Matt 7:12 (§M12.7h)
[12]"So whatever you wish that men would do to you, do so to them; for this is the law and the prophets."

Matt 21:22 ⇨ Matt 7:7–8
[22]*"And whatever you ask in prayer, you will receive, if you have faith."*

Tob 4:15 ⇨ §M12.7h
[15]"And what **you** hate, **do** not **do** to any one. Do not drink wine to excess or let drunkenness go with you on your way."

Sir 31:15 ⇨ §M12.7h
[15]Judge your neighbor's feelings by your own, and in every matter be thoughtful.

JOHN

MARK

Mark 11:24 ⇨ Matt 7:7–8
[24]*"Therefore I tell you, whatever you ask in prayer, believe that you have received it, and it will be yours."*

THOMAS

POxy654 2 ⇨ Matt 7:7
(2) [Jesus says,] "Let him who see[ks] not cease [seeking until] he finds and when he finds, [he will be astounded, and] having been [astoun]ded, he will reign an[d having reigned], he will re[st]."

GThom 2 ⇨ Matt 7:7
(2) Jesus said, "Let him who seeks continue seeking until he finds. When he finds, he will become troubled. When he becomes troubled, he will be astonished, and he will rule over the All."

GThom 92 ⇨ Matt 7:7
(92) Jesus said, **"Seek and you will find.** Yet, what you asked Me about in former times and which I did not tell you then, now I do desire to tell, but you do not inquire after it."

GThom 94 ⇨ Matt 7:7
(94) Jesus [said], "He who seeks **will find,** and [he who knocks] **will be** let in."

POxy654 6 ⇨ §M12.7h
(6) [His disciples] ask him [and s]ay, "How [shall we] fast, [and how shall] we [pray] and how [shall we give alms, a]nd what shall [we] observe [when we sup?"] Jesus says, "[Do not lie and what] you [hate] do not do. [For all things will be full of (?)] truth bef[ore heaven. For there is nothing] hidden [which will not be (made) known. Ha]ppy is [he who does not do these things. For all] will be mani[fest before the Father who] is [in heaven]."

GThom 6 ⇨ §M12.7h
(6) His disciples questioned Him and said to Him, "Do You want us to fast? How shall we pray? Shall we give alms? What diet shall we observe?"

Jesus said, "Do not tell lies, and do not do what you hate, for all things are plain in the sight of Heaven. For nothing hidden will not become manifest, and nothing covered will remain without being uncovered."

LUKE

Luke 11:9–13 (§L50.3) ⇨ §M12.7g
[9]"And I tell you, **Ask, and it will be given you; seek, and you will find; knock, and it will** be opened to you. [10]For every one who asks receives, and he who seeks finds, and to him who knocks it will be opened. [11]What father among you, if his son asks for a fish, will instead of a fish **give him** a serpent; [12]or if he asks for an egg, will give him a scorpion? [13]If you then, who are evil, know how to give good gifts to your children, how much more will the heavenly **Father give** the Holy Spirit **to** those who ask him!"

Luke 6:31 ⇨ §M12.7h
[31]"And as **you wish that men would do to you, do so to them."**

OTHER

Did 1:2 ⇨ §M12.7h
[2]The Way of Life is this: "First, thou shalt love the God who made thee, secondly, thy neighbour as thyself; and whatsoever thou wouldst not have done **to** thyself, **do** not thou to another."

40 **Matt 5:1–7:29**
Matt 5:1–7:29

SERMON ON THE MOUNT
SERMON ON THE MOUNT

M12
S4: M12

M12.8a
M12.8b

THE NARROW GATE
FALSE PROPHETS

Matt 7:13–14
Matt 7:15–20

MATT

Matt 7:13–14 (§M12.8a)
¹³ "Enter by the narrow gate; for the gate is wide and the way is easy, that leads to destruction, and those who enter by it are many. ¹⁴ For[a] the gate is narrow and the way is hard, that leads to life, and those who find it are few."

Matt 7:15–20 (§M12.8b)
¹⁵ "Beware of false prophets, who come to you in sheep's clothing but inwardly are ravenous wolves. ¹⁶ You will know them by their fruits. Are grapes gathered from thorns, or figs from thistles? ¹⁷ So, every sound tree bears good fruit, but the bad tree bears evil fruit. ¹⁸ A sound tree cannot bear evil fruit, nor can a bad tree bear good fruit. ¹⁹ Every tree that does not bear good fruit is cut down and thrown into the fire. ²⁰ Thus you will know them by their fruits."

[a] Text: ℵ* B* X^c al; How (narrow is the gate...): ℵ^c B³ C K L W X* Δ Θ Π f¹ f¹³ 28 al

Matt 12:33–37 ⇨ §M12.8b
³³ "Either make the **tree good**, and its **fruit good**; or make the **tree bad**, and its **fruit** bad; for the tree is known **by its fruit**. ³⁴ You brood of vipers! how can you speak good, when you are evil? For out of the abundance of the heart the mouth speaks. ³⁵ The good man out of his good treasure brings forth **good**, and the evil man out of his evil treasure brings forth **evil**. ³⁶ I tell you, on the day of judgment men will render account for every careless word they utter; ³⁷ for by your words you will be justified, and by your words you will be condemned."

Matt 3:10 ⇨ Matt 7:19
¹⁰ *"Even now the axe is laid to the root of the trees; every tree therefore that does not bear good fruit is cut down and thrown into the fire."*

JOHN

MARK

Mark 13:22 ⇨ Matt 7:15
²² *"False Christs and false prophets will arise and show signs and wonders, to lead astray, if possible, the elect."*

THOMAS

GThom 45 ⇨ Matt 7:16
(45) Jesus said, "**Grapes are** not harvested **from thorns**, nor are **figs** gathered **from thistles**, for they do not produce fruit. A **good** man brings forth **good** from his storehouse; an **evil** man brings forth **evil** things from his **evil** storehouse, which is in his heart, and says evil things. For out of the abundance of the heart he brings forth evil things."

LUKE

Luke 13:22–30 (§L61) ⇨ §M12.8a
²² He went on his way through towns and villages, teaching, and journeying toward Jerusalem. ²³ And some one said to him, "Lord, will those who are saved be few?" And he said to them, ²⁴ "Strive to **enter by the narrow** door; for **many**, I tell you, will seek to **enter** and will not be able. ²⁵ When once the householder has risen up and shut the door, you will begin to stand outside and to knock at the door, saying, 'Lord, open to us.' He will answer you, 'I do not know where you come from.' ²⁶ Then you will begin to say, 'We ate and drank in your presence, and you taught in our streets.' ²⁷ But he will say, 'I tell you, I do not know where you come from; depart from me, all you workers of iniquity!' ²⁸ There you will weep and gnash your teeth, when you see Abraham and Isaac and Jacob and all the prophets in the kingdom of God and you yourselves thrust out. ²⁹ And men will come from east and west, and from north and south, and sit at table in the kingdom of God. ³⁰ And behold, some are last who will be first, and some are first who will be last."

Luke 6:43–45 (§L25.4) ⇨ §M12.8b
⁴³ "For no good **tree** bears bad **fruit, nor** again does a **bad tree** bear good fruit; ⁴⁴ for each tree is known **by its own fruit**. For figs are not **gathered from thorns**, nor **are grapes** picked from a bramble bush. ⁴⁵ The **good** man out of the **good** treasure of his heart produces **good**, and the **evil** man out of his **evil** treasure produces **evil**; for out of the abundance of the heart his mouth speaks."

Luke 3:9 ⇨ Matt 7:19
⁹ *"Even now the axe is laid to the root of the trees; every tree therefore that does not bear good fruit is cut down and thrown into the fire."*

OTHER

M12
S4: M12

SERMON ON THE MOUNT
SERMON ON THE MOUNT

Matt 5:1–7:29
Matt 5:1–7:29

41

MATT

Matt 7:21–23 (§M12.8c)

21 "Not every one who says to me, 'Lord, Lord,' shall enter the kingdom of heaven, but he who does the will of my Father who is in heaven. 22 On that day many will say to me, 'Lord, Lord, did we not prophesy in your name, and cast out demons in your name, and do many mighty works in your name?' 23 And then will I declare to them, 'I never knew you; depart from me, you evildoers.'"

Ps 6:8 ⇨ Matt 7:23

8 **Depart from me**, all you workers of evil;
   for the Lord has heard the sound of my weeping.

MARK

Mark 9:38–40 ⇨ Matt 7:22

38 *John said to him, "Teacher, we saw a man casting* **out demons in your name,** *and we forbade him, because he was not following us." 39 But Jesus said, "Do not forbid him; for no one who does a* **mighty work in my name** *will be able soon after to speak evil of me. 40 For he that is not against us is for us."*

LUKE

Luke 6:46–49 (§L25.5)

46 "Why do you call me '**Lord, Lord,**' and not do what I tell you? 47 Every one who comes to me and hears my words and does them, I will show you what he is like: 48 he is like a man building a house, who dug deep, and laid the foundation upon rock; and when a flood arose, the stream broke against that house, and could not shake it, because it had been well built. 49 But he who hears and does not do them is like a man who built a house on the ground without a foundation; against which the stream broke, and immediately it fell, and the ruin of that house was great."

Luke 13:22–30 (§L60)

22 He went on his way through towns and villages, teaching, and journeying toward Jerusalem. 23 And some one said to him, "**Lord,** will those who are saved be few?" And he said to them, 24 "Strive to enter by the narrow door; for many, I tell you, will seek to enter and will not be able. 25 When once the householder has risen up and shut the door, you will begin to stand outside and to knock at the door, saying, '**Lord,** open to us.' He will answer you, 'I do not know where you come from.' 26 Then you will begin to say, 'We ate and drank in your presence, and you taught in our streets.' 27 But he will say, 'I tell you, I do not know where you come from; depart from me, all you workers of iniquity!' 28 There you will weep and gnash your teeth, when you see Abraham and Isaac and Jacob and all the prophets in **the kingdom of** God and you yourselves thrust out. 29 And men will come from east and west, and from north and south, and sit at table in **the kingdom of** God. 30 And behold, some are last who will be first, and some are first who will be last."

JOHN

THOMAS

OTHER

GNaz 6 ⇨ Matt 7:21

(6) The Jewish Gospel reads here as follows:
If ye be in my bosom and do not **the will of my Father in heaven,** *I will cast you out of my bosom.*
(Variant to Matthew 7:5—or better to Matthew 7:21–23—in the "Zion Gospel" Edition)

2 Clem 4:2 ⇨ Matt 7:21

2 *For he says, "***Not everyone that saith to me Lord, Lord,** *be saved,* **but he that doeth righteousness.***"*

2 Clem 4:5 ⇨ Matt 7:22–23

5 *For this reason, if you do these things, the* **Lord** *said, "If ye be gathred together with me in my bosom, and do not my commandments, I will* **cast you out,** *and will say to you,* **Depart from me, I** *know not whence ye are, ye workers of iniquity."*

MATT

Matt 7:24–27 (§M12.8d)

²⁴"Every one then who hears these words of mine and does them will be like a wise man who built his house upon the rock; ²⁵ and the rain fell, and the floods came, and the winds blew and beat upon that house, but it did not fall, because it had been founded on the rock. ²⁶ And every one who hears these words of mine and does not do them will be like a foolish man who built his house upon the sand; ²⁷ and the rain fell, and the floods came, and the wind blew and beat against that house, and it fell; and great was the fall of it."

Matt 7:28–29 (§M12.9)

²⁸ And when Jesus finished these sayings, the crowds were astonished at his teaching, ²⁹ for he taught them as one who had authority, and not as their scribes.

Matt 13:54 ⇨ §M12.9

*⁵⁴ and coming to his own country he **taught them** in their synagogue, so that they **were astonished**, and said, "Where did this man get this wisdom and these mighty works?"*

Matt 22:33 ⇨ §M12.9

*³³ And **when the crowd heard it**, they **were astonished** at his teaching.*

JOHN

John 7:46 ⇨ §M12.9

⁴⁶ The officers answered, "No man ever spoke like this man!"

MARK

Mark 1:21–22 ⇨ §M12.9

²¹ And they went into Capernaum; and immediately on the sabbath he entered the synagogue and taught. ²² And they were astonished at his teaching, for he taught them as one who had authority, and not as the scribes.

Mark 11:18 ⇨ §M12.9

¹⁸ And the chief priests and the scribes heard it and sought a way to destroy him; for they feared him, because all the multitude was astonished at his teaching.

THOMAS

LUKE

Luke 6:46–49 (§L25.5) ⇨ §M12.8d

⁴⁶"Why do you call me 'Lord, Lord,' and not do what I tell you? ⁴⁷ **Every one who** comes to me and **hears my words and does them**, I will show you what he is **like**: ⁴⁸ he is **like a man** building a **house**, who dug deep, and laid the foundation **upon rock**; **and** when a flood arose, the stream broke against **that house**, and could **not** shake **it**, **because it had been** well built. ⁴⁹ But he **who hears and does not do them** is like **a man who built a house** on the ground without a foundation; against which **the stream broke, and immediately it fell, and** the ruin **of** that **house was great.**"

Luke 4:32 ⇨ §M12.9

³² and they were astonished at his teaching, for his word was with authority.

OTHER

InThom 19:2c ⇨ §M12.9

And all paid attention to him and marvelled how he, a child, put to silence the elders and teachers of the people, expounding the sections of the law and the sayings of the prophets.

MATT	MARK	LUKE

Matt 8:1–4 (§M13)

[1] When he came down from the mountain, great crowds followed him; [2] and behold, a leper came to him and knelt before him, saying, "Lord, if you will, you can make me clean." [3] And he stretched out his hand and touched him, saying, "I will; be clean." And immediately his leprosy was cleansed. [4] And Jesus said to him, "See that you say nothing to any one; but go, show yourself to the priest, and offer the gift that Moses commanded, for a proof to the people."[a]

[a] Greek: *to them*

⇨ Matt 8:4
Cf. Lev 13–14, esp. 14:2–20

Mark 1:40–45 (§K12)

[40] And a leper came to him beseeching him, and kneeling said to him, "If you will, you can make me clean." [41] Moved with pity, he stretched out his hand and touched him, and said to him, "I will; be clean." [42] And immediately the leprosy left him, and he was made clean. [43] And he sternly charged him, and sent him away at once, [44] and said to him, "See that you say nothing to any one; but go, show yourself to the priest, and offer for your cleansing what Moses commanded, for a proof to the people." [45] But he went out and began to talk freely about it, and to spread the news, so that Jesus could no longer openly enter a town, but was out in the country; and people came to him from every quarter.

Luke 5:12–16 (§L18)

[12] While he was in one of the cities, there came a man full of leprosy; and when he saw Jesus, he fell on his face and besought him, "Lord, if you will, you can make me clean." [13] And he stretched out his hand, and touched him, saying, "I will; be clean." And immediately the leprosy left him. [14] And he charged him to tell no one; but "go and show yourself to the priest, and make an offering for your cleansing, as Moses commanded, for a proof to the people." [15] But so much the more the report went abroad concerning him; and great multitudes gathered to hear and to be healed of their infirmities. [16] But he withdrew to the wilderness and prayed.

JOHN	THOMAS	OTHER

PEger2 2

(2) And behold a leper drew near [to him] and said: "Master Jesus, wandering with lepers and eating with [them was I(?)] in the inn; I also [became] a le[per]. If [thou] therefore [wilt], I am made clean." Immediately the Lord [said to him]: "I will, be thou made clean." [And thereupon] the leprosy departed from him. [And the Lord said to him]: "Go [thy way and show th]yself to the [priests] . . ."

MATT	MARK	LUKE

Matt 8:5-13 (§M14)

[5] As he entered Capernaum, a centurion came forward to him, beseeching him [6] and saying, "Lord, my servant is lying paralyzed at home, in terrible distress." [7] And he said to him, "I will come and heal him." [8] But the centurion answered him, "Lord, I am not worthy to have you come under my roof; but only say the word, and my servant will be healed. [9] For I am a man under authority, with soldiers under me; and I say to one, 'Go,' and he goes, and to another, 'Come,' and he comes, and to my slave, 'Do this,' and he does it." [10] When Jesus heard him, he marveled, and said to those who followed him, "Truly, I say to you, not even[a] in Israel have I found such faith. [11] I tell you, many will come from east and west and sit at table with Abraham, Isaac, and Jacob in the kingdom of heaven, [12] while the sons of the kingdom will be thrown into the outer darkness; there men will weep and gnash their teeth." [13] And to the centurion Jesus said, "Go; be it done for you as you have believed." And the servant was healed at that very moment.

[a] *not even:* (cf. Luke 7:9) ℵ C K L X Δ Θ Π 0250 *f*[13] 33 *pm; with no one* B W it (in part) syr[c] *al*

⇨ Matt 8:11
Cf. Ps 107:3

Matt 13:42 ⇨ Matt 8:12
[42] "and throw them into the furnace of fire; there men will weep and gnash their teeth."

JOHN

John 4:45-54 (§J8)

[45] So when **he** came to Galilee, the Galileans welcomed him, having seen all that he had done in Jerusalem at the feast, for they too had gone to the feast.

[46] So **he** came again to Cana in Galilee, where he had made the water wine. And at **Capernaum** there was an official whose son was ill. [47] When he heard that Jesus had come from Judea to Galilee, he went and begged **him** to come down and heal his son, for he was at the point of death. [48] Jesus therefore **said to him**, "Unless you see signs and wonders you will not believe." [49] **The** official said to **him**, "Sir, come down before my child dies." [50] **Jesus said** to him, "Go; your son will live." The man **believed** the word that Jesus spoke to him and went his way. [51] As he was going down, his servants met him and told him that his son was living. [52] So he asked them the hour when he began to mend, and they said to him, "Yesterday at the seventh hour the fever left him." [53] The father knew that was the hour when **Jesus** had **said** to him, "Your son will live"; and he himself **believed**, and all his household. [54] This was now the second sign that Jesus did when he had come from Judea to Galilee.

Matt 13:50 ⇨ Matt 8:12
[50] "and throw them into the furnace of fire; there men will weep and gnash their teeth."

Matt 22:13 ⇨ Matt 8:12
[13] "The the king said to the attendants, 'Bind him hand and foot, and cast him into the outer darkness; there men will weep and gnash their teeth.'"

Matt 24:51 ⇨ Matt 8:12
[51] "and will punish him, and put him with the hypocrites; there men will weep and gnash their teeth."

Matt 25:30 ⇨ Matt 8:12
[30] "'And cast the worthless servant into the outer darkness; there men will weep and gnash their teeth.'"

THOMAS

Luke 7:1-10 (§L26)

[1] After he had ended all his sayings in the hearing of the people **he entered Capernaum.** [2] Now a **centurion** had a slave who was dear to him, who was sick and at the point of death. [3] When he heard of Jesus, he sent to him elders of the Jews, asking him to come and heal his slave. [4] And when they came to Jesus, they besought him earnestly, saying, "He is **worthy to have you** do this for him, [5] for he loves our nation, and he built us our synagogue." [6] And Jesus went with them. When he was not far from the house, the **centurion** sent friends to him, saying to him, "**Lord,** do not trouble yourself, for **I am not worthy to have you come under my roof;** [7] therefore I did not presume to come to you. But say the word, and let my servant be healed. [8] For I am a man set **under authority, with soldiers under me: and I say to one, 'Go,' and he goes; and to another, 'Come,' and he comes; and to my slave, 'Do this,' and he does it."** [9] When **Jesus heard** this **he marveled** at him, and turned **and said to** the multitude that **followed him,** "I tell you, **not even in Israel have I found such faith."** [10] And when those who had been sent returned to the house, they found **the** slave well.

Luke 13:28-30 ⇨ Matt 8:11-12
[28] "There you **will weep and gnash** your **teeth,** when you see **Abraham** and **Isaac and Jacob** and all the prophets **in the kingdom of** God and you yourselves thrust out. [29] And men **will come from east and west,** and from north and south, **and sit at table in the kingdom of** God. [30] And behold, some are last who will be first, and some are first who will be last."

OTHER

MATT	MARK	LUKE

Matt 8:14–15 (§M15)

¹⁴And when Jesus entered Peter's house, he saw his mother-in-law lying sick with a fever; ¹⁵he touched her hand, and the fever left her, and she rose and served him.

Matt 8:16–17 (§M16) °

¹⁶That evening they brought to him many who were possessed with demons; and he cast out the spirits with a word, and healed all who were sick. ¹⁷This was to fulfil what was spoken by the prophet Isaiah, "He took our infirmities and bore our diseases."

°Appendix 3 ⇨ §M16

Isa 53:4 ⇨ Matt 8:17
⁴Surely **he** has borne **our** griefs
　and carried our sorrows;
yet we esteemed him stricken,
　smitten by God, and afflicted.

Mark 1:29–31 (§K9) ⇨ §M15

²⁹And immediately he left the synagogue, and entered the house of Simon and Andrew, with James and John. ³⁰Now Simon's **mother-in-law** lay **sick with a fever**, and immediately they told him of her. ³¹And **he** came and took **her** by the **hand** and lifted her up, **and the fever left her; and she served them.**

Mark 1:32–34 (§K10) ⇨ §M16

³²**That evening**, at sundown, **they brought to him** all **who were** sick or **possessed with demons.** ³³And the whole city was gathered together about the door. ³⁴**And he healed** many **who were sick** with various diseases, **and cast out** many **demons**; and he would not permit the demons to speak, because they knew him.

Luke 4:38–39 (§L14) ⇨ §M15

³⁸And he arose and left the synagogue, and entered Simon's house. Now Simon's **mother-in-law** was ill with a high **fever**, and they besought him for her. ³⁹And **he** stood over **her** and rebuked **the fever**, and it **left her**; and immediately **she rose and served them.**

Luke 4:40–41 (§L15) ⇨ §M16

⁴⁰Now when the sun was setting, all those **who** had any that **were sick** with various diseases **brought** them **to him; and he** laid his hands on every one of them **and healed** them. ⁴¹And **demons** also came **out** of many, crying, "You are the Son of God!" But he rebuked them, and would not allow them to speak, because they knew that he was the Christ.

JOHN	THOMAS	OTHER

MATT

Matt 8:18–22 (§M17)

¹⁸ Now when Jesus saw great crowds around him, he gave orders to go over to the other side. ¹⁹ And a scribe came up and said to him, "Teacher, I will follow you wherever you go." ²⁰ And Jesus said to him, "Foxes have holes, and birds of the air have nests; but the Son of man has nowhere to lay his head." ²¹ Another of the disciplesᵃ said to him, "Lord, let me first go and bury my father." ²² But Jesus said to him, "Follow me, and leave the dead to bury their own dead."

Matt 8:23–27 (§M18)

²³ And when he got into the boat, his disciples followed him. ²⁴ And behold, there arose a great storm on the sea, so that the boat was being swamped by the waves; but he was asleep. ²⁵ And they went and woke him, saying, "Save,ᵇ Lord; we are perishing." ²⁶ And he said to them, "Why are you afraid, O men of little faith?" Then he rose and rebuked the winds and the sea; and there was a great calm. ²⁷ And the men marveled, saying, "What sort of man is this, that even winds and sea obey him?"

ᵃ Add *his:* ℵ B 33 2148 it (in part) cop^sa

ᵇ Text: ℵ B C *f*¹ *f*¹³ 33 892 *al; save us:* K L W X Δ Θ Π *pm*

Matt 6:30 ⇨ Matt 8:26
³⁰ *But if God so clothes the grass of the field, which today is alive and tomorrow is thrown into the oven, will he not much more clothe you, **O men of little faith?***

Matt 14:31 ⇨ Matt 8:26
³¹ *Jesus immediately reached out his hand and caught him, saying to him, "**O man of little faith,** why did you doubt?"*

Matt 16:8 ⇨ Matt 8:26
⁸ *But Jesus, aware of this, said, "**O men of little faith,** why do you discuss among yourselves the fact that you have no bread?*

Ps 65:5–8 ⇨ §M18
⁵ By dread deeds thou dost answer us with deliverance,
    O God of our salvation,
who art the hope of all the ends of the earth,
    and of the farthest seas;
⁶ who by thy strength hast established the mountains,
    being girded with might;
⁷ who dost still the roaring of the seas,
    the roaring of their **waves,**
    the tumult of the peoples;
⁸ so that those who dwell at earth's farthest bounds
    are afraid at thy signs;
thou makest the outgoings of the morning and the evening
    to shout for joy.

JOHN

MARK

Mark 4:35–41 (§K22) ⇨ §M18

³⁵ On that day, when evening had come, he said to them, "Let us go across to the other side." ³⁶ And leaving the crowd, they took him with them in **the boat,** just as he was. And other boats were with him. ³⁷ And **a great storm** of wind **arose, and the waves** beat into the boat, **so that the boat was** already filling. ³⁸ But **he was** in the stern, **asleep** on the cushion; **and they woke him** and said to him, "Teacher, do you not care if **we** perish?" ³⁹ And he awoke **and rebuked the** wind, **and** said to **the sea,** "Peace! Be still!" And the wind ceased, **and there was a great calm.** ⁴⁰ **He said to them,** "**Why are you afraid?** Have you no **faith?**" ⁴¹ And they were filled with awe, and said to one another, "Who then **is this, that even** wind **and** sea obey him?"

THOMAS

GThom 86 ⇨ Matt 8:20
(86) **Jesus said, "[The foxes have their holes] and the birds have** [their] **nests, but the Son of Man has** no place **to lay his head** and rest."

LUKE

Luke 9:57–62 (§L45) ⇨ §M17

⁵⁷ As they were going along the road, a man **said to him, "I will follow you wherever you go."** ⁵⁸ **And Jesus said to him,** "**Foxes have holes, and birds of the air have nests; but the Son of man has nowhere to lay his head."** ⁵⁹ To another he **said, "Follow me."** But he said, "**Lord, let me first go and bury my father."** ⁶⁰ **But he said to him,** "**Leave the dead to bury their own dead;** but as for you, go and proclaim the kingdom of God." ⁶¹ Another said, "I will follow you, Lord; but let me first say farewell to those at my home." ⁶² Jesus said to him, "No one who puts his hand to the plow and looks back is fit for the kingdom of God."

Luke 8:22–25 (§L33) ⇨ §M18

²² One day **he got into a boat** with **his disciples,** and he said to them, "Let us go across to the other side of the lake." So they set out, ²³ and as they sailed **he fell asleep.** And **a storm** of wind came down **on the** lake, and they were filling with water, and were in danger. ²⁴ **And they went and woke him, saying,** "Master, Master, **we are perishing!" And he** awoke **and rebuked the** wind **and the** raging waves; and they ceased, **and there was a calm.** ²⁵ **He said to them,** "Where is your **faith?"** And they were afraid, **and** they **marveled, saying** to one another, "Who then is this, **that he** commands **even** wind **and** water, and they **obey him?"**

OTHER

MATT   MARK   LUKE

HEALING OF THE DEMONIACS

Matt 8:28–33 (§M19.1)

28 And when he came to the other side, to the country of the Gadarenes,[a] two demoniacs met him, coming out of the tombs, so fierce that no one could pass that way. 29 And behold, they cried out, "What have you to do with us, O Son of God? Have you come here to torment us before the time?" 30 Now a herd of swine was feeding at some distance from them. 31 And the demons begged him, "If you cast us out, send us away into the herd of swine." 32 And he said to them, "Go." So they came out and went into the swine; and behold, the whole herd rushed down the steep bank into the sea, and perished in the waters. 33 The herdsmen fled, and going into the city they told everything, and what had happened to the demoniacs.

TOWNSPEOPLE BEG JESUS TO LEAVE

Matt 8:34 (§M19.2)

34 And behold, all the city came out to meet Jesus; and when they saw him, they begged him to leave their neighborhood.

[a] *Gadarenes:* (Cf. Mark 5:1, Luke 8:26) ℵ* B C[txt] Δ Θ sy (in part); *Gerasenes:* it vg cop[sa] sy (in part); *Gergesenes:* ℵ[c] C[mg] K L W *f*[1] *f*[13] cop[bo]

Mark 5:1–14a (§K23.1) ⇨ §M19.1

1 They **came to the other side** of the sea, **to the country of the** Gerasenes. 2 And when he had come out of the boat, there **met him out of the tombs** a man with an unclean spirit, 3 who lived among the tombs; and no one could bind him any more, even with a chain; 4 for he had often been bound with fetters and chains, but the chains he wrenched apart, and the fetters he broke in pieces; and no one had the strength to subdue him. 5 Night and day among the tombs and on the mountains he was always crying out, and bruising himself with stones. 6 And when he saw Jesus from afar, he ran and worshiped him; 7 and crying out with a loud voice, he said, "**What have you to do with me, Jesus, Son** of the Most High **God**? I adjure you by God, do not **torment** me." 8 For he had said to him, "Come out of the man, you unclean spirit!" 9 And Jesus asked him, "What is your name?" He replied, "My name is Legion; for we are many." 10 And he **begged him** eagerly not to send them out of the country. 11 Now a great **herd of swine was feeding** there on the hillside; 12 and they begged him, "**Send us** to **the swine,** let us enter them." 13 So he gave them leave. And the unclean spirits **came out,** and entered **the swine;** and **the herd,** numbering about two thousand, **rushed down the steep bank into the sea, and** were drowned **in the sea.**

14 **The herdsman fled,** and told it in the city and in the country.

Mark 5:14b–20 (§K23.2) ⇨ §M19.2

And people came to see what it was that had happened. 15 And they **came to Jesus, and saw** the demoniac sitting there, clothed and in his right mind, the man who had had the legion; and they were afraid. 16 And those who had seen it told what had happened to the demoniac and to the swine. 17 And **they** began **to** beg Jesus to depart from **their neighborhood.** 18 And as he was getting into the boat, the man who had been possessed with demons begged him that he might be with him. 19 But he refused, and said to him, "Go home to your friends, and tell them how much the Lord has done for you, and how he has had mercy on you." 20 And he went away and began to proclaim in the Decapolis how much Jesus had done for him; and all men marveled.

Mark 1:24 ⇨ Matt 8:29

24 *and he cried out, "What have you to do with us, Jesus of Nazareth? Have you come to destroy us? I know who you are, the Holy One of God."*

Luke 8:26–34 (§L34.1) ⇨ §M19.1

26 Then they arrived at **the country of the** Gerasenes, which is opposite Galilee. 27 And as he stepped out on land, there **met him** a man from the city who had demons; for a long time he had worn no clothes, and he lived not in a house but among the tombs. 28 When he saw Jesus, he **cried out** and fell down before him, and said with a loud voice, "**What have you to do with** me, Jesus, **Son** of the Most High **God**? I beseech you, do not **torment** me." 29 For he had commanded the unclean spirit to come out of the man. (For many a time it had seized him; he was kept under guard, and bound with chains and fetters, but he broke the bonds and was driven by the demon into the desert.) 30 Jesus then asked him, "What is your name?" And he said, "Legion"; for many demons had entered him. 31 And they begged him not to command them to depart into the abyss. 32 Now a large **herd of swine was feeding** there on the hillside; **and** they **begged him** to let them enter these. So he gave them leave. 33 Then the demons **came out** of the man and entered **the swine, and the herd rushed down the steep bank into the** lake and were drowned.

34 When **the herdsmen** saw what had happened, they **fled,** and told it in **the city** and in the country.

Luke 8:35–39 (§L34.2) ⇨ §M19.2

35 Then people went **out to** see what had happened, and they **came to Jesus,** and found the man from whom the demons had gone, sitting at the feet of Jesus, clothed and in his right mind; and they were afraid. 36 And those who had seen it told them how he who had been possessed with demons was healed. 37 Then all the people of the surrounding country of the Gerasenes asked **him to** depart from them; for they were seized with great fear; so he got into the boat and returned. 38 The man from whom the demons had gone begged that he might be with him; but he sent him away, saying, 39 "Return to your home, and declare how much God has done for you." And he went away, proclaiming throughout the whole city how much Jesus had done for him.

JOHN

John 2:4 ⇨ Matt 8:29

4 *And Jesus said to her, "O woman, what have you to do with me? My hour has not yet come."*

THOMAS

OTHER

MATT

Matt 9:1–8 (§M20)

¹ **And getting into a boat he crossed over and came to his own city.** ² **And behold, they brought to him a paralytic, lying on his bed; and when Jesus saw their faith he said to the paralytic, "Take heart, my son; your sins are forgiven."** ³ **And behold, some of the scribes said to themselves, "This man is blaspheming."** ⁴ **But Jesus, knowing their thoughts, said, "Why do you think evil in your hearts?** ⁵ **For which is easier, to say, 'Your sins are forgiven,' or to say, 'Rise and walk'?** ⁶ **But that you may know that the Son of man has authority on earth to forgive sins"—he then said to the paralytic—"Rise, take up your bed and go home."** ⁷ **And he rose and went home.** ⁸ **When the crowds saw it, they were afraid, and they glorified God, who had given such authority to men.**

MARK

Mark 2:1–12 (§K13)

¹ And when he returned to Capernaum after some days, it was reported that he was at home. ² And many were gathered together, so that there was no longer room for them, not even about the door; and he was preaching the word to them. ³ And they came, bringing to **him a paralytic** carried by four men. ⁴ And when they could not get near him because of the crowd, they removed the roof above him; and when they had made an opening, they let down the pallet on which the paralytic lay. ⁵ **And when Jesus saw their faith, he said to the paralytic, "My son, your sins are forgiven."** ⁶ Now **some of the scribes** were sitting there, questioning in their hearts, ⁷ "Why does this man speak thus? It is blasphemy! Who can forgive **sins** but God alone?" ⁸ And immediately **Jesus**, perceiving in his spirit that they thus questioned within themselves, said to them, **"Why do you** question thus **in your hearts?** ⁹ **Which is easier, to say** to the paralytic, **'Your sins are forgiven,' or to say,** 'Rise, take up your pallet **and walk'?** ¹⁰ **But that you may know that the Son of man has authority on earth to forgive sins"—he said to the paralytic—** ¹¹ **"I say to you, rise, take up your** pallet **and go home."** ¹² **And he rose, and** immediately took up the pallet and **went** out before them all; so that **they were** all amazed **and glorified God,** saying, "We never saw anything like this!"

LUKE

Luke 5:17–26 (§L19)

¹⁷ On one of those days, as he was teaching, there were Pharisees and teachers of the law sitting by, who had come from every village of Galilee and Judea and from Jerusalem; and the power of the Lord was with him to heal. ¹⁸ **And behold,** men were bringing **on a bed** a man who was paralyzed, and they sought to bring him in and lay him before **Jesus;** ¹⁹ but finding no way to bring him in, because of the crowd, they went up on the roof and let him down with his bed through the tiles into the midst before Jesus. ²⁰ **And when** he saw their **faith he said, "Man, your sins are forgiven you."** ²¹ And **the scribes** and the Pharisees began to question, saying, "Who is this that speaks blasphemies? Who can forgive **sins** but God only?" ²² When **Jesus** perceived their questionings, he answered them, **"Why do you** question **in your hearts?** ²³ **Which is easier, to say, 'Your sins are forgiven** you,' **or to say, 'Rise and walk'?** ²⁴ **But that you may know that the Son of man has authority on earth to forgive sins"—he said to the** man who was paralyzed—"I say to you, **rise, take up your bed and go home."** ²⁵ And immediately **he rose** before them, and took up that on which he lay, **and went home,** glorifying God. ²⁶ And amazement seized them all, **and they glorified God** and were filled with awe, saying, "We have seen strange things today."

JOHN

John 5:1–9a (§J9.1a)

¹ After this there was a feast of the Jews, and Jesus went up to Jerusalem.

² Now there is in Jerusalem by the Sheep Gate a pool, in Hebrew called Bethzatha, which has five porticoes. ³ In these lay a multitude of invalids, blind, lame, paralyzed. ⁵ One man was there, who had been ill for thirty-eight years. ⁶ **When Jesus saw** him and knew that he had been lying there a long time, **he said to** him, "Do you want to be healed?" ⁷ The sick man answered him, "Sir, I have no man to put me into the pool when the water is troubled, and while I am going another steps before me." ⁸ Jesus **said to** him, **"Rise, take up your** pallet, **and walk."** ⁹ **And** at once the man was healed, **and he** took up his pallet **and** walked.

THOMAS

OTHER

MATT	MARK	LUKE

CALL OF MATTHEW

Matt 9:9 (§M21.1)

⁹ As Jesus passed on from there, he saw a man called Matthew sitting at the tax office; and he said to him, "Follow me." And he rose and followed him.

EATING WITH TAX COLLECTORS

Matt 9:10-13 (§M21.2)

¹⁰ And as he sat at table^a in the house, behold, many tax collectors and sinners came and sat down with Jesus and his disciples. ¹¹ And when the Pharisees saw this, they said to his disciples, "Why does your teacher eat with tax collectors and sinners?" ¹² But when he heard it, he said, "Those who are well have no need of a physician, but those who are sick. ¹³ Go and learn what this means, 'I desire mercy, and not sacrifice.' For I came not to call the righteous, but sinners."

^a Greek: *reclined*

● **Matt 12:7** ⇨ Matt 9:13
⁷ "And if you had known **what this means, 'I desire mercy, and not sacrifice,'** you would not have condemned the guiltless."

Hos 6:6 ⇨ Matt 9:13
⁶ For **I desire** steadfast love **and not sacrifice,**
the knowledge of God, rather than burnt offerings.

Mark 2:14 (§K14.2) ⇨ §M21.1
¹⁴ And as he **passed on, he saw** Levi the son of Alphaeus **sitting at the tax office, and he said to him, "Follow me." And he rose and followed him.**

Mark 2:15-17 (§K14.3) ⇨ §M21.2
¹⁵ And as he sat at table in his **house, many tax collectors and sinners** were sitting **with Jesus and his disciples;** for there were many who followed him. ¹⁶ And the scribes of the **Pharisees, when** they saw that he was eating with sinners and tax collectors, **said to his disciples, "Why does he eat with tax collectors and sinners?"** ¹⁷ And **when Jesus heard it,** he said to them, **"Those who are well have no need of a physician, but those who are sick; I came not to call the righteous, but sinners."**

Luke 5:27-28 (§L20.1) ⇨ §M21.1
²⁷ After this he went out, and **saw a tax** lector, named Levi, **sitting at the tax office; and he said to him, "Follow me."** ²⁸ And he left everything, and **rose and followed him.**

Luke 5:29-32 (§L20.2) ⇨ §M21.2
²⁹ And Levi made him a great feast in his **house;** and there was a large company of **tax collectors** and others sitting **at table** with them. ³⁰ And **the Pharisees** and their scribes murmured against **his disciples,** saying, **"Why do you eat and drink with tax collectors and sinners?"** ³¹ And Jesus answered them, **"Those who are well have no need of a physician, but those who are sick;** ³² I have not **come to call the righteous, but sinners** to repentance."

Luke 15:1-2 ⇨ Matt 9:10-11
¹ *Now the tax collectors and sinners were all drawing near to hear him.* ² *And the Pharisees and the scribes murmured, saying, "This man receives sinners and eats with them."*

JOHN	THOMAS	OTHER

POxy1224 1 ⇨ §M21.2
(1) And the scribes and **[Pharisees]** and priests, when they **sa[w]** him, were angry [that with **sin]ners** in the midst he [reclined] **at table.** But Jesus **heard** [it and **said:**] The he[althy **need** not the **physician.**]

Justin, *Apology* **1.15.8** ⇨ Matt 9:13
¹⁵ *So he said: "I have* **not come to call the righteous but sinners** *to repentance." For the Heavenly Father wishes the repentance of a sinner rather than his punishment.*

MATT

Matt 9:14–17 (§M22)

[14] Then the disciples of John came to him, saying, "Why do we and the Pharisees fast,[a] but your disciples do not fast?" [15] And Jesus said to them, "Can the wedding guests mourn as long as the bridegroom is with them? The days will come, when the bridegroom is taken away from them, and then they will fast. [16] And no one puts a piece of unshrunk cloth on an old garment, for the patch tears away from the garment, and a worse tear is made. [17] Neither is new wine put into old wineskins; if it is, the skins burst, and the wine is spilled, and the skins are destroyed; but new wine is put into fresh wineskins, and so both are preserved."

[a] Text: ℵ* B cop^sa(mg) geo; *fast often:* ℵ^b C D K L W X Δ Θ Π *f*^1 *f*^13 33 *pm*

MARK

Mark 2:18–22 (§K15)

[18] Now John's **disciples** and the Pharisees were fasting; and people came and said **to him**, "Why do John's disciples and the disciples of **the Pharisees fast, but your disciples do not fast?**" [19] And Jesus said to them, "Can the **wedding guests** fast while the **bridegroom is with them?** As long as they have the bridegroom with them, they cannot fast. [20] The **days will come, when the bridegroom is taken away from them, and then they will fast** in that day. [21] **No one sews a piece of unshrunk cloth on an old garment;** if he does, **the patch tears away from** it, the new from the old, **and a worse tear is made.** [22] And no one puts **new wine into old wineskins;** if he does, the wine will **burst the skins, and the wine is** lost, and so are the skins; **but new wine is for fresh** skins."

LUKE

Luke 5:33–39 (§L20.3)

[33] And they said to him, "**The disciples of John fast** often and offer prayers, and so do the disciples of **the Pharisees**, but yours eat and drink." [34] And Jesus said to them, "**Can** you make **wedding guests** fast while the **bridegroom is with them?** [35] **The days will come, when the bridegroom is taken away from them, and then they will fast** in those days." [36] He told them a parable also: "**No one** tears a **piece** from a new garment and puts it upon **an old garment**; if he does, he will tear the new, and the piece from the new will not match the old. [37] And no one puts **new wine into old wineskins;** if he does, the new wine will **burst the skins and** it will be **spilled, and the skins** will be **destroyed.** [38] **But new wine** must be **put into fresh wineskins.** [39] And no one after drinking old wine desires new; for he says, 'The old is good.'"

Luke 7:33–34 ⇨ Matt 9:14

*[33] "For **John** the Baptist has come eating no bread and drinking no wine; and you say, 'He has a demon.' [34] The Son of man has come eating and drinking; and you say, 'Behold, a glutton and a drunkard, a friend of tax collectors and sinners!'"*

Luke 18:12 ⇨ Matt 9:14

*[12] "'I **fast** twice a week, I give tithes of all that I get.'"*

JOHN

THOMAS

GThom 27 ⇨ Matt 9:15

(27) <**Jesus said,**> "If you do not **fast** as regards the world, you will not find the Kingdom. If you do not observe the Sabbath as a Sabbath, you will not see the Father."

GThom 104 ⇨ Matt 9:15

(104) They said [to Jesus], "Come, let us pray today and let us **fast.**"

Jesus said, "What is the sin that I have committed, or wherein have I been defeated? But **when the bridegroom** leaves the bridal chamber, **then** let them **fast** and pray."

GThom 47 ⇨ Matt 9:16–17

(47) **Jesus said,** "It is impossible for a man to mount two horses or to stretch two bows. And it is impossible for a servant to serve two masters; otherwise, he will honor the one and treat the other contemptuously. No man drinks old wine and immediately desires to drink new wine. And **new wine** is not **put into old wineskins**, lest they burst; nor is old wine put into a new wineskin, lest it spoil it. An old patch is not sewn onto a new **garment**, because a tear would result."

OTHER

Did 8:1 ⇨ Matt 9:15

*[1] Let not your fasts be with the hypocrites, for **they fast on Mondays and Thursdays**, but do you fast on Wednesdays and Fridays.*

MATT	MARK	LUKE
RULER'S DAUGHTER: INTRODUCTION	**Mark 5:21–24a (§K24.1)** ⇨ §M23.1	**Luke 8:40–42a (§L35.1)** ⇨ §M23.1
Matt 9:18–19 (§M23.1)	²¹And when Jesus had crossed again in the boat to	⁴⁰Now when Jesus returned, the crowd wel-
¹⁸While he was thus speaking	the other side, a great crowd gathered about him; and	comed him, for they were all waiting for him.
to them, behold, a ruler came in	he was beside the sea. ²²Then **came** one of the rulers of	⁴¹And there came a man named Jairus, who was a
and knelt before him, saying,	the synagogue, Jairus by name; and seeing him, he fell	**ruler** of the synagogue; and falling at Jesus' feet
"My daughter has just died; but	at his feet, ²³and besought **him, saying,** "My little	he besought him to come to his house, ⁴²for he
come and lay your hand on her,	**daughter** is at the point of death. **Come and lay your**	had an only **daughter,** about twelve years of age,
and she will live." ¹⁹And Jesus	hands **on her,** so that **she** may be made well, and **live."**	and she was dying.
rose and followed him, with his	²⁴And he went with **him.**	
disciples.		**Luke 8:42b–48 (§L35.2)** ⇨ §M23.2
	Mark 5:24b–34 (§M24.2) ⇨ §M23.2	As he went, the people pressed round him.
WOMAN WITH THE	And a great crowd followed him and thronged about	⁴³And **a woman who had** had a flow of blood **for**
INTERNAL HEMORRHAGE	him. ²⁵And there was **a woman who had** had **a** flow of	**twelve years** and could not be healed by any one,
	blood **for twelve years,** ²⁶and who had suffered much	⁴⁴**came up behind him, and touched the fringe of**
Matt 9:20–22 (§M23.2)	under many physicians, and had spent all that she had,	**his garment;** and immediately her flow of blood
²⁰And behold, a woman who had	and was no better but rather grew worse. ²⁷She had	ceased. ⁴⁵And Jesus said, "Who was it that
suffered from a hemorrhage for	heard the reports about Jesus, and **came up behind him**	touched me?" When all denied it, Peter said,
twelve years came up behind him	in the crowd **and touched his garment.** ²⁸**For she said,**	"Master, the multitudes surround you and press
and touched the fringe of his gar-	"If I touch even **his** garments, **I shall be made well."**	upon you!" ⁴⁶But Jesus said, "Some one touched
ment; ²¹for she said to herself, "If	²⁹And immediately the hemorrhage ceased; and she	me; for I perceive that power has gone forth from
I only touch his garment, I shall	felt in her body that she was healed of her disease.	me." ⁴⁷And when the woman saw that she was
be made well." ²²Jesus turned,	³⁰And **Jesus,** perceiving in himself that power had	not hidden, she came trembling, and falling
and seeing her he said, "Take	gone forth from him, immediately **turned** about in the	down before him declared in the presence of all
heart, daughter; your faith has	crowd, and said, "Who touched my garments?" ³¹And	the people why she had touched him, and how
made you well." And instantly	his disciples said to him, "You see the crowd pressing	she had been immediately healed. ⁴⁸And **he said**
the woman was made well.	around you, and yet you say, 'Who touched me?'"	to **her, "Daughter, your faith has made you well;**
	³²And he looked around to see who had done it. ³³But	go in peace."
RULER'S DAUGHTER:	the woman, knowing what had been done to her, came	
CONCLUSION	in fear and trembling and fell down before him, and	**Luke 8:49–56 (§L35.3)** ⇨ §M23.3
	told him the whole truth. ³⁴And **he said** to **her,**	⁴⁹While he was still speaking, a man from the
Matt 9:23–26 (§M23.3)	**"Daughter, your faith has made you well**; go in peace,	ruler's house came and said, "Your daughter is
²³And when Jesus came to the	and be healed of your disease."	dead; do not trouble the Teacher any more."
ruler's house, and saw the flute		⁵⁰But Jesus on hearing this answered him, "Do
players, and the crowd making a	**Mark 5:35–43 (§K24.3)** ⇨ §M23.3	not fear; only believe, and she shall be well."
tumult, ²⁴he said, "Depart; for	³⁵While he was still speaking, there came from the	⁵¹And **when** he came **to the house,** he permitted
the girl is not dead but sleeping."	ruler's house some who said, "Your daughter is dead.	no one to enter with him, except Peter and John
And they laughed at him. ²⁵But	Why trouble the Teacher any further?" ³⁶But ignoring	and James, and the father and mother of the
when the crowd had been put	what they said, Jesus said to the ruler of the synagogue,	child. ⁵²And all were weeping and bewailing her;
outside, he went in and took her	"Do not fear, only believe." ³⁷And he allowed no one to	but **he said,** "Do not weep; **for she is not dead but**
by the hand, and the girl arose.	follow him except Peter and James and John the	**sleeping."** ⁵³**And they laughed at him,** knowing
²⁶And the report of this went	brother of James. ³⁸**When** they **came to the house** of the	that she was dead. ⁵⁴But taking her **by the hand**
through all that district.	ruler of the synagogue, he **saw a tumult,** and people	he called, saying, "Child, arise." ⁵⁵And her spirit
	weeping and wailing loudly. ³⁹And when he had	returned, and she got up at once; and he directed
	entered, **he said** to them, "Why do you make **a tumult**	that something should be given her to eat. ⁵⁶And
	and weep? The child **is not dead but sleeping."** ⁴⁰**And**	her parents were amazed; but he charged them to
	they laughed at him. But he **put** them all **outside, and**	tell no one what had happened.
	took the child's father and mother and those who were	
	with him, and **went in** where the child was. ⁴¹Taking	**Luke 7:50** ⇨ Matt 9:22
	her by the hand he said to her, "Talitha cumi"; which	⁵⁰*And he said to the woman, "Your faith has*
	means, "Little girl, I say to you, arise." ⁴²**And** immedi-	*saved you; go in peace."*
	ately **the girl** got up and walked (she was twelve years of	
	age), and they were immediately overcome with	**Luke 17:19** ⇨ Matt 9:22
	amazement. ⁴³And he strictly charged them that no	¹⁹*And he said to him, "Rise and go your way; your*
	one should know this, and told them to give her some-	*faith has made you well."*
	thing to eat.	
		Luke 18:42 ⇨ Matt 9:22
	Mark 10:52 ⇨ Matt 9:22	⁴²*And Jesus said to him, "Receive your sight;*
	⁵²*And Jesus said to him, "Go your way; your faith*	*your faith has made you well."*
	made you well." And immediately he received his sight	
	and followed him on the way.	

JOHN	THOMAS	OTHER

MATT

Matt 9:27–31 (§M24)
²⁷ And as Jesus passed on from there, two blind men followed him, **crying aloud, "Have mercy on us, Son of David."** ²⁸ When he entered the house, the blind men came to him; and Jesus said to them, "Do you believe that I am able to do this?" They said to him, "Yes, Lord." ²⁹ Then he touched their eyes, saying, "According to your faith be it done to you." ³⁰ And their eyes were opened. And Jesus sternly charged them, "See that no one knows it." ³¹ But they went away and spread his fame through all that district.

Matt 9:32–34 (§M25)
³² As they were going away, behold, a dumb demoniac was brought to him. ³³ And when the demon had been cast out, the dumb man spoke; and the crowds marveled, saying, "Never was anything like this seen in Israel." ³⁴ But the Pharisees said, "He casts out demons by the prince of demons." ᵃ

ᵃ Include v. 34: א B C K L W X Δ Θ Π f¹ f¹³ 28 33 *pm;* omit v. 34: D it (in part) sy^s *al*

Matt 20:29–34 (§M70) ⇨ §M24
²⁹ And as they went out of Jericho, a great crowd followed him. ³⁰ And behold, **two blind men** sitting by the roadside, when they heard that **Jesus** was passing by, cried out, **"Have mercy on us, Son of David!"** ³¹ The crowd rebuked them, telling them to be silent; but they cried out the more, "Lord, **have mercy on us, Son of David!"** ³² **And Jesus** stopped and called **them,** saying, "What **do you** want me **to do** for you?" ³³ **They** said to him, "Lord, let our eyes be opened." ³⁴ And Jesus in pity **touched their eyes, and** immediately they received their sight and followed him.

MARK

Mark 10:46–52 (§K56) ⇨ §M24
⁴⁶ And they came to Jericho; and as he was leaving Jericho with his disciples and a great multitude, Bartimaeus, a **blind** beggar, the son of Timaeus, was sitting by the roadside. ⁴⁷ And when he heard that it was **Jesus** of Nazareth, he began to cry out and say, "Jesus, **Son of David, have mercy on me!"** ⁴⁸ And many rebuked him, telling him to be silent; but he cried out all the more, **"Son of David, have mercy on me!"** ⁴⁹ And Jesus stopped and said, "Call him." And they called the blind man, saying to him, "Take heart; rise, he is calling you." ⁵⁰ And throwing off his mantle he sprang up and came to Jesus. ⁵¹ **And Jesus said** to him, "What **do you** want me **to do** for you?" And the blind man **said to him,** "Master, let me receive my sight." ⁵² And Jesus said to him, "Go your way; **your faith** has made you well." **And** immediately he received his sight and followed him on the way.

Mark 3:22 ⇨ Matt 9:34
²² And the scribes who came down from Jerusalem said, "He is possessed by Beelzebul, and **by the prince of demons he casts out** the **demons."**

● **Matt 12:22–24** ⇨ §M25
²² Then a blind and **dumb demoniac was brought to him,** and he healed him, so that the **dumb man spoke** and saw. ²³ **And** all **the** people were amazed, and said, "Can this be the Son of David?" ²⁴ **But** when **the Pharisees** heard it they **said,** "It is only **by** Beelzebul, **the prince of demons,** that this man **casts out demons."**

LUKE

Luke 18:35–43 (§L79) ⇨ §M24
³⁵ As he drew near to Jericho, a **blind** man was sitting by the roadside begging; ³⁶ and hearing a multitude going by, he inquired what this meant. ³⁷ They told him, "Jesus of Nazareth is passing by." ³⁸ And he cried, "Jesus, **Son of David, have mercy on me!"** ³⁹ And those who were in front rebuked him, telling him to be silent; but he cried out all the more, **"Son of David, have mercy on me!"** ⁴⁰ And Jesus stopped, and commanded him to be brought to him; and when he came near, he asked him, ⁴¹ "What **do you** want me **to do** for you?" He **said, "Lord,** let me receive my sight." ⁴² And Jesus said to him, "Receive your sight; **your faith** has made you well." ⁴³ **And** immediately he received his sight and followed him, glorifying God; and all the people, when they saw it, gave praise to God.

Luke 11:14–15 ⇨ §M25
¹⁴ Now he was casting out a demon that was **dumb; when the demon had** gone out, **the dumb man spoke, and the** people **marveled.** ¹⁵ But some of them said, **"He casts out demons by** Beelzebul, **the prince of demons";** . . .

JOHN

John 9:1–7 (§J19.1) ⇨ §M24
*¹ As he passed by, he saw a man **blind** from his birth. ² And his disciples asked him, "Rabbi, who sinned, this man or his parents, that he was born **blind?"** ³ Jesus answered, "It was not that this man sinned, or his parents, but that the works of God might be made manifest in him. ⁴ We must work the works of him who sent me, while it is day; night comes, when no one can work. ⁵ As long as I am in the world, I am the light of the world." ⁶ As he said this, he spat on the ground and made clay of the spittle and anointed the man's eyes with the clay, ⁷ saying to him, "Go, wash in the pool of Siloam" (which means Sent). So he went and washed and came back seeing.*

THOMAS

OTHER

MATT

Matt 9:35–38 (§M26) °

[35] And Jesus went about all the cities and villages, teaching in their synagogues and preaching the gospel of the kingdom, and healing every disease and every infirmity. [36] When he saw the crowds, he had compassion for them, because they were harassed and helpless, like sheep without a shepherd. [37] Then he said to his disciples, "The harvest is plentiful, but the laborers are few; [38] pray therefore the Lord of the harvest to send out laborers into his harvest."

°Appendix 2 ⇨ §M26

°Appendix 3 ⇨ Matt 9:35

Matt 4:23 ⇨ Matt 9:35

[23] And he went about all Galilee teaching in their synagogues and preaching the gospel of the kingdom and healing every disease and every infirmity among the people.

Matt 14:14 ⇨ Matt 9:36

[14] As he went ashore he saw a great throng; and he had compassion on them, and healed their sick.

Matt 15:32 ⇨ Matt 9:36

[32] Then Jesus called his disciples to him and said, "I have compassion on the crowd, because they have been with me now three days, and have nothing to eat; and I am unwilling to send them away hungry, lest they faint on the way."

Num 27:16–17 ⇨ Matt 9:36

[16] "Let the Lord, the God of the Spirits of all flesh, appoint a man over the congregation, [17] who shall go out before them and come in before them, who shall lead them out and bring them in; that the congregation of the Lord may not be as sheep which have no shepherd."

1 Kgs 22:17 ⇨ Matt 9:36

[17] And he said, "I saw all Israel scattered upon the mountains, as sheep that have no shepherd; and the Lord said, 'These have no master; let each return to his home in peace.'"

Zech 10:2 ⇨ Matt 9:36

[2] For the teraphim utter nonsense,
    and the diviners see lies;
the dreamers tell false dreams,
    and give empty consolation.
Therefore the people wander like sheep;
    they are afflicted for want of a shepherd.

MARK

Mark 1:39 ⇨ Matt 9:35

[39] And he went throughout all Galilee, preaching in their synagogues and casting out demons.

Mark 6:6b ⇨ Matt 9:35

And he went about among the villages teaching.

Mark 6:34 ⇨ Matt 9:36

[34] As he went ashore he saw a great throng, and he had compassion on them, because they were like sheep without a shepherd; and he began to teach them many things.

LUKE

Luke 8:1 ⇨ Matt 9:35

[1] Soon afterward he went on through cities and villages, preaching and bringing the good news of the kingdom of God. And the twelve were with him, . . .

Luke 10:2 ⇨ Matt 9:37–38

[2] And he said to them, "The harvest is plentiful, but the laborers are few; pray therefore the Lord of the harvest to send out laborers into his harvest."

JOHN

John 4:35 ⇨ Matt 9:37

[35] "Do you not say, 'There are yet four months, then comes the harvest'? I tell you, lift up your eyes, and see how the fields are already white for harvest."

THOMAS

GThom 73 ⇨ Matt 9:37–38

(73) Jesus said, "The harvest is great but the laborers are few. Beseech the Lord, therefore, to send out laborers to the harvest."

OTHER

MATT

Matt 10:1–4 (§M27) °

[1] And he called to him his twelve disciples and gave them authority over unclean spirits, to cast them out, and to heal every disease and every infirmity. [2] The names of the twelve apostles are these: first, Simon, who is called Peter, and Andrew his brother; James the son of Zebedee, and John his brother; [3] Philip and Bartholomew; Thomas and Matthew the tax collector; James the son of Alphaeus, and Thaddaeus;[a] [4] Simon the Cananaean, and Judas Iscariot, who betrayed him.

[a] *Thaddaeus:* א B *f*[13] 892 *al; Lebbaeus:* D it (in part) *al; Lebbaeus called Thaddaeus:* (C*) C[2] K L W X △ Θ Π *f*[1] 28 33 *pm*

° Appendix 2 ⇨ §M27

MARK

Mark 3:13–19 (§K19)

[13] And he went up on the mountain, and called to him those whom he desired; and they came to him. [14] And he appointed twelve, to be with him, and to be sent out to preach [15] and have authority to cast out demons: [16] Simon whom he surnamed Peter; [17] James the son of Zebedee and John the brother of James, whom he surnamed Boanerges, that is, sons of thunder; [18] Andrew, and Philip, and Bartholomew, and Matthew, and Thomas, and James the son of Alphaeus, and Thaddaeus, and Simon the Cananaean, [19] and Judas Iscariot, who betrayed him.

Then he went home; . . .

Mark 6:7 ⇨ Matt 10:1

[7] And he called to him the twelve, and began to send them out two by two, and gave them authority over the unclean spirits.

LUKE

Luke 6:12–16 (§L23)

[12] In these days he went out to the mountain to pray; and all night he continued in prayer to God. [13] And when it was day, he called his disciples, and chose from them twelve, whom he named apostles; [14] Simon, whom he named Peter, and Andrew his brother, and James and John, and Philip, and Bartholomew, [15] and Matthew, and Thomas, and James the son of Alphaeus, and Simon who was called the Zealot, [16] and Judas the son of James, and Judas Iscariot, who became a traitor.

Luke 9:1 ⇨ Matt 10:1

[1] And he called the twelve together and gave them power and authority over all demons and to cure diseases, . . .

JOHN

John 1:42 ⇨ Matt 10:2

[42] He brought him to Jesus. Jesus looked at him, and said, "So you are Simon the son of John? You shall be called Cephas" (which means Peter).

THOMAS

OTHER

Acts 1:12–14

[12] Then they returned to Jerusalem from the mount called Olivet, which is near Jerusalem, a sabbath day's journey away; [13] and when they had entered, they went up to the upper room, where they were staying, Peter and John and James and Andrew, Philip and Thomas, Bartholomew and Matthew, James the son of Alphaeus and Simon the Zealot and Judas the son of James. [14] All these with one accord devoted themselves to prayer, together with the women and Mary the mother of Jesus, and with his brothers.

GEbi 1

(1) In the Gospel that is in general use amongst them, which is called according to Matthew, which however is not whole (and) complete but forged and mutilated—they call it the Hebrew Gospel—it is reported:

There appeared a certain man named Jesus of about thirty years of age, who chose us. And when he came to Capernaum, he entered into the house of Simon whose surname was Peter, and opened his mouth and said: As I passed along the Lake of Tiberias, I chose John and James the sons of Zebedee, and Simon and Andrew and Thaddaeus and Simon the Zealot and Judas Iscariot, and thee, Matthew, I called as thou didst sit at the receipt of custom, and thou didst follow me. You therefore I will to be twelve apostles for a testimony unto Israel.

MATT

Matt 10:5–15 (§M28.1) °
⁵These twelve Jesus sent out, charging them, "Go nowhere among the Gentiles, and enter no town of the Samaritans, ⁶but go rather to the lost sheep of the house of Israel. ⁷And preach as you go, saying, 'The kingdom of heaven is at hand.' ⁸Heal the sick, raise the dead, cleanse lepers, cast out demons. You received without pay, give without pay. ⁹Take no gold, nor silver, nor copper in your belts, ¹⁰no bag for your journey, nor two tunics, nor sandals, nor a staff; for the laborer deserves his food. ¹¹And whatever town or village you enter, find out who is worthy in it, and stay with him until you depart. ¹²As you enter the house, salute it. ¹³And if the house is worthy, let your peace come upon it; but if it is not worthy, let your peace return to you. ¹⁴And if any one will not receive you or listen to your words, shake off the dust from your feet as you leave that house or town. ¹⁵Truly, I say to you, it shall be more tolerable on the day of judgment for the land of Sodom and Gomorrah than for that town."

°Appendix 2 ⇨ §M28.1

Matt 15:24 ⇨ Matt 10:6
²⁴He answered, "I was sent only to the lost sheep of the house of Israel."

Matt 4:17 ⇨ Matt 10:7
¹⁷From that time Jesus began to **preach**, **saying,** "Repent, for **the kingdom of heaven is at hand.**"

MARK

Mark 6:7–13 (§K26)
⁷And he called to him the **twelve,** and began to send them out two by two, and gave them authority over the unclean spirits. ⁸He charged them to **take** nothing for their **journey** except a **staff;** no bread, **no bag,** no money in their **belts;** ⁹but to wear **sandals** and not put on **two tunics.** ¹⁰And he said to them, "Where **you enter a house,** stay there until you leave the place. ¹¹And if any place **will not receive you** and they refuse to hear you, when **you leave, shake off the dust** that is on **your feet** for a testimony against them." ¹²So they went out and preached that men should repent. ¹³And they **cast out** many **demons,** and anointed with oil many that were sick and healed them.

Mark 1:15 ⇨ Matt 10:7
¹⁵**and saying,** "The time is fulfilled, and **the kingdom of** God **is at hand;** repent, and believe in the gospel."

LUKE

Luke 9:1–6 (§L36)
¹And he called the **twelve** together and gave them power and authority over all **demons** and to cure diseases, ²and he sent them out to **preach the kingdom of** God and to **heal.** ³And he said to them, "**Take** nothing **for your journey,** no **staff,** nor **bag,** nor bread, nor money; and do not have **two tunics.** ⁴**And whatever** house **you enter, stay** there, and from there **depart.** ⁵**And** wherever they do not receive **you,** when **you leave that town shake off the dust** from **your feet as** a testimony against them." ⁶And they departed and went through the villages, preaching the gospel and healing everywhere.

Luke 10:1–16 (§L46)
¹After this the Lord appointed seventy others, and **sent** them on ahead of him, two by two, into every town and place where he himself was about to come. ²And he said to them, "The harvest is plentiful, but the laborers are few; pray therefore the Lord of the harvest to send out laborers into his harvest. ³Go your way; behold, I send you out as lambs in the midst of wolves. ⁴Carry no purse, **no bag,** no **sandals;** and salute no one on the road. ⁵Whatever **house you enter,** first say, 'Peace be to this house!' ⁶And if a son of peace is there, **your peace** shall rest upon him; but if not, it shall **return to you.** ⁷And remain in the same house, eating and drinking what they provide, for the laborer deserves his wages; do not go from house to house. ⁸Whenever **you enter a town** and they receive you, eat what is set before you; ⁹**heal the sick** in it and say to them, '**The kingdom of** God has come near to you.' ¹⁰But whenever you enter a town and they do **not receive you,** go into its streets and say, ¹¹'Even **the dust of your** town that clings to our **feet,** we wipe off against you; nevertheless know this, that **the kingdom of** God has come near.' ¹²I tell you, **it shall be more tolerable on** that **day for Sodom than for that town.**

¹³"Woe to you, Chorazin! woe to you, Bethsaida! for if the mighty works done in you had been done in Tyre and Sidon, they would have repented long ago, sitting in sackcloth and ashes. ¹⁴But **it shall be more tolerable** in the **judgment** for Tyre and Sidon than for you. ¹⁵And you, Capernaum, will you be exalted to heaven? You shall be brought down to Hades.

¹⁶"He who hears you hears me, and he who rejects you rejects me, and he who rejects me rejects him who sent me."

Luke 22:35–36 ⇨ Matt 10:9–10
³⁵And he said to **them,** "When I sent you out with **no** purse or **bag** or **sandals,** did you lack anything?" They said, "Nothing." ³⁶He said to them, "But now, let him who has a purse take it, and likewise a **bag.** And let him who has no sword sell his mantle and buy one."

JOHN

THOMAS

OTHER

1 Cor 9:14 ⇨ Matt 10:10
¹⁴In the same way, the Lord commanded that those who proclaim the gospel should get their living by the gospel.

1 Tim 5:18 ⇨ Matt 10:10
¹⁸for the scripture says, "You shall not muzzle an ox when it is treading out the grain," and, "**The laborer deserves his** wages."

Did 13:1 ⇨ Matt 10:10
¹But every true prophet who wishes to settle among you is "worthy of **his food.**"

MATT

Matt 10:16–23 (§M28.2) °

[16]"Behold, I send you out as sheep in the midst of wolves; so be wise as serpents and innocent as doves. [17]Beware of men; for they will deliver you up to councils, and flog you in their synagogues, [18]and you will be dragged before governors and kings for my sake, to bear testimony before them and the Gentiles. [19]When they deliver you up, do not be anxious how you are to speak or what you are to say; for what you are to say will be given to you in that hour; [20]for it is not you who speak, but the Spirit of your Father speaking through you. [21]Brother will deliver up brother to death, and the father his child, and children will rise against parents and have them put to death; [22]and you will be hated by all for my name's sake. But he who endures to the end will be saved. [23]When they persecute you in one town, flee to the next; for truly, I say to you, you will not have gone through all the towns of Israel, before the Son of man comes."

°Appendix 2 ⇨ §M28.2

Matt 24:9–14

[9]"Then **they will deliver you up to** tribulation, **and put** you **to death; and you will be hated by all** nations **for my name's sake.** [10]And then many will fall away, and betray one another, and hate one another. [11]And many false prophets will arise and lead many astray. [12]And because wickedness is multiplied, most men's love will grow cold. [13]**But he who endures to the end will be saved.** [14]And this gospel of the kingdom will be preached throughout the whole world, as a testimony to all nations; and then the end will come."

MARK

Mark 13:9–13

[9]"But take heed to yourselves; **for they will deliver you up to councils; and you** will be beaten **in synagogues; and you will stand before governors and kings for my sake, to bear testimony before them.** [10]And the gospel must first be preached to all nations. [11]And when they bring you to trial and **deliver you up,** do not be anxious beforehand what **you are** to say; but **say** whatever is **given you in** that hour, for it is not you who speak, but the Holy Spirit. [12]And **brother will deliver up brother to death, and the father his child, and children will rise against parents and have them put to death;** [13]and **you will be hated by all for my name's sake. But he who endures to the end wll be saved."

Mic 7:6 ⇨ Matt 10:21

[6]for the son treats **the father** with contempt,
   the daughter rises **up** against her mother,
   the daughter-in-law **against** her mother-in-law;
   a man's enemies are the men of his own house.

LUKE

Luke 21:12–19

[12]"But before all this they will lay their hands on you and persecute you, delivering **you** up to the **synagogues** and prisons, and **you** will be brought **before kings and governors for my** name's sake. [13]This will be a time for you **to bear testimony.** [14]Settle it therefore in your minds, **not** to meditate beforehand **how to** answer; [15]for I **will give you** a mouth and wisdom, which none of your adversaries will be able to withstand or contradict. [16]You will be delivered **up** even by **parents** and brothers and kinsmen and friends, and some of you they will **put to death;** [17]**you will be hated by all for my name's sake.** [18]But not a hair of your head will perish. [19]By your endurance you will gain your lives."

Luke 10:3 ⇨ Matt 10:16

[3]Go your way; **behold, I send you out as** lambs **in the midst of wolves.**

Luke 12:11–12 ⇨ Matt 10:19–20

[11]"And **when they** bring **you** before the synagogues and the rulers and the authorities, **do not be anxious how** or what **you are to** answer **or what you are to say;** [12]**for** the Holy **Spirit** will teach **you in that** very **hour what you** ought **to say."**

JOHN

John 16:2 ⇨ Matt 10:17

[2]They will put you out of the **synagogues;** indeed, the hour is coming when whoever kills you will think he is offering service to God.

John 14:26 ⇨ Matt 10:19–20

[26]"But the Counselor, **the** Holy **Spirit,** whom the Father will send in my name, he will teach **you** all things, and bring to your remembrance all that I have said to **you."**

John 15:18 ⇨ Matt 10:22

[18]"If the world hates **you,** know that it has **hated** me before it hated you."

THOMAS

POxy655 2 ⇨ Matt 10:16

(2) [Jesus says, "The Pharisees and the scribes have] re[ceived the keys] of [knowledge and] have hid[den them; neither have they] enter[ed nor permitted] those who wo[uld] en[ter. But you] b[ecome **wi]se [as serpents and g]uile[less as do]ve[s]."**

GThom 39 ⇨ Matt 10:16

(39) Jesus said, "The Pharisees and the scribes have taken the keys of Knowledge and hidden them. They themselves have not entered, nor have they allowed to enter those who wish to. **You,** however, **be as wise as serpents and as innocent as doves."**

OTHER

Rom 16:19 ⇨ Matt 10:16

[19]For while your obedience is known to all, so that I rejoice over you, I would have **you** wise as to what is good and guileless as to what is evil; . . .

2 Clem 5:2–4 ⇨ Matt 10:16

[2]for the Lord said, "Ye shall be **as lambs in the midst of wolves,"** [3]and Peter answered and said to him, "If then the wolves tear the lambs?" [4]Jesus said to Peter, "Let the lambs have no fear of the **wolves** after their death; and do ye have no fear of those that slay you, and can do nothing more to you, but fear him who after your death hath power over body and soul, to cast them into the flames of hell."

GNaz 7 ⇨ Matt 10:16

(7) The Jewish Gospel: (**wise**) more than **serpents.** (Variant to Matthew 10:16 in the "Zion Gospel" Edition)

MATT	MARK	LUKE
Matt 10:24–25 (§M28.3) ° ²⁴"A disciple is not above his teacher, nor a servantª above his master; ²⁵it is enough for the disciple to be like his teacher, and the servant like his master. If they have called the master of the house Beelzebul, how much more will they malign those of his household." ª Or: *slave* °Appendix 2 ⇨ §M28.3 **Matt 9:34** ⇨ Matt 10:25 ³⁴But the Pharisees said, "He casts out demons by the prince of demons." **Matt 12:24** ⇨ Matt 10:25 ²⁴But when the Pharisees heard it they said, "It is only by **Beelzebul**, the prince of demons, that this man casts out demons."	**Mark 3:22** ⇨ Matt 10:25 ²²And the scribes who came down from Jerusalem said, "He is possessed by **Beelzebul**, and by the prince of demons he casts out the demons."	**Luke 6:40** ⁴⁰"A disciple is not above his teacher, but every one when he is fully taught will be like his teacher." **Luke 11:15** ⇨ Matt 10:25 ¹⁵But some of them said, "He casts out demons by **Beelzebul**, the prince of demons"; . . .

JOHN	THOMAS	OTHER
John 13:16 ⇨ Matt 10:24 ¹⁶"Truly, truly, I say to you, **a servant** is not greater than **his master**; nor is he who is sent greater than he who sent him." **John 15:20** ⇨ Matt 10:24 ²⁰"Remember the word that I said to you, '**A servant** is not greater than **his master**.' If they persecuted me, they will persecute you; if they kept my word, they will keep yours also."		

MATT

Matt 10:26–33 (§M28.4) °

26 "So have no fear of them; for nothing is covered that will not be revealed, or hidden that will not be known. 27 What I tell you in the dark, utter in the light; and what you hear whispered, proclaim upon the housetops. 28 And do not fear those who kill the body but cannot kill the soul; rather fear him who can destroy both soul and body in hell[a]. 29 Are not two sparrows sold for a penny? And not one of them will fall to the ground without your Father's will. 30 But even the hairs of your head are all numbered. 31 Fear not, therefore; you are of more value than many sparrows. 32 So every one who acknowledges me before men, I also will acknowledge before my Father who is in heaven; 33 but whoever denies me before men, I also will deny before my Father who is in heaven."

[a] Greek: *Gehenna*

° Appendix 2 ⇨ §M28.4

JOHN

MARK

Mark 4:21–23 (§K21.5) ⇨ Matt 10:26

21 And he said to them, "Is a lamp brought in to be put under a bushel, or under a bed, and not on a stand? 22 For there **is nothing** hid, except to **be** made manifest; nor is anything secret, except to come to light. 23 If any man has ears to hear, let him hear."

Mark 8:38 ⇨ Matt 10:33

38 "For **whoever** is ashamed of **me** and of my words in this adulterous and sinful generation, of him will the Son of man **also** be ashamed, when he comes in the glory of his **Father** with the holy angels."

THOMAS

POxy654 5 ⇨ Matt 10:26

(5) Jesus says, "K[now what is be]fore your face, and [that which is hidden] from you will be reveal[ed to you. **For there i]s nothing hidden** which **will not [be made] mani[fest]** and (nothing) buried which will not [be raised up.]"

GThom 5 ⇨ Matt 10:26

(5) Jesus said, "Recognize what is in your sight, and that which is hidden from you will become plain to you. **For there is nothing hidden** which **will not** become manifest."

GThom 6 ⇨ Matt 10:26

(6) His disciples questioned Him and said to Him, "Do You want us to fast? How shall we pray? Shall we give alms? What diet shall we observe?"

Jesus said, "Do not tell lies, and do not do what you hate, for all things are plain in the sight of Heaven. **For nothing hidden will not** become manifest, and **nothing covered will** remain without being uncovered."

POxy1 8 ⇨ Matt 10:27

(8) Jesus says, "**What you hear** in your one ear, preach that **upon** your roof-tops . . ."

GThom 33 ⇨ Matt 10:27

(33) Jesus said, "Preach from your **house-tops** that which **you** will **hear** in your ear [(and) in the other ear]. For no one lights a lamp and puts it under a bushel, nor does he put it in a hidden place, but rather he sets it on a lampstand so that everyone who enters and leaves will see its light."

LUKE

Luke 12:1–12 (§L53)

1 In the meantime, when so many thousands of the multitude had gathered together that they trod upon one another, he began to say to his disciples first, "Beware of the leaven of the Pharisees, which is hypocrisy. 2 **Nothing is covered** up that **will not be revealed, or hidden that will not be known.** 3 Therefore whatever you have said **in the dark** shall be heard **in the light, and what you** have **whispered** in private rooms shall be proclaimed **upon the housetops.**

4 "I tell you, my friends, **do not fear those who kill the body**, and after that have no more that they can do. 5 But I will warn you whom to fear: fear him who, after he has killed, has power to cast into hell; yes, I tell you, fear him! 6 **Are not five sparrows sold for** two pennies? **And not one of them** is forgotten before God. 7 Why, **even the hairs of your head are all numbered. Fear not; you are of more value than many sparrows.**

8 "And I tell you, **every one who acknowledges me before men**, the Son of man **also will acknowledge before** the angels of God; 9 but he who **denies me before men will** be denied **before** the angels of God. 10 And every one who speaks a word against the Son of man will be forgiven; but he who blasphemes against the Holy Spirit will not be forgiven. 11 And when they bring you before the synagogues and the rulers and the authorities, do not be anxious how or what you are to answer or what you are to say; 12 for the Holy Spirit will teach you in that very hour what you ought to say."

Luke 8:16–17 (§L31.4) ⇨ Matt 10:26

16 "No one after lighting a lamp covers it with a vessel, or puts it under a bed, but puts it on a stand, that those who enter may see the light. 17 **For nothing is** hid that shall not **be** made manifest, nor anything secret that shall **not be known** and come to light."

Luke 21:18 ⇨ Matt 10:30

18 "But not a hair **of your head** will perish."

Luke 9:26 ⇨ Matt 10:33

26 "For whoever is ashamed of me and of my words, of him will the Son of man be ashamed when he comes in his glory and the glory of the **Father** and of the holy angels."

OTHER

2 Clem 5:2–4 ⇨ Matt 10:28

2 for the Lord said, "Ye shall be as lambs in the midst of wolves," 3 and Peter answered and said to him, "If then the wolves tear the lambs?" 4 Jesus said to Peter, "Let the lambs have no fear of the wolves after their death; and **do** ye have no **fear** of **those** that slay you, and can do nothing more to you, but **fear him who** after your death hath power over **body and soul**, to cast them into the flames of **hell**."

2 Clem 3:2 ⇨ Matt 10:32

2 And he himself also says, "Whosoever confessed **me before men, I will** confess him **before my Father**"; . . .

MATT

Matt 10:34–39 (§M28.5) °

³⁴"Do not think that I have come to bring peace on earth; I have not come to bring peace, but a sword. ³⁵ For I have come to set a man against his father, and a daughter against her mother, and a daughter-in-law against her mother-in-law; ³⁶ and a man's foes will be those of his own household. ³⁷ He who loves father or mother more than me is not worthy of me; and he who loves son or daughter more than me is not worthy of me; ³⁸ and he who does not take his cross and follow me is not worthy of me. ³⁹ He who finds his life will lose it, and he who loses his life for my sake will find it."

°Appendix 2 ⇨ §M28.5

Matt 16:24–25 ⇨ Matt 10:38–39

²⁴ Then Jesus told his disciples, "If any man would come after me, let him deny himself and **take** up **his cross and follow me**. ²⁵ For whoever would save **his life will lose it, and** whoever **loses his life for my sake will find it**."

Mic 7:5–6 ⇨ Matt 10:35–36
⁵ Put no trust in a neighbor,
   have no confidence in a friend;
guard the doors of your mouth
   from her who lies in your bosom;
⁶ for the son treats the father with contempt,
   the **daughter** rises up **against her mother,**
   the **daughter-in-law against her mother-in-law;**
a **man's enemies are the men of his own** house.

JOHN

John 12:25 ⇨ Matt 10:39
²⁵ "He who loves **his life** loses it, **and he who** hates **his life** in this world **will** keep **it** for eternal life."

MARK

Mark 8:34–35 ⇨ Matt 10:38–39

³⁴ And he called to him the multitude with his disciples, and said to them, "If any man would come after me, let him deny himself and **take** up **his cross and follow me**. ³⁵ For whoever would save **his life will lose it; and** whoever **loses his life for my sake** and the gospel's **will** save **it**."

THOMAS

GThom 16 ⇨ Matt 10:34–36
(16) Jesus said, "Men think, perhaps, that it is **peace** which **I have come to** cast upon the world. They do not know that it is dissension which **I have come to** cast upon the earth: fire, **sword**, and war. For there will be five in a house: three will be against two, and two against three, the father **against** the son, and the son **against** the **father**. And they will stand solitary."

GThom 55 ⇨ Matt 10:37–38
(55) Jesus said, "Whoever does not hate his **father** and his **mother** cannot become a disciple to **Me**. And whoever does not hate his brothers and sisters and **take** up **his cross** in My way will **not** be **worthy of Me**."

GThom 101 ⇨ Matt 10:37–38
(101) <Jesus said,> "Whoever does not hate his **father** and his **mother** as I do cannot become a disciple to **Me**. And whoever does [not] love his father and his mother as I do cannot become a [disciple] to Me. For My mother [gave me falsehood], but [My] true [Mother] gave me life."

LUKE

Luke 12:49–53 (§L56.2) ⇨ Matt 10:34–36

⁴⁹ "I came to cast fire upon the earth; and would that it were already kindled! ⁵⁰ I have a baptism to be baptized with; and how I am constrained until it is accomplished! ⁵¹ **Do** you **think that I have come to give peace on earth**? No, I tell you, but rather division; ⁵² for henceforth in one house there will be five divided, three against two and two against three; ⁵³ they will be divided, father **against** son and son **against father**, mother **against** daughter and **daughter against her mother**, mother-in-law against her daughter-in-law and **daughter-in-law against her mother-in-law**."

Luke 14:25–27 (§L65) ⇨ Matt 10:37–39
²⁵ Now great multitudes accompanied him; and he turned and said to them, ²⁶ "If any one comes to me and does not hate his own **father** and **mother** and wife and children and brothers and sisters, yes, and even his own life, he cannot be my disciple. ²⁷ Whoever **does not** bear **his** own **cross and** come after **me**, cannot be my disciple."

Luke 9:23–24 ⇨ Matt 10:39
²³ And he said to all, "If any man would come after me, let him deny himself and **take** up **his cross** daily **and follow me**. ²⁴ For whoever would save **his life will lose it; and** whoever **loses his life for my sake**, he **will** save **it**."

Luke 17:33 ⇨ Matt 10:39
³³ "Whoever seeks to gain **his life will lose it**, but whoever **loses his life will** preserve **it**."

OTHER

MATT

Matt 10:40–42 (§M28.6) °
⁴⁰"He who receives you receives me, and he who receives me receives him who sent me. ⁴¹ He who receives a prophet because he is a prophet shall receive a prophet's reward, and he who receives a righteous man because he is a righteous man shall receive a righteous man's reward. ⁴² And whoever gives to one of these little ones even a cup of cold water because he is a disciple, truly, I say to you, he shall not lose his reward."

Matt 11:1 (§M28.7) °
¹ And when Jesus had finished instructing his twelve disciples, he went on from there to teach and preach in their cities.

°Appendix 2 ⇨ §M28.6

°Appendix 3 ⇨ §M28.7

Matt 18:5 ⇨ Matt 10:40
⁵ "Whoever receives one such child in my name receives me"; . . .

Matt 7:28 ⇨ §M28.7
²⁸ And when Jesus finished these sayings, the crowds were astonished at his teaching, . . .

Matt 13:53 ⇨ §M28.7
⁵³ And when Jesus had finished these parables, he went away from there, . . .

Matt 19:1 ⇨ §M28.7
¹ Now when Jesus had finished these sayings, he went away from Galilee and entered the region of Judea beyond the Jordan; . . .

Matt 26:1 ⇨ §M28.7
¹ When Jesus had finished all these sayings, he said to his disciples, . . .

MARK

Mark 9:37 ⇨ §M28.6
³⁷ "Whoever receives one such child in my name receives me; and whoever receives me, receives not me but him who sent me."

Mark 9:41 ⇨ Matt 10:42
⁴¹ "For truly, I say to you, whoever gives you a cup of water to drink because you bear the name of Christ, will by no means lose his reward."

LUKE

Luke 9:48 ⇨ Matt 10:40
⁴⁸ and said to them, "Whoever **receives** this child in my name **receives me**, and whoever **receives me receives him who sent me**; for he who is least among you all is the one who is great."

Luke 10:16 ⇨ Matt 10:40
¹⁶ "**He who** hears **you** hears **me, and he who** rejects **you** rejects **me,** and he who rejects me rejects him who sent **me.**"

JOHN

John 12:44–45 ⇨ Matt 10:40
⁴⁴ "And Jesus cried out and said, "**He who** believes in me, believes not in me but in him who sent me. ⁴⁵ And he who sees me sees **him who sent me.**"

John 13:20 ⇨ Matt 10:40
²⁰ "Truly, truly, I say to you, he who receives any one whom I send receives me; and he who receives me receives him who sent me."

THOMAS

OTHER

MATT	MARK	LUKE

Matt 11:1 (§M29) °

[1] And when Jesus had finished instructing his twelve disciples, he went on from there to teach and preach in their cities.

°Appendix 3 ⇨ §M29

Matt 7:28

[28] And when Jesus finished these sayings, the crowds were astonished at his teaching, . . .

Matt 13:53

[53] And when Jesus had finished these parables, he went away from there, . . .

Matt 19:1

[1] Now when Jesus had finished these sayings, he went away from Galilee and entered the region of Judea beyond the Jordan; . . .

Matt 26:1

[1] When Jesus had finished all these sayings, he said to his disciples, . . .

JOHN	THOMAS	OTHER

MATT	MARK	LUKE

Matt 11:2-6 (§M30.1) °

² Now when John heard in prison about the deeds of the Christ, he sent word by his disciples ³ and said to him, "Are you he who is to come, or shall we look for another?" ⁴ And Jesus answered them, "Go and tell John what you hear and see: ⁵ the blind receive their sight and the lame walk, lepers are cleansed and the deaf hear, and the dead are raised up, and the poor have good news preached to them. ⁶ And blessed is he who takes no offense at me."

°Appendix 1 ⇨ §M30.1

Isa 35:5-6 ⇨ Matt 11:5
⁵ Then the eyes of **the blind** shall be opened,
 and the ears of **the deaf** unstopped;
⁶ then shall **the lame** man leap like a hart,
 and the tongue of the dumb sing for joy,
For waters shall break forth in the wilderness,
 and streams in the desert; . . .

⇨ Matt 11:5
Cf. Isa 29:18-19, 61:1

Luke 7:18-23 (§L28.1)

¹⁸ The disciples of **John** told him of all these things. ¹⁹ And **John**, calling to him two of **his disciples, sent** them to the Lord, saying, "**Are you he who is to come, or shall we look for another?**" ²⁰ And when the men had come to him, they **said**, "John the Baptist has sent us to you, saying, '**Are you he who is to come, or shall we look for another?**'" ²¹ In that hour he cured many of diseases and plagues and evil spirits, and on many that were blind he bestowed sight. ²² And he **answered them, "Go and tell John what** you have seen **and** heard: **the blind receive their sight, the lame walk, lepers are cleansed, and the deaf hear, the dead are raised up, the poor have good news preached to them.** ²³ **And blessed is he who takes no offense at me."**

Luke 4:18-19 ⇨ Matt 11:5
¹⁸ "The Spirit of the Lord is upon me,
 because he has anointed me to preach **good news to the poor.**
He has sent me to proclaim release to the captives
and recovering of **sight** to **the blind,**
to set at liberty those who are oppressed,
¹⁹ to proclaim the acceptable year of the Lord."

JOHN	THOMAS	OTHER

John 1:15 ⇨ Matt 11:2-3
¹⁵ *(**John** bore witness **to him,** and cried, "This was he of whom I said, '**He who comes after ranks before me, for he was before me.**'")*

Matt 11:7–15
Matt 11:16–19

JESUS PRAISES JOHN
CHILDREN IN THE MARKETPLACE

M30.2
M30.3

MATT

Matt 11:7–15 (§M30.2) °

⁷ As they went away, Jesus began to speak to the crowds concerning John: "What did you go out into the wilderness to behold? A reed shaken by the wind? ⁸ Why then did you go out? To see[a] a man clothed in soft raiment? Behold, those who wear soft raiment are in kings' houses. ⁹ Why then did you go out? To see a prophet?[b] Yes, I tell you, and more than a prophet. ¹⁰ This is he of whom it is written,

'Behold, I send my messenger before thy face,
who shall prepare thy way before thee.'

¹¹ Truly, I say to you, among those born of women there has risen no one greater than John the Baptist; yet he who is least in the kingdom of heaven is greater than he. ¹² From the days of John the Baptist until now the kingdom of heaven has suffered violence,[c] and men of violence take it by force. ¹³ For all the prophets and the law prophesied until John; ¹⁴ and if you are willing to accept it, he is Elijah who is to come. ¹⁵ He who has ears to hear,[d] let him hear."

Matt 11:16–19 (§M30.3) °

¹⁶ "But to what shall I compare this generation? It is like children sitting in the market places and calling to their playmates,

¹⁷ 'We piped to you, and you did not dance;
we wailed, and you did not mourn.'

¹⁸ For John came neither eating nor drinking, and they say, 'He has a demon'; ¹⁹ the Son of man came eating and drinking, and they say, 'Behold, a glutton and a drunkard, a friend of tax collectors and sinners!' Yet wisdom is justified by her deeds."[e]

[a] Or: *What then did you go out to see? A man . . .*

[b] Or: *What then did you go out to see? A prophet . . .*

[c] Or: *has been coming violently*

[d] Omit *to hear:* B D 700 it (in part) syr[s]

[e] Text: ℵ B* W syr (in part) cop (in part) *al; children:* (cf. Luke 7:35) B² C D K L X Δ Θ Π *f*¹ 28 33 *pm*

°Appendix 1 ⇨ §§M30.2 and M30.3

JOHN

John 1:21 ⇨ Matt 11:14
²¹ *And they asked him, "What then? Are you Elijah?" He said, "I am not." "Are you the prophet?" And he answered, "No."*

MARK

Mark 1:2 ⇨ Matt 11:10
² As it is **written** in Isaiah the prophet,
"**Behold, I send my messenger
before thy face,**
who shall prepare thy way"; . . .

Mark 9:13 ⇨ Matt 11:14
¹³ *"But I tell you that **Elijah has come**, and they did to him whatever they pleased, as it is written of him."*

Mark 4:23 ⇨ Matt 11:15
²³ *"If any man has ears to hear, let him hear."*

⇨Matt 11:9
Cf. Matt 14:5 and 21:26

⇨Matt 11:14
Cf. Matt 17:10–13

Matt 13:9 ⇨ Matt 11:15
⁹ *"He who has ears to hear, let him hear."*

Matt 13:43b ⇨ Matt 11:15
"He who has ears to hear, let him hear."

Mal 3:1a ⇨ Matt 11:10
¹ "**Behold, I send my messenger** to **prepare** the **way before me**, . . ."

Mal 4:5 ⇨ Matt 11:14
⁵ "Behold, I will send you **Elijah** the prophet before the great and terrible day of the Lord comes."

THOMAS

GThom 78 ⇨ Matt 11:7–8
(78) **Jesus** said, "Why have **you** come **out into the desert**? To see **a reed shaken by the wind**? And **to see a man clothed in** fine garments like your **kings** and your great men? Upon them are the fine [garments], and they are unable to discern the truth."

GThom 46 ⇨ Matt 11:11
(46) Jesus said, "**Among those born of women,** from Adam until John the Baptist, **there** is **no one** so superior to **John the Baptist** that his eyes should not be lowered (before him). **Yet** I have said, whichever one of you comes to be a child will be acquainted with **the Kingdom** and will become superior to John."

LUKE

Luke 7:24–30 (§L28.2) ⇨ §M30.2
²⁴ When the messengers of John had gone, he **began to speak to the crowds concerning John**: "**What did you go out into the wilderness to behold? A reed shaken by the wind?** ²⁵ What **then did you go out** to see? A man clothed in soft clothing? Behold, those who are gorgeously apparelled and live in luxury **are in kings'** courts. ²⁶ What **then did you go out** to see? A prophet? Yes, I tell you, and more than a prophet. ²⁷ This is he of whom it is written,

'Behold, I send my messenger before thy face,
who shall prepare thy way before thee.'

²⁸ I tell you, among those born of women none is **greater than John;** yet he who is least in the **kingdom** of God is **greater than he.**" ²⁹ (When they heard this all the people and the tax collectors justified God, having been baptized with the baptism of John; ³⁰ but the Pharisees and the lawyers rejected the purpose of God for themselves, not having been baptized by him.)

Luke 7:31–35 (§L28.3) ⇨ §M30.3
³¹ "**To what** then **shall I compare** the men of **this generation,** and what are they like? ³² They are **like children sitting in the market place and calling to** one another,

'We piped to you, and you did not dance;
we wailed, and you did not weep.'

³³ For **John** the Baptist has come **eating** no bread and **drinking** no wine; **and** you say, '**He has a demon.'** ³⁴ **The Son of man** has come **eating and drinking;** and you say, '**Behold, a glutton and a drunkard, a friend of tax collectors and sinners!'** ³⁵ Yet **wisdom is justified by** all **her** children."

Luke 16:16 ⇨ Matt 11:12–13
¹⁶ "**The law** and **the prophets** were **until John;** since then the good news of the kingdom of God is preached, and every one enters it violently."

⇨ Matt 11:9
Cf. Luke 1:76

OTHER

GNaz 8 ⇨ Matt 11:12
(8) The Jewish Gospel has: (the kingdom of heaven) is plundered. (Variant to Matthew 11:12 in the "Zion Gospel" Edition)

Rev 13:9 ⇨ Matt 11:15
⁹ *If any one has an ear, let him hear:* . . .

64 **Matt 11:2–19**
Matt 11:1–12:21

JESUS AND JOHN THE BAPTIST
THIRD GALILEAN

M30
S9: M29–35

MATT	MARK	LUKE

Matt 11:20–24 (§M31)

²⁰ Then he began to upbraid the cities where most of his mighty works had been done, because they did not repent. ²¹ "Woe to you, Chorazin! woe to you, Bethsaida! for if the mighty works done in you had been done in Tyre and Sidon, they would have repented long ago in sackcloth and ashes. ²² But I tell you, it shall be more tolerable on the day of judgment for Tyre and Sidon than for you. ²³ And you, Capernaum, will you be exalted to heaven? You shall be brought down to Hades. For if the mighty works done in you had been done in Sodom, it would have remained until this day. ²⁴ But I tell you that it shall be more tolerable on the day of judgment for the land of Sodom than for you."

Matt 10:15 ⇨ Matt 11:24

¹⁵ "Truly, I say to you, it shall be more tolerable on the day of judgment for the land of Sodom and Gomorrah than for that town."

Isa 14:13–15 ⇨ Matt 11:23

¹³ "You said in your heart,
     'I will ascend to heaven;
above the stars of God
     I will set my throne on high;
I will sit on the mount of assembly
     in the far north;
¹⁴ I will ascend above the heights of the clouds,
     I will make myself the most High.'
¹⁵ But you are brought down to Sheol,
     to the depths of the Pit."

Luke 10:13–15 ⇨ Matt 11:21–23a

¹³ "Woe to you, Chorazin! woe to you, Bethsaida! for if the mighty works done in you had been done in Tyre and Sidon, they would have repented long ago, sitting in sackcloth and ashes. ¹⁴ But it shall be more tolerable in the judgment for Tyre and Sidon than for you. ¹⁵ And you, Capernaum, will you be exalted to heaven? You shall be brought down to Hades."

Luke 10:12 ⇨ Matt 11:24

¹² "I tell you, it shall be more tolerable on that day for Sodom than for that town."

JOHN	THOMAS	OTHER

GNaz 27 ⇨ Matt 11:20–21

(27) In these cities (namely Chorazin and Bethsaida) many wonders have been wrought, as their number the Gospel according to the Hebrews gives 53. ("Historical Commentary on Luke" on Luke 10:13; cited by Bischoff in *Sacris Erudiri* 6, 1954, p. 262)

MATT	MARK	LUKE

MATT

Matt 11:25–30 (§M32)

²⁵ At that time Jesus declared, "I thank thee, Father, Lord of heaven and earth, that thou hast hidden these things from the wise and understanding and revealed them to babes; ²⁶ yea, Father, for such was thy gracious will.ᵃ ²⁷ All things have been delivered to me by my Father; and no one knows the Son except the Father, and no one knows the Father except the Son and any one to whom the Son chooses to reveal him. ²⁸ Come to me, all who labor and are heavy laden, and I will give you rest. ²⁹ Take my yoke upon you, and learn from me; for I am gentle and lowly in heart, and you will find rest for your souls. ³⁰ For my yoke is easy, and my burden is light."

ᵃ Or: *so it was well-pleasing before thee*

Sir 51:23–27 ⇨ Matt 11:28–29
²³ Draw near to me, you who are untaught,
　　and lodge in my school.
²⁴ Why do you say you are lacking in these things,
　　and why are your souls very thirsty?
²⁵ I opened my mouth and said,
　　Get these things for yourselves without money.
²⁶ Put your neck under the yoke,
　　and let your souls receive instruction;
　　it is to be found close by.
²⁷ See with your eyes that I have labored little
　　and found for myself much rest.

Jer 6:16 ⇨ Matt 11:29
¹⁶ Thus says the Lord:
"Stand by the roads, and look,
　　and ask for the ancient paths,
　where the good way is; and walk in it,
　　and find rest for your souls.
But they said, 'We will not walk in it.'"

JOHN

John 3:35 ⇨ Matt 11:27
³⁵ the Father loves the Son, and has given all things into his hand.

John 7:29 ⇨ Matt 11:27
²⁹ "I know him, for I come from him, and he sent me."

⇨ Matt 11:27
Cf. John 5:20, 10:14–15, 13:3, 17:25

THOMAS

POxy654 3 ⇨ Matt 11:25
(3) Jesus says, ["If] those who draw you on [say to you, 'Behold,] the kingdom (is) in the heav[en,'] the birds of the hea[ven will be (there) before you. But if they say th]at it is under the earth, the fishes of the se[a will enter before you]. And the king[dom of God] is within you [and outside (of you)]. Whoever] knows [himself,] will fin[d] it [and when you] know yourselves, [you will realize that] you are [sons] of the li[ving] Father. [But if you will not] know yourselves, [you are] in [poverty] and you are pov[erty.]"

GThom 4 ⇨ Matt 11:25
(4) Jesus said, "The man old in days will not hesitate to ask a small child seven days old about the place of life, and he will live. For many who are first will become last, and they will become one and the same."

GThom 90 ⇨ Matt 11:28–30
(90) Jesus said, "Come unto Me, for My yoke is easy and My lordship is mild, and you will find repose for yourselves."

POxy654 1 ⇨ Matt 11:29
(1) These are the [secret] words [which] the living Jesus [sp]oke, a[nd Judas who] (is) also (called) Thomas [wrote (them) down]. And he said, ["Whoever who finds the interpre]tation of th[ese] words, shall not taste [death!"]

GThom 2 ⇨ Matt 11:29
(2) Jesus said, "Let him who seeks continue seeking until he finds. When he finds, he will become troubled. When he becomes troubled, he will be astonished, and he will rule over the All."

LUKE

Luke 10:21–22 ⇨ Matt 11:25–27
²¹ In that same hour he rejoiced in the Holy Spirit and said, "I thank thee, Father, Lord of heaven and earth, that thou hast hidden these things from the wise and understanding and revealed them to babes; yea, Father, for such was thy gracious will. ²² All things have been delivered to me by my Father; and no one knows who the Son is except the Father, or who the Father is except the Son and any one to whom the Son chooses to reveal him."

OTHER

GNaz 9 ⇨ Matt 11:25
(9) The Jewish Gospel: I thank thee.
(Variant to Matthew 11:25 in the "Zion Gospel" Edition)

DialSav 141:3–11a ⇨ Matt 11:28–30
Matthew said, "Why do we not put ourselves to rest at once?"
The Lord said, "(You will) when you lay down these burdens."
Matthew said, "In what way does the little one cleave to the great one?"
The Lord said, "When you leave behind you the things that will not be able to follow you, then you will put yourselves to rest."

GHeb 4 ⇨ Matt 11:29
(4a) As also it stands written in the Gospel of the Hebrews:
He that marvels shall reign, and he that has reigned shall rest. (Clement, Stromateis 2.9.45.5)
(4b) To those words (from Plato, Timaeus 90) this is equivalent:
He that seeks will not rest until he finds; and he that has found shall marvel; and he that has marvelled shall reign; and he that has reigned shall rest. (Clement, Stromateis 5.14.96.3)

MATT

Matt 12:1–8 (§M33)
[1] At that time Jesus went through the grainfields on the sabbath; his disciples were hungry, and they began to pluck heads of grain and to eat. [2] But when the Pharisees saw it, they said to him, "Look, your disciples are doing what is not lawful to do on the sabbath." [3] He said to them, "Have you not read what David did, when he was hungry, and those who were with him: [4] how he entered the house of God and ate[a] the bread of the Presence, which it was not lawful for him to eat nor for those who were with him, but only for the priests? [5] Or have you not read in the law how on the sabbath the priests in the temple profane the sabbath, and are guiltless? [6] I tell you, something greater than the temple is here. [7] And if you had known what this means, 'I desire mercy, and not sacrifice,' you would not have condemned the guiltless. [8] For the Son of man is lord of the sabbath."

[a] *And they ate:* ℵ B 481

Matt 9:13 ⇨ Matt 12:7
"Go and learn **what** this **means, 'I desire mercy, and not sacrifice.'** For I came not to call the righteous, but sinners."

Deut 23:25 ⇨ Matt 12:1
[25] "When you go into your neighbor's standing **grain**, you may **pluck the** ears with your hand, but you shall not put a sickle to your neighbor's standing **grain**."

Exod 20:10 ⇨ Matt 12:2
[10] "but the seventh day is a **sabbath** to the Lord your God; in it you shall **not** do any work, you, or your son, or your daughter, or your manservant, or your maidservant, or your cattle, or the sojourner who is within your gates"; . . .

Deut 5:14 ⇨ Matt 12:2
[14] "but the seventh day is a **sabbath** to the Lord your God; in it you shall **not** do any work, you, or your son, or your daughter, or your manservant, or your maidservant, or your ox, or your ass, or any of your cattle, or the sojourner who is within your gates, that your manservant and your maidservant may rest as well as you.'"

1 Sam 21:1–6 ⇨ Matt 12:3–4
[1] Then came **David** to Nob to Ahimelech the priest; and Ahimelech came to meet David trembling, and said to him, "Why are you alone, and no one with you?" [2] And David said to Ahimelech the priest, "The king has charged me with a matter, and said to me, 'Let no one know anything of the matter about which I send you, and with which I have charged you.' I have made an appointment with the young men for such and such a place. [3] Now then, what have you at hand? Give me five loaves of **bread**, or whatever is here." [4] And the priest answered David, "I have no common **bread** at hand, but there is holy **bread**; if only the young men have kept themselves from women." [5] And David answered the priest, "Of a truth women have been kept from us as always when I go on an expedition; the vessels of the young men are holy, even when it is a common journey; how much more today will their vessels be holy?" [6] So the priest gave him the holy **bread**; for there was no **bread** there but **the bread of the Presence, which** is removed from before the Lord, to be replaced by hot **bread** on the day it is taken away.

JOHN

MARK

Mark 2:23–28 (§K16)
[23] One sabbath he was going **through the grainfields**; and as they made their way **his disciples began to pluck heads of grain.** [24] And the Pharisees said to him, "Look, why are they **doing what is not lawful on the sabbath?**" [25] And **he said to them,** "Have you never **read what David did, when he was** in need and was **hungry,** he and those who were with him: [26] how he entered the house of God, when Abiathar was high priest, **and ate the bread of the Presence, which** it is **not lawful for** any but the priests **to eat,** and also gave it to **those who were with him?**" [27] And he said to them, "The sabbath was made for man, not man for the sabbath; [28] so **the Son of man is lord** even **of the sabbath.**"

Lev 24:5–9 ⇨ Matt 12:4
[5] "And you shall take fine flour, and bake twelve cakes of it; two tenths of an ephah shall be in each cake. [6] And you shall set them in two rows, six in a row, upon the table of pure gold. [7] And you shall put pure frankincense with each row, that it may go with the bread as a memorial portion to be offered by fire to the Lord. [8] Every **sabbath** day Aaron shall set it in order before the Lord continually on behalf of the people of Israel as a covenant for ever. [9] And it shall be for Aaron and his sons, and they shall eat it in a holy place, since it is for him a most holy portion out of the offerings by fire to the Lord, a perpetual due."

Num 28:9–10 ⇨ Matt 12:5
[9] "On the sabbath day two male lambs a year old without blemish, and two tenths of an ephah of fine flour for a cereal offering, mixed with oil, and its drink offering: [10] this is the burnt offering of every sabbath, besides the continual burnt offering and its drink offering."

Hos 6:6 ⇨ Matt 12:7
[6] For **I desire** steadfast love **and not sacrifice,** the knowledge of God, rather than burnt offerings.

THOMAS

GThom 27 ⇨ Matt 12:8
(27) <Jesus said,> "If you do not fast as regards the world, you will not find the Kingdom. If you do not observe **the Sabbath as a Sabbath,** you will not see the Father."

LUKE

Luke 6:1–5 (§L21)
[1] On a sabbath, while he was going **through the grainfields, his disciples** plucked and ate some **heads of grain,** rubbing them in their hands. [2] But some of the Pharisees said, "Why are you **doing what is not lawful to do on the sabbath?**" [3] And Jesus answered, "Have you not read what David did when he was hungry, he and those who were with him: [4] how he entered the house of God, and took and ate the bread of Presence, which it is not lawful for any but the priests to eat, and also gave it to those with him?" [5] And he said to them, "The Son of man is lord of the sabbath."

OTHER

GEbi 6 ⇨ Matt 12:7
(6) They say that he (Christ) was not begotten of God the Father, but created as one of the archangels. . . . that he rules over the angels and all the creatures of the Almighty, and that he came and declared, as their Gospel, which is called (according to Matthew? according to the Hebrews?), reports:

I am come to do away with sacrifices, and if ye cease not from sacrificing, the wrath of God will not cease from you. (Epiphanius, *Haer.* 30.16.4f.)

InThom 2:1–5
[1] When this boy Jesus was five years old he was playing at the ford of a brook, and he gathered together into pools the water that flowed by, and made it at once clean, and commanded it by his word alone. [2] He made soft clay and fashioned from it twelve sparrows. And it was the sabbath when he did this. And there were also many other children playing with him. [3] Now when a certain Jew saw what Jesus was doing in his play on the sabbath, he at once went and told his father Joseph: "See, your child is at the brook, and he has taken clay and fashioned twelve birds and has profaned the sabbath." [4] And when Joseph came to the place and saw (it), he cried out to him, saying: "Why do you do on the sabbath what ought not to be done?" But Jesus clapped his hands and cried to the sparrows: "Off with you!" And the sparrows took flight and went away chirping. [5] The Jews were amazed when they saw this, and went away and told their elders what they had seen Jesus do.

MATT	MARK	LUKE

Matt 12:9–14 (§M34)

⁹And he went on from there, and entered their synagogue. ¹⁰And behold, there was a man with a withered hand. And they asked him, "Is it lawful to heal on the sabbath?" so that they might accuse him. ¹¹He said to them, "What man of you, if he has one sheep and it falls into a pit on the sabbath, will not lay hold of it and lift it out? ¹²Of how much more value is a man than a sheep! So it is lawful to do good on the sabbath." ¹³Then he said to the man, "Stretch out your hand." And the man stretched it out, and it was restored, whole like the other. ¹⁴But the Pharisees went out and took counsel against him, how to destroy him.

Mark 3:1–6 (§K17)

¹Again **he entered** the **synagogue, and a man** was there who had **a withered hand.** ²**And they** watched **him,** to see whether he would **heal** him **on the sabbath, so that they might accuse him.** ³And **he said to the man** who had the **withered hand,** "Come here." ⁴And **he said** to them, **"Is it lawful on the sabbath** to do good or to do harm, to save life or to kill?" But they were silent. ⁵And he looked around at them with anger, grieved at their hardness of heart, and **said to the man, "Stretch out your hand."** He stretched it out, **and** his hand **was restored.** ⁶**The Pharisees went out, and** immediately held **counsel** with the Herodians **against him, how to destroy him.**

Luke 6:6–11 (§L22)

⁶On another sabbath, when **he entered** the **synagogue** and taught, **a man was** there whose right **hand** was **withered.** ⁷And the scribes and **the Pharisees** watched him, to see whether he would **heal on the sabbath, so that they might** find an accusation against **him.** ⁸But he knew their thoughts, and he said to the **man** who had the **withered hand,** "Come and stand here." And he rose and stood there. ⁹And Jesus said to them, "I ask you, **is it lawful on the sabbath to** do good or to do harm, to save life or to destroy it?" ¹⁰And he looked around on them all, and **said to him, "Stretch out your hand."** And he did so, **and** his hand **was restored.** ¹¹**But** they were filled with fury and discussed with one another what they might do to Jesus.

Luke 13:15–16 ⇨ Matt 12:11–12

¹⁵Then the Lord answered him, "You hypocrites! Does not each of you on the sabbath untie his ox or his ass from the manger, and lead it away to water it? ¹⁶And ought not this woman, a daughter of Abraham whom Satan bound for eighteen years, be loosed from this bond on the sabbath day?"

Luke 14:3–5 ⇨ Matt 12:11–12

³And Jesus spoke to the lawyers and Pharisees, saying, "Is it lawful to heal on the sabbath, or not?" ⁴But they were silent. Then he took him and healed him, and let him go. ⁵And he said to them, "Which of you, having a son or an ox that has fallen into a well, will not immediately pull him out on a sabbath day?"

JOHN	THOMAS	OTHER

GNaz 10 ⇨ Matt 12:10

(10) In the Gospel which the Nazarenes and the Ebionites use, which we have recently translated out of Hebrew into Greek, and which is called by most people the authentic (Gospel) of Matthew, the **man** who had the **withered hand** is described as a mason who pleaded for help in the following words:

I was a mason and earned (my) livelihood with (my) hands; I beseech thee, Jesus, to restore to me my health that I may not with ignominy have to beg for my bread. (Jerome, *Commentary on Matthew* 2 [on Matthew 12:13])

InThom 2:1–5

*¹When this boy Jesus was five years old he was playing at the ford of a brook, and he gathered together into pools the water that flowed by, and made it at once clean, and commanded it by his word alone. ²He made soft clay and fashioned from it twelve sparrows. And it was **the sabbath** when he did this. And there were also many other children playing with him. ³Now when a certain Jew saw what Jesus was doing in his play **on the sabbath,** he at once went and told his father Joseph: "See, your child is at the brook, and he has taken clay and fashioned twelve birds and has profaned **the sabbath."** ⁴And when Joseph came to the place and saw (it), he cried out to him, saying: "Why do you do on the **sabbath** what ought not to be done?" But Jesus clapped his hands and cried **to the** sparrows: "Off with you!" And the sparrows took flight **and** went away chirping. ⁵**The** Jews were amazed when they saw this, and went away and told their elders what they had seen Jesus do.*

MATT	MARK	LUKE

Matt 12:15–21 (§M35) °

¹⁵ Jesus, aware of this, withdrew from there. And many followed him, and he healed them all, ¹⁶ and ordered them not to make him known. ¹⁷ This was to fulfil what was spoken by the prophet Isaiah:

¹⁸ "Behold, my servant whom I have chosen,
   my beloved with whom my soul is well pleased.
I will put my Spirit upon him,
   and he shall proclaim justice to the Gentiles.
¹⁹ He will not wrangle or cry aloud,
   nor will any one hear his voice in the streets;
²⁰ he will not break a bruised reed
   or quench a smoldering wick,
till he brings justice to victory;
   ²¹ and in his name will the Gentiles hope."

°Appendix 3 ⇨ §M35

Isa 42:1–4 ⇨ Matt 12:18–21
¹ Behold my servant, whom I uphold,
   my chosen, in whom my soul delights;
I have put my Spirit upon him,
   he will bring forth justice to the nations.
² He will not cry or lift up his voice,
   or make it heard in the street;
³ a bruised reed he will not break,
   and a dimly burning wick he will not quench;
   he will faithfully bring forth justice.
⁴ He will not fail or be discouraged
   till he has established justice in the earth;
   and the coastlands wait for his law.

Mark 3:7–12 (§K18)

⁷ Jesus withdrew with his disciples to the sea, and a great multitude from Galilee followed; also from Judea ⁸ and Jerusalem and Idumea and from beyond the Jordan and from about Tyre and Sidon a great multitude, hearing all that he did, came to him. ⁹ And he told his disciples to have a boat ready for him because of the crowd, lest they should crush him; ¹⁰ for he had healed many, so that all who had diseases pressed upon him to touch him. ¹¹ And whenever the unclean spirits beheld him, they fell down before him and cried out, "You are the Son of God." ¹² And he strictly ordered them not to make him known.

Luke 6:17–19 (§L24)

¹⁷ And he came down with them and stood on a level place, with a great crowd of his disciples and a great multitude of people from all Judea and Jerusalem and the seacoast of Tyre and Sidon, who came to hear him and to be healed of their diseases; ¹⁸ and those who were troubled with unclean spirits were cured. ¹⁹ And all the crowd sought to touch him, for power came forth from him and healed them all.

Luke 4:41 ⇨ Matt 12:16
⁴¹ And demons also came out of many, crying, "You are the Son of God!" But he rebuked them, and would not allow them to speak, because they knew that he was the Christ.

JOHN	THOMAS	OTHER

MATT	MARK	LUKE

Matt 12:22–37 (§M36)

²²Then a blind and dumb demoniac was brought to him, and he healed him, so that the dumb man spoke and saw. ²³And all the people were amazed, and said, "Can this be the Son of David?" ²⁴But when the Pharisees heard it they said, "It is only by Beelzebul, the prince of demons, that this man casts out demons." ²⁵Knowing their thoughts, he said to them, "Every kingdom divided against itself is laid waste, and no city or house divided against itself will stand; ²⁶and if Satan casts out Satan, he is divided against himself; how then will his kingdom stand? ²⁷And if I cast out demons by Beelzebul, by whom do your sons cast them out? Therefore they shall be your judges. ²⁸But if it is by the Spirit of God that I cast out demons, then the kingdom of God has come upon you. ²⁹Or how can one enter a strong man's house and plunder his goods, unless he first binds the strong man? Then indeed he may plunder his house. ³⁰He who is not with me is against me, and he who does not gather with me scatters. ³¹Therefore I tell you, every sin and blasphemy will be forgiven men, but the blasphemy against the Spirit will not be forgiven. ³²And whoever says a word against the Son of man will be forgiven, but whoever speaks against the Holy Spirit will not be forgiven, either in this age or in the age to come.

³³"Either make the tree good, and its fruit good; or make the tree bad, and its fruit bad; for the tree is known by its fruit. ³⁴You brood of vipers! how can you speak good, when you are evil? For out of the abundance of the heart the mouth speaks. ³⁵The good man out of his good treasure brings forth good, and the evil man out of his evil treasure brings forth evil. ³⁶I tell you, on the day of judgment men will render account for every careless word they utter; ³⁷for by your words you will be justified, and by your words you will be condemned."

Matt 9:32–34 (§M25) ⇨ Matt 12:22–24

³²*As they were going away, behold, a dumb demoniac was brought to him. ³³And when the demon had been cast out, the dumb man spoke; and the crowds marveled, saying, "Never was anything like this seen in Israel." ³⁴But the Pharisees said, "He casts out demons by the prince of demons."*

Matt 10:25 ⇨ Matt 12:24

²⁵*"it is enough for the disciple to be like his teacher, and the servant like his master. If they have called the master of the house Beelzebul, how much more will they malign those of his household."*

Matt 7:16–20 ⇨ Matt 12:33

¹⁶*"You will know them by their fruits. Are grapes gathered from thorns, or figs from thistles? ¹⁷So, every sound tree bears good fruit, but the bad tree bears evil fruit. ¹⁸A sound tree cannot bear evil fruit, nor can a bad tree bear good fruit. ¹⁹Every tree that does not bear good fruit is cut down and thrown into the fire. ²⁰Thus you will know them by their fruits."*

Matt 15:18 ⇨ Matt 12:34

¹⁸*"But what comes out of the mouth proceeds from the heart, and this defiles a man."*

Mark 3:20–22 (§K20.1)

²⁰and the crowd came together again, so that they could not even eat. ²¹And when his family heard it, they went out to seize him, for people were saying, "He is beside himself." ²²And the scribes who came down from Jerusalem said, "He is possessed by Beelzebul, and by the prince of demons he casts out the demons."

Mark 3:23–30 (§K20.2)

²³And he called them to him, and said to them in parables, "How can Satan cast out Satan? ²⁴If a kingdom is divided against itself, that kingdom cannot stand. ²⁵And if a house is divided against itself, that house will not be able to stand. ²⁶And if Satan has risen up against himself and is divided, he cannot stand, but is coming to an end. ²⁷But no one can enter a strong man's house and plunder his goods, unless he first binds the strong man; then indeed he may plunder his house.

²⁸"Truly, I say to you, all sins will be forgiven the sons of men, and whatever blasphemies they utter; ²⁹but whoever blasphemes against the Holy Spirit never has forgiveness, but is guilty of an eternal sin"— ³⁰for they had said, "He has an unclean spirit."

Mark 9:40 ⇨ Matt 12:30

⁴⁰*"For he that is not against us is for us."*

Luke 11:14–23 (§L51.1)

¹⁴Now he was casting out a demon that was dumb; when the demon had gone out, the dumb man spoke, and the people marveled. ¹⁵But some of them said, "He casts out demons by Beelzebul, the prince of demons"; ¹⁶while others, to test him, sought from him a sign from heaven. ¹⁷But he, knowing their thoughts, said to them, "Every kingdom divided against itself is laid waste, and a divided household falls. ¹⁸And if Satan also is divided against himself, how will his kingdom stand? For you say that I cast out demons by Beelzebul. ¹⁹And if I cast out demons by Beelzebul, by whom do your sons cast them out? Therefore they shall be your judges. ²⁰But if it is by the finger of God that I cast out demons, then the kingdom of God has come upon you. ²¹When a strong man, fully armed, guards his own palace, his goods are in peace; ²²but when one stronger than he assails him and overcomes him, he takes away his armor in which he trusted, and divides his spoil. ²³He who is not with me is against me, and he who does not gather with me scatters."

Luke 9:50 ⇨ Matt 12:30

⁵⁰*But Jesus said to him, "Do not forbid him; for he that is not against you is for you."*

Luke 12:10 ⇨ Matt 12:32

¹⁰*"And every one who speaks a word against the Son of man will be forgiven; but he who blasphemes against the Holy Spirit will not be forgiven."*

Luke 6:43–45 ⇨ Matt 12:33, 35

⁴³*"For no good tree bears bad fruit, nor again does a bad tree bear good fruit; ⁴⁴for each tree is known by its own fruit. For figs are not gathered from thorns, nor are grapes picked from a bramble bush. ⁴⁵The good man out of the good treasure of his heart produces good, and the evil man out of his evil treasure produces evil; for out of the abundance of the heart his mouth speaks."*

JOHN

John 7:20 ⇨ Matt 12:24
²⁰ The people answered, "You have a demon! Who is seeking to kill you?"

John 8:48 ⇨ Matt 12:24
⁴⁸ The Jews answered him, "Are we not right in saying that you are a Samaritan and have a demon?"

John 8:52 ⇨ Matt 12:24
⁵² The Jews said to him, "Now we know that you have a demon. Abraham died, as did the prophets; and you say, 'If any one keeps my word, he will never taste death.'"

John 10:20 ⇨ Matt 12:24
²⁰ Many of them said, "He has a demon, and he is mad; why listen to him?"

THOMAS

GThom 35 ⇨ Matt 12:29
(35) Jesus said, "It is not possible for anyone to **enter** the **house** of **a strong man** and take it by force **unless he binds** his hands; **then he** will (be able to) ransack **his house.**"

GThom 21 ⇨ Matt 12:29
(21) Mary said to Jesus, "Whom are Your disciples like?"
*He said, "They are like children who have settled in a field which is not theirs. When the owners of the field come, they will say, 'Let us have back our field.' They (will) undress in their presence in order to let them have back their field and to give it back to them. Therefore I say to you, if the owner of **a house** knows that the thief is coming, he will begin his vigil before he comes and will not let him dig through into his **house** of his domain to carry away **his** goods. You, then, be on your guard against the world. Arm yourselves with great strength lest the robbers find a way to come to you, for the difficulty which you expect will (surely) materialize. Let there be among you a man of understanding. When the grain ripened, he came quickly with his sickle in his hand and reaped it. Whoever has ears to hear, let him hear."*

GThom 44 ⇨ Matt 12:31–32
(44) Jesus said, "Whoever blasphemes against the Father **will be forgiven, and who-ever** blasphemes **against the Son will be for-given, but whoever** blasphemes **against the Holy Spirit will not be forgiven either** on earth or in heaven."

GThom 45 ⇨ Matt 12:33–35
(45) Jesus said, "Grapes are not harvested from thorns, nor are figs gathered from this-tles, for they do not produce fruit. A **good man brings forth good** from his storehouse; an **evil man brings forth evil** things from **his evil** storehouse, which is in his **heart,** and says **evil** things. **For out of the abundance of the heart** he **brings forth evil** things."

OTHER

POxy1224 2 ⇨ Matt 12:30
(2) And pray for your enemies. For **he who is not [against** you] **is** for you. [He who today] is far-off—tomorrow will be [near to you]. . . .

Matt 12:38–42
Matt 12:43–45

DEMAND FOR A SIGN
RETURN OF THE EVIL SPIRIT

M37
M38

MATT

Matt 12:38–42 (§M37)

³⁸Then some of the scribes and Pharisees said to him, "Teacher, we wish to see a sign from you." ³⁹But he answered them, "An evil and adulterous generation seeks for a sign; but no sign shall be given to it except the sign of the prophet Jonah. ⁴⁰For as Jonah was three days and three nights in the belly of the whale, so will the Son of man be three days and three nights in the heart of the earth. ⁴¹The men of Nineveh will arise at the judgment with this generation and condemn it; for they repented at the preaching of Jonah, and behold, something greater than Jonah is here. ⁴²The queen of the South will arise at the judgment with this generation and condemn it; for she came from the ends of the earth to hear the wisdom of Solomon, and behold, something greater than Solomon is here."

Matt 12:43–45 (§M38)

⁴³"When the unclean spirit has gone out of a man, he passes through waterless places seeking rest, but he finds none. ⁴⁴Then he says, 'I will return to my house from which I came.' And when he comes he finds it empty, swept, and put in order. ⁴⁵Then he goes and brings with him seven other spirits more evil than himself, and they enter and dwell there; and the last state of that man becomes worse than the first. So shall it be also with this evil generation."

Matt 16:1–4 (§M53) ⇨ Matt 12:38–39

¹And the Pharisees and Sadducees came, and to test him they asked him to show them a sign from heaven. ²He answered them, "When it is evening, you say, 'It will be fair weather; for the sky is red.' ³And in the morning, 'It will be stormy today, for the sky is red and threatening.' You know how to interpret the appearance of the sky, but you cannot interpret the signs of the times. ⁴An evil and adulterous generation seeks for a sign, but no sign shall be given to it except the sign of Jonah." So he left them and departed.

Jonah 1:17 ⇨ Matt 12:40

¹⁷And the Lord appointed a great fish to swallow up Jonah; and Jonah was in the belly of the fish three days and three nights.

Jonah 3:5 ⇨ Matt 12:41

⁵And the people of Nineveh believed God; they proclaimed a fast, and put on sackcloth, from the greatest of them to the least of them.

⇨ Matt 12:42
Cf. 1 Kgs 10:1–13

MARK

Mark 8:11–13 (§K38) ⇨ Matt 12:38–39

¹¹The Pharisees came and began to argue with him, seeking from him a sign from heaven, to test him. ¹²And he sighed deeply in his spirit, and said, "Why does this generation seek a sign? Truly, I say to you, no sign shall be given to this generation." ¹³And he left them, and getting into the boat again he departed to the other side.

LUKE

Luke 11:29–32 (§L51.4) ⇨ §M37

²⁹When the crowds were increasing, he began to say, "This generation is an evil generation; it seeks a sign, but no sign shall be given to it except the sign of Jonah. ³⁰For as Jonah became a sign to the men of Nineveh, so will the Son of man be to this generation. ³¹The queen of the South will arise at the judgment with the men of this generation and condemn them; for she came from the ends of the earth to hear the wisdom of Solomon, and behold, something greater than Solomon is here. ³²The men of Nineveh will arise at the judgment with this generation and condemn it; for they repented at the preaching of Jonah, and behold, something greater than Jonah is here."

Luke 11:16 ⇨ Matt 12:38

¹⁶while others, to test him, sought from him a sign from heaven.

Luke 11:24–26 (§L51.2) ⇨ §M38

²⁴"When the unclean spirit has gone out of a man, he passes through waterless places seeking rest; and finding none he says, 'I will return to my house from which I came.' ²⁵And when he comes he finds it swept and put in order. ²⁶Then he goes and brings seven other spirits more evil than himself, and they enter and dwell there; and the last state of that man becomes worse than the first."

JOHN

John 2:18 ⇨ Matt 12:38

¹⁸The Jews then said to him, "What sign have you to show us for doing this?"

John 6:30 ⇨ Matt 12:38

So they said to him, "Then what sign do you do, that we may see, and believe you? What work do you perform?

THOMAS

OTHER

GNaz 11 ⇨ Matt 12:40b

(11) The Jewish Gospel does not have: three d(ays and nights). (Variant to Matthew 12:40 in the "Zion Gospel" Edition)

MATT

Matt 12:46–50 (§M39)
[46] While he was still speaking to the people, behold, his mother and his brothers stood outside, asking to speak to him.[a] [48] But he replied to the man who told him, "Who is my mother, and who are my brothers?" [49] And stretching out his hand toward his disciples, he said, "Here are my mother and my brothers! [50] For whoever does the will of my Father in heaven is my brother, and sister, and mother."

[a] Add v. 47 *Some one told him, "Your mother and your brothers are standing outside, asking to speak to you":* ℵ[a] C D K W X Δ Θ Π (*f*[1]) *f*[13] 28 33 *pm;* omit v. 47: ℵ* B L 1009 it (in part) syr[c,s] cop[sa]

MARK

Mark 3:31–35 (§K20.3)
[31] And his mother and his brothers came; and standing outside they sent to him and called him. [32] And a crowd was sitting about him; and they said to him, "Your mother and your brothers are outside, asking for you." [33] And he replied, "Who are my mother and my brothers?" [34] And looking around on those who sat about him, he said, "Here are my mother and my brothers! [35] Whoever does the will of God is my brother, and sister, and mother."

LUKE

Luke 8:19–21 (§L32)
[19] Then his mother and his brothers came to him, but they could not reach him for the crowd. [20] And he was told, "Your mother and your brothers are standing outside, desiring to see you." [21] But he said to them, "My mother and my brothers are those who hear the word of God and do it."

JOHN

John 15:14 ⇨ Matt 12:50
[14] "You are my friends if you do what I command you."

THOMAS

GThom 99
(99) The disciples said to him, "Your brothers and Your mother are standing outside."

He said to them, "Those here who do the will of My Father are My brothers and My mother. It is they who will enter the Kingdom of My Father."

OTHER

GEbi 5
(5) Moreover they deny that he was a man, evidently on the ground of the word which the Saviour spoke when it was reported to him: "Behold, thy mother and thy brethren stand without," namely:

Who is my mother and who are my brethren? And he stretched forth his hand towards his disciples and said: These are my brethren and mother and sisters, who do the will of my Father. (Epiphanius, *Haer.* 30.14.5)

2 Clem 9:11 ⇨ Matt 12:50
[11] For the Lord said, "My brethren are these who do the will of my Father."

MATT

Matt 13:1–2 (§M40.1)

[1] That same day Jesus went out of the house and sat beside the sea. [2] And great crowds gathered about him, so that he got into a boat and sat there; and the whole crowd stood on the beach.

Matt 13:3–9 (§M40.2)

[3] And he told them many things in parables, saying: "A sower went out to sow. [4] And as he sowed, some seeds fell along the path, and the birds came and devoured them. [5] Other seeds fell on rocky ground, where they had not much soil, and immediately they sprang up, since they had no depth of soil, [6] but when the sun rose they were scorched; and since they had no root they withered away. [7] Other seeds fell upon thorns, and the thorns grew up and choked them. [8] Other seeds fell on good soil and brought forth grain, some a hundredfold, some sixty, some thirty. [9] He who has ears,[a] let him hear."

[a] Some witnesses add *to hear* (cf. Mark 4:9, 23, 7:16, Luke 8:8, 14:35)

MARK

Mark 4:1 (§K21.1) ⇨ §M40.1

Again he began to teach beside **the sea**. And a very large crowd **gathered about him, so that he got into a boat and sat** in it on the sea; **and the whole crowd** was beside the sea on the land.

Mark 4:2–9 (§K21.2) ⇨ §M40.2

[2] And he taught **them many things in parables**, and in his teaching he said to them: [3] "Listen! **A sower went out to sow.** [4] And as he sowed, some seed fell along the path, and the birds came and devoured it. [5] Other seed fell on rocky ground, where it had not much soil, and immediately it sprang up, since it had no depth of soil; [6] and when the sun rose it was scorched, and since it had no root it withered away. [7] Other seed fell among thorns and the thorns grew up and choked it, and it yielded no grain. [8] And other seeds fell into good soil and brought forth grain, growing up and increasing and yielding thirtyfold and sixtyfold and a hundredfold." [9] And he said, "He who has ears to hear, let him hear."

LUKE

Luke 8:4–8 (§L31.1)

[4] And when a **great** crowd came together and people from town after town came to **him**, he said in a parable: [5] "A sower went out to sow his seed; and as he sowed, some fell along the path, and was trodden under foot, and the birds of the air devoured it. [6] And some fell on the rock; and as it grew up, it withered away, because it had no moisture. [7] And some fell among thorns; and the thorns grew with it and choked it. [8] And some fell into good soil and grew, and yielded a hundredfold." As he said this, he called out, "He who has ears to hear, let him hear."

Luke 5:1–3 (§L17.1) ⇨ §M40.1

[1] *While the people pressed upon him to hear the word of God, he was standing by the lake of Gennesaret. [2] And he saw two boats by the lake; but the fishermen had gone out of them and were washing their nets. [3] Getting into one of the boats, which was Simon's, he asked him to put out a little from the land. And he sat down and taught the people from the boat.*

JOHN

THOMAS

GThom 9 ⇨ §M40.2

(9) Jesus said, "Now the **sower went out**, took a handful (of seeds), and scattered them. **Some fell** on the road; **the birds came and** gathered **them** up. **Others fell on** rock, did not take **root** in the **soil**, and did not produce ears. And **others fell** on **thorns**; they **choked** the seed(s) and worms ate them. And others **fell** on the **good soil and** produced good fruit: it bore sixty per measure and a hundred and twenty per measure."

OTHER

InThom 12:1–2 ⇨ §M40.2

[1] *Again, in the time of sowing the child went out with his father to sow wheat in their land. And as his father sowed, the child Jesus also sowed one corn of wheat. [2] And when he had reaped it and threshed it, he brought in a hundred measures; and he called all the poor of the village to the threshing-floor and gave them the wheat, and Joseph took the residue of the wheat. He was eight years old when he worked this miracle.*

ApocJa 12:20–31 ⇨ §M40.2

[20] *he said: "This is why I say this to you (pl.), that you may know yourselves. For the Kingdom of Heaven is like an ear of grain which sprouted in a field. And [25] when it ripened, it scattered its fruit and, in turn, filled the field with ears of grain for another year. You also: be zealous to reap for yourselves an ear of life, in order that [30] you may be filled with the Kingdom."*

MATT

Matt 13:10–17 (§M40.3)
¹⁰ Then the disciples came and said to him, "Why do you speak to them in parables?" ¹¹ And he answered them, "To you it has been given to know the secrets of the kingdom of heaven, but to them it has not been given. ¹² For to him who has will more be given, and he will have abundance; but from him who has not, even what he has will be taken away. ¹³ This is why I speak to them in parables, because seeing they do not see, and hearing they do not hear, nor do they understand. ¹⁴ With them indeed is fulfilled the prophecy of Isaiah which says:

'You shall indeed hear but never understand,
     and you shall indeed see but never perceive.
¹⁵ For this people's heart has grown dull,
     and their ears are heavy of hearing,
     and their eyes they have closed,
lest they should perceive with their eyes,
     and hear with their ears,
and understand with their heart,
     and turn for me to heal them.'

¹⁶ But blessed are your eyes, for they see, and your ears, for they hear. ¹⁷ Truly, I say to you, many prophets and righteous men longed to see what you see, and did not see it, and to hear what you hear, and did not hear it."

Matt 25:29 ⇨ Matt 13:12
²⁹ "'For to every one who has will more be given, and he will have abundance; but from him who has not, even what he has will be taken away.'"

MARK

Mark 4:10–12 (§K21.3)
¹⁰ And when he was alone, those who were about him with the twelve asked him concerning the parables. ¹¹ And he said to them, "To you has been given the secret of the kingdom of God, but for those outside everything is in parables; ¹² so that they may indeed see but not perceive, and may indeed hear but not understand; lest they should turn again, and be forgiven."

Mark 4:25 ⇨ Matt 13:12
²⁵ "For to him who has will more be given; and from him who has not, even what he has will be taken away."

Isa 6:9–10 ⇨ Matt 13:13–17
⁹ And he said, "Go, and say to this people:
'Hear and hear, but do not understand;
     see and see, but do not perceive.'
¹⁰ Make the heart of this people fat,
     and their ears heavy,
     and shut their eyes;
lest they see with their eyes,
     and hear with their ears,
and understand with their hearts,
     and turn and be healed."

LUKE

Luke 8:9–10 (§L31.2)
⁹ And when his disciples asked him what this parable meant, ¹⁰ he said, "To you it has been given to know the secrets of the kingdom of God; but for others they are in parables, so that seeing they may not see, and hearing they may not understand."

Luke 8:18 ⇨ Matt 13:12
¹⁸ "Take heed then how you hear; for to him who has will more be given, and from him who has not, even what he thinks that he has will be taken away."

Luke 19:26 ⇨ Matt 13:12
²⁶ "'I tell you, that to every one who has will more be given; but from him who has not, even what he has will be taken away.'"

Luke 10:23–24 (§L47.3) ⇨ Matt 13:16–17
²³ Then turning to the disciples he said privately, "Blessed are the eyes which see what you see! ²⁴ For I tell you that many prophets and kings desired to see what you see, and did not see it, and to hear what you hear, and did not hear it."

OTHER

Acts 28:25–28
²⁵ So, as they disagreed among themselves, they departed, after Paul had made one statement: "The Holy Spirit was right in saying to your fathers through Isaiah the prophet:
²⁶ 'Go to this people, and say,
You shall indeed hear but never understand,
     and you shall indeed see but never perceive.
²⁷ For this people's heart has grown dull,
     and their ears are heavy of hearing,
     and their eyes they have closed;
lest they should perceive with their eyes,
     and hear with their ears,
and understand with their heart,
     and turn for me to heal them.'
²⁸ Let it be known to you then that this salvation of God has been sent to the Gentiles; they will listen."

ApocJa 7:1–10
I first spoke with you in parables, and you did not understand. Now, in turn, I speak with ⁵ you openly, and you do not perceive. But it is you who were to me a parable in parables and what is apparent ¹⁰ in what are open.

JOHN

John 12:40 ⇨ Matt 13:13–17
⁴⁰ "He has blinded their eyes and hardened their heart,
lest they should see with their eyes and perceive with their heart,
and turn for me to heal them."

THOMAS

GThom 41 ⇨ Matt 13:12
(41) Jesus said, "Whoever has something in his hand will receive more, and whoever has nothing will be deprived of even the little he has."

GThom 38 ⇨ Matt 13:17
(38) Jesus said, "Many times have you desired to hear these words which I am saying to you, and you have no one else to hear them from. There will be days when you will look for Me and will not find Me."

MATT

Matt 13:18–23 (§M40.4)

[18] "Hear then the parable of the sower. [19] When any one hears the word of the kingdom and does not understand it, the evil one comes and snatches away what is sown in his heart; this is what was sown along the path. [20] As for what was sown on rocky ground, this is he who hears the word and immediately receives it with joy; [21] yet he has no root in himself, but endures for a while, and when tribulation or persecution arises on account of the word, immediately he falls away.[a] [22] As for what was sown among thorns, this is he who hears the word, but the cares of the world and the delight in riches choke the word, and it proves unfruitful. [23] As for what was sown on good soil, this is he who hears the word and understands it; he indeed bears fruit, and yields, in one case a hundredfold, in another sixty, and in another thirty."

Matt 13:24–30 (§M40.5)

[24] Another parable he put before them, saying, "The kingdom of heaven may be compared to a man who sowed good seed in his field; [25] but while men were sleeping, his enemy came and sowed weeds among the wheat, and went away. [26] So when the plants came up and bore grain, then the weeds appeared also. [27] And the servants of the householder came and said to him, 'Sir, did you not sow good seed in your field? How then has it weeds?' [28] He said to them, 'An enemy has done this.' The servants[b] said to him, 'Then do you want us to go and gather them?' [29] But he said, 'No, lest in gathering the weeds you root up the wheat along with them. [30] Let both grow together until the harvest; and at harvest time I will tell the reapers, Gather the weeds first and bind them in bundles to be burned, but gather the wheat into my barn.'"

[a] Or: *stumbles*

[b] Or: *slaves*

JOHN

MARK

Mark 4:13–20 (§K21.4) ⇨ §M40.4

[13] And he said to them, "Do you not understand this parable? How then will you understand all the parables? [14] The sower sows the word. [15] And these are the ones **along the path**, where the word **is sown**; when they hear, Satan immediately **comes and** takes **away** the word which **is sown** in them. [16] And these in like manner are the ones **sown** upon **rocky ground, who,** when they hear **the word,** immediately receive **it with joy;** [17] and they have **no root in** themselves, **but** endure **for a while;** then, **when tribulation or persecution arises on account of the word, immediately** they fall **away.** [18] And others are the ones **sown among thorns;** they are those who hear the **word,** [19] **but the cares of the world, and the delight in riches,** and the desire for other things, enter in and **choke the word, and it proves unfruitful.** [20] But those that were **sown** upon the **good soil** are the ones **who** hear **the word** and accept **it** and bear **fruit,** thirtyfold and sixtyfold and **a hundredfold."**

Mark 4:26–29 (§K21.7) ⇨ §M40.5

[26] *And he said, "**The kingdom of** God is as if a man should scatter seed upon the ground, [27] and should sleep and rise night and day, and the seed should sprout and grow, he knows not how. [28] The earth produces of itself, first the blade, then the ear, then the full grain in the ear. [29] But when the grain is ripe, at once he puts in the sickle, because **the harvest has come.**"*

THOMAS

GThom 57 ⇨ §M40.5

(57) Jesus said, "**The Kingdom of** the Father is like **a man who** had [**good**] **seed. His enemy came** by night **and sowed weeds among the** good seed. The man did not allow them to pull up **the weeds;** he said to them, 'I am afraid that you will go intending to pull up **the weeds** and pull **up the wheat along with them.'** For on the day of the harvest **the weeds** will be plainly visible, **and** they will be pulled up and **burned.**"

LUKE

Luke 8:11–15 (§L31.3) ⇨ §M40.4

[11] "Now **the parable** is this: The seed is the word of God. [12] The ones **along the path** are those who have heard; then **the** devil **comes and** takes **away** the word from their hearts, that they may not believe and be saved. [13] And the ones on the rock are those **who,** when they hear **the word,** receive **it with joy;** but these have **no root,** they believe **for a while and** in time of temptation fall **away.** [14] And **as for** what fell **among** the **thorns,** they are those who hear, **but** as they go on their way they are choked by **the cares** and **riches** and pleasures of life, **and** their fruit does not mature. [15] And **as for** that in the **good soil,** they are those who, hearing **the word,** hold it fast in an honest and good heart, and bring forth **fruit** with patience."

OTHER

ApocJa 8:10–27 ⇨ §M40.4

[10] *"Become zealous about **the Word.** For the Word's first condition is faith; the second is love; the third is works. [15] Now from these comes life. For **the Word** is like a grain of wheat. When someone sowed it, he believed in it; and when it sprouted, he loved it, because he looked (forward to) [20] many grains in the place of one; and when he worked (it), he was saved, because he prepared it for food. Again he left (some grains) to sow. Thus it is also possible for you (pl.) to receive [25] the **Kingdom** of Heaven: unless you receive it through knowledge, you will not be able to find it."*

M40.6   PARABLE OF THE MUSTARD SEED   Matt 13:31–32
M40.7   PARABLE OF THE LEAVEN   Matt 13:33
M40.8   SUMMARY: PARABLES FULFIL SCRIPTURE   Matt 13:34–35

MATT

Matt 13:31–32 (§M40.6)
[31] Another parable he put before them, saying, "The kingdom of heaven is like a grain of mustard seed which a man took and sowed in his field; [32] it is the smallest of all seeds, but when it has grown it is the greatest of shrubs and becomes a tree, so that the birds of the air come and make nests in its branches."

Matt 13:33 (§M40.7)
[33] He told them another parable. "The kingdom of heaven is like leaven which a woman took and hid in three measures of flour, till it was all leavened."

Matt 13:34–35 (§M40.8)
[34] All this Jesus said to the crowds in parables; indeed he said nothing to them without a parable. [35] This was to fulfil what was spoken by the prophet:[a]
  "I will open my mouth in parables,
  I will utter what has been hidden since the foundation of the world."

[a] Add *Isaiah:* ℵ* Θ *f*[1] *f*[13] *al*

Dan 4:20–22 ⇨ Matt 13:32
[20] "The **tree** you saw, which grew and bacame strong, so that its top reached to heaven, and it was visible to the end of the whole earth; [21] whose leaves were fair and its fruit abundant, and in which was food for all; under which beasts of the field found shade, and in whose **branches the birds of the air** dwelt—[22] it is you, O king, who have grown and become strong. Your greatness has brown and reaches to heaven, and your dominion to the ends of the earth."

Ps 78:2–3 ⇨ Matt 13:35
[2] **I will open my mouth in** a parable;
  I will utter dark sayings from of old,
[3] things that we have heard and known,
  that our fathers have told us.

MARK

Mark 4:30–32 (§K21.8) ⇨ §M40.6
[30] And **he** said, "With what can we compare **the kingdom of** God, or what parable shall we use for it? It **is like a grain of mustard seed, which,** when sown upon the ground, **is the smallest of all the seeds** on earth; [32] yet **when it** is sown it grows up and becomes **the greatest of all shrubs, and** puts forth large branches, **so that the birds of the air** can **make nests in its** shade."

Mark 4:33–34 (§K21.9) ⇨ §M40.8
[33] With many such **parables** he spoke the word to them, as they were able to hear it; [34] **he** did not speak **to them without a parable,** but privately to his own disciples he explained everything.

LUKE

Luke 13:18–19 (§L59.1) ⇨ §M40.6
[18] **He** said therefore, "What is **the kingdom** of God like? And to what shall I compare it? [19] It **is like a grain of mustard seed which a man took and sowed in his garden;** and it grew and became **a tree, and the birds of the air** made **nests in its branches.**"

Luke 13:20–21 (§L59.2) ⇨ §M40.7
[20] And again **he** said, "To what shall I compare **the kingdom of** God? [21] It **is like leaven which a woman took and hid in three measures,** till it was all leavened."

JOHN

THOMAS

GThom 20 ⇨ §M40.6
(20) The disciples said to Jesus, "Tell us what **the Kingdom of Heaven is like.**"
He said to them, "It **is like a mustard seed, the smallest of all seeds. But when** it falls on tilled soil, it produces a great plant and **becomes a** shelter for **birds of the** sky."

GThom 96 ⇨ §M40.7
(96) Jesus [said], "**The Kingdom of** the Father **is like a** certain **woman.** She **took a** little leaven, [concealed] it in some dough, and made **it** into large loaves. Let him who has ears hear."

OTHER

M40   PARABLES FROM THE BOAT   Matt 13:1–35
S11: M40–41   TEACHING IN PARABLES   Matt 13:1–52
  77

| MATT | MARK | LUKE |

Matt 13:36–43 (§M41.1)

[36] Then he left the crowds and went into the house. And his disciples came to him, saying, "Explain to us the parable of the weeds of the field." [37] He answered, "He who sows the good seed is the Son of man; [38] the field is the world, and the good seed means the sons of the kingdom; the weeds are the sons of the evil one, [39] and the enemy who sowed them is the devil; the harvest is the close of the age, and the reapers are angels. [40] Just as the weeds are gathered and burned with fire, so will it be at the close of the age. [41] The Son of man will send his angels, and they will gather out of his kingdom all causes of sin and all evildoers, [42] and throw them into the furnace of fire; there men will weep and gnash their teeth. [43] Then the righteous will shine like the sun in the kingdom of their Father. He who has ears, [a] let him hear."

Matt 13:44 (§M41.2)

[44] "The kingdom of heaven is like treasure hidden in a field, which a man found and covered up; then in his joy he goes and sells all that he has and buys that field."

[a] Some witnesses add *to hear* (cf. Mark 4:9, 23, 7:16, Luke 8:8, 14:35)

Matt 24:31 ⇨ Matt 13:41
[31] *and he will send out his angels with a loud trumpet call, and they will gather his elect from the four winds, from one end of heaven to the other.*

Matt 8:12 ⇨ Matt 13:42
[12] *"while the sons of the kingdom will be thrown into the outer darkness; there men will weep and gnash their teeth."*

Matt 13:50 ⇨ Matt 13:42
[50] *"and throw them into the furnace of fire; there men will weep and gnash their teeth."*

Matt 22:13 ⇨ Matt 13:42
[13] *"Then the king said to the attendants, 'Bind him hand and foot, and cast him into the outer darkness; there men will weep and gnash their teeth.'"*

Matt 24:51 ⇨ Matt 13:42
[51] *"and will punish him, and put him with the hypocrites; there men will weep and gnash their teeth."*

Matt 25:30 ⇨ Matt 13:42
[30] *"And cast the worthless servant into the outer darkness; there men will weep and gnash their teeth."*

Dan 12:3 ⇨ Matt 13:43
[3] "And those who are wise shall **shine like the** brightness of the firmament; and those who turn many to righteousness, like the stars for ever and ever."

| JOHN | THOMAS | OTHER |

GThom 109 ⇨ §M41.2

(109) Jesus said, "**The Kingdom is like a man** who had a [**hidden**] **treasure in** his **field** without knowing it. And [after] **he** died, **he** left it to his son. The son did not know (about the **treasure**). He inherited the **field** and sold [it]. And the one who bought it went plowing and **found** the **treasure**. He began to lend money at interest to whomever he wished."

| MATT | MARK | LUKE |

Matt 13:45–46 (§M41.3)
[45] "Again, the kingdom of heaven is like a merchant in search of fine pearls, [46] who, on finding one pearl of great value, went and sold all that he had and bought it."

Matt 13:47–50 (§M41.4)
[47] "Again, the kingdom of heaven is like a net which was thrown into the sea and gathered fish of every kind; [48] when it was full, men drew it ashore and sat down and sorted the good into vessels but threw away the bad. [49] So it will be at the close of the age. The angels will come out and separate the evil from the righteous, [50] and throw them into the furnace of fire; there men will weep and gnash their teeth."

Matt 13:51–52 (§M41.5)
[51] "Have you understood all this?" They said to him, "Yes." [52] And he said to them, "Therefore every scribe who has been trained for the kingdom of heaven is like a householder who brings out of his treasure what is new and what is old."

Matt 13:40–42 ⇨ Matt 13:49–50
[40] *"Just as the weeds are gathered and burned with fire, so will it be at the close of the age. [41] The Son of man will send his angels, and they will gather out of his kingdom all causes of sin and all evildoers, [42] and throw them into the furnace of fire; there men will weep and gnash their teeth."*

Matt 8:12 ⇨ Matt 13:50
[12] *"while the sons of the kingdom will be thrown into the outer darkness; there men will weep and gnash their teeth."*

Matt 22:13 ⇨ Matt 13:50
[13] *"Then the king said to the attendants, 'Bind him hand and foot, and cast him into the outer darkness; there men will weep and gnash their teeth.'"*

Matt 24:51 ⇨ Matt 13:50
[51] *"and will punish him, and put him with the hypocrites; there men will weep and gnash their teeth."*

Matt 25:30 ⇨ Matt 13:50
[30] *"And cast the worthless servant into the outer darkness; there men will weep and gnash their teeth.'"*

| JOHN | THOMAS | OTHER |

GThom 76 ⇨ §M41.3
(76) Jesus said, **"The Kingdom of** the Father **is like a merchant** who had a consignment of merchandise and **who** discovered a **pearl.** That merchant was shrewd. He **sold** the merchandise **and bought** the **pearl** alone for himself. You too, seek his unfailing and enduring treasure where no moth comes near to devour and no worm destroys."

GThom 8 ⇨ §M41.4
(8) And He said, "The man is like a wise fisherman who cast his **net into the sea and** drew it up from **the sea full** of small fish. Among them the wise fisherman found a fine large **fish.** He **threw** all the small fish back into the sea and chose the large **fish** without difficulty. Whoever has ears to hear, let him hear."

MATT

Matt 13:53–58 (§M42) °

⁵³ And when Jesus had finished these parables, he went away from there, ⁵⁴ and coming to his own country he taught them in their synagogue, so that they were astonished, and said, "Where did this man get this wisdom and these mighty works? ⁵⁵ Is not this the carpenter's son? Is not his mother called Mary? And are not his brothers James and Joseph and Simon and Judas? ⁵⁶ And are not all his sisters with us? Where then did this man get all this?" ⁵⁷ And they took offense at him. But Jesus said to them, "A prophet is not without honor except in his own country and in his own house." ⁵⁸ And he did not do many mighty works there, because of their unbelief.

°Appendix 3 ⇨ §M42

Matt 7:28–29 (§M12.9) ⇨ Matt 13:54

²⁸ *And when Jesus finished these sayings, the crowds were astonished at his teaching,* ²⁹ *for he taught them as one who had authority, and not as their scribes.*

Matt 22:33 ⇨ Matt 13:54

³³ *And when the crowd heard it, they were astonished at his teaching.*

JOHN

John 7:15 ⇨ Matt 13:54

¹⁵ *The Jews marveled at it, saying, "How is it that this man has learning, when he has never studied?"*

John 6:41–45 ⇨ Matt 13:55–57

The Jews then murmured at him, because he said, "I am the bread which came down from heaven." ⁴² *They said, "Is not this Jesus, the son of Joseph, whose father and mother we know? How does he now say, 'I have come down from heaven'?"* ⁴³ *Jesus answered them, "Do not murmur among yourselves.* ⁴⁴ *No one can come to me unless the Father who sent me draws him; and I will raise him up at the last day.* ⁴⁵ *It is written in the prophets, 'And they shall all be taught by God.' Every one who has heard and learned from the Father comes to me."*

John 4:44 ⇨ Matt 13:57

⁴⁴ *For Jesus himself testified that a prophet has no honor in his own country.*

John 6:61 ⇨ Matt 13:57

⁶¹ *But Jesus, knowing in himself that his disciples murmured at it, said to them, "Do you take offense at this?"*

MARK

Mark 6:1–6 (§K25)

¹ He went away from there and came to his own country; and his disciples followed him. ² And on the sabbath he began to teach in the synagogue; and many who heard him were astonished, saying, "Where did this man get all this? What is the wisdom given to him? What mighty works are wrought by his hands! ³ Is not this the carpenter, the son of Mary and brother of James and Joses and Judas and Simon, and are not his sisters here with us?" And they took offense at him. ⁴ And Jesus said to them, "A prophet is not without honor, except in his own country, and among his own kin, and in his own house." ⁵ And he could do no mighty work there, except that he laid his hands upon a few sick people and healed them. ⁶ And he marveled because of their unbelief.

And he went about among the villages teaching.

THOMAS

POxy1 6 ⇨ Matt 13:57

(6) **Jesus** says, "**A prophet is not** acceptable **in his own** homeland, nor does a physician work cures on those who know him."

GThom 31 ⇨ Matt 13:57

(31) **Jesus** said, "No **prophet is** accepted **in his own** village; no physician heals those who know him."

LUKE

‡ **Luke 4:16–30 (§L12)**

¹⁶ And he came to Nazareth, where he had been brought up; and he went to the synagogue, as his custom was, on the sabbath day. And he stood up to read; ¹⁷ and there was given to him the book of the prophet Isaiah. He opened the book and found the place where it was written,

¹⁸ "The Spirit of the Lord is upon me,
because he has anointed me to preach good
news to the poor.
He has sent me to proclaim release to the
captives
and recovering of sight to the blind,
to set at liberty those who are oppressed,
¹⁹ to proclaim the acceptable year of the
Lord."

²⁰ And he closed the book, and gave it back to the attendant, and sat down; and the eyes of all in the synagogue were fixed on him. ²¹ And he began to say to them, "Today this scripture has been fulfilled in your hearing." ²² And all spoke well of him, and wondered at the gracious words which proceeded out of his mouth; and they said, "Is not this Joseph's son?" ²³ And he said to them, "Doubtless you will quote to me this proverb, 'Physician, heal yourself; what we have heard you did at Capernaum, do here also in your own country.'" ²⁴ And he said, "Truly, I say to you, no prophet is acceptable in his own country. ²⁵ But in truth, I tell you, there were many widows in Israel in the days of Elijah, when the heaven was shut up three years and six months, when there came a great famine over all the land; ²⁶ and Elijah was sent to none of them but only to Zarephath, in the land of Sidon, to a woman who was a widow. ²⁷ And there were many lepers in Israel in the time of the prophet Elisha; and none of them was cleansed, but only Naaman the Syrian." ²⁸ When they heard this, all in the synagogue were filled with wrath. ²⁹ And they rose up and put him out of the city, and led him to the brow of the hill on which their city was built, that they might throw him down headlong. ³⁰ But passing through the midst of them he went away.

OTHER

MATT

Matt 14:1–12 (§M43) °

¹At that time Herod the tetrarch heard about the fame of Jesus; ²and he said to this servants, "This is John the Baptist, he has been raised from the dead; that is why these powers are at work in him." ³For Herod had seized John and bound him and put him in prison, for the sake of Herodias, his brother Philip's[a] wife; ⁴because John said to him, "It is not lawful for you to have her. ⁵And though he wanted to put him to death, he feared the people, because they held him to be a prophet. ⁶But when Herod's birthday came, the daughter of Herodias danced before the company, and pleased Herod, ⁷so that he promised with an oath to give her whatever she might ask. ⁸Prompted by her mother, she said, "Give me the head of John the Baptist here on a platter." ⁹And the king was sorry, but because of his oaths and his guests he commanded it to be given; ¹⁰he sent and had John beheaded in the prison, ¹¹and his head was brought on a platter and given to the girl, and she brought it to her mother. ¹²And his disciples came and took the body and buried it; and they went and told Jesus.

Matt 14:13–14 (§M44) °°

¹³Now when Jesus heard this, he withdrew from there in a boat to a lonely place apart. But when the crowds heard it, they followed him on foot from the towns. ¹⁴As he went ashore he saw a great throng; and he had compassion on them, and healed their sick.

[a] Some witnesses omit *Philip* (cf. Luke 3:19): D it (in part) vg

°Appendix 1 ⇨ §M43

°°Appendix 3 ⇨ §M44

Matt 16:14 ⇨ Matt 14:2, 5
¹⁴And they said, "Some say John the Baptist, others say Elijah, and others Jeremiah or one of the prophets."

Matt 4:12 ⇨ Matt 14:13
¹²Now when he heard that John had been arrested, he withdrew into Galilee; . . .

Matt 9:36 ⇨ Matt 14:14
³⁶When he saw the crowds, he had compassion for them, because they were harassed and helpless, like sheep without a shepherd.

⇨ Matt 14:4
Cf. Lev 18:16, 20:21

JOHN

John 1:19–21, 25 ⇨ Matt 14:2, 5
¹⁹And this is the testimony of John, when the Jews sent priests and Levites from Jerusalem to ask him, "Who are you?" ²⁰He confessed, he did not deny, but confessed, "I am not the Christ." ²¹And they asked him, "What then? Are you Elijah?" He said, "I am not." "Are you the prophet?" And he answered, "No." . . . ²⁵They asked him, "Then why are you baptizing, if you are neither the Christ, nor Elijah, nor the prophet?"

MARK

Mark 6:14–29 (§K27) ⇨ §M43

¹⁴King **Herod heard** of it; for Jesus' name had become known. Some said, "**John the baptizer has been raised from the dead; that is why these powers are at work in him.**" ¹⁵But others said, "It is Elijah." And others said, "It is a prophet, like one of the prophets of old." ¹⁶But when Herod heard of it he said, "John, whom I beheaded, has been raised." ¹⁷**For Herod had** sent and **seized John, and bound him in prison for the sake of Herodias, his brother Philip's wife**; because he had married her. For **John said** to Herod, "**It is not lawful for you to have** your brother's wife." ¹⁹And Herodias had a grudge against him, and wanted to kill him. But she could not, ²⁰for Herod **feared** John, knowing that he was a righteous and holy man, and kept him safe. When he heard him, he was much perplexed; and yet he heard him gladly. ²¹**But** an opportunity came **when** Herod on his **birthday** gave a banquet for his courtiers and officers and the leading men of Galilee. ²²For when Herodias' **daughter** came in and **danced**, she **pleased Herod** and his guests; and the king said to the girl, "Ask me for **whatever** you wish, and I will grant it." ²³And he vowed to her, "**Whatever** you ask me, I will give you, even half of my kingdom." ²⁴And she went out, and said to **her mother**, "What shall I ask?" And she said, "The head of John the baptizer." ²⁵And she came immediately with haste to the king, and asked, saying, "I want you to **give me** at once **the head of John the Baptist on a platter.**" ²⁶**And the king was** exceedingly **sorry; but because of his oaths and his guests he** did not want to break his word to her. ²⁷And immediately the king **sent** a soldier of the guard and gave orders to bring his head. He went and **beheaded** him **in the prison,** ²⁸and **brought his head on a platter, and** gave it **to the girl**; and the girl gave **it to her mother**. ²⁹When **his disciples** heard of it, they **came and took his body,** and laid **it** in a tomb.

Mark 6:30–34 (§K28) ⇨ §M44

³⁰The apostles returned to **Jesus**, and told him all that they had done and taught. ³¹And he said to them, "Come away by yourselves to **a lonely place**, and rest a while." For many were coming and going, and they had no leisure even to eat. ³²And they went away **in the boat to a lonely place** by themselves. ³³Now many saw them going, and knew them, and they ran there **on foot from all the towns**, and got there ahead of them. ³⁴**As he went ashore he saw a great throng, and he had compassion on them**, because they were like sheep without a shepherd; and he began to teach them many things.

Mark 8:28 ⇨ Matt 14:2, 5
²⁸And they told him, "John the Baptist; and others say, Elijah; and others one of the prophets."

THOMAS

LUKE

Luke 9:7–9 (§L37) ⇨ §M43

⁷Now **Herod the tetrarch heard** of all that was done, and he was perplexed, because it was said by some that **John** had **been raised from the dead,** ⁸by some that Elijah had appeared, and by others that one of the old prophets had risen. ⁹**Herod** said, "**John** I beheaded; but who is this about whom I hear such things?" And he sought to see him.

Luke 9:10–11 (§L38)
　⇨ §M44

¹⁰On their return the apostles told him what they had done. And **he** took them and **withdrew apart** to a city called Bethsaida. ¹¹**When the crowds** learned it, **they followed him; and he** welcomed **them** and spoke to them of the kingdom of God, and cured those who had need of healing.

Luke 9:19 ⇨ Matt 14:2, 5
¹⁹And they answered, "John the Baptist; but others say, Elijah; and others, that one of the old prophets has risen."

Luke 3:19–20 ⇨ Matt 14:3–4
*¹⁹But **Herod** the tetrarch, who had been reproved by him for **Herodias, his** brother's **wife,** and for all the evil things that **Herod** had done, ²⁰added this to them all, that he shut up **John in prison**.*

OTHER

MATT	MARK	LUKE

MATT

Matt 14:15–21 (§M45)

[15] When it was evening, the disciples came to him and said, "This is a lonely place, and the day is now over; send the crowds away to go into the villages and buy food for themselves." [16] Jesus said, "They need not go away; you give them something to eat." [17] They said to him, "We have only five loaves here and two fish." [18] And he said, "Bring them here to me." [19] Then he ordered the crowds to sit down on the grass; and taking the five loaves and the two fish he looked up to heaven, and blessed, and broke and gave the loaves to the disciples, and the disciples gave them to the crowds. [20] And they all ate and were satisfied. And they took up twelve baskets full of the broken pieces left over. [21] And those who ate were about five thousand men, besides women and children.

● **Matt 15:32–39 (§M52)**

[32] Then Jesus called his disciples to him and said, "I have compassion on the crowd, because they have been with me now three days, and have nothing to eat; and I am unwilling to send them away hungry, lest they faint on the way." [33] And the disciples said to him, "Where are we to get bread enough in the desert to feed so great a crowd?" [34] And Jesus said to them, "How many loaves have you?" They said, "Seven, and a few small fish." [35] And commanding the crowd to sit down on the ground, [36] he took the seven loaves and the fish, and having given thanks he broke them and gave them to the disciples, and the disciples gave them to the crowds. [37] And they all ate and were satisfied; and they took up seven baskets full of the broken pieces left over. [38] Those who ate were four thousand men, besides women and children. [39] And sending away the crowds, he got into the boat and went to the region of Magadan.

2 Kgs 4:42–44

[42] A man came from Baal-shalishah, bringing the man of God bread of the first fruits, twenty loaves of barley, and fresh ears of grain in his sack. And Elisha said, "Give to the men, that they may eat." [43] But his servant said, "How am I to set this before a hundred men?" So he repeated, "Give them to the men, that they may eat, for thus says the Lord, 'They shall eat and have some left.'" [44] So he set it before them. And they ate, and had some left, according to the word of the Lord.

MARK

Mark 6:35–44 (§K29)

[35] And when it grew late, his disciples came to him and said, "This is a lonely place, and the hour is now late; [36] send them away, to go into the country and villages round about and buy themselves something to eat." [37] But he answered them, "You give them something to eat." And they said to him, "Shall we go and buy two hundred denarii worth of bread, and give it to them to eat?" [38] And he said to them, "How many loaves have you? Go and see." And when they had found out, they said, "Five, and two fish." [39] Then he commanded them all to sit down by companies upon the green grass. [40] So they sat down in groups, by hundreds and by fifties. [41] And taking the five loaves and the two fish he looked up to heaven, and blessed, and broke the loaves, and gave them to the disciples to set before the people; and he divided the two fish among them all. [42] And they all ate and were satisfied. [43] And they took up twelve baskets full of broken pieces and of the fish. [44] And those who ate the loaves were five thousand men.

Mark 8:1–10 (§K37)

[1] In those days, when again a great crowd had gathered, and they had nothing to eat, he called his disciples to him, and said to them, [2] "I have compassion on the crowd, because they have been with me now three days, and have nothing to eat; [3] and if I send them away hungry to their homes, they will faint on the way; and some of them have come a long way." [4] And his disciples answered him, "How can one feed these men with bread here in the desert?" [5] And he asked them, "How many loaves have you?" They said, "Seven." [6] And he commanded the crowd to sit down on the ground; and he took the seven loaves, and having given thanks he broke them and gave them to his disciples to set before the people; and they set them before the crowd. [7] And they had a few small fish; and having blessed them, he commanded that these also should be set before them. [8] And they ate, and were satisfied; and they took up the broken pieces left over, seven baskets full. [9] And there were about four thousand people. [10] And he sent them away and immediately he got into the boat with his disciples, and went to the district of Dalmanutha.

Mark 14:22 ⇨ Matt 14:19

[22] And as they were eating, he took bread, and blessed, and broke it, and gave it to them, and said, "Take; this is my body."

LUKE

Luke 9:12–17 (§L39)

[12] Now the day began to wear away; and the twelve came and said to him, "Send the crowd away, to go into the villages and country round about, to lodge and get provisions; for we are here in a lonely place." [13] But he said to them, "You give them something to eat." They said, "We have no more than five loaves and two fish—unless we are to go and buy food for all these people." [14] For there were about five thousand men. And he said to his disciples, "Make them sit down in companies, about fifty each." [15] And they did so, and made them all sit down. [16] And taking the five loaves and the two fish he looked up to heaven, and blessed and broke them, and gave them to the disciples to set before the crowd. [17] And all ate and were satisfied. And they took up what was left over, twelve baskets of broken pieces.

Luke 22:19 ⇨ Matt 14:19

[19] And he took bread, and when he had given thanks he broke it and gave it to them, saying, "This is my body which is given for you. Do this in remembrance of me."

Luke 24:30 ⇨ Matt 14:19

[30] When he was at table with them, he took the bread and blessed, and broke it, and gave it to them.

| JOHN | THOMAS | OTHER |

JOHN

John 6:1–15 (§J10)

[1] After this Jesus went to the other side of the Sea of Galilee, which is the Sea of Tiberias. [2] And a multitude followed him, because they saw the signs which he did on those who were diseased. [3] Jesus went up on the mountain, and there sat down with his disciples. [4] Now the Passover, the feast of the Jews, was at hand. [5] Lifting up his eyes, then, and seeing that a multitude was coming to him, Jesus said to Philip, "How are we to **buy** bread, so that these people may eat?" [6] This he said to test him, for he himself knew what he would do. [7] Philip answered him, "Two hundred denarii would not buy enough bread for each of them to get a little." [8] One of his disciples, Andrew, Simon Peter's brother, said to him, [9] "There is a lad here who has **five** barley **loaves and two fish**; but what are they among so many?" [10] Jesus **said**, "Make the people sit down." Now there was much **grass** in the place; so the **men** sat down, in number about **five thousand**. [11] Jesus then took **the loaves, and** when **he** had given thanks, **he** distributed them to those who were seated; so also **the fish,** as much as they wanted. [12] **And** when **they** had eaten their fill, he told his disciples, "Gather up the fragments **left over,** that nothing may be lost." [13] So they gathered them up and filled **twelve baskets** with fragments from **the five** barley **loaves, left** by those who had eaten. [14] When the people saw the sign which he had done, they said, "This is indeed the prophet who is to come into the world!"

[15] Perceiving then that they were about to come and take him by force to make him king, Jesus withdrew again to the mountain by himself.

OTHER

Acts 27:35 ⇨ Matt 14:19

[35] *And when **he** had said this, **he** took bread, **and** giving thanks to God in the presence of all he **broke** it and began to eat.*

Matt 14:22–23
Matt 14:24–33

Narrative Transition
Jesus Walks on the Water

M46
M47

Matt	Mark	Luke

Matt 14:22–23 (§M46)

²²Then he made the disciples get into the boat and go before him to the other side, while he dismissed the crowds. ²³And after he had dismissed the crowds, he went up on the mountain by himself to pray. When evening came, he was there alone, . . .

Matt 14:24–33 (§M47)

²⁴but the boat by this time was many furlongs distant from the land,[a] beaten by the waves; for the wind was against them. ²⁵And in the fourth watch of the night he came to them, walking on the sea. ²⁶But when the disciples saw him walking on the sea, they were terrified, saying, "It is a ghost!" And they cried out for fear. ²⁷But immediately he spoke to them, saying, "Take heart, it is I; have no fear." ²⁸And Peter answered him, "Lord, if it is you, bid me come to you on the water." ²⁹He said, "Come." So Peter got out of the boat and walked on the water and came to Jesus; ³⁰but when he saw the wind,[b] he was afraid, and beginning to sink he cried out, "Lord, save me." ³¹Jesus immediately reached out his hand and caught him, saying to him, "O man of little faith, why did you doubt?" ³²And when they got into the boat, the wind ceased. ³³And those in the boat worshiped him, saying, "Truly you are the Son of God."

[a] Some witnesses read *was out on the sea* (cf. Mark 6:47): ℵ C K L P W X Δ Π *pm*

[b] Some witnesses read *(exceedingly) strong wind:* B² C D K L P W X Δ Θ Π 0119 *f*¹ *f*¹³ 28 *pm;* text: ℵ B* 073 33 cop

Matt 15:39 ⇨ Matt 14:23

³⁹And sending away **the crowds, he** got into the boat and **went to** the region of Magadan.

Mark 6:45–46 (§K30) ⇨ §M46

⁴⁵Immediately **he made** his **disciples get into the boat and go before him to the other side,** to Bethsaida, **while he dismissed** the crowd. ⁴⁶**And after he had** taken leave of them, **he went up on the mountain to pray.**

Mark 6:47–52 (§K31) ⇨ §M47

⁴⁷And when evening came, **the boat** was out on the sea, and he was alone on the land. ⁴⁸And he saw that they were making headway painfully, for the wind was against them. **And** about **the fourth watch of the night he came to them, walking on the sea.** He meant to pass by them, ⁴⁹but when they **saw him walking on the sea** they thought it was **a ghost, and cried out;** ⁵⁰for **they** all saw him, and **were terrified. But immediately he spoke to them** and said, **"Take heart, it is I; have no fear."** ⁵¹And he **got into the boat** with them and **the wind ceased. And** they were utterly astounded, ⁵²for they did not understand about the loaves, but their hearts were hardened.

Mark 8:10 ⇨ Matt 14:23

¹⁰**And he** sent them away; and immediately **he** got into the boat with his disciples, and **went to** the district of Dalmanutha.

Luke 24:37 ⇨ Matt 14:26

³⁷*But they were startled and frightened, and supposed that they saw a spirit.*

John	Thomas	Other

John 6:15 ⇨ Matt 14:23

¹⁵Perceiving then that they were about to come and take him by force to make him king, Jesus withdrew again **to the mountain by himself.**

John 6:16–21 (§J11) ⇨ §M47

¹⁶When evening came, his disciples went down to the sea, ¹⁷got into a **boat,** and started across the sea to Capernaum. It was now dark, and Jesus had not yet come to them. ¹⁸The sea rose because a strong **wind was** blowing. ¹⁹When they had rowed about three or four miles, they **saw** Jesus **walking on the sea** and drawing near to the boat. **They were** frightened, ²⁰**but he** said **to them,** "**It is I**; do not be afraid." ²¹Then they were glad to take him **into the boat,** and immediately the boat was at the land to which they were going.

	MATT	MARK	LUKE

MATT

Matt 14:34–36 (§M48) °

³⁴ And when they had crossed over, they came to land at Gennesaret. ³⁵ And when the men of that place recognized him, they sent round to all that region and brought to him all that were sick, ³⁶ and besought him that they might only touch the fringe of his garment; and as many as touched it were made well.

Matt 4:23–25 (§M11)

²³ And he went about all Galilee teaching in their synagogues and preaching the gospel of the kingdom and healing every disease and every infirmity among the people. ²⁴ So his fame spread throughout all Syria, and they **brought him all the sick,** those afflicted with various diseases and pains, demoniacs, epileptics, and paralytics, and he healed them. ²⁵ And great crowds followed him from Galilee and the Decapolis and Jerusalem and Judea and from beyond the Jordan.

Matt 8:16–17 (§M16)

¹⁶ That evening they **brought to him** many who were possessed with demons; and he cast out the spirits with a word, and healed **all who were sick.** ¹⁷ This was to fulfil what was spoken by the prophet Isaiah, "He took our infirmities and bore our diseases."

° Appendix 3 ⇨ §M48

MARK

Mark 6:53–56 (§K32)

⁵³ And when they had crossed over, they came to land at Gennesaret, and moored to the shore. ⁵⁴ And when they got out of the boat, immediately the people **recognized him,** ⁵⁵ and ran about the whole neighborhood and began to bring **sick** people on their pallets to any place where they heard he was. ⁵⁶ And wherever he came, in villages, cities, or country, **they** laid the **sick** in the market places, **and besought him that they might touch** even the **fringe of his garment; and as many as touched it were made well.**

Mark 1:32–34 (§K10)

³² That evening, at sundown, they **brought to him all** who were sick or possessed with demons. ³³ And the whole city was gathered together about the door. ³⁴ And he healed many who were sick with various diseases, and cast out many demons; and he would not permit the demons to speak, because they knew him.

Mark 3:7–12 (§K18)

⁷ Jesus withdrew with his disciples to the sea, and a great multitude from Galilee followed; also from Judea ⁸ and Jerusalem and Idumea and from beyond the Jordan and from about Tyre and Sidon a great multitude, hearing all that he did, came to him. ⁹ And he told his disciples to have a boat ready for him because of the crowd, lest they should crush him; ¹⁰ for he had healed many, so that all who had diseases pressed upon him to **touch** him. ¹¹ And whenever the unclean spirits beheld him, they fell down before him and cried out, "You are the Son of God." ¹² And he strictly ordered them not to make him known.

LUKE

Luke 4:40–41 (§L15)

⁴⁰ Now when the sun was setting, all those who had any that were **sick** with various diseases **brought them to him;** and he laid his hands on every one of them and healed them. ⁴¹ And demons also came out of many, crying, "You are the Son of God!" But he rebuked them, and would not allow them to speak, because they knew that he was the Christ.

Luke 6:17–19 (§L24)

¹⁷ And he came down with them and stood on a level place, with a great crowd of his disciples and a great multitude of people from **all** Judea and Jerusalem and the seacoast of Tyre and Sidon, who came to hear **him** and to be healed of their diseases; ¹⁸ and those who were troubled with unclean spirits were cured. ¹⁹ And all the crowd sought to **touch** him, for power came forth from him and healed them all.

	JOHN	THOMAS	OTHER

MATT	MARK	LUKE

Matt 15:1–9 (§M49.1)

[1] Then **Pharisees and scribes came to Jesus from Jerusalem** and said, [2] "Why do your disciples transgress the tradition of the elders? For they do not wash their hands when they eat." [3] He answered them, "And why do you transgress the commandment of God for the sake of your tradition? [4] For God commanded 'Honor your father and your mother,' and, 'He who speaks evil of father or mother, let him surely die.' [5] But you say, 'If any one tells his father or his mother, What you would have gained from me is given to God,[a] he need not honor his father.' [6] So for the sake of your tradition, you have made void the word[b] of God. [7] You hypocrites! Well did Isaiah prophesy of you, when he said:

[8] 'This people honors me with their lips,
but their heart is far from me;
[9] in vain do they worship me,
teaching as doctrines the precepts of
men.'"

[a] Or: *an offering*

[b] Text (cf. Mark 7:13) ℵ[a] B D Θ 700 892 1230 it (in part) syr (in part) *al; the law* ℵ⋆,[b] C 084 *f*[13] *al; the commandment* (cf. Matt 15:3): K L W X Δ Π 0106 *f*[1] 33 *al*

Exod 20:12 ⇨ Matt 15:4
[12] "**Honor your father and your mother**, that your days may be long in the land which the Lord your God gives you."

Exod 21:17 ⇨ Matt 15:4
[17] "Whoever curses his **father or** his **mother** shall be put to death."

Lev 20:9 ⇨ Matt 15:4
[9] "For every one who curses his **father or** his **mother** shall be put to death; he has cursed his **father or** his **mother**, his blood is upon him."

Deut 5:16 ⇨ Matt 15:4
[16] "'**Honor your father and your mother**, as the Lord your **God commanded** you; that your days may be prolonged, and that it may go well with you, in the land which the Lord your God gives you.'"

Isa 29:13 ⇨ Matt 15:8–9
[13] And the Lord said:
"Because **this people** draw near **with their** mouth
and honor **me with their lips**,
while **their** hearts are **far from me**,
and their fear of **me** is a commandment **of men**
learned by rote"; . . .

Mark 7:1–13 (§K33)

[1] Now when the **Pharisees** gathered together to him, with some of the **scribes**, who had come **from Jerusalem**, [2] they saw that some of his disciples ate with hands defiled, that is, unwashed. [3] (For the Pharisees, and all the Jews, do not eat unless they wash their hands, observing the tradition of the elders; [4] and when they come from the market place, they do not eat unless they purify themselves; and there are many other traditions which they observe, the washing of cups and pots and vessels of bronze.) [5] And the **Pharisees** and the **scribes** asked him, "**Why do your disciples** not live according to **the tradition of the elders**, but **eat** with **hands** defiled?" [6] And he said to **them**, "**Well did Isaiah prophesy of you hypocrites**, as it is written,

'This people honors me with their lips,
but their heart is far from me;
[7] in vain do they worship me,
teaching as doctrines the precepts of
men.'

[8] **You** leave **the commandment of God**, and hold fast the **tradition** of men.

[9] And he said to them, "You have a fine way of rejecting the commandment of **God**, in order to keep your tradition! [10] For Moses said, '**Honor your father and your mother**'; and, '**He who speaks evil of father or mother, let him surely die**'; [11] but you say, 'If a man **tells his father or his mother**, What you would have gained from me is Corban' (that is, **given to God**)— [12] then you no longer permit him to do anything for **his father** or mother, [13] thus making **void the word of God** through your tradition which you hand on. And many such things you do."

OTHER

POxy840 2

(2) And he took them (the disciples) with him into the place of purification itself and walked about in the Temple court. And a Pharisaic chief priest, Levi (?) by name, fell in with them and s[aid] to the Savior: Who gave thee leave to [trea]d this place of purification and to look upon [the]se holy utensils without having bathed thyself and even without thy disciples having [wa]shed their f[eet]? On the contrary, being defi[led], thou hast trodden the Temple court, this clean p[lace], although no [one who] has [not] first bathed himself or [chang]ed his clot[hes] may tread it and [venture] to vi[ew these] holy utensils! Forthwith [the Savior] s[tood] still with h[is] disciples and [answered]: How stands it (then) with thee, thou art forsooth (also) here in the Temple court. Art thou then clean? He said to him: I am clean. For I have bathed myself in the pool of David and have gone down by the one stair and come up by the other and have put on white and clean clothes, and (only) then have I come hither and have viewed these holy utensils. Then said the Savior to him: Woe unto you blind that see not! Thou hast bathed thyself in water that is poured out, in which dogs and swine lie night and day and thou hast washed thyself and hast chafed thine outer skin, which prostitutes also and flute-girls anoint, bathe, chafe and rouge, in order to arouse desire in men, but within they are full of scorpions and of [bad]ness [of every kind]. But I and [my disciples], of whom thou sayest that we have not im[mersed] ourselves, [have been im]mersed in the liv[ing . . .] water which comes down from [. . . B]ut woe unto them that . . .

GNaz 12 ⇨ Matt 15:5

(12) The Jewish Gospel: corban is what you should obtain from us. (Variant to Matthew 15:5 in the "Zion Gospel" Edition)

PEger2 3 ⇨ Matt 15:7–9

(3) . . . [ca]me to him to put him to the pro[of] and to tempt him, whilst [they said]: "Master Jesus, we know that thou art come [from God], for what thou doest bears a test[imony] (to thee which goes) beyond (that) of all the prophets. [Wherefore tell] us: is it admissible [to p]ay to the kings the (charges) appertaining to their rule? [Should we] pay [th]em or not?" But Jesus saw through their [in]tention, became [angry] and said to them: "Why call ye me with yo[ur mou]th Master and yet [do] not what I say? Well has Is[aiah] prophesied [concerning y]ou saying: This [people honours] me with the[ir li]ps but their heart is far from me; [their worship is] vain. [They teach] precepts [of men]." (Fragment 2, recto [lines 43–59])

JOHN	THOMAS	

MATT

Matt 15:10–20 (§M49.2)
[10] And he called the people to him and said to them, "Hear and understand: [11] not what goes into the mouth defiles a man, but what comes out of the mouth, this defiles a man." [12] Then the disciples came and said to him, "Do you know that the Pharisees were offended when they heard this saying?" [13] He answered, "Every plant which my heavenly Father has not planted will be rooted up. [14] Let them alone; they are blind guides. And if a blind man leads a blind man, both will fall into a pit." [15] But Peter said to him, "Explain the parable to us." [16] And he said, "Are you also still without understanding? [17] Do you not see that whatever goes into the mouth passes into the stomach, and so passes on?[a] [18] But what comes out of the mouth proceeds from the heart, and this defiles a man. [19] For out of the heart come evil thoughts, murder, adultery, fornication, theft, false witness, slander. [20] These are what defile a man; but to eat with unwashed hands does not defile a man."

[a] Or: *is evacuated*

Matt 12:34 ⇨ Matt 15:18
[34] *"You brood of vipers! how can you speak good, when you are evil? For out of the abundance of the heart the mouth speaks."*

MARK

Mark 7:14–23 (§K34)
[14] **And he called the people to him** again, **and said to them, "Hear me,** all of you, **and understand:** [15] there is nothing outside a man which by going **into** him can defile him; **but** the things which come **out of** a man are what defile him." [17] And when he had entered the house, and left the people, his **disciples** asked him about **the parable.** [18] And he said to them, "Then **are you also without understanding? Do you not see that whatever goes into** a man from outside cannot defile him, [19] since it enters, not his heart but his **stomach, and so passes on**?" (Thus he declared all foods clean.) [20] And he said, "**What comes out of** a man is what **defiles a man.** [21] **For** from within, **out of the heart** of man, **come evil thoughts, fornication, theft,** murder, **adultery,** [22] coveting, wickedness, deceit, licentiousness, envy, **slander,** pride, foolishness. [23] All **these** evil things come from within, and they **defile a man.**"

LUKE

Luke 6:39 ⇨ Matt 15:14
[39] He also told them a parable: "Can **a blind man** lead **a blind man? Will** they not both **fall into a pit?**"

JOHN

THOMAS

GThom 14 ⇨ Matt 15:11
(14) Jesus said to them, "If you fast, you will give rise to sin for yourselves; and if you pray, you will be condemned; and if you give alms, you will do harm to your spirits. When you go into any land and walk about in the districts, if they receive you, eat what they will set before you, and heal the sick among them. For **what goes into** your **mouth** will **not** defile you, but that which issues from your **mouth**—it is that which will defile you."

GThom 40 ⇨ Matt 15:13
(40) Jesus said, "A grapevine has been planted outside of the **Father,** but being unsound, it will be pulled **up** by its roots and destroyed."

GThom 34 ⇨ Matt 15:14
(34) Jesus said, "**If a blind man leads a blind man,** they **will** both **fall into a pit.**"

OTHER

MATT	MARK	LUKE

Matt 15:21–28 (§M50)

[21] And Jesus "went away from there and withdrew to the district of Tyre and Sidon. [22] And behold, a Canaanite woman from that region came out and cried, "Have mercy on me, O Lord, Son of David; my daughter is severely possessed by a demon." [23] But he did not answer her a word. And his disciples came and begged him, saying, "Send her away, for she is crying after us." [24] He answered, "I was sent only to the lost sheep of the house of Israel." [25] But she came and knelt before him, saying, "Lord, help me." [26] And he answered, "It is not fair to take the children's bread and throw it to the dogs." [27] She said, "Yes, Lord, yet even the dogs eat the crumbs that fall from their master's table." [28] Then Jesus answered her, "O woman, great is your faith! Be it done for you as you desire." And her daughter was healed instantly.

Matt 10:6 ⇨ Matt 15:24

[6] *"but go rather to the lost sheep of the house of Israel."*

Mark 7:24–30 (§K35)

[24] And from there he arose and **went away** to the region **of Tyre and Sidon**. And he entered a house, and would not have any one know it; yet he could not be hid. [25] But immediately a **woman**, whose little **daughter** was **possessed by** an unclean spirit, heard of him, and came and fell down at his feet. [26] Now the woman was a Greek, a Syrophoenician by birth. And **she** begged **him** to cast the demon out of her **daughter**. [27] **And he** said to her, "Let the children first be fed, for it **is not** right **to take the children's bread and throw it to the dogs.**" [28] But she answered him, **"Yes, Lord**; yet **even the dogs** under the table eat the children's crumbs." [29] And he said to **her**, "For this saying you may go your way; the demon has left your **daughter**. [30] And she went home, and found the child lying in bed, and the demon gone."

JOHN	THOMAS	OTHER

MATT	MARK	LUKE

Matt 15:29–31 (§M51) °

²⁹ And Jesus went on from there and passed along the Sea of Galilee. And he went up on the mountain, and sat down there. ³⁰ And great crowds came to him, bringing with them the lame, the maimed, the blind, the dumb, and many others, and they put them at his feet, and he healed them, ³¹ so that the throng wondered, when they saw the dumb speaking, the maimed whole, the lame walking, and the blind seeing; and they glorified the God of Israel.

°Appendix 3 ⇨ §M51

† Mark 7:31–37 (§K36)

³¹ Then he returned **from** the region of Tyre, and **went** through Sidon to **the Sea of Galilee**, through the region of the Decapolis. ³² And they brought to him a man who was deaf and had an impediment in his speech; and they besought him to lay his hand upon him. ³³ And taking him aside from the multitude privately, he put his fingers into his ears, and he spat and touched his tongue; ³⁴ and looking up to heaven, he sighed, and said to him, "Ephphatha," that is, "Be opened." ³⁵ And his ears were opened, his tongue was released, and he spoke plainly. ³⁶ And he charged them to tell no one; but the more he charged them, the more zealously they proclaimed it. ³⁷ **And they** were astonished beyond measure, saying, "He had done all things well; he even makes the deaf hear and **the dumb** speak."

JOHN	THOMAS	OTHER

MATT   MARK   LUKE

Matt 15:32–39 (§M52)

[32] Then Jesus called his disciples to him and said, "I have compassion on the crowd, because they have been with me now three days, and have nothing to eat; and I am unwilling to send them away hungry, lest they faint on the way." [33] And the disciples said to him, "Where are we to get bread enough in the desert to feed so great a crowd?" [34] And Jesus said to them, "How many loaves have you?" They said, "Seven, and a few small fish." [35] And commanding the crowd to sit down on the ground, [36] he took the seven loaves and the fish, and having given thanks he broke them and gave them to the disciples, and the disciples gave them to the crowds. [37] And they all ate and were satisfied; and they took up seven baskets full of the broken pieces left over. [38] Those who ate were four thousand men, besides women and children. [39] And sending away the crowds, he got into the boat and went to the region of Magadan.

● **Matt 14:15–21 (§M45)**

[15] When it was evening, the disciples came to him and said, "This is a lonely place, and the day is now over; send the crowds away to go into the villages and buy food for themselves." [16] Jesus said, "They need not go away; you give them something to eat." [17] They said to him, "We have only five loaves here and two fish." [18] And he said, "Bring them here to me." [19] Then he ordered the crowds to sit down on the grass; and taking the five loaves and the two fish he looked up to heaven, and blessed, and broke and gave the loaves to the disciples, and the disciples gave them to the crowds. [20] And they all ate and were satisfied. And they took up twelve baskets full of the broken pieces left over. [21] And those who ate were about five thousand men, besides women and children.

Matt 9:36 ⇨ Matt 15:32

[36] When he saw the crowds, he had compassion for them, because they were harassed and helpless, like sheep without a shepherd.

2 Kgs 4:42–44

[42] A man came from Baal-shalishah, bringing the man of God **bread** of the first fruits, twenty **loaves** of barley, and fresh ears of grain in his sack. And Elisha said, "Give to the men, that they may eat." [43] But his servant said, "How am I to set this before a hundred men?" So he repeated, "Give them to the men, that they may eat, for thus says the Lord, 'They shall eat and have some **left**.'" [44] So he set it before them. And **they ate**, and had some **left**, according to the word of the Lord.

Mark 8:1–10 (§K37)

[1] In those days, when again a great crowd had gathered, and they had nothing to eat, he called his disciples to him, and said to them, [2] "I have compassion on the crowd, because they have been with me now three days, and have nothing to eat; [3] and if I send them away hungry to their homes, they will faint on the way; and some of them have come a long way." [4] And his disciples answered him, "How can one feed these men with bread here in the desert?" [5] And he asked them, "How many loaves have you?" They said, "Seven." [6] And he commanded the crowd to sit down on the ground; and he took the seven loaves, and having given thanks he broke them and gave them to his disciples to set before the people; and they set them before the crowd. [7] And they had a few small fish; and having blessed them, he commanded that these also should be set before them. [8] And they ate, and were satisfied; and they took up the broken pieces left over, seven baskets full. [9] And there were about four thousand people. [10] And he sent them away and immediately he got into the boat with his disciples, and went to the district of Dalmanutha.

Mark 6:35–44 (§K29)

[35] And when it grew late, his disciples came to him and said, "This is a lonely place, and the hour is now late; [36] send them away, to go into the country and villages round about and buy themselves something to eat." [37] But he answered them, "You give them something to eat." And they said to him, "Shall we go and buy two hundred denarii worth of bread, and give it to them to eat?" [38] And he said to them, "How many loaves have you? Go and see." And when they had found out, they said, "Five, and two fish." [39] Then he commanded them all to sit down by companies upon the green grass. [40] So they sat down in groups, by hundreds and by fifties. [41] And taking the five loaves and the two fish he looked up to heaven, and blessed, and broke the loaves, and gave them to the disciples to set before the people; and he divided the two fish among them all. [42] And they all ate and were satisfied. [43] And they took up twelve baskets full of broken pieces and of the fish. [44] And those who ate the loaves were five thousand men.

Mark 14:22 ⇨ Matt 15:36

[22] And as they were eating, he took bread, and blessed, and broke it, and gave it to them, and said, "Take; this is my body."

Luke 9:12–17 (§L39)

[12] Now the day began to wear away; and the twelve came and said to him, "Send the crowd away, to go into the villages and country round about, to lodge and get provisions; for we are here in a lonely place." [13] But he said to them, "You give them something to eat." They said, "We have no more than five loaves and two fish—unless we are to go and buy food for all these people." [14] For there were about five thousand men. And he said to his disciples, "Make them sit down in companies, about fifty each." [15] And they did so, and made them all sit down. [16] And taking the five loaves and the two fish he looked up to heaven, and blessed and broke them, and gave them to the disciples to set before the crowd. [17] And all ate and were satisfied. And they took up what was left over, twelve baskets of broken pieces.

Luke 22:19 ⇨ Matt 15:36

[19] And he took bread, and when he had given thanks he broke it and gave it to them, saying, "This is my body which is given for you. Do this in remembrance of me."

Luke 24:30 ⇨ Matt 15:36

[30] When he was at table with them, he took the bread and blessed, and broke it, and gave it to them.

JOHN	THOMAS	OTHER

John 6:1–15 (§J10)

[1] After this Jesus went to the other side of the Sea of Galilee, which is the Sea of Tiberias. [2] And a multitude followed him, because they saw the signs which he did on those who were diseased. [3] Jesus went up on the mountain, and there sat down with his disciples. [4] Now the Passover, the feast of the Jews, was at hand. [5] Lifting up his eyes, then, and seeing that a multitude was coming to him, Jesus said to Philip, "How **are we to** buy **bread**, so that these people may eat?" [6] This he said to test him, for he himself knew what he would do. [7] Philip answered him, "Two hundred denarii would not buy enough bread for each of them to get a little." [8] One of his disciples, Andrew, Simon Peter's brother, said to him, [9] "There is a lad here who has five barley loaves and two **fish**; but what are they among so many?" [10] Jesus said, "Make the people **sit down**." Now there was much grass in the place; so the men sat down, in number about five **thousand**. [11] Jesus then **took the loaves, and** when he had **given thanks**, he distributed **them** to those who were seated; so also **the fish**, as much as they wanted. [12] **And** when **they** had eaten their fill, he told his disciples, "Gather up **the** fragments **left over**, that nothing may be lost." [13] So **they** gathered them **up** and filled twelve **baskets** with fragments from the five barley **loaves, left by** those who had eaten. [14] When the people saw the **sign** which he had done, they said, "This is indeed the prophet who is to come into the world!"

[15] Perceiving then that they were about to come and take him by force to make him king, Jesus withdrew again to the mountain by himself.

Acts 27:35 ⇨ Matt 15:36

[35] *And when he had said this, he took bread, and giving **thanks** to God in the presence of all he **broke it and** began to eat.*

MATT	MARK	LUKE

Matt 16:1–4 (§M53)

¹ And the Pharisees and Sadducees came, and to test him they asked him to show them a sign from heaven. ² He answered them,ᵃ "When it is evening, you say, 'It will be fair weather; for the sky is red.' ³ And in the morning, 'It will be stormy today, for the sky is red and threatening.' You know how to interpret the appearance of the sky, but you cannot interpret the signs of the times. ⁴ An evil and adulterous generation seeks for a sign, but no sign shall be given to it except the sign of Jonah." So he left them and departed.

ᵃ Some witnesses omit the words from here to the end of v. 3: ℵ B X *f*¹³ 157 1216 syrᶜ,ˢ copˢᵃ,ᵇᵒ arm; text: C D K L (N) W Δ Θ Π *f*¹ 33 *pm*

Matt 12:38–42 (§M37)

³⁸ Then some of the scribes and **Pharisees** said to him, "Teacher, we wish to see **a sign from you.**" ³⁹ But **he answered them, "An evil and adulterous generation seeks for a sign; but no sign shall be given to it except the sign** of the prophet **Jonah.** ⁴⁰ For as Jonah was three days and three nights in the belly of the whale, so will the Son of man be three days and three nights in the heart of the earth. ⁴¹ The men of Nineveh will arise at the judgment with this generation and condemn it; for they repented at the preaching of **Jonah,** and behold, something greater than **Jonah** is here. ⁴² The queen of the South will arise at the judgment with this generation and condemn it; for she came from the ends of the earth to hear the wisdom of Solomon, and behold, something greater than Solomon is here."

Mark 8:11–13 (§K38)

¹¹ **The Pharisees came and** began **to** argue with **him,** seeking from him **a sign from heaven, to test him.** ¹² And he sighed deeply in his spirit, and said, "Why does this **generation** seek **a sign?** Truly, I say to you, **no sign shall be given** to this generation." ¹³ And **he left them, and** getting into the boat again he **departed** to the other side.

Luke 11:29–32 (§L51.4)

²⁹ When the crowds were increasing, **he** began to say, "This generation is **an evil generation;** it **seeks a sign, but no sign shall be given to it except the sign of Jonah.** ³⁰ For as **Jonah** became a sign to the men of Nineveh, so will the Son of man be to this generation. ³¹ The queen of the South will arise at the judgment with the men of this generation and condemn them; for she came from the ends of the earth to hear the wisdom of Solomon, and behold, something greater than Solomon is here. ³² The men of Nineveh will arise at the judgment with this generation and condemn it; for they repented at the preaching of **Jonah,** and behold, something greater than **Jonah** is here."

Luke 12:54–56 (§L56.3) ⇨ Matt 16:2–3

⁵⁴ **He** also said to the multitudes, "**When** you see a cloud rising in the west, **you say** at once, 'A shower is coming'; and so it happens. ⁵⁵ And when you see the south wind blowing, **you say,** 'There will be scorching heat'; and it happens. ⁵⁶ You hypocrites! **You know how to interpret the appearance of the** earth **and sky; but** why do **you** not know how to **interpret the** present time?"

Luke 11:16 ⇨ Matt 16:1

¹⁶ *while others, to test him, sought from him a sign from heaven.*

JOHN	THOMAS	OTHER

John 6:30 ⇨ Matt 16:1

³⁰ *So they said to him, "Then what sign do you do, that we may see, and believe you? What work do you perform?"*

GThom 91 ⇨ Matt 16:1–3

(91) They said to Him, "Tell us who You are so that we may believe in You."

He said to **them,** "**You** read the face **of the sky** and of the earth, **but you** have not recognized the one who (or: that which) is before you, and you do not know how to read this moment."

GNaz 13 ⇨ Matt 16:2–3

(13) What is marked with an asterisk (i.e., Matthew 16:2–3) is not found in other manuscripts, also it is not found in the Jewish Gospel. (Variant to Matthew 16:2–3 in the "Zion Gospel" Edition)

MATT

MARK

LUKE

Matt 16:5–12 (§M54)

⁵ When the disciples reached the other side, they had forgotten to bring any bread. ⁶ Jesus said to them, "Take heed and beware of the leaven of the Pharisees and Sadducees." ⁷ And they discussed it among themselves, saying, "We brought no bread." ⁸ But Jesus, aware of this, said, "O men of little faith, why do you discuss among yourselves the fact that you have no bread? ⁹ Do you not yet perceive? Do you not remember the five loaves of the five thousand, and how many baskets you gathered? ¹⁰ Or the seven loaves of the four thousand, and how many baskets you gathered? ¹¹ How is it that you fail to perceive that I did not speak about bread? Beware of the leaven of the Pharisees and Sadducees." ¹² Then they understood that he did not tell them to beware of the leaven of bread, but of the teaching of the Pharisees and Sadducees.

Matt 14:15–21 (§M45) ⇨ Matt 16:9

¹⁵ *When it was evening, the disciples came to him and said, "This is a lonely place, and the day is now over; send the crowds away to go into the villages and buy food for themselves." ¹⁶ Jesus said, "They need not go away; you give them something to eat." ¹⁷ They said to him, "We have only five loaves here and two fish." ¹⁸ And he said, "Bring them here to me." ¹⁹ Then he ordered the crowds to sit down on the grass; and taking the five loaves and the two fish he looked up to heaven, and blessed, and broke and gave the loaves to the disciples, and the disciples gave them to the crowds. ²⁰ And they all ate and were satisfied. And they took up twelve baskets full of the broken pieces left over. ²¹ And those who ate were about five thousand men, besides women and children.*

Matt 15:32–39 (§M52) ⇨ Matt 16:10

³² *Then Jesus called his disciples to him and said, "I have compassion on the crowd, because they have been with me now three days, and have nothing to eat; and I am unwilling to send them away hungry, lest they faint on the way." ³³ And the disciples said to him, "Where are we to get bread enough in the desert to feed so great a crowd?" ³⁴ And Jesus said to them, "How many loaves have you?" They said, "Seven, and a few small fish." ³⁵ And commanding the crowd to sit down on the ground, ³⁶ he took the seven loaves and the fish, and having given thanks he broke them and gave them to the disciples, and the disciples gave them to the crowds. ³⁷ And they all ate and were satisfied; and they took up seven baskets full of the broken pieces left over. ³⁸ Those who ate were four thousand men, besides women and children. ³⁹ And sending away the crowds, he got into the boat and went to the region of Magadan.*

Mark 8:14–21 (§K39)

¹⁴ Now **they had forgotten to bring bread;** and they had only one loaf with them in the boat. ¹⁵ And he cautioned them, saying, **"Take heed, beware of the leaven of the Pharisees and** the leaven of Herod." ¹⁶ And **they discussed it** with one another, **saying,** **"We** have **no bread."** ¹⁷ And being **aware of** it, **Jesus said** to them, **"Why do you discuss the fact that you have no bread? Do you not yet perceive** or understand? Are your hearts hardened? ¹⁸ Having eyes do you not see, and having ears do you not hear? And **do you not remember?** ¹⁹ When I broke **the five loaves** for **the five thousand, how many baskets** full of broken pieces did **you** take up?" They said to him, "Twelve." ²⁰ "And the **seven** for **the four thousand, how many baskets** full of broken pieces did **you** take up?" And they said to him, "Seven." ²¹ And he said to them, **"Do you not yet** understand?"

Luke 12:1 ⇨ Matt 16:6

¹ In the meantime, when so many thousands of the multitude had gathered together that they trod upon one another, he began to say to his disciples first, **"Beware of the leaven of the Pharisees,** which is hypocrisy."

JOHN

THOMAS

OTHER

MATT

Matt 16:13–20 (§M55)
[13] Now when Jesus came into the district of Caesarea Philippi, he asked his disciples, "Who do men say that the Son of man is?" [14] And they said, "Some say John the Baptist, others say Elijah, and others Jeremiah or one of the prophets." [15] He said to them, "But who do you say that I am?" [16] Simon Peter replied, "You are the Christ, the Son of the living God." [17] And Jesus answered him, "Blessed are you, Simon Bar-Jona! For flesh and blood has not revealed this to you, but my Father who is in heaven. [18] And I tell you, you are Peter,[a] and on this rock[b] I will build my church, and the powers of death[c] shall not prevail against it. [19] I will give you the keys of the kingdom of heaven, and whatever you bind on earth shall be bound in heaven, and whatever you loose on earth shall be loosed in heaven." [20] Then he strictly charged the disciples to tell no one that he was the Christ.

[a] Greek: *Petros*

[b] Greek: *petra*

[c] Greek: *gates of Hades*

Matt 18:18 ⇨ Matt 16:19
[18] "Truly, I say to you, **whatever you bind on earth shall be bound in heaven, and whatever you loose on earth shall be loosed in heaven."**

MARK

Mark 8:27–30 (§K41)
[27] And **Jesus** went on with **his disciples,** to the villages **of Caesarea Philippi;** and on the way **he asked his disciples, "Who do men say that I am?"** [28] **And they** told him, **"John the Baptist; and others say, Elijah; and others** one of the prophets." [29] And **he** asked **them, "But who do you say that I am?"** Peter answered him, **"You are the Christ."** [30] And **he charged** them **to tell no one** about him.

LUKE

Luke 9:18–22 (§L40.1)
[18] Now it happened that as he was praying alone the **disciples** were with him; and **he** asked them, **"Who do the people say that I am?"** [19] **And they** answered, **"John the Baptist;** but **others** say, Elijah; and **others,** that **one** of the old **prophets** has risen." [20] And **he** said to them, **"But who do you say that I am?"** And Peter answered, **"The Christ of God."** [21] But **he charged** and commanded them **to tell** this **to no one,** [22] saying, "The Son of man must suffer many things, and be rejected by the elders and chief priests and scribes, and be killed, and on the third day be raised."

JOHN

John 1:49 ⇨ Matt 16:16
[49] *Nathanael answered him, "Rabbi, **you are the Son of God! You are the King of Israel!"***

John 6:68–69 ⇨ Matt 16:16
[68] ***Simon Peter** answered him, "Lord, to whom shall we go? You have the words of eternal life;* [69] *and we have believed, and have come to know, that **you are the Holy One of God."***

John 20:22–23 ⇨ Matt 16:19
[22] *And when he had said this, he breathed on them, and said to them, "Receive the Holy Spirit.* [23] *If **you** forgive the sins of any, they are forgiven; if **you** retain the sins of any, they are retained."*

THOMAS

GThom 13
*(13) Jesus said to **His disciples,** "Compare me to someone and tell Me whom I am like."*

*   **Simon Peter** said to Him, "You are like a righteous angel."*

*   Matthew said to Him, "You are like a wise philosopher."*

*   Thomas said to Him, "Master, my mouth is wholly incapable of saying whom You are like."*

*   Jesus said, "I am not your master. Because you have drunk, you have become intoxicated from the bubbling spring which I have measured out."*

*   And He took him and withdrew and told him three things. When Thomas returned to his companions, they asked him, "What did Jesus say to you?"*

*   Thomas said to them, "If I tell you one of the things which he told me, you will pick up stones and throw them at me; a fire will come out of the stones and burn you up."*

OTHER

GNaz 14 ⇨ Matt 16:17
(14) The Jewish Gospel: son of John.
(Variant to Matthew 16:17 in the "Zion Gospel" Edition)

MATT	MARK	LUKE

MATT

Matt 16:21–23 (§M56)

²¹ From that time Jesus began to show his disciples that he must go to Jerusalem and suffer many things from the elders and chief priests and scribes, and be killed, and on the third day be raised. ²² And Peter took him and began to rebuke him, saying, "God forbid, Lord! This shall never happen to you." ²³ But he turned and said to Peter, "Get behind me, Satan! You are a hindrance[a] to me; for you are not on the side of God, but of men."

ᵃ Greek: *stumbling block*

Matt 17:22–23 (§M60)

²² As they were gathering in Galilee, Jesus said to them, "The Son of man is to be delivered into the hands of men, ²³ and they will kill him, and he will be raised on the third day." And they were greatly distressed.

Matt 20:17–19 (§M68)

¹⁷ And as Jesus was going up to Jerusalem, he took the twelve disciples aside, and on the way he said to them, ¹⁸ "Behold, we are going up to Jerusalem; and the Son of man will be delivered to the chief priests and scribes, and they will condemn him to death, ¹⁹ and deliver him to the Gentiles to be mocked and scourged and crucified, and he will be raised on the third day."

MARK

Mark 8:31–33 (§K42)

³¹ And he began to teach them that the Son of man must suffer many things, and be rejected by the elders and the chief priests and the scribes, and be killed, and after three days rise again. ³² And he said this plainly. And Peter took him, and began to rebuke him. ³³ But turning and seeing his disciples, he rebuked Peter, and said, "Get behind me, Satan! For you are not on the side of God, but of men."

Mark 9:30–32 (§K46)

³⁰ They went on from there and passed through Galilee. And he would not have any one know it; ³¹ for he was teaching his disciples, saying to them, "The Son of man will be delivered into the hands of men, and they will kill him; and when he is killed, after three days he will rise." ³² But they did not understand the saying, and they were afraid to ask him.

Mark 10:32–34 (§K54)

³² And they were on the road, going up to Jerusalem, and Jesus was walking ahead of them; and they were amazed, and those who followed were afraid. And taking the twelve again, he began to tell them what was to happen to him, ³³ saying, "Behold, we are going up to Jerusalem; and the Son of man will be delivered to the chief priests and the scribes, and they will condemn him to death, and deliver him to the Gentiles; ³⁴ and they will mock him, and scourge him, and kill him; and after three days he will rise."

LUKE

Luke 9:18–22 (§L40.1)

¹⁸ Now it happened that as he was praying alone the disciples were with him; and he asked them, "Who do the people say that I am?" ¹⁹ And they answered, "John the Baptist; but others say, Elijah; and others, that one of the old prophets has risen." ²⁰ And he said to them, "But who do you say that I am?" And Peter answered, "The Christ of God." ²¹ But he charged and commanded them to tell this to no one, ²² saying, "The Son of man must suffer many things, and be rejected by the elders and chief priests and scribes, and be killed, and on the third day be raised."

Luke 9:43b–45 (§L43.1)

But while they were all marveling at everything he did, he said to his disciples, ⁴⁴ "Let these words sink into your ears; for the Son of man is to be delivered into the hands of men." ⁴⁵ But they did not understand this saying, and it was concealed from them, that they should not perceive it; and they were afraid to ask him about this saying.

Luke 18:31–34 (§L78)

And taking the twelve, he said to them, "Behold, we are going up to Jerusalem, and everything that is written of the Son of man by the prophets will be accomplished. ³² For he will be delivered to the Gentiles, and will be mocked and shamefully treated and spit upon; ³³ they will scourge him and kill him, and on the third day he will rise." ³⁴ But they understood none of these things; this saying was hid from them, and they did not grasp what was said.

JOHN	THOMAS	OTHER

OTHER

ApocJa 5:31–6:11

"Scorn death, therefore, and take concern for life. Remember my cross and my death and you will ³⁵ live."

And I answered and said to him: "Lord, do not mention to us the cross and the death, for they are far from you."

The Lord answered and said: "Truly I say to you (pl.), none will be saved unless they believe in my cross. ⁵ [But] those who have believed in my cross, theirs is the Kingdom of God. Therefore, become seekers for death, just as the dead who seek for life, ¹⁰ for that for which they seek is revealed to them."

MATT

Matt 16:24–28 (§M57)

[24] Then Jesus told his disciples, "If any man would come after me, let him deny himself and take up his cross and follow me. [25] For whoever would save his life will lose it, and whoever loses his life for my sake will find it. [26] For what will it profit a man, if he gains the whole world and forfeits his life? Or what shall a man give in return for his life? [27] For the Son of man is to come with his angels in the glory of his Father, and then he will repay every man for what he has done. [28] Truly, I say to you, there are some standing here who will not taste death before they see the Son of man coming in his kingdom."

• **Matt 10:38–39**

[38] "and he who does not take his cross and follow me is not worthy of me. [39] He who finds his life will lose it, and he who loses his life for my sake will find it."

MARK

Mark 8:34–9:1 (§K43)

[34] And he called to him the multitude with his disciples, and said to them, "If any man would come after me, let him deny himself and take up his cross and follow me. [35] For whoever would save his life will lose it; and whoever loses his life for my sake and the gospel's will save it. [36] For what does it profit a man, to gain the whole world and forfeit his life? [37] For what can a man give in return for his life? [38] For whoever is ashamed of me and of my words in this adulterous and sinful generation, of him will the Son of man also be ashamed, when he comes in the glory of his Father with the holy angels." 9 [1] And he said to them, "Truly, I say to you, there are some standing here who will not taste death before they see that the kingdom of God has come with power."

LUKE

Luke 9:23–27 (§L40.2)

[23] And he said to all, "If any man would come after me, let him deny himself and take up his cross daily and follow me. [24] For whoever would save his life will lose it; and whoever loses his life for my sake, he will save it. [25] For what does it profit a man if he gains the whole world and loses or forfeits himself? [26] For whoever is ashamed of me and of my words, of him will the Son of man be ashamed when he comes in his glory and the glory of the Father and of the holy angels. [27] But I tell you truly, there are some standing here who will not taste death before they see the kingdom of God."

Luke 14:27 ⇨ Matt 16:24

[27] "Whoever does not bear his own cross and come after me, cannot be my disciple."

Luke 17:33 ⇨ Matt 16:25

[33] "Whoever seeks to gain his life will lose it, but whoever loses his life will preserve it."

JOHN

John 12:25 ⇨ Matt 16:25

[25] "He who loves his life loses it, and he who hates his life in this world will keep it for eternal life."

THOMAS

GThom 55 ⇨ Matt 16:24

(55) **Jesus** said, "Whoever does not hate his father and his mother cannot become a disciple to Me. And whoever does not hate his brothers and sisters **and take up his cross** in My way will not be worthy of Me."

GThom 101 ⇨ Matt 16:24

(101) <**Jesus** said,> "Whoever does not hate his father and his mother as I do cannot become a disciple to Me. And whoever does [not] love his father and his mother as I do cannot become a [disciple] to Me. For My mother [gave me falsehood], but [My] true [Mother] gave me life."

OTHER

MATT	MARK	LUKE

JESUS IS TRANSFIGURED

Matt 17:1–8 (§M58.1)

[1] And after six days Jesus took with him Peter and James and John his brother, and led them up a high mountain apart. [2] And he was transfigured before them, and his face shone like the sun, and his garments became white as light. [3] And behold, there appeared to them Moses and Elijah, talking with him. [4] And Peter said to Jesus, "Lord, it is well that we are here; if you wish, I will make three booths here, one for you and one for Moses and one for Elijah." [5] He was still speaking, when lo, a bright cloud overshadowed them, and a voice from the cloud said, "This is my beloved Son, with whom I am well pleased; listen to him." [6] When the disciples heard this, they fell on their faces, and were filled with awe. [7] But Jesus came and touched them, saying, "Rise, and have no fear." [8] And when they lifted up their eyes, they saw no one but Jesus only.

ELIJAH MUST COME FIRST

Matt 17:9–13 (§M58.2)

[9] And as they were coming down the mountain, Jesus commanded them, "Tell no one the vision, until the Son of man is raised from the dead." [10] And the disciples asked him, "Then why do the scribes say that first Elijah must come?" [11] He replied, "Elijah does come, and he is to restore all things; [12] but I tell you that Elijah has already come, and they did not know him, but did to him whatever they pleased. So also the Son of man will suffer at their hands." [13] Then the disciples understood that he was speaking to them of John the Baptist.

Matt 3:16–17 ⇨ Matt 17:5

[16] And when Jesus was baptized, he went up immediately from the water, and behold, the heavens were opened and he saw the Spirit of God descending like a dove, and alighting on him; [17] and lo, a voice from heaven, saying, "This is my beloved Son, with whom I am well pleased."

Ps 2:7 ⇨ Matt 17:5

[7] I will tell of the decree of the Lord: He said to me, "You are my son,
    today I have begotten you."

Isa 42:1 ⇨ Matt 17:5

[1] Behold my servant, whom I uphold,
    my chosen, in whom my soul delights;
I have put my Spirit upon him,
    he will bring forth justice to the nations.

Mal 4:5–6 ⇨ Matt 17:10–11

[5] "Behold, I will send you Elijah the prophet before the great and terrible day of the Lord comes. [6] And he will turn the hearts of fathers to their children and the hearts of children to their fathers, lest I come and smite the land with a curse."

JOHN

Mark 9:2–8 (§K44.1) ⇨ §M58.1

[2] And after six days Jesus took with him Peter and James and John, and led them up a high mountain apart by themselves; and he was transfigured before them, [3] and his garments became glistening, intensely white, as no fuller on earth could bleach them. [4] And there appeared to them Elijah with Moses; and they were talking to Jesus. [5] And Peter said to Jesus, "Master, it is well that we are here; let us make three booths, one for you and one for Moses and one for Elijah." [6] For he did not know what to say, for they were exceedingly afraid. [7] And a cloud overshadowed them, and a voice came out of the cloud, "This is my beloved Son; listen to him." [8] And suddenly looking around they no longer saw any one with them but Jesus only.

Mark 9:9–13 (§K44.2) ⇨ §M58.2

[9] And as they were coming down the mountain, he charged them to tell no one what they had seen, until the Son of man should have risen from the dead. [10] So they kept the matter to themselves, questioning what the rising from the dead meant. [11] And they asked him, "Why do the scribes say that first Elijah must come?" [12] And he said to them, "Elijah does come first to restore all things; and how is it written of the Son of man, that he should suffer many things and be treated with contempt? [13] But I tell you that Elijah has come, and they did to him whatever they pleased, as it is written of him."

Mark 1:10–11 ⇨ Matt 17:5

[10] And when he came up out of the water, immediately he saw the heavens opened and the Spirit descending upon him like a dove; [11] and a voice came from heaven, "Thou art my beloved Son; with thee I am well pleased."

---

1 Kgs 19:1–3, 9–10 ⇨ Matt 17:12

[1] Ahab told Jezebel all that Elijah had done, and how he had slain all the prophets with the sword. [2] Then Jezebel sent a messenger to Elijah, saying, "So may the gods do to me, and more also, if I do not make your life as the life of one of them by this time tomorrow." [3] Then he was afraid, and he arose and went for his life, and came to Beersheba, which belongs to Judah, and left his servant there.... [9] And there he came to a cave, and lodged there; and behold, the word of the Lord came to him, and he said to him, "What are you doing here, Elijah?" [10] He said, "I have been very jealous for the Lord, the God of hosts; for the people of Israel have forsaken thy covenant, thrown down thy altars, and slain thy prophets with the sword; and I, even I only, am left; and they seek my life, to take it away."

THOMAS

GThom 51 ⇨ Matt 17:12

(51) His disciples said to Him, "When will the repose of the dead come about, and when will the new world come?"

He said to them, "What you look forward to has already come, but you do not recognize it."

Luke 9:28–36 (§L41) ⇨ §M58.1

[28] Now about eight days after these sayings he took with him Peter and John and James, and went up on the mountain to pray. [29] And as he was praying, the appearance of his countenance was altered, and his raiment became dazzling white. [30] And behold, two men talked with him, Moses and Elijah, [31] who appeared in glory and spoke of his departure, which he was to accomplish at Jerusalem. [32] Now Peter and those who were with him were heavy with sleep, and when they wakened they saw his glory and the two men who stood with him. [33] And as the men were parting from him, Peter said to Jesus, "Master, it is well that we are here; let us make three booths, one for you and one for Moses and one for Elijah"—not knowing what he said. [34] As he said this, a cloud came and overshadowed them; and they were afraid as they entered the cloud. [35] And a voice came out of the cloud, saying, "This is my Son, my Chosen; listen to him!" [36] And when the voice had spoken, Jesus was found alone. And they kept silence and told no one in those days anything of what they had seen.

Luke 3:22 ⇨ Matt 17:5

[22] and the Holy Spirit descended upon him in bodily form, as a dove, and a voice came from heaven, "Thou art my beloved Son; with thee I am well pleased."

OTHER

MATT

HEALING OF A BOY

Matt 17:14–18 (§M59.1)

[14] And when they came to the crowd, a man came up to him and kneeling before him said, [15] "Lord, have mercy on my son, for he is an epileptic and he suffers terribly; for often he falls into the fire, and often into the water. [16] And I brought him to your disciples, and they could not heal him." [17] And Jesus answered, "O faithless and perverse generation, how long am I to be with you? How long am I to bear with you? Bring him here to me." [18] And Jesus rebuked him, and the demon came out of him, and the boy was cured instantly.

EXPLANATION OF DISCIPLES' FAILURE

Matt 17:19–20 (§M59.2)

[19] Then the disciples came to Jesus privately and said, "Why could we not cast it out?" [20] He said to them, "Because of your little faith. For truly I say to you, if you have faith as a grain of mustard seed, you will say to this mountain, 'Move from here to there,' and it will move; and nothing will be impossible to you."[a]

[a] Some witnesses add v. 21, *"But this kind never comes out except by prayer and* fasting": (cf. Mark 9:29) (ℵ[b]) C D K L W X Δ Π *f*[1] *f*[13] 28 *pm*; text: ℵ* B Θ 33 *al*

Matt 21:21 ⇨ Matt 17:20

[21] And Jesus answered **them**, "**Truly, I say to you**, if **you have faith** and never doubt, you will not only do what has been done to the fig tree, but even if **you say to this mountain,** 'Be taken up and cast into the sea,' **it will** be done."

Matt 18:19 ⇨ Matt 17:20

[19] *"Again **I say to you**, if two of you agree on earth about anything they ask, **it will** be done for them by my Father in heaven."*

MARK

Mark 9:14–27 (§K45.1) ⇨ §M59.1

[14] **And when they came to the** disciples, they saw a great **crowd** about them, and scribes arguing with them. [15] And immediately all the crowd, when they saw him, were greatly amazed, and ran up to him and greeted him. [16] And he asked them, "What are you discussing with them?" [17] And one of the crowd answered **him**, "Teacher, I brought **my son** to you, for **he** has a dumb spirit; [18] and wherever it seizes him, it dashes him down; and he foams and grinds his teeth and becomes rigid; **and I** asked **your disciples** to cast it out, **and they were not** able." [19] And he answered them, "**O faithless generation, how long am I to be with you? How long am I to bear with you? Bring him to me.**" [20] And they brought the boy to him; and when the spirit saw him, immediately it convulsed the boy, and he fell on the ground and rolled about, foaming at the mouth. [21] And Jesus asked his father, "How long has he had this?" And he said, "From childhood. [22] And it has often cast him into the fire and into the water, to destroy him; but if you can do anything, have pity on us and help us." [23] And Jesus said to him, "If you can! All things are possible to him who believes." [24] Immediately the father of the child cried out and said, "I believe; help my unbelief!" [25] And when Jesus saw that a crowd came running together, **he rebuked** the unclean spirit, saying to it, "You dumb and deaf spirit, I command you, come out of him, and never enter him again." [26] And after crying out and convulsing him terribly, **it came out, and the boy was** like a corpse; so that most of them said, "He is dead." [27] But Jesus took him by the hand and lifted him up, and he arose.

Mark 9:28–29 (§K45.2) ⇨ §M59.2

[28] And when he had entered the house, his **disciples** asked him **privately, "Why could we not cast it out?"** [29] And **he said to them,** "This kind cannot be driven out by anything but prayer."

Mark 11:22–23 ⇨ Matt 17:20

[22] And Jesus answered **them**, "Have **faith** in God. [23] **Truly, I say to you**, whoever says **to this mountain,** 'Be taken up and cast into the sea,' and does not doubt in his heart, but believes that what he says will come to pass, **it will** be done for him."

LUKE

Luke 9:37–43a (§L42) ⇨ M59.1

[37] On the next day, **when they** had come down from the mountain, a great **crowd** met **him**. [38] And behold, a man from the crowd cried, "Teacher, I beg you to look upon **my son, for he is** my only child; [39] and behold, a spirit seizes him, and he suddenly cries out; it convulses him till he foams, and shatters him, and will hardly leave him. [40] **And I** begged **your disciples** to cast it out, but **they could not."** [41] Jesus answered, "O faithless and perverse generation, how long am I to be with you and bear with you? **Bring** your son here." [42] While he was coming, the demon tore him and convulsed him. But **Jesus rebuked** the unclean spirit, and healed **the boy,** and gave him back to his father. [43] And all were astonished at the majesty of God.

Luke 17:6 ⇨ Matt 17:20

[6] And the Lord **said,** "If **you** had **faith as a grain of mustard seed, you** could **say to this** sycamine tree, 'Be rooted up, and be planted in the sea,' **and it** would **obey you.**"

JOHN

THOMAS

GThom 48 ⇨ Matt 17:20

(48) Jesus **said,** "If two make peace with each other in this one house, they will say **to the mountain,** '**Move** away,' **and it will move** away."

GThom 106 ⇨ Matt 17:20

(106) Jesus **said,** "When you make the two one, you will become the sons of man, and when you say, '**Mountain, move** away,' **it will move** away."

OTHER

MATT

Matt 17:22–23 (§M60)

²² As they were gathering[a] in Galilee, Jesus said to them, "The Son of man is to be delivered into the hands of men, ²³ and they will kill him, and he will be raised on the third day." And they were greatly distressed.

Matt 17:24–27 (§M61)

²⁴ When they came to Capernaum, the collectors of the half-shekel tax went up to Peter and said, "Does not your teacher pay the tax?" ²⁵ He said "Yes." And when he came home, Jesus spoke to him first, saying, "What do you think, Simon? From whom do kings of the earth take toll or tribute? From their sons or from others?" ²⁶ And when he said, "From others," Jesus said to him, "Then the sons are free. ²⁷ However, not to give offense to them, go to the sea and cast a hook, and take the first fish that comes up, and when you open its mouth you will find a shekel; take that and give it to them for me and for yourself."

[a] Text: ℵ B *f*¹ 892 it (in part) vg *al; abode:* C (D) K L W X Δ Θ Π *f*¹³ 28 33 *pm*

Matt 16:21–23 (§M56) ⇨ §M60

²¹ From that time Jesus began to show his disciples that he must go to Jerusalem and suffer many things from the elders and chief priests and scribes, **and be killed, and on the third day be raised.** ²² And Peter took him and began to rebuke him, saying, "God forbid, Lord! This shall never happen to you." ²³ But he turned and said to Peter, "Get behind me, Satan! You are a hindrance to me; for you are not on the side of God, but of men."

Matt 20:17–19 (§M68) ⇨ §M60

¹⁷ And as Jesus was going up to Jerusalem, he took the twelve disciples aside, and on the way he **said to them**, ¹⁸ "Behold, we are going up to Jerusalem; and **the Son of man** will **be delivered** to the chief priests and scribes, **and they will** condemn him to death, ¹⁹ deliver him to the Gentiles to be mocked and scourged and crucified, **and he will be raised on the third day.**"

Exod 30:13 ⇨ Matt 17:24
¹³ "Each who is numbered in the census shall give this: half a shekel according to the shekel of the sanctuary (the shekel is twenty gerahs), half a shekel as an offering to the Lord."

MARK

Mark 9:30–32 (§K46) ⇨ §M60

³⁰ **They** went on from there and passed through **Galilee**. And he would not have any one know it; ³¹ for he was teaching his disciples, saying **to them**, "**The Son of man** will **be delivered into the hands of men, and they will kill him**; **and** when **he** is killed, after three days he **will rise**." ³² But they did not understand the saying, and they were afraid to ask him.

Mark 8:31–33 (§K42) ⇨ §M60

³¹ And he began **to teach them** that **the Son of man** must suffer many things, and **be** rejected by the elders and the chief priests and the scribes, **and** be killed, **and** after three days rise again. ³² And he said this plainly. And Peter took him, and began to rebuke him. ³³ But turning and seeing his disciples, he rebuked Peter, and said, "Get behind me, Satan! For you are not on the side of God, but of men."

Mark 10:32–34 (§K54) ⇨ §M60

³² And **they were** on the road, going up to Jerusalem, and **Jesus** was walking ahead of them; and they were amazed, and those who followed were afraid. And taking the twelve again, he began to tell them what was to happen to him, ³³ saying, "Behold, we are going up to Jerusalem; and **the Son of man** will **be delivered** to **the** chief priests and the scribes, **and they will** condemn him to death, and deliver him to the Gentiles; ³⁴ and they will mock him, and spit upon him, and scourge him, and kill him; **and** after three days he will rise."

LUKE

Luke 9:43b–45 (§L43.1) ⇨ §M60

But while they were all marveling at everything he did, he **said to** his disciples, ⁴⁴ "Let these words sink into your ears; for **the Son of man is to be delivered into the hands of men.**" ⁴⁵ But **they** did not understand this saying, and it was concealed from them, that they should not perceive it; **and they were** afraid to ask him about this saying.

Luke 9:18–22 (§L40.1) ⇨ §M60

¹⁸ Now it happened that as he was praying alone the disciples were with him; and he asked them, "Who do the people say that I am?" ¹⁹ And they answered "John the Baptist; but others say, Elijah; and others, that one of the old prophets has risen." ²⁰ And he said to them, "But who do you say that I am?" And Peter answered, "The Christ of God." ²¹ But he charged and commanded them to tell this to no one, ²² saying, "**The Son of man** must suffer many things, and be rejected by the elders and chief priests and scribes, and be killed, **and on the third day be raised.**"

Luke 18:31–34 (L78) ⇨ §M60

³¹ And taking the twelve, he **said to them**, "Behold, we are going up to Jerusalem, and everything that is written of **the Son of man** by the prophets will be accomplished. ³² For he will **be delivered** to **the** Gentiles, and will be mocked and shamefully treated and spit upon; ³³ they will scourge him and **kill him, and on the third day he will** rise." ³⁴ But they understood none of these things; this saying was hid from them, **and they** did not grasp what was said.

JOHN

THOMAS

OTHER

MATT	MARK	LUKE

Matt 18:1-10 (§M62.1)

[1] At that time the disciples came to Jesus, saying, "Who is the greatest in the kingdom of heaven? [2] And calling to him a child, he put him in the midst of them, [3] and said, "Truly, I say to you, unless you turn and become like children, you will never enter the kingdom of heaven. [4] Whoever humbles himself like this child, he is the greatest in the kingdom of heaven.

[5] "Whoever receives one such child in my name receives me; [6] but whoever causes one of these little ones who believe in me to sin,[a] it would be better for him to have a great millstone fastened round his neck and to be drowned in the depth of the sea.

[7] "Woe to the world for temptations to sin![b] For it is necessary that temptations come, but woe to the man by whom the temptation comes! [8] And if your hand or your foot causes you to sin,[a] cut it off and throw it away; it is better for you to enter life maimed or lame than with two hands or two feet to be thrown into the eternal fire. [9] And if your eye causes you to sin,[a] pluck it out and throw it away; it is better for you to enter life with one eye than with two eyes to be thrown into the hell[c] of fire.

[10] "See that you do not despise one of these little ones; for I tell you that in heaven their angels always behold the face of my Father who is in heaven."[d]

[a] Greek: *causes . . . to stumble*

[b] Greek: *stumbling blocks*

[c] Greek: *Gehenna*

[d] Some witnesses add v. 11, *For the Son of man came (to seek and) to save the lost:* (cf. Luke 19:10) D K W X Δ Π *pm;* text: ℵ B L* Θ *f¹ f¹³* 33 *al*

●**Matt 5:29-30** ⇨ Matt 18:8-9

[29] "If your right eye causes you to sin, pluck it out and throw it away; it is better that you lose one of your members than that your whole body be thrown into hell. [30] And if your right hand causes you to sin, cut it off and throw it away; it is better that you lose one of your members than that your whole body go into hell."

Matt 23:12 ⇨ Matt 18:4

[12] "whoever exalts himself will be humbled, and whoever humbles himself will be exalted."

Matt 10:40 ⇨ Matt 18:5

[40] "He who receives you receives me, and he who receives me receives him who sent me."

Mark 9:33-37 (§K47)

[33] And they came to Capernaum; and when he was in the house he asked them, "What were you discussing on the way?" [34] But they were silent; for on the way they had discussed with one another **who** was **the greatest.** [35] And he sat down and called the twelve; **and** he **said** to them, "If any one would be first, he must be last of all and servant of all." [36] **And** he took a **child,** and put **him in the midst of them; and** taking him in his arms, he **said** to them, [37] "Whoever receives one such child in my name receives me; and whoever receives me, receives not me but him who sent me."

Mark 9:42-50 (§K49)

[42] "Whoever causes one of these little ones who believe in me to sin, it would be better for him if a great millstone were hung round his neck and he were thrown into the sea. [43] And if your hand causes you to sin, cut it off; it is better for you to enter life maimed than with two hands to go to hell, to the unquenchable fire. [45] And if your foot causes you to sin, cut it off; it is better for you to enter life lame than with two feet to be thrown into hell. [47] And if your eye causes you to sin, pluck it out; it is better for you to enter the kingdom of God with one eye than with two eyes to be thrown into hell, [48] where their worm does not die, and the fire is not quenched. [49] For every one will be salted with fire. [50] Salt is good; but if the salt has lost its saltness, how will you season it? Have salt in yourselves, and be at peace with one another."

Mark 10:13-16 (§K52) ⇨ Matt 18:3-4

[13] And they were bringing children to him, that he might touch them; [13] and the disciples rebuked them. [14] But when Jesus saw it he was indignant, **and said** to them, "Let the **children** come to me, do not hinder them; for to such belongs **the kingdom of** God. [15] **Truly, I say to you,** whoever does not receive **the kingdom of** God like a child shall not **enter** it." [16] And he took them in his arms and blessed them, laying his hands upon them.

Luke 9:46-50 (§L43.2)

[46] And an argument arose among them as to which of them was **the greatest.** [47] But when **Jesus** perceived the thought of their hearts, he took **a child** and **put him** by his side, [48] **and said** to them, "**Whoever receives** this **child in my name receives me,** and **whoever receives me** receives him who sent me; for he who is least among you all is the one who is great."

[49] John answered, "Master, we saw a man casting out demons in your name, and we forbade him, because he does not follow with us." [50] But Jesus said to him, "Do not forbid him; for he that is not against you is for you."

Luke 18:15-17 (§L75.1) ⇨ Matt 18:3-4

[15] Now they were bringing even infants to him that he might touch them; and when the disciples saw it, they rebuked them. [16] But **Jesus** called them **to him,** saying, "Let the **children** come to me, and do not hinder them; for to such belongs **the kingdom of God.** [17] **Truly, I say to you,** whoever does not receive **the kingdom of** God **like a child** shall not **enter it.**"

Luke 10:16 ⇨ Matt 18:5

[16] "He who hears me hears me, and he who rejects you rejects me, and he who rejects me rejects him who sent me."

Luke 17:1-4 (§L71.1) ⇨ Matt 18:6

[1] And he said to his disciples, "Temptations to sin are sure to come; but woe to him by whom they come! [2] It would be better for him if a millstone were hung round his neck and he were cast into the sea, than that he should cause one of these little ones to sin. [3] Take heed to yourselves; if your brother sins, rebuke him, and if he repents, forgive him; [4] and if he sins against you seven times in the day, and turns to you seven times, and says, 'I repent,' you must forgive him."

JOHN	THOMAS	OTHER

John 3:3–5 ⇨ Matt 18:3

³ Jesus answered him, "Truly, truly, I say to you, unless one is born anew, he cannot see the kingdom of God." ⁴ Nicodemus said to him, "How can a man be born when he is old? Can he enter a second time into his mother's womb and be born?" ⁵ Jesus answered, "Truly, truly, I say to you, unless one is born of water and the Spirit, he cannot enter the kingdom of God.

GThom 12 ⇨ Matt 18:1

(12) The disciples said to Jesus, "We know that You will depart from us. Who is to be our leader?"

Jesus said to them, "Wherever you are, you are to go to James the righteous, for whose sake heaven and earth came into being."

GThom 22 ⇨ Matt 18:3

(22) Jesus saw infants being suckled. He said to His disciples, "These infants being suckled are like those who enter the Kingdom."

They said to Him, "Shall we then, as children, enter the Kingdom?"

Jesus said to them, "When you make the two one, and when you make the inside like the outside and the outside like the inside, and the above like the below, and when you make the male and the female one and the same, so that the male not be male nor the female female; and when you fashion eyes in place of an eye, and a hand in place of a hand, and a foot in place of a foot, and a likeness in place of a likeness; then will you enter [the Kingdom]."

MATT	MARK	LUKE

Matt 18:12–14 (§M62.2)

[12] "What do you think? If a man has a hundred sheep, and one of them has gone astray, does he not leave ninety-nine on the mountains and go in search of the one that went astray? [13] And if he finds it, truly, I say to you, he rejoices over it more than over the ninety-nine that never went astray. [14] So it is not the will of my[a] Father who is in heaven that one of these little ones should perish."

[a] Text: B Θ 078 *f*[13] 33 *al; your:* ℵ D^c K L W X △ Π *f*[1] 28 *al*

Luke 15:3–7 (§L66.2)

[3] So he told them this parable: [4] "**What man** of you, having **a hundred sheep**, if he has lost **one of them**, **does not leave the ninety-nine** in the wilderness, **and go** after **the one** which is lost, until he finds it? [5] **And** when **he** has found **it, he** lays it on his shoulders, rejoicing. [6] And when he comes home, he calls together his friends and his neighbors, saying to them, 'Rejoice with me, for I have found my sheep which was lost.' [7] Just **so**, I tell you, there will be more joy **in heaven** over **one** sinner who repents than over **ninety-nine** righteous persons who need no repentance."

JOHN	THOMAS	OTHER

GThom 107

(107) Jesus said, "The Kingdom is like **a** shepherd who had **a hundred sheep. One of them**, the largest, went **astray. He** left the **ninety-nine and** looked for **that one** until **he** found **it**. When he had gone to such trouble, he said to the sheep, 'I care for you more than the **ninety-nine**.'"

MATT	MARK	LUKE

MATT

Matt 18:15–22 (§M63.1)

[15] "If your brother sins against you, go and tell him his fault, between you and him alone. If he listens to you, you have gained your brother. [16] But if he does not listen, take one or two others along with you, that every word may be confirmed by the evidence of two or three witnesses. [17] If he refuses to listen to them, tell it to the church; and if he refuses to listen even to the church, let him be to you as a Gentile and a tax collector. [18] Truly, I say to you, whatever you bind on earth shall be bound in heaven, and whatever you loose on earth shall be loosed in heaven. [19] Again I say to you, if two of you agree on earth about anything they ask, it will be done for them by my Father in heaven. [20] For where two or three are gathered in my name, there am I in the midst of them."

[21] Then Peter came up and said to him, "Lord, how often shall my brother sin against me, and I forgive him? As many as seven times?" [22] Jesus said to him, "I do not say to you seven times, but seventy times seven."[a]

[a] Or: *seventy-seven times*

●**Matt 16:19** ⇨ Matt 18:18
[19] "I will give **you** the keys of the kingdom of heaven, and **whatever you bind on earth shall be bound in heaven, and whatever you loose on earth shall be loosed in heaven.**"

Deut 19:15 ⇨ Matt 18:16
[15] "A single witness shall not prevail against a man for any crime or for any wrong in connection with any offense that he has committed; only on the evidence of **two** witnesses, **or of three witnesses**, shall a charge be sustained."

LUKE

Luke 17:1–4 (§L70.1)

[1] *And he said to his disciples, "Temptations to sin are sure to come; but woe to him by whom they come!* [2] *It would be better for him if a millstone were hung round his neck and he were cast into the sea, than that he should cause one of these little ones to sin.* [3] *Take heed to yourselves; if your brother sins, rebuke him, and if he repents, forgive him;* [4] *and if he sins against you seven times in the day, and turns to you seven times, and says, 'I repent,' you must forgive him."*

JOHN	THOMAS	OTHER

JOHN

John 20:23 ⇨ Matt 18:18
[23] *If you forgive the sins of any, they are forgiven; if you retain the sins of any, they are retained."*

THOMAS

POxy1 5 ⇨ Matt 18:20
(5) [Jesus sa]ys, "[Wh]ere there are [three g]o[ds, they ar]e gods. And where one is all alone to himself, I am with him. Take up the stone and there you will find me; split the wood and I am there."

GThom 30 ⇨ Matt 18:20
(30) Jesus said, "Where there are three gods, they are gods. Where there are two or one, I am with him."

GThom 77 ⇨ Matt 18:20
(77) Jesus said, "It is I who am the light which is above them all. It is I who am the All. From Me did the All come forth, and unto Me did the All extend. Split a piece of wood, and I am there. Lift up the stone, and you will find Me there."

OTHER

GNaz 15 ⇨ Matt 18:21–22
(15a) He (Jesus) said: If thy brother has sinned with a word and has made thee reparation, receive him seven times in a day. Simon his disciple said to him: Seven times in a day? The Lord answered and said to him: Yea, I say unto thee, until seventy times seven times. For in the prophets also after they were anointed with the Holy Spirit, the word of sin (sinful discourse?) was found. (Jerome, *Adversus Pelagianos* 3.2)

(15b) The Jewish Gospel has after "seventy times seven times": For in the prophets also, after they were anointed with the Holy Spirit, the word of sin (sinful discourse?) was found. (Variant to Matthew 18:22 in the "Zion Gospel" Edition)

MATT	MARK	LUKE

Matt 18:23–35 (§M63.2)

[23] "Therefore the kingdom of heaven may be compared to a king who wished to settle accounts with his servants. [24] When he began the reckoning, one was brought to him who owed him ten thousand talents;[a] [25] and as he could not pay, his lord ordered him to be sold, with his wife and children and all that he had, and payment to be made. [26] So the servant fell on his knees, imploring him, 'Lord, have patience with me, and I will pay you everything.' [27] And out of pity for him the lord of that servant released him and forgave him the debt. [28] But that same servant, as he went out, came upon one of his fellow servants who owed him a hundred denarii;[b] and seizing him by the throat he said, 'Pay what you owe.' [29] So his fellow servant fell down and besought him, 'Have patience with me, and I will pay you.' [30] He refused and went and put him in prison till he should pay the debt. [31] When his fellow servants saw what had taken place, they were greatly distressed, and they went and reported to their lord all that had taken place. [32] Then his lord summoned him and said to him, 'You wicked servant! I forgave you all that debt because you besought me; [33] and should not you have had mercy on your fellow servant, as I had mercy on you?' [34] And in anger his lord delivered him to the jailers, till he should pay all his debt. [35] So also my heavenly Father will do to every one of you, if you do not forgive your brother from your heart."

[a] This talent amounted to more than fifteen years' wages of a laborer

[b] The denarius was a day's wage for a laborer (Matt 20:2)

Matt 6:14–15 ⇨ Matt 18:35
[14] *"For if you **forgive** men their trespasses, your heavenly **Father** also will forgive **you**; [15] but if you do not **forgive** men their trespasses, neither will your **Father** forgive your trespasses."*

JOHN	THOMAS	OTHER

MATT	MARK	LUKE

Matt 19:1–2 (§M64) °
¹ Now when Jesus had finished these sayings, he went away from Galilee and entered the region of Judea beyond the Jordan; ² and large crowds followed him, and he healed them there.

°Appendix 3 ⇨ §M64

Mark 10:1 (§K50)
¹ And he left there and went to the region of Judea and beyond the Jordan, and crowds gathered to him again; and again, as his custom was, he taught them.

JOHN	THOMAS	OTHER

MATT

MARK

LUKE

Matt 19:3–9 (§M65.1)

³ And Pharisees came up to him and tested him by asking, "Is it lawful to divorce one's wife for any cause?" ⁴ He answered, "Have you not read that he who made them from the beginning made them male and female, ⁵ and said, 'For this reason a man shall leave his father and mother and be joined to his wife, and the two shall become one flesh'? ⁶ So they are no longer two but one flesh. What therefore God has joined together, let not man put asunder." ⁷ They said to him, "Why then did Moses command one to give a certificate of divorce, and to put her away?" ⁸ He said to them, "For your hardness of heart Moses allowed you to divorce your wives, but from the beginning it was not so. ⁹ And I say to you: whoever divorces his wife, except for unchastity,[a] and marries another, commits adultery."[b]

[a] Some witnesses add, *makes her commit adultery:* (cf. Matt 5:35) P²⁵ (?) B *f*¹ *al*

[b] Some witnesses add, *"and he who marries a divorced woman commits adultery":* (cf. Matt 5:35) B C* K W Δ Θ 078 *f*¹ *f*¹³ 28 33 *pm*

● **Matt 5:31–32 (§M12.5c)** ⇨ Matt 19:7, 9
³¹ "It was also said, 'Whoever divorces his wife, let him give her a certificate of divorce.' ³² But I say to you that every one who divorces his wife, except on the ground of unchastity, makes her an adultress; and whoever marries a divorced woman commits adultery."

Gen 1:27 ⇨ Matt 19:4
²⁷ So God created man in his own image, in the image of God he created him; male and female he created them.

Gen 2:24 ⇨ Matt 19:5
²⁴ Therefore a man leaves his father and his mother and cleaves to his wife, and they become one flesh.

Deut 24:1–4 ⇨ Matt 19:7
¹ "When a man takes a wife and marries her, if then she finds no favor in his eyes because he has found some indecency in her, and he writes her a bill of divorce and puts it in her hand and sends her out of his house, and she departs out of his house, ² and if she goes and becomes another man's wife, ³ and the latter husband dies, who took her to be his wife, ⁴ then her former husband, who sent her away, may not take her again to be his wife, after she has been defiled; for that is an abomination before the Lord, and you shall not bring guilt upon the land which the Lord your God gives you for an inheritance."

Mark 10:2–9 (§K51.1)

² And Pharisees came up and in order to test him asked, "Is it lawful for a man to divorce his wife?" ³ He answered them, "What did Moses command you?" ⁴ They said, "Moses allowed a man to write a certificate of divorce, and to put her away." ⁵ But Jesus said to them, "For your hardness of heart he wrote you this commandment. ⁶ But from the beginning of creation, 'God made them male and female.' ⁷ 'For this reason a man shall leave his father and mother and be joined to his wife, ⁸ and the two shall become one flesh.' So they are no longer two but one flesh. ⁹ What therefore God has joined together, let not man put asunder."

Mark 10:10–12 (§K51.2)

¹⁰ And in the house the disciples asked him again about this matter. ¹¹ And he said to them, "Whoever divorces his wife and marries another, commits adultery against her; ¹² and if she divorces her husband and marries another, she commits adultery."

Luke 16:18 (§L68.2)

¹⁸ "Every one who divorces his wife and marries another commits adultery, and he who marries a woman divorced from her husband commits adultery."

JOHN

THOMAS

OTHER

1 Cor 7:10–11 ⇨ Matt 19:4
¹⁰ *To the married I give charge, not I but the Lord, that the wife should not separate from her husband* ¹¹ *(but if she does, let her remain single or else be reconciled to her husband)—and that the husband should not divorce his wife.*

MATT   MARK   LUKE

OTHER

Matt 19:10–12 (§M65.2)

[10] The disciples said to him, "If such is the case of a man with his wife, it is not expedient to marry." [11] But he said to them, "Not all men can receive this saying, but only those to whom it is given. [12] For there are eunuchs who have been so from birth, and there are eunuchs who have been made eunuchs by men, and there are eunuchs who have made themselves eunuchs for the sake of the kingdom of heaven. He who is able to receive this, let him receive it."

2 Clem 12:1–6

[1] Let us then wait for **the kingdom of God**, from hour to hour, in love and righteousness, seeing that we know not the day of the appearing of God. [2] For when the Lord himself was asked by someone when his kingdom would come, he said: "When the two shall be one, and the outside as the inside, and the male with the female neither male nor female." [3] Now "the two are one" when we speak with one another in truth, and there is but one soul in two bodies without dissimulation. [4] And by "the outside as the inside" he means this, that the inside is the soul, and the outside is the body. Therefore, just as your body is visible, so let your soul be apparent in your good works. [5] And by "the male with the female neither male nor female" he means this, that when a brother sees a sister he should have no thought of her as female, nor she of him as male. [6] When you do this, he says, **the kingdom of my Father will come.**

JOHN   THOMAS

GThom 22

(22) Jesus saw infants being suckled. He said to His disciples, "These infants being suckled are like those who enter the Kingdom."

They said to Him, "Shall we then, as children, enter the Kingdom?"

Jesus said to them, "When you make the two one, and when you make the inside like the outside and the outside like the inside, and the above like the below, and when you make the male and the female one and the same, so that the male not be male nor the female female; and when you fashion eyes in place of an eye, and a hand in place of a hand, and a foot in place of a foot, and a likeness in place of a likeness; then will you enter [the Kingdom]."

GEgy 1–6

(1) When Salome asked, "How long will death have power?" the Lord answered, "So long as you women bear children"—not as if life was something bad and creation evil, but as teaching the sequence of nature. (Clement, Stromateis 3.6.45.3)

(2) Those who are opposed to God's creation because of continence, which has a fair-sounding name, also quote the words addressed to Salome which I mentioned earlier. They are handed down, as I believe, in the Gospel of the Egyptians. For, they say: the Savior himself said, "I am come to undo the works of the female," by the female meaning lust, and by the works birth and decay. (Clement, Stromateis, 3.9.63.1–2)

(3) Since then the Word has alluded to the consummation, Salome saith rightly, "Until when shall men die?" Now Scripture uses the term 'man' in the two senses, of the visible outward form and of the soul, and again of the redeemed man and of him who is not redeemed. And sin is called the death of the soul. Wherefore the Lord answers advisedly, "So long as women bear children," i.e., so long as lusts are powerful. (Clement, Stromateis, 3.9.64.1)

(4) Why do they not also adduce what follows the words spoken to Salome, these people who do anything but walk by the gospel rule according to truth? For when she said, "I have then done well in not bearing children," as if it were improper to engage in procreation, then the Lord answered and said, "Eat every plant, but that which has bitterness eat not." (Clement, Stromateis, 3.9.66.1–2)

(5) Contending further for the impious doctrine he (Julius Cassianus) adds: "And how could a charge not be rightly brought against the Savior, if he has transformed us and freed us from error, and delivered us from sexual intercourse?" In this matter his teaching is similar to that of Tatian. But he emerged from the school of Valentinus. Therefore Cassianus now says, When Salome asked when what she had inquired about would be known, the Lord said, "When you have trampled on the garment of shame and when the two become one and the male with the female (is) neither male nor female." Now in the first place we have not this word in the four Gospels that have been handed down to us, but in the Gospel of the Egyptians. Further he seems to me to fail to recognize that by the male impulse is meant wrath and by the female lust. (Clement, Stromateis, 3.13.92.1–93.1)

(6) And when the Savior says to Salome that death will reign as long as women bear children, he does not thereby slander procreation, for that indeed is necessary for the redemption of believers. (Clement, Excerpta ex Theodoto 67.2)

MATT

Matt 19:13–15 (§M66)

¹³ Then children were brought to him that he might lay his hands on them and pray. The disciples rebuked the people; ¹⁴ but Jesus said, "Let the children come to me, and do not hinder them; for to such belongs the kingdom of heaven." ¹⁵ And he laid his hands on them and went away.

MARK

Mark 10:13–16 (§K52)

¹³ And they were bringing **children to him, that he might** touch **them;** ¹³ and **the disciples rebuked** them. ¹⁴ **But when Jesus** saw it he was indignant, and **said** to them, **"Let the children come to me, do not hinder them; for to such belongs the kingdom of** God. ¹⁵ Truly, I say to you, whoever does not receive the kingdom of God like a child shall not enter it." ¹⁶ **And he** took them in his arms and blessed them, laying **his hands** upon **them.**

LUKE

Luke 18:15–17 (§L76)

¹⁵ Now they **were** bringing even infants **to him that he might** touch **them;** and when **the disciples** saw it, they **rebuked** them. ¹⁶ But Jesus called them to him, saying, **"Let the children come to me, and do not hinder them; for to such belongs the kingdom of** God. ¹⁷ Truly, I say to you, whoever does not receive the kingdom of God like a child shall not enter it."

JOHN

THOMAS

GThom 22

(22) Jesus saw infants being suckled. He said to His disciples, "These infants being suckled are like those who enter the Kingdom."

They said to Him, "Shall we then, as children, enter the Kingdom?"

Jesus said to them, "When you make the two one, and when you make the inside like the outside and the outside like the inside, and the above like the below, and when you make the male and the female one and the same, so that the male not be male nor the female female; and when you fashion eyes in place of an eye, and a hand in place of a hand, and a foot in place of a foot, and a likeness in place of a likeness; then will you enter [the Kingdom]."

OTHER

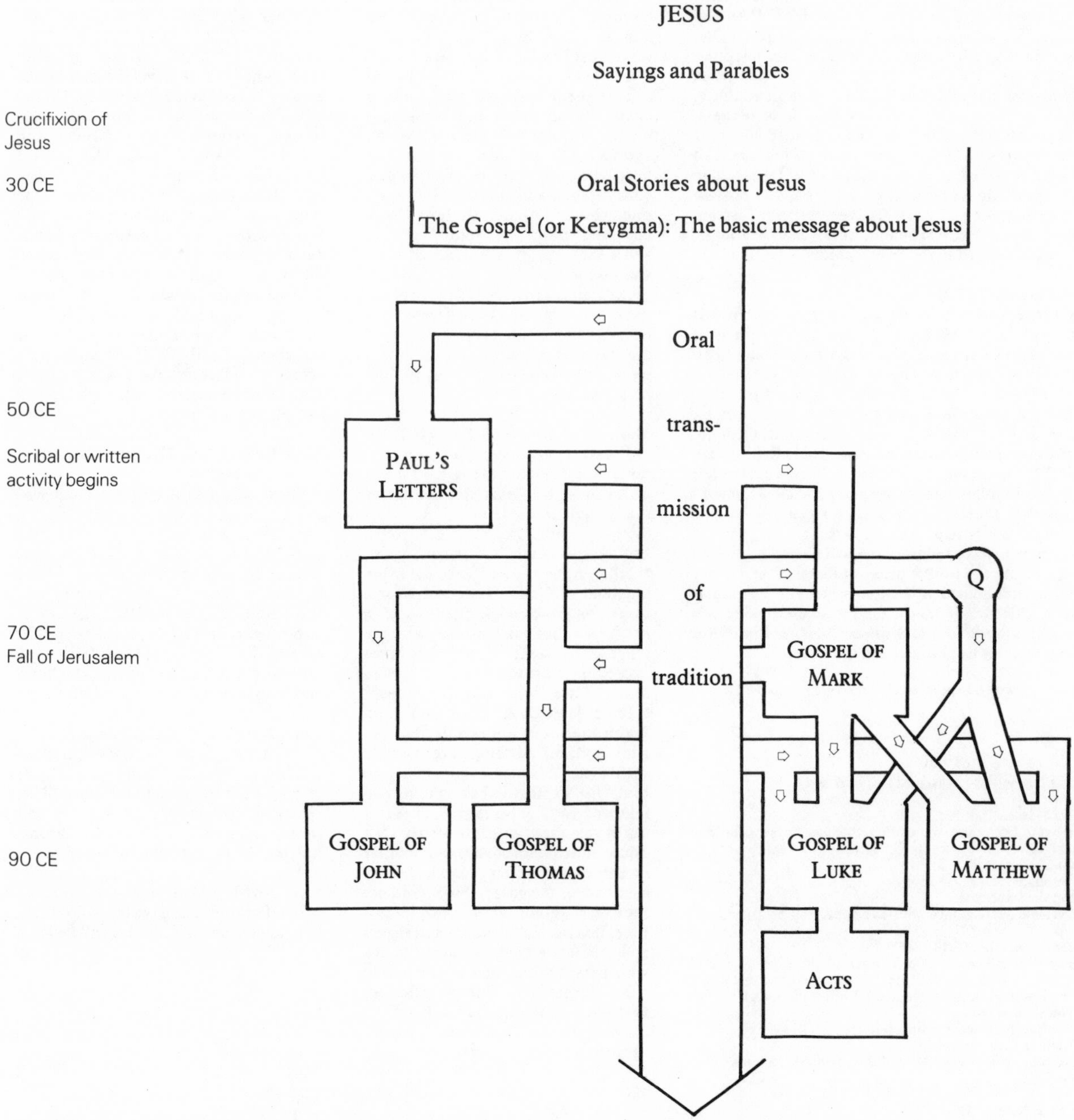

JESUS

Sayings and Parables

Crucifixion of
Jesus

30 CE

Oral Stories about Jesus

The Gospel (or Kerygma): The basic message about Jesus

Oral

trans-

50 CE

Scribal or written
activity begins

PAUL'S
LETTERS

mission

of

70 CE
Fall of Jerusalem

tradition

Q

GOSPEL OF
MARK

90 CE

GOSPEL OF
JOHN

GOSPEL OF
THOMAS

GOSPEL OF
LUKE

GOSPEL OF
MATTHEW

ACTS

| Mᴀᴛᴛ | Mᴀʀᴋ | Lᴜᴋᴇ |

Matt 19:16–22 (§M67.1)

[16] And behold, one came up to him, saying, "Teacher, what good deed must I do, to have eternal life?" [17] And he said to him, "Why do you ask me about what is good? One there is who is good. If you would enter life, keep the commandments." [18] He said to him, "Which?" And Jesus said, "You shall not kill, You shall not commit adultery, You shall not steal, You shall not bear false witness, [19] Honor your father and mother, and, You shall love your neighbor as yourself." [20] The young man said to him, "All these I have observed; what do I still lack?" [21] Jesus said to him, "If you would be perfect, go, sell what you possess and give to the poor, and you will have treasure in heaven; and come, follow me." [22] When the young man heard this he went away sorrowful; for he had great possessions.

Matt 19:23–30 (§M67.2) °

[23] And Jesus said to his disciples, "Truly, I say to you, it will be hard for a rich man to enter the kingdom of heaven. [24] Again I tell you, it is easier for a camel to go through the eye of a needle than for a rich man to enter the kingdom of God." [25] When the disciples heard this they were greatly astonished, saying, "Who then can be saved?" [26] But Jesus looked at them and said to them, "With men this is impossible, but with God all things are possible." [27] Then Peter said in reply, "Lo, we have left everything and followed you. What then shall we have?" [28] Jesus said to them, "Truly, I say to you, in the new world, when the Son of man shall sit on his glorious throne, you who have followed me will also sit on twelve thrones, judging the twelve tribes of Israel. [29] And every one who has left houses or brothers or sisters or father or mother or children or lands, for my name's sake, will receive a hundredfold,[a] and inherit eternal life. [30] But many that are first will be last, and the last first."

[a] Some witnesses read *manifold:* (cf. Luke 18:30) B L 1010 *al*

° Appendix 2 ⇨ Matt 19:27–30

● **Matt 20:16** ⇨ Matt 19:30
[16] "So the last will be first, and the first last."

Exod 20:12–16 ⇨ Matt 19:18–19a
[12] "Honor your father and your mother, that your days may be long in the land which the Lord your God gives you.
[13] "You shall not kill.
[14] "You shall not commit adultery.
[15] "You shall not steal.
[16] "You shall not bear false witness against your neighbor."

Deut 5:16–20 ⇨ Matt 19:18–19a
[16] "'Honor your father and your mother, as the Lord your God commanded you; that your days may be prolonged, and that it may go well with you, in the land which the Lord your God gives you.
[17] "'You shall not kill.
[18] "'Neither shall you commit adultery.
[19] "'Neither shall you steal.
[20] "'Neither shall you bear false witness against your neighbor.'"

Lev 19:18 ⇨ Matt 19:19b
[18] "You shall not take vengeance or bear any grudge against the sons of your own people, but you shall love your neighbor as yourself: I am the Lord."

Mark 10:17–22 (§K53.1) ⇨ §M67.1

[17] And as he was setting out on his journey, a man ran up and knelt before him, and asked him, "Good Teacher, what must I do to inherit eternal life?" [18] And Jesus said to him, "Why do you call me good? No one is good but God alone. [19] You know the commandments: 'Do not kill, Do not commit adultery, Do not steal, Do not bear false witness, Do not defraud, Honor your father and mother.'" [20] And he said to him, "Teacher, all these I have observed from my youth." [21] And Jesus looking upon him loved him, and said to him, "You lack one thing; go, sell what you have, and give to the poor, and you will have treasure in heaven; and come, follow me." [22] At that saying his countenance fell, and he went away sorrowful; for he had great possessions.

Mark 10:23–31 (§K53.2) ⇨ §M67.2

[23] And Jesus looked around and said to his disciples, "How hard it will be for those who have riches to enter the kingdom of God!" [24] And the disciples were amazed at his words. But Jesus said to them again, "Children, how hard it is to enter the kingdom of God! [25] It is easier for a camel to go through the eye of a needle than for a rich man to enter the kingdom of God." [26] And they were exceedingly astonished, and said to him, "Then who can be saved?" [27] Jesus looked at them and said, "With men it is impossible, but not with God; for all things are possible with God." [28] Peter began to say to him, "Lo, we have left everything and followed you." [29] Jesus said, "Truly, I say to you, there is no one who has left house or brothers or sisters or mother or father or children or lands, for my sake and for the gospel, [30] who will not receive a hundredfold now in this time, houses and brothers and sisters and mothers and children and lands, with persecutions, and in the age to come eternal life. [31] But many that are first will be last, and the last first."

Luke 18:18–25 (§L77.1)

[18] And a ruler asked him, "Good Teacher, what shall I do to inherit eternal life?" [19] And Jesus said to him, "Why do you call me good? No one is good but God alone. [20] You know the commandments: 'Do not commit adultery, Do not kill, Do not steal, Do not bear false witness, Honor your father and mother.'" [21] And he said, "All these I have observed from my youth." [22] And when Jesus heard it, he said to him, "One thing you still lack. Sell all that you have and distribute to the poor, and you will have treasure in heaven; and come, follow me." [23] But when he heard this he became sad, for he was very rich. [24] Jesus looking at him said, "How hard it is for those who have riches to enter the kingdom of God! [25] For it is easier for a camel to go through the eye of a needle than for a rich man to enter the kingdom of God."

Luke 18:26–30 (§L77.2)
⇨ Matt 19:25–29

[26] Those who heard it said, "Then who can be saved?" [27] But he said, "What is impossible with men is possible with God." [28] And Peter said, "Lo, we have left our homes and followed you." [29] And he said to them, "Truly, I say to you, there is no man who has left house or wife or brothers or parents or children, for the sake of the kingdom of God, [30] who will not receive manifold more in this time, and in the age to come eternal life."

Luke 22:28–30 ⇨ Matt 19:28

[28] "You are those who have continued with me in my trials; [29] and I assign to you, as my Father assigned to me, a kingdom, [30] that you may eat and drink at my table in my kingdom, and sit on thrones judging the twelve tribes of Israel."

Luke 13:30 ⇨ Matt 19:30
[30] "And behold, some are last who will be first, and some are first who will be last."

JOHN	THOMAS	OTHER

THOMAS

GThom 25 ⇨ Matt 19:19
(25) Jesus said, "Love your brother like your soul, guard him like the pupil of your eye."

GThom 81 ⇨ Matt 19:23
(81) Jesus said, "Let him who has grown rich be king, and let him who possesses power renounce it."

POxy654 4 ⇨ Matt 19:30
(4) [Jesus says,] "A ma[n full of d]ays will not hesitate to ask a ch[ild of seven da]ys about the place of [life and he will live.] For **many (that are) fi[rst] will be [last and] the last** will be **first** and they [will have eternal life]."

GThom 4 ⇨ Matt 19:30
(4) Jesus said, "The man old in days will not hesitate to ask a small child seven days old about the place of life, and he will live. For **many** who **are first will** become **last**, and they will become one and the same."

OTHER

GNaz 16
(16) The other of the two rich men said **to him:** Master, **what good** thing **must I do** that I may live? **He said to him:** Man, fulfil the law and the prophets. He answered **him:** That **have I** done. He **said to him: Go** and **sell** all that thou possessest and distribute it among **the poor, and** then **come** and **follow me.** But the rich man then began to scratch his head and it (the saying) pleased him not. And the Lord said to him: How canst thou say, I have fulfilled the law and the prophets? For it stands written in the law: **Love** thy neighbour as thyself; and behold, many of thy brethren, sons of Abraham, are begrimed with dirt and die of hunger—and thy house is full of many good things and nothing at all comes forth from it to them! And he turned and said to Simon, his disciple, who was sitting by him: Simon, son of Jona, **it is easier for a camel to go through the eye of a needle than for a rich man** to enter into the kingdom of heaven. (Origen, *Commentary on Matthew* 15:14 [on Matthew 19:16–30])

ApocJa 4:22–37 ⇨ Matt 19:27–29
*And I answered and said to him: "Lord, we can obey you [25] if you wish. For **we have** forsaken our forefathers and our mothers and our villages **and have followed you.** Grant us, [therefore], [30] not to be tempted by the wicked devil."*
*The Lord answered and said: "What is your (pl.) merit when **you** do the will of the Father if it is not given to **you** by him [35] as a gift, while **you** are tempted by Satan?"*

MATT	MARK	LUKE
Matt 20:1–16 (§M67.3)	**Mark 10:31** ⇨ Matt 20:16	**Luke 13:30** ⇨ Matt 20:16

MATT

Matt 20:1–16 (§M67.3)

¹"For the kingdom of heaven is like a householder who went out early in the morning to hire laborers for his vineyard. ²After agreeing with the laborers for a denarius[a] a day, he sent them into his vineyard. ³And going out about the third hour he saw others standing idle in the market place; ⁴and to them he said, 'You go into the vineyard too, and whatever is right I will give you.' So they went. ⁵Going out again about the sixth hour and the ninth hour, he did the same. ⁶And about the eleventh hour he went out and found others standing; and he said to them, 'Why do you stand here idle all day? ⁷They said to him, 'Because no one has hired us.' He said to them, 'You go into the vineyard too.' ⁸And when evening came, the owner of the vineyard said to his steward, 'Call the laborers and pay them their wages, beginning with the last, up to the first.' ⁹And when those hired about the eleventh hour came, each of them received a denarius. ¹⁰Now when the first came, they thought they would receive more; but each of them also received a denarius. ¹¹And on receiving it they grumbled at the householder, ¹²saying, 'These last worked only one hour, and you have made them equal to us who have borne the burden of the day and the scorching heat.' ¹³But he replied to one of them, 'Friend, I am doing you no wrong; did you not agree with me for a denarius? ¹⁴Take what belongs to you, and go; I choose to give to this last as I give to you. ¹⁵Am I not allowed to do what I choose with what belongs to me? Or do you begrudge my generosity?'[b] ¹⁶So the last will be first, and the first last."

[a] The denarius was a day's wage for the laborer

[b] Or: *is your eye evil because I am good?*

●**Matt 19:30** ⇨ Matt 20:16
³⁰But many that are **first** will be **last**, and **the last first**.

MARK

Mark 10:31 ⇨ Matt 20:16
³¹"But many that are **first** will be **last**, and **the last first**."

LUKE

Luke 13:30 ⇨ Matt 20:16
³⁰"And behold, some are **last** who **will be first, and** some are **first** who will be **last**."

JOHN	THOMAS	OTHER

JOHN

THOMAS

POxy654 4 ⇨ Matt 20:16
(4) [Jesus says,] "A ma[n full of d]ays will not hesitate to ask a ch[ild of seven da]ys about the place of [life and he will live.] For many (that are) fi[rst] will be [**last and**] **the last will be first** and they [will have eternal life]."

GThom 4 ⇨ Matt 20:16
(4) Jesus said, "The man old in days will not hesitate to ask a small child seven days old about the place of life, and he will live. For many who are **first will** become **last**, and they will become one and the same."

OTHER

MATT

MARK

LUKE

Matt 20:17–19 (§M68) °

¹⁷ And as Jesus was going up to Jerusalem, he took the twelve disciples aside, and on the way he said to them, ¹⁸ "Behold, we are going up to Jerusalem; and the Son of man will be delivered to the chief priests and scribes, and they will condemn him to death, ¹⁹ and deliver him to the Gentiles to be mocked and scourged and crucified, and he will be raised on the third day."

°Appendix 2 ⇨ §M68

Matt 16:21–23 (§M56)

²¹ From that time **Jesus** began to show his disciples that he must go **to Jerusalem** and suffer many things from **the elders and chief priests and scribes, and** be killed, **and on the third day be raised**. ²² And Peter took him and began to rebuke him, saying, "God forbid, Lord! This shall never happen to you." ²³ But he turned and said to Peter, "Get behind me, Satan! You are a hindrance to me; for you are not on the side of God, but of men."

Matt 17:22–23 (§M60)

²² As they were gathering in Galilee, **Jesus said to them, "The Son of man** is to be **delivered** into **the** hands of men, ²³ **and they will** kill **him, and he will be raised on the third day**." And they were greatly distressed.

Mark 10:32–34 (§K54)

³² And they were on the road, going up to Jerusalem, and Jesus was walking ahead of them; and they were amazed, and those who followed were afraid. And taking the twelve again, he began to tell them what was to happen to him, ³³ saying, **"Behold, we are going up to Jerusalem; and the Son of man will be delivered to the chief priests and** the **scribes, and they will condemn him to death, and deliver him to the Gentiles;** ³⁴ and they will mock him, and spit upon him, and scourge him, and kill him; and after three days **he will rise."**

Mark 8:31–33 (§K42)

³¹ **And he** began to teach **them** that **the Son of man** must suffer many things, and be rejected by the elders and **the chief priests and the scribes, and** be killed, **and** after three days rise again. ³² And he said this plainly. And Peter took him, and began to rebuke him. ³³ But turning and seeing his disciples, he rebuked Peter, and said, "Get behind me, Satan! For you are not on the side of God, but of men."

Mark 9:30–32 (§K46)

³⁰ **They** went on from there and passed through **Galilee**. And he would not have any one know it; ³¹ for he was teaching his disciples, saying **to them, "The Son of man** will be **delivered into the hands of men, and they will kill him; and** when **he** is killed, after three days he **will rise."** ³² But they did not understand the saying, and they were afraid to ask him.

Luke 18:31–34 (§L78)

³¹ And taking **the twelve, he said to them, "Behold, we are going up to Jerusalem, and** everything that is written of **the Son of man** by the prophets will be accomplished. ³² For he **will be delivered to the Gentiles, and will be mocked and** shamefully treated and spit upon; ³³ they will scourge him and kill him, and on **the third day he will rise."** ³⁴ But they understood none of these things; this saying was hid from them, and they did not grasp what was said.

Luke 9:18–22 (§L40.1)

¹⁸ Now it happened that as he was praying alone the **disciples** were with him; and he asked them, "Who do the people say that I am?" ¹⁹ And they answered "John the Baptist; but others say, Elijah; and others, that one of the old prophets has risen." ²⁰ And he said to them, "But who do you say that I am?" And Peter answered, "The Christ of God." ²¹ But **he** charged and commanded **them** to tell this to no one, ²² saying, **"The Son of man** must suffer many things, and be rejected by **the** elders and **chief priests and scribes, and** be killed, **and on the third day be raised."**

Luke 9:43b–45 (§L43.1)

But while they were all marveling at everything he did, he **said to** his disciples, ⁴⁴ "Let these words sink into your ears; for **the Son of man is to be delivered into the hands of men."** ⁴⁵ But **they** did not understand this saying, and it was concealed from them, that they should not perceive it; **and they were** afraid to ask him about this saying.

JOHN

THOMAS

OTHER

MATT	MARK	LUKE

MATT

REQUEST FOR POSITIONS OF HONOR

Matt 20:20–23 (§M69.1)

²⁰ Then the mother of the sons of Zebedee came up to him with her sons, and kneeling before him she asked him for something. ²¹ And he said to her, "What do you want?" She said to him, "Command that these two sons of mine may sit, one at your right hand and one at your left, in your kingdom." ²² But Jesus answered, "You do not know what you are asking. Are you able to drink the cup that I am to drink?" They said to him, "We are able." ²³ He said to them, "You will drink my cup, but to sit at my right hand and at my left is not mine to grant, but it is for those for whom it has been prepared by my Father."

THE TEN DISCIPLES ARE INDIGNANT

Matt 20:24–28 (§M69.2)

²⁴ And when the ten heard it, they were indignant at the two brothers. ²⁵ But Jesus called them to him and said, "You know that the rulers of the Gentiles lord it over them, and their great men exercise authority over them. ²⁶ It shall not be so among you; but whoever would be great among you must be your servant, ²⁷ and whoever would be first among you must be your slave; ²⁸ even as the Son of man came not to be served but to serve, and to give his life as a ransom for many."

Matt 23:11–12 ⇨ Matt 20:26–27

¹¹ "He who is greatest **among you** shall **be your servant;** ¹² whoever exalts himself will be humbled, and whoever humbles himself will be exalted."

Matt 18:1–4 ⇨ §M69.2

¹ At that time the disciples came to Jesus, saying, "Who is the greatest in the kingdom of heaven? ² And calling to him a child, he put him in the midst of them, ³ and said, "Truly, I say to you, unless you turn and become like children, you will never enter the kingdom of heaven. ⁴ Whoever humbles himself like this child, he is the greatest in the kingdom of heaven."

MARK

Mark 10:35–40 (§K55.1) ⇨ §M69.1

³⁵ And James and John, **the sons of Zebedee, came** forward **to him,** and said to him, "Teacher, we want you to do for us whatever we ask of you." ³⁶ And **he said to them, "What do you want** me to do for you?" ³⁷ And they said to him, "Grant us to **sit, one at your right hand and one at your** left, in your glory." ³⁸ But Jesus said to them, "You do not know what you are asking. Are you able to drink the cup that I drink, or to be baptized with the baptism with which I am baptized?" ³⁹ And they said to him, "We are able." And Jesus said to them, "The cup that I drink you will drink; and with the baptism with which I am baptized, you will be baptized; ⁴⁰ but to sit at my right hand or at my left is not mine to grant, but it is for those for whom it has been prepared."

Mark 10:41–45 (§K55.2) ⇨ §M69.2

⁴¹ And when the ten heard it, they began to be indignant at James and John. ⁴² And **Jesus called them to him and said** to them, "**You know that** those who are supposed to rule over **the Gentiles lord it over them, and their great men exercise authority over them.** ⁴³ But it shall not be so among you; but whoever would be great among you must be your servant, ⁴⁴ and whoever would be first among you must be slave of all. ⁴⁵ For **the Son of man also came not to be served but to serve, and to give his life as a ransom for many."**

Mark 9:33–37 (§K47) ⇨ §M69.2

³³ And they came to Capernaum; and when he was in the house he asked them, "What were you discussing on the way?" ³⁴ But they were silent; for on the way they had discussed with one another who was the greatest. ³⁵ And he sat down and called the twelve; and he said to them, "If any one would be first, he must be last of all and servant of all." ³⁶ And he took a child, and put him in the midst of them; and taking him in his arms, he said to them, ³⁷ "Whoever receives one such child in my name receives me; and whoever receives me, receives not me but him who sent me."

LUKE

Luke 22:24–27 ⇨ §M69.2

²⁴ A dispute also arose among them, which of them was to be regarded as the greatest. ²⁵ And he **said** to them, "The kings **of the Gentiles** exercise lordship **over them;** and those in **authority over them** are called benefactors. ²⁶ But **not so** with **you;** rather let the greatest **among you** become as the youngest, and the leader as one who serves. ²⁷ For which is the greater, one who sits at table, or one who serves? Is it not the one who sits at table? But I am **among you** as one who serves."

Luke 9:46–50 (§L43.2) ⇨ §M69.2

⁴⁶ And an argument arose among them as to which of them was the greatest. ⁴⁷ But when Jesus perceived the thought of their hearts, he took a child and put him by his side, ⁴⁸ and said to them, "Whoever receives this child in my name receives me, and whoever receives me receives him who sent me; for he who is least among you all is the one who is great."

⁴⁹ John answered, "Master, we saw a man casting out demons in your name, and we forbade him, because he does not follow with us." ⁵⁰ But Jesus said to him, "Do not forbid him; for he that is not against you is for you."

JOHN	THOMAS	OTHER

MATT	MARK	LUKE

Matt 20:29–34 (§M70)

²⁹ And as they went out of Jericho, a great crowd followed him. ³⁰ And behold, two blind men sitting by the roadside, when they heard that Jesus was passing by, cried out, "Have mercy on us, Son of David!" ³¹ The crowd rebuked them, telling them to be silent; but they cried out the more, "Lord, have mercy on us,ᵃ Son of David!" ³² And Jesus stopped and called them, saying, "What do you want me to do for you?" ³³ They said to him, "Lord, let our eyes be opened." ³⁴ And Jesus in pity touched their eyes, and immediately they received their sight and followed him.

ᵃ Some witnesses insert *Lord:* P⁴⁵ (?) C K W X Γ Δ Π ƒ¹ 28 33 *pm;* some insert *Jesus:* (cf. Mark 10:47, Luke 18:38) ℵ Θ ƒ¹³ 700 *al*

● **Matt 9:27–31 (§M24)**

²⁷ And as Jesus passed on from there, two blind men followed him, crying aloud, "Have mercy on us, Son of David." ²⁸ When he entered the house, the blind men came to him; and Jesus said to them, "Do you believe that I am able to do this?" They said to him, "Yes, Lord." ²⁹ Then he touched their eyes, saying, "According to your faith be it done to you." ³⁰ And their eyes were opened. And Jesus sternly charged them, "See that no one knows it." ³¹ But they went away and spread his fame through all that district.

Mark 10:46–52 (§K56)

⁴⁶ And they came to Jericho; and as he was leaving Jericho with his disciples and a great multitude, Bartimaeus, a blind beggar, the son of Timaeus, was sitting by the roadside. ⁴⁷ And when he heard that it was Jesus of Nazareth, he began to cry out and say, "Jesus, Son of David, have mercy on me!" ⁴⁸ And many rebuked him, telling him to be silent; but he cried out all the more, "Son of David, have mercy on me!" ⁴⁹ And Jesus stopped and said, "Call him." And they called the blind man, saying to him, "Take heart; rise, he is calling you." ⁵⁰ And throwing off his mantle he sprang up and came to Jesus. ⁵¹ And Jesus said to him, "What do you want me to do for you?" And the blind man said to him, "Master, let me receive my sight." ⁵² And Jesus said to him, "Go your way; your faith has made you well." And immediately he received his sight and followed him on the way.

Luke 18:35–43 (§L79)

³⁵ As he drew near to Jericho, a blind man was sitting by the roadside begging; ³⁶ and hearing a multitude going by, he inquired what this meant. ³⁷ They told him, "Jesus of Nazareth is passing by." ³⁸ And he cried, "Jesus, Son of David, have mercy on me!" ³⁹ And those who were in front rebuked him, telling him to be silent; but he cried out all the more, "Son of David, have mercy on me!" ⁴⁰ And Jesus stopped, and commanded him to be brought to him; and when he came near, he asked him, ⁴¹ "What do you want me to do for you?" He said, "Lord, let me receive my sight." ⁴² And Jesus said to him, "Receive your sight; your faith has made you well." ⁴³ And immediately he received his sight and followed him, glorifying God; and all the people, when they saw it, gave praise to God.

JOHN	THOMAS	OTHER

MATT	MARK	LUKE

MATT

TWO SENT FOR COLT

Matt 21:1–6 (§M71.1)

[1] And when they drew near to Jerusalem and came to Bethphage, to the Mount of Olives, then Jesus sent two disciples, [2] saying to them, "Go into the village opposite you, and immediately you will find an ass tied, and a colt with her; untie them and bring them to me. [3] If any one says anything to you, you shall say, 'The Lord has need of them,' and he will send them immediately." [4] This took place to fulfil what was spoken by the prophet, saying,

[5] "Tell the daughter of Zion,
Behold, your king is coming to you,
humble, and mounted on an ass,
and on a colt, the foal of an ass."

[6] The disciples went and did as Jesus had directed them; . . .

TRIUMPHAL ENTRY

Matt 21:7–9 (§M71.2)

[7] they brought the ass and the colt, and put their garments on them, and he sat thereon. [8] Most of the crowd spread their garments on the road, and others cut branches from the trees and spread them on the road. [9] And the crowds that went before him and that followed him shouted, "Hosanna to the Son of David! Blessed is he who comes in the name of the Lord! Hosanna in the highest!"

RECOGNIZED AS PROPHET

Matt 21:10–11 (§M71.3)

[10] And when he entered Jerusalem, all the city was stirred, saying, "Who is this?" [11] And the crowds said, "This is the prophet Jesus from Nazareth of Galilee."

Zech 9:9 ⇨ Matt 21:5
[9] Rejoice greatly, O **daughter of Zion**!
Shout aloud, O **daughter** of Jerusalem!
Lo, **your king** comes **to you**;
triumphant and victorious is he,
humble and riding on an ass,
on a colt the foal of an ass.

Ps 118:26 ⇨ Matt 21:9
[26] **Blessed be he who** enters **in the name of the Lord**!
We bless you from the house of the Lord.

MARK

Mark 11:1–3 (§K57.1) ⇨ §M71.1

[1] And when they drew **near** to Jerusalem, to **Bethphage** and Bethany, at **the Mount of Olives**, he **sent two** of his **disciples**, [2] and said to them, "**Go into the village opposite you**, and immediately as you enter it **you will find** a colt **tied**, on which no one has ever sat; **untie** it **and bring** it. [3] **If any** one says to you, 'Why are you doing this?' say, '**The Lord has need of** it **and will send** it back here **immediately**.'"

Mark 11:4–6 (§K57.2) ⇨ §M71.1

[4] And they **went** away, and found a colt tied at the door out in the open street; and they untied it. [5] And those who stood there said to them, "What are you doing, untying the colt?" [6] And they told them what **Jesus had** said; and they let them go.

Mark 11:7–10 (§K57.3) ⇨ §M71.2

[7] And **they brought the colt** to Jesus, and threw **their garments on** it; **and he sat** upon it. [8] And many **spread their garments on the road, and others spread** leafy **branches** which they had **cut from the fields**. [9] **And** those who **went before** and those who **followed** cried out, "**Hosanna! Blessed is he who comes in the name of the Lord!** [10] Blessed is the kingdom of our father David that is coming! **Hosanna in the highest!**"

Mark 11:11 (§K57.4) ⇨ M71.3

[11] And he **entered Jerusalem**, and went into the temple; and when he had looked round at everything, as it was already late, he went out to Bethany with the twelve.

LUKE

Luke 19:28–32 (§L82.1) ⇨ §M71.1

[28] And when he had said this, he went on ahead, going up **to Jerusalem**. [29] When he **drew near to Bethphage** and Bethany, at **the** mount that is called Olivet, he **sent two** of the **disciples**, [30] saying, "**Go into the village opposite**, where on entering **you will find** a colt **tied**, on which no one has ever yet sat; **untie** it **and bring** it here. [31] **If any** one asks **you**, 'Why are you untying it?' **you shall say** this, '**The Lord has need of** it.'" [32] So those who were sent **went** away and found it **as he had** told **them**.

Luke 19:33–34 (§L82.2) ⇨ §M71.1

[33] And as they were untying the colt, its owners said to them, "Why are you untying the colt?" [34] And they said, "**The Lord has need of it.**"

Luke 19:35–40 (§L82.3) ⇨ M71.2

[35] And **they brought** it to Jesus, and throwing **their garments on** the colt they set Jesus upon it. [36] And as he rode along, they **spread their garments on the road**. [37] As he was now drawing near, at the descent of the Mount of Olives, the whole multitude of the disciples began to rejoice and praise God with a loud voice for all the mighty works that they had seen, [38] saying, "**Blessed is** the King **who comes in the name of the Lord!** Peace in heaven and glory **in the highest!**" [39] And some of the Pharisees in the multitude said to him, "Teacher, rebuke your disciples." [40] He answered, "I tell you, if these were silent, the very stones would cry out."

JOHN	THOMAS	OTHER

John 12:12–19 (§J25)

¹²The next day a great crowd who had come to the feast heard that Jesus was coming **to Jerusalem.** ¹³So they took **branches** of palm **trees** and **went** out to meet **him,** crying, "**Hosanna! Blessed is he who comes in the name of the Lord,** even the King of Israel!" ¹⁴And Jesus found a young **ass** and **sat** upon it; as it is written,

¹⁵"Fear not, **daughter of Zion;**
behold, your king is coming,
sitting **on an** ass's **colt!**"

¹⁶His disciples did not understand this at first; but when Jesus was glorified, then they remembered that this had been written of him and had been done to him. ¹⁷**The crowd that** had been with **him** when he called Lazarus out of the tomb and raised him from the dead bore witness. ¹⁸The reason why **the** crowd **went** to meet **him** was that they heard he had done this sign. ¹⁹The Pharisees then said to one another, "You see that you can do nothing; look, the world has gone after him."

MATT

CLEANSING OF THE TEMPLE

Matt 21:12–13 (§M72.1)
[12] And Jesus entered the temple of God[a] and drove out all who sold and bought in the temple, and he overturned the tables of the money-changers and the seats of those who sold pigeons. [13] He said to them, "It is written, 'My house shall be called a house of prayer'; but you make it a den of robbers."

CHILDREN PRAISE JESUS

Matt 21:14–17 (§M72.2)
[14] And the blind and the lame came to him in the temple, and he healed them. [15] But when the chief priests and the scribes saw the wonderful things that he did, and the children crying out in the temple, "Hosanna to the Son of David!" they were indignant; [16] and they said to him, "Do you hear what these are saying?" And Jesus said to them, "Yes, have you never read,

'Out of the mouth of babes and sucklings
thou hast brought perfect praise'?"
[17] And leaving them, he went out of the city to Bethany and lodged there.

[a] Omit *of God:* (cf. Mark 11:15, Luke 19:45) ℵ B L Θ *f*[13] 33 700 *al*

Isa 56:7 ⇨ Matt 21:13
[7] "these I bring to **my** holy mountain,
   and make them joyful in **my house of prayer**;
their burnt offerings and their sacrifices
   will be accepted on my altar;
for **my house** will **be called a house of prayer**
   for all peoples."

MARK

Mark 11:15–19 (§K58.2)
[15] And they came to Jerusalem. **And** he **entered the temple and** began to drive **out** those **who sold and** those who **bought in the temple,** and he overturned the tables of the money-changers and the seats of those who sold pigeons; [16] and he would not allow any one to carry anything through the temple. [17] And **he** taught, and **said to them,** "Is it not written, 'My **house shall be called a house of prayer** for all the nations'? **But you** have made **it a den of robbers."** [18] And **the chief priests and the scribes** heard it and sought a way to destroy him; for **they** feared him, because all the multitude was astonished at his teaching. [19] And when evening came they **went out of the city.**

Jer 7:11 ⇨ Matt 21:13
[11] "Has this **house,** which is called by my name, become **a den of robbers** in your eyes? Behold, I myself have seen it, says the Lord."

Ps 8:1–2 ⇨ Matt 21:16
[1] O Lord, our Lord,
how majestic is thy name in all the earth!
Thou whose glory above the heavens is chanted
   [2] **by the mouth of babes and** infants,
thou hast founded a bulwark because of thy foes,
   to still the enemy and the avenger.

LUKE

Luke 19:45–48 (§L83)
[45] And he **entered the temple and** began to drive **out** those **who sold,** [46] saying **to them,** "It is written, 'My **house shall be a house of prayer'; but you** have made **it a den of robbers."**
[47] And he was teaching daily in the temple. **The chief priests and the scribes** and the principal men of the people sought to destroy him; [48] but they did not find anything they could do, for all the people hung upon his words.

JOHN

John 2:13–22 (§J5.1)
[13] The Passover of the Jews was at hand, **and Jesus** went up to Jerusalem. [14] In **the temple** he found those who were selling oxen and sheep and pigeons, and the money-changers at their business. [15] And making a whip of cords, **he drove** them **all,** with the sheep and oxen, **out** of **the temple;** and he poured out the coins **of the money-changers** and **overturned** their **tables.** [16] And he told **those who sold** the **pigeons,** "Take these things away; you shall not make **my** Father's **house a house of** trade." [17] His disciples remembered that it was written, "Zeal for thy house will consume me." [18] The Jews then **said to him,** "What sign have you to show us for doing this?" [19] **Jesus** answered them, "Destroy this temple, and in three days I will raise it up." [20] The Jews then said, "It has taken forty-six years to build this temple, and will you raise it up in three days?" [21] But he spoke of the temple of his body. [22] When therefore he was raised from the dead, his disciples remembered that he had said this; and they believed the scripture and the word which Jesus had spoken.

THOMAS

OTHER

MATT

Matt 21:18–22 (§M73)

[18] In the morning, as he was returning to the city, he was hungry. [19] And seeing a fig tree by the wayside he went to it, and found nothing on it but leaves only. And he said to it, "May no fruit ever come from you again!" And the fig tree withered at once. [20] When the disciples saw it they marveled, saying, "How did the fig tree wither at once?" [21] And Jesus answered them, "Truly, I say to you, if you have faith and never doubt, you will not only do what has been done to the fig tree, but even if you say to this mountain, 'Be taken up and cast into the sea,' it will be done. [22] And whatever you ask in prayer, you will receive, if you have faith."

Matt 17:19–20 (§M59.2) ⇨ Matt 21:21

[19] Then the disciples came to Jesus privately and said, "Why could we not cast it out?" [20] He said to them, "Because of your little faith. For truly I say to you, if you have faith as a grain of mustard seed, you will say to this mountain, 'Move from here to there,' and it will move; and nothing will be impossible to you."

Matt 18:19 ⇨ Matt 21:22

[19] "Again I say to you, if two of you agree on earth about anything they ask, it will be done for them by my Father in heaven."

JOHN

John 14:13–14 ⇨ Matt 21:21–22

[13] "Whatever you ask in my name, I will do it, that the Father may be glorified in the Son; [14] if you ask anything in my name, I will do it."

John 15:7 ⇨ Matt 21:21–22

[7] "If you abide in me, and my words abide in you, ask whatever you will, and it shall be done for you."

John 16:23 ⇨ Matt 21:21–22

[23] "In that day you will ask nothing of me. Truly, truly, I say to you, if you ask anything of the Father, he will give it to you in my name."

MARK

Mark 11:12–14 (§K58.1)

[12] On the following day, when they came from Bethany, he was hungry. [13] And seeing in the distance a fig tree in leaf, he went to see if he could find anything on it. When he came to it, he found nothing but leaves, for it was not the season for figs. [14] And he said to it, "May no one ever eat fruit from you again." And his disciples heard it.

Mark 11:20–25 (§K59.1)

[20] As they passed by in the morning, they saw the fig tree withered away to its roots. [21] And Peter remembered and said to him, "Master, look! The fig tree which you cursed has withered." [22] And Jesus answered them, "Have faith in God. [23] Truly, I say to you, whoever says to this mountain, 'Be taken up and cast into the sea,' and does not doubt in his heart, but believes that what he says will come to pass, it will be done for him. [24] Therefore I tell you, whatever you ask in prayer, believe that you have received it, and it will be yours. [25] And whenever you stand praying, forgive, if you have anything against any one; so that your Father also who is in heaven may forgive you your trespasses."

THOMAS

GThom 48 ⇨ Matt 21:21

(48) Jesus said, "If two make peace with each other in this one house, they will say to the mountain, 'Move away,' and it will move away."

GThom 106 ⇨ Matt 21:21

(106) Jesus said, "When you make the two one, you will become the sons of man, and when you say, 'Mountain, move away,' it will move away."

LUKE

Luke 13:6–9 (§L57.2)

[6] And he told this parable: "A man had a fig tree planted in his vineyard; and he came seeking fruit on it and found none. [7] And he said to the vinedresser, 'Lo, these three years I have come seeking fruit on this fig tree, and I find none. Cut it down; why should it use up the ground?' [8] And he answered him, 'Let it alone, sir, this year also, till I dig about it and put on manure. [9] And if it bears fruit next year, well and good; but if not, you can cut it down.'"

Luke 17:5–6 (§L70.2) ⇨ Matt 21:21

[5] The apostles said to the Lord, "Increase our faith!" [6] And the Lord said, "If you had faith as a grain of mustard seed, you could say to this sycamine tree, 'Be rooted up, and be planted in the sea,' and it would obey you."

OTHER

InThom 3:1–3

[1] But the son of Annas the scribe was standing there with Joseph; and he took a branch of a willow and (with it) dispersed the water which Jesus had gathered together. [2] When Jesus saw what he had done he was enraged and said to him: "You insolent, godless dunderhead, what harm did the pools and the water do to you? See, now you also shall wither like a tree and shall bear neither leaves nor root nor fruit." [3] And immediately that lad withered up completely; and Jesus departed and went into Joseph's house. But the parents of him that was withered took him away, bewailing his youth, and brought him to Joseph and reproached him: "What a child you have, who does such things."

InThom 4:1–2

[1] After this again he went through the village, and a lad ran and knocked against his shoulder. Jesus was exasperated and said to him: "You shall not go further on your way," and the child immediately fell down and died. But some, who saw what took place, said: "From where does this child spring, since his every word is an accomplished deed?" [2] And the parents of the dead child came to Joseph and blamed him and said: "Since you have such a child, you cannot dwell with us in the village; or else teach him to bless and not to curse. For he is slaying our children."

Matt 21:23–27
Matt 21:28–32

QUESTION OF JESUS' AUTHORITY
PARABLE OF THE TWO SONS

M74.1
M74.2

MATT	MARK	LUKE

Matt 21:23–27 (§M74.1)

²³ And when he entered the temple, the chief priests and the elders of the people came up to him as he was teaching, and said, "By what authority are you doing these things, and who gave you this authority?" ²⁴ Jesus answered them, "I also will ask you a question; and if you tell me the answer, then I also will tell you by what authority I do these things. ²⁵ The baptism of John, whence was it? From heaven or from men?" And they argued with one another, "If we say, 'From heaven,' he will say to us, 'Why then did you not believe him?' ²⁶ But if we say, 'From men,' we are afraid of the multitude; for all hold that John was a prophet." ²⁷ So they answered Jesus, "We do not know." And he said to them, "Neither will I tell you by what authority I do these things."

Matt 21:28–32 (§M74.2)

²⁸ "What do you think? A man had two sons; and he went to the first and said, 'Son, go and work in the vineyard today.' ²⁹ And he answered, 'I will not'; but afterward he repented and went. ³⁰ And he went to the second and said the same; and he answered, 'I go, sir,' but did not go. ³¹ Which of the two did the will of his father?" They said, "The first." Jesus said to them, "Truly, I say to you, the tax collectors and the harlots go into the kingdom of God before you. ³² For John came to you in the way of righteousness, and you did not believe him, but the tax collectors and the harlots believed him; and even when you saw it, you did not afterward repent and believe him."

Mark 11:27–33 (§K59.2) ⇨ §M74.1

²⁷ And they came again to Jerusalem. And as he was walking in the temple, the chief priests and the scribes and the elders came to him, ²⁸ and they said to him, "By what authority are you doing these things, or who gave you this authority to do them?" ²⁹ Jesus said to them, "I will ask you a question; answer me, and I will tell you by what authority I do these things. ³⁰ Was the baptism of John from heaven or from men? Answer me." ³¹ And they argued with one another, "If we say, 'From heaven,' he will say, 'Why then did you not believe him?' ³² But shall we say, 'From men'?"—they were afraid of the people, for all held that John was a real prophet. ³³ So they answered Jesus, "We do not know." And Jesus said to them, "Neither will I tell you by what authority I do these things."

Luke 20:1–8 (§L84) ⇨ §M74.1

¹ One day, as he was teaching the people in the temple and preaching the gospel, the chief priests and the scribes with the elders came up ² and said to him, "Tell us by what authority you do these things, or who it is that gave you this authority." ³ He answered them, "I also will ask you a question; now tell me, ⁴ Was the baptism of John from heaven or from men?" ⁵ And they discussed it with one another, saying, "If we say, 'From heaven,' he will say, 'Why did you not believe him?' ⁶ But if we say, 'From men,' all the people will stone us; for they are convinced that John was a prophet." ⁷ So they answered that they did not know whence it was. ⁸ And Jesus said to them, "Neither will I tell you by what authority I do these things."

Luke 7:29–30 ⇨ Matt 21:32

²⁹ (When they heard this all the people and the tax collectors justified God, having been baptized with the baptism of John; ³⁰ but the Pharisees and the lawyers rejected the purpose of God for themselves, not having been baptized by him.)

OTHER

POxy840 2 ⇨ §M74.1

(2) And he took them (the disciples) with him into the place of purification itself and walked about in the Temple court. And a Pharisaic chief priest, Levi (?) by name, fell in with them and s[aid] to the Savior: Who gave thee leave to [trea]d this place of purification and to look upon [the]se holy utensils without having bathed thyself and even without thy disciples having [wa]shed their f[eet]? On the contrary, being defi[led], thou hast trodden the Temple court, this clean p[lace], although no [one who] has [not] first bathed himself or [chang]ed his clot[hes] may tread it and [venture] to vi[ew these] holy utensils! Forthwith [the Savior] s[tood] still with h[is] disciples and [answered]: How stands it (then) with thee, thou art forsooth (also) here in the Temple court. Art thou then clean? He said to him: I am clean. For I have bathed myself in the pool of David and have gone down by the one stair and come up by the other and have put on white and clean clothes, and (only) then have I come hither and have viewed these holy utensils. Then said the Savior to him: Woe unto you blind that see not! Thou hast bathed thyself in water that is poured out, in which dogs and swine lie night and day and thou hast washed thyself and hast chafed thine outer skin, which prostitutes also and flute-girls anoint, bathe, chafe and rouge, in order to arouse desire in men, but within they are full of scorpions and of [bad]ness [of every kind]. But I and [my disciples], of whom thou sayest that we have not im[mersed] ourselves, [have been im]mersed in the liv[ing . . .] water which comes down from [. . . B]ut woe unto them that . . .

JOHN	THOMAS

John 2:18 ⇨ Matt 21:23

¹⁸ The Jews then said to him, "What sign have you to show us for doing this?"

120
Matt 21:23–46
Matt 21:1–22:46

CONTROVERSIES
IN JERUSALEM

M74
S18: M71–76

MATT

Matt 21:33–46 (§M74.3)

[33] "Hear another parable. There was a householder who planted a vineyard, and set a hedge around it, and dug a wine press in it, and built a tower, and let it out to tenants, and went into another country. [34] When the season of fruit drew near, he sent his servants to the tenants, to get his fruit; [35] and the tenants took his servants and beat one, killed another, and stoned another. [36] Again he sent other servants, more than the first; and they did the same to them. [37] Afterward he sent his son to them, saying 'They will respect my son.' [38] But when the tenants saw the son, they said to themselves, 'This is the heir; come, let us kill him and have his inheritance.' [39] And they took him and cast him out of the vineyard, and killed him. [40] When therefore the owner of the vineyard comes, what will he do to those tenants?" [41] They said to him, "He will put those wretches to a miserable death, and let out the vineyard to other tenants who will give him the fruits in their seasons."

[42] Jesus said to them, "Have you never read in the scriptures:

'The very stone which the builders rejected

has become the head of the corner;

this was the Lord's doing,

and it is marvelous in our eyes'?

[43] Therefore I tell you, the kingdom of God will be taken away from you and given to a nation producing the fruits of it."[a]

[45] When the chief priests and the Pharisees heard his parables, they perceived that he was speaking about them. [46] But when they tried to arrest him, they feared the multitudes, because they held him to be a prophet.

[a] Some witnesses insert v. 44, *"And he who falls on this stone will be broken to pieces; but when it falls on any one, it will crush him":* (cf. Luke 20:18) ℵ B C K L W X △ Π 0138 *f¹ f¹³* 28 *pm*

Isa 5:1–2 ⇨ Matt 21:33

[1] Let me sing for my beloved a love song concerning his vineyard:

My beloved had **a vineyard**

on a very fertile hill.

[2] He digged **it** and cleared it of stones,

and **planted** it with choice vines;

he **built** a watchtower in the midst of it,

and hewed out **a wine** vat **in** it;

and he looked for it to yield grapes,

but it yielded wild grapes.

Ps 118:22–23 ⇨ Matt 21:42

[22] **The stone which the builders rejected**

has become the head of the corner.

[23] **This is the Lord's doing;**

it is marvelous in our eyes.

JOHN

MARK

Mark 12:1–12 (§K59.3)

[1] And he began to speak to them in parables. "A man **planted a vineyard, and set a hedge around it, and dug a** pit for the **wine press, and built a tower, and let it out to tenants, and went into another country.** [2] When the time came, **he sent** a servant **to the tenants, to get** from them some of the **fruit** of the vineyard. [3] **And** they **took** him **and beat** him, and sent him away empty-handed. [4] **Again he sent** to them another servant, **and they** wounded him in the head, and treated him shamefully. [5] And **he sent** another, and him **they** killed; and so with many others, some **they** beat and some **they** killed. [6] **He** had still one other, a beloved **son;** finally **he sent** him to them, saying, '**They will respect my son.**' [7] But those tenants said to one another, '**This is the heir; come, let us kill him, and** the **inheritance** will be ours.' [8] **And they took him and killed him, and cast him out of the vineyard.** [9] **What will the owner of the vineyard do?** He **will** come and destroy the tenants, and give **the vineyard to** others. [10] **Have you** not **read** this scripture:

'**The very stone which the builders rejected**

has become the head of the corner;

[11] this was the Lord's doing,

and it is marvelous in our eyes'?"

[12] And **they tried to arrest him**, but **feared** the multitude, for **they perceived that he** had told the parable against **them**; so they left him and went away.

THOMAS

GThom 65

(65) He said, "There was a good man who owned **a vineyard.** He leased **it to** tenant farmers so that they might work it and he might collect the produce from them. **He sent his** servant so that **the tenants** might give him the produce of the vineyard. They seized **his** servant **and beat** him, all but killing him. The servant went back and told his master. The master said, 'Perhaps <they> did not recognize <him>.' **He sent** another servant. The tenants beat this one as well. Then the owner **sent his son** and said, 'Perhaps **they will** show **respect** to **my son.**' Because **the tenants** knew that it was he who was **the heir** to the vineyard, **they** seized **him and killed him.** Let him who has ears hear."

GThom 66 ⇨ Matt 19:42

(66) Jesus said, "Show me **the stone which the builders** have **rejected.** That one is the cornerstone."

LUKE

Luke 20:9–19 (§L85)

[9] And he began to tell the people this **parable:** "**A** man **planted a vineyard, and let it out to tenants, and went into another country** for a long while. [10] **When the** time came, **he sent** a servant **to the tenants,** that they should give him some of the **fruit** of the vineyard; but **the tenants beat** him, and sent him away empty-handed. [11] **And he sent** another servant; him also **they** beat and treated shamefully, and sent him away empty-handed. [12] **And he sent** yet a third; this one they wounded and cast out. [13] Then the owner of the vineyard said, 'What shall I do? I will send my beloved **son;** it may be **they will respect** him.' [14] **But when the tenants saw** him, **they said to themselves,** 'This is the heir; let us kill him, that the inheritance may be ours.' [15] **And they cast him out of the vineyard and killed him. What** then **will the owner of the vineyard do to them?** [16] **He will** come and destroy those tenants, and give **the vineyard to** others." When they heard this, they said, "God forbid!" [17] But he looked at them and said, "What then is this that is written:

'**The very stone which the builders rejected**

has become the head of the corner'?

[18] Every one who falls on that stone will be broken to pieces; but when it falls on any one it will crush him."

[19] The scribes and **the chief priests tried to** lay hands on **him** at that very hour, but **they feared the** people; for **they perceived that he** had told this parable against **them.**

OTHER

MATT

MARK

LUKE

Matt 22:1–14 (§M75)

¹And again Jesus spoke to them in parables, saying, ²"The kingdom of heaven may be compared to a king who gave a marriage feast for his son, ³and sent his servants to call those who were invited to the marriage feast; but they would not come. ⁴Again he sent other servants, saying, 'Tell those who are invited, Behold, I have made ready my dinner, my oxen and my fat calves are killed, and everything is ready; come to the marriage feast.' ⁵But they made light of it and went off, one to his farm, another to his business, ⁶while the rest seized his servants, treated them shamefully, and killed them. ⁷The king was angry, and he sent his troops and destroyed those murderers and burned their city. ⁸Then he said to his servants, 'The wedding is ready, but those invited were not worthy. ⁹Go therefore to the thoroughfares, and invite to the marriage feast as many as you find.' ¹⁰And those servants went out into the streets and gathered all whom they found, both bad and good; so the wedding hall was filled with guests.

¹¹"But when the king came in to look at the guests, he saw there a man who had no wedding garment; ¹²and he said to him, 'Friend, how did you get in here without a wedding garment?' And he was speechless. ¹³Then the king said to the attendants, 'Bind him hand and foot, and cast him into the outer darkness; there men will weep and gnash their teeth.' ¹⁴For many are called, but few are chosen."

Matt 8:12 ⇨ Matt 22:13

¹²"while the sons of the kingdom will be thrown into the outer darkness; there men will weep and gnash their teeth."

Matt 13:42 ⇨ Matt 22:13

⁴²"and throw them into the furnace of fire; there men will weep and gnash their teeth."

Matt 13:50 ⇨ Matt 22:13

⁵⁰"and throw them into the furnace of fire; there men will weep and gnash their teeth."

Matt 24:51 ⇨ Matt 22:13

⁵¹"and will punish him, and put him with the hypocrites; there men will weep and gnash their teeth."

Matt 25:30 ⇨ Matt 22:13

³⁰"'And cast the worthless servant into the outer darkness; there men will weep and gnash their teeth.'"

JOHN

THOMAS

GThom 64

(64) **Jesus** said, "A man had received visitors. And when he had prepared the dinner, he **sent his** servant **to** invite the guests. He went to the first one and said to him, 'My master invites you.' He said, 'I have claims against some merchants. They are coming to me this evening. I must go and give them my orders. I ask to be excused from the dinner.' He went to another and said to him, 'My master has invited you.' He said to him, 'I have just bought a house and am required for the day. I shall not have any spare time.' He went to another and said to him, 'My master invites you.' He said to him, 'My friend is going to get married, and I am to prepare the banquet. I shall not be able to come. I ask to be excused from the dinner.' He went to another and said to him, 'My master invites you.' He said to him, 'I have just bought a farm, and I am on my way to collect the rent. I shall not be able to come. I ask to be excused.' The servant returned and said to his master, 'Those whom you invited to the dinner have asked to be excused.' **The** master **said to his** servant, '**Go** outside to **the streets and** bring back those **whom** you happen to meet, so that they may dine.' Businessmen and merchants will **not** enter the Places of My Father."

GThom 23 ⇨ Matt 22:14

(23) Jesus said, "I shall choose you, one out of a thousand, and two out of ten thousand, and they shall stand as a single one."

Luke 14:15–24 (§L64)

¹⁵When one of those who sat at table with him heard this, he said to him, "Blessed is he who shall eat bread in the kingdom of God!" ¹⁶But he said to him "**A** man once **gave a** great banquet, and invited many; ¹⁷and at the time for the banquet **he sent his** servant to say to **those who** had been **invited**, 'Come; for all is now ready.' ¹⁸**But they** all alike began to make excuses. The first said to him, 'I have bought a field, and I must go out and see it; I pray you, have me excused.' ¹⁹And another said, 'I have bought five yoke of oxen, and I go to examine them; I pray you, have me excused.' ²⁰And another said, 'I have married a wife, and therefore I cannot come.' ²¹So the servant came and reported this to his master. Then the householder in **anger said to his** servant, '**Go** out quickly to **the streets** and lanes of the city, and bring in the poor and maimed and blind and lame.' ²²And the servant said, 'Sir, what you commanded has been done, and still there is room.' ²³And the master said to the servant, '**Go** out **to the** highways and hedges, **and** compel people to come in, that my house may be **filled**. ²⁴For I tell you, none of those men who were **invited** shall taste my banquet.'"

OTHER

MATT

Matt 22:15–22 (§M76.1)

¹⁵ Then the Pharisees went and took counsel how to entangle him in his talk. ¹⁶ And they sent their disciples to him, along with the Herodians, saying, "Teacher, we know that you are true, and teach the way of God truthfully, and care for no man; for you do not regard the position of men. ¹⁷ Tell us, then, what you think. Is it lawful to pay taxes to Caesar, or not?" ¹⁸ But Jesus, aware of their malice, said, "Why put me to the test, you hypocrites? ¹⁹ Show me the money for the tax." And they brought him a coin.ᵃ ²⁰ And Jesus said to them, "Whose likeness and inscription is this?" ²¹ They said, "Caesar's." Then he said to them, "Render therefore to Caesar the things that are Caesar's, and to God the things that are God's." ²² When they heard it, they marveled; and they left him and went away.

ᵃ Greek: *denarius*

MARK

Mark 12:13–17 (§K59.4)

¹³ And they sent to him some of **the Pharisees** and some of **the Herodians**, to entrap **him in his talk.** ¹⁴ And they came and said to him, **"Teacher, we know that you are true, and care for no man;** for you do not regard the position of men; but truly teach the way of God. **Is it lawful to pay taxes to Caesar, or not?** ¹⁵ Should we pay them, or should we not?" But knowing their hypocrisy, he **said** to them, **"Why put me to the test?** Bring me **a coin,** and let me look at it." ¹⁶ And they brought one. And he said to them, **"Whose likeness and inscription is this?"** They **said** to him, **"Caesar's."** ¹⁷ Jesus **said to them, "Render to Caesar the things that are Caesar's, and to God the things that are God's."** And **they** were amazed at **him.**

LUKE

Luke 20:20–26 (§L86)

²⁰ So they watched him, and sent spies, who pretended to be sincere, that they might take hold of what he said, so as to deliver him up to the authority and jurisdiction of the governor. ²¹ They asked him, **"Teacher, we know that you** speak and teach rightly, and show no partiality, but truly **teach the way of God.** ²² Is it lawful** for **us** to give tribute **to Caesar, or not?"** ²³ But he perceived **their** craftiness, and said to them, ²⁴ **"Show me a coin. Whose likeness and inscription** has it?" They said, **"Caesar's."** ²⁵ He said to them, **"Then render to Caesar the things that are Caesar's, and to God the things that are God's."** ²⁶ And they were not able in the presence of the people to catch him by what he said; but marveling at his answer they were silent.

JOHN

John 3:2 ⇨ Matt 22:16

² *This man came to Jesus by night and said to him, "Rabbi, we know that you are a teacher come from God; for no one can do these signs that you do, unless God is with him."*

THOMAS

GThom 100

(100) **They** showed Jesus **a** gold **coin** and said to Him, "Caesar's men demand **taxes** from us."

He said to them, "Give **Caesar** what belongs to Caesar, give **God** what belongs to God, and give **Me** what is Mine."

OTHER

PEger2 3

(3) . . . [ca]me to him to put **him** to the pro[of] and to tempt **him,** whilst [they said]: "Master Jesus, **we know that** thou art come [from **God**], for what thou doest bears a test[imony] (to thee which goes) beyond (that) of all the prophets. [Wherefore **tell**] **us: is it** admissible [**to p]ay to** the kings the (charges) appertaining to their rule? [Should we] pay [th]em **or not?"** But **Jesus** saw through **their** [in]tention, became [angry] and **said** to them: **"Why** call ye **me** with yo[ur mou]th Master and yet [do] not what I say? Well has Is[aiah] prophesied [concerning y]ou saying: This [people honours] me with the[ir li]ps but their heart is far from me; [their worship is] vain. [They teach] precepts [of men]." (Fragment 2, recto [lines 43–59])

Rom 13:7 ⇨ Matt 22:21

⁷ *Pay all of them their dues, taxes to whom taxes are due, revenue to whom revenue is due, respect to whom respect is due, honor to whom honor is due.*

MATT

Matt 22:23–33 (§M76.2)

²³ The same day Sadducees came to him, who say that there is no resurrection; and they asked him a question, ²⁴ saying, "Teacher, Moses said, 'If a man dies, having no children, his brother must marry the widow, and raise up children for his brother.' ²⁵ Now there were seven brothers among us; the first married, and died, and having no children left his wife to his brother. ²⁶ So too the second and third, down to the seventh. ²⁷ After them all, the woman died. ²⁸ In the resurrection, therefore, to which of the seven will she be wife? For they all had her."

²⁹ But Jesus answered them, "You are wrong, because you know neither the scriptures nor the power of God. ³⁰ For in the resurrection they neither marry nor are given in marriage, but are like angels[a] in heaven. ³¹ And as for the resurrection of the dead, have you not read what was said to you by God, ³² 'I am the God of Abraham, and the God of Isaac, and the God of Jacob'? He is not God of the dead, but of the living." ³³ And when the crowd heard it, they were astonished at his teaching.

[a] Add *of God:* ℵ K L W Δ Π *f*¹³ 28 *al*

Matt 7:28–29 (§M12.9) ⇨ Matt 22:33
²⁸ *And when Jesus finished these sayings, the crowds were astonished at his teaching,* ²⁹ *for he taught them as one who had authority, and not as their scribes.*

Matt 13:54 ⇨ Matt 22:33
⁵⁴ *and coming to his own country he taught them in their synagogue, so that they were astonished and said, "Where did this man get this wisdom and these mighty works?"*

Gen 38:8 ⇨ Matt 22:24
⁸ Then Judah said to Onan, "Go in to your brother's wife, and perform the duty of a brother-in-law to her, **and raise up** offspring **for** your **brother.**"

Deut 25:5–6 ⇨ Matt 22:24
⁵ "If brothers dwell together, and one of them **dies** and has **no** son, the wife of the dead shall not be married outside the family to a stranger; her husband's **brother** shall go in to her, and take her as his wife, and perform the duty of a husband's **brother** to her. ⁶ And the first son whom she bears shall succeed to the name of his brother who is dead, that his name may not be blotted out of Israel."

Exod 3:6 ⇨ Matt 22:32
⁶ And he said, "**I am the God of** your father, **the God of Abraham, the God of Isaac, and the God of Jacob.**" And Moses hid his face, for he was afraid to look at **God.**

JOHN

MARK

Mark 12:18–27 (§K59.5)

¹⁸ And **Sadducees came to him, who say that there is no resurrection;** and they asked him a question, saying, ¹⁹ "Teacher, Moses wrote for us that **if** a man's **brother dies** and leaves a wife, but leaves **no child,** the man **must take the wife, and raise up children for** his brother. ²⁰ There were **seven brothers; the first took a wife, and when he died** left **no children;** ²¹ and **the second** took her, and died, leaving no children; **and the third** likewise; ²² and the seven left no children. Last of all **the** woman also **died.** ²³ In **the resurrection** whose **wife will she be? For** the seven **had her** as wife."

²⁴ **Jesus** said to **them,** "Is not this why **you are wrong,** that **you know neither the scriptures nor the power of God?** ²⁵ For when they rise from the dead, **they neither marry nor are given** in marriage, but are like angels in heaven. ²⁶ And as for the dead being raised, have you **not read** in the book of Moses, in the passage about the bush, how **God said to** him, 'I am the God of Abraham, and the God of Isaac, and the God of Jacob?' ²⁷ He is not God of the dead, but of the living; you are quite wrong."

THOMAS

LUKE

Luke 20:27–40 (§L87)

²⁷ There **came to him** some **Sadducees,** those **who say that there is no resurrection,** ²⁸ and they asked him a question, saying, "Teacher, Moses wrote for us that **if** a man's brother **dies, having** a wife but **no children,** the man **must** take the wife **and raise up children for his brother.** ²⁹ Now **there were seven brothers; the first** took a **wife, and died** without **children;** ³⁰ and **the second** ³¹ and the **third** took her, and likewise all **seven** left no children and died. ³² Afterward **the woman** also died. ³³ In the **resurrection, therefore,** whose wife **will the woman be? For** the seven **had her** as wife."

³⁴ And **Jesus** said to **them,** "The sons of this age marry and are given in marriage; ³⁵ but those who are accounted worthy to attain to that age and to **the resurrection** from the dead **neither marry nor are given in marriage,** ³⁶ for they cannot die any more, because they **are** equal to **angels** and are sons of God, being sons of **the resurrection.** ³⁷ But that **the dead** are raised, even Moses showed, in the passage about the bush, where he calls the Lord **the God of Abraham and the God of Isaac and the God of Jacob.** ³⁸ Now **he is not God of the dead, but of the living;** for all live to him." ³⁹ And some of the scribes answered, "Teacher, you have spoken well." ⁴⁰ For they no longer dared to ask him any question.

OTHER

1 Cor 15:12 ⇨ Matt 22:23, 31–32
¹² *Now if Christ is preached as raised from the dead, how can some of you say that there is no resurrection of the dead?*

MATT	MARK	LUKE

Matt 22:34–40 (§M76.3)

[34] But when the Pharisees heard that he had silenced the Sadducees, they came together. [35] And one of them, a lawyer, asked him a question, to test him. [36] "Teacher, which is the great commandment in the law?" [37] And he said to him, "You shall love the Lord your God with all your heart, and with all your soul, and with all your mind. [38] This is the great and first commandment. [39] And a second is like it, You shall love your neighbor as yourself. [40] On these two commandments depend all the law and the prophets."

Deut 6:5 ⇨ Matt 22:37
[5] "and you shall love the Lord your God with all your heart, and with all your soul, and with all your might."

Lev 19:18 ⇨ Matt 22:39
[18] "You shall not take vengeance or bear any grudge against the sons of your own people, but **you shall love your neighbor as yourself**: I am the Lord."

Mark 12:28–34 (§K59.6)

[28] **And one of** the scribes came up and heard them disputing with one another, and seeing that he answered them well, **asked him, "Which commandment is the first** of all?" [29] Jesus answered, "The first is, 'Hear, O Israel: The Lord our God, the Lord is one; [30] and **you shall love the Lord your God with all your heart, and with all your soul, and with all your mind**, and with all your strength.' [31] The **second is** this, '**You shall love your neighbor as yourself.**' There is no other commandment greater than **these.**" [32] And the scribe said to him, "You are right, Teacher; you have truly said that he is one, and there is no other but he; [33] and to love him **with all the heart, and with all** the understanding, and with all the strength, and to **love** one's **neighbor as** oneself, is much more than all whole burnt offerings and sacrifices." [34] And when Jesus saw that he answered wisely, he said to him, "You are not far from the kingdom of God." And after that no one dared to ask him any question.

Luke 10:25–29 (§L48.1)

[25] And behold, a lawyer stood up to put **him** to the test, saying, "**Teacher**, what shall I do to inherit eternal life?" [26] He said to him, "What is written in the law? How do you read?" [27] And he answered, "**You shall love the Lord your God with all your heart, and with all your soul, and with all your** strength, and with all your mind; and your neighbor as yourself." [28] And he said to him, "You have answered right; do this, and you will live." [29] But he, desiring to justify himself, said to Jesus, "And who is my neighbor?"

JOHN	THOMAS	OTHER

GThom 25 ⇨ Matt 22:39
(25) Jesus said, "**Love your** brother like your soul, guard him like the pupil of your eye."

OTHER

Rom 13:8–10
[8] Owe no one anything, except to **love** one another; for he who loves his **neighbor** has fulfilled **the law**. [9] **The** commandments, "**You shall** not commit adultery, **You shall** not kill, **You shall** not steal, **You shall** not covet," and any other commandment, are summed up in this sentence, "**You shall love your neighbor as yourself.**" [10] **Love** does no wrong to a **neighbor**; therefore **love** is the fulfilling of **the law**.

Gal 5:13–15
[13] For you were called to freedom, brethren; only do not use your freedom as an opportunity for the flesh, but through **love** be servants of one another. [14] For **the** whole **law** is fulfilled in one word, "**You shall love your neighbor as yourself.**" [15] But if you bite and devour one another take heed that you are not consumed by one another.

Did 1:2
[2] The Way of Life is this: "First, thou shalt **love the God** who made thee, secondly, thy neighbour **as** thyself; and whatsoever thou wouldst not have done to thyself, do not thou to another."

Barn 19:5 ⇨ Matt 22:39
[5] Thou shalt not be in two minds whether it shall be or not. "Thou shalt not take the name of the Lord in vain." Thou shalt **love** thy neighbour more than thy own life. Thou shalt not procure abortion, thou shalt not commit infanticide. Thou shalt not withhold thy hand from thy son or from thy daughter, but shalt teach them the fear of God from their youth up.

MATT	MARK	LUKE

Matt 22:41–46 (§M76.4)

[41] Now while the Pharisees were gathered together, Jesus asked them a question, [42] saying, "What do you think of the Christ? Whose son is he?" They said to him, "The son of David." [43] He said to them, "How is it then that David, inspired by the Spirit,[a] calls him Lord, saying,

[44] 'The Lord said to my Lord,
Sit at my right hand,
till I put thy enemies under thy feet'?
[45] If David thus calls him Lord, how is he his son?" [46] And no one was able to answer him a word, nor from that day did any one dare to ask him any more questions.

[a] Or: *David in the Spirit*

Ps 110:1 ⇨ Matt 22:44
[1] The Lord says to my lord:
"Sit at my right hand,
till I make your enemies
your footstool."

2 Sam 7:12–16
[12] "'When your days are fulfilled and you lie down with your fathers, I will raise up your offspring after you, who shall come forth from your body, and I will establish his kingdom. [13] He shall build a house for my name, and I will establish the throne of his kingdom for ever. [14] I will be his father, and he shall be my son. When he commits iniquity, I will chasten him with the rod of men, with the stripes of the sons of men; [15] but I will not take my steadfast love from him, as I took it from Saul, whom I put away from before you. [16] And your house and your kingdom shall be made sure for ever before me; your throne shall be established for ever.'"

Ps 89:3–4
[3] Thou hast said, "I have made a covenant with my chosen one,
I have sworn to **David** my servant:
[4] 'I will establish your descendants for ever,
and build your throne for all generations.'"

Mic 5:2
[2] But you, O Bethlehem Ephrathah,
who are little to be among the clans of Judah,
from you shall come forth for me
one who is to be ruler in Israel,
whose origin is from of old,
from ancient days.

Mark 12:35–37 (§K59.7)

[35] And as **Jesus** taught in the temple, he said, "How can the scribes say that **the Christ** is the **son** of David? [36] **David** himself, **inspired by the** Holy **Spirit**, declared,

'The Lord said to my Lord,
Sit at my right hand,
till I put thy enemies under thy feet.'
[37] David himself **calls him Lord**; so **how is he his son?**" And the great throng heard him gladly.

Mark 12:34 ⇨ Matt 22:46
[34] And when *Jesus saw that he answered wisely, he said to him, "You are not far from the kingdom of God." And after that no one dared to ask him any question.*

Luke 20:41–44 (§L88)

[41] But **he said to them**, "How can they say that **the Christ** is David's **son**? [42] For **David** himself says in the Book of Psalms,

'The Lord said to my Lord,
Sit at my right hand,
[43] till I make thy **enemies** a stool for **thy feet.'**
[44] David thus calls him Lord; so how is he his son?"

Luke 20:40 ⇨ Matt 22:46
[40] *For they no longer dared to ask him any question.*

JOHN	THOMAS	OTHER

John 7:40–44

[40] *When they heard these words, some of the people said, "This is really the prophet." [41] Others said, "This is the Christ." But some said, "Is the Christ to come from Galilee? [42] Has not the scripture said that the Christ is descended from David, and comes from Bethlehem, the village where David was?" [43] So there was a division among the people over him. [44] Some of them wanted to arrest him, but no one laid hands on him.*

1 Cor 15:20–28

[20] *But in fact Christ has been raised from the dead, the first fruits of those who have fallen asleep. [21] For as by a man came death, by a man has come also the resurrection of the dead. [22] For as in Adam all die, so also in Christ shall all be made alive. [23] But each in his own order: Christ the first fruits, then at his coming those who belong to Christ. [24] Then comes the end, when he delivers the kingdom to God the Father after destroying every rule and every authority and power. [25] For he must reign until he has put all his enemies under his feet. [26] The last enemy to be destroyed is death. [27] "For God has put all things in subjection under his feet." But when it says, "All things are put in subjection under him," it is plain that he is excepted who put all things under him. [28] When all things are subjected to him, then the Son himself will also be subjected to him who put all things under him, that God may be everything to every one.*

MATT

MARK

LUKE

Matt 23:1–12 (§M77.1)
[1] Then said Jesus to the crowds and to his disciples, [2] "The scribes and the Pharisees sit on Moses' seat; [3] so practice and observe whatever they tell you, but not what they do; for they preach, but do not practice. [4] They bind heavy burdens, hard to bear,[a] and lay them on men's shoulders; but they themselves will not move them with their finger. [5] They do all their deeds to be seen by men; for they make their phylacteries broad and their fringes long, [6] and they love the place of honor at feasts and the best seats in the synagogues, [7] and salutations in the market places, and being called rabbi by men. [8] But you are not to be called rabbi, for you have one teacher, and you are all brethren. [9] And call no man your father on earth, for you have one Father, who is in heaven. [10] Neither be called masters, for you have one master, the Christ. [11] He who is greatest among you shall be your servant; [12] whoever exalts himself will be humbled, and whoever humbles himself will be exalted."

[a] Omit, *hard to bear:* ℵ L *f*¹ 892 *al*

Matt 18:1–5 ⇨ Matt 23:11–12
[1] At that time the disciples came to Jesus, saying, "Who is the greatest in the kingdom of heaven?" [2] And calling to him a child, he put him in the midst of them, [3] and said, "Truly, I say to you, unless you turn and become like children, you will never enter the kingdom of heaven. [4] Whoever humbles himself like this child, he is the greatest in the kingdom of heaven.
[5] "Whoever receives one such child in my name receives me"; . . .

Matt 20:24–28 (§M69.2) ⇨ Matt 23:11
[24] And when the ten heard it, they were indignant at the two brothers. [25] But Jesus called them to him and said, "You know that the rulers of the Gentiles lord it over them, and their great men exercise authority over them. [26] It shall not be so among you; but whoever would be great among you must be your servant, [27] and whoever would be first among you must be your slave; [28] even as the Son of man came not to be served but to serve, and to give his life as a ransom for many."

⇨ Matt 23:11
Cf. Matt 15:1–9 (§M49.1)

Num 15:37–39 ⇨ Matt 23:5
[37] The Lord said to Moses, [38] "Speak to the people of Israel, and bid them to make tassels on the corners of their garments throughout their generations, and to put upon the tassel of each corner a cord of blue; [39] and it shall be to you a tassel to look upon and remember all the commandments of the Lord, to do them, not to follow after your own heart and your own eyes, which you are inclined to go after wantonly."

Mark 12:38–40 (§K59.8) ⇨ Matt 23:6–7
[38] And in his teaching he said, "Beware of the scribes, who like to go about in long robes, and to have **salutations in the market places** [39] **and the best seats in the synagogues and the** places **of honor at feasts,** [40] who devour widows' houses and for a pretense make long prayers. They will receive the greater condemnation."

Mark 9:33–37 (§K47) ⇨ Matt 23:11
[33] And they came to Capernaum; and when he was in the house he asked them, "What were you discussing on the way?" [34] But they were silent; for on the way they had discussed with one another **who** was the **greatest.** [35] And he sat down and called the twelve; and he said to them, "If any one would be first, he must be last of all and **servant** of all." [36] And he took a child, and put him in the midst of them; and taking him in his arms, he said to them, [37] "Whoever receives one such child in my name receives me; and whoever receives me, receives not me but him who sent me."

Mark 10:41–45 (§K55.2) ⇨ Matt 23:11
[41] And when the ten heard it, they began to be indignant at James and John. [42] And Jesus called them to him and said to them, "You know that those who are supposed to rule over the Gentiles lord it over them, and their great men exercise authority over them. [43] But it shall not be so among you; but whoever would be great **among you** must **be your servant,** [44] and whoever would be first **among you** must **be** slave of all. [45] For the Son of man also came not to be served but to serve, and to give his life as a ransom for many."

Cf. Mark 7:1–13 (§K33)

Luke 20:45–47 (§L89) ⇨ Matt 23:6–7
[45] And in the hearing of all the people he said to his disciples, [46] "Beware of the scribes, who like to go about in long robes, and love **salutations in the market places and the best seats in the synagogues** and the places **of honor at feasts,** [47] who devour widows' houses and for a pretense make long prayers. They will receive the greater condemnation."

Luke 9:46–50 (§L43.2) ⇨ Matt 23:11
[46] And an argument arose among them as to which of them was the **greatest.** [47] But when Jesus perceived the thought of their hearts, he took a child and put him by his side, [48] and said to them, "Whoever receives this child in my name receives me, and whoever receives me receives him who sent me; **for he who is** least **among you** all is the one who is great."
[49] John answered, "Master, we saw a man casting out demons in your name, and we forbade him, because he does not follow with us." [50] But Jesus said to him, "Do not forbid him; for he that is not against you is for you."

Luke 22:24–30 (§L93.3) ⇨ Matt 23:11
[24] A dispute also arose among them, which of them was to be regarded as the **greatest.** [25] And he said to them, "The kings of the Gentiles exercise lordship over them; and those in authority over them are called benefactors. [26] But not so with you; rather let the **greatest among you** become as the youngest, and the leader as one who serves. [27] For which is the greater, one who sits at table, or one who serves? Is it not the one who sits at table? But I am among you as one who serves.
[28] "You are those who have continued with me in my trials; [29] and I assign to you, as my Father assigned to me, a kingdom, [30] that you may eat and drink at my table in my kingdom, and sit on thrones judging the twelve tribes of Israel."

Luke 14:11 ⇨ Matt 23:12
[11] "For every one who **exalts himself will be humbled,** and he who **humbles himself will be exalted.**"

Luke 18:14 ⇨ Matt 23:12
[14] "I tell you, this man went down to his house justified rather than the other; for every one who **exalts himself will be humbled,** but he who **humbles himself will be exalted.**"

JOHN

THOMAS

OTHER

MATT	MARK	LUKE

Matt 23:13–36 (§M77.2)

[13] "But woe to you, scribes and Pharisees, hypocrites! because you shut the kingdom of heaven against men; for you neither enter yourselves, nor allow those who would enter to go in.[a] [15] Woe to you, scribes and Pharisees, hypocrites! for you traverse sea and land to make a single proselyte, and when he becomes a proselyte, you make him twice as much a child of hell[b] as yourselves.

[16] "Woe to you, blind guides, who say, 'If any one swears by the temple, it is nothing; but if any one swears by the gold of the temple, he is bound by his oath.' [17] You blind fools! For which is greater, the gold or the temple that has made the gold sacred? [18] And you say, 'If any one swears by the altar, it is nothing; but if any one swears by the gift that is on the altar, he is bound by his oath.' [19] You blind men! For which is greater, the gift or the altar that makes the gift sacred? [20] So he who swears by the altar, swears by it and by everything on it; [21] and he who swears by the temple, swears by it and by him who dwells in it; [22] and he who swears by heaven, swears by the throne of God and by him who sits upon it.

[23] "Woe to you, scribes and Pharisees, hypocrites! for you tithe mint and dill and cummin, and have neglected the weightier matters of the law, justice and mercy and faith; these you ought to have done, without neglecting the others. [24] You blind guides, straining out a gnat and swallowing a camel!

[25] "Woe to you, scribes and Pharisees, hypocrites! for you cleanse the outside of the cup and of the plate, but inside they are full of extortion and rapacity. [26] You blind Pharisee! first cleanse the inside of the cup and of the plate, that the outside also may be clean.

[27] "Woe to you, scribes and Pharisees, hypocrites! for you are like whitewashed tombs, which outwardly appear beautiful, but within they are full of dead men's bones and all uncleanness. [28] So you also outwardly appear righteous to men, but within you are full of hypocrisy and iniquity.

[29] "Woe to you, scribes and Pharisees, hypocrites! for you build the tombs of the prophets and adorn the monuments of the righteous, [30] saying, 'If we had lived in the days of our fathers, we would not have taken part with them in shedding the blood of the prophets.' [31] Thus you witness against yourselves, that you are sons of those who murdered the prophets. [32] Fill up, then, the measure of your fathers. [33] You serpents, you brood of vipers, how are you to escape being sentenced to hell? [34] Therefore I send you prophets and wise men and scribes, some of whom you will kill and crucify, and some you will scourge in your synagogues and persecute from town to town, [35] that upon you may come all the righteous blood shed on earth, from the blood of innocent Abel to the blood of Zechariah the son of Barachiah, whom you murdered between the sanctuary and the altar. [36] Truly, I say to you, all this will come upon this generation."

Cf. Mark 7:1–13 (§K33)

Cf. Mark 12:38–40 (§K59.8)

---

[a] Some witnesses insert v. 14 here or before v. 12, *"Woe to you, scribes and Pharisees, hypocrites! for you devour widows' houses and for a pretense you make long prayers; therefore you will receive the greater condemnation:* (cf. Mark 12:40, Luke 20:47) K W △ Π 0107 0138 28 *al*

[b] Greek: *Gehenna*

Matt 3:7 ⇨ Matt 23:33

[7] But when he saw many of the Pharisees and Sadducees coming for baptism, he said to them, "**You brood of vipers!** Who warned **you to** flee from the wrath **to** come?"

Gen 4:8 ⇨ Matt 23:35

[8] Cain said to **Abel** his brother, "Let us go out to the field." And when they were in the field, Cain rose up against his brother **Abel**, and killed him.

2 Chr 24:20–21 ⇨ Matt 23:35

[20] Then the Spirit of God took possession of **Zechariah the son of** Jehoiada the priest; and he stood above the people, and said to them, "Thus says God, 'Why do you transgress the commandments of the Lord, so that you cannot prosper? Because you have forsaken the Lord, he has forsaken you.'" [21] But they conspired against him, and by command of the king they stoned him with stones in the court of the house of the Lord.

Zech 1:1 ⇨ Matt 23:35

[1] In the eighth month, in the second year of Darius, the word of the Lord came to **Zechariah the son of** Berechiah, son of Iddo, the prophet, saying, . . .

Luke 11:37–44 (§L52.1)

[37] While he was speaking, a Pharisee asked him to dine with him; so he went in and sat at table. [38] The Pharisee was astonished to see that he did not first wash before dinner. [39] And the Lord said to him, "Now you **Pharisees cleanse the outside of the cup and of the** dish, **but inside** you **are full of extortion and** wickedness. [40] **You** fools! Did not he who made the **outside** make the **inside** also? [41] But give for alms those things which are within; and behold, everything is **clean** for you.

[42] "But **woe to you Pharisees! for you tithe mint and** rue and every herb, and neglect **justice** and the love of God; **these you ought to have done, without neglecting the others.** [43] **Woe to you** Pharisees! for you love the best seat in the synagogues and salutations in the market places. [44] **Woe to you! for you are like** graves **which** are not seen, and men walk over them without knowing it."

Luke 11:45–54 (§L52.2)

[45] One of the lawyers answered him, "Teacher, in saying this you reproach us also." [46] And he said, "**Woe to you** lawyers also! for you load men with burdens hard to bear, and you yourselves do not touch the burdens with one of your fingers. [47] **Woe to you! for you build the tombs of the prophets** whom your **fathers** killed. [48] So **you** are witnesses and consent to the deeds of your **fathers**; for they killed them, and **you build their tombs.** [49] **Therefore** also the Wisdom of God said, 'I will **send** them **prophets and** apostles, **some of whom** they **will kill and** persecute,' [50] **that the blood** of all the prophets, **shed** from the foundation of the world, may be required of **this generation,** [51] **from the blood of Abel to the blood of Zechariah,** who perished **between the altar and the sanctuary.** Yes, **I tell you,** it shall be required of **this generation.** [52] **Woe to you** lawyers! for you have taken away the key of knowledge; you did not enter yourselves, and you hindered those who were entering."

[53] As he went away from there, the scribes and the Pharisees began to press him hard, and to provoke him to speak of many things, [54] lying in wait for him, to catch at something he might say.

Luke 3:7 ⇨ Matt 23:33

[7] He said therefore to the multitudes that came out to be baptized by him, "**You brood of vipers!** Who warned **you to** flee from the wrath to come?"

JOHN	THOMAS	OTHER

THOMAS

POxy655 2 ⇨ Matt 23:13

(2) [Jesus says, "The **Pharisees** and the **scribes** have] re[ceived the keys] of [knowledge and] have hid[den them; **neither** have they] enter[ed **nor** permitted] **those who** wo[uld] en[ter. But you] b[ecome wi]se [as serpents and g]uile[less as do]ve[s]."

GThom 39 ⇨ Matt 23:13

(39) Jesus said, "The **Pharisees and** the **scribes** have taken the keys of Knowledge and hidden them. They themselves have not entered, **nor** have they allowed to **enter those who** wish to. You, however, be as wise as serpents and as innocent as doves."

GThom 102 ⇨ Matt 23:13

(102) Jesus said, "**Woe to** the **Pharisees**, for they are like a dog sleeping in the manger of oxen, **for neither** does he eat **nor** does he let the oxen eat."

GThom 89 ⇨ Matt 23:25–26

(89) Jesus said, "Why do you wash **the outside of the cup**? Do you not realize that he who made **the inside** is the same one who made **the outside?**"

OTHER

POxy840 2 ⇨ Matt 23:25–26

*(2) And he took them (the disciples) with him into the place of purification itself and walked about in the Temple court. And a Pharisaic chief priest, Levi (?) by name, fell in with them and s[aid] to the Savior: Who gave thee leave to [trea]d this place of purification and to look upon [the]se holy utensils without having bathed thyself and even without thy disciples having [wa]shed their f[eet]? On the contrary, being defi[led], thou hast trodden the Temple court, this clean p[lace], although no [one who] has [not] first bathed himself or [chang]ed his clot[hes] may tread it and [venture] to vi[ew these] holy utensils! Forthwith [the Savior] s[tood] still with h[is] disciples and [answered]: How stands it (then) with thee, thou art forsooth (also) here in the Temple court. Art thou then clean? He said to him: I am clean. For I have bathed myself in the pool of David and have gone down by the one stair and come up by the other and have put on white and clean clothes, and (only) then have I come hither and have viewed these holy utensils. Then said the Savior to him: **Woe** unto **you blind** that see not! Thou hast bathed thyself in water that is poured out, in which dogs and swine lie night and day and thou hast washed thyself and hast chafed thine outer skin, which prostitutes also and flute-girls anoint, bathe, chafe and rouge, in order to arouse desire in men, but within they are full of scorpions and of [bad]ness [of every kind]. But I and [my disciples], of whom thou sayest that we have not im[mersed] ourselves, [have been im]mersed in the liv[ing . . .] water which comes down from [. . . B]ut **woe** unto them that . . .*

GNaz 17 ⇨ Matt 23:35

*(17) In the Gospel which the Nazarenes use, instead of "**son of Barachias**" we have found written "**son of Joiada.**" (Jerome, Commentary on Matthew 4 [on Matthew 23:35])*

PJas 24:1–4 ⇨ Matt 23:35

*[1] Rather, at the hour of the salutation the priests were departing, but the blessing of Zacharias did not meet them according to custom. And the priests stood waiting for Zacharias, to greet him with prayer and to glorify the Most High. [2] But when he delayed to come, they were all afraid. But one of them took courage and went into **the sanctuary**. And he saw beside **the altar** congealed blood; and a voice said: "Zacharias has been slain, and his **blood** shall not be wiped away until his avenger comes." And when he heard these words, he was afraid, and went out and told the priests what he had seen. [3] And they heard and saw what had happened. And the panel-work of the ceiling of the temple wailed, and they rent their clothes from the top to the bottom. And they did not find his body, but they found his **blood** turned into stone. And they were afraid, and went out and told all the people: "Zacharias has been slain." And all the tribes of the people heard it and mourned him and lamented three days and three nights. [4] And after the three days the priests took counsel whom they should appoint in his stead. And the lot fell upon Symeon. Now it was he to whom it had been revealed by the Holy Spirit that he should not see death until he had seen the Christ in the flesh.*

MATT	MARK	LUKE

Matt 23:37–39 (§M77.3)

[37] "O Jerusalem, Jerusalem, killing the prophets and stoning those who are sent to you! How often would I have gathered your children together as a hen gathers her brood under her wings, and you would not! [38] Behold, your house is forsaken and desolate.[a] [39] For I tell you, you will not see me again, until you say, 'Blessed is he who comes in the name of the Lord.'"

[a] Omit *and desolate:* B L it (in part) syr[s] cop (in part)

Isa 31:5 ⇨ Matt 23:37
[5] Like birds hovering, so the Lord of hosts
    will protect **Jerusalem**;
he will protect and deliver it,
    he will spare and rescue it.

Ps 118:26 ⇨ Matt 23:39
[26] **Blessed** be **he who** enters **in the name of the Lord**!
    We bless you from the house **of the Lord**.

Luke 13:34–35

[34] "O Jerusalem, Jerusalem, killing the prophets and stoning those who are sent to you! How often would I have gathered your children together as a hen gathers her brood under her wings, and you would not! [35] Behold, your house is forsaken. And I tell you, you will not see me until you say, 'Blessed is he who comes in the name of the Lord!'"

JOHN	THOMAS	OTHER

Matt	Mark	Luke

Matt 24:1–2 (§M78.1)

¹ Jesus left the temple and was going away, when his disciples came to point out to him the buildings of the temple. ² But he answered them, "You see all these, do you not? Truly, I say to you, there will not be left here one stone upon another, that will not be thrown down."

Mark 13:1–2 (§K60.1)

¹ And as he came out of **the temple**, one of **his disciples** said to him, "Look, Teacher, what wonderful stones and what wonderful **buildings!**" ² And Jesus said to him, "Do **you see these** great buildings? **There will not be left here one stone upon another, that will not be thrown down.**"

Luke 21:5–6

⁵ And as some spoke of **the temple**, how it was adorned with noble stones and offerings, he said, ⁶ "As for **these** things which **you see**, the days will come when **there** shall **not be left here one stone upon another that will not be thrown down.**"

John	Thomas	Other

MATT

Matt 24:3–14 (§M78.2)

³As he sat on the Mount of Olives, the disciples came to him privately, saying, "Tell us, when will this be, and what will be the sign of your coming and of the close of the age?" ⁴And Jesus answered them, "Take heed that no one leads you astray. ⁵For many will come in my name, saying, 'I am the Christ,' and they will lead many astray. ⁶And you will hear of wars and rumors of wars; see that you are not alarmed; for this must take place, but the end is not yet. ⁷For nation will rise against nation, and kingdom against kingdom, and there will be famines and earthquakes in various places: ⁸all this is but the beginning of the birth-pangs.

⁹"Then they will deliver you up to tribulation, and put you to death; and you will be hated by all nations for my name's sake. ¹⁰And then many will fall away,ᵃ and betray one another, and hate one another. ¹¹And many false prophets will arise and lead many astray. ¹²And because wickedness is multiplied, most men's love will grow cold. ¹³But he who endures to the end will be saved. ¹⁴And this gospel of the kingdom will be preached throughout the whole world, as a testimony to all nations; and then the end will come."

ᵃ Or: *stumble*

Matt 10:22 ⇨ Matt 24:9, 13

²²"and you will be hated by all for my name's sake. But he who endures to the end will be saved."

Matt 24:23–26 ⇨ Matt 24:5

²³*Then if any one says to you, 'Lo, here is* **the Christ!***' or 'There he is!' do not believe it.* ²⁴*For false Christs and false prophets will arise and show great signs and wonders, so as to* **lead astray***, if possible, even the elect.* ²⁵*Lo, I have told you beforehand.* ²⁶*So, if they say to you, 'Lo, he is in the wilderness,' do not go out; if they say, 'Lo, he is in the inner rooms' do not believe it.*"

Matt 10:18 ⇨ Matt 24:14

¹⁸*"and you will be dragged before governors and kings for my sake, to bear testimony before them and the Gentiles."*

⇨ Matt 24:7
Cf. 2 Chr 15:6, Isa 19:2

MARK

Mark 13:3–13 (§K60.2)

³And **as he sat on the Mount of Olives** opposite the temple, Peter and James and John and Andrew asked **him** privately, ⁴"Tell us, **when will this be, and what will be the sign** when these things are all to be accomplished?" ⁵**And Jesus** began to say to them, "**Take heed that no one leads you astray.** ⁶**Many will come in my name, saying, 'I am he!' and they will lead many astray.** ⁷**And** when **you hear of wars and rumors of wars**, do **not be alarmed; this must take place, but the end is not yet.** ⁸**For nation will rise against nation, and kingdom against kingdom; there will be earthquakes in various places, there will be famines; this is but the beginning of the birth-pangs.**

⁹"But take heed to yourselves; for **they will deliver you up** to councils; **and you will be** beaten in synagogues; **and you will** stand before governors and kings for my sake, to bear testimony before them. ¹⁰And the **gospel** must first **be preached to all nations.** ¹¹And when they bring you to trial and deliver you up, do not be anxious beforehand what you are to say; but say whatever is given you in that hour, for it is not you who speak, but the Holy Spirit. ¹²And brother **will deliver up** brother to death, and the father his child, and children will rise against parents and have them put to death; ¹³**and you will be hated by all for my name's sake. But he who endures to the end will be saved.**"

Mark 13:21–23 ⇨ Matt 24:5

²¹*"And then if any one says to you, 'Look, here is* **the Christ!***' or 'Look, there he is!' do not believe it.* ²²*False Christs and false prophets will arise and show signs and wonders, to* **lead astray***, if possible, the elect.* ²³*But take heed; I have told you all things beforehand."*

LUKE

Luke 21:5–19 (§L91.1)

⁵And as some spoke of the temple, how it was adorned with noble stones and offerings, he said, ⁶"As for these thing which you see, the days will come when there shall not be left here one stone upon another that will not be thrown down." ⁷And they asked him, "Teacher, **when will this be, and what will be the sign** when this is about to take place?" ⁸And he said, "**Take heed that you** are not led astray; **for many will come in my name, saying, 'I am he!'** and, 'The time is at hand!' Do not go after them. ⁹And when **you hear of wars and** tumults, do not be terrified; **for this must first take place, but the end will** not be at once."

¹⁰Then he said to them, "**Nation will rise against nation, and kingdom against kingdom;** ¹¹**there will be great earthquakes, and in various places famines** and pestilences; and there will be terrors and great signs from heaven. ¹²But before all this **they will** lay their hands on **you** and persecute you, delivering **you up** to the synagogues and prisons, and you **will be** brought before kings and governors for my name's sake. ¹³This will be a time for you to bear testimony. ¹⁴Settle it therefore in your minds, not to meditate beforehand how to answer; ¹⁵for I will give you a mouth and wisdom, which none of your adversaries will be able to withstand or contradict. ¹⁶**You will be** delivered up even by parents and brothers and kinsmen and friends, and some of you they will **put to death;** ¹⁷**you will be hated by all for my name's sake.** ¹⁸But not a hair of your head will perish. ¹⁹By your endurance you **will** gain your lives."

Luke 17:23 ⇨ Matt 24:5

²³*"And they will say to you, 'Lo, there!' or 'Lo, here!' Do not go, do not follow them."*

JOHN

John 15:18–21 ⇨ Matt 24:9

¹⁸*"If the world hates* **you***, know that it has* **hated me** *before it* **hated you***.* ¹⁹*If you were of the world, the world would love its own; but because you are not of the world, but I chose you out of the world, therefore the world hates you.* ²⁰*Remember the word that I said to you, 'A servant is not greater than his master.' If they persecuted me, they will persecute you; if they kept my word, they will keep yours also.* ²¹*But all this they will do to you on my account, because they do not know him who sent me."*

THOMAS

OTHER

MATT

Matt 24:15–28 (§M78.3)

[15] "So when you see the desolating sacrilege spoken of by the prophet Daniel, standing in the holy place (let the reader understand), [16] then let those who are in Judea flee to the mountains; [17] let him who is on the housetop not go down to take what is in his house; [18] and let him who is in the field not turn back to take his mantle. [19] And alas for those who are with child and for those who give suck in those days! [20] Pray that your flight may not be in winter or on a sabbath. [21] For then there will be a great tribulation, such as has not been from the beginning of the world until now, no, and never will be. [22] And if those days had not been shortened, no human being would be saved; but for the sake of the elect those days will be shortened. [23] Then if any one says to you, 'Lo, here is the Christ!' or 'There he is!' do not believe it. [24] For false Christs and false prophets will arise and show great signs and wonders, so as to lead astray, if possible, even the elect. [25] Lo, I have told you beforehand. [26] So, if they say to you, 'Lo, he is in the wilderness,' do not go out; if they say, 'Lo, he is in the inner rooms' do not believe it. [27] For as the lightning comes from the east and shines as far as the west, so will be the coming of the Son of man. [28] Wherever the body is, there the eagles[a] will be gathered together."

[a] Or: *vultures*

Matt 24:5 ⇨ Matt 24:23–26
[5] *"For many will come in my name, saying, 'I am the Christ,' and they will lead many astray."*

Dan 9:27 ⇨ Matt 24:15
[27] "And he shall make a strong covenant with many for one week; and for half of the week he shall cause sacrifice and offering to cease; and upon the wing of abominations shall come one who makes desolate, until the decreed end is poured out on the desolator."

Dan 11:31 ⇨ Matt 24:15
[31] "Forces from him shall appear and profane the temple and fortress, and shall take away the continual burnt offering. And they shall set up the abomination that makes desolate."

Dan 12:11 ⇨ Matt 24:15
[11] "And from the time that the continual burnt offering is taken away, and the abomination that makes desolate is set up, there shall be a thousand two hundred and ninety days."

JOHN

MARK

Mark 13:14–23 (§K60.3)

[14] "But when you see the desolating sacrilege set up where it ought not to be (let the reader understand), then let those who are in Judea flee to the mountains; [15] let him who is on the housetop not go down, nor enter his house, to take anything away; [16] and let him who is in the field not turn back to take his mantle. [17] And alas for those who are with child and for those who give suck in those days! [18] Pray that it may not happen in winter. [19] For in those days there will be such tribulation as has not been from the beginning of the creation which God created until now, and never will be. [20] And if the Lord had not shortened the days, no human being would be saved; but for the sake of the elect, whom he chose, he shortened the days. [21] And then if any one says to you, 'Look, here is the Christ!' or 'Look, there he is!' do not believe it. [22] False Christs and false prophets will arise and show signs and wonders, to lead astray, if possible, the elect. [23] But take heed; I have told you all things beforehand."

1 Macc 1:54 ⇨ Matt 24:15
[54] Now on the fifteenth day of Chislev, in the one hundred and forty-fifth year, they erected a desolating sacrilege upon the altar of burnt offering. They also built altars in the surrounding cities of Judah, . . .

⇨ Matt 24:16
Cf. Ezek 7:16

Dan 12:1 ⇨ Matt 24:21
[1] "At that time shall arise Michael, the great prince who has charge of your people. And there shall be a time of trouble, such as never has been since there was a nation till that time; but at that time your people shall be delivered, every one whose name shall be found written in the book."

Deut 13:1–3 ⇨ Matt 24:24
[1] "If a prophet arises among you, or a dreamer of dreams, and gives you a sign or a wonder, [2] and the sign or wonder which he tells you comes to pass, and if he says, 'Let us go after other gods,' which you have not known, 'and let us serve them,' [3] you shall not listen to the words of that prophet or to that dreamer of dreams; for the Lord your God is testing you, to know whether you love the Lord your God with all your heart and with all your soul."

THOMAS

GThom 79 ⇨ Matt 24:19
(79) A woman from the crowd said to Him, "Blessed are the womb which bore You and the breasts which nourished You."

He said to her, "Blessed are those who have heard the word of the Father and have truly kept it. For there will be days when you will say, 'Blessed are the womb which has not conceived and the breasts which have not given milk.'"

GThom 113 ⇨ Matt 24:23
(113) His disciples said to Him, "When will the Kingdom come?"
<Jesus said,> "It will not come by waiting for it. It will not be a matter of saying 'Here it is' or 'There it is.' Rather, the Kingdom of the Father is spread out upon the earth, and men do not see it."

LUKE

Luke 21:20–24 (§L91.2)

[20] "But when you see Jerusalem surrounded by armies, then know that its desolation has come near. [21] Then let those who are in Judea flee to the mountains, and let those who are inside the city depart, and let not those who are out in the country enter it; [22] for these are days of vengeance, to fulfil all that is written. [23] Alas for those who are with child and for those who give suck in those days! For great distress shall be upon the earth and wrath upon this people; [24] they will fall by the edge of the sword, and be led captive among all nations; and Jerusalem will be trodden down by the Gentiles, until the times of the Gentiles are fulfilled."

Luke 17:31 ⇨ Matt 24:17–18
[31] "On that day, let him who is on the housetop, with his goods in the house, not come down to take them away; and likewise let him who is in the field not turn back."

OTHER

MATT	MARK	LUKE

Matt 24:29–36 (§M78.4)

[29] "Immediately after the tribulation of those days the sun will be darkened, and the moon will not give its light, and the stars will fall from heaven, and the powers of the heavens will be shaken; [30] then will appear the sign of the Son of man in heaven, and then all the tribes of the earth will mourn, and they will see the Son of man coming on the clouds of heaven with power and great glory; [31] and he will send out his angels with a loud trumpet call, and they will gather his elect from the four winds, from one end of heaven to the other.

[32] "From the fig tree learn its lesson: as soon as its branch becomes tender and puts forth its leaves, you know that summer is near. [33] So also, when you see all these things, you know that he is near, at the very gates. [34] Truly, I say to you, this generation will not pass away till all these things take place. [35] Heaven and earth will pass away, but my words will not pass away.

[36] "But of that day and hour no one knows, not even the angels of heaven, nor the Son,[a] but the Father only."

[a] Omit *nor the Son:* ℵ[a] K L W Δ Π *f*[1] 33 *pm*

●Matt 26:64 ⇨ Matt 24:30

[64] Jesus said to him, "You have said so. But I tell you, hereafter you **will see the Son of man** seated at the right hand of Power, and **coming on the clouds of heaven.**"

Matt 16:28 ⇨ Matt 24:34

[28] *"Truly, I say to you, there are some standing here who will not taste death before they see the Son of man coming in his kingdom."*

Isa 13:10 ⇨ Matt 24:29

[10] For **the stars** of the heavens and their constellations
will not give their light;
the sun will be dark at its rising
and the moon will not shed **its light.**

Isa 34:4 ⇨ Matt 24:29

[4] All the host of heaven shall rot away,
and the skies roll up like a scroll.
All their host shall fall,
as leaves fall from the vine,
like leaves falling from the fig tree.

Mark 13:24–32 (§K60.4)

[24] "But in **those days,** after that tribulation, the sun will be darkened, and the moon will not give its light, [25] **and the stars will** be falling from heaven, **and the powers in the heavens** will be shaken. [26] **And then they will see the** Son of man coming **in clouds with** great **power and glory.** [27] **And then he will send out** the angels, and gather his elect from the four winds, from the ends of the earth to the ends of heaven.

[28] "From the fig tree learn its lesson: as soon as its branch becomes tender and puts forth its leaves, you know that summer is near. [29] So also, when you see these things taking place, **you know that he is near, at the very gates.** [30] Truly, I say to you, this generation will not pass away before **all these things** take place. [31] Heaven and earth will pass away, but my words will not pass away.

[32] "But of that day or that **hour no one knows,** not even **the angels** in heaven, nor the Son, but only the Father."

Mark 9:1 ⇨ Matt 24:34

[1] *And he said to them, "Truly, I say to you, there are some standing here who will not taste death before they see that the kingdom of God has come with power."*

Dan 7:13–14 ⇨ Matt 24:30–31

[13] "I saw in the night visions,
and behold, with **the clouds of heaven**
there came one like a **son of man,**
and he came to the Ancient of Days
and was presented before him.
[14] And to him was given dominion
and glory and kingdom,
that all peoples, nations, and languages
should serve him;
his dominion is an everlasting dominion,
which shall not pass away,
and his kingdom one
that shall not be destroyed."

Deut 30:3–4 ⇨ Matt 24:31

[3] "then the Lord your God will restore your fortunes, and have compassion upon you, and **he will gather** you again from all the peoples where the Lord your God has scattered you. [4] If your outcasts are in the uttermost parts **of heaven,** from there the Lord your God **will gather** you, and from there he will fetch you"; . . .

Luke 21:25–33 (§L91.3)

[25] "And there will be signs in **sun and moon and stars,** and upon the earth distress of nations in perplexity at the roaring of the sea and the waves, [26] men fainting with fear and with foreboding of what is coming on the world; for **the powers of the heavens will be shaken.** [27] And then they will see the Son of man coming in a cloud **with power and great glory.** [28] Now when these things begin to take place, look up and raise your heads, because your redemption is drawing near."

[29] And he told them a parable: "Look at **the fig tree,** and all the trees; [30] **as soon as** they come out in leaf, **you** see for yourselves and know that **the summer is already near.** [31] So also, **when you see these things** taking place, **you know** that the kingdom of God **is near.** [32] Truly, I say to you, **this generation will not pass away till all** has taken place. [33] Heaven and earth will pass away, but my words will not pass away."

Luke 9:27 ⇨ Matt 24:34

[27] *"But I tell **you truly,** there are some standing here who will not taste death before they see the kingdom of God."*

JOHN	THOMAS	OTHER

Rev 1:7 ⇨ Matt 24:30

[7] *Behold, he is **coming with the clouds,** and every eye will see him, every one who pierced him; and all tribes of the earth will wail on account of him. Even so. Amen.*

1 Thess 4:15–16 ⇨ Matt 24:30–31

[15] *For this we declare to you by the word of the Lord, that we who are alive, who are left until the coming of the Lord, shall not precede those who have fallen asleep. [16] For the Lord himself will descend from **heaven** with a cry of command, with the archangel's **call,** and with the sound of the **trumpet** of God. And the dead in Christ will rise first; . . .*

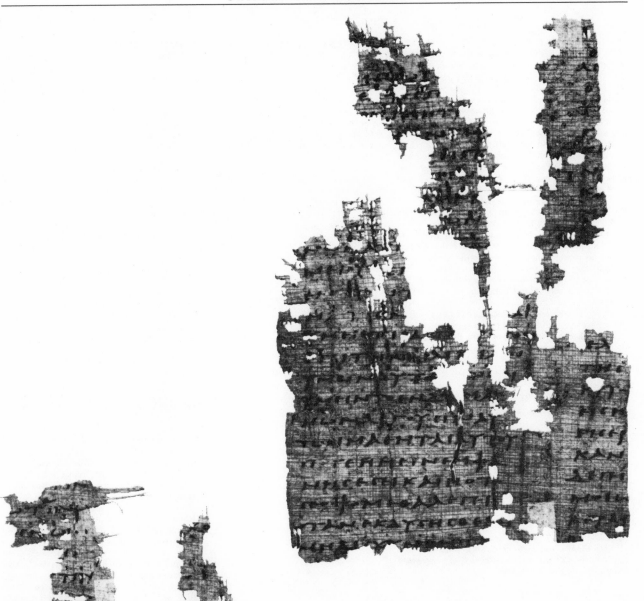

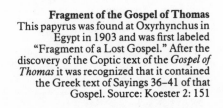

Fragment of the Gospel of Thomas
This papyrus was found at Oxyrhynchus in
Egypt in 1903 and was first labeled
"Fragment of a Lost Gospel." After the
discovery of the Coptic text of the *Gospel of
Thomas* it was recognized that it contained
the Greek text of Sayings 36–41 of that
Gospel. Source: Koester 2: 151

135

MATT

MARK

LUKE

Matt 24:37–51 (§M78.5)
[37] "As were the days of Noah, so will be the coming of the Son of man. [38] For as in those days before the flood they were eating and drinking, marrying and giving in marriage, until the day when Noah entered the ark, [39] and they did not know until the flood came and swept them all away, so will be the coming of the Son of man. [40] Then two men will be in the field; one is taken and one is left. [41] Two women will be grinding at the mill; one is taken and one is left. [42] Watch therefore, for you do not know on what day your Lord is coming. [43] But know this, that if the householder had known in what part of the night the thief was coming, he would have watched and would not have let his house be broken into. [44] Therefore you also must be ready; for the Son of man is coming at an hour you do not expect.

[45] "Who then is the faithful and wise servant, whom his master has set over his household, to give them their food at the proper time? [46] Blessed is that servant whom his master when he comes will find so doing. [47] Truly, I say to you, he will set him over all his possessions. [48] But if that wicked servant says to himself, 'My master is delayed,' [49] and begins to beat his fellow servants, and eats and drinks with the drunken, [50] the master of that servant will come on a day when he does not expect him and at an hour he does not know, [51] and will punish him,[a] and put him with the hypocrites; there men will weep and gnash their teeth."

[a] Or: *cut him in pieces*

Matt 8:12 ⇨ Matt 24:51
[12] *"while the sons of the kingdom will be thrown into the outer darkness; there men will weep and gnash their teeth."*

Matt 13:42 ⇨ Matt 24:51
[42] *"and throw them into the furnace of fire; there men will weep and gnash their teeth."*

Matt 13:50 ⇨ Matt 24:51
[50] *"and throw them into the furnace of fire; there men will weep and gnash their teeth."*

Matt 22:13 ⇨ Matt 24:51
[13] *"Then the king said to the attendants, 'Bind him hand and foot, and cast him into the outer darkness; there men will weep and gnash their teeth.'"*

Matt 25:30 ⇨ Matt 24:51
[30] *"'And cast the worthless servant into the outer darkness; there men will weep and gnash their teeth.'"*

Gen 7:6–10 ⇨ Matt 24:38
[6] **Noah** was six hundred years old when **the flood** of waters came upon the earth. [7] And **Noah** and his sons and his wife and his sons' wives with him went into **the ark**, to escape the waters of **the flood**. [8] Of clean animals, and of animals that are not clean, and of birds, and of everything that creeps on the ground, [9] two and two, male and female, went into **the ark** with **Noah**, as God had commanded Noah. [10] And after seven days the waters of **the flood** came upon the earth.

Mark 13:33–37 (§K60.5)
[33] "Take heed, **watch**; **for you do not know** when the time will come. [34] It is like a man going on a journey, when he leaves home and puts his servants in charge, each with his work, and commands the doorkeeper to be on **watch**. [35] **Watch therefore—for you do not know** when **the master of** the house **will come**, in the evening, or at midnight, or at cockcrow, or in the morning— [36] lest he **come** suddenly and find you asleep. [37] And what I say to you I say to all: **Watch**."

Luke 21:34–36 (§L91.4)
[34] "But take heed to yourselves lest your hearts be weighed down with dissipation and drunkenness and cares of this life, and that day **come** upon you suddenly like a snare; [35] for it **will come** upon all who dwell upon all the face of the whole earth; [36] But **watch** at all times, praying that you may have strength to escape all these things that will take place, and to stand before the Son of man."

Luke 17:26–35 ⇨ Matt 24:37–41
[26] "**As** it was in **the days of Noah, so will it be** in the days **of the Son of man**. [27] **They** ate, they drank, they married, they were given **in marriage, until the day when Noah entered the ark**, and **the flood came and** destroyed **them all**. [28] Likewise as it was in the days of Lot— they ate, they drank, they bought, they sold, they planted, they built, [29] but on the day when Lot went out from Sodom fire and sulphur rained from heaven and destroyed them all— [30] **so will** it **be** on the day when **the Son of man** is revealed. [31] On that day, let him who is on the housetop, with his goods in the house, not come down to take them away; and likewise let him who is **in the field** not turn back. [32] Remember Lot's wife. [33] Whoever seeks to gain his life will lose it, but whoever loses his life will preserve it. [34] I tell you, in that night there will be two in one bed; one will be taken and the other left. [35] There **will be two women grinding** together; **one** will be **taken and** the other **left**."

Luke 12:39–40 ⇨ Matt 24:43–44
[39] "But know this, that if **the householder had known** at what hour **the thief was coming, he** would not have left **his house** to be broken into. [40] You also must be ready; for the Son of man is coming at an unexpected **hour**."

Luke 12:42–46 ⇨ Matt 24:45–51
[42] And the Lord said, "**Who then is the faithful and wise** steward, **whom his master** will **set over his household, to give them their** portion of **food at the proper time?** [43] Blessed is that servant whom his master when he comes will find so doing. [44] Truly, I say to you, he will set him over all his possessions. [45] But if that servant says to himself, 'My master is delayed in coming,' and begins to beat the menservants and the maidservants, and to eat and drink and get drunk, [46] the master of that servant will come on a day when he does not expect him and at an hour he does not know, and will punish him, and put him with the unfaithful."

GThom 21

(21) Mary said to Jesus, "Whom are Your disciples like?"

He said, "They are like children who have settled in a field which is not theirs. When the owners of the field come, they will say, 'Let us have back our field.' They (will) undress in their presence in order to let them have back their field and to give it back to them. **There-fore** I say to you, **if the** owner of a house knows that **the thief** is **coming, he** will begin his vigil before he comes **and** will **not** let him dig through into **his house** of his domain to carry away his goods. **You,** then, be on your guard against the world. Arm yourselves with great strength lest the robbers find a way to come to you, for the difficulty which you expect will (surely) materialize. Let there be among you a man of understanding. When the grain ripened, he came quickly with his sickle in his hand and reaped it. Whoever has ears to hear, let him hear."

GThom 103

(103) Jesus said, "Fortunate is the man who knows where **the** brigands will enter, so that **he** may get up, muster his domain, **and** arm himself before they invade."

1 Thess 5:2 ⇨ Matt 24:42–43

[2] *For you yourselves know well that the **day of the Lord** will come like a **thief in the night.***

Rev 16:15 ⇨ Matt 24:42–43

[15] *("Lo, I am coming like a **thief**! Blessed is he who is awake, keeping his garments that he may not go naked and be seen exposed!")*

GNaz 18 ⇨ Matt 12:48–51

*(18) But since the Gospel (written) in Hebrew characters which has come into our hands enters the threat not against the man who had hid (the talent), but against him who had lived dissolutely—for he (the master) had three servants: one who squandered his master's substance with harlots and flute-girls, one who multiplied the gain, and one who hid the talent; and accordingly one was accepted (with joy), another merely rebuked, and another cast into prison—I wonder whether in Matthew the threat which is uttered after the word against the man who did nothing may refer not to him, but by epanalepsis to the first who had feasted **and drunk with the drunken**. (Eusebius, Theophania 22 [on Matthew 25:14–15])*

MATT	MARK	LUKE

Matt 25:1–13 (§M79.1)

[1]"Then the kingdom of heaven shall be compared to ten maidens who took their lamps and went to meet the bridegroom.[a] [2]Five of them were foolish, and five were wise. [3]For when the foolish took their lamps, they took no oil with them; [4]but the wise took flasks of oil with their lamps. [5]As the bridegroom was delayed, they all slumbered and slept. [6]But at midnight there was a cry, 'Behold, the bridegroom! Come out to meet him.' [7]Then all those maidens rose and trimmed their lamps. [8]And the foolish said to the wise, 'Give us some of your oil, for our lamps are going out.' [9]But the wise replied, 'Perhaps there will not be enough for us and for you; go rather to the dealers and buy for yourselves.' [10]And while they went to buy, the bridegroom came, and those who were ready went in with him to the marriage feast; and the door was shut. [11]Afterward the other maidens came also, saying, 'Lord, lord, open to us.' [12]But he replied, 'Truly, I say to you, I do not know you.' [13]Watch therefore, for you know neither the day nor the hour."

[a]Some witnesses add, *and the bride:* D X* Θ *f*[1] *al*

Mark 13:35–37

[35]*"Watch therefore—for* **you** *do not* **know** *when the master of the house will come, in the evening, or at midnight, or at cockcrow, or in the morning—* [36]*lest he come suddenly and find you asleep.* [37]*And what* **I say to you I** *say to all:* **Watch."**

Luke 12:35–36

[35]*"Let your loins be girded and your* **lamps** *burning,* [36]*and be like men who are waiting for their master to come home from the* **marriage** **feast,** *so that they may open to him at once when he comes and knocks."*

Luke 13:25 ⇨ Matt 25:12

[25]*"When once the householder has risen up and shut the door, you will begin to stand outside and to knock at the door, saying, 'Lord, open to us.' He will answer you, 'I do not* **know** *where you come from.'"*

JOHN	THOMAS	OTHER

Did 16:1 ⇨ Matt 25:13

[1]*"Watch" over your life: "let your lamps" be not quenched "and your loins" be not ungirded, but be "ready," for ye* **know** *not "the hour in which our Lord cometh."*

MATT

Matt 25:14–30 (§M79.2)

14 "For it will be as when a man going on a journey called his servants and entrusted to them his property; 15 to one he gave five talents,[a] to another two, to another one, to each according to his ability. Then he went away. 16 He who had received the five talents went at once and traded with them; and he made five talents more. 17 So also, he who had the two talents made two talents more. 18 But he who had received the one talent went and dug in the ground and hid his master's money. 19 Now after a long time the master of those servants came and settled accounts with them. 20 And he who had received the five talents came forward, bringing five talents more, saying, 'Master, you delivered to me five talents; here I have made five talents more.' 21 His master said to him, 'Well done, good and faithful servant; you have been faithful over a little, I will set you over much; enter into the joy of your master.' 22 And he also who had the two talents came forward, saying, 'Master, you delivered to me two talents; here I have made two talents more.' 23 His master said to him, 'Well done, good and faithful servant; you have been faithful over a little, I will set you over much; enter into the joy of your master.' 24 He also who had received the one talent came forward, saying, 'Master, I knew you to be a hard man, reaping where you did not sow, and gathering where you did not winnow; 25 so I was afraid, and I went and hid your talent in the ground. Here you have what is yours.' 26 But his master answered him, 'You wicked and slothful servant! You knew that I reap where I have not sowed, and gather where I have not winnowed? 27 Then you ought to have invested my money with the bankers, and at my coming I should have received what was my own with interest. 28 So take the talent from him, and give it to him who has the ten talents. 29 For to every one who has will more be given, and he will have abundance; but from him who has not, even what he has will be taken away. 30 And cast the worthless servant into the outer darkness; there men will weep and gnash their teeth.'"

JOHN

MARK

Mark 4:24–25 (§K21.6) ⇨ Matt 25:29

24 And he said to them, "Take heed what you hear; the measure you give will be the measure you get, and still more will be given you. 25 For to him who has will more be given; and from him who has not, even what he has will be taken away."

_____

a This talent amounted to more than fifteen years' wages of a laborer.

Matt 13:10–12 ⇨ Matt 25:29

10 Then the disciples came and said to him, "Why do you speak to them in parables?" 11 And he answered them, "To you it has been given to know the secrets of the kingdom of heaven, but to them it has not been given. 12 For to him who has will more be given, and he will have abundance; but from him who has not, even what he has will be taken away."

Matt 8:12 ⇨ Matt 25:30

12 "while the sons of the kingdom will be thrown into the outer darkness; there men will weep and gnash their teeth."

Matt 13:42 ⇨ Matt 25:30

42 "and throw them into the furnace of fire; there men will weep and gnash their teeth."

Matt 13:50 ⇨ Matt 25:30

50 "and throw them into the furnace of fire; there men will weep and gnash their teeth."

Matt 22:13 ⇨ Matt 25:30

13 "Then the king said to the attendants, 'Bind him hand and foot, and cast him into the outer darkness; there men will weep and gnash their teeth.'"

Matt 24:51 ⇨ Matt 25:30

51 "and will punish him, and put him with the hypocrites; there men will weep and gnash their teeth."

THOMAS

GThom 41 ⇨ Matt 25:29

(41) Jesus said, "Whoever has something in his hand **will** receive **more**, and whoever has nothing will be deprived of **even** the little **he has**."

LUKE

Luke 19:11–27 (§L81)

11 As they heard these things, he proceeded to tell a parable, because he was near to Jerusalem, and because they supposed that the kingdom of God was to appear immediately. 12 He said therefore, "A nobleman went into a far country to receive a kingdom and then return. 13 Calling ten of **his servants, he gave** them ten pounds, and said to them, 'Trade with these till I come.' 14 But his citizens hated him and sent an embassy after him, saying, 'We do not want this man to reign over us.' 15 When he returned, having received the kingdom, he commanded these servants, to whom he had given the money, to be called to him, that he might know what they had gained by trading. 16 The first **came** before him, **saying,** 'Lord, your pound has **made** ten pounds **more.'** 17 And he **said** to him, '**Well done, good servant!** Because **you have been faithful** in a very **little,** you shall have authority over ten cities.' 18 And the second **came, saying,** 'Lord, your pound has **made** five pounds.' 19 And he **said** to him, 'And you are to be over five cities.' 20 Then another **came, saying,** 'Lord, here is your pound, which I kept laid away in a napkin,' 21 for **I was afraid** of you, because **you** are **a** severe **man;** you take up what you did not lay down, and reap what **you did not sow.'** 22 He said to **him,** 'I will condemn you out of your own mouth, **you wicked servant! You knew that I** was a severe man, taking up what I did not lay down and reaping what I did not sow? 23 Why then did you not put **my money** into the bank, **and at my coming I should have** collected it **with interest?'** 24 And he said to those who stood by, '**Take the** pound **from him, and give it to him who has the ten** pounds.' 25 (And they said to him, 'Lord, he has ten pounds!') 26 'I tell you, that **to every one who has will** more **be given; but from him who has not, even what he has will be taken away.** 27 But as for these enemies of mine, who did not want me to reign over them, bring them here and slay them before me.'"

Luke 8:18 (§L32.5) ⇨ Matt 25:29

18 "Take heed then how you hear; for to him who has will more be given, and from him who has not, even what he thinks that he has will be taken away."

Luke 13:28 ⇨ Matt 25:30

28 "There you will weep and gnash your teeth, when you see Abraham and Isaac and Jacob and all the prophets in the kingdom of God and you yourselves thrust out."

OTHER

GNaz 18

(18) But since the Gospel (written) in Hebrew characters which has come into our hands enters the threat not against the man who had hid (the talent), but against him who had lived dissolutely—for he (the master) had three servants: one who squandered his master's substance with harlots and flute-girls, one who multiplied the gain, and one who hid the talent; and accordingly one was accepted (with joy), another merely rebuked, and another cast into prison—I wonder whether in Matthew the threat which is uttered after the word against the man who did nothing may refer not to him, but by epanalepsis to the first who had feasted and drunk with the drunken. (Eusebius, Theophania 22 [on Matthew 25:14–15])

MATT   MARK   LUKE

Matt 25:31–46 (§M79.3)

[31] "When the Son of man comes in his glory, and all the angels with him, then he will sit on his glorious throne. [32] Before him will be gathered all the nations, and he will separate them one from another as a shepherd separates the sheep from the goats, [33] and he will place the sheep at his right hand, but the goats at the left. [34] Then the King will say to those at his right hand, 'Come, O blessed of my Father, inherit the kingdom prepared for you from the foundation of the world; [35] for I was hungry and you gave me food, I was thirsty and you gave me drink, I was a stranger and you welcomed me, [36] I was naked and you clothed me, I was sick and you visited me, I was in prison and you came to me.' [37] Then the righteous will answer him, 'Lord, when did we see thee hungry and feed thee, or thirsty and give thee drink? [38] And when did we see thee a stranger and welcome thee, or naked and clothe thee? [39] And when did we see thee sick or in prison and visit thee?' [40] And the King will answer them, 'Truly, I say to you, as you did it to one of the least of these my brethren, you did it to me.' [41] Then he will say to those at his left hand, 'Depart from me, you cursed, into the eternal fire prepared for the devil and his angels; [42] for I was hungry and you gave me no food, I was thirsty and you gave me no drink, [43] I was a stranger and you did not welcome me, naked and you did not clothe me, sick and in prison and you did not visit me.' [44] Then they also will answer, 'Lord, when did we see thee hungry or thirsty or a stranger or naked or sick or in prison, and did not minister to thee?' [45] Then he will answer them, 'Truly, I say to you, as you did it not to one of the least of these, you did it not to me.' [46] And they will go away into eternal punishment, but the righteous into eternal life."

Dan 12:2 ⇨ Matt 25:46
[2] "And many of those who sleep in the dust of the earth shall awake, some to everlasting **life, and** some to shame and everlasting contempt."

JOHN   THOMAS   OTHER

John 5:28–29 ⇨ Matt 25:46
[28] *"Do not marvel at this; for the hour is coming when all who are in the tombs will hear his voice* [29] *and come forth, those who have done good, to the resurrection of* **life, and** *those who have done evil, to the resurrection of judgment."*

Justin, *Dialogue* **76.5** ⇨ Matt 25:41
Depart into the outer darkness, which the Father has **prepared for** *Satan* **and his angels.**

MATT

Matt 26:1–2 (§M80.1)
¹ When Jesus had finished all these sayings, he said to his disciples, ² "You know that after two days the Passover is coming, and the Son of man will be delivered up to be crucified."

Matt 26:3–5 (§M80.2)
³ Then the chief priests and the elders of the people gathered in the palace of the high priest, who was called Caiaphas, ⁴ and took counsel together in order to arrest Jesus by stealth and kill him. ⁵ But they said, "Not during the feast, lest there be a tumult among the people."

Matt 21:45 ⇨ §M80.2
⁴⁵ *When* **the chief priests and the** *Pharisees heard his parables, they perceived that he was speaking about them.*

JOHN

† **John 11:45–53 (§J23.1)**
⁴⁵ Many of the Jews therefore, who had come with Mary and had seen what he did, believed in him; ⁴⁶ but some of them went to the Pharisees and told them what Jesus had done. ⁴⁷ **So the chief priests and the** Pharisees **gathered** the council, and said, "What are we to do? For this man performs many signs. ⁴⁸ If we let him go on thus, every one will believe in him, and the Romans will come and destroy both our holy place and our nation." ⁴⁹ But one of them, **Caiaphas,** who was **high priest** that year, said to them, "You know nothing at all; ⁵⁰ you do not understand that it is expedient for you that one man should die for the people, and that the whole nation should not perish." ⁵¹ He did not say this of his own accord, but being high priest that year he prophesied that **Jesus** should die for the nation, ⁵² and not for the nation only, but to gather into one the children of God who are scattered abroad. ⁵³ So from that day on they **took counsel** how to put **him** to death.

† **John 11:54 (§J23.2)**
⁵⁴ **Jesus** therefore no longer went about openly among the Jews, but went from there to the country near the wilderness, to a town called Ephraim; and there he stayed with the disciples.

† **John 11:55–57 (§J23.3)**
⁵⁵ Now the Passover of the Jews was at hand, and many went up from the country to Jerusalem before **the Passover,** to purify themselves. ⁵⁶ They were looking for **Jesus** and saying to one another as they stood in the temple, "What do you think? That he will not come to the feast?" ⁵⁷ Now **the chief priests and the** Pharisees had given orders that if any one knew where he was, he should let them know, so that they might **arrest him.**

MARK

Mark 14:1–2 (§K61.1)
¹ It was now **two days** before **the Passover** and the feast of Unleavened Bread. And **the chief priests and the** scribes were seeking how **to arrest** him **by stealth, and kill him;** ² for **they said, "Not during the feast, lest there be a tumult** of **the people."**

Mark 11:18 ⇨ §M80.2
¹⁸ *And* **the chief priests and the scribes heard** *it* **and** *sought a way to destroy* **him;** *for they feared him, because all the multitude was astonished at his teaching.*

Mark 12:12 ⇨ §M80.2
¹² *And they tried* **to arrest him,** *but feared the multitude, for they perceived that he had told the parable against them; so they left him and went away.*

THOMAS

LUKE

Luke 22:1–2 (§L92.1)
¹ Now the feast of Unleavened Bread drew near, which is called **the Passover.** ² And **the chief priests and the** scribes were seeking how to put him to death; for they feared **the people.**

Luke 19:47–48 ⇨ §M80.2
⁴⁷ *And he was teaching daily in the temple.* **The chief priests and the** *scribes and the principal men of the people sought to destroy* **him;** ⁴⁸ *but they did not find anything* **they** *could do, for all* **the people;** *hung upon his words.*

Luke 20:19 ⇨ §M80.2
¹⁹ **The** *scribes and* **the chief priests** *tried to lay hands on* **him** *at that very hour, but they feared* **the people** *for they perceived that he had told this parable against them.*

OTHER

MATT   MARK   LUKE

Matt 26:6–13 (§M80.3)

⁶Now when Jesus was at Bethany in the house of Simon the leper, ⁷a woman came up to him with an alabaster flask of very expensive ointment, and she poured it on his head, as he sat at table. ⁸But when the disciples saw it, they were indignant, saying, "Why this waste? ⁹For this ointment might have been sold for a large sum, and given to the poor." ¹⁰But Jesus, aware of this, said to them, "Why do you trouble the woman? For she has done a beautiful thing to me. ¹¹For you always have the poor with you, but you will not always have me. ¹²In pouring this ointment on my body she has done it to prepare me for burial. ¹³Truly, I say to you, wherever this gospel is preached in the whole world, what she has done will be told in memory of her."

Mark 14:3–9 (§K61.2)

³And while he was at Bethany in the house of Simon the leper, as he sat at table, a woman came with an alabaster flask of ointment of pure nard, very costly, and she broke the flask and poured it over his head. ⁴But there were some who said to themselves indignantly, "Why was the ointment thus wasted? ⁵For this ointment might have been sold for more than three hundred denarii, and given to the poor." And they reproached her. ⁶But Jesus said, "Let her alone; why do you trouble her? She has done a beautiful thing to me. ⁷For you always have the poor with you, and whenever you will, you can do good to them; but you will not always have me. ⁸She has done what she could; she has anointed my body beforehand for burying. ⁹And truly, I say to you, wherever the gospel is preached in the whole world, what she has done will be told in memory of her."

Luke 7:36–50 (§L29)

³⁶One of the Pharisees asked him to eat with him, and he went into the Pharisee's house, and took his place at table. ³⁷And behold, a woman of the city, who was a sinner, when she learned that he was at table in the Pharisee's house, brought an alabaster flask of ointment, ³⁸and standing behind him at his feet, weeping, she began to wet his feet with her tears, and wiped them with the hair of her head, and kissed his feet, and anointed them with the ointment. ³⁹Now when the Pharisee who had invited him saw it, he said to himself, "If this man were a prophet, he would have known who and what sort of woman this is who is touching him, for she is a sinner." ⁴⁰And Jesus answering said to him, "Simon, I have something to say to you." And he answered, "What is it, Teacher?" ⁴¹"A certain creditor had two debtors; one owed five hundred denarii, and the other fifty. ⁴²When they could not pay, he forgave them both. Now which of them will love him more?" ⁴³Simon answered, "The one, I suppose, to whom he forgave more." And he said to him "You have judged rightly." ⁴⁴Then turning toward the woman he said to Simon, "Do you see this woman? I entered your house, you gave me no water for my feet, but she has wet my feet with her tears and wiped them with her hair. ⁴⁵You gave me no kiss, but from the time I came in she has not ceased to kiss my feet. ⁴⁶You did not anoint my head with oil, but she has anointed my feet with ointment. ⁴⁷Therefore I tell you, her sins, which are many, are forgiven, for she loved much; but he who is forgiven little, loves little." ⁴⁸And he said to her, "Your sins are forgiven." ⁴⁹Then those who were at table with him began to say among themselves, "Who is this, who even forgives sins?" ⁵⁰And he said to the woman, "Your faith has saved you; go in peace."

JOHN

† John 12:1–8 (§J24.1)

¹Six days before the Passover, Jesus came to Bethany, where Lazarus was, whom Jesus had raised from the dead. ²There they made him a supper; Martha served, and Lazarus was one of those at table with him. ³Mary took a pound of costly ointment of pure nard and anointed the feet of Jesus and wiped his feet with her hair; and the house was filled with the fragrance of the ointment. ⁴But Judas Iscariot, one of his disciples (he who was to betray him), said, ⁵"Why was this ointment not sold for three hundred denarii and given to the poor?" ⁶This he said, not that he cared for the poor but because he was a thief, and as he had the money box he used to take what was put into it. ⁷Jesus said, "Let her alone, let her keep it for the day of my burial. ⁸The poor you always have with you, but you do not always have me."

THOMAS   OTHER

MATT	MARK	LUKE

Matt 26:14–16 (§M80.4) °
¹⁴ Then one of the twelve, who was called Judas Iscariot, went to the chief priests ¹⁵ and said, "What will you give me if I deliver him to you?" And they paid him thirty pieces of silver. ¹⁶ And from that moment he sought an opportunity to betray him.

°Appendix 2 ⇨ Matt 26:14

Zech 11:12 ⇨ Matt 26:15
¹² Then I said to them, "If it seems right to you, give me my wages; but if not, keep them." And they weighed out as my wages **thirty** shekels of silver.

Mark 14:10–11 (§K61.3)
¹⁰ Then Judas Iscariot, who was one of the twelve, went to the chief priests in order to betray him to them. ¹¹ And when they heard it they were glad, and promised to give him money. And he sought an opportunity to betray him.

Luke 22:3–6 (§L92.2)
³ Then Satan entered into Judas called Iscariot, who was of the number of the twelve; ⁴ he went away and conferred with the chief priests and officers how he might betray him to them. ⁵ And they were glad, and engaged to give him money. ⁶ So he agreed, and sought an opportunity to betray him to them in the absence of the multitude.

JOHN	THOMAS	OTHER

MATT	MARK	LUKE

PREPARATIONS

Matt 26:17–19 (§M81.1)

[17] Now **on the first day of Unleavened Bread the disciples came to Jesus, saying,** "Where will you have us **prepare for you to eat the passover?**" [18] **He said,** "Go into the city to a certain one, and say to him, 'The Teacher says, My time is at hand; I will keep the passover at your house with my disciples.'" [19] And the disciples did as Jesus had directed them, and they prepared the passover.

JESUS FORETELLS HIS BETRAYAL

Matt 26:20–25 (§M81.2) °

[20] When it was evening, he sat at table with **the twelve** disciples;[a] [21] and **as they were eating, he said,** "Truly, I say to you, one of you will betray me." [22] And they were very sorrowful, and began **to say to him one after another,** "Is it I, Lord?" [23] He answered, "He who has dipped his hand in the dish with me, will betray me. [24] The Son of man goes as it is written of him, but woe to that man by whom the Son of man is betrayed! It would have been better for that man if he had not been born." [25] Judas, who betrayed him, said, "Is it I, Master?"[b] He said to him, "You have said so."

THE LAST SUPPER

Matt 26:26–29 (§M81.3)

[26] Now **as they were eating,** Jesus **took bread, and** blessed, **and broke it, and gave it to** the disciples and said, "Take, **eat; this is my body.**" [27] **And he took a cup, and when he had given thanks** he gave it to them, saying, "Drink of it, all of you; [28] for this is my blood of the[c] covenant, which is poured out for many for the forgiveness of sins. [29] I tell you I **shall not drink again of this fruit of the vine until** that day when I **drink it new** with you **in** my Father's **kingdom.**"

[a] Some witnesses omit *disciples:* (𝔓37) (𝔓45) B D K *f*1 *f*13 28 *al*

[b] Or: *Rabbi*

[c] Some witnesses add *new:* (cf. Luke 22:20) A C D K W Δ Π *f*1 *f*13 28 *pm*

° Appendix 2 ⇨ Matt 26:20–21

Exod 24:8 ⇨ Matt 26:28
[8] And Moses took the blood and threw it upon the people, and said, "Behold the **blood of the covenant which** the Lord has made with you in accordance with all these words."

Mark 14:12–16 (§K62.1) ⇨ §M81.1
[12] And **on the first day of Unleavened Bread,** when they sacrificed the passover lamb, his **disciples** said to him, "**Where will you have us** go and **prepare for you to eat the passover?**" [13] And **he** sent two of his disciples, and **said** to them, "**Go into the city,** and a man carrying a jar of water will meet you; follow him, [14] **and** wherever he enters, **say to** the householder, '**The Teacher says,** Where is my guest room, where **I** am **to eat the passover with my disciples?'** [15] And he will show you a large upper room furnished and ready; there prepare for us." [16] **And the disciples** set out and went to the city, and found it **as he had** told **them; and they prepared the passover.**

Mark 14:17–21 (§K62.2) ⇨ §M81.2
[17] And **when it was evening he** came with **the twelve.** [18] **And as they were** at table **eating,** Jesus **said,** "**Truly, I say to you, one of you will betray me,** one who is eating with me." [19] **They began** to be **sorrowful,** and **to say to him one after another,** "Is it I?" [20] **He** said to them, "It is one of the twelve, one **who is** dipping bread into **the dish with me.** [21] For the **Son of man goes as it is written of him,** but **woe to that man by whom the Son of man is betrayed! It would have been better for that man if he had not been born.**"

Mark 14:22–25 (§K62.3) ⇨ §M81.3
[22] And **as they were eating,** he **took bread, and blessed, and broke it, and gave it to** them, **and said,** "**Take; this is my body.**" [23] **And he took a cup, and when he had given thanks he gave it to them,** and they all drank of it. [24] And he said to them, "**This is my blood of the covenant, which is poured out for many.** [25] Truly, **I say to you, I shall not drink again of** the **fruit of the vine until that day when I drink it new in** the **kingdom** of God."

Jer 31:31 ⇨ Matt 26:28
[31] "Behold, the days are coming, says the Lord, when I will make a new **covenant** with the house of Israel and the house of Judah, . . ."

Zech 9:11 ⇨ Matt 26:28
[11] As for you also, because of the **blood of my covenant** with you,
    I will set your captives free from the waterless pit.

Luke 22:7–13 (§L93.1) ⇨ §M81.1
[7] Then came **the day of Unleavened Bread,** on which **the passover** lamb had to be sacrificed. [8] So Jesus sent Peter and John, saying, "Go and **prepare the passover** for us, that we may **eat it.**" [9] They said to him, "**Where will you have us prepare** it?" [10] **He said** to them, "Behold, when you have entered **the city,** a man carrying a jar of water will meet you; follow him into the house which he enters, [11] **and** tell the householder, '**The Teacher says** to you, Where is the guest room, where I am to eat **the passover with my disciples?'** [12] And he will show you a large upper room furnished; there make ready." [13] And they went, and found it as he **had** told **them; and they prepared the passover.**

Luke 22:14–23 (§L93.2) ⇨ §M81.2–3
[14] And when the hour came, **he sat at table,** and the apostles with him. [15] And **he said** to them, "I have earnestly desired to eat this passover with you before I suffer; [16] for **I tell you I shall not** eat it **until** it is fulfilled **in** the **kingdom** of God." [17] **And he took a cup, and when he had given thanks** he said, "Take this, and divide it among yourselves; [18] for **I tell you** that from now on **I shall not drink of the fruit of the vine until** the **kingdom** of God comes." [19] And he **took bread,** and when he had given thanks he **broke it and gave it to** them, saying, "**This is my body** which is given for you. Do this in remembrance of me." [20] And likewise the **cup** after supper, saying, "**This** cup which **is poured out for** you **is the** new **covenant in my blood.** [21] But behold the **hand** of him who betrays **me** is with me on the table. [22] For the **Son of man goes as it** has been determined; **but woe to that man by whom** he **is betrayed!**" [23] And they began to question one another, which of them it was that would do this.

| | JOHN | THOMAS | OTHER |

JOHN

John 13:21–30 (§J29) ⇨ §M81.2
²¹When Jesus had thus spoken, **he** was troubled in spirit, and testified, "Truly, **truly, I say to you, one of you will betray me**." ²²The disciples looked at one another, uncertain of whom he spoke. ²³One of his disciples, whom Jesus loved, was lying close to the breast of Jesus; ²⁴so Simon Peter beckoned to him and said, "Tell us who it is of whom he speaks." ²⁵So lying thus, close to the breast of Jesus, he said to him, "Lord, who is it?" ²⁶Jesus **answered**, "It is **he** to whom I shall give this morsel when I have **dipped** it." So when he had dipped the morsel, he gave it to **Judas**, the son of Simon Iscariot. ²⁷Then after the morsel, Satan entered into him. Jesus **said to him**, "What **you** are going to do, do quickly." ²⁸Now no one at the table knew why he said this to him. ²⁹Some thought that, because Judas had the money box, Jesus was telling him, "Buy what we need for the feast"; or, that he should give something to the poor. ³⁰So, after receiving the morsel, he immediately went out; and it was night.

John 6:48–58 ⇨ §M81.3
⁴⁸"I am the **bread** of life. ⁴⁹Your fathers ate the manna in the wilderness, and they died. ⁵⁰This is the **bread** which comes down from heaven, that a man may eat of it and not die. ⁵¹I am the living **bread** which came down from heaven; if any one eats of this **bread**, he will live for ever; and the **bread** which I shall give for the life of the world **is my** flesh." ⁵²The Jews then disputed among themselves, saying, "How can this man give us his flesh to eat?" ⁵³So **Jesus said** to them, "Truly, truly, I say to you, unless you eat the flesh of the Son of man and **drink** his **blood**, you have no life in you; ⁵⁴he who eats my flesh and drinks **my blood** has eternal life, and I will raise him up at the last day. ⁵⁵For **my** flesh is food indeed, and **my blood is drink** indeed. ⁵⁶He who eats **my** flesh and drinks **my blood** abides in me, and I in him. ⁵⁷As the living Father sent me, and I live because of the Father, so he who eats me will live because of me. ⁵⁸This is the **bread** which came down from heaven, not such as the fathers ate and died; he who eats this **bread** will live for ever."

OTHER

GEbi 7 ⇨ §M81.1
(7) But they abandon the proper sequence of the words and pervert the saying, as is plain to all from the readings attached, and have let the disciples say:
Where wilt thou that we **prepare for thee the passover?** *and him to answer to that:*
Do I desire with desire at this **Passover** *to eat flesh with you?* (Epiphanius, *Haer.* 30.22.4)

1 Cor 11:23–25 ⇨ §M81.3
²³For I received from the Lord what I also delivered to you, that the Lord **Jesus** on the night when he was betrayed **took bread**, ²⁴ **and** when he had given thanks, he **broke it, and** said, "**This is my body** which is for you. Do this in remembrance of me." ²⁵In the same way also the **cup**, after supper, **saying, "This cup is the** new **covenant** in **my blood**. Do this, as often as you drink it, in remembrance of me."

Did 9:1–5 ⇨ §M81.3
¹And concerning the Eucharist, hold Eucharist thus: ²First concerning the **Cup**, "We give **thanks** to thee, our Father, for the Holy Vine of David thy child, which, thou didst make known to us through Jesus thy child; to thee be glory for ever." ³And concerning the broken **Bread**: "We give thee thanks, our Father, for the life and knowledge which thou didst make known to us through Jesus thy child. To thee be glory for ever. ⁴As this broken **bread** is scattered upon the mountains, but was brought together and became one, so let thy Church be gathered together from the ends of the earth into thy kingdom, for thine is the glory and the power through Jesus Christ for ever." ⁵But let none eat or drink of your Eucharist except those who have been baptised in the Lord's Name. For concerning this also did the Lord say, "Give not that which is holy to the dogs."

Justin, *Apology* 1.66.3 ⇨ §M81.3
For the apostles in the memoirs composed by them, which are called Gospels, thus handed down what was commanded them: that **Jesus**, taking **bread** and having given thanks, **said**, "Do this for my memorial, **this is my body**"; **and** likewise taking the **cup** and giving **thanks** he said, "**This is my blood**"; and **gave it to them** alone. **This** also the wicked demons in imitation handed down as something to be done in the mysteries of Mithra; for bread and a cup of water are brought out in their secret rites of initiation, with certain invocations which you either know or can learn.

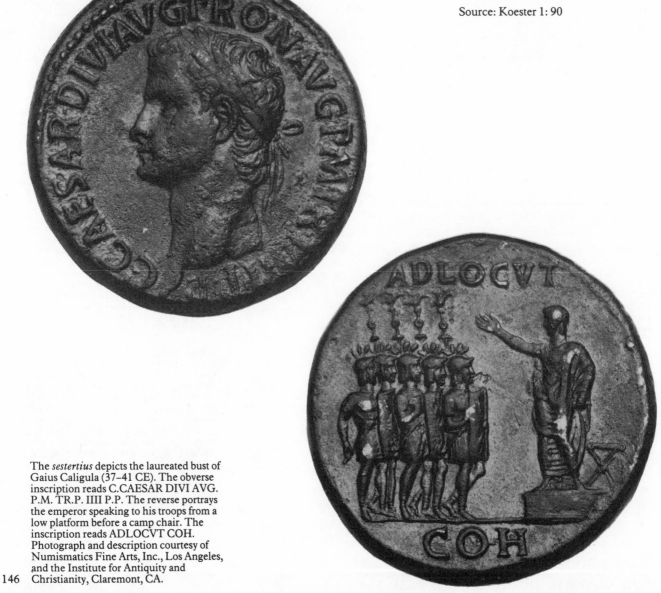

GREEK COINS

1 talent = 60 minas
1 mina = 50 staters (gold)
1 stater = 2 drachmas (silver)
1 drachma = 6 obols (bronze)

ROMAN COINS

1 aureus (gold) = 25 denarii (silver)
1 denarius = 4 sestercia
1 sestertius = 2 dupondii
1 dupondius = 2 asses
1 as = 4 quadrants

1 drachma = 1 denarius

Source: Koester 1: 90

The *sestertius* depicts the laureated bust of Gaius Caligula (37–41 CE). The obverse inscription reads C.CAESAR DIVI AVG. P.M. TR.P. IIII P.P. The reverse portrays the emperor speaking to his troops from a low platform before a camp chair. The inscription reads ADLOCVT COH. Photograph and description courtesy of Numismatics Fine Arts, Inc., Los Angeles, and the Institute for Antiquity and Christianity, Claremont, CA.

MATT

Matt 26:30–35 (§M82.1)
[30] And when they had sung a hymn, they went out to the Mount of Olives. [31] Then Jesus said to them, "You will all fall away because of me this night; for it is written, 'I will strike the shepherd, and the sheep of the flock will be scattered.' [32] But after I am raised up, I will go before you to Galilee." [33] Peter declared to him, "Though they all fall away because of you, I will never fall away." [34] Jesus said to him, "Truly, I say to you, this very night, before the cock crows, you will deny me three times." [35] Peter said to him, "Even if I must die with you, I will not deny you." And so said all the disciples.

Zech 13:7 ⇨ Matt 26:31
[7] "Awake, O sword, against my **shepherd**,
      against the man who stands next to me,"
            says the Lord of hosts.
  "**Strike the shepherd**, that **the sheep** may be **scattered**;
      I will turn my hand against the little ones."

MARK

Mark 14:26–31 (§K63.1)
[26] And when they had sung a hymn, they went out to the Mount of Olives. [27] And Jesus said to them, "You will all fall away; for it is written, 'I will strike the shepherd, and the sheep will be scattered.' [28] But after I am raised up, I will go before you to Galilee." [29] Peter said to him, "Even though they all fall away, I will not." [30] And Jesus said to him, "Truly, I say to you, this very night, before the cock crows twice, you will deny me three times." [31] But he said vehemently, "If I must die with you, I will not deny you." And they all said the same.

LUKE

Luke 22:31–34 (§L93.4)
[31] "Simon, Simon, behold, Satan demanded to have you, that he might sift you like wheat, [32] but I have prayed for you that your faith may not fail; and when you have turned again, strengthen your brethren." [33] And he said to him, "Lord, I am ready to go with you to prison and to death." [34] He said, "I tell you, Peter, the cock will not crow this day, until you three times deny that you know me."

Luke 22:39 (§L94.1a) ⇨ Matt 26:30
[39] And he came out, and went, as was his custom, to the Mount of Olives; and the disciples followed him.

JOHN

John 13:36–38
[36] Simon Peter said to him, "Lord, where are you going?" Jesus answered, "Where I am going you cannot follow me now; but you shall follow afterward." [37] Peter said to him, "Lord, why cannot I follow you now? I will lay down my life for you." [38] Jesus answered, "Will you lay down your life for me? Truly, truly, I say to you, the cock will not crow, till you have denied me three times."

† John 18:1 ⇨ Matt 26:30
[1] When Jesus had spoken these words, he went forth with his disciples across the Kidron valley, where there was a garden, which he and his disciples entered.

John 16:32 ⇨ Matt 26:31
[32] "The hour is coming, indeed it has come, when you will be scattered, every man to his home, and will leave me alone; yet I am not alone, for the Father is with me."

John 11:16 ⇨ Matt 26:35
[16] Thomas, called the Twin, said to his fellow disciples, "Let us also go, that we may die with him."

THOMAS

OTHER

Fayyum Fragment ⇨ Matt 26:31, 33–34
...while he was going **out**, he **said**, "**This night you will all fall away**, as it is written, '**I will strike the shepherd, and the sheep will be scattered.**'" When **Peter** said, "Even **though all, not I**," Jesus said, "Before the cock crows twice, **you will** this day **deny me three times.**"

MATT	MARK	LUKE
INTRODUCTION	**Mark 14:32 (§K63.2a)**	**Luke 22:39 (§L94.1a)**
Matt 26:36 (§M82.2a) [36] Then Jesus went with them to a place called Gethsemane, and he said to his disciples, "Sit here, while I go yonder and pray."	[32] And they **went to a place** which was **called** Gethsemane; **and he said to his disciples**, "**Sit here, while I pray.**"	[39] And he came out, and **went**, as was his custom, to the Mount of Olives; and the **disciples** followed him.
JESUS TAKES THREE	**Mark 14:33–34 (§K63.2b)**	**Luke 22:40–42 (§L94.1b)**
Matt 26:37–38 (§M82.2b) [37] And taking with him Peter and the two sons of Zebedee, he began to be sorrowful and troubled. [38] Then he said to them, "My soul is very sorrowful, even to death; remain here, and watch with me."	[33] And he took **with him Peter and** James and John, and **began to be** greatly distressed **and troubled**. [34] And **he said to them**, "**My soul is very sorrowful, even to death; remain here, and watch.**"	[40] And when he came to the place he said to them, "**Pray that you may not enter into temptation.**" [41] And he withdrew from them about a stone's throw, and knelt down and **prayed**, [42] "**Father**, if thou art willing, remove **this cup from me; nevertheless not** my **will, but** thine, be done."
FIRST PRAYER	**Mark 14:35–36 (§K63.2c)**	**Luke 22:45–46 (§L94.1c)**
Matt 26:39 (§M82.2c) [39] And going a little farther he fell on his face and prayed, "My Father, if it be possible, let this cup pass from me; nevertheless, not as I will, but as thou wilt."	[35] **And going a little farther, he fell on** the ground **and prayed** that, if it were possible, the hour might pass from him. [36] And he said, "**Abba, Father**, all things are **possible** to thee; remove **this cup from me; yet not** what **I will, but** what **thou wilt.**"	[45] **And** when he rose from prayer, **he came to the disciples and found them sleeping** for sorrow, [46] **and he said to them, "Why do you sleep? Rise and pray that you may not enter into temptation.**"
THE THREE SLEEP	**Mark 14:37–38 (§K63.2d)**	
Matt 26:40–41 (§M82.2d) [40] And he came to the disciples and found them sleeping; and he said to Peter, "So, could you not watch[a] with me one hour? [41] Watch and pray that you may not enter into temptation; the spirit indeed is willing, but the flesh is weak."	[37] **And he came and found them sleeping, and said to Peter**, "Simon, are you asleep? **Could you not watch one hour?** [38] **Watch and pray that you may not enter into temptation; the spirit indeed is willing, but the flesh is weak.**"	
SECOND PRAYER	**Mark 14:39 (§K63.2e)**	
Matt 26:42 (§M82.2e) [42] Again, for the second time, he went away and prayed, "My Father, if this cannot pass unless I drink it, thy will be done."	[39] And **again he went away and prayed**, saying the same words.	
THE THREE SLEEP	**Mark 14:40 (§K63.2f)**	
Matt 26:43 (§M82.2f) [43] And again he came and found them sleeping, for their eyes were heavy.	[40] **And again he came and found them sleeping, for their eyes were** very **heavy**; and they did not know what to answer him.	
THIRD PRAYER	**Mark 14:41–42 (§K63.2g)**	
Matt 26:44 (§M82.2g) [44] So, leaving them again, he went away and prayed for the third time, saying the same words.	[41] And **he came** the third time, **and said to them**, "**Are you still sleeping and taking your rest?** It is enough; **the hour** has come; **the Son of man is betrayed into the hands of sinners.** [42] **Rise, let us be going; see, my betrayer is at hand.**"	
THE HOUR HAS COME		
Matt 26:45–46 (§M82.2h) [45] Then he came to the disciples and said to them, "Are you still sleeping and taking your rest? Behold, the hour is at hand, and the Son of man is betrayed into the hands of sinners. [46] Rise, let us be going; see, my betrayer is at hand."		

[a] Or: *keep awake*

JOHN	THOMAS	OTHER

† John 18:1 ⇨ §M82.2a

¹ When **Jesus** had spoken these words, he **went** forth **with** his disciples across the Kidron valley, where there was a garden, which **he** and **his disciples** entered.

John 12:27 ⇨ Matt 26:38–39

²⁷ *"Now **is my soul** troubled. And what shall I say? '**Father**, save **me** from this hour'? No, for this purpose I have come to this hour.*

John 18:11 ⇨ Matt 26:39

¹¹ *Jesus said to Peter, "Put your sword into its sheath; shall **I** not drink the **cup** which the **Father** has given me?"*

John 14:31 ⇨ Matt 26:46

³¹ *"but I do as the Father has commanded me, so that the world may know that I love the Father. **Rise, let us** go hence."*

MATT

Matt 26:47–56 (§M82.3) °

47 While he was still speaking, Judas came, one of the twelve, and with him a great crowd with swords and clubs, from the chief priests and the elders of the people. 48 Now the betrayer had given them a sign, saying, "The one I shall kiss is the man; seize him." 49 And he came up to Jesus at once and said, "Hail, Master!"[a] And he kissed him. 50 Jesus said to him, "Friend, why are you here?"[b] Then they came up and laid hands on Jesus and seized him. 51 And behold, one of those who were with Jesus stretched out his hand and drew his sword, and struck the slave of the high priest, and cut off his ear. 52 Then Jesus said to him, "Put your sword back into its place; for all who take the sword will perish by the sword. 53 Do you think that I cannot appeal to my Father, and he will at once send me more than twelve legions of angels? 54 But how then should the scriptures be fulfilled, that it must be so?" 55 At that hour Jesus said to the crowds, "Have you come out as against a robber, with swords and clubs to capture me? Day after day I sat in the temple teaching, and you did not seize me. 56 But all this has taken place, that the scriptures of the prophets might be fulfilled." Then all the disciples forsook him and fled.

[a] Or: *Rabbi*

[b] Or: *do that for which you have come*

°Appendix 2 ⇨ Matt 26:47

MARK

Mark 14:43–52 (§K63.3)

43 And immediately, **while he was still speaking, Judas came, one of the twelve, and with him a crowd with swords and clubs, from the chief priests** and the scribes **and the elders.** 44 **Now the betrayer had given them a sign, saying, "The one I shall kiss is the man; seize him** and lead him away under guard." 45 **And when he came,** he went up to him at once, **and said, "Master!" And he kissed him.** 46 **And they laid hands on** him **and seized him.** 47 **But one of those who** stood by **drew his sword, and struck the slave of the high priest and cut off his ear.** 48 **And Jesus said to them, "Have you come out as against a robber, with swords and clubs to capture me?** 49 **Day after day I was with you in the temple teaching, and you did not seize me. But let the scriptures be fulfilled."** 50 **And they all forsook him, and fled.**

51 And a young man followed him, with nothing but a linen cloth about his body; and they seized him, 52 but he left the linen cloth and ran away naked.

LUKE

Luke 22:47–54a (§L94.2)

47 **While he was still speaking,** there came **a crowd,** and the man called **Judas, one of the twelve,** was leading them. **He** drew near **to Jesus to kiss him;** 48 but Jesus said to him, "Judas, would you betray the Son of man with a kiss?" 49 And when those who were about him saw what would follow, they said, "Lord, shall we strike with the **sword**?" 50 **And one of** them **struck the slave of the high priest and cut off his** right **ear.** 51 But Jesus said, "No more of this!" And he touched his ear and healed him. 52 Then **Jesus said to the** chief priests and officers of the temple and elders, who had **come out against** him, "**Have you come out as against a robber, with swords and clubs?** 53 When I was with you **day after day in the temple, you did not** lay hands on me. But this is your hour, and the power of darkness."

54 **Then** they seized him and led him away, bringing him into the high priest's house.

JOHN

John 18:1–12 (§J31.1)

1 When Jesus had spoken these words, he went forth with his disciples across the Kidron valley, where there was a garden, which he and his disciples entered. 2 Now **Judas,** who betrayed him, also knew the place; for Jesus often met there with his disciples. 3 So **Judas,** procuring a band of soldiers and some officers from **the chief priests and the** Pharisees, went there with lanterns and torches and weapons. 4 Then Jesus, knowing all that was to befall him, came forward and said to them, "Whom do you seek?" 5 They answered him, "Jesus of Nazareth." **Jesus said to** them, "I am he." Judas, who betrayed him, was standing with them. 6 When he said to them, "I am he," they drew back and fell to the ground. 7 Again he asked them, "Whom do you seek?" And they said, "Jesus of Nazareth." 8 Jesus answered, "I told you that I am he; so, if you seek me, let these men go." 9 This was to fulfil the word which he had spoken, "Of those whom thou gavest me I lost not one." 10 Then Simon Peter, having a **sword, drew** it **and struck the high** priest's **slave and cut off his** right **ear.** The slave's name was Malchus. 11 **Jesus said to** Peter, "**Put your sword into its** sheath; shall I not drink the cup which the Father has given me?"

12 So the band of soldiers and their captain and the officers of the Jews **seized Jesus and** bound **him.**

John 18:20 ⇨ Matt 26:55
20 *Jesus answered him, "I have spoken openly to the world; I have always taught in synagogues and in the temple, where all Jews come together; I have said nothing secretly."*

THOMAS

OTHER

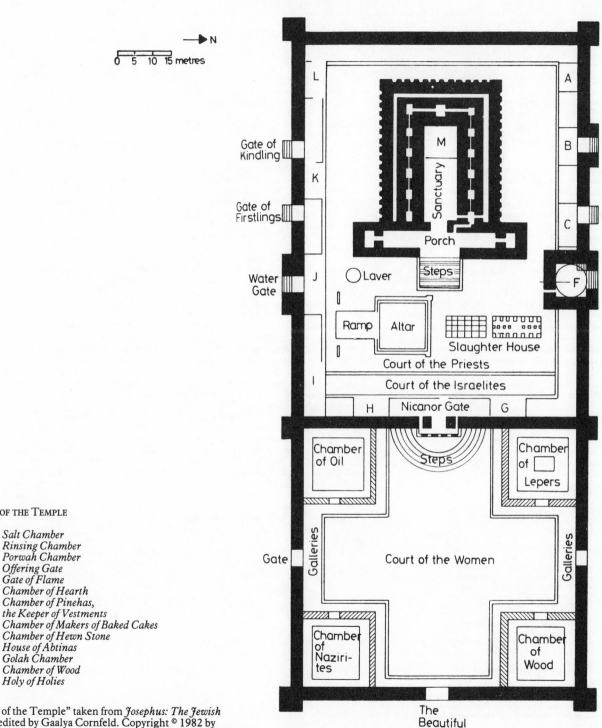

PLAN OF THE TEMPLE

A   Salt Chamber
B   Rinsing Chamber
C   Porwah Chamber
D   Offering Gate
E   Gate of Flame
F   Chamber of Hearth
G   Chamber of Pinehas,
       the Keeper of Vestments
H   Chamber of Makers of Baked Cakes
I   Chamber of Hewn Stone
J   House of Abtinas
K   Golah Chamber
L   Chamber of Wood
M   Holy of Holies

Matt 26:57–58
Matt 26:59–68

INTRODUCTION
TRIAL BEFORE THE COUNCIL

M83.1
M83.2

MATT

Matt 26:57–58 (§M83.1)

[57] Then those who had seized Jesus led him to Caiaphas the high priest, where the scribes and the elders had gathered. [58] But Peter followed him at a distance, as far as the courtyard of the high priest, and going inside he sat with the guards to see the end.

Matt 26:59–68 (§M83.2)

[59] Now the chief priests and the whole council sought false testimony against Jesus that they might put him to death, [60] but they found none, though many false witnesses came forward. At last two came forward [61] and said, "This fellow said, 'I am able to destroy the temple of God, and to build it in three days.'" [62] And the high priest stood up and said, "Have you no answer to make? What is it that these men testify against you?" [63] But Jesus was silent. And the high priest said to him, "I adjure you by the living God, tell us if you are the Christ, the Son of God." [64] Jesus said to him, "You have said so. But I tell you, hereafter you will see the Son of man seated at the right hand of Power, and coming on the clouds of heaven." [65] Then the high priest tore his robes, and said, "He has uttered blasphemy. Why do we still need witnesses? You have now heard his blasphemy. [66] What is your judgment?" They answered, "He deserves death." [67] Then they spat in his face, and struck him; and some slapped him, [68] saying, "Prophesy to us, you Christ! Who is it that struck you?"

•Matt 24:30 ⇨ Matt 26:64

[30] "then will appear the sign of **the Son of man** in heaven, and then all the tribes of the earth will mourn, and they **will see the Son of man coming on the clouds of heaven** with power and great glory";
. . .

Ps 110:1 ⇨ Matt 26:64

[1] The Lord says to my lord:
"Sit **at my right hand,**
till I make your enemies
your footstool."

Dan 7:13–14 ⇨ Matt 26:64

[13] I saw in the night visions,
and behold, with **the clouds of heaven**
there came one like a **son of man,**
and he came to the Ancient of Days
and was presented before him.
[14] And to him was given dominion
and glory and kingdom,
that all peoples, nations, and languages
should serve him;
his dominion is an everlasting dominion,
which shall not pass away,
and his kingdom one
that shall not be destroyed.

Lev 24:16 ⇨ Matt 26:65–66

[16] "**He** who blasphemes the name of the Lord shall be put to **death**; all the congregation shall stone him; the sojourner as well as the native, when **he** blasphemes the Name, shall be put to **death**."

MARK

Mark 14:53–54 (§K64.1) ⇨ §M83.1

[53] And they led **Jesus to the high priest;** and all the chief priests and the elders and the scribes were assembled. [54] And **Peter** had **followed him at a distance,** right into **the courtyard of the high priest;** and **he** was sitting **with the guards,** and warming himself at the fire.

Mark 14:55–65 (§K64.2) ⇨ §M83.2

[55] Now **the chief priests and the whole council sought testimony against Jesus** to put him to death; but **they found none.** [56] For **many** bore **false witness** against him, and their witness did not agree. [57] And some stood up and bore false witness against him, saying, [58] "We heard him say, 'I will **destroy** this **temple** that is made with hands, **and in three days** I will **build** another, not made with hands.'" [59] Yet not even so did their testimony agree. [60] **And the high priest stood up** in the midst, and asked Jesus, "**Have you no answer to make? What is it that these men testify against you?**" [61] But he **was silent** and made no answer. Again **the high priest** asked him, "**Are you the Christ, the Son of** the Blessed?" [62] And **Jesus said,** "I am; and **you will see the Son of man seated at the right hand of Power, and coming with the clouds of heaven.**" [63] And **the high priest tore his** garments, **and said, "Why do we still need witnesses? [64] You have heard his blasphemy. What is your decision?**" And they all condemned him as deserving **death.** [65] And some began to spit on him, and to cover his face, and to strike **him, saying** to him, "**Prophesy!**" And the guards received him with blows.

Mark 13:26 ⇨ Matt 26:64

[26] "And then they **will see the Son of man coming** in **clouds** with great power and glory."

LUKE

Luke 22:54b–62 (§L95.1) ⇨ §M83.1

Peter followed at a distance; [55] and when they had kindled a fire in the middle of **the courtyard** and **sat** down together, Peter **sat** among them. [56] Then a maid, seeing him as he sat in the light and gazing at him, said, "This man also was with him." [57] But he denied it, saying, "Woman, I do not know him." [58] And a little later some one else saw him and said, "You also are one of them." But Peter said, "Man, I am not." [59] And after an interval of about an hour still another insisted, saying, "Certainly this man also was with him; for he is a Galilean." [60] But Peter said, "Man, I do not know what you are saying." And immediately, while he was still speaking, the cock crowed. [61] And the Lord turned and looked at Peter. And Peter remembered the word of the Lord, how he had said to him, "Before the cock crows today, you will deny me three times." [62] And he went out and wept bitterly.

Luke 22:63–65 (§L95.2) ⇨ §M83.2

[63] Now the men who were holding Jesus mocked **him and** beat **him;** [64] **they** also blindfolded him and asked him, "**Prophesy! Who is it that struck you?**" [65] And they spoke many other words against him, reviling him.

Luke 22:66–71 (§L96) ⇨ §M83.2

[66] When day came, the assembly of the elders of the people gathered together, both **chief priests** and scribes; and they led him away to their **council, and they said,** [67] "**If you are the Christ, tell us.**" But he **said to** them, "If **I tell you,** you will not believe; [68] and if I ask you, you will not answer. [69] **But** from now on **the Son of man** shall be **seated at the right hand of** the **power** of God." [70] And they all **said,** "Are you **the Son of God,** then?" And he **said to** them, "**You** say that I am." [71] And they said, "What further testimony do **we need**? We **have heard** it ourselves from his own lips."

Luke 21:27 ⇨ Matt 26:64

[27] "And then they **will see the Son of man coming** in a cloud with power and great glory."

152

Matt 26:57–75
Matt 26:1–27:66

BEFORE THE COUNCIL; PETER'S DENIAL
THE PASSION NARRATIVE

M83
S20: M80–87

<table>
<tr><th>JOHN</th><th>THOMAS</th><th>OTHER</th></tr>
</table>

JOHN	THOMAS	OTHER

John 18:13–14 (§J31.2a)
[13] First they **led him to** Annas; for he was the father-in-law of **Caiaphas**, who was **high priest** that year. [14] It was **Caiaphas** who had given counsel to the Jews that it was expedient that one man should die for the people.

John 18:19–24 (§J31.2c)
[19] The high priest then questioned **Jesus** about his disciples and his teaching. [20] **Jesus** answered **him**, "I have spoken openly to the world; I have always taught in synagogues and in the temple, where all Jews come together; I have said nothing secretly. [21] Why do you ask me? Ask those who have heard me, what I said to them; they know what I said." [22] When he had said this, one of the officers standing by struck Jesus with his hand, saying, "Is that how you answer the high priest?" [23] Jesus answered him, "If I have spoken wrongly, bear witness to the wrong; but if I have spoken rightly, why do you strike me?" [24] Annas then sent **him** bound to **Caiaphas the high priest**.

John 2:19 ⇨ Matt 26:61
[19] Jesus answered them, "**Destroy** this **temple**, and **in three days** I will raise it up."

GThom 71 ⇨ Matt 26:61
(71) Jesus said, "**I** shall **destroy** [this] house, **and** no one will be able **to** rebuild **it**."

GPet 3.9 ⇨ Matt 26:67
[9] And others who stood by **spat** on **his face, and** others buffeted **him** on the cheeks, others nudged **him** with a reed, **and some** scourged him, saying, "With such honour let us honour the Son of God."

MATT	MARK	LUKE

MATT

FIRST DENIAL

Matt 26:69–70 (§M83.3a)

⁶⁹ Now Peter was sitting outside in the courtyard. And a maid came up to him, and said, "You also were with Jesus the Galilean." ⁷⁰ But he denied it before them all, saying, "I do not know what you mean."

SECOND DENIAL

Matt 26:71–72 (§M83.3b)

⁷¹ And when he went out to the porch, another maid saw him, and she said to the bystanders, "This man was with Jesus of Nazareth." ⁷² And again he denied it with an oath, "I do not know the man."

THIRD DENIAL

Matt 26:73–75 (§M83.3c)

⁷³ After a little while the bystanders came up and said to Peter, "Certainly you are also one of them, for your accent betrays you." ⁷⁴ Then he began to invoke a curse on himself and to swear, "I do not know the man." And immediately the cock crowed. ⁷⁵ And Peter remembered the saying of Jesus, "Before the cock crows, you will deny me three times." And he went out and wept bitterly.

MARK

Mark 14:66–72 (§K64.3)

⁶⁶ And as **Peter** was below in the courtyard, one of the maids of the high priest **came**; ⁶⁷ and seeing Peter warming himself, she looked at **him, and said, "You also were with** the Nazarene, **Jesus.**" ⁶⁸ **But he denied it, say-ing, "I** neither **know** nor understand **what you mean.**" And **he went out** into **the** gateway. ⁶⁹ And the **maid saw him,** and began again to say **to the bystanders, "This man** is one of them." ⁷⁰ But **again he denied it. And after a little while** again **the bystanders said to Peter,** "**Certainly you are one of them; for you** are a Galilean." ⁷¹ But **he began to invoke a curse on himself** and to swear, "I **do not know** this **man** of whom you speak." ⁷² **And immediately the cock crowed** a second time. **And Peter remembered** how Jesus had said to him, "**Before the cock** crows twice, **you will deny me three times.**" **And he** broke down and wept.

LUKE

Luke 22:54b–62 (§L95.1)

Peter followed at a distance; ⁵⁵ and when they had kindled a fire in the middle of the court-yard and sat down together, Peter sat among them. ⁵⁶ Then **a maid,** seeing him as he sat in the light and gazing at **him, said,** "This man also was **with him.**" ⁵⁷ **But he denied it, saying,** "Woman, **I do not know** him." ⁵⁸ And a little later some one else **saw him** and **said,** "You also are one of them." But Peter said, "**Man, I am not.**" ⁵⁹ And after an interval of about an hour still another insisted, saying, "**Certainly** this man **also** was with him; **for** he is a Galilean." ⁶⁰ But Peter said, "Man, **I do not know** what you are saying. **And immedi-ately,** while he was still speaking, **the cock crowed.** ⁶¹ And the Lord turned and looked at Peter. **And Peter remembered** the word of the Lord, how he had said to him, "**Before the cock crows** today, **you will deny me three times.**" ⁶² And he went out and wept bitterly.

JOHN	THOMAS	OTHER

JOHN

John 18:15–18 (§J31.2b) ⇨ §M83.3a

¹⁵ Simon **Peter** followed Jesus, and so did another disciple. As this disciple was known to the high priest, he entered the court of the high priest along with Jesus, ¹⁶ while Peter stood outside at the door. So the other disci-ple, who was known to the high priest, went out and spoke to the maid who kept the door, and brought Peter in. ¹⁷ The **maid** who kept the door said to Peter, "Are not **you also** one of this man's disciples?" **He** said, "I am not." ¹⁸ Now the servants and officers had made a charcoal fire, because it was cold, and they were standing and warming themselves; Peter also was with them, standing and warming himself.

John 18:25–27 (§J31.2d) ⇨ §M83.3b–c

²⁵ Now Simon Peter was standing and warming himself. They **said to** him, "Are not you also one of his disciples?" **He denied it** and said, "I am **not.**" ²⁶ One of the servants of the high priest, a kinsman of the man whose ear Peter had cut off, asked, "Did I not see **you** in the garden with him?" ²⁷ Peter again denied it; and at once **the cock crowed.**

OTHER

GNaz 19 ⇨ Matt 26:74

(19) The Jewish Gospel: And he denied and swore and damned himself. (Variant to Matthew 26:74 in the "Zion Gospel" Edition)

M84.1
M84.2

INTRODUCTION
JUDAS REPENTS

Matt 27:1–2
Matt 27:3–10

MATT

Matt 27:1–2 (§M84.1)
¹ When morning came, all the chief priests and the elders of the people took counsel against Jesus to put him to death; ² and they bound him and led him away and delivered him to Pilate the governor.

Matt 27:3–10 (§M84.2)
³ When Judas, his betrayer, saw that he was condemned, he repented and brought back the thirty pieces of silver to the chief priests and the elders, ⁴ saying, "I have sinned in betraying innocent blood." They said, "What is that to us? See to it yourself." ⁵ And throwing down the pieces of silver in the temple, he departed; and he went and hanged himself. ⁶ But the chief priests, taking the pieces of silver, said, "It is not lawful to put them into the treasury, since they are blood money." ⁷ So they took counsel, and bought with them the potter's field, to bury strangers in. ⁸ Therefore that field has been called the Field of Blood to this day. ⁹ Then was fulfilled what had been spoken by the prophet Jeremiah, saying, "And they took the thirty pieces of silver, the price of him on whom a price had been set by some of the sons of Israel, ¹⁰ and they gave them for the potter's field, as the Lord directed me."

Zech 11:12–13 ⇨ Matt 27:9–10
¹² Then I said to them, "If it seems right to you, give me my wages; but if not, keep them." **And they** weighed out as my wages **thirty** shekels **of silver.** ¹³ Then the Lord said to me, "Cast it into the treasury"—the lordly price at which I was paid off by them. So I **took the thirty** shekels **of silver** and cast them into the treasury in the house of the Lord.

⇨ Matt 27:9–10
Cf. Jer 18:2–3, 32:6–15

JOHN

John 18:28 ⇨ §M84.1
²⁸ Then **they led** Jesus from the house of Caiaphas to the praetorium. It was early. They themselves did not enter the praetorium, so that they might not be defiled, but might eat the passover.

MARK

Mark 15:1 ⇨ §M84.1
¹ And as soon as it was **morning the chief priests**, with **the elders** and scribes, and the whole council held a consultation; **and they bound** Jesus **and led him away and delivered him to Pilate.**

THOMAS

LUKE

Luke 23:1 ⇨ §M84.1
¹ Then the whole company of them arose, **and** brought **him** before **Pilate.**

OTHER

Acts 1:15–20 ⇨ §M84.2
¹⁵ In those days Peter stood up among the brethren (the company of persons was in all about a hundred and twenty), and said, ¹⁶ "Brethren, the scripture had to be **fulfilled**, which the Holy Spirit spoke beforehand by the mouth of David, concerning Judas who was guide to those who arrested Jesus. ¹⁷ For he was numbered among us, and was allotted his share in this ministry. ¹⁸ (Now this man **bought a field** with the reward of his wickedness; and falling headlong he burst open in the middle and all his bowels gushed out. ¹⁹ And it became known to all the inhabitants of Jerusalem, so that **the field** was **called** in their language Akeldama, that is, **Field of Blood.**) ²⁰ For it is written in the book of Psalms, 'Let his habitation become desolate, and let there be no one to live in it'; and 'His office let another take.'"

M84
S20: M80–87

BEFORE PILATE
THE PASSION NARRATIVE

Matt 27:1–26
Matt 26:1–27:66

155

MATT	MARK	LUKE

Matt 27:11–14 (§M84.3)

[11] Now Jesus stood before the governor; and the governor asked him, "Are you the King of the Jews?" Jesus said, "You have said so." [12] But when he was accused by the chief priests and elders, he made no answer. [13] Then Pilate said to him, "Do you not hear how many things they testify against you?" [14] But he gave him no answer, not even to a single charge; so that the governor wondered greatly.

Matt 27:15–26 (§M84.4)

[15] Now at the feast the governor was accustomed to release for the crowd any one prisoner whom they wanted. [16] And they had then a notorious prisoner, called Barabbas.[a] [17] So when they had gathered, Pilate said to them, "Whom do you want me to release for you, Barabbas[a] or Jesus who is called Christ?" [18] For he knew that it was out of envy that they had delivered him up. [19] Besides, while he was sitting on the judgment seat, his wife sent word to him, "Have nothing to do with that righteous man, for I have suffered much over him today in a dream." [20] Now the chief priests and the elders persuaded the people to ask for Barabbas and destroy Jesus. [21] The governor again said to them, "Which of the two do you want me to release for you?" And they said, "Barabbas." [22] Pilate said to them, "Then what shall I do with Jesus who is called Christ?" They all said, "Let him be crucified." [23] And he said, "Why, what evil has he done?" But they shouted all the more, "Let him be crucified."

[24] So when Pilate saw that he was gaining nothing, but rather that a riot was beginning, he took water and washed his hands before the crowd, saying, "I am innocent of this man's blood;[b] see to it yourselves." [25] And all the people answered, "His blood be on us and on our children!" [26] Then he released for them Barabbas, and having scourged Jesus, delivered him to be crucified.

[a] Some witnesses read *Jesus Barabbas:* Θ *f*[1] 700* syr (in part) arm geo (in part)

[b] Some witnesses read, *of this righteous man's blood:* ℵ A K L Δ W Π *f*[1] *f*[13] 33 *al*

Mark 15:2–5 ⇨ §M84.3

[2] And Pilate **asked him, "Are you the King of the Jews?"** And he answered him, **"You have said so."** [3] And **the chief priests accused** him of many things. [4] And Pilate again asked **him,** "Have you no answer to make? See **how many** charges **they** bring **against you."** [5] **But** Jesus made **no** further **answer, so that** Pilate **wondered.**

Luke 23:1–7 (§L97) ⇨ §M84.3

[1] Then the whole company of them arose, and brought him before Pilate. [2] And they began to accuse him, saying, "We found this man perverting our nation, and forbidding us to give tribute to Caesar, and saying that he himself is Christ a king." [3] **And** Pilate **asked him, "Are you the King of the Jews?"** And he answered him, **"You have said so."** [4] And Pilate said to **the chief priests** and the multitudes, "I find no crime in this man." [5] But they were urgent, saying, "He stirs up the people, teaching throughout all Judea, from Galilee even to this place."

[6] When Pilate heard this, he asked whether the man was a Galilean. [7] And when he learned that he belonged to Herod's jurisdiction, he sent him over to Herod, who was himself in Jerusalem at that time.

Luke 23:13–25 (§L99) ⇨ §M84.4

[13] Pilate then called together the chief priests and the rulers and the people, [14] and **said to them,** "You brought me this man as one who was perverting the people; and after examining him before you, behold, I did not find this man guilty of any of your charges against him; [15] neither did Herod, for he sent him back to us. Behold, nothing deserving death has been done by him; [16] I will therefore chastise him and release him."

[18] But they all cried out together, "Away with this man, and release to us **Barabbas"**— [19] a man who had been thrown into prison for an insurrection started in the city, and for murder. [20] Pilate addressed them once more, desiring to release Jesus; [21] but **they** shouted out, "Crucify, crucify **him!"** [22] A third time **he said** to them, **"Why, what evil has he done?** I have found in him no crime deserving death; I will therefore chastise him and release him." [23] **But they** were urgent, demanding with loud cries that he should **be crucified.** And their voices prevailed. [24] **So Pilate** gave sentence that their demand should be granted. [25] **He released** the man who had been thrown into prison for insurrection and murder, whom they asked for; but **Jesus** he **delivered** up **to** their will.

JOHN OTHER

John 18:29–19:16

[29] So Pilate went out to them and said, "What accusation do you bring against this man?" [30] They answered him, "If this man were not an evildoer, we would not have handed him over." [31] Pilate said to them, "Take him yourselves and judge him by your own law." The Jews said to him, "Is it not lawful for us to put any man to death." [32] This was to fulfil the word which Jesus had spoken to show by what death he was to die.

[33] Pilate entered the praetorium again and called **Jesus, and** said to **him, "Are you the King of the Jews?"** [34] **Jesus** answered, "Do **you** say this of your own accord, or did others say it to you about me?" [35] Pilate answered, "Am I a Jew? Your own nation and **the chief priests** have handed you over to me; what have you done?" [36] Jesus answered, "My kingship is not of this world; if my kingship were of this world, my servants would fight, that I might not be handed over to the Jews; but my kingship is not from the world." [37] Pilate said to **him**, "So **you are a king?" Jesus** answered, "**You** say that I am a king. For this I was born, and for this I have come into the world, to bear witness to the truth. Every one who is of the truth hears my voice." [38] **Pilate said to him, "What is truth?"**

After he had said this, he went out to the Jews again, and told them, "I find no crime in him. [39] But you have a custom that I should **release one** man **for** you **at the** Passover; will you have **me release for you** the King of the Jews?" [40] They cried out again, "Not this man, but **Barabbas!"** Now **Barabbas** was a robber.

19 [1] Then **Pilate** took **Jesus and scourged** him. [2] And the soldiers plaited a crown of thorns, and put it on his head, and arrayed him in a purple robe; [3] they came up to him, saying, "Hail, King of the Jews!" and struck him with their hands. [4] Pilate went out again, and said to them, "See, I am bringing him out to you, that you may know that I find no crime in him." [5] So Jesus came out, wearing the crown of thorns and the purple robe. **Pilate said to them,** "Behold the man!" [6] When **the chief priests** and the officers saw him, **they** cried out, "Crucify him, crucify **him!" Pilate said to them,** "Take him **yourselves** and crucify **him,** for I find no crime in him." [7] The Jews answered him, "We have a law, and by that law he ought to die, because he has made himself the Son of God." [8] **When Pilate** heard these words, **he was** the more afraid; [9] he entered the praetorium again and **said to** Jesus, "Where are you from?" But Jesus **gave no answer.** [10] **Pilate** therefore **said to him, "You** will **not** speak to me? **Do you not** know that I have power to release you, and power to crucify you?" [11] Jesus answered him, "You would have no power over me unless it had been given you from above; therefore he who delivered me to you has the greater sin."

[12] Upon this **Pilate** sought to release him, but the Jews cried out, "If you release this man, you are not Caesar's friend; every one who makes himself a king sets himself against Caesar." [13] **When Pilate** heard these words, he brought Jesus out and sat down on the judgment seat at a place called The Pavement, and in Hebrew, Gabbatha. [14] Now it was the day of Preparation of the Passover; it was about the sixth hour. He **said to** the Jews, "Behold your King!" [15] They cried out, "Away with him, away with him, crucify **him!" Pilate said to them,** "**Shall** I crucify your King?" The chief priests answered, "We have no king but Caesar." [16] **Then he** handed **him** over to them **to be crucified.**

AcPil 2:1

[1] When **Pilate** saw this he was afraid, and sought to rise from **the judgment-seat.** And while **he was** still thinking of rising up, **his wife sent to him** saying: **Have nothing to do with** this **righteous man. For I have suffered** many things because of **him** by night. And Pilate summoned all the Jews, and stood up and said to them: "You know that my **wife** fears God and favours rather the customs of the Jews, with you." They answered him: "Yes, we know it." Pilate said to them: "See, my **wife sent to** me saying: **Have nothing to do with this righteous man. For I have suffered** many things because of **him** by night." The Jews answered Pilate: "Did we not tell you that he is a sorcerer? Behold, he has sent **a dream** to your **wife."**

AcPil 3:2 ⇨ §M84.3

[2] And Pilate entered the praetorium again and called **Jesus** apart **and asked him: "Are you the king of the Jews?" Jesus** answered Pilate: "Do **you** say this of your own accord, or did others say it to you about me?" **Pilate** answered Jesus: "Am I a Jew? Your own nation and **the chief priests** have handed **you** over to me. What have you done?" Jesus answered: "My kingship is not of this world; for if my kingship were of this world, my servants would fight, that I might not be handed over to the Jews. But now is my kingship not from here." Pilate said to **him:** "So **you are a king?" Jesus** answered him: "**You** say that I am a king. For this cause I was born and have come, that every one who is of the truth should hear my voice." **Pilate said to him:** "What is truth?" Jesus answered him: "Truth is from heaven." **Pilate said:** "Is there not truth upon earth?" Jesus said to Pilate: "You see how those who speak the truth are judged by those who have authority on earth."

AcPil 4:4–5 ⇨ §M84.4

[4] **Pilate said to them:** "Take him **yourselves** and punish him as you wish." The Jews **said** to Pilate: "We wish **him** to **be crucified."** Pilate **said:** "He does not deserve to be crucified." [5] The governor looked at the multitude of Jews standing around, and when he saw many of the Jews weeping, he **said:** "Not all the multitude wishes him to die." But the elders of the Jews said: "For this purpose has the whole multitude of us come, that he should die." Pilate **said** to the Jews: "**Why** should he die?" The Jews said: "Because he called himself the Son of God and a king."

AcPil 9:4–5 ⇨ §M84.4

[4] **When Pilate** heard these words, **he was** afraid. And he silenced the multitudes, because they were crying out, and said to them: "So this is he whom Herod sought?" The Jews replied: "Yes, this is he." And **Pilate took water and washed his hands before the** sun and said: "**I am innocent of the blood of this** righteous man. You **see** to it." Again **the** Jews cried out: **"His blood be on us and on our children."** [5] **Then** Pilate commanded the curtain to be drawn before the judgment-seat on which he sat, and said to **Jesus:** "Your nation has convicted you of claiming to be a king. Therefore I have decreed that you should first be **scourged** according to the law of the pious emperors, and then hanged on the cross in the garden where you were seized. And let Dysmas and Gestas, the two malefactors, be **crucified** with you."

GNaz 20 ⇨ Matt 27:16

(20) **Barabbas** . . . is interpreted in the so-called Gospel according to the Hebrews as "son of their teacher." (Jerome, Commentary on Matthew 4 [on Matthew 27:16])

GPet 1.1–2 ⇨ Matt 27:24

[1] But of the Jews none **washed** their **hands,** neither Herod nor any one of his judges. And as they would not wash, **Pilate** arose. [2] And then Herod the king commanded that the Lord should be marched off, saying to them, "What I have commanded you to do to him, do ye."

MATT

Matt 27:27–31 (§M85.1)

²⁷ Then the soldiers of the governor took Jesus into the praetorium, and they gathered the whole battalion before him. ²⁸ And they stripped him and put a scarlet robe upon him, ²⁹ and plaiting a crown of thorns they put it on his head, and put a reed in his right hand. And kneeling before him they mocked him, saying, "Hail, King of the Jews!" ³⁰ And they spat upon him, and took the reed and struck him on the head. ³¹ And when they had mocked him, they stripped him of the robe, and put his own clothes on him, and led him away to crucify him.

Matt 27:32 (§M85.2)

³² As they went out, they came upon a man of Cyrene, Simon by name; this man they compelled to carry his cross.

MARK

Mark 15:16–20 (§K66.1) ⇨ §M85.1

¹⁶ And the soldiers led him away inside the palace (that is, the praetorium); and they called together the whole battalion. ¹⁷ And they clothed him in a purple cloak, and plaiting a crown of thorns they put it on him. ¹⁸ And they began to salute him, "Hail, King of the Jews!" ¹⁹ And they struck his head with a reed, and spat upon him, and they knelt down in homage to him. ²⁰ And when they had mocked him, they stripped him of the purple cloak, and put his own clothes on him. And they led him out to crucify him.

Mark 15:21 (§K66.2) ⇨ §M85.2

²¹ And they compelled a passer-by, Simon of Cyrene, who was coming in from the country, the father of Alexander and Rufus, to carry his cross.

LUKE

Luke 23:26–32 (§L100.1) ⇨ §M85.2

²⁶ And as they led him away, they seized one Simon of Cyrene, who was coming in from the country, and laid on him the cross, to carry it behind Jesus. ²⁷ And there followed him a great multitude of the people, and of women who bewailed and lamented him. ²⁸ But Jesus turning to them said, "Daughters of Jerusalem, do not weep for me, but weep for yourselves and for your children. ²⁹ For behold, the days are coming when they will say, 'Blessed are the barren, and the wombs that never bore, and the breasts that never gave suck!' ³⁰ Then they will begin to say to the mountains, 'Fall on us'; and to the hills, 'Cover us.' ³¹ For if they do this when the wood is green, what will happen when it is dry?"

³² Two others also, who were criminals, were led away to be put to death with him.

JOHN

John 19:1–3 (§J33.4) ⇨ §M85.1

¹ Then Pilate took Jesus and scourged him. ² And the soldiers plaited a crown of thorns, and put it on his head, and arrayed him in a purple robe; ³ they came up to him, saying, "Hail, King of the Jews!" and struck him with their hands.

THOMAS

OTHER

GPet 2.5b–3.9 ⇨ §M85.1

And he delivered him to the people on the day before the unleavened bread, their feast. 3 ⁶ So they took the Lord and pushed him in great haste and said, "Let us hale the Son of God now that we have gotten power over him." ⁷ And they put upon him a purple robe and set him on the judgment seat and said, "Judge righteously, O King of Israel!" ⁸ And one of them brought a crown of thorns and put it on the Lord's head. ⁹ And others who stood by spat on his face, and others buffeted him on the cheeks, others nudged him with a reed, and some scourged him, saying, "With such honour let us honour the Son of God."

AcPil 10:1a ⇨ §M85.1

¹ And Jesus went out from the praetorium, and the two malefactors with him. And when they came to the place, they stripped him and girded him with a linen cloth and put a crown of thorns on his head.

MATT

Matt 27:33–44 (§M85.3)

³³ And when they came to a place called Golgotha (which means the place of a skull), ³⁴ they offered him wine to drink, mingled with gall; but when he tasted it, he would not drink it. ³⁵ And when they had crucified him, they divided his garments among them by casting lots; ³⁶ then they sat down and kept watch over him there. ³⁷ And over his head they put the charge against him, which read, "This is Jesus the King of the Jews." ³⁸ Then two robbers were crucified with him, one on the right and one on the left. ³⁹ And those who passed by derided him, wagging their heads ⁴⁰ and saying, "You who would destroy the temple and build it in three days, save yourself! If you are the Son of God, come down from the cross." ⁴¹ So also the chief priests, with the scribes and elders, mocked him, saying, ⁴² "He saved others; he cannot save himself. He is the King of Israel; let him come down now from the cross, and we will believe in him. ⁴³ He trusts in God; let God deliver him now, if he desires him; for he said, 'I am the Son of God.'" ⁴⁴ And the robbers who were crucified with him also reviled him in the same way.

Ps 69:21 ⇨ Matt 27:34
²¹ They gave me poison for food,
    and for my thirst **they** gave me vinegar to **drink.**

Ps 22:18 ⇨ Matt 27:35
¹⁸ **they** divide my **garments among them**, and for my
    raiment **they** cast lots.

JOHN

John 19:17–24 (§J34)

¹⁷ So they took Jesus, and he went out, bearing his own cross, **to the place called the place of a skull,** which is called in Hebrew **Golgotha.** ¹⁸ There **they crucified him,** and **with him two** others, **one on** either side, and Jesus between them. ¹⁹ Pilate also wrote a title and **put it on** the cross; it **read,** "**Jesus** of Nazareth, **the King of the Jews.**" ²⁰ Many of the Jews read this title, for the **place** where Jesus was crucified was near the city; and it was written in Hebrew, in Latin, and in Greek. ²¹ **The chief priests** of the Jews then said to Pilate, "Do not write, '**The King of the Jews,**' but 'This man **said, I am King of the Jews.'"** ²² Pilate answered, "What I have written I have written."

²³ **When** the soldiers **had crucified Jesus they** took **his garments** and made four parts, one for each soldier; also his tunic. But the tunic was without seam, woven from top to bottom; ²⁴ so they said to one another, "Let us not tear it, but cast **lots** for it to see whose it shall be." This was to fulfil the scripture, "**They** parted my **garments among them,** and for my clothing **they** cast lots."

John 2:19 ⇨ Matt 27:40
¹⁹ Jesus answered them, "**Destroy** this **temple, and in three days** I will raise it up."

MARK

Mark 15:22–32 (§K66.3)

²² And they brought him to the **place called Golgotha** (which means the place of a skull). ²³ And **they offered him wine mingled with** myrrh; **but he** did not take **it.** ²⁴ And **they crucified him,** and **divided his garments among them, casting lots** for them, to decide what each should take. ²⁵ And it was the third hour, when **they crucified him.** ²⁶ And the inscription of **the charge against him read, "The King of the Jews."** ²⁷ And **with him** they **crucified two robbers, one** on his **right and one on** his left. ²⁹ **And those who passed by derided him, wagging their heads, and saying, "Aha! You who would destroy the temple and build it in three days,** ³⁰ **save yourself, and come down from the cross!"** ³¹ **So also the** chief priests mocked him to one another **with the scribes, saying, "He saved others; he cannot save himself.** ³² Let the Christ, the **King of Israel, come down now from the cross, that we may see and believe."** Those **who were crucified with him also reviled him.**

Ps 22:7 ⇨ Matt 27:39
⁷ All **who** see me mock at me,
    they make mouths at me,
    they wag **their heads;** . . .

Ps 22:8 ⇨ Matt 27:43
⁸ "**He** committed his cause to
    the Lord; let him **deliver**
    him,
    let him rescue **him,** for he
    delights in him!"

THOMAS

GThom 71 ⇨ Matt 27:40
(71) Jesus said, "I shall **destroy** [this] house, and no one will be able to rebuild **it.**"

LUKE

Luke 23:33–43 (§L100.2)

³³ **And when they came to the place** which is **called** The Skull, there **they crucified him,** and the criminals, **one on the right and one on the left.** ³⁴ And Jesus said, "Father, forgive them; for they know not what they do." And **they** cast **lots** to divide **his garments.** ³⁵ And the people stood by, watching; but the rulers scoffed at **him, saying,** "**He saved others,** if **he is** the Christ of God, his Chosen One!" ³⁶ The soldiers also mocked him, coming up and offering **him** vinegar, ³⁷ and saying, "If you are **the King of the Jews, save yourself!**" ³⁸ There was also an inscription over **him, "This is the King of the Jews."**

³⁹ One of **the criminals who were** hanged railed at **him,** saying, "Are you not the Christ? Save yourself and us!" ⁴⁰ But the other rebuked him, saying, "Do you not fear God, since you are under the same sentence of condemnation? ⁴¹ And we indeed justly; for we are receiving the due reward of our deeds; but this man has done nothing wrong." ⁴² And he said, "Jesus, remember me when you come into your kingdom." ⁴³ And he said to him, "Truly, I say to you, today you will be with me in Paradise."

OTHER

GPet 4.10–14

¹⁰ And they brought **two** malefactors and **crucified** the Lord in the midst between them. But he held his peace, as if he felt no pain. ¹¹ **And** when they had set up the cross, **they** wrote upon it: **this is the King of** Israel. ¹² And **they** laid down **his garments** before him and **divided them among** themselves and cast the lot upon them. ¹³ But one of the malefactors rebuked them, saying, "We have landed in suffering for the deeds of wickedness which we have committed, but this man, who has become the saviour of men, what wrong has he done you?" ¹⁴ And they were wroth with him and commanded that his legs should not be broken, so that he might die in torments.

AcPil 10:1b–2

Likewise they hanged up also the **two** malefactors. But Jesus said: "Father, forgive them, for they know not what they do." **And** the soldiers parted **his garments among them.** And the people stood looking at him. And **the chief priests and rulers** with them scoffed at **him, saying:** "**He saved others,** let him **save himself. If he is** the Son of God, **let him come down from the cross."** And the soldiers also mocked him, coming and offering **him** vinegar **with gall,** and they said: "**If you are the king of the Jews, save yourself.**" And Pilate after the sentence commanded the crime brought against him to be written as a title in Greek, Latin and Hebrew, according to the accusation of the Jews that he was **king of the Jews.**

² One of **the** malefactors **who were crucified** said to **him:** "If you are the Christ, **save yourself** and us." But Dysmas answering rebuked him: "Do you not at all fear God, since you are in the same condemnation? And we indeed justly. For we are receiving the due reward of our deeds. But this man has done nothing wrong." And he said to Jesus: "Lord, remember me in your kingdom." And Jesus said to him: "Truly, I say to you, today you will be with me in paradise."

MATT	MARK	LUKE

Matt 27:45–56 (§M85.4)

[45] Now from the sixth hour there was darkness over all the land[a] until the ninth hour. [46] And about the ninth hour Jesus cried with a loud voice, "Eli, Eli, lama sabachthani?" that is, "My God, my God, why hast thou forsaken me?" [47] And some of the bystanders hearing it said, "This man is calling Elijah." [48] And one of them at once ran and took a sponge, filled it with vinegar, and put it on a reed, and gave it to him to drink. [49] But the others said, "Wait, let us see whether Elijah will come to save him."[b] [50] And Jesus cried again with a loud voice and yielded up his spirit.

[51] And behold, the curtain of the temple was torn in two, from top to bottom; and the earth shook, and the rocks were split; [52] the tombs also were opened, and many bodies of the saints who had fallen asleep were raised, [53] and coming out of the tombs after his resurrection they went into the holy city and appeared to many. [54] When the centurion and those who were with him, keeping watch over Jesus, saw the earthquake and what took place, they were filled with awe, and said, "Truly this was the[c] Son of God!"

[55] There were also many women there, looking on from afar, who had followed Jesus from Galilee, ministering to him; [56] among whom were Mary Magdalene, and Mary the mother of James and Joseph, and the mother of the sons of Zebedee.

[a] Or: *the earth*

[b] Some witnesses insert, *And another took a spear and pierced his side, and out came water and blood:* (cf. John 19:34) ℵ B C L *al*

[c] Or: *a son*

Ps 22:1 ⇨ Matt 27:46
[1] My God, my God, why hast thou forsaken me? Why art thou so far from helping me, from the words of my groaning?

Ps 69:21 ⇨ Matt 27:48
[21] They gave me poison for food, and for my thirst they gave me vinegar to drink.

Ps 38:11 ⇨ Matt 22:55–56
[11] My friends and companions stand aloof from my plague, and my kinsmen stand afar off.

Mark 15:33–41 (§K66.4)

[33] And when **the sixth hour** had come, **there was darkness over** the whole **land until** the ninth hour. [34] And at **the ninth hour Jesus cried with a loud voice,** "Eloi, Eloi, **lama sabachthani?**" which means, "**My God, my God, why hast thou forsaken me?**" [35] And some of the bystanders hearing it said, "Behold, **he is calling Elijah.**" [36] And one ran and, filling **a sponge** full of **vinegar, put it on a reed and gave it to him to drink,** saying, "**Wait, let us see whether Elijah will come to take him down.**" [37] **And Jesus** uttered a loud cry, and breathed his last. [38] **And the curtain of the temple was torn in two, from top to bottom.** [39] **And when the centurion,** who stood facing him, **saw** that he thus breathed his last, he said, "**Truly this man was the Son of God!**"

[40] **There were also women looking on from afar, among whom were Mary Magdalene, and Mary the mother of James** the younger and of Joses, and Salome, [41] who, when he was in **Galilee, followed** him, and ministered **to** him; **and also many** other **women who** came up with him to Jerusalem.

Luke 23:44–49 (§L100.3)

[44] It was now about **the sixth hour,** and **there was darkness over** the whole **land until the ninth hour,** [45] while the sun's light failed; and **the curtain of the temple was torn in two.** [46] Then **Jesus,** crying with **a loud voice,** said, "Father, into thy hands I commit my **spirit.**" And having said this he breathed **his** last. [47] Now **when the centurion saw what** had taken **place,** he praised God, **and said,** "Certainly **this** man **was** innocent!" [48] And all the multitudes who assembled to see the sight, when they saw what had taken place, returned home beating their breasts. [49] And all his acquaintances and the **women who had followed** him **from Galilee** stood at a distance and saw these things.

Luke 23:36 ⇨ Matt 27:48
[36] *The soldiers also mocked him, coming up and offering* **him vinegar,** . . .

Luke 8:1–3 (§L30) ⇨ Matt 27:55–56
[1] *Soon afterward he went on through cities and villages, preaching and bringing the good news of the kingdom of God. And the twelve were with him,* [2] *and* **also** *some* **women who had been healed of evil spirits and infirmities:* **Mary,** *called* **Magdalene,** *from whom seven demons had gone out,* [3] *and* **Joanna,** *the wife of Chuza, Herod's steward, and Susanna, and* **many** *others,* **who** *provided for them out of their means.*

Luke 23:55 ⇨ Matt 27:55–56
[55] *The* **women who had come with him from Galilee followed,** *and saw the tomb, and how his body was laid;* . . .

JOHN	THOMAS	OTHER

John 19:25–37 (§J35)

[25] So the soldiers did this. But standing by the cross of Jesus were his mother, and his mother's sister, **Mary** the wife of Clopas, and **Mary Magdalene**. [26] When Jesus saw his mother, and the disciple whom he loved standing near, he said to his mother, "Woman, behold, your son!" [27] Then he said to the disciple, "Behold, your mother!" And from that hour the disciple took her to his own home.

[28] After this Jesus, knowing that all was now finished, said (to fulfil the scripture), "I thirst." [29] A bowl full of **vinegar** stood there; so they put **a sponge** full of the **vinegar** on hyssop and held **it** to his mouth. [30] When **Jesus** had received the **vinegar**, he said, "It is finished"; and he bowed his head **and** gave **up his spirit**.

[31] Since it was the day of Preparation, in order to prevent the bodies from remaining on the cross on the sabbath (for that sabbath was a high day), the Jews asked Pilate that their legs might be broken, and that they might be taken away. [32] So the soldiers came and broke the legs of the first, and of the other who had been crucified with him; [33] but when they came to Jesus and saw that he was already dead, they did not break his legs. [34] But one of the soldeirs pierced his side with a spear, and at once there came out blood and water. [35] He who saw it has borne witness—his testimony is true, and he knows that he tells the truth—that you also may believe. [36] For these things took place that the scripture might be fulfilled, "Not a bone of him shall be broken." [37] And again another scripture says, "They shall look on him whom they have pierced."

GPet 5.15–20

[15] **Now** it **was** midday and a **darkness** covered all Judaea. And they became anxious and uneasy lest the sun had already set, since he was still alive. <For> it stands written for them: the sun should not set on one that has been put to death. [16] And one of them said, "Give **him to drink** gall with **vinegar**." And they mixed it **and gave him to drink**. [17] And they fulfilled all things and completed the measure of their sins on their head. [18] And many went about with lamps, <and> as they supposed that it was night, they went to bed (or: they stumbled). [19] **And** the Lord called out and **cried**, "**My** power, O power, **thou** hast **forsaken me!**" **And** having said this he was taken up. [20] And at the same hour **the veil of the temple** in Jerusalem **was** rent **in two**.

AcPil 11:1–3a

[1] And it was about **the sixth hour**, and **there was darkness over the land until the ninth hour**, for the sun was darkened. **And the curtain of the temple was torn in two. And Jesus cried** with **a loud voice**: "Father, baddach ephkid rouel," which means: "Into thy hands I commit my spirit." **And** having said this he gave **up the ghost. And when the centurion saw what** had happened, he praised God, saying: "**This** man **was** righteous." **And** all the multitudes **who** had come to this sight, when they **saw what** had taken **place**, beat their breasts and returned.

[2] But **the centurion** reported to the governor what had happened. And when the governor and his wife heard, they were greatly grieved, and they neither ate nor drank on that day. And Pilate sent for the Jews and said to them: "Did you see what happened?" But they answered: "There was an eclipse of the sun in the usual way." [3] And his acquaintances had stood far off and the **women who had** come with him **from Galilee**, and saw these things.

GNaz 21 ⇨ Matt 27:51

(21) But in the Gospel which is written in Hebrew characters we read not that the veil of the temple was rent, but that the lintel of the temple of wondrous size collapsed. (Jerome, *Epistula ad Hedybiam* 120.8)

GNaz 36 ⇨ Matt 27:51

*(36) Also in the Gospel of the Nazaraeans we read that at the time of Christ's death **the lintel of the temple**, of immense size, had split (Josephus says the same and adds that overhead awful voices were heard which said: Let us depart from this abode).* ("Historia passionis Domini," MS: Theolog. Sammelhandschrift saec. XIV–XV, foll. 8–71 [saec. XIV] cited by Hennecke in *New Testament Apocrypha,* p. 153)

MATT

Matt 27:57–61 (§M86)

[57] **When it was evening, there came a rich man from Arimathea, named Joseph, who** also was a disciple of Jesus. [58] **He went to Pilate and asked for the body of Jesus. Then Pilate ordered it to be given to him.** [59] **And Joseph took the body, and wrapped it in a clean linen shroud,** [60] **and laid it in his own new tomb, which he had hewn in the rock; and he rolled a great stone to the door of the tomb, and departed.** [61] **Mary Magdalene and the other Mary were there, sitting opposite the sepulchre.**

Deut 21:22–23

[22] "And if a man has committed a crime punishable by death and he is put to death, and you hang him on a tree, [23] his **body** shall not remain all night upon the tree, but you shall bury **him** the same day, for a hanged man is accursed by God; you shall not defile your land which the Lord your God gives you for an inheritance."

Josh 10:18 ⇨ Matt 27:60

[18] And Joshua said, "Roll great stones against **the** mouth **of the** cave, and set men by it to guard them";
. . .

Josh 10:27 ⇨ Matt 27:60

[27] but at the time of the going down of the sun, Joshua commanded, and they took them down from the trees, and threw them into **the** cave where they had hidden themselves, and they set great stones against **the** mouth **of the** cave, which remain to this very day.

JOHN

John 19:38–42 (§J36)

[38] After this **Joseph of Arimathea, who was a disciple of Jesus,** but secretly, for fear of the Jews, **asked Pilate** that he might take away **the body of Jesus,** and **Pilate** gave **him** leave. So he came and **took** away his **body.** [39] Nicodemus also, who had at first come to him by night, came bringing a mixture of myrrh and aloes, about a hundred pounds' weight. [40] They **took the body** of Jesus, and bound **it in linen** cloths with the spices, as is the burial custom of the Jews. [41] Now in the place where he was crucified there was a garden, and in the garden a **new tomb** where no one had ever been laid. [42] So because of the Jewish day of Preparation, as the tomb was close at hand, they **laid** Jesus there.

MARK

Mark 15:42–47 (§K67)

[42] And **when evening** had come, since it was the day of Preparation, that is, the day before the sabbath, [43] **Joseph** of **Arimathea,** a respected member of the council, who was also himself looking for the kingdom of God, took courage and **went to Pilate, and asked for the body of Jesus.** [44] And **Pilate** wondered if he were already dead; and summoning the centurion, he asked him whether he was already dead. [45] And when he learned from the centurion that he was dead, he granted the body to Joseph. [46] And he bought **a linen shroud,** and taking him down, **wrapped** him **in** the **linen shroud, and laid him in a tomb which** had been **hewn** out of the **rock; and he rolled a stone** against **the door of the tomb.** [47] **Mary Magdalene and Mary** the mother of Joses saw where he was laid.

THOMAS

LUKE

Luke 23:50–56 (§L101)

[50] Now there was **a man named Joseph from** the Jewish town of **Arimathea.** He was a member of the council, a good and righteous man, [51] who had not consented to their purpose and deed, and he was looking for the kingdom of God. [52] This man **went to Pilate and asked for the body of Jesus.** [53] Then he **took** it down **and wrapped it in a linen shroud, and laid** him in **a rock-hewn tomb,** where no one had ever yet been laid. [54] It was the day of Preparation, and the sabbath was beginning. [55] The women who had come with him from Galilee followed, and saw the tomb, and how his body was laid; [56] then they returned, and prepared spices and ointments.

On the sabbath they rested according to the commandment.

OTHER

GPet 2.3–5a

[3] Now there stood there **Joseph,** the friend of Pilate and of the Lord, and knowing that they were about to crucify him **he** came **to Pilate** and begged **the body of** the Lord for burial. [4] And **Pilate** sent to Herod and begged his body. [5] And Herod said, "Brother Pilate, even if no one had begged him, we should bury him, since the Sabbath is drawing on. For it stands written in the law: the sun should not set on one that has been put to death."

GPet 6.21–24

[21] And then the Jews drew the nails from the hands of the Lord and laid him on the earth. And the whole earth shook and there came a great fear. [22] Then the sun shone <again>, and it was found to be the ninth hour. [23] And the Jews rejoiced and gave **the body** to **Joseph** that he might bury it, since he had seen all the good that he (Jesus) had done. [24] And he took the Lord, washed him, **wrapped** him **in linen** and brought him into **his own** sepulchre, called Joseph's Garden.

AcPil 11:3b

But **a certain man named Joseph,** a member of the council, from the town of **Arimathaea,** who also was waiting for the kingdom of God, this man **went to Pilate and asked for the body of Jesus.** And he **took** it down, **and wrapped it in a clean linen** cloth, **and** placed **it in** a rock-hewn **tomb,** in which no one had ever yet been laid.

MATT	MARK	LUKE

Matt 27:62–66 (§M87)

⁶²Next day, that is, after the day of Preparation, the chief priests and the Pharisees gathered before Pilate ⁶³and said, "Sir, we remember how that impostor said, while he was still alive, 'After three days I will rise again.' ⁶⁴Therefore order the sepulchre to be made secure until the third day, lest his disciples go and steal him away, and tell the people, 'He has risen from the dead,' and the last fraud will be worse than the first." ⁶⁵Pilate said to them, "You have a guard of soldiers;ᵃ go, make it as secure as you can."ᵇ ⁶⁶So they went and made the sepulchre secure by sealing the stone and setting a guard.

ᵃ Or: *Take a guard*

ᵇ Greek: *know*

JOHN	THOMAS	OTHER

GPet 8.28–9.34

²⁸But the scribes **and Pharisees** and elders, being assembled together and hearing that all the people were murmuring and beating their breasts, saying, "If at his death these exceeding great signs have come to pass, behold how righteous he was!",— ²⁹were afraid and came to **Pilate**, entreating him **and** saying, ³⁰"Give us soldiers that we may watch his **sepulchre** for **three days, lest his disciples** come **and steal him away and the people** suppose that **he is risen from the dead**, and do us harm." ³¹And **Pilate** gave them Petronius the centurion with **soldiers** to watch **the sepulchre**. And with them there came elders and scribes to **the sepulchre**. ³²And all who were there, together with the centurion and the **soldiers**, rolled thither a great **stone** and laid it against the entrance to the **sepulchre** ³³and put on it seven seals, pitched a tent and kept watch. 9 ³⁴Early in the morning, when the Sabbath dawned, there came a crowd from Jerusalem and the country round about to see **the sepulchre** that had been sealed.

GNaz 22 ⇨ Matt 27:65

(22) The Jewish Gospel: And he delivered to them armed men that they might sit over against the cave and guard it day and night. (Variant to Matthew 27:65 in the "Zion Gospel" Edition)

MATT

Matt 28:1–8 (§M88.1)

[1] Now after the sabbath, toward the dawn of the first day of the week, Mary Magdalene and the other Mary went to see the sepulchre. [2] And behold, there was a great earthquake; for an angel of the Lord descended from heaven and came and rolled back the stone, and sat upon it. [3] His appearance was like lightning, and his raiment white as snow. [4] And for fear of him the guards trembled and became like dead men. [5] But the angel said to the women, "Do not be afraid; for I know that you seek Jesus who was crucified. [6] He is not here; for he has risen, as he said. Come, see the place where he[a] lay. [7] Then go quickly and tell his disciples that he has risen from the dead, and behold, he is going before you to Galilee; there you will see him. Lo, I have told you." [8] So they departed quickly from the tomb with fear and great joy, and ran to tell his disciples.

Matt 28:9–10 (§M88.2)

[9] And behold, Jesus met them and said, "Hail!" And they came and took hold of his feet and worshiped him. [10] Then Jesus said to them, "Do not be afraid; go and tell my brethren to go to Galilee, and there they will see me."

Matt 28:11–15 (§M88.3)

[11] While they were going, behold, some of the guard went into the city and told the chief priests all that had taken place. [12] And when they had assembled with the elders and taken counsel, they gave a sum of money to the soldiers [13] and said, "Tell people, 'His disciples came by night and stole him away while we were asleep.' [14] And if this comes to the governor's ears, we will satisfy him and keep you out of trouble." [15] So they took the money and did as they were directed; and this story has been spread among the Jews to this day.

[a] Some witnesses read *The Lord:* A C D K L W Δ Π 0148 *f*[1] *f*[13] 28 *al*

MARK

Mark 16:1–8 (§K68)

[1] And when **the sabbath** was past, **Mary Magdalene, and Mary** the mother of James, and Salome, bought spices, so that they might go and anoint him. [2] And very early on the first day of the week they went to the tomb when the sun had risen. [3] And they were saying to one another, "Who will roll away the stone for us from the door of the tomb?" [4] **And** looking up, they saw that **the stone** was **rolled back**—it was very large. [5] And entering the tomb, they saw a young man sitting on the right side, dressed in a **white** robe; and they were amazed. [6] And he **said to** them, **"Do not be** amazed; **you seek Jesus** of Nazareth, **who was crucified. He has risen, he is not here; see the place where** they laid him. [7] But **go, tell his disciples** and Peter **that he is going before you to Galilee; there you will see him,** as he **told you."** [8] And **they** went out and fled **from the tomb;** for trembling and astonishment had come upon them; and they said nothing to any one, for they were afraid.

LUKE

Luke 24:1–11 (§L102)

[1] But on **the first day of the week**, at early dawn, they **went to** the tomb, taking the spices which they had prepared. [2] **And** they found **the stone rolled** away from the tomb, [3] but when they went in they did not find the body. [4] While they were perplexed about this, behold, two men stood by them in dazzling apparel; [5] and as they were frightened and bowed their faces to the ground, the men **said to** them, "Why do you seek the living among the dead? [6] Remember how he told you, while he was still in Galilee, [7] that the Son of man must be delivered into the hands of sinful men, and be crucified, and on the third day rise." [8] And they remembered his words, [9] and returning from the tomb they told all this to the eleven and to all the rest. [10] Now it was **Mary Magdalene and** Joanna **and Mary** the mother of James and the other women with them who told this **to the apostles;** [11] but these words seemed to them an idle tale, and they did not believe them.

M88.1   TWO WOMEN DISCOVER THE EMPTY TOMB   Matt 28:1–8
M88.2   JESUS MEETS THE TWO WOMEN   Matt 28:9–10
M88.3   THE GUARD IS BRIBED   Matt 28:11–15

JOHN

OTHER

John 20:1–18 (§J37)

[1] Now on the **first day of the week Mary Magdalene** came **to the** tomb early, while it was still dark, and saw that **the stone** had been taken away from the tomb. [2] So she ran, and went to Simon Peter and the other disciple, the one whom Jesus loved, and said to them, "They have taken the Lord out of the tomb, and we do not know where they have laid him." [3] Peter then came out with the other disciple, and they went toward the tomb. [4] They both ran, but the other disciple outran Peter and reached the tomb first; [5] and stooping to look in, he saw the linen cloths lying there, but he did not go in. [6] Then Simon Peter came, following him, and went into the tomb; he saw the linen cloths lying, [7] and the napkin, which had been on his head, not lying with the linen cloths but rolled up in a place by itself. [8] Then the other disciple, who reached the tomb first, also went in, and he saw and believed; [9] for as yet they did not know the scripture, that he must rise from the dead. [10] Then the disciples went back to their homes.

[11] But **Mary** stood weeping outside **the** tomb, and as she wept she stooped to look into the tomb; [12] and she saw two angels in **white**, sitting where the body of Jesus had lain, one at the head and one at the feet. [13] They **said to** her, "Woman, why are you weeping?" She said to them, "Because they have taken away my Lord, and I do not know where they have laid him." [14] Saying this, she turned round and saw **Jesus** standing, but she did not know that it was **Jesus**. [15] **Jesus said** to her, "Woman, why are you weeping? Whom do **you seek**?" Supposing him to be the gardener, she said to him, "Sir, if you have carried him away, tell me where you have laid him, and I will take him away." [16] **Jesus said** to her, "Mary." She turned and said to him in Hebrew, "Rabboni!" (which means Teacher). [17] **Jesus said to** her, "**Do not** hold me, for I have not yet ascended to the Father; but **go to my brethren** and say to them, I am ascending to my Father and your Father, to my God and your God." [18] Mary Magdalene went and said to the **disciples**, "I have seen the Lord"; and she told them that he had said these things to her.

GPet 9.35–13.57

[35] **Now** in the night in which the Lord's day dawned, when the soldiers, two by two in every watch, were keeping guard, there rang out a loud voice in heaven, [36] and they saw the heavens opened and two men come down **from** there in a great brightness and draw nigh to the sepulchre. [37] That **stone** which had been laid against the entrance to the sepulchre started of itself to roll and gave way to the side, and the sepulchre was opened, and both the young men entered in. 10 [38] When now those soldiers saw this, they awakened the centurion and the elders— for they also were there to assist at the watch. [39] And whilst they were relating what they had seen, they saw again three men come out from the sepulchre, and two of them sustaining the other, and a cross following them, [40] and the heads of the two reaching to heaven, but that of him who was led of them by the hand overpassing the heavens. [41] And they heard a voice out of the heavens crying, "Thou has preached to them that sleep," [42] and from the cross there was heard the answer, "Yea." 11 [43] Those men therefore took counsel with one another to go and report this to Pilate. [44] And whilst they were still deliberating, the heavens were again seen to open, and a man **descended** and entered into the sepulchre. [45] When those who were of the centurion's company saw this, they hastened by night to Pilate, abandoning the sepulchre which they were guarding, and reported everything **that** they **had** seen, being full of disquietude and saying, "In truth he was the Son of God." [46] Pilate answered and said, "I am clean from the blood of the Son of God, upon such a thing have you decided." [47] Then all came to him, beseeching him and urgently calling upon him to command the centurion and the soldiers to tell no one what they had seen. [48] "For it better for us," they said, "to make ourselves guilty of the greatest sin before God than to fall into the hands of the people of the Jews and be stoned." [49] Pilate therefore commanded the centurion and the soldiers to say nothing.

12 [50] Early in the morning of the Lord's day **Mary Magdalene**, a woman disciple of the Lord— for fear of the Jews, since [they] were inflamed with wrath, she had not done at the sepulchre of the Lord what women are wont to do for those beloved of them who die—took [51] with her her women friends and came **to the sepulchre** where he was laid. [52] And they feared lest the Jews should see them, and said, "Although we could not weep and lament on that day when he was crucified, yet let us now do so at his sepulchre. [53] But who will roll away for us **the stone** also that is set on the entrance to **the sepulchre**, that we may go in and sit beside him and do what is due?— [54] For the **stone** was great,— and we fear lest any one see us. And if we cannot do so, let us at least put down at the entrance what we bring for a memorial of him and let us weep and lament until we have again gone home."

13 [55] So they **went** and found **the sepulchre** opened. And they came near, stooped down and saw there a young man sitting in the midst of the sepulchre, comely and clothed with a brightly shining robe, who **said to** them, [56] "Wherefore are ye come? Whom **seek** ye? Not him that **was crucified**? **He** is **risen** and gone. But if ye believe not, stoop this way and **see the place where he lay**, for **he is not here**. **For he** is **risen** and is gone thither whence he was sent." [57] Then the women fled affrighted.

AcPil 13:1–3

[1] And while they still sat in the synagogue and marvelled because of Joseph, there came **some of the guard** which the Jews had asked from Pilate to guard the tomb of Jesus, lest his disciples should come and steal him. And they **told the** rulers of the synagogue and **the priests** and the Levites what **had** happened: how **there was a great earthquake**. "And we saw **an angel** descend **from heaven, and** he **rolled** away **the stone** from the mouth of the cave, **and sat upon it**, and he shone **like snow and like lightning**. And we were in great **fear, and lay like dead men**. And we heard the voice of **the angel** speaking **to the women** who waited at the tomb: **Do not be afraid. I know that you seek Jesus who was crucified. He is not here. He has risen, as he said. Come** and **see the place where** the Lord lay. And **go quickly and tell his disciples that he has risen from the dead and is** in **Galilee**."

[2] The Jews asked: "To what women did he speak?" The members of the guard answered: "We do not know who they were." The Jews said: "At what hour was it?" The members of the guard answered: "At midnight." The Jews said: "And why did you not seize the women?" The members of the guard said: "We were **like dead men** through **fear**, and gave up hope of seeing the light of day; how could we then have seized them?" The Jews said: "As the Lord lives, we do not believe you." The members of the guard said to the Jews: "So many signs you saw in that man and you did not believe; and how can you believe us? You rightly swore: As the Lord lives. For he does live." Again the members of the guard said: "We have heard that you shut him up who asked for the body of Jesus, and sealed the door, and that when you opened it you did not find him. Therefore give us Joseph and we will give you Jesus." The Jews said: "Joseph has gone to his own city." And the members of the guard said to the Jews: "And Jesus **has risen**, as we heard from **the angel, and is** in **Galilee**." [3] **And when** the Jews heard these words, they feared greatly and said: "(Take heed) lest this report be heard and all incline to Jesus." **And** the Jews took **counsel**, and offered much **money** and **gave** it **to the soldiers** of the guard, saying: "Say that when you **were** sleeping **his disciples came by night and stole him. And if this** is heard by **the** governor, **we will** persuade **him and keep you out of trouble**."

MATT	MARK	LUKE

Matt 28:16–20 (§M88.4) °

¹⁶ Now the eleven disciples went to Galilee, to the mountain to which Jesus had directed them. ¹⁷ And when they saw him they worshiped him; but some doubted. ¹⁸ And Jesus came and said to them, "All authority in heaven and on earth has been given to me. ¹⁹ Go therefore and make disciples of all nations, baptizing them in the name of the Father and of the Son and of the Holy Spirit, ²⁰ teaching them to observe all that I have commanded you; and lo, I am with you always, to the close of the age."

°Appendix 2 ⇨ §M88.4

JOHN	THOMAS	OTHER

GPet 14.58–60

⁵⁸ Now it was the last day of unleavened bread and many **went** away and repaired to their homes, since the feast was at an end. ⁵⁹ But we, **the** twelve **disciples** of the Lord, wept and mourned, and each one, very grieved for what had come to pass, went to his own home. ⁶⁰ But I, Simon Peter, and my brother Andrew, took our nets and went to the sea. And there was with us Levi, the son of Alphaeus, whom the Lord . . .

AcPil 14:1

¹ **Now** Phineës a priest and Adas a teacher and Angaeus a Levite came from **Galilee** to Jerusalem, and told the rulers of the synagogue and the priests and the Levites: "We **saw** Jesus and his **disciples** sitting upon **the mountain which** is called Mamilch. **And** he **said to** his disciples: **Go** into **all** the world and preach the gospel to the whole creation. He who believes and is baptized will be saved; but he who does not believe will be condemned. And these signs will accompany those who believe: in my name will they cast out demons; they will speak in new tongues; they will pick up serpents; and if they drink any deadly thing, it will not hurt them; they will lay their hands on the sick and they will recover. **And** while **Jesus** was still speaking to his **disciples**, we saw him taken up into heaven."

MARK

K1	TITLE	1:1
	Matt 1:1	InThom 0–1:1
	GThom, title	

S1:K2–4   INTRODUCTION   **1:2–13**

K2	APPEARANCE OF JOHN THE BAPTIST	**1:2–8**
Mal 3:1a	Matt 3:1–12	Luke 3:1–20
Isa 40:3	Matt 11:10	Luke 7:27
2 Kgs 1:8		Acts 13:24–25
John 1:19–28		Acts 19:1–7
John 1:31–32		GEbi 2
		GEbi 3
		Acts 1:5
		Acts 11:16

K3	BAPTISM OF JESUS	**1:9–11**
Ps 2:7	Matt 13:13–17	Luke 3:21–22
Isa 42:1	Matt 17:5	Luke 9:34–35
Isa 44:2		GEbi 4
John 1:29–34		GNaz 2
		GHeb 2

K4	TEMPTATION OF JESUS	**1:12–13**
John 1:51	Matt 4:1–11	Luke 4:1–13

S2:K5–12   FIRST GALILEAN   **1:14–45**

K5	BEGINNING OF JESUS' PUBLIC MINISTRY	**1:14–15**
Mark 6:17	Matt 4:12–17	Luke 4:14–15
John 1:43	Matt 14:3	Luke 4:16–30
John 4:1–3		Luke 3:19–20, 23a
John 4:43		

K6	CALL OF SIMON AND ANDREW	**1:16–18**
K7	CALL OF JAMES AND JOHN	**1:19–20**
John 1:35–42	Matt 4:18–20	Luke 5:1–3
John 1:43–51	Matt 4:21–22	Luke 5:4–11
		GEbi 1

K8	EXORCISM OF AN UNCLEAN SPIRIT	**1:21–28**
Mark 11:18	Matt 13:54	Luke 4:31–37
1 Kgs 17:18	Matt 7:28–29	InThom 19:2b
John 7:46	Matt 22:33	
John 6:69		

K9	HEALING OF SIMON'S MOTHER-IN-LAW	**1:29–31**
	Matt 8:14–15	Luke 4:38–39

K10	SUMMARY: HEALING AND EXORCISMS	**1:32–34**
Mark 3:7–12	Matt 8:16–17	Luke 4:40–41
	Matt 12:16	

K11	WITHDRAWAL AND PREACHING TOUR	**1:35–39**
	Matt 4:23–25	Luke 4:42–44

K12	HEALING OF A LEPER	**1:40–45**
	Matt 8:1–4	Luke 5:12–16
		PEger2 2

S3:K13–17   SECOND GALILEAN   **2:1–3:6**

K13	HEALING OF THE PARALYTIC	**2:1–12**
John 5:8–9a	Matt 9:1–8	Luke 5:17–26

K14   IN THE COMPANY OF TAX COLLECTORS   **2:13–17**

K14.1	TEACHING BESIDE THE SEA	**2:13**
K14.2	CALL OF LEVI	**2:14**
K14.3	EATING WITH TAX COLLECTORS AND SINNERS	**2:15–17**
	Matt 9:9	Luke 5:27–28
	Matt 9:10–13	Luke 5:29–32
		Luke 15:1–2
		POxy1224 1
	Justin, *Apology* 1.15.8	

K15	QUESTION OF FASTING	**2:18–22**
	Matt 9:14–17	Luke 5:33–39
	GThom 27	Luke 7:33–34
	GThom 104	Luke 18:12
	GThom 47	Did 8:1

K16	PLUCKING GRAIN ON THE SABBATH	**2:23–28**
Deut 23:25	Matt 12:1–8	Luke 6:1–5
Exod 20:10	GThom 27	InThom 2:1–5
Deut 5:14		
1 Sam 21:1–6		
Lev 24:5–9		

K17	HEALING OF THE MAN WITH A WITHERED HAND	**3:1–6**
	Matt 12:9–14	Luke 6:6–11
		Luke 14:3
		GNaz 10
		InThom 2:1–5

S4:K18–20   THIRD GALILEAN   **3:7–35**

K18	JESUS HEALS THE MULTITUDES	**3:7–12**
Mark 6:56	Matt 12:15–21	Luke 6:17–19
	Matt 4:25	Luke 4:41
	Matt 14:36	

K19	APPOINTMENT OF THE TWELVE	**3:13–19**
Mark 6:7	Matt 10:1–4	Luke 6:12–16
John 1:42		Luke 9:1–2
		Acts 1:12–14

K20	JESUS IS ACCUSED	**3:20–35**

K20.1	JESUS' FAMILY COMES TO SEIZE HIM	**3:20–22**
K20.2	THE SCRIBES ACCUSE HIM	**3:23–30**
K20.3	TRUE RELATIVES	**3:31–35**

John 15:14	Matt 12:24	Luke 11:15
	Matt 12:25–26	Luke 11:17–18
	Matt 12:29	Luke 11:21
	Matt 12:31–32	Luke 12:10
	Matt 12:46–50	Luke 8:19–21
	GThom 35	GEbi 5
	GThom 21	
	GThom 99	

S5:K21	TEACHING IN PARABLES	**4:1–34**

| **K21.1** | INTRODUCTION | **4:1** |
| **K21.2** | PARABLE OF THE SOWER | **4:2–9** |

	Matt 13:1–2	Luke 8:4–8
	Matt 13:3–9	Luke 5:1–3
	GThom 9	InThom 12:1–2
		ApocJa 12:20–31

K21.3	SECRET OF THE KINGDOM	**4:10–12**

Isa 6:9–10	Matt 13:10–17	Luke 8:9–10
		ApocJa 7:1–10

K21.4	INTERPRETATION OF THE SOWER	**4:13–20**

	Matt 13:18–23	Luke 8:11–15
		ApocJa 8:10–27

K21.5	THE LAMP	**4:21–23**

	Matt 5:15	Luke 8:16–17
	Matt 10:26	Luke 11:33
	GThom 33	Luke 12:2
	POxy654 5	
	GThom 5	
	GThom 6	

K21.6	MEASURE FOR MEASURE AND MORE	**4:24–25**

	Matt 7:2	Luke 8:18
	Matt 13:12	Luke 6:38
	Matt 25:29	Luke 19:26
	GThom 41	

K21.7	SEED AND HARVEST	**4:26–29**

Joel 3:13	Matt 13:24–30	ApocJa 12:20–31
	GThom 21	

K21.8	MUSTARD SEED	**4:30–32**

Dan 4:20–22	Matt 13:31–32	Luke 13:18–19
	GThom 20	

K21.9	CONCLUSION OF TEACHING IN PARABLES	**4:33–34**

	Matt 13:34–35	

S6:K22–24	ACROSS THE SEA	**4:35–5:43**

K22	STILLING OF THE STORM	**4:35–41**

Ps 65:5–8	Matt 8:23–27	Luke 8:22–25
	Matt 8:18	

K23	GERASENE DEMONIAC	**5:1–20**

| **K23.1** | SCENE ONE | **5:1–14a** |
| **K23.2** | SCENE TWO | **5:14b–20** |

Mark 1:24	Matt 8:28–33	Luke 8:26–34
Mark 1:34	Matt 8:34	Luke 8:35–39
Mark 3:11		
John 2:4		

K24	TWO HEALING STORIES	**5:21–43**

K24.1	JAIRUS' DAUGHTER: INTRODUCTION	**5:21–24a**
K24.2	WOMAN WITH THE INTERNAL HEMORRHAGE	**5:24b–34**
K24.3	JAIRUS' DAUGHTER: CONCLUSION	**5:35–43**

Mark 6:56	Matt 9:18–19	Luke 8:40–42a
Mark 10:52	Matt 9:20–22	Luke 8:42b–48
	Matt 9:23–26	Luke 8:49–56
	Matt 14:36	Luke 6:19
		Luke 7:50
		Luke 17:19
		Luke 18:42

S7:K25–32	FOURTH GALILEAN	**6:1–56**

K25	REJECTION AT NAZARETH	**6:1–6**

John 4:44	Matt 13:53–58	Luke 4:16–30
John 7:15	Matt 9:35	
	POxy1 6	
	GThom 31	

K26	MISSION OF THE TWELVE	**6:7–13**

Mark 3:14–15	Matt 10:1	Luke 9:1–6
	Matt 10:9–14	

K27	HEROD THINKS JESUS IS JOHN RISEN	**6:14–29**

Mark 8:28	Matt 14:1–12	Luke 9:7–9
Esth 5:3	Matt 16:14	Luke 9:19
Esth 7:2		Luke 3:19–20
John 1:19–21		

K28	RETURN OF THE TWELVE; NARRATIVE TRANSITION	**6:30–34**

Num 27:15–17	Matt 14:13–14	Luke 9:10–11
1 Kgs 22:17	Matt 9:36	Luke 10:17

K29	FEEDING OF THE FIVE THOUSAND	**6:35–44**

Mark 8:1–10	Matt 14:15–21	Luke 9:12–17
Mark 14:22	Matt 15:32–39	Luke 22:19
2 Kgs 4:42–44	Matt 26:26	Luke 24:30
John 6:1–15		Acts 27:35

K30	DEPARTURES	**6:45–46**
Mark 8:10	Matt 14:22–23	
John 6:15	Matt 15:39	

K31	JESUS WALKS ON THE WATER	**6:47–52**
Mark 8:17	Matt 14:24–33	Luke 24:37
John 6:16–21		

K32	HEALINGS AT GENNESARET	**6:53–56**
Mark 1:32–34	Matt 14:34–36	Luke 4:40–41
Mark 3:7–12	Matt 4:23–25	Luke 6:17–19
Mark 5:27–33	Matt 8:16–17	Luke 8:43–47
	Matt 9:20–21	

S8:K33–34	DISCOURSE ON DEFILEMENT	**7:1–23**

K33	EATING WITH DEFILED HANDS	**7:1–13**
Isa 29:13	Matt 15:1–9	POxy840 2
Exod 20:12		PEger2 3
Exod 21:17		GNaz 12
Lev 20:9		
Deut 5:16		

K34	DEFILEMENT	**7:14–23**

K34.1	TRUE DEFILEMENT	**7:14–15**
	Matt 15:10–11	
	GThom 14	

K34.2	INTERPRETATION	**7:17–23**
	Matt 15:10–20	

S9:K35–36	REGION OF TYRE AND SIDON	**7:24–37**

K35	A SYROPHOENICIAN WOMAN'S DAUGHTER	**7:24–30**
	Matt 15:21–28	

K36	HEALING OF DEAF AND DUMB MAN	**7:31–37**
	Matt 15:29–31	

S10:K37–40	ACROSS THE SEA AND BACK	**8:1–26**

K37	FEEDING OF THE FOUR THOUSAND	**8:1–10**
Mark 6:35–44	Matt 15:32–39	Luke 9:12–17
Mark 6:45–46	Matt 14:15–21	Luke 22:19
Mark 14:22	Matt 15:22–23	Luke 24:30
2 Kgs 4:42–44	Matt 9:36	Acts 27:35
John 6:1–15	Matt 26:26	

K38	THE PHARISEES ASK FOR A SIGN	**8:11–13**
John 6:30	Matt 16:1–4	Luke 11:29–32
	Matt 12:38–42	Luke 11:16

K39	DISCOURSE ON BREAD AND LEAVEN	**8:14–21**
Jer 5:21	Matt 16:5–12	Luke 12:1
Ezek 12:2		
John 6:32–35		

K40	HEALING OF THE BLIND MAN OF BETHSAIDA	**8:22–26**
John 9:1–7		

S11:K41–43	VILLAGES OF CAESAREA PHILIPPI	**8:27–9:1**

K41	PETER'S CONFESSION	**8:27–30**
John 1:49	Matt 16:13–20	Luke 9:18–22
John 6:68–69	GThom 13	

K42	JESUS PREDICTS HIS DEATH AND RESURRECTION	**8:31–33**
Mark 9:30–32	Matt 16:21–23	Luke 9:18–22
Mark 10:32–34	Matt 17:22–23	Luke 9:43b–45
	Matt 20:17–19	Luke 18:31–34
		ApocJa 5:31–6:11

K43	THE WAY OF THE CROSS	**8:34–9:1**
John 12:25	Matt 16:24–28	Luke 9:23–27
	Matt 10:38–39	Luke 14:27
	Matt 10:33	Luke 17:33
	GThom 55	Luke 12:9
	GThom 101	

S12:K44–49	ON THE MOUNTAIN AND AFTER	**9:1–50**

K44	JESUS IS TRANSFIGURED	**9:2–13**

K44.1	JESUS IS TRANSFIGURED	**9:2–8**
Mark 1:10–11	Matt 17:1–8	Luke 9:28–36
Ps 2:7	Matt 3:16–17	Luke 3:22
Isa 42:1		

K44.2	ELIJAH MUST COME FIRST	**9:9–13**
Mal 4:5–6	Matt 17:9–13	
1 Kgs 19:1–3, 9–10	GThom 51	

K45	JESUS EXORCISES A DUMB SPIRIT	**9:14–29**
K45.1	HEALING OF A BOY	**9:14–27**
K45.2	EXPLANATION OF DISCIPLES' FAILURE	**9:28–29**
	Matt 17:14–18	Luke 9:37–43a
	Matt 17:19–20	

K46	JESUS PREDICTS HIS PASSION AGAIN	**9:30–32**
Mark 8:31–33	Matt 17:22–23	Luke 9:43b–45
Mark 10:32–34	Matt 16:21–23	Luke 9:18–22
John 7:1	Matt 20:17–19	Luke 18:31–34

K47	DISPUTE ABOUT GREATNESS	9:33–37
Mark 10:41–45	Matt 18:1–10	Luke 9:46–50
Mark 10:13–16	Matt 20:24–28	Luke 22:24–30
John 12:44–45	Matt 23:11–12	Luke 18:15–17
John 13:20	Matt 10:40	Luke 10:16
	GThom 12	

K48	THE STRANGE EXORCIST	9:38–41
	Matt 12:30	Luke 9:46–50
	Matt 10:42	Luke 11:23
		POxy1224 2

K49	ON TEMPTATIONS	9:42–50
Isa 66:24	Matt 18:1–10	Luke 17:1–4
Lev 2:13	Matt 5:29–30	Luke 14:34–35
	Matt 5:13	

S13:K50–53	JOURNEY TO JERUSALEM	10:1–31

K50	DEPARTURE FOR JUDEA	10:1
	Matt 19:1–2	

K51	ON DIVORCE	10:2–12
K51.1	QUESTION OF DIVORCE	10:2–9
K51.2	EXPLANATION FOR THE DISCIPLES	10:10–12
Deut 24:1–4	Matt 19:3–9	Luke 16:18
Gen 1:27	Matt 5:31–32	1 Cor 7:10–11
Gen 2:24		

K52	ON CHILDREN	10:13–16
John 3:3–5	Matt 19:13–15	Luke 18:15–17
	Matt 18:3	
	GThom 22	

K53	ON RICHES	10:17–31
K53.1	RICH MAN	10:17–22
K53.2	DANGER OF RICHES	10:23–31
Exod 20:12–16	Matt 19:16–22	Luke 18:18–25
Deut 5:16–20	Matt 19:23–30	Luke 18:26–30
	Matt 20:16	Luke 13:30
	POxy654 4	GNaz 16
	GThom 4	ApocJa 4:22–37
	GThom 81	

S14:K54–56	ON THE ROAD TO JERUSALEM	10:32–52

K54	THIRD PREDICTION OF THE PASSION	10:32–34
Mark 8:31–33	Matt 20:17–19	Luke 18:31–34
Mark 9:30–32	Matt 16:21–23	Luke 9:18–22
	Matt 17:22–23	Luke 9:43b–45
		SecMk 1

K55	THE QUESTION OF THE SONS OF ZEBEDEE	10:35–45
K55.1	REQUESTS FOR POSITIONS OF HONOR	10:35–40
K55.2	THE TEN DISCIPLES ARE INDIGNANT	10:41–45
Mark 9:33–37	Matt 20:20–23	Luke 12:49–53
	Matt 20:24–28	Luke 22:24–27
	Matt 18:1–4	Luke 9:46–50

K56	BLIND BARTIMAEUS	10:46–52
	Matt 20:29–34	Luke 18:35–43
	Matt 9:27–31	SecMk 2

S15:K57–60	IN JERUSALEM	11:1–13:37

K57	ENTRY INTO JERUSALEM	11:1–11
K57.1	TWO SENT FOR COLT	11:1–3
K57.2	COLT IS FOUND TIED	11:4–6
K57.3	TRIUMPHAL ENTRY	11:7–10
K57.4	RETURN TO BETHANY	11:11
Zech 9:9	Matt 21:1–6	Luke 19:28–32
Ps 118:26	Matt 21:7–9	Luke 19:33–34
John 12:12–19	Matt 21:10–11	Luke 19:35–40

K58	SECOND DAY	11:12–19

K58.1	CURSING OF FIG TREE	11:12–14
	Matt 21:18–22	Luke 13:6–9
		InThom 3:1–3
		InThom 4:1–2

K58.2	CLEANSING OF TEMPLE	11:15–19
Isa 56:7	Matt 21:12–13	Luke 19:45–48
Jer 7:11	Matt 21:14–17	
John 2:13–22		

K59	THIRD DAY	11:20–12:44

K59.1	LESSON OF THE FIG TREE	11:20–25
Mark 9:28–29	Matt 21:18–22	Luke 13:6–9
John 14:13–14	Matt 17:19–20	Luke 17:5–6
John 15:7	Matt 18:19	
John 16:23	Matt 6:14	
	GThom 48	
	GThom 106	

K59.2	QUESTION OF JESUS' AUTHORITY	11:27–33
John 2:18	Matt 21:23–27	Luke 20:1–8
		POxy840 2

K59.3	PARABLE OF THE WICKED TENANTS	12:1–12
Isa 5:1–2	Matt 21:33–46	Luke 20:9–19
Ps 118:22–23	GThom 65	
	GThom 66	

K59.4   IS IT LAWFUL TO PAY TAXES?   **12:13–17**

| John 3:2 | Matt 22:15–22 | Luke 20:20–26 |
| | GThom 100 | PEger2 3 |

K59.5   WHOSE WIFE WILL SHE BE?   **12:18–27**

Gen 38:8	Matt 22:23–33	Luke 20:27–40
Deut 25:5–6		
Exod 3:6		

K59.6   WHICH IS THE GREATEST COMMANDMENT?   **12:28–34**

Deut 6:4–5	Matt 22:34–40	Luke 10:25–29
Lev 19:18	GThom 25	Luke 20:39
1 Sam 15:22	GThom 82	Luke 20:40
		Did 1:2
		Barn 19:5
		InThom 15:4a

K59.7   WHOSE SON IS THE CHRIST?   **12:35–37**

2 Sam 7:12–16	Matt 22:41–46	Luke 20:41–44
Ps 89:3–4		1 Cor 15:20–28
Mic 5:2		
Ps 110:1		
John 7:40–44		

K59.8   WARNING AGAINST THE SCRIBES   **12:38–40**

	Matt 23:6	Luke 20:45–47
		Luke 11:37–44
		Luke 14:7–11

K59.9   WIDOW'S PENNY   **12:41–44**

| | | Luke 21:1–4 |

K60   THIRD DAY: APOCALYPTIC DISCOURSE   **13:1–37**

K60.1   JESUS PREDICTS THE DESTRUCTION OF THE TEMPLE   **13:1–2**

| | Matt 24:1–2 | Luke 21:5–6 |

K60.2   SIGNS OF THE END   **13:3–13**

Mark 13:21–23	Matt 24:3–14	Luke 21:5–19
John 14:26	Matt 10:16–23	Luke 17:23
John 16:2	Matt 24:23–26	Luke 12:11–12
John 15:18–21		

K60.3   TRIBULATION BEFORE THE END   **13:14–23**

Dan 9:27	Matt 24:15–28	Luke 21:20–24
Dan 11:31	GThom 79	Luke 17:31
Dan 12:11	GThom 113	
1 Macc 1:54		
Dan 12:1		
Deut 13:2		

K60.4   COMING OF THE SON OF MAN   **13:24–32**

Mark 14:62	Matt 24:29–36	Luke 21:25–33
Mark 9:1	Matt 16:28	Luke 9:27
Isa 13:10		1 Thess 4:15–16
Isa 34:4		Rev 1:7
Dan 7:13–14		
Deut 30:3–4		

K60.5   THE NEED FOR WATCHFULNESS   **13:33–37**

	Matt 24:37–51	Luke 21:34–36
	Matt 25:13	Luke 12:35–40
		Did 16:1

S16:K61–68   THE PASSION NARRATIVE   **14:1–16:8**

K61   INTRODUCTION   **14:1–11**

K61.1   THE AUTHORITIES SEEK TO KILL JESUS   **14:1–2**

Mark 11:18	Matt 26:1–2	Luke 22:1–2
Mark 12:12	Matt 26:3–5	Luke 19:47–48
John 11:45–53	Matt 21:45	Luke 20:19
John 11:54		
John 11:55–57		

K61.2   A WOMAN ANOINTS JESUS   **14:3–9**

| John 12:1–8 | Matt 26:6–13 | Luke 7:36–50 |

K61.3   JUDAS MAKES A DEAL   **14:10–11**

| | Matt 26:14–16 | Luke 22:3–6 |

K62   THE PASSOVER MEAL   **14:12–25**

K62.1	THE PASSOVER MEAL	**14:12–16**
K62.2	THE TRAITOR	**14:17–21**
K62.3	THE LAST SUPPER	**14:22–25**

Ps 41:9	Matt 26:17–19	Luke 22:7–13
Exod 24:8	Matt 26:20–25	Luke 22:14–23
Jer 31:31	Matt 26:26–29	GEbi 7
Zech 9:11		1 Cor 11:23–25
John 13:21–30		Did 9:1–5
John 6:48–58	Justin, *Apology* 1.66.3	

K63   EVENTS IN GETHSEMANE   **14:26–52**

K63.1   JESUS PREDICTS PETER'S DENIAL   **14:26–31**

Zech 13:7	Matt 26:30–35	Luke 22:31–34
John 13:36–38		Luke 22:39
John 18:1		Fayyum Fragment
John 16:32		
John 11:16		

K63.2	THE PRAYERS	**14:32–42**
K63.2a	INTRODUCTION	**14:32**
K63.2b	JESUS TAKES THE THREE	**14:33–34**
K63.2c	"ABBA, FATHER"	**14:35–36**
K63.2d	THE THREE SLEEP	**14:37–38**
K63.2e	SECOND PRAYER	**14:39**
K63.2f	THE THREE SLEEP	**14:40**
K63.2g	THE HOUR HAS COME	**14:41–42**

John 18:1	Matt 26:36	Luke 22:39
John 12:27	Matt 26:37–38	Luke 22:40–42
John 18:11	Matt 26:39	Luke 22:45–46
John 14:31	Matt 26:40–41	
	Matt 26:42	
	Matt 26:43	
	Matt 26:44	
	Matt 26:45–46	

K63.3	THE ARREST	**14:43–52**

John 18:1–12	Matt 26:47–56	Luke 22:47–54a
John 18:20		

K64	TRIAL BEFORE THE COUNCIL; PETER'S DENIAL	**14:53–72**

K64.1	INTRODUCTION	**14:53–54**
K64.2	TRIAL BEFORE THE COUNCIL	**14:55–65**

Mark 13:26	Matt 26:57–58	Luke 22:54b–65
Ps 110:1	Matt 26:59–68	Luke 22:66–71
Dan 7:13–14	Matt 24:30	GPet 3.9
Lev 24:16	GThom 71	
John 18:13–14		
John 18:19–24		
John 2:19		

K64.3	PETER'S DENIAL	**14:66–72**

K64.3a	FIRST DENIAL	**14:66–68**
K64.3b	SECOND DENIAL	**14:69–70a**
K64.3c	THIRD DENIAL	**14:70b–72**

John 18:15–18	Matt 26:69–75	Luke 22:54b–62
John 18:25–27		GNaz 19

K65	TRIAL BEFORE PILATE	**15:1–15**

K65.1	PILATE INTERROGATES JESUS	**15:1–5**
K65.2	PILATE CONDEMNS JESUS	**15:6–15**

John 18:28–19:16	Matt 27:1–26	Luke 23:1–7
		Luke 23:13–25
		AcPil 3:2
		AcPil 4:4–5
		AcPil 9:4–5
		GNaz 20

K66	THE CRUCIFIXION	**15:16–41**

K66.1	THE MOCKING	**15:16–20**

John 19:1–3	Matt 27:27–31	GPet 2.5b–3.9
		AcPil 10:1a

K66.2	SIMON OF CYRENE	**15:21**

	Matt 27:32	Luke 23:26–32

K66.3	THE CRUCIFIXION	**15:22–32**

Ps 69:21	Matt 27:33–44	Luke 23:33–43
Ps 22:18	GThom 71	GPet 4.10–14
Ps 22:7		AcPil 10:1b–2
John 19:17–24		
John 2:19		

K66.4	THE DEATH	**15:33–41**

Ps 22:1	Matt 27:45–56	Luke 23:44–49
Ps 69:21		Luke 23:36
Ps 38:11		Luke 8:1–3
John 19:25–37		Luke 23:55
		GPet 5.15–20
		AcPil 11:1–3a
		GNaz 36

K67	THE BURIAL	**15:42–47**

Deut 21:22–23	Matt 27:57–61	Luke 23:50–56
Josh 10:18		GPet 2.3–5a
Josh 10:27		GPet 6.21–24
John 19:38–42		AcPil 11:3b

K68	THE WOMEN DISCOVER THE EMPTY TOMB	**16:1–8**

John 20:1–18	Matt 28:1–8	Luke 24:1–11
		GPet 9.35–13.57
		AcPil 13:1–3

S17:K69–72	THE LONGER ENDING	**16:9–20**

K69	APPEARANCE TO MARY MAGDALENE	**16:9–11**

John 20:11–18		

K70	APPEARANCE TO THE TWO	**16:12–13**

		Luke 24:13–27
		Luke 24:28–33

K71	APPEARANCE TO THE TWELVE	**16:14–18**
K72	ASCENSION AND MISSION	**16:19–20**

W:Freer	Matt 28:16–20	Luke 24:50–53
John 20:19–23		AcPil 14:1

MARK   MATT   LUKE

Mark 1:1 (§K1)
  ¹ **The beginning of the Gospel of Jesus Christ, the Son of God.**ᵃ

ᵃ Omit *Son of God:* ℵ* Θ 28ᶜ *al*

Cf. §L1 and the pars cited there

† Matt 1:1
  ¹ The book of the genealogy **of Jesus Christ, the son of** David, the son of Abraham.

JOHN   THOMAS   OTHER

† GThom, title
  These are the secret sayings which the living **Jesus** spoke and which Didymos Judas Thomas wrote down.

InThom 0–1:1
  The Account of Thomas the Israelite Philosopher concerning the Childhood of the Lord
  1¹ I, Thomas the Israelite, tell and make known to you all, brethren from among the Gentiles, all the works of the childhood of our Lord **Jesus Christ** and his mighty deeds, which he did when he was born in our land. **The beginning** is as follows.

MARK	MATT	LUKE

MARK

Mark 1:2–8 (§K2) °

[2] As it is written in Isaiah the prophet,[a]
"Behold, I send my messenger before thy face,
who shall prepare thy way;
[3] the voice of one crying in the wilderness:
Prepare the way of the Lord,
make his paths straight—"
[4] John the baptizer appeared[b] in the wilderness, preaching a baptism of repentance for the forgiveness of sins. [5] And there went out to him all the country of Judea, and all the people of Jerusalem; and they were baptized by him in the river Jordan, confessing their sins. [6] Now John was clothed in camel's hair, and had a leather girdle around his waist, and ate locusts and wild honey. [7] And he preached, saying, "After me comes he who is mightier than I, the thong of whose sandals I am not worthy to stoop down and untie. [8] I have baptized you with water; but he will baptize you with the Holy Spirit."

[a] Some witnesses read *in the prophets:* A K P W Π *f*[13] 28 *al*

[b] Some witnesses read *John was baptizing:* A K P W Π *f*[1] *f*[13] *al*

° Appendix 1 ⇨ §K2

Mal 3:1a ⇨ Mark 1:2
[1] "Behold, I send my messenger to **prepare** the way before me, . . ."

Isa 40:3 ⇨ Mark 1:3
[3] A voice cries:
"In the wilderness prepare the way of the Lord,
make straight in the desert a highway for our God."

2 Kgs 1:8 ⇨ Mark 1:6
[8] They answered him, "He wore a garment of haircloth, with **a girdle** of **leather** about **his** loins." And he said, "It is Elijah the Tishbite."

MATT

Matt 3:1–12 (§M5)

[1] In those days came **John the** Baptist, **preaching in the wilderness** of Judea, [2] "Repent, for the kingdom of heaven is at hand." [3] For this is he who was spoken of by **the prophet Isaiah** when he said,
"The voice of one crying in the wilderness:
Prepare the way of the Lord,
make his paths straight."
[4] Now John wore a garment of **camel's hair**, and **a leather girdle around his waist**; and his food was **locusts and wild honey**. [5] Then **went out to him Jerusalem** and all **Judea** and all the region about the **Jordan**, [6] **and they were baptized by him in the river Jordan, confessing their sins.** [7] But when he saw many of the Pharisees and Sadducees coming for baptism, he said to them, "You brood of vipers! Who warned you to flee from the wrath to come? [8] Bear fruit that befits **repentance**, [9] and do not presume to say to yourselves, 'We have Abraham as our father'; for I tell you, God is able from these stones to raise up children to Abraham. [10] Even now the axe is laid to the root of the trees; every tree therefore that does not bear good fruit is cut down and thrown into the fire. [11] **I baptize you with water** for repentance, but he who is coming **after me is mightier than I, whose sandals I am not worthy** to carry; **he will baptize you with the Holy Spirit** and with fire. [12] His winnowing fork is in his hand, and he will clear his threshing floor and gather his wheat into the granary, but the chaff he will burn with unquenchable fire."

Matt 11:10 ⇨ Mark 1:2
[10] "This is he of whom it is written,
'Behold, I send my messenger before thy face,
who shall prepare thy way before thee.'"

LUKE

Luke 3:1–20 (§L7)

[1] In the fifteenth year of the reign of Tiberius Caesar, Pontius Pilate being governor of Judea, and Herod being tetrarch of Galilee, and his brother Philip tetrarch of the region of Ituraea and Trachonitis, and Lysanias tetrarch of Abilene, [2] in the high-priesthood of Annas and Caiaphas, the word of God came to **John** the son of Zechariah **in the wilderness**; [3] and he went into all the region about the **Jordan, preaching a baptism of repentance for the forgiveness of sins.** [4] **As it is written in** the book of the words of Isaiah the prophet,
"The voice of one crying in the wilderness:
Prepare the way of the Lord,
make his paths straight.
[5] Every valley shall be filled,
and every mountain and hill shall be brought low,
and the crooked shall be made **straight**,
and the rough ways shall be made smooth;
[6] and all flesh shall see the salvation of God."
[7] He said therefore to the multitudes that came **out to be baptized by him**, "You brood of vipers! Who warned you to flee from the wrath to come? [8] Bear fruits that befit **repentance**, and do not begin to say to yourselves, 'We have Abraham as our father'; for I tell you, God is able from these stones to raise up children to Abraham. [9] Even now the axe is laid to the root of the trees; every tree therefore that does not bear good fruit is cut down and thrown into the fire." [10] And the multitudes asked him, "What then shall we do?" [11] And he answered them, "He who has two coats, let him share with him who has none; and he who has food, let him do likewise." [12] Tax collectors also came to be baptized, and said to him, "Teacher, what shall we do?" [13] And he said to them, "Collect no more than is appointed you." [14] Soldiers also asked him, "And we, what shall we do?" And he said to them, "Rob no one by violence or by false accusation, and be content with your wages." [15] As **the people** were in expectation, and all men questioned in their hearts concerning John, whether perhaps he were the Christ, [16] John answered them all, "I baptize **you with water**; but **he who is mightier than I** is coming, **the thong of whose sandals I am not worthy to untie; he will baptize you with the Holy Spirit** and with fire. [17] His winnowing fork is in his hand, to clear his threshing floor, and to gather the wheat into his granary, but the chaff he will burn with unquenchable fire." [18] So, with many other exhortations, he preached good news to the people. [19] But Herod the tetrarch, who had been reproved by him for Herodias, his brother's wife, and for all the evil things that Herod had done, [20] added this to them all, that he shut up John in prison.

Luke 7:27 ⇨ Mark 1:2
[27] "This is he of whom it is written,
'Behold, I send my messenger before thy face,
who shall prepare thy way before thee.'"

JOHN	THOMAS	OTHER

JOHN

† John 1:19–28 (§J2.1)

¹⁹ And this is the testimony of **John**, when the Jews sent priests and Levites from Jerusalem to ask him, "Who are you?" ²⁰ He confessed, he did not deny, but confessed, "I am not the Christ." ²¹ And they asked him, "What then? Are you Elijah?" He said, "I am not." "Are you the prophet?" And he answered, "No." ²² They said to him then, "Who are you? Let us have an answer for those who sent us. What do you say about yourself?" ²³ He said, "I am **the voice of one crying in the wilderness, 'Make straight the way of the Lord,'** as the prophet Isaiah said."

²⁴ Now they had been sent from the Pharisees. ²⁵ They asked him, "Then why are you baptizing, if you are neither the Christ, nor Elijah, nor the prophet?" ²⁶ John answered them, "I baptize **with water**; but among you stands one whom you do not know, ²⁷ even **he who comes after me, the thong of whose** sandal **I am not worthy to untie.**" ²⁸ This took place in Bethany beyond the **Jordan**, where **John** was baptizing.

John 1:31–32 ⇨ Mark 1:2–3

³¹ "I myself did not know him; but for this I came baptizing with water, that he might be revealed to Israel." ³² And John bore witness, "I saw the Spirit descend as a dove from heaven, and it remained on him."

OTHER

Acts 13:24–25

²⁴ "*Before his coming* **John** *had preached* **a baptism of repentance** *to* **all the people of Israel.** ²⁵ *And as* **John** *was finishing his course, he said, 'What do you suppose that I am? I am not he. No, but* **after me** *one is coming,* **the sandals** *of whose feet* **I am not worthy to untie.**'"

Acts 19:1–7

¹ *While Apollos was at Corinth, Paul passed through the upper country and came to Ephesus. There he found some disciples.* ² *And he said to them, "Did you receive the Holy Spirit when you believed?" And they said, "No, we have never even heard that there is a Holy Spirit."* ³ *And he said, "Into what then were you baptized?" They said, "Into John's baptism."* ⁴ *And Paul said, "* **John** *baptized with the* **baptism of repentance,** *telling the people to believe in the one who was to come* **after him,** *that is, Jesus."* ⁵ *On hearing this, they were baptized in the name of the Lord Jesus.* ⁶ *And when Paul had laid his hands upon them,* **the Holy Spirit** *came on them; and they spoke with tongues and prophesied.* ⁷ *There were about twelve of them in all.*

GEbi 2

(2) And:

It came to pass that **John** *was baptizing; and there went out to him Pharisees and were baptized, and* **all Jerusalem.** *And* **John** *had a garment of* **camel's hair** *and* **a leathern girdle** *about his loins, and his food, as it saith, was* **wild honey,** *the taste of which was that of manna, as a cake dipped in oil.*

Thus they were resolved to pervert the word of truth into a lie and to put a cake in the place of locusts. (Epiphanius, *Haer.* 30.13.4f.)

GEbi 3

(3) And the beginning of their Gospel runs:

It came to pass in the days of Herod the king of **Judaea,** *<when Caiaphas was high priest,> that there came <one>,* **John** *<by name,> and baptized with the* **baptism of repentance in the river Jordan.** *It was said of him that he was of the lineage of Aaron the priest, a son of Zacharias and Elisabeth;* **and all went out to him.** (Epiphanius, *Haer.* 30.13.6)

Acts 1:5 ⇨ Mark 1:8

⁵ "*for* **John** **baptized with water,** *but before many days you shall be baptized* **with the Holy Spirit.**"

Acts 11:16 ⇨ Mark 1:8

¹⁶ "*And I remembered the word of the Lord, how he said, 'John* **baptized with water, but you shall be baptized** **with the Holy Spirit.**'"

MARK

Mark 1:9–11 (§K3) °

⁹ In those days Jesus came from Nazareth of Galilee and was baptized by John in the Jordan. ¹⁰ And when he came up out of the water, immediately he saw the heavens opened and the Spirit descending upon him like a dove; ¹¹ and a voice came from heaven, "Thou art my beloved Son;ᵃ with thee I am well pleased."

ᵃ Or: *my Son, my* (or: *the*) *Beloved*

°Appendix 1 ⇨ §K3

Ps 2:7 ⇨ Mark 1:11
⁷ I will tell of the decree of the Lord:
He said to me, "You are **my son**,
today **I** have begotten you."

Isa 42:1 ⇨ Mark 1:11
¹ Behold **my** servant, whom **I** uphold,
my chosen, in whom **my** soul delights;
I have put my Spirit upon him,
he will bring forth justice to the nations.

Isa 44:2 ⇨ Mark 1:11
² "Thus says the Lord who make you,
who formed you from the womb and will help you:
Fear not, O Jacob **my** servant,
Jeshurun whom **I** have chosen."

JOHN

† **John 1:29–34 (§J2.2)**

²⁹ The next day he saw **Jesus** coming toward him, and said, "Behold, the Lamb of God, who takes away the sin of the world! ³⁰ This is he of whom I said, 'After me comes a man who · ranks before me, for he was before me.' ³¹ I myself did not know him; but for this I came baptizing with water, that he might be revealed to Israel." ³² And **John** bore witness, "**I saw the Spirit** descend as **a dove** from heaven, and it remained on him. ³³ I myself did not know him; but he who sent me to baptize with water said to me, 'He on whom you see **the Spirit** descend and remain, this is he who baptizes with **the** Holy **Spirit**.' ³⁴ And I have seen and have borne witness that this is the **Son** of God."

MATT

Matt 3:13–17 (§M6)

¹³ Then **Jesus came from Galilee** to the **Jordan** to **John**, to be **baptized by** him. ¹⁴ John would have prevented him, saying, "I need to be baptized by you, and do you come to me?" ¹⁵ But Jesus answered him, "Let it be so now; for thus it is fitting for us to fulfil all righteousness." Then he consented. ¹⁶ **And when** Jesus **was baptized, he** went **up immediately** from **the water**, and behold, **the heavens** were **opened** and **he saw** the **Spirit** of God **descending like a dove**, and alighting on **him**; ¹⁷ and lo, **a voice from heaven**, saying, "This is **my beloved Son, with** whom **I am well pleased.**"

Matt 17:5 ⇨ Mark 1:10–11
⁵ *He was still speaking, when lo, a bright cloud overshadowed them, and a voice from the cloud said, "This is my beloved Son, with whom I am well pleased; listen to him."*

THOMAS

LUKE

Luke 3:21–22 (§L8)

²¹ Now when all the people were baptized, **and when Jesus** also had been **baptized and** was praying, **the** heaven was **opened**, ²² and the Holy Spirit descended **upon him** in bodily form, as a dove, and a voice came from heaven, "**Thou art my beloved Son; with thee I am well pleased.**"

Luke 9:34–35 ⇨ Mark 1:10–11
³⁴ *As he said this, a cloud came and overshadowed them; and they were afraid as they entered the cloud.* ³⁵ *And a voice came out of the cloud, saying, "This is my Son, my Chosen; listen to him!"*

OTHER

GEbi 4

(4) And after much has been recorded it proceeds:

When the people were baptized, Jesus also came and was baptized by John. And as he came up from the water, the heavens were opened and he saw the Holy Spirit in the form of a dove that descended and entered into him. And a voice (sounded) from heaven that said: Thou art my beloved Son, in thee I am well pleased. And again: I have this day begotten thee. And immediately a great light shone round about the place. When John saw this, it saith, he saith unto him: Who art thou, Lord? And again a voice from heaven (rang out) to him: This is my beloved Son in whom I am well pleased. And then, it saith, John fell down before him and said: I beseech thee, Lord, baptize thou me. But he prevented him and said: Suffer it; for thus it is fitting that everything should be fulfilled. (Epiphanius, *Haer.* 30.13.7f.)

GNaz 2

(2) Behold, the mother of the Lord and his brethren said to him: John the Baptist baptizes unto the remission of sins, let us go and be baptized by him. But he said to them: Wherein have I sinned that I should go and be baptized by him? Unless what I have said is ignorance (a sin of ignorance). (Jerome, *Adversus Pelagianos* 3.2)

GHeb 2

(2) According to the Gospel written in the Hebrew speech, which the Nazaraeans read, the whole fount of the Holy Spirit shall descend upon him . . . Further in the Gospel which we have just mentioned we find the following written:

And it came to pass when the Lord was come up out of the water, the whole fount of the Holy Spirit descended upon him and rested on him and said to him: My Son, in all the prophets was I waiting for thee that thou shouldest come and I might rest in thee. For thou art my rest; thou art my first-begotten Son that reignest for ever. (Jerome, *Commentary on Isaiah* 4 [on Isaiah 11:2])

MARK

Mark 1:12–13 (§K4)

[12] The Spirit immediately drove him out into the wilderness. [13] And he was in the wilderness forty days, tempted by Satan; and he was with the wild beasts; and the angels ministered to him.

MATT

Matt 4:1–11 (§M7)

[1] Then Jesus was led up by **the Spirit into the wilderness** to be **tempted by** the devil. [2] And he fasted **forty days** and forty nights, and afterward he was hungry. [3] And the tempter came and said to him, "If you are the Son of God, command these stones to become loaves of bread." [4] But he answered, "It is written,

'Man shall not live by bread alone,
but by every word that proceeds from the mouth of God.'"

[5] Then the devil took him to the holy city, and set him on the pinnacle of the temple, [6] and said to him, "If you are the Son of God, throw yourself down; for it is written,

'He will give his angels charge of you,'
and

'On their hands they will bear you up,
lest you strike your foot against a stone.'"

[7] Jesus said to him, "Again it is written, 'You shall not tempt the Lord your God.'" [8] Again, the devil took him to a very high mountain, and showed him all the kingdoms of the world and the glory of them; [9] and he said to him, "All these I will give you, if you will fall down and worship me." [10] Then Jesus said to him, "Begone, Satan! for it is written,

'You shall worship the Lord your God
and him only shall you serve.'"

[11] Then the devil left him, **and behold, angels** came and **ministered to him.**

LUKE

Luke 4:1–13 (§L10)

[1] And Jesus, full of the Holy Spirit, returned from the Jordan, and was led by **the Spirit** [2] for **forty days** in **the wilderness, tempted by** the devil. And he ate nothing in those days; and when they were ended, he was hungry. [3] The devil said to him, "If you are the Son of God, command this stone to become bread." [4] And Jesus answered him, "It is written, 'Man shall not live by bread alone.'" [5] And the devil took him up, and showed him all the kingdoms of the world in a moment of time, [6] and said to him, "To you I will give all this authority and their glory; for it has been delivered to me, and I give it to whom I will. [7] If you, then, will worship me, it shall all be yours." [8] And Jesus answered him, "It is written,

'You shall worship the Lord your God,
and him only shall you serve.'"

[9] And he took him to Jerusalem, and set him on the pinnacle of the temple, and said to him, "If you are the Son of God, throw yourself down from here; [10] for it is written,

'He will give his angels charge of you, to guard you,'

[11] and

'On their hands they will bear you up,
lest you strike your foot against a stone.'"

[12] And Jesus answered him, "It is said, 'You shall not tempt the Lord your God.'" [13] And when the devil had ended every temptation, he departed from him until an opportune time.

JOHN

John 1:51 ⇨ Mark 1:13

[51] *And he said to him, "Truly, truly, I say to you, you will see heaven opened, **and the angels of God ascending and descending upon the Son of man.**"*

THOMAS

OTHER

MARK

Mark 1:14–15 (§K5) °

¹⁴ Now after John was arrested Jesus came into Galilee, preaching the gospel of God, ¹⁵ and saying, "The time is fulfilled, and the kingdom of God is at hand; repent, and believe in the gospel."

°Appendix 3 ⇨ §K5

Mark 6:17 ⇨ Mark 1:14

¹⁷ For Herod had sent and seized **John** and bound him in prison for the sake of Herodias, his brother Philip's wife; because he had married her.

MATT

Matt 4:12–17 (§M8)

¹² Now when he heard that **John** had been **arrested**, he withdrew **into Galilee**; ¹³ and leaving Nazareth he went and dwelt in Capernaum by the sea, in the territory of Zebulun and Naphtali, ¹⁴ that what was spoken by the prophet Isaiah might be fulfilled:

¹⁵ "The land of Zebulun and the land of Naphtali,

toward the sea, across the Jordan, Galilee of the Gentiles—

¹⁶ the people who sat in darkness have seen a great light,

and for those who sat in the region and shadow of death

light has dawned."

¹⁷ From that time Jesus began to preach, **saying, "Repent,** for **the kingdom of** heaven **is at hand."**

Matt 14:3 ⇨ Mark 1:14

³ For Herod had seized **John** and bound him and put him in prison, for the sake of Herodias, his brother Philip's wife; . . .

LUKE

† **Luke 4:14–15 (§L11)**

¹⁴ And **Jesus** returned in the power of the Spirit **into Galilee**, and a report concerning him went out through all the surrounding country. ¹⁵ And he taught in their synagogues, being glorified by all.

† **Luke 4:16–30 (§L12)**

¹⁶ And he came to Nazareth, where he had been brought up; and he went to the synagogue, as his custom was, on the sabbath day. And he stood up to read; ¹⁷ and there was given to him the book of the prophet Isaiah. He opened the book and found the place where it was written,

¹⁸ "The Spirit of the Lord is upon me, because he has anointed me to preach good news to the poor.

He has sent me to proclaim release to the captives

and recovering of sight to the blind, to set at liberty those who are oppressed,

¹⁹ to proclaim the acceptable year of the Lord."

²⁰ And he closed the book, and gave it back to the attendant, and sat down; and the eyes of all in the synagogue were fixed on him. ²¹ And he began to say to them, "Today this scripture has been **fulfilled** in your hearing." ²² And all spoke well of him, and wondered at the gracious words which proceeded out of his mouth; and they said, "Is not this Joseph's son?" ²³ And he said to them, "Doubtless you will quote to me this proverb, 'Physician, heal yourself; what we have heard you did at Capernaum, do here also in your own country.'" ²⁴ And he said, "Truly, I say to you, no prophet is acceptable in his own country. ²⁵ But in truth, I tell you, there were many widows in Israel in the days of Elijah, when the heaven was shut up three years and six months, when there came a great famine over all the land; ²⁶ and Elijah was sent to none of them but only to Zarephath, in the land of Sidon, to a woman who was a widow. ²⁷ And there were many lepers in Israel in the time of the prophet Elisha; and none of them was cleansed, but only Naaman the Syrian." ²⁸ When they heard this, all in the synagogue were filled with wrath. ²⁹ And they rose up and put him out of the city, and led him to the brow of the hill on which their city was built, that they might throw him down headlong. ³⁰ But passing through the midst of them he went away.

JOHN

John 1:43 ⇨ Mark 1:14

⁴³ The next day *Jesus decided to go to Galilee. And he found Philip and said to him, "Follow me."*

John 4:1–3 ⇨ Mark 1:14

¹ Now when the Lord knew that the Pharisees had heard that *Jesus was making and baptizing more disciples than John* ² (although Jesus himself did not baptize, but only his disciples), ³ he left Judea and departed again to *Galilee*.

John 4:43 ⇨ Mark 1:14

⁴³ After the two days he departed to *Galilee*.

THOMAS

Luke 3:19–20, 23a

¹⁹ But Herod the tetrarch, who had been reproved by him for Herodias, his brother's wife, and for all the evil things that Herod had done, ²⁰ added this to them all, that he shut up **John** in prison. . . .

²³ **Jesus**, when he began his ministry, was about thirty years of age, . . .

OTHER

MARK   MATT   LUKE

Mark 1:16–18 (§K6) °

[16] And passing along by **the Sea of Galilee**, he saw **Simon** and **Andrew** the brother of Simon casting a **net** in the sea; for they were **fishermen**. [17] And Jesus said to them, "**Follow me** and I will make you become **fishers of men**." [18] And immediately they left their **nets and followed him**.

Mark 1:19–20 (§K7) °

[19] And going on a little farther, he saw James the son of Zebedee and John his brother, who were in their boat mending the nets. [20] And immediately he called them; and they left their father Zebedee in the boat with the hired servants, and followed him.

°Appendix 2 ⇨ §§K6 and K7

JOHN

† John 1:35–42 (§J3.1)

[35] The next day again John was standing with two of his disciples; [36] and he looked at Jesus as he walked, and said, "Behold, the Lamb of God!" [37] The two disciples heard him say this, **and they followed** Jesus. [38] Jesus turned, and saw them following, **and said to them**, "What do you seek?" And they said to him, "Rabbi" (which means Teacher), "where are you staying?" [39] He said to them, "Come and see." They came and saw where he was staying; and they stayed with him that day, for it was about the tenth hour. [40] One of the two who heard John speak, **and followed him**, was **Andrew**, Simon Peter's **brother**. [41] He first found his brother **Simon**, and said to him, "We have found the Messiah" (which means Christ). [42] He brought him to Jesus. **Jesus** looked at him, **and said**, "So you are Simon the son of John? You shall be called Cephas" (which means Peter).

† John 1:43–51 (§J3.2)

[43] The next day Jesus decided to go to **Galilee**. And **he** found Philip **and said to him, "Follow me."** [44] Now Philip was from Bethsaida, the city of **Andrew** and Peter. [45] Philip found Nathanael, and said to him, "We have found him of whom Moses in the law and also the prophets wrote, Jesus of Nazareth, the son of Joseph." [46] Nathanael said to him, "Can anything good come out of Nazareth?" Philip said to him, "Come and see." [47] **Jesus saw** Nathanael coming to him, **and said of** him, "Behold, an Israelite indeed, in whom is no guile!" [48] Nathanael said to him, "How do you know me?" Jesus answered him, "Before Philip called you, when you were under the fig tree, I **saw** you." [49] Nathanael answered him, "Rabbi, you are the Son of God! You are the King of Israel!" [50] Jesus answered him, "Because I said to you, I saw you under the fig tree, do you believe? You shall see greater things than these." [51] **And he said to** him, "Truly, truly, I say to you, you will see heaven opened, and the angels of God ascending and descending upon the Son of man."

Matt 4:18–20 (§M9) ⇨ §K6

[18] As he walked **by the Sea of Galilee**, **he saw** two brothers, **Simon** who is called Peter and **Andrew** his **brother**, **casting a net** into **the sea; for they were fishermen**. [19] **And** he **said to them**, "**Follow me, and I will make you fishers of men**." [20] **Immediately they left their nets and followed him**.

Matt 4:21–22 (§M10) ⇨ §K7

[21] **And going on** from there **he saw** two other brothers, **James the son of Zebedee and John his brother, in** the **boat** with Zebedee their father, **mending their nets, and he called them.** [22] Immediately **they left the boat** and **their father, and followed him.**

THOMAS

OTHER

GEbi 1

(1) In the Gospel that is in general use amongst them, which is called according to Matthew, which however is not whole (and) complete but forged and mutilated—they call it the Hebrew Gospel—it is reported:

*There appeared a certain man named **Jesus** of about thirty years of age, who chose us. And when he came to Capernaum, he entered into the house of **Simon** whose surname was Peter, and opened his mouth **and said:** As I passed along **the Lake of Tiberias, I** chose **John** and **James** the sons of **Zebedee**, and **Simon and Andrew** and Thaddaeus and Simon the Zealot and Judas Iscariot, and thee, Matthew, I **called** as thou didst sit at the receipt of custom, and thou didst follow me. You therefore **I will** to be twelve apostles for a testimony unto Israel. (Epiphanius, Haer. 30.13.2f.)*

† Luke 5:1–3 (§L17.1)

[1] While the people pressed upon him to hear the word of God, he was standing by **the lake of** Gennesaret. [2] And he saw two boats by the lake; but the **fishermen** had gone out of them and were washing their **nets**. [3] Getting into one of the boats, which was Simon's, he asked him to put out a little from the land. And he sat down and taught the people from the boat.

† Luke 5:4–11 (§L17.2)

[4] And when he had ceased speaking, he **said to Simon**, "Put out into the deep and let down your nets for a catch." [5] And Simon answered, "Master, we toiled all night and took nothing! But at your word I will let down the nets." [6] And when they had done this, they enclosed a great shoal of fish; and as their nets were breaking, [7] they beckoned to their partners in the other boat to come and help them. And they came and filled both the boats, so that they began to sink. [8] But when **Simon** Peter **saw** it, he fell down at Jesus' knees, saying, "Depart from me, for I am a sinful man, O Lord." [9] For he was astonished, and all that were with him, at the catch of fish which they had taken; [10] and so also were **James** and **John**, sons **of Zebedee**, who were partners with Simon. **And Jesus said to** Simon, "Do not be afraid; henceforth you **will** be catching **men**." [11] **And** when they had brought their boats to land, **they left** everything **and followed him.**

MARK

Mark 1:21–28 (§K8)

²¹ And they went into Capernaum; and immediately on the sabbath he entered the synagogue and taught. ²² And they were astonished at his teaching, for he taught them as one who had authority, and not as the scribes. ²³ And immediately there was in their synagogue a man with an unclean spirit; ²⁴ and he cried out, "What have you to do with us, Jesus of Nazareth? Have you come to destroy us? I know who you are, the Holy One of God." ²⁵ But Jesus rebuked him, saying, "Be silent, and come out of him!" ²⁶ And the unclean spirit, convulsing him and crying with a loud voice, came out of him. ²⁷ And they were all amazed, so that they questioned among themselves, saying, "What is this? A new teaching! With authority he commands even the unclean spirits, and they obey him." ²⁸ And at once his fame spread everywhere throughout all the surrounding region of Galilee.

Mark 11:18 ⇨ Mark 1:22

¹⁸ And the chief priests and **the scribes** heard it and sought a way to destroy him; for they feared him, because all the multitude was **astonished at his teaching**.

1 Kgs 17:18 ⇨ Mark 1:24

¹⁸ And she said to Elijah, "**What have you** against me, O man of God? **You have come to** me **to** bring my sin to rememberance, and **to** cause the death of my son!"

MATT

Matt 13:54 ⇨ Mark 1:21–22

⁵⁴ and coming to his own country **he taught them in their synagogue**, so that **they were astonished**, and said, "Where did this man get this wisdom and these mighty works?"

Matt 7:28–29 ⇨ Mark 1:22

²⁸ And when Jesus finished these sayings, the crowds were astonished at his teaching, ²⁹ for he taught them as one who had authority, and not as their scribes.

Matt 22:33 ⇨ Mark 1:22

³³ And when the crowd heard it, **they were astonished at his teaching**.

LUKE

Luke 4:31–37 (§L13)

³¹ And he went down to **Capernaum**, a city of Galilee. **And** he was teaching them **on the sabbath;** ³² **and they were astonished at his teaching,** for his word was with **authority.** ³³ And in the **synagogue** there was **a man** who had the **spirit** of an **unclean** demon; **and he cried out** with a loud voice, ³⁴ "Ah! **What have you to do with us, Jesus of Nazareth? Have you come to destroy us? I know who you are, the Holy One of God."** ³⁵ **But Jesus rebuked him, saying,** "Be silent, **and come out of him!"** And when **the** demon had thrown **him** down in the midst, he **came out of him**, having done him no harm. ³⁶ **And they were all amazed** and said to one another, "**What is this** word? For with **authority** and power **he commands the unclean spirits, and they** come out." ³⁷ And reports of him went out into every place in the surrounding region.

JOHN

John 7:46 ⇨ Mark 1:22

⁴⁶ The officers answered, "No man ever spoke like this man!"

John 6:69 ⇨ Mark 1:24

⁶⁹ "and we have believed, and have **come to know**, that **you are the Holy One of God**."

THOMAS

OTHER

InThom 19:2b ⇨ Mark 1:22

And all paid attention to him and marvelled how he, a child, put to silence **the** elders and teachers of the people, expounding the sections of the law and the sayings of the prophets.

MARK

Mark 1:29–31 (§K9)

²⁹ And immediately he[a] left the synagogue, and entered the house of Simon and Andrew, with James and John. ³⁰ Now Simon's mother-in-law lay sick with a fever, and immediately they told him of her. ³¹ And he came and took her by the hand and lifted her up, and the fever left her; and she served them.

Mark 1:32–34 (§K10) °

³² That evening, at sundown, they brought to him all who were sick or possessed with demons. ³³ And the whole city was gathered together about the door. ³⁴ And he healed many who were sick with various diseases, and cast out many demons; and he would not permit the demons to speak, because they knew him.

[a] Some witnesses read *they:* ℵ A C K L Δ Π 28 33 *al;* text: B D Θ *f¹ f¹³ al*

°Appendix 3 ⇨ §K10

Mark 3:7–12 (§K18) ⇨ §K10
⁷ *Jesus withdrew with his disciples to the sea, and a great multitude from Galilee followed; also from Judea ⁸ and Jerusalem and Idumea and from beyond the Jordan and from about Tyre and Sidon a great multitude, hearing all that he did, came to him. ⁹ And he told his disciples to have a boat ready for him because of the crowd, lest they should crush him; ¹⁰ for he had **healed many**, so that all who had **diseases** pressed upon him to touch him. ¹¹ And whenever the unclean spirits beheld **him**, they fell down before him and cried out, "You are the Son of God." ¹² And he strictly ordered them **not** to make **him** known.*

MATT

Matt 8:14–15 (§M15) ⇨ §K9

¹⁴ And when Jesus **entered** Peter's **house,** he saw his **mother-in-law** lying **sick** with a **fever;** ¹⁵ he touched **her hand, and the fever left her, and she** rose and **served** him.

Matt 8:16–17 (§M16) ⇨ §K10

¹⁶ That **evening they brought to him** many **who were possessed with demons; and he cast out** the spirits with a word, and **healed** all **who were sick.** ¹⁷ This was to fulfil what was spoken by the prophet Isaiah, "He took our infirmities and bore our diseases."

Matt 12:16 ⇨ Mark 1:34
¹⁶ *and ordered them not to make **him** known.*

LUKE

Luke 4:38–39 (§L14) ⇨ §K9

³⁸ And he arose and **left the synagogue, and** entered Simon's **house. Now Simon's mother-in-law** was ill **with a** high **fever, and** they besought **him** for **her.** ³⁹ And he stood over **her and** rebuked **the fever, and it left her;** and immediately **she** rose and **served them.**

Luke 4:40–41 (§L15) ⇨ §K10

⁴⁰ Now when the sun was setting, all those **who** had any that **were sick** with various diseases **brought** them **to him; and he** laid his hands on every one of them and **healed** them. ⁴¹ And **demons** also came **out** of **many,** crying, "You are the Son of God!" But **he** rebuked them, and **would not** allow them **to speak, because they knew** that he was the Christ.

JOHN

THOMAS

OTHER

MARK

Mark 1:35–39 (§K11) °
[35] And in the morning, a great while before day, he rose and went out to a lonely place, and there he prayed. [36] And Simon and those who were with him pursued him, [37] and they found him and said to him, "Every one is searching for you." [38] And he said to them, "Let us go on to the next towns, that I may preach there also; for that is why I came out." [39] And he went throughout all Galilee, preaching in their synagogues and casting out demons.

Mark 1:40–45 (§K12)
[40] And a leper came to him beseeching him, and kneeling said to him, "If you will, you can make me clean." [41] Moved with pity,[a] he stretched out his hand and touched him, and said to him, "I will; be clean." [42] And immediately the leprosy left him, and he was made clean. [43] And he sternly charged him, and sent him away at once, [44] and said to him, "See that you say nothing to any one; but go, show yourself to the priest, and offer for your cleansing what Moses commanded, for a proof to the people."[b] [45] But he went out and began to talk freely about it, and to spread the news, so that Jesus[c] could no longer openly enter a town, but was out in the country; and people came to him from every quarter.

[a] Text: ℵ A B C K L W Δ Θ Π 090 *f*[1] *f*[13] 28 33 *pm*; *Being angry:* D it (in part)

[b] Greek: *to them*

[c] Greek: *he*

° Appendix 3 ⇨ §K11

⇨ Mark 1:44
Cf. Lev 13–14, esp. 14:2–20

MATT

Matt 4:23–25 (§M11) ⇨ §K11
[23] And he went about **all Galilee** teaching **in their synagogues and preaching** the gospel of the kingdom and healing every disease and every infirmity among the people. [24] So his fame spread throughout all Syria, and they brought him all the sick, those afflicted with various diseases and pains, demoniacs, epileptics, and paralytics, and he healed them. [25] And great crowds followed him from Galilee and the Decapolis and Jerusalem and Judea and from beyond the Jordan.

Matt 8:1–4 (§M13) ⇨ §K12
[1] When he came down from the mountain, great crowds followed him; [2] and behold, a leper came to him and knelt before him, saying, "Lord, if you will, you can make me clean." [3] And he stretched out his hand and touched him, saying, "I will; be clean." And immediately his **leprosy** was cleansed. [4] And Jesus said to him, "See that you say nothing to any one; but go, show yourself to the priest, and offer the gift that Moses commanded, for a proof to the people."

LUKE

Luke 4:42–44 (§L16) ⇨ §K11
[42] And when it was day he departed and went into a lonely place. And the people sought him and came to him, and would have kept him from leaving them; [43] but he said to them, "I must preach the good news of the kingdom of God to the other cities also; for I was sent for this purpose." [44] And he was preaching in the synagogues of Judea.

Luke 5:12–16 (§L18) ⇨ §K12
[12] While he was in one of the cities, there came a man full of leprosy; and when he saw Jesus, he fell on his face and besought him, "Lord, if you will, you can make me clean." [13] And he stretched out his hand, and touched him, saying, "I will; be clean." And immediately the leprosy left him. [14] And he charged him to tell no one; but "go and show yourself to the priest, and make an offering for your cleansing, as Moses commanded, for a proof to the people." [15] But so much the more the report went abroad concerning him; and great multitudes gathered to hear and to be healed of their infirmities. [16] But he withdrew to the wilderness and prayed.

JOHN

THOMAS

OTHER

PEger2 2 ⇨ §K12
(2) **And behold a leper** drew near *[to him]* and said: "Master Jesus, wandering with lepers and eating with [them was I(?)] in the inn; I also [became] a le[per]. **If** [thou] therefore [wilt], I am made clean." Immediately the Lord [said to him]: "**I will, be thou made clean.**" [And thereupon] the leprosy departed from him. [And the Lord said to him]: "**Go** [thy way and show th]yself to the [priests] . . ."

MARK	MATT	LUKE

Mark 2:1-12 (§K13)

[1] And when he returned to Capernaum after some days, it was reported that he was at home. [2] And many were gathered together, so that there was no longer room for them, not even about the door; and he was preaching the word to them. [3] And they came, bringing to him a paralytic carried by four men. [4] And when they could not get near him because of the crowd, they removed the roof above him; and when they had made an opening, they let down the pallet on which the paralytic lay. [5] And when Jesus saw their faith, he said to the paralytic, "My son, your sins are forgiven." [6] Now some of the scribes were sitting there, questioning in their hearts, [7] "Why does this man speak thus? It is blasphemy! Who can forgive sins but God alone?" [8] And immediately Jesus, perceiving in his spirit that they thus questioned within themselves, said to them, "Why do you question thus in your hearts? [9] Which is easier, to say to the paralytic, 'Your sins are forgiven,' or to say, 'Rise, take up your pallet and walk'? [10] But that you may know that the Son of man has authority on earth to forgive sins"—he said to the paralytic— [11] "I say to you, rise, take up your pallet and go home." [12] And he rose, and immediately took up the pallet and went out before them all; so that they were all amazed and glorified God, saying, "We never saw anything like this!"

Matt 9:1-8 (§M20)

[1] And getting into a boat he crossed over and came to his own city. [2] And behold, they brought to him a paralytic, lying on his bed; and when Jesus saw their faith he said to the paralytic, "Take heart, my son; your sins are forgiven." [3] And behold, some of the scribes said to themselves, "This man is blaspheming." [4] But Jesus, knowing their thoughts, said, "Why do you think evil in your hearts? [5] For which is easier, to say, 'Your sins are forgiven,' or to say, 'Rise and walk'? [6] But that you may know that the Son of man has authority on earth to forgive sins"—he then said to the paralytic—"Rise, take up your bed and go home." [7] And he rose and went home. [8] When the crowds saw it, they were afraid, and they glorified God, who had given such authority to men.

Luke 5:17-26 (§L19)

[17] On one of those days, as he was teaching, there were Pharisees and teachers of the law sitting by, who had come from every village of Galilee and Judea and from Jerusalem; and the power of the Lord was with him to heal. [18] And behold, men were bringing on a bed a man who was paralyzed, and they sought to bring him in and lay him before Jesus; [19] but finding no way to bring him in, because of the crowd, they went up on the roof and let him down with his bed through the tiles into the midst before Jesus. [20] And when he saw their faith he said, "Man, your sins are forgiven you." [21] And the scribes and the Pharisees began to question, saying, "Who is this that speaks blasphemies? Who can forgive sins but God only?" [22] When Jesus perceived their questionings, he answered them, "Why do you question in your hearts? [23] Which is easier, to say, 'Your sins are forgiven you,' or to say, 'Rise and walk'? [24] But that you may know that the Son of man has authority on earth to forgive sins"—he said to the man who was paralyzed—"I say to you, rise, take up your bed and go home." [25] And immediately he rose before them, and took up that on which he lay, and went home, glorifying God. [26] And amazement seized them all, and they glorified God and were filled with awe, saying, "We have seen strange things today."

JOHN	THOMAS	OTHER

John 5:8-9a ⇨ Mark 2:11-12

[8] Jesus said to him, "Rise, take up your pallet, and walk." [9] And at once the man was healed, and he took up his pallet and walked.

MARK	MATT	LUKE

MARK

TEACHING BESIDE THE SEA

Mark 2:13 (§K14.1)

[13] He went out again beside the sea; and all the crowd gathered about him, and he taught them.

CALL OF LEVI

Mark 2:14 (§K14.2) °

[14] And as he passed on, he saw Levi[a] the son of Alphaeus sitting at the tax office, and he said to him, "Follow me." And he rose and followed him.

EATING WITH
TAX COLLECTORS AND SINNERS

Mark 2:15-17 (§K14.3)

[15] And as he sat at table in his house, many tax collectors and sinners were sitting with Jesus and his disciples; for there were many who followed him. [16] And the scribes of the Pharisees,[b] when they saw that he was eating with sinners and tax collectors, said to his disciples, "Why does he eat[c] with tax collectors and sinners?" [17] And when Jesus heard it, he said to them, "Those who are well have no need of a physician, but those who are sick; I came not to call the righteous, but sinners."

[a] Some witnesses read *James:* (cf. Matt 3:18) D Θ *f*[13] 565 it (in part) *al*

[b] Some witnesses read *and the Pharisees:* A C (D) K Θ Π *f*[1] *f*[13] *al*

[c] Some witnesses add *and drink:* (cf. Luke 5:30) A K Π *f*[1] 28 33 *al*

° Appendix 2 ⇨ §K14.2

MATT

Matt 9:9 (§M21.1) ⇨ §K14.2

[9] As Jesus **passed on** from there, **he saw a** man called Matthew **sitting at the tax office; and he said to him, "Follow me." And he rose and followed him.**

Matt 9:10-13 (§M21.2) ⇨ §K14.3

[10] **And as he sat at table in the house,** behold, **many tax collectors and sinners** came and sat down **with Jesus and his disciples.** [11] And **when the Pharisees saw** this, they **said to his disciples, "Why does** your teacher **eat with tax collectors and sinners?"** [12] But **when** he **heard it, he said, "Those who are well have no need of a physician, but those who are sick.** [13] Go and learn what this means, 'I desire mercy, and not sacrifice.' For **I came not to call the righteous, but sinners."**

LUKE

Luke 5:27-28 (§L20.1) ⇨ §K14.2

[27] After this **he** went out, and **saw a** tax collector, named **Levi, sitting at the tax office; and he said to him, "Follow me."** [28] And he left everything, and **rose and followed him.**

Luke 5:29-32 (§L20.2) ⇨ §K14.3

[29] And **Levi** made him a great feast **in his house;** and there was a large company of **tax collectors** and others sitting **at table** with them. [30] **And the Pharisees** and their **scribes** murmured against **his disciples,** saying, "Why do you **eat and drink with tax collectors and sinners?"** [31] **And Jesus** answered them, **"Those who are well have no need of a physician, but those who are sick;** [32] I have **not come to call the righteous, but sinners** to repentance."

Luke 15:1-2 ⇨ Mark 2:15-16

[1] *Now the **tax collectors and sinners** were all drawing near to hear him.* [2] *And the **Pharisees and the scribes** murmured, saying, "This man receives **sinners and eats with them."***

JOHN	THOMAS	OTHER

OTHER

POxy1224 1 ⇨ §K14.3

(1) **And the scribes** and **[Pharisees]** and priests, when **they sa[w]** him, were angry [that with **sin]ners** ners in the midst he [reclined] **at table.** But **Jesus heard** [it and **said:**] The he[althy **need** not the **physician.**]

Justin, *Apology* **1.15.8** ⇨ Mark 2:17

[15] *So he said: "I have **not come to call the righteous but sinners** to repentance." For the Heavenly Father wishes the repentance of a sinner rather than his punishment.*

MARK

Mark 2:18–22 (§K15) °

[18] Now John's disciples and the Pharisees were fasting; and people came and said to him, "Why do John's disciples and the disciples of the Pharisees fast, but your disciples do not fast?" [19] And Jesus said to them, "Can the wedding guests fast while the bridegroom is with them? As long as they have the bridegroom with them, they cannot fast. [20] The days will come, when the bridegroom is taken away from them, and then they will fast in that day. [21] No one sews a piece of unshrunk cloth on an old garment; if he does, the patch tears away from it, the new from the old, and a worse tear is made. [22] And no one puts new wine into old wineskins; if he does, the wine will burst the skins, and the wine is lost, and so are the skins; but new wine is for fresh skins."[a]

[a] Some witnesses omit *but new wine is for fresh skins:* D it (in part)

° Appendix 1 ⇨ Mark 2:18

MATT

Matt 9:14–17 (§M22)

[14] Then the disciples of John came to him, saying, "Why do we and the Pharisees fast, but your disciples do not fast?" [15] And Jesus said to them, "Can the wedding guests mourn as long as the bridegroom is with them? The days will come, when the bridegroom is taken away from them, and then they will fast0 [16] And no one puts a piece of unshrunk cloth on an old garment, for the patch tears away from the garment, and a worse tear is made. [17] Neither is new wine put into old wineskins; if it is, the skins burst, and the wine is spilled, and the skins are destroyed; but new wine is put into fresh wineskins, and so both are preserved."

LUKE

Luke 5:33–39 (§L20.3)

[33] And they said to him, "The disciples of John fast often and offer prayers, and so do the disciples of the Pharisees, but yours eat and drink." [34] And Jesus said to them, "Can you make wedding guests fast while the bridegroom is with them? [35] The days will come, when the bridegroom is taken away from them, and then they will fast in those days." [36] He told them a parable also: "No one tears a piece from a new garment and puts it upon an old garment; if he does, he will tear the new, and the piece from the new will not match the old. [37] And no one puts new wine into old wineskins; if he does, the new wine will burst the skins and it will be spilled, and the skins will be destroyed. [38] But new wine must be put into fresh wineskins. [39] And no one after drinking old wine desires new; for he says, 'The old is good.'"

Luke 7:33–34 ⇨ Mark 2:18
[33] *"For John the Baptist has come eating no bread and drinking no wine; and you say, 'He has a demon.' [34] The Son of man has come eating and drinking; and you say, 'Behold, a glutton and a drunkard, a friend of tax collectors and sinners!'"*

Luke 18:12 ⇨ Mark 2:18
[12] *"'I fast twice a week, I give tithes of all that I get.'"*

JOHN

THOMAS

GThom 27 ⇨ Mark 2:19–20
(27) <Jesus said,> "If you do not fast as regards the world, you will not find the Kingdom. If you do not observe the Sabbath as a Sabbath, you will not see the Father."

GThom 104 ⇨ Mark 2:19–20
(104) They said [to Jesus], "Come, let us pray today and let us fast."
Jesus said, "What is the sin that I have committed, or wherein have I been defeated? But when the bridegroom leaves the bridal chamber, then let them fast and pray."

GThom 47 ⇨ Mark 2:21–23
(47) Jesus said, "It is impossible for a man to mount two horses or to stretch two bows. And it is impossible for a servant to serve two masters; otherwise, he will honor the one and treat the other contemptuously. No man drinks old wine and immediately desires to drink new wine. And new wine is not put into old wineskins, lest they burst; nor is old wine put into a new wineskin, lest it spoil it. An old patch is not sewn onto a new garment, because a tear would result."

OTHER

Did 8:1 ⇨ Mark 2:20
[1] *Let not your fasts be with the hypocrites, for they fast on Mondays and Thursdays, but do you fast on Wednesdays and Fridays.*

MARK	MATT	LUKE

MARK

Mark 2:23–28 (§K16)

²³ One sabbath he was going through the grain-fields; and as they made their way his disciples began to pluck heads of grain. ²⁴ And the Pharisees said to him, "Look, why are they doing what is not lawful on the sabbath?" ²⁵ And he said to them, "Have you never read what David did, when he was in need and was hungry, he and those who were with him: ²⁶ how he entered the house of God, when Abiathar was high priest, and ate the bread of the Presence, which it is not lawful for any but the priests to eat, and also gave it to those who were with him?" ²⁷ And he said to them, "The sabbath was made for man, not man for the sabbath; ²⁸ so the Son of man is lord even of the sabbath."

Deut 23:25 ⇨ Mark 2:23

²⁵ "When you go into your neighbor's standing grain, you may **pluck** the ears with your hand, but you shall not put a sickle to your neighbor's standing **grain.**"

Exod 20:10 ⇨ Mark 2:24

¹⁰ "but the seventh day is a **sabbath** to the Lord your God; in it you shall not do any work, you, or your son, or your daughter, your manservant, or your maidservant, or your cattle, or the sojourner who is within your gates"; . . .

Deut 5:14 ⇨ Mark 2:24

¹⁴ "but the seventh day is a **sabbath** to the Lord your God; in it you shall not do any work, you, or your son, or your daughter, or your manservant, or your maidservant, or your ox, or your ass, or any of your cattle, or the sojourner who is within your gates, that your manservant and your maidservant may rest as well as you."

1 Sam 21:1–6 ⇨ Mark 5:25–26

¹ Then came **David** to Nob to Ahimelech the **priest**; and Ahimelech came to meet David trembling, and said to him, "Why are you alone, and no one with you?" ² And David said to Ahimelech the **priest**, "The king has charged me with a matter, and said to me, 'Let no one know anything of the matter about which I send you, and with which I have charged you.' I have made an appointment with the young men for such and such a place. ³ Now then, what have you at hand? Give me five loaves of **bread**, or whatever is here." ⁴ And the priest answered David, "I have no common bread at hand, but there is holy **bread**; if only the young men have kept themselves from women." ⁵ And David answered the priest, "Of a truth women have been kept from us as always when I go on an expedition; the vessels of the young men are holy, even when it is a common journey; how much more today will their vessels be holy?" ⁶ So the priest **gave** him the holy **bread**; for there was no bread there but the **bread of the Presence**, which is removed from before the Lord, to be replaced by hot **bread** on the day it is taken away.

Lev 24:5–9 ⇨ Mark 2:26

⁵ "And you shall take fine flour, and bake twelve cakes of it; two tenths of an ephah shall be in each cake. ⁶ And you shall set them in two rows, six in a row, upon the table of pure gold. ⁷ And you shall put pure frankincense with each row, that it may go with **the bread** as a memorial portion to be offered by fire to the Lord. ⁸ Every sabbath day Aaron shall set it in order before the Lord continually on behalf of the people of Israel as a covenant for ever. ⁹ And it shall be for Aaron and his sons, and they shall **eat** it in a holy place, since it is for him a most holy portion out of the offerings by fire to the Lord, a perpetual due."

JOHN

MATT

Matt 12:1–8 (§M33)

¹ At that time Jesus went **through the grainfields** on the **sabbath; his disciples** were hungry, and they **began to pluck heads of grain** and to eat. ² But when the **Pharisees** saw it, they **said to him**, "Look, your disciples **are doing what is not lawful** to do **on the sabbath.**" ³ **He said to them**, "Have you not **read what David did, when he was** hungry, and those who were with him: ⁴ how he entered the house of God and ate the bread of the Presence, which it was not lawful for him to eat nor for those who were with him, but only for the priests? ⁵ Or have you not read in the law how on **the sabbath** the priests in the temple profane **the sabbath**, and are guiltless? ⁶ I tell you, something greater than the temple is here. ⁷ And if you had known what this means, 'I desire mercy, and not sacrifice,' you would not have condemned the guiltless. ⁸ For **the Son of man is lord of the sabbath.**"

THOMAS

GThom 27 ⇨ Mark 2:27–28

(27) <Jesus said,> "If you do not fast as regards the world, you will not find the Kingdom. If you do not observe the Sabbath as a Sabbath, you will not see the Father."

LUKE

Luke 6:1–5 (§L21)

¹ On a **sabbath**, while **he was going through the grainfields, his disciples** plucked and ate some **heads of grain**, rubbing them in their hands. ² But some of **the Pharisees** said, "**Why are** you **doing what is not lawful** to do **on the sabbath?**" ³ And Jesus answered, "**Have you** not **read what David did when he was** hungry, he and **those who were with him:** ⁴ **how he entered the house of God**, and took **and ate the bread of the Presence, which it is not lawful for any but the priests to eat, and also gave it to those with him?**" ⁵ **And he said to them, "The Son of man is lord of the sabbath.**"

OTHER

InThom 2:1–5

¹ When this boy Jesus was five years old he was playing at the ford of a brook, and he gathered together into pools the water that flowed by, and made it at once clean, and commanded it by his word alone. ² He made soft clay and fashioned from it twelve sparrows. And it was the sabbath when he did this. And there were also many other children playing with him. ³ Now when a certain Jew saw what Jesus was doing in his play on the sabbath, he at once went and told his father Joseph: "See, your child is at the brook, and he has taken clay and fashioned twelve birds and has profaned the sabbath." ⁴ And when Joseph came to the place and saw (it), he cried out to him, saying: "Why do you do on the sabbath what ought not to be done?" But Jesus clapped his hands and cried to the sparrows: "Off with you!" And the sparrows took flight and went away chirping. ⁵ The Jews were amazed when they saw this, and went away and told their elders what they had seen Jesus do.

MARK	MATT	LUKE

Mark 3:1–6 (§K17)

¹ Again he entered the synagogue, and a man was there who had a withered hand. ² And they watched him, to see whether he would heal him on the sabbath, so that they might accuse him. ³ And he said to the man who had the withered hand, "Come here." ⁴ And he said to them, "Is it lawful on the sabbath to do good or to do harm, to save life or to kill?" But they were silent. ⁵ And he looked around at them with anger, grieved at their hardness of heart, and said to the man, "Stretch out your hand." He stretched it out, and his hand was restored. ⁶ The Pharisees went out, and immediately held counsel with the Herodians against him, how to destroy him.

Matt 12:9–14 (§M34)

⁹ And he went on from there, and **entered** their **synagogue**. ¹⁰ And behold, **there was a man** with **a withered hand**. And they asked him, "**Is it lawful to heal on the sabbath?**" so that they might accuse him. ¹¹ He said to them, "What man of you, if he has one sheep and it falls into a pit on the sabbath, will not lay hold of it and lift it out? ¹² Of how much more value is a man than a sheep! So **it is lawful to do good on the sabbath.**" ¹³ Then he **said to the man, "Stretch out your hand."** And the man **stretched it out, and** it **was restored,** whole like the other. ¹⁴ But **the Pharisees went out and** took **counsel against him, how to destroy him.**

Luke 6:6–11 (§L22)

⁶ On another sabbath, when **he entered the synagogue** and taught, **a man was there** whose right **hand** was **withered.** ⁷ **And** the scribes and the Pharisees **watched him, to see whether he would heal on the sabbath, so that they might** find an accusation against **him.** ⁸ But he knew their thoughts, **and he said to the man who had the withered hand, "Come** and stand **here."** And he rose and stood there. ⁹ **And** Jesus **said to them,** "I ask you, **is it lawful on the sabbath to do good or to do harm, to save life or to destroy it?** ¹⁰ **And he looked around** on them all, **and said to him, "Stretch out your hand."** And **he** did so, **and his hand was restored.** ¹¹ But they were filled **with** fury and discussed with one another what they might do to Jesus.

Luke 14:3 ⇨ Mark 3:4

³ And Jesus spoke to the lawyers and Pharisees, saying, "**Is it lawful to** heal **on the sabbath, or** not?"

JOHN	THOMAS	OTHER

GNaz 10 ⇨ Mark 3:1

(10) In the Gospel which the Nazarenes and the Ebionites use, which we have recently translated out of Hebrew into Greek, and which is called by most people the authentic (Gospel) of Matthew, the **man who had** the **withered hand** is described as a mason who pleaded for help in the following words:

I was a mason and earned (my) livelihood with (my) hands; I beseech thee, Jesus, to restore to me my health that I may not with ignominy have to beg for my bread. (Jerome, *Commentary on Matthew* 2 [on Matthew 12:13])

InThom 2:1–5

¹ When this boy Jesus was five years old he was playing at the ford of a brook, and he gathered together into pools the water that flowed by, and made it at once clean, and commanded it by his word alone. ² He made soft clay and fashioned from it twelve sparrows. And it was the sabbath when he did this. And there were also many other children playing with him. ³ Now when a certain Jew saw what Jesus was doing in his play on the sabbath, he at once went and told his father Joseph: "See, your child is at the brook, and he has taken clay and fashioned twelve birds and has profaned the sabbath." ⁴ And when Joseph came to the place and saw (it), he cried out to him, saying: "Why do you do on the sabbath what ought not to be done?" But Jesus clapped his hands and cried to the sparrows: "Off with you!" And the sparrows took flight and went away chirping. ⁵ The Jews were amazed when they saw this, and went away and told their elders what they had seen Jesus do.

MARK

Mark 3:7–12 (§K18) °

⁷ Jesus withdrew with his disciples to the sea, and a great multitude from Galilee followed; also from Judea ⁸ and Jerusalem and Idumea and from beyond the Jordan and from about Tyre and Sidon a great multitude, hearing all that he did, came to him. ⁹ And he told his disciples to have a boat ready for him because of the crowd, lest they should crush him; ¹⁰ for he had healed many, so that all who had diseases pressed upon him to touch him. ¹¹ And whenever the unclean spirits beheld him, they fell down before him and cried out, "You are the Son of God." ¹² And he strictly ordered them not to make him known.

°Appendix 3 ⇨ §K18

Mark 6:56 ⇨ Mark 3:10

⁵⁶ And wherever he came, in villages, cities, or country, they laid the sick in the market places, and besought **him** that they might **touch** even the fringe of his garment; and as many as touched it were made well.

MATT

Matt 12:15–21 (§M35)

¹⁵ Jesus, aware of this, **withdrew** from there. And many **followed** him, and **he healed** them all, ¹⁶ **and ordered them not to make him known**. ¹⁷ This was to fulfil what was spoken by the prophet Isaiah:
¹⁸ "Behold, my servant whom I have chosen,
  my beloved with whom my soul is well pleased.
I will put my Spirit upon him,
  and he shall proclaim justice to the Gentiles.
¹⁹ He will not wrangle or cry aloud,
  nor will any one hear his voice in the streets;
²⁰ he will not break a bruised reed
  or quench a smoldering wick,
till he brings justice to victory;
  ²¹ and in his name will the Gentiles hope."

Matt 4:25 ⇨ Mark 3:7–8

²⁵ **And great** crowds **followed** him **from Galilee** and the Decapolis **and Jerusalem** and **Judea and from beyond the Jordan**.

Matt 14:36 ⇨ Mark 3:10

³⁶ and besought **him** that they might only **touch** the fringe of his garment; and as many as touched it were made well.

LUKE

Luke 6:17–19 (§L24)

¹⁷ And he came down with them and stood on a level place, with a great crowd of **his disciples and a great multitude** of people **from** all **Judea and Jerusalem** and the seacoast of **Tyre and Sidon**, who **came to** hear **him** and to be **healed** of their **diseases**; ¹⁸ and those who were troubled with **unclean spirits** were cured. ¹⁹ And all the crowd sought **to touch him**, for power came forth from him and **healed** them all.

Luke 4:41 ⇨ Mark 3:11–12

⁴¹ And demons also came out of many, crying, "You are the Son of God!" But **he** rebuked **them**, and would **not** allow **them to** speak, because they knew that he was the Christ.

JOHN

THOMAS

OTHER

MARK

Mark 3:13–19 (§K19) °

¹³ And he went up on the mountain, and called to him those whom he desired; and they came to him. ¹⁴ And he appointed twelve,^a to be with him, and to be sent out to preach ¹⁵ and have authority to cast out demons: ¹⁶ Simon^b whom he surnamed Peter; ¹⁷ James the son of Zebedee and John the brother of James, whom he surnamed Boanerges, that is, sons of thunder; ¹⁸ Andrew, and Philip, and Bartholomew, and Matthew, and Thomas, and James the son of Alphaeus, and Thaddaeus, and Simon the Cananaean, ¹⁹ and Judas Iscariot, who betrayed him.

Then he went home; ...

^a Text: A C² (D) K L P Π *f*¹ 33 *pm*; ℵ B C* Θ *f*¹³ 28 1195 syr (in part) cop (in part) eth add (from Luke 6:13): *whom also he named apostles*

^b ℵ B C* 565 insert: *So he appointed the twelve: Simon*

° Appendix 2 ⇨ K19

Mark 6:7 ⇨ Mark 3:13–15

⁷ And he called to him the twelve, and began to send them out two by two, and gave them authority over the unclean spirits.

JOHN

John 1:42 ⇨ Mark 3:16

⁴² He brought him to Jesus. Jesus looked at him, and said, "So you are Simon the son of John? You shall be called Cephas" (which means Peter).

MATT

Matt 10:1–4 (§M27)

¹ And he called to him his twelve disciples and gave them authority over unclean spirits, to cast them out, and to heal every disease and every infirmity. ² The names of the twelve apostles are these: first, Simon, who is called Peter, and Andrew his brother; James the son of Zebedee, and John his brother; ³ Philip and Bartholomew; Thomas and Matthew the tax collector; James the son of Alphaeus, and Thaddaeus; ⁴ Simon the Cananaean, and Judas Iscariot, who betrayed him.

THOMAS

LUKE

Luke 6:12–16 (§L23)

¹² In these days he went out to the mountain to pray; and all night he continued in prayer to God. ¹³ And when it was day, he called his disciples, and chose from them twelve, whom he named apostles; ¹⁴ Simon, whom he named Peter, and Andrew his brother, and James and John, and Philip, and Bartholomew, ¹⁵ and Matthew, and Thomas, and James the son of Alphaeus, and Simon who was called the Zealot, ¹⁶ and Judas the son of James, and Judas Iscariot, who became a traitor.

Luke 9:1–2 ⇨ Mark 3:13–15

¹ And he called the twelve together and gave them power and authority over all demons and to cure diseases, ² and he sent them out to preach the kingdom of God and to heal.

OTHER

Acts 1:12–14 ⇨ Mark 3:16–19

¹² Then they returned to Jerusalem from the mount called Olivet, which is near Jerusalem, a sabbath day's journey away; ¹³ and when they had entered, they went up to the upper room, where they were staying, Peter and John and James and Andrew, Philip and Thomas, Bartholomew and Matthew, James the son of Alphaeus and Simon the Zealot and Judas the son of James. ¹⁴ All these with one accord devoted themselves to prayer, together with the women and Mary the mother of Jesus, and with his brothers.

MARK

JESUS' FAMILY COMES TO SEIZE HIM

Mark 3:20–22 (§K20.1)

²⁰ and the crowd came together again, so that they could not even eat. ²¹ And when his family heard it, they went out to seize him, for people were saying, "He is beside himself." ²² And the scribes who came down from Jerusalem said, "He is possessed by Beelzebul, and by the prince of demons he casts out the demons."

THE SCRIBES ACCUSE HIM

Mark 3:23–30 (§K20.2)

²³ And he called them to him, and said to them in parables, "How can Satan cast out Satan? ²⁴ If a kingdom is divided against itself, that kingdom cannot stand. ²⁵ And if a house is divided against itself, that house will not be able to stand. ²⁶ And if Satan has risen up against himself and is divided, he cannot stand, but is coming to an end. ²⁷ But no one can enter a strong man's house and plunder his goods, unless he first binds the strong man; then indeed he may plunder his house. ²⁸ "Truly, I say to you, all sins will be forgiven the sons of men, and whatever blasphemies they utter; ²⁹ but whoever blasphemes against the Holy Spirit never has forgiveness, but is guilty of an eternal sin"— ³⁰ for they had said, "He has an unclean spirit."

TRUE RELATIVES

Mark 3:31–35 (§K20.3)

³¹ And his mother and his brothers came; and standing outside they sent to him and called him. ³² And a crowd was sitting about him; and they said to him, "Your mother and your brothers[a] are outside, asking for you." ³³ And he replied, "Who are my mother and my brothers?" ³⁴ And looking around on those who sat about him, he said, "Here are my mother and my brothers! ³⁵ Whoever does the will of God is my brother, and sister, and mother."

[a] A D *al* add: *and your sisters*

JOHN

John 15:14 ⇨ Mark 3:35
¹⁴ "You are my friends if you do what I command you."

MATT

Matt 12:24 ⇨ Mark 3:22
²⁴ But when the Pharisees heard it they **said,** "It is only **by Beelzebul, the prince of demons,** that this man **casts out demons."**

Matt 12:25–26 ⇨ Mark 3:23–26
²⁵ Knowing their thoughts, **he said to them,** "Every **kingdom divided against itself** is laid waste, and no city or **house divided against itself will stand;** ²⁶ and if **Satan** casts out Satan, he **is divided against himself;** how then will his kingdom **stand?"**

Matt 12:29 ⇨ Mark 3:27
²⁹ "Or how **can one enter a strong man's house and plunder his goods, unless he first binds the strong man? Then indeed he may plunder his house."**

Matt 12:31–32 ⇨ Mark 3:28–29
³¹ "Therefore I tell **you,** every sin and blasphemy **will be forgiven men,** but the blasphemy **against the Spirit** will not be forgiven. ³² And whoever says a word against the Son of man will be forgiven, but whoever speaks **against the Holy Spirit** will not be forgiven, either in this age or in the age to come."

Matt 12:46–50 (§M39) ⇨ §K20.3
⁴⁶ While he was still speaking to the people, behold, **his mother and his brothers** stood **outside,** asking to speak **to him.** ⁴⁸ But **he** replied to the man who told him, **"Who** is my mother, **and** who are **my brothers?"** ⁴⁹ And stretching out his hand toward his disciples, **he said, "Here are my mother and my brothers!** ⁵⁰ For **whoever does the will of** my Father in heaven **is my brother, and sister, and mother."**

THOMAS

GThom 35 ⇨ Mark 3:27
(35) Jesus said, "It is not possible for anyone to enter the **house** of **a strong man** and take it by force **unless he binds** his hands; **then he** will (be able to) ransack **his house."**

GThom 21 ⇨ Mark 3:27
(21) Mary said to Jesus, "Whom are Your disciples like?"

He said, "They are like children who have settled in a field which is not theirs. When the owners of the field come, they will say, 'Let us have back our field.' They (will) undress in their presence in order to let them have back their field and to give it back to them. Therefore I say to you, if the owner of a house knows that the thief is coming, he will begin his vigil before he comes and will not let him dig through into his house of his domain to carry away his goods. You, then, be on your guard against the world. Arm yourselves with great strength lest the robbers find a way to come to you, for the difficulty which you expect will (surely) materialize. Let there be among you a man of understanding. When the grain ripened, he came quickly with his sickle in his hand and reaped it. Whoever has ears to hear, let him hear."

LUKE

Luke 11:15 ⇨ Mark 3:22
¹⁵ But some of them **said, "He** casts out **demons by Beelzebul, the prince of demons";** . . .

Luke 11:17–18 ⇨ Mark 3:23–26
¹⁷ But he, knowing their thoughts, **said to them,** "Every **kingdom divided against itself** is laid waste, and a divided household falls. ¹⁸ **And if Satan** also is divided **against himself,** how will his kingdom **stand?** For you say that I cast out demons by Beelzebul."

Luke 11:21 ⇨ Mark 3:27
²¹ When a **strong man,** fully armed, guards his own palace, his goods are in peace; . . .

Luke 12:10 ⇨ Mark 3:29
¹⁰ "And every one who speaks a word against the Son of man **will be forgiven; but** he who **blasphemes against the Holy Spirit** will not be forgiven."

Luke 8:19–21 (§L32) ⇨ §K20.3
¹⁹ Then **his mother and his brothers came to him,** but they could not reach **him** for the crowd. ²⁰ And he was told, **"Your mother and your brothers are standing outside,** desiring to see **you."** ²¹ But **he** said to them, **"My mother and my brothers** are those who hear the word of God and do it."

OTHER

GEbi 5 ⇨ §K20.3
*(5) Moreover they deny that he was a man, evidently on the ground of the word which the Saviour spoke when it was reported to him: "Behold, thy **mother and thy brethren stand without," namely:***

***Who** is my mother **and** who are my brethren? And **he** stretched forth his hand towards his disciples and **said: These are my brethren and mother and sisters, who do the will of my Father.** (Epiphanius, Haer. 30.14.5)*

GThom 99 ⇨ §K20.3
(99) The disciples said to him, "Your brothers and Your mother are standing outside."

He said to them, "Those here who do the will of My Father are My brothers and My mother. It is they who will enter the Kingdom of My Father."

MARK

Mark 4:1 (§K21.1)

[1] Again he began to teach beside the sea. And a very large **crowd** gathered about him, so that he got into a boat and sat in it on the sea; and the whole crowd was beside the sea on the land.

Mark 4:2–9 (§K21.2)

[2] And he taught them many things in parables, and in his teaching he said to them: [3] "Listen! **A sower went out to sow.** [4] And as he sowed, **some** seed **fell along the path**, and **the birds came and devoured it.** [5] **Other** seed **fell on rocky ground, where it had not much soil, and immediately it sprang up, since it had no depth of soil;** [6] **and when the sun rose it was scorched**, and since it had no root it **withered away.** [7] **Other** seed **fell among thorns and the thorns grew up and choked it,** and it yielded no grain. [8] And other seeds **fell into good soil and brought forth grain**, growing up and increasing and yielding thirtyfold and sixtyfold and **a hundredfold.**" [9] And he said, "**He who has ears to hear, let him hear.**"

MATT

Matt 13:1–2 (§M40.1) ⇨ §K21.1

[1] That same day Jesus went out of the house and sat **beside the sea.** [2] And great **crowds gathered about him, so that he got into a boat and sat** there; **and the whole crowd** stood **on** the beach.

Matt 13:3–9 (§M40.2) ⇨ §K21.2

[3] And he told **them many things in parables**, saying: "**A sower went out to sow.** [4] **And as he** sowed, **some** seeds **fell along the path, and the birds came and devoured them.** [5] **Other** seeds **fell on rocky ground, where** they **had not much soil, and immediately** they **sprang up, since** they **had no depth of soil,** [6] but **when the sun rose** they were **scorched; and since** they **had no root** they **withered away.** [7] **Other** seeds **fell upon thorns, and the thorns grew up and choked** them. [8] **Other** seeds **fell on good soil and brought forth grain**, some **a** hundredfold, some sixty, some thirty. [9] **He who has ears, let him hear.**"

LUKE

Luke 8:4–8 (§L31.1)

[4] And when **a** great **crowd** came together and people from town after town came to him, he **said** in a parable: [5] "**A sower went out to sow** his seed; **and as he sowed, some fell along the path**, and was trodden under foot, **and the birds** of the air **devoured it.** [6] And some **fell on** the rock; and as it grew **up, it withered away**, because it **had** no moisture. [7] And some **fell among thorns; and the thorns grew** with it **and choked it.** [8] And some **fell into good soil** and grew, and yielded **a hundredfold.**" As he said this, he called out, "**He who has ears to hear, let him hear.**"

Luke 5:1–3 (§L17.1) ⇨ §K21.1

[1] *While the people pressed upon* **him** *to hear the word of God, he was standing by the lake of Gennesaret.* [2] *And he saw two boats by the lake; but the fishermen had gone out of them and were washing their nets.* [3] *Getting* **into** *one of the boats, which was Simon's, he asked him to put out a little from the land.* **And he sat down and taught** *the people from the boat.*

JOHN

THOMAS

GThom 9 ⇨ §K21.2

(9) Jesus **said**, "Now the **sower went out**, took a handful (of seeds), and scattered them. **Some fell** on the road; **the birds came and** gathered them up. Others **fell on** rock, did not take **root** in the **soil**, and did not produce ears. And others **fell on thorns**; they **choked** the seed(s) and worms ate them. **And** others **fell** on the **good soil and** produced good fruit: it bore sixty per measure **and a** hundred and twenty per measure."

OTHER

InThom 12:1–2 ⇨ §K21.2

[1] *Again, in the time of sowing the child* **went** *out with his father* **to sow wheat in their land.** *And as his father* **sowed**, *the child Jesus also sowed one corn of wheat.* [2] *And when he had reaped it and threshed it, he brought in a hundred measures; and he called all the poor of the village to the threshing-floor and gave them the wheat, and Joseph took the residue of the wheat. He was eight years old when he worked this miracle.*

ApocJa 12:20–31 ⇨ §K21.2

[20] *he said: "This is why I say this to you, that you may know yourselves. For the Kingdom of Heaven is like an ear of* **grain** *which sprouted in a field. And* [25] *when it ripened, it scattered its fruit and, in turn, filled the field with ears of* **grain** *for another year. You also: be zealous to reap for yourselves an ear of life, in order that* [30] *you may be filled with the Kingdom."*

MARK

Mark 4:10–12 (§K21.3) °

[10] And when he was alone, those who were about him with the twelve asked him concerning the parables. [11] And he said to them, "To you has been given the secret of the kingdom of God, but for those outside everything is in parables; [12] so that they may indeed see but not perceive, and may indeed hear but not understand; lest they should turn again, and be forgiven."

Mark 4:13–20 (§K21.4)

[13] And he said to them, "Do you not understand this parable? How then will you understand all the parables? [14] The sower sows the word. [15] And these are the ones along the path, where the word is sown; when they hear, Satan immediately comes and takes away the word which is sown in them. [16] And these in like manner are the ones sown upon rocky ground, who, when they hear the word, immediately receive it with joy; [17] and they have no root in themselves, but endure for a while; then, when tribulation or persecution arises on account of the word, immediately they fall away.[a] [18] And others are the ones sown among thorns; they are those who hear the word, [19] but the cares of the world, and the delight in riches, and the desire for other things, enter in and choke the word, and it proves unfruitful. [20] But those that were sown upon the good soil are the ones who hear the word and accept it and bear fruit, thirtyfold and sixtyfold and a hundredfold."

[a] Or: *stumble*

° Appendix 2 ⇨ §K21.3

Isa 6:9–10 ⇨ **Mark 4:12**

[9] And he said, "Go, and say to this people:
  'Hear and **hear,** but do **not understand;**
  see and **see,** but do **not perceive.'**
[10] Make the heart of this people fat,
    and their ears heavy,
    and shut their eyes;
  lest they see with their eyes,
    and hear with their ears,
    and understand with their hearts,
    and **turn and** be healed."

JOHN

MATT

Matt 13:10–17 (§M40.3) ⇨ §K21.3

[10] Then the disciples came and said to **him,** "Why do you speak to them in parables?" [11] **And** he answered **them, "To you** it **has been given** to know **the secrets of the kingdom of** heaven, **but** to them it has not been given. [12] For to him who has will more be given, and he will have abundance; but from him who has not, even what he has will be taken away. [13] This is why I speak to them **in parables,** because seeing they do **not see,** and hearing they do **not hear,** nor do they **understand.** [14] With them indeed is fulfilled the prophecy of Isaiah which says:

'You shall **indeed hear but** never **understand,**
  and you shall **indeed see but** never **perceive.**
[15] For **this** people's **heart** has grown dull,
  and their ears are heavy of hearing,
  and their eyes they have closed,
lest they should perceive with their eyes,
  and **hear** with their ears,
and **understand** with their heart,
  and **turn** for me to heal them.'

[16] But blessed are your eyes, for they see, and your ears, for they hear. [17] Truly, I say to you, many prophets and righteous men longed to see what you see, and did not see it, and to hear what you hear, and did not hear it."

Matt 13:18–23 (§M40.4) ⇨ §K21.4

[18] "Hear **then** the **parable of the sower.** [19] When any one hears **the word** of the kingdom and does not understand it, the evil one **comes and** snatches **away** what **is sown in** his heart; this is what was sown **along the path.** [20] As for what was **sown** on **rocky ground,** this is he who hears **the word** and **immediately** receives it **with joy;** [21] yet he has **no root in** himself, **but** endures **for a while,** and **when tribulation or persecution arises on account of the word, immediately** he falls **away.** [22] As for what was **sown among thorns,** this is he **who** hears **the word, but the cares of the world and the delight in riches** choke **the word, and it proves unfruitful.** [23] As for what was **sown** on **good soil,** this is he **who** hears **the word and** understands **it;** he indeed bears **fruit,** and yields, in one case **a hundredfold,** in another sixty, and in another thirty."

THOMAS

LUKE

Luke 8:9–10 (§L31.2) ⇨ §K21.3

[9] **And when** his disciples **asked him** what this parable meant, [10] **he** said, **"To you** it **has been given** to know **the secrets of the kingdom of God; but for** others they are **in parables, so that** seeing they may **not see,** and hearing they may **not understand."**

Luke 8:11–15 (§L31.3) ⇨ §K21.4

[11] "Now the **parable** is this: The seed is **the word** of God. [12] **The ones along the path** are those who have heard; then the devil **comes and takes away the word** from their hearts, that they may not believe and be saved. [13] **And the ones** on the rock are those **who, when they hear the word, receive it with joy;** but these **have no root,** they believe **for a while** and in time of temptation **fall away.** [14] **And** as for what fell **among** the **thorns, they are those who hear, but** as they go on their way they are choked by **the cares** and **riches** and pleasures of life, and their fruit does not mature. [15] And as for that in **the good soil,** they are those **who,** hearing **the word,** hold it fast in an honest and good heart, **and** bring forth **fruit** with patience."

OTHER

ApocJa 7:1–10 ⇨ §K21.3

*"I first spoke with you **in parables,** and you did **not understand.** Now, in turn, I speak with [5] you openly, and you do **not perceive.** But it is you who were to me a parable **in parables** and what is apparent [10] in what are open."*

ApocJa 8:10–27 ⇨ §K21.4

[10] *"Become zealous about **the Word.** For the Word's first condition is faith; the second is love; the third is works. [15] Now from these comes life. For **the Word** is like a grain of wheat. When someone sowed it, he believed in it; and when it sprouted, he loved it, because he looked (forward to) [20] many grains in the place of one; and when he worked (it), he was saved, because he prepared it for food. Again he left (some grains) to sow. Thus it is also possible for you (pl.) to receive [25] the Kingdom of Heaven: unless you receive it through knowledge, you will not be able to find it."*

MARK	MATT	LUKE

Mark 4:21–23 (§K21.5)

21 And he said to them, "Is a lamp brought in to be put under a bushel, or under a bed, and not on a stand? 22 For there is nothing hid, except to be made manifest; nor is anything secret, except to come to light. 23 If any man has ears to hear, let him hear."

Matt 5:15 ⇨ Mark 4:21

15 "Nor do men light **a lamp** and put it **under a bushel**, but **on a stand**, and it gives light to all in the house."

Matt 10:26 ⇨ Mark 4:22

26 "So have no fear of them; for **nothing is** covered that will not **be** revealed, or hidden that will not **be** known."

Luke 8:16–17 (§L31.4)

16 "No one after lighting **a lamp** covers it with a vessel, or puts it **under a bed**, but puts it **on a stand**, that those who enter may see the light. 17 **For nothing is hid** that shall not **be made manifest, nor anything secret** that shall not be known and **come to light**."

Luke 11:33 ⇨ Mark 4:21

33 "No one after lighting **a lamp** puts it in a cellar or **under a bushel**, but **on a stand**, that those who enter may see the light."

Luke 12:2 ⇨ Mark 4:22

2 "**Nothing is** covered up that will not **be** revealed, or hidden that will not be known."

JOHN	THOMAS	OTHER

GThom 33 ⇨ Mark 4:21–22

(33) Jesus said, "Preach from your house-tops that which you will hear in your ear {(and) in the other ear}. For no one lights **a lamp** and puts it **under a bushel**, nor does he put it in a hidden place, but rather he sets it **on a** lampstand so that everyone who enters and leaves will see its **light**."

POxy654 5 ⇨ Mark 4:22

(5) Jesus says, "K[now what is be]fore your face, and [that which is hidden] from you will be reveal[ed to you. **For there i]s nothing** hidden which will not [**be made] mani[fest]** and (nothing) buried which will not [be raised up.]"

GThom 5 ⇨ Mark 4:22

(5) Jesus said, "Recognize what is in your sight, and that which is hidden from you will become plain to you. **For there is nothing** hidden which will not become **manifest**."

GThom 6 ⇨ Mark 4:22

(6) His disciples questioned Him and said to Him, "Do You want us to fast? How shall we pray? Shall we give alms? What diet shall we observe?"

Jesus said, "Do not tell lies, and do not do what you hate, for all things are plain in the sight of Heaven. **For nothing** hidden will not become **manifest**, and nothing covered will remain without being uncovered."

MARK	MATT	LUKE

Mark 4:24–25 (§K21.6)
²⁴ And he said to them, "Take heed what you hear; the measure you give will be the measure you get, and still more will be given you. ²⁵ For to him who has will more be given; and from him who has not, even what he has will be taken away."

Matt 7:2 ⇨ Mark 4:24
² "For with the judgment you pronounce you will be judged, and **the measure you give will be the measure you get.**"

Matt 13:12 ⇨ Mark 4:25
¹² "**For to him who has will more be given,** and he will have abundance; but **from him who has not, even what he has will be taken away.**"

Matt 25:29 ⇨ Mark 4:25
²⁹ "**For to every one who has will more be given, and** he will have abundance; but **from him who has not, even what he has will be taken away.**"

Luke 8:18 (§L31.5)
¹⁸ "**Take heed** then how **you hear; for to him who has will more be given, and from him who has not, even what he** thinks that **he has will be taken away.**"

Luke 6:38 ⇨ Mark 4:24
³⁸ "give, and it will be given to you; good measure, pressed down, shaken together, running over, will be put into your lap. For **the measure you give will be the measure you get** back."

Luke 19:26 ⇨ Mark 4:25
²⁶ "'I tell you, that **to every one who has will more be given;** but **from him who has not, even what he has will be taken away.**'"

JOHN	THOMAS	OTHER

GThom 41 ⇨ Mark 4:25
(41) Jesus said, "Whoever **has** something in his hand **will** receive **more, and** whoever **has** nothing **will be** deprived of **even** the little **he has.**"

MARK	MATT	LUKE

Mark 4:26–29 (§K21.7)

²⁶ And he said, "The kingdom of God is as if a man should scatter seed upon the ground, ²⁷ and should sleep and rise night and day, and the seed should sprout and grow, he knows not how. ²⁸ The earth produces of itself, first the blade, then the ear, then the full grain in the ear. ²⁹ But when the grain is ripe, at once he puts in the sickle, because the harvest has come."

Joel 3:13 ⇨ Mark 4:29
¹³ Put **in the sickle**,
    for **the harvest** is ripe.
Go in, tread,
    for the wine press is full.
The vats overflow,
    for their wickedness is great.

Matt 13:24–30 (§M40.5)

²⁴ Another parable he put before them, saying, *"The kingdom* of heaven may be compared to *a man who sowed good seed in his field;* ²⁵ but while men were sleeping, his enemy came and sowed weeds among the wheat, and went away. ²⁶ So when the plants came up and bore grain, then the weeds appeared also. ²⁷ And the servants of the householder came and said to him, 'Sir, did you not sow good seed in your field? How then has it weeds?' ²⁸ He said to them, 'An enemy has done this.' The servants said to him, 'Then do you want us to go and gather them?' ²⁹ But he said, 'No, lest in gathering the weeds you root up the wheat along with them. ³⁰ Let both grow together until the harvest; and at* harvest *time I will tell the reapers, Gather the weeds first and bind them in bundles to be burned, but gather the wheat into my barn.'"*

JOHN	THOMAS	OTHER

GThom 21 ⇨ Mark 4:29

(21) Mary said to Jesus, "Whom are Your disciples like?"

He said, "They are like children who have settled in a field which is not theirs. When the owners of the field come, they will say, 'Let us have back our field.' They (will) undress in their presence in order to let them have back their field and to give it back to them. Therefore I say to you, if the owner of a house knows that the thief is coming, he will begin his vigil before he comes and will not let him dig through into his house of his domain to carry away his goods. You, then, be on your guard against the world. Arm yourselves with great strength lest the robbers find a way to come to you, for the difficulty which you expect will (surely) materialize. Let there be among you a man of understanding. When the grain ripened, he came quickly with his *sickle* in his hand and reaped it. Whoever has ears to hear, let him hear."

ApocJa 12:20–31

²⁰ *he said: "This is why I say this to you (pl.), that you may know yourselves. For the* **King-** **dom** *of Heaven is like an* **ear** *of* **grain** *which sprouted in a field. And* ²⁵ **when** *it ripened, it scattered its fruit and, in turn, filled the field with ears of* **grain** *for another year. You also: be zealous to reap for yourselves and ear of life, in order that* ³⁰ *you may be filled with* **the** **Kingdom.**"

MARK

Mark 4:30–32 (§K21.8)

³⁰And he said, "With what can we compare the kingdom of God, or what parable shall we use for it? ³¹It is like a grain of mustard seed, which, when sown upon the ground, is the smallest of all the seeds on earth; ³²yet when it is sown it grows up and becomes the greatest of all shrubs, and puts forth large branches, so that the birds of the air can make nests in its shade."

Mark 4:33–34 (§K21.9)

³³With many such parables he spoke the word to them, as they were able to hear it; ³⁴he did not speak to them without a parable, but privately to his own disciples he explained everything.

Dan 4:20–22 ⇨ Mark 4:32

²⁰"The tree you saw, which grew and became strong, so that its top reached to heaven, and it was visible to the end of the whole earth; ²¹ whose leaves were fair and its fruit abundant, and in which was food for all; under which beasts of the field found **shade**, and in whose **branches the birds of the air** dwelt—²²it is you, O king, who have grown and become strong. Your greatness has grown and reaches to heaven, and your dominion to the ends of the earth."

MATT

Matt 13:31–32 (§M40.6) ⇨ §K21.8

³¹Another parable **he** put before them, saying, "**The kingdom** of heaven **is like a grain of mustard seed which** a man took and sowed in his field; ³²it **is the smallest of all seeds**, but **when** it has grown it is **the greatest of shrubs** and becomes a tree, **so that the birds of the air** come and **make nests in its** branches."

Matt 13:34–35 (§M40.8) ⇨ §K21.9

³⁴All this Jesus said **to** the crowds in **parables**; indeed **he** said nothing **to them without a parable**. ³⁵This was to fulfil what was spoken by the prophet:

"I will open my mouth in **parables**,
I will utter what has been hidden since the foundation of the world."

LUKE

Luke 13:18–19 (§L59.1) ⇨ §K21.8

¹⁸**He said** therefore, "**What is the kingdom of God** like? And to what shall I **compare** it? ¹⁹It **is like a grain of mustard seed which** a man took and sowed in his garden; and it grew and became a tree, and **the birds of the air** made **nests in its** branches."

JOHN

THOMAS

GThom 20 ⇨ §K21.8

(20) The disciples **said** to Jesus, "Tell us **what the Kingdom of** Heaven is like."

He said to them, "**It is like a mustard seed, the smallest of all seeds**. But **when** it falls on tilled soil, **it** produces a great plant **and** becomes a shelter for **birds of the** sky."

OTHER

MARK

Mark 4:35–41 (§K22)
[35] On that day, when evening had come, he said to them, "Let us go across to the other side." [36] And leaving the crowd, they took him with them in the boat, just as he was. And other boats were with him. [37] And a great storm of wind arose, and the waves beat into the boat, so that the boat was already filling. [38] But he was in the stern, asleep on the cushion; and they woke him and said to him, "Teacher, do you not care if we perish?" [39] And he awoke and rebuked the wind, and said to the sea, "Peace! Be still!" And the wind ceased, and there was a great calm. [40] He said to them, "Why are you afraid? Have you no faith?" [41] And they were filled with awe, and said to one another, "Who then is this, that even wind and sea obey him?"

Ps 65:5–8
[5] By dread deeds thou dost answer us with deliverance,
    O God of our salvation,
who art the hope of all the ends of the earth,
    and of the farthest seas;
[6] who by thy strength hast established the mountains,
    being girded with might;
[7] who dost still the roaring of the seas,
    the roaring of their waves,
    the tumult of the peoples;
[8] so that those who dwell at earth's farthest bounds
    are afraid at thy signs;
thou makest the outgoings of the morning and the evening
    to shout for joy.

MATT

Matt 8:23–27 (§M18)
[23] And when he got into the boat, his disciples followed him. [24] And behold, there arose a great storm on the sea, so that the boat was being swamped by the waves; but he was asleep. [25] And they went and woke him, saying, "Save, Lord; we are perishing." [26] And he said to them, "Why are you afraid, O men of little faith?" Then he rose and rebuked the winds and the sea; and there was a great calm. [27] And the men marveled, saying, "What sort of man is this, that even winds and sea obey him?"

Matt 8:18 ⇨ Mark 4:35
[18] Now when Jesus saw great crowds around him, he gave orders to go over to the other side.

LUKE

Luke 8:22–25 (§L33)
[22] One day he got into a boat with his disciples, and he said to them, "Let us go across to the other side of the lake." So they set out, [23] and as they sailed he fell asleep. And a storm of wind came down on the lake, and they were filling with water, and were in danger. [24] And they went and woke him, saying, "Master, Master, we are perishing!" And he awoke and rebuked the wind and the raging waves; and they ceased, and there was a calm. [25] He said to them, "Where is your faith?" And they were afraid, and they marveled, saying to one another, "Who then is this, that he commands even wind and water, and they obey him?"

JOHN

THOMAS

OTHER

MARK

SCENE ONE

Mark 5:1–14a (§K23.1)

[1] They came to the other side of the sea, to the country of the Gerasenes.[a] [2] And when he had come out of the boat, there met him out of the tombs a man with an unclean spirit, [3] who lived among the tombs; and no one could bind him any more, even with a chain; [4] for he had often been bound with fetters and chains, but the chains he wrenched apart, and the fetters he broke in pieces; and no one had the strength to subdue him. [5] Night and day among the tombs and on the mountains he was always crying out, and bruising himself with stones. [6] And when he saw Jesus from afar, he ran and worshiped him; [7] and crying out with a loud voice, he said, "What have you to do with me, Jesus, Son of the Most High God? I adjure you by God, do not torment me." [8] For he had said to him, "Come out of the man, you unclean spirit!" [9] And Jesus[b] asked him, "What is your name?" He replied, "My name is Legion; for we are many." [10] And he begged him eagerly not to send them out of the country. [11] Now a great herd of swine was feeding there on the hillside; [12] and they begged him, "Send us to the swine, let us enter them." [13] So he gave them leave. And the unclean spirits came out, and entered the swine; and the herd, numbering about two thousand, rushed down the steep bank into the sea, and were drowned in the sea.

[14] The herdsman fled, and told it in the city and in the country.

SCENE TWO

Mark 5:14b–20 (§K23.2)

And people came to see what it was that had happened. [15] And they came to Jesus, and saw the demoniac sitting there, clothed and in his right mind, the man who had had the legion; and they were afraid. [16] And those who had seen it told what had happened to the demoniac and to the swine. [17] And they began to beg Jesus[c] to depart from their neighborhood. [18] And as he was getting into the boat, the man who had been possessed with demons begged him that he might be with him. [19] But he refused, and said to him, "Go home to your friends, and tell them how much the Lord has done for you, and how he has had mercy on you." [20] And he went away and began to proclaim in the Decapolis how much Jesus had done for him; and all men marveled.

[a] *Gerasenes:* (cf. Matt 8:28, Luke 8:26) ℵ* B D it vg cop[sa]; *Gadarenes:* A C K *f*[13] sy (in part); *Gergesenes:* ℵ[c] L Δ Θ *f*[1] sy (in part) cop[bo]

JOHN

John 2:4 ⇨ Mark 5:7
[4] And Jesus said to her, "O woman, what have you to do with me? My hour has not yet come."

MATT

Matt 8:28–33 (§M19.1) ⇨ §K23.1

[28] And when he **came to the other side,** to **the country of the** Gadarenes, two demoniacs met him, coming **out of the tombs,** so fierce that no one could pass that way. [29] And behold, they cried **out,** "What **have you to do with** us, O **Son of God?** Have you come here to torment us before the time?" [30] **Now a herd of swine was feeding** at some distance from them. [31] And the demons **begged him,** "If you cast us **out, send us** away into **the herd of swine."** [32] And **he said to them, "Go." So they came out and** went into **the swine; and** behold, the whole **herd rushed down the steep bank into the sea, and** perished **in the** waters. [33] **The herdsmen fled, and** going into **the city** they **told** everything, and what had happened to the demoniacs.

Matt 8:34 (§M19.2) ⇨ §K23.2

[34] **And** behold, all the city **came** out **to** meet **Jesus;** and when they **saw** him, **they** begged him **to** leave **their neighborhood.**

---

[b] Greek: *he*

[c] Greek: *him*

Mark 1:24 ⇨ Mark 5:7
[24] and he cried out, "What have you to do with us, Jesus of Nazareth? Have you come to destroy us? I know who you are, the Holy One of God."

Mark 1:34 ⇨ Mark 5:7
[34] And he healed many who were sick with various diseases, and cast out many demons; and he would not permit the demons to speak, because they knew him.

Mark 3:11 ⇨ Mark 5:7
[11] And whenever the unclean spirits beheld him, they fell down before him and cried out, "You are the Son of God."

THOMAS

LUKE

Luke 8:26–34 (§L34.1) ⇨ §K23.1

[26] Then **they** arrived at **the country of the Gerasenes,** which is opposite Galilee. [27] **And** as he stepped **out** on land, **there met him a man** from the city who had demons; for a long time he had worn no clothes, and he **lived** not in a house but **among the tombs.** [28] **When he saw Jesus,** he cried out and fell down before him, and **said with a loud voice,** "What **have you to do with me, Jesus, Son of the Most High God? I** beseech **you, do not torment me."** [29] **For he** had commanded **the unclean spirit** to **come out of the man.** (For many a time it had seized him; **he** was kept under guard, and **bound with chains and fetters, but he broke** the bonds and was driven by the demon into the desert.) [30] **Jesus** then **asked him, "What is your name?"** And he said, **"Legion"; for many** demons had entered him. [31] **And** they **begged him not to** command **them** to depart into the abyss. [32] **Now a large herd of swine was feeding** there on **the hillside; and they begged him** to let **them enter** these. **So he gave** them **leave.** [33] Then **the demons came out** of the man **and entered the swine, and the herd rushed down the steep bank into the** lake **and were drowned.**

[34] When **the herdsmen** saw what had happened, they **fled, and told it in the city and in the country.**

Luke 8:35–39 (§L34.2) ⇨ §K23.2

[35] Then **people** went out **to see what had happened, and they came to Jesus, and** found **the man** from whom the demons had gone, **sitting** at the feet of Jesus, **clothed and in his right mind; and they were afraid.** [36] **And those who had seen it told** them how he who had been possessed with demons was healed. [37] Then all the people of the surrounding country of the Gerasenes asked him **to depart from** them; for they were seized with great fear; so **he** got **into the boat** and returned. [38] **The man** from whom the **demons** had gone **begged that he might be with him; but he** sent him away, saying, [39] "Return **to your home, and** declare **how much** God **has done for you."** **And he went away,** proclaiming throughout the whole city **how much Jesus had done for him.**

OTHER

MARK	MATT	LUKE

MARK

JAIRUS' DAUGHTER: INTRODUCTION

Mark 5:21–24a (§K24.1)

21 And when Jesus had crossed again in the boat to the other side, a great crowd gathered about him; and he was beside the sea. 22 Then came one of the rulers of the synagogue, Jairus by name; and seeing him, he fell at his feet, 23 and besought him, saying, "My little daughter is at the point of death. Come and lay your hands on her, so that she may be made well, and live." 24 And he went with him.

WOMAN WITH THE INTERNAL HEMORRHAGE

Mark 5:24b–34 (§K24.2)

And a great crowd followed him and thronged about him. 25 And there was a woman who had had a flow of blood for twelve years, 26 and who had suffered much under many physicians, and had spent all that she had, and was no better but rather grew worse. 27 She had heard the reports about Jesus, and came up behind him in the crowd and touched his garment. 28 For she said, "If I touch even his garments, I shall be made well." 29 And immediately the hemorrhage ceased; and she felt in her body that she was healed of her disease. 30 And Jesus, perceiving in himself that power had gone forth from him, immediately turned about in the crowd, and said, "Who touched my garments?" 31 And his disciples said to him, "You see the crowd pressing around you, and yet you say, 'Who touched me?'" 32 And he looked around to see who had done it. 33 But the woman, knowing what had been done to her, came in fear and trembling and fell down before him, and told him the whole truth. 34 And he said to her, "Daughter, your faith has made you well; go in peace, and be healed of your disease."

JAIRUS' DAUGHTER: CONCLUSION

Mark 5:35–43 (§K24.3)

35 While he was still speaking, there came from the ruler's house some who said, "Your daughter is dead. Why trouble the Teacher any further?" 36 But ignoring[a] what they said, Jesus said to the ruler of the synagogue, "Do not fear, only believe." 37 And he allowed no one to follow him except Peter and James and John the brother of James. 38 When they came to the house of the ruler of the synagogue, he saw a tumult, and people weeping and wailing loudly. 39 And when he had entered, he said to them, "Why do you make a tumult and weep? The child is not dead but sleeping." 40 And they laughed at him. But he put them all outside, and took the child's father and mother and those who were with him, and went in where the child was. 41 Taking her by the hand he said to her, "Talitha cumi"; which means, "Little girl, I say to you, arise." 42 And immediately the girl got up and walked (she was twelve years of age), and they were immediately overcome with amazement. 43 And he strictly charged them that no one should know this, and told them to give her something to eat.

[a] Or: overhearing; ℵ[a] A C D K Θ Π al read: hearing (from Luke 8:50)

MATT

Matt 9:18–19 (§M23.1)

18 While he was thus speaking to them, behold, a ruler came in and knelt before him, saying, "My daughter has just died; but come and lay your hand on her, and she will live." 19 And Jesus rose and followed him, with his disciples.

Matt 9:20–22 (§M23.2)

20 And behold, a woman who had suffered from a hemorrhage for twelve years came up behind him and touched the fringe of his garment; 21 for she said to herself, "If I only touch his garment, I shall be made well." 22 Jesus turned, and seeing her he said, "Take heart, daughter; your faith has made you well." And instantly the woman was made well.

Matt 9:23–26 (§M23.3)

23 And when Jesus came to the ruler's house, and saw the flute players, and the crowd making a tumult, 24 he said, "Depart; for the girl is not dead but sleeping." And they laughed at him. 25 But when the crowd had been put outside, he went in and took her by the hand, and the girl arose. 26 And the report of this went through all that district.

Matt 14:36 ⇨ Mark 5:27–33
36 *and besought him that they might only touch the fringe of his garment; and as many as touched it were made well.*

Mark 6:56 ⇨ Mark 5:27–33
56 *And wherever he came, in villages, cities, or country, they laid the sick in the market places, and besought him that they might touch even the fringe of his garment; and as many as touched it were made well.*

Mark 10:52 ⇨ Mark 5:34
52 *And Jesus said to him, "Go your way; your faith has made you well." And immediately he received his sight and followed him on the way.*

LUKE

Luke 8:40–42a (§L35.1)

40 Now when Jesus returned, the crowd welcomed him, for they were all waiting for him. 41 And there came a man named Jairus, who was a ruler of the synagogue; and falling at Jesus' feet he besought him to come to his house, 42 for he had an only daughter, about twelve years of age, and she was dying.

Luke 8:42b–48 (§L35.2)

As he went, the people pressed round him. 43 And a woman who had had a flow of blood for twelve years and could not be healed by any one, 44 came up behind him, and touched the fringe of his garment; and immediately her flow of blood ceased. 45 And Jesus said, "Who was it that touched me?" When all denied it, Peter said, "Master, the multitudes surround you and press upon you!" 46 But Jesus said, "Some one touched me; for I perceive that power has gone forth from me." 47 And when the woman saw that she was not hidden, she came trembling, and falling down before him declared in the presence of all the people why she had touched him, and how she had been immediately healed. 48 And he said to her, "Daughter, your faith has made you well; go in peace."

Luke 8:49–56 (§L35.3)

49 While he was still speaking, a man from the ruler's house came and said, "Your daughter is dead; do not trouble the Teacher any more." 50 But Jesus on hearing this answered him, "Do not fear; only believe, and she shall be well." 51 And when he came to the house, he permitted no one to enter with him, except Peter and John and James, and the father and mother of the child. 52 And all were weeping and bewailing her; but he said, "Do not weep; for she is not dead but sleeping." 53 And they laughed at him, knowing that she was dead. 54 But taking her by the hand he called, saying, "Child, arise." 55 And her spirit returned, and she got up at once; and he directed that something should be given her to eat. 56 And her parents were amazed; but he charged them to tell no one what had happened.

Luke 6:19 ⇨ Mark 5:27–33
19 *And all the crowd sought to touch him, for power came forth from him and healed them all.*

Luke 7:50 ⇨ Mark 5:34
50 *And he said to the woman, "Your faith has saved you; go in peace."*

Luke 17:19 ⇨ Mark 5:34
19 *And he said to him, "Rise and go your way; your faith has made you well."*

Luke 18:42 ⇨ Mark 5:34
42 *And Jesus said to him, "Receive your sight; your faith has made you well."*

JOHN	THOMAS	OTHER

MARK　　　　　　　　　MATT　　　　　　　　　LUKE

Mark 6:1–6 (§K25) °

[1] He went away from there and came to his own country; and his disciples followed him. [2] And on the sabbath he began to teach in the synagogue; and many who heard him were astonished, saying, "Where did this man get all this? What is the wisdom given to him? What mighty works are wrought by his hands! [3] Is not this the carpenter, the son of Mary and brother of James and Joses and Judas and Simon, and are not his sisters here with us?" And they took offense[a] at him. [4] And Jesus said to them, "A prophet is not without honor, except in his own country, and among his own kin, and in his own house." [5] And he could do no mighty work there, except that he laid his hands upon a few sick people and healed them. [6] And he marveled because of their unbelief.

And he went about among the villages teaching.

[a] Or: *stumbled*

°Appendix 3 ⇨ §K25

Matt 13:53–58 (§M42)

[53] And when Jesus had finished these parables, **he went away from there,** [54] **and** coming to **his own country** he taught them **in** their **synagogue,** so that they **were astonished,** and said, "**Where did this man get this wisdom** and these mighty works? [55] **Is not this** the carpenter's **son?** Is not his mother called **Mary?** And are not his brothers **James and** Joseph **and Simon and Judas?** [56] **And are not** all **his sisters with us?** **Where** then **did this man get all this?**" [57] **And they took offense at him.** But Jesus said to them, "**A prophet is not without honor except in his own country and in his own house.**" [58] **And he** did not **do many** mighty works **there, because of their unbelief.**

Matt 9:35 ⇨ Mark 6:6

[35] *And Jesus went about all the cities and villages, teaching in their synagogues and preaching the gospel of the kingdom, and healing every disease and every infirmity.*

‡ **Luke 4:16–30 (§L12)**

[16] And **he came to** Nazareth, where he had been brought up; **and he** went to the **synagogue,** as his custom was, **on the sabbath** day. And he stood up to read; [17] and there was given to him the book of the prophet Isaiah. He opened the book and found the place where it was written,
[18] "The Spirit of the Lord is upon me,
because he has anointed me to preach good
　news to the poor.
He has sent me to proclaim release to the
　captives
and recovering of sight to the blind,
to set at liberty those who are oppressed,
[19] to proclaim the acceptable year of the
　Lord."
[20] And he closed the book, and gave it back to the attendant, and sat down; **and** the eyes of all in the synagogue were fixed on **him.** [21] And he began to say to them, "Today this scripture has been fulfilled in your hearing." [22] **And** all spoke well of **him,** and wondered at the gracious words which proceeded out of his mouth; and they said, "Is not this Joseph's **son?**" [23] **And** he **said to them,** "Doubtless you will quote to me this proverb, 'Physician, heal yourself; what we have heard you did at Capernaum, do here also in your own country.'" [24] **And** he **said,** "Truly, I say to you, no **prophet is** acceptable **in his own country.** [25] But in truth, I tell you, there were many widows in Israel in the days of Elijah, when the heaven was shut up three years and six months, when there came a great famine over all the land; [26] and Elijah was sent to none of them but only to Zarephath, in the land of Sidon, to a woman who was a widow. [27] And there were many lepers in Israel in the time of the prophet Elisha; and none of them was cleansed, but only Naaman the Syrian." [28] When they heard this, all in the synagogue were filled with wrath. [29] And they rose up and put him out of the city, and led him to the brow of the hill on which their city was built, that they might throw him down headlong. [30] But passing through the midst of them **he went** away.

JOHN　　　　　　　　　THOMAS　　　　　　　　　OTHER

John 7:15 ⇨ Mark 6:2
[15] *The Jews marveled at it, saying, "How is it that this man has learning, when he has never studied?"*

John 4:44 ⇨ Mark 6:4
[44] For **Jesus** himself testified that **a prophet** has no **honor in his own country.**

POxyl 6 ⇨ Mark 6:4
(6) **Jesus** says, "**A prophet is not** acceptable **in his own** homeland, nor does a physician work cures on those who know him."

GThom 31 ⇨ Mark 6:4
(31) **Jesus** said, "No **prophet is** accepted in **his own** village; no physician heals those who know him."

MARK

Mark 6:7–13 (§K26) °
⁷ And he called to him the twelve, and began to send them out two by two, and gave them authority over the unclean spirits. ⁸ He charged them to take nothing for their journey except a staff; no bread, no bag, no money in their belts; ⁹ but to wear sandals and not put on two tunics. ¹⁰ And he said to them, "Where you enter a house, stay there until you leave the place. ¹¹ And if any place will not receive you and they refuse to hear you, when you leave, shake off the dust that is on your feet for a testimony against them." ¹² So they went out and preached that men should repent. ¹³ And they cast out many demons, and anointed with oil many that were sick and healed them.

°Appendix 2 ⇨ §K26

Mark 3:14–15 ⇨ Mark 6:7
¹⁴ And he appointed twelve, to be with him, and to be sent out to preach ¹⁵ and have authority to cast out demons: . . .

MATT

Matt 10:1 ⇨ Mark 6:7
¹ And he called to him his twelve disciples and gave them authority over unclean spirits, to cast them out, and to heal every disease and every infirmity.

Matt 10:9–14 ⇨ Mark 6:8–12
⁹ "Take no gold, nor silver, nor copper in your belts, ¹⁰ no bag for your journey, nor two tunics, nor sandals, nor a staff; for the laborer deserves his food. ¹¹ And whatever town or village you enter, find out who is worthy in it, and stay with him until you depart. ¹² As you enter the house, salute it. ¹³ And if the house is worthy, let your peace come upon it; but if it is not worthy, let your peace return to you. ¹⁴ And if any one will not receive you or listen to your words, shake off the dust from your feet as you leave that house or town."

LUKE

Luke 9:1–6 (§L36)
¹ And he called the twelve together and gave them power and authority over all demons and to cure diseases, ² and he sent them out to preach the kingdom of God and to heal. ³ And he said to them, "Take nothing for your journey, no staff, nor bag, nor bread, nor money; and do not have two tunics. ⁴ And whatever house you enter, stay there, and from there depart. ⁵ And wherever they do not receive you, when you leave that town shake off the dust from your feet as a testimony against them." ⁶ And they departed and went through the villages, preaching the gospel and healing everywhere.

Cf. Luke 10:1–16 (§L46)

JOHN

THOMAS

OTHER

MARK | MATT | LUKE

Mark 6:14–29 (§K27) °

[14] King Herod heard of it; for Jesus'[a] name had become known. Some[b] said, "John the baptizer has been raised from the dead; that is why these powers are at work in him." [15] But others said, "It is Elijah." And others said, "It is a prophet, like one of the prophets of old." [16] But when Herod heard of it he said, "John, whom I beheaded, has been raised." [17] For Herod had sent and seized John, and bound him in prison for the sake of Herodias, his brother Philip's wife; because he had married her. [18] For John said to Herod, "It is not lawful for you to have your brother's wife." [19] And Herodias had a grudge against him, and wanted to kill him. But she could not, [20] for Herod feared John, knowing that he was a righteous and holy man, and kept him safe. When he heard him, he was much perplexed; and yet he heard him gladly. [21] But an opportunity came when Herod on his birthday gave a banquet for his courtiers and officers and the leading men of Galilee. [22] For when Herodias' daughter came in and danced, she pleased Herod and his guests; and the king said to the girl, "Ask me for whatever you wish, and I will grant it." [23] And he vowed to her, "Whatever you ask me, I will give you, even half of my kingdom." [24] And she went out, and said to her mother, "What shall I ask?" And she said, "The head of John the baptizer." [25] And she came immediately with haste to the king, and asked, saying, "I want you to give me at once the head of John the Baptist on a platter." [26] And the king was exceedingly sorry; but because of his oaths and his guests he did not want to break his word to her. [27] And immediately the king sent a soldier of the guard and gave orders to bring his head. He went and beheaded him in the prison, [28] and brought his head on a platter, and gave it to the girl; and the girl gave it to her mother. [29] When his disciples heard of it, they came and took his body, and laid it in a tomb.

[a] Greek: *his*

[b] Text: B W it (in part); *he said:* א A C K L Δ Θ Π *f*[1] *f*[13] 28 33 *pm*

° Appendix 1 ⇨ §K27

Mark 8:28 ⇨ Mark 6:14–15
[28] And they told him, "**John the** Baptist; and **others** say, **Elijah; and others one of the prophets.**"

⇨ Mark 6:18
Cf. Lev. 18:16, 20:21

Matt 14:1–12 (§M43)

[1] At that time **Herod** the tetrarch **heard** about the fame of **Jesus**; [2] and he **said** to this servants, "This is **John the** Baptist, he **has been raised from the dead; that is why these powers are at work in him.**" [3] For Herod had seized John and bound him and put him **in prison, for the sake of Herodias, his brother Philip's wife;** [4] **because John** said to him, "**It is not lawful for you to have** her." [5] **And** though he wanted to put **him** to death, he **feared** the people, because they held him to be a prophet. [6] **But when** Herod's **birthday** came, the **daughter** of Herodias **danced** before the company, and **pleased Herod,** [7] so that he promised her with an oath to give her **whatever** she might ask. [8] Prompted by **her mother, she said, "Give me the head of John the Baptist** here **on a platter.**" [9] **And the king was sorry, but because of his oaths and his guests he** commanded it to be given; [10] he **sent** and had John **beheaded in the prison,** [11] and **his head** was **brought on a platter and** given **to the girl, and** she brought it **to her mother.** [12] **And his disciples came and took** the **body** and buried **it;** and they went and told Jesus.

Matt 16:14 ⇨ Mark 6:14–15
[14] And they **said,** "**Some** say **John the** Baptist, **others** say **Elijah, and others** Jeremiah or **one of the prophets.**"

Esth 5:3 ⇨ Mark 6:23
[3] **And** the king said **to her,** "What is it, Queen Esther? What is your request? It shall be given **you, even** to the **half of my kingdom.**"

Esth 7:2 ⇨ Mark 6:23
[2] **And** on the second day, as they were drinking wine, the king again said **to** Esther, "What is your petition, Queen Esther? It shall be granted **you.** And what is your request? **Even** to the **half of my kingdom,** it shall be fulfilled."

Luke 9:7–9 (§L37)

[7] Now **Herod** the tetrarch **heard of** all that was done, and he was perplexed, because it was **said** by some that **John** had **been raised from the dead,** [8] by some that **Elijah** had appeared, and by others that **one of the old prophets** had risen. [9] **Herod** said, "**John I beheaded;** but who is this about whom I hear such things?" And he sought to see him.

Luke 9:19 ⇨ Mark 6:14–15
[19] And they answered, "**John the** Baptist; **but others** say, **Elijah; and others,** that **one of the old prophets** has risen."

Luke 3:19–20 ⇨ Mark 6:17–18
[19] But **Herod** the tetrarch, who had been reproved by him for **Herodias, his** brother's **wife,** and for all the evil things that **Herod** had done, [20] added this to them all, that he shut up **John in prison.**

JOHN | THOMAS | OTHER

John 1:19–21 ⇨ Mark 6:14–15
[19] and this is the testimony of **John,** when the Jews sent priests and Levites from Jerusalem to ask him, "Who are you?" [20] He confessed, "I am not the Christ." [21] And they asked him, "What then? Are you **Elijah**?" He said, "I am not." "Are you the **prophet**?" And he answered, "No."

MARK

MATT

LUKE

Mark 6:30–34 (§K28) °

³⁰ The apostles returned to Jesus, and told him all that they had done and taught. ³¹ And he said to them, "Come away by yourselves to a lonely place, and rest a while." For many were coming and going, and they had no leisure even to eat. ³² And they went away in the boat to a lonely place by themselves. ³³ Now many saw them going, and knew them, and they ran there on foot from all the towns, and got there ahead of them. ³⁴ As he went ashore he saw a great throng, and he had compassion on them, because they were like sheep without a shepherd; and he began to teach them many things.

°Appendix 2 ⇨ K28

Num 27:15–17 ⇨ Mark 6:34
¹⁵ Moses said to the Lord, ¹⁶ "Let the Lord, the God of the Spirits of all flesh, appoint a man over the congregation, ¹⁷ who shall go out before them and come in before them, who shall lead them out and bring them in; that the congregation of the Lord may not be as **sheep** which have no **shepherd**."

1 Kgs 22:17 ⇨ Mark 6:34
¹⁷ And he said, "I saw all Israel scattered upon the mountains, as **sheep** that have no **shepherd**; and the Lord said, 'These have no master; let each return to his home in peace.'"

Matt 14:13–14 (§M44)

¹³ Now when **Jesus** heard this, he withdrew from there **in a boat to a lonely place** apart. But when the crowds heard it, **they** followed him **on foot from the towns**. ¹⁴ As he went ashore he saw a great throng; **and he had compassion on them**, and healed their sick.

Matt 9:36 ⇨ Mark 6:34
³⁶ *When he saw the crowds, he had compassion for them, because they were harassed and helpless, like sheep without a shepherd.*

Luke 9:10–11 (§L38)

¹⁰ On their return **the apostles told him** what **they had done. And he** took them and withdrew apart to a city called Bethsaida. ¹¹ When the crowds learned it, **they** followed him; and **he** welcomed **them** and spoke **to them** of the kingdom of God, and cured those who had need of healing.

Luke 10:17 ⇨ Mark 6:30
¹⁷ *The seventy* ***returned*** *with joy, saying, "Lord, even the demons are subject to us in your name!"*

JOHN

THOMAS

OTHER

MARK

Mark 6:35–44 (§K29)

[35] And when it grew late, his disciples came to him and said, "This is a lonely place, and the hour is now late; [36] send them away, to go into the country and villages round about and buy themselves something to eat." [37] But he answered them, "You give them something to eat." And they said to him, "Shall we go and buy two hundred denarii[a] worth of bread, and give it to them to eat?" [38] And he said to them, "How many loaves have you? Go and see." And when they had found out, they said, "Five, and two fish." [39] Then he commanded them all to sit down by companies upon the green grass. [40] So they sat down in groups, by hundreds and by fifties. [41] And taking the five loaves and the two fish he looked up to heaven, and blessed, and broke the loaves, and gave them to the disciples to set before the people; and he divided the two fish among them all. [42] And they all ate and were satisfied. [43] And they took up twelve baskets full of broken pieces and of the fish. [44] And those who ate the loaves were five thousand men.

[a] The denarius was a day's wage for a laborer

● Mark 8:1–10 (§K37)

[1] In those days, when again a great crowd had gathered, and they had nothing to eat, he called his disciples to him, and said to them, [2] "I have compassion on the crowd, because they have been with me now three days, and have nothing to eat; [3] and if I send them away hungry to their homes, they will faint on the way; and some of them have come a long way." [4] And his disciples answered him, "How can one feed these men with bread here in the desert?" [5] And he asked them, "How many loaves have you?" They said, "Seven." [6] And he commanded the crowd to sit down on the ground; and he took the seven loaves, and having given thanks he broke them and gave them to his disciples to set before the people; and they set them before the crowd. [7] And they had a few small fish; and having blessed them, he commanded that these also should be set before them. [8] And they ate, and were satisfied; and they took up the broken pieces left over, seven baskets full. [9] And there were about four thousand people. [10] And he sent them away and immediately he got into the boat with his disciples, and went to the district of Dalmanutha.

Mark 14:22 ⇨ Mark 6:41

[22] And as they were eating, he took bread, and blessed, and broke it, and gave it to them, and said, "Take; this is my body."

2 Kgs 4:42–44

[42] A man came from Baal-shalishah, bringing the man of God bread of the first fruits, twenty loaves of barley, and fresh ears of grain in his sack. And Elisha said, "Give to the men, that they may eat." [43] But his servant said, "How am I to set this before a hundred men?" So he repeated, "Give them to the men, that they may eat, for thus says the Lord, 'They shall eat and have some left.'" [44] So he set it before them. And they ate, and had some left, according to the word of the Lord.

MATT

Matt 14:15–21 (§M45)

[15] When it was evening, the disciples came to him and said, "This is a lonely place, and the day is now over; send the crowds away to go into the villages and buy food for themselves." [16] Jesus said, "They need not go away; you give them something to eat." [17] They said to him, "We have only five loaves here and two fish." [18] And he said, "Bring them here to me." [19] Then he ordered the crowds to sit down on the grass; and taking the five loaves and the two fish he looked up to heaven, and blessed, and broke and gave the loaves to the disciples, and the disciples gave them to the crowds. [20] And they all ate and were satisfied. And they took up twelve baskets full of the broken pieces left over. [21] And those who ate were about five thousand men, besides women and children.

Matt 15:32–39 (§M52)

[32] Then Jesus called his disciples to him and said, "I have compassion on the crowd, because they have been with me now three days, and have nothing to eat; and I am unwilling to send them away hungry, lest they faint on the way." [33] And the disciples said to him, "Where are we to get bread enough in the desert to feed so great a crowd?" [34] And Jesus said to them, "How many loaves have you?" They said, "Seven, and a few small fish." [35] And commanding the crowd to sit down on the ground, [36] he took the seven loaves and the fish, and having given thanks he broke them and gave them to the disciples, and the disciples gave them to the crowds. [37] And they all ate and were satisfied; and they took up seven baskets full of the broken pieces left over. [38] Those who ate were four thousand men, besides women and children. [39] And sending away the crowds, he got into the boat and went to the region of Magadan.

Matt 26:26 ⇨ Mark 6:41

[26] Now as they were eating, Jesus took bread, and blessed, and broke it, and gave it to the disciples and said, "Take, eat; this is my body."

LUKE

Luke 9:12–17 (§L39)

[12] Now the day began to wear away; and the twelve came and said to him, "Send the crowd away, to go into the villages and country round about, to lodge and get provisions; for we are here in a lonely place." [13] But he said to them, "You give them something to eat." They said, "We have no more than five loaves and two fish—unless we are to go and buy food for all these people." [14] For there were about five thousand men. And he said to his disciples, "Make them sit down in companies, about fifty each." [15] And they did so, and made them all sit down. [16] And taking the five loaves and the two fish he looked up to heaven, and blessed and broke them, and gave them to the disciples to set before the crowd. [17] And all ate and were satisfied. And they took up what was left over, twelve baskets of broken pieces.

Luke 22:19 ⇨ Mark 6:41

[19] And he took bread, and when he had given thanks he broke it and gave it to them, saying, "This is my body which is given for you. Do this in remembrance of me."

Luke 24:30 ⇨ Mark 6:41

[30] When he was at table with them, he took the bread and blessed, and broke it, and gave it to them.

JOHN	THOMAS	OTHER

John 6:1–15 (§J10)

[1] After this Jesus went to the other side of the Sea of Galilee, which is the Sea of Tiberias. [2] And a multitude followed him, because they saw the signs which he did on those who were diseased. [3] Jesus went up on the mountain, and there sat down with **his disciples**. [4] Now the Passover, the feast of the Jews, was at hand. [5] Lifting up his eyes, then, and seeing that a multitude was coming to him, Jesus said to Philip, "How are **we** to **buy bread**, so that these people may **eat**?" [6] This he said to test him, for he himself knew what he would do. [7] Philip answered him, **"Two hundred denarii** would not **buy** enough **bread** for each of **them to** get a little." [8] One of his disciples, Andrew, Simon Peter's brother, said to him, [9] "There is a lad here who has **five** barley **loaves** and **two fish**; but what are they among so many?" [10] Jesus said, "Make the people **sit down**." Now there was much **grass** in the place; **so** the men **sat down, in** number about **five thousand**. [11] Jesus then took **the loaves, and** when **he** had given thanks, he distributed **them to** those who were seated; so also the **fish**, as much as they wanted. [12] **And** when **they** had eaten their fill, he told his disciples, "Gather up the fragments left over, that nothing may be lost." [13] So **they** gathered them **up** and filled **twelve baskets** with fragments from the **five** barley **loaves**, left by those who had eaten. [14] When the people saw the sign which he had done, they said, "This is indeed the prophet who is to come into the world!"

[15] Perceiving then that they were about to come and take him by force to make him king, Jesus withdrew again to the mountain by himself.

Acts 27:35 ⇨ Mark 6:41

[35] *And when he had said this,* **he** *took bread, and giving thanks* **to** *God in the presence of all he* **broke it and** *began to eat.*

| MARK | MATT | LUKE |

MARK

Mark 6:45–46 (§K30)

⁴⁵ Immediately **he made his disciples get into the boat and go before him to the other side,** to Bethsaida, **while he dismissed the crowd.** ⁴⁶ **And after** he had taken leave of them, **he went up on the mountain to pray.**

Mark 8:10

¹⁰ And **he** sent **them** away; and **immediately he** got **into the boat** with **his disciples,** and **went to** the district of Dalmanutha.

MATT

Matt 14:22–23 (§M46)

²² Then **he made** the **disciples get into the boat and go before him to the other side,** while **he dismissed the** crowds. ²³ **And after he** had dismissed the crowds, **he went up on the mountain** by himself **to pray.** When evening came, he was there alone, . . .

Matt 15:39

³⁹ **And** sending away **the** crowds, **he** got **into the boat** and **went to** the region of Magadan.

JOHN

John 6:15

¹⁵ Perceiving then that they were about to come and take him by force to make him king, Jesus withdrew again to **the mountain** by himself.

THOMAS

OTHER

MARK	MATT	LUKE

Mark 6:47–52 (§K31)

⁴⁷ And when evening came, the boat was out on the sea, and he was alone on the land. ⁴⁸ And he saw that they were making headway painfully, for the wind was against them. And about the fourth watch of the night he came to them, walking on the sea. He meant to pass by them, ⁴⁹ but when they saw him walking on the sea they thought it was a ghost, and cried out; ⁵⁰ for they all saw him, and were terrified. But immediately he spoke to them and said, "Take heart, it is I; have no fear." ⁵¹ And he got into the boat with them and the wind ceased. And they were utterly astounded, ⁵² for they did not understand about the loaves, but their hearts were hardened.

Mark 8:17 ⇨ Mark 6:52

*¹⁷ And being aware of it, Jesus said to them, "Why do you discuss the fact that you have no bread? Do you not yet perceive or **understand**? Are your **hearts hardened**?"*

Matt 14:24–33 (§M47)

²⁴ but **the boat** by this time was many furlongs distant from the land, beaten by the waves; for the wind was against them. ²⁵ **And** in **the fourth watch of the night he came to them, walking on the sea.** ²⁶ **But when** the disciples **saw him walking on the sea, they were terrified**, saying, "**It** is **a ghost!**" And they **cried** out for fear. ²⁷ **But immediately he spoke to** them, saying, "**Take heart, it is I; have no fear.**"

²⁸ And Peter answered him, "Lord, if it is you, bid me come to you on the water." ²⁹ He said, "Come." So Peter got out of the boat and walked on the water and came to Jesus; ³⁰ but when he saw the wind, he was afraid, and beginning to sink he cried out, "Lord, save me." ³¹ Jesus immediately reached out his hand and caught him, saying to him, "O man of little faith, why did you doubt?" ³² **And** when they **got into the boat, the wind ceased.** ³³ **And** those in the boat worshiped him, saying, "Truly you are the Son of God."

Luke 24:37 ⇨ Mark 6:49

*³⁷ But **they** were startled and frightened, and supposed that **they saw a spirit.***

JOHN	THOMAS	OTHER

John 6:16–21 (§J11)

¹⁶ **When evening came**, his disciples went down to the sea, ¹⁷ got into **a boat**, and started across **the sea** to Capernaum. It was now dark, and Jesus had not yet come to them. ¹⁸ The sea rose because a strong **wind was** blowing. ¹⁹ When they had rowed about three or four miles, they saw Jesus **walking on the sea** and drawing near to the boat. **They were** frightened, ²⁰ but **he said to them**, "**It is I**; do not be afraid." ²¹ Then they were glad to take him **into the boat**, and immediately the boat was at the land to which they were going.

MARK	MATT	LUKE

Mark 6:53–56 (§K32) °

⁵³ And when they had crossed over, they came to land at Gennesaret, and moored to the shore. ⁵⁴ And when they got out of the boat, immediately the people recognized him, ⁵⁵ and ran about the whole neighborhood and began to bring sick people on their pallets to any place where they heard he was. ⁵⁶ And wherever he came, in villages, cities, or country, they laid the sick in the market places, and besought him that they might touch even the fringe of his garment; and as many as touched it were made well.

°Appendix 3 ⇨ §K32

Mark 1:32–34 (§K10)

³² That evening, at sundown, they brought to him all who were sick or possessed with demons. ³³ And the whole city was gathered together about the door. ³⁴ And he healed many who were sick with various diseases, and cast out many demons; and he would not permit the demons to speak, because they knew him.

Mark 3:7–12 (§K18)

⁷ Jesus withdrew with his disciples to the sea, and a great multitude from Galilee followed; also from Judea ⁸ and Jerusalem and Idumea and from beyond the Jordan and from about Tyre and Sidon a great multitude, hearing all that he did, came to him. ⁹ And he told his disciples to have a boat ready for him because of the crowd, lest they should crush him; ¹⁰ for he had healed many, so that all who had diseases pressed upon him to touch him. ¹¹ And whenever the unclean spirits beheld him, they fell down before him and cried out, "You are the Son of God." ¹² And he strictly ordered them not to make him known.

Mark 5:27–33 ⇨ Mark 6:56

²⁷ She had heard the reports about Jesus, and came up behind him in the crowd and touched his garment. ²⁸ For she said, "If I touch even his garments, I shall be made well." ²⁹ And immediately the hemorrhage ceased; and she felt in her body that she was healed of her disease. ³⁰ And Jesus, perceiving in himself that power had gone forth from him, immediately turned about in the crowd, and said, "Who touched my garments?" ³¹ And his disciples said to him, "You see the crowd pressing around you, and yet you say, 'Who touched me?'" ³² And he looked around to see who had done it. ³³ But the woman, knowing what had been done to her, came in fear and trembling and fell down before him, and told him the whole truth.

Matt 14:34–36 (§M48)

³⁴ And when they had crossed over, they came to land at Gennesaret. ³⁵ And when the men of that place recognized him, they sent round to all that region and brought to him all that were sick, ³⁶ and besought him that they might only touch the fringe of his garment; and as many as touched it were made well.

Matt 4:23–25 (§M11)

²³ And he went about all Galilee teaching in their synagogues and preaching the gospel of the kingdom and healing every disease and every infirmity among the people. ²⁴ So his fame spread throughout all Syria, and they brought him all the sick, those afflicted with various diseases and pains, demoniacs, epileptics, and paralytics, and he healed them. ²⁵ And great crowds followed him from Galilee and the Decapolis and Jerusalem and Judea and from beyond the Jordan.

Matt 8:16–17 (§M16)

¹⁶ That evening they brought to him many who were possessed with demons; and he cast out the spirits with a word, and healed all who were sick. ¹⁷ This was to fulfil what was spoken by the prophet Isaiah, "He took our infirmities and bore our diseases."

Matt 9:20–21 ⇨ Mark 6:56

²⁰ And behold, a woman who had suffered from a hemorrhage for twelve years came up behind him and touched the fringe of his garment; ²¹ for she said to herself, "If I only touch his garment, I shall be made well."

Luke 4:40–41 (§L15)

⁴⁰ Now when the sun was setting, all those who had any that were sick with various diseases brought them to him; and he laid his hands on every one of them and healed them. ⁴¹ And demons also came out of many, crying, "You are the Son of God!" But he rebuked them, and would not allow them to speak, because they knew that he was the Christ.

Luke 6:17–19 (§L24)

¹⁷ And he came down with them and stood on a level place, with a great crowd of his disciples and a great multitude of people from all Judea and Jerusalem and the seacoast of Tyre and Sidon, who came to hear him and to be healed of their diseases; ¹⁸ and those who were troubled with unclean spirits were cured. ¹⁹ And all the crowd sought to touch him, for power came forth from him and healed them all.

Luke 8:43–47 ⇨ Mark 6:56

⁴³ And a woman who had had a flow of blood for twelve years and could not be healed by any one, ⁴⁴ came up behind him, and touched the fringe of his garment; and immediately her flow of blood ceased. ⁴⁵ And Jesus said, "Who was it that touched me?" When all denied it, Peter said, "Master, the multitudes surround you and press upon you!" ⁴⁶ but Jesus said, "Some one touched me; for I perceive that power has gone forth from me." ⁴⁷ And when the woman saw that she was not hidden, she came forth trembling, and falling down before him declared in the presence of all the people why she had touched him, and how she had been immediately healed.

JOHN	THOMAS	OTHER

MARK	MATT	LUKE

LUKE — OTHER

MARK

Mark 7:1–13 (§K33)

¹Now when the Pharisees gathered together to him, with some of the scribes, who had come from Jerusalem, ²they saw that some of his disciples ate with hands defiled, that is, unwashed. ³(For the Pharisees, and all the Jews, do not eat unless they wash their hands,ᵃ observing the tradition of the elders; ⁴and when they come from the market place, they do not eat unless they purifyᵇ themselves;ᶜ and there are many other traditions which they observe, the washing of cups and pots and vessels of bronze.)ᵈ ⁵And the Pharisees and the scribes asked him, "Why do your disciples not liveᵉ according to the tradition of the elders, but eat with hands defiled?" ⁶And he said to them, "Well did Isaiah prophesy of you hypocrites, as it is written,

'This people honors me with their lips,
but their heart is far from me;
⁷in vain do they worship me,
teaching as doctrines the precepts of men.'

⁸You leave the commandment of God, and hold fast the tradition of men."

⁹And he said to them, "You have a fine way of rejecting the commandment of God, in order to keep your tradition! ¹⁰For Moses said, 'Honor your father and your mother'; and, 'He who speaks evil of father or mother, let him surely die'; ¹¹but you say, 'If a man tells his father or his mother, What you would have gained from me is Corban' (that is, given to God)ᶠ— ¹²then you no longer permit him to do anything for his father or mother, ¹³thus making void the word of God through your tradition which you hand on. And many such things you do."

ᵃ One Greek word of uncertain meaning ("with a fist") is left untranslated

ᵇ Some witnesses read *baptize*: A D K L W X Δ Θ Π *f*¹ *f*¹³ 28 33 *pm*; text: ℵ B cop^sa geo

ᶜ Text: D W 1009 it (in part) arm geo; *and they do not eat anything from the market unless they purify it*: 𝔓⁴⁵ ℵ B K L X Δ Θ Π *f*¹ *f*¹³ 28 33 *pm*

ᵈ Some witnesses add *and beds*: A D K W X Θ Π *f*¹ *f*¹³ 28ᶜ 33 *pm*

ᵉ Greek: *walk*

ᶠ Or: *an offering*

Isa 29:13 ⇨ Mark 7:6–7
¹³And the Lord said:
"Because **this people** draw near with their mouth
and honor **me with their lips**,
while their hearts are **far from me**,
and their fear of me is a commandment **of men**
learned by rote"; . . .

JOHN

MATT

Matt 15:1–9 (§M49.1)

¹Then **Pharisees and scribes** came to Jesus from Jerusalem and said, ²"Why do your disciples transgress **the tradition of the elders**? For they do not wash their hands when they **eat**." ³**He** answered them, "And why do **you** transgress **the commandment of God** for the sake of **your tradition**? ⁴**For** God commanded 'Honor your father and your mother,' and, 'He who speaks evil of father or mother, let him surely die.' ⁵But you say, 'If any one tells his father or his mother, What you would have gained from me is given to God, he need not honor his father.' ⁶So for the sake of **your tradition**, you have made void the word of God. ⁷You hypocrites! Well did Isaiah prophesy of you, when he said:

⁸'This people honors me with their lips,
but their heart is far from me;
⁹in vain do they worship me,
teaching as doctrines the precepts of men.'"

Exod 20:12 ⇨ Mark 7:10
¹²"Honor your **father and your mother**, that your days may be long in the land which the Lord your God gives you."

Exod 21:17 ⇨ Mark 7:10
¹⁷"Whoever curses his **father or** his **mother** shall be put to death."

Lev 20:9 ⇨ Mark 7:10
⁹"For every one who curses his **father or** his **mother** shall be put to death; he has cursed his **father or** his **mother**, his blood is upon **him**."

Deut 5:16 ⇨ Mark 7:10
¹⁶"Honor your **father and your mother**, as the Lord your God commanded you; that your days may be prolonged, and that it may go well with you, in the land which the Lord your God gives you."

THOMAS

OTHER

POxy840 2

(2) And he took them (the disciples) with him into the place of purification itself and walked about in the Temple court. And a Pharisaic chief priest, Levi (?) by name, fell in with them and s[aid] to the Savior: Who gave thee leave to [trea]d this place of purification and to look upon [the]se holy utensils without having bathed thyself and even without thy disciples having [wa]shed their f[eet]? On the contrary, being defi[led], thou hast trodden the Temple court, this clean p[lace], although no [one who] has [not] first bathed himself or [chang]ed his clot[hes] may tread it and [venture] to vi[ew these] holy utensils! Forthwith [the Savior] s[tood] still with h[is] disciples and [answered]: How stands it (then) with thee, thou art forsooth (also) here in the Temple court. Art thou then clean? He said to him: I am clean. For I have bathed myself in the pool of David and have gone down by the one stair and come up by the other and have put on white and clean clothes, and (only) then have I come hither and have viewed these holy utensils. Then said the Savior to him: Woe unto you blind that see not! Thou hast bathed thyself in water that is poured out, in which dogs and swine lie night and day and thou hast washed thyself and hast chafed thine outer skin, which prostitutes also and flute-girls anoint, bathe, chafe and rouge, in order to arouse desire in men, but within they are full of scorpions and of [bad]ness [of every kind]. But I and [my disciples], of whom thou sayest that we have not im[mersed] ourselves, [have been im]mersed in the liv[ing . . .] water which comes down from [. . . B]ut woe unto them that . . .

PEger2 3 ⇨ Mark 7:6–7

(3) . . . [ca]me to him to put him to the pro[of] and to tempt him, whilst [they said]: "Master Jesus, we know that thou art come [from God], for what thou doest bears a test[imony] (to thee which goes) beyond (that) of all the prophets. [Wherefore tell] us: is it admissible [to p]ay to the kings the (charges) appertaining to their rule? [Should we] pay [th]em or not?" But Jesus saw through their [in]tention, became [angry] and said to them: "Why call ye me with yo[ur mou]th Master and yet [do] not what I say? Well has Is[aiah] prophesied [concerning y]ou saying: This [people honours] me with the[ir li]ps but their heart is far from me; [their worship is] vain. [They teach] precepts [of men]." (Fragment 2, recto [lines 43–59])

GNaz 12 ⇨ Mark 7:11

(12) The Jewish Gospel: corban is what you should obtain from us. (Variant to Matthew 15:5 in the "Zion Gospel" Edition)

MARK	MATT	LUKE

MARK

TRUE DEFILEMENT

Mark 7:14–15 (§K34.1)

[14] And he called the people to him again, and said to them, "Hear me, all of you, and understand: [15] there is nothing outside a man which by going into him can defile him; but the things which come out of a man are what defile him."[a]

INTERPRETATION

Mark 7:17–23 (§K34.2)

[17] And when he had entered the house, and left the people, his disciples asked him about the parable. [18] And he said to them, "Then are you also without understanding? Do you not see that whatever goes into a man from outside cannot defile him, [19] since it enters, not his heart but his stomach, and so passes on?"[b] (Thus he declared all foods clean.) [20] And he said, "What comes out of a man is what defiles a man. [21] For from within, out of the heart of man, come evil thoughts, fornication, theft, murder, adultery, [22] coveting, wickedness, deceit, licentiousness, envy, slander, pride, foolishness. [23] All these evil things come from within, and they defile a man."

[a] Some witnesses add *If any man has ears to hear, let him hear* (Cf. Mark 4:9, 23): A D K W X Δ^c Θ Π *f*[1] *f*[13] 33 *pm*; ℵ B L Δ* 28 *al* omit

[b] Or: *is evacuated*

MATT

Matt 15:10–11 ⇨ §K34.1

[10] And he called the people to him and said to them, "Hear and understand: [11] not what goes **into** the mouth defiles a man, **but** what comes **out of** the mouth, this defiles a man."

Matt 15:10–20 (§M49.2) ⇨ §K34.2

[10] And he called the people to him and said to them, "Hear and understand: [11] not what goes into the mouth defiles a man, but what comes out of the mouth, this defiles a man." [12] Then the **disciples** came and said to **him**, "Do you know that the Pharisees were offended when they heard this saying?" [13] He answered, "Every plant which my heavenly Father has not planted will be rooted up. [14] Let them alone; they are blind guides. And if a blind man leads a blind man, both will fall into a pit." [15] But Peter said to him, "Explain **the parable** to us." [16] **And he said, "Are you also** still **without understanding?** [17] **Do you not see that whatever goes into** the mouth **passes into the stomach, and so passes on?** [18] But **what comes out of** the mouth proceeds **from the heart**, and this **defiles a man.** [19] **For out of the heart come evil thoughts, murder, adultery, fornication, theft,** false witness, slander. [20] **These** are what **defile a man**; but to eat with unwashed hands does not **defile a man.**"

JOHN

THOMAS

GThom 14 ⇨ Mark 7:15

(14) Jesus **said to them,** "If you fast, you will give rise to sin for yourselves; and if you pray, you will be condemned; and if you give alms, you will do harm to your spirits. When you go into any land and walk about in the districts, if they receive you, eat what they will set before you, and heal the sick among them. For what goes **into** your mouth will not **defile** you, **but** that **which** issues from your mouth—it is that which will **defile** you."

OTHER

MARK	MATT	LUKE

Mark 7:24–30 (§K35)

24 And from there he arose and went away to the region of Tyre and Sidon.[a] And he entered a house, and would not have any one know it; yet he could not be hid. 25 But immediately a woman, whose little daughter was possessed by an unclean spirit, heard of him, and came and fell down at his feet. 26 Now the woman was a Greek, a Syrophoenician by birth. And she begged him to cast the demon out of her daughter. 27 And he said to her, "Let the children first be fed, for it is not right to take the children's bread and throw it to the dogs." 28 But she answered him, "Yes, Lord; yet even the dogs under the table eat the children's crumbs." 29 And he said to her, "For this saying you may go your way; the demon has left your daughter." 30 And she went home, and found the child lying in bed, and the demon gone.

Mark 7:31–37 (§K36)

31 Then he returned from the region of Tyre, and went through Sidon to the Sea of Galilee, through the region of the Decapolis. 32 And they brought to him a man who was deaf and had an impediment in his speech; and they besought him to lay his hand upon him. 33 And taking him aside from the multitude privately, he put his fingers into his ears, and he spat and touched his tongue; 34 and looking up to heaven, he sighed, and said to him, "Ephphatha," that is, "Be opened." 35 And his ears were opened, his tongue was released, and he spoke plainly. 36 And he charged them to tell no one; but the more he charged them, the more zealously they proclaimed it. 37 And they were astonished beyond measure, saying, "He had done all things well; he even makes the deaf hear and the dumb speak."

[a] Omit *and Sidon:* D L W Δ Θ 28 *al;* text: (cf. Matt 15:21) ℵ A B K X Π *f¹ f¹³* 33 *al*

Matt 15:21–28 (§M50) ⇨ §K35

21 And Jesus **went away from there** and withdrew **to the** district **of Tyre and Sidon.** 22 **And** behold, a Canaanite **woman** from that region **came** out and cried, "Have mercy on me, O Lord, Son of David; my **daughter** is severely **possessed by a demon.**" 23 But he did not answer her a word. And his disciples came and begged him, saying, "Send her away, for she is crying after us." 24 He answered, "I was sent only to the lost sheep of the house of Israel." 25 But she **came and** knelt before him, saying, "Lord, help me." 26 **And he** answered, "It is not fair **to take the children's bread and throw it to the dogs.**" 27 **She** said, **"Yes, Lord, yet even the dogs eat** the **crumbs** that fall from their master's **table.**" 28 Then Jesus answered **her,** "O woman, great is your faith! Be it done for you as you desire." **And** her **daughter** was healed instantly.

† Matt 15:29–31 (§M51) ⇨ §K36

29 And Jesus **went** on from there and passed along **the Sea of Galilee.** And he went up on the mountain, and sat down there. 30 **And** great crowds came **to him,** bringing with them the lame, the maimed, the blind, the dumb, and many others, **and they** put them at his feet, and he healed them, 31 so that the throng wondered, when **they** saw **the dumb** speaking, the maimed whole, the lame walking, and the blind seeing; **and they** glorified the God of Israel.

JOHN	THOMAS	OTHER

MARK	MATT	LUKE

MARK

Mark 8:1–10 (§K37)

[1] In those days, when again a great crowd had gathered, and they had nothing to eat, he called his disciples to him, and said to them, [2] "I have compassion on the crowd, because they have been with me now three days, and have nothing to eat; [3] and if I send them away hungry to their homes, they will faint on the way; and some of them have come a long way." [4] And his disciples answered him, "How can one feed these men with bread here in the desert?" [5] And he asked them, "How many loaves have you?" They said, "Seven." [6] And he commanded the crowd to sit down on the ground; and he took the seven loaves, and having given thanks he broke them and gave them to his disciples to set before the people; and they set them before the crowd. [7] And they had a few small fish; and having blessed them, he commanded that these also should be set before them. [8] And they ate, and were satisfied; and they took up the broken pieces left over, seven baskets full. [9] And there were about four thousand people. [10] And he sent them away and immediately he got into the boat with his disciples, and went to the district of Dalmanutha.[a]

[a] Some witnesses read *Magadan* or *Magdala*: D Θ *f*¹ *f*¹³ 28 it (in part) syr (in part) *pc*

● **Mark 6:35–44 (§K29)**

[35] And when it grew late, his disciples came to him and said, "This is a lonely place, and the hour is now late; [36] send them away, to go into the country and villages round about and buy themselves something to eat." [37] But he answered them, "You give them something to eat." And they said to him, "Shall we go and buy two hundred denarii worth of bread, and give it to them to eat?" [38] And he said to them, "How many loaves have you? Go and see." And when they had found out, they said, "Five, and two fish." [39] Then he commanded them all to sit down by companies upon the green grass. [40] So they sat down in groups, by hundreds and by fifties. [41] And taking the five loaves and the two fish he looked up to heaven, and blessed, and broke the loaves, and gave them to the disciples to set before the people; and he divided the two fish among them all. [42] And they all ate and were satisfied. [43] And they took up twelve baskets full of broken pieces and of the fish. [44] And those who ate the loaves were five thousand men.

● **Mark 6:45–46 (§K30)** ⇨ Mark 8:10

[45] Immediately he made his disciples get into the boat and go before him to the other side, to Bethsaida, while he dismissed the crowd. [46] And after he had taken leave of them, he went up on the mountain to pray.

Mark 14:22 ⇨ Mark 8:6

[22] *And as they were eating, he took bread, and blessed, and broke it, and gave it to them, and said, "Take; this is my body."*

2 Kgs 4:42–44

[42] A man came from Baal-shalishah, bringing the man of God bread of the first fruits, twenty loaves of barley, and fresh ears of grain in his sack. And Elisha said, "Give to the men, that they may eat." [43] But his servant said, "How am I to set this before a hundred men?" So he repeated, "Give them to the men, that they may eat, for thus says the Lord, 'They shall eat and have some left.'" [44] So he set it before them. And they ate, and had some left, according to the word of the Lord.

MATT

Matt 15:32–39 (§M52)

[32] Then Jesus called his disciples to him and said, "I have compassion on the crowd, because they have been with me now three days, and have nothing to eat; and I am unwilling to send them away hungry, lest they faint on the way." [33] And the disciples said to him, "Where are we to get bread enough in the desert to feed so great a crowd?" [34] And Jesus said to them, "How many loaves have you?" They said, "Seven, and a few small fish." [35] And commanding the crowd to sit down on the ground, [36] he took the seven loaves and the fish, and having given thanks he broke them and gave them to the disciples, and the disciples gave them to the crowds. [37] And they all ate and were satisfied; and they took up seven baskets full of the broken pieces left over. [38] Those who ate were four thousand men, besides women and children. [39] And sending away the crowds, he got into the boat and went to the region of Magadan.

Matt 14:15–21 (§M45)

[15] When it was evening, the disciples came to him and said, "This is a lonely place, and the day is now over; send the crowds away to go into the villages and buy food for themselves." [16] Jesus said, "They need not go away; you give them something to eat." [17] They said to him, "We have only five loaves here and two fish." [18] And he said, "Bring them here to me." [19] Then he ordered the crowds to sit down on the grass; and taking the five loaves and the two fish he looked up to heaven, and blessed, and broke and gave the loaves to the disciples, and the disciples gave them to the crowds. [20] And they all ate and were satisfied. And they took up twelve baskets full of the broken pieces left over. [21] And those who ate were about five thousand men, besides women and children.

Matt 15:22–23 (§M46)

[22] And behold, a Canaanite woman from that region came out and cried, "Have mercy on me, O Lord, Son of David; my daughter is severely possessed by a demon." [23] But he did not answer her a word. And his disciples came and begged him, saying, "send her away, for she is crying after us."

Matt 9:36 ⇨ Mark 8:1–3

[36] *When he saw the crowds, he had compassion for them, because they were harassed and helpless, like sheep without a shepherd.*

Matt 26:26 ⇨ Mark 8:6

[26] *Now as they were eating, Jesus took bread, and blessed, and broke it, and gave it to the disciples and said, "Take, eat; this is my body."*

LUKE

Luke 9:12–17 (§L39)

[12] Now the day began to wear away; and the twelve came and said to him, "Send the crowd away, to go into the villages and country round about, to lodge and get provisions; for we are here in a lonely place." [13] But he said to them, "You give them something to eat." They said, "We have no more than five loaves and two fish—unless we are to go and buy food for all these people." [14] For there were about five thousand men. And he said to his disciples, "Make them sit down in companies, about fifty each." [15] And they did so, and made them all sit down. [16] And taking the five loaves and the two fish he looked up to heaven, and blessed and broke them, and gave them to the disciples to set before the crowd. [17] And all ate and were satisfied. And they took up what was left over, twelve baskets of broken pieces.

Luke 22:19 ⇨ Mark 8:6

[19] *And he took bread, and when he had given thanks he broke it and gave it to them, saying, "This is my body which is given for you. Do this in remembrance of me."*

Luke 24:30 ⇨ Mark 8:6

[30] *When he was at table with them, he took the bread and blessed, and broke it, and gave it to them.*

JOHN	THOMAS	OTHER

John 6:1–15 (§J10)

¹ After this Jesus went to the other side of the Sea of Galilee, which is the Sea of Tiberias. ² And a multitude followed him, because they saw the signs which he did on those who were diseased. ³ Jesus went up on the mountain, and there sat down with **his disciples**. ⁴ Now the Passover, the feast of the Jews, was at hand. ⁵ Lifting up his eyes, then, and seeing that a multitude was coming to him, Jesus **said to** Philip, "**How** are we to buy **bread**, so that **these** people may eat?" ⁶ This he said to test him, for he himself knew what he would do. ⁷ Philip answered him, "Two hundred denarii would not buy enough **bread** for each of them to get a little." ⁸ One of his disciples, Andrew, Simon Peter's brother, said to him, ⁹ "There is a lad here who has five barley **loaves** and two **fish**; but what are they among so many?" ¹⁰ Jesus said, "Make **the** people **sit down**." Now there was much grass in the place; so the men sat **down**, in number about five **thousand**. ¹¹ Jesus then **took the loaves, and** when he had **given thanks, he** distributed **them** to those who were seated; so also the **fish**, as much as they wanted. ¹² **And** when **they** had eaten their fill, he told his disciples, "Gather **up the** fragments **left over**, that nothing may be lost." ¹³ So **they** gathered them **up** and filled twelve **baskets** with fragments from the five barley loaves, **left** by those who had eaten. ¹⁴ When the people saw the sign which he had done, they said, "This is indeed the prophet who is to come into the world!"

¹⁵ Perceiving then that they were about to come and take him by force to make him king, Jesus withdrew again **to the** mountain by himself.

Acts 27:35 ⇨ Mark 8:6

³⁵ *And when he had said this,* **he took bread,** *and giving* **thanks** *to God in the presence of all he broke it and* **began to eat.**

MARK	MATT	LUKE

MARK

Mark 8:11–13 (§K38)

[11] The Pharisees came and began to argue with him, seeking from him a sign from heaven, to test him. [12] And he sighed deeply in his spirit, and said, "Why does this generation seek a sign? Truly, I say to you, no sign shall be given to this generation." [13] And he left them, and getting into the boat again he departed to the other side.

MATT

Matt 16:1–4 (§M53)

[1] And **the Pharisees** and Sadducees **came**, and **to test him** they asked **him** to show them **a sign from heaven.** [2] **He** answered them, "When it is evening, you say, 'It will be fair weather; for the sky is red.' [3] And in the morning, 'It will be stormy today, for the sky is red and threatening.' You know how to interpret the appearance of the sky, but you cannot interpret the signs of the times. [4] An evil and adulterous **generation** seeks for **a sign,** but **no sign shall be given to** it except the sign of Jonah." So **he left them** and **departed.**

Matt 12:38–42 (§M37)

[38] Then some of the scribes and **Pharisees** said to **him,** "Teacher, we wish to see **a sign from** you." [39] But **he** answered them, "An evil and adulterous **generation** seeks for **a sign;** but **no sign shall be given to** it except the sign of the prophet Jonah. [40] For as Jonah was three days and three nights in the belly of the whale, so will the Son of man be three days and three nights in the heart of the earth. [41] The men of Nineveh will arise at the judgment with **this generation** and condemn it; for they repented at the preaching of Jonah, and behold, something greater than Jonah is here. [42] The queen of the South will arise at the judgment with **this generation** and condemn it; for she came from the ends of the earth to hear the wisdom of Solomon, and behold, something greater than Solomon is here."

LUKE

Luke 11:29–32 (§L51.4)

[29] When the crowds were increasing, **he** began to say, "**This generation** is an evil **generation;** it seeks **a sign,** but **no sign shall be given to** it except the sign of Jonah. [30] For as Jonah became a sign to the men of Nineveh, so will the Son of man be to this generation. [31] The queen of the South will arise at the judgment with the men of **this generation** and condemn them; for she came from the ends of the earth to hear the wisdom of Solomon, and behold, something greater than Solomon is here. [32] The men of Nineveh will arise at the judgment with **this generation** and condemn it; for they repented at the preaching of Jonah, and behold, something greater than Jonah is here."

Luke 11:16 ⇨ Mark 8:11

[16] *while others, to test him, sought from him a sign from heaven.*

JOHN	THOMAS	OTHER

John 6:30 ⇨ Mark 8:11

[30] *So they said to him, "Then what sign do you do, that we may see, and believe you? What work do you perform?"*

MARK

Mark 8:14–21 (§K39)

[14] Now they had forgotten to bring bread; and they had only one loaf with them in the boat. [15] And he cautioned them, saying, "Take heed, beware of the leaven of the Pharisees and the leaven of Herod."[a] [16] And they discussed it with one another, saying, "We have no bread." [17] And being aware of it, Jesus said to them, "Why do you discuss the fact that you have no bread? Do you not yet perceive or understand? Are your hearts hardened? [18] Having eyes do you not see, and having ears do you not hear? And do you not remember? [19] When I broke the five loaves for the five thousand, how many baskets full of broken pieces did you take up?" They said to him, "Twelve." [20] "And the seven for the four thousand, how many baskets full of broken pieces did you take up?" And they said to him, "Seven." [21] And he said to them, "Do you not yet understand?"

[a] Some witnesses read *the Herodians* (cf. Mark 3:6): $\mathfrak{P}^{45}$ W Θ f^1 f^{13} 28 *pc*

⇨ Mark 8:19
Cf. Mark 6:35–44 (§K29)

⇨ Mark 8:20
Cf. Mark 8:1–10 (§K37)

Jer 5:21 ⇨ Mark 8:18
[21] "Hear this, O foolish and senseless people,
    who have **eyes**, but **see not**,
    who have **ears**, but **hear not**."

Ezek 12:2 ⇨ Mark 8:18
[2] "Son of man, **you** dwell in the midst of a rebellious house, who have **eyes** to see, but **see not**, who have **ears** to hear, but **hear not**"; . . .

MATT

Matt 16:5–12 (§M54)

[5] When the disciples reached the other side, **they had forgotten to bring** any **bread**. [6] Jesus said to them, "**Take heed** and **beware of the leaven of the Pharisees and** Sadducees." [7] **And they discussed it** among themselves, **saying, "We** brought **no bread."** [8] But **Jesus, aware of** this, **said**, "O men of little faith, **why do you discuss** among yourselves **the fact that you have no bread?** [9] **Do you not yet perceive? Do you not remember the five loaves** of **the five thousand**, and **how many baskets you** gathered? [10] Or **the seven** loaves of **the four thousand**, and **how many baskets you** gathered? [11] How is it that you fail to **perceive** that I did not speak about **bread**? **Beware of the leaven of the Pharisees and** Sadducees." [12] Then they understood that he did not tell them to **beware of the leaven of** bread, but of the teaching **of the Pharisees and** Sadducees.

LUKE

Luke 12:1 ⇨ Mark 8:15

[1] In the meantime, when so many thousands of the multitude had gathered together that they trod upon one another, **he** began to say to his disciples first, "**Beware of the leaven of the Pharisees**, which is hypocrisy."

JOHN

John 6:32–35

[32] *Jesus then said to them,* "Truly, truly, I say to *you,* it was not Moses who gave *you* the *bread from heaven; my Father gives* **you** the *true bread from heaven.* [33] For the *bread* of God is that which comes down from heaven, and gives life to the world." [34] They said to *him,* "Lord, give us this bread always."

[35] *Jesus* **said to them,** "I am the bread of life; he who comes to me shall not hunger, and he who believes in me shall never thirst."

THOMAS

OTHER

MATT	MATT	LUKE

Mark 8:22–26 (§K40)

²² And they came to Bethsaida. And some people brought to him a blind man, and begged him to touch him. ²³ And he took the blind man by the hand, and led him out of the village; and when he had spit on his eyes and laid his hands upon him, he asked him, "Do you see anything?" ²⁴ And he looked up and said, "I see men; but they look like trees, walking." ²⁵ Then again he laid his hands upon his eyes; and he looked intently and was restored, and saw everything clearly. ²⁶ And he sent him away to his home, saying, "Do not even enter the village."

JOHN	THOMAS	OTHER

John 9:1–7 (§J19.1)

¹ As he passed by, he saw a **man blind** *from his birth. ² And his disciples asked him, "Rabbi, who sinned, this man or his parents, that he was born blind?" ³ Jesus answered, "It was not that this man sinned, or his parents, but that the works of God might be made manifest in him. ⁴ We must work the works of him who sent me, while it is day; night comes, when no one can work. ⁵ As long as I am in the world, I am the light of the world." ⁶ As he said this,* **he spat on** *the ground and made clay of the spittle and anointed the man's* **eyes** *with the clay, ⁷ saying to* **him,** *"Go, wash in the pool of Siloam" (which means Sent). So he went and washed and came back seeing.*

MARK

Mark 8:27–30 (§K41) °

²⁷ And Jesus went on with his disciples, to the villages of Caesarea Philippi; and on the way he asked his disciples, "Who do men say that I am?" ²⁸ And they told him, "John the Baptist; and others say, Elijah; and others one of the prophets." ²⁹ And he asked them, "But who do you say that I am?" Peter answered him, "You are the Christ." ³⁰ And he charged them to tell no one about him.

° Appendix 1 ⇨ Mark 8:27–28

MATT

Matt 16:13–20 (§M55)

¹³ Now when **Jesus** came into **the** district **of Caesarea Philippi, he** asked **his disciples,** "Who do men say that the Son of man is?" ¹⁴ And they said, "Some say **John the Baptist, others say Elijah, and others** Jeremiah or **one of the prophets.**" ¹⁵ **He** said to **them, "But who do you say that I am?**" ¹⁶ Simon **Peter** replied, "**You are the Christ,** the Son of the living God." ¹⁷ **And** Jesus answered him, "Blessed are you, Simon Bar-Jona! For flesh and blood has not revealed this to you, but my Father who is in heaven. ¹⁸ And I tell you, you are Peter, and on this rock I will build my church, and the powers of death shall not prevail against it. ¹⁹ I will give you the keys of the kingdom of heaven, and whatever you bind on earth shall be bound in heaven, and whatever you loose on earth shall be loosed in heaven." ²⁰ Then **he** strictly **charged** the disciples **to tell no one** that he was **the Christ.**

LUKE

Luke 9:18–22 (§L40.1)

¹⁸ Now it happened that as he was praying alone the **disciples** were with him; and **he** asked them, "**Who do** the people **say that I am?**" ¹⁹ **And they** answered, "**John the Baptist;** but **others say, Elijah; and others,** that **one of the** old **prophets** has risen." ²⁰ **And he** said to them, "**But who do you say that I am?**" And **Peter answered,** "**The Christ** of God." ²¹ But **he charged** and commanded **them to tell** this to **no one,** ²² saying, "The Son of man must suffer many things, and be rejected by the elders and chief priests and scribes, and be killed, and on the third day be raised."

JOHN

John 1:49 ⇨ Mark 8:29
⁴⁹ *Nathanael* **answered** *him, "Rabbi,* **you are** *the Son of God!* **You are the king of Israel!"**

John 6:68–69 ⇨ Mark 8:29
⁶⁸ *Simon* **Peter** *answered* **him,** *"Lord, to whom shall we go? You have the words of eternal life;* ⁶⁹ *and we have believed, and have come to know, that* **you are the** *Holy One of God."*

THOMAS

GThom 13

(13) Jesus said to **His disciples,** *"Compare me to someone and tell Me whom* **I am** *like."*

Simon **Peter** *said to* **Him,** *"***You are** *like a righteous angel."*

Matthew said to Him, "You are like a wise philosopher."

Thomas said to Him, "Master, my mouth is wholly incapable of saying whom You are like."

Jesus said, "I am not your master. Because you have drunk, you have become intoxicated from the bubbling spring which I have measured out."

And He took him and withdrew and told him three things. When Thomas returned to his companions, they asked him, "What did Jesus say to you?"

Thomas said to them, "If I tell you one of the things which he told me, you will pick up stones and throw them at me; a fire will come out of the stones and burn you up."

OTHER

MARK	MATT	LUKE

MARK

Mark 8:31–33 (§K42)

[31] And he began to teach them that the Son of man must suffer many things, and be rejected by the elders and the chief priests and the scribes, and be killed, and after three days rise again. [32] And he said this plainly. And Peter took him, and began to rebuke him. [33] But turning and seeing his disciples, he rebuked Peter, and said, "Get behind me, Satan! For you are not on the side of God, but of men."

Mark 9:30–32 (§K46)

[30] They went on from there and passed through Galilee. And he would not have any one know it; [31] for **he** was teaching his disciples, saying to **them**, "The Son of man will be delivered into the hands of men, and they will kill him; **and** when he is killed, **after three days** he will **rise**." [32] But they did not understand the saying, and they were afraid to ask him.

Mark 10:32–34 (§K54)

[32] And they were on the road, going up to Jerusalem, and Jesus was walking ahead of them; and they were amazed, and those who followed were afraid. **And** taking the twelve again, **he began to** tell **them what** was to happen to him, [33] saying, "Behold, we are going up to Jerusalem; and **the Son of man** will be delivered to **the chief priests and the scribes**, and they will condemn him to death, and deliver him to the Gentiles; [34] and they will mock him, and spit upon him, and scourge him, **and** kill **him**; **and after three days** he will **rise**."

MATT

Matt 16:21–23 (§M56)

[21] From that time Jesus **began to** show his disciples that he must go to Jerusalem and **suffer many things** from **the elders and chief priests and scribes, and be killed, and** on the third day be raised. [22] **And Peter took him and began to rebuke him**, saying, "God forbid, Lord! This shall never happen to you." [23] **But** he turned **and said** to **Peter, "Get behind me, Satan! You are** a hindrance to me; **for you are not on the side of God, but of men."**

Matt 17:22–23 (§M60)

[22] As they were gathering in Galilee, Jesus said to **them, "The Son of man** is to **be** delivered into the hands of men, [23] **and they** will kill him, **and** he will be raised on the third day." **And** they were greatly distressed.

Matt 20:17–19 (§M68)

[17] **And** as Jesus was going up to Jerusalem, **he** took the twelve disciples aside, and on the way **he** said to **them**, [18] "Behold, we are going up to Jerusalem; and **the Son of man** will **be** delivered to **the chief priests and scribes, and** they will condemn him to death, [19] and deliver him to the Gentiles to be mocked and scourged and crucified, **and** he will be raised on the third day."

LUKE

Luke 9:18–22 (§L40.1)

[18] Now it happened that as he was praying alone the disciples were with him; and he asked them, "Who do the people say that I am?" [19] And they answered, "John the Baptist; but others say, Elijah; and others, that one of the old prophets has risen." [20] And he said to them, "But who do you say that I am?" And Peter answered, "The Christ of God." [21] But he charged and commanded them to tell this to no one, [22] saying, "**The Son of man must suffer many things, and be rejected by the elders and chief priests and scribes, and be killed, and** on the third day be raised."

Luke 9:43b–45 (§L43.1)

But while they were all marveling at everything he did, **he** said to his disciples, [44] "Let these words sink into your ears; for **the Son of man** is to **be** delivered into the hands of men." [45] But they did not understand this saying, and it was concealed from them, that they should not perceive it; and they were afraid to ask him about this saying.

Luke 18:31–34 (§L78)

[31] **And** taking the twelve, **he** said to **them**, "Behold, we are going up to Jerusalem, and everything that is written of **the Son of man** by the prophets will be accomplished. [32] For he will **be** delivered to the Gentiles, **and** will **be** mocked and shamefully treated and spit upon; [33] they will scourge him **and** kill him, **and** on the third day he will **rise**." [34] But they understood none of these things; this saying was hid from them, and they did not grasp what was said.

JOHN	THOMAS	OTHER

OTHER

ApocJa 5:31–6:11

"Scorn death, therefore, and take concern for life. Remember my cross and my death and you will [35] live."

And I answered and said to him: "Lord, do not mention to us the cross and the death, for they are far from you."

The Lord answered and said: "Truly I say to you, none will be saved unless they believe in my cross. [5] [But] those who have believed in my cross, theirs is the Kingdom of God. Therefore, become seekers for death, just as the dead who seek for life, [10] for that for which they seek is revealed to them."

MARK

Mark 8:34–9:1 (§K43)

[34] And he called to him the multitude with his disciples, and said to them, "If any man would come after me, let him deny himself and take up his cross and follow me. [35] For whoever would save his life will lose it; and whoever loses his life for my sake and the gospel's will save it. [36] For what does it profit a man, to gain the whole world and forfeit his life? [37] For what can a man give in return for his life? [38] For whoever is ashamed of me and of my words in this adulterous and sinful generation, of him will the Son of man also be ashamed, when he comes in the glory of his Father with the holy angels." 9 [1] And he said to them, "Truly, I say to you, there are some standing here who will not taste death before they see that the kingdom of God has come with power."

MATT

Matt 16:24–28 (§M57)

[24] Then Jesus told **his disciples**, "If any man would come after me, let him deny himself and take up his cross and follow me. [25] For whoever would save his life will lose it, and whoever loses his life for my sake will find it. [26] For what will it profit a man, if he gains the whole world and forfeits his life? Or what shall a man give in return for his life? [27] For the Son of man is to come with his angels in the glory of his Father, and then he will repay every man for what he has done. [28] Truly, I say to you, there are some standing here who will not taste death before they see the Son of man coming in his kingdom."

Matt 10:38–39 ⇨ Mark 8:34–35

[38] "and he who does not take his cross and follow me is not worthy of me. [39] He who finds his life will lose it, and he who loses his life for my sake will find it."

Matt 10:33 ⇨ Mark 8:38

[33] "but whoever denies me before men, I also will deny before my Father who is in heaven."

LUKE

Luke 9:23–27 (§L40.2)

[23] And he said to all, "If any man would come after me, let him deny himself and take up his cross daily and follow me. [24] For whoever would save his life will lose it; and whoever loses his life for my sake, he will save it. [25] For what does it profit a man if he gains the whole world and loses or forfeits himself? [26] For whoever is ashamed of me and of my words, of him will the Son of man be ashamed when he comes in his glory and the glory of the Father and of the holy angels. [27] But I tell you truly, there are some standing here who will not taste death before they see the kingdom of God."

Luke 14:27 ⇨ Mark 8:34

[27] "Whoever does not bear his own cross and come after me, cannot be my disciple."

Luke 17:33 ⇨ Mark 8:35

[33] "Whoever seeks to gain his life will lose it, but whoever loses his life will preserve it."

Luke 12:9 ⇨ Mark 8:38

[9] "but he who denies me before men will be denied before the angels of God."

JOHN

John 12:25 ⇨ Mark 8:35

[25] "He who loves his life loses it, and he who hates his life in this world will keep it for eternal life."

THOMAS

GThom 55 ⇨ Mark 8:34

(55) Jesus said, "Whoever does not hate his father and his mother cannot become a disciple to Me. And whoever does not hate his brothers and sisters and take up his cross in My way will not be worthy of Me."

GThom 101 ⇨ Mark 8:34

(101) <Jesus said,> "Whoever does not hate his father and his mother as I do cannot become a disciple to Me. And whoever does [not] love his father and his mother as I do cannot become a [disciple] to Me. For My mother [gave me falsehood], but [My] true [Mother] gave me life."

OTHER

MARK

MATT

LUKE

Mark 9:2–8 (§K44.1)

[2] And after six days Jesus took with him Peter and James and John, and led them up a high mountain apart by themselves; and he was transfigured before them, [3] and his garments became glistening, intensely white, as no fuller on earth could bleach them. [4] And there appeared to them Elijah with Moses; and they were talking to Jesus. [5] And Peter said to Jesus, "Master,[a] it is well that we are here; let us make three booths, one for you and one for Moses and one for Elijah." [6] For he did not know what to say, for they were exceedingly afraid. [7] And a cloud overshadowed them, and a voice came out of the cloud, "This is my beloved Son;[b] listen to him." [8] And suddenly looking around they no longer saw any one with them but Jesus only.

[a] Or: *Rabbi*

[b] Or: *my Son, my* (or *the*) *Beloved*

Mark 1:10–11 ⇨ Mark 9:7
[10] *And when he came up out of the water, immediately he saw the heavens opened and the Spirit descending upon him like a dove;* [11] *and a voice came from heaven, "Thou art my beloved Son; with thee I am well pleased."*

Ps 2:7 ⇨ Mark 9:7
[7] I will tell of the decree of the Lord:
He said to me, "You are **my son**,
today I have begotten you."

Isa 42:1 ⇨ Mark 9:7
[1] Behold **my** servant, whom I uphold,
my chosen, in whom **my** soul delights;
I have put **my** Spirit upon **him**,
he will bring forth justice to the nations.

Matt 17:1–8 (§M58.1)

[1] And after six days Jesus took with him Peter and James and John his brother, and led them up a high mountain apart. [2] And he was transfigured before them, and his face shone like the sun, and his garments became white as light. [3] And behold, there appeared to them Moses and Elijah, talking with him. [4] And Peter said to Jesus, "Lord, it is well that we are here; if you wish, I will make three booths here, one for you and one for Moses and one for Elijah." [5] He was still speaking, when lo, a bright cloud overshadowed them, and a voice from the cloud said, "This is my beloved Son, with whom I am well pleased; listen to him." [6] When the disciples heard this, they fell on their faces, and were filled with awe. [7] But Jesus came and touched them, saying, "Rise, and have no fear." [8] And when they lifted up their eyes, they saw no one but Jesus only.

Matt 3:16–17 ⇨ Mark 9:7
[16] *And when Jesus was baptized, he went up immediately from the water, and behold, the heavens were opened and he saw the Spirit of God descending like a dove, and alighting on him;* [17] *and lo, a voice from heaven, saying, "This is my beloved Son, with whom I am well pleased."*

Luke 9:28–36 (§L41)

[28] Now about eight **days** after these sayings he **took with him** Peter and John and James, and went **up** on the **mountain** to pray. [29] **And** as he was praying, the appearance of his countenance was altered, **and his** raiment **became** dazzling **white**. [30] **And** behold, two men talked with him, **Moses and Elijah**, [31] who **appeared** in glory and spoke of his departure, which he was to accomplish at Jerusalem. [32] Now Peter and those who were with him were heavy with sleep, and when they wakened they saw his glory and the two men who stood with him. [33] And as the men were parting from him, **Peter said to Jesus, "Master, it is well that we are here; let us make three booths, one for you and one for Moses and one for Elijah"**—not knowing **what** he said. [34] As he said this, **a cloud** came **and overshadowed them**; and **they were afraid** as they entered the cloud. [35] **And a voice came out of the cloud,** saying, **"This is my Son, my** Chosen; **listen to him!"** [36] **And** when the voice had spoken, **Jesus** was found alone. And they kept silence and told no one in those days anything of what they had seen.

Luke 3:22 ⇨ Mark 9:7
[22] *and the Holy Spirit descended upon him in bodily form, as a dove, and a voice came from heaven, "Thou art my beloved Son; with thee I am well pleased."*

JOHN

THOMAS

OTHER

MARK

Mark 9:9–13 (§K44.2) °

⁹ And as they were coming down the mountain, he charged them to tell no one what they had seen, until the Son of man should have risen from the dead. ¹⁰ So they kept the matter to themselves, questioning what the rising from the dead meant. ¹¹ And they asked him, "Why do the scribes say that first Elijah must come?" ¹² And he said to them, "Elijah does come first to restore all things; and how is it written of the Son of man, that he should suffer many things and be treated with contempt? ¹³ But I tell you that Elijah has come, and they did to him whatever they pleased, as it is written of him."

°Appendix 1 ⇨ Mark 9:11–13

Mal 4:5–6 ⇨ Mark 9:11–12

⁵ "Behold, I will send you **Elijah** the prophet before the great and terrible day of the Lord comes. ⁶ And he will turn the hearts of fathers to their children and the hearts of children to their fathers, lest I come and smite the land with a curse."

1 Kgs 19:1–3, 9–10 ⇨ Mark 9:13

¹ Ahab told Jezebel all that **Elijah** had done, and how he had slain all the prophets with the sword. ² Then Jezebel sent a messenger to **Elijah**, saying, "So may the gods do to me, and more also, if I do not make your life as the life of one of them by this time tomorrow." ³ Then he was afraid, and he arose and went for his life, and came to Beersheba, which belongs to Judah, and left his servant there. . . .

⁹ And there he came to a cave, and lodged there; and behold, the word of the Lord came to him, and he said to him, "What are you doing here, **Elijah**?" ¹⁰ He said, "I have been very jealous for the Lord, the God of hosts; for the people of Israel have forsaken thy covenant, thrown down thy altars, and slain thy prophets with the sword; and I, even I only, am left; and they seek my life, to take it away."

MATT

Matt 17:9–13 (§M58.2)

⁹ And as they were coming down the mountain, Jesus commanded them, "Tell no one the vision, **until the Son of man** is raised from the dead." ¹⁰ And the disciples **asked** him, "Then **why do the scribes say that first Elijah must come?**" ¹¹ He replied, "Elijah does come, and he is **to restore all things;** ¹² but I tell you that Elijah has already **come, and they** did not know **him,** but **did to him whatever they pleased.** So also **the Son of man** will **suffer** at their hands." ¹³ Then the disciples understood that he was speaking to them of John the Baptist.

LUKE

JOHN

THOMAS

GThom 51 ⇨ Mark 9:13

(51) His disciples said to Him, "When will the repose of the dead come about, and when will the new world come?"

*He said to them, "What you look forward to **has already come,** but you do not recognize it."*

OTHER

MARK

HEALING OF A BOY

Mark 9:14–27 (§K45.1)

[14] And when they came to the disciples, they saw a great crowd about them, and scribes arguing with them. [15] And immediately all the crowd, when they saw him, were greatly amazed, and ran up to him and greeted him. [16] And he asked them, "What are you discussing with them?" [17] And one of the crowd answered him, "Teacher, I brought my son to you, for he has a dumb spirit; [18] and wherever it seizes him, it dashes him down; and he foams and grinds his teeth and becomes rigid; and I asked your disciples to cast it out, and they were not able." [19] And he answered them, "O faithless generation, how long am I to be with you? How long am I to bear with you? Bring him to me." [20] And they brought the boy to him; and when the spirit saw him, immediately it convulsed the boy, and he fell on the ground and rolled about, foaming at the mouth. [21] And Jesus[a] asked his father, "How long has he had this?" And he said, "From childhood. [22] And it has often cast him into the fire and into the water, to destroy him; but if you can do anything, have pity on us and help us." [23] And Jesus said to him, "If you can! All things are possible to him who believes." [24] Immediately the father of the child cried out[b] and said, "I believe; help my unbelief!" [25] And when Jesus saw that a crowd came running together, he rebuked the unclean spirit, saying to it, "You dumb and deaf spirit, I command you, come out of him, and never enter him again." [26] And after crying out and convulsing him terribly, it came out, and the boy was like a corpse; so that most of them said, "He is dead." [27] But Jesus took him by the hand and lifted him up, and he arose.

EXPLANATION OF DISCIPLES' FAILURE

Mark 9:28–29 (§K45.2)

[28] And when he had entered the house, his disciples asked him privately, "Why could we not cast it out?" [29] And he said to them, "This kind cannot be driven out by anything but prayer."[c]

[a] Greek: *he*

[b] Some witnesses add *with tears:* A[2] C[3] D K X Θ Π *f*[1] *f*[13] 33 *pm*

[c] Text: ℵ* B it (in part) *pc;* add *and fasting:* 𝔓[45] ℵ[b] A C D K L W X Δ Θ Π Ψ *f*[1] *f*[13] 28 33 *pm*

MATT

Matt 17:14–18 (§M59.1) ⇨ §K45.1

[14] And when they came to the crowd, a man came up to him and kneeling before him said, [15] "Lord, have mercy on my son, for he is an epileptic and he suffers terribly; for often he falls into the fire, and often into the water. [16] And I brought him to your disciples, and they could not heal him." [17] And Jesus answered, "O faithless and perverse generation, how long am I to be with you? How long am I to bear with you? Bring him here to me." [18] And Jesus rebuked him, and the demon came out of him, and the boy was cured instantly.

Matt 17:19–20 (§M59.2) ⇨ §K45.2

[19] Then the disciples came to Jesus privately and said, "Why could we not cast it out?" [20] He said to them, "Because of your little faith. For truly I say to you, if you have faith as a grain of mustard seed, you will say to this mountain, 'Move from here to there,' and it will move; and nothing will be impossible to you."

LUKE

Luke 9:37–43a (§L42) ⇨ §K45.1

[37] On the next day, when they had come down from the mountain, a great crowd met him. [38] And behold, a man from the crowd cried, "Teacher, I beg you to look upon my son, for he is my only child; [39] and behold, a spirit seizes him, and he suddenly cries out; it convulses him till he foams, and shatters him, and will hardly leave him. [40] And I begged your disciples to cast it out, but they could not." [41] Jesus answered, "O faithless and perverse generation, how long am I to be with you and bear with you? Bring your son here." [42] While he was coming, the demon tore him and convulsed him. But Jesus rebuked the unclean spirit, and healed the boy, and gave him back to his father. [43] And all were astonished at the majesty of God.

JOHN

THOMAS

OTHER

MARK

Mark 9:30–32 (§K46)
[30] They went on from there and passed through Galilee. And he would not have any one know it; [31] for he was teaching his disciples, saying to them, "The Son of man will be delivered into the hands of men, and they will kill him; and when he is killed, after three days he will rise." [32] But they did not understand the saying, and they were afraid to ask him.

Mark 8:31–33 (§K42)
[31] And he began to teach them that the Son of man must suffer many things, and be rejected by the elders and the chief priests and the scribes, and be killed, and after three days rise again. [32] And he said this plainly. And Peter took him, and began to rebuke him. [33] But turning and seeing his disciples, he rebuked Peter, and said, "Get behind me, Satan! For you are not on the side of God, but of men."

Mark 10:32–34 (§K54)
[32] And they were on the road, going up to Jerusalem, and Jesus was walking ahead of them; and they were amazed, and those who followed were afraid. And taking the twelve again, he began to tell them what was to happen to him, [33] saying, "Behold, we are going up to Jerusalem; and the Son of man will be delivered to the chief priests and the scribes, and they will condemn him to death, and deliver him to the Gentiles; [34] and they will mock him, and spit upon him, and scourge him, and kill him; and after three days he will rise."

MATT

Matt 17:22–23 (§M60)
[22] As they were gathering in Galilee, Jesus said to them, "The Son of man is to be delivered into the hands of men, [23] and they will kill him, and he will be raised on the third day." And they were greatly distressed.

Matt 16:21–23 (§M56)
[21] From that time Jesus began to show his disciples that he must go to Jerusalem and suffer many things from the elders and chief priests and scribes, and be killed, and on the third day be raised. [22] And Peter took him and began to rebuke him, saying, "God forbid, Lord! This shall never happen to you." [23] But he turned and said to Peter, "Get behind me, Satan! You are a hindrance to me; for you are not on the side of God, but of men."

Matt 20:17–19 (§M68)
[17] And as Jesus was going up to Jerusalem, he took the twelve disciples aside, and on the way he said to them, [18] "Behold, we are going up to Jerusalem; and the Son of man will be delivered to the chief priests and scribes, and they will condemn him to death, [19] and deliver him to the Gentiles to be mocked and scourged and crucified, and he will be raised on the third day."

LUKE

Luke 9:43b–45 (§L43.1)
But while they were all marveling at everything he did, he said to his disciples, [44] "Let these words sink into your ears; for the Son of man is to be delivered into the hands of men." [45] But they did not understand this saying, and it was concealed from them, that they should not perceive it; and they were afraid to ask him about this saying.

Luke 9:18–22 (§L40.1)
[18] Now it happened that as he was praying alone the disciples were with him; and he asked them, "Who do the people say that I am?" [19] And they answered, "John the Baptist; but others say, Elijah; and others, that one of the old prophets has risen." [20] And he said to them, "But who do you say that I am?" And Peter answered, "The Christ of God." [21] But he charged and commanded them to tell this to no one, [22] saying, "The Son of man must suffer many things, and be rejected by the elders and chief priests and scribes, and be killed, and on the third day be raised."

Luke 18:31–34 (§L78)
[31] And taking the twelve, he said to them, "Behold, we are going up to Jerusalem, and everything that is written of the Son of man by the prophets will be accomplished. [32] For he will be delivered to the Gentiles, and will be mocked and shamefully treated and spit upon; [33] they will scourge him and kill him, and on the third day he will rise." [34] But they understood none of these things; this saying was hid from them, and they did not grasp what was said.

JOHN

John 7:1 ⇨ Mark 9:30
[1] *After this Jesus went about in Galilee; he would not go about in Judea, because the Jews sought to kill him.*

THOMAS

OTHER

MARK	MATT	LUKE

MARK

Mark 9:33–37 (§K47) °

[33] And they came to Capernaum; and when he was in the house he asked them, "What were you discussing on the way?" [34] But they were silent; for on the way they had discussed with one another who was the greatest. [35] And he sat down and called the twelve; and he said to them, "If any one would be first, he must be last of all and servant of all." [36] And he took a child, and put him in the midst of them; and taking him in his arms, he said to them, [37] "Whoever receives one such child in my name receives me; and whoever receives me, receives not me but him who sent me."

°Appendix 2 ⇨ §K47

Mark 10:41–45 (§K56.2) ⇨ Mark 9:35

[41] And when the ten heard it, they began to be indignant at James and John. [42] And Jesus called them to him and said to them, "You know that those who are supposed to rule over the Gentiles lord it over them, and their great men exercise authority over them. [43] But it shall not be so among you; but whoever would be great among you must be your servant, [44] and whoever would be first among you must be slave of all. [45] For the Son of man also came not to be served but to serve, and to give his life as a ransom for many."

Mark 10:13–16 (§K52) ⇨ Mark 9:36–37

[13] And they were bringing children to him, that he might touch them; [13] and the disciples rebuked them. [14] But when Jesus saw it he was indignant, and said to them, "Let the children come to me, do not hinder them; for to such belongs the kingdom of God. [15] Truly, I say to you, whoever does not receive the kingdom of God like a child shall not enter it." [16] And he took them in his arms and blessed them, laying his hands upon them.

JOHN

John 12:44–45 ⇨ Mark 9:37

[44] And Jesus cried out and said, "He who believes in me, believes not in me but in him who sent me. [45] And he who sees me sees him who sent me."

John 13:20 ⇨ Mark 9:37

[20] "Truly, truly, I say to you, he who receives any one whom I send receives me; and he who receives me receives him who sent me."

MATT

Matt 18:1–10 (§M62.1)

[1] At that time the disciples came to Jesus, saying, "Who is the greatest in the kingdom of heaven? [2] And calling to him a child, he put him in the midst of them, [3] and said, "Truly, I say to you, unless you turn and become like children, you will never enter the kingdom of heaven. [4] Whoever humbles himself like this child, he is the greatest in the kingdom of heaven.

[5] "Whoever receives one such child in my name receives me; [6] but whoever causes one of these little ones who believe in me to sin, it would be better for him to have a great millstone fastened round his neck and to be drowned in the depth of the sea. [7] "Woe to the world for temptations to sin! For it is necessary that temptations come, but woe to the man by whom the temptation comes! [8] And if your hand or your foot causes you to sin, cut it off and throw it away; it is better for you to enter life maimed or lame than with two hands or two feet to be thrown into the eternal fire. [9] And if your eye causes you to sin, pluck it out and throw it away; it is better for you to enter life with one eye than with two eyes to be thrown into the hell of fire.

[10] "See that you do not despise one of these little ones; for I tell you that in heaven their angels always behold the face of my Father who is in heaven."

Matt 20:24–28 (§M69.2) ⇨ Mark 9:35

[24] And when the ten heard it, they were indignant at the two brothers. [25] But Jesus called them to him and said, "You know that the rulers of the Gentiles lord it over them, and their great men exercise authority over them. [26] It shall not be so among you; but whoever would be great among you must be your servant, [27] and whoever would be first among you must be your slave; [28] even as the Son of man came not to be served but to serve, and to give his life as a ransom for many."

Matt 23:11–12 ⇨ Mark 9:35

[11] "He who is greatest among you shall be your servant; [12] whoever exalts himself will be humbled, and whoever humbles himself will be exalted."

Matt 10:40 ⇨ Mark 9:37

[40] "He who receives you receives me, and he who receives me receives him who sent me."

THOMAS

GThom 12 ⇨ Mark 9:34

(12) The disciples said to Jesus, "We know that You will depart from us. Who is to be our leader?"

Jesus said to them, "Wherever you are, you are to go to James the righteous, for whose sake heaven and earth came into being."

LUKE

Luke 9:46–50 (§L43.2)

[46] And an argument arose among them as to which of them was the greatest. [47] But when Jesus perceived the thought of their hearts, he took a child and put him by his side, [48] and said to them, "Whoever receives this child in my name receives me, and whoever receives me receives him who sent me; for he who is least among you all is the one who is great."

[49] John answered, "Master, we saw a man casting out demons in your name, and we forbade him, because he does not follow with us." [50] But Jesus said to him, "Do not forbid him; for he that is not against you is for you."

Luke 22:24–30 (§L93.3) ⇨ Mark 9:35

[24] A dispute also arose among them, which of them was to be regarded as the greatest. [25] And he said to them, "The kings of the Gentiles exercise lordship over them; and those in authority over them are called benefactors. [26] But not so with you; rather let the greatest among you become as the youngest, and the leader as one who serves. [27] For which is the greater, one who sits at table, or one who serves? Is it not the one who sits at table? But I am among you as one who serves.

[28] "You are those who have continued with me in my trials; [29] and I assign to you, as my Father assigned to me, a kingdom, [30] that you may eat and drink at my table in my kingdom, and sit on thrones judging the twelve tribes of Israel."

Luke 18:15–17 (§L76) ⇨ Mark 9:36–37

[15] Now they were bringing even infants to him that he might touch them; and when the disciples saw it, they rebuked them. [16] But Jesus called them to him, saying, "Let the children come to me, and do not hinder them; for to such belongs the kingdom of God. [17] Truly, I say to you, whoever does not receive the kingdom of God like a child shall not enter it."

Luke 10:16 ⇨ Mark 9:37

[16] "He who hears you hears me, and he who rejects you rejects me, and he who rejects me rejects him who sent me."

OTHER

MARK

Mark 9:38–41 (§K48)

[38] John said to him, "Teacher, we saw a man casting out demons in your name, and we forbade him, because he was not following us." [39] But Jesus said, "Do not forbid him; for no one who does a mighty work in my name will be able soon after to speak evil of me. [40] For he that is not against us is for us. [41] For truly, I say to you, whoever gives you a cup of water to drink because you bear the name of Christ, will by no means lose his reward."

MATT

Matt 12:30 ⇨ Mark 9:40

[30] "**He** who **is not** with me **is** against me, and he who does **not** gather with me scatters."

Matt 10:42 ⇨ Mark 9:41

[42] "And **whoever gives** to one of these little ones even **a cup of** cold **water because** he is a disciple, **truly, I say to you,** he shall not **lose his reward.**"

LUKE

Luke 9:46–50 (§L43.2)

[46] And an argument arose among them as to which of them was the greatest. [47] But when Jesus perceived the thought of their hearts, he took a child and put him by his side, [48] and said to them, "Whoever receives this child in my name receives me, and whoever receives me receives him who sent me; for he who is least among you all is the one who is great." [49] John answered, "Master, **we saw a man casting out demons in your name, and we forbade him, because he** does **not** follow with **us**." [50] But Jesus said to him, "**Do not forbid him; for he that is not against** you **is for** you."

Luke 11:23 ⇨ Mark 9:40

[23] "**He** who **is not** with me **is** against me, and he who does **not** gather with me scatters."

JOHN

THOMAS

OTHER

POxy1224 2 ⇨ Mark 9:40

(2) And pray for your enemies. **For he** who **is not [against** you] **is for** you. [He who today] is far-off—tomorrow will be [near to you]. . . .

MARK	MATT	LUKE

Mark 9:42–50 (§K49)

[42] "Whoever causes one of these little ones who believe in me to sin,[a] it would be better for him if a great millstone were hung round his neck and he were thrown into the sea. [43] And if your hand causes you to sin,[a] cut it off; it is better for you to enter life maimed than with two hands to go to hell,[b] to the unquenchable fire.[c] [45] And if your foot causes you to sin,[a] cut it off; it is better for you to enter life lame than with two feet to be thrown into hell.[b][d] [47] And if your eye causes you to sin,[a] pluck it out; it is better for you to enter the kingdom of God with one eye than with two eyes to be thrown into hell, [48] where their worm does not die, and the fire is not quenched. [49] For every one will be salted with fire.[e] [50] Salt is good; but if the salt has lost its saltness, how will you season it? Have salt in yourselves, and be at peace with one another."

[a] Greek: *stumble*

[b] Greek: *Gehenna*

[c] Omit v. 44: ℵ B C L W Δ Ψ *f*[1] 28 *pc;* include v. 44 (identical with v. 48) (cf. Isa 66:24): A D K X Θ Π *f*[13] *al*

[d] Omit v. 46: ℵ B C L W Δ Ψ *f*[1] 28 *pc;* include v. 46 (identical with v. 48) (cf. Isa 66:24): A D K X Θ Π *f*[13] *al*

[e] Some witnesses add *and every sacrifice will be salted with salt:* A C K X Θ Π Ψ 28[c] *pm;* text: ℵ B L W Δ *f*[1] *f*[13] 28★ *pc*

Isa 66:24 ⇨ Mark 9:48

[24] "And they shall go forth and look on the dead bodies of the men that have rebelled against me; for **their worm** shall **not die**, their **fire** shall **not** be **quenched**, and they shall be an abhorrence to all flesh."

Lev 2:13 ⇨ Mark 9:49

[13] "You shall season all your cereal offerings with salt; you shall not let the salt of the covenant with your God be lacking from your cereal offering; with all your offerings you shall offer salt."

Matt 18:1–10 (§M62.1)

[1] At that time the disciples came to Jesus, saying, "Who is the greatest in the kingdom of heaven? [2] And calling to him a child, he put him in the midst of them, [3] and said, "Truly, I say to you, unless you turn and become like children, you will never enter the kingdom of heaven. [4] Whoever humbles himself like this child, he is the greatest in the kingdom of heaven.

[5] "Whoever receives one such child in my name receives me; [6] but **whoever causes one of these little ones who believe in me to sin**, **it would be better for him** to have **a great millstone** fastened **round his neck and** to be drowned in the depth of **the sea.**

[7] "Woe to the world for temptations to sin! For it is necessary that temptations come, but woe to the man by whom the temptation comes! [8] **And if your hand** or **your foot causes you to sin, cut it off** and throw it away; **it is better for you to enter life maimed** or **lame than with two hands** or **two feet to be thrown into** the eternal fire. [9] **And if your eye causes you to sin, pluck it out** and throw it away; **it is better for you to enter** life **with one eye than with two eyes to be thrown into** the **hell** of fire.

[10] "See that you do not despise one of these little ones; for I tell you that in heaven their angels always behold the face of my Father who is in heaven."

Matt 5:29–30 ⇨ Mark 9:43–47

[29] "**If your right eye causes you to sin, pluck it out** and throw it away; **it is better** that **you** lose **one** of your members than that your whole **body be thrown into hell**. [30] **And if your** right **hand causes you to sin, cut it off** and throw it away; **it is better** that **you** lose one of your members **than** that your whole **body go into hell.**"

Matt 5:13 ⇨ Mark 9:50

[13] "You are the **salt** of the earth; **but if salt has lost its** taste, **how** shall its **saltness** be restored? It is no longer good for anything except to be thrown out and trodden under foot by men."

Luke 17:1–4 (§L70.1) ⇨ Mark 9:42

[1] And he said to his disciples, "Temptations to sin are sure to come; but woe to him by whom they come! [2] **It would be better for him if a millstone were hung round his neck and he were** cast **into the sea**, than that he should cause **one of these little ones to sin**. [3] Take heed to yourselves; if your brother sins, rebuke him, and if he repents, forgive him; [4] and if he sins against you seven times in the day, and turns to you seven times, and says, 'I repent,' you must forgive him."

Luke 14:34–35 ⇨ Mark 9:50

[34] "**Salt is good; but if salt has lost its taste, how** shall **its saltness** be restored? [35] It is fit neither for the land nor for the dunghill; men throw it away. He who has ears to hear, let him hear."

JOHN	THOMAS	OTHER

MARK	MATT	LUKE

Mark 10:1 (§K50) °
¹ And he left there and went to the region of Judea and beyond the Jordan, and crowds gathered to him again; and again, as his custom was, he taught them.

°Appendix 3 ⇨ §K50

Matt 19:1–2 (§M64)
¹ Now when Jesus had finished these sayings, **he went** away from Galilee and entered **the region of Judea beyond the Jordan;** ² **and** large **crowds** followed **him**, and **he** healed **them** there.

JOHN	THOMAS	OTHER

MARK	MATT	LUKE

QUESTION OF DIVORCE

Mark 10:2–9 (§K51.1)

[2] And Pharisees came up and in order to test him asked, "Is it lawful for a man to divorce his wife?" [3] He answered them, "What did Moses command you?" [4] They said, "Moses allowed a man to write a certificate of divorce, and to put her away." [5] But Jesus said to them, "For your hardness of heart he wrote you this commandment. [6] But from the beginning of creation, 'God made them male and female.' [7] 'For this reason a man shall leave his father and mother and be joined to his wife.[a] [8] and the two shall become one flesh.' So they are no longer two but one flesh. [9] What therefore God has joined together, let not man put asunder."

EXPLANATION FOR THE DISCIPLES

Mark 10:10–12 (§K51.2)

[10] And in the house the disciples asked him again about this matter. [11] And he said to them, "Whoever divorces his wife and marries another, commits adultery against her; [12] and if she divorces her husband and marries another, she commits adultery."

[a] A few witnesses omit *and be joined to his wife:* א B Ψ *pc*

Deut 24:1–4 ⇨ Mark 10:4

[1] "When a man takes a wife and marries her, if then she finds no favor in his eyes because he has found some indecency in her, and he writes her a bill of divorce and puts it in her hand and sends her out of his house, and she departs out of his house, [2] and if she goes and becomes another man's wife, [3] and the latter husband dislikes her and writes her a bill of divorce and puts it in her hand and sends her out of his house, or if the latter husband dies, who took her to be his wife, [4] then her former husband, who sent her away, may not take her again to be his wife, after she has been defiled; for that is an abomination before the Lord, and you shall not bring guilt upon the land which the Lord your God gives you for an inheritance."

Gen 1:27 ⇨ Mark 10:6

[27] So God created man in his own image, in the image of God he created him; male and female he created them.

Gen 2:24 ⇨ Mark 10:7–8

[24] Therefore a man leaves his father and his mother and cleaves to his wife, and they become one flesh.

Matt 19:3–9 (§M65.1)

[3] And Pharisees came up to him and tested him by asking, "Is it lawful to divorce one's wife for any cause?" [4] He answered, "Have you not read that he who made them from the beginning made them male and female, [5] and said, 'For this reason a man shall leave his father and mother and be joined to his wife, and the two shall become one flesh'? [6] So they are no longer two but one flesh. What therefore God has joined together, let not man put asunder." [7] They said to him, "Why then did Moses command one to give a certificate of divorce, and to put her away?" [8] He said to them, "For your hardness of heart Moses allowed you to divorce your wives, but from the beginning it was not so. [9] And I say to you: whoever divorces his wife, except for unchastity, and marries another, commits adultery."

Matt 5:31–32 (§M12.5c) ⇨ §K51.2

[31] "It was also said, 'Whoever divorces his wife, let him give her a certificate of divorce.' [32] But I say to you that every one who divorces his wife, except on the ground of unchastity, makes her an adultress; and whoever marries a divorced woman commits adultery."

Luke 16:18 (§L68.2) ⇨ §K51.2

[18] "Every one who divorces his wife and marries another commits adultery, and he who marries a woman divorced from her husband commits adultery."

JOHN	THOMAS	OTHER

1 Cor 7:10–11 ⇨ Mark 10:6

[10] To the married I give charge, not I but the Lord, that the wife should not separate from her husband [11] (but if she does, let her remain single or else be reconciled to her husband)—and that the husband should not divorce his wife.

MARK

Mark 10:13–16 (§K52)

[13] And they were bringing children to him, that he might touch them; and the disciples rebuked them. [14] But when Jesus saw it he was indignant, and said to them, "Let the children come to me, do not hinder them; for to such belongs the kingdom of God. [15] Truly, I say to you, whoever does not receive the kingdom of God like a child shall not enter it." [16] And he took them in his arms and blessed them, laying his hands upon them.

MATT

Matt 19:13–15 (§M66)

[13] Then **children** were brought **to him that** he might lay his hands on **them** and pray. **The disciples rebuked** the people; [14] but **Jesus said, "Let the children come to me, and do not hinder them; for to such belongs the kingdom** of heaven." [15] And he laid **his hands** on **them** and went away.

Matt 18:3 ⇨ Mark 10:15

[3] and said, **"Truly, I say to you,** unless **you** turn and become **like** children, **you** will never **enter the kingdom of** heaven."

LUKE

Luke 18:15–17 (§L76)

[15] Now **they were** bringing even infants **to him that he might touch them; and** when **the disciples** saw it, they **rebuked them.** [16] But **Jesus** called them to him, saying, **"Let the children come to me, and do not hinder them; for to such belongs the kingdom of God.** [17] Truly, I say to you, whoever does not receive the kingdom of God like a child shall not enter it."

JOHN

John 3:3–5 ⇨ Mark 10:15

[3] Jesus answered him, "Truly, truly, I say to you, unless one is born anew, he cannot see the kingdom of God." [4] Nicodemus said to him, "How can a man be born when he is old? Can he enter a second time into his mother's womb and be born?" [5] Jesus answered, "Truly, truly, I say to you, unless one is born of water and the Spirit, he cannot enter the kingdom of God."

THOMAS

GThom 22

(22) Jesus saw infants being suckled. He said to His disciples, "These infants being suckled are like those who enter the Kingdom."

They said to Him, "Shall we then, as children, enter the Kingdom?"

Jesus said to them, "When you make the two one, and when you make the inside like the outside and the outside like the inside, and the above like the below, and when you make the male and the female one and the same, so that the male not be male nor the female female; and when you fashion eyes in place of an eye, and a hand in place of a hand, and a foot in place of a foot, and a likeness in place of a likeness; then will you enter [the Kingdom]."

OTHER

MARK	MATT	LUKE

MARK

RICH MAN

Mark 10:17–22 (§K53.1)

[17] And as he was setting out on his journey, a man ran up and knelt before him, and asked him, "Good Teacher, what must I do to inherit eternal life?" [18] And Jesus said to him, "Why do you call me good? No one is good but God alone. [19] You know the commandments: 'Do not kill, Do not commit adultery, Do not steal, Do not bear false witness, Do not defraud, Honor your father and mother.'" [20] And he said to him, "Teacher, all these I have observed from my youth." [21] And Jesus looking upon him loved him, and said to him, "You lack one thing; go, sell what you have, and give to the poor, and you will have treasure in heaven; and come, follow me." [22] At that saying his countenance fell, and he went away sorrowful; for he had great possessions.

DANGER OF RICHES

Mark 10:23–31 (§K53.2)

[23] And Jesus looked around and said to his disciples, "How hard it will be for those who have riches to enter the kingdom of God!" [24] And the disciples were amazed at his words. But Jesus said to them again, "Children, how hard it is[a] to enter the kingdom of God! [25] It is easier for a camel to go through the eye of a needle than for a rich man to enter the kingdom of God." [26] And they were exceedingly astonished, and said to him,[b] "Then who can be saved?" [27] Jesus looked at them and said, "With men it is impossible, but not with God; for all things are possible with God." [28] Peter began to say to him, "Lo, we have left everything and followed you." [29] Jesus said, "Truly, I say to you, there is no one who has left house or brothers or sisters or mother or father or children or lands, for my sake and for the gospel, [30] who will not receive a hundredfold now in this time, houses and brothers and sisters and mothers and children and lands, with persecutions, and in the age to come eternal life. [31] But many that are first will be last, and the last first."

[a] Some witnesses insert *for those who trust in riches:* A C D Θ *f*[1] *f*[13] *al*

[b] Some witnesses read *to one another:* A D W Θ *f*[1] *f*[13] it vg goth arm *al;* text: ℵ B C Δ Ψ 892 cop

Exod 20:12–16 ⇨ Mark 10:19
[12] "**Honor your father** and your **mother,** that your days may be long in the land which the Lord your God gives you.
[13] "You shall **not kill.**
[14] "You shall **not commit adultery.**
[15] "You shall **not steal.**
[16] "You shall **not bear false witness** against your neighbor."

Deut 5:16–20 ⇨ Mark 10:19
[16] "**Honor your father and** your **mother,** as the Lord your God commanded you; that your days may be prolonged, and that it may go well with you, in the land which the Lord your God gives you.
[17] "You shall **not kill.**
[18] "Neither shall you **commit adultery.**
[19] "Neither shall you **steal.**
[20] "Neither shall you **bear false witness** against your neighbor.'"

MATT

Matt 19:16–22 (§M67.1) ⇨ §K53.1

[16] And behold, one came **up** to him, saying, "**Teacher, what** good deed **must I do,** to have **eternal life?**" [17] And he said to him, "**Why do you ask me** about what is **good? One** there is who is **good.** If you would enter life, keep the **commandments.**" [18] He said to him, "**Which?**" And Jesus said, "You shall **not kill,** You shall **not commit adultery,** You shall **not steal,** You shall **not bear false witness,** [19] **Honor your father and mother,** and, You shall **love your neighbor as yourself.**" [20] The young man said to him, "**All these I have observed;** what do I still lack?" [21] Jesus said to him, "If you would be perfect, **go, sell what you possess and give to the poor, and you will have treasure in heaven; and come, follow me.**" [22] When the young man heard this **he went away sorrowful; for he had great possessions.**

Matt 19:23–30 (§M67.2) ⇨ §K53.2

[23] And Jesus said to his disciples, "Truly, I say to you, **it will be hard for** a rich man to **enter the kingdom** of heaven. [24] Again I tell you, **it is easier for a camel to go through the eye of a needle than for a rich man to enter the kingdom of God.**" [25] When the disciples heard this **they were** greatly astonished, saying, "**Who then can be saved?**" [26] But **Jesus looked at them and said to them, "With men** this is **impossible, but with God all things are possible.**" [27] Then **Peter** said in reply, "**Lo, we have left everything and followed you.** What then shall we have?" [28] **Jesus said to them,** "**Truly, I say to you,** in the new world, when the Son of man shall sit on his glorious throne, you who have followed me will also sit on twelve thrones, judging the twelve tribes of Israel. [29] And every **one who has left houses or brothers or sisters or father or mother or children or lands,** for my name's **sake, will receive a hundredfold,** and **inherit eternal life.** [30] **But many that are first will be last, and the last first.**"

Matt 20:16 ⇨ Mark 10:31
[16] "So **the last** will be **first,** and the **first last.**"

LUKE

Luke 18:18–25 (§L77.1)

[18] And a ruler **asked him, "Good Teacher, what** shall **I do to inherit eternal life?**" [19] And Jesus said to him, "**Why do you call me good?** No one is good but **God alone.** [20] You know the commandments: 'Do not **commit adultery,** Do not **kill,** Do not **steal,** Do not **bear false witness, Honor your father and mother.**'" [21] And he said, "**All these I have observed from my youth.**" [22] And when **Jesus** heard it, he said to him, "**One thing you** still **lack.** Sell all that you have and distribute to the poor, and you will have treasure in heaven; and **come, follow me.**" [23] But when he heard this he became sad, for he was very rich. [24] **Jesus** looking at him said, "**How hard it is for those who have riches to enter the kingdom of God!** [25] For **it is easier for a camel to go through the eye of a needle than for a rich man to enter the kingdom of God.**"

Luke 18:26–30 (§L77.2) ⇨ Mark 10:26–30

[26] Those who heard it **said, "Then who can be saved?**" [27] But he **said, "What is impossible with men is possible with God.**" [28] And **Peter** said, "**Lo, we have left** our homes **and followed you.**" [29] And he **said** to them, "**Truly, I say to you, there is no man who has left house** or wife or **brothers** or parents **or children, for the sake** of the kingdom of God, [30] **who will not receive** manifold more in this time, and **in the age to come eternal life.**"

Luke 13:30 ⇨ Mark 10:31
[30] "And behold, some are **last** who will be **first,** and some **are first** who **will be last.**"

JOHN	THOMAS	OTHER

THOMAS

GThom 81 ⇨ Mark 10:23

(81) Jesus said,"Let him who has grown rich be king, and let him who possesses power renounce it."

POxy654 4 ⇨ Mark 10:31

(4) [Jesus says,] "A ma[n full of d]ays will not hesitate to ask a ch[ild of seven da]ys about the place of [life and he will live.] For **many (that are) fi[rst] will be [last and] the last** will be **first** and they [will have eternal life]."

GThom 4 ⇨ Mark 10:31

(4) Jesus said, "The man old in days will not hesitate to ask a small child seven days old about the place of life, and he will live. For **many** who **are first will** become **last**, and they will become one and the same."

OTHER

GNaz 16 ⇨ §K53.1

(16) The other of the two rich men said to **him**: Master, **what** good thing **must I do** that I may live? He **said to him**: Man, fulfil the law and the prophets. He answered him: That **have I** done. He **said to him**: **Go** and **sell** all that thou possessest and distribute it among **the poor, and** then **come** and **follow me**. But the rich man then began to scratch his head and it (the **saying**) pleased him not. And the Lord said to him: How canst thou say, I have fulfilled the law and the prophets? For it stands written in the law: Love they neighbour as thyself; and behold, many of thy brethren, sons of Abraham, are begrimed with dirt and die of hunger—and thy house is full of many good things and nothing at all comes forth from it to them! And he turned **and said to** Simon, **his** disciple, who was sitting by him: Simon, son of Jona, **it is easier for a camel to go through the eye of a needle than for a rich man to enter into the kingdom of** heaven. (Origen, *Commentary on Matthew* 15:14 [on Matthew 19:16–30])

ApocJa 4:22–37 ⇨ Mark 10:28–30

And I answered and said to him: "Lord, we can obey you [25]if you wish. For we have forsaken our forefathers and our mothers and our villages and have followed you. Grant us, [therefore], [30]not to be tempted by the wicked devil."

The Lord answered and said: "What is your (pl.) merit when you do the will of the Father if it is not given to you by him [35]as a gift, while you are tempted by Satan?"

MARK	MATT	LUKE

MARK

Mark 10:32–34 (§K54) °

³² And they were on the road, going up to Jerusalem, and Jesus was walking ahead of them; and they were amazed, and those who followed were afraid. And taking the twelve again, he began to tell them what was to happen to him, ³³ saying, "Behold, we are going up to Jerusalem; and the Son of man will be delivered to the chief priests and the scribes, and they will condemn him to death, and deliver him to the Gentiles; ³⁴ and they will mock him, and spit upon him, and scourge him, and kill him; and after three days he will rise."

°Appendix 2 ⇨ §K54

Mark 8:31–33 (§K42)

³¹ And he began to teach them that the Son of man must suffer many things, and be rejected by the elders and the chief priests and the scribes, and be killed, and after three days rise again. ³² And he said this plainly. And Peter took him, and began to rebuke him. ³³ But turning and seeing his disciples, he rebuked Peter, and said, "Get behind me, Satan! For you are not on the side of God, but of men."

Mark 9:30–32 (§K46)

³⁰ They went on from there and passed through Galilee. And he would not have any one know it; ³¹ for he was teaching his disciples, saying to them, "The Son of man will be delivered into the hands of men, and they will kill him; and when he is killed, after three days he will rise." ³² But they did not understand the saying, and they were afraid to ask him.

JOHN

MATT

Matt 20:17–19 (§M68)

¹⁷ And as Jesus was going up to Jerusalem, he took the twelve disciples aside, and on the way he said to them, ¹⁸ "Behold, we are going up to Jerusalem; and the Son of man will be delivered to the chief priests and scribes, and they will condemn him to death, ¹⁹ and deliver him to the Gentiles to be mocked and scourged and crucified, and he will be raised on the third day."

Matt 16:21–23 (§M56)

²¹ From that time Jesus began to show his disciples that he must go to Jerusalem and suffer many things from the elders and chief priests and scribes, and be killed, and on the third day be raised. ²² And Peter took him and began to rebuke him, saying, "God forbid, Lord! This shall never happen to you." ²³ But he turned and said to Peter, "Get behind me, Satan! You are a hindrance to me; for you are not on the side of God, but of men."

Matt 17:22–23 (§60)

²² As they were gathering in Galilee, Jesus said to them, "The Son of man is to be delivered into the hands of men, ²³ and they will kill him, and he will be raised on the third day." And they were greatly distressed.

THOMAS

LUKE

Luke 18:31–34 (§L78)

³¹ And taking the twelve, he said to them, "Behold, we are going up to Jerusalem, and everything that is written of the Son of man by the prophets will be accomplished. ³² For he will be delivered to the Gentiles, and will be mocked and shamefully treated and spit upon; ³³ they will scourge him and kill him, and on the third day he will rise." ³⁴ But they understood none of these things; this saying was hid from them, and they did not grasp what was said.

Luke 9:18–22 (§L40.1)

¹⁸ Now it happened that as he was praying alone the disciples were with him; and he asked them, "Who do the people say that I am?" ¹⁹ And they answered, "John the Baptist; but others say, Elijah; and others, that one of the old prophets has risen." ²⁰ And he said to them, "But who do you say that I am?" And Peter answered, "The Christ of God." ²¹ But he charged and commanded them to tell this to no one, ²² saying, "The Son of man must suffer many things, and be rejected by the elders and chief priests and scribes, and be killed, and on the third day be raised."

Luke 9:43b–45 (§L43.1)

But while they were all marveling at everything he did, he said to his disciples, ⁴⁴ "Let these words sink into your ears; for the Son of man is to be delivered into the hands of men." ⁴⁵ But they did not understand this saying, and it was concealed from them, that they should not perceive it; and they were afraid to ask him about this saying.

OTHER

SecMk 1 (follows on Mark 10:34)

"And they come into Bethany. And a certain woman whose brother had died was there. And, coming, she prostrated herself before Jesus and says to him, 'Son of David, have mercy on me.' But the disciples rebuked her. And Jesus, being angered, went off with her into the garden where the tomb was, and straightway a great cry was heard from the tomb. And going near Jesus rolled away the stone from the door of the tomb. And straightway, going in where the youth was, he stretched forth his hand and raised him, seizing his hand. But the youth, looking upon him, loved him and began to beseech him that he might be with him. And going out of the tomb they came into the house of the youth, for he was rich. And after six days Jesus told him what to do and in the evening the youth comes to him, wearing a linen cloth over his naked body. And he remained with him that night, for Jesus taught him the mystery of the kingdom of God. And thence, arising, he returned to the other side of the Jordan."

MARK	MATT	LUKE

MARK

REQUESTS FOR POSITIONS OF HONOR

Mark 10:35–40 (§K55.1)

³⁵ And James and John, the sons of Zebedee, came forward to him, and said to him, "Teacher, we want you to do for us whatever we ask of you." ³⁶ And he said to them, "What do you want me to do for you?" ³⁷ And they said to him, "Grant us to sit, one at your right hand and one at your left, in your glory." ³⁸ But Jesus said to them, "You do not know what you are asking. Are you able to drink the cup that I drink, or to be baptized with the baptism with which I am baptized?" ³⁹ And they said to him, "We are able." And Jesus said to them, "The cup that I drink you will drink; and with the baptism with which I am baptized, you will be baptized; ⁴⁰ but to sit at my right hand or at my left is not mine to grant, but it is for those for whom it has been prepared."

THE TEN DISCIPLES ARE INDIGNANT

Mark 10:41–45 (§K55.2)

⁴¹ And when the ten heard it, they began to be indignant at James and John. ⁴² And Jesus called them to him and said to them, "You know that those who are supposed to rule over the Gentiles lord it over them, and their great men exercise authority over them. ⁴³ But it shall not be so among you; but whoever would be great among you must be your servant, ⁴⁴ and whoever would be first among you must be slave of all. ⁴⁵ For the Son of man also came not to be served but to serve, and to give his life as a ransom for many."

Mark 9:33–37 (§K47) ⇨ §K55.2

³³ And they came to Capernaum; and when he was in the house he asked them, "What were you discussing on the way?" ³⁴ But they were silent; for on the way they had discussed with one another who was the greatest. ³⁵ And he sat down and called the twelve; and he said to them, "If any one would be first, he must be last of all and servant of all." ³⁶ And he took a child, and put him in the midst of them; and taking him in his arms, he said to them, ³⁷ "Whoever receives one such child in my name receives me; and whoever receives me, receives not me but him who sent me."

MATT

Matt 20:20–23 (§M69.1) ⇨ §K55.1

²⁰ Then the mother of **the sons of Zebedee came** up **to him** with her sons, and kneeling before him she asked **him** for something. ²¹ And he said to her, "**What do you want?**" She **said to him,** "Command that these two sons of mine may **sit, one at your right hand** and one at your left, in your **kingdom." ²² But Jesus** answered, "**You do not know what you are asking. Are you able to drink the cup that** I am to **drink?**" They said to him, "**We are able." ²³** He said to them, "**You will drink** my cup, but to sit at **my right hand** and at **my left** is not mine to grant, but it is **for those for whom it has been prepared** by my Father."

Matt 20:24–28 (§M69.2) ⇨ §K55.2

²⁴ And when the ten heard it, they were **indignant** at the two brothers. ²⁵ But **Jesus called** them to him and said, "**You know** that the rulers of **the Gentiles lord it over them,** and their great men exercise authority over them. ²⁶ It shall not be so among you; but whoever would be great among you must be your servant, ²⁷ and whoever would be first among you must be your **slave;** ²⁸ even as **the Son of man came not to be served but to serve,** and to give his life as a ransom for many."

Matt 18:1–4 ⇨ §K55.2

¹ At that time the disciples came to Jesus, saying, "Who is the greatest in the kingdom of heaven?" ² And calling to him a child, he put him in the midst of them, ³ and said, "Truly, I say to you, unless you turn and become like children, you will never enter the kingdom of heaven. ⁴ Whoever humbles himself like this child, he is the greatest in the kingdom of heaven."

LUKE

Luke 12:49–53 (§L56.2) ⇨ Mark 10:38–40

⁴⁹ "I came to cast fire upon the earth; and would that it were already kindled! ⁵⁰ I have a **baptism to be baptized with;** and how I am constrained until it is accomplished! ⁵¹ Do you think that I have come to give peace on earth? No, I tell you, but rather division; ⁵² for henceforth in one house there will be five divided, three against two and two against three; ⁵³ they will be divided, father against son and son against father, mother against daughter and daughter against her mother, mother-in-law against her daughter-in-law and daughter-in-law against her mother-in-law."

Luke 9:46–50 (§L43.2) ⇨ §K55.2

⁴⁶ And an argument arose among them as to which of them was the greatest. ⁴⁷ But when Jesus perceived the thought of their hearts, he took a child and put him by his side, ⁴⁸ and said to them, "Whoever receives this child in my name receives me, and **whoever** receives me receives him who sent me; for he who is least **among you** all is the one who is **great.**"

⁴⁹ John answered, "Master, we saw a man casting out demons in your name, and we forbade him, because he does not follow with us." ⁵⁰ But Jesus said to him, "Do not forbid him; for he that is not against you is for you."

Luke 22:24–27 ⇨ §K55.2

²⁴ A dispute also arose among them, which of them was to be regarded as the greatest. ²⁵ And he **said to them,** "The kings of **the Gentiles** exercise lordship **over them;** and those in **authority** over them are called benefactors. ²⁶ **But not so** with **you;** rather let the greatest **among you** become as the youngest, and the leader as one who serves. ²⁷ For which is the greater, one who sits at table, or one who serves? Is it not the one who sits at table? But I am among you as one who serves."

JOHN	THOMAS	OTHER

MARK

Mark 10:46–52 (§K56)

[46] And they came to Jericho; and as he was leaving Jericho with his disciples and a great multitude, Bartimaeus, a blind beggar, the son of Timaeus, was sitting by the roadside. [47] And when he heard that it was Jesus of Nazareth, he began to cry out and say, "Jesus, Son of David, have mercy on me!" [48] And many rebuked him, telling him to be silent; but he cried out all the more, "Son of David, have mercy on me!" [49] And Jesus stopped and said, "Call him." And they called the blind man, saying to him, "Take heart; rise, he is calling you." [50] And throwing off his mantle he sprang up and came to Jesus. [51] And Jesus said to him, "What do you want me to do for you?" And the blind man said to him, "Master,[a] let me receive my sight." [52] And Jesus said to him, "Go your way; your faith has made you well." And immediately he received his sight and followed him on the way.

[a] Or: *Rabbi*

MATT

Matt 20:29–34 (§M70)

[29] And as they went out of Jericho, a great crowd followed him. [30] And behold, two blind men sitting by the roadside, when they heard that Jesus was passing by, cried out, "Have mercy on us, Son of David!" [31] The crowd rebuked them, telling them to be silent; but they cried out the more, "Lord, have mercy on us, Son of David!" [32] And Jesus stopped and called them, saying, "What do you want me to do for you?" [33] They said to him, "Lord, let our eyes be opened." [34] And Jesus in pity touched their eyes, and immediately they received their sight and followed him.

Matt 9:27–31 (§M24)

[27] And as Jesus passed on from there, two blind men followed him, crying aloud, "Have mercy on us, Son of David." [28] When he entered the house, the blind men came to him; and Jesus said to them, "Do you believe that I am able to do this?" They said to him, "Yes, Lord." [29] Then he touched their eyes, saying, "According to your faith be it done to you." [30] And their eyes were opened. And Jesus sternly charged them, "See that no one knows it." [31] But they went away and spread his fame through all that district.

LUKE

Luke 18:35–43 (§L79)

[35] As he drew near to Jericho, a blind man was sitting by the roadside begging; [36] and hearing a multitude going by, he inquired what this meant. [37] They told him, "Jesus of Nazareth is passing by." [38] And he cried, "Jesus, Son of David, have mercy on me!" [39] And those who were in front rebuked him, telling him to be silent; but he cried out all the more, "Son of David, have mercy on me!" [40] And Jesus stopped, and commanded him to be brought to him; and when he came near, he asked him, [41] "What do you want me to do for you?" He said, "Lord, let me receive my sight." [42] And Jesus said to him, "Receive your sight; your faith has made you well." [43] And immediately he received his sight and followed him, glorifying God; and all the people, when they saw it, gave praise to God.

JOHN

THOMAS

OTHER

SecMk 2 (follows on Mark 10:46a)

"*And the sister of the youth whom Jesus loved and his mother and Salome were there, and Jesus did not receive them.*"

MARK

TWO SENT FOR COLT

Mark 11:1–3 (§K57.1)

[1] And when they drew near to Jerusalem, to Bethphage and Bethany, at the Mount of Olives, he sent two of his disciples, [2] and said to them, "Go into the village opposite you, and immediately as you enter it you will find a colt tied, on which no one has ever sat; untie it and bring it. [3] If any one says to you, 'Why are you doing this?' say, 'The Lord has need of it and will send it back here immediately.'"

COLT IS FOUND TIED

Mark 11:4–6 (§K57.2)

[4] And they went away, and found a colt tied at the door out in the open street; and they untied it. [5] And those who stood there said to them, "What are you doing, untying the colt?" [6] And they told them what Jesus had said; and they let them go.

TRIUMPHAL ENTRY

Mark 11:7–10 (§K57.3)

[7] And they brought the colt to Jesus, and threw their garments on it; and he sat upon it. [8] And many spread their garments on the road, and others spread leafy branches which they had cut from the fields. [9] And those who went before and those who followed cried out, "Hosanna! Blessed is he who comes in the name of the Lord! [10] Blessed is the kingdom of our father David that is coming! Hosanna in the highest!"

RETURN TO BETHANY

Mark 11:11 (§K57.4) °

[11] And he entered Jerusalem, and went into the temple; and when he had looked round at everything, as it was already late, he went out to Bethany with the twelve.

°Appendix 2 ⇨ Mark 11:11

JOHN

John 12:12–19 (§J25)

[12] The next day a great crowd who had come to the feast heard that Jesus was coming to Jerusalem. [13] So they took branches of palm trees and went out to meet him, crying, "Hosanna! Blessed is he who comes in the name of the Lord, even the King of Israel!" [14] And Jesus found a young ass and sat upon it; as it is written,

[15] "Fear not, daughter of Zion;
behold, your king is coming,
sitting on an ass's colt!"

[16] His disciples did not understand this at first; but when Jesus was glorified, then they remembered that this had been written of him and had been done to him. [17] The crowd that had been with him when he called Lazarus out of the tomb and raised him from the dead bore witness. [18] The reason why the crowd went to meet him was that they heard he had done this sign. [19] The Pharisees then said to one another, "You see that you can do nothing; look, the world has gone after him."

MATT

Matt 21:1–6 (§M71.1) ⇨ §K57.1–2

[1] And when they drew near to Jerusalem and came to Bethphage, to the Mount of Olives, then Jesus sent two disciples, [2] saying to them, "Go into the village opposite you, and immediately you will find an ass tied, and a colt with her; untie them and bring them to me. [3] If any one says anything to you, you shall say, 'The Lord has need of them,' and he will send them immediately." [4] This took place to fulfil what was spoken by the prophet, saying,

[5] "Tell the daughter of Zion,
Behold, your king is coming to you,
humble, and mounted on an ass,
and on a colt, the foal of an ass."

[6] The disciples went and did as Jesus had directed them; . . .

Matt 21:7–9 (§M71.2) ⇨ §K57.3

[7] they brought the ass and the colt, and put their garments on them, and he sat thereon. [8] Most of the crowd spread their garments on the road, and others cut branches from the trees and spread them on the road. [9] And the crowds that went before him and that followed him shouted, "Hosanna to the Son of David! Blessed is he who comes in the name of the Lord! Hosanna in the highest!"

Matt 21:10–11 (§M71.3) ⇨ §K57.4

[10] And when he entered Jerusalem, all the city was stirred, saying, "Who is this?" [11] And the crowds said, "This is the prophet Jesus from Nazareth of Galilee."

Zech 9:9 ⇨ Mark 11:2, 7, 8
[9] Rejoice greatly, O daughter of Zion!
Shout aloud, O daughter of Jerusalem!
Lo, your king comes to you;
triumphant and victorious is he,
humble and riding on an ass,
on a colt the foal of an ass.

Ps 118:26 ⇨ Mark 11:9–10
[26] Blessed be he who enters in the name of the Lord!
We bless you from the house of the Lord.

THOMAS

LUKE

Luke 19:28–32 (§L82.1) ⇨ §K57.1–2

[28] And when he had said this, he went on ahead, going up to Jerusalem. [29] When he drew near to Bethphage and Bethany, at the mount that is called Olivet, he sent two of the disciples, [30] saying, "Go into the village opposite, where on entering you will find a colt tied, on which no one has ever yet sat; untie it and bring it here. [31] If any one asks you, 'Why are you untying it?' you shall say this, 'The Lord has need of it.'" [32] So those who were sent went away and found it as he had told them.

Luke 19:33–34 (§L82.2) ⇨ §K57.2

[33] And as they were untying the colt, its owners said to them, "Why are you untying the colt?" [34] And they said, "The Lord has need of it."

Luke 19:35–40 (§L82.3) ⇨ §K57.3

[35] And they brought it to Jesus, and throwing their garments on the colt they set Jesus upon it. [36] And as he rode along, they spread their garments on the road. [37] As he was now drawing near, at the descent of the Mount of Olives, the whole multitude of the disciples began to rejoice and praise God with a loud voice for all the mighty works that they had seen, [38] saying, "Blessed is the King who comes in the name of the Lord! Peace in heaven and glory in the highest!" [39] And some of the Pharisees in the multitude said to him, "Teacher, rebuke your disciples." [40] He answered, "I tell you, if these were silent, the very stones would cry out."

OTHER

MARK	MATT	LUKE

Mark 11:12–14 (§K58.1)

[12] On the following day, when they came from Bethany, he was hungry. [13] And seeing in the distance a fig tree in leaf, he went to see if he could find anything on it. When he came to it, he found nothing but leaves, for it was not the season for figs. [14] And he said to it, "May no one ever eat fruit from you again." And his disciples heard it.

Cf. Mark 11:20–21

Matt 21:18–22 (§M73)

[18] In the morning, as he was returning to the city, **he was hungry.** [19] **And seeing a fig tree** by the wayside **he went to** it, and **found nothing** on it **but leaves** only. **And he said to** it, "May no fruit ever come **from you again!**" And the **fig tree** withered at once. [20] When the disciples saw it they marveled, saying, "How did the **fig tree** wither at once?" [21] And Jesus answered them, "Truly, I say to you, if you have faith and never doubt, you will not only do what has been done to the **fig tree**, but even if you say to this mountain, 'Be taken up and cast into the sea,' it will be done. [22] And whatever you ask in prayer, you will receive, if you have faith."

Luke 13:6–9 (§L57.2)

[6] *And he told this parable: "A man had a fig tree planted in his vineyard; and he came seeking fruit on it and found none. [7] And he said to the vinedresser, 'Lo, these three years I have come seeking fruit on this fig tree, and I find none. Cut it down; why should it use up the ground?' [8] And he answered him, 'Let it alone, sir, this year also, till I dig about it and put on manure. [9] And if it bears* **fruit** *next year, well and good; but if not, you can cut it down.'"*

JOHN	THOMAS	OTHER

InThom 3:1–3

[1] *But the son of Annas the scribe was standing there with Joseph; and he took a branch of a willow and (with it) dispersed the water which Jesus had gathered together. [2] When Jesus saw what he had done he was enraged* **and said** *to him: "You insolent, godless dunderhead, what harm did the pools and the water do to you? See, now you also shall wither like* **a tree** *and shall bear neither* **leaves** *nor root nor* **fruit.**" [3] *And immediately that lad withered up completely; and Jesus departed and went into Joseph's house. But the parents of him that was withered took him away, bewailing his youth, and brought him to Joseph and reproached him: "What a child you have, who does such things."*

InThom 4:1–2

[1] *After this again he went through the village, and a lad ran and knocked against his shoulder. Jesus was exasperated* **and said** *to him: "You shall not go further on your way," and the child immediately fell down and died. But some, who saw what took place, said: "From where does this child spring, since his every word is an accomplished deed?" [2] And the parents of the dead child came to Joseph and blamed him and said: "Since you have such a child, you cannot dwell with us in the village; or else teach him to bless and not to curse. For he is slaying our children."*

MARK

Mark 11:15–19 (§K58.2)

15 And they came to Jerusalem. And he entered the temple and began to drive out those who sold and those who bought in the temple, and he overturned the tables of the money-changers and the seats of those who sold pigeons; 16 and he would not allow any one to carry anything through the temple. 17 And he taught, and said to them, "Is it not written, 'My house shall be called a house of prayer for all the nations'? But you have made it a den of robbers." 18 And the chief priests and the scribes heard it and sought a way to destroy him; for they feared him, because all the multitude was astonished at his teaching. 19 And when evening came they[a] went out of the city.

[a] he: ℵ C (D) X Θ f¹ f¹³ al; they: A B K W Δ Π Ψ 28 pc

Mark 12:12 ⇨ Mark 11:18

12 And they tried to arrest him, but feared the multitude, for they perceived that he had told the parable against them; so they left him and went away.

Mark 14:1–2 (§K61.1) ⇨ Mark 11:18

1 It was now two days before the Passover and the feast of Unleavened Bread. And the chief priests and the scribes were seeking how to arrest him by stealth, and kill him; 2 for they said, "Not during the feast, lest there be a tumult of the people."

Isa 56:7 ⇨ Mark 11:7

7 "these I bring to my holy mountain,
and make them joyful in my house of prayer;
their burnt offerings and their sacrifices
will be accepted on my altar;
for my house will be called a house of prayer
for all peoples."

Jer 7:11 ⇨ Mark 11:17

11 "Has this house, which is called by my name, become a den of robbers in your eyes? Behold, I myself have seen it, says the Lord."

JOHN

John 2:13–22 (§J5.1)

13 The Passover of the Jews was at hand, and Jesus went up to Jerusalem. 14 In the temple he found those who were selling oxen and sheep and pigeons, and the money-changers at their business. 15 And making a whip of cords, he drove them all, with the sheep and oxen, out of the temple; and he poured out the coins of the money-changers and overturned their tables. 16 And he told those who sold the pigeons, "Take these things away; you shall not make my Father's house a house of trade." 17 His disciples remembered that it was written, "Zeal for thy house will consume me." 18 The Jews then said to him, "What sign have you to show us for doing this?" 19 Jesus answered them, "Destroy this temple, and in three days I will raise it up." 20 The Jews then said, "It has taken forty-six years to build this temple, and will you raise it up in three days?" 21 But he spoke of the temple of his body. 22 When therefore he was raised from the dead, his disciples remembered that he had said this; and they believed the scripture and the word which Jesus had spoken.

MATT

Matt 21:12–13 (§M72.1)

12 And Jesus entered the temple of God and drove out all who sold and bought in the temple, and he overturned the tables of the money-changers and the seats of those who sold pigeons. 13 He said to them, "It is written, 'My house shall be called a house of prayer'; but you make it a den of robbers."

Matt 21:14–17 (§M72.2)

14 And the blind and the lame came to him in the temple, and he healed them. 15 But when the chief priests and the scribes saw the wonderful things that he did, and the children crying out in the temple, "Hosanna to the Son of David!" they were indignant; 16 and they said to him, "Do you hear what these are saying?" And Jesus said to them, "Yes, have you never read,

'Out of the mouth of babes and sucklings
thou hast brought perfect praise'?"
17 And leaving them, he went out of the city to Bethany and lodged there.

THOMAS

LUKE

Luke 19:45–48 (§L83)

45 And he entered the temple and began to drive out those who sold, 46 saying to them, "It is written, 'My house shall be a house of prayer'; but you have made it a den of robbers."

47 And he was teaching daily in the temple. The chief priests and the scribes and the principal men of the people sought to destroy him; 48 but they did not find anything they could do, for all the people hung upon his words.

OTHER

MARK

Mark 11:20–25 (§K59.1)

²⁰ As they passed by in the morning, they saw the fig tree withered away to its roots. ²¹ And Peter remembered and said to him, "Master,ᵃ look! The fig tree which you cursed has withered." ²² And Jesus answered them, "Have faith in God. ²³ Truly, I say to you, whoever says to this mountain, 'Be taken up and cast into the sea,' and does not doubt in his heart, but believes that what he says will come to pass, it will be done for him. ²⁴ Therefore I tell you, whatever you ask in prayer, believe that you have receivedᵇ it, and it will be yours. ²⁵ And whenever you stand praying, forgive, if you have anything against any one; so that your Father also who is in heaven may forgive you your trespasses."ᶜ

ᵃ Or *Rabbi*

ᵇ Text: ℵ B C L W Δ Ψ *pc*; *are receiving*: A K X Π *f*¹³ 28 33 *al*

ᶜ V. 26 does not appear in: ℵ B L W Δ Ψ *al*; add v. 26, *But if you do not forgive, neither will your Father who is in heaven forgive your trespasses (cf. Matt 6:15)*: A (C) (D) K X Θ Π (*f*¹) 28 (33) *al*

⇨ Mark 11:20–21
Cf. Mark 11:12–14 (§K58.1)

Mark 9:28–29 (§K45.2) ⇨ Mark 11:24
²⁸ And when he had entered the house, his disciples asked him privately, "Why could we not cast it out?" ²⁹ And he said to them, "This kind cannot be driven out by anything but **prayer**."

MATT

Matt 21:18–22 (§M73)

¹⁸ In the **morning**, as he was returning to the city, he was hungry. ¹⁹ And seeing a fig tree by the wayside he went to it, and found nothing on it but leaves only. And he said to it, "May no fruit ever come from you again!" And the fig tree **withered** at once. ²⁰ When the disciples saw it they marveled, saying, "How did the fig tree wither at once?" ²¹ **And Jesus answered them, "Truly, I say to you,** if you **have faith** and never **doubt**, you will not only do what has been done to the fig tree, but even if you say to **this mountain,** 'Be taken up and cast into the sea,' it will be done. ²² And whatever you ask in prayer, you** will receive, if you have faith."

Matt 17:19–20 (§M59.2) ⇨ Mark 11:23
¹⁹ *Then the disciples came to Jesus privately and said, "Why could we not cast it out?"* ²⁰ *He said to them, "Because of your little faith. For* **truly I** *say to you, if you have faith as a grain of mustard seed, you will say to* **this mountain,** *'Move from here to there,' and* **it** *will move; and nothing* **will** *be impossible to you."*

Matt 18:19 ⇨ Mark 11:24
¹⁹ *"Again* **I** *say to* **you,** *if two of* **you** *agree on earth about anything they ask, it will be done for them by my Father in heaven."*

Matt 6:14 ⇨ Mark 11:25
¹⁴ *"For* **if you forgive** *men their trespasses,* **your** *heavenly* **Father** *also will forgive you";* . . .

LUKE

Luke 13:6–9 (§L57.2)

⁶ *And he told this parable: "A man had a* **fig** *tree planted in his vineyard; and he came seeking fruit on it and found none.* ⁷ *And he said to the vinedresser, 'Lo, these three years I have come seeking fruit on this fig tree, and I find none. Cut it down; why should it use up the ground?'* ⁸ *And he answered him, 'Let it alone, sir, this year also, till I dig about it and put on manure.* ⁹ *And if it bears fruit next year, well and good; but if not, you can cut it down.'"*

Luke 17:5–6 (§L70.2) ⇨ Mark 11:22–23
⁵ *The apostles said to the Lord, "Increase our faith!"* ⁶ *And the Lord said, "If you had faith as a grain of mustard seed, you could say* **to this** *sycamine tree, '* **Be rooted up,** *and be planted in the sea,' and it would obey you."*

JOHN

John 14:13–14 ⇨ Mark 11:24
¹³ *"* **Whatever you ask in my name, I will do it,** *that the Father may be glorified in the Son;* ¹⁴ *if* **you ask** *anything in my name, I will do* **it.** *"*

John 15:7 ⇨ Mark 11:24
⁷ *"If you abide in me, and my words abide in* **you, ask** *whatever* **you** *will,* **and it shall be done** *for you."*

John 16:23 ⇨ Mark 11:24
²³ *"In that day* **you** *will* **ask** *nothing of me. Truly, truly,* **I** *say to* **you,** *if* **you ask** *anything of the Father, he will give* **it** *to* **you** *in my name."*

THOMAS

GThom 48 ⇨ Mark 11:22–23
(48) **Jesus** said, "If two make peace with each other in this one house, they will say **to** the **mountain,** 'Move away,' and **it will** move away."

GThom 106 ⇨ Mark 11:22–23
(106) Jesus said, "When you make the two one, you will become the sons of man, and when you say, '**Mountain,** move away,' **it will** move away."

OTHER

MARK

Mark 11:27–33 (§K59.2)°

²⁷ And they came again to Jerusalem. And as he was walking in the temple, the chief priests and the scribes and the elders came to him, ²⁸ and they said to him, "By what authority are you doing these things, or who gave you this authority to do them?" ²⁹ Jesus said to them, "I will ask you a question; answer me, and I will tell you by what authority I do these things. ³⁰ Was the baptism of John from heaven or from men? Answer me." ³¹ And they argued with one another, "If we say, 'From heaven,' he will say, 'Why then did you not believe him?' ³² But shall we say, 'From men'?"—they were afraid of the people, for all held that John was a real prophet. ³³ So they answered Jesus, "We do not know." And Jesus said to them, "Neither will I tell you by what authority I do these things."

°Appendix 1 ⇨ Mark 11:29–33

MATT

Matt 21:23–27 (§M74.1)

²³ And when he entered the temple, the chief priests and the elders of the people came up to him as he was teaching, and said, "By what authority are you doing these things, and who gave you this authority?" ²⁴ Jesus answered them, "I also will ask you a question; and if you tell me the answer, then I also will tell you by what authority I do these things. ²⁵ The baptism of John, whence was it? From heaven or from men?" And they argued with one another, "If we say, 'From heaven,' he will say to us, 'Why then did you not believe him?' ²⁶ But if we say, 'From men,' we are afraid of the multitude; for all hold that John was a prophet." ²⁷ So they answered Jesus, "We do not know." And he said to them, "Neither will I tell you by what authority I do these things."

LUKE

Luke 20:1–8 (§L84)

¹ One day, as he was teaching the people in the temple and preaching the gospel, the chief priests and the scribes with the elders came up ² and said to him, "Tell us by what authority you do these things, or who it is that gave you this authority." ³ He answered them, "I also will ask you a question; now tell me, ⁴ Was the baptism of John from heaven or from men?" ⁵ And they discussed it with one another, saying, "If we say, 'From heaven,' he will say, 'Why did you not believe him?' ⁶ But if we say, 'From men,' all the people will stone us; for they are convinced that John was a prophet." ⁷ So they answered that they did not know whence it was. ⁸ And Jesus said to them, "Neither will I tell you by what authority I do these things."

JOHN

John 2:18 ⇨ Mark 11:28
¹⁸ The Jews then said to him, "What sign have you to show us for doing this?"

THOMAS

OTHER

POxy840 2

(2) *And he took them (the disciples) with him into the place of purification itself and walked about in the Temple court. And a Pharisaic chief priest, Levi (?) by name, fell in with them and s[aid] to the Savior: Who gave thee leave to [trea]d this place of purification and to look upon [the]se holy utensils without having bathed thyself and even without thy disciples having [wa]shed their f[eet]? On the contrary, being defi[led], thou hast trodden the Temple court, this clean p[lace], although no [one who] has [not] first bathed himself or [chang]ed his clot[hes] may tread it and [venture] to vi[ew these] holy utensils! Forthwith [the Savior] s[tood] still with h[is] disciples and [answered]: How stands it (then) with thee, thou art forsooth (also) here in the Temple court. Art thou then clean? He said to him: I am clean. For I have bathed myself in the pool of David and have gone down by the one stair and come up by the other and have put on white and clean clothes, and (only) then have I come hither and have viewed these holy utensils. Then said the Savior to him: Woe unto you blind that see not! Thou hast bathed thyself in water that is poured out, in which dogs and swine lie night and day and thou hast washed thyself and hast chafed thine outer skin, which prostitutes also and flute-girls anoint, bathe, chafe and rouge, in order to arouse desire in men, but within they are full of scorpions and of [bad]ness [of every kind]. But I and [my disciples], of whom thou sayest that we have not im[mersed] ourselves, [have been im]mersed in the liv[ing . . .] water which comes down from [. . . B]ut woe unto them that . . .*

MARK

Mark 12:1–12 (§K59.3)

¹And he began to speak to them in parables. "A man planted a vineyard, and set a hedge around it, and dug a pit for the wine press, and built a tower, and let it out to tenants, and went into another country. ²When the time came, he sent a servant to the tenants, to get from them some of the fruit of the vineyard. ³And they took him and beat him, and sent him away empty-handed. ⁴Again he sent to them another servant, and they wounded him in the head, and treated him shamefully. ⁵And he sent another, and him they killed; and so with many others, some they beat and some they killed. ⁶He had still one other, a beloved son; finally he sent him to them, saying, 'They will respect my son.' ⁷But those tenants said to one another, 'This is the heir; come, let us kill him, and the inheritance will be ours.' ⁸And they took him and killed him, and cast him out of the vineyard. ⁹What will the owner of the vineyard do? He will come and destroy the tenants, and give the vineyard to others. ¹⁰Have you not read this scripture:

'The very stone which the builders rejected
   has become the head of the corner;
¹¹this was the Lord's doing,
   and it is marvelous in our eyes'?"

¹²And they tried to arrest him, but feared the multitude, for they perceived that he had told the parable against them; so they left him and went away.

Isa 5:1–2 ⇨ Mark 12:1
¹Let me sing for my beloved
   a love song concerning his vineyard:
My beloved had a vineyard
   on a very fertile hill.
²He digged it and cleared it of stones,
   and planted it with choice vines;
he built a watchtower in the midst of it,
   and hewed out a wine vat in it;
and he looked for it to yield grapes,
   but it yielded wild grapes.

Ps 118:22–23 ⇨ Mark 12:10
²²The stone which the builders rejected
   has become the head of the corner.
²³This is the Lord's doing;
   it is marvelous in our eyes.

JOHN

MATT

Matt 21:33–46 (§M74.3)

³³"Hear another parable. There was a householder who planted a vineyard, and set a hedge around it, and dug a wine press in it, and built a tower, and let it out to tenants, and went into another country. ³⁴When the season of fruit drew near, he sent his servants to the tenants, to get his fruit; ³⁵and the tenants took his servants and beat one, killed another, and stoned another. ³⁶Again he sent other servants, more than the first; and they did the same to them. ³⁷Afterward he sent his son to them, saying 'They will respect my son.' ³⁸But when the tenants saw the son, they said to themselves, 'This is the heir; come, let us kill him and have his inheritance.' ³⁹And they took him and cast him out of the vineyard, and killed him. ⁴⁰When therefore the owner of the vineyard comes, what will he do to those tenants?" ⁴¹They said to him, "He will put those wretches to a miserable death, and let out the vineyard to other tenants who will give him the fruits in their seasons."

⁴²Jesus said to them, "Have you never read in the scriptures:

'The very stone which the builders rejected
   has become the head of the corner;
this was the Lord's doing,
   and it is marvelous in our eyes'?
⁴³Therefore I tell you, the kingdom of God will be taken away from you and given to a nation producing the fruits of it."

⁴⁵When the chief priests and the Pharisees heard his parables, they perceived that he was speaking about them. ⁴⁶But when they tried to arrest him, they feared the multitudes, because they held him to be a prophet.

THOMAS

GThom 65

(65) He said, "There was a good man who owned a vineyard. He leased it to tenant farmers so that they might work it and he might collect the produce from them. He sent his servant so that the tenants might give him the produce of the vineyard. They seized his servant and beat him, all but killing him. The servant went back and told his master. The master said, 'Perhaps <they> did not recognize <him>.' He sent another servant. The tenants beat this one as well. Then the owner sent his son and said, 'Perhaps they will show respect to my son.' Because the tenants knew that it was he who was the heir to the vineyard, they seized him and killed him. Let him who has ears hear."

GThom 66 ⇨ Mark 12:10

(66) Jesus said, "Show me the stone which the builders have rejected. That one is the cornerstone."

LUKE

Luke 20:9–19 (§L85)

⁹And he began to tell the people this parable: "A man planted a vineyard, and let it out to tenants, and went into another country for a long while. ¹⁰When the time came, he sent a servant to the tenants, that they should give him some of the fruit of the vineyard; but the tenants beat him, and sent him away empty-handed. ¹¹And he sent another servant; him also they beat and treated shamefully, and sent him away empty-handed. ¹²And he sent yet a third; this one they wounded and cast out. ¹³Then the owner of the vineyard said, 'What shall I do? I will send my beloved son; it may be they will respect him.' ¹⁴But when the tenants saw him, they said to themselves, 'This is the heir; let us kill him, that the inheritance may be ours.' ¹⁵And they cast him out of the vineyard and killed him. What then will the owner of the vineyard do to them? ¹⁶He will come and destroy those tenants, and give the vineyard to others." When they heard this, they said, "God forbid!" ¹⁷But he looked at them and said, "What then is this that is written:

'The very stone which the builders rejected
   has become the head of the corner'?
¹⁸Every one who falls on that stone will be broken to pieces; but when it falls on any one it will crush him."

¹⁹The scribes and the chief priests tried to lay hands on him at that very hour, but they feared the people; for they perceived that he had told this parable against them.

OTHER

MARK	MATT	LUKE

Mark 12:13–17 (§K59.4)
[13] And they sent to him some of the Pharisees and some of the Herodians, to entrap him in his talk. [14] And they came and said to him, "Teacher, we know that you are true, and care for no man; for you do not regard the position of men; but truly teach the way of God. Is it lawful to pay taxes to Caesar, or not? [15] Should we pay them, or should we not?" But knowing their hypocrisy, he said to them, "Why put me to the test? Bring me a coin,[a] and let me look at it." [16] And they brought one. And he said to them, "Whose likeness and inscription is this?" They said to him, "Caesar's." [17] Jesus said to them, "Render to Caesar the things that are Caesar's, and to God the things that are God's." And they were amazed at him.

[a] Greek: *denarius*

Matt 22:15–22 (§M76.1)
[15] Then **the Pharisees** went and took counsel how **to entangle him in his talk**. [16] And **they** sent their disciples to him, along with the Herodians, saying, **"Teacher, we know that you are true**, and teach **the way of God** truthfully, **and care for no man; for you do not regard the position of men**. [17] Tell us, then, what you think. **Is it lawful to pay taxes to Caesar, or not?"** [18] But Jesus, aware of **their** malice, **said**, **"Why put me to the test**, you hypocrites? [19] Show me the money for the tax." **And they brought** him a coin. [20] And Jesus **said to them, "Whose likeness and inscription is this?"** [21] **They said, "Caesar's."** Then he **said to them, "Render** therefore to **Caesar the things that are Caesar's, and to God the things that are God's."** [22] When **they** heard it, **they** marveled; and they left him and went away.

Luke 20:20–26 (§L86)
[20] So **they** watched him, and **sent** spies, who pretended to be sincere, that they might take hold of what he said, so as to deliver him up to the authority and jurisdiction of the governor. [21] They asked **him**, **"Teacher, we know that you speak and teach rightly, and show no** partiality, **but truly teach the way of God**. [22] Is it lawful for us to give tribute **to Caesar, or not?"** [23] But he perceived **their** craftiness, and **said to them**, [24] **"Show me a coin**. Whose likeness **and inscription** has it?" **They said, "Caesar's."** [25] He said to them, **"Then render to Caesar the things that are Caesar's, and to God the things that are God's."** [26] And they were not able in the presence of the people to catch him by what he said; but marveling at his answer **they were** silent.

JOHN	THOMAS	OTHER

John 3:2 ⇨ Mark 12:14
[2] *This man came to Jesus by night and said to him, "Rabbi, we know that you are a teacher come from God; for no one can do these signs that you do, unless God is with him."*

GThom 100
(100) **They** showed Jesus **a** gold **coin** and said to Him, "Caesar's men demand **taxes** from us."

He **said to them**, "Give **Caesar** what belongs to Caesar, give **God** what belongs to God, and give **Me** what is Mine."

PEger2 3
(3) . . . [ca]me **to him** to put him to the pro[of] and **to** tempt **him**, whilst [they **said**]: "Master Jesus, **we know that** thou art come [from God], for what thou doest bears a test[imony] (to thee which goes) beyond (that) of all the prophets. [Wherefore tell] us: is it admissible [**to p]ay** to the kings the (charges) appertaining to their rule? [Should we] pay [th]em **or not?**" But Jesus saw through **their** [in]tention, became [angry] and **said to them**: **"Why** call ye **me** with yo[ur mou]th Master and yet [do] not what I say? Well has Is[aiah] prophesied [concerning y]ou saying: This [people honours] me with the[ir li]ps but their heart is far from me; [their worship is] vain. [They teach] precepts [of men]." (Fragment 2, recto [lines 43–59])

MARK	MATT	LUKE

MARK

Mark 12:18–27 (§K59.5)

[18] And Sadducees came to him, who say that there is no resurrection; and they asked him a question, saying, [19] "Teacher, Moses wrote for us that if a man's brother dies and leaves a wife, but leaves no child, the man[a] must take the wife, and raise up children for his brother. [20] There were seven brothers; the first took a wife, and when he died left no children; [21] and the second took her, and died, leaving no children; and the third likewise; [22] and the seven left no children. Last of all the woman also died. [23] In the resurrection whose wife will she be? For the seven had her as wife."

[24] Jesus said to them, "Is not this why you are wrong, that you know neither the scriptures nor the power of God? [25] For when they rise from the dead, they neither marry nor are given in marriage, but are like angels in heaven. [26] And as for the dead being raised, have you not read in the book of Moses, in the passage about the bush, how God said to him, 'I am the God of Abraham, and the God of Isaac, and the God of Jacob?' [27] He is not God of the dead, but of the living; you are quite wrong."

[a] Greek: *his brother*

Gen 38:8 ⇨ Mark 12:19
[8] Then Judah said to Onan, "Go in to your brother's **wife,** and perform the duty of a brother-in-law to her, **and raise up** offspring for your **brother.**"

Deut 25:5–6 ⇨ Mark 12:19
[5] "If brothers dwell together, and one of them **dies** and has **no son, the wife** of the dead shall not be married outside the family to a stranger; her husband's **brother** shall go in to her, and **take** her as his **wife,** and perform the duty of a husband's **brother** to her. [6] And the first son whom she bears shall succeed to the name of his brother who is dead, that his name may not be blotted out of Israel."

Exod 3:6 ⇨ Mark 12:26
[6] And he **said, "I am the God of** your father, **the God of Abraham, the God of Isaac, and the God of Jacob."** And Moses hid his face, for he was afraid to look at God.

MATT

Matt 22:23–33 (§M76.2)

[23] The same day **Sadducees came to him,** who say that there is no resurrection; and they asked him a question, [24] saying, "Teacher, Moses said, 'If a man **dies,** having no children, his brother **must** marry the widow, **and raise up children for his brother.'** [25] Now **there were seven brothers** among us; the first married, and **died,** and having **no** children left his wife to his brother. [26] So too **the second and third,** down to **the seventh.** [27] After them **all, the woman died.** [28] In the **resurrection,** therefore, to which of the seven **will she be wife? For they all had her."**

[29] But **Jesus** answered **them, "You are wrong, because you know neither the scriptures nor the power of God. [30] For** in the resurrection **they neither marry nor are given in marriage, but are like angels in heaven.** [31] And as for the resurrection of the **dead,** have **you not read** what was said to you by God, [32] 'I am the God of Abraham, and the God of Isaac, and the God of Jacob'? He is not God of the dead, but of the living." [33]** And when the crowd heard it, they were astonished at his teaching.

LUKE

Luke 20:27–40 (§L87)

[27] There came to him some **Sadducees,** those who say that there is no resurrection, [28] and they asked him a question, saying, "Teacher, Moses wrote for us that if a man's brother dies, having a wife but no children, the man must take the wife and raise up children for his brother. [29] Now there were seven brothers; the first took a wife, and died without children; [30] and the second [31] and the third took her, and likewise all seven left no children and died. [32] Afterward the woman also died. [33] In the resurrection, therefore, whose wife will the woman be? For the seven had her as wife."

[34] And **Jesus said to them,** "The sons of this age marry and are given in marriage; [35] but those who are accounted worthy to attain to that age and to the resurrection from the dead neither marry nor are given in marriage, [36] for they cannot die any more, because they are equal to angels and are sons of God, being sons of the resurrection. [37] But that the dead are raised, even Moses showed, in the passage about the bush, where he calls the Lord the God of Abraham and the God of Isaac and the God of Jacob. [38] Now he is not God of the dead, but of the living; for all live to him." [39] And some of the scribes answered, "Teacher, you have spoken well." [40] For they no longer dared to ask him any question.

JOHN	THOMAS	OTHER

MARK

Mark 12:28–34 (§K59.6)

[28] And one of the scribes came up and heard them disputing with one another, and seeing that he answered them well, asked him, "Which commandment is the first of all?" [29] Jesus answered, "The first is, 'Hear, O Israel: The Lord our God, the Lord is one; [30] and you shall love the Lord your God with all your heart, and with all your soul, and with all your mind, and with all your strength.' [31] The second is this, 'You shall love your neighbor as yourself.' There is no other commandment greater than these." [32] And the scribe said to him, "You are right, Teacher; you have truly said that he is one, and there is no other but he; [33] and to love him with all the heart, and with all the understanding, and with all the strength, and to love one's neighbor as oneself, is much more than all whole burnt offerings and sacrifices." [34] And when Jesus saw that he answered wisely, he said to him, "You are not far from the kingdom of God." And after that no one dared to ask him any question.

Deut 6:4–5 ⇨ Mark 12:29–30

[4] "Hear, O Israel: The Lord our God is one Lord; [5] and you shall love the Lord your God with all your heart, and with all your might."

Lev 19:18 ⇨ Mark 12:31

[18] "You shall not take vengeance or bear any grudge against the sons of your own people, but **you shall love your neighbor as yourself**: I am the Lord."

1 Sam 15:22 ⇨ Mark 12:33

[22] And Samuel said,

"Has the Lord as great delight in **burnt offerings and sacrifices**,
    as in obeying the voice of the Lord?
Behold, to obey is better than sacrifice,
    and to hearken than the fat of rams."

JOHN

MATT

Matt 22:34–40 (§M76.3)

[34] But when the Pharisees heard that he had silenced the Sadducees, they came together. [35] **And one of** them, a lawyer, **asked him** a question, to test him. [36] "Teacher, **which is** the great **commandment** in the law?" [37] And he said to him, "**You shall love the Lord your God with all your heart, and with all your soul, and with all your mind.** [38] This is the great and first commandment. [39] And a second is like it, **You shall love your neighbor as yourself.** [40] On these two commandments depend all the law and the prophets."

THOMAS

GThom 25 ⇨ Mark 12:31

(25) Jesus said, "Love your brother like your soul, guard him like the pupil of your eye."

GThom 82 ⇨ Mark 12:34

(82) Jesus said, "He who is near Me is near the fire, and he who is far from Me is far from the Kingdom."

LUKE

Luke 10:25–29 (§L48.1)

[25] And behold, a lawyer stood up to put him to the test, saying, "Teacher, what shall I do to inherit eternal life?" [26] He said to him, "What is written in the law? How do you read?" [27] And he answered, "You shall love the Lord your God with all your heart, and with all your soul, and with all your strength, and with all your mind; and your neighbor as yourself." [28] And he said to him, "You have answered right; do this, and you will live."

[29] But he, desiring to justify himself, said to Jesus, "And who is my neighbor?"

Luke 20:39 ⇨ Mark 12:32

[39] And some of the scribes answered, "Teacher, you have spoken well."

Luke 20:40 ⇨ Mark 12:34

[40] For they no longer dared to ask him any question.

OTHER

Did 1:2 ⇨ Mark 12:30–31

[2] The Way of Life is this: "First, thou shalt **love the God** who made thee, secondly, thy **neighbour as** thyself; and whatsoever thou wouldst not have had done to thyself, do not thou to another."

Barn 19:5 ⇨ Mark 12:31

[5] Thou shalt not be in two minds whether it shall be or not. "Thou shalt not take the name of the Lord in vain." Thou shalt **love** thy neighbour more than thy own life. Thou shalt not procure abortion, thou shalt not commit infanticide. Thou shalt not withhold thy hand from thy son or from thy daughter, but shalt teach them the fear of God from their youth up.

InThom 15:4a ⇨ Mark 12:34

[4] *And when the child heard this, he at once smiled on him and said: "Since you have spoken well and have testified rightly, for your sake shall he also that was smitten be healed."*

MARK	MATT	LUKE

Mark 12:35–37 (§K59.7)

³⁵ And as Jesus taught in the temple, he said, "How can the scribes say that the Christ is the son of David? ³⁶ David himself, inspired by[a] the Holy Spirit, declared,

'The Lord said to my Lord,
Sit at my right hand,
till I put thy enemies under thy feet.'

³⁷ David himself calls him Lord; so how is he his son?" And the great throng heard him gladly.

[a] Or: *himself, in*

Ps 110:1 ⇨ Mark 12:36
¹ **The Lord** says to **my lord**:
"**Sit at my right hand**,
till I make your **enemies**
your footstool."

2 Sam 7:12–16
¹² "'When your days are fulfilled and you lie down with your fathers, I will raise up your offspring after you, who shall come forth from your body, and I will establish his kingdom. ¹³ He shall build a house for my name, and I will establish the throne of his kingdom for ever. ¹⁴ I will be his father, and he shall be my **son**. When he commits iniquity, I will chasten him with the rod of men, with the stripes of the sons of men; ¹⁵ but I will not take my steadfast love from him, as I took it from Saul, whom I put away from before you. ¹⁶ And your house and your kingdom shall be made sure for ever before me; your throne shall be established for ever.'"

Ps 89:3–4
³ Thou hast said, "I have made a covenant with **my** chosen one,
I have sworn to **David my** servant:
⁴ 'I will establish your descendants for ever,
and build your throne for all generations.'"

Mic 5:2
² But you, O Bethlehem Ephrathah,
who are little to be among the clans of Judah,
from you shall come forth for me
one who is to be ruler in Israel,
whose origin is from of old,
from ancient days.

Matt 22:41–46 (§M76.4)

⁴¹ Now while the Pharisees were gathered together, **Jesus** asked them a question, ⁴² saying, "What do you think of **the Christ**? Whose **son** is he?" They said to him, "The son of David." ⁴³ He said to them, "How is it then that **David**, **inspired by the Spirit**, calls him Lord, saying,

⁴⁴ 'The Lord said to my Lord,
Sit at my right hand,
till I put thy enemies under thy feet'?

⁴⁵ If **David** thus **calls him Lord, how is he his son?**" ⁴⁶ And no one was able to answer him a word, nor from that day did any one dare to ask him any more questions.

Luke 20:41–44 (§L88)

⁴¹ But **he said** to them, "**How can** they **say that the Christ is** David's **son**? ⁴² For **David himself** says in the Book of Psalms,

'The Lord said to my Lord,
Sit at my right hand,
⁴³ till I make **thy enemies** a stool for **thy feet**.'

⁴⁴ **David** thus **calls him Lord; so how is he his son?**"

THOMAS	OTHER

1 Cor 15:20–28

²⁰ *But in fact Christ has been raised from the dead, the first fruits of those who have fallen asleep. ²¹ For as by a man came death, by a man has come also the resurrection of the dead. ²² For as in Adam all die, so also in Christ shall all be made alive. ²³ But each in his own order: Christ the first fruits, then at his coming those who belong to Christ. ²⁴ Then comes the end, when he delivers the kingdom to God the Father after destroying every rule and every authority and power. ²⁵ For he must reign until he has put all his enemies under his feet. ²⁶ The last enemy to be destroyed is death. ²⁷ "For God has put all things in subjection under his feet." But when it says, "All things are put in subjection under him," it is plain that he is excepted who put all things under him. ²⁸ When all things are subjected to him, then the Son himself will also be subjected to him who put all things under him, that God may be everything to every one.*

JOHN

John 7:40–44

⁴⁰ *When they heard these words, some of the people said, "This is really the prophet." ⁴¹ Others said, "This is the Christ." But some said, "Is the Christ to come from Galilee? ⁴² Has not the scripture said that the Christ is descended from David, and comes from Bethlehem, the village where David was?" ⁴³ So there was a division among the people over him. ⁴⁴ Some of them wanted to arrest him, but no one laid hands on him.*

MARK	MATT	LUKE

MARK

Mark 12:38–40 (§K59.8)

[38] And in his teaching he said, "Beware of the scribes, who like to go about in long robes, and to have salutations in the market places [39] and the best seats in the synagogues and the places of honor at feasts, [40] who devour widows' houses and for a pretense make long prayers. They will receive the greater condemnation."

MATT

Matt 23:6 ⇨ Mark 12:39

[6] "and they love the place of honor at feasts and the best seats in the synagogues, . . ."

LUKE

Luke 20:45–47 (§L89)

[45] And in the hearing of all the people he said to his disciples, [46] "Beware of the scribes, who like to go about in long robes, and love salutations in the market places and the best seats in the synagogues and the places of honor at feasts, [47] who devour widows' houses and for a pretense make long prayers. They will receive the greater condemnation."

Luke 11:37–44 (§L52.1)

[37] *While he was speaking, a Pharisee asked him to dine with him; so he went in and sat at table.* [38] *The Pharisee was astonished to see that he did not first wash before dinner.* [39] *And the Lord said to him, "Now you Pharisees cleanse the outside of the cup and of the dish, but inside you are full of extortion and wickedness.* [40] *You fools! Did not he who made the outside make the inside also?* [41] *But give for alms those things which are within; and behold, everything is clean for you.*

[42] *"But woe to you Pharisees! for you tithe mint and rue and every herb, and neglect justice and the love of God; these you ought to have done, without neglecting the others.* [43] *Woe to you Pharisees! for you love the best seat in the synagogues and salutations in the market places.* [44] *Woe to you! for you are like graves which are not seen, and men walk over them without knowing it."*

Luke 14:7–11 (§L63.1)

[7] *Now he told a parable to those who were invited, when he marked how they chose the places of honor, saying to them,* [8] *"When you are invited by any one to a marriage feast, do not sit down in a place of honor, lest a more eminent man than you be invited by him;* [9] *and he who invited you both will come and say to you, 'Give place to this man,' and then you will begin with shame to take the lowest place.* [10] *But when you are invited, go and sit in the lowest place, so that when your host comes he may say to you, 'Friend, go up higher'; then you will be honored in the presence of all who sit at table with you.* [11] *For every one who exalts himself will be humbled, and he who humbles himself will be exalted."*

JOHN	THOMAS	OTHER

MARK	MATT	LUKE

Mark 12:41–44 (§K59.9)

⁴¹ And he sat down opposite the treasury, and watched the multitude putting money into the treasury. Many rich people put in large sums. ⁴² And a poor widow came, and put in two copper coins, which make a penny. ⁴³ And he called his disciples to him, and said to them, "Truly, I say to you, this poor widow has put in more than all those who are contributing to the treasury. ⁴⁴ For they all contributed out of their abundance; but she out of her poverty has put in everything she had, her whole living."

Luke 21:1–4 (§L90)

¹ He looked up and saw the rich putting their gifts into the treasury; ² and he saw a poor widow put in two copper coins. ³ And he said, "Truly I tell you, this poor widow has put in more than all of them; ⁴ for they all contributed out of their abundance, but she out of her poverty put in all the living that she had."

JOHN	THOMAS	OTHER

MARK	MATT	LUKE

Mark 13:1–2 (§K60.1)
¹ And as he came out of the temple, one of his disciples said to him, "Look, Teacher, what wonderful stones and what wonderful buildings!" ² And Jesus said to him, "Do you see these great buildings? There will not be left here one stone upon another, that will not be thrown down."

Matt 24:1–2 (§M78.1)
¹ Jesus left **the temple** and was going away, when **his disciples** came to point out to him the buildings of **the temple**. ² But he answered them, "You **see** all these, **do you** not? Truly, I say to you, **there will not be left here one stone upon another, that will not be thrown down.**"

Luke 21:5–6
⁵ And as some spoke **of the temple**, how it was adorned with noble **stones** and offerings, he said, ⁶ "As for **these** things which **you see**, the days will come when **there** shall **not be left here one stone upon another that will not be thrown down.**"

JOHN	THOMAS	OTHER

MARK

Mark 13:3–13 (§K60.2)

³And as he sat on the Mount of Olives opposite the temple, Peter and James and John and Andrew asked him privately, ⁴"Tell us, when will this be, and what will be the sign when these things are all to be accomplished?" ⁵And Jesus began to say to them, "Take heed that no one leads you astray. ⁶Many will come in my name, saying, 'I am he!' and they will lead many astray. ⁷And when you hear of wars and rumors of wars, do not be alarmed; this must take place, but the end is not yet. ⁸For nation will rise against nation, and kingdom against kingdom; there will be earthquakes in various places, there will be famines; this is but the beginning of the birth-pangs.

⁹"But take heed to yourselves; for they will deliver you up to councils; and you will be beaten in synagogues; and you will stand before governors and kings for my sake, to bear testimony before them. ¹⁰And the gospel must first be preached to all nations. ¹¹And when they bring you to trial and deliver you up, do not be anxious beforehand what you are to say; but say whatever is given you in that hour, for it is not you who speak, but the Holy Spirit. ¹²And brother will deliver up brother to death, and the father his child, and children will rise against parents and have them put to death; ¹³and you will be hated by all for my name's sake. But he who endures to the end will be saved."

Mark 13:21–23 ⇨ Mark 13:6

²¹*"And then if any one says to you, 'Look, here is the Christ!' or 'Look, there he is!' do not believe it. ²²False Christs and false prophets will arise and show signs and wonders, to lead astray, if possible, the elect. ²³But take heed; I have told you all things beforehand."*

⇨ Mark 13:8
Cf. 2 Chr 15:6, Isa 19:2

⇨ Mark 13:12
Cf. Mic 7:6

MATT

Matt 24:3–14 (§M78.2)

³As he sat on the Mount of Olives, the disciples came to him privately, saying, "Tell us, when will this be, and what will be the sign of your coming and of the close of the age?" ⁴And Jesus answered them, "Take heed that no one leads you astray. ⁵For many will come in my name, saying, 'I am the Christ,' and they will lead many astray. ⁶And you will hear of wars and rumors of wars; see that you are not alarmed; for this must take place, but the end is not yet. ⁷For nation will rise against nation, and kingdom against kingdom, and there will be famines and earthquakes in various places: ⁸all this is but the beginning of the birth-pangs.

⁹"Then they will deliver you up to tribulation, and put you to death; and you will be hated by all nations for my name's sake. ¹⁰And then many will fall away, and betray one another, and hate one another. ¹¹And many false prophets will arise and lead many astray. ¹²And because wickedness is multiplied, most men's love will grow cold. ¹³But he who endures to the end will be saved. ¹⁴And this gospel of the kingdom will be preached throughout the whole world, as a testimony to all nations; and then the end will come."

Matt 24:23–26 ⇨ Mark 13:6

²³*"Then if any one says to you, 'Lo, here is the Christ!' or 'There he is!' do not believe it. ²⁴For false Christs and false prophets will arise and show great signs and wonders, so as to lead astray, if possible, even the elect. ²⁵Lo, I have told you beforehand. ²⁶So, if they say to you, 'Lo, he is in the wilderness,' do not go out; if they say, 'Lo, he is in the inner rooms' do not believe it."*

Matt 10:16–23 (§M28.2) ⇨ Mark 13:9–13

¹⁶"Behold, I send you out as sheep in the midst of wolves; so be wise as serpents and innocent as doves. ¹⁷Beware of men; for they will deliver you up to councils, and flog you in their synagogues, ¹⁸and you will be dragged before governors and kings for my sake, to bear testimony before them and the Gentiles. ¹⁹When they deliver you up, do not be anxious how you are to speak or what you are to say; for what you are to say will be given to you in that hour; ²⁰for it is not you who speak, but the Spirit of your Father speaking through you. ²¹Brother will deliver up brother to death, and the father his child, and children will rise against parents and have them put to death; ²²and you will be hated by all for my name's sake. But he who endures to the end will be saved. ²³When they persecute you in one town, flee to the next; for truly, I say to you, you will not have gone through all the towns of Israel, before the Son of man comes."

LUKE

Luke 21:5–19 (§L91.1)

⁵And as some spoke of the temple, how it was adorned with noble stones and offerings, he said, ⁶"As for these things which you see, the days will come when there shall not be left here one stone upon another that will not be thrown down." ⁷And they asked him, "Teacher, when will this be, and what will be the sign when this is about to take place?" ⁸And he said, "Take heed that you are not led astray; for many will come in my name, saying, 'I am he!' and, 'The time is at hand!' Do not go after them. ⁹And when you hear of wars and tumults, do not be terrified; for this must first take place, but the end will not be at once."

¹⁰Then he said to them, "Nation will rise against nation, and kingdom against kingdom; ¹¹there will be great earthquakes, and in various places famines and pestilences; and there will be terrors and great signs from heaven. ¹²But before all this they will lay their hands on you and persecute you, delivering you up to the synagogues and prisons, and you will be brought before kings and governors for my name's sake. ¹³This will be a time for you to bear testimony. ¹⁴Settle it therefore in your minds, not to meditate beforehand how to answer; ¹⁵for I will give you a mouth and wisdom, which none of your adversaries will be able to withstand or contradict. ¹⁶You will be delivered up even by parents and brothers and kinsmen and friends, and some of you they will put to death; ¹⁷you will be hated by all for my name's sake. ¹⁸But not a hair of your head will perish. ¹⁹By your endurance you will gain your lives."

Luke 17:23 ⇨ Mark 13:6

²³*"And they will say to you, 'Lo, there!' or 'Lo, here!' Do not go, do not follow them."*

Luke 12:11–12 ⇨ Mark 13:11

¹¹*"And when they bring you before the synagogues and the rulers and the authorities, do not be anxious how or what you are to answer or what you are to say; ¹²for the Holy Spirit will teach you in that very hour what you ought to say."*

JOHN	THOMAS	OTHER

John 14:26 ⇨ Mark 13:11

*26 "But the Counselor, **the Holy Spirit**, whom the Father will send in my name, he will teach you all things, and bring to your remembrance all that I have said to you."*

John 16:2 ⇨ Mark 13:12

2 "They will put you out of the synagogues; indeed, the hour is coming when whoever kills you will think he is offering service to God."

John 15:18–21 ⇨ Mark 13:13

*18 "If the world hates **you**, know that it has hated me before it hated **you**. 19 If **you** were of the world, the world would love its own; but because **you** are not of the world, but I chose **you** out of the world, therefore the world hates you. 20 Remember the word that I said to **you**, 'A servant is not greater than his master.' If they persecuted me, they will persecute **you**; if they kept my word, they will keep yours also. 21 But all this they will do to **you** on **my** account, because they do not know him who sent me."*

MARK

Mark 13:14–23 (§K60.3)

¹⁴ "But when you see the desolating sacrilege set up where it ought not to be (let the reader understand), then let those who are in Judea flee to the mountains; ¹⁵ let him who is on the housetop not go down, nor enter his house, to take anything away; ¹⁶ and let him who is in the field not turn back to take his mantle. ¹⁷ And alas for those who are with child and for those who give suck in those days! ¹⁸ Pray that it may not happen in winter. ¹⁹ For in those days there will be such tribulation as has not been from the beginning of the creation which God created until now, and never will be. ²⁰ And if the Lord had not shortened the days, no human being would be saved; but for the sake of the elect, whom he chose, he shortened the days. ²¹ And then if any one says to you, 'Look, here is the Christ!' or 'Look, there he is!' do not believe it. ²² False Christs and false prophets will arise and show signs and wonders, to lead astray, if possible, the elect. ²³ But take heed; I have told you all things beforehand."

Dan 9:27 ⇨ Mark 13:14a

²⁷ "And he shall make a strong covenant with many for one week; and for half of the week he shall cause sacrifice and offering to cease; and upon the wing of abominations shall come one who makes desolate, until the decreed end is poured out on the desolator."

Dan 11:31 ⇨ Mark 13:14a

³¹ "Forces from him shall appear and profane the temple and fortress, and shall take away the continual burnt offering. And they shall set up the abomination that makes desolate."

Dan 12:11 ⇨ Mark 13:14a

¹¹ "And from the time that the continual burnt offering is taken away, and the abomination that makes desolate is set up, there shall be a thousand two hundred and ninety days."

1 Macc 1:54 ⇨ Mark 13:14a

⁵⁴ Now on the fifteenth day of Chislev, in the one hundred and forty-fifth year, they erected a **desolating sacrilege** upon the altar of burnt offering. They also built altars in the surrounding cities of Judah, . . .

⇨ Mark 13:14b
Cf. Ezek 7:16

Dan 12:1 ⇨ Mark 13:19

¹ "At that time shall arise Michael, the great prince who has charge of your people. And there shall be a time of trouble, **such as** never **has been** since there was a nation till that time; but at that time your people shall be delivered, every one whose name shall be found written in the book."

Deut 13:2 ⇨ Mark 13:22

² "and the sign or wonder which he tells you comes to pass, and if he says, 'Let us go after other gods,' which you have not known, 'and let us serve them, . . .'"

JOHN

MATT

Matt 24:15–28 (§M78.3)

¹⁵ "So **when you see the desolating sacrilege** spoken of by the prophet Daniel, standing in the holy place (let the reader understand), ¹⁶ then let those who are in Judea flee to the mountains; ¹⁷ let him who is on the housetop not go down to take what is in his house; ¹⁸ and let him who is in the field not turn back to take his mantle. ¹⁹ And alas for those who are with child and for those who give suck in those days! ²⁰ Pray that your flight may not be in winter or on a sabbath. ²¹ For then there will be a great tribulation, such as has not been from the beginning of the world until now, no, and never will be. ²² And if those days had not been shortened, no human being would be saved; but for the sake of the elect those days will be shortened. ²³ Then if any one says to you, 'Lo, here is the Christ!' or 'There he is!' do not believe it. ²⁴ For false Christs and false prophets will arise and show great signs and wonders, so as to lead astray, if possible, even the elect. ²⁵ Lo, I have told you beforehand. ²⁶ So, if they say to you, 'Lo, he is in the wilderness,' do not go out; if they say, 'Lo, he is in the inner rooms' do not believe it. ²⁷ For as the lightning comes from the east and shines as far as the west, so will be the coming of the Son of man. ²⁸ Wherever the body is, there the eagles will be gathered together."

THOMAS

GThom 79 ⇨ Mark 13:17

(79) A woman from the crowd said to Him, "Blessed are the womb which bore You and the breasts which nourished You."

*He said to her, "Blessed are **those who have** heard the word of the Father and have truly kept it. For there will be days when you will say, 'Blessed are the womb which has not conceived **and the breasts which have not given milk.'"***

GThom 113 ⇨ Mark 13:21

(113) His disciples said to Him, "When will the Kingdom come?"

*<Jesus said,> "It will **not** come by waiting for it. It will **not** be a matter of saying '**Here** it is' or '**There** it is.' Rather, the Kingdom of the Father is spread out upon the earth, and men do not see it."*

LUKE

Luke 21:20–24 (§L91.2)

²⁰ "But when you see Jerusalem surrounded by armies, then know that its desolation has come near. ²¹ Then let those who are in Judea flee to the mountains, and let those who are inside the city depart, and let not those who are out in the country enter it; ²² for these are days of vengeance, to fulfil all that is written. ²³ Alas for those who are with child and for those who give suck in those days! For great distress shall be upon the earth and wrath upon this people; ²⁴ they will fall by the edge of the sword, and be led captive among all nations; and Jerusalem will be trodden down by the Gentiles, until the times of the Gentiles are fulfilled."

Luke 17:31 ⇨ Mark 13:15–16

³¹ "On that day, **let him who is on the housetop**, with his goods in the house, not come **down** to take them **away**; and likewise **let him who is in the field not turn back.**"

OTHER

MARK	MATT	LUKE

MARK

Mark 13:24–32 (§K60.4)

²⁴ "But in those days, after that tribulation, the sun will be darkened, and the moon will not give its light, ²⁵ and the stars will be falling from heaven, and the powers in the heavens will be shaken. ²⁶ And then they will see the Son of man coming in clouds with great power and glory. ²⁷ And then he will send out the angels, and gather his elect from the four winds, from the ends of the earth to the ends of heaven.

²⁸ "From the fig tree learn its lesson: as soon as its branch becomes tender and puts forth its leaves, you know that summer is near. ²⁹ So also, when you see these things taking place, you know that he is near, at the very gates. ³⁰ Truly, I say to you, this generation will not pass away before all these things take place. ³¹ Heaven and earth will pass away, but my words will not pass away.

³² "But of that day or that hour no one knows, not even the angels in heaven, nor the Son, but only the Father."

●**Mark 14:62** ⇨ Mark 13:26
⁶² And Jesus said, "I am; and you will see the Son of man seated at the right hand of Power, and coming with the clouds of heaven."

Mark 9:1 ⇨ Mark 13:30
¹ And he said to them, "*Truly, I say to you*, there are some standing here who *will not taste death before they see that the kingdom of God has come with power.*"

Isa 13:10 ⇨ Mark 13:24
¹⁰ For the stars of the heavens and their constellations
will not give their light;
the sun will be dark at its rising
and the moon will not shed **its light.**

Isa 34:4 ⇨ Mark 13:24
⁴ All the host of heaven shall rot away,
and the skies roll up like a scroll.
All their host shall fall,
as leaves fall from the vine,
like leaves falling from the fig tree.

Dan 7:13–14 ⇨ Mark 13:26–27
¹³ I saw in the night visions,
and behold, with the **clouds** of heaven
there came one like a **son of man**,
and he came to the Ancient of Days
and was presented before him.
¹⁴ And to him was given dominion
and glory and kingdom,
that all peoples, nations, and languages
should serve him;
his dominion is an everlasting dominion,
which shall not pass away,
and his kingdom one
that shall not be destroyed.

JOHN

MATT

Matt 24:29–36 (§M78.4)

²⁹ "Immediately **after** the **tribulation** of those days the sun will be darkened, and the moon will not give its light, **and the stars will fall from heaven, and the powers of the heavens will be shaken;** ³⁰ then will appear the sign of **the Son of man** in heaven, and then all the tribes of the earth will mourn, **and they will see the Son of man coming** on the **clouds** of heaven **with power and great glory;** ³¹ and **he will send out** his **angels** with a loud trumpet call, and they will **gather his elect from the four winds, from** one end **of heaven to the** other.

³² "From the fig tree learn its lesson: as soon as its branch becomes tender and puts forth its leaves, you know that summer is near. ³³ So also, when you see all these things, you know that he is near, at the very gates. ³⁴ Truly, I say to you, this generation will not pass away till all these things take place. ³⁵ Heaven and earth will pass away, but my words will not pass away.

³⁶ "But of that day and hour no one knows, not even the angels of heaven, nor the Son, but the Father only."

Matt 16:28 ⇨ Mark 13:30
²⁸ "*Truly, I say to you*, there are some standing here who *will not taste death before they see the Son of man coming in his kingdom.*"

Deut 30:3–4 ⇨ Mark 13:27
³ "then the Lord your God will restore your fortunes, and have compassion upon you, and **he will gather** you again **from** all the peoples where the Lord your God has scattered you. ⁴ If your outcasts are in the uttermost parts **of heaven,** from there the Lord your God **will gather** you, and from there **he will** fetch you"; . . .

THOMAS

LUKE

Luke 21:25–33 (§L91.3)

²⁵ "And there will be signs in **sun and moon and stars**, and upon the earth distress of nations in perplexity at the roaring of the sea and the waves, ²⁶ men fainting with fear and with foreboding of what is coming on the world; for **the powers of the heavens will be shaken.** ²⁷ **And then they will see the Son of man coming in** a cloud **with power and great glory.** ²⁸ Now when these things begin to take place, look up and raise your heads, because your redemption is drawing near."

²⁹ And he told them a parable: "Look at the **fig tree**, and all the trees; ³⁰ as soon as they come out in leaf, **you** see for yourselves and **know that the summer is** already **near.** ³¹ So also, when you see these **things taking place, you know that** the kingdom of God is **near.** ³² Truly, I say to you, this generation will not pass away till all has taken place. ³³ Heaven and earth will pass away, but my words will not pass away."

Luke 9:27 ⇨ Mark 13:30
²⁷ "*But I tell you truly, there are some standing here who will not taste death before they see the kingdom of God.*"

OTHER

1 Thess 4:15–16 ⇨ Mark 13:26–27
¹⁵ *For this we declare to you by the word of the Lord, that we who are alive, who are left until the **coming** of the Lord, shall not precede those who have fallen asleep.* ¹⁶ *For the Lord himself will descend from heaven **with** a cry of command, **with** the archangel's call, and **with** the sound of the trumpet of God. And the dead in Christ will rise first;* . . .

Rev 1:7 ⇨ Mark 13:26
⁷ *Behold, he is **coming with the clouds**, and every eye will see him, every one who pierced him; and all tribes of the earth **will** wail on account of him. Even so. Amen.*

MARK

MATT

LUKE

Mark 13:33–37 (§K60.5)

[33] "Take heed, watch;[a] for you do not know when the time will come. [34] It is like a man going on a journey, when he leaves home and puts his servants in charge, each with his work, and commands the doorkeeper to be on watch. [35] Watch therefore—for you do not know when the master of the house will come, in the evening, or at midnight, or at cockcrow, or in the morning— [36] lest he come suddenly and find you asleep. [37] And what I say to you I say to all: Watch."

[a] Some witnesses add, *and pray:* (cf. Mark 14:38) ℵ A C K L W X Δ Θ Π Ψ *f*[1] *f*[13] 28 *al*

Matt 24:37–51 (§M78.5)

[37] "As were the days of Noah, so will be the coming of the Son of man. [38] For as in those days before the flood they were eating and drinking, marrying and giving in marriage, until the day when Noah entered the ark, [39] and they did **not know** until the flood came and swept them all away, so **will** be the coming of the Son of man. [40] Then two men will be in the field; one is taken and one is left. [41] Two women will be grinding at the mill; one is taken and one is left. [42] **Watch therefore, for you do not know** on what day your Lord is coming. [43] But know this, that if the householder had known in what part of the night the thief was coming, he would have watched and would not have let his house be broken into. [44] Therefore **you** also must be ready; for the Son of man is coming at an hour **you do not** expect.

[45] "Who then is the faithful and wise servant, whom his **master** has set over **his** household, to give them their food at the proper time? [46] Blessed is that servant whom his **master** when he comes will find so doing. [47] Truly, I say to you, he will set him over all his possessions. [48] But if that wicked servant says to himself, 'My **master** is delayed,' [49] and begins to beat his fellow servants, and eats and drinks with the drunken, [50] the **master of** that servant **will come** on a day when he does **not** expect him and at an hour he does **not know**, [51] and will punish him, and put him with the hypocrites; there men will weep and gnash their teeth."

Matt 25:13 ⇨ Mark 13:35
[13] "**Watch therefore, for you know** neither the day nor the hour."

Luke 21:34–36 (§L91.4)

[34] "But **take heed** to yourselves lest your hearts be weighed down with dissipation and drunkenness and cares of this life, and that day **come** upon **you suddenly** like a snare; [35] for it **will come** upon all who dwell upon the face of the whole earth. [36] But **watch** at all times, praying that you may have strength to escape all these things that will take place, and to stand before the Son of man."

Luke 12:35–40

[35] *"Let your loins be girded and your lamps burning, [36] and be like men who are waiting for their **master** to come home from the marriage feast, so that they may open to him at once when he comes and knocks. [37] Blessed are those servants whom the **master** finds awake when he comes; truly, I say to you, he will gird himself and have them sit at table, and he **will come** and serve them. [38] If he comes in the second watch, or in the third, and finds them so, blessed are those servants! [39] But **know** this, that if the householder had **known** at what hour the thief was coming, he would not have left his house to be broken into. [40] You also must be ready; for the Son of man is coming at an unexpected hour."*

JOHN

THOMAS

OTHER

Did 16:1
[1] *"**Watch**" over your life: "let your lamps" be not quenched "and your loins" be not ungirded, but be "ready," **for** ye **know not** "the hour in which our Lord cometh."*

MARK

Mark 14:1–2 (§K61.1)

[1] It was now two days before the Passover and the feast of Unleavened Bread. And the chief priests and the scribes were seeking how to arrest him by stealth, and kill him; [2] for they said, "Not during the feast, lest there be a tumult of the people."

Mark 11:18

[18] *And the chief priests and the scribes heard it and sought a way to destroy him; for they feared him, because all the multitude was astonished at his teaching.*

Mark 12:12

[12] *And they tried to arrest him, but feared the multitude, for they perceived that he had told the parable against them; so they left him and went away.*

JOHN

† John 11:45–53 (§J23.1)

[45] Many of the Jews therefore, who had come with Mary and had seen what he did, believed in him; [46] but some of them went to the Pharisees and told them what Jesus had done. [47] So the chief priests and the Pharisees gathered the council, and said, "What are we to do? For this man performs many signs. [48] If we let him go on thus, every one will believe in him, and the Romans will come and destroy both our holy place and our nation." [49] But one of them, Caiaphas, who was high priest that year, said to them, "You know nothing at all; [50] you do not understand that it is expedient for you that one man should die for the people, and that the whole nation should not perish." [51] He did not say this of his own accord, but being high priest that year he prophesied that Jesus should die for the nation, [52] and not for the nation only, but to gather into one the children of God who are scattered abroad. [53] So from that day on they took counsel how to put him to death.

† John 11:54 (§J23.2)

[54] Jesus therefore no longer went about openly among the Jews, but went from there to the country near the wilderness, to a town called Ephraim; and there he stayed with the disciples.

† John 11:55–57 (§J23.3)

[55] Now the Passover of the Jews was at hand, and many went up from the country to Jerusalem before the Passover, to purify themselves. [56] They were looking for Jesus and saying to one another as they stood in the temple, "What do you think? That he will not come to the feast?" [57] Now the chief priests and the Pharisees had given orders that if any one knew where he was, he should let them know, so that they might arrest him.

MATT

Matt 26:1–2 (§M80.1)

[1] When Jesus had finished all these sayings, he said to his disciples, [2] "You know that after two days the Passover is coming, and the Son of man will be delivered up to be crucified."

Matt 26:3–5 (§M80.2)

[3] Then the chief priests and the elders of the people gathered in the palace of the high priest, who was called Caiaphas, [4] and took counsel together in order to arrest Jesus by stealth and kill him. [5] But they said, "Not during the feast, lest there be a tumult among the people."

Matt 21:45

[45] *When the chief priests and the Pharisees heard his parables, they perceived that he was speaking about them.*

THOMAS

LUKE

Luke 22:1–2 (§L92.1)

[1] Now the feast of Unleavened Bread drew near, which is called the Passover. [2] And the chief priests and the scribes were seeking how to put him to death; for they feared the people.

Luke 19:47–48

[47] *And he was teaching daily in the temple. The chief priests and the scribes and the principal men of the people sought to destroy him;* [48] *but they did not find anything they could do, for all the people hung upon his words.*

Luke 20:19

[19] *The scribes and the chief priests tried to lay hands on him at that very hour, but they feared the people; for they perceived that he had told this parable against them.*

OTHER

MARK	MATT	LUKE

MARK

Mark 14:3–9 (§K61.2)

³ And while he was at Bethany in the house of Simon the leper, as he sat at table, a woman came with an alabaster flask of ointment of pure nard, very costly, and she broke the flask and poured it over his head. ⁴ But there were some who said to themselves indignantly, "Why was the ointment thus wasted? ⁵ For this ointment might have been sold for more than three hundred denarii,ᵃ and given to the poor." And they reproached her. ⁶ But Jesus said, "Let her alone; why do you trouble her? She has done a beautiful thing to me. ⁷ For you always have the poor with you, and whenever you will, you can do good to them; but you will not always have me. ⁸ She has done what she could; she has anointed my body beforehand for burying. ⁹ And truly, I say to you, wherever the gospel is preached in the whole world, what she has done will be told in memory of her."

ᵃ A denarius was a day's wage for a laborer

MATT

Matt 26:6–13 (§M80.3)

⁶ Now when Jesus was at Bethany in the house of Simon the leper, ⁷ a woman came up to him with an alabaster flask of very expensive ointment, and she poured it on his head, as he sat at table. ⁸ But when the disciples saw it, they were indignant, saying, "Why this waste? ⁹ For this ointment might have been sold for a large sum, and given to the poor." ¹⁰ But Jesus, aware of this, said to them, "Why do you trouble the woman? For she has done a beautiful thing to me. ¹¹ For you always have the poor with you, but you will not always have me. ¹² In pouring this ointment on my body she has done it to prepare me for burial. ¹³ Truly, I say to you, wherever this gospel is preached in the whole world, what she has done will be told in memory of her."

LUKE

Luke 7:36–50 (§L29)

³⁶ One of the Pharisees asked him to eat with him, and he went into the Pharisee's house, and took his place at table. ³⁷ And behold, a woman of the city, who was a sinner, when she learned that he was at table in the Pharisee's house, brought an alabaster flask of ointment, ³⁸ and standing behind him at his feet, weeping, she began to wet his feet with her tears, and wiped them with the hair of her head, and kissed his feet, and anointed them with the ointment. ³⁹ Now when the Pharisee who had invited him saw it, he said to himself, "If this man were a prophet, he would have known who and what sort of woman this is who is touching him, for she is a sinner." ⁴⁰ And Jesus answering said to him, "Simon, I have something to say to you." And he answered, "What is it, Teacher?" ⁴¹ "A certain creditor had two debtors; one owed five hundred denarii, and the other fifty. ⁴² When they could not pay, he forgave them both. Now which of them will love him more?" ⁴³ Simon answered, "The one, I suppose, to whom he forgave more." And he said to him "You have judged rightly." ⁴⁴ Then turning toward the woman he said to Simon, "Do you see this woman? I entered your house, you gave me no water for my feet, but she has wet my feet with her tears and wiped them with her hair. ⁴⁵ You gave me no kiss, but from the time I came in she has not ceased to kiss my feet. ⁴⁶ You did not anoint my head with oil, but she has anointed my feet with ointment. ⁴⁷ Therefore I tell you, her sins, which are many, are forgiven, for she loved much; but he who is forgiven little, loves little." ⁴⁸ And he said to her, "Your sins are forgiven." ⁴⁹ Then those who were at table with him began to say among themselves, "Who is this, who even forgives sins?" ⁵⁰ And he said to the woman, "Your faith has saved you; go in peace."

JOHN

† John 12:1–8 (§J24.1)

¹ Six days before the Passover, Jesus came to Bethany, where Lazarus was, whom Jesus had raised from the dead. ² There they made him a supper; Martha served, and Lazarus was one of those at table with him. ³ Mary took a pound of costly ointment of pure nard and anointed the feet of Jesus and wiped his feet with her hair; and the house was filled with the fragrance of the ointment. ⁴ But Judas Iscariot, one of his disciples (he who was to betray him), said, ⁵ "Why was this ointment not sold for three hundred denarii and given to the poor?" ⁶ This he said, not that he cared for the poor but because he was a thief, and as he had the money box he used to take what was put into it. ⁷ Jesus said, "Let her alone, let her keep it for the day of my burial. ⁸ The poor you always have with you, but you do not always have me."

THOMAS

OTHER

MARK	MATT	LUKE
Mark 14:10–11 (§K61.3) °	**Matt 26:14–16 (§M80.4)**	**Luke 22:3–6 (§L92.2)**
¹⁰ Then **Judas Iscariot, who was one of the twelve, went to the chief priests** in order to betray him to them. ¹¹ **And when they heard it they were glad, and** promised **to give him** money. **And he sought an opportunity to betray him.**	¹⁴ **Then** one of the twelve, who was called **Judas Iscariot, went to the chief priests** ¹⁵ and said, "What will you give me if I deliver **him to** you?" **And they** paid **him** thirty pieces of silver. ¹⁶ **And** from that moment **he sought an opportunity to betray him.**	³ Then Satan entered into **Judas** called **Iscariot, who was** of the number **of the twelve;** ⁴ **he went** away and conferred with **the chief priests** and officers how he might **betray him to them.** ⁵ **And they were glad, and** engaged to **give him money.** ⁶ So **he** agreed, **and sought an opportunity to betray him** to them in the absence of the multitude.

°Appendix 2 ⇨ Mark 14:10

JOHN	THOMAS	OTHER

MARK	MATT	LUKE

THE PASSOVER MEAL

Mark 14:12–16 (§K62.1)

[12] And on the first day of Unleavened Bread, when they sacrificed the passover lamb, his disciples said to him, "Where will you have us go and prepare for you to eat the passover?" [13] And he sent two of his disciples, and said to them, "Go into the city, and a man carrying a jar of water will meet you; follow him, [14] and wherever he enters, say to the householder, 'The Teacher says, Where is my guest room, where I am to eat the passover with my disciples?' [15] And he will show you a large upper room furnished and ready; there prepare for us." [16] And the disciples set out and went to the city, and found it as he had told them; and they prepared the passover.

THE TRAITOR

Mark 14:17–21 (§K62.2) °

[17] And when it was evening he came with the twelve. [18] And as they were at table eating, Jesus said, "Truly, I say to you, one of you will betray me, one who is eating with me." [19] They began to be sorrowful, and to say to him one after another, "Is it I?" [20] He said to them, "It is one of the twelve, one who is dipping bread into the dish with me. [21] For the Son of man goes as it is written of him, but woe to that man by whom the Son of man is betrayed! It would have been better for that man if he had not been born."

THE LAST SUPPER

Mark 14:22–25 (§K62.3)

[22] And as they were eating, he took bread, and blessed, and broke it, and gave it to them, and said, "Take; this is my body." [23] And he took a cup, and when he had given thanks he gave it to them, and they all drank of it. [24] And he said to them, "This is my blood of the[a] covenant, which is poured out for many. [25] Truly, I say to you, I shall not drink again of the fruit of the vine until that day when I drink it new in the kingdom of God."

[a] Some witnesses insert *new:* A K P X Δ Π *f¹ f¹³* 28 *al;* text: ℵ B C L Θ Ψ *al*

° Appendix 2 ⇨ Mark 14:17, 20

Ps 41:9 ⇨ Mark 14:18
[9] Even my bosom friend in whom I trusted, who ate of my bread, has lifted his heel against **me.**

Matt 26:17–19 (§M81.1) ⇨ §K62.1
[17] Now **on the first day of Unleavened Bread** the **disciples** came to Jesus, saying, "Where will you have us prepare for you to eat the passover?" [18] He said, "Go into the city to a certain one, **and say to him,** 'The Teacher says, My time is at hand; I will keep the passover at your house **with my disciples.'"** [19] And the disciples did as Jesus had directed them, and they prepared the passover.

Matt 26:20–25 (§M81.2) ⇨ §K62.2
[20] When it was evening, he sat at table with the twelve disciples; [21] and as they were eating, he said, "Truly, I say to you, one of you will betray me." [22] And they were very sorrowful, and began to say to him one after another, "Is it I, Lord?" [23] He answered, "He who has dipped his hand in **the dish with me,** will betray me. [24] The Son of man goes as it is written of him, but woe to that man by whom the Son of man is betrayed! It would have been better for that man if he had not been born." [25] Judas, who betrayed him, said, "Is it I, Master?" He said to him, "You have said so."

Matt 26:26–29 (§M81.3) ⇨ §K62.3
[26] Now **as they were eating,** Jesus took bread, and blessed, and broke it, and gave it to the disciples **and said,** "Take, eat; **this is my body."** [27] And he took a cup, and when he had given thanks he gave it to them, saying, "Drink of it, all of you; [28] for **this is my blood of the covenant, which is poured out for many** for the forgiveness of sins. [29] I tell **you** I shall not drink again of this **fruit of the vine until that day when** I drink it new with you in my Father's **kingdom."**

Exod 24:8 ⇨ Mark 14:24
[8] And Moses took the **blood** and threw it upon the people, and said, "Behold the **blood of the covenant which** the Lord has made with you in accordance with all these words."

Jer 31:31 ⇨ Mark 14:24
[31] "Behold, the days are coming, says the Lord, when I will make a new **covenant** with the house of Israel and the house of Judah, . . .

Zech 9:11 ⇨ Mark 14:24
[11] As for you also, because of **the blood of my covenant** with you,
    I will set your captives free from the waterless pit.

Luke 22:7–13 (§L93.1) ⇨ §K62.1
[7] Then came the **day of Unleavened Bread,** on which **the passover lamb** had to be **sacrificed.** [8] So Jesus sent Peter and John, saying, "Go and **prepare the passover for us,** that we may eat it." [9] They said to him, "**Where will you have us prepare it?**" [10] He said to them, "Behold, when you have entered **the city,** a **man carrying a jar of water will meet you;** follow **him** into the house which **he enters,** [11] and tell **the householder,** 'The Teacher says to you, **Where is** the guest room, where I am to eat the passover with my disciples?' [12] And he will show you a large **upper room furnished;** there make ready." [13] And they went, and **found** it as he had told them; and they prepared the passover.

Luke 22:14–23 (§L93.2) ⇨ §K62.2–3
[14] And when the hour **came, he** sat at table, and the apostles with him. [15] And he **said** to them, "I have earnestly desired to eat this passover with you before I suffer; [16] for I tell **you I shall not** eat it **until it is** fulfilled in **the kingdom of God."** [17] And he took a cup, and when he had given thanks he said, "Take this, and divide it among yourselves; [18] for I tell **you** that from now on I shall not drink **of the fruit of the vine until the kingdom of God** comes." [19] And he took bread, and when he had given thanks he **broke it and gave it to** them, saying, "**This is my body** which is given for you. Do this in remembrance of me." [20] And likewise the **cup** after supper, saying, "**This cup which is poured out for** you **is the new covenant in my blood.** [21] But behold the hand of him who betrays **me is with me on the table.** [22] For the Son of man goes as it **has been determined; but woe to that man by whom** he **is betrayed!"** [23] And **they began to** question one another, which of them it was that would do this.

| | JOHN | THOMAS | OTHER |

JOHN   THOMAS   OTHER

John 13:21–30 (§J29) ⇨ §K62.2

²¹ When **Jesus** had thus spoken, he was troubled in spirit, and testified, "Truly, **truly, I say to you, one of you will betray me**." ²² The disciples looked at one another, uncertain of whom he spoke. ²³ One of his disciples, whom Jesus loved, was lying close to the breast of Jesus; ²⁴ so Simon Peter beckoned to him and said, "Tell us who it is of whom he speaks." ²⁵ So lying thus, close to the breast of Jesus, he said to him, "Lord, who is it?" ²⁶ Jesus answered, "**It is** he to whom I shall give this morsel when I have dipped it." So when he had dipped the morsel, he gave it to Judas, the son of Simon Iscariot. ²⁷ Then after the morsel, Satan entered into him. Jesus said to him, "What you are going to do, do quickly." ²⁸ Now no one at the table knew why he said this to him. ²⁹ Some thought that, because Judas had the money box, Jesus was telling him, "Buy what we need for the feast"; or, that he should give something to the poor. ³⁰ So, after receiving the morsel, he immediately went out; and it was night.

John 6:48–58 ⇨ §K62.3

⁴⁸ "I am the **bread** of life. ⁴⁹ Your fathers ate the manna in the wilderness, and they died. ⁵⁰ This is the **bread** which comes down from heaven, that a man may eat of it and not die. ⁵¹ I am the living **bread** which came down from heaven; if any one eats of this **bread**, he will live for ever; and the **bread** which I shall give for the life of the world is my flesh." ⁵² The Jews then disputed among themselves, saying, "How can this man give us his flesh to eat?" ⁵³ So Jesus **said to them**, "Truly, truly, I say to you, unless you eat the flesh of the Son of man and drink his **blood**, you have no life in you; ⁵⁴ he who eats **my** flesh and drinks **my blood** has eternal life, and I will raise him up at the last day. ⁵⁵ For **my** flesh is food indeed, and **my blood** is drink indeed. ⁵⁶ He who eats my flesh and drinks **my blood** abides in me, and I in him. ⁵⁷ As the living Father sent me, and I live because of the Father, so he who eats me will live because of me. ⁵⁸ This is the **bread** which came down from heaven, not such as the fathers ate and died; he who eats this **bread** will live for ever."

GEbi 7 ⇨ §K62.1

(7) But they abandon the proper sequence of the words and pervert the saying, as is plain to all from the readings attached, and have let the disciples say:
Where wilt thou that we prepare for thee the passover? *and him to answer to that:*
Do I desire with desire at this Passover to eat flesh with you? (Epiphanius, *Haer.* 30.22.4)

1 Cor 11:23–25 ⇨ §K62.3

²³ For I received from the Lord what I also delivered to you, that the Lord Jesus on the night when **he** was betrayed **took bread**, ²⁴ **and** when he had given thanks, he **broke it, and said**, "**This is my body** which is for you. Do this in remembrance of me." ²⁵ In the same way also the **cup**, after supper, saying, "**This cup is the** new **covenant** in **my blood**. Do this, as often as you drink **it**, in remembrance of me."

Did 9:1–5 ⇨ §K62.3

¹ And concerning the Eucharist, hold Eucharist thus: ² First concerning the **Cup**, "We give thanks to thee, our Father, for the Holy Vine of David thy child, which, thou didst make known to us through Jesus thy child; to thee be glory for ever." ³ And concerning the broken **Bread**: "We give thee thanks, our Father, for the life and knowledge which thou didst make known to us through Jesus thy child. To thee be glory for ever. ⁴ As this broken **bread** is scattered upon the mountains, but was brought together and became one, so let thy Church be gathered together from the ends of the earth into thy kingdom, for thine is the glory and the power through Jesus Christ for ever." ⁵ But let none eat or drink of your Eucharist except those who have been baptised in the Lord's Name. For concerning this also did the Lord say, "Give not that which is holy to the dogs."

Justin, *Apology* 1.66.3 ⇨ §K62.3

For the apostles in the memoirs composed by them, which are called Gospels, thus handed down what was commanded them: that Jesus, taking **bread** and having given thanks, said, "Do this for my memorial, **this my body**"; and likewise taking the **cup** and giving **thanks he said**, "**This is my blood**"; and gave it to them alone. This also the wicked demons in imitation handed down as something to be done in the mysteries of Mithra; for **bread** and **a cup** of water are brought out in their secret rites of initiation, with certain invocations which you either know or can learn.

MEASURES OF LENGTH IN THE NEW TESTAMENT

Greek	RSV	U.S. Measures
pēchus	cubit	ca. 1.5 feet
orguia	fathom	ca. 72.44 inches
stadion	furlong, stadia,	ca. 606 feet =
	or the equivalent in miles	.1148 of a mile
milion	mile	ca. 4,879 feet
	day's journey	ca. 20–25 miles
	sabbath day's journey	6 stadia or ca. 3,636 feet

MEASURES OF CAPACITY IN THE NEW TESTAMENT

Greek	RSV	Equivalence	U.S. Measures
batos	measure	bath (Hebrew)	6.073 gallons
koros	measure	kōr (Hebrew)	60.738 gallons
saton	measure	şe'āh (Hebrew)	6.959 dry quarts
metrētēs	measure		10.3 gallons
choinix	quart		0.98 dry quart
modios	bushel	modius (Latin)	7.68 dry quarts
xestēs	pot	sextarius (Latin)	0.96 dry pint = 1.12 fluid pints

WEIGHTS IN THE NEW TESTAMENT

Greek	RSV	Equivalence	U.S. Avoirdupois
talenton	talent	talent (Hebrew)	75.558 pounds
mna	pound	mina (Hebrew)	20.148 ounces
litra	pound	libra (Latin)	0.719 pound = 11.504 ounces

U.S. Dry Measures

Bushel	4 pecks
peck	8 quarts
quart	2 pints
pint	.5 quart

Adapted from: *The New Oxford Annotated Bible* (New York: Oxford University Press, 1977), pp. 1546–47 and O. R. Sellers, "Weights and Measures," *Interpreter's Dictionary of the Bible,* ed. G. A. Buttrick, et al. (Nashville: Abingdon Press, 1962), pp. 828–39.

NEW GOSPEL PARALLELS

MARK	MATT	LUKE

MARK

Mark 14:26–31 (§K63.1)

²⁶ And when they had sung a hymn, they went out to the Mount of Olives. ²⁷ And Jesus said to them, "You will all fall away; for it is written, 'I will strike the shepherd, and the sheep will be scattered.' ²⁸ But after I am raised up, I will go before you to Galilee." ²⁹ Peter said to him, "Even though they all fall away, I will not." ³⁰ And Jesus said to him, "Truly, I say to you, this very night, before the cock crows twice, you will deny me three times." ³¹ But he said vehemently, "If I must die with you, I will not deny you." And they all said the same.

Zech 13:7 ⇨ Mark 14:27

⁷ "Awake, O sword, against my **shepherd**, against the man who stands next to me," says the Lord of hosts. "**Strike the shepherd**, that **the sheep** may **be scattered**; I will turn my hand against the little ones."

MATT

Matt 26:30–35 (§M82.1)

³⁰ And when they had sung a hymn, they went out to the Mount of Olives. ³¹ Then Jesus said to them, "You will all fall away because of me this night; for it is written, 'I will strike the shepherd, and the sheep of the flock will be scattered.' ³² But after I am raised up, I will go before you to Galilee." ³³ Peter declared to him, "Though they all fall away because of you, I will never fall away." ³⁴ Jesus said to him, "Truly, I say to you, this very night, before the cock crows, you will deny me three times." ³⁵ Peter said to him, "Even if I must die with you, I will not deny you." And so said all the disciples.

LUKE

Luke 22:31–34 (§L93.4)

³¹ "Simon, Simon, behold, Satan demanded to have you, that he might sift you like wheat, ³² but I have prayed for you that your faith may not fail; and when you have turned again, strengthen your brethren." ³³ And he said to him, "Lord, I am ready to go with you to prison and to death." ³⁴ He said, "I tell you, Peter, the cock will not crow this day, until you three times deny that you know me."

Luke 22:39 (§L94.1a) ⇨ Mark 14:26

³⁹ And he came out, and went, as was his custom, to the Mount of Olives; and the disciples followed him.

JOHN	THOMAS	OTHER

JOHN

John 13:36–38 ⇨ Mark 14:29–30

³⁶ Simon **Peter said to him,** "Lord, where are you going?" Jesus answered, "Where I am going you cannot follow me now; but you shall follow afterward." ³⁷ **Peter said to him,** "Lord, why cannot I follow you now? I will lay down my life for **you.**" ³⁸ **Jesus** answered, "Will you lay down your life for me? **Truly, truly, I say to you, the cock will** not crow, till **you** have denied **me three times.**"

† John 18:1 ⇨ Mark 14:26

¹ **When** Jesus had spoken these words, he **went** forth with his disciples across the Kidron valley, where there was a garden, which he and his disciples entered.

John 16:32 ⇨ Mark 14:27

³² *"The hour is coming, indeed it has come, when **you will be scattered**, every man to his home, and will leave me alone; yet I am not alone, for the Father is with me."*

John 11:16 ⇨ Mark 14:31

¹⁶ *Thomas, called the Twin, **said** to his fellow disciples, "Let us also go, that we may **die with him.**"*

OTHER

Fayyum Fragment ⇨ Mark 14:27, 29–30

. . . while he was going **out** he **said,** "This night **you will all fall away,** as **it is written,** '**I will strike the shepherd, and the sheep will be scattered.**'" When **Peter** said, "**Even though all, not I,**" Jesus said, "**Before the cock crows twice, you will** this day **deny me three times.**"

MARK	MATT	LUKE

MARK

INTRODUCTION

Mark 14:32 (§K63.2a)

³² And they went to a place which was called Gethsemane; and he said to his disciples, "Sit here, while I pray."

JESUS TAKES THE THREE

Mark 14:33–34 (§K63.2b)

³³ And he took with him Peter and James and John, and began to be greatly distressed and troubled. ³⁴ And he said to them, "My soul is very sorrowful, even to death; remain here, and watch."[a]

"ABBA, FATHER"

Mark 14:35–36 (§K63.2c)

³⁵ And going a little farther, he fell on the ground and prayed that, if it were possible, the hour might pass from him. ³⁶ And he said, "Abba, Father, all things are possible to thee; remove this cup from me; yet not what I will, but what thou wilt."

THE THREE SLEEP

Mark 14:37–38 (§K63.2d)

³⁷ And he came and found them sleeping, and he said to Peter, "Simon, are you asleep? Could you not watch[a] one hour? ³⁸ Watch[a] and pray that you may not enter into temptation; the spirit indeed is willing, but the flesh is weak."

SECOND PRAYER

Mark 14:39 (§K63.2e)

³⁹ And again he went away and prayed, saying the same words.

THE THREE SLEEP

Mark 14:40 (§K63.2f)

⁴⁰ And again he came and found them sleeping, for their eyes were very heavy; and they did not know what to answer him.

THE HOUR HAS COME

Mark 14:41–42 (§K63.2g)

⁴¹ And he came the third time, and said to them, "Are you still sleeping and taking your rest? It is enough; the hour has come; the Son of man is betrayed into the hands of sinners. ⁴² Rise, let us be going; see, my betrayer is at hand."

[a] Or: *keep awake*

MATT

Matt 26:36 (§M82.2a)

³⁶ Then Jesus went with them to a place called Gethsemane, and he said to his disciples, "Sit here, while I go yonder and pray."

Matt 26:37–38 (§M82.2b)

³⁷ And taking with him Peter and the two sons of Zebedee, he began to be sorrowful and troubled. ³⁸ Then he said to them, "My soul is very sorrowful, even to death; remain here, and watch with me."

Matt 26:39 (§M82.2c)

³⁹ And going a little farther he fell on his face and prayed, "My father, if it be possible, let this cup pass from me; nevertheless, not as I will, but as thou wilt."

Matt 26:40–41 (§M82.2d)

⁴⁰ And he came to the disciples and found them sleeping; and he said to Peter, "So, could you not watch with me one hour? ⁴¹ Watch and pray that you may not enter into temptation; the spirit indeed is willing, but the flesh is weak."

Matt 26:42 (§M82.2e)

⁴² Again, for the second time, he went away and prayed, "My Father, if this cannot pass unless I drink it, thy will be done."

Matt 26:43 (§M82.2f)

⁴³ And again he came and found them sleeping, for their eyes were heavy.

Matt 26:44 (§M82.2g)

⁴⁴ So, leaving them again, he went away and prayed for the third time, saying the same words.

Matt 26:45–46 (§M82.2h)

⁴⁵ Then he came to the disciples and said to them, "Are you still sleeping and taking your rest? Behold, the hour is at hand, and the Son of man is betrayed into the hands of sinners. ⁴⁶ Rise, let us be going; see, my betrayer is at hand."

LUKE

Luke 22:39 (§L94.1a)

³⁹ And he came out, and went, as was his custom, to the Mount of Olives; and the disciples followed him.

Luke 22:40–42 (§L94.1b)

⁴⁰ And when he came to the place he said to them, "Pray that you may not enter into temptation." ⁴¹ And he withdrew from them about a stone's throw, and knelt down and prayed, ⁴² "Father, if thou art willing, remove this cup from me; nevertheless not my will, but thine, be done."

Luke 22:45–46 (§L94.1c)

⁴⁵ And when he rose from prayer, he came to the disciples and found them sleeping for sorrow, ⁴⁶ and he said to them, "Why do you sleep? Rise and pray that you may not enter into temptation."

JOHN	THOMAS	OTHER

† John 18:1 ⇨ §K63.2a
¹ When Jesus had spoken these words, he **went** forth with **his disciples** across the Kidron valley, where there was a garden, which he and **his disciples** entered.

John 12:27 ⇨ Mark 14:34
²⁷ *"Now **is my soul** troubled. And what shall I say? 'Father, save me from this hour'? No, for this purpose I have come to this hour."*

John 18:11 ⇨ Mark 14:36
¹¹ *Jesus said to Peter, "Put your sword into its sheath; shall **I** not drink the **cup** which the **Father** has given me?"*

John 14:31 ⇨ Mark 14:42
³¹ *"but I do as the Father has commanded me, so that the world may know that I love the Father. **Rise, let us** go hence."*

MARK

Mark 14:43–52 (§K63.3) °

[43] And immediately, while he was still speaking, Judas came, one of the twelve, and with him a crowd with swords and clubs, from the chief priests and the scribes and the elders. [44] Now the betrayer had given them a sign, saying, "The one I shall kiss is the man; seize him and lead him away under guard." [45] And when he came, he went up to him at once, and said, "Master!"[a] And he kissed him. [46] And they laid hands on him and seized him. [47] But one of those who stood by drew his sword, and struck the slave of the high priest and cut off his ear. [48] And Jesus said to them, "Have you come out as against a robber, with swords and clubs to capture me? [49] Day after day I was with you in the temple teaching, and you did not seize me. But let the scriptures be fulfilled." [50] And they all forsook him, and fled.

[51] And a young man followed him, with nothing but a linen cloth about his body; and they seized him, [52] but he left the linen cloth and ran away naked.

[a] Or: *Rabbi*

° Appendix 2 ⇨ Mark 14:43

JOHN

John 18:1–12 (§J31.1)

[1] When Jesus had spoken these words, he went forth with his disciples across the Kidron valley, where there was a garden, which he and his disciples entered. [2] Now **Judas**, who betrayed him, also knew the place; for Jesus often met there with his disciples. [3] So **Judas**, procuring **a** band of soldiers and some officers **from the chief priests and the** Pharisees, went there **with** lanterns **and** torches and weapons. [4] Then Jesus, knowing all that was to befall him, came forward and said to them, "Whom do you seek?" [5] They answered him, "Jesus of Nazareth." Jesus said to them, "I am he." **Judas**, who betrayed him, was standing with them. [6] When he said to them, "I am he," they drew back and fell to the ground. [7] Again he asked them, "Whom do you seek?" And they said, "Jesus of Nazareth." [8] Jesus answered, "I told you that I am he; so, if you seek me, let these men go." [9] This was to fulfil **the** word which he had spoken, "Of those whom thou gavest me I lost not one." [10] Then Simon Peter, having **a sword, drew** it **and struck the high** priest's **slave and cut off his** right **ear**. The slave's name was Malchus. [11] **Jesus said to** Peter, "Put your sword into its sheath; shall I not drink the cup which the Father has given me?"

[12] So the band of soldiers and their captain **and the** officers of the Jews **seized** Jesus and bound **him**.

John 18:20 ⇨ Mark 14:49
[20] *Jesus answered him, "I have spoken openly to the world; I have always taught in synagogues and in the temple, where all Jews come together; I have said nothing secretly."*

MATT

Matt 26:47–56 (§M82.3)

[47] While he was still speaking, Judas came, one of the twelve, and with him a great crowd with swords and clubs, from the chief priests and the elders of the people. [48] Now the betrayer had given them a sign, saying, "The one I shall kiss is the man; seize him." [49] And he came up to Jesus at once and said, "Hail, **Master!**" And he kissed him. [50] Jesus said to him, "Friend, why are you here?" Then **they** came up and **laid hands** on Jesus **and seized him.** [51] And behold, **one of those who** were with Jesus stretched out his hand and **drew his sword, and struck the slave of the high priest, and cut off his ear.** [52] Then **Jesus said to** him, "Put your sword back into its place; for all who take the sword will perish by the sword. [53] Do you think that I cannot appeal to my Father, and he will at once send me more than twelve legions of angels? [54] **But** how then should **the scriptures be fulfilled**, that it must be so?" [55] At that hour **Jesus said to** the crowds, "**Have you come out as against a robber, with swords and clubs to capture me? Day after day** I sat **in the temple teaching, and you did not seize me.** [56] **But** all this has taken place, that **the scriptures** of the prophets might **be fulfilled.**" Then **all** the disciples **forsook him and fled.**

THOMAS

LUKE

Luke 22:47–54a (§L94.2)

[47] While he was still speaking, there came a crowd, and the man called **Judas, one of the twelve,** was leading them. **He** drew near to Jesus to **kiss him;** [48] but Jesus said to him, "**Judas,** would you betray the Son of man with a **kiss?**" [49] And when those who were about him saw what would follow, they said, "Lord, shall we strike with the **sword?**" [50] And **one** of them **struck the slave of the high priest and cut off his right ear.** [51] But **Jesus said,** "No more of this!" And he touched his ear and healed him. [52] Then **Jesus said to** the chief priests and officers of the temple and elders, who had come out against him, "**Have you come out as against a robber, with swords and clubs?** [53] When **I was with you day after day in the temple, you did not lay hands on me.** But this is your hour, and the power of darkness."

[54] Then **they seized him** and led him away, bringing him into the high priest's house.

OTHER

Dome of the Rock (a Muslim shrine built on the site of the Herodian Temple) with the
Mount of Olives in the background. Photo courtesy of John C. Trever.

| MARK | MATT | LUKE |

MARK

Mark 14:53–54 (§K64.1)

⁵³And they led Jesus to the high priest; and all the chief priests and the elders and the scribes were assembled. ⁵⁴And Peter had followed him at a distance, right into the courtyard of the high priest; and he was sitting with the guards, and warming himself at the fire.

Mark 14:55–65 (§K64.2)

⁵⁵Now the chief priests and the whole council sought testimony against Jesus to put him to death; but they found none. ⁵⁶For many bore false witness against him, and their witness did not agree. ⁵⁷And some stood up and bore false witness against him, saying, ⁵⁸"We heard him say, 'I will destroy this temple that is made with hands, and in three days I will build another, not made with hands.'" ⁵⁹Yet not even so did their testimony agree. ⁶⁰And the high priest stood up in the midst, and asked Jesus, "Have you no answer to make? What is it that these men testify against you?" ⁶¹But he was silent and made no answer. Again the high priest asked him, "Are you the Christ, the Son of the Blessed?" ⁶²And Jesus said, "I am; and you will see the Son of man seated at the right hand of Power, and coming with the clouds of heaven." ⁶³And the high priest tore his garments, and said, "Why do we still need witnesses? ⁶⁴You have heard his blasphemy. What is your decision?" And they all condemned him as deserving death. ⁶⁵And some began to spit on him, and to cover his face, and to strike him, saying to him, "Prophesy!" And the guards received him with blows.

•**Mark 13:26** ⇨ Mark 14:62

²⁶"And then they **will see the Son of man coming** in **clouds with** great power and glory."

Ps 110:1 ⇨ Mark 14:62
¹The Lord says to my lord:
"Sit **at my right hand,**
till I make your enemies
your footstool."

Dan 7:13–14 ⇨ Mark 14:62
¹³I saw in the night vision,
and behold, **with the clouds of heaven**
   there came one like a **son of man,**
and he came to the Ancient of Days
   and was presented before him.
¹⁴And to him was given dominion
   and glory and kingdom,
that all peoples, nations, and languages
   should serve him;
his dominion is an everlasting dominion,
   which shall not pass away,
and his kingdom one
   that shall not be destroyed.

Lev 24:16 ⇨ Mark 14:64
¹⁶"He who blasphemes the name of the Lord shall be put to **death**; all the congregation shall stone him; the sojourner as well as the native, when he blasphemes the Name, shall be put to **death.**"

MATT

Matt 26:57–58 (§M83.1) ⇨ §K64.1

⁵⁷Then those who had seized **Jesus led** him to Caiaphas **the high priest,** where **the scribes and the elders** had gathered. ⁵⁸But **Peter followed him at a distance,** as far as **the courtyard of the high priest,** and going inside **he** sat **with the guards** to see the end.

Matt 26:59–68 (§M83.2) ⇨ §K64.2

⁵⁹Now **the chief priests and the whole council sought** false **testimony against Jesus** that they might **put him to death,** ⁶⁰but **they found none,** though **many false** witnesses came forward. At last two came forward ⁶¹and said, "This fellow said, 'I am able to **destroy** the **temple** of God, and to **build** it **in three days.'"** ⁶²**And the high priest stood up** and said, **"Have you no answer to make? What is it that these men testify against you?"** ⁶³But **Jesus was silent. And the high priest** said to **him,** "I adjure you by the living God, tell us if **you are the Christ, the Son of God."** ⁶⁴**Jesus said** to **him,** "**You have said** so. But I tell you, hereafter **you will see the Son of man seated at the right hand of Power, and coming on the clouds of heaven."** ⁶⁵Then **the high priest tore his** robes, **and said,** "He has uttered **blasphemy. Why do we still need witnesses?** ⁶⁶**What is your** judgment?" **They** answered, "He deserves **death."** ⁶⁷Then **they spat in his face, and** struck **him;** and some slapped **him,** ⁶⁸saying, **"Prophesy** to us, you Christ! Who is it that struck you?"

Matt 24:30 ⇨ Mark 14:62

³⁰"then will appear the sign of **the Son of man** in heaven, and then all the tribes of the earth will mourn, **and they will see the Son of man coming** on **the clouds of heaven** with power and great glory"; . . .

LUKE

Luke 22:54b–65 (§L95)

Peter followed at a distance; ⁵⁵and when they had kindled a fire in the middle of the **courtyard** and sat down together, Peter sat among them. ⁵⁶Then a maid, seeing him as he sat in the light and gazing at him, said, "This man also was with him." ⁵⁷But he denied it, saying, "Woman, I do not know him." ⁵⁸And a little later some one else saw him and said, "You also are one of them." But Peter said, "Man, I am not." ⁵⁹And after an interval of about an hour still another insisted, saying, "Certainly this man also was with him; for he is a Galilean." ⁶⁰But Peter said, "Man, I do not know what you are saying." And immediately, while he was still speaking, the cock crowed. ⁶¹And the Lord turned and looked at Peter. And Peter remembered the word of the Lord, how he had said to him, "Before the cock crows today, you will deny me three times." ⁶²And he went out and wept bitterly.

⁶³Now the men who were holding Jesus mocked **him** and beat **him;** ⁶⁴they also blindfolded **him** and asked **him,** **"Prophesy!** Who is it that struck you?" ⁶⁵And they spoke many other words against **him,** reviling **him.**

Luke 22:66–71 (§L96) ⇨ §K64.2

⁶⁶When day came, the assembly of the elders of the people gathered together, both **chief priests and** scribes; and they led him away to their **council, and** they said, ⁶⁷"If **you are the Christ,** tell us." But he **said** to them, "If I tell you, you will not believe; ⁶⁸and if I ask you, you will not answer. ⁶⁹But from now on **the Son of man** shall be **seated at the right hand** of the **power** of God." ⁷⁰And they all said, **"Are you the Son of** God, then?" **And** he **said** to them, "You say that **I am."** ⁷¹**And** they **said,** "What further testimony do **we need? We have heard** it ourselves from **his** own lips."

JOHN

John 18:13–14 (§J31.2a)
[13] First **they led** him to Annas; for he was the father-in-law of Caiaphas, who was **high priest** that year. [14] It was Caiaphas who had given counsel to the Jews that it was expedient that one man should die for the people.

John 18:19–24 (§J31.2c)
[19] **The high priest** then questioned **Jesus** about his disciples and his teaching. [20] **Jesus** answered him, "I have spoken openly to the world; I have always taught in synagogues and in the temple, where all Jews come together; I have said nothing secretly. [21] Why do you ask me? Ask those who have heard me, what I said to them; they know what I said." [22] When he had said this, one of the officers standing by struck Jesus with his hand, saying, "Is that how you answer the high priest?" [23] Jesus answered him, "If I have spoken wrongly, bear witness to the wrong; but if I have spoken rightly, why do you strike me?" [24] Annas then sent him bound to Caiaphas **the high priest**.

John 2:19 ⇨ Mark 14:58
[19] Jesus answered them, **"Destroy this temple, and in three days I will** raise it up."

THOMAS

GThom 71 ⇨ Mark 14:58
(71) Jesus said, "**I** shall **destroy** [this] house, and no one will be able to rebuild it."

OTHER

GPet 3.9 ⇨ Mark 14:65
[9] **And** others who stood by spat **on his face, and** others buffeted **him** on the cheeks, others nudged **him** with a reed, and some scourged **him, saying,** "With such honour let us honour the Son of God."

MARK

FIRST DENIAL

Mark 14:66–68 (§K64.3a)

⁶⁶ And as Peter was below in the courtyard, one of the maids of the high priest came; ⁶⁷ and seeing Peter warming himself, she looked at him, and said, "You also were with the Nazarene, Jesus." ⁶⁸ But he denied it, saying, "I neither know nor understand what you mean." And he went out into the gateway.ᵃ

SECOND DENIAL

Mark 14:69–70a (§K64.3b)

⁶⁹ And the maid saw him, and began again to say to the bystanders, "This man is one of them." ⁷⁰ But again he denied it.

THIRD DENIAL

Mark 14:70b–72 (§K64.3c)

And after a little while again the bystanders said to Peter, "Certainly you are one of them; for you are a Galilean." ⁷¹ But he began to invoke a curse on himself and to swear, "I do not know this man of whom you speak." ⁷² And immediately the cock crowed a second time. And Peter remembered how Jesus had said to him, "Before the cock crows twice, you will deny me three times." And he broke down and wept.

ᵃ Or: *fore-court*. Some witnesses add, *and the cock crowed* (cf. 14:72): A C D K X △ Θ Π Ψᶜ *f*¹ *f*¹³ 28 33 *al;* text: ℵ B L W Ψ* *pc* (cf. Matt 26:71, Luke 22:57, John 18:25)

MATT

Matt 26:69–75 (§M83.3)

⁶⁹ Now Peter was sitting outside in the courtyard. And a maid came up to him, and said, "You also were with Jesus the Galilean." ⁷⁰ But he denied it before them all, saying, "I do not know what you mean." ⁷¹ And when he went out to the porch, another maid saw him, and she said to the bystanders, "This man was with Jesus of Nazareth." ⁷² And again he denied it with an oath, "I do not know the man." ⁷³ After a little while the bystanders came up and said to Peter, "Certainly you are also one of them, for your accent betrays you." ⁷⁴ Then he began to invoke a curse on himself and to swear, "I do not know the man." And immediately the cock crowed. ⁷⁵ And Peter remembered the saying of Jesus, "Before the cock crows, you will deny me three times." And he went out and wept bitterly.

LUKE

Luke 22:54b–62 (§L95.1)

Peter followed at a distance; ⁵⁵ and when they had kindled a fire in the middle of the courtyard and sat down together, Peter sat among them. ⁵⁶ Then a maid, seeing him as he sat in the light and gazing at him, said, "This man also was with him." ⁵⁷ But he denied it, saying, "Woman, I do not know him. " ⁵⁸ And a little later some one else saw him and said, "You also are one of them." But Peter said, "Man, I am not." ⁵⁹ And after an interval of about an hour still another insisted, saying, "Certainly this man also was with him; for he is a Galilean." ⁶⁰ But Peter said, "Man, I do not know what you are saying." And immediately, while he was still speaking, the cock crowed. ⁶¹ And the Lord turned and looked at Peter. And Peter remembered the word of the Lord, how he had said to him, "Before the cock crows today, you will deny me three times." ⁶² And he went out and wept bitterly.

JOHN

John 18:15–18 (§J31.2b) ⇨ §K64.3a

¹⁵ Simon Peter followed Jesus, and so did another disciple. As this disciple was known to the high priest, he entered the court of the high priest along with Jesus, ¹⁶ while Peter stood outside at the door. So the other disciple, who was known to the high priest, went out and spoke to the maid who kept the door, and brought Peter in. ¹⁷ The maid who kept the door said to Peter, "Are not you also one of this man's disciples?" He said, "I am not." ¹⁸ Now the servants and officers had made a charcoal fire, because it was cold, and they were standing and warming themselves; Peter also was with them, standing and warming himself.

John 18:25–27 (§J31.2d) ⇨ §K64.3b–c

²⁵ Now Simon Peter was standing and warming himself. They said to him, "Are not you also one of his disciples?" He denied it and said, "I am not." ²⁶ One of the servants of the high priest, a kinsman of the man whose ear Peter had cut off, asked, "Did I not see you in the garden with him?" ²⁷ Peter again denied it; and at once the cock crowed.

THOMAS

OTHER

GNaz 19 ⇨ Mark 14:71

(19) The Jewish Gospel: And he denied and swore and damned himself. (Variant to Matthew 26:74 in the "Zion Gospel" Edition)

The silver *denarius* depicts the bare head of Octavian with a small lituus or priest's staff behind. It was minted in 28 BCE, one year before Octavian received the title of Augustus, an event that marks the beginning of imperial Rome. The obverse inscription records his then current rank as CAESAR and his sixth year as consul (COS VI). The reverse depicts a crocodile with open jaws and bears the inscription AEGYPTO CAPTA. The coin commemorates Octavian's defeat of Cleopatra VII of Egypt in 31 BCE and the subsequent annexation by Rome of Ptolemaic Egypt. Once proud Egypt was henceforth administered as a private estate of the Roman emperor. Photo and description courtesy of Numismatic Fine Arts, Inc., Los Angeles, and the Institute for Antiquity and Christianity, Claremont, CA.

The silver *denarius* depicts the bearded, laureated bust of the youthful Emperor Nero. The obverse inscription reads NERO CAESAR, continuing on the reverse with the words AVGVSTVS GERMANICVS. The reverse depicts a togate and radiate standing figure of Nero. He faces forward, holding a branch in his right hand and a figure of Victory on a globe in his left. This figure very possibly represents the colossal statue of Nero as the sun-god Sol which the emperor set up before his Golden House *(Domus Aurea)* in Rome. The statue, executed in gilt bronze by Zenodorus, stood 30 meters tall. When it was moved during the reign of Hadrian, the task required 24 elephants. While the statue no longer exists, memory of it may be preserved in the name of the Colosseum which was built on the site of the Golden House. Photo and description courtesy of Numismatic Fine Arts, Inc., Los Angeles, and the Institute for Antiquity and Christianity, Claremont, CA.

MARK   MATT   LUKE

PILATE INTERROGATES JESUS

Mark 15:1-5 (§K65.1)

[1] And as soon as it was morning the chief priests, with the elders and scribes, and the whole council held a consultation; and they bound Jesus and led him away and delivered him to Pilate. [2] And Pilate asked him, "Are you the King of the Jews?" And he answered him, "You have said so." [3] And the chief priests accused him of many things. [4] And Pilate again asked him, "Have you no answer to make? See how many charges they bring against you." [5] But Jesus made no further answer, so that Pilate wondered.

PILATE CONDEMNS JESUS

Mark 15:6-15 (§K65.2)

[6] Now at the feast he used to release for them one prisoner for whom they asked. [7] And among the rebels in prison, who had committed murder in the insurrection, there was a man called Barabbas. [8] And the crowd came up and began to ask Pilate to do as he was wont to do for them. [9] And he answered them, "Do you want me to release for you the King of the Jews?" [10] For he perceived that it was out of envy that the chief priests had delivered him up. [11] But the chief priests stirred up the crowd to have him release for them Barabbas instead. [12] And Pilate again said to them, "Then what shall I do with the man whom you call the King of the Jews?" [13] And they cried out again, "Crucify him." [14] And Pilate said to them, "Why, what evil has he done?" But they shouted all the more, "Crucify him." [15] So Pilate, wishing to satisfy the crowd, released for them Barabbas; and having scourged Jesus, he delivered him to be crucified.

Matt 27:1-26 (§M84)

[1] When **morning** came, all **the chief priests** and **the elders** of the people took counsel against Jesus to put him to death; [2] **and they bound** him **and led him away and delivered him to Pilate** the governor.

[3] When Judas, his betrayer, saw that he was condemned, he repented and brought back the thirty pieces of silver to the chief priests and the elders, [4] saying, "I have sinned in betraying innocent blood." They said, "What is that to us? See to it yourself." [5] And throwing down the pieces of silver in the temple, he departed; and he went and hanged himself. [6] But the chief priests, taking the pieces of silver, said, "It is not lawful to put them into the treasury, since they are blood money." [7] So they took counsel, and bought with them the potter's field, to bury strangers in. [8] Therefore that field has been called the Field of Blood to this day. [9] Then was fulfilled what had been spoken by the prophet Jeremiah, saying, "And they took the thirty pieces of silver, the price of him on whom a price had been set by some of the sons of Israel, [10] and they gave them for the potter's field, as the Lord directed me."

[11] Now Jesus stood before the governor; **and the** governor **asked him, "Are you the King of the Jews?"** Jesus said, **"You have said so."** [12] But when he was **accused** by **the chief priests** and elders, he **made no answer.** [13] Then **Pilate** said to **him,** "Do you not hear **how many** things **they** testify **against you?"** [14] But he gave him **no answer,** not even to a single charge; **so that** the governor **wondered** greatly.

[15] **Now at the feast** the governor was accustomed **to release for** the crowd any **one prisoner whom they** wanted. [16] **And** they had then a notorious prisoner, **called Barabbas.** [17] So when they had gathered, Pilate said to **them,** "Whom **do you want me to release for you,** Barabbas or Jesus who is called Christ?" [18] **For he** knew **that it was out of** envy that they **had delivered him up.** [19] Besides, while he was sitting on the judgment seat, his wife sent word to him, "Have nothing to do with that righteous man, for I have suffered much over him today in a dream." [20] Now **the chief priests** and the elders persuaded **the** people to ask **for Barabbas** and destroy Jesus. [21] The governor **again said to them,** "Which of the two do you want me to release for you?" And they said, "Barabbas." [22] **Pilate said to them, "Then what shall I do with** Jesus who is called Christ?" **They** all said, "Let **him** be crucified." [23] **And he said, "Why, what evil has he done?"** But they shouted all the more, "Let **him** be crucified."

[24] **So** when **Pilate** saw that he was gaining nothing, but rather that a riot was beginning, he took water and washed his hands before the crowd, saying, "I am innocent of this man's blood; see to it yourselves." [25] And all the people answered, "His blood be on us and on our children!" [26] Then **he released for them Barabbas, and having scourged Jesus, delivered him to be crucified.**

Luke 23:1-7 (§L97) ⇨ §K65.1

[1] Then **the** whole company of them arose, **and** brought **him** before **Pilate.** [2] And they began to accuse **him,** saying, "We found this man perverting our nation, and forbidding us to give tribute to Caesar, and saying that he himself is Christ a king." [3] **And Pilate asked him, "Are you the King of the Jews?" And he answered him, "You have said so."** [4] **And Pilate** said to the chief priests and the multitudes, "I find no crime in this man." [5] But they were urgent, saying, "He stirs up the people, teaching throughout all Judea, from Galilee even to this place."

[6] When Pilate heard this, he asked whether the man was a Galilean. [7] And when he learned that he belonged to Herod's jurisdiction, he sent him over to Herod, who was himself in Jerusalem at that time.

Luke 23:13-25 (§L99) ⇨ §K65.2

[13] Pilate then called together the chief priests and the rulers and the people, [14] and said to them, "You brought me this man as one who was perverting the people; and after examining him before you, behold, I did not find this man guilty of any of your charges against him; [15] neither did Herod, for he sent him back to us. Behold, nothing deserving death has been done by him; [16] I will therefore chastise him and **release** him."

[18] But they all cried out together, "Away with this man, and release to us **Barabbas"**— [19] **a man** who had been thrown into prison for an **insurrection** started in the city, and for **murder.** [20] Pilate addressed them once more, desiring to **release** Jesus; [21] but **they** shouted **out, "Crucify, crucify him!"** [22] A third time he **said to them, "Why, what evil has he done?** I have found in him no crime deserving death; I will therefore chastise him and **release** him." [23] **But they** were urgent, demanding with loud cries that he should be crucified. And their voices prevailed. [24] **So Pilate** gave sentence that their demand should be granted. [25] He **released** the man who had been thrown into prison for **insurrection** and **murder,** whom they asked for; but **Jesus he delivered** up to their will.

JOHN   THOMAS   OTHER

JOHN

John 18:28–19:16 (§J33)

[28]Then **they led Jesus** from the house of Caiaphas **to the** praetorium. **It was** early. They themselves did not enter the praetorium, so that they might not be defiled, but might eat the passover. [29]So **Pilate** went out to them and said, "What accusation do you bring against this man?" [30]They answered him, "If this man were not an evildoer, we would not have handed him over." [31]Pilate said to them, "Take him yourselves and judge him by your own law." The Jews said to him, "It is not lawful for us to put any man to death." [32]This was to fulfil the word which Jesus had spoken to show by what death he was to die.

[33]**Pilate** entered the praetorium again and called Jesus, and said to **him**, **"Are you the King of the Jews?"** [34]Jesus **answered**, "Do you say this of your own accord, or did others say it to you about me?" [35]**Pilate** answered, "Am I a Jew? Your own nation and **the chief priests** have handed you over to me; what have you done?" [36]Jesus answered, "My kingship is not of this world; if my kingship were of this world, my servants would fight, that I might not be handed over to the Jews; but my kingship is not from the world." [37]**Pilate** said to **him**, "So **you are** a **king**?" Jesus answered, "**You** say that I am a **king**. For this I was born, and for this I have come into the world, to bear witness to the truth. Every one who is of the truth hears my voice." [38]Pilate said to him, "What is truth?"

After he had said this, he went out to the Jews again, and told them, "I find no crime in him. [39]But you have a custom that I should **release one** man for you **at the** Passover; will you have **me release for you the King of the Jews**?" [40]They cried out again, "Not this man, but **Barabbas!**" Now **Barabbas** was a robber.

19 [1]Then **Pilate** took Jesus **and scourged** him. [2]And the soldiers plaited a crown of thorns, and put it on his head, and arrayed him in a purple robe; [3]they came up to him, saying, "Hail, **King of the Jews!**" and struck him with their hands. [4]**Pilate** went out again, and **said to them**, "See, I am bringing him out to you, that you may know that I find no crime in him." [5]So Jesus came out, wearing the crown of thorns and the purple robe. **Pilate said to them**, "Behold the man!" [6]When the chief priests and the officers saw him, **they cried out, "Crucify him, crucify him!" Pilate said to them**, "Take him yourselves and crucify him, for I find no crime in him." [7]The Jews answered him. "We have a law, and by that law he ought to die, because he has made himself the Son of God." [8]When Pilate heard these words, he was the more afraid; [9]he entered the praetorium again and said to Jesus, "Where are you from?" **But Jesus** gave **no answer.** [10]**Pilate** therefore said to **him**, "**You** will not speak to me? Do you not know that I have power to **release** you, and power to **crucify** you?" [11]Jesus answered him, "You would have no power over me unless it had been given you from above; therefore he who delivered me to you has the greater sin."

[12]Upon this **Pilate** sought to **release** him, **but** the Jews **cried out,** "If you release this man, you are not Caesar's friend; every one who makes himself a king sets himself against Caesar." [13]When **Pilate** heard these words, he brought Jesus out and sat down on the judgment seat at a place called The Pavement, and in Hebrew, Gabbatha. [14]Now it was the day of Preparation of the Passover; it was about the sixth hour. He **said to** the Jews, "Behold your **King!**" [15]**They** cried out, "Away with him, away with him, **crucify him!**" **Pilate** said to them, "Shall I **crucify** your **King?**" The chief priests answered, "We have no king but Caesar." [16]Then he handed **him** over to them **to be crucified.**

OTHER

AcPil 3:2 ⇒ §K65.1

[2]**And Pilate** entered the praetorium again and called Jesus apart **and asked him: "Are you the king of the Jews?"** Jesus **answered** Pilate: "Do **you** say this of your own accord, or did others say it to you about me?" Pilate answered Jesus: "Am I a Jew? Your own nation and **the chief priests** have handed you over to me. What have you done?" Jesus answered: "My kingship is not of this world; for if my kingship were of this world, my servants would fight, that I might not be handed over to the Jews. But now is my kingship not from here." **Pilate** said to **him**: "So **you are** a **king**?" Jesus **answered him**: "**You** say that I am a **king**. For this cause I was born and have come, that every one who is of the truth should hear my voice." **Pilate** said to **him**: "What is truth?" Jesus answered him: "Truth is from heaven." Pilate said: "Is there not truth upon earth?" Jesus said to Pilate: "You see how those who speak the truth are judged by those who have authority on earth."

AcPil 4:4–5 ⇒ §K65.2

[4]Pilate said to them: "Take him yourselves and punish him as you wish." The Jews said to Pilate: "We wish **him** to be crucified." **Pilate said: "He** does not deserve to be crucified." [5]The governor looked at **the** multitude of Jews standing around, and when he saw many of the Jews weeping, he said: "Not all the multitude wishes him to die." But the elders of the Jews said: "For this purpose has the whole multitude of us come, that he should die." **Pilate said to** the Jews: **"Why** should he die?" The Jews said: "Because he called himself the Son of God and a **king**."

AcPil 9:4–5 ⇒ §K65.2

[4]When **Pilate** heard these words, he was afraid. And he silenced the multitudes, because **they** were crying **out**, and said to them: "So this is he whom Herod sought?" The Jews replied: "Yes, this is he." And **Pilate** took water and washed his hands before the sun and said: "I am innocent of the blood of this righteous man. You see to it." Again the Jews **cried out:** "His blood be on us and on our children." [5]Then **Pilate** commanded the curtain to be drawn before the judgment-seat on which he sat, and said to Jesus: "Your nation has convicted you of claiming to be a **king**. Therefore I have decreed that you should first be **scourged** according to the law of the pious emperors, and then hanged on the cross in the garden where you were seized. And let Dysmas and Gestas, the two malefactors, **be crucified** with you."

GNaz 20 ⇒ Mark 15:7

(20) Barabbas ... is interpreted in the so-called Gospel according to the Hebrews as "son of their teacher." (Jerome, *Commentary on Matthew* 4 [on Matthew 27:16])

MARK	MATT	LUKE

Mark 15:16–20 (§K66.1)

¹⁶ And the soldiers led him away inside the palace (that is, the praetorium); and they called together the whole battalion. ¹⁷ And they clothed him in a purple cloak, and plaiting a crown of thorns they put it on him. ¹⁸ And they began to salute him, "Hail, King of the Jews!" ¹⁹ And they struck his head with a reed, and spat upon him, and they knelt down in homage to him. ²⁰ And when they had mocked him, they stripped him of the purple cloak, and put his own clothes on him. And they led him out to crucify him.

Matt 27:27–31 (§M85.1)

²⁷ Then **the soldiers** of the governor took Jesus into **the praetorium, and they** gathered **the whole battalion** before him. ²⁸ **And they** stripped **him** and put a scarlet robe upon **him,** ²⁹ and **plaiting a crown of thorns they put it on** his head, and put **a reed** in his right hand. **And** kneeling before him **they** mocked **him,** saying, **"Hail, King of the Jews!"** ³⁰ **And they spat upon him,** and took the **reed** and **struck** him on the **head.** ³¹ **And when they had mocked** him, **they stripped him of the** robe, **and put his own clothes on him, and led him** away to **crucify him.**

JOHN	THOMAS	OTHER

John 19:1–3 (§J33.4)

¹ Then Pilate took Jesus and scourged him. ² And the soldiers **plaited a crown of thorns,** and **put it on** his head, and arrayed **him in a purple** robe; ³ they came up to **him,** saying, **"Hail, King of the Jews!" and struck** him with their hands.

GPet 2.5b–3.9

And he delivered **him** to the people on the day before the unleavened bread, their feast. 3⁶ So they took the Lord and pushed him in great haste and said, "Let us hale the Son of God now that we have gotten power over him." ⁷ **And they** put upon **him a purple** robe and set him on the judgment seat and said, "Judge righteously, O **King of** Israel!" ⁸ And one of them brought **a crown of thorns** and **put it on** the Lord's head. ⁹ **And** others who stood by **spat on** his face, **and** others buffeted him on the cheeks, others nudged him **with a reed,** and some scourged **him,** saying, "With such honour let us honour the Son of God."

AcPil 10:1a

¹ And Jesus went out from **the praetorium,** and the two malefactors with him. And when they came to the place, they stripped him **and** girded **him** with a linen cloth **and** put **a crown of thorns on** his head.

MARK	MATT	LUKE
Mark 15:21 (§K66.2)	**Matt 27:32 (§M85.2)**	**Luke 23:26–32 (§L100.1)**

Mark 15:21 (§K66.2)

²¹ And they compelled a passer-by, **Simon of Cyrene, who was coming in from the country,** the father of Alexander and Rufus, **to carry his cross.**

Matt 27:32 (§M85.2)

³² As they went out, they came upon a man **of Cyrene, Simon** by name; this man **they compelled to carry his cross.**

Luke 23:26–32 (§L100.1)

²⁶ And as they led him away, **they** seized one **Simon of Cyrene, who was coming in from the country,** and laid on him the **cross, to carry** it behind Jesus. ²⁷ And there followed him a great multitude of the people, and of women who bewailed and lamented him. ²⁸ But Jesus turning to them said, "Daughters of Jerusalem, do not weep for me, but weep for yourselves and for your children. ²⁹ For behold, the days are coming when they will say, 'Blessed are the barren, and the wombs that never bore, and the breasts that never gave suck!' ³⁰ Then they will begin to say to the mountains, 'Fall on us'; and to the hills, 'Cover us.' ³¹ For if they do this when the wood is green, what will happen when it is dry?"

³² Two others also, who were criminals, were led away to be put to death with him.

JOHN   THOMAS   OTHER

MARK	MATT	LUKE

Mark 15:22–32 (§K66.3)

[22] And they brought him to the place called Golgotha (which means the place of a skull). [23] And they offered him wine mingled with myrrh; but he did not take it. [24] And they crucified him, and divided his garments among them, casting lots for them, to decide what each should take. [25] And it was the third hour, when they crucified him. [26] And the inscription of the charge against him read, "The King of the Jews." [27] And with him they crucified two robbers, one on his right and one on his left.[a] [29] And those who passed by derided him, wagging their heads, and saying, "Aha! You would destroy the temple and build it in three days, [30] save yourself, and come down from the cross!" [31] So also the chief priests mocked him to one another with the scribes, saying, "He saved others; he cannot save himself. [32] Let the Christ, the King of Israel, come down now from the cross, that we may see and believe." Those who were crucified with him also reviled him.

[a] V. 28 is lacking in: ℵ A B C D X Ψ *pc;* insert, *And the scripture was fulfilled which says, "He was reckoned with the transgressors"* (cf. Luke 22:37, Isa 53:12): K L P (Δ) Θ Π *f¹ f¹³* 28 33 *pm*

Ps 69:21 ⇨ Mark 15:23
[21] They gave me poison for food,
    and for my thirst they gave me vinegar to drink.

Ps 22:18 ⇨ Mark 15:24
[18] **they** divide my **garments among them,**
    and **for** my raiment they cast **lots.**

Ps 22:7 ⇨ Mark 15:29
[7] All who see me mock at me,
    they make mouths at me, they wag **their heads;**
    . . .

Matt 27:33–44 (§M85.3)

[33] And **when** they came **to a place called Golgotha (which means the place of a skull),** [34] **they offered him wine** to drink, **mingled with gall; but** when he tasted it, **he** would **not** drink it. [35] **And** when **they** had **crucified him,** they **divided his garments among them** by **casting lots;** [36] then they sat down and kept watch over him there. [37] And over his head they put **the charge against him,** which **read,** "This is Jesus **the King of the Jews."** [38] **Then two robbers** were **crucified with him, one on the right and one** on the left. [39] **And those who** passed by **derided him, wagging their heads** [40] **and saying, "You who would destroy the temple and build it in three days, save yourself!** If you are the Son of God, **come down from the cross."** [41] **So also the chief priests, with the scribes** and elders, **mocked him,** saying, [42] **"He saved others; he cannot save himself.** He is **the King of Israel; let** him **come down now from the cross, and we will believe** in him. [43] He trusts in God; let God deliver him now, if he desires him; for he said, 'I am the Son of God.'" [44] And the robbers **who were crucified with him also reviled him** in the same way.

Luke 23:33–43 (§L100.2)

[33] And when **they** came **to the place** which is **called The Skull,** there **they crucified him,** and the criminals, **one on** the **right and one** on the **left.** [34] And Jesus said, "Father, forgive them; for they know not what they do." And **they** cast **lots** to **divide his garments.** [35] And the people stood by, watching; but the rulers scoffed at **him, saying, "He saved others;** let him **save himself,** if he is **the Christ** of God, his Chosen One!" [36] The soldiers also mocked him, coming up **and** offering **him** vinegar, [37] and saying, "If you are the **King of the Jews, save yourself!"** [38] There was also an **inscription** over **him,** "This is **the King of the Jews."**

[39] One of the criminals who were hanged railed at him, saying, "Are you not the Christ? Save yourself and us!" [40] But the other rebuked him, saying, "Do you not fear God, since you are under the same sentence of condemnation? [41] And we indeed justly; for we are receiving the due reward of our deeds; but this man has done nothing wrong." [42] And he said, "Jesus, remember me when you come into your kingdom." [43] And he said to him, "Truly, I say to you, today you will be with me in Paradise."

John 19:17–24 (§J34)

[17]So **they** took Jesus, and he went out, bearing his own cross, **to the place** called **the place of a skull**, which is **called** in Hebrew **Golgotha**. [18]There **they crucified him, and with him two** others, **one on** either side, and Jesus between them. [19]Pilate also wrote a title and put it on the cross; it **read**, "Jesus of Nazareth, **the King of the Jews**." [20]Many of the Jews read this title, for the place where Jesus was **crucified** was near the city; and it was written in Hebrew, in Latin, and in Greek. [21]The chief priests of the Jews then said to Pilate, "Do not write, 'The **King of the Jews**,' but 'This man said, I am **King of the Jews**.'" [22]Pilate answered, "What I have written I have written."

[23]When the soldiers had **crucified** Jesus **they** took **his garments** and made four parts, one for each soldier; also his tunic. But the tunic was without seam, woven from top to bottom; [24]so they said to one another, "Let us not tear it, but cast **lots for** it to see whose it shall be." This was to fulfil the scripture,

"They parted my **garments among them**, and for my clothing they cast **lots**."

John 2:19 ⇨ Mark 15:29–30

[19]Jesus answered them, **"Destroy** this **temple, and in three days** I will raise it up."

GThom 71 ⇨ Mark 15:29–30

(71) Jesus said, "I shall **destroy** [this] house, and no one will be able to rebuild **it**."

GPet 4.10–14

[10]**And they brought two** malefactors and **crucified** the Lord in the midst between them. But he held his peace, as if he felt no pain. [11]**And** when they had set up the cross, they wrote upon it: this is **the King of** Israel. [12]And **they** laid down **his garments** before him **and divided** them **among** themselves and cast the lot upon **them**. [13]But one of the malefactors rebuked them, saying, "We have landed in suffering for the deeds of wickedness which we have committed, but this man, who has become the saviour of men, what wrong has he done you?" [14]And they were wroth with him and commanded that his legs should not be broken, so that he might die in torments.

AcPil 10:1b–2

Likewise they hanged up also the two malefactors. But Jesus said: "Father, forgive them, for they know not what they do." And the soldiers parted his garments among them. And the people stood looking at him. And the chief priests and rulers with them scoffed at him, saying: "He saved others, let him save himself. If he in the Son of God, let him come down from the cross." And the soldiers also mocked him, coming and offering him vinegar with gall, and they said: "If you are the king of the Jews, save yourself." And Pilate after the sentence commanded the crime brought against him to be written as a title in Greek, Latin and Hebrew, according to the accusation of the Jews that he was king of the Jews.

[2]*One of the malefactors who were crucified said to him: "If you are the Christ, save yourself and us." But Dysmas answering rebuked him: "Do you not at all fear God, since you are in the same condemnation? And we indeed justly. For we are receiving the due reward of our deeds. But this man has done nothing wrong." And he said to Jesus: "Lord, remember me in your kingdom." And Jesus said to him: "Truly, I say to you, today you will be with me in paradise."*

MARK	MATT	LUKE

Mark 15:33–41 (§K66.4)

[33] And when the sixth hour had come, there was darkness over the whole land[a] until the ninth hour. [34] And at the ninth hour Jesus cried with a loud voice, "Eloi, Eloi, lama sabachthani?" which means, "My God, my God, why hast thou forsaken me?" [35] And some of the bystanders hearing it said, "Behold, he is calling Elijah." [36] And one ran and, filling a sponge full of vinegar, put it on a reed and gave it to him to drink, saying, "Wait, let us see whether Elijah will come to take him down." [37] And Jesus uttered a loud cry, and breathed his last. [38] And the curtain of the temple was torn in two, from top to bottom. [39] And when the centurion, who stood facing him, saw that he thus[b] breathed his last, he said, "Truly this man was the[c] Son of God!"

[40] There were also women looking on from afar, among whom were Mary Magdalene, and Mary the mother of James the younger and of Joses, and Salome, [41] who, when he was in Galilee, followed him, and ministered to him; and also many other women who came up with him to Jerusalem.

[a] Or: *earth*

[b] Some witnesses insert, *cried out and:* A C D K X W Δ Θ Π *f*¹ *f*¹³ 28 33 *al;* text: ℵ B L Ψ *pc*

[c] Or: *a*

Ps 22:1 ⇨ Mark 15:34
[1] My God, my God, why hast thou forsaken me? Why art thou so far from helping me, from the words of my groaning?

Ps 69:21 ⇨ Mark 15:36
[21] They gave me poison for food, and for my thirst they gave me vinegar to drink.

Ps 38:11 ⇨ Mark 15:40–41
[11] My friends and companions stand aloof from my plague, and my kinsmen stand afar off.

Matt 27:45–56 (§M85.4)

[45] Now from the sixth hour there was darkness over all the land until the ninth hour. [46] And about the ninth hour Jesus cried with a loud voice, "Eli, Eli, lama sabachthani?" that is, "My God, my God, why hast thou forsaken me?" [47] And some of the bystanders hearing it said, "This man is calling Elijah." [48] And one of them at once ran and took a sponge, filled it with vinegar, and put it on a reed, and gave it to him to drink. [49] But the others said, "Wait, let us see whether Elijah will come to save him." [50] And Jesus cried again with a loud voice and yielded up his spirit.

[51] And behold, the curtain of the temple was torn in two, from top to bottom; and the earth shook, and the rocks were split; [52] the tombs also were opened, and many bodies of the saints who had fallen asleep were raised, [53] and coming out of the tombs after his resurrection they went into the holy city and appeared to many. [54] When the centurion and those who were with him, keeping watch over Jesus, saw the earthquake and what took place, they were filled with awe, and said, "Truly this was the Son of God!"

[55] There were also many women there, looking on from afar, who had followed Jesus from Galilee, ministering to him; [56] among whom were Mary Magdalene, and Mary the mother of James and Joseph, and the mother of the sons of Zebedee.

Luke 23:44–49 (§L100.3)

[44] It was now about the sixth hour, and there was darkness over the whole land until the ninth hour, [45] while the sun's light failed; and the curtain of the temple was torn in two. [46] Then Jesus, crying with a loud voice, said, "Father, into thy hands I commit my spirit!" And having said this he breathed his last. [47] Now when the centurion saw what had taken place, he praised God, and said, "Certainly this man was innocent!" [48] And all the multitudes who assembled to see the sight, when they saw what had taken place, returned home beating their breasts. [49] And all his acquaintances and the women who had followed him from Galilee stood at a distance and saw these things.

Luke 23:36 ⇨ Mark 15:36
[36] The soldiers also mocked him, coming up and offering him vinegar, . . .

Luke 8:1–3 (§L30) ⇨ Mark 15:40–41
[1] Soon afterward he went on through cities and villages, preaching and bringing the good news of the kingdom of God. And the twelve were with him, [2] and also some women who had been healed of evil spirits and infirmities: Mary, called Magdalene, from whom seven demons had gone out, [3] and Joanna, the wife of Chuza, Herod's steward, and Susanna, and many others, who provided for them out of their means.

Luke 23:55 ⇨ Mark 15:40–41
[55] The women who had come with him from Galilee followed, and saw the tomb, and how his body was laid; . . .

JOHN	THOMAS	OTHER

JOHN

John 19:25–37 (§J35)

²⁵ So the soldiers did this. But standing by the cross of Jesus were his mother, and his mother's sister, **Mary the** wife of Clopas, and **Mary Magdalene**. ²⁶ When Jesus saw his mother, and the disciple whom he loved standing near, he said to his mother, "Woman, behold, your son!" ²⁷ Then he said to the disciple, "Behold, your mother!" And from that hour the disciple took her to his own home.

²⁸ After this Jesus, knowing that all was now finished, said (to fulfil the scripture), "I thirst." ²⁹ A bowl **full of vinegar** stood there; so they put a **sponge full of the vinegar** on hyssop and held it to his mouth. ³⁰ When **Jesus** had received the vinegar, he said, "It is finished"; and he bowed his head **and** gave up **his** spirit.

³¹ Since it was the day of Preparation, in order to prevent the bodies from remaining on the cross on the sabbath (for that sabbath was a high day), the Jews asked Pilate that their legs might be broken, and that they might be taken away. ³² So the soldiers came and broke the legs of the first, and of the other who had been crucified with him; ³³ but when they came to Jesus and saw that he was already dead, they did not break his legs. ³⁴ But one of the soldeirs pierced his side with a spear, and at once there came out blood and water. ³⁵ He who saw it has borne witness—his testimony is true, and he knows that he tells the truth—that you also may believe. ³⁶ For these things took place that the scripture might be fulfilled, "Not a bone of him shall be broken." ³⁷ And again another scripture says, "They shall look on him whom they have pierced."

OTHER

GPet 5.15–20

¹⁵ Now it was midday and a **darkness** covered all Judaea. And they became anxious and uneasy lest the sun had already set, since he was still alive. <For> it stands written for them: the sun should not set on one that has been put to death. ¹⁶ **And one** of them said, "Give him to drink gall with **vinegar**." **And** they mixed **it** and **gave him to drink**. ¹⁷ And they fulfilled all things and completed the measure of their sins on their head. ¹⁸ And many went about with lamps, <and> as they supposed that it was night, they went to bed (or: they stumbled). ¹⁹ **And** the Lord called out and **cried**, "**My** power, O power, **thou** hast **forsaken me!**" And having said this he was taken up. ²⁰ **And** at the same hour **the veil of the temple** in Jerusalem **was** rent **in two**.

AcPil 11:1–3a

¹ **And** it was about **the sixth hour**, and **there was darkness over the land until the ninth hour**, for the sun was darkened. **And the curtain of the temple was torn in two. And Jesus cried with a loud voice:** "Father, baddach ephkid rouel," which means: "Into thy hands I commit my spirit." **And** having said this he gave up the ghost. **And when the centurion saw** what had happened, **he** praised God, saying: "**This man was** righteous." And all the multitudes who had come to this sight, when they saw what had taken place, beat their breasts and returned.

² But the centurion reported to the governor what had happened. And when the governor and his wife heard, they were greatly grieved, and they neither ate nor drank on that day. And Pilate sent for the Jews and said to them: "Did you see what happened?" But they answered: "There was an eclipse of the sun in the usual way." ³ And his acquaintances had stood far off and the **women who** had come **with him** from **Galilee**, and saw these things.

GNaz 36 ⇨ Mark 15:38

*(36) Also in the Gospel of the Nazaraeans we read that at the time of Christ's death **the lintel of the temple**, of immense size, had split (Josephus says the same and adds that overhead awful voices were heard which said: Let us depart from this abode).* ("Historia passionis Domini," MS: Theolog. Sammelhandschrift saec. XIV–XV, foll. 8–71 [saec. XIV] cited by Hennecke in *New Testament Apocrypha,* p. 153)

MARK

Mark 15:42-47 (§K67)

[42] And when evening had come, since it was the day of Preparation, that is, the day before the sabbath, [43] Joseph of Arimathea, a respected member of the council, who was also himself looking for the kingdom of God, took courage and went to Pilate, and asked for the body of Jesus. [44] And Pilate wondered if he were already dead; and summoning the centurion, he asked him whether he was already dead.[a] [45] And when he learned from the centurion that he was dead, he granted the body to Joseph. [46] And he bought a linen shroud, and taking him down, wrapped him in the linen shroud, and laid him in a tomb which had been hewn out of the rock; and he rolled a stone against the door of the tomb. [47] Mary Magdalene and Mary the mother of Joses saw where he was laid.

[a] Some witnesses read, *whether he had been dead for some time:* ℵ A C K L X Π Ψ *f*[1] *f*[13] 28 33 *al;* text: B D W Θ *pc*

Deut 21:22-23

[22] "And if a man has committed a crime punishable by death and he is put to death, and you hang him on a tree, [23] his **body** shall not remain all night upon the tree, but you shall bury **him** the same day, for a hanged man is accursed by God; you shall not defile your land which the Lord your God gives you for an inheritance."

Josh 10:18 ⇨ Mark 15:46

[18] And Joshua said, "Roll great stones **against the** mouth **of the** cave, and set men by it to guard them"; . . .

Josh 10:27 ⇨ Mark 15:46

[27] but at the time of the going down of the sun, Joshua commanded, and they took them down from the trees, and threw them into **the** cave where they had hidden themselves, and they set great stones **against the** mouth **of the** cave, which remain to this very day.

JOHN

John 19:38-42 (§J36)

[38] After this **Joseph of Arimathea, who was** a disciple of Jesus, but secretly, for fear of the Jews, asked **Pilate** that he might take away **the body of Jesus,** and Pilate gave him leave. So he came and took away his body. [39] Nicodemus also, who had at first come to him by night, came bringing a mixture of myrrh and aloes, about a hundred pounds' weight. [40] They took the body of Jesus, and bound it **in linen** cloths with the spices, as is the burial custom of the Jews. [41] Now in the place where he was crucified there was a garden, and in the garden **a** new **tomb** where no one had ever been **laid.** [42] So because of the Jewish day of Preparation, as the tomb was close at hand, they **laid** Jesus there.

MATT

Matt 27:57-61 (§M86)

[57] When it was **evening,** there came a rich man from **Arimathea,** named **Joseph, who** also **was** a disciple of Jesus. [58] He **went to Pilate and asked for the body of Jesus.** Then Pilate ordered it to be given to him. [59] And Joseph took the body, and **wrapped** it **in a** clean **linen shroud,** [60] and **laid** it **in** his own new **tomb, which** he **had hewn** in the **rock; and** he **rolled a great stone** to **the door of the tomb,** and departed. [61] **Mary Magdalene and** the other **Mary** were there, sitting opposite the sepulchre.

THOMAS

LUKE

Luke 23:50-56 (§L101)

[50] Now there was a man named **Joseph** from the Jewish town **of Arimathea.** He was **a member of the council,** a good and righteous man, [51] who had not consented to their purpose and deed, and he **was looking for the kingdom of God.** [52] This man **went to Pilate and asked for the body of Jesus.** [53] Then **he** took it **down** and **wrapped** it **in a linen shroud, and laid him in** a rock-hewn **tomb,** where no one had ever yet been **laid.** [54] **It was the day of Preparation,** and **the sabbath** was beginning. [55] The women who had come with him from Galilee followed, and **saw** the tomb, and how his body **was laid;** [56] then they returned, and prepared spices and ointments.

On the sabbath they rested according to the commandment.

OTHER

GPet 2.3-5a

[3] Now there stood there **Joseph,** the friend of Pilate and of the Lord, and knowing that they were about to crucify him he came **to Pilate and** begged **the body of** the Lord for burial. [4] And Pilate sent to Herod **and** begged his **body.** [5] And Herod said, "Brother Pilate, even if no one had begged him, we should bury him, since the Sabbath is drawing on. For it stands written in the law: the sun should not set on one that has been put to death."

GPet 6.21-24

[21] And then the Jews drew the nails from the hands of the Lord and laid him on the earth. And the whole earth shook and there came a great fear. [22] Then the sun shone <again>, and it was found to be the ninth hour. [23] And the Jews rejoiced and gave **the body to Joseph** that he might bury it, since he had seen all the good that he (Jesus) had done. [24] And he took the Lord, washed him, **wrapped him in linen** and brought **him** into his own sepulchre, called Joseph's Garden.

AcPil 11:3b

But a certain man named **Joseph, a member of the council,** from the twon **of Arimathaea, who also was** waiting **for the kingdom of God,** this man **went to Pilate and asked for the body of Jesus. And** he took it **down,** and **wrapped** it **in** a clean **linen** cloth, **and** placed it **in a** rock-hewn **tomb,** in which no one had ever yet been laid.

Model of the Herodian temple (on display at the Holy Land Hotel, Jerusalem). Cf. the plan of the Herodian temple, p. 151. Photo courtesy of John C. Trever.

MARK	MATT	LUKE

Mark 16:1–8 (§K68)

[1] And when the sabbath was past, Mary Magdalene, and Mary the mother of James, and Salome, bought spices, so that they might go and anoint him. [2] And very early on the first day of the week they went to the tomb when the sun had risen. [3] And they were saying to one another, "Who will roll away the stone for us from the door of the tomb?" [4] And looking up, they saw that the stone was rolled back—it was very large. [5] And entering the tomb, they saw a young man sitting on the right side, dressed in a white robe; and they were amazed. [6] And he said to them, "Do not be amazed; you seek Jesus of Nazareth, who was crucified. He has risen, he is not here; see the place where they laid him. [7] But go, tell his disciples and Peter that he is going before you to Galilee; there you will see him, as he told you." [8] And they went out and fled from the tomb; for trembling and astonishment had come upon them; and they said nothing to any one, for they were afraid.[a]

[a] The Gospel of Mark ends with v. 8 in: ℵ B 304 syr[s] cop (in part), arm (in part) geo (in part) Clement Origen Eusebius Jerome *pc*. The so-called shorter ending to Mark, *But they reported briefly to Peter and those with him all that they had been told. And after this, Jesus himself sent out by means of them, from east to west, the sacred and imperishable proclamation of eternal salvation,* is found in it[k]; L Ψ *pc* combine the shorter and the longer endings (see on §K72)

Matt 28:1–8 (§M88.1)

[1] Now after **the sabbath**, toward the dawn of **the first day of the week**, **Mary Magdalene** and the other **Mary went to** see **the** sepulchre. [2] And behold, there was a great earthquake; for an angel of the Lord descended from heaven and came and **rolled back the stone,** and sat upon it. [3] His appearance was like lightning, and his raiment **white** as snow. [4] And for fear of him the guards trembled and became like dead men. [5] But the angel **said to** the women, "**Do not be** afraid; for I know that **you seek Jesus who was crucified.** [6] **He is not here**; for **he has risen,** as he said. Come, **see the place where** he lay. [7] Then **go** quickly and **tell his disciples that** he has risen from the dead, and behold, **he is going before you to Galilee; there you will see him.** Lo, I have told you." [8] So **they** departed quickly **from the tomb** with fear and great joy, and ran to tell his disciples.

Luke 24:1–11 (§L102)

[1] But **on the first day of the week**, at early dawn, **they went to the tomb**, taking the **spices** which they had prepared. [2] And **they** found **the stone rolled** away from the tomb, [3] but when they went in they did not find the body. [4] While **they** were perplexed about this, behold, two men stood by them in dazzling apparel; [5] and as **they were** frightened and bowed their faces to the ground, the men **said to them,** "Why do **you seek** the living among the dead? [6] Remember how he told you, while he was still in Galilee, [7] that the Son of man must be delivered into the hands of sinful men, and be **crucified**, and on the third day rise." [8] And they remembered his words, [9] **and** returning **from the tomb they** told all this to the eleven and to all the rest. [10] Now it was **Mary Magdalene** and Joanna **and Mary the mother of James** and the other women with them who told this to the apostles; [11] but these words seemed to them an idle tale, and they did not believe them.

JOHN   OTHER

John 20:1–18 (§J37)

[1] Now **on the first day of the week Mary Magdalene** came **to the tomb** early, while it was still dark, and **saw that the stone** had been taken away from **the tomb**. [2] So she ran, and went to Simon Peter and the other disciple, the one whom Jesus loved, and said to them, "They have taken the Lord out of **the tomb**, and we do not know where **they** have **laid him**." [3] Peter then came out with the other disciple, and they went toward the tomb. [4] They both ran, but the other disciple outran Peter and reached **the tomb** first; [5] and stooping to look in, he **saw** the linen cloths lying there, but he did not go in. [6] Then Simon Peter came, following him, and went into **the tomb**; he **saw** the linen cloths lying, [7] and the napkin, which had been on his head, not lying with the linen cloths but rolled up in a place by itself. [8] Then the other disciple, who reached **the tomb** first, also went in, and he **saw** and believed; [9] for as yet they did not know the scripture, that he must rise from the dead. [10] Then the disciples went back to their homes.

[11] But **Mary** stood weeping outside **the tomb, and** as she wept she stooped to look into **the tomb**; [12] and she **saw** two angels **in white, sitting** where the body of Jesus had lain, one at the head and one at the feet. [13] They **said to** her, "Woman, why are you weeping?" She said to them, "Because they have taken away my Lord, and I do not know where **they** have **laid him**." [14] Saying this, she turned round and saw **Jesus** standing, but she did not know that it was **Jesus**. [15] **Jesus** said to her, "Woman, why are you weeping? Whom do **you seek**?" Supposing him to be the gardener, she said to him, "Sir, if you have carried him away, tell me where you have **laid him**, and I will take him away." [16] **Jesus** said to her, "Mary." She turned and said to him in Hebrew, "Rabboni!" (which means Teacher). [17] Jesus said to her, "Do not hold me, for I have not yet ascended to the Father; **but go** to my brethren and say to them, 'I am ascending to my Father and your Father, to my God and your God.'" [18] Mary Magdalene **went and said** to the disciples, "I have seen the Lord"; and she told them that he had said these things to her.

GPet 9.35–13.57

[35] Now in the night in which the Lord's day dawned, when the soldiers, two by two in every watch, were keeping guard, there rang out a loud voice in heaven, [36] and they saw the heavens opened and two men come down from there **in** a great brightness and draw nigh to the sepulchre. [37] That **stone** which had been laid against the entrance to **the** sepulchre started of itself to **roll** and gave way to the side, and **the** sepulchre was opened, and both the **young** men entered in. 10 [38] When now those soldiers saw this, they awakened the centurion and the elders— for they also were there to assist at the watch. [39] And whilst they were relating what they had seen, they saw again three men come out from the sepulchre, and two of them sustaining the other, and a cross following them, [40] and the heads of the two reaching to heaven, but that of him who was led of them by the hand overpassing the heavens. [41] And they heard a voice out of the heavens crying, "Thou has preached to them that sleep," [42] and from the cross there was heard the answer, "Yea." 11 [43] Those men therefore took counsel with one another to go and report this to Pilate. [44] And whilst they were still deliberating, the heavens were again seen to open, and **a man** descended and entered into **the** sepulchre. [45] When those who were of the centurion's company **saw** this, they hastened by night to Pilate, abandoning **the** sepulchre which they were guarding, and reported everything that they had seen, being full of disquietude and saying, "In truth he was the Son of God." [46] Pilate answered and said, "I am clean from the blood of the Son of God, upon such a thing have you decided." [47] Then all came to him, beseeching him and urgently calling upon him to command the centurion and the soldiers to tell no one what they had seen. [48] "For it better for us," they said, "to make ourselves guilty of the greatest sin before God than to fall into the hands of the people of the Jews and be stoned." [49] Pilate therefore commanded the centurion and the soldiers to say nothing.

12 [50] **Early** in the morning of the Lord's day **Mary Magdalene**, a woman disciple of the Lord— for fear of the Jews, since [they] were inflamed with wrath, she had not done at the sepulchre of the Lord what women are wont to do for those beloved of them who die—took [51] with her her women friends and came to **the** sepulchre where he was **laid**. [52] **And they** feared lest the Jews should see them, and said, "Although we could not weep and lament on that day when he **was crucified**, yet let us now do so at his sepulchre. [53] But **who will roll away for us the stone** also that is set on **the** entrance to **the** sepulchre, that we may go in and sit beside him and do what is due?— [54] For **the stone was** great,— and we fear lest any one see us. And if we cannot do so, let us at least put down at the entrance what we bring for a memorial of him and let us weep and lament until we have again gone home."

13 [55] So **they** went and found the sepulchre opened. **And they** came near, stooped down and **saw** there **a young man sitting** in the midst of the sepulchre, comely and clothed with **a** brightly shining **robe**, who **said to them**, [56] "Wherefore are ye come? Whom **seek** ye? Not him that **was crucified? He is risen** and gone. But if ye believe not, stoop this way and **see the place where** he lay, for **he is not here**. For **he is risen** and is gone thither whence he was sent." [57] Then the women **fled** affrighted.

AcPil 13:1–3

[1] And while they still sat in the synagogue and marvelled because of Joseph, there came some of the guard which the Jews had asked from Pilate to guard the tomb of Jesus, lest his disciples should come and steal him. And they told the rulers of the synagogue and the priests and the Levites what had happened: how there was a great earthquake. "And we saw an angel descend from heaven, and he **rolled away the stone from** the mouth **of** the cave, **and** sat upon it, and he shone like snow and like lightning. **And** we **were** in great fear, and lay like dead men. And we heard the voice of the angel speaking to the women who waited at **the tomb: Do not be afraid.** I know that **you seek Jesus who was crucified. He is not here. He has risen,** as he said. Come and **see the place where** the Lord lay. And **go** quickly and **tell his disciples that he** has risen from the dead and **is in Galilee**." [2] The Jews asked: "To what women did he speak?" The members of the guard answered: "We do not know who they were." The Jews said: "At what hour was it?" The members of the guard answered: "At midnight." The Jews said: "And why did you not seize the women?" The members of the guard said: "We were like dead men through fear, and gave up hope of seeing the light of day; how could we then have seized them?" The Jews said: "As the Lord lives, we do not believe you." The members of the guard said to the Jews: "So many signs you saw in that man and you did not believe; and how can you believe us? You rightly swore: As the Lord lives. For he does live." Again the members of the guard said: "We have heard that you shut him up who asked for the body of Jesus, and sealed the door, and that when you opened it you did not find him. Therefore give us Joseph and we will give you Jesus." The Jews said: "Joseph has gone to his own city." And the members of the guard said to the Jews: "And **Jesus has risen,** as we heard from the angel, and **is in Galilee.**" [3] And when the Jews heard these words, they feared greatly and said: "(Take heed) lest this report be heard and all incline to Jesus." And the Jews took counsel, and offered much money and gave it to the soldiers of the guard, saying: "Say that when you were sleeping his disciples came by night and stole him. And if this is heard by the governor, we will persuade him and keep you out of trouble." [57] Then the women **fled** affrighted.

MARK

Mark 16:9–11 (§K69)

9 Now when he rose early on the first day of the week, he appeared first to Mary Magdalene, from whom he had cast out seven demons. 10 She went and told those who had been with him, as they mourned and wept. 11 But when they heard that he was alive and had been seen by her, they would not believe it.

Mark 16:12–13 (§K70)

12 After this he appeared in another form to two of them, as they were walking into the country. 13 And they went back and told the rest, but they did not believe them.

JOHN

† John 20:11–18 (§J37.1c) ⇨ §K69

11 But Mary stood weeping outside the tomb, and as she wept she stooped to look into the tomb; 12 and she saw two angels in white, sitting where the body of Jesus had lain, one at the head and one at the feet. 13 They said to her, "Woman, why are you weeping?" She said to them, "Because they have taken away my Lord, and I do not know where they have laid him." 14 Saying this, she turned round and saw Jesus standing, but she did not know that it was Jesus. 15 Jesus said to her, "Woman, why are you weeping? Whom do you seek?" Supposing him to be the gardener, she said to him, "Sir, if you have carried him away, tell me where you have laid him, and I will take him away." 16 Jesus said to her, "**Mary**." She turned and said to him in Hebrew, "Rabboni!" (which means Teacher). 17 Jesus said to her, "Do not hold me, for I have not yet ascended to the Father; but go to my brethren and say to them, I am ascending to my Father and your Father, to my God and your God." 18 **Mary Magdalene went and** said to the disciples, "I have seen the Lord"; **and** she **told** them that he had said these things to her.

MARK

THOMAS

LUKE

Luke 24:13–27 (§L103.1) ⇨ §K70

13 That very day **two of them** were going to a village named Emmaus, about seven miles from Jerusalem, 14 and talking with each other about all these things that had happened. 15 While they were talking and dicussing together, Jesus himself drew near and went with them. 16 But their eyes were kept from recognizing him. 17 And he said to them, "What is this conversation which you are holding with each other as you walk?" And they stood still, looking sad. 18 Then one of them, named Cleopas, answered him, "Are you the only visitor to Jerusalem who does not know the things that have happened there in these days?" 19 And he said to him, "What things?" And they said to him, "Concerning Jesus of Nazareth, who was a prophet mighty in deed and word before God and all the people, 20 and how our chief priests and rulers delivered him up to be condemned to death, and crucified him. 21 But we had hoped that he was the one to redeem Israel. Yes, and besides all this, it is now the third day since this happened. 22 Moreover, some women of our company amazed us. They were at the tomb early in the morning 23 and did not find his body; and they came back saying that they had even seen a vision of angels, who said that he was alive. 24 Some of those who were with us went to the tomb, and found it just as the women had said; but him they did not see." 25 And he said to them, "O foolish men, and slow of heart to believe all that the prophets have spoken! 26 Was it not necessary that the Christ should suffer these things and enter into his glory?" 27 And beginning with Moses and all the prophets, he interpreted to them in all the scriptures the things concerning himself.

Luke 24:28–33 (§L103.2) ⇨ §K70

28 So they drew near to the village to which they were going. He appeared to be going further, 29 but they constrained him, saying, "Stay with us, for it is toward evening and the day is now far spent." So he went in to stay with them. 30 When he was at table with them, he took the bread and blessed, and broke it, and gave it to them. 31 And their eyes were opened and they recognized him; and he vanished out of their sight. 32 They said to each other, "Did not our hearts burn within us while he talked to us on the road, while he opened to us the scriptures?" 33 And they rose that same hour and returned to Jerusalem; and they found the eleven gathered together and those who were with them, . . .

OTHER

MARK

Mark 16:14–18 (§K71) °

¹⁴ Afterward he appeared to the eleven themselves as they sat at table; and he upbraided them for their unbelief and hardness of heart, because they had not believed those who saw him after he had risen.ᵃ ¹⁵ And he said to them, "Go into all the world and preach the gospel to the whole creation. ¹⁶ He who believes and is baptized will be saved; but he who does not believe will be condemned. ¹⁷ And these signs will accompany those who believe: in my name they will cast out demons; they will speak in new tongues; ¹⁸ they will pick up serpents, and if they drink any deadly thing, it will not hurt them; they will lay their hands on the sick, and they will recover."

Mark 16:19–20 (§K72) °

¹⁹ So then the Lord Jesus, after he had spoken to them, was taken up into heaven, and sat down at the right hand of God. ²⁰ And they went forth and preached everywhere, while the Lord worked with them and confirmed the message by the signs that attended it. Amen.ᵇ

ᵃ W contains the longer ending expanded by the Freer logion (see below)

ᵇ The following witnesses contain the longer ending to the Gospel of Mark (16:9–20): A C D K (W) X Δ Θ Π ƒ¹³ 28 33 *pm*

° Appendix 2 ⇨ §§K71 and K72

W:Freer ⇨ Mark 16:14
1. And they excused themselves with the words, "This aeon of lawlessness and unbelief is under Satan, who through the unclean spirits does not allow the true power of God to be comprehended. Therefore," they said to Christ, "reveal your righteousness now." And Christ replied to them, "The measure of the years of Satan's power is filled up. But other fearful things draw near, also (for those) for whom I, because they have sinned, was delivered to death, that they might turn back to the truth and sin no more in order to inherit the spiritual and imperishable glory of righteousness (preserved) in heaven."

JOHN

† John 20:19–23 (§J37.2a) ⇨ Mark 16:14

¹⁹ On the evening of that day, the first day of the week, the doors being shut where the disciples were, for fear of the Jews, Jesus came and stood among them and said to them, "Peace be with you." ²⁰ When **he** had said this, he showed them his hands and his side. Then the disciples were glad when they saw the Lord. ²¹ Jesus said to them again, "Peace be with you. As the Father has sent me, even so I send you." ²² And when he had said this, he breathed on them, and said to them, "Receive the Holy Spirit. ²³ If you forgive the sins of any, they are forgiven; if you retain the sins of any, they are retained."

MATT

† Matt 28:16–20 (§M88.4) ⇨ Mark 16:14–16

¹⁶ Now the eleven disciples went to Galilee, to the mountain to which Jesus had directed them. ¹⁷ And when they saw him they worshiped him; but some doubted. ¹⁸ And Jesus came **and said to them**, "All authority in heaven and on earth has been given to me. ¹⁹ **Go** therefore and make disciples of all nations, baptizing them in the name of the Father and of the Son and of the Holy Spirit, ²⁰ teaching them to observe all that I have commanded you; and lo, I am with you always, to the close of the age."

THOMAS

LUKE

† Luke 24:50–53 (§L104) ⇨ Mark 16:19

⁵⁰ Then he led them out as far as Bethany, and lifting up his hands he blessed them. ⁵¹ While he blessed them, he parted from them, and **was** carried **up into heaven**. ⁵² And they returned to Jerusalem with great joy, ⁵³ and were continually in the temple blessing God.

OTHER

AcPil 14:1

¹ Now Phineës a priest and Adas a teacher and Angaeus a Levite came from Galilee to Jerusalem, and told the rulers of the synagogue and the priests and the Levites: "We saw Jesus and his disciples sitting upon the mountain which is called Mamilch. **And he said to** his disciples: **Go into all the world and preach the gospel to the whole creation. He who believes and is baptized will be saved; but he who does not believe will be condemned. And these signs will accompany those who believe: in my name will they cast out demons; they will speak in new tongues; they will pick up serpents; and if they drink any deadly thing, it will not hurt them; they will lay their hands on the sick and they will recover.** And while **Jesus** was still speaking to his disciples, we saw him **taken up into heaven**."

LUKE

L1	PROLOGUE	**1:1–4**
John 15:27	GThom, title	Mark 1:1
		Acts 1:1–2
		Josephus, *Against Apion* 1.1.1–3
		Josephus, *Against Apion* 2.1.1
		Philo, *On the Life of Moses* 1.1.1–4
		InThom 0–1:1

S1:L2	INTRODUCTION TO THE BIRTH OF JOHN AND JESUS	**1:5–56**

L2	INTRODUCTION TO THE BIRTH OF JOHN AND JESUS	**1:5–56**

L2.1	THE PREDICTION OF JOHN'S BIRTH	**1:5–25**
L2.1a	INTRODUCTION	**1:5–7**
L2.1b	ZECHARIAH'S VISION	**1:8–23**
L2.1c	CONCEPTION OF JOHN	**1:24–25**

Luke 1:26–38		PJas 8:3
Luke 1:76		PJas 10:2
Gen 16:1–16		PJas 23:1–24:2
Judg 13:2–21		
Gen 17:19		
Num 6:1–3		
Mal 4:5–6		
Gen 15:8		

L2.2	THE ANNUNCIATION TO MARY	**1:26–38**
Luke 1:8–23		PJas 11:1–3
Isa 7:14		Acts 2:30
2 Sam 7:12–16		Acts 13:23
Isa 9:6–7		PCairo 2

L2.3	MARY'S VISIT TO ELIZABETH	**1:39–56**
Luke 6:21,24		PJas 12:2–3
1 Sam 2:1–10		
Hab 3:18		
1 Sam 1:11		
Ps 113:56		
Deut 10:21		
Ps 111:9		
Ps 103:17		
Ps 89:11		
1 Sam 2:4, 7		
Sir 10:14		
Ps 107:9		
1 Sam 2:5		
Job 22:9		
Isa 41:8–9		
Ps 98:3		
Mic 7:20		

S2:L3	THE BIRTH AND CHILDHOOD OF JOHN	**1:57–80**

L3	THE BIRTH AND CHILDHOOD OF JOHN	**1:57–80**
Luke 1:17		Acts 3:21
Luke 3:4		InThom 19:5b
Luke 7:27		
Luke 2:40		
Luke 2:52		
Lev 12:3		
Ps 41:3		
Ps 111:9		
Ps 18:2		
Ps 132:17		
Ps 18:17		
2 Sam 22:18		
Ps 106:10		
Gen 24:12		
Mic 7:20		
Ps 105:8		
Ps 106:45		
Gen 26:3		
Jer 11:5		
Josh 24:14		
Isa 38:20		
Mal 3:1		
Isa 40:3		
Ps 107:10		
Isa 59:8		

S3:L4–6	BIRTH AND CHILDHOOD OF JESUS	**2:1–52**

L4	THE BIRTH OF JESUS	**2:1–21**

L4.1	THE BIRTH OF JESUS	**2:1–7**
	Matt 1:18–25	PJas 17:1–3
		PJas 22:2

L4.2	THE SHEPHERDS	**2:8–20**
L4.2a	THE ANNUNCIATION TO THE SHEPHERDS	**2:8–14**
L4.2b	THE VISIT OF THE SHEPHERDS	**2:15–20**

Luke 19:38	Matt 2:1–12	Acts 13:23
Luke 2:51		InThom 19:5a
		InThom 11:2c

L4.3	THE CIRCUMCISION OF JESUS	**2:21**

L5	THE PRESENTATION OF JESUS IN JERUSALEM	2:22–40
L5.1	THE PRESENTATION OF JESUS	2:22–24
L5.2	SIMEON BLESSES JESUS	2:25–35
L5.3	ANNA THE PROPHETESS	2:36–38
L5.4	RETURN TO NAZARETH	2:39–40

Luke 3:6	Matt 2:19–23	PJas 24:4
Luke 1:80		Acts 13:47
Luke 2:52		Acts 26:23
Lev 12:6		Acts 28:28
Exod 13:2, 12, 15		InThom 19:5b
Lev 12:8		
Isa 40:5		
Isa 52:10		
Isa 49:6		

L6	JESUS VISITS JERUSALEM AT TWELVE	2:41–52
L6.1	JESUS' PARENTS TAKE HIM TO JERUSALEM	2:41–45
L6.2	JESUS AMONG THE TEACHERS IN THE TEMPLE	2:46–52

Luke 2:19	InThom 19:1–5b
Luke 1:80	InThom 15:2
Luke 2:40	InThom 11:2c
1 Sam 2:26	
Prov 3:4	

S4:L7–10	INTRODUCTION TO THE MINISTRY OF JESUS	3:1–4:13

L7	APPEARANCE OF JOHN THE BAPTIST	3:1–20

Luke 1:76	Matt 3:1–12	GEbi 2
Luke 7:27	Matt 7:19	GEbi 3
Luke 2:30–32	Matt 14:3–4	Mark 1:2–8
Luke 6:43–44		Mark 1:15
Luke 13:6–9		Mark 6:17–18
Luke 13:31		Acts 2:38
Luke 23:8		Acts 13:10
Isa 40:3–6		Acts 13:47
John 1:19–28		Acts 28:28
John 8:39		ApocJa 9:24–10:6
		Acts 26:20
		Acts 1:5
		Acts 11:16
		Acts 13:24–25
		Acts 19:1–7

L8	BAPTISM OF JESUS	3:21–22

Luke 9:35	Matt 3:13–17	Mark 1:9–11
Ps 2:7	Matt 17:5	Mark 9:7
Isa 42:1		GEbi 4
Isa 44:2		GHeb 2
John 1:29–34		GNaz 2

L9	GENEALOGY OF JESUS	3:23–38

John 1:45	Matt 1:1–17	GEbi 1
John 8:57		
John 6:42		

L10	THE TEMPTATIONS OF JESUS	4:1–13
L10.1	INTRODUCTION	4:1–2
L10.2	FIRST TEMPTATION	4:3–4
L10.3	SECOND TEMPTATION	4:5–8
L10.4	THIRD TEMPTATION	4:9–12
L10.5	CONCLUSION	4:13

Exod 34:28	Matt 4:1–11	Mark 1:12–13
Deut 9:9		
Deut 8:3		
Deut 6:13		
Ps 91:11–12		
Deut 6:16		

S5:L11–12	FIRST GALILEAN	4:14–30

L11	RETURN TO GALILEE	4:14–15

Luke 4:37	Matt 4:12–17	Mark 1:14–15
John 1:43	Matt 9:26	
John 4:1–3		
John 4:43		

L12	SERMON AT NAZARETH AND REJECTION	4:16–30

Luke 7:22	Matt 13:53–58	Mark 6:1–6
Luke 4:43	POxy1 6	Acts 10:36–38
Isa 61:1–2	GThom 31	Acts 7:54, 58a
John 4:44		
John 1:45		
John 6:42		
John 8:59		

S6:L13–16	SECOND GALILEAN	4:31–44

L13	EXORCISM OF AN UNLCEAN SPIRIT	4:31–37

1 Kgs 17:18	Matt 7:28–29	Mark 1:21–28
John 7:46	Matt 13:54	Mark 11:18
John 6:69	Matt 22:33	

L14	HEALING OF SIMON'S MOTHER-IN-LAW	4:38–39

	Matt 8:14–15	Mark 1:29–31

L15	SUMMARY: HEALING AND EXORCISMS	4:40–41

	Matt 8:16–17	Mark 1:32–34
	Matt 12:15–16	Mark 3:12

L16	WITHDRAWAL AND PREACHING TOUR	4:42–44

Luke 4:18	Matt 4:23–25	Mark 1:35–39
Luke 7:22		Acts 10:36–38

S7:L17–22	THIRD GALILEAN	5:1–6:11

L17	ON THE SEA OF GALILEE	5:1–11

L17.1	TEACHING FROM A BOAT	5:1–3
L17.2	MIRACULOUS CATCH OF FISH	5:4–11

Luke 5:28	Matt 4:18–20	Mark 1:16–18
Luke 18:28	Matt 4:21–22	Mark 1:19–20
John 1:35–42		GEbi 1
John 1:43–51		
John 21:1–14		

L18	HEALING OF A LEPER	5:12–16

Luke 17:14	Matt 8:1–4	Mark 1:40–45
		PEger2 2

L19	HEALING OF THE PARALYTIC	5:17–26

Luke 7:48–49	Matt 9:1–8	Mark 2:1–12
John 5:1–9a		

L20	TAX COLLECTORS AND FASTING	5:27–39

L20.1	CALL OF LEVI	5:27–28

Luke 5:11	Matt 9:9	Mark 2:14
Luke 18:28		

L20.2	QUESTION OF TABLE COMPANY	5:29–32

Luke 7:34	Matt 9:10–13	Mark 2:15–17
Luke 15:1–2		POxy1224 1
Luke 19:7		Justin, *Apology* 1.15.8

L20.3	QUESTION OF FASTING	5:33–39

Luke 7:33–34	Matt 9:14–17	Mark 2:18–22
Luke 18:12	GThom 27	Did 8:1
	GThom 104	
	GThom 47	

L21	PLUCKING GRAIN ON THE SABBATH	6:1–5

Deut 23:25	Matt 12:1–8	Mark 2:23–28
Exod 20:10	GThom 27	InThom 2:1–5
Deut 5:14		
1 Sam 21:1–6		
Lev 24:5–9		

L22	HEALING OF THE MAN WITH THE WITHERED HAND	6:6–11

Luke 14:1	Matt 12:9–14	Mark 3:1–6
Luke 14:3		GNaz 10
		InThom 2:1–5

S8:L23–25	FOURTH GALILEAN	6:12–49

L23	APPOINTMENT OF THE TWELVE	6:12–16

John 1:42	Matt 10:1–4	Mark 3:13–19
		Acts 1:12–14

L24	RETURN TO THE PLAIN: NARRATIVE TRANSITION	6:17–19

Luke 8:43–47	Matt 12:15–21	Mark 3:7–12
	Matt 4:25	Mark 5:27–33
	Matt 9:20–21	Mark 6:56
	Matt 14:36	Acts 5:12–16

L25	SERMON ON THE PLAIN	6:20–49

L25.1	FOUR BEATITUDES AND WOES	6:20–26

Luke 11:47–48	Matt 5:3–12	1 Pet 4:15–16
Ps 126:1–2	GThom 54	Acts 7:52
	GThom 68–69	

L25.2	LOVE OF ENEMIES	6:27–36

Tob 4:15	Matt 5:38–42	Did 1:2
Sir 31:15	Matt 5:43–48	POxy1224 2
	Matt 7:12	2 Clem 13:4
	GThom 95	

L25.3	JUDGE NOT	6:37–42

John 13:16	Matt 7:1–5	Mark 4:24–25
John 15:20	GThom 34	1 Clem 13:2
	GThom 26	
	POxy1 1	

L25.4	BY THEIR FRUITS	6:43–45

Luke 3:9	Matt 7:15–20	
Luke 13:6–9	Matt 12:33–37	
	GThom 45	
	GThom 43	

L25.5	ADMONITION: THE TWO HOUSES	6:46–49

	Matt 7:24–27	PEger2 3

S9:L26–29	FIFTH GALILEAN	7:1–50

L26	THE CENTURION'S SLAVE	7:1–10

John 4:45–54	Matt 8:5–13	Acts 10:1–2

L27	WIDOW'S SON AT NAIN	7:11–17

1 Kgs 17:17–24		Acts 20:7–12

L28	EXCHANGE WITH JOHN	7:18–35

L28.1	JOHN'S QUESTION OF JESUS	7:18–23

Luke 3:15–16	Matt 11:2–6	
Luke 4:18		
Isa 35:5–6		
John 1:15		

L28.2	Jesus Speaks of John	7:24–30
Luke 1:76	Matt 11:7–15	Mark 1:2
Luke 3:4	Matt 21:32	
Luke 9:51–52	GThom 78	
Luke 10:1	GThom 46	
Luke 20:4–6		
Mal 3:1a		

L28.3	Children in the Marketplace	7:31–35
Luke 5:29–30	Matt 11:16–19	
Luke 15:1–2		
Luke 19:7		

L29	A Woman Anoints Jesus' Feet	7:36–50
Luke 11:37	Matt 26:6–13	Mark 14:3–9
Luke 14:1	Matt 9:22	Mark 5:34
Luke 5:20–21		Mark 10:52
Luke 8:48		
Luke 17:19		
Luke 18:42		
John 12:1–8		

S10:L30–32	Sixth Galilean	8:1–21

L30	Narrative Summary	8:1–3
Luke 23:49	Matt 27:55–56	Mark 15:40–41
Luke 23:55		Mark 16:9

L31	Teaching in Parables	8:4–18

L31.1	Parable of the Sower	8:4–8
	Matt 13:1–2	Mark 4:2–9
	Matt 13:3–9	InThom 12:1–2
	GThom 9	ApocJa 12:20–31

L31.2	Why Jesus Speaks in Parables	8:9–10
Isa 6:9–10	Matt 13:10–17	Mark 4:10–12
		Acts 28:26–27
		ApocJa 7:1–10

L31.3	Interpretation of the Sower	8:11–15
	Matt 13:18–23	Mark 4:13–20
		ApocJa 8:10–27

L31.4	Lamp on the Stand	8:16–17
Luke 11:33	Matt 5:15	Mark 4:21–23
Luke 12:2	Matt 10:26	
	GThom 33	
	POxy654 5	
	GThom 5	
	GThom 6	

L31.5	Dangers of Hearing	8:18
Luke 19:26	Matt 13:12	Mark 4:24–25
	Matt 25:29	
	GThom 41	

L32	Jesus' Relatives	8:19–21
Luke 11:27–28	Matt 12:46–50	Mark 3:31–35
John 15:14	GThom 99	GEbi 5
		2 Clem 9:11

S11:L33–35	Seventh Galilean	8:22–56

L33	Stilling of the Storm	8:22–25
Ps 65:5–8	Matt 8:23–27	Mark 4:35–41
	Matt 8:18	

L34	Gerasene Demoniac	8:26–39

L34.1		Scene One	8:26–34
L34.2		Scene Two	8:35–39
John 2:4		Matt 8:28–33	Mark 5:1–14a
		Matt 8:34	Mark 5:14b–20
			Mark 1:24

L35	Two Healing Stories	8:40–56

L35.1	Jairus' Daughter: Introduction	8:40–42a
L35.2	Woman with the Internal Hemorrhage	8:42b–48
L35.3	Jairus' Daughter: Conclusion	8:49–56
Luke 6:19	Matt 9:18–19	Mark 5:21–24a
Luke 7:50	Matt 9:20–22	Mark 5:24b–34
Luke 17:19	Matt 9:23–26	Mark 5:35–43
Luke 18:42	Matt 14:36	Mark 6:56
		Mark 10:52

S12:L36–40	Eighth Galilean	9:1–27

L36	Mission of the Twelve	9:1–6
Luke 22:35–36	Matt 10:1	Mark 6:7–13
Luke 10:11	Matt 10:9–14	Mark 3:14–15
		Acts 13:57
		Acts 18:6

L37	Herod Is Perplexed	9:7–9
Luke 13:31–33	Matt 14:1–12	Mark 6:14–29
Luke 23:8	Matt 16:14	Mark 8:28
Luke 9:19		
John 1:19–21, 25		

L38	Return of the Twelve; Narrative Transition	9:10–11
Luke 10:17	Matt 14:13–14	Mark 6:30–34

L39 FEEDING OF THE FIVE THOUSAND **9:12–17**

Luke 22:19	Matt 14:15–21	Mark 6:35–44
Luke 24:30	Matt 15:32–39	Mark 8:1–10
2 Kgs 4:42–44		Mark 14:22
John 6:1–15		Acts 27:35

L40 THE CHRIST AND THE CROSS **9:18–27**

L40.1 PETER'S CONFESSION; JESUS PREDICTS HIS PASSION **9:18–22**

Luke 9:43b–45	Matt 16:13–20	Mark 8:27–30
Luke 18:31–34	Matt 16:21–23	Mark 8:31–33
Luke 9:7–8	Matt 17:22–23	Mark 9:30–32
Luke 17:25	Matt 20:17–19	Mark 10:32–34
Luke 22:22	GThom 13	ApocJa 5:31–6:11
Luke 24:6–8		
Luke 24:26		
Luke 24:46		
John 1:49		
John 6:68–69		

L40.2 THE WAY OF THE CROSS **9:23–27**

Luke 14:27	Matt 16:24–28	Mark 8:34–9:1
Luke 17:33	Matt 10:38–39	
Luke 12:9	Matt 10:33	
Luke 21:32	GThom 55	
John 12:25	GThom 101	

S13:L41–43 ON THE MOUNTAIN **9:28–50**

L41 JESUS IS TRANSFIGURED **9:28–36**

Luke 3:22	Matt 17:1–13	Mark 9:2–8
Ps 2:7	Matt 3:16–17	Mark 1:10–11
Isa 42:1		
John 1:14		

L42 JESUS EXORCISES AN UNCLEAN SPIRIT **9:37–43a**

	Matt 17:14–18	Mark 9:14–27
	Matt 17:19–20	Mark 9:28–29

L43 PASSION AND POSITION **9:43b–50**

L43.1 JESUS PREDICTS HIS PASSION AGAIN **9:43b–45**

Luke 9:18–22	Matt 17:22–23	Mark 9:30–32
Luke 18:31–34	Matt 16:21–23	Mark 8:31–33
Luke 17:25	Matt 20:17–19	Mark 10:32–34
Luke 22:22		
Luke 24:6–8		
Luke 24:26		
Luke 24:46		
Luke 18:34		
Luke 24:25–27		
Luke 24:44–45		

L43.2 THE DISCIPLES DISPUTE **9:46–50**

Luke 11:23	Matt 18:1–10	Mark 9:33–37
Luke 22:24–27	Matt 20:24–28	Mark 9:38–41
Luke 10:16	Matt 23:11–12	Mark 10:13–16
John 12:44–45	Matt 12:30	POxy1224 2
John 13:20	Matt 10:40	
	GThom 12	

S14:L44–45 JOURNEY TO JERUSALEM ONE **9:51–62**

L44 JESUS DEPARTS FOR JERUSALEM **9:51–56**

Luke 1:76		
Luke 3:4		
Luke 7:27		
Luke 10:1		
Luke 13:22		
Luke 13:33		
Luke 17:11		
Luke 18:31		
Luke 19:11		
2 Kgs 1:9–12		

L45 WOULD-BE FOLLOWERS OF JESUS **9:57–62**

Luke 14:25–33	Matt 8:18–22	
	GThom 86	

S15:L46–47 JOURNEY TO JERUSALEM TWO **10:1–24**

L46 THE SEVENTY: COMMISSIONING AND CHARGE **10:1–16**

Luke 9:1–6	Matt 9:35–38	Mark 6:7–13
Luke 1:76	Matt 10:5–15	Mark 9:37
Luke 3:4	Matt 11:20–24	2 Clem 5:2
Luke 7:27	Matt 10:16	Acts 13:51
Luke 9:51–52	Matt 10:40	Acts 18:6
Luke 22:35–36	Matt 18:5	GNaz 27
Luke 9:48	GThom 73	
John 4:35	GThom 14	
John 5:23		
John 12:44–45		
John 12:48		
John 13:20		
John 15:23		

L47 RETURN OF THE SEVENTY **10:17–24**

L47.1 THE SEVENTY REPORT VICTORY **10:17–20**

Luke 9:10		Mark 16:14–18
Ps 9:13		Mark 6:30
John 12:31		

L47.2 JESUS THANKS THE FATHER **10:21–22**

John 3:35	Matt 11:25–27	GNaz 9
John 10:14–15	POxy654 3	
John 17:25–26	GThom 4	
	GThom 61	

| **L47.3** | THE DISCIPLES ARE BLESSED | **10:23–24** |

Matt 13:10–17
GThom 38

| **S16:L48–49** | JOURNEY TO JERUSALEM THREE | **10:25–42** |

| **L48** | THE GOOD SAMARITAN | **10:25–37** |

| **L48.1** | INTRODUCTION: THE LAWYER'S QUESTION | **10:25–29** |

Luke 18:18–21	Matt 22:34–40	Mark 12:28–34
Lev 19:18	Matt 19:16–21	Mark 10:17–20
Deut 6:5	GThom 25	Did 1:2
Lev 18:5		Barn 19:5
		Rom 13:8–10
		Jas 2:8
		Gal 5:14

| **L48.2** | THE GOOD SAMARITAN | **10:30–35** |

| **L48.3** | CONCLUSION | **10:36–37** |

| **L49** | MARY AND MARTHA | **10:38–42** |

John 11:1–6
John 11:17–37
John 12:2

| **S17:L50–52** | JOURNEY TO JERUSALEM FOUR | **11:1–54** |

| **L50** | PRAYER | **11:1–13** |

| **L50.1** | JESUS TEACHES THE DISCIPLES TO PRAY | **11:1–4** |

Matt 6:5–15	Mark 11:25
	Did 8:2
	GNaz 5

| **L50.2** | THE FRIEND AT MIDNIGHT | **11:5–8** |

Luke 18:1–5

| **L50.3** | GOD ANSWERS PRAYER | **11:9–13** |

Matt 7:7–11
POxy654 2
GThom 2
GThom 92
GThom 94

| **L51** | DEMONS AND SIGNS | **11:14–36** |

| **L51.1** | ON EXORCISMS | **11:14–23** |

Luke 9:50	Matt 9:32–34	Mark 3:22
John 7:20	Matt 12:22–24	POxy1224 2
John 8:48	GThom 21	
John 8:52	GThom 35	
John 10:20		

| **L51.2** | AN UNCLEAN SPIRIT RETURNS | **11:24–26** |

Matt 12:43–45

| **L51.3** | A WOMAN BLESSES JESUS | **11:27–28** |

| Luke 8:19–21 | GThom 79 |

| **L51.4** | THE SIGN OF JONAH | **11:29–32** |

Luke 11:16	Matt 12:38–42	Mark 8:11–13
1 Kgs 10:1–13	Matt 16:1–4	
Jonah 3:5		

| **L51.5** | THE LAMP OF THE BODY | **11:33–36** |

Luke 8:16–17	Matt 5:13–16	Mark 4:21–23
	Matt 6:22–23	DialSav 125:18–126:2
	GThom 33	
	GThom 24	

| **L52** | PHARISEES AND LAWYERS | **11:37–54** |

| **L52.1** | WOES AGAINST THE PHARISEES | **11:37–44** |

Luke 7:36	Matt 23:25–26	Mark 12:38–40
Luke 14:1	Matt 23:23–24	POxy840 2
Luke 20:45–47	Matt 23:5–7	
Luke 14:7–11	Matt 23:27–28	
Mic 6:8	GThom 89	

| **L52.2** | WOES AGAINST THE LAWYERS | **11:45–54** |

Luke 13:33–34	Matt 23:4	Acts 7:51–52
Zech 1:1–6	Matt 23:29–31	PJas 24:1–4
Gen 4:8	Matt 23:32–36	GNaz 17
2 Chr 24:20–21	Matt 23:13	
	POxy655 2	
	GThom 39	
	GThom 102	

| **S18:L53–57** | JOURNEY TO JERUSALEM FIVE | **12:1–13:9** |

| **L53** | JESUS ADVISES THE DISCIPLES | **12:1–12** |

Luke 8:16–17	Matt 10:26–33	Mark 4:21–23
Luke 12:24	Matt 12:32	Mark 8:38
Luke 21:18	Matt 10:19–20	Mark 3:28–29
Luke 9:26	POxy654 5	Mark 13:11
Luke 21:14–15	GThom 5	2 Clem 5:2–4
John 14:26	GThom 6	Acts 27:34
	POxy1 8	2 Clem 3:2
	GThom 33	Acts 4:5–8
	GThom 44	

| **L54** | THE RICH FOOL | **12:13–21** |

| Luke 12:33–34 | GThom 72 | 1 Cor 15:32 |
| Luke 18:22 | GThom 63 | |

L55	ANXIETIES ABOUT EARTHLY THINGS	**12:22–34**
Luke 12:7	Matt 6:25–34	Clem., *Strom.* 1.24.158
Luke 12:21	Matt 6:19–21	Phil 4:6
Luke 18:22	GThom 36	
	GThom 76	

L56	COMPENDIUM OF SAYINGS	**12:35–59**

L56.1	WATCHFUL SERVANTS	**12:35–48**
John 13:3–5	Matt 24:43–51	Mark 13:33–37
	Matt 25:1–13	GNaz 18
	GThom 21	
	GThom 103	

L56.2	THE MESSIAH BRINGS DIVISION	**12:49–53**
Mic 7:5–6	Matt 10:34–39	Mark 10:38
John 15:18–21	GThom 10	Mark 13:12–13
	GThom 16	

L56.3	INTERPRETING THE TIME	**12:54–56**
	Matt 16:2–3	
	GThom 91	

L56.4	SETTLING WITH AN ACCUSER	**12:57–59**
	Matt 5:25–26	
	Matt 18:34–35	

L57	REPENTANCE OR DESTRUCTION	**13:1–9**

L57.1	THE GALILEANS AS SINNERS	**13:1–5**

L57.2	THE PARABLE OF THE FIG TREE	**13:6–9**
Luke 3:9	Matt 21:18–22	Mark 11:12–14
Luke 6:43–44	Matt 7:17–20	Mark 11:20–25

S19:L58–59	JOURNEY TO JERUSALEM SIX	**13:10–21**

L58	THE INFIRM WOMAN	**13:10–17**
Luke 14:5	Matt 12:11–12	InThom 2:1–5
Exod 20:9		
Deut 5:13		

L59	TWO PARABLES	**13:18–21**

L59.1	MUSTARD SEED	**13:18–19**
Dan 4:20–22	Matt 13:31–32	Mark 4:30–32
	GThom 20	

L59.2	LEAVEN	**13:20–21**
	Matt 13:33	
	GThom 96	

S20:L60–61	JOURNEY TO JERUSALEM SEVEN	**13:22–35**

L60	THE KINGDOM HAS A NARROW ENTRANCE	**13:22–30**
Luke 9:51	Matt 7:13–14	Mark 10:31
Luke 13:33	Matt 25:10–12	
Luke 17:11	Matt 7:21–23	
Luke 18:31	Matt 8:11–12	
Luke 19:11	Matt 19:30	
Ps 6:8	Matt 20:16	
Ps 107:3	POxy654 4	
	GThom 4	

L61	A PROPHET MUST PERISH IN JERUSALEM	**13:31–35**
Luke 9:7–9	Matt 23:37–39	Acts 7:51–52
Luke 3:19–20		
Luke 23:8		
Luke 11:47–51		
Luke 9:51		
Luke 13:22		
Luke 17:11		
Luke 18:31		
Luke 19:11		
Luke 19:41–44		
Luke 21:20–24		
Luke 23:27–31		
Luke 19:37–38		
Isa 31:5		
Ps 118:26		

S21:L62–64	JOURNEY TO JERUSALEM EIGHT	**14:1–24**

L62	A MAN WITH DROPSY ·	**14:1–6**
Luke 6:6–11	Matt 12:11–12	Mark 3:1–6
Luke 13:10–17	Matt 12:9–14	InThom 2:1–5

L63	ON HUMILITY	**14:7–14**

L63.1	HUMILITY AS GUESTS	**14:7–11**
L63.2	HUMILITY AS HOSTS	**14:12–14**
Luke 18:14	Matt 23:12	
Luke 11:43	Matt 18:4	
Luke 20:46		
Luke 14:21		

L64	PARABLE OF THE GREAT SUPPER	**14:15–24**
Luke 14:13	Matt 22:1–14	
	GThom 64	

S22:L65–66   JOURNEY TO JERUSALEM NINE   **14:25–15:32**

L65   THE WAY OF THE CROSS   **14:25–35**

Luke 9:23–27	Matt 10:34–39	Mark 8:34–9:1
Luke 9:57–62	Matt 16:24–28	Mark 9:50
Luke 18:29–30	Matt 5:13–16	
	Matt 8:18–22	
	GThom 55	
	GThom 101	

L66   TAX COLLECTORS AND SINNERS LISTEN   **15:1–32**

L66.1   INTRODUCTION   **15:1–2**

Luke 5:29–32	Matt 9:10–13	Mark 2:15–17
Luke 7:34		POxy1224 1
Luke 19:7		

L66.2   PARABLE OF THE LOST SHEEP   **15:3–7**

| | Matt 18:12–14 | Justin, *Apology* 1.15.8 |
| | GThom 107 | |

L66.3   PARABLE OF THE LOST COIN   **15:8–10**

| Luke 19:10 | | |

L66.4   PARABLE OF THE PRODIGAL SON   **15:11–32**

S23:L67–70   JOURNEY TO JERUSALEM TEN   **16:1–17:10**

L67   PARABLE OF THE UNJUST STEWARD   **16:1–15**

L67.1   PARABLE OF THE UNJUST STEWARD   **16:1–9**
L67.2   TRUE STEWARDSHIP   **16:10–13**
L67.3   THE PHARISEES SCOFF   **16:14–15**

Luke 10:29	Matt 6:24	2 Clem 8:5
Luke 14:11	GThom 47	
Luke 18:9		Ireneaus, *Adv. haer.* 2.34.3
Luke 18:14		

L68   ON LAW AND DIVORCE   **16:16–18**

L68.1   ON LAW   **16:16–17**
L68.2   ON DIVORCE   **16:18**

	Matt 11:12–13	Mark 10:10–12
	Matt 5:18	
	Matt 5:31–32	
	Matt 19:3–9	
	GThom 11	

L69   THE RICH MAN AND LAZARUS   **16:19–31**

| Luke 3:8 | | |

L70   CONVERSATIONS WITH THE DISCIPLES   **17:1–10**

L70.1   SIN AND FORGIVENESS   **17:1–4**
L70.2   ON FAITH   **17:5–6**
L70.3   THE WORTHY SERVANT   **17:7–10**

Matt 18:6–7	Mark 9:42
Matt 18:35	Mark 11:22–23
Matt 18:21–22	
Matt 17:20	
Matt 21:21	
GThom 48	
GThom 106	

S24:L71–78   JOURNEY TO JERUSALEM ELEVEN   **17:11–18:34**

L71   TEN LEPERS   **17:11–19**

L71.1   SCENE ONE   **17:11–14**
L71.2   SCENE TWO   **17:15–19**

Luke 9:51	PEger2 2
Luke 13:22	
Luke 13:33	
Luke 18:31	
Luke 19:11	
Luke 18:38–39	
Luke 5:14	
Luke 7:50	
Luke 8:48	
Luke 18:42	

L72   WHEN WILL THE KINGDOM COME?   **17:20–21**

Matt 24:23	Mark 13:21
POxy654 3	
GThom 3	
GThom 113	

L73   THE DAYS OF THE SON OF MAN   **17:22–37**

Luke 9:22	Matt 24:26–27	Mark 13:15–16
Luke 9:44	Matt 24:37–41	Mark 8:35
Luke 13:31–33	Matt 24:17–18	Mark 13:21
Luke 22:22	Matt 10:39	
Luke 24:6–8	Matt 16:25	
Luke 24:26	Matt 24:28	
Luke 24:46	GThom 38	
Luke 9:24	GThom 113	
Gen 7:6–10	GThom 61	

L74   PARABLE OF THE UNJUST JUDGE   **18:1–8**

| Luke 11:5–8 | | |

L75   PARABLE OF THE PHARISEE AND THE PUBLICAN   **18:9–14**

Luke 14:11	Matt 23:12
Luke 16:15	Matt 18:4
Luke 10:29	

L76	THE KINGDOM BELONGS TO CHILDREN	**18:15–17**
Luke 9:48	Matt 19:13–15	Mark 10:13–16
John 3:3–5	Matt 18:2–6	Mark 9:36–37
	GThom 22	

L77	ON RICHES	**18:18–30**

L77.1	RICH RULER	**18:18–25**
L77.2	DANGER OF RICHES	**18:26–30**
Luke 10:25	Matt 19:16–22	Mark 10:17–22
Luke 12:21	Matt 19:23–30	Mark 10:23–31
Luke 12:33–34		GNaz 16
Luke 5:11		Acts 4:34–35
Luke 5:28		ApocJa 4:32–37
Luke 14:26		
Exod 20:12–16		
Deut 5:16–20		

L78	THIRD PREDICTION OF THE PASSION	**18:31–34**
Luke 9:18–22	Matt 20:17–19	Mark 10:32–34
Luke 9:43b–45	Matt 16:21–23	Mark 8:31–33
Luke 17:25	Matt 17:22–23	Mark 9:30–32
Luke 22:22		
Luke 24:6–8		
Luke 24:26		
Luke 24:46		
Luke 9:51		
Luke 13:22		
Luke 13:33		
Luke 17:11		
Luke 19:11		
Luke 24:25–27		
Luke 24:44–45		

S25:L79–81	JOURNEY TO JERUSALEM TWELVE	**18:35–19:27**

L79	JESUS HEALS A BLIND MAN	**18:35–43**
Luke 17:13	Matt 9:27–31	Mark 10:46–52
Luke 7:50	Matt 20:29–34	
Luke 8:48		
Luke 17:19		

L80	ZACCHAEUS THE RICH TAX COLLECTOR	**19:1–10**
Luke 5:29–30		
Luke 7:34		
Luke 15:1–2		
Luke 18:22		
Luke 15:3–7		
Luke 15:8–10		

L81	PARABLE OF THE POUNDS	**19:11–27**
Luke 9:51	Matt 25:14–30	Mark 4:24–25
Luke 3:22	Matt 13:10–12	GNaz 18
Luke 13:33	GThom 41	
Luke 17:11		
Luke 18:31		
Luke 8:18		

S26:L82	ENTRY INTO JERUSALEM	**19:28–44**

L82	ENTRY INTO JERUSALEM	**19:28–44**

L82.1	TWO SENT FOR COLT	**19:28–32**
L82.2	COLT FOUND TIED	**19:33–34**
L82.3	TRIUMPHAL ENTRY	**19:35–40**
Luke 2:14	Matt 21:1–6	Mark 11:1–3
Luke 13:35	Matt 21:7–9	Mark 11:4–6
Ps 118:26	Matt 21:10–11	Mark 11:7–10
Hab 2:11		Mark 11:11
John 12:12–19		

L82.4	LAMENT OVER JERUSALEM	**19:41–44**
Luke 1:68–79		
Luke 13:34–35		
Luke 21:20–24		
Luke 23:27–31		
Luke 21:6		
Ps 137:9		

S27:L83–91	IN THE TEMPLE AREA	**19:45–21:38**

L83	CLEANSING THE TEMPLE	**19:45–48**
Luke 20:19	Matt 21:12–13	Mark 11:15–19
Luke 22:2	Matt 21:14–17	Mark 12:12
Isa 56:7	Matt 21:45	Mark 14:1–2
Jer 7:11	Matt 26:3–5	
John 2:13–22		
John 7:43–44		

L84	QUESTION OF JESUS' AUTHORITY	**20:1–8**
Luke 7:29–30	Matt 21:23–27	Mark 11:27–33
John 2:18		POxy840 2

L85	PARABLE OF THE WICKED TENANTS	**20:9–19**
Luke 3:22	Matt 21:33–46	Mark 12:1–12
Luke 19:47–48	Matt 26:3–5	Mark 14:1–2
Luke 22:2	GThom 65	Acts 4:11
Isa 5:1–2	GThom 66	
Ps 118:22		
John 7:43–44		

L86	IS IT LAWFUL TO GIVE TRIBUTE?	**20:20–26**
John 3:2	Matt 22:15–22	Mark 12:13–17
	GThom 100	PEger2 3
		Rom 13:7

L87	WHOSE WIFE WILL SHE BE?	**20:27–40**
Gen 38:8	Matt 22:23–33	Mark 12:18–27
Deut 25:5–6	Matt 22:46	Mark 12:32
Exod 3:6		Mark 12:34
		1 Cor 15:12

L88　　　　WHOSE SON IS THE CHRIST?　　　**20:41–44**

Luke 22:69	Matt 22:41–46	Mark 12:35–37
Ps 110:1		Acts 2:34–35
2 Sam 7:12–16		Acts 7:55–56
Mic 5:2		1 Cor 15:20–28
Ps 89:3–4		
John 7:40–44		

L89　　　WARNING AGAINST THE SCRIBES　　　**20:45–47**

| Luke 11:37–44 | Matt 23:6 | Mark 12:38–40 |
| Luke 14:7–11 | | |

L90　　　　　WIDOW'S COINS　　　　**21:1–4**

| | | Mark 12:41–44 |

L91　　　　APOCALYPTIC DISCOURSE　　　**21:5–38**

L91.1　　　　SIGNS OF THE END　　　**21:5–19**

Luke 19:44	Matt 24:3–14	Mark 13:3–13
Luke 12:11–12	Matt 10:16–23	Acts 27:34
Luke 12:7	Matt 10:22	
John 14:26	Matt 10:30	
John 16:2		
John 15:18–21		

L91.2　　　TRIBULATION BEFORE THE END　　　**21:20–24**

Luke 17:31	Matt 24:15–28	Mark 13:14–23
Luke 13:34–35	GThom 79	
Luke 19:41–44		
Luke 23:27–31		

L91.3　　　COMING OF THE SON OF MAN　　　**21:25–33**

| Luke 9:27 | Matt 24:29–36 | Mark 13:24–32 |
| Dan 7:13–14 | Matt 16:28 | Mark 9:1 |

L91.4　　　THE NEED FOR WATCHFULNESS　　　**21:34–36**

| Luke 12:45–46 | Matt 24:37–51 | Mark 13:33–37 |

L91.5　　　NARRATIVE CONCLUSION　　　**21:37–38**

| Luke 19:47–48 | Matt 21:17 | Mark 11:19 |

S28:L92–101　　THE PASSION NARRATIVE　　**22:1–23:56**

L92　　　　INTRODUCTION　　　　**22:1–6**

L92.1　　　　INTRODUCTION　　　　**22:1–2**

Luke 19:47–48	Matt 26:1–2	Mark 14:1–2
Luke 20:19	Matt 26:3–5	Mark 12:12
John 11:45–53	Matt 21:45	
John 11:54		
John 11:55–57		

L92.2　　　JUDAS AGREES TO BETRAY JESUS　　　**22:3–6**

| | Matt 26:14–16 | Mark 14:10–11 |
| | | Acts 1:16–20 |

L93　　　　THE PASSOVER MEAL　　　　**22:7–38**

L93.1　　PREPARATION FOR THE PASSOVER MEAL　　**22:7–13**

| | Matt 26:17–19 | Mark 14:12–16 |
| | | GEbi 7 |

L93.2　　LAST SUPPER; JESUS FORETELLS BETRAYAL　　**22:14–23**

Luke 9:16	Matt 26:20–25	Mark 14:17–21
Luke 24:30	Matt 26:26–29	Mark 14:22–25
Luke 9:22		1 Cor 11:23–25
Luke 9:44		Did 9:1–5
Luke 17:25		Justin, *Apology* 1.66.3
Luke 18:31–33		GEbi 7
Luke 24:6–8		
Luke 24:26		
Luke 24:46		
Exod 24:8		
Jer 31:31		
Zech 9:11		
John 13:21–30		
John 6:48–58		

L93.3　　DISPUTE OVER WHO IS GREATEST　　**22:24–30**

Luke 9:48	Matt 20:24–28	Mark 10:41–45
Luke 12:37	Matt 19:28	Mark 9:35
Luke 23:42–43	Matt 23:11–12	Acts 10:41
John 13:1–20	GThom 12	

L93.4　　JESUS PREDICTS PETER'S DENIAL　　**22:31–34**

Luke 22:54b–62	Matt 26:30–35	Mark 14:26–31
John 13:36–38		Fayyum Fragment
		Acts 21:13

L93.5　　　　TWO SWORDS　　　　**22:35–38**

Luke 9:3	Matt 10:9–10	Mark 6:8–9
Luke 10:4		
Luke 22:49–50		
Isa 53:12		

L94　　EVENTS ON THE MOUNT OF OLIVES　　**22:39–54a**

L94.1　　　　THE PRAYER　　　　**22:39–46**

L94.1a	INTRODUCTION	**22:39**
L94.1b	THE PRAYER	**22:40–42**
L94.1c	THE DISCIPLES SLEEP	**22:45–46**

John 18:1	Matt 26:36	Mark 14:32
John 18:11	Matt 26:37–38	Mark 14:33–34
	Matt 26:39	Mark 14:35–36
	Matt 26:40–41	Mark 14:37–38
	Matt 26:42	Mark 14:39
	Matt 26:43	Mark 14:40
	Matt 26:44	Mark 14:41–42
	Matt 26:45–46	Acts 21:14

L94.2	THE ARREST	**22:47–54a**
Luke 22:36–38	Matt 26:47–56	Mark 14:43–52
John 18:1–12	Matt 26:57	Mark 14:53
John 18:20		

L95	AT THE HIGH PRIEST'S HOUSE	**22:54b–65**

L95.1	PETER'S DENIAL	**22:54b–62**
L95.2	THE GUARDS MOCK JESUS	**22:63–65**
Luke 22:31–34	Matt 26:57–58	Mark 14:53–54
John 18:13–14	Matt 26:69–75	Mark 14:66–72
John 18:15–18	Matt 26:67–68	Mark 14:65
John 18:25–27		

L96	TRIAL BEFORE THE COUNCIL	**22:66–71**
Luke 20:42–43	Matt 26:59–68	Mark 14:55–65
Luke 21:27	Matt 24:30	Mark 13:26
Ps 110:1		Acts 2:34–35
John 18:13–14		Acts 7:55–56
John 18:19–24		

L97	TRIAL BEFORE PILATE	**Luke 23:1–7**
L98	TRIAL BEFORE HEROD	**Luke 23:8–12**
L99.1–2	TRIAL BEFORE PILATE RESUMED	**Luke 23:13–25**
John 18:28–19:16	Matt 27:1–2	Mark 15:1–5
	Matt 27:11–14	Mark 15:6–15
	Matt 27:15–26	AcPil 3:2
		AcPil 4:4–5
		AcPil 9:4–5
		Acts 3:13–15
		Acts 21:36

L100	THE CRUCIFIXION	**23:26–49**

L100.1	JESUS IS LED AWAY	**23:26–32**
Luke 13:34–35	Matt 27:32	Mark 15:21
Luke 19:41–44	GThom 79	
Luke 21:20–24		
Hos 10:8		

L100.2	THE CRUCIFIXION	**23:33–43**
Luke 22:29–30	Matt 27:33–44	Mark 15:22–32
Ps 22:18	Matt 27:47–48	Mark 15:35–36
Ps 22:7		GPet 4.10–14
Ps 69:21		AcPil 10:1–2
John 19:17–24		GPet 5.16
John 19:28–30		GNaz 24
		GNaz 35
		Acts 7:60

L100.3	THE DEATH	**23:44–49**
Luke 23:55	Matt 27:45–56	Mark 15:33–41
Luke 8:2–3		GPet 5.15–20
Ps 31:5		AcPil 11:1–3a
Ps 38:11		GNaz 36
John 19:25–37		Acts 7:59
		GPet 7.25

L101	THE BURIAL	**23:50–56**
Luke 8:2–3	Matt 27:57–61	Mark 15:42–47
Luke 23:49		GPet 2.3–5a
Deut 21:22–23		GPet 6.21–24
Josh 10:18		AcPil 11:3b
Josh 10:27		
Exod 20:8–10		
John 19:38–42		

S29:L102–104	RESURRECTION AND DEPARTURE	**24:1–53**

L102	THE WOMEN DISCOVER THE EMPTY TOMB	**24:1–11**
Luke 9:22	Matt 28:1–8	Mark 16:1–8
Luke 9:44	Matt 27:55–56	Mark 15:40–41
Luke 17:25		GPet 9.35–13.57
Luke 18:31–33		AcPil 13:1–3
Luke 22:22		
Luke 24:26		
Luke 24:46		
Luke 8:1–3		
Luke 23:49		
Luke 23:55		
John 20:1–18		

L103	EMMAUS AND JERUSALEM	**24:13–49**

L103.1	TWO ON THE ROAD TO EMMAUS	**24:13–27**
Luke 7:16		
Luke 1:68		
Luke 2:38		
Luke 9:45		
Luke 18:34		
Luke 24:44–45		
Luke 9:22		
Luke 9:44		
Luke 17:25		
Luke 18:31–33		
Luke 22:22		
Luke 24:6–8		
Luke 24:46		

L103.2	IN EMMAUS	**24:28–33a**

GHeb 7

| **L103.3** | IN JERUSALEM | **24:33b–49** |

L103.3a	THE TWO REPORT TO THE ELEVEN	**24:28–33a**
L103.3b	JESUS APPEARS	**24:36–43**
L103.3c	JESUS INSTRUCTS THE DISCIPLES	**24:44–49**

Luke 9:45	AcPil 14:1
Luke 18:34	Ign, *Smyr.* 3.2
Luke 24:25–27	Acts 1:4–8
Luke 9:22	
Luke 9:44	
Luke 17:25	
Luke 18:31–33	
Luke 22:22	
Luke 24:6–8	
Luke 24:26	
Hos 6:2	
John 20:19–23	
John 20:24–29	

| **L104** | BETHANY: JESUS DEPARTS | **24:50–53** |

AcPil 14:1
Acts 1:9–12

LUKE	MATT

LUKE

Luke 1:1–4 (§L1)
[1] Inasmuch as many have undertaken to compile a narrative of the things which have been accomplished among us, [2] just as they were delivered to us by those who from the beginning were eyewitnesses and ministers of the word, [3] it seemed good to me also, having followed all things closely[a] for some time past, to write an orderly account for you, most excellent Theophilus, [4] that you may know the truth concerning the things of which you have been informed.

[a] Or *accurately*

MATT

Cf. Matt 1:1

MARK

Mark 1:1
[1] The beginning of the gospel of Jesus Christ, the Son of God.

OTHER

† Acts 1:1–2
[1] In the first book, O **Theophilus**, I have dealt with all that Jesus began to do and teach, [2] until the day when he was taken up, after he had given commandment through the Holy Spirit to the apostles whom he had chosen.

Josephus, *Against Apion* 1.1.1–3
(1) In my history of our Antiquities, *most excellent Epaphroditus, I have, I think, made sufficiently clear to any who may peruse that work the extreme antiquity of our Jewish race, the purity of the original stock, and the manner in which it established itself in the country which we occupy to-day. That history embraces a period of five thousand years, and was written by me in Greek on the basis of our sacred books. Since, however, I observe that a considerable number of persons, influenced by the malicious calumnies of certain individuals, discredit the statements in my history concerning our antiquity, and adduce as proof of the comparative modernity of our race the fact that it has not been thought worthy of mention by the best known Greek historians, I consider it my duty to devote a brief treatise to all these points; in order at once to convict our detractors of malignity and deliberate falsehood, to correct the ignorance of others, and to instruct all who desire to* **know the truth concerning the** *antiquity of our race.*

Josephus, *Against Apion* 2.1.1
(1) In the first volume of this work, my **most** *esteemed Epaphroditus, I demonstrated the antiquity of our race, corroborating my statements by the writings of Phoenicians, Chaldaeans, and Egyptians, besides citing as witnesses numerous Greek historians; I also challenged the statement of Manetho, Chaeremon, and some others.*

Philo, *On the Life of Moses* 1.1.1–4
(I) I purpose to write the life of Moses, whom some describe as the legislator of the Jews, others as the interpreter of the Holy Laws. I hope to bring the story of this greatest and most perfect of men to the knowledge of such as deserve not to remain in ignorance of it; for, while the fame of the laws which he left behind him has travelled throughout the civilized world and reached the ends of the earth, the man himself as he really was is known to few. Greek men of letters have refused to treat him as worthy of memory, possibly through envy, and also because in many cases the ordinances of the legislators of the different states are opposed to his. Most of these authors have abused the powers which education gave them, by composing in verse or prose comedies and pieces of voluptuous licence, to their widespread disgrace, when they should have used their natural gifts to the full on the lessons taught by good men and their lives. In this way they might have ensured that nothing of excellence, old or new, should be consigned to oblivion and to the extinction of the light which it could give, and also save themselves from seeming to neglect the better themes and prefer others unworthy of attention, in which all their efforts to express bad matter in good language served to confer distinction on shameful subjects. But I will disregard their malice and tell the story of Moses as I have learned it, both from the sacred books, the wonderful monuments of his wisdom which he has left behind him, and from some of the elders of the nation; for I always interwove what I was told with what I read, and thus believed myself to have a closer knowledge than others of his life's history.

InThom 0–1:1
The Account of Thomas the Israelite Philosopher concerning the Childhood of the Lord
1 [1] I, Thomas the Israelite, tell and make known to **you** *all, brethren from among the Gentiles, all the works of the childhood of our Lord Jesus Christ and his mighty deeds,* **which** *he did when he was born in our land. The beginning is as follows.*

JOHN	THOMAS

JOHN

John 15:27 ⇨ Luke 1:2
[27] and you also are witnesses, because you have been with me *from the beginning.*

THOMAS

GThom, title
These are the secret sayings which the living Jesus spoke and which Didymos Judas Thomas wrote down.

LUKE	MATT	MARK

LUKE

INTRODUCTION

Luke 1:5–7 (§L2.1a) °

⁵ In the days of Herod, king of Judea, there was a priest named Zechariah[a], of the division of Abijah; and he had a wife of the daughters of Aaron, and her name was Elizabeth. ⁶ And they were both righteous before God, walking in all the commandments and ordinances of the Lord blameless. ⁷ But they had no child, because Elizabeth was barren, and both were advanced in years.

ZECHARIAH'S VISION

Luke 1:8–23 (§L2.1b) °

⁸ Now while he was serving as priest before God when his division was on duty, ⁹ according to the custom of the priesthood, it fell to him by lot to enter the temple of the Lord and burn incense. ¹⁰ And the whole multitude of the people were praying outside at the hour of incense. ¹¹ And there appeared to him an angel of the Lord standing on the right side of the altar of incense. ¹² And Zechariah was troubled when he saw him, and fear fell upon him. ¹³ But the angel said to him, "Do not be afraid, Zechariah, for your prayer is heard, and your wife Elizabeth will bear you a son, and you shall call his name John.

¹⁴ And you will have joy and gladness,
and many will rejoice at his birth;
¹⁵ for he will be great before the Lord,
and he shall drink no wine nor strong drink,
and he will be filled with the Holy Spirit,
even from his mother's womb.
¹⁶ And he will turn many of the sons of Israel to the
Lord their God,
¹⁷ and he will go before him in the spirit and power of
Elijah,
to turn the hearts of the fathers to the children,
and the disobedient to the wisdom of the just,
to make ready for the Lord a people prepared."

¹⁸ And Zechariah said to the angel, "How shall I know this? For I am an old man, and my wife is advanced in years." ¹⁹ And the angel answered him, "I am Gabriel, who stand in the presence of God; and I was sent to speak to you, and to bring you this good news. ²⁰ And behold, you will be silent and unable to speak until the day that these things come to pass, because you did not believe my words, which will be fulfilled in their time." ²¹ And the people were waiting for Zechariah, and they wondered at his delay in the temple. ²² And when he came out, he could not speak to them, and they perceived that he had seen a vision in the temple; and he made signs to them and remained dumb. ²³ And when his time of service was ended, he went to his home.

CONCEPTION OF JOHN

Luke 1:24–25 (§L2.1c) °

²⁴ After these days his wife Elizabeth conceived, and for five months she hid herself, saying, ²⁵ "Thus the Lord has done to me in the days when he looked on me, to take away my reproach among men."

MATT

[a] Greek: *Zacharias*

°Appendix 1 ⇨ §L2.1a–c

Luke 1:26–38 (§L2.2) ⇨ §L2.1b

²⁶ *In the sixth month the angel Gabriel was sent from God to a city of Galilee named Nazareth,* ²⁷ *to a virgin betrothed to a man whose name was Joseph, of the house of David; and the virgin's name was Mary.* ²⁸ *And he came to her and said, "Hail, O favored one, the Lord is with you!"* ²⁹ *But she was greatly troubled at the saying, and considered in her mind what sort of greeting this might be.* ³⁰ *And the angel said to her, "Do not be afraid, Mary, for you have found favor with God.* ³¹ *And behold, you will conceive in your womb and bear a son, and you shall call his name Jesus.*

³² *He will be great, and will be called the
Son of the Most High;*
*and the Lord God will give to him the
throne of his father David,*
³³ *and he will reign over the house of
Jacob for ever;*
and of his kingdom there will be no end."
³⁴ *And Mary said to the angel, "How shall this be, since I have no husband?"*
³⁵ *And the angel said to her,*
*"The Holy Spirit will come upon you,
and the power of the Most High will
overshadow you;*
*therefore the child to be born will be
called holy,
the Son of God.*
³⁶ *And behold, your kinswoman* **Elizabeth** *in her old age has also conceived a son; and this is the sixth month with her who was called barren.* ³⁷ *For with God nothing will be impossible."* ³⁸ *And Mary said, "Behold, I am the handmaid of the Lord; let it be to me according to your word." And the angel departed from her.*

Luke 1:76 ⇨ Luke 1:17

⁷⁶ *And you, child, will be called the prophet of the Most High;*
for you **will go before the Lord** *to prepare his ways, . . .*

MARK

Gen 16:1–16 ⇨ §L2.1b

¹ Now Sarai, Abram's wife, bore him no children. She had an Egyptian maid whose name was Hagar; ² and Sarai said to Abram, "Behold now, the Lord has prevented me from bearing children; go in to my maid; it may be that I shall obtain children by her." And Abram hearkened to the voice of Sarai. ³ So, after Abram had dwelt ten years in the land of Canaan, Sarai, Abram's wife, took Hagar the Egyptian, her maid, and gave her to Abram her husband as a wife. ⁴ And he went in to Hagar, and she conceived; and when she saw that she had conceived, she looked with contempt on her mistress. ⁵ And Sarai said to Abram, "May the wrong done to me be on you! I gave my maid to your embrace, and when she saw that she had conceived, she looked on me with contempt. May the Lord judge between you and me!" ⁶ But Abram said to Sarai "Behold, your maid is in your power; do to you as you please." Then Sarai dealt harshly with her, and she fled from her.

⁷ **The angel of the Lord** found her by a spring of water in the wilderness, the spring on the way to Shur. ⁸ And he **said**, "Hagar, maid of Sarai, where have you come from and where are you going?" She said, "I am fleeing from my mistress Sarai." ⁹ **The angel of the Lord said to** her, "Return to your mistress, and submit to her." ¹ **The angel of the Lord** also **said to** her, "I will so greatly multiply your descendants that they cannot be numbered for multitude." ¹¹ And **the angel of the Lord said to** her, "Behold, you are with child, and shall **bear a son; you shall call his name** Ishmael; because the Lord has given heed to **your** affliction. ¹² He shall be a wild ass of a man, his hand against every man and every man's hand against him; and he shall dwell over against all his kinsmen." ¹³ So she called the name of the Lord who spoke to her, "Thou art a God of seeing"; for she said, "Have I really seen God and remained alive after seeing him?" ¹⁴ Therefore the well was called Beerlahairoi; it lies between Kadesh and Bered.

¹⁵ And Hagar bore Abram **a son**; and Abram called the name of his **son**, whom Hagar bore, Ishmael. ¹⁶ Abram was eighty-six years old when Hagar bore Ishmael to Abram.

Judg 13:2–21 ⇨ §L2.1b

² And there was a certain man of Zorah, of the tribe of the Danites, whose name was Manoah; **and** his **wife** was barren and had no children. ³ **And the angel of the Lord appeared to** the woman and **said to** her, "Behold, you are barren and have no children; but you shall conceive and **bear a son**. ⁴ Therefore beware, and **drink no wine** or **strong drink** and eat nothing unclean, ⁵ for lo, you shall conceive and **bear a**

JOHN	THOMAS	OTHER

PJas 8:3 ⇨ Luke 1:8–11

[3] *And the high* **priest** *took the vestment with the twelve bells and went into* **the Holy of Holies** *and prayed concerning her.* **And behold, an angel of the Lord** *(suddenly) stood before* **him** *and said to him: "Zacharias, Zacharias, go out and assemble the widowers of the people, [who shall each bring a rod,] and to whomsoever the Lord shall give a (miraculous) sign, his wife she shall be." And the heralds went forth and spread out through all the country round about Judaea; the trumpet of the Lord sounded, and all ran to it.*

PJas 10:2 ⇨ Luke 1:20

[2] *Then they brought them into the temple of the Lord, and the priest said: "Cast me lots, who shall weave the gold, the amiant, the linen, the silk, the hyacinth-blue, the scarlet and the pure purple." And to Mary fell the lot of the "pure purple" and "scarlet." And she took them and worked them in her house. At that time Zacharias became dumb, and Samuel took his place until Zacharias was able to speak (again). But Mary took the scarlet and spun it.*

son. No razor shall come upon his head, for the boy shall be a Nazirite to God from birth; and he shall begin to deliver Israel from the hand of the Philistines." [6] Then the woman came and told her husband, "A man of God came to me, and his countenance was like the countenance of the **angel of** God, very terrible; I did not ask him whence he was, and he did not tell me his name; [7] **but** he **said to** me, 'Behold, you shall conceive and **bear a son**;' so then **drink no wine** or **strong drink**, and eat nothing unclean, for the boy **shall** be a Nazirite to God from birth to the day of his death.'"

[8] Then Manoah entreated the Lord, and said, "O, Lord, I pray thee, let the man of God whom thou didst send come again to us, and teach us what we are to do with the boy that will be born." [9] And God listened to the voice of Manoah, **and the angel of** God came again **to** the woman as she sat in the field; but Manoah her husband was not with her. [10] And the woman ran in haste and told her husband, "Behold, the man who came to me the other day has **appeared to** me." [11] And Manah arose and sent after his **wife**, and came to the man **and said to** him, "Are you the man who spoke to this woman?" **And** he **said**, "I am." [12] And Manoah **said**, "Now when your words come true, what is to be the boy's manner of life, and what is he to do?" [13] **And the angel of the Lord** said to Manoah, "Of all that I said to the woman let her beware. [14] She may not eat of anything that comes from the vine, neither let her **drink wine** or **strong drink**, or eat any unclean thing; all that I commanded her let her observe."

[15] Manoah **said to the angel of the Lord**, "Pray, let us detain you, and prepare a kid for you." [16] And the **angel of the Lord** said to Manoah, "If you detain me, I will not eat of your food; but if you make ready a burnt offering, then offer it to **the Lord**." (For Manoah did not know that he was the **angel of God**.) [17] And Manoah said to **the angel of the Lord**, "What is your name, so that, when your words come true, we may honor you?" [18] And **the angel of the Lord** said to him, "Why do you ask my name, seeing it is wonderful?" [19] So Manoah took the kid with the cereal offering, and offered it upon the rock to the Lord, to him who works wonders. [20] And when the flame went up toward heaven from the altar, **the angel of the Lord** ascended in the flame of the altar while Manoah and his wife looked on and they fell on their faces to the ground.

[21] **The angel of the Lord** appeared no more to Manoah and to his wife. Then Manoah knew that he was **the angel of the Lord**.

⇨ Luke 1:5
Cf. 1 Chr 24:10

Gen 17:19 ⇨ Luke 1:13

[19] God **said**, "No, but Sarah **your wife** shall **bear you a son, and you shall call his name** Isaac. I will establish my covenant with him as an everlasting covenant for his descendants after him."

⇨ Luke 1:13
Cf. Gen 15:1, Dan 10:12

Num 6:1–3 ⇨ Luke 1:15

[1] And the Lord said to Moses, [2] "Say to the people of Israel, When either a man or a woman makes a special vow, the vow of a Nazirite, to separate himself to **the Lord**, [3] **he shall** separate himself from **wine and strong drink**; **he shall drink no** vinegar made from **wine** or **strong drink**, and **shall** not **drink** any juice of grapes or eat grapes, fresh or dried."

⇨ Luke 1:15
Cf. Judg 13:2–5, 1 Sam 1:11 (LXX)

Mal 4:5–6 ⇨ Luke 1:16

[5] "Behold, I will send you Elijah the prophet before the great and terrible day of the Lord comes. [6] **And he will turn** the hearts **of** fathers **to their** children and the hearts **of** children **to their** fathers, lest I come and smite the land with a curse."

⇨ Luke 1:16
Cf. Sir 48:10

Gen 15:8 ⇨ Luke 1:18

[8] But he **said**, "O Lord God, **how** am **I** to **know** that **I shall** possess it?"

PJas 23:1–24:2 ⇨ Luke 1:21

[1] *Now Herod was searching for John, and sent officers to Zacharias at the altar to ask him: "Where have you hidden your son?" And he answered and said to them: "I am a minister of God and attend continually upon his* **temple.** *How should I know where my son is?" [2] And the officers departed and told all this to Herod. Then Herod was angry and said, "Is his son to be king over Israel?" And he sent the officers to him again with the command: "Tell the truth. Where is your son? You know that your blood is under my hand." And the officers departed and told him all this. [3] And Zacharias said: "I am a martyr of God. Take my blood! But my spirit the Lord will receive, for you shed innocent blood in the forecourt of* **the temple** *of the Lord." And about the dawning of the day Zacharias was slain. And the children of Israel did not know that he had been slain.*

24 [1] *Rather, at the hour of the salutation the priests were departing, but the blessing of Zacharias did not meet them according to custom.* **And the priests stood waiting for Zacharias, to** *greet him with prayer and to glorify the Most High. [2] But when he delayed to come, they were all afraid. But one of them took courage and went into* **the** *sanctuary. And he saw beside the altar congealed blood; and a voice said: "Zacharias has been slain, and his blood shall not be wiped away until his avenger comes." And when he heard these words, he was afraid, and went out and told the priests what he had seen.*

LUKE	MATT	MARK

Luke 1:26–38 (§L2.2) °

26 In the sixth month the angel Gabriel was sent from God to a city of Galilee named Nazareth, 27 to a virgin betrothed to a man whose name was Joseph, of the house of David; and the virgin's name was Mary. 28 And he came to her and said, "Hail, O favored one, the Lord is with you!"ᵃ 29 But she was greatly troubled at the saying, and considered in her mind what sort of greeting this might be. 30 And the angel said to her, "Do not be afraid, Mary, for you have found favor with God. 31 And behold, you will conceive in your womb and bear a son, and you shall call his name Jesus.

32 He will be great, and will be called the
     Son of the Most High;
and the Lord God will give to him the
     throne of his father David,
33 and he will reign over the house of Jacob
     for ever;
and of his kingdom there will be no end."
34 And Mary said to the angel, "How shall this be, since I have no husband?" 35 And the angel said to her,

"The Holy Spirit will come upon you,
and the power of the Most High will over-
     shadow you;
therefore the child to be bornᵇ will be
     called holy,
the Son of God.
36 And behold, your kinswoman Elizabeth in her old age has also conceived a son; and this is the sixth month with her who was called barren. 37 For with God nothing will be impossible." 38 And Mary said, "Behold, I am the handmaid of the Lord; let it be to me according to your word." And the angel departed from her.

ᵃ Some witnesses add *Blessed are you among women!* (see v. 42): A C D K X Δ Θ Π *pm*; text: ℵ B L W Ψ *f*¹ *pc*

ᵇ A few witnesses add *of you:* C⋆ Θ *f*¹ 33 *pc*

°Appendix 1 ⇨ §L2.2

Luke 1:8–23 (§L2.1b)

8 *Now while he was serving as priest before God when his division was on duty,* 9 *according to the custom of the priesthood, it fell to him by lot to enter the temple of the Lord and burn incense.* 10 *And the whole multitude of the people were praying outside at the hour of incense.* 11 *And there appeared to him an* **angel** *of the Lord standing on the right side of the altar of incense.* 12 *And Zechariah was* **troubled** *when he saw him, and fear fell upon him.* 13 *But the angel said to him,* **"Do not be afraid,** *Zechariah, for your prayer is heard, and your wife Elizabeth* **will bear** *you* **a son, and you shall** *call his name John.*

14 *And you will have joy and gladness,
and many will rejoice at his birth;
15 for* **he will be great** *before the Lord,
and he shall drink no wine nor strong drink,
and he will be filled with* **the Holy Spirit,**
even from his mother's **womb.**
16 *And he will turn many of the sons of Israel
     to the Lord their God,
17 and he will go before him in the spirit and
     power of Elijah,
to turn the hearts of the fathers to the chil-
     dren,
and the disobedient to the wisdom of the just,
to make ready for the Lord a people pre-
     pared."*
18 *And Zechariah said to the angel,* **"How shall I know this? For I** *am an old man, and my wife is advanced in years."* 19 *And the angel answered him, "I am Gabriel, who stand in the presence of* **God;** *and I* **was sent** *to speak* **to** *you, and to bring you this good news.* 20 *And behold, you will be silent and unable to speak until the day that these things come to pass, because you did not believe my words, which will be fulfilled in their time."* 21 *And the people were waiting for Zechariah, and they wondered at his delay in the temple.* 22 *And when he came out, he could not speak to them, and they perceived that he had seen a vision in the temple; and he made signs to them and remained dumb.* 23 *And when his time of service was ended, he went to his home.*

Isa 7:14 ⇨ Luke 1:31
14 Therefore the Lord himself will give you a sign. **Behold,** a young woman shall **conceive and bear a son, and he shall call his name** Immanuel.

2 Sam 7:12–16 ⇨ Luke 1:32–33
12 "'When your days are fulfilled and you lie down with your fathers, I will raise up your offspring after you, who shall come forth from your body, and I will establish **his kingdom.** 13 He shall build a **house** for my name, and I will establish **the throne** of **his king-dom** for ever. 14 I will be his father, and he shall be my son. When he commits iniquity, I will chasten him with the rod of men, with the stripes of the sons of men; 15 but I will not take my steadfast love from him, as I took it from Saul, whom I put away from before you. 16 And your **house** and your **kingdom** shall be made sure **for ever** before me; your **throne** shall be established **for ever.**'"

Isa 9:6–7 ⇨ Luke 1:32–33
6 For to us a child is born,
     to us a son is given;
and the government will be upon his shoulder,
     and his name **will be called**
"Wonderful Counselor, Mighty God,
     Everlasting Father, Prince of Peace."
7 Of the increase of his government and of peace
     there will be no end,
upon **the throne of David, and over his kingdom,**
     to establish it, and to uphold it
with justice and with righteousness
     from this time forth and **for** evermore.
The zeal of **the Lord** of hosts **will** do this.

⇨ Luke 1:37
Cf. Gen 18:14 (LXX)

JOHN	THOMAS	OTHER

PJas 11:1–3

¹And she took the pitcher and went forth to draw water, and behold, a voice said: "Hail, thou that art highly favored, [the Lord is with thee, blessed art thou] among women." And she looked around on the right and on the left to see whence this voice came. And trembling she went to her house and put down the pitcher and took the purple and sat down on her seat and drew out (the thread). ²And behold, an angel of the Lord (suddenly) stood before her and said: "Do not fear, Mary; for you have found grace before the Lord of all things and shall conceive of his Word." When she heard this she doubted in herself and said: "Shall I conceive of the Lord, the living God, [and bear] as every woman bears?" ³And the angel of the Lord said: "Not so, Mary; for a power of the Lord shall overshadow you; Wherefore also that holy thing which is born of you shall be called the Son of the Highest. And you shall call his name Jesus; for he shall save his people from their sins." And Mary said: "Behold, (I am) the handmaid of the Lord before him: be it to me according to your word."

Acts 2:30 ⇨ Luke 1:32

*³⁰Being therefore a prophet, and knowing that **God** had sworn with an oath to him that he would set one of **his** descendants upon **his** throne, . . .*

Acts 13:23 ⇨ Luke 1:32

*²³Of this man's posterity **God** has brought to Israel a Savior, Jesus, as he promised.*

PCairo 2 ⇨ Luke 1:36

(2) [. . .] should interpret to thee. The [archistrategus however] said to the virgin: Behold, [Elisabeth, thy relat]ive has also con[ceived, and it is the s]ixth month for her who [was called barren. In] the sixth, that is [in the month Thoth, did his mother] conceive John. [But it behoved] the archistra[tegus to an] nounce [beforehand John, the] servant who go[es before his Lord's] coming . . .

LUKE	MATT	MARK

Luke 1:39–56 (§L2.3) °

[39] In those days Mary arose and went with haste into the hill country, to a city of Judah, [40] and she entered the house of Zechariah and greeted Elizabeth. [41] And when Elizabeth heard the greeting of Mary, the babe leaped in her womb; and Elizabeth was filled with the Holy Spirit [42] and she exclaimed with a loud cry, "Blessed are you among women, and blessed is the fruit of your womb! [43] And why is this granted me, that the mother of my Lord should come to me? [44] For behold, when the voice of your greeting came to my ears, the babe in my womb leaped for joy. [45] And blessed is she who believed that there would be[a] a fullfilment of what was spoken to her from the Lord." [46] And Mary said,

"My soul magnifies the Lord,
[47] and my spirit rejoices in God my Savior,
[48] for he has regarded the low estate of his
    handmaiden.
For behold, henceforth all generations will
    call me blessed;
[49] for he who is mighty has done great
    things for me,
and holy is his name.
[50] And his mercy is on those who fear him
from generation to generation.
[51] He has shown strength with his arm,
he has scattered the proud in the imagina-
    tion of their hearts,
[52] he has put down the mighty from their
    thrones,
and exalted those of low degree;
[53] he has filled the hungry with good things,
and the rich he has sent empty away.
[54] He has helped his servant Israel,
in remembrance of his mercy,
[55] as he spoke to our fathers,
to Abraham and to his posterity for ever."
[56] And Mary remained with her about three months, and returned to her home.

[a] Or *believed, for there will be*

° Appendix 1 ⇨ §L2.3

Luke 6:21, 24 ⇨ Luke 1:53
[21] *"Blessed are you that hunger now, for you shall be satisfied.*
"Blessed are you that weep now, for you shall laugh. . . .
[24] *"But woe to you that are rich, for you have received your consolation."*

1 Sam 2:1–10 ⇨ Luke 1:46–55
Hannah also prayed **and said,**
"My heart exults in the **Lord;**
    my strength is exalted in the Lord.
My mouth derides my enemies,
    because I rejoice in thy salvation.
[2] "There is none holy like the Lord,
    there is none besides thee;
    there is no rock like our God.

[3] Talk no more so very proudly,
    let not arrogance come from your mouth;
for the Lord is a God of knowledge,
    and by him actions are weighed.
[4] The bows of **the mighty** are broken,
    but the feeble gird on strength.
[5] Those who were full have hired themselves out
    for bread,
    but those who were **hungry** have ceased to
    hunger.
The barren has borne seven,
    but she who has many children is forlorn.
[6] The Lord kills and brings to life;
    he brings down to Sheol and raises up.
[7] The Lord makes poor and makes **rich;**
    he brings **low, he** also exalts.
[8] **He** raises up the poor from the dust;
    he lifts the needy from the ash heap,
to make them sit with princes and inherit a seat of
    honor.
For the pillars of the earth are the Lord's,
    and on them he has set the world.
[9] "**He** will guard the feet of his faithful ones;
    but the wicked shall be cut off in darkness;
    for not by might shall a man prevail.
[10] **The** adversaries of the Lord shall be broken to
    pieces;
    against them **he** will thunder in heaven.
The Lord will judge the ends of the earth;
    he will give strength to his king,
    and exalt the power of **his** anointed."

⇨ Luke 1:46
Cf. Ps 25:5 (LXX)

Hab 3:18 ⇨ Luke 1:47
[18] yet I will rejoice **in** the Lord,
    I will joy **in the God of my** salvation.

1 Sam 1:11 ⇨ Luke 1:48
[11] And she vowed a vow and said, "O Lord of hosts, if thou wilt indeed look on the affliction of thy maid-servant, and remember **me,** and not forget thy maid-servant, but wilt give to thy maidservant a son, then I will give him to the Lord all the days of his life, and no razor shall touch his head."

Ps 113:5–6 ⇨ Luke 1:48
[5] Who is like the Lord our God,
    who is seated on high,
[6] who looks far down
    upon the heavens and the earth?

⇨ Luke 1:48
Cf. Gen 30:13

Deut 10:21 ⇨ Luke 1:49
[21] "**He is** your praise; **he is** your God, **who has done for** you these **great** and terrible **things** which your eyes have seen."

Ps 111:9 ⇨ Luke 1:49
[9] **He** sent redemption to his people;
    he has commanded his covenant for ever.
    Holy and terrible **is his name**!

Ps 103:17 ⇨ Luke 1:50
[17] But the steadfast love of the Lord is from ever-
    lasting to everlasting
    upon **those who fear him,**
    and his righteousness to children's children,
    . . .

Ps 89:11 ⇨ Luke 1:51
[11] The heavens are thine, the earth also is thine;
    the world and all that is in it, thou hast founded
    them.

1 Sam 2:4, 7 ⇨ Luke 1:52
[4] The laws of **the mighty** are broken,
    but the feeble gird on strength.
[7] The Lord makes poor and makes rich;
    he brings **low, he** also exalts.

Sir 10:14 ⇨ Luke 1:52
[14] The Lord **has** cast **down the thrones** of rulers,
    and has seated the lowly in their place.

⇨ Luke 1:52
Cf. Job 12:19, Ezek 21:31

Ps 107:9 ⇨ Luke 1:53
[9] For **he** satisfies him who is thirsty,
    and **the hungry he** fills **with good things.**

1 Sam 2:5 ⇨ Luke 1:53
[5] Those who were full have hired themselves out
    for bread,
    but those who were **hungry** have ceased to
    hunger.
The barren has borne seven,
    but she who has many children is forlorn.

Job 22:9 ⇨ Luke 1:53
[9] "You have **sent** widows **away empty,**
    and the arms of the fatherless were crushed."

Isa 41:8–9 ⇨ Luke 1:54
[8] But you, **Israel,** my **servant,**
    Jacob, whom I have chosen,
    the offspring of Abraham, my friend;
[9] you whom I took from the ends of the earth,
    and called from its farthest corners,
saying to you, "You are my **servant,**
    I have chosen you and not cast you off"; . . .

Ps 98:3 ⇨ Luke 1:54
[3] **He has** remembered **his** steadfast love and faith-
    fulness
    to the house of **Israel.**
All the ends of the earth have seen
    the victory of our God.

Mic 7:20 ⇨ Luke 1:55
[20] Thou wilt show faithfulness to Jacob
    and steadfast love **to Abraham,**
as thou hast sworn **to our fathers**
    from the days of old.

⇨ Luke 1:55
Cf. 2 Sam 22:51

| JOHN | THOMAS | OTHER |

PJas 12:2–3

[2] *And Mary rejoiced, and went to Elizabeth her kinswoman, and knocked on the door. When Elizabeth heard it, she put down the scarlet, and ran to the door and opened it, [and when she saw Mary], she blessed her and said: "Whence is this to me, that the mother of my Lord should come to me? For behold, that which is in me leaped and blessed thee." But Mary forgot the mysteries which the [arch]angel Gabriel had told her, and raised a sigh towards heaven and said: "Who am I, Lord, that all the women [generations] of the earth count me blessed?"* [3] *And she remained three months with Elizabeth. Day by day her womb grew, and Mary was afraid and went into her house and hid herself from the children of Israel. And Mary was sixteen years old when all these mysterious things happened.*

LUKE	MATT	MARK

Luke 1:57–80 (§L3) °

⁵⁷ Now the time came for Elizabeth to be delivered, and she gave birth to a son. ⁵⁸ And her neighbors and kinsfolk heard that the Lord had shown great mercy to her, and they rejoiced with her. ⁵⁹ And on the eighth day they came to circumcise the child; and they would have named him Zechariah after his father, ⁶⁰ but his mother said, "Not so, he shall be called John." ⁶¹ And they said to her, "None of your kindred is called by this name." ⁶² And they made signs to his father, inquiring what he would have him called. ⁶³ And he asked for a writing tablet, and wrote, "His name is John." And they all marveled. ⁶⁴ And immediately his mouth was opened and his tongue loosed, and he spoke, blessing God. ⁶⁵ And fear came on all their neighbors. And all these things were talked about through all the hill country of Judea; ⁶⁶ and all who heard them laid them up in their hearts, saying, "What then will this child be?" For the hand of the Lord was with him.

⁶⁷ And his father Zechariah was filled with the Holy Spirit, and prophesied, saying,

⁶⁸ "Blessed be the Lord God of Israel,
  for he has visited and redeemed his people,
⁶⁹ and has raised up a horn of salvation for us
  in the house of his servant David,
⁷⁰ as he spoke by the mouth of his holy
    prophets from of old,
⁷¹ that we should be saved from our ene-
    mies,
  and from the hand of all who hate us;
⁷² to perform the mercy promised to our
    fathers,
  and to remember his holy covenant,
⁷³ the oath which he swore to our father
    Abraham, ⁷⁴ to grant us
  that we, being delivered from the hand of
    our enemies,
  might serve him without fear,
⁷⁵ in holiness and righteousness before him
    all the days of our life.
⁷⁶ And you, child, will be called the prophet
    of the Most High;
  for you will go before the Lord to prepare
    his ways,
⁷⁷ to give knowledge of salvation to his peo-
    ple
  in the forgiveness of their sins,
⁷⁸ through the tender mercy of our God,
  when the day shall dawn upon us ᵃ from on
    high
⁷⁹ to give light to those who sit in darkness
    and in the shadow of death,
  to guide our feet into the way of peace."
⁸⁰ And the child grew and became strong in spirit, and he was in the wilderness till the day of his manifestation to Israel.

ᵃ Or *whereby the dayspring will visit;* some witnesses read *since the dayspring has visited:* ℵᶜ A C D K Δ Ξ Ψ *f¹ f* ¹³ 28 33 *pm*

°Appendix 1 ⇨ §L3

Luke 1:17 ⇨ Luke 1:76
¹⁷ *"and he will go before him in the spirit
    and power of Elijah,
  to turn the hearts of the fathers to the chil-
    dren,
  and the disobedient to the wisdom of the just,
  to make ready for the Lord a people
    prepared."*

Luke 3:4 ⇨ Luke 1:76
⁴ *As it is written in the book of the words of
Isaiah the prophet,*
  *"The voice of one crying in the wilderness;
  Prepare the way of the Lord,
  make his paths straight."*

Luke 7:27 ⇨ Luke 1:76
²⁷ *"This is he of whom it is written,
  'Behold, I send my messenger before thy face,
  who shall prepare thy way before thee.'"*

Luke 2:40 ⇨ Luke 1:80
⁴⁰ *And the child grew and became strong, filled
with wisdom; and the favor of God was upon
him.*

Luke 2:52 ⇨ Luke 1:80
⁵² *And Jesus increased in wisdom and in
stature, and in favor with God and man.*

Lev 12:3 ⇨ Luke 1:59
³ *"And on the eighth day* the flesh of his foreskin
shall be circumcised."

Ps 41:3 ⇨ Luke 1:68
¹³ **Blessed be the Lord,** the **God of Israel,**
  from everlasting to everlasting!
  Amen and Amen.

⇨ Luke 1:68
Cf. Ps 72:18, 106:48

Ps 111:9 ⇨ Luke 1:68
⁹ **He sent redemption to his people;**
  he has commanded his covenant for ever.
  Holy and terrible is his name!

Ps 18:2 ⇨ Luke 1:69
² The Lord is my rock, and my fortress, and my
    deliverer,
  my God, my rock, in whom I take refuge,
  my shild, and the **horn of** my **salvation,** my
    stronghold.

Ps 132:17 ⇨ Luke 1:69
¹⁷ There I will make **a horn** to sprout for **David;**
  I have prepared a lamp for my anointed.

⇨ Luke 1:69
Cf. 1 Sam 2:10

Ps 18:17 ⇨ Luke 1:71
¹⁷ He delivered me **from** my strong enemy,
  and **from** those **who** hated me;
  for they were too mighty for me.

2 Sam 22:18 ⇨ Luke 1:71
¹⁸ He delivered me **from** my strong enemy,
  from those **who** hated me;
  for they were too mighty for me.

Ps 106:10 ⇨ Luke 1:71
¹⁰ So he **saved them from the hand of** the foe,
  and delivered them **from the** power **of** the
    enemy.

Gen 24:12 ⇨ Luke 1:72
¹² And he said, "O Lord, God of my master Abraham,
grant me success tody, I pray thee, and show steadfast love **to** my master Abraham."

Mic 7:20 ⇨ Luke 1:72
²⁰ Thou wilt show faithfulness **to** Jacob
  and steadfast love **to** Abraham,
  as thou hast sworn **to our fathers**
  from the days of old.

Ps 105:8 ⇨ Luke 1:72
⁸ He is mindful of **his covenant** for ever,
  of the word that he commanded, for a thousand
    generations, . . .

Ps 106:45 ⇨ Luke 1:72
⁴⁵ He remembered for their sake **his covenant,**
  and relented according to the abundance of **his**
    steadfast love.

JOHN	THOMAS	OTHER

Acts 3:21 ⇨ Luke 1:70
[21] *"whom heaven must receive until the time for establishing all that God spoke by the mouth of his holy prophets from of old."*

InThom 19:5b ⇨ Luke 1:80
And Jesus increased in wisdom and stature and grace.

Gen 26:3 ⇨ Luke 1:73
[3] "Sojourn in this land, and I will be with you, and will bless you; for to you and to your descendants I will give all these lands, and I will fulfil **the oath which** I **swore to Abraham** your **father.**"

Jer 11:5 ⇨ Luke 1:73
[5] "that I may perform **the oath which** I **swore to** your fathers, to give them a land flowing with milk and honey, as at this day." Then I answered, "So be it, Lord."

⇨ Luke 1:73
Cf. Gen 22:16

Josh 24:14 ⇨ Luke 1:75
[14] "Now therefore fear the Lord, and serve **him in** sincerity **and in** faithfulness; put away the gods which your fathers served beyond the River, and in Egypt, and serve the Lord."

Isa 38:20 ⇨ Luke 1:75
[20] The Lord will save me,
    and we will sing to stringed instruments
all the days of our life,
    at the house of the Lord.

Mal 3:1 ⇨ Luke 1:76
[1] "Behold, I send my messenger **to prepare** the way **before** me, and **the Lord** whom you seek will suddenly come to his temple; **the** messenger of the covenant in whom you delight, behold, he is coming, says **the Lord** of hosts."

Isa 40:3 ⇨ Luke 1:76
[3] A voice cries:
"In the wilderness **prepare** the way of **the Lord,**
make straight in the desert a highway for our
    God."

Ps 107:10 ⇨ Luke 1:79
[10] Some sat **in darkness and in** gloom,
    prisoners in affliction and in irons, . . .

Isa 59:8 ⇨ Luke 1:79
[8] **The way of peace** they know not,
    and there is no justice **in** their paths;
they have made their roads crooked,
    no one who goes **in** them knows **peace.**

LUKE	MATT	MARK

LUKE

Luke 2:1–7 (§L4.1)

¹ In those days a decree went out from Caesar Augustus that all the world should be enrolled. ² This was the first enrollment, when Quirinius was governor of Syria. ³ And all went to be enrolled, each to his own city. ⁴ And Joseph also went up from Galilee, from the city of Nazareth, to Judea, to the city of David, which is called Bethlehem, because he was of the house and lineage of David, ⁵ to be enrolled with Mary, his betrothed, who was with child. ⁶ And while they were there, the time came for her to be delivered. ⁷ And she gave birth to her first-born son and wrapped him in swaddling cloths, and laid him in a manger, because there was no place for them in the inn.

MATT

† Matt 1:18–25 (§M2)

¹⁸ Now the birth of Jesus Christ took place in this way. When his mother **Mary** had been **betrothed** to **Joseph**, before they came together she **was** found to be **with child** of the Holy Spirit; ¹⁹ and her husband **Joseph**, being a just man and unwilling to put her to shame, resolved to divorce her quietly. ²⁰ But as he considered this, behold, an angel of the Lord appeared to him in a dream, saying, **"Joseph,** son **of David,** do not fear to take Mary your wife, for that which is conceived in her is of the Holy Spirit; ²¹ she will bear a **son,** and you shall call his name Jesus, for he will save his people from their sins." ²² All this took place to fulfil what the Lord had spoken by the prophet:

²³ "Behold, a virgin shall conceive and bear
   a **son,**

and his name shall be called Emmanuel"
(which means, God with us). ²⁴ When **Joseph** woke from sleep, he did as the angel of the Lord commanded him; he took **his** wife, ²⁵ but knew her not until **she** had borne a **son**; and he called his name Jesus.

MARK

JOHN	THOMAS	OTHER

OTHER

PJas 17:1–3

¹ *Now there went out a decree from the king Augustus that all (inhabitants) of Bethlehem in Judaea should be enrolled. And Joseph said: "I shall enroll my sons, but what shall I do with this **child**? How shall I enroll her? As my wife? I am ashamed to do that. Or as my daughter? But all the children of Israel know that she is not my daughter. The day of the Lord himself will do as [t]he [Lord] wills." ² And he saddled his ass [his she-ass] and sat her on it; his son led it, and Samuel [Joseph] followed. And they drew near to the third mile(stone). And Joseph turned round and saw her sad, and said within himself: "Perhaps that which is within her is paining her." And again Joseph turned round and saw her laughing. And he said to her: "Mary, why is it that I see your face at one time laughing and at another sad?" And she said to him: "Joseph, I see with my eyes two peoples, one weeping and lamenting and another rejoicing and exulting." ³ And they came half the way, and Mary said to him: "Joseph, take me down from the ass [from the she-ass], for the **child** within me presses me, to come forth." And he took her down there and said to her: "Where shall I take you and hide your shame?" For the place is desert.*

PJas 22:2 ⇨ Luke 2:7
² *When Mary heard that the children were to be killed, she was afraid and took the child and **wrapped him in swaddling clothes and laid him** in an ox-manger.*

L4.2a–b
L4.3

THE SHEPHERDS
THE CIRCUMCISION OF JESUS

Luke 2:8–20
Luke 2:21

LUKE

THE ANNUNCIATION TO THE SHEPHERDS

Luke 2:8–14 (§L4.2a)

[8] And in that region there were shepherds out in the field, keeping watch over their flock by night. [9] And an angel of the Lord appeared to them, and the glory of the Lord shone around them, and they were filled with fear. [10] And the angel said to them, "Be not afraid; for behold, I bring you good news of a great joy which will come to all the people; [11] for to you is born this day in the city of David a Savior, who is Christ the Lord. [12] And this will be a sign for you: you will find a babe wrapped in swaddling cloths and lying in a manger." [13] And suddenly there was with the angel a multitude of the heavenly host praising God and saying,

[14] "Glory to God in the highest,
and on earth peace among men with whom he is pleased!"[a]

THE VISIT OF THE SHEPHERDS

Luke 2:15–20 (§L4.2b)

[15] When the angels went away from them into heaven, the shepherds said to one another, "Let us go over to Bethlehem and see this thing that has happened, which the Lord has made known to us." [16] And they went with haste, and found Mary and Joseph, and the babe lying in a manger. [17] And when they saw it they made known the saying which had been told them concerning this child; [18] and all who heard it wondered at what the shepherds told them. [19] But Mary kept all these things, pondering them in her heart. [20] And the shepherds returned, glorifying and praising God for all they had heard and seen, as it had been told them.

Luke 2:21 (§L4.3)

[21] And at the end of eight days, when he was circumcised, he was called Jesus, the name given by the angel before he was conceived in the womb.

[a] Some witnesses read *peace, goodwill among men*: ℵ* A B* D W *al*; text: ℵᶜ B³ K L P Δ Θ Ξ Ψ *f*¹ *f*¹³ 28 *al*

Luke 19:38 ⇨ Luke 2:14
[38] saying, "Blessed is the King who comes in the name of the Lord! **Peace** in heaven and **glory in the highest!**"

Luke 2:51 ⇨ Luke 2:19
[51] And he went down with them and came to Nazareth, and was obedient to them; and his mother **kept all these things in her heart.**

JOHN

MATT

† Matt 2:1–12 (§M3) ⇨ §L4.2
[1] Now when Jesus was born in **Bethlehem** of Judea in the days of Herod the king, behold, wise men from the East came to Jerusalem, saying, [2] "Where is he who has been born king of the Jews? For we have seen his star in the East, and have come to worship him." [3] When Herod the king heard this, he was troubled, and all Jerusalem with him; [4] and assembling all the chief priests and scribes of the people, he inquired of them where the **Christ** was to be **born**. [5] They told him, "In **Bethlehem** of Judea; for so it is written by the prophet:

[6] 'And you, O **Bethlehem**, in the land of Judah,
are by no means least among the rulers of Judah,
for from you shall come a ruler
who will govern my people Israel.'"

[7] Then Herod summoned the wise men secretly and ascertained from them what time the star appeared; [8] and he sent them **to Bethlehem**, saying, "Go and search diligently for the child, and when you have found him bring me word, that I too may come and worship him." [9] When they had heard the king **they went** their way; and lo, the star which they had seen in the East went before them, till it came to rest over the place where the child was. [10] **When they saw** the star, they rejoiced exceedingly with great joy; [11] and going into the house **they saw** the child with **Mary** his mother, and they fell down and worshiped him. Then, opening their treasures, they offered him gifts, gold and frankincense and myrrh. [12] And being warned in a dream not to return to Herod, they departed to their own country by another way.

THOMAS

MARK

OTHER

Acts 13:23 ⇨ Luke 2:11
[23] Or this man's posterity God has brought to Israel *a Savior, Jesus,* as he promised.

InThom 11:2c ⇨ Luke 2:19
And when his mother saw miracle, she kissed him, and **kept** within herself the mysteries which she had seen him do.

InThom 19:5a ⇨ Luke 2:19
[5] And Jesus arose and followed his mother and was subject to his parents; **but his mother kept (in her heart)** all that had taken place.

L4
S3: L4–6

THE BIRTH OF JESUS
BIRTH AND CHILDHOOD OF JESUS

Luke 2:1–21
Luke 2:1–52

309

LUKE	MATT	MARK

LUKE

THE PRESENTATION OF JESUS

Luke 2:22–24 (§L5.1)

²²And when the time came for their purification according to the law of Moses, they brought him up to Jerusalem to present him to the Lord. ²³as it is written in the law of the Lord, "Every male that opens the womb shall be called holy to the Lord") ²⁴and to offer a sacrifice according to what is said in the law of the Lord, "a pair of turtledoves, or two young pigeons."

SIMEON BLESSES JESUS

Luke 2:25–35 (§L5.2)

²⁵Now there was a man in Jerusalem, whose name was Simeon, and this man was righteous and devout, looking for the consolation of Israel, and the Holy Spirit was upon him. ²⁶And it had been revealed to him by the Holy Spirit that he should not see death before he had seen the Lord's Christ. ²⁷And inspired by the Spirit[a] he came into the temple; and when the parents brought in the child Jesus, to do for him according to the custom of the law, ²⁸he took him up in his arms and blessed God and said,

²⁹"Lord, now lettest thou thy servant depart in peace,

according to thy word;

³⁰for mine eyes have seen thy salvation

³¹which thou hast prepared in the presence of all peoples,

³²a light for revelation to the Gentiles, and for glory to thy people Israel."

³³And his father and his mother marveled at what was said about him; ³⁴and Simeon blessed them and said to Mary his mother,

"Behold, this child is set for the fall and rising of many in Israel,

and for a sign that is spoken against

³⁵(and a sword will pierce through your own soul also),

that thoughts out of many hearts may be revealed."

ANNA THE PROPHETESS

Luke 2:36–38 (§L5.3)

³⁶And there was a prophetess, Anna, the daughter of Phanuel, of the tribe of Asher; she was of a great age, having lived with her husband seven years from her virginity, ³⁷and as a widow till she was eighty-four. She did not depart from the temple, worshiping with fasting and prayer night and day. ³⁸And coming up at that very hour she gave thanks to God, and spoke of him to all who were looking for the redemption of Jerusalem.

RETURN TO NAZARETH

Luke 2:39–40 (§L5.4)

³⁹And when they had performed everything according to the law of the Lord, they returned into Galilee, to their own city, Nazareth. ⁴⁰And the child grew and became strong, filled with wisdom; and the favor of God was upon him.

MATT

† **Matt 2:19–23 (§M4.3)**

¹⁹But when Herod died, behold, an angel of the Lord appeared in a dream to Joseph in Egypt, saying, ²⁰"Rise, take the child and his mother, and go to the land of **Israel**, for those who sought the child's life are dead." ²¹And he rose and took the child and his mother, and went to the land of Israel. ²²But when he heard that Archelaus reigned over Judea in place of his father Herod, he was afraid to go there, and being warned in a dream he withdrew to the district of **Galilee**. ²³And he went and dwelt in a **city** called **Nazareth**, that what was spoken by the prophets might be fulfilled, "He shall be called a Nazarene."

---

[a] Or *in the Spirit*

Luke 3:6 ⇨ Luke 2:30–32
⁶*"and all flesh shall see the **salvation** of God."*

Luke 1:80 ⇨ Luke 2:40
⁸⁰*And the child grew and became strong in spirit, and he was in the wilderness till the day of his manifestation to Israel.*

Luke 2:52 ⇨ Luke 2:40
⁵²*And Jesus increased in **wisdom** and in stature, and in favor with **God** and man.*

Lev 12:6 ⇨ Luke 2:22
⁶"And **when the** days of her purifying are completed, whether for a son or for a daughter, she shall bring **to** the priest at the door of the tent of meeting a lamb a year old for a burnt offering, and a young pigeon or turtledove for a sin offering", . . .

Exod 13:2, 12, 15 ⇨ Luke 2:23
²"Consecrate to me all the first-born; whatever is the first to open **the womb** among the people of Israel, both of man and of beast, is mine. . . ." ¹²you shall set apart to **the Lord** all that first **opens the womb**. All the firstlings of your cattle that are males shall be **the Lord's**. . . . ¹⁵"'For when Pharaoh stubbornly refused to let us go, **the Lord** slew all the first-born of man and the first-born of cattle. Therefore I sacrifice to **the Lord** all the males **that** first open **the womb**; but all the first-born of my sons I redeem.'"

MARK

Lev 12:8 ⇨ Luke 2:24
⁸"And if she cannot afford a lamb, then she shall take two **turtledoves or two young pigeons**, one for a burnt offering and the other for a sin offering; and the priest shall make atonement for her, and she shall be clean."

Isa 40:5 ⇨ Luke 2:30
⁵"And the glory of the Lord shall be revealed,
and all flesh shall see it together,
for the mouth of the Lord has spoken."

Isa 52:10 ⇨ Luke 2:31
¹⁰The Lord has bared his holy arm
before the eyes of all the nations;
and **all** the ends of the earth shall see
the salvation of our God.

Isa 49:6 ⇨ Luke 2:32
⁶he says:
"It is too **light** a thing that you should be my servant
to raise up the tribes of Jacob
and to restore the preserved of **Israel**;
I will give you as a **light to the** nations,
that my salvation may reach **to** the end of the earth."

JOHN	THOMAS	OTHER
		PJas 24:4 ⇨ Luke 2:26 *4 And after the three days the priests took counsel whom they should appoint in his stead. And the lot fell upon Symeon. Now it was he to whom it had been revealed by the Holy Spirit that he should not see death until he had seen the Christ in the flesh.* **Acts 13:47** ⇨ Luke 2:30–32 *47 "For so the Lord has commanded us, saying, 'I have set you to be a light for the Gentiles, that you may bring salvation to the uttermost parts of the earth.'"* **Acts 26:23** ⇨ Luke 2:30–32 *23 "that the Christ must suffer, and that, by being the first to rise from the dead, he would proclaim light both to the people and to the Gentiles."* **Acts 28:28** ⇨ Luke 2:30–32 *28 "Let it be known to you thou that this salvation of God has been sent to the Gentiles; they will listen."* **InThom 19:5b** ⇨ Luke 2:40 *And Jesus increased in wisdom and stature and grace.*

LUKE	MATT	MARK

JESUS' PARENTS TAKE HIM TO JERUSALEM

Luke 2:41–45 (§L6.1)

⁴¹Now his parents went to Jerusalem every year at the feast of the Passover. ⁴²And when he was twelve years old, they went up according to custom; ⁴³and when the feast was ended, as they were returning, the boy Jesus stayed behind in Jerusalem. His parents did not know it, ⁴⁴but supposing him to be in the company they went a day's journey, and they sought him among their kinsfolk and acquaintances; ⁴⁵and when they did not find him, they returned to Jerusalem, seeking him.

JESUS AMONG THE TEACHERS IN THE TEMPLE

Luke 2:46–52 (§L6.2)

⁴⁶After three days they found him in the temple, sitting among the teachers, listening to them and asking them questions; ⁴⁷and all who heard him were amazed at his understanding and his answers. ⁴⁸And when they saw him they were astonished; and his mother said to him, "Son, why have you treated us so? Behold, your father and I have been looking for you anxiously." ⁴⁹And he said to them, "How is it that you sought me? Did you not know that I must be in my Father's house?" ⁵⁰And they did not understand the saying which he spoke to them. ⁵¹And he went down with them and came to Nazareth, and was obedient to them; and his mother kept all these things in her heart. ⁵²And Jesus increased in wisdom and in stature,[a] and in favor with God and man.

[a] Or *years*

Luke 2:19 ⇨ Luke 2:51
¹⁹*But Mary kept all these things, pondering them in her heart.*

Luke 1:80 ⇨ Luke 2:52
⁸⁰*And the child grew and became strong in spirit, and he was in the wilderness till the day of his manifestation to Israel.*

Luke 2:40 ⇨ Luke 2:52
⁴⁰*And the child grew and became strong, filled with wisdom; and the favor of God was upon him.*

1 Sam 2:26 ⇨ Luke 1:52
²⁶Now the boy Samuel continued to grow both in stature and in favor with the Lord and with men.

Prov 3:4 ⇨ Luke 1:52
⁴So you will find **favor** and good repute in the sight of **God and man.**

JOHN

THOMAS

OTHER

InThom 19:1–5b
¹And when he was twelve years old his parents went according to the custom to Jerusalem to the feast of the passover with their company, and after the passover they returned to go to their house. And while they were returning the child Jesus went back to Jerusalem. But his parents supposed that he was in the company. ²And when they had gone a day's journey, they sought him among their kinsfolk, and when they did not find him, they were troubled, and returned again to the city seeking him. And after the third day they found him in the temple sitting among the teachers, listening to the law and asking them questions. And all paid attention to him and marvelled how he, a child, put to silence the elders and teachers of the people, expounding the sections of the law and the sayings of the prophets. ³And his mother Mary came near and said to him: "Why have you done this to us, child? Behold, we have sought you sorrowing." Jesus said to them: "Why do you seek me? Do you not know that I must be in my Father's house? ⁴But the scribes and Pharisees said: "Are you the mother of this child?" And she said: "I am." And they said to her: "Blessed are you among women, because the Lord has blessed the fruit of your womb. For such glory and such excellence and wisdom we have never seen nor heard." ⁵And Jesus arose and followed his mother and was subject to his parents; but his mother kept (in her heart) all that had taken place. And Jesus increased in wisdom and stature and grace.

InThom 15:2 ⇨ Luke 2:47–48
²*And he went boldly into the school and found a book lying on the reading-desk and took it, but did not read the letters in it, but opened his mouth and spoke by the Holy Spirit and taught the law to those that stood by. And a large crowd assembled and stood there listening to him, wondering at the grace of his teaching and the readiness of his words, that although an infant he made such utterances.*

InThom 11:2c ⇨ Luke 2:51
And when his mother saw the miracle, she kissed him, and kept within herself the mysteries which she had seen him do.

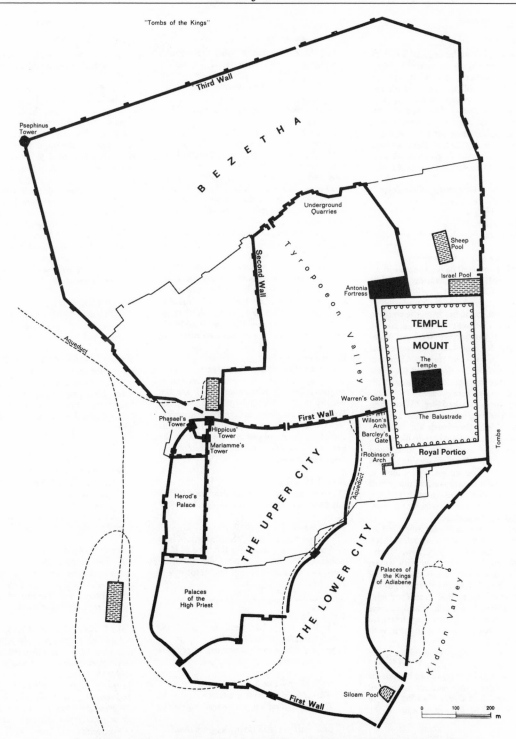

Jerusalem in the period of the Second Temple; Source: *Jerusalem Revealed:
Archaeology in the Holy City, 1968–1974,* edited by Yigael Yadin; Copyright © 1975
The Israel Exploration Society (New Haven: Yale University Press, 1976), 10.

LUKE	MATT	MARK

Luke 3:1–20 (§L7) °

¹ In the fifteenth year of the reign of Tiberius Caesar, Pontius Pilate being governor of Judea, and Herod being tetrarch of Galilee, and his brother Philip tetrarch of the region of Ituraea and Trachonitis, and Lysanias tetrarch of Abilene, ² in the high-priesthood of Annas and Caiaphas, the word of God came to John the son of Zechariah in the wilderness; ³ and he went into all the region about the Jordan, preaching a baptism of repentance for the forgiveness of sins. ⁴ As it is written in the book of the words of Isaiah the prophet,

"The voice of one crying in the wilderness:
Prepare the way of the Lord,
make his paths straight.
⁵ Every valley shall be filled,
and every mountain and hill shall be brought
low,
and the crooked shall be made straight,
and the rough ways shall be made smooth;
⁶ and all flesh shall see the salvation of God."

⁷ He said therefore to the multitudes that came out to be baptized by him, "You brood of vipers! Who warned you to flee from the wrath to come? ⁸ Bear fruits that befit repentance, and do not begin to say to yourselves, 'We have Abraham as our father'; for I tell you, God is able from these stones to raise up children to Abraham. ⁹ Even now the axe is laid to the root of the trees; every tree therefore that does not bear good fruit is cut down and thrown into the fire."

¹⁰ And the multitudes asked him, "What then shall we do?" ¹¹ And he answered them, "He who has two coats, let him share with him who has none; and he who has food, let him do likewise." ¹² Tax collectors also came to be baptized, and said to him, "Teacher, what shall we do?" ¹³ And he said to them, "Collect no more than is appointed you." ¹⁴ Soldiers also asked him, "And we, what shall we do?" And he said to them, "Rob no one by violence or by false accusation, and be content with your wages."

¹⁵ As the people were in expectation, and all men questioned in their hearts concerning John, whether perhaps he were the Christ, ¹⁶ John answered them all, "I baptize you with water; but he who is mightier than I is coming, the thong of whose sandals I am not worthy to untie; he will baptize you with the Holy Spirit and with fire. ¹⁷ His winnowing fork is in his hand, to clear his threshing floor, and to gather the wheat into his granary, but the chaff he will burn with unquenchable fire."

¹⁸ So, with many other exhortations, he preached good news to the people. ¹⁹ But Herod the tetrarch, who had been reproved by him for Herodias, his brother's wife, and for all the evil things that Herod had done, ²⁰ added this to them all, that he shut up John in prison.

°Appendix 1 ⇨ §L7

Matt 3:1–12 (§M5)

¹ In those days came **John the** Baptist, preaching **in the wilderness** of Judea, ² "Repent, **for the** kingdom of heaven is at hand." ³ For this is he who was spoken of by **the prophet Isaiah** when he said,

"The voice of one crying in the wilderness:
Prepare the way of the Lord,
make his paths straight."

⁴ Now John wore a garment of camel's hair, and a leather girdle around his waist; and his food was locusts and wild honey. ⁵ Then **went** out to him Jerusalem and all Judea and **all the region about the Jordan,** ⁶ and they were baptized by him in the river Jordan, confessing their sins.

⁷ But when he saw many of the Pharisees and Sadducees coming for baptism, **he said** to them, "**You brood of vipers! Who warned you to flee from the wrath to come?** ⁸ **Bear** fruit that befits **repentance,** ⁹ and do not presume to say to yourselves, 'We have Abraham as our father'; for I tell you, God is able from these stones to raise up children to Abraham. ¹⁰ Even now the axe is laid to the root of the trees; every tree therefore that does not bear good fruit is cut down and thrown into the fire.

¹¹ "**I baptize you with water** for repentance, **but he who is coming** after me is **mightier than I, whose sandals I am not worthy to carry; he will baptize you with the Holy Spirit** and with fire. ¹² **His winnowing fork is in his hand,** and he will **clear his** threshing floor and gather his **wheat into the granary, but the chaff he will burn with** unquenchable fire."

Matt 7:19 ⇨ Luke 3:9

¹⁹ "**Every tree that does not bear good fruit is cut down and thrown into the fire.**"

Matt 14:3–4 ⇨ Luke 3:19–20

³ For **Herod** had seized **John** and bound him and put him **in prison,** for the sake of **Herodias, his** brother Philip's **wife;** ⁴ because John said to him, "It is not lawful for you to have her."

Luke 1:76 ⇨ Luke 3:4

⁷⁶ "And you, child, will be called **the prophet** of the Most High;
for you will go before **the Lord** to **prepare** his ways, . . ."

Luke 7:27 ⇨ Luke 3:4

²⁷ "This is he of whom **it is written,**
'Behold, I send my messenger before thy face,
who shall **prepare thy way** before thee.'"

Mark 1:2–8 (§K2)

² As it is written in Isaiah the prophet,
"Behold, I send my messenger before thy face,
who hall prepare thy way;
³ the voice of one crying in the wilderness:
Prepare the way of the Lord,
make his paths straight—"

⁴ **John the** baptizer appeared **in the wilderness, preaching a baptism of repentance for the forgiveness of sins.** ⁵ And there went out to him all the country of Judea, and all the people of Jerusalem; and they were baptized by him in the river **Jordan,** confessing their sins. ⁶ Now John was clothed in camel's hair, and had a leather girdle around his waist, and ate locusts and wild honey. ⁷ And he preached, saying, "After me comes **he who is mightier than I, the thong of whose sandals I am not worthy to** stoop down and **untie.** ⁸ **I have baptized you with water;** but **he will baptize you with the Holy Spirit.**"

Mark 1:15 ⇨ Luke 3:3

¹⁵ and saying, "The time is fulfilled, and the kingdom of God is at hand; repent, and believe in the gospel."

Mark 6:17–18 ⇨ Luke 3:19–20

¹⁷ For **Herod** had sent and seized **John,** and bound him **in prison for** the sake of **Herodias, his** brother Philip's **wife;** because he had married her. For John said to Herod, "It is not lawful for you to have your **brother's wife.**"

Luke 2:30–32 ⇨ Luke 3:6

³⁰ "for mine eyes have seen thy **salvation**
³¹ which thou hast prepared in the presence of **all** peoples,
³² a light for revelation to the Gentiles, and for glory to thy people Israel."

Luke 6:43–44 ⇨ Luke 3:9

⁴³ "For no **good tree** bears bad **fruit,** nor again does a bad **tree** bear **good fruit;** ⁴⁴ for each **tree** is know by its own **fruit.** For figs are not gathered from thorns, nor are grapes picked from a bramble bush."

Luke 13:6–9 (§L57.2) ⇨ Luke 3:9

⁶ And he told this parable: "A man had a fig tree planted in his vineyard; and he came seeking **fruit** on it and found none. ⁷ And he said to the vinedresser, 'Lo, these three years I have come seeking **fruit** on this fig tree, and I find none. **Cut it down;** why should it use up the ground?' ⁸ And he answered him, 'Let it alone, sir, this year also, till I dig about it and put on manure. ⁹ And if it bears **fruit** next year, well and good; but if not, you can **cut it down.**'"

JOHN

† John 1:19–28 (§J2.1)

¹⁹ And this is the testimony of **John**, when the Jews sent priests and Levites from Jerusalem to ask him, "Who are you?" ²⁰ He confessed, he did not deny, but confessed, "I am not the Christ." ²¹ And they asked him, "What then? Are you Elijah?" He said, "I am not." "Are you the prophet?" And he answered, "No." ²² They said to him then, "Who are you? Let us have an answer for those who sent us. What do you say about yourself?" ²³ He said, "I am **the voice of one crying in the wilderness, 'Make straight the way of the Lord,'** as **the prophet Isaiah** said." ²⁴ Now they had been sent from the Pharisees. ²⁵ They asked him, "Then why are you baptizing, if you are neither the Christ, nor Elijah, nor the prophet?" ²⁶ **John answered them, "I baptize with water**; **but** among you stands one whom you do not know, ²⁷ even **he** who comes after me, **the thong of whose sandal I am not worthy to untie.**" ²⁸ This took place in Bethany beyond the Jordan, where John was baptizing.

John 8:39 ⇨ Luke 3:8

³⁹ They answered him, "**Abraham** is **our father.**" Jesus said to them, "If you were Abraham's children, you would do what **Abraham** did, . . ."

Luke 13:31 ⇨ Luke 3:19–20

³¹ At that very hour some Pharisees came, and said to him, "Get away from here, for **Herod** wants to kill you."

Luke 23:8 ⇨ Luke 3:19–20

⁸ When **Herod** saw Jesus, he was very glad, for he had long desired to see **him**, because **he** had heard about **him**, and **he** was hoping to see some sign done **by him.**

Isa 40:3–6 ⇨ Luke 3:4–6

³ A **voice** cries:
   "**In the wilderness prepare the way of the Lord,**
     make straight in the desert a highway for our God.
⁴ **Every valley shall be** lifted up,
     and every mountain and hill be made **low**;
the uneven ground **shall** become level,
     and the rough places a plain.
⁵ And the glory of the Lord shall be revealed,
     and all flesh shall see it together,
for the mouth of the Lord has spoken."
⁶ A **voice** says, "Cry!"
   And I said, "What shall I cry?"
All flesh is grass,
     and all its beauty is like the flower of the field.

OTHER

GEbi 2 ⇨ Luke 3:1–6

(2) And:

It came to pass that **John** *was baptizing; and there went* **out to him** *Pharisees and were* **baptized**, *and all Jerusalem. And* **John** *had a garment of camel's hair and a leathern girdle about his loins, and his food, as it saith, was wild honey, the taste of which was that of manna, as a cake dipped in oil.*

Thus they were resolved to pervert the word of truth into a lie and to put a cake in the place of locusts. (Epiphanius, *Haer.* 30.13.4f.)

GEbi 3 ⇨ Luke 3:1–6

(3) And the beginning of their Gospel runs:

It came to pass in the days of **Herod** *the king of Judaea, <when* **Caiaphas** *was high priest,> that there came <one>,* **John** *<by name,> and baptized with the* **baptism of repentance** *in the river* **Jordan**. *It was said of him that he was of the lineage of Aaron the priest, a son of Zacharias and Elisabeth; and all went out to him.* (Epiphanius, *Haer.* 30.13.6)

Acts 2:38 ⇨ Luke 3:3

³⁸ And Peter said to them, "Repent, and be baptized every one of you in the name of Jesus Christ **for the forgiveness of** your sins; and you shall receive the gift of the Holy Spirit."

Acts 13:10 ⇨ Luke 3:4

¹⁰ and said, "You son of the devil, you enemy of all righteousness, full of all deceit and villainy, will you not stop making crooked the **straight paths** of the Lord?"

Acts 13:47 ⇨ Luke 3:6

⁴⁷ "For so the Lord has commanded us, saying,
   'I have set you to be a light for the Gentiles,
   that you may bring **salvation** to the uttermost parts of the earth.'"

Acts 28:28 ⇨ Luke 3:6

²⁸ "Let it be known to you then that this **salvation of God** has been sent to the Gentiles; they will listen."

ApocJa 9:24–10:6 ⇨ Luke 3:7–9

"*O* **you** *(pl.) wretched! O* **you** ²⁵ *unfortunates! O* **you** *falsifiers of knowledge! O* **you** *sinners against the spirit! Do* **you** *even now dare* ³⁰ *to listen, when it behooved* **you** *to speak from the beginning? Do* **you** *even now dare to sleep, when it behooved* **you** *to be awake from the beggining, in order that* ³⁵ *the Kingdom of Heaven might receive* **you***? 10 In truth I say to* **you***, it is easier for a holy one to sink into defilement, and for a man of light to sink into* ⁵ *darkness, than for* **you** *to reign— or (even) not to (reign)!*"

Acts 26:20 ⇨ Luke 3:8

²⁰ but declared first to those at Damascus, then at Jerusalem and throughout all the country of Judea, and also to the Gentiles, **that** they should repent and turn to God and perform deeds worthy of their **repentance**.

Acts 1:5 ⇨ Luke 3:16

⁵ "for John baptized **with water, but** before many days you shall be baptized **with the Holy Spirit.**"

Acts 11:16 ⇨ Luke 3:16

¹⁶ "And I remembered the word of the Lord, how he said, 'John baptized **with water, but you** shall be baptized **with the Holy Spirit.**'"

Acts 13:24–25 ⇨ Luke 3:3, 16

²⁴ "Before his coming John had preached **a baptism of repentance** to all the people of Israel. ²⁵ And as **John** was finishing his course, he said, 'What do you suppose that I am? I am not he. No, but after me one is coming, **the sandals** of whose feet **I am not worthy to untie.**'"

Acts 19:1–7 ⇨ Luke 3:3, 16

¹ While Apollos was at Corinth, Paul passed through the upper country and came to Ephesus. There he found some disciples. ² And he said to them, "Did **you** receive **the Holy Spirit** when you believed?" And they said, "No, we have never even heard that there is a Holy Spirit." ³ And he said, "Into what then were you baptized?" They said, "Into John's baptism." ⁴ And Paul said, "John baptized with the baptism of repentance, telling the people to believe in the one who was to come after him, that is, Jesus." ⁵ On hearing this, they were baptized in the name of the Lord Jesus. ⁶ And when Paul had laid his hands upon them, **the Holy Spirit** came on them; and they spoke with tongues and prophesied. ⁷ There were about twelve of them in all.

LUKE

Luke 3:21–22 (§L8) °
[21] Now when all the people were baptized, and when Jesus also had been baptized and was praying, the heaven was opened, [22] and the Holy Spirit descended upon him in bodily form, as a dove, and a voice came from heaven, "Thou art my beloved Son;[a] with thee I am well pleased."[b]

[a] Or *my Son, my* (or *the*) *Beloved*

[b] A few witnesses read *today I have begotten thee* (from Ps 2:7): D it (in part) *pc*

° Appendix 1 ⇨ §L8

Luke 9:35 ⇨ Luke 3:22
[35] And a voice came out of the cloud, saying, "This is my Son, my Chosen; listen to him!"

Ps 2:7 ⇨ Luke 3:22
[7] I will tell of the decree of the Lord:
He said to me, "You are my son,
     today I have begotten you."

Isa 42:1 ⇨ Luke 3:22
[1] Behold my servant, whom I uphold,
   my chosen, in whom my soul delights;
I have put my Spirit upon him,
   he will bring forth justice to the nations.

Isa 44:2 ⇨ Luke 3:22
[2] "Thus says the Lord who made you,
   who formed you from the womb and will
     help you:
Fear not, O Jacob my servant,
   Jeshurun whom I have chosen."

MATT

Matt 3:13–17 (§M6)
[13] Then Jesus came from Galilee to the Jordan to John, to be baptized by him. [14] John would have prevented him, saying, "I need to be baptized by you, and do you come to me?" [15] But Jesus answered him, "Let it be so now; for thus it is fitting for us to fulfil all righteousness." Then he consented. [16] **And when Jesus** was **baptized,** he went up immediately from the water, **and** behold, **the** heavens were **opened** and he saw **the Spirit** of God descending like **a dove,** and alighting on **him;** [17] **and** lo, a **voice from heaven,** saying, "This is **my beloved Son, with** whom **I am well pleased."**

Matt 17:5 ⇨ Luke 3:22
[5] *He was still speaking, when lo, a bright cloud overshadowed them, and a voice from the cloud said, "This is my beloved Son, with whom I am well pleased; listen to him."*

MARK

Mark 1:9–11 (§K3)
[9] In those days **Jesus** came from Nazareth of Galilee and was **baptized** by John in the Jordan. [10] And when he came up out of the water, immediately he saw **the** heavens **opened and the Spirit descending upon him** like **a dove;** [11] and a **voice came from heaven,** "Thou art **my beloved Son; with thee I am well pleased."**

Mark 9:7 ⇨ Luke 3:22
[7] *And a cloud overshadowed them, and a voice came out of the cloud, "This is my beloved Son; listen to him."*

OTHER

GEbi 4
(4) And after much has been recorded it proceeds: **When the people were baptized, Jesus also** came and was **baptized** by John. And as he came up from the water, the heavens were **opened** and he saw **the Holy Spirit** in the form of **a dove** that **descended** and entered into **him. And a voice** (sounded) **from heaven** that said: Thou art **my beloved Son,** in **thee I am well pleased.** And again: I have this day begotten thee. And immediately a great light shone round about the place. When John saw this, it saith, he saith unto him: Who art thou, Lord? And again a **voice from heaven** (rang out) to him: This is **my beloved Son** in whom **I am well pleased.** And then, it saith, John fell down before him and said: I beseech thee, Lord, baptize thou me. But he prevented him and said: Suffer it; for thus it is fitting that everything should be fulfilled. (Epiphanius, *Haer.* 30.13.7f.)

GHeb 2
(2) According to the Gospel written in the Hebrew speech, which the Nazaraeans read, **the** whole fount of **the Holy Spirit** shall descend upon **him** . . . Further in the Gospel which we have just mentioned we find the following written:
     And it came to pass **when** the Lord was come up out of the water, the whole fount of **the Holy Spirit descended upon him** and rested on **him** and said to him: **My Son,** in all the prophets was I waiting for thee that thou shouldest come and I might rest in thee. For thou art my rest; thou art **my** first-begotten **Son** that reignest for ever. (Jerome, *Commentary on Isaiah 4* [on Isaiah 11:2])

GNaz 2
(2) Behold, the mother of the Lord and his brethren said to him: John the Baptist baptizes unto the remission of sins, let us go and be baptized by him. But he said to them: Wherein have I sinned that I should go and be baptized by him? Unless what I have said is ignorance (a sin of ignorance). (Jerome, *Adversus Pelagianos* 3.2)

JOHN

† **John 1:29–34 (§J2.2)**
[29] The next day he saw Jesus coming toward him, and said, "Behold, the Lamb of God, who takes away the sin of the world! [30] This is he of whom I said, 'After me comes a man who ranks before me, for he was before me.' [31] I myself did not know him; but for this I came baptizing with water, that he might be revealed to Israel." [32] And John bore witness, "I saw **the Spirit** descend as **a dove from heaven,** and it remained on **him.** [33] I myself did not know him; but he who sent me to baptize with water said to me, 'He on whom you see the **Spirit** descend and remain, this is he who baptizes with **the Holy Spirit.**' [34] And I have seen and have borne witness that this is the **Son** of God."

THOMAS

LUKE

Luke 3:23–38 (§L9)

[23] Jesus, when he began his ministry, was about thirty years of age, being the son (as was supposed) of Joseph, the son of Heli, [24] the son of Matthat, the son of Levi, the son of Melchi, the son of Jannai, the son of Joseph, [25] the son of Mattathias, the son of Amos, the son of Nahum, the son of Esli, the son of Naggai, [26] the son of Maath, the son of Mattathias, the son of Semein, the son of Josech, the son of Joda, [27] the son of Joanan, the son of Rhesa, the son of Zerubbabel, the son of Shealtiel,[a] the son of Neri, [28] the son of Melchi, the son of Addi, the son of Cosam, the son of Elmadam, the son of Er, [29] the son of Joshua, the son of Eliezer, the son of Jorim, the son of Matthat, the son of Levi, [30] the son of Simeon, the son of Judah, the son of Joseph, the son of Jonam, the son of Eliakim, [31] the son of Melea, the son of Menna, the son of Mattatha, the son of Nathan, the son of David, [32] the son of Jesse, the son of Obed, the son of Boaz, the son of Sala, the son of Nahshon, [33] the son of Amminadab, the son of Admin, the son of Arni, the son of Hezron, the son of Perez, the son of Judah, [34] the son of Jacob, the son of Isaac, the son of Abraham, the son of Terah, the son of Nahor, [35] the son of Peleg, the son of Eber, the son of Shelah, [36] the son of Cainan, the son of Arphaxad, the son of Shem, the son of Noah, the son of Lamech, [37] the son of Methuselah, the son of Enoch, the son of Jared, the son of Mahalaleel, the son of Cainan, [38] the son of Enos, the son of Seth, the son of Adam, the son of God.

[a] Greek: *Salathiel*

Cf. Gen 5:1–32, 11:10–26, 1 Chr 1–3, Ruth 4:18–22

MATT

Matt 1:1–17 (§M1)

[1] The book of the genealogy of **Jesus** Christ, the son **of David**, the son **of Abraham**.

[2] **Abraham** was the father **of Isaac**, and Isaac the father **of Jacob**, and **Jacob** the father **of Judah** and his brothers, [3] and **Judah** the father **of Perez** and Zerah by Tamar, and **Perez** the father of **Hezron**, and **Hezron** the father of Ram, [4] and Ram the father **of Amminadab**, and **Amminadab** the father **of Nahshon**, and **Nahshon** the father of Salmon, [5] and Salmon the father of **Boaz** by Rahab, and **Boaz** the father **of Obed** by Ruth, and **Obed** the father of **Jesse**, [6] and **Jesse** the father of **David** the king.

And **David** was the father of Solomon by the wife of Uriah, [7] and Solomon the father of Rehoboam, and Rehoboam the father of Abijah, and Abijah the father of Asa, [8] and Asa the father of Jehoshaphat, and Jehoshaphat the father of Joram, and Joram the father of Uzziah, [9] and Uzziah the father of Jotham, and Jotham the father of Ahaz, and Ahaz the father of Hezekiah, [10] and Hezekiah the father of Manasseh, and Manasseh the father of Amos, and Amos the father of Josiah, [11] and Josiah the father of Jechoniah and his brothers, at the time of the deportation to Babylon.

[12] And after the deportation to Babylon: Jechoniah was the father **of Shealtiel**, and **Shealtiel** the father **of Zerubbabel**, [13] and **Zerubbabel** the father of Abiud, and Abiud the father of Eliakim, and Eliakim the father of Azor, [14] and Azor the father of Zadok, and Zadok the father of Achim, and Achim the father of Eliud, [15] and Eliud the father of Eleazar, and Eleazar the father of Matthan, and Matthan the father of Jacob, [16] and Jacob the father **of Joseph** the husband of Mary, of whom **Jesus** was born, who is called Christ.

[17] So all the generations from **Abraham** to **David** were fourteen generations, and from **David** to the deportation to Babylon fourteen generations, and from the deportation to Babylon to the Christ fourteen generations.

THOMAS

MARK

OTHER

GEbi 1

(1) In the Gospel that is in general use amongst them, which is called according to Matthew, which however is not whole (and) complete but forged and mutilated—they call it the Hebrew Gospel—it is reported:

There appeared a certain man named Jesus of about thirty years of age, who chose us. And when he came to Capernaum, he entered into the house of Simon whose surname was Peter, and opened his mouth and said: As I passed along the Lake of Tiberias, I chose John and James the sons of Zebedee, and Simon and Andrew and Thaddaeus and Simon the Zealot and Judas Iscariot, and thee, Matthew, I called as thou didst sit at the receipt of custom, and thou didst follow me. You therefore I will to be twelve apostles for a testimony unto Israel. (Epiphanius, *Haer.* 30.13.2f.)

JOHN

John 1:45 ⇨ Luke 3:23

[45] *Philip found Nathanael, and said to him, "We have found him of whom Moses in the law and also the prophets wrote, Jesus of Nazareth, the son of Joseph."*

John 8:57 ⇨ Luke 3:23

[57] *The Jews then said to him, "You are not yet fifty years old, and have you seen Abraham?"*

John 6:42 ⇨ Luke 3:23

[42] *They said, "Is not this Jesus, the son of Joseph, whose father and mother we know? How does he now say, 'I have come down from heaven'?"*

LUKE	MATT	MARK

LUKE

INTRODUCTION

Luke 4:1–2 (§L10.1)
[1] And Jesus, full of the Holy Spirit, returned from the Jordan, and was led by the Spirit [2] for forty days in the wilderness, tempted by the devil. And he ate nothing in those days; and when they were ended, he was hungry.

FIRST TEMPTATION

Luke 4:3–4 (§L10.2)
[3] The devil said to him, "If you are the Son of God, command this stone to become bread." [4] And Jesus answered him, "It is written, 'Man shall not live by bread alone.'"

SECOND TEMPTATION

Luke 4:5–8 (§L10.3)
[5] And the devil took him up, and showed him all the kingdoms of the world in a moment of time, [6] and said to him, "To you I will give all this authority and their glory; for it has been delivered to me, and I give it to whom I will. [7] If you, then, will worship me, it shall all be yours." [8] And Jesus answered him, "It is written,
'You shall worship the Lord your God,
and him only shall you serve.'"

THIRD TEMPTATION

Luke 4:9–12 (§L10.4)
[9] And he took him to Jerusalem, and set him on the pinnacle of the temple, and said to him, "If you are the Son of God, throw yourself down from here; [10] for it is written,
'He will give his angels charge of you, to
guard you,'
[11] and 'On their hands they will bear you up,
lest you strike your foot against a stone.'"
[12] And Jesus answered him, "It is said, 'You shall not tempt the Lord your God.'"

CONCLUSION

Luke 4:13 (§L10.5)
[13] And when the devil had ended every temptation, he departed from him until an opportune time.

Exod 34:28 ⇨ Luke 4:2
[28] And he was there with the Lord **forty days** and forty nights; **he** neither **ate** bread nor drank water. And he wrote upon the tables the words of the covenant, the ten commandments.

⇨ Luke 4:2
Cf. Exod 24:18, 1 Kgs 19:8

JOHN

MATT

Matt 4:1–11 (§M7)
[1] Then **Jesus was led** up **by the Spirit** into **the wilderness** to be tempted by the devil. [2] And he fasted **forty days** and forty nights, and afterward **he was hungry**. [3] And the tempter came and **said to him**, "If you are the Son of God, command these stones **to become** loaves of **bread**." [4] But he answered, "**It is written**,
'**Man shall not live by bread alone**,
but by every word that proceeds from the
mouth of God.'"
[5] Then the devil **took him to** the holy city, **and set him on the pinnacle of the temple**, [6] **and said to him, "If you are the Son of God, throw yourself down**; for it is written,
'**He will give his angels charge of you**,'
and
'**On their hands they will bear you up**,
lest you strike your foot against a stone.'"
[7] **Jesus** said to **him**, "Again it is written, '**You shall not tempt the Lord your God**.'" [8] Again, the devil took **him** to a very high mountain, and **showed him all the kingdoms of the world** and the glory of them; [9] **and he said to him**, "All these **I will give** you, if you will fall down and **worship me**." [10] Then **Jesus** said to him, "Begone, Satan! for **it** is written,
'**You shall worship the Lord your God
and him only shall you serve**.'"
[11] Then **the devil** left **him**, and behold, angels came and ministered to him.

Deut 9:9 ⇨ Luke 4:2
[9] "When I went up the mountain to receive the tables of stone, the tables of the covenant which the Lord made with you, I remained on the mountain **forty days** and forty nights; I neither **ate** bread nor drank water."

Deut 8:3 ⇨ Luke 4:4
[3] "And he humbled you and let you hunger and fed you with manna, which you did not know, nor did your fathers know; that he might make you know that **man** does **not live by bread alone**, but that **man** lives by everything that proceeds out of the mouth of the Lord."

Deut 6:13 ⇨ Luke 4:8
[13] "**You shall** fear **the Lord your god; you shall serve him**, and swear by his name."

Ps 91:11–12 ⇨ Luke 4:10–11
[11] For **he will give his angels charge of you
to guard you** in all your ways,
[12] **On their hands they will bear you up**,
lest you dash **your foot against a stone**.

Deut 6:16 ⇨ Luke 4:12
[16] "**You shall not** put **the Lord your God** to the test, as you tested him at Massah."

THOMAS

MARK

Mark 1:12–13 (§K4)
[12] **The Spirit** immediately drove him out into **the wilderness**. [13] And he was **in the wilderness forty days**, **tempted by** Satan; and he was with the wild beasts; and the angels ministered to him.

OTHER

LUKE

Luke 4:14–15 (§L11) °

¹⁴ And Jesus returned in the power of the Spirit into Galilee, and a report concerning him went out through all the surrounding country. ¹⁵ And he taught in their synagogues, being glorified by all.

°Appendix 3 ⇨ §L11

Luke 4:37 ⇨ Luke 4:14b

³⁷ *And reports of* ***him*** *went out into every place in the surrounding region.*

MATT

† Matt 4:12–17 (§M8)

¹² Now when he heard that John had been arrested, he withdrew **into Galilee**; ¹³ and leaving Nazareth he went and dwelt in Capernaum by the sea, in the territory of Zebulun and Naphtali, ¹⁴ that what was spoken by the prophet Isaiah might be fulfilled:

¹⁵ "The land of Zebulun and the land of Naphtali,
toward the sea, across the Jordan,
Galilee of the Gentiles—
¹⁶ the people who sat in darkness
have seen a great light,
and for those who sat in the region and shadow of death
light has dawned."
¹⁷ From that time Jesus began to preach, saying, "Repent, for the kingdom of heaven is at hand."

Matt 9:26 ⇨ Luke 4:14b

²⁶ *And the report of this went* ***through all*** *that district.*

MARK

† Mark 1:14–15 (§K5)

¹⁴ Now after John was arrested **Jesus** came **into Galilee**, preaching the gospel of God, ¹⁵ and saying, "The time is fulfilled, and the kingdom of God is at hand; repent, and believe in the gospel."

JOHN

John 1:43 ⇨ Luke 4:14a

⁴³ *The next day* ***Jesus*** *decided to go to* ***Galilee***. *And he found Philip and said to him, "Follow me."*

John 4:1–3 ⇨ Luke 4:14a

¹ *Now when the Lord knew that the Pharisees had heard that* ***Jesus*** *was making and baptizing more disciples than John* ² *(although Jesus himself did not baptize, but only his disciples),* ³ *he left Judea and departed again to* ***Galilee***.

John 4:43 ⇨ Luke 4:14a

⁴³ *After the two days he departed to* ***Galilee***.

THOMAS

OTHER

LUKE	MATT	MARK

Luke 4:16–30 (§L12)

¹⁶ And he came to Nazareth, where he had been brought up; and he went to the synagogue, as his custom was, on the sabbath day. And he stood up to read; ¹⁷ and there was given to him the book of the prophet Isaiah. He opened the book and found the place where it was written,

¹⁸ "The Spirit of the Lord is upon me,
because he has anointed me to preach good news to the poor.
He has sent me to proclaim release to the captives
and recovering of sight to the blind,
to set at liberty those who are oppressed,
¹⁹ to proclaim the acceptable year of the Lord."

²⁰ And he closed the book, and gave it back to the attendant, and sat down; and the eyes of all in the synagogue were fixed on him. ²¹ And he began to say to them, "Today this scripture has been fulfilled in your hearing." ²² And all spoke well of him, and wondered at the gracious words which proceeded out of his mouth; and they said, "Is not this Joseph's son?" ²³ And he said to them, "Doubtless you will quote to me this proverb, 'Physician, heal yourself; what we have heard you did at Capernaum, do here also in your own country.'" ²⁴ And he said, "Truly, I say to you, no prophet is acceptable in his own country. ²⁵ But in truth, I tell you, there were many widows in Israel in the days of Elijah, when the heaven was shut up three years and six months, when there came a great famine over all the land; ²⁶ and Elijah was sent to none of them but only to Zarephath, in the land of Sidon, to a woman who was a widow. ²⁷ And there were many lepers in Israel in the time of the prophet Elisha; and none of them was cleansed, but only Naaman the Syrian." ²⁸ When they heard this, all in the synagogue were filled with wrath. ²⁹ And they rose up and put him out of the city, and led him to the brow of the hill on which their city was built, that they might throw him down headlong. ³⁰ But passing through the midst of them he went away.

Luke 7:22 ⇨ Luke 4:18

²² And he answered them, "Go and tell John what you have seen and heard: *the blind receive their sight, the lame walk, lepers are cleansed, and the deaf hear, the dead are raised up, the poor have good news preached to them*."

Luke 4:43 ⇨ Luke 4:18

⁴³ but he said to them, "I must **preach the good news** of the kingdom of God to the other cities also; for I was sent for this purpose."

‡ **Matt 13:53–58 (§M42)**

⁵³ And when Jesus had finished these parables, he went away from there, ⁵⁴ and coming to his own country **he** taught them in their **synagogue**, so that they were astonished, and said, "Where did this man get this wisdom and these mighty works? ⁵⁵ **Is not this** the carpenter's son? Is not his mother called Mary? And are not his brothers James and Joseph and Simon and Judas? ⁵⁶ And are not all his sisters with us? Where then did this man get all this?" ⁵⁷ And they took offense at him. But Jesus **said** to them, "**A prophet is** not without honor except **in his own country** and in his own house." ⁵⁸ And he did not do many mighty works there, because of their unbelief.

Isa 61:1–2 ⇨ Luke 4:18–19

¹ **The Spirit of the Lord** God **is upon me,**
because the Lord **has anointed me**
to bring **good** tidings **to the** afflicted;
he has sent me to bind up the brokenhearted,
to proclaim liberty to the captives,
and the opening of the prison **to those who are** bound; . . .

⇨ Luke 4:25–26
Cf. 1 Kgs 17:1–16

⇨ Luke 4:27
Cf. 2 Kgs 5:1–14

‡ **Mark 6:1–6 (§K25)**

¹ He went away from there and came to his own country; and his disciples followed him. ² And **on the sabbath** he began to teach in **the synagogue**; and many who heard him were astonished, saying, "Where did this man get all this? What is the wisdom given to him? What mighty works are wrought by his hands! ³ **Is not this** the carpenter, the **son** of Mary and brother of James and Joses and Judas and Simon, and are not his sisters here with us?" And they took offense at him. ⁴ **And** Jesus **said** to them, "**A prophet is** not without honor, except **in his own country**, and among his own kin, and in his own house." ⁵ And he could do no mighty work there, except that he laid his hands upon a few sick people and healed them. ⁶ And he marveled because of their unbelief.

And **he went** about among the villages teaching.

JOHN

John 4:44 ⇨ Luke 4:24

⁴⁴ For Jesus himself testified that **a prophet** has **no** honor **in his own country**.

John 1:45 ⇨ Luke 4:22

⁴⁵ *Philip found Nathanael, and said to him, "We have found **him** of whom Moses in the law and also the prophets wrote, Jesus of Nazareth, the son of Joseph."*

John 6:42 ⇨ Luke 4:22

⁴² *They said, "**Is not this** Jesus, the son of Joseph, whose father and mother we know? How does he now say, 'I have come down from heaven'?"*

John 8:59 ⇨ Luke 4:30

⁵⁹ *So they took up stones to throw at him; but Jesus hid himself, and **went** out of the temple.*

THOMAS

POxy1 6 ⇨ Luke 4:23–24

(6) Jesus says, "**A prophet is** not **acceptable in his own** homeland, nor does **a physician** work cures on those who know him."

GThom 31 ⇨ Luke 4:23–24

(31) Jesus said, "No **prophet is** accepted **in his own** village; no **physician** heals those who know him."

OTHER

Acts 10:36–38 ⇨ Luke 4:18

³⁶ *"You know the word which **he sent to Israel**, preaching **good news** of peace by Jesus Christ (he is Lord of all), ³⁷ the word which was proclaimed throughout all Judea, beginning from Galilee after the baptism which John preached: ³⁸ how God anointed Jesus of Nazareth with the Holy **Spirit** and with power; how **he** went about doing good and healing all that were **oppressed** by the devil, for God was with him."*

Acts 7:54, 58a ⇨ Luke 4: 28–29

⁵⁴ *Now **when they heard** these things they were enraged, **and they ground their teeth** against **him**. . . . ⁵⁸ Then they cast **him out of the city** and stoned **him**; . . .*

Cf. Acts 13:13–43

LUKE

Luke 4:31–37 (§L13)
[31] And he went down to Capernaum, a city of Galilee. And he was teaching them on the sabbath; [32] and they were astonished at his teaching, for his word was with authority. [33] And in the synagogue there was a man who had the spirit of an unclean demon; and he cried out with a loud voice, [34] "Ah!ᵃ What have you to do with us, Jesus of Nazareth? Have you come to destroy us? I know who you are, the Holy One of God." [35] But Jesus rebuked him, saying, "Be silent, and come out of him!" And when the demon had thrown him down in the midst, he came out of him, having done him no harm. [36] And they were all amazed and said to one another, "What is this word? For with authority and power he commands the unclean spirits, and they come out." [37] And reports of him went out into every place in the surrounding region.

Luke 4:38–39 (§L14)
[38] And he arose and left the synagogue, and entered Simon's house. Now Simon's mother-in-law was ill with a high fever, and they besought him for her. [39] And he stood over her and rebuked the fever, and it left her; and immediately she rose and served them.

ᵃ Or *Let us alone*

1 Kgs 17:18 ⇨ Luke 4:34
[18] And she said to Elijah, "**What have you** against me, O man of God? **You have come to** me to bring my sin to remembrance, and to cause the death of my son!"

MATT

Matt 7:28–29 ⇨ Luke 4:31–32
[28] *And when Jesus finished these sayings, the crowds were astonished at his teaching,* [29] *for he taught them as one who had* **authority,** *and not as their scribes.*

Matt 13:54 ⇨ Luke 4:32
[54] *and coming to his own country he taught them in their synagogue, so that* **they were astonished,** *and said, "Where did this man get this wisdom and these mighty works?"*

Matt 22:33 ⇨ Luke 4:32
[33] *And when the crowd heard it,* **they were astonished at his teaching.**

Matt 8:14–15 (§M15) ⇨ §L14
[14] **And** when Jesus **entered** Peter's **house,** he saw his **mother-in-law** lying sick with a **fever;** [15] he touched her hand, and **the fever left her,** and **she rose and served** him.

MARK

Mark 1:21–28 (§K8) ⇨ §L13
[21] **And** they **went** into **Capernaum;** and immediately **on the sabbath** he entered the synagogue and taught. [22] **And they were astonished at his teaching, for** he taught them as one who had **authority,** and not as the scribes. [23] And immediately **there was in** their **synagogue a man** with **an unclean spirit;** [24] and he **cried out, "What have you to do with us, Jesus of Nazareth? Have you come to destroy us? I know who you are, the Holy One of God."** [25] **But Jesus rebuked him, saying, "Be silent, and come out of him!"** [26] **And** the unclean spirit, convulsing **him** and crying with a loud voice, **came out of him.** [27] **And they were all amazed,** so that they questioned among themselves, saying, **"What is this?** A new teaching! **With authority he commands** even **the unclean spirits, and they obey him."** [28] And at once his fame spread everywhere throughout all **the surrounding region** of Galilee.

Mark 11:18 ⇨ Luke 4:32
[18] *And the chief priests and the scribes heard it and sought a way to destroy him; for they feared him, because all the multitude was* **astonished at his teaching.**

Mark 1:29–31 (§K9) ⇨ §L14
[29] **And** immediately **he left the synagogue, and entered** the **house** of Simon and Andrew, with James and John. [30] **Now Simon's mother-in-law** lay sick with **a fever,** and immediately **they** told **him** of her. [31] **And** he came and took **her** by the hand and lifted her up, and **the fever left her; and she served** them.

JOHN

John 7:46 ⇨ Luke 4:32
[46] *The officers answered, "No man ever spoke like this man!"*

John 6:69 ⇨ Luke 4:34
[69] *"and we have believed, and have come to know, that* **you are the Holy One of God."**

THOMAS

OTHER

LUKE

Luke 4:40–41 (§L15)°

[40] Now when the sun was setting, all those who had any that were sick with various diseases brought them to him; and he laid his hands on every one of them and healed them. [41] And demons also came out of many, crying, "You are the Son of God!" But he rebuked them, and would not allow them to speak, because they knew that he was the Christ.

Luke 4:42–44 (§L16)°

[42] And when it was day he departed and went into a lonely place. And the people sought him and came to him, and would have kept him from leaving them; [43] but he said to them, "I must preach the good news of the kingdom of God to the other cities also; for I was sent for this purpose." [44] And he was preaching in the synagogues of Judea.[a]

[a] Some witnesses read *Galilee* (see Matt 4:23, Mark 1:39): A D K X Δ Θ Π Ψ *f*¹ 28 33 *al*

° Appendix 3 ⇨ §§L15 and L16

Luke 4:18 ⇨ Luke 4:43
[18] *"The Spirit of the Lord is upon me, because he has anointed me to **preach good news** to the poor.*
*He has **sent** me to proclaim release to the captives*
and recovering of sight to the blind,
to set at liberty those who are oppressed, . . ."

Luke 7:22 ⇨ Luke 4:43
[22] *And he answered **them**, "Go and tell John what you have seen and heard: the blind receive their sight, the lame walk, lepers are cleansed, and the deaf hear, the dead are raised up, the poor have **good news preached** to them."*

MATT

Matt 8:16–17 (§M16) ⇨ §L15
[16] That evening they **brought to him** many who were possessed with demons; and he cast out the spirits with a word, and healed all who **were sick**. [17] This was to fulfil what was spoken by the prophet Isaiah, "He took our infirmities and bore our diseases."

Matt 12:15–16 ⇨ Luke 1:41
[15] Jesus, aware of this, withdrew from there. And many followed him, and he healed them all, [16] and ordered **them not to** make him known.

Matt 4:23–25 (§M11) ⇨ §L16
[23] And **he went** about all Galilee teaching **in** their **synagogues** and **preaching** the gospel of **the kingdom** and healing every disease and every infirmity among the people. [24] So his fame spread throughout all Syria, and they brought **him** all the sick, those afflicted with various diseases and pains, demoniacs, epileptics, and paralytics, and he healed them. [25] And great crowds followed him from Galilee and the Decapolis and Jerusalem and **Judea** and from beyond the Jordan.

MARK

Mark 1:32–34 (§K10) ⇨ §L15
[32] That evening, at sundown, they **brought to him all who were sick** or possessed with **demons**. [33] And the whole city was gathered together about the door. [34] **And he healed** many who **were sick with various diseases, and** cast out many **demons**; and **he** would **not** permit the demons **to speak, because they knew** him.

Mark 3:12 ⇨ Luke 1:41
[12] And he strictly ordered **them not to** make him known.

Mark 1:35–39 (§K11) ⇨ §L16
[35] And in the morning, a great while before day, **he** rose and **went** out to **a lonely place**, and there he prayed. [36] And Simon and those who were with him pursued him, [37] and they found him and said to him, "Every one is searching for you." [38] And **he said to them**, "Let us go on **to the** next towns, that **I** may **preach** there **also; for** that is why **I** came out." [39] And **he** went throughout all Galilee, **preaching in** their **synagogues** and casting out demons.

JOHN

THOMAS

OTHER

Acts 10:36–38 ⇨ §L16
[36] *"You know the word which he sent to Israel, preaching **good news** of peace by Jesus Christ (he is Lord of all), [37] the word which was proclaimed throughout all Judea, beginning from Galilee after the baptism which John preached: [38] how God anointed Jesus of Nazareth with the Holy Spirit and with power; how he went about doing good and healing all that were oppressed by the devil, for God was with him."*

LUKE

TEACHING FROM A BOAT

Luke 5:1–3 (§L17.1) °

[1] While the people **pressed upon him to hear the word of God, he was standing by the lake of Gennesaret.** [2] **And he saw two boats by the lake; but the fishermen had gone out of them and were washing their nets.** [3] Getting into one of the boats, which was Simon's, he asked him to put out a little from the land. And he sat down and taught the people from the boat.

MIRACULOUS CATCH OF FISH

Luke 5:4–11 (§L17.2) °

[4] And when he had ceased speaking, he said to Simon, "Put out into the deep and let down your nets for a catch." [5] And Simon answered, "Master, we toiled all night and took nothing! But at your word I will let down the nets." [6] And when they had done this, they enclosed a great shoal of fish; and as their nets were breaking, [7] they beckoned to their partners in the other boat to come and help them. And they came and filled both the boats, so that they began to sink. [8] But when Simon Peter saw it, he fell down at Jesus' knees, saying, "Depart from me, for I am a sinful man, O Lord." [9] For he was astonished, and all that were with him, at the catch of fish which they had taken; [10] and so also were **James and John, sons of Zebedee, who were partners with Simon. And Jesus said to Simon, "Do not be afraid; henceforth you will be catching men."** [11] **And when they had brought their boats to land, they left everything and followed him.**

°Appendix 2 ⇨ §§L17.1 and L17.2

Luke 5:28 ⇨ Luke 5:11
[28] And he left everything, and rose and followed him.

Luke 18:28 ⇨ Luke 5:11
[28] And Peter said, "Lo, we have left our homes and followed you."

MATT

† Matt 4:18–20 (§M9)

[18] As he walked by **the** Sea **of** Galilee, he saw two brothers, **Simon** who is called **Peter** and Andrew his brother, casting a net into the sea; for they were **fishermen.** [19] And **he said to** them, "Follow me, and I **will** make **you** fishers of **men.**" [20] Immediately **they left** their nets **and followed him.**

† Matt 4:21–22 (§M10)

[21] And going on from there he saw two other brothers, **James** the son **of Zebedee and John** his brother, in the boat with **Zebedee** their father, mending their nets, **and** he called them. [22] Immediately **they left** the boat and their father, **and followed him.**

MARK

† Mark 1:16–18 (§K6)

[16] And passing along by **the** Sea **of** Galilee, he saw **Simon** and Andrew the brother of **Simon** casting a net in the sea; for they were **fishermen.** [17] And Jesus **said to** them, "Follow me and I **will** make **you** become fishers of **men.**" [18] **And** immediately **they left** their nets **and followed him.**

† Mark 1:19–20 (§K7)

[19] And going on a little farther, he saw **James** the son **of Zebedee** and **John** his brother, **who were** in their boat mending the **nets.** [20] **And** immediately he called them; and **they left** their father **Zebedee** in the boat with the hired servants, **and followed him.**

JOHN   THOMAS   OTHER

† John 1:35–42 (§J3.1)

35 The next day again **John** was standing with two of his disciples; 36 and he looked at Jesus as he walked, and said, "Behold, the Lamb of God!" 37 The two disciples heard him say this, and they followed Jesus. 38 Jesus turned, and saw them following, and said to them, "What do you seek?" And they said to him, "Rabbi" (which means Teacher), "where are you staying?" 39 He said to them, "Come and see." They came and saw where he was staying; and they stayed with him that day, for it was about the tenth hour. 40 One of the two who heard **John** speak, and followed him, was Andrew, **Simon** Peter's brother. 41 He first found his brother **Simon**, and said to him, "We have found the Messiah" (which means Christ). 42 He brought him to Jesus. **Jesus** looked at him, and **said**, "So you are **Simon** the son **of** John? You shall be called Cephas" (which means **Peter**).

† John 1:43–51 (§J3.2)

43 The next day Jesus decided to go to Galilee. And he found Philip and said to him, "Follow me." 44 Now Philip was from Bethsaida, the city of Andrew and **Peter**. 45 Philip found Nathanael, and said to him, "We have found him of whom Moses in the law and also the prophets wrote, Jesus of Nazareth, the son of Joseph." 46 Nathanael said to him, "Can anything good come out of Nazareth?" Philip said to him, "Come and see." 47 Jesus saw Nathanael coming to him, and said of him, "Behold, an Israelite indeed, in whom is no guile!" 48 Nathanael said to him, "How do you know me?" **Jesus** answered him, "Before Philip called you, when you were under the fig tree, I saw you." 49 Nathanael answered him, "Rabbi, you are the Son of God! You are the King of Israel!" 50 Jesus answered him, "Because I said to you, I saw you under the fig tree, do you believe? You shall see greater things than these." 51 And he said to him, "Truly, truly, I say to you, you will see heaven opened, and the angels of God ascending and descending upon the Son of man."

‡John 21:1–14 (§J39)

1 After this Jesus revealed himself again to the disciples **by the** Sea **of** Tiberias; and he revealed himself in this way. 2 **Simon Peter**, Thomas called the Twin, Nathanael of Cana in Galilee, the **sons of Zebedee**, and two others of his disciples **were** together. 3 **Simon Peter** said to them, "I am going fishing." They said to him, "We will go with you." They went out and got **into the** boat; but that **night** they caught **nothing**.

4 Just as day was breaking, Jesus stood on the beach; yet the disciples did not know that it was Jesus. 5 Jesus **said to** them, "Children have you any fish?" They answered him, "No." 6 **He said to** them, "Cast the net on the right side of the boat, and you will find some." So they cast it, and now they were not able to haul it in, for the quantity of **fish**. 7 That disciple whom Jesus loved said to **Peter**, "It is the Lord!" When **Simon Peter** heard that **it** was the Lord, he put on his clothes, for he was stripped for work, and sprang into the sea. 8 But the other disciples came in the boat, dragging the net full **of fish**, for they were not far from the land, but about a hundred yards off.

9 When they got out on land, they saw a charcoal fire there, with **fish** lying on it, and bread. 10 Jesus said to them, "Bring some **of the fish** that you have just caught." 11 So Simon Peter went aboard and hauled the net ashore, full of large **fish**, a hundred and fifty-three of them; and although there were so many, the net was not torn. 12 Jesus **said to** them, "Come and have breakfast." Now none of the disciples dared ask him, "Who are you?" They knew it was the Lord. 13 Jesus came and took the bread and gave it to them, and so with the **fish**. 14 This was now the third time that Jesus was revealed to the disciples after he was raised from the dead.

GEbi 1

(1) In the Gospel that is in general use amongst them, which is called according to Matthew, which however is not whole (and) complete but forged and mutilated—they call it the Hebrew Gospel—it is reported:

*There appeared a certain man named Jesus of about thirty years of age, who chose us. And when he came to Capernaum, he entered into the house of **Simon** whose surname was **Peter**, and opened his mouth and said: As I passed along **the Lake of Tiberias**, I chose **John and James** the sons of **Zebedee**, and **Simon** and Andrew and Thaddaeus and Simon the Zealot and Judas Iscariot, and thee, Matthew, I called as thou didst sit at the receipt of custom, and thou didst **follow** me. You therefore I will to be twelve apostles for a testimony unto Israel.* (Epiphanius, *Haer.* 30.13.2f.)

LUKE

Luke 5:12-16 (§L18)
[12] While he was in one of the cities, there came a man full of leprosy; and when he saw Jesus, he fell on his face and besought him, "Lord, if you will, you can make me clean." [13] And he stretched out his hand, and touched him, saying, "I will; be clean." And immediately the leprosy left him. [14] And he charged him to tell no one; but "go and show yourself to the priest, and make an offering for your cleansing, as Moses commanded, for a proof to the people.[a]" [15] But so much the more the report went abroad concerning him; and great multitudes gathered to hear and to be healed of their infirmities. [16] But he withdrew to the wilderness and prayed.

[a] Greek: *to them*

Luke 17:14 ⇨ Luke 5:14
[14] *When he saw them he said to them, "Go and show yourselves to the priests." And as they went they were cleansed.*

⇨ Luke 5:14
Cf. Lev 13-14, esp. 14:2-20

MATT

Matt 8:1-4 (§M13)
[1] When he came down from the moutain, great crowds followed him; [2] and behold, a leper came to him and knelt before him, saying, "Lord, if you will, you can make me clean." [3] And he stretched out his hand and touched him, saying, "I will; be clean." And immediately his leprosy was cleansed. [4] And Jesus said to him, "See that you say nothing to any one; but go, show yourself to the priest, and offer the gift that Moses commanded, for a proof to the people."

MARK

Mark 1:40-45 (§K12)
[40] And a leper came to him beseeching him, and kneeling said to him, "If you will, you can make me clean." [41] Moved with pity, he stretched out his hand and touched him, and said to him, "I will; be clean." [42] And immediately the leprosy left him, and "If you will, you can make me clean." [43] And he sternly charged him, and sent him away at to him, "I will; be clean." [44] and said to him, "See that you say nothing to any one; but go, show yourself to the priest, and offer for your cleansing what Moses commanded, for a proof to the people." [45] But he went out and began to talk freely about it, and to spread the news, so that Jesus could no longer openly enter a town, but was out in the country; and people came to him from every quarter.

JOHN

THOMAS

OTHER

PEger2 2
(2) And behold a leper drew near [to him] and said: "Master Jesus, wandering with lepers and eating with [them was I(?)] in the inn; I also [became] a le[per]. If [thou] therefore [wilt], I am made clean." Immediately the Lord [said to him]: "I will, be thou made clean." [And thereupon] the leprosy departed from him. [And the Lord said to him]: "Go [thy way and show th]yself to the [priests] . . ."

LUKE

Luke 5:17–26 (§L19)

[17] On one of those days, as he was teaching, there were Pharisees and teachers of the law sitting by, who had come from every village of Galilee and Judea and from Jerusalem; and the power of the Lord was with him to heal.[a] [18] And behold, men were bringing on a bed a man who was paralyzed, and they sought to bring him in and lay him before Jesus;[b] [19] but finding no way to bring him in, because of the crowd, they went up on the roof and let him down with his bed through the tiles into the midst before Jesus. [20] And when he saw their faith he said, "Man, your sins are forgiven you." [21] And the scribes and the Pharisees began to question, saying, "Who is this that speaks blasphemies? Who can forgive sins but God only?" [22] When Jesus perceived their questionings, he answered them, "Why do you question in your hearts? [23] Which is easier, to say, 'Your sins are forgiven you,' or to say, 'Rise and walk'? [24] But that you may know that the Son of man has authority on earth to forgive sins"—he said to the man who was paralyzed—"I say to you, rise, take up your bed and go home." [25] And immediately he rose before them, and took up that on which he lay, and went home, glorifying God. [26] And amazement seized them all, and they glorified God and were filled with awe, saying, "We have seen strange things today."

[a] Some witnesses read *was present to heal them:* A C D X Δ Θ Π Ψ *f¹ f¹³* 28 33 *pm*

[b] Greek: *him*

Luke 7:48–49 ⇨ Luke 5:20–21
[48] *And He said to her, "Your sins are forgiven." * [49] *Then those who were at table with him began to say among themselves, "Who is this, who even forgives sins?"*

MATT

Matt 9:1–8 (§M20)

[1] And getting into a boat he crossed over and came to his own city. [2] And behold, they brought to him a paralytic, lying on his bed; and when Jesus saw their faith he said to the paralytic, "Take heart, my son; your sins are forgiven." [3] And behold, some of the scribes said to themselves, "This man is blaspheming." [4] But Jesus, knowing their thoughts, said, "Why do you think evil in your hearts? [5] For which is easier, to say, 'Your sins are forgiven,' or to say, 'Rise and walk'? [6] But that you may know that the Son of man has authority on earth to forgive sins"—he then said to the paralytic—"Rise, take up your bed and go home." [7] And he rose and went home. [8] When the crowds saw it, they were afraid, and they glorified God, who had given such authority to men.

MARK

Mark 2:1–12 (§K13)

[1] And when he returned to Capernaum after some days, it was reported that he was at home. [2] And many were gathered together, so that there was no longer room for them, not even about the door; and he was preaching the word to them. [3] And they came, bringing to him a paralytic carried by four men. [4] And when they could not get near him because of the crowd, they removed the roof above him; and when they had made an opening, they let down the pallet on which the paralytic lay. [5] And when Jesus saw their faith, he said to the paralytic, "My son, your sins are forgiven." [6] Now some of the scribes were sitting there, questioning in their hearts, [7] "Why does this man speak thus? It is blasphemy! Who can forgive sins but God alone?" [8] And immediately Jesus, perceiving in his spirit that they thus questioned within themselves, said to them, "Why do you question thus in your hearts? [9] Which is easier, to say to the paralytic, 'Your sins are forgiven,' or to say, 'Rise, take up your pallet and walk'? [10] But that you may know that the Son of man has authority on earth to forgive sins"—he said to the paralytic— [11] "I say to you, rise, take up your pallet and go home." [12] And he rose, and immediately took up the pallet and went out before them all; so that they were all amazed and glorified God, saying, "We never saw anything like this!"

JOHN

John 5:1–9a (§J9.1a)

[1] After this there was a feast of the Jews, and Jesus went up to Jerusalem.

[2] Now there is in Jerusalem by the Sheep Gate a pool, in Hebrew called Bethzatha, which has five porticoes. [3] In these lay a multitude of invalids, blind, lame, paralyzed. [5] One man was there, who had been ill for thirty-eight years. [6] When Jesus saw him and knew that he had been lying there a long time, he said to him, "Do you want to be healed?" [7] The sick man answered him, "Sir, I have no man to put me into the pool when the water is troubled, and while I am going another steps down before me." [8] Jesus said to him, "Rise, take up your pallet, and walk." [9] And at once the man was healed, and he took up his pallet and walked.

THOMAS

OTHER

Luke 5:27–28
Luke 5:29–32

CALL OF LEVI
QUESTION OF TABLE COMPANY

L20.1
L20.2

LUKE	MATT	MARK
Luke 5:27–28 (§L20.1)	**Matt 9:9 (§M21.1)** ⇨ §L20.1	**Mark 2:14 (§K14.2)** ⇨ §L20.1
27 After this he went out, and saw a tax collector, named Levi, sitting at the tax office; and he said to him, "Follow me." 28 And he left everything, and rose and followed him.	9 As Jesus passed on from there, **he saw a man** called Matthew **sitting at the tax office; and he said to him, "Follow me." And he rose and followed him.**	14 And as he passed on, **he saw** Levi the son of Alphaeus **sitting at the tax office, and he said to him, "Follow me." And he rose and followed him.**
Luke 5:29–32 (§L20.2)	**Matt 9:10–13 (§M21.2)** ⇨ §L20.2	**Mark 2:15–17 (§K14.3)** ⇨ §L20.2
29 And Levi made him a great feast in his house; and there was a large company of tax collectors and others sitting at table[a] with them. 30 And the Pharisees and their scribes murmured against his disciples, saying, "Why do you eat and drink with tax collectors and sinners?" 31 And Jesus answered them, "Those who are well have no need of a physician, but those who are sick; 32 I have not come to call the righteous, but sinners to repentance."	10 And as he sat **at table** in the **house,** behold, many **tax collectors and sinners** came and sat down with Jesus and his disciples. 11 And when **the Pharisees** saw this, they said to **his disciples, "Why** does your teacher **eat with tax collectors and sinners?"** 12 But when he heard it, he said, **"Those who are well have no need of a physician, but those who are sick.** 13 Go and learn what this means, 'I desire mercy, and not sacrifice.' For **I** came **not to call the righteous, but sinners."**	15 And as he sat **at table in his house,** many **tax collectors and** sinners were **sitting with** Jesus and his disciples; for there were many who followed him. 16 **And the scribes** of the **Pharisees,** when they saw that he was eating **with sinners and tax collectors,** said to his **disciples, "Why does he** eat **with tax collectors and sinners?"** 17 **And** when Jesus heard it, he said to them, **"Those who are well have no need of a physician, but those who are sick; I came not to call the righteous, but sinners."**

[a] Greek: *reclining at table*

Luke 5:11 ⇨ Luke 5:28
11 and when they had brought their boats to land, they left everything and followed him.

Luke 18:28 ⇨ Luke 5:28
28 And Peter said, "Lo, we have left our homes and followed you."

Luke 7:34 ⇨ Luke 5:29–30
34 "The Son of man has come eating and drinking; and you say, 'Behold, a glutton and a drunkard, a friend of tax collectors and sinners!"

Luke 15:1–2 (§L66.1) ⇨ Luke 5:29–30
1 Now the tax collectors and sinners were all drawing near to hear him. 2 And the Pharisees and the scribes murmured, saying, "This man receives sinners and eats with them."

Luke 19:7 ⇨ Luke 5:29–30
7 And when they saw it they all murmured, "He has gone in to be the guest of a man who is a sinner."

JOHN	THOMAS	OTHER
-		**POxy1224 1** ⇨ Luke 5:29–31

POxy1224 1 ⇨ Luke 5:29–31
(1) **And the scribes** and **[Pharisees]** and priests, when they sa[w] him, were angry [that with **sin]ners** in the midst he [reclined] at **table.** But **Jesus** heard [it and said:] The he[althy **need** not the **physician.**]

Justin, *Apology* 1.15.8 ⇨ Luke 5:32
15 So he said: "I have not come to call the righteous but sinners to repentance." For the Heavenly Father wishes the repentance of a sinner rather than his punishment.

328
Luke 5:27–39
Luke 5:1–6:11

TAX COLLECTORS AND FASTING
THIRD GALILEAN

L20
S7: L17–22

LUKE	MATT	MARK

LUKE

Luke 5:33–39 (§L20.3)

[33] And they said to him, "The disciples of John fast often and offer prayers, and so do the disciples of the Pharisees, but yours eat and drink." [34] And Jesus said to them, "Can you make wedding guests fast while the bridegroom is with them? [35] The days will come, when the bridegroom is taken away from them, and then they will fast in those days." [36] He told them a parable also: "No one tears a piece from a new garment and puts it upon an old garment; if he does, he will tear the new, and the piece from the new will not match the old. [37] And no one puts new wine into old wineskins; if he does, the new wine will burst the skins and it will be spilled, and the skins will be destroyed. [38] But new wine must be put into fresh wineskins. [39] And no one after drinking old wine desires new; for he says, 'The old is good.'"[a]

[a] Some witnesses read *better*: A C K X Δ Θ Π *f*¹ *f*¹³ 28 33 *al*

Luke 7:33–34 ⇨ Luke 5:33
[33] "For *John* the Baptist has come eating no bread and drinking no wine; and you say, 'He has a demon.' [34] The Son of man has come eating and drinking; and you say, 'Behold, a glutton and a drunkard, a friend of tax collectors and sinners!'"

Luke 18:12 ⇨ Luke 5:33
[12] "'I *fast* twice a week, I give tithes of all that I get.'"

JOHN

MATT

Matt 9:14–17 (§M22)

[14] Then the disciples of John came to him, saying, "Why do we and the Pharisees fast, but your disciples do not fast?" [15] And Jesus said to them, "Can the wedding guests mourn as long as the bridegroom is with them? The days will come, when the bridegroom is taken away from them, and then they will fast. [16] And no one puts a piece of unshrunk cloth on an old garment, for the patch tears away from the garment, and a worse tear is made. [17] Neither is new wine put into old wineskins; if it is, the skins burst, and the wine is spilled, and the skins are destroyed; but new wine is put into fresh wineskins, and so both are preserved."

MARK

Mark 2:18–22 (§K15)

[18] Now John's disciples and the Pharisees were fasting; and people came and said to him, "Why do John's disciples and the disciples of the Pharisees fast, but your disciples do not fast?" [19] And Jesus said to them, "Can the wedding guests fast while the bridegroom is with them? As long as they have the bridegroom with them, they cannot fast. [20] The days will come, when the bridegroom is taken away from them, and then they will fast in that day. [21] No one sews a piece of unshrunk cloth on an old garment; if he does, the patch tears away from it, the new from the old, and a worse tear is made. [22] And no one puts new wine into old wineskins; if he does, the wine will burst the skins, and the wine is lost, and so are the skins; but new wine is for fresh skins."

THOMAS

GThom 27 ⇨ Luke 5:34–35
(27) <*Jesus said*,> "*If you do not fast as regards the world, you will not find the Kingdom. If you do not observe the Sabbath as a Sabbath, you will not see the Father.*"

GThom 104 ⇨ Luke 5:34–35
(104) *They said [to Jesus], "Come, let us pray today and let us fast."*
Jesus said, "What is the sin that I have committed, or wherein have I been defeated? But when the bridegroom leaves the bridal chamber, then let them fast and pray."

GThom 47 ⇨ Luke 5:36–39
(47) Jesus said, "It is impossible for a man to mount two horses or to stretch two bows. And it is impossible for a servant to serve two masters; otherwise, he will honor the one and treat the other contemptuously. No man drinks old wine and immediately desires to drink new wine. And new wine is not put into old wineskins, lest they burst; nor is old wine put into a new wineskin, lest it spoil it. An old patch is not sewn onto a new garment, because a tear would result."

OTHER

Did 8:1 ⇨ Luke 5:35
[1] *Let not your fasts be with the hypocrites, for they fast on Mondays and Thursdays, but do you fast on Wednesdays and Fridays.*

LUKE

Luke 6:1–5 (§L21)

[1] On a sabbath,[a] while he was going through the grainfields, his disciples plucked and ate some heads of grain, rubbing them in their hands. [2] But some of the Pharisees said, "Why are you doing what is not lawful to do on the sabbath?" [3] And Jesus answered, "Have you not read what David did when he was hungry, he and those who were with him: [4] how he entered the house of God, and took and ate the bread of the Presence, which it is not lawful for any but the priests to eat, and also gave it to those with him?" [5] And he said to them, "The Son of man is lord of the sabbath."

[a] some witnesses read *On the second first sabbath* (i.e., on the second sabbath after the first): A C D K X Δ Θ Π Ψ *f*[13] 28 pm

Deut 23:25 ⇨ Luke 6:1
[25] "When you go into your neighbor's standing **grain**, you may pluck the ears with your hand, but you shall not put a sickle to your neighbor's standing **grain**."

Exod 20:10 ⇨ Luke 6:2
[10] "but the seventh day is a **sabbath** to the Lord your God; in it you shall **not do** any work, **you**, or your son, or your daughter, or your manservant, or your maidservant, or your cattle, or the sojourner who is within your gates"; . . .

Deut 5:14 ⇨ Luke 6:2
[14] "'but the seventh day is a **sabbath** to the Lord your God; in it you shall **not do** any work, **you**, or your son, or your daughter, or your manservant, or your maidservant, or your ox, or your ass, or any of your cattle, or the sojourner who is within your gates, that your manservant and your maidservant may rest as well as **you**.'"

1 Sam 21:1–6 ⇨ Luke 6:3–4
[1] Then came **David** to Nob to Ahimelech the priest; and Ahimelech came to meet David trembling, and said to him, "Why are you alone, and no one with you?" [2] And **David** said to Ahimelech the priest, "The king has charged me with a matter, and said to me, 'Let no one know anything of the matter about which I send you, and with which I have charged you.' I have made an appointment with the young men for such and such a place. [3] Now then, what have you at hand? Give me five loaves of **bread**, or whatever is here." [4] And the priest answered David, "I have no common **bread** at hand, but there is holy bread; if only the young men have kept themselves from women." [5] And **David** answered the priest, "Of a truth women have been kept from us as always when I go on an expedition; the vessels of the young men are holy, even when it is a common journey; how much more today will their vessels be holy?" [6] So **the** priest gave him the holy **bread**; for there was no **bread** there but **the bread of the Presence**, which is removed from before the Lord, to be replaced by hot **bread** on the day it is taken away.

JOHN

MATT

Matt 12:1–8 (§M33)

[1] At that time Jesus went **through the grainfields on** the **sabbath; his disciples** were hungry, and they began to pluck **heads of grain** and to eat. [2] But when **the Pharisees** saw it, they **said** to him, "Look, your **disciples are doing what is not lawful to do on the** sabbath." [3] He said to them, "Have you not read what David did, when he was hungry, and those who were with him: [4] how he entered the house of God and ate the bread of the Presence, which it was not lawful for** him to eat** nor for those who were with him, but only for **the priests**? [5] Or **have you not read** in the law how **on the sabbath the priests** in the temple profane **the sabbath**, and are guiltless? [6] I tell you, something greater than **the temple** is here. [7] And if you had known what this means, 'I desire mercy, and not sacrifice,' you would not have condemned the guiltless. [8] For **the Son of man is lord of the sabbath**."

Lev 24:5–9 ⇨ Luke 6:4
[5] "And you shall take fine flour, and bake twelve cakes of it; two tenths of an ephah shall be in each cake. [6] And you shall set them in two rows, six in a row, upon the table of pure gold. [7] And you shall put pure frankincense with each row, that it may go with **the bread** as a memorial portion to be offered by fire to the Lord. [8] Every sabbath day Aaron shall set it in order before the Lord continually on behalf of the people of Israel as a covenant for ever. [9] And it shall be for Aaron and his sons, and they shall eat it in a holy place, since it is for him a most holy portion out of the offerings by fire to the Lord, a perpetual due."

THOMAS

GThom 27 ⇨ Luke 6:5

(27) <Jesus said,> "If you do not fast as regards the world, you will not find the Kingdom. If you do not observe the Sabbath as a Sabbath, you will not see the Father."

MARK

Mark 2:23–28 (§K16)

[23] One **sabbath** he was going through the **grainfields**; and as they made their way **his disciples** began to pluck **heads of grain**. [24] And **the Pharisees said** to him, "Look, **why are** they **doing what is not lawful to do on the sabbath?**" [25] And he said to them, "**Have you never read what David did, when he was** in need and was hungry, he and those who were with him: [26] how he entered the house of God**, when Abiathar was high priest, **and ate the bread of the Presence, which it is not lawful for any but the priests to eat, and also gave it to those who were with him?**" [27] And he said to them, "**The sabbath** was made for man, not man for **the sabbath;** [28] so the Son of man is lord** even **of the sabbath.**"

OTHER

InThom 2:1–5

[1] When this boy Jesus was five years old he was playing at the ford of a brook, and he gathered together into pools the water that flowed by, and made it at once clean, and commanded it by his word alone. [2] He made soft clay and fashioned from it twelve sparrows. And it was the sabbath when he did this. And there were also many other children playing with him. [3] Now when a certain Jew saw what Jesus was doing in his play on the sabbath, he at once went and told his father Joseph: "See, your child is at the brook, and he has taken clay and fashioned twelve birds and has profaned the sabbath." [4] And when Joseph came to the place and saw (it), he cried out to him, saying: "Why do you do on the sabbath what ought not to be done?" But Jesus clapped his hands and cried to the sparrows: "Off with you!" And the sparrows took flight and went away chirping. [5] The Jews were amazed when they saw this, and went away and told their elders what they had seen Jesus do.

LUKE

Luke 6:6–11 (§L22)

[6] On another sabbath, when he entered the synagogue and taught, a man was there whose **right hand was withered**. [7] And the scribes and the Pharisees watched him, to see whether he would heal on the sabbath, so that they might find an accusation against him. [8] But he knew their thoughts, and he said to the man who had the withered hand, "Come and stand here." And he rose and stood there. [9] And Jesus said to them, "I ask you, is it lawful on the sabbath to do good or to do harm, to save life or to destroy it?" [10] And he looked around on them all, and said to him, "Stretch out your hand." And he did so, and his hand was restored. [11] But they were filled with fury and discussed with one another what they might do to Jesus.

Luke 14:1 ⇨ Luke 6:7

[1] One **sabbath** when he went to dine at the house of a ruler who belonged to **the Pharisees**, they were watching **him**.

Luke 14:3 ⇨ Luke 6:9

[3] And **Jesus** spoke to the lawyers and Pharisees, saying, "**Is it lawful to** heal **on the sabbath**, or not?"

JOHN

MATT

Matt 12:9–14 (§M34)

[9] And **he** went on from there, and **entered** their **synagogue**. [10] And behold, there was **a man** with a **withered hand**. And they asked him, "Is it lawful to heal **on the sabbath**?" so that **they might** accuse **him**. [11] **He** said to them, "What man of you, if he has one sheep and it falls into a pit on the sabbath, will not lay hold of it and lift it out? [12] Of how much more value is a man than a sheep! So **it is lawful to do good on the sabbath**." [13] Then **he** said to the man, "**Stretch out your hand**." And the man stretched it out, **and** it **was restored**, whole like the other. [14] **But** the Pharisees went out and took counsel against him, how **to** destroy him.

THOMAS

MARK

Mark 3:1–6 (§K17)

[1] Again **he entered the synagogue**, and **a man was there** who had a **withered hand**. [2] And they **watched him**, to see whether he **would heal** him **on the sabbath, so that they might** accuse **him**. [3] **And he said to the man who had the withered hand**, "Come here." [4] **And** he said to them, "**Is it lawful on the sabbath to do good or to do harm, to save life or to kill?**" But they were silent. [5] **And he looked around** at **them** with anger, grieved at their hardness of heart, **and said** to the man, "**Stretch out your hand**." **He** stretched it out, **and his hand was restored**. [6] The Pharisees went out, and immediately held counsel **with** the Herodians against him, how **to** destroy him.

OTHER

GNaz 10 ⇨ Luke 6:6

(10) In the Gospel which the Nazarenes and the Ebionites use, which we have recently translated out of Hebrew into Greek, and which is called by most people the authentic (Gospel) of Matthew, the **man** who had the **withered hand** is described as a mason who pleaded for help in the following words:

I was a mason and earned (my) livelihood with (my) hands; I beseech thee, Jesus, to restore to me my health that I may not with ignominy have to beg for my bread. (Jerome, *Commentary on Matthew* 2 [on Matthew 12:13])

InThom 2:1–5

[1] When this boy Jesus was five years old he was playing at the ford of a brook, and he gathered together into pools the water that flowed by, and made it at once clean, and commanded it by his word alone. [2] He made soft clay and fashioned from it twelve sparrows. And it was **the sabbath** when he did this. And there were also many other children playing with him. [3] Now when a certain Jew saw what Jesus was doing in his play **on the sabbath**, he at once went and told his father Joseph: "See, your child is at the brook, and he has taken clay and fashioned twelve birds and has profaned **the sabbath**." [4] And when Joseph came to the place and saw (it), he cried out to him, saying: "Why do **you do on the sabbath** what ought not to be done?" But Jesus clapped his hands and cried to the sparrows: "Off with you!" And the sparrows took flight and went away chirping. [5] The Jews were amazed when they saw this, **and** went away and told their elders **what they had seen Jesus do**.

LUKE

Luke 6:12–16 (§L23) °

[12] In these days he went out to the mountain to pray; and all night he continued in prayer to God. [13] And when it was day, he called his disciples, and chose from them twelve, whom he named apostles; [14] Simon, whom he named Peter, and Andrew his brother, and James and John, and Philip, and Bartholomew, [15] and Matthew, and Thomas, and James the son of Alphaeus, and Simon who was called the Zealot, [16] and Judas the son of James, and Judas Iscariot, who became a traitor.

°Appendix 2 ⇨ §L23

MATT

Matt 10:1–4 (§M27)

[1] And he called to him **his twelve disciples** and gave them authority over unclean spirits, to cast them out, and to heal every disease and every infirmity. [2] The names of the **twelve apostles** are these: first, **Simon**, who is called **Peter, and Andrew his brother; James** the son of Zebedee, **and John** his brother; [3] **Philip and Bartholomew; Thomas and Matthew** the tax collector; **James the son of Alphaeus, and** Thaddaeus; [4] **Simon** the Cananaean, **and Judas Iscariot, who** betrayed him.

MARK

Mark 3:13–19 (§K19)

[13] And **he went** up on **the mountain, and called** to him those whom he desired; and they came to him. [14] **And** he appointed **twelve,** to be with him, and to be sent out to preach [15] and have authority to cast out demons: [16] **Simon whom he** surnamed **Peter;** [17] **James** the son of Zebedee **and John** the brother of James, whom he surnamed Boanerges, that is, sons of thunder; [18] **Andrew, and Philip, and Bartholomew, and Matthew, and Thomas, and James the son of Alphaeus,** and Thaddaeus, **and Simon** the Cananaean, [19] **and Judas Iscariot, who** betrayed him.

Then he went home; . . .

JOHN

John 1:42 ⇨ Luke 6:14

[42] *He brought him to Jesus. Jesus looked at him, and said, "So you are **Simon** the son of John? You shall be called Cephas" (which means* **Peter***).*

THOMAS

OTHER

Acts 1:12–14 ⇨ Luke 6:14–16

[12] *Then they returned to Jerusalem from the mount called Olivet, which is near Jerusalem, a sabbath day's journey away;* [13] *and when they had entered, they went up to the upper room, where they were staying,* **Peter and John and James and Andrew, Philip and Thomas, Bartholomew and Matthew, James the son of Alphaeus and Simon the Zealot and Judas the son of James.** [14] *All these with one accord devoted themselves to prayer, together with the women and Mary the mother of Jesus, and with his brothers.*

LUKE

Luke 6:17–19 (§L24) °

¹⁷ **And he came down with them and stood on a level place, with a great crowd of his disciples and a great multitude of people from all Judea and Jerusalem and the seacoast of Tyre and Sidon, who came to hear him and to be healed of their diseases;** ¹⁸ **and those who were troubled with unclean spirits were cured.** ¹⁹ **And all the crowd sought to touch him, for power came forth from him and healed them all.**

°Appendix 3 ⇨ §L24

Luke 8:43–47 ⇨ Luke 6:19
⁴³ *And a woman who had had a flow of blood for twelve years and could not be healed by any one,* ⁴⁴ *came up behind him, and touched the fringe of his garment; and immediately her flow of blood ceased.* ⁴⁵ *And Jesus said, "Who was it that touched me?" When all denied it, Peter said, "Master, the multitudes surround you and press upon you!"* ⁴⁶ *But Jesus said, "Some one touched me; for I perceive that* **power** *has gone forth* **from me."** ⁴⁷ *And when the woman saw that she was not hidden, she came trembling, and falling down before him declared in the presence of all the people why she had touched* **him,** *and how she had been immediately* **healed.**

MATT

Matt 12:15–21 (§M35)

¹⁵ Jesus, aware of this, withdrew from there. And many followed **him, and** he **healed them all,** ¹⁶ and ordered them not to make him known. ¹⁷ This was to fulfil what was spoken by the prophet Isaiah:
¹⁸ "Behold, my servant whom I have chosen,
   my beloved with whom my soul is well pleased.
I will put my Spirit upon him,
   and he shall proclaim justice to the Gentiles.
¹⁹ He will not wrangle or cry aloud,
   nor will any one hear his voice in the streets;
²⁰ he will not break a bruised reed
   or quench a smoldering wick,
till he brings justice to victory;
   ²¹ and in his name will the Gentiles hope."

Matt 4:25 ⇨ Luke 6:17
²⁵ *And great crowds followed him from Galilee and the Decapolis and* **Jerusalem** *and* **Judea** *and from beyond the Jordan.*

Matt 9:20–21 ⇨ Luke 6:19
²⁰ *And behold, a woman who had suffered from a hemorrhage for twelve years came up behind him and touched the fringe of his garment;* ²¹ *for she said to herself, "If I only* **touch** *his garment, I shall be made well."*

Matt 14:36 ⇨ Luke 6:19
³⁶ *and besought him that they might only* **touch** *the fringe of his garment; and as many as touched it were made well.*

MARK

Mark 3:7–12 (§K18)

⁷ Jesus withdrew with his disciples to the sea, **and a great multitude from** Galilee followed; also **from Judea** ⁸ **and Jerusalem** and Idumea and from beyond the Jordan and from about **Tyre and Sidon a great multitude,** hearing all that he did, **came to him.** ⁹ And he told his disciples to have a boat ready for him because of the crowd, lest they should crush him; ¹⁰ for he had **healed** many, so that all who had diseases pressed upon him **to touch him.** ¹¹ And whenever the **unclean spirits** beheld him, they fell down before him and cried out, "You are the Son of God." ¹² And he strictly ordered them not to make him known.

Mark 5:27–33 ⇨ Luke 6:19
²⁷ *She had heard the reports about Jesus, and came up behind him in* **the crowd** *and touched his garment.* ²⁸ *For she said, "If I* **touch** *even his garments, I shall be made well."* ²⁹ *And immediately the hemorrhage ceased; and she felt in her body that she was* **healed** *of her disease.* ³⁰ *And Jesus, perceiving in himself that* **power** *had gone* **forth** *from him, immediately turned about in the crowd, and said, "Who touched my garments?"* ³¹ *And his disciples said to him, "You see* **the crowd** *pressing around you, and yet you say, 'Who touched me?'"* ³² *And he looked around to see who had done it.* ³³ *But the woman, knowing what had been done to her, came in fear and trembling and fell down before him, and told him the whole truth.*

Mark 6:56 ⇨ Luke 6:19
⁵⁶ *And wherever he came, in villages, cities, or country, they laid the sick in the market places, and besought him that they might* **touch** *even the fringe of his garment; and as many as touched it were made well.*

JOHN

THOMAS

OTHER

Acts 5:12–16
¹² *Now many signs and wonders were done among the* **people** *by the hands of the apostles. And they were all together in Solomon's Portico.* ¹³ *None of the rest dared join them, but the* **people** *held them in high honor.* ¹⁴ *And more than ever believers were added to the Lord, multitudes both of men and women,* ¹⁵ *so that they even carried out the sick into the streets, and laid them on beds and pallets, that as Peter came by at least his shadow might fall on some of them.* ¹⁶ *The* **people** *also gathered* **from the towns around Jerusalem,** *bringing the sick and those afflicted* **with unclean spirits,** *and they were* **all healed.**

LUKE	MATT	MARK

Luke 6:20–26 (§L25.1)

20 And he lifted up his eyes on his disciples, and said:

"Blessed are you poor, for yours is the kingdom of God.

21 "Blessed are you that hunger now, for you shall be satisfied.

"Blessed are you that weep now, for you shall laugh.

22 "Blessed are you when men hate you, and when they exclude you and revile you, and cast out your name as evil, on account of the Son of man! 23 Rejoice in that day, and leap for joy, for behold, your reward is great in heaven; for so their fathers did to the prophets.

24 "But woe to you that are rich, for you have received your consolation.

25 "Woe to you that are full now, for you shall hunger.

"Woe to you that laugh now, for you shall mourn and weep.

26 "Woe to you, when all men speak well of you, for their fathers did to the false prophets."

Luke 11:47–48 ⇨ Luke 6:23

47 *"Woe to you! for you build the tombs of the prophets whom your fathers killed.* 48 *So you are witnesses and consent to the deeds of your fathers; for they killed them, and you build their tombs."*

Ps 126:1–2 ⇨ Luke 6:21b

1 When the Lord restored the fortunes of Zion, we were like those who dream.
2 Then our mouth was filled with laughter, and our tongue with shouts of joy; then they said among the nations, "The Lord has done great things for them."

Matt 5:3–12 (§M12.2)

3 "Blessed are the poor in spirit, for theirs is the kingdom of heaven.

4 "Blessed are those who mourn, for they shall be comforted.

5 "Blessed are the meek, for they shall inherit the earth.

6 "Blessed are those who hunger and thirst for righteousness, for they shall be satisfied.

7 "Blessed are the merciful, for they shall obtain mercy.

8 "Blessed are the pure in heart, for they shall see God.

9 "Blessed are the peacemakers, for they shall be called sons of God.

10 "Blessed are those who are persecuted for righteousness' sake, for theirs is the kingdom of heaven.

11 "Blessed are you when men revile you and persecute you and utter all kinds of evil against you falsely on my account. 12 Rejoice and be glad, for your reward is great in heaven, for so men persecuted the prophets who were before you."

JOHN	THOMAS	OTHER

GThom 54 ⇨ Luke 6:20

(54) Jesus said, "Blessed are the poor, for yours is the Kingdom of Heaven."

GThom 68–69 ⇨ Luke 21a, 22

(68) *Jesus said, "Blessed are you when you are hated and persecuted. Wherever you have been persecuted they will find no Place."*

(69) *Jesus said, "Blessed are they who have been persecuted within themselves. It is they who have truly come to know the Father. Blessed are the hungry, for the belly of him who desires will be filled."*

1 Pet 4:15–16 ⇨ Luke 6:22–23

15 *But let none of you suffer as a murderer, or a thief, or a wrongdoer, or a mischief-maker;* 16 *yet if one suffers as a Christian, let him not be ashamed, but under that name let him glorify God.*

Acts 7:52 ⇨ Luke 6:23

52 *"Which of the prophets did not your fathers persecute? And they killed those who announced beforehand the coming of the Righteous One, whom you have now betrayed and murdered, . . ."*

LUKE

Luke 6:27–36 (§L25.2)

27 "But I say to you that hear, Love your enemies, do good to those who hate you, 28 bless those who curse you, pray for those who abuse you. 29 To him who strikes you on the cheek, offer the other also; and from him who takes away your coat do not withhold even your shirt. 30 Give to every one who begs from you; and of him who takes away your goods do not ask them again. 31 And as you wish that men would do to you, do so to them.

32 "If you love those who love you, what credit is that to you? For even sinners love those who love them. 33 And if you do good to those who do good to you, what credit is that to you? For even sinners do the same. 34 And if you lend to those from whom you hope to receive, what credit is that to you? Even sinners lend to sinners, to receive as much again. 35 But love your enemies, and do good, and lend, expecting nothing in return;[a] and your reward will be great, and you will be sons of the Most High; for he is kind to the ungrateful and the selfish. 36 Be merciful, even as your Father is merciful."

a A few witnesses read *despairing of no man:* ℵ W X* Ξ Π* *pc*

Tob 4:15 ⇨ Luke 6:31

15 "And what you hate, do not do to any one. Do not drink wine to excess or let drunkenness go with you on your way."

Sir 31:15 ⇨ Luke 6:31

15 Judge your neighbor's feelings by your own, and in every matter be thoughtful.

MATT

Matt 5:38–42 (§M12.5e)

38 "You have heard that it was said, 'An eye for an eye and a tooth for a tooth.' 39 But I say to you, do not resist one who is evil. But if any one **strikes you on the** right **cheek,** turn to him **the other also;** 40 **and** if any one would sue you and take **your coat,** let him have **your** cloak as well; 41 and if any one forces you to go one mile, go with him two miles. 42 **Give to** him **who begs from you,** and do not refuse him who would borrow from you."

Matt 5:43–48 (§M12.5f)

43 "You have heard that it was said, 'You shall **love** your neighbor and **hate** your enemy.' 44 **But I say to** you, **Love your enemies** and pray for **those who** persecute **you,** 45 so that you may be sons of your Father who is in heaven; for he makes his sun rise on the evil and on the good, and sends rain on the just and on the unjust. 46 For **if you love those who love you, what** reward have **you?** Do not **even** the tax collectors **do the same?** 47 **And if you** salute only your brethren, **what** more are **you** doing than others? Do not **even** the Gentiles **do the same?** 48 You, therefore, must **be** perfect, **as your** heavenly **Father is** perfect."

Matt 7:12 (§M12.7h)

12 "So whatever **you wish that men would do to you, do so to them;** for this is the law and the prophets."

MARK

JOHN

THOMAS

GThom 95 ⇨ Luke 6:30, 34–35

(95) [Jesus said], "**If you** have money, do not **lend** it at interest, but **give** [it] **to** one from whom **you** will not get it back."

OTHER

Did 1:2 ⇨ Luke 6:31

2 The Way of Life is this: "First, thou shalt love the God who made thee, secondly, thy neighbour as thyself; and whatsoever thou wouldst not have done **to** thyself, **do** not thou **to** another."

POxy1224 2 ⇨ Luke 6:27

(2) And pray for **your enemies.** *For he who is not [against you] is for you. [He who today] is far-off—tomorrow will be [near to you] . . . .*

2 Clem 13:4 ⇨ Luke 6:27

4 *For when they hear from us that God says: "It is no credit to you, if ye* **love** *them that love you, but it is a credit to you, if ye* **love your enemies,** *and those that hate you";—when they hear this they wonder at this extraordinary goodness; but when they see that we not only do not* **love** *those that hate us, but not even* **those who love** *us, they laugh us to scorn, and the name is blasphemed.*

LUKE

Luke 6:37–42 (§L25.3)

37"Judge not, and you will not be judged; condemn not, and you will not be condemned; forgive, and you will be forgiven; 38give, and it will be given to you; good measure, pressed down, shaken together, running over, will be put into your lap. For the measure you give will be the measure you get back."

39He also told them a parable: "Can a blind man lead a blind man? Will they not both fall into a pit? 40A disciple is not above his teacher, but every one when he is fully taught will be like his teacher. 41Why do you see the speck that is in your brother's eye, but do not notice the log that is in your own eye? 42Or how can you say to your brother, 'Brother, let me take out the speck that is in your eye,' when you yourself do not see the log that is in your own eye? You hypocrite, first take the log out of your own eye, and then you will see clearly to take out the speck that is in your brother's eye."

MATT

Matt 7:1–5 (§M12.7e)

1"Judge not, that **you be not judged.** 2For with the judgment you pronounce you will be judged, and **the measure you give will be the measure you get.** 3Why do you see the speck that is in your brother's eye, but do not notice the log that is in your own eye? 4Or how can you say to your brother, 'Let me take the speck out of your eye,' when there is the log in your own eye? 5You hypocrite, first take the log out of your own eye, and then you will see clearly to take the speck out of your brother's eye.

MARK

Mark 4:24–25 ⇨ Luke 6:38

24And he said to them, "Take heed what you hear; **the measure you give will be the measure you get, and** still more **will be given you.** 25For to him who has **will** more **be given;** and from him who has not, even what he has **will** be taken away."

JOHN

John 13:16 ⇨ Luke 6:40

16"Truly, truly, I say to you, **a servant is not** greater than **his** master; nor **is he** who **is** sent greater than he who sent him."

John 15:20 ⇨ Luke 6:40

20"Remember the word that I said to you, '**A** servant **is not** greater than **his** master,' If they persecuted me, they will persecute you; if they kept my word, they will keep yours also."

THOMAS

GThom 34 ⇨ Luke 6:39

(34)Jesus said, "If **a blind man** leads **a blind man,** they will both **fall into a pit.**"

GThom 26 ⇨ Luke 6:41–42

(26) Jesus said, "**You see the** mote **in your brother's eye, but** you **do not see the** beam **in your own eye.** When you cast **the** beam **out of your own eye, then you will see clearly to** cast **the** mote **from your brother's eye.**"

POxy1 1 ⇨ Luke 6:42

(1) [Jesus says, "You see the splinter in your brother's eye, but the beam in your own eye you do not see. Hypocrite, cast the beam out of your eye,] and then you will see in order to cast out the splinter which (is) in your brother's eye."

OTHER

1 Clem 13:2 ⇨ Luke 6:37–38

2For he spoke thus: "Be merciful, that ye may obtain mercy. Forgive, that ye may be forgiven. As ye do, so shall it be given unto you. As ye judge, so shall ye be judged. As ye are kind, so shall kindness be shewn you. With what measure ye mete, it shall be measured to you."

LUKE

Luke 6:43–45 (§L25.4)
43 "For no good tree bears bad fruit, nor again does a bad tree bear good fruit; 44 for each tree is known by its own fruit. For figs are not gathered from thorns, nor are grapes picked from a bramble bush. 45 The good man out of the good treasure of his heart produces good, and the evil man out of his evil treasure produces evil; for out of the abundance of the heart his mouth speaks."

Luke 3:9 ⇨ Luke 6:43–44
9 "Even now the axe is laid to the root of the trees; every tree therefore that does not bear good fruit is cut down and thrown into the fire."

Luke 13:6–9 (§L57.2) ⇨ Luke 6:43–44
6 And he told this parable: "A man had a fig tree planted in his vineyard; and he came seeking fruit on it and found none. 7 And he said to the vinedresser, 'Lo, these three years I have come seeking fruit on this fig tree, and I find none. Cut it down; why should it use up the ground?' 8 And he answered him, 'Let it alone, sir, this year also, till I dig about it and put on manure. 9 And if it bears fruit next year, well and good; but if not, you can cut it down.'"

MATT

Matt 7:15–20 (§M12.8b)
15 "Beware of false prophets, who come to you in sheep's clothing but inwardly are ravenous wolves. 16 You will know them **by** their fruits. Are **grapes** gathered **from thorns**, or **figs from** thistles? 17 So, every sound **tree** bears **good fruit**, but the **bad tree** bears evil **fruit**. 18 A sound **tree** cannot bear evil **fruit, nor** can a **bad tree** bear **good fruit**. 19 Every **tree** that does not bear **good fruit** is cut down and thrown into the fire. 20 Thus you will know them by their fruits."

Matt 12:33–37
33 "Either make the **tree good**, and its **fruit good**; or make the **tree bad**, and its **fruit bad**; for the **tree is known by its fruit**. 34 You brood of vipers! how can you speak good, when you are evil? **For out of the abundance of the heart the mouth speaks**. 35 **The good man out of** his **good treasure** brings forth **good, and the evil man out of his evil treasure** brings forth **evil**. 36 I tell you, on the day of judgment men will render account for every careless word they utter; 37 for by your words you will be justified, and by your words you will be condemned."

MARK

JOHN

THOMAS

GThom 45
(45) Jesus said, **"Grapes are** not harvested **from thorns**, nor are **figs** gathered **from** thistles, for they do not produce fruit. A **good man** brings forth **good** from his storehouse; an **evil man** brings forth **evil** things from his **evil** storehouse, which is in his heart, and says evil things. **For out of the abundance of the heart** he brings forth evil things."

GThom 43
(43) His disciples said to him, "Who are You, that You should say these things to us?"
<Jesus said to them,> "You do not realize who I am from what I say to you, but you have become like the Jews, for they (either) love the tree and hate its fruit (or) love the fruit and hate the tree."

OTHER

LUKE   MATT   MARK

Luke 6:46–49 (§L25.5)

[46] "Why do you call me 'Lord, Lord,' and not do what I tell you? [47] Every one who comes to me and hears my words and does them, I will show you what he is like: [48] he is like a man building a house, who dug deep, and laid the foundation upon rock; and when a flood arose, the stream broke against that house, and could not shake it, because it had been well built.[a] [49] But he who hears and does not do them is like a man who built a house on the ground without a foundation; against which the stream broke, and immediately it fell, and the ruin of that house was great."

[a] Some witnesses read *founded upon the rock* (see Matt 7:25): A C D K X Δ Θ Π Ψ f^1 f^{13} 28 *al*

Matt 7:24–27 (§M12.8d)

[24] "Every one then who **hears** these **words** of mine **and does them** will be **like a** wise **man** who built his **house upon the rock**; [25] and the rain fell, **and** the floods came, and the winds blew and beat upon **that house**, but it did not fall, **because it had been** founded on the rock. [26] And every one **who hears** these words of mine **and does not do them** will be **like a** foolish **man who built** his **house** upon **the** sand; [27] and the rain fell, and the floods came, and the wind blew and beat against that house, **and it fell**; and **great** was **the** fall of it."

JOHN   THOMAS   OTHER

PEger2 3 ⇨ Luke 6:46

(3) . . . [ca]me to him to put him to the pro[of] and to tempt him, whilst [they said]: "Master Jesus, we know that thou art come [from God], for what thou doest bears a test[imony] (to thee which goes) beyond (that) of all the prophets. [Wherefore tell] us: is it admissible [to p]ay to the kings the (charges) appertaining to their rule? [Should we] pay [th]em or not?" But Jesus saw through their [in]tention, became [angry] and said to them: "Why call ye me with yo[ur mou]th Master and yet [do] not what I say? Well has Is[aiah] prophesied [concerning y]ou saying: This [people honours] me with the[ir li]ps but their heart is far from me; [their worship is] vain. [They teach] precepts [of men]." (Fragment 2, recto [lines 43–59])

LUKE

Luke 7:1–10 (§L26)

[1] After he had ended all his sayings in the hearing of the people he entered Capernaum. [2] Now a centurion had a slave who was dear[a] to him, who was sick and at the point of death. [3] When he heard of Jesus, he sent to him elders of the Jews, asking him to come and heal his slave. [4] And when they came to Jesus, they besought him earnestly, saying, "He is worthy to have you do this for him, [5] for he loves our nation, and he built us our synagogue." [6] And Jesus went with them. When he was not far from the house, the centurion sent friends to him, saying to him, "Lord, do not trouble yourself, for I am not worthy to have you come under my roof; [7] therefore I did not presume to come to you. But say the word, and let my servant be healed. [8] For I am a man set under authority, with soldiers under me: and I say to one, 'Go,' and he goes; and to another, 'Come,' and he comes; and to my slave, 'Do this,' and he does it." [9] When Jesus heard this he marveled at him, and turned and said to the multitude that followed him, "I tell you, not even in Israel have I found such faith." [10] And when those who had been sent returned to the house, they found the slave well.

[a] Or *valuable*

MATT

Matt 8:5–13 (§M14)

[5] As he entered Capernaum, a centurion came forward to him, beseeching him [6] and saying, "Lord, my servant is lying paralyzed at home, in terrible distress." [7] And he said to him, "I will come and heal him." [8] But the centurion answered him, "Lord, I am not worthy to have you come under my roof; but only say the word, and my servant will be healed. [9] For I am a man under authority, with soldiers under me; and I say to one, 'Go,' and he goes, and to another, 'Come,' and he comes, and to my slave, 'Do this,' and he does it." [10] When Jesus heard him, he marveled, and said to those who followed him, "Truly, I say to you, not even in Israel have I found such faith. [11] I tell you, many will come from east and west and sit at table with Abraham, Isaac, and Jacob in the kingdom of heaven, [12] while the sons of the kingdom will be thrown into the outer darkness; there men will weep and gnash their teeth." [13] And to the centurion Jesus said, "Go; be it done for you as you have believed." And the servant was healed at that very moment.

MARK

JOHN

John 4:45–54 (§J8)

[45] So when he came to Galilee, the Galileans welcomed him, having seen all that he had done in Jerusalem at the feast, for they too had gone to the feast.

[46] So he came again to Cana in Galilee, where he had made the water wine. And at **Capernaum** there was an official whose son was ill. [47] **When he heard** that **Jesus** had come from Judea to Galilee, **he** went and begged him **to come** down and **heal his** son, for he **was at the point of death.** [48] **Jesus** therefore **said** to him, "Unless you see signs and wonders you will not believe." [49] The official said to him, "Sir, come down before my child dies." [50] **Jesus said** to him, "Go; your son will live." The man believed the word that Jesus spoke to him and went his way. [51] As he was going down, his servants met him and told him that his son was living. [52] So he asked them the hour when he began to mend, and they said to him, "Yesterday at the seventh hour the fever left him." [53] The father knew that was the hour when **Jesus** had **said** to him, "Your son will live"; and he himself believed, and all his household. [54] This was now the second sign that Jesus did when he had come from Judea to Galilee.

THOMAS

OTHER

Acts 10:1–2 ⇨ Luke 7:4–5

[1] *At Caesarea there was a man named Cornelius, a centurion of what was known as the Italian Cohort, [2] a devout man who feared God with all his household, gave alms liberally to the people, and prayed constantly to God.*

LUKE   MATT   MARK

Luke 7:11-17 (§L27)

[11] Soon afterward[a] he went to a city called Nain, and his disciples and a great crowd went with him. [12] As he drew near to the gate of the city, behold, a man who had died was being carried out, the only son of his mother, and she was a widow; and a large crowd from the city was with her. [13] And when the Lord saw her, he had compassion on her and said to her, "Do not weep." [14] And he came and touched the bier, and the bearers stood still. And he said, "Young man, I say to you, arise." [15] And the dead man sat up, and began to speak. And he gave him to his mother. [16] Fear seized them all; and they glorified God, saying, "A great prophet has arisen among us!" and "God has visited his people!" [17] And this report concerning him spread through the whole of Judea and all the surrounding country.

[a] Some witnesses read *Next day:* ℵ* C D K W II 28 *al*

1 Kgs 17:17-24

[17] After this **the son of** the woman, the mistress of the house, became ill; and his illness was so severe that there was no breath left in him. [18] And she said to Elijah, "What have you against me, O man of God? You have come to me to bring my sin to remembrance, and to cause the death of my son!" [19] And he said to her, "Give me your son." And he took him from her bosom, and carried him up into the upper chamber, where he lodged, and laid him upon his own bed. [20] And he cried to the Lord, "O Lord my God, hast thou brought calamity even upon the **widow** with whom I sojourn, by slaying her son?" [21] Then he stretched himself upon the child three times, and cried to the Lord, "O Lord my God, let this child's soul come into him again." [22] And the Lord hearkened to the voice of Elijah; and the soul of the child came into him again, and he revived. [23] And Elijah took the child, and brought him down from the upper chamber into the house, **and** delivered **him to his mother**; and Elijah said, "See, your son lives." [24] And the woman said to Elijah, "Now I know that you are a man of God, and that the word of the Lord in your mouth is truth."

JOHN   THOMAS   OTHER

Acts 20:7-12

[7] *On the first day of the week, when we were gathered together to break bread, Paul talked with them, intending to depart on the morrow; and he prolonged his speech until midnight.* [8] *There were many lights in the upper chamber where we were gathered.* [9] *And a **young man** named Eutychus was sitting in the window. He sank into a deep sleep as Paul talked still longer; and being overcome by sleep, he fell down from the third story and was taken up dead.* [10] *But Paul went down and bent over him, and embracing him said, "**Do not be alarmed**, for his life is in him."* [11] *And when Paul had gone up and had broken bread and eaten, he conversed with them a long while, until daybreak, and so departed.* [12] *And they took **the lad** away alive, and were not a little comforted.*

LUKE

Luke 7:18–23 (§L28.1) °

[18] The disciples of John told him of all these things. [19] And John, calling to him two of his disciples, sent them to the Lord, saying, "Are you he who is to come, or shall we look for another?" [20] And when the men had come to him, they said, "John the Baptist has sent us to you, saying, 'Are you he who is to come, or shall we look for another?'" [21] In that hour he cured many of diseases and plagues and evil spirits, and on many that were blind he bestowed sight. [22] And he answered them, "Go and tell John what you have seen and heard: the blind receive their sight, the lame walk, lepers are cleansed, and the deaf hear, the dead are raised up, the poor have good news preached to them. [23] And blessed is he who takes no offense at me."

°Appendix 1 ⇨ §L28.1

Luke 3:15–16 ⇨ Luke 7:20

[15] *As the people were in expectation, and all men questioned in their hearts concerning John, whether perhaps he were the Christ,* [16] *John answered them all, "I baptize you with water; but he who is mightier than I is coming, the thong of whose sandals I am not worthy to untie; he will baptize you with the Holy Spirit and with fire."*

Luke 4:18 ⇨ Luke 7:22

[18] *"The Spirit of the Lord is upon me,*
because he has anointed me to preach good
    news to the poor.
He has sent me to proclaim release to the
    captives
and recovering of sight to the blind,
to set at liberty those who are oppressed, . . ."

Isa 35:5–6 ⇨ Luke 7:22

[5] Then the eyes of **the blind** shall be opened,
    and the ears of **the deaf** unstopped;
[6] then shall **the lame** man leap like a hart,
    and the tongue of the dumb sing for joy,
For waters shall break forth in the wilderness,
    and streams in the desert; . . .

⇨ Luke 7:22
Cf. Isa 29:18–19, 61:1

JOHN

John 1:15 ⇨ Luke 7:20

[15] *(John bore witness to him, and cried, "This was he of whom I said, 'He who comes after me ranks before me, for he was before me.'")*

MATT

Matt 11:2–6 (§M30.1)

[2] Now when **John** heard in prison about the deeds of the Christ, he sent word by **his disciples** [3] and said to him, "**Are you he who is to come, or shall we look for another?**" [4] And Jesus **answered them,** "**Go and tell John what** you hear **and see:** [5] **the blind receive their sight and the lame walk, lepers are cleansed and the deaf hear, and the dead are raised up, and the poor have good news preached to** them. [6] **And blessed is he who takes no offense at me.**"

THOMAS

MARK

OTHER

LUKE

Luke 7:24–30 (§L28.2) °
²⁴When the messengers of John had gone, he began to speak to the crowds concerning John: "What did you go out into the wilderness to behold? A reed shaken by the wind? ²⁵What then did you go out to see? A man clothed in soft clothing? Behold, those who are gorgeously appareled and live in luxury are in kings' courts. ²⁶What then did you go out to see? A prophet? Yes, I tell you, and more than a prophet. ²⁷This is he of whom it is written,
'Behold, I send my messenger before thy face, who shall prepare thy way before thee.'
²⁸I tell you, among those born of women none is greater than John; yet he who is least in the kingdom of God is greater than he." ²⁹(When they heard this all the people and the tax collectors justified God, having been baptized with the baptism of John; ³⁰but the Pharisees and the lawyers rejected the purpose of God for themselves, not having been baptized by him.)

°Appendix 1 ⇨ §L28.2

Luke 1:76 ⇨ Luke 7:27
⁷⁶"And you, child, will be called the prophet of the Most High;
for you will go **before** the Lord to **prepare** his ways, . . ."

Luke 3:4 ⇨ Luke 7:27
⁴As **it is written** in the book of the words of Isaiah the prophet,
"The voice of one crying in the wilderness:
Prepare the **way** of the Lord,
make his paths straight."

Luke 9:51–52 ⇨ Luke 7:27
⁵¹When the days drew near for him to be received up, he set his face to go to Jerusalem. ⁵²And he sent messengers ahead of him, who went and entered a village of the Samaritans, to make ready for him; . . .

Luke 10:1 ⇨ Luke 7:27
¹After this the Lord appointed seventy others, and sent them on ahead of him, two by two, into every town and place where he himself was about to come.

Luke 20:4–6 ⇨ Luke 7:29–30
⁴"Was **the baptism of John** from heaven or from me?" ⁵And they discussed it with one another, saying, "If we say, 'From heaven,' he will say, 'Why did you **not** believe him?' ⁶But if we say, 'From men,' all the people will stone us; for they are convinced that **John** was a prophet."

Mal 3:1a ⇨ Luke 7:27
¹"**Behold, I send my messenger** to **prepare** the **way** before me, . . ."

JOHN

MATT

Matt 11:7–15 (§M30.2)
⁷As they went away, Jesus **began to speak** to the crowds concerning John: "What did you go out into the wilderness to behold? A reed shaken by the wind? ⁸Why then did you go out? To see a man clothed in soft raiment? Behold, those who wear soft raiment **are in kings'** houses. ⁹Why **then did you go out?** To see a prophet? Yes, I tell you, and more than a prophet. ¹⁰This is he of whom it is written,
'Behold, I send my messenger before thy face,
who shall prepare thy way before thee.'
¹¹Truly, I say to **you,** among **those born of women** there has risen no one **greater than John** the Baptist; **yet he who is least in the kingdom of** heaven **is greater than he.** ¹²From the days of John the Baptist until now the kingdom of heaven has suffered violence, and men of violence take it by force. ¹³For all the prophets and the law prophesied until John; ¹⁴and if you are willing to accept it, he is Elijah who is to come. ¹⁵He who has ears to hear, let him hear."

Matt 21:32 ⇨ Luke 7:27, 29–30
³²"For John came to you in the **way** of righteousness, and you did not believe him, but **the tax collectors** and the harlots believed him; and even when you saw it, you did **not** afterward repent and believe **him.**"

THOMAS

GThom 78 ⇨ Luke 7:24–25
(78) Jesus said, "Why have **you** come **out into the** desert? To see a **reed shaken by the wind**? And to see a **man clothed in** fine garments like your **kings** and your great men? Upon them are the fine [garments], and they are unable to discern the truth."

GThom 46 ⇨ Luke 7:28
(46) Jesus said, "**Among those born of women,** from Adam until John the Baptist, there is no one so superior to **John** the Baptist that his eyes should not be lowered (before him). **Yet** I have said, whichever one of you comes to be a child will be acquainted with **the Kingdom** and will become superior to John."

MARK

Mark 1:2 ⇨ Luke 7:27
²As it is written in Isaiah the prophet,
"Behold, I send my messenger before thy face,
who shall prepare thy way; . . ."

OTHER

LUKE	MATT	MARK

Luke 7:31–35 (§L28.3) °

[31] "To what then shall I compare the men of this generation, and what are they like? [32] They are like children sitting in the market place and calling to one another,

'We piped to you, and you did not dance; we wailed, and you did not weep.'

[33] For John the Baptist has come eating no bread and drinking no wine; and you say, 'He has a demon.' [34] The Son of man has come eating and drinking; and you say, 'Behold, a glutton and a drunkard, a friend of tax collectors and sinners!' [35] Yet wisdom is justified by all her children."

°Appendix 1 ⇨ §L28.3

Luke 5:29–30 ⇨ Luke 7:34

[29] *And Levi made him a great feast in his house; and there was a large company of tax collectors and others sitting at table with them. [30] And the Pharisees and their scribes murmured against his disciples, saying, "Why do you eat and drink with tax collectors and sinners?"*

Luke 15:1–2 (§L66.1) ⇨ Luke 7:34

[1] *Now the tax collectors and sinners were all drawing near to hear him. [2] And the Pharisees and the scribes murmured, saying, "This man receives sinners and eats with them."*

Luke 19:7 ⇨ Luke 7:34

[7] *And when they saw it they all murmured, "He has gone in to be the guest of a man who is a sinner."*

Matt 11:16–19 (§M30.3)

[16] "But to what shall I compare this generation? It is like children sitting in the market places and calling to their playmates,

[17] 'We piped to you, and you did not dance; we wailed, and you did not mourn.'

[18] For John came neither eating nor drinking, and they say, 'He has a demon'; [19] the Son of man came eating and drinking, and they say, 'Behold, a glutton and a drunkard, a friend of tax collectors and sinners!' Yet wisdom is justified by her deeds."

JOHN	THOMAS	OTHER

LUKE	MATT	MARK

Luke 7:36–50 (§L29)

³⁶ One of the Pharisees asked him to eat with him, and he went into the Pharisee's house, and took his place at table, ³⁷ And behold, a woman of the city, who was a sinner, when she learned that he was at table in the Pharisee's house, brought an alabaster flask of ointment, ³⁸ and standing behind him at his feet, weeping, she began to wet his feet with her tears, and wiped them with the hair of her head, and kissed his feet, and anointed them with the ointment. ³⁹ Now when the Pharisee who had invited him saw it, he said to himself, "If this man were a prophet, he would have known who and what sort of woman this is who is touching him, for she is a sinner." ⁴⁰ And Jesus answering said to him, "Simon, I have something to say to you." And he answered, "What is it, Teacher?" ⁴¹ "A certain creditor had two debtors; one owed five hundred denarii, and the other fifty. ⁴² When they could not pay, he forgave them both. Now which of them will love him more?" ⁴³ Simon answered, "The one, I suppose, to whom he forgave more." And he said to him "You have judged rightly." ⁴⁴ Then turning toward the woman he said to Simon, "Do you see this woman? I entered your house, you gave me no water for my feet, but she has wet my feet with her tears and wiped them with her hair. ⁴⁵ You gave me no kiss, but from the time I came in she has not ceased to kiss my feet. ⁴⁶ You did not anoint my head with oil, but she has anointed my feet with ointment. ⁴⁷ Therefore I tell you, her sins, which are many, are forgiven, for she loved much; but he who is forgiven little, loves little." ⁴⁸ And he said to her, "Your sins are forgiven." ⁴⁹ Then those who were at table with him began to say among themselves, "Who is this, who even forgives sins?" ⁵⁰ And he said to the woman, "Your faith has saved you; go in peace."

Luke 11:37 ⇨ Luke 7:36
³⁷ While he was speaking, a Pharisee asked him to dine with him; so he went in and sat at table.

Luke 14:1 ⇨ Luke 7:36
¹ One sabbath when he went to dine at the house of a ruler who belonged to the Pharisees, they were watching him.

Luke 5:20–21 ⇨ Luke 7:48–49
²⁰ And when he saw their faith he said, "Man, your sins are forgiven you." ²¹ And the scribes and the Pharisees began to question, saying, "Who is this that speaks blasphemies? Who can forgive sins but God only?"

Matt 26:6–13 (§M80.3)

⁶ Now when Jesus was at Bethany in the house of Simon the leper, ⁷ a woman came up to him with an alabaster flask of very expensive ointment, and she poured it on his head, as he sat at table. ⁸ But when the disciples saw it, they were indignant, saying, "Why this waste? ⁹ For this ointment might have been sold for a large sum, and given to the poor." ¹⁰ But Jesus, aware of this, said to them, "Why do you trouble the woman? For she has done a beautiful thing to me. ¹¹ For you always have the poor with you, but you will not always have me. ¹² In pouring this ointment on my body she has done it to prepare me for burial. ¹³ Truly, I say to you, wherever this gospel is preached in the whole world, what she has done will be told in memory of her."

Matt 9:22 ⇨ Luke 7:50
²² Jesus turned, and seeing her he said, "Take heart, daughter; your faith has made you well." And instantly the woman was made well.

Luke 8:48 ⇨ Luke 7:50
⁴⁸ And he said to her, "Daughter, your faith has made you well; go in peace."

Luke 17:19 ⇨ Luke 7:50
¹⁹ And he said to him, "Rise and go your way; your faith has made you well."

Luke 18:42 ⇨ Luke 7:50
⁴² And Jesus said to him, "Receive your sight; your faith has made you well."

Mark 14:3–9 (§K62.2)

³ And while he was at Bethany in the house of Simon the leper, as he sat at table, a woman came with an alabaster flask of ointment of pure nard, very costly, and she broke the flask and poured it over his head. ⁴ But there were some who said to themselves indignantly, "Why was the ointment thus wasted? ⁵ For this ointment might have been sold for more than three hundred denarii, and given to the poor." And they reproached her. ⁶ But Jesus said, "Let her alone; why do you trouble her? She has done a beautiful thing to me. ⁷ For you always have the poor with you, and whenever you will, you can do good to them; but you will not always have me. ⁸ She has done what she could; she has anointed my body beforehand for burying. ⁹ And truly, I say to you, wherever the gospel is preached in the whole world, what she has done will be told in memory of her."

Mark 5:34 ⇨ Luke 7:50
³⁴ And he said to her, "Daughter, your faith has made you well; go in peace, and be healed of your disease."

Mark 10:52 ⇨ Luke 7:50
⁵² And Jesus said to him, "Go your way; your faith has made you well." And immediately he received his sight and followed him on the way.

JOHN	THOMAS	OTHER

John 12:1–8 (§J24.1)

*¹ Six days before the Passover, Jesus came to Bethany, where Lazarus was, whom Jesus had raised from the dead. ² There they made him a supper; Martha served, and Lazarus was one of those **at table** with him. ³ Mary took a pound of costly **ointment** of pure nard **and anointed the feet** of Jesus **and wiped** his feet with her **hair;** and the house was filled with the fragrance of the ointment. ⁴ But Judas Iscariot, one of his disciples (he who was to betray him), said, ⁵ "Why was this **ointment** not sold for three hundred denarii and given to the poor?" ⁶ This he said, not that he cared for the poor but because he was a thief, and as he had the money box he used to take what was put into it. ⁷ **Jesus said,** "Let her alone, let her keep it for the day of my burial. ⁸ The poor you always have with you, but you do not always have me."*

LUKE

Luke 8:1–3 (§L30) °

[1] Soon afterward he went on through cities and villages, preaching and bringing the good news of the kingdom of God. And the twelve were with him, [2] and also some women who had been healed of evil spirits and infirmities: Mary, called Magdalene, from whom seven demons had gone out, [3] and Joanna, the wife of Chuza, Herod's steward, and Susanna, and many others, who provided for them[a] out of their means.

[a] Some witnesses read *him* (cf. Matt 27:55, Mark 15:41): ℵ A L X Π Ψ *f*[1] 33 *al*

° Appendix 3 ⇨ §L30

° Appendix 2 ⇨ Luke 8:1

Luke 23:49 ⇨ Luke 8:2–3
[49] And all his acquaintances **and the women who had** followed him from Galilee stood at a distance and saw these things.

Luke 23:55 ⇨ Luke 8:2–3
[55] The **women who had** come with him from Galilee followed, and saw the tomb, and how his body was laid; . . .

MATT

Matt 27:55–56 ⇨ Luke 8:2–3
[55] There were also many **women** there, looking on from afar, who had followed Jesus from Galilee, ministering to him; [56] among whom were **Mary Magdalene**, and Mary the mother of James and Joseph, and the mother of the sons of Zebedee.

MARK

Mark 15:40–41 ⇨ Luke 8:2–3
[40] There were **also women** looking on from afar, among whom were **Mary Magdalene**, and Mary the mother of James the younger and of Joses, and Salome, [41] who, when he was in Galilee, followed him, and ministered to him; **and** also **many** other women who came up with him to Jerusalem.

Mark 16:9 ⇨ Luke 8:2
[9] Now when he rose early on the first day of the week, he appeared first to **Mary Magdalene, from whom he had** cast out seven demons.

JOHN

THOMAS

OTHER

LUKE

Luke 8:4–8 (§L31.1)

⁴ **And when a great crowd came together and people from town after town came to him, he said in a parable:** ⁵ "**A sower went out to sow his seed; and as he sowed, some fell along the path, and was trodden under foot, and the birds of the air devoured it.** ⁶ **And some fell on the rock; and as it grew up, it withered away, because it had no moisture.** ⁷ **And some fell among thorns; and the thorns grew with it and choked it.** ⁸ **And some fell into good soil and grew, and yielded a hundredfold." As he said this, he called out, "He who has ears to hear, let him hear."**

MATT

Matt 13:1–2 (§M40.1)

¹ That same day Jesus went out of the house and sat beside the sea. ² **And great** crowds gathered about **him**, so that he got into a boat and sat there; and the whole **crowd** stood on the beach.

Matt 13:3–9 (§M40.2)

³ And **he** told them many things in parables, saying: "**A sower went out to sow.** ⁴ **And as he sowed, some seeds fell along the path, and the birds** came and **devoured** them. ⁵ Other seeds **fell on** rocky ground, where they had not much soil, and immediately they sprang up, since they **had no** depth of soil, ⁶ but when the sun rose they were scorched; and since they **had no** root they **withered away.** ⁷ Other seeds **fell** upon **thorns, and the thorns grew** up and **choked** them. ⁸ Other seeds **fell** on **good soil** and brought forth grain, some a **hundredfold**, some sixty, some thirty. ⁹ **He who has ears, let him hear."**

MARK

Mark 4:2–9 (§K21.2)

² **And** he taught them many things **in** parables, and in his teaching **he said** to them: ³ "**Listen! A sower went out to sow.** ⁴ **And as he sowed, some seed fell along the path, and the birds** came and **devoured it.** ⁵ Other seed **fell on** rocky ground, where it had not much soil, and immediately it sprang up, since it **had no** depth of soil; ⁶ and when the sun rose it was scorched, and since it **had no** root it **withered away.** ⁷ Other seed **fell among thorns and the thorns grew** up **and choked it,** and it yielded no grain. ⁸ **And** other seeds **fell into good soil and** brought forth grain, growing up and increasing **and** yielding thirtyfold and sixtyfold and a **hundredfold."** ⁹ And **he** said, "**He who has ears to hear, let him hear."**

JOHN

THOMAS

GThom 9

(9) Jesus **said,** "Now the **sower went out,** took a handful (of seeds), and scattered them. **Some fell** on **the** road; **the birds** came and gathered them up. Others **fell on rock,** did not take root in the soil, and did not produce ears. And others **fell** on **thorns;** they **choked** the seed(s) and worms ate them. And others **fell** on the **good soil and** produced good fruit: it bore sixty per measure **and a** hundred and twenty per measure."

OTHER

InThom 12:1–2

¹ *Again, in the time of sowing the child went out with his father to sow wheat in their land. And as his father sowed, the child Jesus also sowed one corn of wheat.* ² *And when he had reaped it and threshed it, he brought in a hundred measures; and he called all the poor of the village to the threshing-floor and gave them the wheat, and Joseph took the residue of the wheat. He was eight years old when he worked this miracle.*

ApocJa 12:20–31

²⁰ *he said: "This is why I say this to you (pl.), that you may know yourselves. For the Kingdom of Heaven is like an ear of grain which sprouted in a field. And* ²⁵ *when it ripened, it scattered its fruit and, in turn, filled the field with ears of grain for another year. You also: be zealous to reap for yourselves an ear of life, in order that* ³⁰ *you may be filled with the Kingdom."*

LUKE

Luke 8:9–10 (§L31.2)

⁹And when his disciples asked him what this parable meant, ¹⁰he said, "To you it has been given to know the secrets of the kingdom of God; but for others they are in parables, so that seeing they may not see, and hearing they may not understand."

Isa 6:9–10 ⇨ Luke 8:10

⁹And he said, "Go, and say to this people:
'Hear and hear, but do **not understand**;
see and see, but do **not** perceive.'
¹⁰Make the heart of this people fat,
   and their ears heavy,
   and shut their eyes;
lest **they see** with their eyes,
   and hear with their ears,
and **understand** with their hearts,
   and turn and be healed."

MATT

Matt 13:10–17 (§M40.3)

¹⁰Then the **disciples** came and said to **him,** "Why do you speak to them in parables?" ¹¹And **he** answered them, **"To you it has been given to know the secrets of the kingdom of** heaven, **but** to them it has not been given. ¹²For to him who has will more be given, and he will have abundance; but from him who has not, even what he has will be taken away. ¹³This is why I speak to them in parables, because **seeing they** do **not see, and hearing they** do **not** hear, nor do they **understand.** ¹⁴With them indeed is fulfilled the prophecy of Isaiah which says:

'You shall indeed hear but never **understand,**

   and you shall indeed **see** but never perceive.

¹⁵For this people's heart has grown dull,
   and their ears are heavy of hearing,
   and their eyes they have closed,
lest they should perceive with their eyes,
   and hear with their ears,
and **understand** with their heart,
   and turn for me to heal them.'

¹⁶But blessed are your eyes, for they **see,** and your ears, for they hear. ¹⁷Truly, I say to you, many prophets and righteous men longed to **see** what you **see,** and did **not see** it, **and** to hear what you hear, and did **not** hear it."

MARK

Mark 4:10–12 (§K21.3)

¹⁰And **when** he was alone, those who were about him with the twelve **asked him** concerning the parables. ¹¹And **he said** to them, **"To you has been given the** secret **of the kingdom of God, but for those** outside everything is **in parables;** ¹²**so that** they may indeed see but **not** perceive, and may indeed hear but **not understand;** lest they should **turn again, and be** forgiven."

JOHN

THOMAS

OTHER

Acts 28:26–27 ⇨ Luke 8:10

²⁶ "'Go to this people, and say,
You shall indeed hear but never **understand,**
and you shall indeed see but never perceive.
²⁷ For this people's heart has grown dull,
and their ears are heavy of hearing,
and their eyes they have closed;
lest they should perceive with their eyes,
and hear with their ears,
and **understand** with their heart,
and turn for me to heal them.'"

ApocJa 7:1–10

⁷ "I first spoke with **you in parables,** and you did **not understand.** Now, in turn, I speak with ⁵ **you** openly, and **you** do not perceive. But it is **you** who were to me a parable **in parables** and what is apparent ¹⁰ in what are open."

LUKE	MATT	MARK

Luke 8:11–15 (§L31.3)

[11] "Now the parable is this: The seed is the word of God. [12] The ones along the path are those who have heard; then the devil comes and takes away the word from their hearts, that they may not believe and be saved. [13] And the ones on the rock are those who, when they hear the word, receive it with joy; but these have no root, they believe for a while and in time of temptation fall away. [14] And as for what fell among the thorns, they are those who hear, but as they go on their way they are choked by the cares and riches and pleasures of life, and their fruit does not mature. [15] And as for that in the good soil, they are those who, hearing the word, hold it fast in an honest and good heart, and bring forth fruit with patience."

Matt 13:18–23 (§M40.4)

[18] "Hear then **the parable** of the sower. [19] When any one hears **the word of** the kingdom and does not understand it, **the** evil one **comes and** snatches **away** what is sown in his heart; this is what was sown **along the path.** [20] As for what was sown on rocky ground, this is he **who** hears **the word** and immediately receives it **with joy;** [21] yet he has **no root** in himself, but endures **for a while,** and when tribulation or persecution arises on account of the word, immediately he falls **away.** [22] **As for what** was sown **among thorns,** this is he who hears the word, **but the cares** of the world and the delight in **riches** choke the word, and it proves unfruitful. [23] **As for** what was sown on **good soil,** this is he **who** hears **the word** and understands **it;** he indeed bears **fruit,** and yields, in one case a hundredfold, in another sixty, and in another thirty."

Mark 4:13–20 (§K21.4)

[13] And he said to them, "Do you not understand **this parable?** How then will you understand all **the parables?** [14] The sower sows **the word.** [15] And these are **the ones along the path,** where the word is sown; when they hear, Satan immediately **comes and takes away the word** which is sown in them. [16] **And** these in like manner are **the ones** sown upon rocky ground, **who, when they hear the word,** immediately **receive it with joy;** [17] and they **have no root** in themselves, but endure **for a while;** then, when tribulation or persecution arises on account of the word, immediately they **fall away.** [18] **And** others are the ones sown **among thorns; they are those who hear** the word, [19] **but the cares of** the world, **and the** delight in **riches,** and the desire for other things, enter in and choke the word, **and** it proves unfruitful. [20] But those that were sown upon **the good soil are** the ones **who hear the word** and accept it and bear **fruit,** thirtyfold and sixtyfold and a hundredfold."

JOHN	THOMAS	OTHER

ApocJa 8:10–27

[10] *"Become zealous about **the Word.** For the Word's first condition is faith; the second is love; the third is works.* [15] *Now from these comes life. For **the Word** is like a grain of wheat. When someone sowed it, he believed in **it;** and when it sprouted, he loved **it,** because he looked (forward to)* [20] *many grains in the place of one; and when he worked (**it**), he was saved, because he prepared **it** for food. Again he left (some grains) to sow. Thus it is also possible for you (pl.) to receive* [25] ***the Kingdom of Heaven:** unless you receive **it** through knowledge, you will not be able to find **it.**"*

LUKE

Luke 8:16–17 (§L31.4)
[16]"No one after lighting a lamp covers it with a vessel, or puts it under a bed, but puts it on a stand, that those who enter may see the light. [17]For nothing is hid that shall not be made manifest, nor anything secret that shall not be known and come to light."

Luke 8:18 (§L31.5)
[18]"Take heed then how you hear; for to him who has will more be given, and from him who has not, even what he thinks that he has will be taken away."

Luke 11:33 ⇨ Luke 8:16
[33]"No one after lighting a lamp puts it in a cellar or under a bushel, but on a stand, that those who enter may see the light."

Luke 12:2 ⇨ Luke 8:17
[2]"Nothing is covered up that will not be revealed, or hidden that will not be known."

Luke 19:26 ⇨ §L31.5
[26]"'I tell you, that to every one who has will more be given; but from him who has not, even what he has will be taken away.'"

JOHN

MATT

Matt 5:15 ⇨ Luke 8:16
[15]"Nor do men light a lamp and put it under a bushel, but on a stand, and it gives light to all in the house."

Matt 10:26 ⇨ Luke 8:17
[26]"So have no fear of them; for nothing is covered that will not be revealed, or hidden that will not be known."

Matt 13:12 ⇨ §L31.5
[12]"For to him who has will more be given, and he will have abundance; but from him who has not, even what he has will be taken away."

Matt 25:29 ⇨ §L31.5
[29]"'For to every one who has will more be given, and he will have abundance; but from him who has not, even what he has will be taken away.'"

THOMAS

GThom 33 ⇨ §L31.4
(33) Jesus said, "Preach from your housetops that which you will hear in your ear {(and) in the other ear}. For no one lights a lamp and puts it under a bushel, nor does he put it in a hidden place, but rather he sets it on a lampstand so that everyone who enters and leaves will see its light."

POxy654 5 ⇨ Luke 8:17
(5) Jesus says, "K[now what is be]fore your face, and [that which is hidden] from you will be reveal[ed to you. For there i]s nothing hidden which will not [be made] mani[fest] and (nothing) buried which will not [be raised up.]"

GThom 5 ⇨ Luke 8:17
(5) Jesus said, "Recognize what is in your sight, and that which is hidden from you will become plain to you. For there is nothing hidden which will not become manifest."

GThom 6 ⇨ Luke 8:17
(6) His disciples questioned Him and said to Him, "Do You want us to fast? How shall we pray? Shall we give alms? What diet shall we observe?"
Jesus said, "Do not tell lies, and do not do what you hate, for all things are plain in the sight of Heaven. For nothing hidden will not become manifest, and nothing covered will remain without being uncovered."

GThom 41 ⇨ §L31.5
(41) Jesus said, "Whoever has something in his hand will receive more, and whoever has nothing will be deprived of even the little he has."

MARK

Mark 4:21–23 (§K21.5) ⇨ §L31.4
[21]And he said to them, "Is a lamp brought in to be put under a bushel, or under a bed, and not on a stand? [22]For there is nothing hid, except to be made manifest; nor is anything secret, except to come to light. [23]If any man has ears to hear, let him hear."

Mark 4:24–25 (§K21.6) ⇨ §L31.5
[24]And he said to them, "Take heed what you hear; the measure you give will be the measure you get, and still more will be given you. [25]For to him who has will more be given; and from him who has not, even what he has will be taken away."

OTHER

LUKE

Luke 8:19–21 (§L32)

[19] Then his mother and his brothers came to him, but they could not reach him for the crowd. [20] And he was told, "Your mother and your brothers are standing outside, desiring to see you." [21] But he said to them, "My mother and my brothers are those who hear the word of God and do it."

Luke 11:27–28

[27] As he said this, a woman in the crowd raised her voice and said to him, "Blessed is the womb that bore you, and the breasts that you sucked!" [28] But he said, "blessed rather are those who hear the word of God and keep it!"

MATT

Matt 12:46–50 (§M39)

[46] While he was still speaking to the people, behold, **his mother and his brothers** stood outside, asking to speak **to him.** [48] But **he** replied to the man who **told** him, "Who is **my mother, and** who are **my brothers?**" [49] And stretching out his hand toward his disciples, **he said,** "Here are **my mother and my brothers!** [50] For whoever does **the** will **of** my Father in heaven is **my** brother, and sister, **and mother.**"

MARK

Mark 3:31–35 (§K20.3)

[31] And **his mother and his brothers came;** and standing outside they sent to him and called him. [32] And a crowd was sitting about him; and they said to him, "**Your mother and your brothers are outside,** asking for you." [33] And **he** replied, "Who are my mother and my brothers?" [34] And looking around on those who sat about him, **he said,** "Here are **my mother and my brothers!** [35] Whoever does the will **of God** is my brother, and sister, and mother."

JOHN

John 15:14 ⇨ Luke 8:21

[14] "You are my friends if you do what I command you."

THOMAS

GThom 99 ⇨ Luke 8:20–21

(99) The disciples said to him, "**Your brothers and Your mother are standing outside.**"

He said to them, "**Those** here **who** do **the** will **of** My Father **are My brothers and My mother.** It is they **who** will enter the Kingdom of My Father."

OTHER

GEbi 5

(5) Moreover they deny that he was a man, evidently on the ground of the word which the Saviour spoke when it was reported to him: "Behold, thy **mother** and thy **brethren** stand without," namely:

Who is **my mother** and who are **my brethren?** And he stretched forth his hand towards his disciples and said: These are **my brethren** and **mother** and sisters, **who do the** will **of my** Father. (Epiphanius, Haer. 30.14.5)

2 Clem 9:11 ⇨ Luke 8:21

[11] For the Lord said, "**My brethren are these who** do **the** will **of** my Father."

LUKE

Luke 8:22–25 (§L33)

[22] One day he got into a boat with his disciples, and he said to them, "Let us go across to the other side of the lake." So they set out, [23] and as they sailed he fell asleep. And a storm of wind came down on the lake, and they were filling with water, and were in danger. [24] And they went and woke him, saying, "Master, Master, we are perishing!" And he awoke and rebuked the wind and the raging waves; and they ceased, and there was a calm. [25] He said to them, "Where is your faith?" And they were afraid, and they marveled, saying to one another, "Who then is this, that he commands even wind and water, and they obey him?"

Ps 65:5–8

[5] By dread deeds thou dost answer us with deliverance,
     O God of our salvation,
who are the hope of all the ends of the earth,
     and of the farthest seas;
[6] who by thy strength hast established the mountains,
     being girded with might;
[7] who dost still the roaring of the seas;
     the roaring of their **waves**,
     the tumult of the peoples;
[8] so that those who dwell at earth's farthest bounds
     are afraid at thy signs;
thou makest the outgoings of the morning and the evening
     to shout for joy.

MATT

Matt 8:23–27 (§M18)

[23] And when he **got into** the **boat, his disciples** followed him. [24] **And** behold, there arose a great **storm on the** sea, so that the boat was being swamped by the waves; but he was asleep. [25] **And they went and woke him, saying,** "Save, Lord; **we are perishing**." [26] And **he said to them,** "Why are you afraid, O men of little **faith**?" Then **he** rose and **rebuked the** winds **and the** sea; **and there was** a great **calm.** [27] **And** the men **marveled, saying,** "What sort of man **is this, that even** winds **and** sea **obey him**?"

Matt 8:18 ⇨ Luke 8:22

[18] Now when Jesus saw great crowds around him, he gave orders to **go** over **to the other side.**

MARK

Mark 4:35–41 (§K22)

[35] On that **day,** when evening had come, **he said to them,** "Let us go across to the other side." [36] And leaving the crowd, **they** took him with them in the **boat,** just as he was. And other boats were with him. [37] **And a** great **storm of wind** arose, **and** the waves beat into the boat, so that the boat was already **filling.** [38] But he was in the stern, **asleep** on the cushion; **and they woke him** and said to him, "Teacher, do you not care if **we** perish?" [39] **And he awoke and rebuked the wind,** and said to the sea, "Peace! Be still!" And the wind **ceased, and there was** a great **calm.** [40] He said to them, "Why are you afraid? Have you no **faith**?" [41] **And they were** filled with awe, and said **to one another,** "**Who then is this, that even wind and sea obey him**?"

JOHN

THOMAS

OTHER

LUKE

SCENE ONE

Luke 8:26–34 (§L34.1)

[26] Then they arrived at the country of the Gerasenes,[a] which is opposite Galilee. [27] And as he stepped out on land, there met him a man from the city who had demons; for a long time he had worn no clothes, and he lived not in a house but among the tombs. [28] When he saw Jesus, he cried out and fell down before him, and said with a loud voice, "What have you to do with me, Jesus, Son of the Most High God? I beseech you, do not torment me." [29] For he had commanded the unclean spirit to come out of the man. (For many a time it had seized him; he was kept under guard, and bound with chains and fetters, but he broke the bonds and was driven by the demon into the desert.) [30] Jesus then asked him, "What is your name?" And he said, "Legion"; for many demons had entered him. [31] And they begged him not to command them to depart into the abyss. [32] Now a large herd of swine was feeding there on the hillside; and they begged him to let them enter these. So he gave them leave. [33] Then the demons came out of the man and entered the swine, and the herd rushed down the steep bank into the lake and were drowned.

[34] When the herdsmen saw what had happened, they fled, and told it in the city and in the country.

SCENE TWO

Luke 8:35–39 (§L34.2)

[35] Then people went out to see what had happened, and they came to Jesus, and found the man from whom the demons had gone, sitting at the feet of Jesus, clothed and in his right mind; and they were afraid. [36] And those who had seen it told them how he who had been possessed with demons was healed. [37] Then all the people of the surrounding country of the Gerasenes asked him to depart from them; for they were seized with great fear; so he got into the boat and returned. [38] The man from whom the demons had gone begged that he might be with him; but he sent him away, saying, [39] "Return to your home, and declare how much God has done for you." And he went away, proclaiming throughout the whole city how much Jesus had done for him.

[a] Text (see Mark 5:1): 𝔓⁷⁵ B D it (in part) *pc*; *Gergesenes* (see Luke 8:37): ℵ L X Θ Ξ *f*¹ 33 *pc*; *Gadarenes* (see Matt 8:28): A K W Δ ᵍʳ Π Ψ *f*¹³ 28 *al*

JOHN

John 2:4 ⇨ Luke 8:28

[4] *And Jesus said to her, "O woman, what have you to do with me? My hour has not yet come."*

MATT

Matt 8:28–33 (§M19.1)

[28] And when he came to the other side, to the country of the Gadarenes, two demoniacs met him, coming out of the tombs, so fierce that no one could pass that way. [29] And behold, they cried out, "What have you to do with us, O Son of God? Have you come here to torment us before the time?" [30] Now a herd of swine was feeding at some distance from them. [31] And the demons begged him, "If you cast us out, send us away into the herd of swine." [32] And he said to them, "Go." So they came out and went into the swine; and behold, the whole herd rushed down the steep bank into the sea, and perished in the waters. [33] The herdsmen fled, and going into the city they told everything, and what had happened to the demoniacs.

Matt 8:34 (§M19.2)

[34] And behold, all the city came out to meet Jesus; and when they saw him, they begged him to leave their neighborhood.

MARK

Mark 5:1–14a (§K23.1)

[1] They came to the other side of the sea, to the country of the Gerasenes. [2] And when he had come out of the boat, there met him out of the tombs a man with an unclean spirit, [3] who lived among the tombs; and no one could bind him any more, even with a chain; [4] for he had often been bound with fetters and chains, but the chains he wrenched apart, and the fetters he broke in pieces; and no one had the strength to subdue him. [5] Night and day among the tombs and on the mountains he was always crying out, and bruising himself with stones. [6] And when he saw Jesus from afar, he ran and worshiped him; [7] and crying out with a loud voice, he said, "What have you to do with me, Jesus, Son of the Most High God? I adjure you by God, do not torment me." [8] For he had said to him, "Come out of the man, you unclean spirit!" [9] And Jesus asked him, "What is your name?" He replied, "My name is Legion; for we are many." [10] And he begged him eagerly not to send them out of the country. [11] Now a great herd of swine was feeding there on the hillside; [12] and they begged him, "Send us to the swine, let us enter them." [13] So he gave them leave. And the unclean spirits came out, and entered the swine; and the herd, numbering about two thousand, rushed down the steep bank into the sea, and were drowned in the sea.

[14] The herdsman fled, and told it in the city and in the country.

Mark 5:14b–20 (§K23.2)

And people came to see what it was that had happened. [15] And they came to Jesus, and saw the demoniac sitting there, clothed and in his right mind, the man who had had the legion; and they were afraid. [16] And those who had seen it told what had happened to the demoniac and to the swine. [17] And they began to beg Jesus to depart from their neighborhood. [18] And as he was getting into the boat, the man who had been possessed with demons begged him that he might be with him. [19] But he refused, and said to him, "Go home to your friends, and tell them how much the Lord has done for you, and how he has had mercy on you." [20] And he went away and began to proclaim in the Decapolis how much Jesus had done for him; and all men marveled.

Mark 1:24 ⇨ Luke 8:28

[24] *and he cried out, "What have you to do with us, Jesus of Nazareth? Have you come to destroy us? I know who you are, the Holy One of God."*

THOMAS

OTHER

LUKE

JAIRUS' DAUGHTER: INTRODUCTION

Luke 8:40–42a (§L35.1)

[40] Now when Jesus returned, the crowd welcomed him, for they were all waiting for him. [41] And there came a man named Jairus, who was a ruler of the synagogue; and falling at Jesus' feet he besought him to come to his house, [42] for he had an only daughter, about twelve years of age, and she was dying.

WOMAN WITH THE INTERNAL HEMORRHAGE

Luke 8:42b–48 (§L35.2)

As he went, the people pressed round him. [43] And a woman who had had a flow of blood for twelve years[a] and could not be healed by any one, [44] came up behind him, and touched the fringe of his garment; and immediately her flow of blood ceased. [45] And Jesus said, "Who was it that touched me?" When all denied it, Peter[b] said, "Master, the multitudes surround you and press upon you!" [46] But Jesus said, "Some one touched me; for I perceive that power has gone forth from me." [47] And when the woman saw that she was not hidden, she came trembling, and falling down before him declared in the presence of all the people why she had touched him, and how she had been immediately healed. [48] And he said to her, "Daughter, your faith has made you well; go in peace."

JAIRUS' DAUGHTER: CONCLUSION

Luke 8:49–56 (§L35.3)

[49] While he was still speaking, a man from the ruler's house came and said, "Your daughter is dead; do not trouble the Teacher any more." [50] But Jesus on hearing this answered him, "Do not fear; only believe, and she shall be well." [51] And when he came to the house, he permitted no one to enter with him, except Peter and John and James, and the father and mother of the child. [52] And all were weeping and bewailing her; but he said, "Do not weep; for she is not dead but sleeping." [53] And they laughed at him, knowing that she was dead. [54] But taking her by the hand he called, saying, "Child, arise." [55] And her spirit returned, and she got up at once; and he directed that something should be given her to eat. [56] And her parents were amazed; but he charged them to tell no one what had happened.

[a] Some witnesses add *and had spent all her living upon physicians:* ℵ A C K L P W X Δ Θ Π Ψ *f*[1] *f*[13] 28 33 *al*; text: 𝔓[75] B (D) (it[d]) *pc*

[b] Some witnesses add *and those who were with him* (see Mark 5:31): ℵ A C D K L P W X Δ Θ Ξ Ψ *f*[1] *f*[13] 28 33 *pm*; text: 𝔓[75] B Π *pc*

Luke 6:19 ⇨ Luke 8:43–47
[19] And all the crowd sought to touch him, for power came forth from him and healed them all.

MATT

Matt 9:18–19 (§M23.1)

[18] While he was thus speaking to them, behold, **a ruler came in and** knelt before him, saying, "My **daughter** has just died; but come and lay your hand on her, and she will live." [19] And Jesus rose and followed him, with his disciples.

Matt 9:20–22 (§M23.2)

[20] **And behold, a woman who had** suffered from a hemorrhage **for twelve years came up behind him and touched the fringe of his garment;** [21] for she said to herself, "If I only touch **his garment,** I **shall be made well.**" [22] Jesus turned, and seeing her **he said,** "Take heart, **daughter; your faith has made you well." And** instantly the woman was **made well.**

Matt 9:23–26 (§M23.3)

[23] And when Jesus **came to** the ruler's **house,** and saw the flute players, and the crowd making a tumult, [24] **he said,** "Depart; **for the girl is not dead but sleeping." And they laughed at him.** [25] But when the crowd had been put outside, he went in and took **her by the hand,** and the girl arose. [26] And the report of this went through all that district.

Matt 14:36 ⇨ Luke 8:43–47
*[36] and besought **him** that they might only touch **the fringe of his garment; and** as many as touched it were made well.*

Luke 7:50 ⇨ Luke 8:48
[50] And he said to the woman, "Your faith has saved you; go in peace."

Luke 17:19 ⇨ Luke 8:48
[19] And he said to him, "Rise and go your way; your faith has made you well."

Luke 18:42 ⇨ Luke 8:48
[42] And Jesus said to him, "Receive your sight; your faith has made you well."

MARK

Mark 5:21–24a (§K24.1)

[21] And **when Jesus** had crossed again in the boat to the other side, a great **crowd** gathered about **him;** and he was beside the sea. [22] Then **came** one of the rulers **of the synagogue, Jairus** by name; and seeing him, he fell **at his feet,** [23] and **besought him,** saying, "My little **daughter** is at the point of death. Come and lay your hands on her, so that she may be made well, and live." [24] And he went with him.

Mark 5:24b–34 (§K24.2)

And a great crowd followed him and thronged about **him.** [25] **And** there was **a woman who had had a flow of blood for twelve years,** [26] and who had suffered much under many physicians, and had spent all that she had, and was no better but rather grew worse. [27] She had heard the reports about Jesus, and **came up behind him** in the crowd **and touched his garment.** [28] For she said, "If I touch even **his** garments, I shall be made well." [29] **And immediately** the hemorrhage **ceased;** and she felt in her body that she was healed of her disease. [30] **And Jesus,** perceiving in himself **that power** had gone forth from him, immediately turned about in the crowd, and **said,** "**Who touched** my garments?" [31] And his disciples **said** to him, "You see **the** crowd pressing around **you,** and yet you say, '**Who touched me?'**" [32] And he looked around to see who had done it. [33] But **the woman,** knowing what had been done to her, **came** in fear and **trembling and** fell **down before him,** and told him the whole truth. [34] **And he said to her, "Daughter, your faith has made you well; go in peace,** and be healed of your disease."

Mark 5:35–43 (§K24.3)

[35] While he was still speaking, there **came from the ruler's house** some who **said, "Your daughter is dead.** Why **trouble the Teacher any** further?" [36] **But** ignoring what they said, Jesus said to the ruler of the synagogue, "**Do not fear, only believe.**" [37] And **he** allowed **no one to** follow **him except Peter and James and John** the brother of James. [38] **When** they **came to the house** of the ruler of the synagogue, he saw a tumult, and people **weeping and** wailing loudly. [39] And when he had entered, **he said to** them, "Why **do** you make a tumult and **weep?** The child is **not dead but sleeping.**" [40] **And they laughed at him.** But he put them all outside, and took **the** child's **father and mother** and those who were with him, and went in where the child was. [41] **Taking her by the hand** he **said** to her, "Talitha cumi"; which means, "Little girl, I say to you, **arise.**" [42] And immediately the girl **got up** and walked (she was **twelve years of age**), and they **were** immediately overcome with amazement. [43] And **he** strictly **charged them** that **no one** should know this, and told them to give **her something to eat.**

Mark 6:56 ⇨ Luke 8:43–47
*[56] And wherever he came, in villages, cities, or country, they laid the sick in the market places, and besought **him** that they might touch even **the fringe of his garment; and** as many as touched it were made well.*

Mark 10:52 ⇨ Luke 8:48
[52] And Jesus said to him, "Go your way; your faith has made you well." And immediately he received his sight and followed him on the way.

JOHN	THOMAS	OTHER

LUKE	MATT	MARK

LUKE

Luke 9:1-6 (§L36) °

¹ **And he called the twelve together and gave them power and authority over all demons and to cure diseases,** ² **and he sent them out to preach the kingdom of God and to heal.** ³ **And he said to them, "Take nothing for your journey, no staff, nor bag, nor bread, nor money; and do not have two tunics.** ⁴ **And whatever house you enter, stay there, and from there depart.** ⁵ **And wherever they do not receive you, when you leave that town shake off the dust from your feet as a testimony against them."** ⁶ **And they departed and went through the villages, preaching the gospel and healing everywhere.**

°Appendix 2 ⇨ §L36

Luke 22:35-36 ⇨ Luke 9:3

³⁵ *And he said to them, "When I sent you out with no purse or **bag** or sandals, did you lack anything?" They said, "**Nothing**." ³⁶ He said to them, "But now, let him who has a purse take it, and likewise a **bag**. And let him who has no sword sell his mantle and buy one."*

Luke 10:11 ⇨ Luke 9:5

¹¹ *"Even **the dust** of **your town** that clings to our feet, we wipe off **against** you; nevertheless know this, that the kingdom of God has come near."*

Cf. Luke 10:1-16 (§L46)

MATT

Matt 10:1 ⇨ Luke 9:1

¹ **And he called** to him his **twelve** disciples **and gave them authority over** unclean spirits, to cast them out, **and to** heal every disease and every infirmity.

Matt 10:9-14 ⇨ Luke 9:3-6

⁹ **"Take** no gold, nor silver, nor copper in your belts, ¹⁰ **no bag** for your journey, nor **two tunics**, nor sandals, nor a **staff**; for the laborer deserves his food. ¹¹ **And whatever** town or village **you enter**, find out who is worthy in it, and **stay** with him until you **depart**. ¹² As **you enter** the **house**, salute it. ¹³ And if the house is worthy, let your peace come upon it; but if it is not worthy, let your peace return to you. ¹⁴ And if any one will **not receive you** or listen to your words, **shake off the dust from your feet** as **you leave that** house or **town**."

MARK

Mark 6:7-13 (§K26)

⁷ **And he called** to him **the twelve**, and began to send **them out** two by two, **and gave them authority over** the unclean spirits. ⁸ He charged **them to take nothing for** their journey except a **staff**; no **bread**, no bag, no **money** in their belts; ⁹ but to wear sandals **and not** put on **two tunics**. ¹⁰ And he said to them, "Where **you enter a house, stay there** until you leave the place. ¹¹ And if any place will not **receive you** and they refuse to hear you, **when you leave, shake off the dust** that is on **your feet** for **a testimony against them**." ¹² So **they went** out and preached that men should repent. ¹³ And they cast out many demons, and anointed with oil many that were sick and healed them.

Mark 3:14-15 ⇨ Luke 9:1

¹⁴ **And he** appointed **twelve**, to be with him, **and** to be **sent out to preach** ¹⁵ **and** have **authority** to cast out **demons**: . . .

JOHN	THOMAS	OTHER

OTHER

Acts 13:57 ⇨ Luke 9:5

⁵¹ *But they shook **off the dust from their feet against them**, and went to Iconium.*

Acts 18:6 ⇨ Luke 9:5

⁶ *And when **they** opposed and reviled him, he shook out his garments and said to them, "Your blood be upon your heads! I am innocent. From now on I will go to the Gentiles."*

LUKE

Luke 9:7–9 (§L37) °

⁷ Now Herod the tetrarch heard of all that was done, and he was perplexed, because it was said by some that John had been raised from the dead, ⁸ by some that Elijah had appeared, and by others that one of the old prophets had risen. ⁹ Herod said, "John I beheaded; but who is this about whom I hear such things?" And he sought to see him.

Luke 9:10–11 (§L38) °°

¹⁰ On their return the apostles told him what they had done. And he took them and withdrew apart to a city called Bethsaida. ¹¹ When the crowds learned it, they followed him; and he welcomed them and spoke to them of the kingdom of God, and cured those who had need of healing.

° Appendix 1 ⇨ §L37

°° Appendices 2 and 3 ⇨ §L38

Luke 13:31–33 ⇨ §L37

³¹ At that very hour some Pharisees came, and said to him, "Get away from here, for Herod wants to kill you." ³² And he said to them, "Go and tell that fox, 'Behold, I cast out demons and perform cures today and tomorrow, and the third day I finish my course. ³³ Nevertheless I must go on my way today and tomorrow and the day following; for it cannot be that a prophet should perish away from Jerusalem.'"

Luke 23:8 ⇨ §L37

⁸ When Herod saw Jesus, he was very glad, for he had long desired to see him, because he had heard about him, and he was hoping to see some sign done by him.

Luke 9:19 ⇨ Luke 9:7–8

¹⁹ And they answered, "John the Baptist; but others say, Elijah; and others, that one of the old prophets has risen."

Luke 10:17 ⇨ Luke 9:10

¹⁷ The seventy returned with joy, saying, "Lord, even the demons are subject to us in your name!"

JOHN

John 1:19–21, 25 ⇨ Luke 9:7–8

¹⁹ And this is the testimony of John, when the Jews sent priests and Levites from Jerusalem to ask him, ²Who are you?" ²⁰ He confessed, he did not deny, but confessed, "I am not the Christ." ²¹ And they asked him, "What then?" Are you Elijah?" He said, "I am not." "Are you the prophet?" And he answered, "No. . . ." ²⁵ They asked him, "Then why are you baptizing, if you are neither the Christ, nor Elijah, nor the prophet?"

MATT

Matt 14:1–12 (§L43) ⇨ §L37

¹ At that time Herod the tetrarch heard about the fame of Jesus; ² and he said to this servants, "This is John the Baptist, he has been raised from the dead; that is why these powers are at work in him." ³ For Herod had seized John and bound him and put him in prison, for the sake of Herodias, his brother Philip's wife; ⁴ because John said to him, "It is not lawful for you to have her. ⁵ And though he wanted to put him to death, he feared the people, because they held him to be a prophet. ⁶ But when Herod's birthday came, the daughter of Herodias danced before the company, and pleased Herod, ⁷ so that he promised with an oath to give her whatever she might ask. ⁸ Prompted by her mother, she said, "Give me the head of John the Baptist here on a platter." ⁹ And the king was sorry, but because of his oaths and his guests he commanded it to be given; ¹⁰ he sent and had John beheaded in the prison, ¹¹ and his head was brought on a platter and given to the girl, and she brought it to her mother. ¹² And his disciples came and took the body and buried it; and they went and told Jesus.

Matt 16:14 ⇨ Luke 9:7–8

¹⁴ And they said, "Some say John the Baptist, others say Elijah, and others Jeremiah or one of the prophets."

Matt 14:13–14 (§M44) ⇨ §L38

¹³ Now when Jesus heard this, he withdrew from there in a boat to a lonely place apart. But when the crowds heard it, they followed him on foot from the towns. ¹⁴ As he went ashore he saw a great throng; and he had compassion on them, and healed their sick.

THOMAS

MARK

Mark 6:14–29 (§K27) ⇨ §L37

¹⁴ King Herod heard of it; for Jesus' name had become known. Some said, "John the baptizer has been raised from the dead; that is why these powers are at work in him." ¹⁵ But others said, "It is Elijah." And others said, "It is a prophet, like one of the prophets of old." ¹⁶ But when Herod heard of it he said, "John, whom I beheaded, has been raised." ¹⁷ For Herod had sent and seized John, and bound him in prison for the sake of Herodias, his brother Philip's wife; because he had married her. For John said to Herod, "It is not lawful for you to have your brother's wife." ¹⁹ And Herodias had a grudge against him, and wanted to kill him. But she could not, ²⁰ for Herod feared John, knowing that he was a righteous and holy man, and kept him safe. When he heard him, he was much perplexed; and yet he heard him gladly. ²¹ But an opportunity came when Herod on his birthday gave a banquet for his courtiers and officers and the leading men of Galilee. ²² For when Herodias' daughter came in and danced, she pleased Herod and his guests; and the king said to the girl, "Ask me for whatever you wish, and I will grant it." ²³ And he vowed to her, "Whatever you ask me, I will give you, even half of my kingdom." ²⁴ And she went out, and said to her mother, "What shall I ask?" And she said, "The head of John the baptizer." ²⁵ And she came immediately with haste to the king, and asked, saying, "I want you to give me at once the head of John the Baptist on a platter." ²⁶ And the king was exceedingly sorry; but because of his oaths and his guests he did not want to break his word to her. ²⁷ And immediately the king sent a soldier of the guard and gave orders to bring his head. He went and beheaded him in the prison, ²⁸ and brought his head on a platter, and gave it to the girl; and the girl gave it to her mother. ²⁹ When his disciples heard of it, they came and took his body, and laid it in a tomb.

Mark 8:28 ⇨ Luke 9:7–8

²⁸ And they told him, "John the Baptist; and others say, Elijah; and others one of the prophets."

Mark 6:30–34 (§K28) ⇨ §L38

³⁰ The apostles returned to Jesus, and told him all that they had done and taught. ³¹ And he said to them, "Come away by yourselves to a lonely place, and rest a while." For many were coming and going, and they had no leisure even to eat. ³² And they went away in the boat to a lonely place by themselves. ³³ Now many saw them going, and knew them, and they ran there on foot from all the towns, and got there ahead of them. ³⁴ As he went ashore he saw a great throng, and he had compassion on them, because they were like sheep without a shepherd; and he began to teach them many things.

OTHER

LUKE	MATT	MARK

Luke 9:12–17 (§L39) °
¹²Now the day began to wear away; and the twelve came and said to him, "Send the crowd away, to go into the villages and country round about, to lodge and get provisions; for we are here in a lonely place." ¹³But he said to them, "You give them something to eat." They said, "We have no more than five loaves and two fish—unless we are to go and buy food for all these people." ¹⁴For there were about five thousand men. And he said to his disciples, "Make them sit down in companies, about fifty each." ¹⁵And they did so, and made them all sit down. ¹⁶And taking the five loaves and the two fish he looked up to heaven, and blessed and broke them, and gave them to the disciples to set before the crowd. ¹⁷And all ate and were satisfied. And they took up what was left over, twelve baskets of broken pieces.

°Appendix 2 ⇨ Luke 9:12

Luke 22:19 ⇨ Luke 9:16
¹⁹And he took bread, and when he had given thanks he broke it and gave it to them, saying, "This is my body which is given for you. Do this in remembrance of me."

Luke 24:30 ⇨ Luke 9:16
³⁰When he was at table with them, he took the bread and blessed, and broke it, and gave it to them.

2 Kgs 4:42–44
⁴²A man came from Baal-shalishah, bringing the man of God bread of the first fruits, twenty **loaves** of barley, and fresh ears of grain in his sack. And Elisha said, "**Give** to the men, that they may **eat**." ⁴³But his servant **said**, "How am I to set this before a hundred **men**?" So he repeated, "**Give them** to the men, that they may eat, for thus says the Lord, 'They shall eat and have some left.'" ⁴⁴So he **set** it **before** them. **And** they **ate**, and had some **left**, according to the word of the Lord.

Matt 14:15–21 (§M45)
¹⁵When it was evening, the disciples **came to him and said,** "This is **a lonely place,** and the day is now over; **send the crowds away to go into the villages** and buy food for themselves." ¹⁶Jesus **said,** "They need not go away; **you give them something to eat.**" ¹⁷**They said** to him, "**We have** only **five loaves** here **and two fish.**" ¹⁸And he said, "Bring them here to me." ¹⁹Then he ordered the crowds to **sit down** on the grass; **and taking the five loaves and the two fish he looked up to heaven, and blessed, and broke and gave** the loaves **to the disciples,** and **the disciples** gave them **to the** crowds. ²⁰**And they all ate and were satisfied. And they took up twelve baskets** full **of the broken pieces left over.** ²¹And those who ate were about five thousand **men,** besides women and children.

Matt 15:32–39 (§M52)
³²Then Jesus called his disciples to him and **said,** "I have compassion on the crowd, because they have been with me now three days, and have nothing **to eat**; and I am unwilling to **send** them **away** hungry, lest they faint on the way." ³³And the disciples **said** to him, "Where **are we** to get bread enough in the desert to feed so great a crowd?" ³⁴And Jesus **said to them,** "How many loaves have you?" **They said,** "Seven, and a few small **fish.**" ³⁵And commanding the crowd to **sit down** on the ground, ³⁶he took the seven **loaves and the fish,** and having given thanks **he broke them and gave them to the disciples,** and **the disciples** gave them **to the** crowds. ³⁷**And they all ate and were satisfied; and they** took up seven **baskets** full **of the broken pieces left over.** ³⁸Those who ate **were** four **thousand men,** besides women and children. ³⁹And sending away the crowds, he got into the boat and went to the region of Magadan.

Mark 6:35–44 (§K29)
³⁵And when it grew late, his disciples **came to him and said,** "This is **a lonely place,** and the hour is now late; ³⁶**send** them **away, to go into the country and villages round about** and buy themselves something to eat." ³⁷**But he** answered **them,** "**You give them something to eat.**" And **they said** to him, "Shall **we go and buy** two hundred denarii worth of bread, and give it to them to eat?" ³⁸**And he said to** them, "**How many loaves have you? Go and see.**" And when they had found out, **they said,** "**Five, and two fish.**" ³⁹Then he commanded them all to **sit down** by companies upon the green grass. ⁴⁰So they sat **down** in groups, by hundreds and by fifties. ⁴¹**And taking the five loaves and the two fish he looked up to heaven, and blessed, and broke** the loaves, **and gave them to the disciples to set before the** people; and **he** divided **the two fish** among them all. ⁴²**And** they **all ate and were satisfied.** ⁴³**And they took up twelve baskets full of broken pieces** and of the fish. ⁴⁴And those who ate the loaves **were five thousand men.**

Mark 8:1–10 (§K37)
¹In those days, when again a great crowd had gathered, and they had nothing to eat, he called his disciples to him, and **said to them,** ²"I have compassion on the crowd, because they have been with me now three days, and have nothing **to eat**; ³and if I **send** them **away** hungry to their homes, they will faint on the way; and some of them have come a long way." ⁴And his disciples answered him, "How can one feed these men with bread here in the desert?" ⁵And **he** asked **them,** "How many loaves have you?" **They said,** "Seven." ⁶So **he** commanded the crowd to **sit down** on the ground; **and** he took **the** seven **loaves,** and having given thanks **he broke them and gave them to his disciples to set before the** people; and they **set** them **before the crowd.** ⁷And they had a few small **fish**; and having **blessed them,** he commanded that these also should be **set before** them. ⁸**And they** ate, **and were** satisfied; and **they took up** the broken pieces left over, seven **baskets** full. ⁹**And there were about** four **thousand** people. ¹⁰And he sent them away and immediately he got into the boat with his disciples, and went to the district of Dalmanutha.

Mark 14:22 ⇨ Luke 9:16
²²And as they were eating, he took bread, and blessed, and broke it, and gave it to them, and said, "Take; this is my body."

JOHN	THOMAS	OTHER

John 6:1–15 (§J10)

[1] After this Jesus went to the other side of the Sea of Galilee, which is the Sea of Tiberias. [2] And a multitude followed him, because they saw the signs which he did on those who were diseased. [3] Jesus went up on the mountain, and there sat down with his disciples. [4] Now the Passover, the feast of the Jews, was at hand. [5] Lifting up his eyes, then, and seeing that a multitude was coming to him, Jesus **said** to Philip, "How are **we to buy** bread, so that **these people** may **eat**?" [6] This he said to test him, for he himself knew what he would do. [7] Philip answered him, "Two hundred denarii would not **buy** enough bread for each of them to get a little." [8] One of his disciples, Andrew, Simon Peter's brother, **said** to him, [9] "There is a lad here who has **five** barley **loaves and two fish**; but what are they among so many?" [10] Jesus **said**, "**Make** the people **sit down**." Now there was much grass in the place; **so** the men sat **down**, in number **about five thousand**. [11] Jesus then took **the loaves**, and when **he** had given thanks, **he** distributed **them to** those who were seated; so also the **fish**, as much as they wanted. [12] **And** when they had eaten their fill, he told his disciples, "Gather **up** the fragments **left over**, that nothing may be lost." [13] So **they** gathered them **up** and filled **twelve baskets** with fragments from the **five** barley **loaves**, left by those who had eaten. [14] When the people saw the sign which he had done, they said, "This is indeed the prophet who is to come into the world!"

[15] Perceiving then that they were about to come and take him by force to make him king, Jesus withdrew again to the mountain by himself.

Acts 27:35 ⇨ Luke 9:16
[35] *And when* **he** *had said this,* **he** *took bread, and giving thanks to God in the presence of all he broke it and began to eat.*

LUKE	MATT	MARK

LUKE

Luke 9:18–22 (§L40.1)

[18] Now it happened that as he was praying alone the disciples were with him; and he asked them, "Who do the people say that I am?" [19] And they answered, "John the Baptist; but others say, Elijah; and others, that one of the old prophets has risen." [20] And he said to them, "But who do you say that I am?" And Peter answered, "The Christ of God." [21] But he charged and commanded them to tell this to no one, [22] saying, "The Son of man must suffer many things, and be rejected by the elders and chief priests and scribes, and be killed, and on the third day be raised."

Luke 9:43b–45 (§L43.1)

But while they were all marveling at everything he did, he said to his disciples, [44] "Let these words sink into your ears; for **the Son of man** is to be delivered into the hands of men." [45] But they did not understand this saying, and it was concealed from them, that they should not perceive it; and they were afraid to ask him about this saying.

Luke 18:31–34 (§L78)

[31] And taking the twelve, he said to them, "Behold, we are going up to Jerusalem, and everything that is written of **the Son of man** by the prophets will be accomplished. [32] For he will **be** delivered to the Gentiles, and will be mocked and shamefully treated and spit upon; [33] they will scourge him **and** kill him, **and on the third day** he will rise." [34] But they understood none of these things; this saying was hid from them, and they did not grasp what was said.

Luke 9:7–8 ⇨ Luke 9:19

[7] *Now Herod the tetrarch heard of all that was done, and he was perplexed, because it was said by some that* **John** *had been raised from the dead,* [8] *by some that* **Elijah** *had appeared,* **and by others that** *one of the old prophets had risen.*

Luke 17:25 ⇨ Luke 9:22

[25] *"But first he* **must suffer many things and be rejected by this generation.***"*

Luke 22:22 ⇨ Luke 9:22

[22] *"For* **the Son of man** *goes as it has been determined; but woe to that man by whom he is betrayed!"*

Luke 24:6–8 ⇨ Luke 9:22

[6] *"Remember how he told you, while he was still in Galilee,* [7] *that* **the Son of man must** *be delivered into the hands of sinful men,* **and be crucified, and on the third day rise."** [8] *And they remembered his words,* . . .

Luke 24:26 ⇨ Luke 9:22

[26] *"Was it not necessary that the Christ should* **suffer** *these* **things** *and enter into his glory?"*

MATT

Matt 16:13–20 (§M55)

[13] Now when Jesus came into the district of Caesarea Philippi, **he asked** his disciples, **"Who do** men **say that** the Son of man is?" [14] **And they** said, "Some say **John the Baptist**, others say **Elijah, and** others Jeremiah or **one of the prophets."** [15] **He said to them, "But who do you say that I am?"** [16] Simon **Peter** replied, "You are **the Christ**, the Son **of** the living **God."** [17] And Jesus answered him, "Blessed are you, Simon Bar-Jona! For flesh and blood has not revealed this to you, but my Father who is in heaven. [18] And I tell you, you are Peter, and on this rock I will build my church, and the powers of death shall not prevail against it. [19] I will give you the keys of the kingdom of heaven, and whatever you bind on earth shall be bound in heaven, and whatever you loose on earth shall be loosed in heaven." [20] Then **he** strictly **charged** the disciples **to tell no one** that he was the Christ.

Matt 16:21–23 (§M56)

[21] From that time Jesus began to show his disciples that he must go to Jerusalem and **suffer many things** from **the elders and chief priests and scribes, and be killed, and on the third day be raised**. [22] And Peter took him and began to rebuke him, saying, "God forbid, Lord! This shall never happen to you." [23] But he turned and said to Peter, "Get behind me, Satan! You are a hindrance to me; for you are not on the side of God, but of men."

Matt 17:22–23 (§M60)

[22] **And he said to** the disciples, "The days are coming when you will desire to see one of the days of **the Son of man**, and you will not see it. [23] And they will say to you, 'Lo, there!' or 'Lo, here!' Do not go, do not follow them."

Matt 20:17–19 (§M68)

[17] But **he** looked at **them** and said, "What then is this that is written:

'The very stone which the builders rejected has become the head of the corner'?

[18] Every one who falls on that stone will be broken to pieces; but when it falls on any one it will crush him."

[19] The **scribes and** the **chief priests** tried to lay hands on him at that very hour, but they feared the people; for they perceived that he had told this parable against them.

Luke 24:46 ⇨ Luke 9:22

[46] *and said to them, "Thus it is written, that the Christ should* **suffer and on the third day rise** *from the dead, . . ."*

MARK

Mark 8:27–30 (§K41)

[27] And Jesus went on with his **disciples**, to the villages of Caesarea Philippi; and on the way **he asked** his disciples, **"Who do** men **say that I am?"** [28] **And they** told him, **"John the Baptist; and others say, Elijah; and others one of the prophets."** [29] **And he** asked **them, "But who do you say that I am?" Peter answered** him, "You are **the Christ."** [30] And **he charged them** to **tell no one** about him.

Mark 8:31–33 (§K42)

[31] And he began to teach them that **the Son of man must suffer many things, and be rejected by the elders and** the **chief priests and** the **scribes, and be killed, and** after three days rise again. [32] And he said this plainly. And Peter took him, and began to rebuke him. [33] But turning and seeing his disciples, he rebuked Peter, and said, "Get behind me, Satan! For you are not on the side of God, but of men."

Mark 9:30–32 (§K46)

[30] They went on from there and passed through Galilee. And he would not have any one know it; [31] for he was teaching his **disciples**, saying to **them, "The Son of man** will **be** delivered into the hands of men, **and** they will kill him; **and** when he is **killed**, after three days he will rise."

Mark 10:32–34 (§K54)

[32] And they were on the road, going up to Jerusalem, and Jesus was walking ahead of them; and they were amazed, and those who followed were afraid. And taking the twelve again, he began to tell them what was to happen to him, [33] **saying**, "Behold, we are going up to Jerusalem; and **the Son of man** will **be** delivered to the **chief priests and** the **scribes**, and they will condemn him to death, and deliver him to **the** Gentiles; [34] **and** they will mock him, and spit upon him, and scourge him, **and** kill him; **and** after three days he will rise."

JOHN	THOMAS	OTHER

JOHN

John 1:49 ⇨ Luke 9:20

[49] *Nathanael* **answered** *him, "Rabbi, you are the Son of God! You are the King of Israel!"*

John 6:68–69 ⇨ Luke 9:20

[68] *Simon* **Peter** **answered** *him, "Lord, to whom shall we go? You have the words of eternal life;* [69] *and we have believed, and have come to know, that you are* **the Holy One** *of* **God**.*"*

THOMAS

GThom 13

(13) Jesus said to His disciples, "Compare me to someone and tell Me whom **I am** *like."*

Simon **Peter** *said to Him, "You are like a righteous angel."*

Matthew said to Him, "You are like a wise philosopher."

Thomas said to Him, "Master, my mouth is wholly incapable of saying whom You are like."

Jesus said, "I am not your master. Because you have drunk, you have become intoxicated from the bubbling spring which I have measured out."

And He took him and withdrew and told him three things. When Thomas returned to his companions, they asked him, "What did Jesus say to you?"

Thomas said to them, "If I tell you one of the things which he told me, you will pick up stones and throw them at me; a fire will come out of the stones and burn you up."

OTHER

ApocJa 5:31–6:11

"Scorn death, therefore, and take concern for life. Remember my cross and my death and you will [35] *live."*

And I answered and said to him: "Lord, do not mention to us the cross and the death, for they are far from you."

The Lord answered and said: "Truly I say to you (pl.), none will be saved unless they believe in my cross. [5] *[But] those who have believed in my cross, theirs is the Kingdom of God. Therefore, become seekers for death, just as the dead who seek for life,* [10] *for that for which they seek is revealed to them."*

LUKE

Luke 9:23–27 (§L40.2)

23 And he said to all, "If any man would come after me, let him deny himself and take up his cross daily and follow me. 24 For whoever would save his life will lose it; and whoever loses his life for my sake, he will save it. 25 For what does it profit a man if he gains the whole world and loses or forfeits himself? 26 For whoever is ashamed of me and of my words, of him will the Son of man be ashamed when he comes in his glory and the glory of the Father and of the holy angels. 27 But I tell you truly, there are some standing here who will not taste death before they see the kingdom of God."

●**Luke 14:27** ⇨ Luke 9:23

27 "Whoever does not bear his own cross and come after me, cannot be my disciple."

●**Luke 17:33** ⇨ Luke 9:24

33 "Whoever seeks to gain his life will lose it, but whoever loses his life will preserve it."

●**Luke 12:9** ⇨ Luke 9:26

9 "but he who denies me before men will be denied before the angels of God."

Luke 21:32 ⇨ Luke 9:27

32 *"Truly, I say to you, this generation will not pass away till all has taken place."*

MATT

Matt 16:24–28 (§M57)

24 Then Jesus told his disciples, "If any man would come after me, let him deny himself and take up his cross and follow me. 25 For whoever would save his life will lose it, and whoever loses his life for my sake will find it. 26 For what will it profit a man, if he gains the whole world and forfeits his life? Or what shall a man give in return for his life? 27 For the Son of man is to come with his angels in the glory of his Father, and then he will repay every man for what he has done. 28 Truly, I say to you, there are some standing here who will not taste death before they see the Son of man coming in his kingdom."

Matt 10:38–39 ⇨ Luke 9:23–24

38 "and he who does not take his cross and follow me is not worthy of me. 39 He who finds his life will lose it, and he who loses his life for my sake will find it."

Matt 10:33 ⇨ Luke 9:26

33 "but whoever denies me before men, I also will deny before my Father who is in heaven."

MARK

Mark 8:34–9:1 (§K43)

34 And he called to him the multitude with his disciples, and said to them, "If any man would come after me, let him deny himself and take up his cross and follow me. 35 For whoever would save his life will lose it; and whoever loses his life for my sake and the gospel's will save it. 36 For what does it profit a man, to gain the whole world and forfeit his life? 37 For what can a man give in return for his life? 38 For whoever is ashamed of me and of my words in this adulterous and sinful generation, of him will the Son of man also be ashamed, when he comes in the glory of his Father with the holy angels." 9 1 And he said to them, "Truly, I say to you, there are some standing here who will not taste death before they see that the kingdom of God has come with power."

JOHN

John 12:25 ⇨ Luke 9:24

25 "He who loves his life loses it, and he who hates his life in this world will keep it for eternal life."

THOMAS

GThom 55 ⇨ Luke 9:23

(55) Jesus said, "Whoever does not hate his father and his mother cannot become a disciple to Me. And whoever does not hate his brothers and sisters and take up his cross in My way will not be worthy of Me."

GThom 101 ⇨ Luke 9:23

(101) <Jesus said,> "Whoever does not hate his father and his mother as I do cannot become a disciple to Me. And whoever does [not] love his father and his mother as I do cannot become a [disciple] to Me. For My mother [gave me falsehood], but [My] true [Mother] gave me life."

OTHER

Luke	Matt	Mark

Luke

Luke 9:28–36 (§L41)

²⁸Now about eight days after these sayings he took with him Peter and John and James, and went up on the mountain to pray. ²⁹And as he was praying, the appearance of his countenance was altered, and his raiment became dazzling white. ³⁰And behold, two men talked with him, Moses and Elijah, ³¹who appeared in glory and spoke of his departure, which he was to accomplish at Jerusalem. ³²Now Peter and those who were with him were heavy with sleep, and when they wakened they saw his glory and the two men who stood with him. ³³And as the men were parting from him, Peter said to Jesus, "Master, it is well that we are here; let us make three booths, one for you and one for Moses and one for Elijah"—not knowing what he said. ³⁴As he said this, a cloud came and overshadowed them; and they were afraid as they entered the cloud. ³⁵And a voice came out of the cloud, saying, "This is my Son, my Chosen;ᵃ listen to him!" ³⁶And when the voice had spoken, Jesus was found alone. And they kept silence and told no one in those days anything of what they had seen.

ᵃ Some witnesses read *my Beloved* (see Mark 9:7, Luke 3:22): A C* K P W X △ Π *f*¹³ 28 33 *al;* text 𝔓⁴⁵ 𝔓⁷⁵ ℵ B L ⊖ Ξ *f*¹ *pc*

Luke 3:22 ⇨ Luke 9:34–35
²²*and the Holy Spirit descended upon him in bodily form, as a dove, and a voice came from heaven, "Thou art my beloved Son; with thee I am well pleased."*

Ps 2:7 ⇨ Luke 9:35
⁷I will tell of the decree of the Lord:
He said to me, "You are **my son**,
   today I have begotten you."

Isa 42:1 ⇨ Luke 9:35
¹Behold **my** servant, whom I uphold,
   my chosen, in whom my soul delights;
I have put my Spirit upon **him**,
   he will bring forth justice to the nations.

Matt

Matt 17:1–13 (§M58)

¹And after six **days** Jesus **took with him** Peter and James and John his brother, and led them **up** a **high mountain** apart. ²**And he was** transfigured before them, and his face shone like the sun, **and his** garments **became white** as light. ³**And behold**, there **appeared** to them **Moses and Elijah**, talking **with him**. ⁴**And** Peter said to Jesus, "Lord, **it is well that we are here**; if you wish, I will **make three booths** here, **one for you and one for Moses and one for Elijah**." ⁵**He** was still speaking, when lo, a bright **cloud overshadowed them, and a voice** from **the cloud** said, **"This is my** beloved **Son**, with whom I am well pleased; **listen to him."** ⁶**When** the disciples heard this, they fell on their faces, and were filled with awe. ⁷But Jesus came and touched them, saying, "Rise, and have no fear." ⁸**And when** they lifted up their eyes, they saw no one but **Jesus** only.

⁹**And** as **they** were coming down the mountain, Jesus commanded them, "Tell **no one** the vision, until the Son of man is raised from the dead." ¹⁰And the disciples asked him, "Then why do the scribes say that first **Elijah** must come?" ¹¹He replied, **"Elijah** does come, and he is to restore all things; ¹²but I tell you that **Elijah** has already come, and they did not know him, but did to him whatever they pleased. So also the **Son** of man will suffer at their hands." ¹³Then the disciples understood that he was speaking to them of John the Baptist.

Matt 3:16–17 ⇨ Luke 9:34–35
¹⁶*And when Jesus was baptized, he went up immediately from the water, and behold, the heavens were opened and he saw the Spirit of God descending like a dove, and alighting on him;* ¹⁷*and lo, a voice from heaven, saying, "This is my beloved Son, with whom I am well pleased."*

Mark

Mark 9:2–8 (§K44.1)

²And after six **days** Jesus **took with him** Peter and James and John, and led them **up** a high **mountain** apart by themselves; **and he** was transfigured before them, ³**and his** garments **became** glistening, intensely **white**, as no fuller on earth could bleach them. ⁴**And** there **appeared** to them **Elijah** with **Moses**; and they were talking to Jesus. ⁵and **Peter said** to **Jesus**, "Master, it is well that we are here; let us make three booths, one for you and one for Moses and one for Elijah." ⁶For **he** did **not** know **what** to say, for they were exceedingly afraid. ⁷And **a cloud overshadowed them, and a voice came out of the cloud, "This is my** beloved **Son; listen to him."** ⁸**And** suddenly looking around they no longer saw any one with them but **Jesus** only.

Mark 1:10–11 ⇨ Luke 9:34–35
¹⁰*And when he came up out of the water, immediately he saw the heavens opened and the spirit descending upon him like a dove;* ¹¹*and a voice came from heaven, "Thou art my beloved Son; with thee I am well pleased."*

John	Thomas	Other

John

John 1:14 ⇨ Luke 9:32
¹⁴*And the Word became flesh and dwelt among us, full of grace and truth; we have beheld **his glory, glory** as of the only Son from the Father.*

LUKE	MATT	MARK

Luke 9:37–43a (§L42)

[37] On the next day, when they had come down from the mountain, a great crowd met him. [38] And behold, a man from the crowd cried, "Teacher, I beg you to look upon my son, for he is my only child; [39] and behold, a spirit seizes him, and he suddenly cries out; it convulses him till he foams, and shatters him, and will hardly leave him. [40] And I begged your disciples to cast it out, but they could not." [41] Jesus answered, "O faithless and perverse generation, how long am I to be with you and bear with you? Bring your son here." [42] While he was coming, the demon tore him and convulsed him. But Jesus rebuked the unclean spirit, and healed the boy, and gave him back to his father. [43] And all were astonished at the majesty of God.

Matt 17:14–18 (§M59.1)

[14] And when they came to the crowd, a man came up to him and kneeling before him said, [15] "Lord, have mercy on my son, for he is an epileptic and he suffers terribly; for often he falls into the fire, and often into the water. [16] And I brought him to your disciples, and they could not heal him." [17] And Jesus answered, "O faithless and perverse generation, how long am I to be with you? How long am I to bear with you? Bring him here to me." [18] And Jesus rebuked him, and the demon came out of him, and the boy was cured instantly.

Matt 17:19–20 (§M59.2)

[19] Then the disciples came to Jesus privately and said, "Why could we not cast it out?" [20] He said to them, "Because of your little faith. For truly I say to you, if you have faith as a grain of mustard seed, you will say to this mountain, 'Move from here to there,' and it will move; and nothing will be impossible to you."

Mark 9:14–27 (§K45.1)

[14] And when they came to the disciples, they saw a great crowd about them, and scribes arguing with them. [15] And immediately all the crowd, when they saw him, were greatly amazed, and ran up to him and greeted him. [16] And he asked them, "What are you discussing with them?" [17] And one of the crowd answered him, "Teacher, I brought my son to you, for he has a dumb spirit; [18] and wherever it seizes him, it dashes him down; and he foams and grinds his teeth and becomes rigid; and I asked your disciples to cast it out, and they were not able." [19] And he answered them, "O faithless generation, how long am I to be with you? How long am I to bear with you? Bring him to me." [20] And they brought the boy to him; and when the spirit saw him, immediately it convulsed the boy, and he fell on the ground and rolled about, foaming at the mouth. [21] And Jesus asked his father, "How long has he had this?" And he said, "From childhood. [22] And it has often cast him into the fire and into the water, to destroy him; but if you can do anything, have pity on us and help us." [23] And Jesus said to him, "If you can! All things are possible to him who believes." [24] Immediately the father of the child cried out and said, "I believe; help my unbelief!" [25] And when Jesus saw that a crowd came running together, he rebuked the unclean spirit, saying to it, "You dumb and deaf spirit, I command you, come out of him, and never enter him again." [26] And after crying out and convulsing him terribly, it came out, and the boy was like a corpse; so that most of them said, "He is dead." [27] But Jesus took him by the hand and lifted him up, and he arose.

Mark 9:28–29 (§K45.2)

[28] And when he had entered the house, his disciples asked him privately, "Why could we not cast it out?" [29] And he said to them, "This kind cannot be driven out by anything but prayer."

JOHN	THOMAS	OTHER

| LUKE | MATT | MARK |

LUKE

Luke 9:43b–45 (§L43.1)

But while they were all marveling at everything he did, he said to his disciples, ⁴⁴"Let these words sink into your ears; for the Son of man is to be delivered into the hands of men." ⁴⁵But they did not understand this saying, and it was concealed from them, that they should not perceive it; and they were afraid to ask him about this saying.

Luke 9:18–22 (§L40.1)

¹⁸Now it happened that as he was praying alone the **disciples** were with him; and **he** asked them, "Who do the people say that I am?" ¹⁹And they answered, "John the Baptist; but others say, Elijah; and others, that one of the old prophets has risen." ²⁰And he said to them, "But who do you say that I am?" And Peter answered, "The Christ of God." ²¹But he charged and commanded them to tell this to no one, ²²saying, "**The Son of man** must suffer many things, and be rejected by the elders and chief priests and scribes, and be killed, and on the third day be raised."

Luke 18:31–34 (§L78)

³¹And taking the twelve, **he said to** them, "Behold, we are going up to Jerusalem, and everything that is written of **the Son of man** by the prophets **will be** accomplished. ³²For he will **be delivered** to the Gentiles, and will be mocked and shamefully treated and spit upon; ³³they will scourge him and kill him, and on the third day he will rise." ³⁴**But they** understood none of these things; this saying was hid **from them**, and **they** did **not** grasp what was said.

Luke 17:25 ⇨ Luke 9:44

²⁵*"But first he must suffer many things and be rejected by this generation."*

Luke 22:22 ⇨ Luke 9:44

²²*"For the son of man goes as it has been determined; but woe to that man by whom he is betrayed!"*

Luke 24:6–8 ⇨ Luke 9:44

⁶*"Remember how he told you, while he was still in Galilee, ⁷that* **the Son of man must be delivered into the hands of sinful men, and crucified, and on the third day rise."** ⁸*And they remembered his words, . . .*

Luke 24:26 ⇨ Luke 9:44

²⁶*"Was it not necessary that* **the Christ should suffer these things and enter into his glory?"**

MATT

Matt 17:22–23 (§M60)

²²As they were gathering in Galilee, Jesus said to them, "**The Son of man is to be delivered into the hands of men,** ²³and they will kill him, and he will be raised on the third day." And they were greatly distressed.

Matt 16:21–23 (§M56)

²¹From that time Jesus began to show **his disciples** that he must go to Jerusalem and suffer many things from **the** elders and chief priests and scribes, and be killed, and on the third day be raised. ²²And Peter took him and began to rebuke him, saying, "God forbid, Lord! This shall never happen to you." ²³But he turned and said to Peter, "Get behind me, Satan! You are a hindrance to me; for you are not on the side of God, but of men."

Matt 20:17–19 (§M68)

¹⁷And as Jesus was going up to Jerusalem, he took the twelve **disciples** aside, and on the way **he said to** them, ¹⁸"Behold, we are going up to Jerusalem; and **the Son of man** will **be delivered** to **the** chief priests and scribes, and they will condemn him to death, ¹⁹and deliver him to the Gentiles to be mocked and scourged and crucified, and he will be raised on the third day."

Luke 24:46 ⇨ Luke 9:44

⁴⁶*and said to them, "Thus it is written, that the Christ should suffer and on the third day rise from the dead, . . ."*

Luke 18:34 ⇨ Luke 9:45

³⁴*But they understood none of these things; this saying was hid from them, and they did not grasp what was said.*

Luke 24:25–27 ⇨ Luke 9:45

²⁵*And he said to them, "O foolish men, and slow of heart to believe all that the prophets have spoken! ²⁶Was it not necessary that the Christ should suffer these things and enter into his glory?" ²⁷And beginning with Moses and all the prophets, he interpreted to them in all the scriptures the things concerning himself.*

Luke 24:44–45 ⇨ Luke 9:45

⁴⁴*Then he said to them, "These are my words which I spoke to you, while I was still with you, that everything written about me in the law of Moses and the prophets and the psalms must be fulfilled." Then he opened their minds to* **understand** *the scriptures, . . .*

MARK

Mark 9:30–32 (§K46)

³⁰They went on from there and passed through Galilee. And he would not have any one know it; ³¹for **he** was teaching his **disciples,** saying to them, "**The Son of man** will **be delivered into the hands of men,** and they will kill him; and when he is killed, after three days he will rise." ³²**But they did not understand** the **saying, and they were afraid to ask him.**

Mark 8:31–33 (§K42)

³¹And **he** began **to** teach them that **the Son of man** must suffer many things, and **be** rejected by **the** elders and the chief priests and the scribes, and be killed, and after three days rise again. ³²And he said this plainly. And Peter took him, and began to rebuke him. ³³But turning and seeing his disciples, he rebuked Peter, and said, "Get behind me, Satan! For you are not on the side of God, but of men."

Mark 10:32–34 (§54)

³²And **they were** on the road, going up to Jerusalem, and Jesus was walking ahead of them; and **they were** amazed, and those who followed were afraid. And taking the twelve again, **he** began to tell them what was to happen to him, ³³saying, "Behold, we are going up to Jerusalem; and **the Son of man** will **be delivered** to the chief priests and the scribes, and they will condemn him to death, and deliver him to the Gentiles; ³⁴and they will mock him, and spit upon him, and scourge him, and kill him; and after three days he will rise."

| JOHN | THOMAS | OTHER |

L43

S13: L41–43

PASSION AND POSITION

ON THE MOUNTAIN

Luke 9:43b–50

Luke 9:28–50

365

LUKE

Luke 9:46–50 (§L43.2)

⁴⁶ And an argument arose among them as to which of them was the greatest. ⁴⁷ But when Jesus perceived the thought of their hearts, he took a child and put him by his side, ⁴⁸ and said to them, "Whoever receives this child in my name receives me, and whoever receives me receives him who sent me; for he who is least among you all is the one who is great."

⁴⁹ John answered, "Master, we saw a man casting out demons in your name, and we forbade him, because he does not follow with us." ⁵⁰ But Jesus said to him, "Do not forbid him; for he that is not against you is for you."

Luke 11:23 ⇨ Luke 9:50

²³ "He who **is not** with me is **against** me, and he who does not gather with me scatters."

Luke 22:24–27 ⇨ Luke 9:46–48

²⁴ *A dispute also **arose among them**, **which of them was to be regarded as the greatest**. ²⁵ And he said to them, "The kings of the Gentiles exercise lordship over them; and those in authority over them are called benefactors. ²⁶ But not so with you; rather let the greatest **among you** become as the youngest, and the leader as one who serves. ²⁷ which is the greater, one who sits at table, or one who serves? Is it not the one who sits at table? But I am among you as one who serves."*

Luke 10:16 ⇨ Luke 9:48a

¹⁶ *"He who hears you hears **me**, and he who rejects you rejects me, and he who rejects me rejects **him who sent me**."*

JOHN

John 12:44–45 ⇨ Luke 9:48

⁴⁴ *And Jesus cried out and said, "He who believes in me, believes not in me but in him who sent me. ⁴⁵ And he who sees me sees him who sent me."*

John 13:20 ⇨ Luke 9:48

²⁰ *"Truly, truly, I say to you, he who receives any one whom I send receives me; and he who receives me receives him who sent me."*

MATT

Matt 18:1–10 (§M62.1)

¹ At that time the disciples came to Jesus, saying, "Who is **the greatest** in the kingdom of heaven? ² And calling to him **a child**, he **put him** in the midst of them, ³ **and said**, "Truly, I say to you, unless you turn and become like children, you will never enter the kingdom of heaven. ⁴ Whoever humbles himself like this child, he is the greatest in the kingdom of heaven.

⁵ **"Whoever receives** one such **child in my name receives me**; ⁶ but **whoever** causes one of these little ones who believe in me to sin, it would be better for him to have a great millstone fastened round his neck and to be drowned in the depth of the sea.

⁷ "Woe to the world for temptations to sin! For it is necessary that temptations come, but woe to the man by whom the temptation comes! ⁸ And if your hand or your foot causes you to sin, cut it off and throw it away; it is better for you to enter life maimed or lame than with two hands or two feet to be thrown into the eternal fire. ⁹ And if your eye causes you to sin, pluck it out and throw it away; it is better for you to enter life with one eye than with two eyes to be thrown into the hell of fire.

¹⁰ "See that you do not despise one of these little ones; for I tell you that in heaven their angels always behold the face of my Father who is in heaven."

Matt 20:24–28 ⇨ Luke 9:48b

²⁴ And when the ten heard it, they were indignant at the two brothers. ²⁵ But Jesus called **them** to him and **said**, "You know that the rulers of the Gentiles lord it over them, and their great men exercise authority over them. ²⁶ It shall not be so among you; but whoever would be **great among you** must be your servant, ²⁷ and whoever would be first among you must be your slave; ²⁸ even as the Son of man came not to be served but to serve, and to give his life as a ransom for many."

Matt 23:11–12 ⇨ Luke 9:48b

¹¹ **"He who** is greatest **among you** shall be your servant; ¹² whoever exalts himself will be humbled, and whoever humbles himself will be exalted."

Matt 12:30 ⇨ Luke 9:50

³⁰ **"He** who **is not** with me is against me, and he who does not gather with me scatters."

Matt 10:40 ⇨ Luke 9:48a

⁴⁰ *"He who receives you receives me, and he who receives me receives him who sent me."*

THOMAS

GThom 12 ⇨ Luke 9:46

(12) The disciples said to Jesus, "We know that You will depart from us. Who is to be our leader?"

Jesus said to them, "Wherever you are, you are to go to James the righteous, for whose sake heaven and earth came into being."

MARK

Mark 9:33–37 (§K47)

³³ **And** they came to Capernaum; and when he was in the house he asked **them**, "What were you discussing on the way?" ³⁴ But they were silent; for on the way they had discussed with one another who **was the greatest**. ³⁵ And he sat down and called the twelve; **and he said to them**, "If any one would be first, he must be last of all and servant of all." ³⁶ And **he took a child, and put him** in the midst of them; and taking him in his arms, he **said to them**, ³⁷ "Who**ever receives** one such **child in my name receives me; and whoever receives me, receives** not me but **him who sent me.**"

Mark 9:38–41 (§K48)

³⁸ **John** said to him, "Teacher, **we saw a man casting out demons in your name, and we forbade him,** because he **was not following us.**" ³⁹ **But Jesus said, "Do not forbid him; for** no one who does a mighty work in my name will be able soon after to speak evil of me. ⁴⁰ **For he that is not against** us **is for** us. ⁴¹ For truly, I say to you, whoever gives you a cup of water to drink because you bear the name of Christ, will by no means lose his reward."

Mark 10:13–16 (§K52)

¹³ *And they were bringing children to him, that he might touch them; ¹³ and the disciples rebuked them. ¹⁴ **But when Jesus** saw it he was indignant, and **said to them**, "Let the children come to me, do not hinder them; for to such belongs the kingdom of God. ¹⁵ Truly, I say to you, **whoever** does not receive the kingdom of God like a **child** shall not enter it." ¹⁶ And **he took them in his arms and blessed them, laying his hands upon them.*

OTHER

POxy1224 2 ⇨ Luke 9:50

(2) And pray for your enemies. **For he** who **is not [against you] is for you.** [He who today] is far-off—tomorrow will be [near to you].....

LUKE   MATT   MARK

Luke 9:51–56 (§L44)

⁵¹ When the days drew near for him to be received up, he set his face to go to Jerusalem. ⁵² And he sent messengers ahead of him, who went and entered a village of the Samaritans, to make ready for him; ⁵³ but the people would not receive him, because his face was set toward Jerusalem. ⁵⁴ And when his disciples James and John saw it, they said, "Lord, do you want us to bid fire come down from heaven and consume them?"ᵃ ⁵⁵ But he turned and rebuked them.ᵇ ⁵⁶ And they went on to another village.

ᵃ Some witnesses add *as Elijah did:* A C D K W X Δ Θ Π Ψ *f¹ f¹³* 28 33 *pm*

ᵇ Some witnesses add *and he said, "You do not know what manner of spirit you are of; for the Son of man came not to destroy men's lives but to save them":* (D) K Θ Π *f¹ f¹³ pc*

Luke 1:76 ⇨ Luke 9:51–52
⁷⁶ *"And you, child, will be called the prophet of the Most High;*
for you will go before the Lord to prepare his ways, . . ."

Luke 3:4 ⇨ Luke 9:51–52
⁴ *As it is written in the book of the words of Isaiah the prophet,*
"The voice of one crying in the wilderness:
Prepare the way of the Lord,
make his paths straight."

Luke 7:27 ⇨ Luke 9:51–52
²⁷ *"This is he of whom it is written,*
'Behold, I send my messenger before thy face,
who shall prepare thy way before thee.'"

Luke 10:1 ⇨ Luke 9:51–52
¹ *After this the Lord appointed seventy others, and sent them on ahead of him, two by two, into every town and place where he himself was about to come.*

Luke 13:22 ⇨ Luke 9:51
²² *He went on his way through towns and villages, teaching, and journeying toward Jerusalem.*

Luke 13:33 ⇨ Luke 9:51
³³ *"'Nevertheless I must go on my way today and tomorrow and the day following; for it cannot be that a prophet should perish away from Jerusalem.'"*

Luke 17:11 ⇨ Luke 9:51
¹¹ *On the way to Jerusalem he was passing along between Samaria and Galilee.*

Luke 18:31 ⇨ Luke 9:51
³¹ *And taking the twelve, he said to them, "Behold, we are going up to Jerusalem, and everything that is written of the Son of man by the prophets will be accomplished."*

Luke 19:11 ⇨ Luke 9:51
¹¹ *As they heard these things, he proceeded to tell a parable, because he was near to Jerusalem, and because they supposed that the kingdom of God was to appear immediately.*

2 Kgs 1:9–12 ⇨ Luke 9:54
⁹ Then the king sent to him a captain of fifty men with his fifty. He went up to Elijah, who was sitting on the top of a hill, and said to him, "O man of God, the king says, 'Come down.'" ¹⁰ But Elijah answered the captain of fifty, "If I am a man of God, let **fire come down from heaven and consume** you and your fifty." Then **fire** came **down from heaven**, and consumed him and his fifty.
¹¹ Again the king sent to him another captain of fifty men with his fifty. And he went up and said to him, "O man of God, this is the king's order, 'Come down quickly!'" ¹² But Elijah answered them, "If I am a man of God, let **fire come down from heaven and consume** you and your fifty." Then the fire of God came **down from heaven and** consumed him and his fifty.

JOHN   THOMAS   OTHER

LUKE   MATT   MARK

Luke 9:57–62 (§L45)

[57] As they were going along the road, a man said to him, "I will follow you wherever you go." [58] And Jesus said to him, "Foxes have holes, and birds of the air have nests; but the Son of man has nowhere to lay his head." [59] To another he said, "Follow me." But he said, "Lord, let me first go and bury my father." [60] But he said to him, "Leave the dead to bury their own dead; but as for you, go and proclaim the kingdom of God." [61] Another said, "I will follow you, Lord; but let me first say farewell to those at my home." [62] Jesus said to him, "No one who puts his hand to the plow and looks back is fit for the kingdom of God."

Luke 14:25–33

[25] *Now great multitudes accompanied* **him;** *and he turned* **and said to** *them,* [26] *"If any one comes to me and does not hate his own father and mother and wife and children and brothers and sisters, yes, and even his own life, he cannot be my disciple.* [27] *Whoever does not bear his own cross and come after me, cannot be my disciple.* [28] *For which of you, desiring to build a tower, does not first sit down and count the cost, whether he has enough to complete it?* [29] *Otherwise, when he has laid a foundation, and is not able to finish, all who see it begin to mock him,* [30] *saying, 'This man began to build, and was not able to finish.'* [31] *Or what king, going to encounter another king in war, will not sit down first and take counsel whether he is able with ten thousand to meet him who comes against him with twenty thousand?* [32] *And if not, while the other is yet a great way off, he sends an embassy and asks terms of peace.* [33] *So therefore, whoever of you does not renounce all that he has cannot be my disciple."*

Matt 8:18–22 (§M17)

[18] Now when Jesus saw great crowds around him, he gave orders to go over to the other side. [19] And a scribe came up and **said to him,** "Teacher, **I will follow you wherever you go."** [20] And **Jesus said to him,** "Foxes have holes, and birds of the air have nests; but the Son of man has nowhere to lay his head." [21] Another of the disciples **said to him,** "Lord, let me first go and bury my father." [22] But Jesus said to him, "Follow me, and **leave the dead to bury their own dead."**

JOHN   THOMAS   OTHER

GThom 86 ⇨ Luke 9:58

(86) **Jesus said,** "[The **foxes have** their **holes**] **and the birds have** [their] **nests, but the Son of Man has** no place **to lay his head** and rest."

The synagogue at Capernaum is usually dated II/III CE. The main building, rectangular in shape, was bordered on the east by a courtyard. The main building had a second story which functioned as a gallery for the hall below. On the main floor, stone benches ran along the walls to provide seats for the congregation. Source: *Ancient Synagogues Revealed*, edited by Lee I. Levine; Copyright © 1982 The Israel Exploration Society (Detroit: Wayne State University Press, 1982), 6.

LUKE	MATT	MARK

Luke 10:1–16 (§L46) °

[1] After this the Lord appointed seventy[a] others, and sent them on ahead of him, two by two, into every town and place where he himself was about to come. [2] And he said to them, "The harvest is plentiful, but the laborers are few; pray therefore the Lord of the harvest to send out laborers into his harvest. [3] Go your way; behold, I send you out as lambs in the midst of wolves. [4] Carry no purse, no bag, no sandals; and salute no one on the road. [5] Whatever house you enter, first say, 'Peace be to this house!' [6] And if a son of peace is there, your peace shall rest upon him; but if not, it shall return to you. [7] And remain in the same house, eating and drinking what they provide, for the laborer deserves his wages; do not go from house to house. [8] Whenever you enter a town and they receive you, eat what is set before you; [9] heal the sick in it and say to them, 'The kingdom of God has come near to you.' [10] But whenever you enter a town and they do not receive you, go into its streets and say, [11] 'Even the dust of your town that clings to our feet, we wipe off against you; nevertheless know this, that the kingdom of God has come near.' [12] I tell you, it shall be more tolerable on that day for Sodom than for that town.

[13] "Woe to you, Chorazin! woe to you, Bethsaida! for if the mighty works done in you had been done in Tyre and Sidon, they would have repented long ago, sitting in sackcloth and ashes. [14] But it shall be more tolerable in the judgment for Tyre and Sidon than for you. [15] And you, Capernaum, will you be exalted to heaven? You shall be brought down to Hades.

[16] "He who hears you hears me, and he who rejects you rejects me, and he who rejects me rejects him who sent me."

[a] A few witnesses read *seventy-two* (cf. Luke 10:17): 𝔓75 B D *pc*

°Appendix 2 ⇨ §L46

Luke 9:1–6 (§L36)

[1] And he called the twelve together and gave them power and authority over all demons and to cure diseases, [2] and he sent them out to preach the kingdom of God and to heal. [3] and he said to them, "Take nothing for your journey, no staff, nor bag, nor bread, nor money; and do not have two tunics. [4] And whatever house you enter, stay there, and from there depart. [5] And wherever they do not receive you, when you leave that town shake off the dust from your feet as a testimony against them." [6] And they departed and went through the villages, preaching the gospel and healing everywhere.

Matt 9:35–38 (§M26)

[35] And Jesus went about all the cities and villages, teaching in their synagogues and preaching the gospel of the kingdom, and healing every disease and every infirmity. [36] When he saw the crowds, he had compassion for them, because they were harassed and helpless, like sheep without a shepherd. [37] Then **he said to** his disciples, "**The harvest is plentiful, but the laborers are few;** [38] **pray therefore the Lord of the harvest to send out laborers into his harvest."**

Matt 10:5–15 (§M28.1)

[5] These twelve Jesus **sent** out, charging **them,** "Go nowhere among the Gentiles, and enter no town of the Samaritans, [6] but go rather to the lost sheep of the house of Israel. [7] And preach as you go, saying, '**The kingdom of** heaven is at hand.' [8] **Heal the sick,** raise the dead, cleanse lepers, cast out demons. You received without pay, give without pay. [9] Take **no** gold, nor silver, nor copper in your belts, [10] **no bag** for your journey, nor two tunics, nor **san**dals, nor a staff; **for the laborer deserves his** food. [11] And whatever **town** or village **you enter,** find out who is worthy in it, and stay with **him** until you depart. [12] As **you enter** the **house,** salute it. [13] And if the **house** is worthy, let **your peace** come upon it; **but if** it is **not** worthy, let your peace **return to you.** [14] **And** if any one will **not receive you** or listen to your words, shake off **the dust** from your **feet** as you leave that house or town. [15] Truly, **I** say to **you, it shall be more tolerable on** the **day** of judgment **for** the land of **Sodom** and Gomorrah **than for that town."**

Matt 11:20–24 (§M31)

[20] Then he began to upbraid the cities where most of his mighty works had been done, because they did not repent. [21] "Woe to you, Chorazin! woe to you, Bethsaida! for if the mighty works done in you had been done in Tyre and Sidon, they would have repented long ago in sackcloth and ashes. [22] But I tell you, it shall be more tolerable on the day of judgment for Tyre and Sidon than for you. [23] And you, Capernaum, will you be exalted to heaven? You shall be brought down to Hades. For if the mighty works done in you had been done in Sodom, it would have remained until this day. [24] But I tell you that it shall be more tolerable on** the **day** of judgment **for** the land of **Sodom than for** you."

Matt 10:16 ⇨ Luke 10:3

[16] "Behold, **I send you** out as sheep **in the midst of wolves;** so be wise as serpents and innocent as doves."

Matt 10:40 ⇨ Luke 10:16

[40] "He who receives you receives me, and he who receives me receives him who sent me."

Matt 18:5 ⇨ Luke 10:16

[5] "Whoever receives one such child in my name receives me; . . ."

Luke 1:76 ⇨ Luke 10:1

[76] "And you, child, will be called the prophet of the Most High;
for you will go before the Lord to prepare his ways, . . ."

Mark 6:7–13 (§K26)

[7] And he called to him the twelve, and began to send **them** out **two by two,** and gave them authority over the unclean spirits. [8] He charged them to take nothing for their journey except a staff; no bread, **no bag, no** money in their belts; [9] but to wear **sandals** and not put on two tunics. [10] And he said to them, "Where **you enter a house,** stay there until you leave the place. [11] And if any place will **not receive you** and they refuse to hear you, when you leave, shake off **the dust** that is on your **feet** for a testimony **against** them." [12] So they went out and preached that men should repent. [13] And they cast out many demons, and anointed with oil many that were **sick** and healed them.

Mark 9:37 ⇨ Luke 10:16

[37] "Whoever receives one such child in my name receives me; and whoever receives me, receives not me but him who sent me."

Luke 3:4 ⇨ Luke 10:1

[4] As it is written in the book of the words of Isaiah the prophet,
"The voice of one crying in the wilderness:
Prepare the way of the Lord,
make his paths straight."

Luke 7:27 ⇨ Luke 10:1

[27] "This is he of whom it is written,
'Behold, I send my messenger before thy face,
who shall prepare thy way before thee.'"

Luke 9:51–52 ⇨ Luke 10:1

[51] When the days drew near for him to be received up, he set his face to go to Jerusalem. [52] And he sent messengers ahead of him, who went and entered a village of the Samaritans, to make ready for him; . . .

JOHN

John 4:35 ⇨ Luke 10:2
35 "Do you not say, 'There are yet four months, then comes the harvest'? I tell you, lift up your eyes, and see how the fields are already white for harvest."

John 5:23 ⇨ Luke 10:16
23 "that all may honor the Son, even as they honor the Father. He who does not honor the Son does not honor the Father who sent him."

John 12:44–45 ⇨ Luke 10:16
44 And Jesus cried out and said, "He who believes in me, believes not in me but in him who sent me. 45 And he who sees me sees him who sent me."

John 12:48 ⇨ Luke 10:16
48 "He who rejects me and does not receive my sayings has a judge; the word that I have spoken will be his judge on the last day."

John 13:20 ⇨ Luke 10:16
20 "Truly, truly, I say to you, he who receives any one whom I send receives me; and he who receives me receives him who sent me."

John 15:23 ⇨ Luke 10:16
23 "He who hates me hates my Father also."

THOMAS

GThom 73 ⇨ Luke 10:2
(73) Jesus **said, "The harvest is** great **but the laborers are few**. Beseech **the Lord**, therefore, **to send out laborers** to the **harvest."**

GThom 14 ⇨ Luke 10:8
(14) Jesus said to them, "If you fast, you will give rise to sin for yourselves; and if you pray, you will be condemned; and if you give alms, you will do harm to your spirits. When **you** go into any land and walk about in the districts, if **they receive you, eat what** they will **set before you,** and heal the sick among them. For what goes into your mouth will not defile you, but that which issues from your mouth—it is that which will defile you."

OTHER

2 Clem 5:2 ⇨ Luke 10:3
2 for the Lord said, "Ye shall be as lambs in the midst of wolves, . . ."

Acts 13:51 ⇨ Luke 10:11
51 But they shook off the dust from their feet against them, and went to Iconium.

Acts 18:6 ⇨ Luke 10:11
6 And when they opposed and reviled him, he shook out his garments and said to them, "Your blood be upon your heads! I am innocent. From now on I will go to the Gentiles."

GNaz 27 ⇨ Luke 10:13
(27) In these cities (namely Chorazin and Bethsaida) many wonders have been wrought, as their number the Gospel according to the Hebrews gives 53. ("Historical Commentary on Luke" on Luke 10:13; cited by Bischoff in *Sacris Erudiri* 6, 1954, p. 262)

Luke 22:35–36 ⇨ Luke 10:4
35 And he said to them, "When I sent you out with no purse or bag or sandals, did you lack anything?" They said, "Nothing." 36 He said to them, "But now, let him who has a purse take it, and likewise a bag. And let him who has no sword sell his mantle and buy one."

Luke 9:48 ⇨ Luke 10:16
48 and said to them, "Whoever receives this child in my name receives me, and whoever receives me receives him who sent me; for he who is least among you all is the one who is great."

LUKE	MATT	MARK

Luke 10:17–20 (§L47.1)°

[17] The seventy[a] returned with joy, saying, "Lord, even the demons are subject to us in your name!" [18] And he said to them, "I saw Satan fall like lightning from heaven. [19] Behold, I have given you authority to tread upon serpents and scorpions, and over all the power of the enemy; and nothing shall hurt you. [20] Nevertheless do not rejoice in this, that the spirits are subject to you; but rejoice that your names are written in heaven."

[a] A few witnesses read *seventy-two* (see Luke 10:1): 𝔓⁴⁵ 𝔓⁷⁵ B D *pc*

°Appendix 2 ⇨ §L47.1

Luke 9:10 ⇨ Luke 10:17
[10] On their return *the* apostles told him what they had done. And he took them and withdrew apart to a city called Bethsaida.

Ps 9:13 ⇨ Luke 10:19
[13] You will **tread** on lion **and** the adder, the young lion **and** the serpent **you** will trample under foot.

Mark 16:14–18 (§K72)

[14] Afterward he appeared to **the** eleven themselves as they sat at table; and he upbraided them for their unbelief and hardness of heart, because they had not believed those who saw him after he had risen. [15] And he said to them, "Go into all the world and preach the gospel to the whole creation. [16] He who believes and is baptized will be saved; but he who does not believe will be condemned. [17] And these signs will accompany those who believe: in my name they will cast out **demons;** they will speak in new tongues; [18] they will pick up **serpents,** and if they drink any deadly thing, it will not hurt them; they will lay their hands on the sick, and they will recover."

Mark 6:30 ⇨ Luke 10:17
[30] **The** apostles **returned** to Jesus, and told him all that they had done and taught.

JOHN	THOMAS	OTHER

John 12:31 ⇨ Luke 10:18
[31] "Now is the judgment of this world, now shall the ruler of this world be cast out"; . . .

LUKE

Luke 10:21–22 (§L47.2) °
²¹ In that same hour he rejoiced in the Holy Spirit and said, "I thank thee, Father, Lord of heaven and earth, that thou hast hidden these things from the wise and understanding and revealed them to babes; yea, Father, for such was thy gracious will.ᵃ ²² All things have been delivered to me by my Father; and no one knows who the Son is except the Father, or who the Father is except the Son and any one to whom the Son chooses to reveal him."

ᵃ Or *so it was well-pleasing before thee*

° Appendix 2 ⇨ §L47.2

MATT

Matt 11:25–27
²⁵ At that time Jesus declared, "I thank thee, Father, Lord of heaven and earth, that thou hast hidden these things from the wise and understanding and revealed them to babes; ²⁶ yea, Father, for such was thy gracious will. ²⁷ All things have been delivered to me by my Father; and no one knows the Son except the Father, and no one knows the Father except the Son and any one to whom the Son chooses to reveal him."

MARK

JOHN

John 3:35 ⇨ Luke 10:22
³⁵ the **Father** loves **the Son**, **and** has given **all things** into his hand.

John 10:14–15 ⇨ Luke 10:22
¹⁴ "I am the good shepherd; I know my own and my own know me, ¹⁵ as **the Father** knows me and I know **the Father**; and I lay down my life for the sheep."

John 17:25–26 ⇨ Luke 10:22
²⁵ "O righteous **Father**, the world has not known thee, but I have known thee; and these know that thou hast sent **me**. ²⁶ I made known to them thy name, and I will make it known, that the love with which thou hast loved **me** may be in them, and I in them."

THOMAS

POxy654 3 ⇨ Luke 10:21
(3) Jesus says, ["If] those who draw you on [say to you, 'Behold,] the kingdom (is) in the heav[en,'] the birds of the hea[ven will be (there) before you. But if they th]at it is under the earth, the fishes of the se[a will enter before you]. And the king[dom of God] is within you [and outside (of you). Whoever] knows [himself,] will fin[d] it [and when you] know yourselves, [you will realize that] you are [sons] of the li[ving] Father. [But if you will not] know yourselves, [you are] in [poverty] and you are pov[erty.]"

GThom 4 ⇨ Luke 10:21
(4) Jesus said, "The man old in days will not hesitate to ask a small child seven days old about the place of life, and he will live. For many who are first will become last, and they will become one and the same."

GThom 61 ⇨ Luke 10:22
(61) Jesus said, "Two will rest on a bed: the one will die, the other will live."
Salome said, "Who are You, man, that You, as though from the One, (or: as<whose son>, that You) have come up on my couch and eaten from my table?"
*Jesus said to her, "I am He who exists from the Undivided. I was given some of the **things** of **My father**."*
<Salome said,> "I am Your disciple."
<Jesus said to her,> "Therefore I say, if he is <undivided>, he will be filled with light, but if he is divided, he will be filled with darkness."

OTHER

GNaz 9 ⇨ Luke 10:21
*(9) The Jewish Gospel: **I thank thee**.*
(Variant to Matthew 11:25 in the "Zion Gospel" Edition)

LUKE	MATT	MARK

LUKE

Luke 10:23–24 (§L47.3) °

²³ Then turning to the disciples he said privately, "Blessed are the eyes which see what you see! ²⁴ For I tell you that many prophets and kings desired to see what you see, and did not see it, and to hear what you hear, and did not hear it."

°Appendix 2 ⇨ §L47.3

MATT

Matt 13:10–17 (§M40.3)

¹⁰ Then **the disciples** came and said to him, "Why do you speak to them in parables?" ¹¹ And **he** answered them, "To you it has been given to know the secrets of the kingdom of heaven, but to them it has not been given. ¹² For to him who has will more be given, and he will have abundance; but from him who has not, even what he has will be taken away. ¹³ This is why I speak to them in parables, because seeing they do **not see**, and hearing they do **not hear**, nor do they understand. ¹⁴ With them indeed is fulfilled the prophecy of Isaiah which says:

'**You** shall indeed **hear** but never understand,

  and you shall indeed **see** but never perceive.

¹⁵ For this people's heart has grown dull, and their ears are heavy of hearing, and their eyes they have closed, lest they should perceive with their eyes, and hear with their ears, and understand with their heart, and turn for me to heal them.'

¹⁶ But **blessed are** your **eyes**, for they **see**, and your ears, for they **hear**. ¹⁷ Truly, **I** say to **you**, **many prophets and** righteous men longed **to see what you see, and did not see it, and to hear what you hear, and did not hear it.**"

MARK

JOHN	THOMAS	OTHER

THOMAS

GThom 38 ⇨ Luke 10:24

*(38) Jesus said, "Many times have **you** desired to hear these words which I am saying to **you**, and **you** have no one else to **hear** them from. There will be days when **you** will look for Me and will not find Me."*

LUKE

Luke 10:25–29 (§L48.1)

²⁵ And behold, a lawyer stood up to put him to the test, saying, "Teacher, what shall I do to inherit eternal life?" ²⁶ He said to him, "What is written in the law? How do you read?" ²⁷ And he answered, "You shall love the Lord your God with all your heart, and with all your soul, and with all your strength, and with all your mind; and your neighbor as yourself." ²⁸ And he said to him, "You have answered right; do this, and you will live."

²⁹ But he, desiring to justify himself, said to Jesus, "And who is my neighbor?"

Luke 18:18–21

¹⁸ And a ruler asked him, "Good Teacher, what shall I do to inherit eternal life?" ¹⁹ And Jesus said to him, "Why do you call me good? No one is good but God alone. ²⁰ You know the commandments: 'Do not commit adultery, Do not kill, Do not steal, Do not bear false witness, Honor your father and mother.'" ²¹ And he said, "All these I have observed from my youth."

Lev 19:18 ⇨ Luke 10:27

¹⁸ "You shall not take vengeance or bear any grudge against the sons of your own people, but **you shall love your neighbor as yourself**: I am **the Lord**."

Deut 6:5 ⇨ Luke 10:27

⁵ "and **you shall love the Lord your God with all your heart, and with all your might**."

Lev 18:5 ⇨ Luke 10:28

⁵ "You shall therefore keep my statutes and walk in them. I am the Lord your God."

MATT

Matt 22:34–40 (§M76.3)

³⁴ But when the Pharisees heard that he had silenced the Sadducees, they came together. ³⁵ And one of them, a lawyer, asked **him** a question, to test him. ³⁶ "Teacher, which is the great commandment in the law?" ³⁷ And he said to him, "**You shall love the Lord your God with all your heart, and with all your soul, and with all your mind.** ³⁸ This is the great and first commandment. ³⁹ And a second is like it, **You shall love your neighbor as yourself.** ⁴⁰ On these two commandments depend all **the law** and the prophets."

Matt 19:16–21

*¹⁶ And behold, one came **up to** him, saying, "Teacher, what good deed must I do, to have eternal life?" ¹⁷ And he said to him, "Why do you ask me about what is good? One there is who is good. If you would enter life, keep the commandments." ¹⁸ He said to him, "Which?" And Jesus said, "**You shall not kill, You shall not commit adultery, You shall not steal, You shall not bear false witness,** ¹⁹ Honor your father and mother, and, **You shall love your neighbor as yourself.**" ²⁰ The young man said to him, "All these I have observed; what do I still lack?" ²¹ Jesus said to him, "If you would be perfect, go, sell what you possess and give to the poor, and you will have treasure in heaven; and come, follow me."*

MARK

Mark 12:28–34 (§M59)

²⁸ And one of the scribes came up and heard them disputing with one another, and seeing that he answered them well, asked him, "Which commandment is the first of all?" ²⁹ Jesus **answered**, "The first is, 'Hear, O Israel: **The Lord** our **God, the Lord** is one; ³⁰ and **you shall love the Lord your God with all your heart, and with all your soul, and with all your mind, and with all your strength.'** ³¹ The second is this, 'You shall love your **neighbor as yourself.**' There is no other commandment greater than these." ³² And the scribe said to him, "You are right, Teacher; you have truly said that he is one, and there is no other but he; ³³ and to **love** him **with all the heart**, and with all the understanding, **and with all the strength**, and to **love** one's **neighbor as** oneself, is much more than all whole burnt offerings and sacrifices." ³⁴ And when Jesus saw that he **answered** wisely, **he said to him,** "You are not far from the kingdom of God." And after that no one dared to ask him any question.

Mark 10:17–20

*¹⁷ And as he was setting out on his journey, a man ran **up** and knelt before **him**, and asked **him**, "Good **Teacher, what must I do to inherit eternal life?**" ¹⁸ And Jesus said to him, "Why do you call me good? No one is good but God alone. ¹⁹ You know the commandments: 'Do not kill, Do not commit adultery, Do not steal, Do not bear false witness, Do not defraud, Honor your father and mother.'" ²⁰ And he said to him, "Teacher, all these I have observed from my youth."*

OTHER

Did 1:2 ⇨ Luke 10:27

*² The Way of Life is this: "First, thou shalt **love** the **God** who made thee, secondly, thy neighbour as thyself; and whatsoever thou wouldst not have done to thyself, do not thou to another."*

Barn 19:5 ⇨ Luke 10:27

*⁵ Thou shalt not be in two minds whether it shall be or not. "Thou shalt not take the name of **the Lord** in vain." Thou shalt **love** thy neighbour more than thy own life. Thou shalt not procure abortion, thou shalt not commit infanticide. Thou shalt not withhold thy hand from thy son or from thy daughter, but shalt teach them the fear of God from their youth up.*

Rom 13:8–10 ⇨ Luke 10:27

*⁸ Owe no one anything, except to love one another; for he who loves his **neighbor** has fulfilled **the law**. ⁹ The commandments, "**You shall** not commit adultery, **You shall** not kill, **You shall** not steal, **You shall** not covet," and any other commandment, are summed up in this sentence, "**You shall love your neighbor as yourself.**" ¹⁰ Love does no wrong to a **neighbor**; therefore **love** is the fulfilling of **the law**.*

Jas 2:8 ⇨ Luke 10:27

*⁸ If you really fulfil the royal law, according to the scripture, "**You shall love your neighbor as yourself**," you do well.*

Gal 5:14 ⇨ Luke 10:27

*¹⁴ For the whole law is fulfilled in one word, "**You shall love your neighbor as yourself.**"*

JOHN

THOMAS

GThom 25 ⇨ Luke 10:27

*(25) Jesus said, "**Love** your brother like your soul, guard him like the pupil of your eye."*

LUKE   MATT   MARK

Luke 10:30–35 (§L48.2)
[30] Jesus replied, "A man was going down from Jerusalem to Jericho, and he fell among robbers, who stripped him and beat him, and departed, leaving him half dead. [31] Now by chance a priest was going down that road; and when he saw him he passed by on the other side. [32] So likewise a Levite, when he came to the place and saw him, passed by on the other side. [33] But a Samaritan, as he journeyed, came to where he was; and when he saw him, he had compassion, [34] and went to him and bound up his wounds, pouring on oil and wine; then he set him on his own beast and brought him to an inn, and took care of him. [35] And the next day he took out two denarii[a] and gave them to the innkeeper, saying, 'Take care of him; and whatever more you spend, I will repay you when I come back.'"

Luke 10:36–37 (§L48.3)
[36] "Which of these three, do you think, proved neighbor to the man who fell among the robbers?" [37] He said, "The one who showed mercy on him." And Jesus said to him "Go and do likewise."

[a] The denarius was a day's wage for a laborer

JOHN   THOMAS   OTHER

LUKE	MATT	MARK

LUKE

Luke 10:38-42 (§L49)

[38] Now as they went on their way, he entered a village; and a woman named Martha received him into her house. [39] And she had a sister called Mary, who sat at the Lord's feet and listened to his teaching. [40] But Martha was distracted with much serving; and she went to him and said, "Lord, do you not care that my sister has left me to serve alone? Tell her then to help me." [41] But the Lord answered her, "Martha, Martha, you are anxious and troubled about many things; [42] one thing is needful.[a] Mary has chosen the good portion, which shall not be taken away from her."

[a] Some witnesses read *few things are needful, or only one:* 𝔓³ ℵ B L *f¹* 33 *pc*

JOHN

THOMAS	OTHER

John 11:1-6 (§J22.1)

[1] *Now a certain man was ill, Lazarus of Bethany, the village of Mary and her sister **Martha**. [2] It was **Mary** who anointed **the** Lord with ointment and wiped his feet with her hair, whose brother Lazarus was ill. [3] So the sisters sent to him, saying, "Lord, he whom you love is ill." [4] But when Jesus heard it he said, "This illness is not unto death; it is for the glory of God, so that the Son of God may be glorified by means of it."*

[5] *Now Jesus loved **Martha** and her sister and Lazarus. [6] So when he heard that he was ill, he stayed two days longer in the place where he was.*

John 11:17-37 (§J22.3)

[17] *Now when Jesus came, he found that Lazarus had already been in the tomb four days. [18] Bethany was near Jerusalem, about two miles off, [19] and many of the Jews had come to **Martha** and **Mary** to console them concerning their brother. [20] When **Martha** heard that Jesus was coming, she went and met him, while **Mary** sat in the house. [21] **Martha** said to Jesus, "Lord if you had been here, my brother would not have died. [22] And even now I know that whatever you ask from God, God will give you." [23] Jesus said to her, "Your brother will rise again." [24] **Martha** said to him, "I know that he will rise again in the resurrection at the last day." [25] Jesus said to **her**, "I am the resurrection and the life; he who believes in me, though he die, yet shall he live, [26] and whoever lives and believes in me shall never die. Do you believe this?" [27] She said to him, "Yes, Lord; I believe that you are the Christ, the Son of God, he who is coming into the world."*

[28] *When she said this, she went and called her sister **Mary**, saying quietly, "The Teacher is here and is calling for you." [29] And when she heard it, she rose quickly and went to him. [30] Now Jesus had not yet come to the **village**, but was still in the place where **Martha** had met him. [31] When the Jews who were with her in the house, consoling her, saw **Mary** rise quickly and go out, they followed her, supposing that she was going to the tomb to weep there. [32] Then **Mary**, when she came where Jesus was and saw him, fell **at his feet**, saying to him, "Lord, if you had been here, my brother would not have died." [33] When Jesus saw her weeping, and the Jews who came with her also weeping, he was deeply moved in spirit and troubled; [34] and he said, "Where have you laid him?" They said to him, "Lord, come and see." [35] Jesus wept. [36] So the Jews said, "See how he loved him!" [37] But some of them said, "Could not he who opened the eyes of the blind man have kept this man from dying?"*

John 12:2 ⇨ Luke 10:40
[2] *There they made him a supper; **Martha** served, and Lazarus was one of those at table with **him**.*

LUKE

Luke 11:1–4 (§L50.1)

[1] He was praying in a certain place, and when he ceased, one of his disciples said to him, "Lord teach us to pray, as John taught his disciples." [2] And he said to them, "When you pray, say:

"Father, hallowed be thy name. Thy kingdom come. [3] Give us each day our daily bread;[a] [4] and forgive us our sins, for we ourselves forgive every one who is indebted to us; and lead us not into temptation."

[a] Or *our bread for the morrow*

MATT

Matt 6:5–15 (§M12.6c)

[5] "And **when you pray**, you must not be like the hypocrites; for they love to stand and **pray** in the synagogues and at the street corners, that they may be seen by men. Truly, I say to you, they have received their reward. [6] But **when you pray**, go into your room and shut the door and **pray** to your Father who is in secret; and your Father who sees in secret will reward you.

[7] "And in praying do not heap up empty phrases as the Gentiles do; for they think that they will be heard for their many words. [8] Do not be like them, for your Father knows what you need before you ask him. [9] **Pray** then like this:

Our **Father** who art in heaven,
Hallowed be thy name.
[10] **Thy kingdom come,**
Thy will be done,
　On earth as it is in heaven.
[11] **Give us** this **day our daily bread;**
[12] **And forgive us our** debts,
　As **we** also have forgiven our debtors;
[13] **And lead us not into temptation,**
　But deliver us from evil.

[14] For if you **forgive** men their trespasses, your heavenly **Father** also will **forgive** you; [15] but if you do not **forgive** men their trespasses, neither will your **Father forgive** your trespasses."

MARK

Mark 11:25 ⇨ Luke 11:4

[25] "And whenever you stand praying, **forgive**, if you have anything against any **one**; so that your Father also who is in heaven may **forgive** you your trespasses."

JOHN

THOMAS

OTHER

Did 8:2

[2] And do not pray as the hypocrites, but as the Lord commanded in his Gospel, **pray** thus: "Our **Father**, who art in Heaven, **hallowed be thy Name, thy Kingdom come**, thy will be done, as in Heaven so also upon earth; **give us** to-day **our daily bread, and forgive us our** debt as **we forgive** our debtors, **and lead us not into** trial, but deliver us from the Evil One, for thine is the power and the glory for ever."

GNaz 5 ⇨ Luke 11:3

(5) In the so-called Gospel according to the Hebrews instead of "essential to existence" I found "mahar," which means "of tomorrow," so that the sense is:

Our bread *of tomorrow—that is, of the future—***give us** *this* **day.** (Jerome, *Commentary on Matthew* 1 [on Matthew 6:11])

LUKE

Luke 11:5–8 (§L50.2)

5 And he said to them, "Which of you who has a friend will go to him at midnight and say to him, 'Friend, lend me three loaves; 6 for a friend of mine has arrived on a journey, and I have nothing to set before him'; 7 and he will answer from within, 'Do not bother me; the door is now shut, and my children are with me in bed; I cannot get up and give you anything'? 8 I tell you, though he will not get up and give him anything because he is his friend, yet because of his importunity he will rise and give him whatever he needs."

Luke 11:9–13 (§L50.3)

9 "And I tell you, Ask, and it will be given you; seek, and you will find; knock, and it will be opened to you. 10 For every one who asks receives, and he who seeks finds, and to him who knocks it will be opened. 11 What father among you, if his son asks for a fish,[a] will instead of a fish give him a serpent; 12 or if he asks for an egg, will give him a scorpion? 13 If you then, who are evil, know how to give good gifts to your children, how much more will the heavenly Father give the Holy Spirit to those who ask him!"

[a] Some witnesses insert *bread, will give him a stone; or if he asks for* (see Matt 7:9): ℵ C (D) K L W X Δ Θ Π Ψ *f*[1] *f*[13] 28 33 *al;* text 𝔓[45] 𝔓[75] B 1241 *pc*

Luke 18:1–5 ⇨ §L50.2

1 *And he told them a parable, to the effect that they ought always to pray and not lose heart.* 2 *He said, "In a certain city there was a judge who neither feared God nor regarded man;* 3 *and there was a widow in that city who kept coming to him and saying, 'Vindicate me against my adversary.'* 4 *For a while he refused; but afterward he said to himself, 'Though I neither fear God nor regard man,* 5 *yet because this widow bothers me, I will vindicate her, or she will wear me out by her continual coming.'"*

JOHN

MATT

Matt 7:7–11 (§M12.7g) ⇨ §L50.3

7 "Ask, and it will be given you; seek, and you will find; knock, and it will be opened to you. 8 For every one who asks receives, and he who seeks finds, and to him who knocks it will be opened. 9 Or what man of you, if his son asks him for bread, will give him a stone? 10 Or if he asks for a fish, will give him a serpent? 11 If you then, who are evil, know how to give good gifts to your children, how much more will your Father who is in heaven give good things to those who ask him!"

THOMAS

POxy654 2 ⇨ Luke 11:9–10

(2) [*Jesus says,*] *"Let him who see[ks] not cease [seeking until] he finds and when he finds, [he will be astounded, and] having been [astoun]ded, he will reign an[d having reigned], he will re[st]."*

GThom 2 ⇨ Luke 11:9–10

(2) Jesus said, "Let him who seeks continue seeking until he finds. When he finds, he will become troubled. When he becomes troubled, he will be astonished, and he will rule over the All."

GThom 94 ⇨ Luke 11:9

(94) Jesus [said], "He who seeks will find, and [he who knocks] will be let in."

GThom 92 ⇨ Luke 11:9

(92) Jesus said, "Seek and you will find. Yet, what you asked Me about in former times and which I did not tell you then, now I do desire to tell, but you do not inquire after it."

MARK

OTHER

LUKE

Luke 11:14–23 (§L51.1)

[14] Now he was casting out a demon that was dumb; when the demon had gone out, the dumb man spoke, and the people marveled. [15] But some of them said, "He casts out demons by Beelzebul, the prince of demons"; [16] while others, to test him, sought from him a sign from heaven. [17] But he, knowing their thoughts, said to them, "Every kingdom divided against itself is laid waste, and a divided household falls. [18] And if Satan also is divided against himself, how will his kingdom stand? For you say that I cast out demons by Beelzebul. [19] And if I cast out demons by Beelzebul, by whom do your sons cast them out? Therefore they shall be your judges. [20] But if it is by the finger of God that I cast out demons, then the kingdom of God has come upon you. [21] When a strong man, fully armed, guards his own palace, his goods are in peace; [22] but when one stronger than he assails him and overcomes him, he takes away his armor in which he trusted, and divides his spoil. [23] He who is not with me is against me, and he who does not gather with me scatters."

Luke 9:50 ⇨ Luke 11:23

[50] But Jesus said to him, "Do not forbid him; for he that is not against you is for you."

MATT

Matt 9:32–34 (§M25)

[32] As they were going away, behold, a **dumb** demoniac was brought to him. [33] And **when the demon had** been cast **out, the dumb man spoke; and the** crowds **marveled**, saying, "Never was anything like this seen in Israel." [34] But the Pharisees **said,** "He casts out demons by the prince of demons."

Matt 12:22–24 ⇨ Luke 11:14–15

[22] Then a blind and **dumb** demoniac was brought to him, and he healed him, so that **the dumb man spoke** and saw. [23] **And** all **the people** were amazed, and said, "Can this be the Son of David?" [24] **But** when the Pharisees heard it they **said,** "It is only **by Beelzebul, the prince of demons**, that this man **casts out demons**."

MARK

Mark 3:22 ⇨ Luke 11:15

[22] And the scribes who came down from Jerusalem **said,** "He is possessed **by Beelzebul, and by the prince of demons he casts out the demons.**"

JOHN

John 7:20 ⇨ Luke 11:15

[20] *The people answered, "You have a demon! Who is seeking to kill you?"*

John 8:48 ⇨ Luke 11:15

[48] *The Jews answered him, "Are we not right in saying that you are a Samaritan and have a demon?"*

John 8:52 ⇨ Luke 11:15

[52] *The Jews* **said** *to him, "Now we know that you have a demon. Abraham died, as did the prophets; and you say, 'If any one keeps my word, he will never taste death.'"*

John 10:20 ⇨ Luke 11:15

[20] *Many* **of them said,** *"He has a demon, and he is mad; why listen to him?"*

THOMAS

GThom 21 ⇨ Luke 11:21–22

(21) Mary said to Jesus, "Whom are Your disciples like?"

He said, "They are like children who have settled in a field which is not theirs. **When** *the owners of the field come, they will say, 'Let us have back our field.' They (will) undress in their presence in order to let them have back their field and to give it back to them. Therefore I say to you, if the owner of a house knows that the thief is coming, he will begin his vigil before he comes and will not let him dig through into his house of his domain to carry away his goods. You, then, be on your guard against the world. Arm yourselves with great strength lest the robbers find a way to come to you, for the difficulty which you expect will (surely) materialize. Let there be among you a man of understanding. When the grain ripened, he came quickly with his sickle in his hand and reaped it. Whoever has ears to hear, let him hear."*

GThom 35 ⇨ Luke 11:21–22

(35) Jesus said, "It is not possible for anyone to enter the house of **a strong man and** *take it by force unless he binds his hands; then he will (be able to) ransack* **his** *house."*

OTHER

POxy1224 2 ⇨ Luke 11:23

(2) And pray for your enemies. For **he who is not [against** you**] is** for you. **[He who** today] is far-off—tomorrow will be [near to you]. . . .

LUKE

Luke 11:24–26 (§L51.2)

24 "When the unclean spirit has gone out of a man, he passes through waterless places seeking rest; and finding none he says, 'I will return to my house from which I came.' 25 And when he comes he finds it swept and put in order. 26 Then he goes and brings seven other spirits more evil than himself, and they enter and dwell there; and the last state of that man becomes worse than the first."

Luke 11:27–28 (§L51.3)

27 As he said this, a woman in the crowd raised her voice and said to him, "Blessed is the womb that bore you, and the breasts that you sucked!" 28 But he said, "Blessed rather are those who hear the word of God and keep it!"

Luke 8:19–21 ⇨ §L51.3

19 Then his mother and his brothers came to him, but they could not reach him for the crowd. 20 And he was told, "Your mother and your brothers are standing outside, desiring to see you." 21 But he said to them, "My mother and my brothers are those who hear the word of God and do it."

MATT

Matt 12:43–45 (§M38) ⇨ §L51.2

43 "When the unclean spirit has gone out of a man, he passes through waterless places seeking rest, but he finds none. 44 Then he says, 'I will return to my house from which I came.' And when he comes he finds it empty, swept, and put in order. 45 Then he goes and brings with him seven other spirits more evil than himself, and they enter and dwell there; and the last state of that man becomes worse than the first. So shall it be also with this evil generation."

MARK

JOHN

THOMAS

GThom 79 ⇨ §L51.3

(79) A woman from the crowd said to Him, "Blessed are the womb which bore You and the breasts which nourished You."

He said to her, "Blessed are those who have heard the word of the Father and have truly kept it. For there will be days when you will say, 'Blessed are the womb which has not conceived and the breasts which have not given milk.'"

OTHER

LUKE	MATT	MARK

LUKE

Luke 11:29–32 (§L51.4)

²⁹ When the crowds were increasing, he began to say, "This generation is an evil generation; it seeks a sign, but no sign shall be given to it except the sign of Jonah. ³⁰ For as Jonah became a sign to the men of Nineveh, so will the Son of man be to this generation. ³¹ The queen of the South will arise at the judgment with the men of this generation and condemn them; for she came from the ends of the earth to hear the wisdom of Solomon, and behold, something greater than Solomon is here. ³² The men of Nineveh will arise at the judgment with this generation and condemn it; for they repented at the preaching of Jonah, and behold, something greater than Jonah is here.

Luke 11:16 ⇨ Luke 11:29

¹⁶ while others, to test him, sought from him a sign from heaven.

1 Kgs 10:1–13 ⇨ Luke 11:31

¹ Now when **the queen of** Sheba heard of the fame of **Solomon** concerning the name of the Lord, **she came** to test him with hard questions. ² **She came** to Jerusalem with a very great retinue, with camels bearing spices, and very much gold, and precious stones; and when **she came** to **Solomon**, she told him all that was on her mind. ³ And Solomon answered all her quesions; there was nothing hidden from the king which he could not explain to her. ⁴ And when **the queen of** Sheba had seen all **the wisdom of Solomon**, the house that he had built, ⁵ the food of his table, the seating of his officials, and the attendance of his servants, their clothing, his cupbearers, and his burnt offerings which he offered at the house of the Lord, there was no more spirit in her.

⁶ And she said to the king, "The report was true which I heard in my own land of your affairs and of your **wisdom**, ⁷ but I did not believe the reports until I **came** and my own eyes had seen it; and, behold, the half was not told me; your **wisdom** and prosperity surpass the report which I had heard. ⁸ Happy are your wives! Happy are your servants, who continually stand before you and hear your **wisdom**! ⁹ Blessed be the Lord your God, who has delighted in you and set you on the throne of Israel! Because the Lord loved Israel for ever, he has made you king, that you may execute justice and righteousness." ¹⁰ Then she gave the king a hundred and twenty talents of gold, and a very great quantity of spices, and precious stones; never again came such an abundance of spices as these which **the queen of** Sheba gave to King **Solomon**.

¹¹ Moreover the fleet of Hiram, which brought gold from Ophir, brought from Ophir a very great amount of almug wood and precious stones. ¹² And the king made of the almug wood supports for the house of the Lord, and for the king's house, lyres also and harps for the singers; no such almug wood has come or been seen, to this day.

¹³ And King **Solomon** gave to **the queen of** Sheba all that she desired, whatever she asked besides what was given her by the bounty of King **Solomon**. So she turned and went back to her own land, with her servants.

Jonah 3:5 ⇨ Luke 11:32

⁵ And **the** people **of Nineveh** believed God; **they** proclaimed a fast, and put on sackcloth, from the greatest of them to the least of them.

MATT

Matt 12:38–42 (§M37)

³⁸ Then some of the scribes and Pharisees said to him, "Teacher, we wish to see a sign from you." ³⁹ But **he** answered them, "An evil and adulterous **generation seeks** for a sign; but no sign shall be given to it except the sign of the prophet **Jonah**. ⁴⁰ For as Jonah was three days and three nights in the belly of the whale, **so will the** Son of man be three days and three nights in the heart of the earth. ⁴¹ The men of Nineveh will arise at the judgment with this generation and condemn it; for they repented at the preaching of Jonah, and behold, something greater than Jonah is here. ⁴² The queen of the South will arise at the judgment with this generation and condemn it; for she came from the ends of the earth to hear the wisdom of Solomon, and behold, something greater than Solomon is here.

Matt 16:1–4 (§M53) ⇨ Luke 11:29

¹ And the Pharisees and Sadducees came, and to test him they asked him to show them a sign from heaven. ² **He** answered them, "When it is evening, you say, 'It will be fair weather; for the sky is red.' ³ And in the morning, 'It will be stormy today, for the sky is red and threatening.' You know how to interpret the appearance of the sky, but you cannot interpret the signs of the times. ⁴ **An evil** and adulterous **generation seeks** for a sign, **but no sign shall be given to it except the sign of Jonah.**" So he left them and departed.

MARK

Mark 8:11–13 (§38) ⇨ Luke 11:29

¹¹ The Pharisees came and began to argue with him, seeking from him **a sign** from heaven, to test him. ¹² And **he** sighed deeply in his spirit, and said, "Why does **this generation** seek a sign? Truly, I say to you, **no sign shall be given to** this generation." ¹³ And he left them, and getting into the boat again he departed to the other side.

JOHN	THOMAS	OTHER

LUKE

Luke 11:33–36 (§L51.5)

³³ "No one after lighting a lamp puts it in a cellar or under a bushel, but on a stand, that those who enter may see the light. ³⁴ Your eye is the lamp of your body; when your eye is sound, your whole body is full of light; but when it is not sound, your body is full of darkness. ³⁵ Therefore be careful lest the light in you be darkness. ³⁶ If then your whole body is full of light, having no part dark, it will be wholly bright, as when a lamp with its rays gives you light."

● **Luke 8:16–17 (§L31.4)**

¹⁶ "No one after lighting a lamp covers it with a vessel, or puts it under a bed, but puts it on a stand, that those who enter may see the light. ¹⁷ For nothing is hid that shall not be made manifest, nor anything secret that shall not be known and come to light."

MATT

Matt 5:13–16 (§M12.3)

¹³ "You are the salt of the earth; but if salt has lost its taste, how shall its saltness be restored? It is no longer good for anything except to be thrown out and trodden under foot by men.

¹⁴ "You are the light of the world. A city set on a hill cannot be hid. ¹⁵ Nor do men light a lamp and put it under a bushel, but on a stand, and it gives light to all in the house. ¹⁶ Let your light so shine before men, that they may see your good works and give glory to your Father who is in heaven."

Matt 6:22–23 (§M12.7b)

²² "The eye is the lamp of the body. So, if your eye is sound, your whole body will be full of light; ²³ but if your eye is not sound, your whole body will be full of darkness. If then the light in you is darkness, how great is the darkness!"

MARK

Mark 4:21–23 (§21.5)

²¹ And he said to them, "Is a lamp brought in to be put under a bushel, or under a bed, and not on a stand? ²² For there is nothing hid, except to be made manifest; nor is anything secret, except to come to light. ²³ If any man has ears to hear, let him hear."

JOHN

THOMAS

GThom 33 ⇨ Luke 11:33

(33) Jesus said, "Preach from your housetops that which you will hear in your ear {(and) in the other ear}. For no one lights a lamp and puts it under a bushel, nor does he put it in a hidden place, but rather he sets it on a lampstand so that everyone who enters and leaves will see its light."

GThom 24 ⇨ Luke 11:34–36

(24) His disciples said to Him, "Show us the place where You are, since it is necessary for us to seek it."

He said to them, "Whoever has ears, let him hear. There is light within a man of light, and he (or: it) lights up the whole world. If he (or: it) does not shine, he (or: it) is darkness."

OTHER

DialSav 125:18–126:2 ⇨ Luke 11:34–36

The Savior said, "The lamp [of the] body is the mind; as long as ²⁰ you (sing.) are upright [of heart] —which is [. . .] —then your (pl.) bodies are [lights]. As long as your mind is [darkness], your light which you. wait for [will not be]."

LUKE

Luke 11:37–44 (§L52.1)
[37] While he was speaking, a Pharisee asked him to dine with him; so he went in and sat at table. [38] The Pharisee was astonished to see that he did not first wash before dinner. [39] And the Lord said to him, "Now you Pharisees cleanse the outside of the cup and of the dish, but inside you are full of extortion and wickedness. [40] You fools! Did not he who made the outside make the inside also? [41] But give for alms those things which are within; and behold, everything is clean for you.

[42] "But woe to you Pharisees! for you tithe mint and rue and every herb, and neglect justice and the love of God; these you ought to have done, without neglecting the others. [43] Woe to you Pharisees! for you love the best seat in the synagogues and salutations in the market places. [44] Woe to you! for you are like graves which are not seen, and men walk over them without knowing it."

Luke 7:36 ⇨ Luke 11:37
[36] One of the Pharisees asked him to eat with him, and he went into the Pharisee's house, and took his place at table, . . .

Luke 14:1 ⇨ Luke 11:37
[1] One sabbath when he went to dine at the house of a ruler who belonged to the Pharisees, they were watching him.

Luke 20:45–47 ⇨ Luke 11:42–43
[45] And in the hearing of all the people he said to his disciples, [46] "Beware of the scribes, who like to go about in long robes, and **love salutations in the market places and the best** seats **in the synagogues** and the places of honor at feasts, [47] who devour widows' houses and for a pretense make long prayers. They will receive the greater condemnation."

Luke 14:7–11 ⇨ Luke 11:43
[7] Now he told a parable to those who were invited, when he marked how they chose the places of honor, saying to them, [8] "When you are invited by any one to a marriage feast, do not sit down in a place of honor, lest a more eminent man than you be invited by him; [9] and he who invited you both will come and say to you, 'Give place to this man,' and then you will begin with shame to take the lowest place. [10] But when you are invited, go and sit in the lowest place, so that when your host comes he may say to you, 'Friend, go up higher'; then you will be honored in the presence of all who sit at table with you. [11] For every one who exalts himself will be humbled, and he who humbles himself will be exalted."

JOHN

MATT

Matt 23:25–26 ⇨ Luke 11:39–41
[25] "Woe to **you**, scribes and **Pharisees**, hypocrites! for you **cleanse the outside of the cup and of the** plate, **but inside** they **are full of extortion** and rapacity. [26] **You** blind Pharisee! first cleanse the **inside** of the cup and of the plate, that the **outside** also may be clean."

Matt 23:23–24 ⇨ Luke 11:42
[23] "**Woe to you**, scribes and **Pharisees**, hypocrites! **for you tithe mint and** dill and cummin, **and** have neglected the weightier matters of the law, **justice and** mercy and faith; **these you ought to have done, without neglecting the others**. [24] You blind guides, straining out a gnat and swallowing a camel!"

Matt 23:5–7 ⇨ Luke 11:43
[5] "They do all their deeds to be seen by men; for they make their phylacteries broad and their fringes long, [6] and they **love** the place of honor at feasts and **the best** seats **in the synagogues**, [7] **and salutations in the market places**, and being called rabbi by men."

Matt 23:27–28 ⇨ Luke 11:44
[27] "**Woe to you**, scribes and Pharisees, hypocrites! **for you are like** whitewashed tombs, **which** outwardly appear beautiful, but within they **are** full of dead men's bones and all uncleanness. [28] So you also outwardly appear righteous to **men**, but within **you are** full of hypocrisy and iniquity."

Cf. Matt 15:1–9 (§M49.1), Matt 23:1–12 (§M77.1), Matt 23:13–16 (§M77.2)

Mic 6:8 ⇨ Luke 11:42
[8] He has showed **you**, O man, what is good; and what does the Lord require of **you** but to do **justice, and** to **love** kindness, and to walk humbly with your **God**?

THOMAS

GThom 89 ⇨ Luke 11:39–41
(89) Jesus said, "Why do you wash the outside of the cup? Do you not realize that he who made the inside is the same one who made the outside?"

MARK

Mark 12:38–40 (§59.8) ⇨ Luke 11:42–43
[38] And in his teaching he said, "Beware of the scribes, who like to go about in long robes, and to have **salutations in the market places** [39] **and the best** seats **in the synagogues** and the places of honor at feasts, [40] who devour widows' houses and for a pretense make long prayers. They will receive the greater condemnation."

Cf. Mark 7:1–13 (§K33)

OTHER

POxy840 2 ⇨ Luke 11:39–41
*(2) And he took them (the disciples) with him into the place of purification itself and walked about in the Temple court. And a Pharisaic chief priest, Levi (?) by name, fell in with them and s[aid] to the Savior: Who gave thee leave to [trea]d this place of purification and to look upon [the]se holy utensils without having bathed thyself and even without thy disciples having [wa]shed their f[eet]? On the contrary, being defi[led], thou hast trodden the Temple court, this clean p[lace], although no [one who] has [not] first bathed himself or [chang]ed his clot[hes] may tread it and [venture] to vi[ew these] holy utensils! Forthwith [the Savior] s[tood] still with h[is] disciples and [answered]: How stands it (then) with thee, thou art forsooth (also) here in the Temple court. Art thou then **clean?** He said to him: I am **clean.** For I have bathed myself in the pool of David and have gone down by the one stair and come up by the other and have put on white and clean clothes, and (only) then have I come hither and have viewed these holy utensils. Then **said** the Savior **to him:** Woe unto **you** blind that see not! Thou hast bathed thyself in water that is poured out, in which dogs and swine lie night and day and thou hast washed thyself and hast chafed thine outer skin, which prostitutes also and flute-girls anoint, bathe, chafe and rouge, in order to arouse desire in men, **but** within they **are full of** scorpions **and** of [bad]ness [of every kind]. But I and [my disciples], of whom thou sayest that we have not im[mersed] ourselves, [have been im]mersed in the liv[ing . . .] water which comes down from [. . . B]ut woe unto them that . . .*

LUKE

Luke 11:45-54 (§L52.2)

45 One of the lawyers answered him, "Teacher, in saying this you reproach us also." 46 And he said, "Woe to you lawyers also! for you load men with burdens hard to bear, and you yourselves do not touch the burdens with one of your fingers. 47 Woe to you! for you build the tombs of the prophets whom your fathers killed. 48 So you are witnesses and consent to the deeds of your fathers; for they killed them, and you build their tombs. 49 Therefore also the Wisdom of God said, 'I will send them prophets and apostles, some of whom they will kill and persecute,' 50 that the blood of all the prophets, shed from the foundation of the world, may be required of this generation, 51 from the blood of Abel to the blood of Zechariah, who perished between the altar and the sanctuary. Yes, I tell you, it shall be required of this generation. 52 Woe to you lawyers! for you have taken away the key of knowledge; you did not enter yourselves, and you hindered those who were entering."

53 As he went away from there, the scribes and the Pharisees began to press him hard, and to provoke him to speak of many things, 54 lying in wait for him, to catch at something he might say.

Luke 13:33-34 ⇨ Luke 11:47-51

33 "'Nevertheless I must go on my way today and tomorrow and the day following; for it cannot be that a prophet should perish away from Jerusalem.' 34 O Jerusalem, Jerusalem, killing the prophets and stoning those who are sent to you! How often would I have gathered your children together as a hen gathers her brood under her wings, and you would not!"

Zech 1:1-6 ⇨ Luke 11:49-51

1 In the eighth month, in the second year of Darius, the word of the Lord came to Zechariah the son of Berechiah, son of Iddo, the prophet, saying, 2 "The Lord was very angry with your fathers. 3 Therefore say to them, Thus says the Lord of hosts: Return to me, says the Lord of hosts, and I will return to you, says the Lord of hosts. 4 Be not like your fathers, to whom the former prophets cried out, 'Thus says the Lord of hosts, Return from your evil ways and from your evil deeds.' but they did not hear or heed me, says the Lord. 5 Your fathers, where are they? And the prophets, do they live for ever? 6 But my words and my statutes, which I commanded my servants the prophets, did they not overtake your fathers? So they repented and said, As the Lord of hosts purposed to deal with us for our ways and deeds, so has he dealt with us."

Gen 4:8 ⇨ Luke 11:50-51

8 Cain said to Abel his brother, "Let us go out to the field." And when they were in the field, Cain rose up against his brother Abel, and killed him.

2 Chr 24:20-21 ⇨ Luke 11:50-51

20 Then the Spirit of God took possession of Zechariah the son of Jehoiada the priest; and he stood above the people, and said to them, "Thus says God, 'Why do you transgress the commandments of the Lord, so that you cannot prosper? Because you have forsaken the Lord, he has forsaken you.'" 21 But they conspired against him, and by command of the king they stoned him with stones in the court of the house of the Lord.

JOHN

MATT

Matt 23:4 ⇨ Luke 11:46

4 "They bind heavy burdens, hard to bear, and lay them on men's shoulders; but they themselves will not move them with their finger."

Matt 23:29-31 ⇨ Luke 11:47-48

29 "Woe to you, scribes and Pharisees, hypocrites! for you build the tombs of the prophets and adorn the monuments of the righteous, 30 saying, 'If we had lived in the days of our fathers, we would not have taken part with them in shedding the blood of the prophets.' 31 Thus you witness against yourselves, that you are sons of those who murdered the prophets."

Matt 23:32-36 ⇨ Luke 11:49-51

32 "Fill up, then, the measure of your fathers. 33 You serpents, you brood of vipers, how are you to escape being sentenced to hell? 34 Therefore I send you prophets and wise men and scribes, some of whom you will kill and crucify, and some you will scourge in your synagogues and persecute from town to town, 35 that upon you may come all the righteous blood shed on earth, from the blood of innocent Abel to the blood of Zechariah the son of Barachiah, whom you murdered between the sanctuary and the altar. 36 Truly, I say to you, all this will come upon this generation."

Matt 23:13 ⇨ Luke 11:52

13 "But woe to you, scribes and Pharisees, hypocrites! because you shut the kingdom of heaven against men; for you neither enter yourselves, nor allow those who would enter to go in."

Cf. Matt 15:1-9 (§M49.1), Matt 23:1-12 (§M77.1), Matt 23:13-26 (§M77.2)

THOMAS

POxy655 2 ⇨ Luke 11:52

(2) [Jesus says, "The Pharisees and the scribes have] re[ceived the keys] of [knowledge and] have hid[den them; neither have they] enter[ed nor permitted] those who wo[uld] en[ter. But you] b[ecome wi]se [as serpents and g]uile[less as do]ve[s]."

GThom 39 ⇨ Luke 11:52

(39) Jesus said, "The Pharisees and the scribes have taken the keys of Knowledge and hidden them. They themselves have not entered, nor have they allowed to enter those who wish to. You, however, be as wise as serpents and as innocent as doves."

GThom 102 ⇨ Luke 11:52

(102) Jesus said, "Woe to the Pharisees, for they are like a dog sleeping in the manger of oxen, for neither does he eat nor does he let the oxen eat."

MARK

Cf. Mark 7:1-13 (§K33)

OTHER

Acts 7:51-52 ⇨ Luke 11:47-51

51 "You stiff-necked people, uncircumcised in heart and ears, you always resist the Holy Spirit. As your fathers did, so do you. 52 Which of the prophets did not your fathers persecute? And they killed those who announced beforehand the coming of the Righteous One, whom you have now betrayed and murdered, . . ."

PJas 24:1-4 ⇨ Luke 11:50-51

1 Rather, at the hour of the salutation the priests were departing, but the blessing of Zacharias did not meet them according to custom. And the priests stood waiting for Zacharias, to greet him with prayer and to glorify the Most High. 2 But when he delayed to come, they were all afraid. But one of them took courage and went into the sanctuary. And he saw beside the altar congealed blood; and a voice said: "Zacharias has been slain, and his blood shall not be wiped away until his avenger comes." And when he heard these words, he was afraid, and went out and told the priests what he had seen. 3 And they heard and saw what had happened. And the panelwork of the ceiling of the temple wailed, and they rent their clothes from the top to the bottom. And they did not find his body, but they found his blood turned into stone. And they were afraid, and went out and told all the people: "Zacharias has been slain." And all the tribes of the people heard it and mourned him and lamented three days and three nights. 4 And after the three days the priests took counsel whom they should appoint in his stead. And the lot fell upon Symeon. Now it was he to whom it had been revealed by the Holy Spirit that he should not see death until he had seen the Christ in the flesh.

GNaz 17 ⇨ Luke 11:50

(17) In the Gospel which the Nazarenes use, instead of "son of Barachias" we have found written "son of Joiada." (Jerome, Commentary on Matthew 4 [on Matthew 23:35])

L52

S17: L50-52

PHARISEES AND LAWYERS

JOURNEY TO JERUSALEM FOUR

Luke 11:37-54

Luke 11:1-54

385

LUKE	MATT	MARK

Luke 12:1–12 (§L53)

¹In the meantime, when so many thousands of the multitude had gathered together that they trod upon one another, he began to say to his disciples first, "Beware of the leaven of the Pharisees, which is hypocrisy. ²Nothing is covered up that will not be revealed, or hidden that will not be known. ³Therefore whatever you have said in the dark shall be heard in the light, and what you have whispered in private rooms shall be proclaimed upon the housetops.

⁴"I tell you, my friends, do not fear those who kill the body, and after that have no more that they can do. ⁵But I will warn you whom to fear: fear him who, after he has killed, has power to cast into hell;ᵃ yes, I tell you, fear him! ⁶Are not five sparrows sold for two pennies? And not one of them is forgotten before God. ⁷Why, even the hairs of your head are all numbered. Fear not; you are of more value than many sparrows.

⁸"And I tell you, every one who acknowledges me before men, the Son of man also will acknowledge before the angels of God; ⁹but he who denies me before men will be denied before the angels of God. ¹⁰And every one who speaks a word against the Son of man will be forgiven; but he who blasphemes against the Holy Spirit will not be forgiven. ¹¹And when they bring you before the synagogues and the rulers and the authorities, do not be anxious how or what you are to answer or what you are to say; ¹²for the Holy Spirit will teach you in that very hour what you ought to say."

ᵃ Greek: *Gehenna*

Luke 8:16–17 (§L31.4) ⇨ Luke 12:2

¹⁶"No one after lighting a lamp covers it with a vessel, or puts it under a bed, but puts it on a stand, that those who enter may see the light. ¹⁷For **nothing is** hid **that** shall **not be** made manifest, nor anything secret **that** shall **not be known** and come to light."

Luke 12:24 ⇨ Luke 12:7

²⁴*"Consider the ravens: they neither sow nor reap, they had neither storehouse nor barn, and yet God feeds them. Of how much **more value** are you **than** the birds!"*

Luke 21:18 ⇨ Luke 12:7

¹⁸*"But not a hair of your head will perish."*

Matt 10:26–33 (§M28.4) ⇨ Luke 12:1–9

²⁶"So have no fear of them; for **nothing is covered** that **will not be revealed, or hidden that will not be known.** ²⁷What I tell you **in the dark**, utter **in the light; and what you hear** whispered, proclaim **upon the housetops.** ²⁸And **do not fear those who kill the body** but cannot kill the soul; rather **fear him who** can destroy both soul and body in **hell.** ²⁹**Are not** two **sparrows sold for** a penny? **And not one of them** will fall to the ground without your Father's will. ³⁰But **even the hairs of your head are all numbered.** ³¹**Fear not**, therefore; **you are of more value than many sparrows.** ³²So **every one who acknowledges me before men, I also will acknowledge before** my Father who is in heaven; ³³but whoever **denies me before men, I also will deny before** my Father who is in heaven."

Matt 12:32 ⇨ Luke 12:10

³²"And whoever says **a word against the Son of man will be forgiven, but** whoever speaks **against the Holy Spirit will not be forgiven,** either in this age or in the age to come."

Matt 10:19–20 ⇨ Luke 12:11–12

¹⁹"**When they** deliver **you up, do not be anxious how** you are to speak **or what you are to say; for what you** are **to say will** be given to **you in that hour;** ²⁰for **it is not you who speak,** but **the Spirit** of your Father speaking through **you.**"

Luke 9:26 ⇨ Luke 12:8–9

²⁶"For whoever is ashamed of **me** and of my words, of him **will** the Son of man be ashamed when he comes in his glory and the glory **of** the Father and of **the** holy **angels.**"

Luke 21:14–15 ⇨ Luke 12:11–12

¹⁴"Settle it therefore in your minds, **not** to meditate beforehand **how to answer;** ¹⁵**for I will** give **you** a mouth and wisdom, which none of your adversaries will be able to withstand or contradict."

Mark 4:21–23 (§K21.5) ⇨ Luke 12:2

²¹And he said to thm, "Is a lamp brought in to be put under a bushel, or under a bed, and not on a stand? ²²For there **is nothing** hid, except to **be** made manifest; nor is anything secret, except to come to light. ²³If any man has ears to hear, let him hear."

Mark 8:38 ⇨ Luke 12:8–9

³⁸"For whoever is ashamed of **me** and of my words in this adulterous and sinful generation, of him will the **Son of man** also be ashamed, when he comes in the glory of his Father with **the** holy **angels.**"

Mark 3:28–29 ⇨ Luke 12:10

²⁸"Truly, I say to you, all sins **will be forgiven** the sons of men, and whatever blasphemies they utter; ²⁹but whoever **blasphemes against the Holy Spirit** never has forgiveness, but is guilty of an eternal sin"—

Mark 13:11 ⇨ Luke 12:12

¹¹"**And when they bring you** to trial and deliver you up, **do not be anxious** beforehand **what you are to say;** but **say** whatever is given **you in that hour, for** it is not you who speak, but **the Holy Spirit.**"

JOHN

John 14:26 ⇨ Luke 12:12
²⁶"But the Counselor, **the Holy Spirit**, whom the Father will send in my name, he **will teach you** all things, and bring to your remembrance all that I have said to you."

THOMAS

POxy654 5 ⇨ Luke 12:2
(5) Jesus says, "K[now what is be]fore your face, and [that which **is hidden**] from you **will be reveal[ed** to you. For there i]s **nothing hidden** which **will not** [be made] mani[fest] and (**nothing**) buried which **will not** [be raised up.]"

GThom 5 ⇨ Luke 12:2
(5) Jesus said, "Recognize what is in your sight, and that which **is hidden** from you **will** become plain to you. For there **is nothing hidden** which **will not** become manifest."

GThom 6 ⇨ Luke 12:2
(6) His disciples questioned Him and said to Him, "Do You want us to fast? How shall we pray? Shall we give alms? What diet shall we observe?"
Jesus said, "Do not tell lies, and do not do what you hate, for all things are plain in the sight of Heaven. For **nothing hidden will not** become manifest, and **nothing covered will** remain without being uncovered."

POxy1 8 ⇨ Luke 12:3
(8) Jesus says, "What **you** hear your one ear, preach that **upon** your roof-tops . . ."

GThom 33 ⇨ Luke 12:3
(33) Jesus said, "Preach from your **housetops** that which you will hear in your ear {(and) in the other ear}. For no one lights a lamp and puts it under a bushel, nor does he put it in a hidden place, but rather he sets it on a lampstand so that everyone who enters and leaves will see its light."

GThom 44 ⇨ Luke 12:10
(44) Jesus said, "Whoever blasphemes against the Father **will be forgiven**, and whoever blasphemes **against the Son will be forgiven,** but whoever blasphemes **against the Holy Spirit will not be forgiven** either on earth or in heaven."

OTHER

2 Clem 5:2–4 ⇨ Luke 12:4–5
²*for the Lord said, "Ye shall be as lambs in the midst of wolves,"* ³*and Peter answered and said to him, "If then the wolves tear the lambs?"* ⁴*Jesus said to Peter, "Let the lambs have no fear of the wolves after their death; and do ye have no fear of those that slay you, and can do nothing more to you, but fear him who after your death hath power over body and soul, to cast them into the flames of hell."*

Acts 27:34 ⇨ Luke 12:7
³⁴*"Therefore I urge you to take some food; it will give you strength, since not a hair is to perish from the head of any of you."*

2 Clem 3:2 ⇨ Luke 12:8
²**And** *he himself also says, "Whosoever confessed* **me before men,** *I* **will** *confess him* **before** *my Father";* . . .

Acts 4:5–8 ⇨ Luke 12:11–12
⁵*On the morrow their* **rulers and** *elders and scribes were gathered together in Jerusalem,* ⁶*with Annas the high priest and Caiaphas and John and Alexander, and all who were of the high-priestly family.* ⁷**And** *when they had set them in the midst, they inquired, "By what power or by what name did you do this?"* ⁸*Then Peter, filled with* **the Holy Spirit,** *said to them, "rulers of the people and elders, . . ."*

LUKE	MATT	MARK

LUKE

Luke 12:13–21 (§L54)

¹³One of the multitude said to him, "Teacher, bid my brother divide the inheritance with me." ¹⁴But he said to him, "Man, who made me a judge or divider over you?" ¹⁵And he said to them, "Take heed, and beware of all covetousness; for a man's life does not consist in the abundance of his possessions." ¹⁶And he told them a parable, saying, "The land of a rich man brought forth plentifully; ¹⁷and he thought to himself, 'What shall I do, for I have nowhere to store my crops?' ¹⁸And he said, 'I will do this: I will pull down my barns, and build larger ones; and there I will store all my grain and my goods. ¹⁹And I will say to my soul, Soul, you have ample goods laid up for many years; take your ease, eat, drink, be merry.' ²⁰But God said to him, 'Fool! This night your soul is required of you; and the things you have prepared, whose will they be?' ²¹So is he who lays up treasure for himself, and is not rich toward God."

Luke 12:33–34 ⇨ Luke 12:21

*³³"Sell your possessions, and give alms; provide yourselves with purses that do not grow old, with a **treasure** in the heavens that does not fail, where no thief approaches and no moth destroys. ³⁴For where your **treasure** is, there will your heart be also."*

Luke 18:22 ⇨ Luke 12:21

*²²And when Jesus heard it, he said to him, "One thing you still lack. Sell all that you have and distribute to the poor, and you will have **treasure** in heaven; and come, follow me."*

JOHN	THOMAS	OTHER

THOMAS

GThom 72 ⇨ Luke 12:13–14

(72) [A man **said**] **to Him**, "Tell **my** brothers to **divide** my father's possessions **with me**." hers to

He said to him, "O **man, who** has **made Me a divider**?"

He turned to His disciples and said to them, "I am not a divider, am I?"

GThom 63 ⇨ Luke 12:16–21

(63) Jesus said, "There was **a rich man** who had much money. **He** said, 'I shall put **my** money to use so that I may sow, reap, plant, and fill my storehouse with produce, with the result that **I** shall lack nothing.' Such were his intentions, but that same **night** he died. Let him who has ears hear."

OTHER

1 Cor 15:32 ⇨ Luke 12:19

*³²What do I gain if, humanly speaking, I fought with beasts at Ephesus? If the dead are not raised, "Let us **eat** and **drink**, for tomorrow we die."*

LUKE

Luke 12:22–34 (§L55)

[22] And he said to his disciples, "Therefore I tell you, do not be anxious about your life, what you shall eat, nor about your body, what you shall put on. [23] For life is more than food, and the body more than clothing. [24] Consider the ravens: they neither sow nor reap, they have neither storehouse nor barn, and yet God feeds them. Of how much more value are you than the birds! [25] And which of you by being anxious can add a cubit to his span of life?[a] [26] If then you are not able to do as small a thing as that, why are you anxious about the rest? [27] Consider the lilies, how they grow; they neither toil nor spin;[b] yet I tell you, even Solomon in all his glory was not arrayed like one of these. [28] But if God so clothes the grass which is alive in the field today and tomorrow is thrown into the oven, how much more will he clothe you, O men of little faith! [29] And do not seek what you are to eat and what you are to drink, nor be of anxious mind. [30] For all the nations of the world seek these things; and your Father knows that you need them. [31] Instead, seek his[c] kingdom, and these things shall be yours as well.

[32] "Fear not, little flock, for it is your Father's good pleasure to give you the kingdom. [33] Sell your possessions, and give alms; provide yourselves with purses that do not grow old, with a treasure in the heavens that does not fail, where no thief approaches and no moth destroys. [34] For where your treasure is, there will your heart be also."

[a] Or *to his stature*

[b] A few witnesses read *Consider the lilies; they neither spin nor weave:* D it[d] syr[c,s] *al*

[c] Some witnesses read *God's:* 𝔓[45] A D[b] K W X Δ Θ Π *f*[1] *f*[13] 28 33 *pm*

Luke 12:7 ⇨ Luke 12:24
[7] "Why, even the hairs of your head are all numbered. Fear not; *you are of more value than many sparrows.*"

Luke 12:21 ⇨ Luke 12:33–34
[21] "So is he who lays up *treasure* for himself, and is not rich toward God."

Luke 18:22 ⇨ Luke 12:33–34
[22] And when Jesus heard it, he said to him, "One thing you still lack. *Sell all that you have and distribute to the poor, and you will have treasure in heaven; and come, follow me.*"

JOHN

MATT

Matt 6:25–34 (§M12.7d)

[25] "Therefore I tell you, **do not be anxious about your life, what you shall eat** or what you shall drink, **nor about your body, what you shall put on.** Is not **life more than food, and the body more than clothing?** [26] Look at the birds of the air: **they neither sow nor reap** nor gather into barns, **and yet** your heavenly Father **feeds them.** Are you not of **more value** than they? [27] **And which of you by being** anxious can add one **cubit to his span of life?** [28] And **why are you anxious about clothing?** Consider the lilies of the field, how they grow; **they neither toil nor spin;** [29] yet I tell you, **even Solomon in all his glory was not arrayed like one of these.** [30] But if God so clothes the **grass of the field, which today is alive and tomorrow is thrown into the oven, will he** not much more clothe you, **O men of little faith?** [31] Therefore **do not be anxious,** saying, '**What** shall we **eat?**' or '**What** shall we **drink?**' or 'What shall we wear?' [32] **For the** Gentiles **seek** all **these things; and your** heavenly **Father knows that you need them** all. [33] But **seek** first **his kingdom** and his righteousness, **and** all **these things shall be yours as well.**

[34] "Therefore **do not be anxious about** tomorrow, for tomorrow will **be anxious** for itself. Let the day's own trouble be sufficient for the day."

Matt 6:19–21 (§M12.7a) ⇨ Luke 12:33–34
[19] "Do not lay up for yourselves treasures on earth, where **moth** and rust consume and where thieves break in and steal, [20] but lay up for **yourselves** treasures **in** heaven, where neither moth nor rust consumes and where thieves do not break in and steal. [21] **For where your treasure is, there will your heart be also.**"

THOMAS

GThom 36 ⇨ Luke 12:22–23
(36) Jesus said, "**Do not be** concerned from morning until evening and from evening until morning **about what you** will wear."

GThom 76 ⇨ Luke 12:32–34
(76) Jesus said, "The Kingdom of the Father is like a merchant who had a consignment of merchandise and who discovered a pearl. That merchant was shrewd. He sold the merchandise and bought the pearl alone for himself. You too, seek his unfailing and enduring **treasure where no moth** comes near to devour and **no** worm **destroys.**"

MARK

OTHER

Clement, *Stromateis* **1.24.158** ⇨ Luke 12:31
"Ask for the great things, and God will add unto you the little things."

Phil 4:6 ⇨ Luke 12:29
[6] *Have no anxiety about anything, but in everything by prayer and supplication with thanksgiving let your requests be made known to God.*

LUKE

Luke 12:35–48 (§L56.1)

[35]"Let your loins be girded and your lamps burning, [36] and be like men who are waiting for their master to come home from the marriage feast, so that they may open to him at once when he comes and knocks. [37] Blessed are those servants whom the master finds awake when he comes; truly, I say to you, he will gird himself and have them sit at table, and he will come and serve them. [38] If he comes in the second watch, or in the third, and finds them so, blessed are those servants! [39] But know this, that if the householder had known at what hour the thief was coming, he[a] would not have left his house to be broken into. [40] You also must be ready; for the Son of man is coming at an unexpected hour."

[41] Peter said, "Lord, are you telling this parable for us or for all?" [42] And the Lord said, "Who then is the faithful and wise steward, whom his master will set over his household, to give them their portion of food at the proper time? [43] Blessed is that servant whom his master when he comes will find so doing. [44] Truly, I say to you, he will set him over all his possessions. [45] But if that servant says to himself, 'My master is delayed in coming,' and begins to beat the menservants and the maidservants, and to eat and drink and get drunk, [46] the master of that servant will come on a day when he does not expect him and at an hour he does not know, and will punish him,[b] and put him with the unfaithful. [47] And that servant who knew his master's will, but did not make ready or act according to his will, shall receive a severe beating. [48] But he who did not know, and did what deserved a beating, shall receive a light beating. Every one to whom much is given, of him will much be required; and of him to whom men commit much they will demand the more."

[a] Some witnesses add *would have watched and* (see Matt 24:43): ℵ^c A B K L P W X Δ Θ Π Ψ f¹ f¹³ 28 33 pm

[b] Or *cut him in pieces*

JOHN

John 13:3–5 ⇨ Luke 12:37

[3] *Jesus, knowing that the Father had given all things into his hands, and that he had come from God and was going to God, [4] rose from supper, laid aside his garments, and girded himself with a towel. [5] Then he poured water into a basin, and began to wash the disciples' feet and to wipe them with the towel with which he was girded.*

MATT

Matt 24:43–51

[43]"But know this, that if the householder had known in what part of the night the thief was coming, he would have watched and would not have let his house be broken into. [44] Therefore you also must be ready; for the Son of man is coming at an hour you do not expect.

[45]"Who then is the faithful and wise servant, whom his master has set over his household, to give them their food at the proper time? [46] Blessed is that servant whom his master when he comes will find so doing. [47] Truly, I say to you, he will set him over all his possessions. [48] But if that wicked servant says to himself, 'My master is delayed,' [49] and begins to beat his fellow servants, and eats and drinks with the drunken, [50] the master of that servant will come on a day when he does not expect him and at an hour he does not know, [51] and will punish him, and put him with the hypocrites; there men will weep and gnash their teeth."

Matt 25:1–13 (§M79.1)

[1] *"Then the kingdom of heaven shall be compared to ten maidens who took their lamps and went to meet the bridegroom. [2] Five of them were foolish, and five were wise. [3] For when the foolish took their lamps, they took no oil with them; [4] but the wise took flasks of oil with their lamps. [5] As the bridegroom was delayed, they all slumbered and slept. [6] But at midnight there was a cry, 'Behold, the bridegroom! Come out to meet him.' [7] Then all those maidens rose and trimmed their lamps. [8] And the foolish said to the wise, 'Give us some of your oil, for our lamps are going out.' [9] But the wise replied, 'Perhaps there will not be enough for us and for you; go rather to the dealers and buy for yourselves.' [10] And while they went to buy, the bridegroom came, and those who were ready went in with him to the marriage feast; and the door was shut. [11] Afterward the other maidens came also, saying, 'Lord, lord, open to us.' [12] But he replied, 'Truly, I say to you, I do not know you.' [13] Watch therefore, for you know neither the day nor the hour."*

THOMAS

GThom 21 ⇨ Luke 12:39

(21) Mary said to Jesus, "Whom are Your disciples like?"

He said, "They are like children who have settled in a field which is not theirs. When the owners of the field come, they will say, 'Let us have back our field.' They (will) undress in their presence in order to let them have back their field and to give it back to them. Therefore I say to you, if the owner of a house knows that the thief is coming, he will begin his vigil before he comes and will not let him dig through into his house of his domain to carry away his goods. You, then, be on your guard against the world. Arm yourselves with great strength lest the robbers find a way to come to you, for the difficulty which you expect will (surely) materialize. Let there be among you a man of understanding. When the grain ripened, he came quickly with his sickle in his hand and reaped it. Whoever has ears to hear, let him hear."

GThom 103 ⇨ Luke 12:39

(103) Jesus said, "Fortunate is the man who knows where the brigands will enter, so that he may get up, muster his domain, and arm himself before they invade."

MARK

Mark 13:33–37 (§K60.5)

[33] Take heed, watch; for you do not know when the time will come. [34] It is like a man going on a journey, when he leaves home and puts his servants in charge, each with his work, and commands the doorkeeper to be on watch. [35] Watch therefore—for you do not know when the master of the house will come, in the evening, or at midnight, or at cockcrow, or in the morning— [36] lest he come suddenly and find you asleep. [37] And what I say to you I say to all: Watch."

OTHER

GNaz 18 ⇨ Luke 12:45–46

(18) But since the Gospel (written) in Hebrew characters which has come into our hands enters the threat not the against man who had hid (the talent), but against him who had lived dissolutely—for he (the master) had three servants: one who squandered his master's substance with harlots and flute-girls, one who multiplied the gain, and one who hid the talent; and accordingly one was accepted (with joy), another merely rebuked, and another cast into prison—I wonder whether in Matthew the threat which is uttered after the word against the man who did nothing may refer not to him, but by epanalepsis to the first who had feasted and drunk with the drunken. (Eusebius, Theophania 22 [on Matthew 25:14–15])

LUKE

Luke 12:49–53 (§L56.2)

⁴⁹"I came to cast fire upon the earth; and would that it were already kindled! ⁵⁰ I have a baptism to be baptized with; and how I am constrained until it is accomplished! ⁵¹ Do you think that I have come to give peace on earth? No, I tell you, but rather division; ⁵² for henceforth in one house there will be five divided, three against two and two against three; ⁵³ they will be divided, father against son and son against father, mother against daughter and daughter against her mother, mother-in-law against her daughter-in-law and daughter-in-law against her mother-in-law."

Mic 7:5–6 ⇨ Luke 12:53

⁵ Put no trust in a neighbor,
    have no confidence in a friend;
guard the doors of your mouth
    from her who lies in your bosom;
⁶ for the son treats the **father** with contempt,
    the **daughter** rises up **against** her **mother**,
    the **daughter-in-law against her mother-in-law**;
a man's enemies are the men of his own house.

MATT

Matt 10:34–39 (§M28.5)

³⁴"**Do** not **think that I have come** to bring **peace on earth**; **I have** not **come** to bring **peace**, but a sword. ³⁵ **For** I have come to set a man **against** his **father**, and a **daughter against** her **mother**, and a **daughter-in-law against her mother-in-law**; ³⁶ and a man's foes will be those of his own household. ³⁷ He who loves father or mother more than me is not worthy of me; and he who loves son or daughter more than me is not worthy of me; ³⁸ and he who does not take his cross and follow me is not worthy of me. ³⁹ He who finds his life will lose it, and he who loses his life for my sake will find it."

MARK

Mark 10:38 ⇨ Luke 12:50

³⁸ *But Jesus said to them, "You do not know what you are asking. Are you able to drink the cup that I drink, or to be baptized with the baptism with which I am baptized?"*

Mark 13:12–13 ⇨ Luke 12:51–53

¹² *"And brother will deliver up brother to death, and the **father** his child, and children will rise **against** parents and have them put to death; ¹³ and you will be hated by all for my name's sake. But he who endures to the end will be saved."*

JOHN

John 15:18–21 ⇨ 12:51–53

¹⁸ *"If the world hates you, know that it has hated me before it hated you. ¹⁹ If you were of the world, the world would love its own; but because you are not of the world, but I chose you out of the world, therefore the world hates you. ²⁰ Remember the word that I said to you, 'A servant is not greater than his master.' If they persecuted me, they will persecute **you**; if they kept my word, they will keep yours also. ²¹ But all this they will do to **you** on my account, because they do not know him who sent me."*

THOMAS

GThom 10 ⇨ Luke 12:49

(10) Jesus said, "**I** have **cast fire upon the** world, and see, I am guarding it until it blazes."

GThom 16 ⇨ Luke 12:51–53

(16) Jesus said, "Men think, perhaps, that it is **peace** which **I have come to** cast upon the world. They do not know that it is dissension which I have come **to cast** upon the earth: **fire**, sword, and war. For **there will be five** in a house: **three** will be **against two, and two against three**, the **father against** the **son, and** the **son against** the **father**. And they will stand solitary."

OTHER

LUKE

MATT

MARK

Luke 12:54–56 (§L56.3)

⁵⁴He also said to the multitudes, "**When you see** a cloud rising in the west, **you say** at once, 'A shower is coming'; and so it happens. ⁵⁵And when you see the south wind blowing, you say, 'There will be scorching heat'; and it happens. ⁵⁶**You** hypocrites! **You know how to interpret the** appearance **of the** earth and **sky;** but why do **you** not know how to **interpret the** present time?"

Luke 12:57–59 (§L56.4)

⁵⁷"And why do you not judge for yourselves what is right? ⁵⁸As you go **with your accuser** before the magistrate, make an effort to settle with him on the way, **lest** he drag **you to the judge, and the** judge hand **you** over to the officer, and the officer **put you in prison.** ⁵⁹I tell **you, you will never get out till you have paid** the very last copper."

Matt 16:2–3 ⇨ §L56.3

²**He** answered them, "**When** it is evening, **you say,** 'It will be fair weather; for the sky is red.' ³**And** in the morning, 'It will be stormy today, for the sky is red and threatening.' **You know how to interpret the appearance of the sky, but you cannot interpret the** signs **of the** times."

Matt 5:25–26 ⇨ §L56.4

²⁵"**Make** friends quickly **with your accuser,** while **you** are going **with** him to court, **lest** your accuser hand **you** over **to the judge, and the** judge to the guard, and **you be put in prison;** ²⁶truly, **I** say to **you, you will never get out till you have paid the last** penny."

Matt 18:34–35 ⇨ §L56.4

³⁴"*And in anger his lord delivered him to the jailers, till he should pay all his debt.* ³⁵*So also my heavenly Father will* **do** *to every one of you, if* **you do** *not forgive your brother from your heart.*"

JOHN

THOMAS

OTHER

GThom 91 ⇨ §L56.3

(91) They said to Him, "Tell us who You are so that we may believe in You."

He said to them, "**You** read the face of the **sky** and **of the earth, but you** have **not** recognized the one who (or: that which) is before **you, and you do not know how to** read this moment."

LUKE

THE GALILEANS AS SINNERS

Luke 13:1–5 (§L57.1)
¹ There were some present at that very time who told him of the Galileans whose blood Pilate had mingled with their sacrifices. ² And he answered them, "Do you think that these Galileans were worse sinners than all the other Galileans, because they suffered thus? ³ I tell you, No; but unless you repent you will all likewise perish. ⁴ Or those eighteen upon whom the tower in Siloam fell and killed them, do you think that they were worse offenders than all the others who dwelt in Jerusalem? ⁵ I tell you, No; but unless you repent you will all likewise perish."

THE PARABLE OF THE FIG TREE

Luke 13:6–9 (§L57.2)
⁶ And he told this parable: "A man had a fig tree planted in his vineyard; and he came seeking fruit on it and found none. ⁷ And he said to the vinedresser, 'Lo, these three years I have come seeking fruit on this fig tree, and I find none. Cut it down; why should it use up the ground?' ⁸ And he answered him, 'Let it alone, sir, this year also, till I dig about it and put on manure. ⁹ And if it bears fruit next year, well and good; but if not, you can cut it down.'"

Luke 3:9 ⇨ §L57.2
⁹ *"Even now the axe is laid to the root of the trees; every tree therefore that does not bear good **fruit** is **cut down** and thrown into the fire."*

Luke 6:43–44 ⇨ §L57.2
⁴³ *"For no good **tree** bears bad **fruit**, nor again does a bad **tree** bear good **fruit**; ⁴⁴ for each **tree** is known by its own **fruit**. For figs are not gathered from thorns, nor are grapes picked from a bramble bush."*

MATT

Matt 21:18–22 (§M73) ⇨ §L57.2
¹⁸ *In the morning, as he was returning to the city, he was hungry. ¹⁹ And seeing **a fig tree** by the wayside he went to it, **and found** nothing on it but leaves only. **And he said to it,** "May no **fruit** ever come from you again!" And the **fig** tree withered at once. ²⁰ When the disciples saw it they marveled, saying, "How did the **fig** tree wither at once?" ²¹ And Jesus answered them, "Truly, I say to you, if you have faith and never doubt, you will not only do what has been done to the **fig** tree, but even if you say to this mountain, 'Be taken up and cast into the sea,' it will be done. ²² And whatever you ask in prayer, you will receive, if you have faith."*

Matt 7:17–20 ⇨ §L57.2
¹⁷ *"So, every sound **tree** bears good **fruit**, but the bad **tree** bears evil **fruit**, nor can a bad **tree** bear good **fruit**. ¹⁹ Every **tree** that does not bear good **fruit** is **cut down** and thrown into the fire. ²⁰ Thus you will know them by their fruits."*

MARK

Mark 11:12–14 (§K58.1) ⇨ §L57.2
¹² *On the following day, when they came from Bethany, he was hungry. ¹³ And seeing in the distance **a fig tree** in leaf, he went to see if he could **find** anything on it. When **he came** to it, **he found** nothing but leaves, for it was not the season for figs. ¹⁴ **And he said to it,** "May no one ever eat **fruit** from you again." And his disciples heard it.*

Mark 11:20–25 (§K59.1) ⇨ §L57.2
²⁰ *As they passed by in the morning, they saw the **fig tree** withered away to its roots. ²¹ And Peter remembered and said to him, "Master, look! The **fig tree** which you cursed has withered." ²² And Jesus answered them, "Have faith in God. ²³ Truly, I say to you, whoever says to this mountain, 'Be taken up and cast into the sea,' and does not doubt in his heart, but believes that what he says will come to pass, it will be done for him. ²⁴ Therefore I tell you, whatever you ask in prayer, believe that you have received it, and it will be yours. ²⁵ And whenever you stand praying, forgive, if you have anything against any one; so that your Father also who is in heaven may forgive you your trespasses."*

JOHN

THOMAS

OTHER

LUKE	MATT	MARK

Luke 13:10–17 (§L58)

¹⁰ Now he was teaching in one of the synagogues on the sabbath. ¹¹ And there was a woman who had had a spirit of infirmity for eighteen years; she was bent over and could not fully straighten herself. ¹² And when Jesus saw her, he called her and said to her, "Woman, you are freed from your infirmity." ¹³ And he laid his hands upon her, and immediately she was made straight, and she praised God. ¹⁴ But the ruler of the synagogue, indignant because Jesus had healed on the sabbath, said to the people, "There are six days on which work ought to be done; come on those days and be healed, and not on the sabbath day." ¹⁵ Then the Lord answered him, "You hypocrites! Does not each of you on the sabbath untie his ox or his ass from the manger, and lead it away to water it? ¹⁶ And ought not this woman, a daughter of Abraham whom Satan bound for eighteen years, be loosed from this bond on the sabbath day?" ¹⁷ As he said this, all his adversaries were put to shame; and all the people rejoiced at all the glorious things that were done by him.

Luke 14:5 ⇨ Luke 13:15–16
⁵ *And he said to them, "Which of you, having a son or an* **ox** *that has fallen into a well, will not immediately pull him out* **on a sabbath day?"**

Exod 20:9 ⇨ Luke 13:14
⁹ **"Six days** you shall labor, and do all your **work";** . . .

Deut 5:13 ⇨ Luke 13:14
¹³ **"'Six days** you shall labor, and do all your **work'";** . . .

Matt 12:11–12 ⇨ Luke 13:15–16
¹¹ *He said to them, "What man* **of you,** *if he has one sheep and it falls into a pit on the sabbath, will not lay hold of* **it** *and lift* **it** *out?* ¹² *Of how much more value is a man than a sheep! So it is lawful to do good* **on the sabbath."**

JOHN	THOMAS	OTHER

InThom 2:1–5

¹ *When this boy Jesus was five years old he was playing at the ford of a brook, and he gathered together into pools the water that flowed by, and made it at once clean, and commanded it by his word alone.* ² *He made soft clay and fashioned from it twelve sparrows. And it was* **the sabbath** *when he did this. And there were also many other children playing with him.* ³ *Now when a certain Jew saw what Jesus was doing in his play on* **the sabbath,** *he at once went and told his father Joseph: "See, your child is at the brook, and he has taken clay and fashioned twelve birds and has profaned* **the sabbath."** ⁴ *And when Joseph came to the place and saw (it), he cried out to him, saying: "Why do you do* **on the sabbath** *what ought* **not** *to be done?" But Jesus clapped his hands and cried to the sparrows: "Off with you!" And the sparrows took flight and went away chirping.* ⁵ *The Jews* **were** *amazed when they saw* **this,** *and went away* **and** *told their elders what they had seen Jesus do.*

LUKE

MUSTARD SEED

Luke 13:18–19 (§L59.1)

[18] He said therefore, "What is the kingdom of God like? And to what shall I compare it? [19] It is like a grain of mustard seed which a man took and sowed in his garden; and it grew and became a tree, and the birds of the air made nests in its branches."

LEAVEN

Luke 13:20–21 (§L59.2)

[20] And again he said, "To what shall I compare the kingdom of God? [21] It is like leaven which a woman took and hid in three measures of flour, till it was all leavened."

Dan 4:20–22 ⇨ Luke 13:19

[20]"The **tree** you saw, which **grew and became** strong, so that **its** top reached to heaven, and **it** was visible to the end of the whole earth; [21] whose leaves were fair and **its** fruit abundant, and in which was food for all; under which beasts of the field found shade, **and in** whose **branches the birds of the air** dwelt—[22]it is you, O king, who have grown and become strong. Your greatness has grown and reaches to heaven, and your dominion to the ends of the earth."

MATT

Matt 13:31–32 (§M40.6) ⇨ §L59.1

[31] Another parable he put before them, saying, **"The kingdom of** heaven **is like a grain of mustard seed which a man took and sowed in** his field; [32]it is the smallest of all seeds, but when it has grown it is the greatest of shrubs **and** becomes **a tree,** so that **the birds of the air** come and make **nests in its branches."**

Matt 13:33 (§M40.7) ⇨ §L59.2

[33]He told them another parable. **"The kingdom of** heaven **is like leaven which a woman took and hid in three measures of flour, till it was all leavened."**

MARK

Mark 4:30–32 (§K21.8) ⇨ §L59.1

[30] And **he said,** "With **what** can we compare **the kingdom of God,** or what parable shall we use for it? [31] **It is like a grain of mustard seed, which,** when sown upon the ground, is the smallest of all the seeds on earth; [32] yet when **it** is sown it grows up **and** becomes the greatest of all shrubs, and puts forth large **branches,** so that **the birds of the air** can make **nests in its** shade."

JOHN

THOMAS

GThom 20 ⇨ §L59.1

(20) The disciples **said** to Jesus, "Tell us **what the Kingdom of** Heaven **is like."**

He **said** to them, **"It is like a mustard seed,** the smallest of all seeds. But when **it** falls on tilled soil, **it** produces a great plant **and** becomes a shelter for **birds of the** sky."

GThom 96 ⇨ §L59.2

(96) Jesus [**said**], **"The Kingdom of** the Father **is like a** certain **woman.** She **took** a little **leaven,** [concealed] it **in** some dough, and made it into large loaves. Let him who has ears hear."

OTHER

LUKE	MATT	MARK

LUKE

Luke 13:22–30 (§L60) °

²² He went on his way through towns and villages, teaching, and journeying toward Jerusalem. ²³ And some one said to him, "Lord, will those who are saved be few?" And he said to them, ²⁴ "Strive to enter by the narrow door; for many, I tell you, will seek to enter and will not be able. ²⁵ When once the householder has risen up and shut the door, you will begin to stand outside and to knock at the door, saying, 'Lord, open to us.' He will answer you, 'I do not know where you come from.' ²⁶ Then you will begin to say, 'We ate and drank in your presence, and you taught in our streets.' ²⁷ But he will say, 'I tell you, I do not know where you come from; depart from me, all you workers of iniquity!' ²⁸ There you will weep and gnash your teeth, when you see Abraham and Isaac and Jacob and all the prophets in the kingdom of God and you yourselves thrust out. ²⁹ And men will come from east and west, and from north and south, and sit at table in the kingdom of God. ³⁰ And behold, some are last who will be first, and some are first who will be last."

°Appendix 3 ⇨ Luke 13:22

Luke 9:51 ⇨ Luke 13:22
⁵¹ *When the days drew near for him to be received up, he set his face to go to Jerusalem.*

Luke 13:33 ⇨ Luke 13:22
³³ *"Nevertheless I must go on my way today and tomorrow and the day following; for it cannot be that a prophet should perish away from Jerusalem."*

Luke 17:11 ⇨ Luke 13:22
¹¹ *On the way to Jerusalem he was passing along between Samaria and Galilee.*

Luke 18:31 ⇨ Luke 13:22
³¹ *And taking the twelve, he said to them, "Behold, we are going up to Jerusalem, and everything that is written of the Son of man by the prophets will be accomplished."*

Luke 19:11 ⇨ Luke 13:22
¹¹ *As they heard these things, he proceeded to tell a parable, because he was near to Jerusalem, and because they supposed that the kingdom of God was to appear immediately.*

Ps 6:8 ⇨ Luke 13:27
⁸ *Depart from me, all you workers of evil; for the Lord has heard the sound of my weeping.*

Ps 107:3 ⇨ Luke 13:29
³ *and gathered in from the lands, from the east and from the west, from the north and from the south.*

JOHN

MATT

Matt 7:13–14 ⇨ Luke 13:23–24
¹³ "Enter by the narrow gate; for the gate is wide and the way is easy, that leads to destruction, and those who enter by it are many. ¹⁴ For the gate is narrow and the way is hard, that leads to life, and those who find it are few."

Matt 25:10–12 ⇨ Luke 13:25
¹⁰ "And while they went to buy, the bridegroom came, and those who were ready went in with him to the marriage feast; and the door was shut. ¹¹ Afterward the other maidens came also, saying, 'Lord, lord, open to us,' ¹² but he replied, 'Truly, I say to you, I do not know you.'"

Matt 7:21–23 ⇨ Luke 13:26–27
²¹ "Not every one who says to me, 'Lord, Lord,' shall enter the kingdom of heaven, but he who does the will of my Father who is in heaven. ²² On that day many will say to me, 'Lord, Lord, did we not prophesy in your name, and cast out demons in your name, and do many mighty works in your name?' ²³ And then will I declare to them, 'I never knew you; depart from me, you evildoers.'"

Matt 8:11–12 ⇨ Luke 13:28–29
¹¹ "I tell you, many will come from east and west and sit at table with Abraham, Isaac, and Jacob in the kingdom of heaven, ¹² while the sons of the kingdom will be thrown into the outer darkness; there men will weep and gnash their teeth."

Matt 19:30 ⇨ Luke 13:30
³⁰ "But many that are first will be last, and the last first."

Matt 20:16 ⇨ Luke 13:30
¹⁶ "So the last will be first, and the first last."

THOMAS

POxy654 4 ⇨ Luke 13:30
(4) [Jesus says,] "A ma[n full of d]ays will not hesitate to ask a ch[ild of seven da]ys about the place of [life and he will live.] For many (that are) fi[rst] will be [last and] the last will be first and they [will have eternal life]."

GThom 4 ⇨ Luke 13:30
(4) Jesus said, "The man old in days will not hesitate to ask a small child seven days old about the place of life, and he will live. For many who are first will become last, and they will become one and the same."

MARK

Mark 10:31 ⇨ Luke 13:30
³¹ "But many that are first will be last, and the last first."

OTHER

LUKE

Luke 13:31–35 (§L61)
³¹ At that very hour some Pharisees came, and said to him, "Get away from here, for Herod wants to kill you." ³² And he said to them, "Go and tell that fox, 'Behold, I cast out demons and perform cures today and tomorrow, and the third day I finish my course. ³³ Nevertheless I must go on my way today and tomorrow and the day following; for it cannot be that a prophet should perish away from Jerusalem.' ³⁴ O Jerusalem, Jerusalem, killing the prophets and stoning those who are sent to you! How often would I have gathered your children together as a hen gathers her brood under her wings, and you would not! ³⁵ Behold, your house is forsaken. And I tell you, you will not see me until you say, 'Blessed is he who comes in the name of the Lord!'"

Luke 9:7–9 (§L37) ⇨ Luke 13:31
⁷ Now **Herod** the tetrarch heard of all that was done, and he was perplexed, because it was said by some that John had been raised from the dead, ⁸ by some that Elijah had appeared, and by others that one of the old prophets had risen. ⁹ **Herod** said, "John I beheaded; but who is this about whom I hear such things?" And he sought to see him.

Luke 3:19–20 ⇨ Luke 13:31
¹⁹ But Herod the tetrarch, who had been reproved by him for Herodias, his brother's wife, and for all the evil things that **Herod** had done, ²⁰ added this to them all, that he shut up John in prison.

Luke 23:8 ⇨ Luke 13:31
⁸ When **Herod** saw Jesus, he was very glad, for he had long desired to see him, because he had heard about him, and he was hoping to see some sign done by him.

Luke 11:47–51 ⇨ Luke 13:33–34
⁴⁷ "Woe to you! for **you** build the tombs of the **prophets** whom your fathers killed. ⁴⁸ So you are witnesses and consent to the deeds of your fathers; for they killed them, and **you** build their tombs. ⁴⁹ Therefore also the Wisdom of God said, 'I will send them **prophets** and apostles, some of whom they will kill and persecute,' ⁵⁰ that the blood of all **the prophets**, shed from the foundation of the world, may be required of this generation, ⁵¹ from the blood of Abel to the blood of Zechariah, who perished between the altar and the sanctuary. Yes, I tell you, it shall be required of this generation."

JOHN

MATT

Matt 23:37–39 (§M77.3) ⇨ Luke 13:34–35
³⁷ "O Jerusalem, Jerusalem, killing the prophets and stoning those who are sent to you! How often would I have gathered your children together as a hen gathers her brood under her wings, and you would not! ³⁸ Behold, your house is forsaken and desolate. ³⁹ For I tell you, you will not see me again, until you say, 'Blessed is he who comes in the name of the Lord.'"

Luke 9:51 ⇨ Luke 13:33
⁵¹ When the days drew near for him to be received up, he set his face to go to Jerusalem.

Luke 13:22 ⇨ Luke 13:33
²² He went on his way through towns and villages, teaching, and journeying toward Jerusalem.

Luke 17:11 ⇨ Luke 13:33
¹¹ On the way to Jerusalem he was passing along between Samaria and Galilee.

Luke 18:31 ⇨ Luke 13:33
³¹ And taking the twelve, he said to them, "Behold, we are going up to Jerusalem, everything that is written of the Son of man by the prophets will be accomplished."

Luke 19:11 ⇨ Luke 13:33
¹¹ As they heard these things, he proceeded to tell a parable, because he was near to Jerusalem, and because they supposed that the kingdom of God was to appear immediately.

Luke 19:41–44 (§L82.4) ⇨ Luke 13:34–35
⁴¹ And when he drew near and saw the city he wept over it, ⁴² saying, "Would that even today you knew the things that make for peace! But now they are hid from your eyes. ⁴³ For the days shall come upon you, when your enemies will cast up a bank about you and surround you, and hem you in on every side, ⁴⁴ and dash you to the ground, you and your children within you, and they will not leave one stone upon another in you; because you did not know the time of your visitation."

Luke 21:20–24 (§L91.2) ⇨ Luke 13:34–35
²⁰ "But when you see Jerusalem surrounded by armies, then know that its desolation has come near. ²¹ Then let those who are in Judea flee to the mountains, and let those who are inside the city depart, and let not those who are out in the country enter it; ²² for these are days of vengeance, to fulfil all that is written. ²³ Alas for

THOMAS

MARK

those who are with child and for those who give suck in those days! For great distress shall be upon the earth and wrath upon this people; ²⁴ they will fall by the edge of the sword, and be led captive among all nations; and Jerusalem will be trodden down by the Gentiles, until the times of the Gentiles are fulfilled."

Luke 23:27–31 ⇨ Luke 13:34–35
²⁷ And there followed him a great multitude of the people, and of women who bewailed and lamented him. ²⁸ But Jesus turning to them said, "Daughters of Jerusalem, do not weep for me, but weep for yourselves and for your children. ²⁹ For behold, the days are coming when they will say, 'Blessed are the barren, and the wombs that never bore, and the breasts that never gave suck!' ³⁰ Then they will begin to say to the mountains, 'Fall on us'; and to the hills, 'Cover us.' ³¹ For if they do this when the wood is green, what will happen when it is dry?"

Luke 19:37–38 ⇨ Luke 13:35
³⁷ As he was now drawing near, at the descent of the Mount of Olives, the whole multitude of the disciples began to rejoice and praise God with a loud voice for all the mighty works that they had seen, ³⁸ saying, "Blessed is the King who comes in the name of the Lord! Peace in heaven and glory in the highest!"

Isa 31:5 ⇨ Luke 13:34
⁵ Like birds hovering, so the Lord of hosts
    will protect Jerusalem;
he will protect and deliver it,
    he will spare and rescue it.

Ps 118:26 ⇨ Luke 13:35
²⁶ Blessed be he who enters in the name of the Lord!
    We bless you from the house of the Lord.

OTHER

Acts 7:51–52 ⇨ Luke 13:33–34
⁵¹ "You stiff-necked people, uncircumcised in heart and ears, **you** always resist the Holy Spirit. As your fathers did, so do **you**. ⁵² Which of **the prophets** did not your fathers persecute? And they killed **those who** announced beforehand the coming of the Righteous One, whom **you** have now betrayed and murdered, . . ."

LUKE	MATT	MARK

Luke 14:1–6 (§L62)

¹One sabbath when he went to dine at the house of a ruler who belonged to the Pharisees, they were watching him. ²And behold, there was a man before him who had dropsy. ³And Jesus spoke to the lawyers and Pharisees, saying, "Is it lawful to heal on the sabbath, or not?" ⁴But they were silent. Then he took him and healed him, and let him go. ⁵And he said to them, "Which of you, having a son[a] or an ox that has fallen into a well, will not immediately pull him out on a sabbath day?" ⁶And they could not reply to this.

ᵃ Some witnesses read *an ass:* ℵ K L X Π Ψ *f*¹ *f*¹³ 33 *al*

Luke 6:6–11 (§L22)

⁶*On another* **sabbath, when he entered the** synagogue and taught, *a man was there whose right hand was withered.* ⁷*And the scribes and* **the Pharisees** *watched* **him,** *to see whether he would* **heal on the sabbath,** *so that they might find an accusation against him.* ⁸*But he knew their thoughts, and he said to the* **man who had** *the withered hand,* "Come and stand here." *And he rose and stood there.* ⁹**And** *Jesus said to them,* "I ask you, is it **lawful on the sabbath to** do good *or* **to do harm, to save life** or **to destroy** it?" ¹⁰*And* **he** *looked around on them all, and said to* **him,** "Stretch out your hand." *And he did so,* **and his hand was restored.** ¹¹*But they were filled with fury and discussed with one another what they might do to Jesus.*

Luke 13:10–17 (§L58)

¹⁰*Now* **he** *was teaching in one of the synagogues on the* **sabbath.** ¹¹*And* **there was a woman who had** *had a spirit of infirmity for eighteen years; she was bent over and could not fully straighten herself.* ¹²*And when* **Jesus** *saw her,* **he** *called her* **and said to her,** "Woman, you are freed from your infirmity." ¹³*And he laid his hands upon her, and immediately she was made straight, and she praised God.* ¹⁴*But the ruler of the synagogue, indignant because* **Jesus** *had healed* **on the sabbath,** *said to the people,* "There are six days on which work ought to be done; come on those days and be healed, and not **on the sabbath** day." ¹⁵*Then the Lord answered him,* "You hypocrites! Does not each **of you on the sabbath** untie his ox or his ass from the manger, and lead it away to water it? ¹⁶And ought not this woman, a daughter of Abraham whom Satan bound for eighteen years, be loosed from this bond **on the sabbath** day?" ¹⁷*As he said this, all his adversaries were put to shame; and all the people rejoiced at all the glorious things that were done by him.*

Matt 12:11–12 ⇨ **Luke 14:5**

¹¹**He said to them,** "What man **of you,** if he has one sheep and it falls **into a** pit **on the sabbath, will not** lay hold of it and lift it **out?** ¹²Of how much more value is a man than a sheep! So it is lawful to do good **on the sabbath.**"

Matt 12:9–14 (§M34)

⁹*And* **he** *went on from there, and entered their synagogue.* ¹⁰**And behold, there was a man** *with a withered hand. And they asked him,* "Is it lawful to heal on the sabbath?" *so that they might accuse him.* ¹¹**He said to them,** "What man **of you,** if he has one sheep and it falls **into a** pit **on the sabbath, will not** lay hold of it and lift it **out?** ¹²Of how much more value is a man than a sheep! So **it is lawful to** do good **on the sabbath.**" ¹³**Then** he said to the man, "Stretch out your hand." And the man stretched it out, and it was restored, whole like the other. ¹⁴*But* **the Pharisees** *went out and took counsel against him, how to destroy him.*

Mark 3:1–6 (§K17)

¹*Again he entered the synagogue, and* **a man** *was there who had a withered hand.* ²*And they watched* **him,** *to see whether he would* **heal him on the sabbath,** *so that they might accuse him.* ³*And he said to the* **man who had the withered** *hand,* "Come here." ⁴*And he said to them,* "Is it **lawful on the sabbath to do good or to do harm, to save life or to kill?** But they were silent." ⁵*And* **he** *looked around at them with anger, grieved at their hardness of heart, and said to the man,* "Stretch out your hand." *He stretched it out,* **and his hand was restored.** ⁶*The Pharisees went out, and immediately held counsel with the Herodians against him, how to destroy him.*

JOHN	THOMAS	OTHER

InThom 2:1–5

¹*When this boy* **Jesus** *was five years old he was playing at the ford of a brook, and he gathered together into pools the water that flowed by, and made it at once clean, and commanded it by his word alone.* ²*He made soft clay and fashioned from it twelve sparrows. And it was* **the sabbath when** *he did this. And there were also many other children playing with* **him.** ³*Now when a certain Jew saw what* **Jesus** *was doing in his play* **on the sabbath,** *he at once went and told his father Joseph:* "See, your child is at the brook, and he has taken clay and fashioned twelve birds and has profaned the sabbath." ⁴*And when Joseph came to the place and saw (it), he cried out to him, saying:* "Why do you do **on the sabbath** what ought not to be done?" *But* **Jesus** *clapped his hands and cried to the sparrows:* "Off with you!" *And the sparrows took flight and went away chirping.* ⁵*The Jews were amazed when* **they saw this,** *and went away and told their elders what they had seen Jesus do.*

LUKE   MATT   MARK

HUMILITY AS GUESTS

Luke 14:7–11 (§L63.1)

⁷ Now he told a parable to those who were invited, when he marked how they chose the places of honor, saying to them, ⁸ "When you are invited by any one to a marriage feast, do not sit down in a place of honor, lest a more eminent man than you be invited by him; ⁹ and he who invited you both will come and say to you, 'Give place to this man,' and then you will begin with shame to take the lowest place. ¹⁰ But when you are invited, go and sit in the lowest place, so that when your host comes he may say to you, 'Friend, go up higher'; then you will be honored in the presence of all who sit at table with you. ¹¹ For every one who exalts himself will be humbled, and he who humbles himself will be exalted."

HUMILITY AS HOSTS

Luke 14:12–14 (§L63.2)

¹² He said also to the man who had invited him, "When you give a dinner or a banquet, do not invite your friends or your brothers or your kinsmen or rich neighbors, lest they also invite you in return, and you be repaid. ¹³ But when you give a feast, invite the poor, the maimed, the lame, the blind, ¹⁴ and you will be blessed, because they cannot repay you. You will be repaid at the resurrection of the just."

Luke 18:14 ⇨ Luke 14:11

¹⁴ "I tell you, this man went down to his house justified rather than the other; **for every one who exalts himself will be humbled,** but **he who humbles himself will be exalted.**"

Luke 11:43 ⇨ §L63.1

⁴³ *"Woe to you Pharisees! for **you** love **the** best seat in the synagogues and salutations **in** the market places."*

Luke 20:46 ⇨ §L63.1

⁴⁶ *"Beware of the scribes, who like to go about in long robes, and love salutations **in** the market places and **the best seats in** the synagogues and the places **of honor** at feasts, . . ."*

Luke 14:21 ⇨ Luke 14:13

²¹ *"So the servant came and reported this to his master. Then the householder in anger said to his servant, 'Go out quickly to the streets and lanes of the city, and bring in **the poor** and maimed and blind and lame.'"*

Matt 23:12 ⇨ Luke 14:11

¹² "whoever **exalts himself will be humbled,** and whoever **humbles himself will be exalted.**"

Matt 18:4 ⇨ Luke 14:11

⁴ *"Whoever **humbles himself** like this child, he is the greatest in the kingdom of heaven."*

JOHN   THOMAS   OTHER

LUKE	MATT	MARK

Luke 14:15–24 (§L64)

[15] When one of those who sat at table with him heard this, he said to him, "Blessed is he who shall eat bread in the kingdom of God!" [16] But he said to him "A man once gave a great banquet, and invited many; [17] and at the time for the banquet he sent his servant to say to those who had been invited, 'Come; for all is now ready.' [18] But they all alike began to make excuses. The first said to him, 'I have bought a field, and I must go out and see it; I pray you, have me excused.' [19] And another said, 'I have bought five yoke of oxen, and I go to examine them; I pray you, have me excused.' [20] And another said, 'I have married a wife, and therefore I cannot come.' [21] So the servant came and reported this to his master. Then the householder in anger said to his servant, 'Go out quickly to the streets and lanes of the city, and bring in the poor and maimed and blind and lame.' [22] And the servant said, 'Sir, what you commanded has been done, and still there is room.' [23] And the master said to the servant, 'Go out to the highways and hedges, and compel people to come in, that my house may be filled. [24] For I tell you,[a] none of those men who were invited shall taste my banquet.'"

[a] Greek: *you* is plural

Luke 14:13 ⇨ Luke 14:21
[13] *"But when you give a feast, invite the poor, the maimed, the lame, and blind, . . ."*

Matt 22:1–14 (§M75)

[1] And again Jesus spoke to them in parables, saying, [2] "The kingdom of heaven may be compared to a king who **gave a** marriage feast for his son, [3] **and sent his** servants to call **those who** were **invited** to the marriage feast; **but they** would not come. [4] Again **he sent** other servants, saying, 'Tell **those who** are **invited**, Behold, I have made ready my dinner, my oxen and my fat calves are killed, and everything **is ready; come** to the marriage feast.' [5] **But they** made light of it and went off, one to his farm, another to his business, [6] while the rest seized his servants, treated them shamefully, and killed them. [7] **The** king was angry, and he sent his troops and destroyed those murderers and burned their city. [8] **Then he said to his** servants, 'The wedding is ready, but those invited were not worthy. [9] **Go** therefore **to the** thoroughfares, **and** invite to the marriage feast as many as you find.' [10] And those servants went **out** into **the** streets **and** gathered all whom they found, both bad and good; so the wedding hall was **filled** with guests.

[11] "But when the king came in to look at the guests, he saw there a man who had no wedding garment; [12] and he said to him, 'Friend, how did you get in here without a wedding garment?' And he was speechless. [13] Then the king said to the attendants, 'Bind him hand and foot, and cast him into the outer darkness; there men will weep and gnash their teeth.' [14] For many are called, but few are chosen."

JOHN	THOMAS	OTHER

GThom 64

(64) Jesus **said**, "**A man** had received visitors. And when he had prepared the dinner, **he sent his servant to** invite the guests. He went to **the first** one and said to him, 'My master invites you.' He **said**, '**I have** claims against some merchants. They are coming to me this evening. **I must go and** give them my orders. I ask to be **excused** from the dinner.' He went to **another** and said to him, 'My master has invited you.' He **said** to him, '**I have** just **bought** a house **and** am required for the day. I shall not have any spare time.' He went to **another** and said to him, 'My master invites you.' He **said** to him, 'My friend is going to get **married, and** I am to prepare the banquet. I shall not be able to **come**. I ask to be excused from the dinner.' He went to another and said to him, 'My master invites you.' He **said** to him, '**I have** just **bought** a farm, **and I** am on my way to collect the rent. I shall not be able to come. I ask to be **excused**.' **The servant** returned and said **to his master**, 'Those whom you invited to the dinner have asked to be **excused**.' **The** master **said to his servant**, '**Go** outside **to the streets and bring** back those whom you happen to meet, so that they may dine.' Businessmen and merchants will not enter the Places of My Father."

LUKE

Luke 14:25–35 (§L65)

²⁵ Now great multitudes accompanied him; and he turned and said to them, ²⁶ "If any one comes to me and does not hate his own father and mother and wife and children and brothers and sisters, yes, and even his own life, he cannot be my disciple. ²⁷ Whoever does not bear his own cross and come after me, cannot be my disciple. ²⁸ For which of you, desiring to build a tower, does not first sit down and count the cost, whether he has enough to complete it? ²⁹ Otherwise, when he has laid a foundation, and is not able to finish, all who see it begin to mock him, ³⁰ saying, 'This man began to build, and was not able to finish.' ³¹ Or what king, going to encounter another king in war, will not sit down first and take counsel whether he is able with ten thousand to meet him who comes against him with twenty thousand? ³² And if not, while the other is yet a great way off, he sends an embassy and asks terms of peace. ³³ So therefore, whoever of you does not renounce all that he has cannot be my disciple.

³⁴ "Salt is good; but if salt has lost its taste, how shall its saltness be restored? ³⁵ It is fit neither for the land nor for the dunghill; men throw it away. He who has ears to hear, let him hear."

Luke 9:23–27 (§L40.2) ⇨ Luke 14:25–33

²³ *And he said to all, "If any man would **come after me**, let him deny himself and take up **his cross** daily and follow me. ²⁴ For whoever would save his life will lose it; and whoever loses his life for my sake, he will save it. ²⁵ For what does it profit a man if he gains the whole world and loses or forfeits himself? ²⁶ For **whoever** is ashamed of me and of my words, of him will the Son of man be ashamed when he comes in his glory and the glory of the Father and of the holy angels. ²⁷ But I tell you truly, there are some standing here who will not taste death before they see the kingdom of God."*

Luke 9:57–62 (§L45) ⇨ Luke 14:25–33

⁵⁷ *As they were going along the road, a man said to him, "I will follow you wherever you go." ⁵⁸ And Jesus said to him, "Foxes have holes, and birds of the air have nests; but the Son of man has nowhere to lay his head." ⁵⁹ To another **he said**, "Follow me." But he said, "Lord, let me first go and bury my father." ⁶⁰ But **he said to him**, "Leave the dead to bury their own dead; but as for you, go and proclaim the kingdom of God." ⁶¹ Another said, "I will follow you, Lord; but let me first say farewell to those at my home." ⁶² Jesus **said to him**, "No one who puts his hand to the plow and looks back is fit for the kingdom of God."*

Luke 18:29–30 ⇨ Luke 14:25–33

²⁹ *And he said to them, "Truly, I say to you, there is no man who has left house or wife or **brothers** or parents or **children**, for the sake of the kingdom of God, ³⁰ who will not receive manifold more in this time, and in the age to come eternal life."*

JOHN

MATT

Matt 10:34–39 (§M28.5)

³⁴ "Do not think that I have come to bring peace on earth; I have not come to bring peace, but a sword. ³⁵ For I have come to set a man against **his father**, and a daughter against her **mother**, and a daughter-in-law against her mother-in-law; ³⁶ and a man's foes will be those of his own household. ³⁷ He who loves **father** or **mother** more than me is not worthy of me; and he who loves son or daughter more than me is not worthy of me; ³⁸ and he who **does not** take **his cross and** follow **me** is not worthy of **me**. ³⁹ He who finds his life will lose it, and he who loses his life for my sake will find it."

Matt 16:24–28 (§M57)

²⁴ Then Jesus told his disciples, "**If any** man would **come after me**, let him deny himself and take up **his cross and** follow **me**. ²⁵ For **whoever** would save his life will lose it, and whoever loses his life for my sake will find it. ²⁶ For what will it profit a man, if he gains the whole world and forfeits his life? Or what shall a man give in return for his life? ²⁷ For the Son of man is to come with his angels in the glory of his Father, and then he will repay every man for what he has done. ²⁸ Truly, I say to you, there are some standing here who will not taste death before they see the Son of man coming in his kingdom."

Matt 5:13–16 (§M12.3)

¹³ "You are the **salt** of the earth; **but if salt has lost its taste, how shall its saltness be restored**? It is no longer good for anything except to be thrown out and trodden under foot by **men**.

¹⁴ "You are the light of the world. A city set on a hill cannot be hid. ¹⁵ Nor do men light a lamp and put it under a bushel, but on a stand, and it gives light to all in the house. ¹⁶ Let your light so shine before men, that they may see your good works and give glory to your Father who is in heaven."

Matt 8:18–22 (§M17) ⇨ Luke 4:25–33

¹⁸ *Now when Jesus saw **great** crowds around **him**, he gave orders to go over to the other side. ¹⁹ And a scribe came up and said to him, "Teacher, I will follow you wherever you go." ²⁰ **And Jesus said to him**, "Foxes have holes, and birds of the air have nests; but the Son of man has nowhere to lay his head." ²¹ Another of the disciples said to him, "Lord, let me first go and bury my father." ²² But Jesus **said to him**, "Follow **me**, and leave the dead to bury their own dead."*

THOMAS

GThom 55 ⇨ Luke 14:26–27

(55) Jesus **said**, "Whoever **does not hate his father and** his **mother cannot** become a **disciple** to **Me**. And whoever **does not hate his brothers and sisters** and take up **his cross in My** way will not be worthy of **Me**."

GThom 101 ⇨ Luke 14:26–27

(101) <Jesus said,> "Whoever **does not hate his father and** his **mother** as I do **cannot** become a **disciple** to **Me**. And whoever **does [not]** love **his father and** his **mother** as I do **cannot** become a [**disciple**] to **Me**. For My **mother** [gave me falsehood], but [My] true [**Mother**] gave me life."

MARK

Mark 8:34–9:1 (§K43)

³⁴ And he called to **him** the multitude with his disciples, **and said to them, "If any** man would **come after me**, let him deny himself and take up **his cross and** follow **me**. ³⁵ For **whoever** would save his life will lose it; and whoever loses his life for my sake and the gospel's will save it. ³⁶ For what does it profit a man, to gain the whole world and forfeit his life? ³⁷ For what can a man give in return for his life? ³⁸ For **whoever** is ashamed of me and of my words in this adulterous and sinful generation, of him will the Son of man also be ashamed, when he comes in the glory of his Father with the holy angels." 9 ¹ And he said to them, "Truly, I say to you, there are some standing here who will not taste death before they see that the kingdom of God has come with power."

Mark 9:50 ⇨ Luke 14:34–35

⁵⁰ "**Salt is good; but if the salt has lost its** saltness, **how** will you season it? Have **salt** in yourselves, and be at peace with one another."

OTHER

Luke 15:1–2   INTRODUCTION   **L66.1**
Luke 15:3–7   PARABLE OF THE LOST SHEEP   **L66.2**
Luke 15:8–10   PARABLE OF THE LOST COIN   **L66.3**

LUKE

Luke 15:1–2 (§L66.1)
[1] Now the tax collectors and sinners were all drawing near to hear him. [2] And the Pharisees and the scribes murmured, saying, "This man receives sinners and eats with them."

Luke 15:3–7 (§L66.2)
[3] So he told them this parable: [4] "What man of you, having a hundred sheep, if he has lost one of them, does not leave the ninety-nine in the wilderness, and go after the one which is lost, until he finds it? [5] And when he has found it, he lays it on his shoulders, rejoicing. [6] And when he comes home, he calls together his friends and his neighbors, saying to them, 'Rejoice with me, for I have found my sheep which was lost.' [7] Just so, I tell you, there will be more joy in heaven over one sinner who repents than over ninety-nine righteous persons who need no repentance."

Luke 15:8–10 (§L66.3)
[8] "Or what woman, having ten silver coins,[a] if she loses one coin, does not light a lamp and sweep the house and seek diligently until she finds it? [9] And when she has found it, she calls together her friends and neighbors, saying, 'Rejoice with me, for I have found the coin which I had lost.' [10] Just so, I tell you, there is joy before the angels of God over one sinner who repents."

[a] Greek: *drachma*, here translated *silver coin*, was about a day's wage for a laborer

Luke 5:29–32 (§L20.2) ⇨ §L66.1
[29] *And Levi made him a great feast in his house; and there was a large company of* **tax collectors and** *others sitting at table with them.* [30] *And the Pharisees and their scribes mur-* **mured** *against his disciples, saying, "Why do you eat and drink* **with** *tax collectors and* **sinners?"** [31] *And Jesus answered them, "Those who are well have no need of a physician, but those who are sick;* [32] *I have not come to call the righteous, but sinners to repentance."*

JOHN

MATT

Matt 9:10–13 (§M21.2) ⇨ §L66.1
[10] *And as he sat at table in the house, behold, many* **tax collectors and sinners** *came and sat down with Jesus and his disciples.* [11] *And when* **the Pharisees** *saw this, they said to his disciples, "Why does your teacher eat* **with** *tax collectors and* **sinners?"** [12] *But when he heard it, he said, "Those who are well have no need of a physician, but those who are sick.* [13] *Go and learn what this means, 'I desire mercy, and not sacrifice.' For I came not to call the righteous, but sinners."*

Matt 18:12–14 (§M62.2) ⇨ §L66.2
[12] **"What** *do you think? If a* **man** *has a* **hundred sheep,** *and* **one of them has** *gone astray,* **does** *he* **not leave the ninety-nine** *on the mountains* **and go** *in search of* **the one** *that went astray?* [13] *And if he* **finds it,** *truly, I say to you,* **he** *rejoices over it more* **than over** *the* **ninety- nine** *that never went astray.* [14] **So** *it is not the will of my Father who is in heaven that one of these little ones should perish."*

Luke 7:34 ⇨ §L66.1
[34] *"The Son of man has come eating and drink- ing; and you say, 'Behold, a glutton and a drunkard, a friend of* **tax collectors and sinners!'"**

Luke 19:7 ⇨ §L66.1
[7] *And when they saw it they all* **murmured,** *"He has gone in to be the guest of a man who is a sinner."*

Luke 19:10 ⇨ §L66.3
[10] *"For the Son of man came to* **seek** *and to save the lost."*

THOMAS

GThom 107 ⇨ §L66.2
(107) Jesus said, "The Kingdom is like a shepherd who had a hundred sheep. One of them, the largest, went astray. He left the ninety-nine and looked for that one until he found it. When he had gone to such trouble, he said to the sheep, 'I care for you more than the ninety-nine.'"

MARK

Mark 2:15–17 (§K14.3) ⇨ §L66.1
[15] *And as he sat at table in his house, many* **tax collectors and sinners** *were sitting with Jesus and his disciples; for there were many who followed him.* [16] *And the scribes of the Phari- sees, when they saw that he was eating with sinners and tax collectors, said to his disciples, "Why does he eat with tax collectors and sin- ners?"* [17] *And when Jesus heard it, he said to them, "Those who are well have no need of a physician, but those who are sick; I came not to call the righteous, but sinners."*

OTHER

POxy1224 1 ⇨ §L66.1
(1) **And the scribes and [Pharisees] and** *priests, when they sa[w] him, were angry [that with sin] ners in the midst he [reclined] at table. But Jesus heard [it and said:] The he[althy need not the physician.]*

Justin, *Apology* 1.15.8 ⇨ §L66.2
So he said: "I have not come to call the **righteous** *but sinners to* **repentance."** *For the Heavenly Father wishes the* **repentance** *of a sinner rather* **than his punishment.**

LUKE	MATT	MARK

Luke 15:11-32 (§L66.4)

¹¹ And he said, "There was a man who had two sons; ¹² and the younger of them said to his father, 'Father, give me the share of property that falls to me.' And he divided his living between them. ¹³ Not many days later, the younger son gathered all he had and took his journey into a far country, and there he squandered his property in loose living. ¹⁴ And when he had spent everything, a great famine arose in that country, and he began to be in want. ¹⁵ So he went and joined himself to one of the citizens of that country, who sent him into his fields to feed swine. ¹⁶ And he would gladly have fed on^a the pods that the swine ate; and no one gave him anything. ¹⁷ But when he came to himself he said, 'How many of my father's hired servants have bread enough and to spare, but I perish here with hunger! ¹⁸ I will arise and go to my father, and I will say to him, "Father, I have sinned against heaven and before you; ¹⁹ I am no longer worthy to be called your son; treat me as one of your hired servants."' ²⁰ And he arose and came to his father. But while he was yet at a distance, his father saw him and had compassion, and ran and embraced him and kissed him. ²¹ And the son said to him, 'Father, I have sinned against heaven and before you; I am no longer worthy to be called your son.'^b ²² But the father said to his servants, 'Bring quickly the best robe, and put it on him; and put a ring on his hand, and shoes on his feet; ²³ and bring the fatted calf and kill it, and let us eat and make merry; ²⁴ for this my son was dead, and is alive again; he was lost, and is found.' And they began to make merry.

²⁵ "Now his elder son was in the field; and as he came and drew near to the house, he heard music and dancing. ²⁶ And he called one of the servants and asked what this meant. ²⁷ And he said to him, 'Your brother has come, and your father has killed the fatted calf, because he has received him safe and sound.' ²⁸ But he was angry and refused to go in. His father came out and entreated him, ²⁹ but he answered his father, 'Lo, these many years I have served you, and I never disobeyed your command; yet you never gave me a kid, that I might make merry with my friends. ³⁰ But when this son of yours came, who has devoured your living with harlots, you killed for him the fatted calf!' ³¹ And he said to him, 'Son, you are always with me, and all that is mine is yours. ³² It was fitting to make merry and be glad, for this your brother was dead, and is alive; he was lost, and is found.'"

^a Some witnesses read *filled his belly with:* A K P X Δ Θ Π Ψ 28 *pm;* text: 𝔓⁷⁵ ℵ B D L *f*¹ *f*¹³ *pc*

^b Some witnesses add *treat me as one of your hired servants* (see Luke 15:19): ℵ B D X (33) *al*

JOHN	THOMAS	OTHER

LUKE	MATT	MARK

LUKE

PARABLE OF THE UNJUST STEWARD

Luke 16:1–9 (§L67.1)
[1] He also said to the disciples, "There was a rich man who had a steward, and charges were brought to him that this man was wasting his goods. [2] And he called him and said to him, 'What is this that I hear about you? Turn in the account of your stewardship, for you can no longer be steward.' [3] And the steward said to himself, 'What shall I do, since my master is taking the stewardship away from me? I am not strong enough to dig, and I am ashamed to beg. [4] I have decided what to do, so that people may receive me into their houses when I am put out of the stewardship.' [5] So, summoning his master's debtors one by one, he said to the first, 'How much do you owe my master?'; [6] He said, 'A hundred measures of oil.' And he said to him, 'Take your bill, and sit down quickly and write fifty.' [7] Then he said to another, 'And how much do you owe?' He said, 'A hundred measures of wheat.' He said to him, 'Take your bill, and write eighty.' [8] The master commended the dishonest steward for his shrewdness; for the sons of this world[a] are more shrewd in dealing with their own generation than the sons of light. [9] And I tell you, make friends for yourselves by means of unrighteous mammon,[b] so that when it fails they may receive you into the eternal habitations."

TRUE STEWARDSHIP

Luke 16:10–13 (§L67.2)
[10] "He who is faithful in a very little is faithful also in much; and he who is dishonest in a very little is dishonest also in much. [11] If then you have not been faithful in the unrighteous mammon, who will entrust to you the true riches? [12] And if you have not been faithful in that which is another's, who will give you that which is your own? [13] No servant can serve two masters; for either he will hate the one and love the other, or he will be devoted to the one and despise the other. You cannot serve God and mammon."[b]

THE PHARISEES SCOFF

Luke 16:14–15 (§L67.3)
[14] The Pharisees, who were lovers of money, heard all this, and they scoffed at him. [15] But he said to them, "You are those who justify yourselves before men, but God knows your hearts; for what is exalted among men is an abomination in the sight of God."

JOHN

MATT

Matt 6:24 (§12.7c) ⇨ Luke 16:13
[24] "No one **can serve two masters**; for either he will hate the one and love the other, or he will be devoted to one and despise the other. You cannot serve God and mammon."

---

[a] Greek: *age*

[b] *Mammon* is a Semitic word for money or riches

Luke 10:29 ⇨ Luke 16:15
[29] *But he, desiring to* **justify** *himself, said to Jesus, "And who is my neighbor?"*

Luke 14:11 ⇨ Luke 16:15
[11] *"For every one* **who exalts himself will be** *humbled, and he who humbles himself will be exalted."*

Luke 18:9 ⇨ Luke 16:15
[9] *He also told this parable to some* **who** *trusted in themselves that they were righteous and despised others: . . .*

Luke 18:14 ⇨ Luke 16:15
[14] *"I tell you, this man went down to his house justified rather than the other; for every one* **who exalts himself will be humbled, but he who** *humbles himself will be exalted."*

THOMAS

GThom 47 ⇨ Luke 16:13
(47) Jesus said, "It is impossible for a man to mount two horses or to stretch two bows. And it is impossible for a **servant** to **serve two masters**; otherwise, **he will** honor **the one and** treat **the other** contemptuously. No man drinks old wine and immediately desires to drink new wine. And new wine is not put into old wineskins, lest they burst; nor is old wine put into a new wineskin, lest it spoil it. An old patch is not sewn onto a new garment, because a tear would result."

OTHER

2 Clem 8:5 ⇨ Luke 16:10–11
For the Lord says in the Gospel, "**If** ye did not guard that which is small, **who** shall give **you** that which is great? For I tell you that **he who is faithful in** that which is least, **is faithful also in** that which is **much**."

Ireneaus, *Adv. haer.* 2.34.3
⇨ Luke 16:10–11
Therefore the Lord said to those who were ungrateful to him, "**If you have not been faithful in** a little, **who will** give **you** what is great?"

MARK

LUKE

ON LAW

Luke 16:16–17 (§L68.1) °
[16] "The law and the prophets were until John; since then the good news of the kingdom of God is preached, and every one enters it violently. [17] But it is easier for heaven and earth to pass away, than for one dot of the law to become void."

ON DIVORCE

Luke 16:18 (§L68.2)
[18] "Every one who divorces his wife and marries another commits adultery, and he who marries a woman divorced from her husband commits adultery."

°Appendix 1 ⇨ §L68.1

MATT

Matt 11:12–13 ⇨ Luke 16:16
[12] "From the days of John the Baptist until now **the kingdom of** heaven has suffered violence, and men of violence take **it** by force. [13] For all **the prophets and the law** prophesied **until John**"; . . .

Matt 5:18 ⇨ Luke 16:17
[18] "For truly, I say to you, till **heaven and earth pass away**, not an iota, not a **dot**, will pass from **the law** until all is accomplished."

Matt 5:31–32 (§M12.5c) ⇨ §L68.2
[31] "It was also said, 'Whoever **divorces his wife**, let him give her a certificate of divorce.' [32] But I say to you that every one who **divorces his wife**, except on the ground of unchastity, makes her an adultress; **and** whoever **marries a divorced woman commits adultery**."

Matt 19:3–9 (§M65.1) ⇨ §L68.2
[3] And Pharisees came up to him and tested him by asking, "Is it lawful to divorce one's wife for any cause?" [4] He answered, "Have you not read that he who made them from the beginning made them male and female, [5] and said, 'For this reason a man shall leave his father and mother and be joined to his wife, and the two shall become one flesh'? [6] So they are no longer two but one flesh. What therefore God has joined together, let not man put asunder." [7] They said to him, "Why then did Moses command one to give a certificate of divorce, and to put her away?" [8] He said to them, "For your hardness of heart Moses allowed you to divorce your wives, but from the beginning it was not so. [9] And I say to you: whoever divorces his wife, except for unchastity, and marries another, commits adultery."

MARK

Mark 10:10–12 (§K51.2) ⇨ §L68.2
[10] And in the house the disciples asked him again about this matter. [11] And he said to them, "Whoever divorces his wife and marries another, commits adultery against her; [12] and if she divorces her husband and marries another, she commits adultery."

JOHN

THOMAS

GThom 11 ⇨ Luke 16:17
*(11) Jesus said, "This **heaven will pass away**, and the one above it will **pass away**. The dead are not alive, and the living will not die. In the days when you consumed what is dead, you made it what is alive. When you come to dwell in the light, what will you do? On the day when you were one you became two. But when you become two, what will you do?"*

OTHER

LUKE	MATT	MARK

Luke 16:19–31 (§L69)

19 "There was a rich man, who was clothed in purple and fine linen and who feasted sumptuously every day. 20 And at his gate lay a poor man named Lazarus, full of sores, 21 who desired to be fed with what fell from the rich man's table; moreover the dogs came and licked his sores. 22 The poor man died and was carried by the angels to Abraham's bosom. The rich man also died and was buried; 23 and in Hades, being in torment, he lifted up his eyes, and saw Abraham far off and Lazarus in his bosom. 24 And he called out, 'Father Abraham, have mercy upon me, and send Lazarus to dip the end of his finger in water and cool my tongue; for I am in anguish in this flame.' 25 But Abraham said, 'Son, remember that you in your lifetime received your good things, and Lazarus in like manner evil things; but now he is comforted here, and you are in anguish. 26 And besides all this, between us and you a great chasm has been fixed, in order that those who would pass from here to you may not be able, and none may cross from there to us.' 27 And he said, 'Then I beg you, father, to send him to my father's house, 28 for I have five brothers, so that he may warn them, lest they also come into this place of torment.' 29 But Abraham said, 'They have Moses and the prophets; let them hear them.' 30 And he said, 'No, father Abraham; but if some one goes to them from the dead, they will repent.' 31 He said to him, 'If they do not hear Moses and the prophets, neither will they be convinced if some one should rise from the dead.'"

Luke 3:8 ⇨ Luke 16:24, 27, 30
*8 "Bear fruits that befit repentance, and do not begin to say to yourselves, 'We have **Abraham** as our **father**'; for I tell you, God is able from these stones to raise up children to **Abraham**."*

JOHN	THOMAS	OTHER

LUKE

SIN AND FORGIVENESS

Luke 17:1–4 (§L70.1)
¹ And he said to his disciples, "Temptations to sin[a] are sure to come; but woe to him by whom they come! ² It would be better for him if a millstone were hung round his neck and he were cast into the sea, than that he should cause one of these little ones to sin.[b] ³ Take heed to yourselves; if your brother sins, rebuke him, and if he repents, forgive him; ⁴ and if he sins against you seven times in the day, and turns to you seven times, and says, 'I repent,' you must forgive him."

ON FAITH

Luke 17:5–6 (§L70.2)
⁵ The apostles said to the Lord, "Increase our faith!" ⁶ And the Lord said, "If you had faith as a grain of mustard seed, you could say to this sycamine tree, 'Be rooted up, and be planted in the sea,' and it would obey you."

THE WORTHY SERVANT

Luke 17:7–10 (§L70.3)
⁷ "Will any one of you, who has a servant plowing or keeping sheep, say to him when he has come in from the field, 'Come at once and sit down at table'? ⁸ Will he not rather say to him, 'Prepare supper for me, and gird yourself and serve me, till I eat and drink; and afterward you shall eat and drink'? ⁹ Does he thank the servant because he did what was commanded? ¹⁰ So you also, when you have done all that is commanded you, say, 'We are unworthy servants; we have only done what was our duty.'"

[a] Greek: *stumbling blocks*

[b] Greek: *stumble*

MATT

Matt 18:6–7 ⇨ Luke 17:1–2
⁶ "but whoever causes **one of these little ones** who believe in me **to sin, it would be better for** him to have a great **millstone** fastened **round his neck and** to be drowned in the depth of **the sea.**
⁷ "Woe to the world for temptations to sin! For it is necessary that **temptations come, but woe to** the man **by whom** the temptation comes!"

Matt 18:35 ⇨ Luke 17:3
³⁵ "So also my heavenly Father will do to every one of you, if you do not **forgive your brother** from your heart."

Matt 18:21–22 ⇨ Luke 17:4
²¹ Then Peter came up and said to him, "Lord, how often shall my brother sin **against** me, and I **forgive** him? As many as **seven times?**" ²² Jesus said to him, "I do not say to you **seven times,** but seventy **times seven.**"

Matt 17:20 ⇨ §L70.2
²⁰ He **said** to them, "Because of your little **faith.** For truly I say to you, **if you** have **faith as a grain of mustard seed, you** will **say to this** mountain, 'Move from here to there,' **and it** will move; and nothing will be impossible to **you.**"

Matt 21:21 ⇨ §L70.2
²¹ And Jesus answered them, "Truly, I say to **you, if you** have **faith** and never doubt, **you** will not only do what has been done to the fig **tree,** but even if **you say to this** mountain, '**Be** taken **up and** cast into **the sea,**' it will be done."

MARK

Mark 9:42 ⇨ Luke 17:1–2
⁴² "Whoever causes **one of these little ones** who believe in me **to sin, it would be better for** him if a great **millstone** were hung round his neck and he were thrown **into the sea.**"

Mark 11:22–23 ⇨ §L70.2
²² And Jesus answered them, "Have **faith** in God. ²³ Truly, I say to you, whoever says **to this** mountain, '**Be** taken **up and** cast into **the sea,**' and does not doubt in his heart, but believes that what he says will come to pass, **it** will be done for him."

JOHN

THOMAS

GThom 48 ⇨ Luke 17:6
(48) Jesus **said,** "If two make peace with each other in this one house, they will **say to** the mountain, 'Move away,' **and it** will move away."

GThom 106 ⇨ Luke 17:6
(106) Jesus **said,** "When you make the two one, you will become the sons of man, and when **you say,** 'Mountain, move away,' **it** will move away."

OTHER

LUKE   MATT   MARK

SCENE ONE

Luke 17:11–14 (§L71.1)
[11] On the way to Jerusalem he was passing along between Samaria and Galilee. [12] And as he entered a village, he was met by ten lepers, who stood at a distance [13] and lifted up their voices and said, "Jesus, Master, have mercy on us." [14] When he saw them he said to them, "Go and show yourselves to the priests." And as they went they were cleansed.

SCENE TWO

Luke 17:15–19 (§L71.2)
[15] Then one of them, when he saw that he was healed, turned back, praising God with a loud voice; [16] and he fell on his face at Jesus' feet, giving him thanks. Now he was a Samaritan. [17] Then said Jesus, "Were not ten cleansed? Where are the nine? [18] Was no one found to return and give praise to God except this foreigner?" [19] And he said to him, "Rise and go your way; your faith has made you well."

Luke 9:51 ⇨ Luke 17:11
[51] *When the days drew near for him to be received up, he set his face to go to Jerusalem.*

Luke 13:22 ⇨ Luke 17:11
[22] *He went on his way through towns and villages, teaching, and journeying toward Jerusalem.*

Luke 13:33 ⇨ Luke 17:11
[33] *"Nevertheless I must go on my way today and tomorrow and the day following; for it cannot be that a prophet should perish away from Jerusalem."*

Luke 18:31 ⇨ Luke 17:11
[31] *And taking the twelve, he said to them, "Behold, we are going up to Jerusalem, and everything that is written of the Son of man by the prophets will be accomplished."*

Luke 19:11 ⇨ Luke 17:11
[11] *As they heard these things, he proceeded to tell a parable, because **he was near to Jerusalem**, and because they supposed that the kingdom of God was to appear immediately.*

Luke 18:38–39 ⇨ Luke 17:13
[38] *And he cried, "Jesus, Son of David, **have mercy on me!**" [39] And those who were in front rebuked him, telling him to be silent; but he cried out all the more, "Son of David, **have mercy on me!**"*

Luke 5:14 ⇨ Luke 17:14
[14] *And he charged him to tell no one; but "**go and show yourself to the** priest, **and make an** offering for your cleansing, as Moses commanded, for proof to the people."*

Luke 7:50 ⇨ Luke 17:19
[50] *And he said to the woman, "**Your faith has saved you; go in peace.**"*

Luke 8:48 ⇨ Luke 17:19
[48] *And he said to her, "Daughter, **your faith has made you well; go in peace.**"*

Luke 18:42 ⇨ Luke 17:19
[42] *And Jesus said to him, "Receive your sight; **your faith has made you well.**"*

JOHN   THOMAS   OTHER

PEger2 2
*(2) **And** behold a leper drew near [to him] and said: "**Master Jesus**, wandering with lepers and eating with [them was I(?)] in the inn; I also [became] a le[per]. If [thou] therefore [wilt], I am made clean." Immediately the Lord [said to him]: "I will, be thou made clean." [And thereupon] the leprosy departed from him. [And the Lord said to him]: "**Go** [thy way and show th]yself to the [priests] . . ."*

LUKE

Luke 17:20–21 (§L72)

[20] Being asked by the Pharisees when the kingdom of God was coming, he answered them, "The kingdom of God is not coming with signs to be observed; [21] nor will they say, 'Lo, here it is!' or 'There!' for behold, the kingdom of God is in the midst of you."[a]

a Or *within you*

MATT

Matt 24:23 ⇨ Luke 17:21

[23] "Then if any one says to you, '**Lo, here is** the Christ!' **or** '**There** he is!' do not believe it."

MARK

Mark 13:21 ⇨ Luke 17:21

[21] "And then if any one says to you, 'Look, **here is** the Christ!' **or** 'Look, **there** he is!' do not believe it."

JOHN

THOMAS

POxy654 3

(3) Jesus says, ["If] those who draw you on [say to you, 'Behold,] **the kingdom** (**is**) in the heav[en,'] the birds of the hea[ven will be (there) before you. But if **they say** th]at it is under the earth, the fishes of the se[a will enter before you]. And **the king[dom of God] is** within **you** [and outside (of **you**). Whoever] knows [himself,] will fin[d] it [and when **you**] know yourselves, [**you** will realize that] **you** are [sons] of the li[ving] Father. [But if **you** will not] know yourselves, [**you** are] in [poverty] and **you** are pov[erty.]"

GThom 3

(3) Jesus said, "If those who lead you say to you, 'See, the Kingdom is in the sky,' then the birds of the sky will precede you. If **they say** to you, 'It is in the sea,' then the fish will precede you. Rather, **the Kingdom is** inside **of you**, and it **is** outside **of you**. When **you** come to know yourselves, then **you** will become known, and **you** will realize that it is **you** who are the sons of the living Father. But if **you** will not know yourselves, **you** dwell in poverty and it is **you** who are that poverty."

GThom 113

(113) His disciples said to Him, "When will **the Kingdom** come?"

<Jesus said,> "It will **not** come by waiting for it. It will not be a matter of saying '**Here it is**' **or** '**There** it is.' Rather, **the Kingdom of** the Father **is** spread out upon the earth, and men do not see it."

OTHER

LUKE	MATT	MARK

Luke 17:22-37 (§L73)

²² And he said to the disciples, "The days are coming when you will desire to see one of the days of the Son of man, and you will not see it. ²³ And they will say to you, 'Lo, there!' or 'Lo, here!' Do not go, do not follow them. ²⁴ For as lightning flashes and lights up the sky from one side to the other, so will the Son of man be in his day.[a] ²⁵ But first he must suffer many things and be rejected by this generation. ²⁶ As it was in the days of Noah, so will it be in the days of the Son of man. ²⁷ They ate, they drank, they married, they were given in marriage, until the day when Noah entered the ark, and the flood came and destroyed them all. ²⁸ Likewise as it was in the days of Lot—they ate, they drank, they bought, they sold, they planted, they built, ²⁹ but on the day when Lot went out from Sodom fire and sulphur rained from heaven and destroyed them all— ³⁰ so will it be on the day when the Son of man is revealed. ³¹ On that day, let him who is on the housetop, with his goods in the house, not come down to take them away; and likewise let him who is in the field not turn back. ³² Remember Lot's wife. ³³ Whoever seeks to gain his life will lose it, but whoever loses his life will preserve it. ³⁴ I tell you, in that night there will be two in one bed; one will be taken and the other left. ³⁵ There will be two women grinding together; one will be taken and the other left."[b] ³⁷ And they said to him, "Where Lord?" He said to them, "Where the body is, there the eagles[c] will be gathered together."

[a] Some witnesses omit *in his day:* 𝔓⁴⁵ B D it (in part)

[b] Some witnesses add v. 36, *Two men will be in the field; one will be taken and the other left* (see Matt 24:40): D *f*¹³ it (in part) *al;* omit v. 36: 𝔓⁷⁵ ℵ B K L W X Δ Θ Π Ψ *f*¹ 28 33 *al*

[c] Or *vultures*

Luke 9:22 ⇨ Luke 17:25
²² saying, "The Son of man *must suffer many things, and be rejected by the elders and chief priests and scribes, and be killed, and on the third day be raised.*"

Luke 9:44 ⇨ Luke 17:25
⁴⁴ "*Let these words sink into your ears; for the Son of man is to be delivered into the hands of men.*"

Luke 18:31-33 ⇨ Luke 17:25
³¹ And taking the twelve, he said to them, *"Behold, we are going up to Jerusalem, and everything that is written of the Son of man by the prophets will be accomplished. *³² *For he will be delivered to the Gentiles, and will be mocked and shamefully treated and spit upon; *³³ *they will scourge him and kill him, and on the thrid day he will rise.*"

Matt 24:26-27 ⇨ Luke 17:23-24
²⁶ "So, if **they say to you,** '**Lo,** he is in the wilderness,' **do not go** out; if they say, '**Lo,** he is in the inner rooms' **do not** believe it. ²⁷ **For as** the **lightning** comes from the east and shines as far as the west, **so will** be the coming of **the Son of man.**"

Matt 24:37-41 ⇨ Luke 17:26-30, 34-35
³⁷ "**As** were **the days of Noah, so will** be the coming **of the Son of man**. ³⁸ For as in those days before the flood **they** were eating and drinking, marrying and giving **in marriage, until the day when Noah entered the ark,** ³⁹ **and** they did not know until the **flood came** and swept **them all** away, **so will** be the coming of **the Son of man**. ⁴⁰ Then **two** men **will be** in the field; **one** is **taken and** one is **left**. ⁴¹ **Two women will be grinding** at the mill; **one** is **taken and** one is **left**."

Matt 24:17-18 ⇨ Luke 17:31
¹⁷ "**let him who is on the housetop not** go **down** to take what is **in his house;** ¹⁸ **and let him who is in the field not turn back** to take his mantle."

Matt 10:39 ⇨ Luke 17:33
³⁹ "He who finds **his life will lose it,** and he who **loses his life** for my sake **will find it.**"

Matt 16:25 ⇨ Luke 17:33
²⁵ "For **whoever** would save **his life will lose it,** and **whoever loses his life** for my sake **will find it.**"

Matt 24:28 ⇨ Luke 17:37
²⁸ Wherever **the body is, there the eagles will be gathered together.**

Mark 13:15-16 ⇨ Luke 17:31
¹⁵ "**let him who is on the housetop not** go **down,** nor enter his **house, to take** anything **away;** ¹⁶ **and let him who is in the field not turn back** to take his mantle."

Mark 8:35 ⇨ Luke 17:33
³⁵ "For **whoever** would save **his life will lose it; and whoever loses his life** for my sake and the gospel's **will save it.**"

Mark 13:21 ⇨ Luke 17:23
²¹ "*And then if any one says to you, 'Look, here is the Christ!' or 'Look, there he is!' do not believe it.*"

Luke 22:22 ⇨ Luke 17:25
²² "*For the Son of man goes as it has been determined; but woe to that man by whom he is betrayed!*"

Luke 24:6-8 ⇨ Luke 17:25
⁶ "*Remember how he told you, while he was still in Galilee, *⁷ *that the Son of man **must be** delivered into the hands of sinful men, and be crucified, and on the third day rise." *⁸ *And they remembered his words, . . .*

Luke 24:26 ⇨ Luke 17:25
²⁶ "*Was it not necessary that the Christ should **suffer** these **things and** enter into his glory?*"

Luke 24:46 ⇨ Luke 17:25
⁴⁶ and said to them, "*Thus it is written, that the Christ should **suffer** and on the third day rise from the dead, . . .*"

Luke 9:24 ⇨ Luke 17:33
²⁴ "For **whoever** would save **his life will lose it; and whoever loses his life** for my sake, he **will save it.**"

Gen 7:6-10 ⇨ Luke 17:26-27
⁶ **Noah** was six hundred years old when **the flood** of waters **came** upon the earth. ⁷ And **Noah** and his sons and his wife and his sons' wives with him went into **the ark,** to escape the waters of **the flood.** ⁸ Of clean animals, and of animals that are not clean, and of birds, and of everything that creeps on the ground, ⁹ two and two, male and female, went into **the ark** with **Noah,** as God had commanded **Noah.** ¹⁰ And after seven days the waters of **the flood came** upon the earth.

⇨ Luke 17:28-29, 32
Cf. Gen 19:1-29

JOHN	THOMAS	OTHER

GThom 38 ⇨ Luke 17:22

*(38) Jesus **said**, "Many times have you desired to hear these words which I am saying to you, and you have no one else to hear them from. There will be **days when you will** look for Me **and will not** find Me."*

GThom 113 ⇨ Luke 17:22-23

(113) His disciples said to Him, "When will the Kingdom come?"

*<Jesus said,> "**It** will not come by waiting for **it**. It will not be a matter of saying '**Here it is**' or '**There it is**.' Rather, the Kingdom of the Father is spread out upon the earth, and men do **not see it**."*

GThom 61 ⇨ Luke 17:34

*(61) Jesus said, "**Two will** rest on a **bed**: the **one will** die, the **other** will live."*

Salome said, "Who are You, man, that You, as though from the One, (or: as<whose son>, that You) have come up on my couch and eaten from my table?"

Jesus said to her, "I am He who exists from the Undivided. I was given some of the things of My father."

<Salome said,> "I am Your disciple."

<Jesus said to her,> "Therefore I say, if he is <undivided>, he will be filled with light, but if he is divided, he will be filled with darkness."

LUKE	MATT	MARK

LUKE

Luke 18:1–8 (§L74)

¹ And he told them a parable, to the effect that they ought always to pray and not lose heart. ² He said, "In a certain city there was a judge who neither feared God nor regarded man; ³ and there was a widow in that city who kept coming to him and saying, 'Vindicate me against my adversary.' ⁴ For a while he refused; but afterward he said to himself, 'Though I neither fear God nor regard man, ⁵ yet because this widow bothers me, I will vindicate her, or she will wear me out by her continual coming.'" ⁶ And the Lord said, "Hear what the unrighteous judge says. ⁷ And will not God vindicate his elect, who cry to him day and night? Will he delay long over them? ⁸ I tell you, he will vindicte them speedily. Nevertheless, when the Son of man comes, will he find faith on earth?"

Luke 18:9–14 (§L75)

⁹ He also told this parable to some who trusted in themselves that they were righteous and despised others: ¹⁰ "Two men went up into the temple to pray, one a Pharisee and the other a tax collector. ¹¹ The Pharisee stood and prayed thus with himself, 'God, I thank thee that I am not like other men, extortioners, unjust, adulterers, or even like this tax collector. ¹² I fast twice a week, I give tithes of all that I get.' ¹³ But the tax collector, standing far off, would not even lift up his eyes to heaven, but beat his breast, saying, 'God, be merciful to me a sinner!' ¹⁴ I tell you, this man went down to his house justified rather than the other; for every one who exalts himself will be humbled, but he who humbles himself will be exalted."

Luke 11:5–8 ⇨ Luke 18:1–5

⁵ *And he said to them, "Which of you who has a friend will go to him at midnight and say to him, 'Friend, lend me three loaves; ⁶ for a friend of mine has arrived on a journey, and I have nothing to set before him'; ⁷ and he will answer from within, 'Do not bother me; the door is now shut, and my children are with me in bed; I cannot get up and give you anything'? ⁸ I tell you, though he will not get up and give him anything because he is his friend, yet because of his importunity he will rise and give him whatever he needs."*

Luke 10:29 ⇨ Luke 18:9

²⁹ *But he, desiring to justify himself, said to Jesus, "And who is my neighbor?"*

Luke 16:15 ⇨ Luke 18:9, 14

¹⁵ *But he said to them, "You are those who justify yourselves before men, but God knows your hearts; for what is exalted among men is an abomination in the sight of God."*

●**Luke 14:11** ⇨ Luke 18:14

¹¹ "For every one who exalts himself will be humbled, and he who humbles himself will be exalted."

MATT

Matt 23:12 ⇨ Luke 18:14

¹² "whoever **exalts himself will be humbled**, and whoever **humbles himself will be exalted**."

Matt 18:4 ⇨ Luke 18:14

⁴ *"Whoever **humbles himself** like this child, he is the greatest in the kingdom of heaven."*

JOHN	THOMAS	OTHER

LUKE

Luke 18:15–17 (§L76)
¹⁵ Now they were bringing even infants to him that he might touch them; and when the disciples saw it, they rebuked them. ¹⁶ But Jesus called them to him, saying, "Let the children come to me, and do not hinder them; for to such belongs the kingdom of God. ¹⁷ Truly, I say to you, whoever does not receive the kingdom of God like a child shall not enter it."

Luke 9:48
⁴⁸ and said to them, "Whoever receives this child in my name receives me, and whoever receives me receives him who sent me; for he who is least among you all is the one who is great."

MATT

Matt 19:13–15 (§M66)
¹³ Then children were brought **to him that he might** lay his hands on **them** and pray. **The disciples rebuked** the people; ¹⁴ **but Jesus** said, **"Let the children come to me, and do not hinder them; for to such belongs the kingdom** of heaven." ¹⁵ And he laid his hands on them and went away.

Matt 18:2–6
² And calling **to him** a child, he put him in the midst of them, ³ and said, **"Truly, I say to you,** unless you turn and become like **children,** you will never enter **the kingdom** of heaven. ⁴ Whoever humbles himself **like this child,** he is the greatest in **the kingdom of** heaven.

⁵ **"Whoever receives one such child in my name receives me;** ⁶ but **whoever** causes one of these little ones who believe **in me** to sin, it would be better for him to have a great millstone fastened round his neck and to be drowned in the depth of the sea."

MARK

Mark 10:13–16 (§K52)
¹³ And **they were bringing** children **to him, that he might touch them;** ¹³ **and the disciples rebuked them.** ¹⁴ **But** when **Jesus** saw it he was indignant, and said to them, **"Let the children come to me, do not hinder them; for to such belongs the kingdom of God.** ¹⁵ **Truly, I say to you, whoever does not receive the kingdom of God like a child shall not enter it."** ¹⁶ And he took them in his arms and blessed them, laying his hands upon them.

Mark 9:36–37
³⁶ And he took **a child,** and put him in the midst of them; and taking him in his arms, he said to them, ³⁷ "Whoever receives one such **child in** my name receives **me;** and **whoever receives me,** receives not me but him who sent **me."**

JOHN

John 3:3–5 ⇨ Luke 18:17
³ Jesus answered him, **"Truly, truly, I say to you,** unless one is born anew, he cannot see the **kingdom of God."** ⁴ Nicodemus said to him, "How can a man be born when he is old? Can he enter a second time into his mother's womb and be born?" ⁵ Jesus answered, **"Truly, truly, I say to you,** unless one is born of water and the Spirit, he cannot **enter the kingdom of God."**

THOMAS

GThom 22
(22) Jesus saw **infants** being suckled. He said to His disciples, "These infants being suckled are like those who **enter the Kingdom.**"

They said to Him, "Shall we then, as children, enter the Kingdom?"

Jesus said to them, "When you make the two one, and when you make the inside like the outside and the outside like the inside, and the above like the below, and when you make the male and the female one and the same, so that the male not be male nor the female female; and when you fashion eyes in place of an eye, and a hand in place of a hand, and a foot in place of a foot, and a likeness in place of a likeness; then will you enter [the Kingdom]."

OTHER

LUKE

RICH RULER

Luke 18:18–25 (§L77.1)
[18] And a ruler asked him, "Good Teacher, what shall I do to inherit eternal life?" [19] And Jesus said to him, "Why do you call me good? No one is good but God alone. [20] You know the commandments: 'Do not commit adultery, Do not kill, Do not steal, Do not bear false witness, Honor your father and mother.'" [21] And he said, "All these I have observed from my youth." [22] And when Jesus heard it, he said to him, "One thing you still lack. Sell all that you have and distribute to the poor, and you will have treasure in heaven; and come, follow me." [23] But when he heard this he became sad, for he was very rich. [24] Jesus looking at him said, "How hard it is for those who have riches to enter the kingdom of God! [25] For it is easier for a camel to go through the eye of a needle than for a rich man to enter the kingdom of God."

DANGER OF RICHES

Luke 18:26–30 (§L77.2)
[26] Those who heard it said, "Then who can be saved?" [27] But he said, "What is impossible with men is possible with God." [28] And Peter said, "Lo, we have left our homes and followed you." [29] And he said to them, "Truly, I say to you, there is no man who has left house or wife or brothers or parents or children, for the sake of the kingdom of God, [30] who will not receive manifold more in this time, and in the age to come eternal life."

Luke 10:25 ⇨ Luke 18:18–21
[25] And behold, a lawyer stood up to put him to the test, saying, "Teacher, what shall I do to inherit eternal life?" [26] He said to him, "What is written in the law? How do you read?" [27] And he answered, "You shall love the Lord your God with all your heart, and with all your soul, and with all your strength, and with all your mind; and your neighbor as yourself." [28] And he said to him, "You have answered right; do this, and you will live."

Luke 12:21 ⇨ Luke 18:22
[21] "So is he who lays up treasure for himself, and is not rich toward God."

Luke 12:33–34 ⇨ Luke 18:22
[33] "Sell your possessions, and give alms; provide yourselves with purses that do not grow old, with a treasure in the heavens that does not fail, where no thief approaches and no moth destroys. [34] For where your treasure is, there will your heart be also."

Luke 5:11 ⇨ Luke 18:28
[11] And when they had brought their boats to land, they left everything and followed him.

MATT

Matt 19:16–22 (§M67.1) ⇨ Luke 18:18–23
[16] And behold, one came up to him, saying, "Teacher, **what** good deed must **I do**, **to** have eternal life?" [17] And he **said to him**, "Why do you ask me about what is **good**? One there is who **is good**. If you would enter life, keep the **commandments**." [18] He said to him, "Which?" And Jesus said, "You shall **not kill**, You shall **not commit adultery**, You shall **not** steal, You shall **not bear false witness**, [19] Honor **your father and mother**, and, You shall love your neighbor as yourself." [20] The young man **said** to him, "**All these I have observed**; what do I still lack?" [21] **Jesus** said to him, "If **you** would be perfect, go, **sell** what you possess and give **to the poor, and you will have treasure in heaven; and come, follow me**." [22] **When** the young man **heard this he** went away sorrowful; **for he** had great possessions.

Matt 19:23–30 (§M67.2) ⇨ Luke 18:24–30
[23] And **Jesus** said to his disciples, "Truly, I say to you, **it** will be **hard** for a rich man **to enter the kingdom** of heaven. [24] Again I tell you, **it is easier for a camel to go through the eye of a needle than for a rich man to enter the kingdom of God**." [25] When the disciples **heard** this they were greatly astonished, saying, "**Who then can be saved?**" [26] **But** Jesus looked at them and **said** to them, "**With men** this **is impossible**, but **with God** all things are **possible**." [27] Then **Peter** said in reply, "**Lo, we have left** everything **and followed you**. What then shall we have?" [28] Jesus **said to them**, "**Truly, I say to you,** in the new world, when the Son of man shall sit on his glorious throne, you who have followed me will also sit on twelve thrones, judging the twelve tribes of Israel. [29] And every one **who has left** houses **or brothers or** sisters **or** father **or** mother **or children** or lands, **for** my name's **sake, will receive** a hundredfold and inherit **eternal life**. [30] But many that are first will be last, and the last first."

Luke 5:28 ⇨ Luke 18:28
[28] And he left everything, and rose and followed him.

Luke 14:26 ⇨ Luke 18:29
[26] "If any one comes to me and does not hate his own father and mother and wife and children and brothers and sisters, yes, even his own life, he cannot be my disciple."

Exod 20:12–16 ⇨ Luke 18:20
[12] "**Honor your father and** your **mother**, that your days may be long in the land which the Lord your God gives you.
[13] "You shall **not kill.**
[14] "You shall **not commit adultery.**
[15] "You shall **not steal.**
[16] "You shall **not bear false witness** against your neighbor."

MARK

Mark 10:17–22 (§K53.1) ⇨ Luke 18:18–23
[17] And as he was setting out on his journey, a man ran up and knelt before him, and **asked** him, "Good Teacher, **what** must **I do** to **inherit eternal life**?" [18] And Jesus said to him, "**Why do you call me good? No one is good but God alone.** [19] **You know the commandments:** 'Do **not kill, Do not commit adultery, Do not steal, Do not bear false witness,** Do not defraud, **Honor your father and mother.**'" [20] **And he said** to him, "Teacher, **all these I have observed from my youth.**" [21] **And Jesus** looking upon him loved him, and **said to him,** "**You lack one thing;** go, **sell** what **you have, and** give **to the poor, and you will have treasure in heaven; and come, follow me.**" [22] At that saying his countenance fell, and **he** went away sorrowful; **for he** had great possessions.

Mark 10:23–31 (§K53.2) ⇨ Luke 18:24–30
[23] And **Jeus** looked around and **said** to his disciples, "**How hard** it will be **for those who have riches to enter the kingdom of God!**" [24] And the disciples were amazed at his words. But Jesus said to them again, "Children, **how hard it is to enter the kingdom of God! [25] It is easier for a camel to go through the eye of a needle than for a rich man to enter the kingdom of God.**" [26] And they were exceedingly astonished, and **said** to him, "**Then who can be saved?**" [27] Jesus looked at them and **said**, "**With men it is impossible**, but not **with God;** for all things are **possible with God.**" [28] **Peter** began to say to him, "**Lo, we have left** everything **and followed you.**" [29] Jesus **said**, "**Truly, I say to you, there is no** one **who has left house or brothers or** sisters **or** mother **or** father **or children** or lands, **for** my **sake** and for the gospel, [30] **who will not receive** a hundredfold now **in this time,** houses and brothers and sisters and mothers and children and lands, with persecutions, **and in the age to come eternal life.** [31] But many that are first will be last, and the last first."

Deut 5:16–20 ⇨ Luke 18:20
[16] "**Honor your father and** your **mother**, as the Lord your God commanded you; that your days may be prolonged, and that it may go well with you, in the land which the Lord your God gives you.
[17] "You shall **not kill.**
[18] "Neither shall you **commit adultery.**
[19] "Neither shall you **steal.**
[20] "Neither shall you **bear false witness** against your neighbor."

JOHN	THOMAS	OTHER

GNaz 16 ⇨ §L77.1

(16) The other of the two rich men said to **him**: Master, **what** good thing must **I do** that I may live? He **said to him**: Man, fulfil the law and the prophets. **He** answered him: That **have I** done. **He said to him**: Go and **sell all that** thou possessest **and distribute** it among **the poor, and** then **come** and **follow me. But** the rich man then began to scratch his head and it (the saying) pleased him not. And the Lord said to him: How canst thou say, I have fulfilled the law and the prophets? For it stands written in the law: Love thy neighbour as thyself; and behold, many of thy brethren, sons of Abraham, are begrimed with dirt and die of hunger—and thy house is full of many good things and nothing at all comes forth from it to them! And he turned and **said** to Simon, his disciple, who was sitting by him: Simon, son of Jona, **it is easier for a camel to go through the eye of a needle than for a rich man to enter** into **the kingdom of** heaven. (Origen, *Commentary on Matthew* 15:14 [on Matthew 19:16–30])

Acts 4:34–35 ⇨ Luke 18:22

34 There was not a needy person among them, for as many as were possessors of lands or houses sold them, and brought the proceeds of what was sold 35 and laid it at the apostles' feet; and distribution was made to each as any had need.

ApocJa 4:32–37 ⇨ Luke 18:28–30

And I answered and said to him: "Lord, we can obey you 25 if you wish. For we have forsaken our forefathers and our mothers and our villages and have followed you. Grant us, [therefore], 30 not to be tempted by the wicked devil."

The Lord answered and said: "What is your (pl.) merit when you do the will of the Father if it is not given to you by him 35 as a gift, while you are tempted by Satan?"

LUKE	MATT	MARK

LUKE

Luke 18:31–34 (§L78) °

[31] **And taking the twelve, he said to them,** "Behold, we are going up to Jerusalem, and everything that is written of the Son of man by the prophets will be accomplished. [32] For he will be delivered to the Gentiles, and will be mocked and shamefully treated and spit upon; [33] they will scourge him and kill him, and on the third day he will rise." [34] But they understood none of these things; this saying was hid from them, and they did not grasp what was said.

°Appendix 2 ⇨ §L78

Luke 9:18–22 (§L40.1)

[18] Now it happened that as he was praying along the disciples were with him; and **he** asked **them,** "Who do the people say that I am?" [19] and they answered, "John the Baptist; but others say, Elijah; and others, that one of the old prophets has risen." [20] And he said to them, "but who do you say that I am?" and Peter answered, "The Christ of God." [21] But he charged and commanded them to tell this to no one, [22] saying, "**The Son of man** must suffer many things, **and be** rejected by **the** elders chief priests and scribes, **and** be killed, **and on the third day** be raised."

Luke 9:43b–45 (§43.1)

But while they were all marveling at everything he did, **he said to** his disciples, [44] "Let these words sink into your ears; for **the Son of man** is to **be delivered** into **the** hands of men." [45] But they did not understand **this saying,** and it **was** concealed **from them,** that **they** should not perceive it; and they were afraid to ask him about **this saying.**

Luke 17:25 ⇨ Luke 18:31–33

[25] "But first **he must suffer many things and be** rejected by this generation."

Luke 22:22 ⇨ Luke 18:31–33

[22] "For **the Son of man** goes as it has been determined; but woe to that man by whom **he** is betrayed!"

Luke 24:6–8 ⇨ Luke 18:31–33

[6] "Remember how he told you, while he was still in Galilee, [7] that the Son of man must be delivered into the hands of sinful men, and be crucified, **and on the third day** rise." [8] And they remembered his words, . . .

Luke 24:26 ⇨ Luke 18:31–33

[26] "Was it not necessary that **the Christ should** suffer these things **and enter into his glory?"**

MATT

Matt 20:17–19 (§M68)

[17] **And as Jesus was going up to Jerusalem,** he took **the twelve** disciples aside, and on the way **he said to them,** [18] "Behold, **we are going up to Jerusalem;** and **the Son of man will be delivered to the** chief priests and scribes, and **they will** condemn **him** to death, [19] and deliver him **to the Gentiles to be mocked** and scourged and crucified, **and he will** be raised **on the third day.**"

Matt 16:21–23 (§M56)

[21] From that time Jesus began to show his disciples that he must go **to Jerusalem** and suffer many things from **the** elders and chief priests and scribes, **and** be killed, **and on the third day** be raised. [22] And Peter took him and began to rebuke him, saying, "God forbid, Lord! This shall never happen to you." [23] But he turned and said to Peter, "Get behind me, Satan! You are a hindrance to me; for you are not on the side of God, but of men."

Matt 17:22–23 (§M60)

[22] As they were gathering in Galilee, Jesus **said to them,** "**The Son of man is to be delivered** into **the** hands of men, [23] **and they will kill him, and he will** be raised **on the third day.**" And **they** were greatly distressed.

Luke 24:46 ⇨ Luke 18:31–33

[46] and said to them, "Thus it is written, that the Christ should suffer and on the third day rise from the dead, . . ."

Luke 9:51 ⇨ Luke 18:31

[51] When the days drew near for him to be received up, he set his face to go **to Jerusalem.**

Luke 13:22 ⇨ Luke 18:31

[22] He went on his way through towns and villages, teaching, and journeying toward **Jerusalem.**

Luke 13:33 ⇨ Luke 18:31

[33] "Nevertheless I must go on my way today and tomorrow and the day following; for it cannot be that a prophet should perish away from **Jerusalem.**'"

Luke 17:11 ⇨ Luke 18:31

[11] On the way **to Jerusalem** he was passing along between Samaria and Galilee.

Luke 19:11 ⇨ Luke 18:31

[11] As they heard these things, **he** proceeded to tell a parable, because he was near **to Jerusalem, and** because they supposed that the kingdom of God was to appear immediately.

MARK

Mark 10:32–34 (§K54)

[32] **And they were on the road, going up to Jerusalem,** and Jesus was walking ahead of them; and they were amazed, and those who followed were afraid. **And taking the twelve** again, he began to tell **them** what was to happen to him, [33] saying, "Behold, **we are going up to Jerusalem;** and **the Son of man will be delivered to the** chief priests and the scribes, **and** they **will** condemn him to death, and deliver him **to the Gentiles;** [34] **and they will** mock him, **and spit upon him,** and **scourge him, and kill him; and** after three days **he will rise.**"

Mark 8:31–33 (§K42)

[31] **And he** began to teach **them** that **the Son of man** must suffer many things, and **be** rejected by **the** elders and the chief priests and the scribes, **and be killed, and** after three days **rise** again. [32] And he said this plainly. And Peter took him, and began to rebuke him. [33] But turning and seeing his disciples, he rebuked Peter, and said, "Get behind me, Satan! For you are not on the side of God, but of men."

Mark 9:30–32 (§K46)

[30] They went on from there and passed through Galilee. And he would not have any one know it; [31] for **he** was teaching his disciples, saying **to them,** "**The Son of man will be delivered** into **the** hands of men, **and they will kill him; and** when **he** is killed, after three days **he will rise.**" [32] **But they did not** understand the **saying,** and they were afraid to ask him.

Luke 24:25–27 ⇨ Luke 18:34

[25] And he said to them, "O foolish men, and slow of heart to believe all that the prophets have spoken! [26] Was it not necessary that the Christ should suffer **these things** and enter into his glory?" [27] And beginning with Moses and all the prophets, he interpreted to **them** in all the scriptures the things concerning himself.

Luke 24:44–45 ⇨ Luke 18:34

[44] Then he said to them, "**These** are my words which I spoke to you, while I was still with you, that everything written about me in the law of Moses and the prophets and the psalms must be fulfilled." [45] Then he opened their minds to understand the scriptures, . . .

JOHN	THOMAS	OTHER

LUKE

Luke 18:35–43 (§L79)

³⁵ As he drew near to Jericho, a blind man was sitting by the roadside begging; ³⁶ and hearing a multitude going by, he inquired what this meant. ³⁷ They told him, "Jesus of Nazareth is passing by." ³⁸ And he cried, "Jesus, Son of David, have mercy on me!" ³⁹ And those who were in front rebuked him, telling him to be silent; but he cried out all the more, "Son of David, have mercy on me!" ⁴⁰ And Jesus stopped, and commanded him to be brought to him; and when he came near, he asked him, ⁴¹ "What do you want me to do for you?" He said, "Lord, let me receive my sight." ⁴² And Jesus said to him, "Receive your sight; your faith has made you well." ⁴³ And immediately he received his sight and followed him, glorifying God; and all the people, when they saw it, gave praise to God.

Luke 17:13 ⇨ Luke 18:38–39
¹³ and lifted up their voices and said, "Jesus, Master, have mercy on us."

Luke 7:50 ⇨ Luke 18:42
⁵⁰ And he said to the woman, "Your faith has saved you; go in peace."

Luke 8:48 ⇨ Luke 18:42
⁴⁸ And he said to her, "Daughter, your faith has made you well; go in peace."

Luke 17:19 ⇨ Luke 18:42
¹⁹ And he said to him, "Rise and go your way; your faith has made you well."

JOHN

MATT

Matt 9:27–31 (§M24)

²⁷ And as **Jesus** passed on from there, two **blind** men followed him, crying aloud, **"Have mercy on us, Son of David."** ²⁸ When he entered the house, the blind men came to him; **and Jesus said** to them, **"Do you** believe that I am able to **do this?"** They **said** to him, "Yes, **Lord.**" ²⁹ Then he touched their eyes, saying, "According to **your faith** be it done to you." ³⁰ **And** their eyes were opened. And Jesus sternly charged them, "See that no one knows it." ³¹ But they went away and spread his fame through all that district.

Matt 20:29–34 (§M70)

²⁹ And **as** they went out of **Jericho,** a great crowd followed him. ³⁰ And behold, two **blind** men **sitting by the roadside,** when they heard that **Jesus** was **passing by, cried** out, **"Have mercy on us, Son of David!"** ³¹ The crowd **rebuked** them, **telling** them **to be silent; but** they **cried out the more,** "Lord, **have mercy on us, Son of David!"** ³² **And Jesus stopped** and **called** them, saying, **"What do you want me to do for you?"** ³³ They **said** to him, **"Lord,** let our eyes be opened." ³⁴ **And Jesus** in pity touched their eyes, **and immediately** they **received** their **sight and followed him.**

THOMAS

MARK

Mark 10:46–52 (§K56)

⁴⁶ And they came **to Jericho;** and as he was leaving Jericho with his disciples and a great multitude, Bartimaeus, a **blind** beggar, the son of Timaeus, **was sitting by the roadside.** ⁴⁷ **And** when **he** heard that it was **Jesus of Nazareth, he** began to cry out and say, **"Jesus, Son of David, have mercy on me!"** ⁴⁸ **And** many **rebuked him, telling him to be silent; but he cried out all the more, "Son of David, have mercy on me!"** ⁴⁹ **And Jesus stopped and** said, "Call **him.**" And they called the blind man, saying to him, "Take heart; rise, he is calling you." ⁵⁰ And throwing off his mantle he sprang up and came to Jesus. ⁵¹ And Jesus said to **him, "What do you want me to do for you?"** And the blind man **said** to him, "Master, **let me receive my sight."** ⁵² **And Jesus said to him,** "Go your way; **your faith has made you well." And immediately he received his sight and followed him** on the way.

OTHER

LUKE   MATT   MARK

Luke 19:1–10 (§L80)

¹He entered Jericho and was passing through. ²And there was a man named Zacchaeus; he was a chief tax collector, and rich. ³And he sought to see who Jesus was, but could not, on account of the crowd, because he was small of stature. ⁴So he ran on ahead and climbed up into a sycamore tree to see him, for he was to pass that way. ⁵And when Jesus came to the place, he looked up and said to him, "Zacchaeus, make haste and come down; for I must stay at your house today." ⁶So he made haste and came down, and received him joyfully. ⁷And when they saw it they all murmured, "He has gone in to be the guest of a man who is a sinner." ⁸And Zacchaeus stood and said to the Lord, "Behold, Lord, the half of my goods I give to the poor; and if I have defrauded any one of anything, I restore it fourfold." ⁹And Jesus said to him, "Today salvation has come to this house, since he also is a son of Abraham. ¹⁰For the Son of man came to seek and to save the lost."

Luke 5:29–30 ⇨ Luke 19:7

²⁹*And Levi made him a great feast in his house; and there was a large company of tax collectors and others sitting at table with them.* ³⁰*And the Pharisees and their scribes **murmured** against his disciples, saying, "Why do you eat and drink with tax collectors and sinners?"*

Luke 7:34 ⇨ Luke 19:7

³⁴*"The Son of man **has** come eating and drinking; and you say, 'Behold, a glutton and a drunkard, **a** friend of tax collectors and sinners!'"*

Luke 15:1–2 (§L66.1) ⇨ Luke 19:7

¹*Now the tax collectors and sinners were all drawing near to hear him.* ²*And the Pharisees and the scribes **murmured**, saying, "This man receives sinners and eats with them."*

Luke 18:22 ⇨ Luke 19:8

²²*And when Jesus heard it, he said to him, "One thing you still lack. Sell all that you have and distribute **to the poor**, and you will have treasure in heaven; and come, follow me."*

Luke 15:3–7 (§L66.2) ⇨ Luke 19:10

³*So he told them this parable:* ⁴*"What man of you, haveing a hundred sheep, if he has **lost** one of them, does not leave the ninety-nine in the wilderness, and go after the one which is **lost** until he finds it?* ⁵*And when he has found it, he lays it on his shoulders, rejoicing.* ⁶*And when he comes home, he calls together his friends and his neighbors, saying to them, 'Rejoice with me, for I have found my sheep which was **lost**.'* ⁷*Just so, I tell you, there will be more joy in heaven over one sinner who repents than over ninety-nine righteous persons who need no repentance."*

Luke 15:8–10 (§L66.3) ⇨ Luke 19:10

⁸*"Or what woman, having ten silver coins, if she loses one coin, does not light a lamp and sweep the house and **seek** diligently until she finds it?* ⁹*And when she has found it, she calls together her friends and neighbors, saying, 'Rejoice with me, for I have found the coin which I had **lost**.'* ¹⁰*Just so, I tell you, there is joy before the angels of God over one sinner who repents."*

JOHN   THOMAS   OTHER

LUKE

Luke 19:11–27 (§L81)

[11] As they heard these things, he proceeded to tell a parable, because he was near to Jerusalem, and because they supposed that the kingdom of God was to appear immediately. [12] He said therefore, "A nobleman went into a far country to receive a kingdom and then return. [13] Calling ten of his servants, he gave them ten pounds,[a] and said to them, 'Trade with these till I come.' [14] But his citizens hated him and sent an embassy after him, saying, 'We do not want this man to reign over us.' [15] When he returned, having received the kingdom, he commanded these servants, to whom he had given the money, to be called to him, that he might know what they had gained by trading. [16] The first came before him, saying, 'Lord, your pound has made ten pounds more.' [17] And he said to him, 'Well done, good servant! Because you have been faithful in a very little, you shall have authority over ten cities.' [18] And the second came, saying, 'Lord, your pound has made five pounds.' [19] And he said to him, 'And you are to be over five cities.' [20] Then another came, saying, 'Lord, here is your pound, which I kept laid away in a napkin; [21] for I was afraid of you, because you are a severe man; you take up what you did not lay down, and reap what you did not sow.' [22] He said to him, 'I will condemn you out of your own mouth, you wicked servant! You knew that I was a severe man, taking up what I did not lay down and reaping what I did not sow? [23] Why then did you not put my money into the bank, and at my coming I should have collected it with interest?' [24] And he said to those who stood by, 'Take the pound from him, and give it to him who has the ten pounds.' [25] (And they said to him, 'Lord, he has ten pounds!') [26] I tell you, that to every one who has will more be given; but from him who has not, even what he has will be taken away. [27] But as for these enemies of mine, who did not want me to reign over them, bring them here and slay them before me.'"

[a] The mina, here translated by *pound,* was about three months' wages for a laborer

Luke 9:51 ⇨ Luke 19:11
[51] *When the days drew near for him to be received up, he set his face to go* **to** *Jerusalem.*

Luke 3:22 ⇨ Luke 19:11
[22] *He went on his way through towns and villages, teaching, and journeying toward* **Jerusalem.**

Luke 13:33 ⇨ Luke 19:11
[33] *"'Nevertheless I must go on my way today and tomorrow and the day following; for it cannot be that a prophet should perish away from* **Jerusalem.**'"

Luke 17:11 ⇨ Luke 19:11
[11] *On the way* **to** *Jerusalem he was passing along between Samaria and Galilee.*

Luke 18:31 ⇨ Luke 19:11
[31] *And taking the twelve, he said to them, "Behold, we are going up* **to** *Jerusalem, and everything that is written of the Son of man by the prophets will accomplished."*

JOHN

MATT

Matt 25:14–30 (§M79.2)

[14] "For it will be as when **a** man going on a journey called **his servants** and entrusted to them his property; [15] to one **he gave** five talents, to another two, to another one, to each according to his ability. Then he went away. [16] He who had received the five talents went at once and traded with them; and he made five talents more. [17] So also, he who had the two talents made two talents more. [18] But he who had received the one talent went and dug in the ground and hid his master's money. [19] Now after a long time the master of those servants came and settled accounts with them. [20] And he who had received the five talents **came** forward, bringing five talents **more, saying,** 'Master, you delivered to me five talents; here I have **made** five talents **more.'** [21] His master **said to him, 'Well done, good** and faithful **servant; you have been faithful** over **a** little, I will set **you** over much; enter into the joy of your master.' [22] And he also who had the two talents **came** forward, **saying,** 'Master, you delivered to me two talents; here I have **made** two talents **more.'** [23] His master **said to him, 'Well done, good** and faithful **servant; you have been faithful** over **a** little, I will set **you** over much; enter into the joy of your master.' [24] He also who had received the one talent **came** forward, **saying,** 'Master, I knew **you** to be a hard **man,** reaping where **you did not sow, and** gathering where **you did not** winnow; [25] so **I was afraid,** and I went and hid your talent in the ground. **Here** you have what **is** yours.' [26] But his master answered him, **'You wicked** and slothful **servant! You knew that** I reap where I have **not** sowed, and gather where I have **not** winnowed? [27] **Then you** ought to have invested **my money** with **the** bankers, **and at my coming I should have** received what was my own **with interest.** [28] So take the talent from **him, and give it to him** who has **the ten** talents. [29] For **to every one who has will more be given,** and he will have abundance; **but from him who has not, even what he has will be taken away.** [30] And cast the worthless servant into the outer darkness; there men will weep and gnash their teeth.'"

Matt 13:10–12 ⇨ Luke 19:26
[10] *Then the disciples came and said to him, "Why do you speak to them in parables?"* [11] *And he answered them, "To you it has been given to know the secrets of the kingdom of heaven, but to them it has not been given.* [12] *For to* **him who has will more be given, and he will have abundance; but from him who has not, even what he has will be taken away."**

Luke 8:18 (§L32.5) ⇨ Luke 19:26
[18] *"Take heed then how you hear; for to* **him who has will more be given, and from him who has not, even what he** *thinks that* **he has will be taken away."**

THOMAS

GThom 41 ⇨ Luke 19:26
(41) Jesus said, "Whoever **has** something in his hand will receive **more,** and whoever **has** nothing **will be** deprived of **even** the little **he has."**

MARK

Mark 4:24–25 (§K21.6)
⇨ Luke 19:26
[24] *And he said to them, "Take heed what you hear; the measure you give will be the measure you get, and still more will be given you.* [25] *For to him who has will more be given; and from him who has not, even what he has will be taken away."*

OTHER

GNaz 18
(18) But since the Gospel (written) in Hebrew characters which has come into our hands enters the threat not against the man who had hid (the talent), but against him who had lived dissolutely—for he (the master) had three servants: one who squandered his master's substance with harlots and flute-girls, one who multiplied the gain, and one who hid the talent; and accordingly one was accepted (with joy), another merely rebuked, and another cast into prison—I wonder whether in Matthew the threat which is uttered after the word against the man who did nothing may refer not to him, but by epanalepsis to the first who had feasted and drunk with the drunken. (Eusebius, Theophania 22 [on Matthew 25:14–15])

LUKE

Luke 19:28–32 (§L82.1)

²⁸ And when he had said this, he went on ahead, going up to Jerusalem. ²⁹ When he drew near to Bethphage and Bethany, at the mount that is called Olivet, he sent two of the disciples, ³⁰ saying, "Go into the village opposite, where on entering you will find a colt tied, on which no one has ever yet sat; untie it and bring it here. ³¹ If any one asks you, 'Why are you untying it?' you shall say this, 'The Lord has need of it.'" ³² So those who were sent away and found it as he had told them.

Luke 19:33–34 (§L82.2)

³³ And as they were untying the colt, its owners said to them, "Why are you untying the colt?" ³⁴ And they said, "The Lord has need of it."

Luke 19:35–40 (§L82.3)

³⁵ And they brought it to Jesus, and throwing their garments on the colt they set Jesus upon it. ³⁶ And as he rode along, they spread their garments on the road. ³⁷ As he was now drawing near, at the descent of the Mount of Olives, the whole multitude of the disciples began to rejoice and praise God with a loud voice for all the mighty works that they had seen, ³⁸ saying, "Blessed is the King who comes in the name of the Lord! Peace in heaven and glory in the highest!" ³⁹ And some of the Pharisees in the multitude said to him, "Teacher, rebuke your disciples." ⁴⁰ He answered, "I tell you, if these were silent, the very stones would cry out."

Luke 2:14 ⇨ Luke 19:38

¹⁴ *"Glory to God in the highest,*
  and on earth peace among men with whom he is
  pleased!"

JOHN

John 12:12–19 (§J25)

¹² The next day a great crowd who had come to the feast heard that Jesus was coming **to Jerusalem.** ¹³ So they took branches of palm trees and went out to meet him, crying, "Hosanna! **Blessed is** he **who comes in the name of the Lord,** even the King of Israel!" ¹⁴ And **Jesus** found **a** young ass and sat **upon it;** as it is written,

¹⁵ "Fear not, daughter of Zion;
  behold, your king is coming,
  sitting **on an ass's colt!"**

¹⁶ His **disciples** did not understand this at first; but when Jesus was glorified, then they remembered that this had been written of him and had been done to him. ¹⁷ The crowd that had been with him when he called Lazarus out of the tomb and raised him from the dead bore witness. ¹⁸ The reason why the crowd went to meet him was that they heard he had done this sign. ¹⁹ The **Pharisees** then said to one another, "You see that you can do nothing; look, the world has gone after him."

MATT

Matt 21:1–6 (§M71.1) ⇨ §L82.1–2

¹ **And when** they **drew near to Jerusalem** and came **to Bethphage,** to the **Mount** of Olives, then Jesus **sent two disciples,** ² **saying** to them, **"Go into the village opposite** you, and immediately **you will find** an ass **tied,** and **a colt** with her; **untie** them and bring them to me. ³ **If any one** says anything to **you, you shall say,** 'The Lord has need of them,' and he will send them immediately." ⁴ This took place to fulfil what was spoken by the prophet, saying,

⁵ "Tell the daughter of Zion,
  Behold, your king is coming to you,
  humble, and mounted on an ass,
  and on **a colt,** the foal of an ass."

⁶ The disciples **went** and did **as** Jesus **had** directed **them;** . . .

Matt 21:7–9 (§M71.2) ⇨ §L82.3

⁷ **they brought** the ass and the colt, **and** put **their garments on** them, and he sat thereon. ⁸ Most of the crowd **spread their garments on the road,** and others cut branches from the trees and **spread** them **on the road.** ⁹ And the crowds that went before him and that followed him shouted, "Hosanna to the Son of David! **Blessed is** he **who comes in the name of the Lord!** Hosanna **in the highest!"**

Matt 21:10–11 (§M71.3)

¹⁰ And when he entered Jerusalem, all the city was stirred, saying, "Who is this?" ¹¹ And the crowds said, "This is the prophet Jesus from Nazareth of Galilee."

Luke 13:35 ⇨ Luke 19:38

³⁵ *"Behold, your house is forsaken. And I tell you, you will not see me until you say, 'Blessed is he who comes in the name of the Lord!'"*

Ps 118:26 ⇨ Luke 19:38

²⁶ **Blessed** be he **who** enters **in the name of the Lord!**
  We bless you from the house **of the Lord.**

Hab 2:11 ⇨ Luke 19:40

¹¹ For **the** stone will **cry out** from the wall,
  and the beam from the woodwork respond.

THOMAS

MARK

Mark 11:1–3 (§K57.1) ⇨ §L82.1

¹ **And when** they **drew near to Jerusalem, to Bethphage and Bethany, at the Mount** of Olives, **he sent two of his disciples,** ² and said to them, **"Go into the village opposite** you, and immediately as you enter it **you will find a colt tied, on which no one has ever sat; untie it and bring it.** ³ **If any one** says to you, 'Why are you doing this?' say, 'The Lord has need of it and will send it back here immediately.'"

Mark 11:4–6 (§K57.2) ⇨ §L82.1–2

⁴ And they **went away, and found** a colt tied at the door out in the open street; **and they** untied it. ⁵ And those who stood there **said to them,** "What **are** you doing, **untying the colt?"** ⁶ **And they** told them what Jesus had said; and they let them go.

Mark 11:7–10 (§K57.3) ⇨ §L82.3

⁷ **And they brought** the colt **to Jesus, and** threw **their garments on** it; and he sat **upon it.** ⁸ And many **spread their garments on the road,** and others spread leafy branches which they had cut from the fields. ⁹ And those who went before and those who followed cried out, "Hosanna! **Blessed is** he **who comes in the name of the Lord!** ¹⁰ **Blessed is** the kingdom of our father David that is coming! Hosanna **in the highest!"**

Mark 11:11 (§K57.4)

¹¹ And he entered Jerusalem, and went into the temple; and when he had looked round at everything, as it was already late, he went out to Bethany with the twelve.

OTHER

LUKE   MATT   MARK

Luke 19:41–44 (§L82.4)

⁴¹ And when he drew near and saw the city he wept over it, ⁴² saying, "Would that even today you knew the things that make for peace! But now they are hid from your eyes. ⁴³ For the days shall come upon you, when your enemies will cast up a bank about you and surround you, and hem you in on every side, ⁴⁴ and dash you to the ground, you and your children within you, and they will not leave one stone upon another in you; because you did not know the time of your visitation."

Luke 1:68–79

⁶⁸ *"Blessed be the Lord God of Israel,*
for he has visited and redeemed his people,
⁶⁹ *and has raised up a horn of salvation for us*
in the house of his servant David,
⁷⁰ *as he spoke by the mouth of his holy pro-*
phets from of old,
⁷¹ *that we should be saved from our* **enemies**,
and from the hand of all who hate us;
⁷² *to perform the mercy promised to our*
fathers,
and to remember his holy covenant,
⁷³ *the oath which he swore to our father Abra-*
ham, ⁷⁴ *to grant us*
that we, being delivered from the hand of our
enemies,
might serve him without fear,
⁷⁵ *in holiness and righteousness before him all*
the days of our life.
⁷⁶ *And* **you**, *child, will be called the prophet of*
the Most High;
for **you** *will go before the Lord to prepare his*
ways,
⁷⁷ *to give knowledge of salvation to his people*
in the forgiveness of their sins,
⁷⁸ *through the tender mercy of our God,*
when **the** *day shall dawn upon us from on*
high
⁷⁹ *to give light to those who sit in darkness*
and in the shadow of death,
to guide our feet into the way of **peace**.*"

Luke 13:34–35

³⁴ *"O Jerusalem, Jerusalem, killing the pro-*
phets and stoning those who are sent to you!
How often would I have gathered **your children**
together as a hen gathers her brood under her
wings, and you would not! ³⁵ *Behold, your house*
is forsaken. And I tell **you**, **you** *will not see me*
until you say, 'Blessed is he who comes in the
name of the Lord!'"

Luke 21:20–24

²⁰ *"But* **when** *you see Jerusalem surrounded*
by armies, then **know** *that its desolation has*
come near. ²¹ *Then let those who are in Judea*
flee to the mountains, and let those who are
inside the city depart, and let not those who are
out in the country enter it; ²² *for these are* **days**
of vengeance, to fulfil all that is written. ²³ *Alas*
for those who are with child and for those who
give suck in those days! For great distress shall
be upon the earth and wrath upon this people;
²⁴ *they will fall by the edge of the sword, and be*
led captive among all nations; and Jerusalem
will be trodden down by the Gentiles, until the
times of the Gentiles are fulfilled."

Luke 23:27–31

²⁷ **And** *there followed him a great multitude of*
the people, and of women who bewailed and
lamented him. ²⁸ *But Jesus turning to them*
said, "Daughters of Jerusalem, do not weep for
me, but weep for yourselves **and** *for* **your chil-**
dren. ²⁹ *For behold, the days are coming when*
they will say, 'Blessed are the barren, and the
wombs that never bore, and the breasts that
never gave suck!' ³⁰ *Then they will begin to say*
to *the mountains, 'Fall on us'; and* **to the** *hills,*
'Cover us.' ³¹ *For if they do this when the wood*
is green, what will happen when it is dry?"

Luke 21:6 ⇨ Luke 19:44

⁶ *"As for these things which* **you** *see, the days*
will come when there shall **not** *be left here* **one**
stone upon *another* **that will not** *be thrown*
down.*"

Ps 137:9 ⇨ Luke 19:44

⁹ Happy shall he be who takes **your** little ones
and dashes them against **the** rock!

JOHN   THOMAS   OTHER

LUKE

Luke 19:45–48 (§L83)

⁴⁵ And he entered the temple and began to drive out those who sold, ⁴⁶ saying to them, "It is written, 'My house shall be a house of prayer'; but you have made it a den of robbers."

⁴⁷ And he was teaching daily in the temple. The chief priests and the scribes and the principal men of the people sought to destroy him; ⁴⁸ but they did not find anything they could do, for all the people hung upon his words.

Luke 20:19 ⇨ Luke 19:47–48

¹⁹ The scribes and the chief priests tried to lay hands on him at that very hour, but they feared the people; for they perceived that he had told this parable against them.

Luke 22:2 ⇨ Luke 19:47–48

² And the chief priests and the sribes were seeking how to put him to death; for they feared the people.

Isa 56:7 ⇨ Luke 19:46

⁷ "these I bring to **my** holy mountain,
    and make them joyful in **my house of prayer**;
their burnt offerings and their sacrifices
    will be accepted on **my** altar;
for **my house** will be called a **house of prayer**
    for all peoples."

Jer 7:11 ⇨ Luke 19:46

¹¹ "Has this **house**, which is called by my name, become a **den of robbers** in your eyes? Behold, I myself have seen it, says the Lord."

JOHN

John 2:13–22 (§J5.1)

¹³ The Passover of the Jews was at hand, and Jesus went up to Jerusalem. ¹⁴ In **the temple** he found **those who** were selling oxen and sheep and pigeons, and the money-changers at their business. ¹⁵ And making a whip of cords, **he** drove them all, with the sheep and oxen, **out** of **the temple**; and he poured out the coins of the money-changers and overturned their tables. ¹⁶ And he told **those who sold** the pigeons, "Take these things away; you shall not make **my** Father's **house a house of** trade." ¹⁷ His disciples remembered that **it** was **written**, "Zeal for thy **house** will consume me." ¹⁸ **The** Jews then said to him, "What sign have you to show us for doing this?" ¹⁹ Jesus answered them, "Destroy this **temple**, and in three days I will raise it up." ²⁰ **The** Jews then said, "It has taken forty-six years to build this **temple**, and will you raise it up in three days?" ²¹ But he spoke of **the temple** of his body. ²² When therefore he was raised from the dead, his disciples remembered that he had said this; and they believed the scripture and the word which Jesus had spoken.

John 7:43–44 ⇨ Luke 19:47–48

⁴³ So there was a division among the people over him. ⁴⁴ Some of them wanted to arrest him, but no one laid hands on him.

MATT

Matt 21:12–13 (§M72.1)

¹² And Jesus **entered the temple** of God and drove **out** all **who sold** and bought in **the temple**, and he overturned the tables of the money-changers and the seats of **those who sold** pigeons. ¹³ He said **to them, "It is written, 'My house shall be** called **a house of prayer'; but you** make **it a den of robbers."**

Matt 21:14–17 (§M72.2)

¹⁴ **And** the blind and the lame came to him **in the temple**, and he healed them. ¹⁵ But when **the chief priests and the scribes** saw the wonderful things that he did, and the children crying out in **the temple**, "Hosanna to the Son of David!" they were indignant; ¹⁶ and they said to him, "Do you hear what these are saying?" And Jesus said to them, "Yes, have you never read,

    'Out of the mouth of babes and sucklings
      thou hast brought perfect praise'?"
¹⁷ And leaving them, he went out of the city to Bethany and lodged there.

Matt 21:45 ⇨ Luke 19:47–48

⁴⁵ When the chief priests and the Pharisees heard his parables, they perceived that he was speaking about them.

Matt 26:3–5 (§M77.2) ⇨ Luke 19:47–48

³ Then the chief preists and the elders of the people gathered in the palace of the high priest, who was called Caiaphas, ⁴ took counsel together in order to arrest Jesus by stealth and kill him. ⁵ But they said, "Not during the feast, lest there be a tumult among the people.

THOMAS

MARK

Mark 11:15–19 (§K58.2)

¹⁵ And they came to Jerusalem. **And he entered the temple and began to drive out those who sold** and **those who** bought in **the temple**, and he overturned the tables of the money-changers and the seats of **those who sold** pigeons; ¹⁶ and he would not allow any one to carry anything through **the temple**. ¹⁷ And he taught, and said **to them, "Is it not written, 'My house shall be called a house of prayer** for all the nations'? **But you have made it a den of robbers."** ¹⁸ And **the chief priests and the scribes** heard it and **sought** a way **to destroy him**; for **they** feared him, because **all the** multitude was astonished at **his** teaching. ¹⁹ And when evening came they went out of the city.

Mark 12:12 ⇨ Luke 19:47–48

¹² And they tried to arrest him, but feared the multitude, for they perceived that he had told the parable against them; so they left him and went away.

Mark 14:1–2 (§K61.1) ⇨ Luke 19:47–48

It was now two days before the Passover and the feast of Unleavened Bread. And the chief priests and the scribes were seeking how to arrest him by stealth, and kill him; ²for they said, "Not during the feast, lest there be a tumult of the people."

OTHER

LUKE

Luke 20:1–8 (§L84)

[1] One day, as he was teaching the people in the temple and preaching the gospel, the chief priests and the scribes with the elders came up [2] and said to him, "Tell us by what authority you do these things, or who it is that gave you this authority." [3] He answered them, "I also will ask you a question; now tell me, [4] Was the baptism of John from heaven or from men?" [5] And they discussed it with one another, saying, "If we say, 'From heaven,' he will say, 'Why did you not believe him?' [6] But if we say, 'From men,' all the people will stone us; for they are convinced that John was a prophet." [7] So they answered that they did not know whence it was. [8] And Jesus said to them, "Neither will I tell you by what authority I do these things."

Luke 7:29–30

[29] *(When they heard this all the people and the tax collectors justified God, having been baptized with the baptism of John; [30] but the Pharisees and the lawyers rejected the purpose of God for themselves, not haveing been baptized by him.)*

JOHN

John 2:18 ⇨ Luke 20:2

[18] *The Jews then said to him, "What sign have you to show us for doing this?"*

MATT

Matt 21:23–27 (§M74.1)

[23] And when he entered the temple, the chief priests and the elders of the people came up to him as he was teaching, and said, "By what authority are you doing these things, and who gave you this authority?" [24] Jesus answered them, "I also will ask you a question; and if you tell me the answer, then I also will tell you by what authority I do these things. [25] The baptism of John, whence was it? From heaven or from men?" And they argued with one another, "If we say, 'From heaven,' he will say to us, 'Why then did you not believe him?' [26] But if we say, 'From men,' we are afraid of the multitude; for all hold that John was a prophet." [27] So they answered Jesus, "We do not know." And he said to them, "Neither will I tell you by what authority I do these things."

THOMAS

MARK

Mark 11:27–33 (§K59.2)

[27] And they came again to Jerusalem. And as he was walking in the temple, the chief priests and the scribes and the elders came to him, [28] and they said to him, "By what authority are you doing these things, or who gave you this authority to do them?" [29] Jesus said to them, "I will ask you a question; answer me, and I will tell you by what authority I do these things. [30] Was the baptism of John from heaven or from men? Answer me." [31] And they argued with one another, "If we say, 'From heaven,' he will say, 'Why then did you not believe him?' [32] But shall we say, 'From men'?"—they were afraid of the people, for all held that John was a real prophet. [33] So they answered Jesus, "We do not know." And Jesus said to them, "Neither will I tell you by what authority I do these things."

OTHER

POxy840 2

(2) And he took them (the disciples) with him into the place of purification itself and walked about in the Temple court. And a Pharisaic chief priest, Levi (?) by name, fell in with them and s[aid] to the Savior: Who gave thee leave to [trea]d this place of purification and to look upon [the]se holy utensils without having bathed thyself and even without thy disciples having [wa]shed their f[eet]? On the contrary, being defi[led], thou hast trodden the Temple court, this clean p[lace], although no [one who] has [not] first bathed himself or [chang]ed his clot[hes] may tread it and [venture] to vi[ew these] holy utensils! Forthwith [the Savior] s[tood] still with h[is] disciples and [answered]: How stands it (then) with thee, thou art forsooth (also) here in the Temple court. Art thou then clean? He said to him: I am clean. For I have bathed myself in the pool of David and have gone down by the one stair and come up by the other and have put on white and clean clothes, and (only) then have I come hither and have viewed these holy utensils. Then said the Savior to him: Woe unto you blind that see not! Thou hast bathed thyself in water that is poured out, in which dogs and swine lie night and day and thou hast washed thyself and hast chafed thine outer skin, which prostitutes also and flute-girls anoint, bathe, chafe and rouge, in order to arouse desire in men, but within they are full of scorpions and of [bad]ness [of every kind]. But I and [my disciples], of whom thou sayest that we have not im[mersed] ourselves, [have been im]mersed in the liv[ing . . .] water which comes down from [. . . B]ut woe unto them that . . .

LUKE	MATT	MARK

Luke 20:9–19 (§L85)

⁹ And he began to tell the people this parable: "A man planted a vineyard, and let it out to tenants, and went into another country for a long while. ¹⁰ When the time came, he sent a servant to the tenants, that they should give him some of the fruit of the vineyard; but the tenants beat him, and sent him away empty-handed. ¹¹ And he sent another servant; him also they beat and treated shamefully, and sent him away empty-handed. ¹² And he sent yet a third; this one they wounded and cast out. ¹³ Then the owner of the vineyard said, 'What shall I do? I will send my beloved son; it may be they will respect him.' ¹⁴ But when the tenants saw him, they said to themselves, 'This is the heir; let us kill him, that the inheritance may be ours.' ¹⁵ And they cast him out of the vineyard and killed him. What then will the owner of the vineyard do to them? ¹⁶ He will come and destroy those tenants, and give the vineyard to others." When they heard this, they said, "God forbid!" ¹⁷ But he looked at them and said, "What then is this that is written:

'The very stone which the builders rejected
    has become the head of the corner'?

¹⁸ Every one who falls on that stone will be broken to pieces; but when it falls on any one it will crush him."

¹⁹ The scribes and the chief priests tried to lay hands on him at that very hour, but they feared the people; for they perceived that he had told this parable against them.

Luke 3:22 ⇨ Luke 20:13

²² and the Holy Spirit descended upon him in bodily form, as a dove, and a voice came from heaven, "Thou art my beloved Son; with thee I am well pleased."

Luke 19:47–48 ⇨ Luke 20:19

⁴⁷ And he was teaching daily in the temple. The chief priests and the scribes and the principal men of the people sought to destroy him; ⁴⁸ but they did not find anything they could do, for all the people hung upon his words.

Luke 22:2 ⇨ Luke 20:19

² And the chief priests and the scribes were seeking how to put him to death; for they feared the people.

Isa 5:1–2 ⇨ Luke 20:9

¹ Let me sing for my beloved a song concerning his
    vineyard:
My beloved had a vineyard
    on a very fertile hill.
² He digged it and cleared it of stones,
    and planted it with choice vines;
he built a watchtower in the midst of it,
    and hewed out a wine vat in it;
and he looked for it to yield grapes,
    but it yielded wild grapes.

Ps 118:22 ⇨ Luke 20:17

²² The stone which the builders rejected
    has become the head of the corner.

Matt 21:33–46 (§M74.3)

³³ "Hear another **parable**. There was a householder who **planted a vineyard**, and set a hedge around it, and dug a wine press in it, and built a tower, **and let it out to tenants, and went into another country.** ³⁴ When the season of fruit drew near, **he sent** his servants **to the tenants**, to get his **fruit**; ³⁵ and **the tenants** took his servants and **beat** one, killed another, and stoned another. ³⁶ Again **he sent** other servants, more than the first; and they did the same to them. ³⁷ Afterward he sent his **son** to them, saying '**They will respect** my son.' ³⁸ But when the tenants saw the son, **they said to themselves, 'This is the heir; come, let us kill him** and have his **inheritance.'** ³⁹ And they took him and **cast him out of the vineyard, and killed him.** ⁴⁰ When therefore **the owner of the vineyard** comes, **what will** he **do to** those tenants?" ⁴¹ They said to him, "He will put those wretches to a miserable death, and let out **the vineyard to** other tenants who will give him the fruits in their seasons."

⁴² Jesus **said** to **them,** "Have you never read in the scriptures:

'The very **stone which the builders rejected**
    has become the head of the corner;
    this was the Lord's doing,
    and it is marvelous in our eyes'?

⁴³ Therefore I tell you, the kingdom of God will be taken away from you and given to a nation producing the fruits of it."

⁴⁵ When **the chief priests and the** Pharisees heard his parables, **they perceived that he** was speaking about **them.** ⁴⁶ But when they **tried** to arrest **him, they feared** the multitudes, because they held him to be a prophet.

Matt 26:3–5 (§M72.2) ⇨ Luke 20:19

³ Then the chief priests and the elders of the people gathered in the palace of the high priest, who was called Caiaphas, ⁴ and took counsel together in order to arrest Jesus by stealth and kill him. ⁵ But they said, "Not during the feast, lest there be a tumult among the people."

Mark 12:1–12 (§K59.3)

¹ And he began to speak to them in parables. "**A man planted a vineyard,** and set a hedge around it, and dug a pit for the wine press, and built a tower, **and let it out to tenants, and went into another country.** ² When the time came, he sent a servant to the tenants, to get from them some of the fruit of the vineyard. ³ And they took him and beat him, and sent him away empty-handed. ⁴ Again he sent to them another servant, and they wounded him in the head, and treated him shamefully. ⁵ And he sent another, and him they killed; and so with many others, some they beat and some they killed. ⁶ He had still one other, a beloved son; finally he sent him to them, saying, 'They will respect my son.' ⁷ But those tenants said to one another, 'This is the heir; come, let us kill him, and the inheritance will be ours.' ⁸ And they took him and killed him, and cast him out of the vineyard. ⁹ What will the owner of the vineyard do? He will come and destroy the tenants, and give the vineyard to others. ¹⁰ Have you not read this scripture:

'The very stone which the builders rejected
    has become the head of the corner;
    ¹¹ this was the Lord's doing,
    and it is marvelous in our eyes'?"

¹² And they **tried** to arrest **him, but feared the** multitude, **for they perceived that he had told** the **parable against them;** so they left him and went away.

Mark 14:1–2 (§K61.1) ⇨ Luke 20:19

¹ It was not two days before the Passover and the feast of Unleavened Bread. And the chief priests and the scribes were seeking how to arrest him by stealth, and kill him; ² for they said, "Not during the feast, lest there be a tumult of the people."

JOHN	THOMAS	OTHER

John 7:43–44 ⇨ Luke 20:19
*43 So there was a division among **the people** over **him**. 44 Some of them wanted to arrest **him**, but no one laid hands on **him**.*

GThom 65
(65) **He** said, "There was **a** good **man** who owned **a vineyard**. He leased **it** to tenant farmers so that they might work it and he might collect the produce from them. **He sent** his **servant** so that **the tenants** might **give him** the produce **of the vineyard**. They seized his **servant** and **beat him**, all but killing him. The **servant** went back and told his master. **The** master **said**, 'Perhaps <they> did not recognize <him>.' **He sent another servant**. The tenants beat **this one** as well. **Then the owner** sent his **son** and **said**, 'Perhaps **they will** show **respect** to **my son**.' Because **the tenants** knew that it was he who was **the heir** to the vineyard, **they** seized **him and killed him**. Let him who has ears hear."

GThom 66 ⇨ Luke 20:17
(66) Jesus **said**, "Show me **the stone which the builders** have **rejected**. That one is the cornerstone."

Acts 4:11 ⇨ Luke 20:17
*11 "This is **the stone which was rejected by you builders, but which has become the head of the corner."***

LUKE

Luke 20:20–26 (§L86)

²⁰ So they watched him, and sent spies, who pretended to be sincere, that they might take hold of what he said, so as to deliver him up to the authority and jurisdiction of the governor. ²¹ They asked him, "Teacher, we know that you speak and teach rightly, and show no partiality, but truly teach the way of God. ²² Is it lawful for us to give tribute to Caesar, or not?" ²³ But he perceived their craftiness, and said to them, ²⁴ "Show me a coin.ᵃ Whose likeness and inscription has it?" They said, "Caesar's." ²⁵ He said to them, "Then render to Caesar the things that are Caesar's, and to God the things that are God's." ²⁶ And they were not able in the presence of the people to catch him by what he said; but marveling at his answer they were silent.

ᵃ Greek: *denarius*

MATT

Matt 22:15–22 (§M76.1)

¹⁵ Then the Pharisees went and took counsel how to entangle him in his talk. ¹⁶ And **they sent** their disciples to him, along with the Herodians, saying, **"Teacher, we know that you** are true, **and teach the way of God** truthfully, and care for no man; for you do not regard the position of men. ¹⁷ Tell us, then, what you think. **Is it lawful to** pay taxes **to Caesar, or not?"** ¹⁸ But Jesus, aware of **their** malice, **said,** "Why put me to the test, you hypocrites? ¹⁹ **Show me** the money for the tax." And they brought him a coin. ²⁰ And Jesus **said to them, "Whose likeness and inscription** is this?" ²¹ **They said, "Caesar's."** Then **he said to them, "Render** therefore **to Caesar the things that are Caesar's, and to God the things that are God's."** ²² When **they** heard it, **they** marveled; and they left him and went away.

MARK

Mark 12:13–17 (§K59.4)

¹³ And **they sent** to him some of the Pharisees and some of the Herodians, to entrap him in his talk. ¹⁴ And **they came and said to him, "Teacher, we know that you** are true, and care for no man; for you do not regard the position of men; **but truly teach the way of God. Is it lawful to** pay taxes to **Caesar, or not?** ¹⁵ Should we pay them, **or should we not?"** But knowing **their** hypocrisy, **he said to them,** "Why put me to the test? Bring **me a coin,** and let me look at it." ¹⁶ And they brought one. And he **said to them, "Whose likeness and inscription** is this?" **They said** to him, "Caesar's." ¹⁷ Jesus **said to them, "Render to Caesar the things that are Caesar's, and to God the things that are God's." And they were** amazed at **him.**

JOHN

John 3:2 ⇨ Luke 20:21

² *This man came to Jesus by night and said to him, "Rabbi, we know that you are a teacher come from God; for no one can do these signs that you do, unless God is with him.*

THOMAS

GThom 100

(100) They showed Jesus a gold coin and said to Him, "Caesar's men demand taxes from us."

He said to them, "Give **Caesar** what belongs to Caesar, give **God** what belongs to God, and give Me what is Mine."

OTHER

PEger2 3

(3) . . . [ca]me to **him** to put him to the pro[of] and to tempt him, whilst [they] said: "Master Jesus, **we know that** thou art come [from **God**], for what thou doest bears a test[i-mony] (to thee which goes) beyond (that) of all the prophets. [Wherefore tell] us: **is it** admissible [to p]ay **to** the kings the (charges) appertaining to their rule? [Should we] pay [th]em **or not?"** But Jesus saw through their [in]tention, became [angry] **and said to them**: "Why call ye me with yo[ur mou]th Master and yet [do] not what I say? Well has Is[aiah] prophesied [concerning y]ou saying: This [people honours] me with the[ir li]ps but their heart is far from me; [their worship is] vain. [They teach] precepts [of men]." (Fragment 2, recto [lines 43–59])

Rom 13:7 ⇨ Luke 20:25

⁷ *Pay all of them their dues, taxes to whom taxes are due, revenue to whom revenue is due, respect to whom respect is due, honor to whom honor is due.*

LUKE

Luke 20:27–40 (§L87)

²⁷ There came to him some **Sadducees,** those who say that there is no resurrection, ²⁸ and they asked him a question, saying, "Teacher, Moses wrote for us that if a man's brother dies, having a wife but no children, the manᵃ must take the wife and raise up children for his brother. ²⁹ Now there were seven brothers; the first took a wife, and died without children; ³⁰ and the second ³¹ and the third took her, and likewise all seven left no children and died. ³² Afterward the woman also died. ³³ In the resurrection, therefore, whose wife will the woman be? For the seven had her as wife."

³⁴ And Jesus said to them, "The sons of this age marry and are given in marriage; ³⁵ but those who are accounted worthy to attain to that age and to the resurrection from the dead neither marry nor are given in marriage, ³⁶ for they cannot die any more, because they are equal to angels and are sons of God, being sons of the resurrection. ³⁷ But that the dead are raised, even Moses showed, in the passage about the bush, where he calls the Lord the God of Abraham and the God of Isaac and the God of Jacob. ³⁸ Now he is not God of the dead, but of the living; for all live to him." ³⁹ And some of the scribes answered, "Teacher, you have spoken well." ⁴⁰ For they no longer dared to ask him any question.

ᵃ Greek: *his brother*

Gen 38:8 ⇨ Luke 20:28
⁸ Then Judah said to Onan, "Go in to your **brother's wife,** and perform the duty of a brother-in-law to her, **and raise up** offspring **for** your **brother.**"

Deut 25:5–6 ⇨ Luke 20:28
⁵ "If brothers dwell together, and one of them **dies** and has **no** son, the **wife** of the dead shall not be married outside the family to a stranger; her husband's **brother** shall go in to her, and **take** her as his **wife, and** perform the duty of a husband's **brother** to her. ⁶ And the first son whom she bears shall succeed to the name of his **brother** who is dead, that his name may not be blotted out of Israel."

Exod 3:6 ⇨ Luke 20:37
⁶ And he said, "I am the God of your father, **the God of Abraham, the God of Isaac, and the God of Jacob.**" And **Moses** hid his face, for he was afraid to look at God.

MATT

Matt 22:23–33 (§M76.2)

²³ The same day **Sadducees came to him,** **who say that there is no resurrection;** and they asked him a question, ²⁴ saying, "**Teacher, Moses** said, 'If a man **dies, having no children,** his **brother** must marry the widow, **and raise up children for his brother.'** ²⁵ **Now there were seven brothers** among us; the **first** married, **and died,** and having no **children** left his wife to his brother. ²⁶ So too **the second and third,** down to the seventh. ²⁷ After them all, **the woman died.** ²⁸ **In the resurrection, therefore,** to which of the seven will she **be wife? For** they all **had her.**"

²⁹ But **Jesus** answered **them,** "You are wrong, because you know neither the scriptures nor the power of God. ³⁰ For in **the resurrection** they **neither marry nor are given in marriage,** but **are** like **angels** in heaven. ³¹ And as for **the resurrection** of **the dead,** have you not read what was said to you by God, ³² 'I am **the God of Abraham, and the God of Isaac, and the God of Jacob'?** He is not God of the **dead, but of the living.**" ³³ And when the crowd heard it, **they** were astonished at his teaching.

Matt 22:46 ⇨ Luke 20:40
⁴⁶ *And no one was able to answer* **him** *a word, nor from that day did any one dare* **to ask him** *any more questions.*

MARK

Mark 12:18–27 (§K59.5)

¹⁸ And **Sadducees came to him, who say** that there is no resurrection; and they asked him a question, saying, ¹⁹ "Teacher, Moses wrote for us that if a man's brother dies and leaves a wife, but leaves no child, the man must take the wife, and raise up children for his brother. ²⁰ There were seven brothers; the first took a wife, and when he died left no children; ²¹ and the second took her, and died, leaving no children; and the third likewise; ²² and the seven left no children. Last of all the woman also died. ²³ In the resurrection whose wife will she be? For the seven had her as wife.

²⁴ **Jesus said to them,** "Is not this why you are wrong, that you know neither the scriptures nor the power of God? ²⁵ For when they rise **from the dead,** they **neither marry nor are given in marriage,** but **are** like **angels** in heaven. ²⁶ And as for **the dead** being **raised,** have you not read in the book of **Moses, in the passage about the bush,** how God said to him, 'I am **the God of Abraham, and the God of Isaac, and the God of Jacob?'** ²⁷ He is not God of the dead, but of the living; you are quite wrong."

Mark 12:32 ⇨ Luke 20:39
³² *And the scribe said to him,* **"You are right, Teacher; you have truly said that he is one, and there is no other but he";** . . .

Mark 12:34 ⇨ Luke 20:40
³⁴ *And when Jesus saw that he answered wisely, he said to him, "You are not far from the kingdom of God." And after that no one dared to ask him any question.*

JOHN

THOMAS

OTHER

1 Cor 15:12 ⇨ Luke 20:27, 37–38
¹² *Now if Christ is preached as* **raised from the dead,** *how can some of you say* **that there is no resurrection of the dead?**

LUKE	MATT	MARK

LUKE

Luke 20:41–44 (§L88)

⁴¹ But he said to them, "How can they say that the Christ is David's son? ⁴² For David himself says in the Book of Psalms,

'The Lord said to my Lord,

Sit at my right hand,

⁴³ till I make thy enemies a stool for thy feet.'

⁴⁴ David thus calls him Lord; so how is he his son?"

Luke 22:69 ⇨ Luke 20:42–43

⁶⁹ *"But from now on the Son of man shall be seated at the right hand of the power of God."*

Ps 110:1 ⇨ Luke 20:42–43

¹ **The Lord** says to my lord:

"**Sit at my right hand,**

till **I make** your **enemies** your footstool."

2 Sam 7:12–16

¹² "'When your days are fulfilled and you lie down with your fathers, I will raise up your offspring after you, who shall come forth from your body, and I will establish his kingdom. ¹³ He shall build a house for **my** name, and I will establish the throne of his kingdom for ever. ¹⁴ I will be **his** father, and **he** shall be my **son**. When he commits iniquity, I will chasten him with the rod of men, with the stripes of the sons of men; ¹⁵ but I will not take my steadfast love from him, as I took it from Saul, whom I put away from before you. ¹⁶ And your house and your kingdom shall be made sure for ever before me; your throne shall be established for ever.'"

Mic 5:2

² But you, O Bethlehem Ephrathah,

who are little to be among the clans of Judah,

from you shall come forth for me

one who is to be ruler in Israel,

whose origin is from of old,

from ancient days.

Ps 89:3–4

³ Thou hast **said**, "I have made covenant with **my** chosen one.

I have sworn to **David my** servant:

⁴ 'I will establish your descendants for ever,

and build your throne for all generations.'"

JOHN

John 7:40–44

⁴⁰ *When they heard these words, some of the people said, "This is really the prophet." ⁴¹ Others said, "This is the Christ." But some said, "Is the Christ to come from Galilee? ⁴² Has not the scripture said that the Christ is descended from David, and comes from Bethlehem, the village where David was?" ⁴³ So there was a division among the people over him. ⁴⁴ Some of them wanted to arrest him, but no one laid hands on him.*

MATT

Matt 22:41–46 (§M76.4)

⁴¹ Now while the Pharisees were gathered together, Jesus asked **them** a question, ⁴² saying, "What do you think of **the Christ**? Whose **son** is he?" They said to him, "The son of David." ⁴³ He said to them, "How is it then that **David**, inspired by the Spirit, calls him Lord, saying,

⁴⁴ 'The Lord said to my Lord,

Sit at my right hand,

till I put **thy enemies** under **thy feet**'?

⁴⁵ If **David** thus calls him Lord, how is he his son?" ⁴⁶ And no one was able to answer him a word, nor from that day did any one dare to ask him any more questions.

THOMAS

MARK

Mark 12:35–37 (§K59.7)

³⁵ And as Jesus taught in the temple, **he said**, "How can the scribes **say that the Christ is the son** of David? ³⁶ **David himself**, inspired by the Holy Spirit, declared,

'**The Lord said to my Lord,**

Sit at my right hand,

till I put **thy enemies** under **thy feet**.'

³⁷ **David** himself **calls him Lord; so how is he his son?"** And the great throng heard him gladly.

OTHER

Acts 2:34–35 ⇨ Luke 20:42–43

³⁴ "**For David** did not ascend into the heavens; but he **himself says**,

'The Lord said to my Lord, Sit at my right hand,

³⁵ till **I make thy** enemies a stool for thy feet.'"

Acts 7:55–56 ⇨ Luke 20:42–43

⁵⁵ *But he, full of the Holy Spirit, gazed into heaven and saw the glory of God, and Jesus standing at the right hand of God; ⁵⁶ and he said, "Behold, I see the heavens opened, and the Son of man standing at the right hand of God."*

1 Cor 15:20–28

²⁰ *But in fact Christ has been raised from the dead, the first fruits of those who have fallen asleep. ²¹ For as by a man came death, by a man has come also the resurrection of the dead. ²² For as in Adam all die, so also in Christ shall all be made alive. ²³ But each in his own order: Christ the first fruits, then at his coming those who belong to Chirst. ²⁴ Then comes the end, when he delivers the kingdom to God the Father after destroying every rule and every authority and power. ²⁵ For he must reign until he has put all his enemies under his feet. ²⁶ The last enemy to be destoryed is death. ²⁷ For God has put all things in subjection under his feet." But when it says, "All things are put in subjection under him," it is plain that he is excepted who put all things under him. ²⁸ When all things are subjected to him, then the Son himself will also be subjected to him who put all things under him, that God may be everything to everyone.*

L89
L90
WARNING AGAINST THE SCRIBES
WIDOW'S COINS
Luke 20:45–47
Luke 21:1–4

LUKE

Luke 20:45–47 (§L89)

45 And in the hearing of all the people he said to his disciples, 46 "Beware of the scribes, who like to go about in long robes, and love salutations in the market places and the best seats in the synagogues and the places of honor at feasts, 47 who devour widows' houses and for a pretense make long prayers. They will receive the greater condemnation."

Luke 21:1–4 (§L90)

1 He looked up and saw the rich putting their gifts into the treasury; 2 and he saw a poor widow put in two copper coins. 3 And he said, "Truly I tell you, this poor widow has put in more than all of them; 4 for they all contributed out of their abundance, but she out of her poverty put in all the living that she had."

Luke 11:37–44 (§L52.1) ⇨ §L89

37 *While he was speaking, a Pharisee asked him to dine with him; so he went in and sat at table.* 38 *The Pharisee was astonished to see that he did not first wash before dinner.* 39 *And the Lord* said to *him, "Now you Pharisees cleanse the outside of the cup and of the dish, but inside you are full of extortion and wickedness.* 40 *You fools! Did not he who made the outside make the inside also?* 41 *But give for alms those things which are within; and behold, everything is clean for you.*

42 *"But woe to you Pharisees! for you tithe mint and rue and every herb, and neglect justice and the love of God; these you ought to have done, without neglecting the others.* 43 *Woe to you Pharisees! for you* love the best seat in the synagogues and salutations in the market places. 44 *Woe to you! for you are like graves which are not seen, and men walk over them without knowing it."*

Luke 14:7–11 (§L63.1) ⇨ §L89

7 *Now* he *told a parable to those who were invited, when he marked how they chose* the places of honor, *saying* to them, 8 *"When you are invited by any one to a marriage feast, do not sit down in a place of* honor, *lest a more eminent man than you be invited by him;* 9 *and he who invited you both will come and say to you, 'Give place to this man,' and then you will begin with shame to take the lowest place.* 10 *But when you are invited, go and sit in the lowest place, so that when your host comes he may say to you, 'Friend, go up higher'; then you will be honored in the presence of all who sit at table with you.* 11 *For every one who exalts himself will be humbled, and he who humbles himself will be exalted."*

JOHN

MATT

Matt 23:6 ⇨ Luke 20:46
6 "and they love the place of honor at feasts and the best seats in the synagogues, . . ."

THOMAS

MARK

Mark 12:38–40 (§K59.8) ⇨ §L89

38 And in his teaching he said, "Beware of the scribes, who like to go about in long robes, and to have salutations in the market places 39 and the best seats in the synagogues and the places of honor at feasts, 40 who devour widows' houses and for a pretense make long prayers. They will receive the greater condemnation."

Mark 12:41–44 (§K59.9) ⇨ §L90

41 And he sat down opposite the treasury, and watched the Y multitude putting money into the treasury. Many rich people put in large sums. 42 And a poor widow came, and put in two copper coins, which make a penny. 43 And he called his disciples to him, and said to them, "Truly, I say to you, this poor widow has put in more than all those who are contributing to the treasury. 44 For they all contributed out of their abundance; but she out of her poverty has put in everything she had, her whole living."

OTHER

LUKE	MATT	MARK

LUKE

Luke 21:5–19 (§L91.1)

5 And as some spoke of the temple, how it was adorned with noble stones and offerings, he said, 6 "As for these things which you see, the days will come when there shall not be left here one stone upon another that will not be thrown down." 7 And they asked him, "Teacher, when will this be, and what will be the sign when this is about to take place?" 8 And he said, "Take heed that you are not led astray; for many will come in my name, saying, 'I am he!' and, 'The time is at hand!' Do not go after them. 9 And when you hear of wars and tumults, do not be terrified; for this must first take place, but the end will not be at once."

10 Then he said to them, "Nation will rise against nation, and kingdom against kingdom; 11 there will be great earthquakes, and in various places famines and pestilences; and there will be terrors and great signs from heaven. 12 But before all this they will lay their hands on you and persecute you, delivering you up to the synagogues and prisons, and you will be brought before kings and governors for my name's sake. 13 This will be a time for you to bear testimony. 14 Settle it therefore in your minds, not to meditate beforehand how to answer; 15 for I will give you a mouth and wisdom, which none of your adversaries will be able to withstand or contradict. 16 You will be delivered up even by parents and brothers and kinsmen and friends, and some of you they will put to death; 17 you will be hated by all for my name's sake. 18 But not a hair of your head will perish. 19 By your endurance you will gain your lives."

Luke 19:44 ⇨ Luke 21:6

44 "and dash you to the ground, you and your children within you, and they will not leave one stone upon another in you; because you did not know the time of your visitation."

Luke 12:11–12 ⇨ Luke 21:14–15

11 "And when they bring you before the synagogues and the rulers and the authorities, do not be anxious how or what you are to answer or what you are to say; 12 for the Holy Spirit will teach you in that very hour what you ought to say."

Luke 12:7 ⇨ Luke 21:18

7 "Why, even the hairs of your head are all numbered. Fear not; you are of more value than many sparrows."

⇨ Luke 21:10
Cf. 2 Chr 15:6, Isa 19:2

MATT

Matt 24:3–14 (§M78.2)

3 As he sat on the Mount of Olives, the disciples came to him privately, saying, "Tell us, when will this be, and what will be the sign of your coming and of the close of the age?" 4 And Jesus answered them, "Take heed that no one leads you astray. 5 For many will come in my name, saying, 'I am the Christ,' and they will lead many astray. 6 And you will hear of wars and rumors of wars; see that you are not alarmed; for this must take place, but the end is not yet. 7 For nation will rise against nation, and kingdom against kingdom, and there will be famines and earthquakes in various places: 8 all this is but the beginning of the birth-pangs.

9 "Then they will deliver you up to tribulation, and put you to death; and you will be hated by all nations for my name's sake. 10 And then many will fall away, and betray one another, and hate one another. 11 And many false prophets will arise and lead many astray. 12 And because wickedness is multiplied, most men's love will grow cold. 13 But he who endures to the end will be saved. 14 And this gospel of the kingdom will be preached throughout the whole world, as a testimony to all nations; and then the end will come."

Matt 10:16–23 (§M28.2) ⇨ Luke 21:12–17

16 "Behold, I send you out as sheep in the midst of wolves; so be wise as serpents and innocent as doves. 17 Beware of men; for they will deliver you up to councils, and flog you in their synagogues, 18 and you will be dragged before governors and kings for my sake, to bear testimony before them and the Gentiles. 19 When they deliver you up, do not be anxious how you are to speak or what you are to say; for what you are to say will be given to you in that hour; 20 for it is not you who speak, but the Spirit of your Father speaking through you. 21 Brother will deliver up brother to death, and the father his child, and children will rise against parents and have them put to death; 22 and you will be hated by all for my name's sake. But he who endures to the end will be saved. 23 When they persecute you in one town, flee to the next; for truly, I say to you, you will not have gone through all the towns of Israel, before the Son of man comes."

Matt 10:22 ⇨ Luke 21:17, 19

22 "and you will be hated by all for my name's sake. But he who endures to the end will be saved."

Matt 10:30 ⇨ Luke 21:18

30 "But even the hairs of your head are all numbered."

MARK

Mark 13:3–13 (§K60.2)

3 And as he sat on the Mount of Olives opposite the temple, Peter and James and John and Andrew asked him privately, 4 "Tell us, when will this be, and what will be the sign when these things are all to be accomplished?" 5 And Jesus began to say to them, "Take heed that no one leads you astray. 6 Many will come in my name, saying, 'I am he!' and they will lead many astray. 7 And when you hear of wars and rumors of wars, do not be alarmed; this must take place, but the end is not yet. 8 For nation will rise against nation, and kingdom against kingdom; there will be earthquakes in various places, there will be famines; this is but the beginning of the birth-pangs.

9 "But take heed to yourselves; for they will deliver you up to councils; and you will be beaten in synagogues; and you will stand before governors and kings for my sake, to bear testimony before them. 10 And the gospel must first be preached to all nations. 11 And when they bring you to trial and deliver you up, do not be anxious beforehand what you are to say; but say whatever is given you in that hour, for it is not you who speak, but the Holy Spirit. 12 And brother will deliver up brother to death, and the father his child, and children will rise against parents and have them put to death; 13 and you will be hated by all for my name's sake. But he who endures to the end will be saved."

| JOHN | THOMAS | OTHER |

JOHN

John 14:26 ⇨ Luke 21:14–15
*26 "But the Counselor, the Holy Spirit, whom the Father will send in my name, he will teach **you** all things, and bring to your remembrance all that I have said to **you**."*

John 16:2 ⇨ Luke 21:16
*2 "They will put **you** out of the synagogues; indeed, the hour is coming when whoever kills **you** will think he is offering service to God."*

John 15:18–21 ⇨ Luke 21:17
*18 "If the world hates **you**, know that it has hated me before it **hated you**. 19 If **you** were of the world, the world would love its own; but because **you** are not of the world, but I chose **you** out of the world, therefore the world hates **you**. 20 Remember the word that I said to **you**, 'A servant is not greater than his master.' If they persecuted me, they will persecute **you**; if they kept my word, they will keep yours also. 21 But all this they will do to **you** on my account, because they do not know him who sent me."*

THOMAS

OTHER

Acts 27:34 ⇨ Luke 21:18
*34 "Therefore I urge you to take some food; it will give you strength, since **not a hair** is to **perish** from the **head** of any of you."*

LUKE

Luke 21:20–24 (§L91.2)

²⁰ "But when you see Jerusalem surrounded by armies, then know that its desolation has come near. ²¹ Then let those who are in Judea flee to the mountains, and let those who are inside the city depart, and let not those who are out in the country enter it; ²² for these are days of vengeance, to fulfil all that is written. ²³ Alas for those who are with child and for those who give suck in those days! For great distress shall be upon the earth and wrath upon this people; ²⁴ they will fall by the edge of the sword, and be led captive among all nations; and Jerusalem will be trodden down by the Gentiles, until the times of the Gentiles are fulfilled."

Luke 17:31 ⇨ Luke 21:21

³¹ *"On that day, let him who is on the housetop, with his goods in the house, not come down to take them away; and likewise let him who is in the field not turn back."*

Luke 13:34–35

³⁴ *"O Jerusalem, Jerusalem, killing the prophets and stoning those who are sent to you! How often would I have gathered your children together as a hen gathers her brood under her wings, and you would not! ³⁵ Behold, your house is forsaken. And I tell you, you will not see me until you say, 'Blessed is he who comes in the name of the Lord!'"*

Luke 19:41–44

⁴¹ *And when he drew near and saw the city he wept over it, ⁴² saying, "Would that even today you knew the things that make for peace! But now they are hid from your eyes. ⁴³ For the days shall come upon you, when your enemies will cast up a bank about you and surround you, and hem you in on every side, ⁴⁴ and dash you to the ground, you and your children within you, and they will not leave one stone upon another in you; because you did not know the time of your visitation."*

Luke 23:27–31

²⁷ *And there followed him a great multitude of the people, and of women who bewailed and lamented him. ²⁸ But Jesus turning to them said, "Daughters of Jerusalem, do not weep for me, but weep for yourselves and for your children. ²⁹ For behold, the days are coming when they will say, 'Blessed are the barren, and the wombs that never bore, and the breasts that never gave suck!' ³⁰ Then they will begin to say to the mountains, 'Fall on us'; and to the hills, 'Cover us.' ³¹ For if they do this when the wood is green, what will happen when it is dry?"*

⇨ Luke 21:22
Cf. Deut 32:35

JOHN

MATT

Matt 24:15–28 (§M78.3)

¹⁵ "So **when you see** the desolating sacrilege spoken of by the prophet Daniel, standing in the holy place (let the reader understand), ¹⁶ **then let those who are in Judea flee to the mountains**; ¹⁷ **let** him **who** is on the housetop not go down to take what is in his house; ¹⁸ and **let** him **who** is in the field **not** turn back to take his mantle. ¹⁹ And **alas for those who are with child and for those who give suck in those days!** ²⁰ Pray that your flight may not be in winter or on a sabbath. ²¹ **For** then there will **be a great** tribulation, such as has not been from the beginning of the world until now, no, and never will be. ²² And if those days had not been shortened, no human being would be saved; but for the sake of the elect those days will be shortened. ²³ Then if any one says to you, 'Lo, here is the Christ!' or 'There he is!' do not believe it. ²⁴ For false Christs and false prophets will arise and show great signs and wonders, so as to lead astray, if possible, even the elect. ²⁵ Lo, I have told you beforehand. ²⁶ So, if they say to you, 'Lo, he is in the wilderness,' do not go out; if they say, 'Lo, he is in the inner rooms' do not believe it. ²⁷ For as the lightning comes from the east and shines as far as the west, so will be the coming of the Son of man. ²⁸ Wherever the body is, there the eagles will be gathered together."

THOMAS

GThom 79 ⇨ Luke 21:23

(79) A woman from the crowd said to Him, "Blessed are the womb which bore You and the breasts which nourished You."

He said to her, "Blessed are those who have heard the word of the Father and have truly kept it. For there will be days when you will say, 'Blessed are the womb which has not conceived and the breasts which have not given milk.'"

MARK

Mark 13:14–23 (§K60.3)

¹⁴ "But **when you see** the desolating sacrilege set up where it ought not to be (let the reader understand), then **let those who are in Judea flee to the mountains**; ¹⁵ **let** him **who** is on the housetop not go down, nor enter his house, to take anything away; ¹⁶ and **let** him **who** is in the field not turn back to take his mantle. ¹⁷ And **alas for those who are with child and for those who give suck in those days!** ¹⁸ Pray that it may not happen in winter. ¹⁹ **For** in those days there will be such tribulation as has not been from the beginning of the creation which God created until now, and never will be. ²⁰ And if the Lord had not shortened the days, no human being would be saved; but for the sake of the elect, whom he chose, he shortened the days. ²¹ And then if any one says to you, 'Look, here is the Christ!' or 'Look, there he is!' do not believe it. ²² False Christs and false prophets will arise and show signs and wonders, to lead astray, if possible, the elect. ²³ But take heed; I have told you all things beforehand."

OTHER

LUKE

Luke 21:25–33 (§L91.3)

²⁵ "And there will be signs in sun and moon and stars, and upon the earth distress of nations in perplexity at the roaring of the sea and the waves, ²⁶ men fainting with fear and with foreboding of what is coming on the world; for the powers of the heavens will be shaken. ²⁷ And then they will see the Son of man coming in a cloud with power and great glory. ²⁸ Now when these things begin to take place, look up and raise your heads, because your redemption is drawing near."

²⁹ And he told them a parable: "Look at the fig tree, and all the trees; ³⁰ as soon as they come out in leaf, you see for yourselves and know that the summer is already near. ³¹ So also, when you see these things taking place, you know that the kingdom of God is near. ³² Truly, I say to you, this generation will not pass away till all has taken place. ³³ Heaven and earth will pass away, but my words will not pass away."

Luke 9:27 ⇨ Luke 21:32

²⁷ "But I tell you truly, there are some standing here who will not taste death before they see the kingdom of God."

Dan 7:13–14 ⇨ Luke 21:27

¹³ I saw in the night visions,
     and behold, with the clouds of heaven
         there came one like a son of man,
     and he came to the Ancient of Days
         and was presented before him.
¹⁴ And to him was given dominion
     and glory and kingdom,
     that all peoples, nations, and languages
         should serve him;
     his dominion is an everlasting dominion,
         which shall not pass away,
     and his kingdom one
         that shall not be destroyed.

MATT

Matt 24:29–36 (§M78.4)

²⁹ "Immediately after the tribulation of those days the **sun** will be darkened, **and the moon** will not give its light, **and** the **stars** will fall from heaven, and **the powers of the heavens will be shaken;** ³⁰ then will appear the sign of **the Son of man** in heaven, **and then** all the tribes of the earth will mourn, and they **will see the Son of man coming** on the clouds of heaven **with power and great glory;** ³¹ and he will send out his angels with a loud trumpet call, and they will gather his elect from the four winds, from one end of heaven to the other.

³² "From **the fig tree** learn its lesson: **as soon** as its branch becomes tender and puts forth its leaves, **you know that summer is near.** ³³ **So also, when you see** all **these things, you know that** he **is near,** at the very gates. ³⁴ **Truly, I say to you, this generation will not pass away till** all these things take **place.** ³⁵ **Heaven and earth will pass away, but my words will not pass away.**

³⁶ "But of that day and hour no one knows, not even the angels of heaven, nor the Son, but the Father only."

Matt 16:28 ⇨ Luke 21:32

²⁸ *"Truly, I say to you, there are some standing here who will not taste death before they see the Son of man coming in his kingdom."*

MARK

Mark 13:24–32 (§K60.4)

²⁴ "But in those days, after that tribulation, the **sun** will be darkened, **and the moon** will not give its light, ²⁵ **and** the **stars** will be falling from heaven, and **the powers in the heavens will be shaken.** ²⁶ **And then they will see the Son of man coming in** clouds **with great power and glory.** ²⁷ And then he will send out the angels, and gather his elect from the four winds, from the ends of the earth to the ends of heaven.

²⁸ "From **the fig tree** learn its lesson: **as soon as** its branch becomes tender and puts forth its leaves, **you know that summer is near.** ²⁹ So also, **when you see these things taking place, you know that** he **is near,** at the very gates. ³⁰ **Truly, I say to you, this generation will not pass away** before **all** these things take **place.** ³¹ **Heaven and earth will pass away, but my words will not pass away.**

³² "But of that day or that hour no one knows, not even the angels in heaven, nor the Son, but only the Father."

Mark 9:1 ⇨ Luke 21:32

¹ *"And he said to them, "Truly, I say to you, there are some standing here who will not taste death before they see that the kingdom of God has come with power."*

JOHN

THOMAS

OTHER

LUKE

Luke 21:34–36 (§L91.4)

³⁴"But take heed to yourselves lest your hearts be weighed down with dissipation and drunkenness and cares of this life, and that day come upon you suddenly like a snare; ³⁵for it will come upon all who dwell upon the face of the whole earth; ³⁶But watch at all times, praying that you may have strength to escape all these things that will take place, and to stand before the Son of man."

Luke 21:37–38 (§L91.5)

³⁷And every day he was teaching in the temple, but at night he went out and lodged on the mount called Olivet. ³⁸And early in the morning all the people came to him in the temple to hear him.

Luke 12:45–46 ⇨ Luke 21:34

⁴⁵*"But if that servant says to himself, 'My master is delayed in coming,' and begins to beat the menservants and the maidservants, and to eat and drink and get drunk,* ⁴⁶*the master of that servant will* **come** *on a* **day** *when he does not expect him and at an hour he does not know, and will punish him, and put him with the unfaithful."*

Luke 19:47–48 ⇨ §L91.5

⁴⁷*And he was teaching daily in the temple. The chief priests and the scribes and the principal men of the people sought to destroy him;* ⁴⁸*but they did not find anything they could do, for* **all the people** *hung upon his words.*

MATT

Matt 24:37–51 (§M78.5) ⇨ §L91.4

³⁷"As were the days of Noah, so will be the coming of the Son of man. ³⁸For as in those days before the flood they were eating and drinking, marrying and giving in marriage, until the day when Noah entered the ark, ³⁹and they did not know until the flood came and swept them all away, so will be the coming of **the Son of man.** ⁴⁰Then two men will be in the field; one is taken and one is left. ⁴¹Two women will be grinding at the mill; one is taken and one is left. ⁴²**Watch** therefore, for **you** do not know on what **day** your Lord is coming. ⁴³But know this, that if the householder had known in what part of the night the thief was coming, he would have watched and would not have let his house be broken into. ⁴⁴Therefore you also must be ready; for **the Son of man** is coming at an hour **you** do not expect.

⁴⁵"Who then is the faithful and wise servant, whom his master has set over his household, to give them their food at the proper time? ⁴⁶Blessed is that servant whom his master when he comes will find so doing. ⁴⁷Truly, I say to you, he will set him over all his possessions. ⁴⁸But if that wicked servant says to himself, 'My master is delayed,' ⁴⁹and begins to beat his fellow servants, and eats and drinks with the drunken, ⁵⁰the master of that servant **will come** on a **day** when he does not expect him and at an hour he does not know, ⁵¹and will punish him, and put him with the hypocrites; there men will weep and gnash their teeth."

† Matt 21:17 ⇨ §L91.5

¹⁷**And** leaving them, **he went out** of the city to Bethany **and lodged** there.

MARK

Mark 13:33–37 (§K60.5) ⇨ §L91.4

³³"**Take heed, watch**; for **you** do not know when the time will come. ³⁴It is like a man going on a journey, when he leaves home and puts his servants in charge, each with his work, and commands the doorkeeper to be on watch. ³⁵**Watch** therefore—for **you** do not know when the master of the house **will come**, in the evening, or at midnight, or at cockcrow, or in the morning— ³⁶lest he **come suddenly** and find you asleep. ³⁷And what I say to **you** I say to all: **Watch**."

† Mark 11:19 ⇨ §L91.5

¹⁹**And** when evening came they **went out** of the city.

JOHN

THOMAS

OTHER

LUKE

Luke 22:1–2 (§L92.1)

[1] Now the feast of Unleavened Bread drew near, which is called the Passover. [2] And the chief priests and the scribes were seeking how to put him to death; for they feared the people.

Luke 22:3–6 (§L92.2) °

[3] Then Satan entered into Judas called Iscariot, who was of the number of the twelve; [4] he went away and conferred with the chief priests and officers how he might betray him to them. [5] And they were glad, and engaged to give him money. [6] So he agreed, and sought an opportunity to betray him to them in the absence of the multitude.

°Appendix 2 ⇨ Luke 22:3

Luke 19:47–48 ⇨ §L92.1

[47] *And he was teaching daily in the temple.* **The chief priests and the scribes and the principal men of the people sought to destroy him;** [48] *but* **they** *did not find anything they could do, for* **all the people** *hung upon his words.*

Luke 20:19 ⇨ §L92.1

[19] *The scribes and the chief priests tried to lay hands on him at that very hour, but* **they feared the people;** *for they perceived that he had told this parable against them.*

JOHN

† **John 11:45–53 (§J23.1) ⇨ L92.1**

[45] Many of the Jews therefore, who had come with Mary and had seen what he did, believed in him; [46] but some of them went to the Pharisees and told them what Jesus had done. [47] So **the chief priests and the** Pharisees gathered the council, and said, "What are we to do? For this man performs many signs. [48] If we let him go on thus, every one will believe in him, and the Romans will come and destroy both our holy place and our nation." [49] But one of them, Caiaphas, who was high priest that year, said to them, "You know nothing at all; [50] you do not understand that it is expedient for you that one man should die for the people, and that the whole nation should not perish." [51] He did not say this of his own accord, but being high priest that year he prophesied that Jesus should die for the nation, [52] and not for the nation only, but to gather into one the children of God who are scattered abroad. [53] So from that day on they took counsel **how to put him to death.**

† **John 11:54 (§J23.2) ⇨ §L92.1**

[54] Jesus therefore no longer went about openly among the Jews, but went from there to the country near the wilderness, to a town called Ephraim; and there he stayed with the disciples.

† **John 11:55–57 (§J23.3) ⇨ §L92.1**

[55] Now **the Passover** of the Jews was at hand, and many went up from the country to Jerusalem before **the Passover,** to purify themselves. [56] They were looking for Jesus and saying to one another as they stood in the temple, "What do you think? That he will not come to **the feast?"** [57] Now **the chief priests and the** Pharisees had given orders that if any one knew where he was, he should let them know, so that they might arrest **him.**

MATT

Matt 26:1–2 (§M80.1) ⇨ §L92.1

[1] When Jesus had finished all these sayings, he said to his disciples, [2] "You know that after two days **the Passover** is coming, and the Son of man will be delivered up to be crucified."

Matt 26:3–5 (§M80.2) ⇨ §L92.1

[3] Then **the chief priests and the** elders of the people gathered in the palace of the high priest, who was called Caiaphas, [4] and took counsel together in order **to** arrest Jesus by stealth and kill **him.** [5] But they said, "Not during the feast, lest there be a tumult among **the people."**

Matt 21:45 ⇨ §L92.1

[45] *When the chief priests and the Pharisees heard his parables, they perceived that he was speaking about them.*

Matt 26:14–16 (§M80.4) ⇨ §L92.2

[14] Then one **of the twelve,** who was called **Judas Iscariot, went** to **the chief priests** [15] **and** said, "What will you give me if I deliver **him to** you?" And they paid **him** thirty pieces of silver. [16] And from that moment **he sought an opportunity to betray him.**

THOMAS

MARK

Mark 14:1–2 (§K61.1) ⇨ §L92.1

[1] It was now two days before **the Passover** and **the feast of Unleavened Bread. And the chief priests and the scribes were seeking how to** arrest him by stealth, and kill **him;** [2] **for they** said, "Not during the feast, lest there be a tumult of **the people."**

Mark 12:12 ⇨ §L92.1

[12] *And they tried to arrest him, but feared the multitude, for they perceived that he had told the parable against them; so they left him and went away.*

Mark 14:10–11 (§K61.3) ⇨ §L92.2

[10] Then **Judas Iscariot, who was one of the twelve, went to the chief priests** in order to **betray him to them.** [11] **And** when they heard it **they were glad, and** promised **to give him money. And he sought an opportunity to betray him.**

OTHER

Acts 1:16–20 ⇨ §L92.2

[16] *"Brethren, the scripture had to be fulfilled, which the Holy Spirit spoke beforehand by the mouth of David, concerning* **Judas who was guide to** *those who arrested Jesus.* [17] *For he was numbered among us, and was allotted his share in this ministry.* [18] *(Now this man bought a field with the reward of his wickedness; and falling headlong he burst open in the middle and all his bowels gushed out.* [19] *And it became known to all the inhabitants of Jerusalem, so that the field was called in their language Akeldama, that is, Field of Blood.)* [20] *For it is written in the book of Psalms,*

'Let his habitation become desolate, and let there be no one to live in it'; *and*

'His office let another take.'"

LUKE	MATT	MARK

Luke 22:7–13 (§L93.1)

[7] Then came the day of Unleavened Bread, on which the passover lamb had to be sacrificed. [8] So Jesus[a] sent Peter and John, saying, "Go and prepare the passover for us, that we may eat it." [9] They said to him, "Where will you have us prepare it?" [10] He said to them, "Behold, when you have entered the city, a man carrying a jar of water will meet you; follow him into the house which he enters, [11] and tell the householder, 'The Teacher says to you, Where is the guest room, where I am to eat the passover with my disciples?' [12] And he will show you a large upper room furnished; there make ready." [13] And they went, and found it as he had told them; and they prepared the passover.

Luke 22:14–23 (§L93.2) °

[14] And when the hour came, he sat at table, and the apostles with him. [15] And he said to them, "I have earnestly desired to eat this passover with you before I suffer; [16] for I tell you I shall not eat it[b] until it is fulfilled in the kingdom of God." [17] And he took a cup, and when he had given thanks he said, "Take this, and divide it among yourselves; [18] for I tell you that from now on I shall not drink of the fruit of the vine until the kingdom of God comes." [19] And he took bread, and when he had given thanks he broke it and gave it to them, saying, "This is my body which is given for you. Do this in remembrance of me." [20] And likewise the cup after supper, saying, "This cup which is poured out for you is the new covenant in my blood.[c] [21] But behold the hand of him who betrays me is with me on the table. [22] For the Son of man goes as it has been determined; but woe to that man by whom he is betrayed!" [23] And they began to question one another, which of them it was that would do this.

[a] Greek: *he*

[b] Some witnesses read *never eat it again* (see Mark 14:25): (C) K P W X Δ Π Ψ *f*[13] it (in part) *al;* text: (𝔓[75]) ℵ A B L *f*[1] *pc*

[c] Some witnesses omit vv. 19b–20 (*which is given . . . in my blood*): D it (in part)

° Appendix 2 ⇨ Luke 22:14

Luke 9:16 ⇨ Luke 22:19
[16] *And taking the five loaves and the two fish he looked up to heaven, and blessed and broke them, and gave them to the disciples to set before the crowd.*

Matt 26:17–19 (§M81.1) ⇨ §L93.1

[17] Now on the first day of Unleavened Bread the disciples came to Jesus, saying, "Where will you have us prepare for you to eat the passover?" [18] He said, "Go into the city to a certain one, and say to him, 'The Teacher says, My time is at hand; I will keep the passover at your house with my disciples.'" [19] And the disciples did as Jesus had directed them, and they prepared the passover.

Matt 26:20–25 (§M81.2) ⇨ §L93.2

[20] When it was evening, he sat at table with the twelve disciples; [21] and as they were eating, he said, "Truly, I say to you, one of you will betray me." [22] And they were very sorrowful, and began to say to him one after another, "Is it I, Lord?" [23] He answered, "He who has dipped his hand in the dish with me, will betray me. [24] The Son of man goes as it is written of him, but woe to that man by whom the Son of man is betrayed! It would have been better for that man if he had not been born." [25] Judas, who betrayed him, said, "Is it I, Master?" He said to him, "You have said so."

Matt 26:26–29 (§M81.3) ⇨ §L93.2

[26] Now as they were eating, Jesus took bread, and blessed, and broke it, and gave it to the disciples and said, "Take, eat; this is my body." [27] And he took a cup, and when he had given thanks he gave it to them, saying, "Drink of it, all of you; [28] for this is my blood of the covenant, which is poured out for many for the forgiveness of sins. [29] I tell you I shall not drink again of this fruit of the vine until that day when I drink it new with you in my Father's kingdom."

Luke 24:30 ⇨ Luke 22:19
[30] *When he was at table with them, he took the bread and blessed, and broke it, and gave it to them.*

Luke 9:22 ⇨ Luke 22:22
[22] *saying, "The Son of man must suffer many things, and be rejected by the elders and chief priests and scribes, and be killed, and on the third day be raised."*

Luke 9:44 ⇨ Luke 22:22
[44] *"Let these words sink into your ears; for the Son of man is to be delivered into the hands of men."*

Mark 14:12–16 (§K62.1) ⇨ §L93.1

[12] And on the first day of Unleavened Bread, when they sacrificed the passover lamb, his disciples said to him, "Where will you have us go and prepare for you to eat the passover?" [13] And he sent two of his disciples, and said to them, "Go into the city, and a man carrying a jar of water will meet you; follow him, [14] and wherever he enters, say to the householder, 'The Teacher says, Where is my guest room, where I am to eat the passover with my disciples?' [15] And he will show you a large upper room furnished and ready; there prepare for us." [16] And the disciples set out and went to the city, and found it as he had told them; and they prepared the passover.

Mark 14:17–21 (§K62.2) ⇨ §L93.2

[17] And when it was evening he came with the twelve. [18] And as they were at table eating, Jesus said, "Truly, I say to you, one of you will betray me, one who is eating with me." [19] They began to be sorrowful, and to say to him one after another, "Is it I?" [20] He said to them, "It is one of the twelve, one who is dipping bread into the dish with me. [21] For the Son of man goes as it is written of him, but woe to that man by whom the Son of man is betrayed! It would have been better for that man if he had not been born."

Mark 14:22–25 (§K62.3) ⇨ §L93.2

[22] And as they were eating, he took bread, and blessed, and broke it, and gave it to them, and said, "Take; this is my body." [23] And he took a cup, and when he had given thanks he gave it to them, and they all drank of it. [24] And he said to them, "This is my blood of the covenant, which is poured out for many. [25] Truly, I say to you, I shall not drink again of the fruit of the vine until that day when I drink it new in the kingdom of God."

Luke 17:25 ⇨ Luke 22:22
[25] *"But first he must suffer many things and be rejected by this generation."*

Luke 18:31–33 ⇨ Luke 22:22
[31] *And taking the twelve, he said to them, "Behold, we are going up to Jerusalem, and everything that is written of the Son of man by the prophets will be accomplished. [32] For he will be delivered to the Gentiles, and will be mocked and shamefully treated and spit upon; [33] they will scourge him and kill him, and on the third day he will rise."*

JOHN

John 13:21–30 (§J29) ⇨ Luke 22:21–23

[21] When Jesus had thus spoken, he was troubled in spirit, and testified, "Truly, truly, I say to you, one of you will betray **me**." [22] The disciples looked at **one another**, uncertain of whom he spoke. [23] One of his disciples, whom Jesus loved, was lying close to the breast of Jesus; [24] so Simon Peter beckoned to him and said, "Tell us who it is of whom he speaks." [25] So lying thus, close to the breast of Jesus, he said to him, "Lord, who is it?" [26] Jesus answered, "It is he to whom I shall give this morsel when I have dipped it." So when he had dipped the morsel, he gave it to Judas, the son of Simon Iscariot. [27] Then after the morsel, Satan entered into him. Jesus said to him, "What you are going to do, do quickly." [28] Now no one at the table knew why he said this to him. [29] Some thought that, because Judas had the money box, Jesus was telling him, "Buy what we need for the feast"; or, that he should give something to the poor. [30] So, after receiving the morsel, he immediately went out; and it was night.

John 6:48–58 ⇨ §L93.2

[48] "I am the **bread** of life. [49] Your fathers ate the manna in the wilderness, and they died. [50] This is the **bread** which comes down from heaven, that a man may **eat** of it and not die. [51] I am the living **bread** which came down from heaven; if any one eats of this **bread**, he will live for ever; and the **bread** which I shall give **for** the life of the world **is my** flesh."

[52] The Jews then disputed among themselves, saying, "How can this man give us his flesh to **eat**?" [53] So Jesus **said to them**, "Truly, truly, I say to you, unless you **eat** the flesh of **the Son of man** and **drink** his **blood**, you have no life in you; [54] he who eats **my** flesh and drinks **my blood** has eternal life, and I will raise him up at the last day. [55] For **my** flesh is food indeed, and **my blood** is drink indeed. [56] He who eats **my** flesh and drinks **my blood** abides in me, and I in him. [57] As the living Father sent me, and I live because of the Father, so he who eats me will live because of me. [58] This is **the bread** which came down from heaven, not such as the fathers ate and died; he who eats this **bread** will live for ever."

Luke 24:6–8 ⇨ Luke 22:22

[6] *"Remember how he told you, while he was still in Galilee, [7] that the Son of man must be delivered into the hands of sinful men, and be crucified, and on the third day rise."* [8] *And they remembered his words, . . .*

Luke 24:26 ⇨ Luke 22:22

[26] *"Was it not necessary that the Christ should suffer these things and enter into his glory?"*

Luke 24:46 ⇨ Luke 22:22

[46] *and said to them, "Thus it is written, that the Christ should suffer and on the thrid day rise from the dead, . . ."*

THOMAS

Exod 24:8 ⇨ Luke 22:20

[8] And Moses took the **blood** and threw it upon the people, and said, "Behold the **blood** of **the covenant** which the Lord has made with **you** in accordance with all these words."

Jer 31:31 ⇨ Luke 22:20

[31] "Behold, the days are coming, says the Lord, when I will make a **new covenant** with the house of Israel and the house of Judah, . . ."

Zech 9:11 ⇨ Luke 22:20

[11] As for you also, because of the **blood** of **my covenant** with **you,**
I will set your captives free from the waterless pit.

OTHER

1 Cor 11:23–25 ⇨ Luke 22:14–20

[23] For I received from the Lord what I also delivered to you, that the Lord Jesus on the night when he was betrayed **took bread,** [24] and when he had given thanks, he broke it, and said, "This is my body which is for you. Do this in remembrance of me." [25] In the same way also **the cup, after supper, saying, "This cup is the new covenant in my blood**. Do this, as often as you drink it, in remembrance of me."

Did 9:1–5 ⇨ Luke 22:14–20

[1] And concerning the Eucharist, hold Eucharist thus: [2] First concerning **the Cup,** "We give thanks to thee, our Father, for the Holy Vine of David thy child, which, thou didst make known to us through Jesus thy child; to thee be glory for ever." [3] And concerning the broken **Bread**: "We give thee thanks, our Father, for the life and knowledge which thou didst make known to us through Jesus thy child. To thee be glory for ever. [4] As this broken **bread** is scattered upon the mountains, but was brought together and became one, so let thy Church be gathered together from the ends of the earth into thy **kingdom**, for thine is the glory and the power through Jesus Christ for ever." [5] But let none **eat** or **drink** of your Eucharist except those who have been baptised in the Lord's Name. For concerning this also did the Lord say, "Give not that which is holy to the dogs."

Justin, *Apology* 1.66.3 ⇨ Luke 22:14–20

For the apostles in the memoirs composed by them, which are called Gospels, thus handed down what was commanded them: that Jesus, taking **bread and** having **given thanks**, said, "**Do this** for my memorial, **this is my body**"; **and likewise** taking **the cup** and giving **thanks** he said, "**This is my blood**"; and gave it to them alone. This also the wicked demons in imitation handed down as something to be done in the mysteries of Mithra; for **bread** and a **cup** of water are brought out in their secret rites of initiation, with certain invocations which you either know or can learn.

GEbi 7 ⇨ §L93.1, Luke 22:15

(7) But they abandon the proper sequence of the words and pervert the saying, as is plain to all from the readings attached, and have let the disciples say:

*Where wilt thou that we **prepare** for thee the passover? and him to answer to that:*

*Do **I** desire with desire at **this Passover** to eat flesh with you?* (Epiphanius, *Haer.* 30.22.4)

LUKE	MATT	MARK
Luke 22:24–30 (§L93.3) ° ²⁴ A dispute also arose among them, which of them was to be regarded as the greatest. ²⁵ And he said to them, "The kings of the Gentiles exercise lordship over them; and those in authority over them are called benefactors. ²⁶ But not so with you; rather let the greatest among you become as the youngest, and the leader as one who serves. ²⁷ For which is the greater, one who sits at table, or one who serves? Is it not the one who sits at table? But I am among you as one who serves. ²⁸ "You are those who have continued with me in my trials; ²⁹ and I assign to you, as my Father assigned to me, a kingdom, ³⁰ that you may eat and drink at my table in my kingdom, and sit on thrones judging the twelve tribes of Israel." °Appendix 2 ⇨ Luke 22:28–30 **Luke 9:48** ⇨ Luke 22:26 *⁴⁸ and said to them, "Whoever receives this child in my name receives me, and whoever receives me receives him who sent me; for he who is least among you all is the one who is great."* **Luke 12:37** ⇨ Luke 22:27 *³⁷ "Blessed are those servants whom the master finds awake when he comes; truly, I say to you, he will gird himself and have them sit at table, and he will come and serve them."* **Luke 23:42–43** ⇨ Luke 22:29–30 *⁴² And he said, "Jesus, remember me when you come into your kingdom." ⁴³ And he said to him, "Truly, I say to you, today you will be with me in Paradise."*	**Matt 20:24–28 (§M69.2)** ²⁴ And when the ten heard it, they were indignant at the two brothers. ²⁵ But Jesus called **them** to him **and said,** "You know that the rulers **of the Gentiles** lord it **over them, and** their great men exercise **authority over them.** ²⁶ It shall **not** be **so** among **you**; but whoever would be great **among you** must be your servant, ²⁷ and whoever would be first **among you** must be your slave; ²⁸ even as the Son of man came not to be served but to serve, and to give his life as a ransom for many." **Matt 19:28** ⇨ Luke 22:28–30 *²⁸ Jesus said to them, "Truly, I say to you, in the new world, when the Son of man shall sit on his glorious throne,* **you** *who have followed me will also* **sit on** *twelve* **thrones, judging the twelve tribes of Israel."** **Matt 23:11–12** ⇨ Luke 22:26 *¹¹ "He who is* **greatest among you** *shall be your servant; ¹² whoever exalts himself will be humbled, and whoever humbles himself will be exalted."*	**Mark 10:41–45 (§K55.2)** ⁴¹ And when the ten heard it, they began to be indignant at James and John. ⁴² **And** Jesus called them to him and **said to them,** "You know that those who are supposed to rule over **the Gentiles** lord it **over them, and** their great men exercise **authority over them.** ⁴³ But it shall not be so among you; but whoever would be great **among you** must be your servant, ⁴⁴ and whoever would be first among you must be slave of all. ⁴⁵ For the Son of man also came not to be served but to serve, and to give his life as a ransom for many." **Mark 9:35** ⇨ Luke 22:26 *³⁵ And he sat down and called the twelve; and he said to them, "If any one would be first, he must be last of all and servant of all."*

JOHN	THOMAS	OTHER

John 13:1–20 (§J28)

¹Now before the feast of the Passover, when Jesus knew that his hour had come to depart out of this world to the Father, having loved his own who were in the world, he loved them to the end. ²And during supper, when the devil had already put it into the heart of Judas Iscariot, Simon's son, to betray him, ³Jesus, knowing that the Father had given all things into his hands, and that he had come from God and was going to God, ⁴rose from supper, laid aside his garments, and girded himself with a towel. ⁵Then he poured water into a basin, and began to wash the disciples' feet and to wipe them with the towel with which he was girded. ⁶He came to Simon Peter; and Peter said to him, "Lord, do you wash my feet?" ⁷Jesus answered him, "What I am doing you do not know now, but afterward you will understand." ⁸Peter said to him, "You shall never wash my feet." Jesus answered him, "If I do not wash you, you have no part in me." ⁹Simon Peter said to him, "Lord, not my feet only but also my hands and my head!" ¹⁰Jesus said to him, "He who has bathed does not need to wash, except for his feet, but he is clean all over; and you are clean, but not every one of you." ¹¹For he knew who was to betray him; that was why he said, "You are not all clean."

*¹²When he had washed their feet, and taken his garments, and resumed his place, he said to them, "Do you know what I have done to you? ¹³You call me Teacher and Lord; and you are right, for so I am. ¹⁴If I then, your Lord and Teacher, have washed your feet, you also ought to wash one another's feet. ¹⁵For I have given you an example, that you also should do as I have done to you. ¹⁶Truly, truly, I say to **you**, a servant is not **greater** than his master; nor is he who is sent **greater** than he who sent him. ¹⁷If you know these things, blessed are you if you do them. ¹⁸I am not speaking of you all; I know whom I have chosen; it is that that the scripture may be fulfilled, 'He who ate my bread has lifted his heel against me.' ¹⁹I tell you this now, before it takes place, that when it does take place you may believe that I am he. ²⁰Truly, truly, I say to you, he who receives any one whom I send receives me; and he who receives me receives him who sent me."*

GThom 12 ⇨ Luke 22:24

(12) The disciples said to Jesus, "We know that You will depart from us. Who is to be our leader?"

Jesus said to them, "Wherever you are, you are to go to James the righteous, for whose sake heaven and earth came into being."

Acts 10:41 ⇨ Luke 22:29–30

*⁴¹"not to all the people but to us who were chosen by God as witnesses, who ate **and** drank with him after he rose from the dead."*

LUKE

Luke 22:31–34 (§L93.4)
[31] "Simon, Simon, behold, Satan demanded to have you,[a] that he might sift you like wheat, [32] but I have prayed for you that your faith may not fail; and when you have turned again, strengthen your brethren." [33] And he said to him, "Lord, I am ready to go with you to prison and to death." [34] He said, "I tell you, Peter, the cock will not crow this day, until you three times deny that you know me."

[a] The Greek word for *you* here is plural; in v. 32 it is singular

Luke 22:54b–62 (§L95.1)
Peter followed at a distance; [55] and when they had kindled a fire in the middle of the courtyard and sat down together, **Peter** sat among them. [56] Then a maid, seeing him as he sat in the light and gazing at him, said, "This man also was with him." [57] But he denied it, saying, "Woman, I do not know him." [58] And a little later some one else saw him and said, "You also are one of them." But **Peter** said, "Man, I am not." [59] And after an interval of about an hour still another insisted, saying, "Certainly this man also was with him; for he is a Galilean." [60] But Peter said, "Man, I do not know what you are saying." And immediately, while he was still speaking, **the cock** crowed. [61] And the Lord turned and looked at **Peter**. And **Peter** remembered the word of the Lord, how **he** had **said** to him, "Before **the cock** crows today, **you** will **deny me three times**." [62] And he went out and wept bitterly.

MATT

Matt 26:30–35 (§M82.1)
[30] And when they had sung a hymn, they went out to the Mount of Olives. [31] Then Jesus said to them, "You will all fall away because of me this night; for it is written, 'I will strike the shepherd, and the sheep of the flock will be scattered.' [32] But after I am raised up, I will go before you to Galilee." [33] Peter declared **to him**, "Though they all fall away because of you, I will never fall away." [34] Jesus **said** to him, "Truly, **I** say to **you, this** very night, before **the cock** crows, **you** will **deny me three times**." [35] Peter said to him, "Even if I must die with you, I will not deny you." And so said all the disciples.

MARK

Mark 14:26–31 (§K63.1)
[26] And when they had sung a hymn, they went out to the Mount of Olives. [27] And Jesus said to them, "You will all fall away; for it is written, 'I will strike the shepherd, and the sheep will be scattered.' [28] But after I am raised up, I will go before you to Galilee." [29] Peter **said to him**, "Even though they all fall away, I will not." [30] And Jesus **said** to him, "Truly, I say to **you, this** very night, before **the cock** crows twice, **you** will **deny me three times**." [31] But he said vehemently, "If I must die with you, I will not deny you." And they all said the same.

JOHN

John 13:36–38
[36] Simon Peter said to him, "Lord, where are you going?" Jesus answered, "Where I am going you cannot follow me now; but you shall follow afterward." [37] Peter **said to him**, "Lord, why cannot I follow you now? **I** will lay down my life for **you**." [38] Jesus answered, "Will you lay down your life for me? Truly, truly, **I** say to **you, the cock will not crow**, till **you** have denied **me three times**.

THOMAS

OTHER

Fayyum Fragment ⇨ Luke 22:33–34
... while he was going out he said, "This night you will all fall away as it is written, 'I will strike the shepherd, and the sheep will be scattered.'" When Peter **said**, "Even though all, not **I**," Jesus **said**, "Before **the cock** crows twice, **you** will **this day deny me three times**."

Acts 21:13 ⇨ Luke 22:33
*[13] Then Paul answered, "What are you doing, weeping and breaking my heart? For **I am ready** not only to be imprisoned but even to die at Jerusalem for the name of the Lord Jesus."*

LUKE

Luke 22:35–38 (§L93.5)

³⁵ And he said to them, "When I sent you out with no purse or bag or sandals, did you lack anything?" They said, "Nothing." ³⁶ He said to them, "But now, let him who has a purse take it, and likewise a bag. And let him who has no sword sell his mantle and buy one. ³⁷ For I tell you that this scripture must be fulfilled in me, 'And he was reckoned with transgressors'; for what is written about me has its fulfilment." ³⁸ And they said, "Look, Lord, here are two swords." And he said to them, "It is enough."

Luke 9:3 ⇨ Luke 22:35–36

³ *And he said to them, "Take nothing for your journey, no staff, nor* **bag**, *nor bread, nor money; and do not have two tunics."*

Luke 10:4 ⇨ Luke 22:35–36

⁴ *"Carry* **no purse, no bag, no sandals**; *and salute* **no** *one on the road."*

Luke 22:49–50 ⇨ Luke 22:36–38

⁴⁹ *And when those who were about him saw what would follow, they said, "Lord, shall we strike with the* **sword**?" ⁵⁰ *And one of them struck the slave of the high priest and cut off his right ear.*

Isa 53:12 ⇨ Luke 22:37

¹² Therefore I will divide him a portion
with the great,
    and he shall divide the spoil with the strong;
    because **he** poured out his soul to death,
    and was numbered **with** the **transgressors**;
    yet he bore the sin of many,
    and made intercession for the **transgressors**.

MATT

Matt 10:9–10 ⇨ Luke 22:35–36

⁹ *"Take* **no gold**, *nor* **silver**, *nor* **copper** *in your belts*, ¹⁰ *no* **bag** *for your journey, nor two* **tunics**, *nor* **sandals**, *nor a* **staff**; *for the laborer deserves his food."*

MARK

Mark 6:8–9 ⇨ Luke 22:35–36

⁸ *He charged them to take nothing for their journey except a staff; no bread, no* **bag**, *no* money *in their* belts; ⁹ *but to wear* **sandals** *and not put on two* **tunics**.

JOHN

THOMAS

OTHER

LUKE

INTRODUCTION

Luke 22:39 (§L94.1a)
[39] And he came out, and went, as was his custom, to the Mount of Olives; and the disciples followed him.

THE PRAYER

Luke 22:40–42 (§L94.1b)
[40] And when he came to the place he said to them, "Pray that you may not enter into temptation." [41] And he withdrew from them about a stone's throw, and knelt down and prayed, [42] "Father, if thou art willing, remove this cup from me; nevertheless not my will, but thine, be done."[a]

THE DISCIPLES SLEEP

Luke 22:45–46 (§L94.1c)
[45] And when he rose from prayer, he came to the disciples and found them sleeping for sorrow, [46] and he said to them, "Why do you sleep? Rise and pray that you may not enter into temptation."

[a] Some witnesses add vv. 43–44, [43] *And there appeared to him an angel from heaven, strengthening him.* [44] *And being in an agony he prayed more earnestly; and his sweat became like great drops of blood falling down upon the ground:* ℵ*,b D K L X Δ* Θ Π* Ψ *f*[1] *pm;* include vv. 43–44 with obeli or asterisks: Δc Πc *pc;* transpose vv. 43–44 after Matt 26:39: *f*[13]; omit vv. 43–44: 𝔓[75] ℵa A B T W *al*

MATT

Matt 26:36 (§M82.2a)
[36] Then Jesus **went** with them **to** a place called Gethsemane, and he said to his **disciples**, "Sit here, while I go yonder and pray."

Matt 26:37–38 (§M82.2b)
[37] And taking with him Peter and the two sons of Zebedee, he began to be sorrowful and troubled. [38] Then **he said to them**, "My soul is very sorrowful, even to death; remain here, and watch with me."

Matt 26:39 (§M82.2c)
[39] **And** going a little farther **he** fell on his face **and prayed**, "My father, if it be possible, let **this cup** pass **from me; nevertheless**, **not** as I **will, but** as thou wilt."

Matt 26:40–41 (§M82.2d)
[40] **And he came to the disciples and found them sleeping;** and **he said to** Peter, "So, could you not watch with me one hour? [41] Watch **and pray that you may not enter into temptation;** the spirit indeed is willing, but the flesh is weak."

Matt 26:42 (§M82.2e)
[42] Again, for the second time, **he** went away **and prayed**, "My **Father**, if this cannot pass unless I drink it, thy will **be done**."

Matt 26:43 (§M82.2f)
[43] **And** again **he came and found them sleeping, for** their eyes were heavy.

Matt 26:44 (§M82.2g)
[44] So, leaving them again, **he** went away **and prayed** for the third time, saying the same words.

Matt 26:45–46 (§M82.2h)
[45] Then **he came to the disciples** and **said to them**, "Are **you** still **sleeping** and taking your rest? Behold, the hour is at hand, and the Son of man is betrayed into the hands of sinners. [46] **Rise**, let us be going; see, my betrayer is at hand."

MARK

Mark 14:32 (§K63.2a)
[32] And they **went to** a place which was called Gethsemane; and he said to his **disciples**, "Sit here, while I pray."

Mark 14:33–34 (§K63.2b)
[33] **And he** took with him Peter and James and John, and began to be greatly distressed and troubled. [34] **And he said to them**, "My soul is very sorrowful, even to death; remain here, and watch."

Mark 14:35–36 (§K63.2c)
[35] **And** going a little farther, **he** fell on the ground **and prayed** that, if it were possible, the hour might pass from him. [36] And he said, "Abba, **Father**, all things are possible to thee; **remove this cup from me;** yet **not** what **I will, but** what thou wilt."

Mark 14:37–38 (§K63.2d)
[37] And **he came and found them sleeping, and he said to** Peter, "Simon, are you asleep? Could you not watch one hour? [38] Watch **and pray that you may not enter into temptation;** the spirit indeed is willing, but the flesh is weak."

Mark 14:39 (§K63.2e)
[39] **And** again **he** went away **and prayed**, saying the same words.

Mark 14:40 (§K63.2f)
[40] **And** again **he came and found them sleeping,** for their eyes were very heavy; and they did not know what to answer him.

Mark 14:41–42 (§K63.2g)
[41] **And he came** the third time, and **said to them**, "Are **you** still **sleeping** and taking your rest? It is enough; the hour has come; the Son of man is betrayed into the hands of sinners. [42] **Rise**, let us be going; see, my betrayer is at hand."

JOHN

† **John 18:1** ⇨ Luke 22:39
[1] When Jesus had spoken these words, **he went** forth with his **disciples** across the Kidron valley, where there was a garden, which he and his **disciples** entered.

† **John 18:11** ⇨ Luke 22:42
[11] Jesus said to Peter, "Put your sword into its sheath; shall I not drink the **cup** which the **Father** has given me?"

THOMAS

OTHER

Acts 21:14 ⇨ Luke 22:42
[14] *And when he would not be persuaded, we ceased and said, "The **will** of the Lord **be done**."*

LUKE

Luke 22:47–54a (§L94.2) °
⁴⁷ While he was still speaking, there came a crowd, and the man called Judas, one of the twelve, was leading them. He drew near to Jesus to kiss him; ⁴⁸ but Jesus said to him, "Judas, would you betray the Son of man with a kiss?" ⁴⁹ And when those who were about him saw what would follow, they said, "Lord, shall we strike with the sword?" ⁵⁰ And one of them struck the slave of the high priest and cut off his right ear. ⁵¹ But Jesus said, "No more of this!" And he touched his ear and healed him. ⁵² Then Jesus said to the chief priests and officers of the temple and elders, who had come out against him, "Have you come out as against a robber, with swords and clubs? ⁵³ When I was with you day after day in the temple, you did not lay hands on me. But this is your hour, and the power of darkness."
⁵⁴ Then they seized him and led him away, bringing him into the high priest's house.

°Appendix 2 ⇨ Luke 22:47

Luke 22:36–38 ⇨ Luke 22:49–50
³⁶ *He said to them, "But now, let him who has a purse take it, and likewise a bag. And let him who has no sword sell his mantle and buy one. ³⁷ For I tell you that this scripture must be fulfilled in me, 'And he was reckoned with transgressors'; for what is written about me has its fulfillment." ³⁸ And they said, "Look, Lord, here are two swords." And he said to them, "It is enough."*

JOHN

John 18:1–12 (§J31.1)
¹ When Jesus had spoken these words, he went forth with his disciples across the Kidron valley, where there was a garden, which he and his disciples entered. ² Now Judas, who betrayed him, also knew the place; for Jesus often met there with his disciples. ³ So **Judas**, procuring a band of soldiers and some officers from **the chief priests** and the Pharisees, went there with lanterns and torches and weapons. ⁴ Then Jesus, knowing all that was to befall him, came forward and said to them, "Whom do you seek?" ⁵ They answered him, "Jesus of Nazareth." Jesus said to them, "I am he." Judas, who betrayed him, was standing with them. ⁶ When he said to them, "I am he," they drew back and fell to the ground. ⁷ Again he asked them, "Whom do you seek?" And they said, "Jesus of Nazareth." ⁸ Jesus answered, "I told you that I am he; so, if you seek me, let these men go." ⁹ This was to fulfil the word which he had spoken, "Of those whom thou gavest me I lost not one." ¹⁰ Then Simon Peter, having a **sword**, drew it and **struck the high** priest's **slave and cut off his right ear**. The slave's name was Malchus. ¹¹ **Jesus said** to Peter, "Put your sword into its sheath; shall I not drink the cup which the Father has given me?"
¹² So the band of soldiers and their captain and the officers of the Jews **seized** Jesus and bound **him**.

John 18:20 ⇨ Luke 22:53
²⁰ *Jesus answered him, "I have spoken openly to the world; I have always taught in synagogues and in the temple, where all Jews come together; I have said nothing secretly."*

MATT

Matt 26:47–56 (§M82.3)
⁴⁷ **While he was still speaking, Judas came, one of the twelve,** and with him **a** great **crowd** with swords and clubs, from the chief priests and the elders of the people. ⁴⁸ Now the betrayer had given them a sign, saying, "The one I shall **kiss** is the man; seize him." ⁴⁹ And **he** came up **to Jesus** at once and said, "Hail, Master!" And he kissed **him**. ⁵⁰ **Jesus said to him,** "Friend, why are you here?" **Then they** came up and laid hands on Jesus and **seized him**. ⁵¹ **And** behold, **one** of those who were with Jesus stretched out his hand and drew his **sword, and struck the slave of the high priest, and cut off his ear**. ⁵² Then **Jesus said** to him, "Put your sword back into its place; for all who take the sword will perish by the sword. ⁵³ Do you think that I cannot appeal to my Father, and he will at once send me more than twelve legions of angels? ⁵⁴ But how then should the scriptures be fulfilled, that it must be so?" ⁵⁵ At that hour **Jesus said to the** crowds, **"Have you come out as against a robber, with swords and clubs** to capture me? **Day after day I sat in the temple** teaching, and **you did not seize me**. ⁵⁶ **But all this** has taken place, that the scriptures of the prophets might be fulfilled." Then all the disciples forsook him and fled.

Matt 26:57 ⇨ Luke 22:54a
⁵⁷ **Then** those who had **seized** Jesus **led him** to Caiaphas **the high** priest, where the scribes and the elders had gathered.

THOMAS

MARK

Mark 14:43–52 (§K63.3)
⁴³ And immediately, **while he was still speaking, Judas came, one of the twelve,** and with him **a crowd** with swords and clubs, from the chief priests and the scribes and the elders. ⁴⁴ Now the betrayer had given them a sign, saying, "The one I shall **kiss** is the man; seize him and lead him away under guard." ⁴⁵ And when he came, **he** went up to him at once, and said, "Master!" And he kissed **him**. ⁴⁶ And **they** laid hands on him **and seized him**. ⁴⁷ But **one** of those **who** stood by drew his **sword, and struck the slave of the high priest and cut off his ear**. ⁴⁸ And **Jesus said to them, "Have you come out as against a robber, with swords and clubs** to capture me? ⁴⁹ **Day after day I was with you in the temple** teaching, and **you did not seize me. But** let the scriptures be fulfilled." ⁵⁰ And they all forsook him, and fled.
⁵¹ And a young man **followed** him, with nothing but a linen cloth about his body; and they seized him, ⁵² but he left the linen cloth and ran away naked.

Mark 14:53 ⇨ Luke 22:54a
⁵³ **And they led** Jesus to **the high** priest; and all the chief priests and the elders and the scribes were assembled.

OTHER

LUKE

PETER'S DENIAL

Luke 22:54b–62 (§L95.1)
Peter followed at a distance; [55] and when they had kindled a fire in the middle of the courtyard and sat down together, Peter sat among them. [56] Then a maid, seeing him as he sat in the light and gazing at him, said, "This man also was with him." [57] But he denied it, saying, "Woman, I do not know him." [58] And a little later some one else saw him and said, "You also are one of them." But Peter said, "Man, I am not." [59] And after an interval of about an hour still another insisted, saying, "Certainly this man also was with him; for he is a Galilean." [60] But Peter said, "Man, I do not know what you are saying." And immediately, while he was still speaking, the cock crowed. [61] And the Lord turned and looked at Peter. And Peter remembered the word of the Lord, how he had said to him, "Before the cock crows today, you will deny me three times." [62] And he went out and wept bitterly.

THE GUARDS MOCK JESUS

Luke 22:63–65 (§L95.2)
[63] Now the men who were holding Jesus mocked him and beat him; [64] they also blindfolded him and asked him, "Prophesy! Who is it that struck you?" [65] And they spoke many other words against him, reviling him.

Luke 22:31–34 (§L93.4) ⇨ §L95.1
[31] "Simon, Simon, behold, Satan demanded to have you, that he might sift you like wheat, [32] but I have prayed for you that your faith may not fail; and when you have turned again, strengthen your brethren." [33] And he said to him, "Lord, I am ready to go with you to prison and to death." [34] He said, "I tell you, **Peter, the cock** will not crow this day, until **you three times deny** that you know **me**."

JOHN

John 18:13–14 (§J31.2a) ⇨ §L95.1
[13] First they led **him** to Annas; for he was the father-in-law of Caiaphas, who was **high** priest that year. [14] It was Caiaphas who had given counsel to the Jews that it was expedient that one man should die for the people.

John 18:15–18 (§J31.2b) ⇨ §L95.1
[15] Simon **Peter followed** Jesus, and so did another disciple. As this disciple was known to the high priest, he entered the court of the high priest along with Jesus, [16] while Peter stood outside at the door. So the other disciple, who was known to the high priest, went out and spoke to the **maid** who kept the door, and brought Peter in. [17] The **maid** who kept the door **said** to Peter, "Are not you also one of this man's disciples?" He said, "**I am not**." [18] Now the servants and officers had made a charcoal **fire**, because it was cold, and they were standing and warming themselves; **Peter** also was with **them**, standing and warming himself.

John 18:25–27 (§J31.2d) ⇨ §L95.1
[25] Now Simon **Peter** was standing and warming himself. They **said** to him, "**Are** not **you also one of** his disciples?" He denied it and **said**, "**I am not**." [26] One of the servants of the high priest, a kinsman of the man whose ear Peter had cut off, asked, "Did I not see you in the garden **with him**?" [27] Peter again denied it; and at once **the cock crowed**.

MATT

Matt 26:57–58 (§M83.1) ⇨ §L95.1
[57] Then those who had seized Jesus led him to Caiaphas the high priest, where the scribes and the elders had gathered. [58] But **Peter followed** him at **a distance**, as far as **the courtyard** of the high priest, **and** going inside he sat with the guards to see the end.

Matt 26:69–75 (§M83.3) ⇨ §L95.1
[69] Now **Peter** was sitting outside **in the courtyard**. And **a maid** came up to him, and **said**, "You **also** were **with** Jesus the Galilean." [70] **But he denied it** before them all, **saying, "I do not know** what you mean." [71] **And** when he went out to the porch, another maid **saw him, and** she **said** to the bystanders, "This man was with Jesus of Nazareth." [72] And again he denied it with an oath, "**I do not** know the **man**." [73] **After** a little while the bystanders came up and said to Peter, "**Certainly** you are **also** one of them, **for** your accent betrays you." [74] Then he began to invoke a curse on himself and to swear, "**I do not** know the **man**." **And immediately the cock crowed**. [75] **Peter remembered** the **saying** of Jesus, "**Before the cock crows, you will deny me three times**." **And he went out and wept bitterly**.

Matt 26:67–68 ⇨ §L95.2
[67] Then they spat in his face, **and** struck **him**; **and** some slapped **him**, [68] saying, "**Prophesy** to us, you Christ! **Who is it that struck you?**"

MARK

Mark 14:53–54 (§K64.1) ⇨ §L95.1
[53] And they led Jesus to the high priest; and all the chief priests and the elders and the scribes were assembled. [54] And **Peter** had **followed** him **at a distance**, right into **the courtyard** of the high priest; **and** he was sitting with the guards, and warming himself at the **fire**.

Mark 14:66–72 (§64.3) ⇨ §L95.1
[66] **And as Peter** was below **in the courtyard**, one of the maids of the high priest came; [67] **and seeing** Peter warming himself, she looked **at him**, and **said**, "You **also** were **with** the Nazarene, Jesus." [68] **But he denied it, saying**, "I neither **know** nor understand what you mean." And he went out into the gateway. [69] **And** the maid **saw him**, and began again to say to the bystanders, "This man is **one of them**." [70] But again he denied it. **And after a** little while again the bystanders said to Peter, "**Certainly** you are one of them; **for you are a Galilean**." [71] But he began to invoke a curse on himself and to swear, "**I do not know** this man of whom **you** speak." [72] **And immediately the cock crowed** a second time. **And Peter remembered** how Jesus **had said to him, "Before the cock crows** twice, **you will deny me three times**." **And he** broke down **and wept**.

Mark 14:65 ⇨ §L95.2
[65] And some began to spit on **him**, and to cover his face, **and** to strike **him**, saying to **him**, "**Prophesy!**" And the guards received **him** with blows.

THOMAS

OTHER

LUKE

Luke 22:66–71 (§L96)

⁶⁶**When day came, the assembly of the elders of the people gathered together, both chief priests and scribes; and they led him away to their council, and they said,** ⁶⁷**"If you are the Christ, tell us." But he said to them, "If I tell you, you will not believe;** ⁶⁸**and if I ask you, you will not answer.** ⁶⁹**But from now on the Son of man shall be seated at the right hand of the power of God."** ⁷⁰**And they all said, "Are you the Son of God, then?" And he said to them, "You say that I am."** ⁷¹**And they said, "What further testimony do we need? We have heard it ourselves from his own lips."**

Luke 20:42–43 ⇨ Luke 22:69
⁴²*"For David himself says in the Book of Psalms,*

'The Lord said to my Lord,
Sit at my right hand,
⁴³*till I make thy enemies a stool for thy feet.'"*

Luke 21:27 ⇨ Luke 22:69
²⁷*"And then they will see the Son of man coming in a cloud with power and great glory."*

Ps 110:1 ⇨ Luke 22:69
¹The Lord says to my lord:
"Sit at my **right hand**, till I make your enemies your footstool."

JOHN

John 18:13–14 (§J31.2a)
¹³First **they led him** to Annas; for he was the father-in-law of Caiaphas, who was the high priest that year. ¹⁴It was Caiaphas who had given counsel to the Jews that it was expedient that one man should die for the people.

John 18:19–24 (§J31.2c)
¹⁹The high priet then questioned Jesus about his disciples and his teaching. ²⁰Jesus answered him, "I have spoken openly to the world; I have always taught in synagogues and in the temple, where all Jews come together; I have said nothing secretly. ²¹Why do you ask me? Ask those who have heard me, what I said to them; they know what I said." ²²When he had said this, one of the officers standing by struck Jesus with his hand, saying, "Is that how you answer the high priest?" ²³Jesus answered him, "If I have spoken wrongly, bear witness to the wrong; but if I have spoken rightly, why do you strike me?" ²⁴Annas then sent him bound to Caiaphas the high priest.

MATT

Matt 26:59–68 (§M83.2)
⁵⁹Now the **chief priests and** the whole council sought false testimony against Jesus that they might put him to death, ⁶⁰but they found none, though many false witnesses came forward. At last two came forward ⁶¹and said, "This fellow said, 'I am able to destroy the temple of God, and to build it in three days.'" ⁶²And the high priest stood up and said, "Have you no answer to make? What is it that these men testify against you?" ⁶³But Jesus was silent. **And** the high priest **said** to him, "I adjure you by the living God, tell us if **you are** the Christ, **the Son of God."** ⁶⁴Jesus **said** to him, "**You** have said so. **But** I tell you, hereafter you will see **the Son of man seated at the right hand of Power**, and coming on the clouds of heaven." ⁶⁵Then the high priest tore his robes, and **said**, "He has uttered blasphemy. Why **do we** still **need** witnesses? You **have** now **heard his** blasphemy. ⁶⁶What is your judgment?" They answered, "He deserves death." ⁶⁷Then they spat in his face, and struck him; and some slapped him, ⁶⁸saying, "Prophesy to us, you Christ! Who is it that struck you?"

Matt 24:30 ⇨ Luke 22:69
³⁰*"then will appear the sign of the Son of man in heaven, and then all the tribes of the earth will mourn, and they will see the Son of man coming on the clouds of heaven with power and great glory";...*

THOMAS

MARK

Mark 14:55–65 (§K64.2)
⁵⁵Now **the chief priests and** the whole council sought testimony against Jesus to put him to death; but they found none. ⁵⁶For many bore false witness against him, and their witness did not agree. ⁵⁷And some stood up and bore false witness against him, saying, ⁵⁸"We heard him say, 'I will destroy this temple that is made with hands, and in three days I will build another, not made with hands.'" ⁵⁹Yet not even so did their testimony agree. ⁶⁰And the high priest stood up in the midst, and asked Jesus, "Have you no answer to make? What is it that these men testify against you?" ⁶¹But he was silent and made no answer. Again the high priest asked him, **"Are you the** Christ, **the Son of** the Blessed?" ⁶²And Jesus said, "**I am**; and **you** will see **the Son of man seated at the right hand of Power**, and coming with the clouds of heaven." ⁶³And the high priest tore his garments, and **said**, "Why **do we** still **need** witnesses? ⁶⁴You have heard his blasphemy. What is your decision?" And they all condemned him as deserving death. ⁶⁵And some began to spit on him, and to cover his face, and to strike him, saying to him, "Prophesy!" And the guards received him with blows.

Mark 13:26 ⇨ Luke 22:69
²⁶*"And then they will see the Son of man coming in clouds with great power and glory."*

OTHER

Acts 2:34–35 ⇨ Luke 22:69
³⁴*"For David did not ascend into the heavens; but he himelf says,*

'The Lord said to my Lord, Sit at my right hand,
³⁵*till I make thy enemies a stool for thy feet.'"*

Acts 7:55–56 ⇨ Luke 22:69
⁵⁵*But he, full of the Holy Spirit, gazed into heaven and saw the glory of God, and Jesus standing at the right hand of God;* ⁵⁶*and he said, "Behold, I see the heavens opened, and the Son of man standing at the right hand of God."*

LUKE	MATT	MARK

LUKE

Luke 23:1–7 (§L97)

[1] Then the whole company of them arose, and brought him before Pilate. [2] And they began to accuse him, saying, "We found this man perverting our nation, and forbidding us to give tribute to Caesar, and saying that he himself is Christ a king." [3] And Pilate asked him, "Are you the King of the Jews?" And he answered him, "You have said so." [4] And Pilate said to the chief priests and the multitudes, "I find no crime in this man." [5] But they were urgent, saying, "He stirs up the people, teaching throughout all Judea, from Galilee even to this place."

[6] When Pilate heard this, he asked whether the man was a Galilean. [7] And when he learned that he belonged to Herod's jurisdiction, he sent him over to Herod, who was himself in Jerusalem at that time.

Luke 23:8–12 (§L98)

[8] When Herod saw Jesus, he was very glad, for he had long desired to see him, because he had heard about him, and he was hoping to see some sign done by him. [9] So he questioned him at some length; but he made no answer. [10] The chief priests and the scribes stood by, vehemently accusing him. [11] And Herod with his soldiers treated him with contempt and mocked him; then, arraying him in gorgeous apparel, he sent him back to Pilate. [12] And Herod and Pilate became friends with each other that very day, for before this they had been at enmity with each other.

PILATE FINDS JESUS INNOCENT

Luke 23:13–16 (§L99.1)

[13] Pilate then called together the chief priests and the rulers and the people, [14] and said to them, "You brought me this man as one who was perverting the people; and after examining him before you, behold, I did not find this man guilty of any of your charges against him; [15] neither did Herod, for he sent him back to us. Behold, nothing deserving death has been done by him; [16] I will therefore chastise him and release him."[a]

RELEASE OF BARABBAS; JESUS CONDEMNED

Luke 23:18–25 (§L99.2)

[18] But they all cried out together, "Away with this man, and release to us Barabbas"— [19] a man who had been thrown into prison for an insurrection started in the city, and for murder.[b] [20] Pilate addressed them once more, desiring to release Jesus; [21] but they shouted out, "Crucify, crucify him!" [22] A third time he said to them, "Why, what evil has he done? I have found in him no crime deserving death; I will therefore chastise him and release him." [23] But they were urgent, demanding with loud cries that he should be crucified. And their voices prevailed. [24] So Pilate gave sentence that their demand should be granted. [25] He released the man who had been thrown into prison for insurrection and murder, whom they asked for; but Jesus he delivered up to their will.

[a] Some witnesses add v. 17, *Now he was obliged to release one man to them at the festival* (see Matt 27:15, Mark 15:6): א W X Δ (Θ) (Ψ) *f*¹ *f*¹³ 28 *al;* omit v. 17: 𝔓⁷⁵ A B K L T Π *al*

[b] Add v. 17 after v. 19: D it* (in part) syr (in part) eth

MATT

Matt 27:1–2 (§M84.1) ⇨ §L97

[1] When morning came, all the chief priests and the elders of the people took counsel against Jesus to put him to death; [2] and they bound him and led him away and delivered him to **Pilate** the governor.

Matt 27:11–14 (§M84.3) ⇨ §L97

[11] Now Jesus stood before the governor; and the governor asked him, "Are you the King of the Jews?" Jesus said, "You have said so." [12] But when he was accused by the chief priests and elders, he made no answer. [13] Then Pilate said to him, "Do you not hear how many things they testify against you?" [14] But he gave him no answer, not even to a single charge; so that the governor wondered greatly.

Matt 27:15–26 (§M84.4) ⇨ §L99.1–2

[15] Now at the feast the goveror was accustomed to release for the crowd any one prisoner whom they wanted. [16] And they had then a notorious prisoner, called Barabbas. [17] So when they had gathered, Pilate said to them, "Whom do you want me to release for you, Barabbas or Jesus who is called Christ?" [18] For he knew that it was out of envy that they had delivered him up. [19] Besides, while he was sitting on the judgment seat, his wife sent word to him, "Have nothing to do with that righteous man, for I have suffered much over him today in a dream." [20] Now the chief priests and the elders persuaded the people to ask for Barabbas and destroy Jesus. [21] The governor again said to them, "Which of the two do you want me to release for you?" And they said, "Barabbas." [22] Pilate said to them, "Then what shall I do with Jesus who is called Christ?" They all said, "Let him be crucified." [23] And he said, "Why, what evil has he done?" But they shouted all the more, "Let him be crucified."

[24] So when Pilate saw that he was gaining nothing, but rather that a riot was beginning, he took water and washed his hands before the crowd, saying, "I am innocent of this man's blood; see to it yourselves." [25] And all the people answered, "His blood be on us and on our children!" [26] Then he released for them Barabbas, and having scourged Jesus, delivered him to be crucified.

MARK

Mark 15:1–5 (§K65.1) ⇨ §L97

[1] And as soon as it was morning the chief priests, with the elders and scribes, and the whole council held a consultation; and they bound Jesus and led him away and delivered him to Pilate. [2] And Pilate asked him, "Are you the King of the Jews?" And he answered him, "You have said so." [3] And the chief priests accused him of many things. [4] And Pilate again asked him, "Have you no answer to make? See how many charges they bring against you." [5] But Jesus made no further answer, so that Pilate wondered.

Mark 15:6–15 (§K65.2) ⇨ §L99.1–2

[6] Now at the feast he used to release for them one prisoner for whom they asked. [7] And among the rebels in prison, who had committed murder in the insurrection, there was a man called Barabbas. [8] And the crowd came up and began to ask Pilate to do as he was wont to do for them. [9] And he answered them, "Do you want me to release for you the King of the Jews?" [10] For he perceived that it was out of envy that the chief priests had delivered him up. [11] But the chief priests stirred up the crowd to have him release for them Barabbas instead. [12] And Pilate again said to them, "Then what shall I do with the man whom you call the King of the Jews?" [13] And they cried out again, "Crucify him." [14] And Pilate said to them, "Why, what evil has he done?" But they shouted all the more, "Crucify him." [15] So Pilate, wishing to satisfy the crowd, released for them Barabbas; and having scourged Jesus, he delivered him to be crucified.

L97
L98
L99.1–2

TRIAL BEFORE PILATE
TRIAL BEFORE HEROD
TRIAL BEFORE PILATE RESUMED

Luke 23:1–7
Luke 23:8–12
Luke 23:13–25

JOHN

John 18:28–19:16 (§J33)

²⁸ **Then** they led Jesus from the house of Caiaphas to the praetorium. It was early. They themselves did not enter the praetorium, so that they might not be defiled, but might eat the passover. ²⁹ So **Pilate** went out to them and said, "What accusation do you bring against this man?" ³⁰ **They** answered him, "If **this man** were not an evildoer, we would not have handed him over." ³¹ Pilate said to them, "Take him yourselves and judge him by your own law." The Jews said to him, "Is it not lawful for us to put any man to death." ³² This was to fulfil the word which Jesus had spoken to show by what death he was to die.

³³ **Pilate** entered the praetorium again and called Jesus, and said to him, **"Are you the King of the Jews?"** ³⁴ Jesus **answered**, "Do **you** say this of your own accord, or did others say it to you about me?" ³⁵ Pilate answered, "Am I a Jew? Your own nation and the chief priests have handed you over to me; what have you done?" ³⁶ Jesus answered, "My kingship is not of this world; if my kingship were of this world, my servants would fight, that I might not be handed over to the Jews; but my kingship is not from the world." ³⁷ Pilate said to him, "So you are a king?" Jesus **answered**, **"You** say that I am a king. For this I was born, and for this I have come into the world, to bear witness to the truth. Every one who is of the truth hears my voice." ³⁸ Pilate said to him, "What is truth?"

After he had said this, he went out to the Jews again, and told them, **"I find no crime** in him. ³⁹ **But** you have a custom that I should release one man for you at the Passover; will you have me release for you the King of the Jews?" ⁴⁰ **They cried out** again, "Not **this man**, but **Barabbas!"** Now Barabbas was a robber.

19 ¹ **Then Pilate** took Jesus and scourged **him**. ² And the soldiers plaited a crown of thorns, and put it on his head, and arrayed him in a purple robe; ³ they came up to him, saying, "Hail, King of the Jews!" and struck him with their hands. ⁴ Pilate went out again, and said to them, "See, I am bringing him out to you, that you may know that I find no crime in him." ⁵ So Jesus came out, wearing the crown of thorns and the purple robe. **Pilate** said to **them,** "Behold the man!" ⁶ When the chief priests and the officers saw him, **they** cried **out,** **"Crucify** him, **crucify him!"** Pilate **said to them,** "Take him yourselves and crucify him, for **I find no crime in him."** ⁷ The Jews answered him. "We have a law, and by that law he ought to die, because he has made himself the Son of God." ⁸ When Pilate heard these words, he was the more afraid; ⁹ he entered the praetorium again and said to Jesus, "Where are you from?" **But** Jesus gave **no answer.** ¹⁰ Pilate therefore said to him, "You will not speak to me? Do you not know that I have power to release you, and power to crucify you?" ¹¹ Jesus answered him, "You would have no power over me unless it had been given you from above; therefore he who delivered me to you has the greater sin."

¹² Upon this Pilate sought to **release him,** but the Jews cried out, "If you release this man, you are not Caesar's friend; every one who makes himself a king sets himself against Caesar." ¹³ When Pilate heard these words, he brought Jesus out and sat down on the judgment seat at a place called The Pavement, and in Hebrew, Gabbatha. ¹⁴ Now it was the day of Preparation of the Passover; it was about the sixth hour. **He said to** the Jews, "Behold your King!" ¹⁵ **They** cried out, "Away with him, away with him, crucify him!" **Pilate** said to them, "Shall I crucify your King?" The chief priests answered, "We have no king but Caesar." ¹⁶ Then **he** handed him over **to** them to be crucified.

OTHER

AcPil 3:2 ⇨ §L97

² **And Pilate** entered the praetorium again and called Jesus apart and **asked him: "Are you the king of the Jews?"** Jesus **answered** Pilate: "Do **you** say this of your own accord, or did others say it to you about me?" **Pilate** answered Jesus: "Am I a Jew? Your own nation and the chief priests have handed you over to me. What have you done?" Jesus answered: "My kingship is not of this world; for if my kingship were of this world, my servants would fight, that I might not be handed over to the Jews. But now is my kingship not from here." **Pilate** said to **him:** "So you are a **king?"** Jesus **answered him: "You** say that I am a king. For this cause I was born and have come, that every one who is of the truth should hear my voice." **Pilate said** to him: "What is truth?" Jesus **answered him:** "Truth is from heaven." **Pilate said:** "Is there not truth upon earth?" Jesus said to Pilate: "You see how those who speak the truth are judged by those who have authority on earth."

AcPil 4:4–5 ⇨ §L99.1–2

⁴ **Pilate said to them:** "Take him yourselves and punish him as you wish." The Jews said to Pilate: "We wish him to be crucified." Pilate said: "He does not deserve to be crucified." ⁵ The governor looked at the multitude of Jews standing around, and when he saw many of the Jews weeping, he said: "Not all the multitude wishes him to die." But the elders of the Jews said: "For this purpose has the whole multitude of us come, that he should die." Pilate **said to** the Jews: **"Why** should he die?" The Jews said: "Because he called himself the Son of God and a king."

AcPil 9:4–5 ⇨ §L99.1–2

⁴ When **Pilate** heard these words, he was afraid. And he silenced the multitudes, because they were crying out, and said to them: "So this is he whom Herod sought?" The Jews replied: "Yes, this is he." And Pilate took water and washed his hands before the sun and said: "I am innocent of the blood of this righteous man. You see to it." Again the Jews **cried out:** "His blood be on us and on our children." ⁵ Then **Pilate** commanded the curtain to be drawn before the judgment-seat on which he sat, and said to Jesus: "Your nation has convicted you of claiming to be a king. Therefore I have decreed that you should first be scourged according to the law of the pious emperors, and then hanged on the cross in the garden where you were seized. And let Dysmas and Gestas, the two malefactors, be crucified with you."

Acts 3:13–15 ⇨ §L99.1–2

¹³ *"The God of Abraham and of Isaac and of Jacob, the God of our fathers, glorified his servant Jesus, whom you delivered up and denied in the presence of* **Pilate,** *when he had decided to* **release him.** ¹⁴ *But you denied the Holy and Righteous One, and asked for a murderer to be granted to you,* ¹⁵ *and killed the Author of life, whom God raised from the dead. To this we are witnesses."*

Acts 21:36 ⇨ Luke 23:18

³⁶ *for the mob of the people followed, crying,* "**Away with him!**"

This inscription was found during excavations in Jerusalem 1913–1914. The text may be translated: Theodotus, son of Vettenos the priest and *archisynagogos,* son of a *archisynagogos* and grandson of a *archisynagogos,* who built the synagogue for purposes of reciting the Law and studying the commandments, and the hostel, chambers and water installations to provide for the needs of itinerants from abroad, and whose father, with the elders and Simonidus, founded the synagogue. Source: *Ancient Synagogues Revealed,* edited by Lee I. Levine; Copyright © 1982 The Israel Exploration Society (Detroit: Wayne State University Press, 1982), 11.

LUKE

Luke 23:26–32 (§L100.1)

²⁶ And as they led him away, they seized one Simon of Cyrene, who was coming in from the country, and laid on him the cross, to carry it behind Jesus. ²⁷ And there followed him a great multitude of the people, and of women who bewailed and lamented him. ²⁸ But Jesus turning to them said, "Daughters of Jerusalem, do not weep for me, but weep for yourselves and for your children. ²⁹ For behold, the days are coming when they will say, 'Blessed are the barren, and the wombs that never bore, and the breasts that never gave suck!' ³⁰ Then they will begin to say to the mountains, 'Fall on us'; and to the hills, 'Cover us.' ³¹ For if they do this when the wood is green, what will happen when it is dry?"

³² Two others also, who were criminals, were led away to be put to death with him.

Luke 13:34–35 ⇨ Luke 23:27–31

³⁴ *"O Jerusalem, Jerusalem, killing the prophets and stoning those who are sent to you! How often would I have gathered your children together as a hen gathers her brood under her wings, and you would not!* ³⁵ *Behold, your house is forsaken. And I tell you, you will not see me until you say, 'Blessed is he who comes in the name of the Lord!'"*

Luke 19:41–44 (§L82.4) ⇨ Luke 23:27–31

⁴¹ *And when he drew near and saw the city he wept over it,* ⁴² *saying, "Would that even today you knew the things that make for peace! But now they are hid from your eyes.* ⁴³ *For the days shall come upon you, when your enemies will cast up a bank about you and surround you, and hem you in on every side,* ⁴⁴ *and dash you to the ground, you and your children within you, and they will not leave one stone upon another in you; because you did not know the time of your visitation."*

Luke 21:20–24 (§L91.2) ⇨ Luke 23:27–31

²⁰ *"But when you see Jerusalem surrounded by armies, then know that its desolation has come near.* ²¹ *Then let those who are in Judea flee to the mountains, and let those who are inside the city depart, and let not those who are out in the country enter it;* ²² *for these are days of vengeance, to fulfil all that is written.* ²³ *Alas for those who are with child and for those who give suck in those days! For great distress shall be upon the earth and wrath upon this people;* ²⁴ *they will fall by the edge of the sword, and be led captive among all nations; and Jerusalem will be trodden down by the Gentiles, until the times of the Gentiles are fulfilled."*

Hos 10:8 ⇨ Luke 23:30

⁸ The high places of Aven, the sin of Israel,
     shall be destroyed.
Thorn and thistle shall grow up
     on their altars;
and **they shall say to the mountains,**
     Cover us,
     and to the hills, **Fall** upon **us.**

JOHN

MATT

Matt 27:32 (§M85.2) ⇨ Luke 23:26

³² **As they** went out, **they** came upon a man **of Cyrene, Simon** by name; this man they compelled **to carry** his **cross.**

THOMAS

GThom 79 ⇨ Luke 23:29

(79) A woman from the crowd said to Him, **"Blessed are the** womb which **bore** You **and the breasts** which nourished You."

He said to her, **"Blessed are** those who have heard the word of the Father and have truly kept it. For there will be **days when** you **will say,** 'Blessed are the womb which has not conceived **and the breasts** which have not given milk.'"

MARK

Mark 15:21 (§K66.2) ⇨ Luke 23:26

²¹ And **they** compelled a passer-by, **Simon of Cyrene, who was coming in from the country,** the father of Alexander and Rufus, **to carry** his **cross.**

OTHER

LUKE	MATT	MARK

Luke 23:33–43 (§L100.2)

[33] And when they came to the place which is called The Skull, there they crucified him, and the criminals, one on the right and one on the left. [34] And Jesus said, "Father, forgive them; for they know not what they do."[a] And they cast lots to divide his garments. [35] And the people stood by, watching; but the rulers scoffed at him, saying, "He saved others; let him save himself, if he is the Christ of God, his Chosen One!" [36] The soldiers also mocked him, coming up and offering him vinegar, [37] and saying, "If you are the King of the Jews, save yourself!" [38] There was also an inscription over him,[b] "This is the King of the Jews."

[39] One of the criminals who were hanged railed at him, saying, "Are you not the Christ? Save yourself and us!" [40] But the other rebuked him, saying, "Do you not fear God, since you are under the same sentence of condemnation? [41] And we indeed justly; for we are receiving the due reward of our deeds; but this man has done nothing wrong." [42] And he said, "Jesus, remember me when you come into[c] your kingdom." [43] And he said to him, "Truly, I say to you, today you will be with me in Paradise."

[a] Some witnesses omit this sentence: 𝔓[75] (ℵ[a]) B D⋆ W Θ it (in part) syr[s] cop (in part); text: ℵ⋆,[c] (A) C D[b] (K) L X Δ Π Ψ f[1] (f[13]) 28 33 pm

[b] Some witnesses add *in letters of Greek and Latin and Hebrew* (see John 19:20): ℵ⋆,[b] A C[3] D K W Δ Θ Π X Ψ f[1] f[13] 28 33 al; text 𝔓[75] ℵ[a] B L pc

[c] Some witnesses read *in:* ℵ A C K W X Δ Θ Π Ψ f[1] f[13] 28 33 al; text: 𝔓[75] B L it (in part) pc

Luke 22:29–30 ⇨ Luke 23:42–43

[29] *"and I assign to you, as my Father assigned to me, a* **kingdom**, [30] *that you may eat and drink at my table in my* **kingdom**, *and sit on thrones judging the twelve tribes of Israel."*

Ps 22:18 ⇨ Luke 23:34b

[18] **they divide** my **garments** among them, and for my raiment **they cast lots**.

Ps 22:7 ⇨ Luke 23:35

[7] All who see me mock **at me**, they make mouths **at me**, they wag their heads; . . .

Ps 69:21 ⇨ Luke 23:36

[21] They gave me poison for food, and for my thirst they gave me **vinegar** to drink.

Matt 27:33–44 (§M85.3)

[33] **And when they came to a place called** Golgotha (which means the place of a **skull**), [34] they offered **him** wine to drink, mingled with gall; but when he tasted it, he would not drink it. [35] And when **they** had **crucified him, they** divided **his garments** among them by casting **lots**; [36] then they sat down and kept watch over him there. [37] And **over** his head they put the charge against him, which read, "This is Jesus **the King of the Jews.**" [38] Then two robbers were crucified with him, **one on the right and one on the left.** [39] **And** those who passed by derided him, wagging their heads [40] and saying, "You who would destroy the temple and build it in three days, **save yourself! If you are the** Son **of God**, come down from the cross." [41] So also the chief priests, with the scribes and elders, mocked **him, saying,** [42] "**He saved others**; he cannot **save himself. He is the** King of Israel; let him come down now from the cross, and we will believe in him. [43] He trusts in **God**; let **God** deliver him now, if he desires him; for he said, 'I am **the** Son **of God.**'" [44] And **the robbers who were** crucified with **him** also reviled him in the same way.

Matt 27:47–48 ⇨ Luke 23:36

[47] And some of the bystanders hearing it said, "This man is calling Elijah." [48] And one of them at once ran and took a sponge, filled it with **vinegar**, and put it on a reed, **and** gave it to **him** to drink.

Mark 15:22–32 (§K66.3)

[22] **And they** brought him **to the place called** Golgotha (which means the place of a **skull**). [23] And they offered **him** wine mingled with myrrh; but he did not take it. [24] And **they crucified him, and** divided **his garments** among them, casting lots for them, to decide what each should take. [25] And it was the third hour, when **they crucified him.** [26] And the **inscription** of the charge against **him** read, "**The King of the Jews.**" [27] **And** with him they crucified two robbers, **one on** his **right and one on** his **left.** [29] **And** those who passed by derided him, wagging their heads, and **saying,** "Aha! You who would destroy the temple and build it in three days, [30] **save yourself,** and come down from the cross!" [31] So also **the** chief priests mocked him to one another with the scribes, **saying, "He saved others**; he cannot **save himself.** [32] Let **the Christ, the King of** Israel, come down now from the cross, that we may see and believe." Those **who were** crucified with him also reviled **him.**

Mark 15:35–36 ⇨ Luke 23:36

[35] And some of the bystanders hearing it said, "Behold, he is calling Elijah." [36] And one ran and, filling a sponge full of **vinegar**, put it on a reed **and** gave it to **him** to drink, saying, "Wait, let us see whether Elijah will come to take him down."

JOHN   THOMAS   OTHER

John 19:17–24 (§J34)

17 So **they** took Jesus, and he went out, bearing his own cross, to **the place called** the place of a **skull**, which is called in Hebrew Golgotha. 18 **There they crucified him, and** with him two others, **one on** either side, **and Jesus** between them. 19 Pilate **also** wrote a title and put it on the cross; it read, "Jesus of Nazareth, **the King of the Jews.**" 20 Many of the Jews read this title, for the place where Jesus was crucified was near the city; and it was written in Hebrew, in Latin, and in Greek. 21 The chief priests of the Jews then said to Pilate, "Do not write, '**The King of the Jews**,' but 'This man said, I am **King of the Jews.**'" 22 Pilate answered, "What I have written I have written."

23 When **the soldiers** had crucified Jesus **they** took **his garments** and made four parts, one for each soldier; also his tunic. But the tunic was without seam, woven from top to bottom; 24 so they said to one another, "Let us not tear it, but **cast lots** for it **to** see whose it shall be." This was to fulfil the scripture,

"**They** parted my **garments** among them,
and for my clothing **they cast lots.**"

John 19:28–30 ⇨ Luke 23:36

28 After this Jesus, knowing that all was not finished, said (to fulfil the scripture), "I thirst." 29 A bowl full of **vinegar** stood there; so they put a sponge full of the **vinegar** on hyssop and held it to his mouth. 30 When Jesus had received the **vinegar**, he said, "It is finished"; and he bowed his head and gave up his spirit.

GPet 4.10–14

10 **And they** brought two malefactors and **crucified** the Lord in the midst between them. But he held his peace, as if he felt no pain. 11 And when they had set up the cross, they wrote upon it: **this is the King of** Israel. 12 **And they** laid down **his garments** before him and divided them among themselves and **cast** the lot upon them. 13 But **one of the** malefactors **rebuked** them, **saying,** "**We** have landed in suffering for the deeds of wickedness which **we** have committed, **but this man**, who **has** become the saviour of men, what wrong has he done you?" 14 And they were wroth with him and commanded that his legs should not be broken, so that he might die in torments.

AcPil 10:1–2

1 And Jesus went out from the praetorium, and the two malefactors with him. **And when they came to the place,** they stripped him and girded him with a linen cloth and put a crown of thorns on his head. Likewise they hanged up also the two malefactors. But **Jesus said: "Father, forgive them, for they know not what they do." And** the soldiers parted **his garments** among them. **And the people stood** looking at him. **And the** chief priests and **rulers** with them **scoffed at him, saying: "He saved others, let him save himself. If he is the Son of** God, let him come down from the cross." And **the soldiers also mocked him, coming and offering him vinegar** with gall, **and** they said: "**If you are the king of the Jews, save yourself."** And Pilate after the sentence commanded the crime brought against him to be written as a title in Greek, Latin and Hebrew, according to the accusation of the Jews that he was **king of the Jews.**

2 **One of the** malefactors **who were** crucified said to **him:** "If **you are the Christ, save yourself and us."** But Dysmas answering **rebuked him: "Do you not at all fear God, since you are in the same condemnation? And we indeed justly. For we are receiving the due reward of our deeds. But this man has done nothing wrong." And he said** to Jesus: "Lord, **remember me** in **your kingdom." And** Jesus **said to him: "Truly, I say to you, today you will be with me in paradise."**

GPet 5.16 ⇨ Luke 23:36

16 And one of them said, "Give **him** to drink gall with **vinegar**." And they mixed it **and** gave **him** to drink.

GNaz 24 ⇨ Luke 23:34a

(24) As it is said in the Gospel of the Nazaraeans:

At this word of the Lord many thousands of the Jews who were standing round the cross became believers. (Haimo of Auxerre, *Comm. on Is.* [on 53:2])

GNaz 35 ⇨ Luke 23:34a

(35) [Father, forgive them, for they know not what they do.] Note that in the Gospel of the Nazaraeans we have to read that at this virtuous discourse of Christ eight thousand were later converted to the faith; namely three thousand on the day of Pentecost as stated in the Acts of the Apostles ii, and subsequently five thousand about whom we are informed in the Acts of the Apostles x [?]. ("Historia passionis Domini," MS: Theolog. Sammelhandschrift saec. XIV–XV, foll. 8–71 [saec. XIV] cited by Hennecke in *New Testament Apocrypha,* p. 153)

Acts 7:60 ⇨ Luke 23:34

60 **And** he knelt down and cried with a loud voice, "Lord, **do not hold this sin against them."** And when he had said this, he fell asleep.

LUKE	MATT	MARK

LUKE

Luke 23:44–49 (§L100.3)

44 It was now about the sixth hour, and there was darkness over the whole land[a] until the ninth hour, **45** while the sun's light failed;[b] and the curtain of the temple was torn in two. **46** Then Jesus, crying with a loud voice, said, "Father, into thy hands I commit my spirit!" And having said this he breathed his last. **47** Now when the centurion saw what had taken place, he praised God, and said, "Certainly this man was innocent!" **48** And all the multitudes who assembled to see the sight, when they saw what had taken place, returned home beating their breasts. **49** And all his acquaintances and the women who had followed him from Galilee stood at a distance and saw these things.

[a] Or *earth*

[b] Or *the sun was eclipsed*

Luke 8:2–3 ⇨ Luke 23:49
2 *and also some women who had been healed of evil spirits and infirmities: Mary, called Magdalene, from whom seven demons had gone out,* **3** *and Joanna, the wife of Chuza, Herod's steward, and Susanna, and many others, who provided for them out of their means.*

Luke 23:55 ⇨ Luke 23:49
55 *The women who had come with him from Galilee followed, and saw the tomb, and how his body was laid; . . .*

Ps 31:5 ⇨ Luke 23:46
5 *Into thy* hand **I commit my spirit;**
     thou hast redeemed me, O Lord, faithful God.

Ps 38:11 ⇨ Luke 23:49
11 My friends **and** companions stand aloof from my
     plague,
     and my kinsmen stand afar off.

MATT

Matt 27:45–56 (§M85.4)

45 Now from **the sixth hour there was darkness over** all **the land until the ninth hour**. **46** And about the ninth hour Jesus cried with a loud voice, "Eli, Eli, lama sabachthani?" that is, "My God, my God, why hast thou forsaken me?" **47** And some of the bystanders hearing it said, "This man is calling Elijah." **48** And one of them at once ran and took a sponge, filled it with vinegar, and put it on a reed, and gave it to him to drink. **49** But the others said, "Wait, let us see whether Elijah will come to save him." **50** And **Jesus** cried again **with a loud voice** and yielded up his spirit.

51 And behold, **the curtain of the temple was torn in two**, from top to bottom; and the earth shook, and the rocks were split; **52** the tombs also were opened, and many bodies of the saints who had fallen asleep were raised, **53** and coming out of the tombs after his resurrection they went into the holy city and appeared to many. **54** **When the centurion** and those who were with him, keeping watch over Jesus, **saw** the earthquake and **what** took **place**, they were filled with awe, **and said**, "Truly **this** was the Son of God!"

55 There were also many **women** there, looking on from afar, **who had followed** Jesus **from Galilee**, ministering to him; **56** among whom were Mary Magdalene, and Mary the mother of James and Joseph, and the mother of the sons of Zebedee.

MARK

Mark 15:33–41 (§K66.4)

33 And when **the sixth hour** had come, **there was darkness over the whole land until the ninth hour**. **34** And at the ninth hour **Jesus** cried **with a loud voice**, "Eloi, Eloi, lama sabachthani?" which means, "My God, my God, why hast thou forsaken me?" **35** And some of the bystanders hearing it said, "Behold, he is calling Elijah." **36** And one ran and, filling a sponge full of vinegar, put it on a reed and gave it to him to drink, saying, "Wait, let us see whether Elijah will come to take him down." **37** And **Jesus** uttered **a loud** cry, and **breathed his last**. **38** And **the curtain of the temple was torn in two**, from top to bottom. **39** And **when the centurion**, who stood facing him, **saw** that he thus breathed his last, he **said**, "Truly **this man was** the Son of God!"

40 There were also **women** looking on from afar, among whom were Mary Magdalene, and Mary the mother of James the younger and of Joses, and Salome, **41** who, when he was in **Galilee**, **followed him**, and ministered to him; and also many other **women who** came up with **him** to Jerusalem.

JOHN	THOMAS	OTHER

JOHN

John 19:25–37 (§J35)

²⁵ So the soldiers did this. But standing by the cross of Jesus were his mother, and his mother's sister, Mary the wife of Clopas, and Mary Magdalene. ²⁶ When Jesus saw his mother, and the disciple whom he loved standing near, he said to his mother, "Woman, behold, your son!" ²⁷ Then he said to the disciple, "Behold, your mother!" And from that hour the disciple took her to his own home.

²⁸ After this Jesus, knowing that all was now finished, said (to fulfil the scripture), "I thirst." ²⁹ A bowl full of vinegar stood there; so they put a sponge full of the vinegar on hyssop and held it to his mouth. ³⁰ When **Jesus** had received the vinegar, he **said**, "It is finished"; **and he** bowed **his** head and gave up his spirit.

³¹ Since it was the day of Preparation, in order to prevent the bodies from remaining on the cross on the sabbath (for that sabbath was a high day), the Jews asked Pilate that their legs might be broken, and that they might be taken away. ³² So the soldiers came and broke the legs of the first, and of the other who had been crucified with him; ³³ but when they came to Jesus and saw that he was already dead, they did not break his legs. ³⁴ But one of the soldeirs pierced his side with a spear, and at once there came out blood and water. ³⁵ He who saw it has borne witness—his testimony is true, and he knows that he tells the truth—that you also may believe. ³⁶ For these things took place that the scripture might be fulfilled, "Not a bone of him shall be broken." ³⁷ And again another scripture says, "They shall look on him whom they have pierced."

OTHER

GPet 5.15–20

¹⁵ Now it was midday and a darkness covered all Judaea. And they became anxious and uneasy lest the sun had already set, since he was still alive. <For> it stands written for them: the sun should not set on one that has been put to death. ¹⁶ And one of them said, "Give him to drink gall with vinegar." And they mixed it and gave him to drink. ¹⁷ And they fulfilled all things and completed the measure of their sins on their head. ¹⁸ And many went about with lamps, <and> as they supposed that it was night, they went to bed (or: they stumbled). ¹⁹ And the Lord called out and cried, "My power, O power, thou hast forsaken me!" And having said this he was taken up. ²⁰ And at the same hour the veil of the temple in Jerusalem was rent in two.

AcPil 11:1–3a

¹ And **it was** about **the sixth hour, and there was darkness over the land until the ninth hour,** for the sun was darkened. **And the curtain of the temple was torn in two.** And **Jesus** cried **with a loud voice: "Father,** baddach ephkid rouel," which means: **"Into thy hands I commit my spirit." And having said this he** gave up the ghost. And **when the centurion saw what had** happened, **he praised God,** saying: **"This man was** righteous." **And all the multitudes who** had come **to** this **sight, when they saw what had taken place,** beat **their breasts** and **returned.**

² But **the centurion** reported to the governor what had happened. And when the governor and his wife heard, they were greatly grieved, and they neither ate nor drank on that day. And Pilate sent for the Jews and said to them: "Did you see what happened?" But they answered: "There was an eclipse of the sun in the usual way." ³ **And his acquaintances** had **stood** far off **and the women who had** come with **him from Galilee, and saw these things.** But a certain man named Joseph, a member of the council, from the town of Arimathaea, who also was waiting for the kingdom of God, this man went to Pilate and asked for the body of Jesus. And he took it down, and wrapped it in a clean linen cloth, and placed it in a rock-hewn tomb, in which no one had ever yet been laid.

GNaz 36 ⇨ Luke 23:45

*(36) Also in the Gospel of the Nazaraeans we read that at the time of Christ's death **the lintel of the temple,** of immense size, had split (Josephus says the same and adds that overhead awful voices were heard which said: Let us depart from this abode).* ("Historia passionis Domini," MS: Theolog. Sammelhandschrift saec. XIV–XV, foll. 8–71 [saec. XIV] cited by Hennecke in *New Testament Apocrypha,* p. 153)

Acts 7:59 ⇨ Luke 23:46

*⁵⁹ And as they were stoning Stephen, he prayed, "Lord **Jesus** receive **my spirit.**"*

GPet 7.25 ⇨ Luke 23:48

*²⁵ Then **the** Jews and the elders and the priests perceiving what great evil **they** had done to themselves, began to lament and to say, "Woe on our sins, the judgment and the end of Jerusalem is drawn nigh."*

LUKE

Luke 23:50–56 (§L101)

[50] Now there was a man named Joseph from the Jewish town of Arimathea. He was a member of the council, a good and righteous man, [51] who had not consented to their purpose and deed, and he was looking for the kingdom of God. [52] This man went to Pilate and asked for the body of Jesus. [53] Then he took it down and wrapped it in a linen shroud, and laid him in a rock-hewn tomb, where no one had ever yet been laid. [54] It was the day of Preparation, and the sabbath was beginning.[a] [55] The women who had come with him from Galilee followed, and saw the tomb, and how his body was laid; [56] then they returned, and prepared spices and ointments.

On the sabbath they rested according to the commandment.

[a] Greek: *was dawning*

Luke 8:2–3 ⇨ Luke 23:55

[2] *and also some women who had been healed of evil spirits and infirmities: Mary, called Magdalene, from whom seven demons had gone out,* [3] *and Joanna, the wife of Chuza, Herod's steward, and Susanna, and many others, who provided for them out of their means.*

Luke 23:49 ⇨ Luke 23:55

[49] *And all his acquaintances and the women who had followed him from Galilee stood at a distance and saw these things.*

Deut 21:22–23

[22] "And if a man has committed a crime punishable by death and he is put to death, and you hang him on a tree, [23] his **body** shall not remain all night upon the tree, but you shall bury him the same day, for a hanged man is accursed by God; you shall not defile your land which the Lord your God gives you for an inheritance."

Josh 10:18 ⇨ Luke 23:53

[18] And Joshua said, "Roll great stones against the mouth of the cave, and set men by it to guard them"; . . .

Josh 10:27 ⇨ Luke 23:53

[27] but at the time of the going down of the sun, Joshua commanded, and they **took** them **down** from the trees, **and** threw them into the cave where they had hidden themselves, and they set great stones against the mouth of the cave, which remain to this very day.

JOHN

John 19:38–42 (§J36)

[38] After this **Joseph of Arimathea**, who **was a** disciple of Jesus, but secretly, for fear of the Jews, **asked Pilate** that he might take away **the body of Jesus**, and Pilate gave him leave. So **he** came and **took** away his body. [39] Nicodemus also, who had at first come to him by night, came bringing a mixture of myrrh and aloes, about a hundred pounds' weight. [40] They **took** the body of Jesus, **and** bound **it in linen** cloths with the spices, as is the burial custom of the Jews. [41] Now in the place where he was crucified there was a garden, and in the garden a new **tomb where no one had ever been laid.** [42] So because of **the** Jewish **day of Preparation**, as the **tomb** was close at hand, they **laid** Jesus there.

MATT

Matt 27:57–61 (§M86)

[57] When it was evening, **there** came **a** rich **man from Arimathea, named Joseph**, who also **was a** disciple of Jesus. [58] He went to Pilate and asked for the **body of Jesus**. Then Pilate ordered it to be given to him. [59] And Joseph **took** the body, **and wrapped it in** a clean **linen shroud,** [60] **and laid** it **in** his own new **tomb**, which he had hewn in the rock; and he rolled a great stone to the door of the tomb, and departed. [61] Mary Magdalene and the other Mary were there, sitting opposite the sepulchre.

Exod 20:8–10 ⇨ Luke 23:56b

[8] "Remember **the sabbath** day, to keep it holy. [9] Six days you shall labor and do all your work; [10] but the seventh day is a **sabbath** to the Lord your God; in it you shall not do any work, you, or your son, or your daughter, your manservant, or your maidservant, or your cattle, or the sojourner who is within your gates"; . . .

⇨ Luke 23:56
Cf. Exod 12:16, Deut 5:12–14

THOMAS

.

MARK

Mark 15:42–47 (§K67)

[42] And when evening had come, since **it was the day of Preparation**, that is, the day before **the sabbath**, [43] Joseph of Arimathea, a respected **member of the council**, who was also himself looking for the kingdom of God, took courage and **went to Pilate, and asked for the body of Jesus.** [44] And Pilate wondered if he were already dead; and summoning the centurion, asked him whether he was already dead. [45] And when he learned from the centurion that he was dead, he granted **the body** to Joseph. [46] And **he** bought a **linen shroud,** and taking him **down, wrapped** him **in the linen shroud, and laid him in a tomb** which had been hewn out of the rock; and he rolled a stone against the door of the **tomb.** [47] Mary Magdalene and Mary the mother of Joses **saw** where he was laid.

OTHER

GPet 2.3–5a

[3] Now there stood there **Joseph**, the friend of Pilate and of the Lord, and knowing that they were about to crucify him he came **to Pilate and** begged **the body of** the Lord for burial. [4] And Pilate sent to Herod and begged his body. [5] And Herod said, "Brother Pilate, even if no one had begged him, we should bury him, since **the Sabbath** is drawing on. For it stands written in the law: the sun should not set on one that has been put to death."

GPet 6.21–24

[21] And then the Jews drew the nails from the hands of the Lord and laid him on the earth. And the whole earth shook and there came a great fear. [22] Then the sun shone <again>, and it was found to be the ninth hour. [23] And the Jews rejoiced and gave **the body** to **Joseph** that he might bury it, since he had seen all the good that he (Jesus) had done. [24] And **he took** the Lord, washed him, **wrapped** him **in linen and** brought **him** into his own sepulchre, called Joseph's Garden.

AcPil 11:3b

But **a** certain **man named Joseph, a member of the council, from the town of Arimathaea**, who also **was** waiting **for the kingdom of God**, this man went to Pilate **and asked for the body of Jesus. And he took it down, and wrapped it in a** clean **linen** cloth, **and** placed it **in a rock-hewn tomb**, in which **no one had ever yet been laid.**

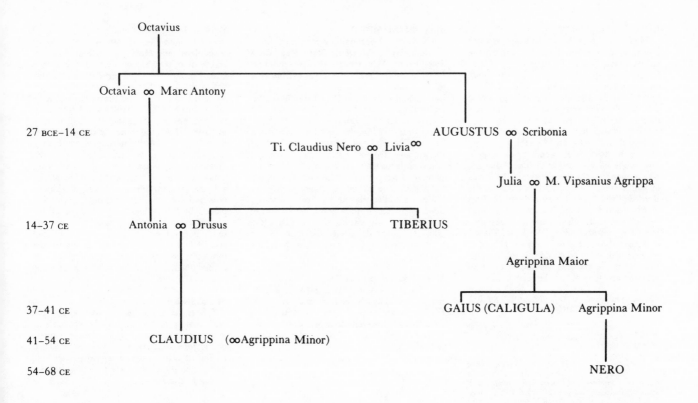

Source: Koester 1: 309

LUKE	MATT	MARK

Luke 24:1-11 (§L102) °

¹But on the first day of the week, at early dawn, they went to the tomb, taking the spices which they had prepared. ²And they found the stone rolled away from the tomb, ³but when they went in they did not find the body.ᵃ ⁴While they were perplexed about this, behold, two men stood by them in dazzling apparel; ⁵and as they were frightened and bowed their faces to the ground, the men said to them, "Why do you seek the living among the dead?ᵇ ⁶Remember how he told you, while he was still in Galilee, ⁷that the Son of man must be delivered into the hands of sinful men, and be crucified, and on the third day rise." ⁸And they remembered his words, ⁹and returning from the tomb they told all this to the eleven and to all the rest. ¹⁰Now it was Mary Magdalene and Joanna and Mary the mother of James and the other women with them who told this to the apostles; ¹¹but these words seemed to them an idle tale, and they did not believe them.ᶜ

ᵃSome witnesses add *of the Lord Jesus*: 𝔓⁷⁵ ℵ A B C W Θ f¹ f¹³ 33 *al*; text: D it (in part)

ᵇSome witnesses add *He is not here, but has risen*: 𝔓⁷⁵ ℵ A B C³ K L (W) X Δ Θ Π Ψ f¹ f¹³ 28 33 *pm*; text: D it (in part)

ᶜSome witnesses add v. 12, *But Peter rose and ran to the tomb; stooping and looking in, he saw the linen cloths by themselves; and he went home wondering at what had happened* (see John 20:3, 5, 6, 10): 𝔓⁷⁵ ℵ A B K L W X Δ Θ Π Ψ f¹ f¹³ 28 33 *pm*; text: D it (in part) syr (in part)

°Appendix 2 ⇨ Luke 24:9

Luke 9:22 ⇨ Luke 24:6-8

²²saying, *"The Son of man must suffer many things, and be rejected by the elders and chief priests and scribes, and be killed, and on the third day be raised."*

Luke 9:44 ⇨ Luke 24:6-8

⁴⁴*"Let these words sink into your ears; for the Son of man is to be delivered into the hands of men."*

Luke 17:25 ⇨ Luke 24:6-8

²⁵*"But first he must suffer many things and be rejected by this generation."*

Luke 18:31-33 ⇨ Luke 24:6-8

³¹*And taking the twelve, he said to them, "Behold, we are going up to Jerusalem, and everything that is written of the Son of man by the prophets will be accomplished. ³²For he will be delivered to the Gentiles, and will be mocked and shamefully treated and spit upon; ³³they will scourge him and kill him, and on the third day he will rise."*

Matt 28:1-8 (§M88.1)

¹Now after the sabbath, toward the dawn of **the first day of the week**, **Mary Magdalene** and the other **Mary went to see the** sepulchre. ²And behold, there was a great earthquake; for an angel of the Lord descended from heaven and came and **rolled** back **the stone**, and sat upon it. ³His appearance was like lightning, and his raiment white as snow. ⁴And for fear of him the guards trembled and became like dead men. ⁵But the angel **said to** the women, **"Do** not be afraid; for I know that **you seek** Jesus who was **crucified**. ⁶He is not here; for he has risen, as **he** said. Come, see the place where he lay. ⁷Then go quickly and tell his disciples that he has risen from the dead, and behold, he is going before you to Galilee; there you will see him. Lo, I have told you." ⁸So they departed quickly from the tomb with fear and great joy, and ran **to** tell his disciples.

Matt 27:55-56 ⇨ Luke 24:10

⁵⁵*There were also many **women** there, looking on from afar, who had followed Jesus from Galilee, ministering to him; ⁵⁶among whom were **Mary Magdalene, and Mary the mother of James** and Joseph, **and** the mother of the sons of Zebedee.*

Luke 22:22 ⇨ Luke 24:6-8

²²*"For **the Son of man** goes as it has been determined; but woe to that man by whom he is betrayed!"*

Luke 24:26 ⇨ Luke 24:6-8

²⁶*"Was it not necessary **that the Christ should** suffer these things and enter **into his glory?"***

Luke 24:46 ⇨ Luke 24:6-8

⁴⁶*and said to them, "Thus it is written, **that the Christ should suffer and on the third day rise** from the dead, . . ."*

Luke 8:1-3 (§L30) ⇨ Luke 24:10

¹*Soon afterward he went on through cities and villages, preaching and bringing the good news of the kingdom of God. And the twelve were with him, ²and also some **women** who had been healed of evil spirits and infirmities: **Mary**, called **Magdalene**, from whom seven demons had gone out, ³**and Joanna**, the wife of Chuza, Herod's steward, **and Susanna**, and many others, who provided for them out of their means.*

Mark 16:1-8 (§K68)

¹And when the sabbath was past, **Mary Magdalene, and Mary the mother of James**, and Salome, bought **spices**, so that they might go and anoint him. ²And very **early on the first day of the week they went to the tomb** when the sun had risen. ³And they were saying to one another, "Who will roll away the stone for us from the door of the tomb?" ⁴And looking up, **they** saw that **the stone** was **rolled** back—it was very large. ⁵And entering the tomb, they saw a young man sitting on the right side, dressed in a white robe; **and they were** amazed. ⁶And he **said to them**, "Do not be amazed; **you seek** Jesus of Nazareth, who was **crucified**. He has risen, he is not here; see the place where they laid him. ⁷But go, tell his disciples and Peter that he is going before you to Galilee; there you will see him, as he told you." ⁸And **they** went out and fled from the tomb; for trembling and astonishment had come upon them; and they said nothing **to** any one, for they were afraid.

Mark 15:40-41 ⇨ Luke 24:10

⁴⁰*There were also **women** looking on from afar, among whom were **Mary Magdalene, and Mary the mother of James** the younger and of Joses, **and Salome**, ⁴¹who, when he was in Galilee, followed him, and ministered to him; and also many **other women** who came up **with** him to Jerusalem.*

Luke 23:49 ⇨ Luke 24:10

⁴⁹*And all his acquaintances **and the women** who had followed him from Galilee stood at a distance and saw these things.*

Luke 23:55 ⇨ Luke 24:10

⁵⁵*The **women** who had come with him from Galilee followed, and saw the tomb, and how his body was laid; . . .*

JOHN

OTHER

John 20:1–18 (§J37)

[1] Now **on the first day of the week Mary Magdalene** came **to the tomb early**, while it was still dark, and saw that **the stone** had been taken **away from the tomb**. [2] So she ran, and went to Simon Peter and the other disciple, the one whom Jesus loved, and said to them, "They have taken the Lord out of **the tomb**, and we do not know where they have laid him." [3] Peter then came out with the other disciple, and **they went** toward **the tomb**. [4] They both ran, but the other disciple outran Peter and reached **the tomb** first; [5] and stooping to look **in**, he saw the linen cloths lying there, but he did not go **in**. [6] Then Simon Peter came, following him, and **went** into **the tomb**; he saw the linen cloths lying, [7] and the napkin, which had been on his head, not lying with the linen cloths but rolled up in a place by itself. [8] Then the other disciple, who reached **the tomb** first, also **went in**, and he saw and believed; [9] for as yet they did not know the scripture, that he must **rise** from the dead. [10] Then the disciples went back to their homes.

[11] But Mary stood weeping outside **the tomb**, and as she wept she stooped to look into the tomb; [12] and she saw **two** angels **in** white, sitting where the body of Jesus had lain, one at the head and one at the feet. [13] They **said to** her, "Woman, **why** are **you** weeping?" She said to them, "Because they have taken away my Lord, and I do not know where they have laid him." [14] Saying this, she turned round and saw Jesus standing, but she did not know that it was Jesus. [15] Jesus **said to** her, "Woman, **why** are **you** weeping? Whom **do you seek**?" Supposing him to be the gardener, she said to him, "Sir, if you have carried him away, tell me where you have laid him, and I will take him away." [16] Jesus **said to** her, "Mary." She turned and said to him in Hebrew, "Rabboni!" (which means Teacher). [17] Jesus **said to** her, "Do not hold me, for I have not yet ascended to the Father; but go to my brethren and say to them, I am ascending to my Father and your Father, to my God and your God." [18] **Mary Magdalene** went and said **to the** disciples, "I have seen the Lord"; and she **told** them that he had said these things to her.

GPet 9.35–13.57

[35] Now in the night in which the Lord's day dawned, when the soldiers, two by two in every watch, were keeping guard, there rang out a loud voice in heaven, [36] and they saw the heavens opened and **two men** come down from there in a great brightness and draw nigh to **the** sepulchre. [37] That **stone** which had been laid against the entrance to **the** sepulchre started of itself to roll and gave way to the side, and **the** sepulchre was opened, and both the young **men** entered in.

10 [38] When now those soldiers saw this, they awakened the centurion and the elders— for they also were there to assist at the watch. [39] And whilst they were relating what they had seen, they saw again three **men** come out from **the** sepulchre, and two of them sustaining the other, and a cross following them, [40] and the heads of the two reaching to heaven, but that of him who was led of them by the hand overpassing the heavens. [41] And they heard a voice out of the heavens crying, "Thou has preached to them that sleep," [42] and from the cross there was heard the answer, "Yea."

11 [43] Those men therefore took counsel with one another to go and report this to Pilate. [44] And whilst they were still deliberating, the heavens were again seen to open, and a man descended and entered into **the** sepulchre. [45] When those who were of the centurion's company saw this, they hastened by night to Pilate, abandoning **the** sepulchre which they were guarding, and reported everything that they had seen, being full of disquietude and saying, "In truth he was the Son of God." [46] Pilate answered and said, "I am clean from the blood of the Son of God, upon such a thing have you decided." [47] Then all came to him, beseeching him and urgently calling upon him to command the centurion and the soldiers to tell no one what they had seen. [48] "For it is better for us," they said, "to make ourselves guilty of the greatest sin before God than to fall into the hands of the people of the Jews and be stoned." [49] Pilate therefore commanded the centurion and the soldiers to say nothing.

12 [50] **Early** in the morning of the Lord's day **Mary Magdalene**, a woman disciple of the Lord— for fear of the Jews, since [they] were inflamed with wrath, she had not done at **the** sepulchre of the Lord what women are wont to do for those beloved of them who die—took [51] with her her **women** friends and came **to the** sepulchre where he was laid. [52] And they feared lest the Jews should see them, and said, "Although we could not weep and lament on that day when he was crucified, yet let us now do so at his sepulchre. [53] But who will roll **away** for us **the stone** also that is set on the entrance to **the** sepulchre, that we may go in and sit beside him and do what is due?— [54] For **the stone** was great,— and we fear lest any one see us. And if we cannot do so, let us at least put down at the entrance what we bring for a memorial of him and let us weep and lament until we have again gone home."

13 [55] So **they** went and **found the** sepulchre opened. And **they** came near, stooped down and saw there a young man sitting in the midst of **the** sepulchre, comely and clothed with a brightly shining robe, who **said to them**, [56] "Wherefore are ye come? Whom seek ye? Not him that was **crucified**? he is risen and gone. But if ye believe not, stoop this way and see the place where he lay, for he is **not** here. For he is risen and is gone thither whence he was sent." [57] Then **the women** fled affrighted.

AcPil 13:1–3

[1] And while they still sat in the synagogue and marvelled because of Joseph, there came some of the guard which the Jews had asked from Pilate to guard **the tomb** of Jesus, lest his disciples should come and steal him. And they told the rulers of the synagogue and the priests and the Levites what had happened: how there was a great earthquake. "And we saw an angel descend from heaven, and he **rolled away the stone from the** mouth of **the** cave, and sat upon it, and he shone like snow and like lightning. **And we were** in great fear, and lay like dead men. And we heard the voice of the angel speaking to **the women** who waited at the tomb: Do not be afraid. I know that **you seek** Jesus who was crucified. He is not here. He has risen, as he said. Come and see the place where the Lord lay. And go quickly and tell his disciples that he has risen from the dead and is in Galilee."

[2] The Jews asked: "To what **women** did he speak?" The members of the guard answered: "We do not know who they were." The Jews said: "At what hour was it?" The members of the guard answered: "At midnight." The Jews said: "And why did you not seize **the women**?" The members of the guard said: "We **were** like dead men through fear, and gave up hope of seeing the light of day; how could we then have seized them?" The Jews said: "As the Lord lives, we do not believe you." The members of the guard said to the Jews: "So many signs you saw in that man and you did not believe; and how can you believe us? You rightly swore: As the Lord lives. For he does live." Again the members of the guard said: "We have heard that you shut him up who asked for the body of Jesus, and sealed the door, and that when you opened it you did not find him. Therefore give us Joseph and we will give you Jesus." The Jews said: "Joseph has gone to his own city." And the members of the guard said to the Jews: "And Jesus has risen, as we heard from the angel, and is in Galilee." [3] And when the Jews heard these words, they feared greatly and said: "(Take heed) lest this report be heard and all incline to Jesus." And the Jews took counsel, and offered much money and gave it to the soldiers of the guard, saying: "Say that when you were sleeping his disciples came by night and stole him. And if this is heard by the governor, we will persuade him and keep you out of trouble."

The copper *as* depicts the emperor Antoninus Pius (138–161 CE). The obverse reads ANTONINVS AVG PIVS P P. The reverse records his titles, TR POT COS III. The coin shown here depicts Mars, holding a spear and shield, descending through the air to the sleeping Rhea Silvia, a vestal virgin of royal lineage who, through this nocturnal violation, became the mother of Romulus and Remus.

The gold *aureus* depicts Faustina Junior, the wife of the Roman emperor Marcus Aurelius (161–180 CE). The reverse features the great mother goddess Cybele (MATRI MAGNAE) seated on a throne flanked by two sacred lions. Goddess of nature and mistress of wild beasts, her cult festival involved ecstatic dancing and self-emasculation. Phrygian in origin, she was introduced at Rome in 204 BCE to aid in Hannibal's defeat. The conservative Romans did not easily adjust to her cult. Roman citizens were forbidden to participate in her services on the Palatine, and she did not become an acceptable subject for Roman coinage until the 2nd century CE.

The silver *shekel* depicts the facade of the Temple at Jerusalem with the Ark of the Covenant in its interior. The name Simon appears in Hebrew characters. The coin was struck over a "pagan" tetradrachm during the Second Jewish Revolt against Rome (132–135 CE). Led by Simon bar Kochba, this nationalistic movement included in its programs the reconstruction of the Jewish Temple destroyed by Titus during the First Revolt in 70 CE. The reverse depicts the lulav, a bundle of myrtle, palm, and willow branches, and an etrog or citron fruit, both used in the Temple ritual. The inscription translates "Year Two of the Freedom of Israel."

Photographs and descriptions courtesy of Numismatics Fine Arts, Inc., Los Angeles, and the Institute for Antiquity and Christianity, Claremont, CA.

LUKE   MATT   MARK

Luke 24:13–27 (§L103.1)

[13] That very day two of them were going to a village named Emmaus, about seven miles[a] from Jerusalem, [14] and talking with each other about all these things that had happened. [15] While they were talking and discussing together, Jesus himself drew near and went with them. [16] But their eyes were kept from recognizing him. [17] And he said to them, "What is this conversation which you are holding with each other as you walk?" And they stood still, looking sad. [18] Then one of them, named Cleopas, answered him, "Are you the only visitor to Jerusalem who does not know the things that have happened there in these days?" [19] And he said to him, "What things?" And they said to him, "Concerning Jesus of Nazareth, who was a prophet mighty in deed and word before God and all the people, [20] and how our chief priests and rulers delivered him up to be condemned to death, and crucified him. [21] But we had hoped that he was the one to redeem Israel. Yes, and besides all this, it is now the third day since this happened. [22] Moreover, some women of our company amazed us. They were at the tomb early in the morning [23] and did not find his body; and they came back saying that they had even seen a vision of angels, who said that he was alive. [24] Some of those who were with us went to the tomb, and found it just as the women had said; but him they did not see." [25] And he said to them, "O foolish men, and slow of heart to believe all that the prophets have spoken! [26] Was it not necessary that the Christ should suffer these things and enter into his glory?" [27] And beginning with Moses and all the prophets, he interpreted to them in all the scriptures the things concerning himself.

[a] Greek: *sixty stadia;* some witnesses read *a hundred and sixty stadia:* ℵ K⋆ Θ Π *pc*

Luke 7:16 ⇨ Luke 24:19
[16] *Fear seized them all; and they glorified **God**, saying, "A great **prophet** has arisen among us!" and "**God** has visited his **people!**"*

Luke 1:68 ⇨ Luke 24:21
[68] *"Blessed be the Lord God of **Israel**, for he has visited and redeemed his people, . . ."*

Luke 2:38 ⇨ Luke 24:21
[38] *coming up at that very hour she gave thanks to God, and spoke of him to all who were looking for the redemption of Jerusalem.*

Luke 9:45 ⇨ Luke 24:25–27
[45] *But they did not understand this saying, and it was concealed from them, that they should not perceive it; and they were afraid to ask him about this saying.*

Luke 18:34 ⇨ Luke 24:25–27
[34] *But they understood none of these **things**; this saying was hid from **them**, and they did not grasp what was said.*

Luke 24:44–45 ⇨ Luke 24:25–27
[44] *Then he said to them, "These are my words which I spoke to you, while I was still with you, that everything written about me in the law of **Moses and the prophets** and the psalms must be fulfilled." [45] Then **he** opened their minds to understand **the scriptures,** . . .*

Luke 9:22 ⇨ Luke 24:26
[22] *saying, "**The Son of man must suffer** many **things, and** be rejected by the elders and chief priests and scribes, **and** be killed, **and** on the third day be raised."*

Luke 9:44 ⇨ Luke 24:26
[44] *"Let these words sink into your ears; for **the** Son of man is to be delivered into the hands of men."*

Luke 17:25 ⇨ Luke 24:26
[25] *"But first he must **suffer** many **things and** be rejected by this generation."*

Luke 18:31–33 ⇨ Luke 24:26
[31] *And taking the twelve, he said to them, "Behold, we are going up to Jerusalem, and everything that is written of **the** Son of man by the prophets will be accomplished. [32] For he will be delivered to the Gentiles, **and** will be mocked **and** shamefully treated **and** spit upon; [33] they will scourge him **and** kill him, **and** on the thrid day he will rise."*

Luke 22:22 ⇨ Luke 24:26
[22] *"For the Son of man goes as it has been determined; but woe to that man by whom he is betrayed!"*

Luke 24:6–8 ⇨ Luke 24:26
[6] *"Remember how he told you, while he was still in Galilee, [7] that the Son of man must be delivered into the hands of sinful men, **and** be crucified, **and** on the thrid day rise." [8] And they remembered his words,* . . .

Luke 24:46 ⇨ Luke 24:26
[46] *and said to them, "Thus it is written, **that the Christ should suffer and** on the third day rise from the dead, . . ."*

JOHN   THOMAS   OTHER

Luke 24:28–33a
Luke 24:33b–49

IN EMMAUS
IN JERUSALEM

L103.2
L103.3a–c

LUKE	MATT	MARK

LUKE

Luke 24:28–33a (§L103.2)

²⁸ So they drew near to the village to which they were going. He appeared to be going further, ²⁹ but they constrained him, saying, "Stay with us, for it is toward evening and the day is now far spent." So he went in to stay with them. ³⁰ When he was at table with them, he took the bread and blessed, and broke it, and gave it to them. ³¹ And their eyes were opened and they recognized him; and he vanished out of their sight. ³² They said to each other, "Did not our hearts burn within us[a] while he talked to us on the road, while he opened to us the scriptures?" ³³ And they rose that same hour and returned to Jerusalem; . . .

THE TWO REPORT TO THE ELEVEN

Luke 24:33b–35 (§L103.3a) °

. . .and they found the eleven gathered together and those who were with them, ³⁴ who said, "The Lord has risen indeed, and has appeared to Simon!" ³⁵ Then they told what had happened on the road, and how he was known to them in the breaking of the bread.

JESUS APPEARS

Luke 24:36–43 (§L103.3b)

³⁶ As they were saying this, Jesus himself stood among them.[b] ³⁷ But they were startled and frightened, and supposed that they saw a spirit. ³⁸ And he said to them, "Why are you troubled, and why do questionings rise in your hearts? ³⁹ See my hands and my feet, that it is I myself; handle me, and see; for a spirit has not flesh and bones as you see that I have."[c] ⁴¹ And while they still disbelieved for joy, and wondered, he said to them, "Have you anything here to eat?" ⁴² They gave him a piece of broiled fish, ⁴³ and he took it and ate before them.

JESUS INSTRUCTS THE DISCIPLES

Luke 24:44–49 (§L103.3c)

⁴⁴ Then he said to them, "These are my words which I spoke to you, while I was still with you, that everything written about me in the law of Moses and the prophets and the psalms must be fulfilled." ⁴⁵ Then he opened their minds to understand the scriptures, ⁴⁶ and said to them, "Thus it is written, that the Christ should suffer and on the third day rise from the dead, ⁴⁷ and that repentance and forgiveness of sins should be preached in his name to all nations,[d] beginning from Jerusalem. ⁴⁸ You are witnesses of these things. ⁴⁹ And behold, I send the promise of my Father upon you; but stay in the city, until you are clothed with power from on high."

MATT

[a] Some witnesses omit *within us:* 𝔓⁷⁵ B D *pc;* text: ℵ (A)(K) L P W X Δ Θ Π Ψ *f¹ f¹³* 28 33 *pm*

[b] Some witnesses add *and said to them, "Peace to you!"* (see John 20:19, 26): 𝔓⁷⁵ ℵ A B K L X Δ Θ Π Ψ *f¹ f¹³* (28) 33 *al;* text: D it (in part)

[c] Some witnesses add v. 40, *And when he had said this, he showed them his hands and his feet* (see John 20:20): 𝔓⁷⁵ ℵ A B K L W X Δ Θ Π Ψ *f¹ f¹³* 28 33 *al;* omit: D it (in part) syr (in part)

[d] Or *nations. Beginning from Jerusalem you are witnesses*

° Appendix 2 ⇨ Luke 24:33b

Luke 9:45 ⇨ Luke 24:44–45
⁴⁵ *But they did not understand this saying, and it was concealed from them, that they should not perceive it; and they were afraid to ask him about this saying.*

Luke 18:34 ⇨ Luke 24:44–45
³⁴ *But they understood none of these things; this saying was hid from them, and they did not grasp what was said.*

Luke 24:25–27 ⇨ Luke 24:44–45
²⁵ *And he said to them, "O foolish men, and slow of heart to believe all that the prophets have spoken! ²⁶ Was it not necessary that the Christ should suffer these things and enter into his glory?" ²⁷ And beginning with Moses and all the prophets, he interpreted to them in all the scriptures the things concerning himself.*

Luke 9:22 ⇨ Luke 24:46
²² *saying, "The Son of man must suffer many things, and be rejected by the elders and chief priests and scribes, and be killed, and on the third day be raised."*

MARK

Luke 9:44 ⇨ Luke 24:46
⁴⁴ *"Let these words sink into your ears; for the Son of man is to be delivered into the hands of men."*

Luke 17:25 ⇨ Luke 24:46
²⁵ *"But first he must suffer many things and be rejected by this generation."*

Luke 18:31–33 ⇨ Luke 24:46
³¹ *And taking the twelve, he said to them, "Behold, we are going up to Jerusalem, and everything that is written of the Son of man by the prophets will be accomplished. ³² For he will be delivered to the Gentiles, and will be mocked and shamefully treated and spit upon; ³³ they will scourge him and kill him, and on the third day he will rise."*

Luke 22:22 ⇨ Luke 24:46
²² *"For the Son of man goes as it has been determined; but woe to that man by whom he is betrayed!"*

Luke 24:6–8 ⇨ Luke 24:46
⁶ *"Remember how he told you, while he was still in Galilee, ⁷ that the Son of man must be delivered into the hands of sinful men, and be crucified, and on the third day rise." ⁸ And they remembered his words, . . .*

Luke 24:26 ⇨ Luke 24:46
²⁶ *"Was it not neccessary that the Christ should suffer these things and enter into his glory?"*

Hos 6:2 ⇨ Luke 24:46
² *After two days he will revive us;*
on the third day he will raise us up,
that we may live before him.

460
Luke 24:13–49
Luke 24:1–53

EMMAUS AND JERUSALEM
RESURRECTION AND DEPARTURE

L103
S28: L102–104

L103.2
L103.3a–c

IN EMMAUS
IN JERUSALEM

Luke 24:28–33a
Luke 24:33b–49

JOHN

THOMAS

OTHER

John 20:19–23 (§J37.2a) ⇨ §L103.3

[19] On the evening of that day, the first day of the week, the doors being shut where the disciples were, for fear of the Jews, **Jesus** came and **stood among them and said to them**, "Peace be with **you**." [20] When he had said this, he showed them his **hands** and his side. Then the disciples were glad when they **saw** the Lord. [21] Jesus **said to them** again, "Peace be with you. As the Father has sent me, even so I send you." [22] And when he had said this, he breathed on them, and said to them, "Receive the Holy Spirit. [23] If you forgive the sins of any, they are forgiven; if you retain the sins of any, they are retained."

John 20:24–29 (§J37.2b) ⇨ §L103.3

[24] Now Thomas, one of the twelve, called the Twin, was not with them when Jesus came. [25] So the other disciples told him, "We have seen the Lord." But he said to them, "Unless I see in his hands the print of the nails, and place my finger in the mark of the nails, and place my hand in his side, I will not believe."

[26] Eight days later, his disciples were again in the house, and Thomas was with them. The doors were shut, but **Jesus** came and **stood among them, and said**, "Peace be with **you**." [27] Then he said to Thomas, "Put your finger here, and **see my hands**; and put out your hand, and place it in my side; do not be faithless, but believing." [28] Thomas answered him, "My Lord and my God!" [29] Jesus **said to** him, "Have you believed because you have seen me? Blessed are those who have not seen and yet believe."

GHeb 7 ⇨ §L103.2

(7) The Gospel called according to the Hebrews which was recently translated by me into Greek and Latin, which Origen frequently uses, records after the resurrection of the Savior:

And when the Lord had given the linen cloth to the servant of the priest, he went to James and appeared to him. For James had sworn that he would not eat **bread** *from that hour in which he had drunk the cup of the Lord until he should see him risen from among them that sleep. And shortly thereafter the Lord said: Bring a* **table** *and* **bread!** *And immediately it is added:* **he took the bread, blessed it and brake it and gave it to James the Just and said to him: My brother, eat thy bread,** *for the Son of man is risen from among them that sleep.* (Jerome, *De viris inlustribus 2*)

AcPil 14:1 ⇨ §L103.3c

[1] Now Phineës a priest and Adas a teacher and Angaeus a Levite came from Galilee to Jerusalem, and told the rulers of the synagogue and the priests and the Levites: "We saw Jesus and his disciples sitting upon the mountain which is called Mamilch. And **he said to** his disciples: Go into all the world and preach the gospel **to** the whole creation. He who believes and is baptized will be saved; but he who does not believe will be condemned. And these signs will accompany those who believe: in my name will they cast out demons; they will speak in new tongues; they will pick up serpents; and if they drink any deadly thing, it will not hurt them; they will lay their hands on the sick and they will recover. And while Jesus was still speaking to his disciples, we saw him taken up into heaven."

Ign. *Smyr.* 3.2 ⇨ Luke 24:39

And when he came to those with Peter he said to them: "Take, **handle me and see that I am not a** *phantom without a body." And they immediately touched him and believed, being mingled both with his* **flesh and spirit.** *Therefore they despised even death, and were proved to be above death.*

Acts 1:4–8 ⇨ Luke 24:47–49

[4] **And** *while staying with them he charged them not to depart* **from Jerusalem,** *but to wait for* **the promise of the Father,** *which, he said, "you heard from me,* [5] *for John baptized with water, but before many days you shall be baptized with the Holy Spirit."*

[6] *So when they had come together, they asked him, "Lord, will you at this time restore the kingdom to Israel?"* [7] *He said to them, "It is not for you to know times or seasons which the* **Father** *has fixed by his own authority.* [8] *But you shall receive* **power** *when the Holy Spirit has come upon* **you;** *and* **you** *shall be my* **witnesses in Jerusalem** *and in* **all** *Judea and Samaria and to the end of the earth."*

L103
S28: L102–104

EMMAUS AND JERUSALEM
RESURRECTION AND DEPARTURE

Luke 24:13–49
Luke 24:1–53

461

| LUKE | MATT | MARK |

Luke 24:50–53 (§L104)

⁵⁰ Then he led them out as far as Bethany, and lifting up his hands he blessed them. ⁵¹ While he blessed them, he parted from them, and was carried up into heaven.ᵃ ⁵² and theyᵇ returned to Jerusalem with great joy, ⁵³ and were continually in the temple blessing God.

ᵃ Some witnesses omit *and was carried up into heaven:* ℵ* D it (in part) (syrˢ) *pc*

ᵇ Some witnesses insert *worshiped him, and:* 𝔓⁷⁵ ℵ A B C K L W X Δ Θ Π Ψ ƒ¹ ƒ¹³ 28 33 *al;* text: D it (in part) syrˢ

| JOHN | THOMAS | OTHER |

AcPil 14:1

¹ Now Phineës a priest and Adas a teacher and Angaeus a Levite came from Galilee to Jerusalem, and told the rulers of the synagogue and the priests and the Levites: "We saw Jesus and his disciples sitting upon the mountain which is called Mamilch. And he said to his disciples: Go into all the world and preach the gospel to the whole creation. He who believes and is baptized will be saved; but he who does not believe will be condemned. And these signs will accompany those who believe: in my name will they cast out demons; they will speak in new tongues; they will pick up serpents; and if they drink any deadly thing, it will not hurt them; they will lay their hands on the sick and they will recover. And **while** Jesus was still speaking to his disciples, we saw him taken **up into heaven**."

Acts 1:9–12

⁹ *And when **he** had said this, as they were look-ing on, **he** was lifted up, **and** a cloud took him out of their sight.* ¹⁰ *And while they were gazing **into heaven** as he went, behold, two men stood by them in white robes,* ¹¹ *and said, "Men of Galilee, why do you stand looking **into heaven?** This Jesus, who was taken up **from** you **into heaven,** will come in the same way as you saw him go **into heaven.***"

¹² *Then **they** returned to **J**erusalem from the mount called **J**livet, which is near **J**eru-salem, a sabbath day's journey away; . . .*

LUKE	JOHN	OTHER

PROLOGUE

John 1:6–8, 15

⁶There was a man sent from God, whose name was John. ⁷He came for testimony, to bear witness to the light, that all might believe through him. ⁸He was not the light, but came to bear witness to the light.

¹⁵(John bore witness to him and cried, "This was he of whom I said, 'He who comes after me ranks before me, for he was before me.'")

THE PREDICTION OF JOHN'S BIRTH

Luke 1:5–25 (§L2.1)

⁵In the days of Herod, king of Judea, there was a priest named Zechariah, of the division of Abijah; and he had a wife of the daughters of Aaron, and her name was Elizabeth. ⁶And they were both righteous before God, walking in all the commandments and ordinances of the Lord blameless. ⁷But they had no child, because Elizabeth was barren, and both were advanced in years.

⁸Now while he was serving as priest before God when his division was on duty, ⁹according to the custom of the priesthood, it fell to him by lot to enter the temple of the Lord and burn incense. ¹⁰And the whole multitude of the people were praying outside at the hour of incense. ¹¹And there appeared to him an angel of the Lord standing on the right side of the altar of incense. ¹²And Zechariah was troubled when he saw him, and fear fell upon him. ¹³But the angel said to him, "Do not be afraid, Zechariah, for your prayer is heard, and your wife Elizabeth will bear you a son, and you shall call his name John.

¹⁴And you will have joy and gladness,
and many will rejoice at his birth;
¹⁵for he will be great before the Lord,
and he shall drink no wine nor strong drink,
and he will be filled with the Holy Spirit,
even from his mother's womb.
¹⁶And he will turn many of the sons of Israel to the Lord their
　　God,
¹⁷and he will go before him in the spirit and power of Elijah,
to turn the hearts of the fathers to the children,
and the disobedient to the wisdom of the just,
to make ready for the Lord a people prepared."

¹⁸And Zechariah said to the angel, "How shall I know this? For I am an old man, and my wife is advanced in years." ¹⁹And the angel answered him, "I am Gabriel, who stand in the presence of God; and I was sent to speak to you, and to bring you this good news. ²⁰And behold, you will be silent and unable to speak until the day that these things come to pass, because you did not believe my words, which will be fulfilled in their time." ²¹And the people were waiting for Zechariah, and they wondered at his delay in the temple. ²²And when he came out, he could not speak to them, and they perceived that he had seen a vision in the temple; and he made signs to them and remained dumb. ²³And when his time of service was ended, he went to his home.

LUKE	JOHN	OTHER

LUKE

[24] After these days his wife Elizabeth conceived, and for five months she hid herself, saying, [25] "Thus the Lord has done to me in the days when he looked on me, to take away my reproach among men."

THE ANNUCIATION TO MARY

Luke 1:26–38 (§L2.2)

[26] In the sixth month the angel Gabriel was sent from God to a city of Galilee named Nazareth, [27] to a virgin betrothed to a man whose name was Joseph, of the house of David; and the virgin's name was Mary. [28] And he came to her and said, "Hail, O favored one, the Lord is with you!" [29] But she was greatly troubled at the saying, and considered in her mind what sort of greeting this might be. [30] And the angel said to her, "Do not be afraid, Mary, for you have found favor with God. [31] And behold, you will conceive in your womb and bear a son, and you shall call his name Jesus.

[32] He will be great, and will be called the Son of the Most High;
and the Lord God will give to him the throne of his father David,
[33] and he will reign over the house of Jacob for ever;
and of his kingdom there will be no end."

[34] And Mary said to the angel, "How shall this be, since I have no husband?" [35] And the angel said to her,

"The Holy Spirit will come upon you,
and the power of the Most High will overshadow you;
therefore the child to be born will be called holy,
the Son of God.

[36] And behold, your kinswoman Elizabeth in her old age has also conceived a son; and this is the sixth month with her who was called barren. [37] For with God nothing will be impossible." [38] And Mary said, "Behold, I am the handmaid of the Lord; let it be to me according to your word." And the angel departed from her.

MARY'S VISIT TO ELIZABETH

Luke 1:39–56 (§L2.3)

[39] In those days Mary arose and went with haste into the hill country, to a city of Judah, [40] and she entered the house of Zechariah and greeted Elizabeth. [41] And when Elizabeth heard the greeting of Mary, the babe leaped in her womb; and Elizabeth was filled with the Holy Spirit [42] and she exclaimed with a loud cry, "Blessed are you among women, and blessed is the fruit of your womb! [43] And why is this granted me, that the mother of my Lord should come to me? [44] For behold, when the voice of your greeting came to my ears, the babe in my womb leaped for joy. [45] And blessed is she who believed that there would be a fulfilment of what was spoken to her from the Lord." [46] And Mary said,

"My soul magnifies the Lord,
[47] and my spirit rejoices in God my Savior,
[48] for he has regarded the low estate of his handmaiden.
For behold, henceforth all generations will call me blessed;
[49] for he who is mighty has done great things for me,
and holy is his name.
[50] And his mercy is on those who fear him
from generation to generation.
[51] He has shown strength with his arm,
he has scattered the proud in the imagination of their hearts,
[52] he has put down the mighty from their thrones,
and exalted those of low degree;

MARY'S VISIT TO ELIZABETH

PJas 12:1–3

[1] And she made (ready) the purple and the scarlet and brought (them) to the priest. And the priest took (them), and blessed (Mary) and said: "Mary, the Lord God has magnified your name, and you shall be blessed among all generations of the earth." [2] And Mary rejoiced, and went to Elizabeth her kinswoman, and knocked on the door. When Elizabeth heard it, she put down the scarlet, and ran to the door and opened it, [and when she saw Mary], she blessed her and said: "Whence is this to me, that the mother of my Lord should come to me? For behold, that which is in me leaped and blessed thee." But Mary forgot the mysteries which the [arch]angel Gabriel had told her, and raised a sigh towards heaven and said: "Who am I, Lord, that all the women [generations] of the earth count me blessed?" [3] And she remained three months with Elizabeth. Day by day her womb grew, and Mary was afraid and went into her house and hid herself from the children of Israel. And Mary was sixteen years old when all these mysterious things happened.

LUKE	JOHN	OTHER

LUKE

[53] he has filled the hungry with good things,
and the rich he has sent empty away.
[54] He has helped his servant Israel,
in remembrance of his mercy,
[55] as he spoke to our fathers,
to Abraham and to his posterity for ever."
[56] And Mary remained with her about three months, and returned to her home.

THE BIRTH AND CHILDHOOD OF JOHN

Luke 1:57–80 (§L3)

[57] Now the time came for Elizabeth to be delivered, and she gave birth to a son. [58] And her neighbors and kinsfolk heard that the Lord had shown great mercy to her, and they rejoiced with her. [59] And on the eighth day they came to circumcise the child; and they would have named him Zechariah after his father, [60] but his mother said, "Not so, he shall be called John." [61] And they said to her, "None of your kindred is called by this name." [62] And they made signs to his father, inquiring what he would have him called. [63] And he asked for a writing tablet, and wrote, "His name is John." And they all marveled. [64] And immediately his mouth was opened and his tongue loosed, and he spoke, blessing God. [65] And fear came on all their neighbors. And all these things were talked about through all the hill country of Judea; [66] and all who heard them laid them up in their hearts, saying, "What then will this child be?" For the hand of the Lord was with him.

[67] And his father Zechariah was filled with the Holy Spirit, and prophesied, saying,

[68] "Blessed be the Lord God of Israel,
for he has visited and redeemed his people,
[69] and has raised up a horn of salvation for us
in the house of his servant David,
[70] as he spoke by the mouth of his holy prophets from of old,
[71] that we should be saved from our enemies,
and from the hand of all who hate us;
[72] to perform the mercy promised to our fathers,
and to remember his holy covenant,
[73] the oath which he swore to our father Abraham, [74] to grant
us
that we, being delivered from the hand of our enemies,
might serve him without fear,
[75] in holiness and righteousness before him all the days of our
life.
[76] And you, child, will be called the prophet of the Most High;
for you will go before the Lord to prepare his ways,
[77] to give knowledge of salvation to his people
in the forgiveness of their sins,
[78] through the tender mercy of our God,
when the day shall dawn upon us from on high
[79] to give light to those who sit in darkness and in the shadow of
death,
to guide our feet into the way of peace."
[80] And the child grew and became strong in spirit, and he was in the wilderness till the day of his manifestation to Israel.

OTHER

ELIZABETH HIDES JOHN

PJas 22:3

[3] But Elizabeth, when she heard that John was sought for, took him and went up into the hill-country. And she looked around (to see) where she could hide him, and there was no hiding-place. And Elizabeth groaned aloud and said: "O mountain of God, receive me, a mother, with my child." For Elizabeth could not go up (further) for fear. And immediately the mountain was rent asunder and received her. And that mountain made a light to gleam for her; for an angel of the Lord was with them and protected them.

ZACHARIAS IS SLAIN

PJas 23:1–24:4

[1] Now Herod was searching for John, and sent officers to Zacharias at the altar to ask him: "Where have you hidden your son?" And he answered and said to them: "I am a minister of God and attend continually upon his temple. How should I know where my son is?" [2] And the officers departed and told all this to Herod. Then Herod was angry and said, "Is his son to be king over Israel?" And he sent the officers to him again with the command: "Tell the truth. Where is your son? You know that your blood is under my hand." And the officers departed and told him all this. [3] And Zacharias said: "I am a martyr of God. Take my blood! But my spirit the Lord will receive, for you shed innocent blood in the forecourt of the temple of the Lord." And about the dawning of the day Zacharias was slain. And the children of Israel did not know that he had been slain.

[24] [1] Rather, at the hour of the salutation the priests were departing, but the blessing of Zacharias did not meet them according to custom. And the priests stood waiting for Zacharias, to greet him with prayer and to glorify the Most High. [2] But when he delayed to come, they were all afraid. But one of them took courage and went into the sanctuary. And he saw beside the altar congealed blood; and a voice said: "Zacharias has been slain, and his blood shall not be wiped away until his avenger comes." And when he heard these words, he was afraid, and went out and told the priests what he had seen. [3] And they heard and saw what had happened. And the panel-work of the ceiling of the temple wailed, and they rent their clothes from the top to the bottom. And they did not find his body, but they found his blood turned into stone. And they were afraid, and went out and told all the people: "Zacharias has been slain." And all the tribes of the people heard it and mourned him and lamented three days and three nights. [4] And after the three days the priests took counsel whom they should appoint in his stead. And the lot fell upon Symeon. Now it was he to whom it had been revealed by the Holy Spirit that he should not see death until he had seen the Christ in the flesh.

MATT

APPEARANCE OF JOHN THE BAPTIST

Matt 3:1–12 (§M5)

[1] In those days came John the Baptist, preaching in the wilderness of Judea, [2] "Repent, for the kingdom of heaven is at hand." [3] For this is he who was spoken of by the prophet Isaiah when he said,

"The voice of one crying in the wilderness:
Prepare the way of the Lord,
make his paths straight."

[4] Now John wore a garment of camel's hair, and a leather girdle around his waist; and his food was locusts and wild honey. [5] Then went out to him Jerusalem and all Judea and all the region about the Jordan, [6] and they were baptized by him in the river Jordan, confessing their sins.

[7] But when he saw many of the Pharisees and Sadducees coming for baptism, he said to them, "You brood of vipers! Who warned you to flee from the wrath to come? [8] Bear fruit that befits repentance, [9] and do not presume to say to yourselves, 'We have Abraham as our father'; for I tell you, God is able from these stones to raise up children to Abraham. [10] Even now the axe is laid to the root of the trees; every tree therefore that does not bear good fruit is cut down and thrown into the fire.

[11] "I baptize you with water for repentance, but he who is coming after me is mightier than I, whose sandals I am not worthy to carry; he will baptize you with the Holy Spirit and with fire. [12] His winnowing fork is in his hand, and he will clear his threshing floor and gather his wheat into the granary, but the chaff he will burn with unquenchable fire."

BAPTISM OF JESUS

Matt 3:13–17 (§M6)

[13] Then Jesus came from Galilee to the Jordan to John, to be baptized by him. [14] John would have prevented him, saying, "I need to be baptized by you, and do you come to me?" [15] But Jesus answered him, "Let it be so now; for thus it is fitting for us to fulfil all righteousness." Then he consented. [16] And when Jesus was baptized, he went up immediately from the water, and behold, the heavens were opened and he saw the Spirit of God descending like a dove, and alighting on him; [17] and lo, a voice from heaven, saying, "This is my beloved Son, with whom I am well pleased."

MARK

APPEARANCE OF JOHN THE BAPTIST

Mark 1:2–8 (§K2)

[2] As it is written in Isaiah the prophet,
"Behold, I send my messenger before thy face,
who shall prepare thy way;
[3] the voice of one crying in the wilderness:
Prepare the way of the Lord,
make his paths straight—"

[4] John the baptizer appeared in the wilderness, preaching a baptism of repentance for the forgiveness of sins. [5] And there went out to him all the country of Judea, and all the people of Jerusalem; and they were baptized by him in the river Jordan, confessing their sins. [6] Now John was clothed in camel's hair, and had a leather girdle around his waist, and ate locusts and wild honey. [7] And he preached, saying, "After me comes he who is mightier than I, the thong of whose sandals I am not worthy to stoop down and untie. [8] I have baptized you with water; but he will baptize you with the Holy Spirit."

BAPTISM OF JESUS

Mark 1:9–11 (§K3)

[9] In those days Jesus came from Nazareth of Galilee and was baptized by John in the Jordan. [10] And when he came up out of the water, immediately he saw the heavens opened and the Spirit descending upon him like a dove; [11] and a voice came from heaven, "Thou art my beloved Son; with thee I am well pleased."

LUKE

APPEARANCE OF JOHN THE BAPTIST

Luke 3:1–20 (§L7)

[1] In the fifteenth year of the reign of Tiberius Caesar, Pontius Pilate being governor of Judea, and Herod being tetrarch of Galilee, and his brother Philip tetrarch of the region of Ituraea and Trachonitis, and Lysanias tetrarch of Abilene, [2] in the high-priesthood of Annas and Caiaphas, the word of God came to John the son of Zechariah in the wilderness; [3] and he went into all the region about the Jordan, preaching a baptism of repentance for the forgiveness of sins. [4] As it is written in the book of the words of Isaiah the prophet,

"The voice of one crying in the wilderness:
Prepare the way of the Lord,
make his paths straight.
[5] Every valley shall be filled,
and every mountain and hill shall be brought low,
and the crooked shall be made straight,
and the rough ways shall be made smooth;
[6] and all flesh shall see the salvation of God."

[7] He said therefore to the multitudes that came out to be baptized by him, "You brood of vipers! Who warned you to flee from the wrath to come? [8] Bear fruits that befit repentance, and do not begin to say to yourselves, 'We have Abraham as our father'; for I tell you, God is able from these stones to raise up children to Abraham. [9] Even now the axe is laid to the root of the trees; every tree therefore that does not bear good fruit is cut down and thrown into the fire."

[10] And the multitudes asked him, "What then shall we do?" [11] And he answered them, "He who has two coats, let him share with him who has none; and he who has food, let him do likewise." [12] Tax collectors also came to be baptized, and said to him, "Teacher, what shall we do?" [13] And he said to them, "Collect no more than is appointed you." [14] Soldiers also asked him, "And we, what shall we do?" And he said to them, "Rob no one by violence or by false accusation, and be content with your wages."

[15] As the people were in expectation, and all men questioned in their hearts concerning John, whether perhaps he were the Christ, [16] John answered them all, "I baptize you with water; but he who is mightier than I is coming, the thong of whose sandals I am not worthy to untie; he will baptize you with the Holy Spirit and with fire. [17] His winnowing fork is in his hand, to clear his threshing floor, and to gather the wheat into his granary, but the chaff he will burn with unquenchable fire."

[18] So, with many other exhortations, he preached good news to the people. [19] But Herod the tetrarch, who had been reproved by him for Herodias, his brother's wife, and for all the evil things that Herod had done, [20] added this to them all, that he shut up John in prison.

BAPTISM OF JESUS

Luke 3:21–22 (§L8)

[21] Now when all the people were baptized, and when Jesus also had been baptized and was praying, the heaven was opened, [22] and the Holy Spirit descended upon him in bodily form, as a dove, and a voice came from heaven, "Thou art my beloved Son; with thee I am well pleased."

John

John's Confession

John 1:19–28 (§J2.1)

¹⁹ And this is the testimony of John, when the Jews sent priests and Levites from Jerusalem to ask him, "Who are you?" ²⁰ He confessed, he did not deny, but confessed, "I am not the Christ." ²¹ And they asked him, "What then? Are you Elijah?" He said, "I am not." "Are you the prophet?" And he answered, "No." ²² They said to him then, "Who are you? Let us have an answer for those who sent us. What do you say about yourself?" ²³ He said, "I am the voice of one crying in the wilderness, 'Make straight the way of the Lord,' as the prophet Isaiah said."

²⁴ Now they had been sent from the Pharisees. ²⁵ They asked him, "Then why are you baptizing, if you are neither the Christ, nor Elijah, nor the prophet?" ²⁶ John answered them, "I baptize with water; but among you stands one whom you do not know, ²⁷ even he who comes after me, the thong of whose sandal I am not worthy to untie." ²⁸ This took place in Bethany beyond the Jordan, where John was baptizing.

John's Testimony

John 1:29–34 (§J2.2)

²⁹ The next day he saw Jesus coming toward him, and said, "Behold, the Lamb of God, who takes away the sin of the world! ³⁰ This is he of whom I said, 'After me comes a man who ranks before me, for he was before me.' ³¹ I myself did not know him; but for this I came baptizing with water, that he might be revealed to Israel." ³² And John bore witness, "I saw the Spirit descend as a dove from heaven, and it remained on him. ³³ I myself did not know him; but he who sent me to baptize with water said to me, 'He on whom you see the Spirit descend and remain, this is he who baptizes with the Holy Spirit.' ³⁴ And I have seen and have borne witness that this is the Son of God."

Thomas

Other

GEbi 2, 3, 4

(2) And:

It came to pass that John was baptizing; and there went out to him Pharisees and were baptized, and all Jerusalem. And John had a garment of camel's hair and a leathern girdle about his loins, and his food, as it saith, was wild honey, the taste of which was that of manna, as a cake dipped in oil.

Thus they were resolved to pervert the word of truth into a lie and to put a cake in the place of locusts. (Epiphanius, *Haer.* 30.13.4f.)

(3) And the beginning of their Gospel runs:

It came to pass in the days of Herod the king of Judaea, <when Caiaphas was high priest,> that there came <one>, John <by name,> and baptized with the baptism of repentance in the river Jordan. It was said of him that he was of the lineage of Aaron the priest, a son of Zacharias and Elisabeth; and all went out to him. (Epiphanius, *Haer.* 30.13.6)

(4) And after much has been recorded it proceeds:

When the people were baptized, Jesus also came and was baptized by John. And as he came up from the water, the heavens were opened and he saw the Holy Spirit in the form of a dove that descended and entered into him. And a voice (sounded) from heaven that said: Thou art my beloved Son, in thee I am well pleased. And again: I have this day begotten thee. And immediately a great light shone round about the place. When John saw this, it saith, he saith unto him: Who art thou, Lord? And again a voice from heaven (rang out) to him: This is my beloved Son in whom I am well pleased. And then, it saith, John fell down before him and said: I beseech thee, Lord, baptize thou me. But he prevented him and said: Suffer it; for thus it is fitting that everything should be fulfilled. (Epiphanius, *Haer.* 30.13.7f.)

GNaz 2

(2) Behold, the mother of the Lord and his brethren said to him: John the Baptist baptizes unto the remission of sins, let us go and be baptized by him. But he said to them: Wherein have I sinned that I should go and be baptized by him? Unless what I have said is ignorance (a sin of ignorance). (Jerome, *Adversus Pelagianos* 3.2)

GHeb 2

(2) According to the Gospel written in the Hebrew speech, which the Nazaraeans read, the whole fount of the Holy Spirit shall descend upon him . . . Further in the Gospel which we have just mentioned we find the following written:

And it came to pass when the Lord was come up out of the water, the whole fount of the Holy Spirit descended upon him and rested on him and said to him: My Son, in all the prophets was I waiting for thee that thou shouldest come and I might rest in thee. For thou art my rest; thou art my first-begotten Son that reignest for ever. (Jerome, *Commentary on Isaiah* 4 [on Isaiah 11:2])

MATT	MARK	LUKE

JOHN	THOMAS	OTHER

JOHN'S DISCIPLES GO OVER TO JESUS

John 1:35–42 (§J3.1)

[35] The next day again John was standing with two of his disciples; [36] and he looked at Jesus as he walked, and said, "Behold, the Lamb of God!" [37] The two disciples heard him say this, and they followed Jesus. [38] Jesus turned, and saw them following, and said to them, "What do you seek?" And they said to him, "Rabbi" (which means Teacher), "where are you staying?" [39] He said to them, "Come and see." They came and saw where he was staying; and they stayed with him that day, for it was about the tenth hour. [40] One of the two who heard John speak, and followed him, was Andrew, Simon Peter's brother. [41] He first found his brother Simon, and said to him, "We have found the Messiah" (which means Christ). [42] He brought him to Jesus. Jesus looked at him, and said, "So you are Simon the son of John? You shall be called Cephas" (which means Peter).

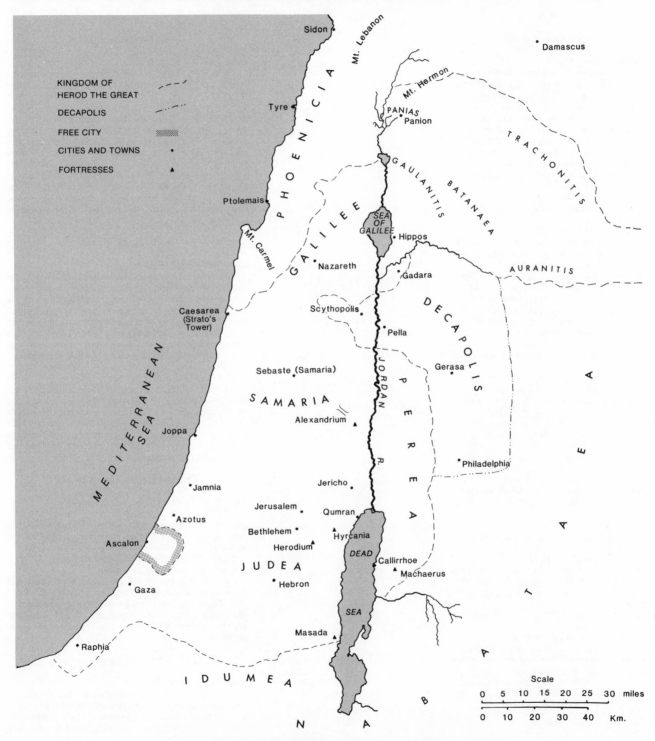

KINGDOM OF
HEROD THE GREAT

DECAPOLIS

FREE CITY

CITIES AND TOWNS

FORTRESSES

Sidon

Damascus

Mt. Lebanon

Mt. Hermon

Tyre

PHOENICIA

PANIAS
Panion

TRACHONITIS

GAULANITIS

BATANAEA

Ptolemais

Mt. Carmel

SEA
OF
GALILEE

GALILEE

Hippos

AURANITIS

Nazareth

Gadara

DECAPOLIS

Scythopolis

Caesarea
(Strato's
Tower)

Pella

JORDAN R.

Sebaste (Samaria)

Gerasa

MEDITERRANEAN SEA

SAMARIA

PEREA

Joppa

Alexandrium

Philadelphia

Jamnia

Jericho

Jerusalem

Qumran

Azotus

Bethlehem

Hyrcania

Ascalon

Herodium

JUDEA

DEAD

Callirrhoe

Machaerus

Gaza

Hebron

SEA

Masada

Raphia

IDUMEA

N   A

B

A

Scale

0   5 10 15 20 25 30 miles

0   10   20   30   40 Km.

Source: George W. E. Nickelsburg, *Jewish Literature Between the Bible and the Mishnah* (Philadelphia: Fortress Press, 1981), end papers.

MATT	MARK	LUKE

MATT

JOHN QUERIES JESUS

Matt 11:2–6 (§M30.1)

[2] Now when John heard in prison about the deeds of the Christ, he sent word by his disciples [3] and said to him, "Are you he who is to come, or shall we look for another?" [4] And Jesus answered them, "Go and tell John what you hear and see: [5] the blind receive their sight and the lame walk, lepers are cleansed and the deaf hear, and the dead are raised up, and the poor have good news preached to them. [6] And blessed is he who takes no offense at me."

JESUS PRAISES JOHN

Matt 11:7–15 (§M30.2)

[7] As they went away, Jesus began to speak to the crowds concerning John: "What did you go out into the wilderness to behold? A reed shaken by the wind? [8] Why then did you go out? To see a man clothed in soft raiment? Behold, those who wear soft raiment are in kings' houses. [9] Why then did you go out? To see a prophet? Yes, I tell you, and more than a prophet. [10] This is he of whom it is written,

'Behold, I send my messenger before thy face,

who shall prepare thy way before thee.'

[11] Truly, I say to you, among those born of women there has risen no one greater than John the Baptist; yet he who is least in the kingdom of heaven is greater than he. [12] From the days of John the Baptist until now the kingdom of heaven has suffered violence, and men of violence take it by force. [13] For all the prophets and the law prophesied until John; [14] and if you are willing to accept it, he is Elijah who is to come. [15] He who has ears to hear, let him hear."

CHILDREN IN THE MARKETPLACE

Matt 11:16–19 (§M30.3)

[16] "But to what shall I compare this generation? It is like children sitting in the market places and calling to their playmates,

[17] 'We piped to you, and you did not dance;

we wailed, and you did not mourn.'

[18] For John came neither eating nor drinking, and they say, 'He has a demon'; [19] the Son of man came eating and drinking, and they say, 'Behold, a glutton and a drunkard, a friend of tax collectors and sinners!' Yet wisdom is justified by her deeds."

LUKE

JOHN'S QUESTION OF JESUS

Luke 7:18–23 (§L28.1)

[18] The disciples of John told him of all these things. [19] And John, calling to him two of his disciples, sent them to the Lord, saying, "Are you he who is to come, or shall we look for another?" [20] And when the men had come to him, they said, "John the Baptist has sent us to you, saying, 'Are you he who is to come, or shall we look for another?'" [21] In that hour he cured many of diseases and plagues and evil spirits, and on many that were blind he bestowed sight. [22] And he answered them, "Go and tell John what you have seen and heard: the blind receive their sight, the lame walk, lepers are cleansed, and the deaf hear, the dead are raised up, the poor have good news preached to them. [23] And blessed is he who takes no offense at me."

JESUS SPEAKS OF JOHN

Luke 7:24–30 (§L28.2)

[24] When the messengers of John had gone, he began to speak to the crowds concerning John: "What did you go out into the wilderness to behold? A reed shaken by the wind? [25] What then did you go out to see? A man clothed in soft clothing? Behold, those who are gorgeously appareled and live in luxury are in kings' courts. [26] What then did you go out to see? A prophet? Yes, I tell you, and more than a prophet. [27] This is he of whom it is written,

'Behold, I send my messenger before thy face,

who shall prepare thy way before thee.'

[28] I tell you, among those born of women none is greater than John; yet he who is least in the kingdom of God is greater than he." [29] (When they heard this all the people and the tax collectors justified God, having been baptized with the baptism of John; [30] but the Pharisees and the lawyers rejected the purpose of God for themselves, not having been baptized by him.)

CHILDREN IN THE MARKETPLACE

Luke 7:31–35 (§L28.3)

[31] "To what then shall I compare the men of this generation, and what are they like? [32] They are like children sitting in the market place and calling to one another,

'We piped to you, and you did not dance;

we wailed, and you did not weep.'

[33] For John the Baptist has come eating no bread and drinking no wine; and you say, 'He has a demon.' [34] The Son of man has come eating and drinking; and you say, 'Behold, a glutton and a drunkard, a friend of tax collectors and sinners!' [35] Yet wisdom is justified by all her children."

ON LAW

Luke 16:16–17 (§L68.1)

[16] "The law and the prophets were until John; since then the good news of the kingdom of God is preached, and every one enters it violently. [17] But it is easier for heaven and earth to pass away, than for one dot of the law to become void."

JOHN THE BAPTIST

JOHN

JOHN'S FINAL TESTIMONY

John 3:22–30 (§J6.2)

[22] After this Jesus and his disciples went into the land of Judea; there he remained with them and baptized. [23] John also was baptizing at Aenon near Salim, because there was much water there; and people came and were baptized. [24] For John had not yet been put in prison.

[25] Now a discussion arose between John's disciples and a Jew over purifying. [26] And they came to John, and said to him, "Rabbi, he who was with you beyond the Jordan, to whom you bore witness, here he is, baptizing, and all are going to him." [27] John answered, "No one can receive anything except what is given him from heaven. [28] You yourselves bear me witness, that I said, I am not the Christ, but I have been sent before him. [29] He who has the bride is the bridegroom; the friend of the bridegroom, who stands and hears him, rejoices greatly at the bridegroom's voice; therefore this joy of mine is now full. [30] He must increase, but I must decrease."

THOMAS

GThom 78

(78) Jesus said, "Why have you come out into the desert? To see a reed shaken by the wind? And to see a man clothed in fine garments like your kings and your great men? Upon them are the fine [garments], and they are unable to discern the truth."

GThom 46

(46) Jesus said, "Among those born of women, from Adam until John the Baptist, there is no one so superior to John the Baptist that his eyes should not be lowered (before him). Yet I have said, whichever one of you comes to be a child will be acquainted with the Kingdom and will become superior to John."

OTHER

MATT

HEROD BEHEADS JOHN

Matt 14:1–12 (§M43)

¹At that time Herod the tetrarch heard about the fame of Jesus; ²and he said to this servants, "This is John the Baptist, he has been raised from the dead; that is why these powers are at work in him." ³For Herod had seized John and bound him and put him in prison, for the sake of Herodias, his brother Philip's wife; ⁴because John said to him, "It is not lawful for you to have her. ⁵And though he wanted to put him to death, he feared the people, because they held him to be a prophet. ⁶But when Herod's birthday came, the daughter of Herodias danced before the company, and pleased Herod, ⁷so that he promised with an oath to give her whatever she might ask. ⁸Prompted by her mother, she said, "Give me the head of John the Baptist here on a platter." ⁹And the king was sorry, but because of his oaths and his guests he commanded it to be given; ¹⁰he sent and had John beheaded in the prison, ¹¹and his head was brought on a platter and given to the girl, and she brought it to her mother. ¹²And his disciples came and took the body and buried it; and they went and told Jesus.

MARK

HEROD THINKS JESUS IS JOHN RISEN

Mark 6:14–29 (§K27)

¹⁴King Herod heard of it; for Jesus' name had become known. Some said, "John the baptizer has been raised from the dead; that is why these powers are at work in him." ¹⁵But others said, "It is Elijah." And others said, "It is a prophet, like one of the prophets of old." ¹⁶But when Herod heard of it he said, "John, whom I beheaded, has been raised." ¹⁷For Herod had sent and seized John, and bound him in prison for the sake of Herodias, his brother Philip's wife; because he had married her. For John said to Herod, "It is not lawful for you to have your brother's wife." ¹⁹And Herodias had a grudge against him, and wanted to kill him. But she could not, ²⁰for Herod feared John, knowing that he was a righteous and holy man, and kept him safe. When he heard him, he was much perplexed; and yet he heard him gladly. ²¹But an opportunity came when Herod on his birthday gave a banquet for his courtiers and officers and the leading men of Galilee. ²²For when Herodias' daughter came in and danced, she pleased Herod and his guests; and the king said to the girl, "Ask me for whatever you wish, and I will grant it." ²³And he vowed to her, "Whatever you ask me, I will give you, even half of my kingdom." ²⁴And she went out, and said to her mother, "What shall I ask?" And she said, "The head of John the baptizer." ²⁵And she came immediately with haste to the king, and asked, saying, "I want you to give me at once the head of John the Baptist on a platter." ²⁶And the king was exceedingly sorry; but because of his oaths and his guests he did not want to break his word to her. ²⁷And immediately the king sent a soldier of the guard and gave orders to bring his head. He went and beheaded him in the prison, ²⁸and brought his head on a platter, and gave it to the girl; and the girl gave it to her mother. ²⁹When his disciples heard of it, they came and took his body, and laid it in a tomb.

LUKE

HEROD IS PERPLEXED

Luke 9:7–9 (§L37)

⁷Now Herod the tetrarch heard of all that was done, and he was perplexed, because it was said by some that John had been raised from the dead, ⁸by some that Elijah had appeared, and by others that one of the old prophets had risen. ⁹Herod said, "John I beheaded; but who is this about whom I hear such things?" And he sought to see him.

JOHN

THOMAS

OTHER

JOHN THE BAPTIST

Matt	Mark	Luke

Mark 2:18

[18] Now John's disciples and the Pharisees were fasting; and people came and said to him, "Why do John's disciples and the disciples of the Pharisees fast, but your disciples do not fast?"

Mark 8:27-28

[27] And Jesus went on with his disciples, to the villages of Caesarea Philippi; and on the way he asked his disciples, "Who do men say that I am?" [28] And they told him, "John the Baptist; and others say, Elijah; and others one of the prophets."

Mark 9:11-13

[11] And they asked him, "Why do the scribes say that first Elijah must come?" [12] And he said to them, "Elijah does come first to restore all things; and how is it written of the Son of man, that he should suffer many things and be treated with contempt? [13] But I tell you that Elijah has come, and they did to him whatever they pleased, as it is written of him."

Mark 11:29-33

[29] Jesus said to them, "I will ask you a question; answer me, and I will tell you by what authority I do these things. [30] Was the baptism of John from heaven or from men? Answer me." [31] And they argued with one another, "If we say, 'From heaven,' he will say, 'Why then did you not believe him?' [32] But shall we say, 'From men'?"— they were afraid of the people, for all held that John was a real prophet. [33] So they answered Jesus, "We do not know." And Jesus said to them, "Neither will I tell you by what authority I do these things."

John	Thomas	Other

John 4:1

[1] Now when the Lord knew that the Pharisees had heard that Jesus was making and baptizing more disciples than John . . .

John 5:33-36

[33] "You sent to John, and he has borne witness to the truth. [34] Not that the testimony which I receive is from man; but I say this that you may be saved. [35] He was a burning and shining lamp, and you were willing to rejoice for a while in his light. [36] But the testimony which I have is greater than that of John; for the works which the Father has granted me to accomplish, these very works which I am doing, bear me witness that the Father has sent me."

John 10:40-41

[40] He went away again across the Jordan to the place where John at first baptized, and there he remained. [41] And many came to him; and they said, "John did no sign, but everything that John said about this man was true."

MATT	MARK	LUKE

JOHN	THOMAS	OTHER

Acts 1:5

[5] "for John baptized with water, but before many days you shall be baptized with the Holy Spirit."

Acts 1:21–22

[21] "So one of the men who have accompanied us during all the time that the Lord Jesus went in and out among us, [22] beginning from the baptism of John until the day when he was taken up from us—one of these men must become with us a witness to his resurrection."

Acts 11:16

[16] "And I remembered the word of the Lord, how he said, 'John baptized with water, but you shall be baptized with the Holy Spirit.'"

Acts 13:24–25

[24] "Before his coming John had preached a baptism of repentance to all the people of Israel. [25] And as John was finishing his course, he said, 'What do you suppose that I am? I am not he. No, but after me one is coming, the sandals of whose feet I am not worthy to untie.'"

Acts 19:1–7

[1] While Apollos was at Corinth, Paul passed through the upper country and came to Ephesus. There he found some disciples. [2] And he said to them, "Did you receive the Holy Spirit when you believed?" And they said, "No, we have never even heard that there is a Holy Spirit." [3] And he said, "Into what then were you baptized?" They said, "Into John's baptism." [4] And Paul said, "John baptized with the baptism of repentance, telling the people to believe in the one who was to come after him, that is, Jesus." [5] On hearing this, they were baptized in the name of the Lord Jesus. [6] And when Paul had laid his hands upon them, the Holy Spirit came on them; and they spoke with tongues and prophesied. [7] There were about twelve of them in all.

Josephus, *Antiquites* 18.5.2

(2) But to some of the Jews the destruction of Herod's army seemed to be divine vengeance, and certainly a just vengeance, for his treatment of John, surnamed the Baptist. For Herod had put him to death, though he was a good man and had exhorted the Jews to lead righteous lives, to practise justice towards their fellows and piety towards God, and so doing to join in baptism. In his view this was a necessary preliminary if baptism was to be acceptable to God. They must not employ it to gain pardon for whatever sins they committed, but as a consecration of the body implying that the soul was already thoroughly cleansed by right behaviour. When others too joined the crowds about him, because they were aroused to the highest degree by his sermons, Herod became alarmed. Eloquence that had so great an effect on mankind might lead to some form of sedition, for it looked as if they would be guided by John in everything that they did. Herod decided therefore that it would be much better to strike first and be rid of him before his work led to an uprising, than to wait for an upheaval, get involved in a difficult situation and see his mistake. Though John, because of Herod's suspicions, was brought in chains to Machaerus, the stronghold that we have previously mentioned, and there put to death, yet the verdict of the Jews was that the destruction visited upon Herod's army was a vindication of John, since God saw fit to inflict such a blow on Herod.

JOHN THE BAPTIST

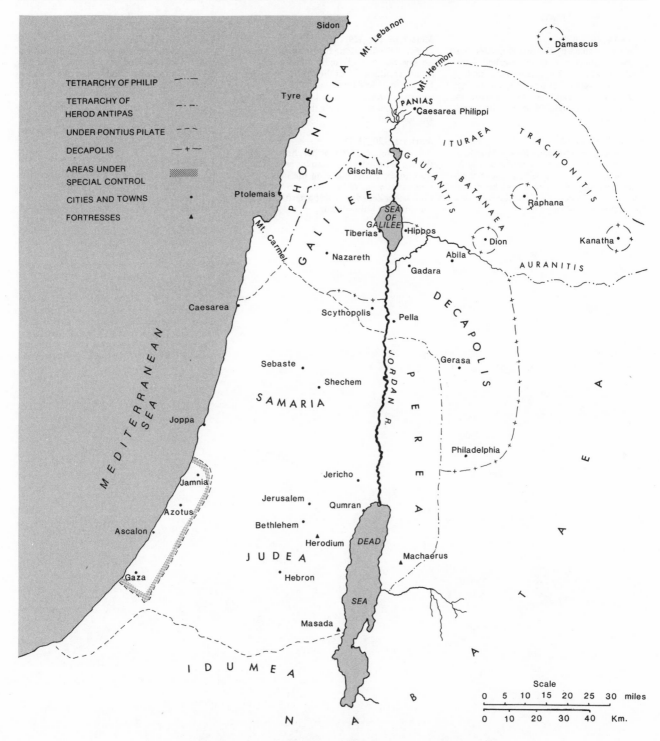

Source: George W. E. Nickelsburg, *Jewish Literature Between the Bible and the Mishnah* (Philadelphia: Fortress Press, 1981), end papers.

MATT	MARK	LUKE

Matt 4:18–20 (§M9)

[18] As he walked by the Sea of Galilee, he saw two brothers, Simon who is called Peter and Andrew his brother, casting a net into the sea; for they were fishermen. [19] And he said to them, "Follow me, and I will make you fishers of men." [20] Immediately they left their nets and followed him.

Matt 4:21–22 (§K10)

[21] And going on from there he saw two other brothers, James the son of Zebedee and John his brother, in the boat with Zebedee their father, mending their nets, and he called them. [22] Immediately they left the boat and their father, and followed him.

Mark 1:16–18 (§K6)

[16] And passing along by the Sea of Galilee, he saw Simon and Andrew the brother of Simon casting a net in the sea; for they were fishermen. [17] And Jesus said to them, "Follow me and I will make you become fishers of men." [18] And immediately they left their nets and followed him.

Mark 1:19–20 (§K7)

[19] And going on a little farther, he saw James the son of Zebedee and John his brother, who were in their boat mending the nets. [20] And immediately he called them; and they left their father Zebedee in the boat with the hired servants, and followed him.

Luke 5:1–3 (§L17.1)

[1] While the people pressed upon him to hear the word of God, he was standing by the lake of Gennesaret. [2] And he saw two boats by the lake; but the fishermen had gone out of them and were washing their nets. [3] Getting into one of the boats, which was Simon's, he asked him to put out a little from the land. And he sat down and taught the people from the boat.

Luke 5:4–11 (§L17.2)

[4] And when he had ceased speaking, he said to Simon, "Put out into the deep and let down your nets for a catch." [5] And Simon answered, "Master, we toiled all night and took nothing! But at your word I will let down the nets." [6] And when they had done this, they enclosed a great shoal of fish; and as their nets were breaking, [7] they beckoned to their partners in the other boat to come and help them. And they came and filled both the boats, so that they began to sink. [8] But when Simon Peter saw it, he fell down at Jesus' knees, saying, "Depart from me, for I am a sinful man, O Lord." [9] For he was astonished, and all that were with him, at the catch of fish which they had taken; [10] and so also were James and John, sons of Zebedee, who were partners with Simon. And Jesus said to Simon, "Do not be afraid; henceforth you will be catching men." [11] And when they had brought their boats to land, they left everything and followed him.

JOHN THOMAS OTHER

John 1:35–42 (§J3.1)

[35] The next day again John was standing with two of his disciples; [36] and he looked at Jesus as he walked, and said, "Behold, the Lamb of God!" [37] The two disciples heard him say this, and they followed Jesus. [38] Jesus turned, and saw them following, and said to them, "What do you seek?" And they said to him, "Rabbi" (which means Teacher), "where are you staying?" [39] He said to them, "Come and see." They came and saw where he was staying; and they stayed with him that day, for it was about the tenth hour. [40] One of the two who heard John speak, and followed him, was Andrew, Simon Peter's brother. [41] He first found his brother Simon, and said to him, "We have found the Messiah" (which means Christ). [42] He brought him to Jesus. Jesus looked at him, and said, "So you are Simon the son of John? You shall be called Cephas" (which means Peter).

John 1:43–51 (§J3.2)

[43] The next day Jesus decided to go to Galilee. And he found Philip and said to him, "Follow me." [44] Now Philip was from Bethsaida, the city of Andrew and Peter. [45] Philip found Nathanael, and said to him, "We have found him of whom Moses in the law and also the prophets wrote, Jesus of Nazareth, the son of Joseph." [46] Nathanael said to him, "Can anything good come out of Nazareth?" Philip said to him, "Come and see." [47] Jesus saw Nathanael coming to him, and said of him, "Behold, an Israelite indeed, in whom is no guile!" [48] Nathanael said to him, "How do you know me?" Jesus answered him, "Before Philip called you, when you were under the fig tree, I saw you." [49] Nathanael answered him, "Rabbi, you are the Son of God! You are the King of Israel!" [50] Jesus answered him, "Because I said to you, I saw you under the fig tree, do you believe? You shall see greater things than these." [51] And he said to him, "Truly, truly, I say to you, you will see heaven opened, and the angels of God ascending and descending upon the Son of man."

John 6:66–71

[66] After this many of his disciples drew back and no longer went about with him. [67] Jesus said to the twelve, "Do you also wish to go away?" [68] Simon Peter answered him, "Lord, to whom shall we go? You have the words of eternal life; [69] and we have believed, and have come to know, that you are the Holy One of God." [70] Jesus answered them, "Did I not choose you, the twelve, and one of you is a devil?" [71] He spoke of Judas the son of Simon Iscariot, for he, one of the twelve, was to betray him.

Acts 1:12–26

[12] Then they returned to Jerusalem from the mount called Olivet, which is near Jerusalem, a sabbath day's journey away; [13] and when they had entered, they went up to the upper room, where they were staying, Peter and John and James and Andrew, Philip and Thomas, Bartholomew and Matthew, James the son of Alphaeus and Simon the Zealot and Judas the son of James. [14] All these with one accord devoted themselves to prayer, together with the women and Mary the mother of Jesus, and with his brothers.

[15] In those days Peter stood up among the brethren (the company of persons was in all about a hundred and twenty), and said, [16] "Brethren, the scripture had to be fulfilled, which the Holy Spirit spoke beforehand by the mouth of David, concerning Judas who was guide to those who arrested Jesus. [17] For he was numbered among us, and was allotted his share in this ministry. [18] (Now this man bought a field with the reward of his wickedness; and falling headlong he burst open in the middle and all his bowels gushed out. [19] And it became known to all the inhabitants of Jerusalem, so that the field was called in their language Akeldama, that is, Field of Blood.) [20] For it is written in the book of Psalms,

'Let his habitation become desolate,
and let there be no one to live in it';
and
'His office let another take.'

[21] So one of the men who have accompanied us during all the time that the Lord Jesus went in and out among us, [22] beginning from the baptism of John until the day when he was taken up from us—one of these men must become with us a witness to his resurrection." [23] And they put forward two, Joseph called Barsabbas, who was surnamed Justus, and Matthias. [24] And they prayed and said, "Lord, who knowest the hearts of all men, show which one of these two thou hast chosen [25] to take the place in this ministry and apostleship from which Judas turned aside, to go to his own place." [26] And they cast lots for them, and the lot fell on Matthias; and he was enrolled with the eleven apostles.

MATT

Matt 9:35–38 (§M26)

[35] And Jesus went about all the cities and villages, teaching in their synagogues and preaching the gospel of the kingdom, and healing every disease and every infirmity. [36] When he saw the crowds, he had compassion for them, because they were harassed and helpless, like sheep without a shepherd. [37] Then he said to his disciples, "The harvest is plentiful, but the laborers are few; [38] pray therefore the Lord of the harvest to send out laborers into his harvest."

Matt 10:1–4 (§M27)

[1] And he called to him his twelve disciples and gave them authority over unclean spirits, to cast them out, and to heal every disease and every infirmity. [2] The names of the twelve apostles are these: first, Simon, who is called Peter, and Andrew his brother; James the son of Zebedee, and John his brother; [3] Philip and Bartholomew; Thomas and Matthew the tax collector; James the son of Alphaeus, and Thaddaeus; [4] Simon the Cananaean, and Judas Iscariot, who betrayed him.

Matt 10:5–15 (§M28.1)

[5] These twelve Jesus sent out, charging them, "Go nowhere among the Gentiles, and enter no town of the Samaritans, [6] but go rather to the lost sheep of the house of Israel. [7] And preach as you go, saying, 'The kingdom of heaven is at hand.' [8] Heal the sick, raise the dead, cleanse lepers, cast out demons. You received without pay, give without pay. [9] Take no gold, nor silver, nor copper in your belts, [10] no bag for your journey, nor two tunics, nor sandals, nor a staff; for the laborer deserves his food. [11] And whatever town or village you enter, find out who is worthy in it, and stay with him until you depart. [12] As you enter the house, salute it. [13] And if the house is worthy, let your peace come upon it; but if it is not worthy, let your peace return to you. [14] And if any one will not receive you or listen to your words, shake off the dust from your feet as you leave that house or town. [15] Truly, I say to you, it shall be more tolerable on the day of judgment for the land of Sodom and Gomorrah than for that town."

Matt 10:16–23 (§M28.2)

[16] "Behold, I send you out as sheep in the midst of wolves; so be wise as serpents and innocent as doves. [17] Beware of men; for they will deliver you up to councils, and flog you in their synagogues, [18] and you will be dragged before governors and kings for my sake, to bear testimony before them and the Gentiles. [19] When they deliver you up, do not be anxious how you are to speak or what you are to say; for what you are to say will be given to you in that hour; [20] for it is not you who speak, but the Spirit of your Father speaking through you. [21] Brother will

MARK

Mark 3:13–19 (§K19)

[13] And he went up on the mountain, and called to him those whom he desired; and they came to him. [14] And he appointed twelve, to be with him, and to be sent out to preach [15] and have authority to cast out demons: [16] Simon whom he surnamed Peter; [17] James the son of Zebedee and John the brother of James, whom he surnamed Boanerges, that is, sons of thunder; [18] Andrew, and Philip, and Bartholomew, and Matthew, and Thomas, and James the son of Alphaeus, and Thaddaeus, and Simon the Cananaean, [19] and Judas Iscariot, who betrayed him.

Then he went home; . . .

Mark 6:7–13 (§K26)

[7] And he called to him the twelve, and began to send them out two by two, and gave them authority over the unclean spirits. [8] He charged them to take nothing for their journey except a staff; no bread, no bag, no money in their belts; [9] but to wear sandals and not put on two tunics. [10] And he said to them, "Where you enter a house, stay there until you leave the place. [11] And if any place will not receive you and they refuse to hear you, when you leave, shake off the dust that is on your feet for a testimony against them." [12] So they went out and preached that men should repent. [13] And they cast out many demons, and anointed with oil many that were sick and healed them.

Mark 6:30–34 (§K28)

[30] The apostles returned to Jesus, and told him all that they had done and taught. [31] And he said to them, "Come away by yourselves to a lonely place, and rest a while." For many were coming and going, and they had no leisure even to eat. [32] And they went away in the boat to a lonely place by themselves. [33] Now many saw them going, and knew them, and they ran there on foot from all the towns, and got there ahead of them. [34] As he went ashore he saw a great throng, and he had compassion on them, because they were like sheep without a shepherd; and he began to teach them many things.

Mark 4:10–12 (§K21.3)

[10] And when he was alone, those who were about him with the twelve asked him concerning the parables. [11] And he said to them, "To you has been given the secret of the kingdom of God, but for those outside everything is in parables; [12] so that they may indeed see but not perceive, and may indeed hear but not understand; lest they should turn again, and be forgiven."

LUKE

Luke 6:12–16 (§L23)

[12] In these days he went out to the mountain to pray; and all night he continued in prayer to God. [13] And when it was day, he called his disciples, and chose from them twelve, whom he named apostles; [14] Simon, whom he named Peter, and Andrew his brother, and James and John, and Philip, and Bartholomew, [15] and Matthew, and Thomas, and James the son of Alphaeus, and Simon who was called the Zealot, [16] and Judas the son of James, and Judas Iscariot, who became a traitor.

Luke 9:1–6 (§L36)

[1] And he called the twelve together and gave them power and authority over all demons and to cure diseases, [2] and he sent them out to preach the kingdom of God and to heal. [3] And he said to them, "Take nothing for your journey, no staff, nor bag, nor bread, nor money; and do not have two tunics. [4] And whatever house you enter, stay there, and from there depart. [5] And wherever they do not receive you, when you leave that town shake off the dust from your feet as a testimony against them." [6] And they departed and went through the villages, preaching the gospel and healing everywhere.

Luke 9:10–11 (§L38)

[10] On their return the apostles told him what they had done. And he took them and withdrew apart to a city called Bethsaida. [11] When the crowds learned it, they followed him; and he welcomed them and spoke to them of the kingdom of God, and cured those who had need of healing.

Luke 10:1–16 (§L46)

[1] After this the Lord appointed seventy others, and sent them on ahead of him, two by two, into every town and place where he himself was about to come. [2] And he said to them, "The harvest is plentiful, but the laborers are few; pray therefore the Lord of the harvest to send out laborers into his harvest. [3] Go your way; behold, I send you out as lambs in the midst of wolves. [4] Carry no purse, no bag, no sandals; and salute no one on the road. [5] Whatever house you enter, first say, 'Peace be to this house!' [6] And if a son of peace is there, your peace shall rest upon him; but if not, it shall return to you. [7] And remain in the same house, eating and drinking what they provide, for the laborer deserves his wages; do not go from house to house. [8] Whenever you enter a town and they receive you, eat what is set before you; [9] heal the sick in it and say to them, 'The kingdom of God has come near to you.' [10] But whenever you enter a town and they do not receive you, go into its streets and say, [11] 'Even the dust of your town that clings to our feet, we wipe off against you; nevertheless know this, that the kingdom of God has come near.' [12] I tell you, it

THE INNER CIRCLE OF DISCIPLES: THE TWELVE AND THE SEVENTY

MATT

deliver up brother to death, and the father his child, and children will rise against parents and have them put to death; [22] and you will be hated by all for my name's sake. But he who endures to the end will be saved. [23] When they persecute you in one town, flee to the next; for truly, I say to you, you will not have gone through all the towns of Israel, before the Son of man comes."

Matt 10:24–25 (§M28.3)

[24] "A disciple is not above his teacher, nor a servant above his master; [25] it is enough for the disciple to be like his teacher, and the servant like his master. If they have called the master of the house Beelzebul, how much more will they malign those of his household."

Matt 10:26–33 (§M28.4)

[26] "So have no fear of them; for nothing is covered that will not be revealed, or hidden that will not be known. [27] What I tell you in the dark, utter in the light; and what you hear whispered, proclaim upon the housetops. [28] And do not fear those who kill the body but cannot kill the soul; rather fear him who can destroy both soul and body in hell. [29] Are not two sparrows sold for a penny? And not one of them will fall to the ground without your Father's will. [30] But even the hairs of your head are all numbered. [31] Fear not, therefore; you are of more value than many sparrows. [32] So every one who acknowledges me before men, I also will acknowledge before my Father who is in heaven; [33] but whoever denies me before men, I also will deny before my Father who is in heaven."

Matt 10:34–39 (§M28.5)

[34] "Do not think that I have come to bring peace on earth; I have not come to bring peace, but a sword. [35] For I have come to set a man against his father, and a daughter against her mother, and a daughter-in-law against her mother-in-law; [36] and a man's foes will be those of his own household. [37] He who loves father or mother more than me is not worthy of me; and he who loves son or daughter more than me is not worthy of me; [38] and he who does not take his cross and follow me is not worthy of me. [39] He who finds his life will lose it, and he who loses his life for my sake will find it."

Matt 10:40–42 (§M28.6)

[40] "He who receives you receives me, and he who receives me receives him who sent me. [41] He who receives a prophet because he is a prophet shall receive a prophet's reward, and he who receives a righteous man because he is a righteous man shall receive a righteous man's reward. [42] And whoever gives to one of these little ones even a cup of cold water because he is a disciple, truly, I say to you, he shall not lose his reward."

MARK

Mark 9:33–37 (§K47)

[33] And they came to Capernaum; and when he was in the house he asked them, "What were you discussing on the way?" [34] But they were silent; for on the way they had discussed with one another who was the greatest. [35] And he sat down and called the twelve; and he said to them, "If any one would be first, he must be last of all and servant of all." [36] And he took a child, and put him in the midst of them; and taking him in his arms, he said to them, [37] "Whoever receives one such child in my name receives me; and whoever receives me, receives not me but him who sent me."

LUKE

shall be more tolerable on that day for Sodom than for that town.

[13] "Woe to you, Chorazin! woe to you, Bethsaida! for if the mighty works done in you had been done in Tyre and Sidon, they would have repented long ago, sitting in sackcloth and ashes. [14] But it shall be more tolerable in the judgment for Tyre and Sidon than for you. [15] And you, Capernaum, will you be exalted to heaven? You shall be brought down to Hades. [16] "He who hears you hears me, and he who rejects you rejects me, and he who rejects me rejects him who sent me."

Luke 10:17–20 (§L47.1)

[17] The seventy returned with joy, saying, "Lord, even the demons are subject to us in your name!" [18] And he said to them, "I saw Satan fall like lightning from heaven. [19] Behold, I have given you authority to tread upon serpents and scorpions, and over all the power of the enemy; and nothing shall hurt you. [20] Nevertheless do not rejoice in this, that the spirits are subject to you; but rejoice that your names are written in heaven."

Luke 10:21–22 (§L47.2)

[21] In that same hour he rejoiced in the Holy Spirit and said, "I thank thee, Father, Lord of heaven and earth, that thou hast hidden these things from the wise and understanding and revealed them to babes; yea, Father, for such was thy gracious will. [22] All things have been delivered to me by my Father; and no one knows who the Son is except the Father, or who the Father is except the Son and any one to whom the Son chooses to reveal him."

Luke 10:23–24 (§L47.3)

[23] Then turning to the disciples he said privately, "Blessed are the eyes which see what you see! [24] For I tell you that many prophets and kings desired to see what you see, and did not see it, and to hear what you hear, and did not hear it."

Luke 8:1

[1] Soon afterward he went on through cities and villages, preaching and bringing the good news of the kingdom of God. And the twelve were with him, . . .

Luke 9:12

[12] Now the day began to wear away; and the twelve came and said to him, "Send the crowd away, to go into the villages and country round about, to lodge and get provisions; for we are here in a lonely place."

MATT

Matt 19:27–30
[27] Then Peter said in reply, "Lo, we have left everything and followed you. What then shall we have?" [28] Jesus said to them, "Truly, I say to you, in the new world, when the Son of man shall sit on his glorious throne, you who have followed me will also sit on twelve thrones, judging the twelve tribes of Israel. [29] And every one who has left houses or brothers or sisters or father or mother or children or lands, for my name's sake, will receive a hundredfold, and inherit eternal life. [30] But many that are first will be last, and the last first."

Matt 20:17–19 (§M68)
[17] And as Jesus was going up to Jerusalem, he took the twelve disciples aside, and on the way he said to them, [18] "Behold, we are going up to Jerusalem; and the Son of man will be delivered to the chief priests and scribes, and they will condemn him to death, [19] and deliver him to the Gentiles to be mocked and scourged and crucified, and he will be raised on the third day."

Matt 26:14, 20–21, 47
[14] Then one of the twelve, who was called Judas Iscariot, went to the chief priests . . .

[20] When it was evening, he sat at table with the twelve disciples; [21] and as they were eating, he said, "Truly, I say to you, one of you will betray me."

[47] While he was still speaking, Judas came, one of the twelve, and with him a great crowd with swords and clubs, from the chief priests and the elders of the people.

Matt 28:16–20 (§M88.4)
[16] Now the eleven disciples went to Galilee, to the mountain to which Jesus had directed them. [17] And when they saw him they worshiped him; but some doubted. [18] And Jesus came and said to them, "All authority in heaven and on earth has been given to me. [19] Go therefore and make disciples of all nations, baptizing them in the name of the Father and of the Son and of the Holy Spirit, [20] teaching them to observe all that I have commanded you; and lo, I am with you always, to the close of the age."

MARK

Mark 10:32–34 (§K54)
[32] And they were on the road, going up to Jerusalem, and Jesus was walking ahead of them; and they were amazed, and those who followed were afraid. And taking the twelve again, he began to tell them what was to happen to him, [33] saying, "Behold, we are going up to Jerusalem; and the Son of man will be delivered to the chief priests and the scribes, and they will condemn him to death, and deliver him to the Gentiles; [34] and they will mock him, and spit upon him, and scourge him, and kill him; and after three days he will rise."

Mark 11:11
[11] And he entered Jerusalem, and went into the temple; and when he had looked round at everything, as it was already late, he went out to Bethany with the twelve.

Mark 14:10, 17, 20, 43
[10] Then Judas Iscariot, who was one of the twelve, went to the chief priests in order to betray him to them.

[17] And when it was evening he came with the twelve.

[20] He said to them, "It is one of the twelve, one who is dipping bread into the dish with me."

[43] And immediately, while he was still speaking, Judas came, one of the twelve, and with him a crowd with swords and clubs, from the chief priests and the scribes and the elders.

Mark 16:14–18 (§K71)
[14] Afterward he appeared to the eleven themselves as they sat at table; and he upbraided them for their unbelief and hardness of heart, because they had not believed those who saw him after he had risen. [15] And he said to them, "Go into all the world and preach the gospel to the whole creation. [16] He who believes and is baptized will be saved; but he who does not believe will be condemned. [17] And these signs will accompany those who believe: in my name they will cast out demons; they will speak in new tongues; [18] they will pick up serpents, and if they drink any deadly thing, it will not hurt them; they will lay their hands on the sick, and they will recover."

Mark 16:19–20 (§K72)
[19] So then the Lord Jesus, after he had spoken to them, was taken up into heaven, and sat down at the right hand of God. [20] And they went forth and preached everywhere, while the Lord worked with them and confirmed the message by the signs that attended it. Amen.

LUKE

Luke 18:31–34 (§L78)
[31] And taking the twelve, he said to them, "Behold, we are going up to Jerusalem, and everything that is written of the Son of man by the prophets will be accomplished. [32] For he will be delivered to the Gentiles, and will be mocked and shamefully treated and spit upon; [33] they will scourge him and kill him, and on the third day he will rise." [34] But they understood none of these things; this saying was hid from them, and they did not grasp what was said.

Luke 22:28–30
[28] "You are those who have continued with me in my trials; [29] and I assign to you, as my Father assigned to me, a kingdom, [30] that you may eat and drink at my table in my kingdom, and sit on thrones judging the twelve tribes of Israel."

Luke 22:3, 14, 47
[3] Then Satan entered into Judas called Iscariot, who was of the number of the twelve;
. . .

[14] And when the hour came, he sat at table, and the apostles with him.

[47] While he was still speaking, there came a crowd, and the man called Judas, one of the twelve, was leading them. He drew near to Jesus to kiss him; . . .

Luke 24:9, 33b
[9] and returning from the tomb they told all this to the eleven and to all the rest.

. . . and they found the eleven gathered together and those who were with them, . . .

THE INNER CIRCLE OF DISCIPLES: THE TWELVE AND THE SEVENTY

JOHN	THOMAS	OTHER

John 20:24

[24] Now Thomas, one of the twelve, called the Twin, was not with them when Jesus came.

AcPil 14:1

[1] Now Phinees a priest and Adas a teacher and Angaeus a Levite came from Galilee to Jerusalem, and told the rulers of the synagogue and the priests and the Levites: "We saw Jesus and his disciples sitting upon the mountain which is called Mamilch. And he said to his disciples: Go into all the world and preach the gospel to the whole creation. He who believes and is baptized will be saved; but he who does not believe will be condemned. And these signs will accompany those who believe: in my name will they cast out demons; they will speak in new tongues; they will pick up serpents; and if they drink any deadly thing, it will not hurt them; they will lay their hands on the sick and they will recover. And while Jesus was still speaking to his disciples, we saw him taken up into heaven."

1 Cor 15:5

[5] and that he appeared to Cephas, then to the twelve.

Acts 2:14

[14] But Peter, standing with the eleven, lifted up his voice and addressed them, "Men of Judea and all who dwell in Jerusalem, let this be known to you, and give ear to my words."

THE INNER CIRCLE OF DISCIPLES: THE TWELVE AND THE SEVENTY

MATT	MARK	LUKE
Matt 4:12–17 (§M8)	**Mark 1:14–15 (§K5)**	**Luke 4:14–15 (§L11)**
[12] Now when he heard that John had been arrested, he withdrew into Galilee; [13] and leaving Nazareth he went and dwelt in Capernaum by the sea, in the territory of Zebulun and Naphtali, [14] that what was spoken by the prophet Isaiah might be fulfilled: [15] "The land of Zebulun and the land of Naphtali, toward the sea, across the Jordan, Galilee of the Gentiles— [16] the people who sat in darkness have seen a great light, and for those who sat in the region and shadow of death light has dawned." [17] From that time Jesus began to preach, saying, "Repent, for the kingdom of heaven is at hand."	[14] Now after John was arrested Jesus came into Galilee, preaching the gospel of God, [15] and saying, "The time is fulfilled, and the kingdom of God is at hand; repent, and believe in the gospel."	[14] And Jesus returned in the power of the Spirit into Galilee, and a report concerning him went out through all the surrounding country. [15] And he taught in their synagogues, being glorified by all.
Cf. §M16	**Mark 1:32–34 (§K10)**	**Luke 4:40–41 (§L15)**
	[32] That evening, at sundown, they brought to him all who were sick or possessed with demons. [33] And the whole city was gathered together about the door. [34] And he healed many who were sick with various diseases, and cast out many demons; and he would not permit the demons to speak, because they knew him.	[40] Now when the sun was setting, all those who had any that were sick with various diseases brought them to him; and he laid his hands on every one of them and healed them. [41] And demons also came out of many, crying, "You are the Son of God!" But he rebuked them, and would not allow them to speak, because they knew that he was the Christ.
Matt 4:23–25 (§M11)	**Mark 1:35–39 (§K11)**	**Luke 4:42–44 (§L16)**
[23] And he went about all Galilee teaching in their synagogues and preaching the gospel of the kingdom and healing every disease and every infirmity among the people. [24] So his fame spread throughout all Syria, and they brought him all the sick, those afflicted with various diseases and pains, demoniacs, epileptics, and paralytics, and he healed them. [25] And great crowds followed him from Galilee and the Decapolis and Jerusalem and Judea and from beyond the Jordan.	[35] And in the moring, a great while before day, he rose and went out to a lonely place, and there he prayed. [36] And Simon and those who were with him pursued him, [37] and they found him and said to him, "Every one is searching for you." [38] And he said to them, "Let us go on to the next towns, that I may preach there also; for that is why I came out." [39] And he went throughout all Galilee, preaching in their synagogues and casting out demons. they brought to him all who were sick or possessed with demons.	[42] And when it was day he departed and went into a lonely place. And the people sought him and came to him, and would have kept him from leaving them; [43] but he said to them, "I must preach the good news of the kingdom of God to the other cities also; for I was sent for this purpose." [44] And he was preaching in the synagogues of Judea.
Matt 8:16–17 (§M16)	Cf. §K10	Cf. §L16
[16] That evening they brought to him many who were possessed with demons; and he cast out the spirits with a word, and healed all who were sick. [17] This was to fulfil what was spoken by the prophet Isaiah, "He took our infirmities and bore our diseases."		
Matt 9:35	Cf. Mark 6:6b	
[35] And Jesus went about all the cities and villages, teaching in their synagogues and preaching the gospel of the kingdom, and healing every disease and every infirmity.		

MATT	MARK	LUKE

Matt 11:1 (§§M28.7, M29)

¹ And when Jesus had finished instructing his twelve disciples, he went on from there to teach and preach in their cities.

Matt 12:15–21 (§M35)

¹⁵ Jesus, aware of this, withdrew from there. And many followed him, and he healed them all, ¹⁶ and ordered them not to make him known. ¹⁷ This was to fulfil what was spoken by the prophet Isaiah:

¹⁸ "Behold, my servant whom I have chosen,
 my beloved with whom my soul is well pleased,
I will put my Spirit upon him,
 and he shall proclaim justice to the Gentiles.
¹⁹ He will not wrangle or cry aloud,
 nor will any one hear his voice in the streets;
²⁰ he will not break a bruised reed
 or quench a smoldering wick,
till he brings justice to victory;
²¹ and in his name will the Gentiles hope."

Mark 3:7–12 (§K18)

⁷ Jesus withdrew with his disciples to the sea, and a great multitude from Galilee followed; also from Judea ⁸ and from Jerusalem and Idumea and from beyond the Jordan and from about Tyre and Sidon a great multitude, hearing all that he did, came to him. ⁹ And he told his disciples to have a boat ready for him because of the crowd, lest they should crush him; ¹⁰ for he had healed many, so that all who had diseases pressed upon him to touch him. ¹¹ And whenever the unclean spirits beheld him, they fell down before him and cried out, "You are the Son of God." ¹² And he strictly ordered them not to make him known.

Luke 6:17–19 (§L24)

¹⁷ And he came down with them and stood on a level place, with a great crowd of his disciples and a great multitude of people from all Judea and Jerusalem and the seacoast of Tyre and Sidon, who came to hear him and to be healed of their diseases; ¹⁸ and those who were troubled with unclean spirits were cured. ¹⁹ And all the crowd sought to touch him, for power came forth from him and healed them all.

Luke 8:1–3 (§L30)

¹ Soon afterward he went on through cities and villages, preaching and bringing the good news of the kingdom of God. And the twelve were with him, ² and also some women who had been healed of evil spirits and infirmities: Mary, called Magdalene, from whom seven demons had gone out, ³ and Joanna, the wife of Chuza, Herod's steward, and Susanna, and many others, who provided for them out of their means.

Matt 13:53–58 (§M42)

⁵³ And when Jesus had finished these parables, he went away from there, ⁵⁴ and coming to his own country he taught them in their synagogue, so that they were astonished, and said, "Where did this man get this wisdom and these mighty works? ⁵⁵ Is not this the carpenter's son? Is not his mother called Mary? And are not his brothers James and Joseph and Simon and Judas? ⁵⁶ And are not all his sisters with us? Where then did this man get all this?" ⁵⁷ And they took offense at him. But Jesus said to them, "A prophet is not without honor except in his own country and in his own house." ⁵⁸ And he did not do many mighty works there, because of their unbelief.

Mark 6:1–6 (§K25)

¹ He went away from there and came to his own country; and his disciples followed him. ² And on the sabbath he began to teach in the synagogue; and many who heard him were astonished, saying, "Where did this man get all this? What is the wisdom given to him? What mighty works are wrought by his hands! ³ Is not this the carpenter, the son of Mary and brother of James and Joses and Judas and Simon, and are not his sisters here with us?" And they took offense at him. ⁴ And Jesus said to them, "A prophet is not without honor, except in his own country, and among his own kin, and in his own house." ⁵ And he could do no mighty work there, except that he laid his hands upon a few sick people and healed them. ⁶ And he marveled because of their unbelief.

And he went about among the villages teaching.

MATT	MARK	LUKE
Matt 14:13–14 (§M44) ¹³Now when Jesus heard this, he withdrew from there in a boat to a lonely place apart. But when the crowds heard it, they followed him on foot from the towns. ¹⁴As he went ashore he saw a great throng; and he had compassion on them, and healed their sick.	**Mark 6:30–34 (§K28)** ³⁰The apostles returned to Jesus, and told him all that they had done and taught. ³¹And he said to them, "Come away by yourselves to a lonely place, and rest a while." For many were coming and going, and they had no leisure even to eat. ³²And they went away in the boat to a lonely place by themselves. ³³Now many saw them going, and knew them, and they ran there on foot from all the towns, and got there ahead of them. ³⁴As he went ashore he saw a great throng, and he had compassion on them, because they were like sheep without a shepherd; and he began to teach them many things.	**Luke 9:10–11 (§L38)** ¹⁰On their return the apostles told him what they had done. And he took them and withdrew apart to a city called Bethsaida. ¹¹When the crowds learned it, they followed him; and he welcomed them and spoke to them of the kingdom of God, and cured those who had need of healing.
Matt 14:34–36 (§M48) ³⁴And when they had crossed over, they came to land at Gennesaret. ³⁵And when the men of that place recognized him, they sent round to all that region and brought to him all that were sick, ³⁶and besought him that they might only touch the fringe of his garment; and as many as touched it were made well.	**Mark 6:53–56 (§K32)** ⁵³And when they had crossed over, they came to land at Gennesaret, and moored to the shore. ⁵⁴And when they got out of the boat, immediately the people recognized him, ⁵⁵and ran about the whole neighborhood and began to bring sick people on their pallets to any place where they heard he was. ⁵⁶And wherever he came, in villages, cities, or country, they laid the sick in the market places, and besought him that they might touch even the fringe of his garment; and as many as touched it were made well.	
Matt 15:29–31 (§M51) ²⁹And Jesus went on from there and passed along the Sea of Galilee. And he went up on the mountain, and sat down there. ³⁰And great crowds came to him, bringing with them the lame, the maimed, the blind, the dumb, and many others, and they put them at his feet, and he healed them, ³¹so that the throng wondered, when they saw the dumb speaking, the maimed whole, the lame walking, and the blind seeing; and they glorified the God of Israel.		
		Luke 13:22 ²²He went on his way through towns and villages, teaching, and journeying toward Jerusalem.
Matt 19:1–2 (§M64) ¹Now when Jesus had finished these sayings, he went away from Galilee and entered the region of Judea beyond the Jordan; ²and large crowds followed him, and he healed them there.	**Mark 10:1 (§K50)** ¹And he left there and went to the region of Judea and beyond the Jordan, and crowds gathered to him again; and again, as his custom was, he taught them.	

11:1–6, L49
11:16, M82.1, K63.1
11:17–37, L49
11:45–53, M80.1–2, K61.1,
  L92.1
11:54, M80.1–2, K61.1, L92.1
11:55–57, M80.1–2, K61.1,
  L92.1
12:1–8, M80.3, K61.2, L29
12:2, L49
12:12–19, M71, K57, L82.1–3
12:25, M28.5, M57, K43, L40.2
12:27, M82.2, K63.2
12:31, L47.1
12:40, M40.3
12:44–45, M28.6, K47, L43.2,
  L46
12:48, L46
13:1–20, L93.3
13:3–5, L56.1
13:16, M28.3, L25.3
13:20, M28.6, K47, L43.2, L46
13:21–30, M81, K62, L93.2
13:36–38, M82.1, K63.1, L93.4
14:13–14, M73, K59.1
14:26, M28.2, K60.2, L53, L91.1
14:31, M82.2, K63.2
15:7, M73, K59.1
15:14, M39, K20.1–3, L32
15:18–21, M78.2, K60.2, L56.2,
  L91.1
15:18, M28.2
15:20, M28.3, L25.3
15:23, L46
15:27, L1
16:2, M28.2, K60.2, L91.1
16:23, M73, K59.1
16:32, M82.1, K63.1
17:25–26, L47.2
18:1–12, M82.3, K63.3, L94.2
18:1, M82.1, M82.2, K63.1,
  K63.2, L94.1
18:11, M82.2, K63.2, L94.1
18:13–14, M83.1–2, K64.1–2,
  L95, L96
18:15–18, M83.3, K64.3, L95
18:19–24, M83.1–2, K64.1–2,
  L96
18:20, M82.3, K63.3, L94.2
18:25–27, M83.3, K64.3, L95
18:28–19:16, K65, L97–99
18:28, M84.1
18:29–19:16, M84.3–4
19:1–3, M85.1, K66.1
19:17–24, M85.3, K66.3, L100.2
19:25–37, M85.4, K66.4, L100.3

19:28–30, L100.2
19:38–42, M86, K67, L101
20:1–18, M88.1–3, K68, L102
20:11–18, K69
20:19–23, K71–72, L103.3
20:22–23, M55
20:23, M63.1
20:24–29, L103.3
21:1–14, L17

Acts
1:1–2, L1
1:4–8, L103.3
1:5, M5, K2, L7
1:9–12, L104
1:12–14, M27, K19, L23
1:15–20, M84.2
1:16–20, L92.2
2:30, L2.2
2:34–35, L88, L96
2:38, L7
3:13–15, L99.1–2
3:21, L3
4:5–8, L53
4:11, L85
4:34–35, L77
5:12–16, L24
7:51–52, L52.2, L61
7:52, L25.1
7:54, 58a, L12
7:55–56, L88, L96
7:59, L100.3
7:60, L100.2
10:1–2, L26
10:36–38, L12, L16
10:41, L93.3
11:16, M5, K2, L7
13:10, L7
13:23, L2.2, L4.2
13:24–25, M5, K2, L7
13:47, L5, L7
13:51, L46
13:57, L36
18:6, L36, L46
19:1–7, M5, K2, L7
20:7–12, L27
21:13, L93.4
21:14, L94.1
21:26, L99.1–2
26:20, L7
26:23, L5
27:34, L53, L91.1
27:35, M45, M52, K29, K37, L39
28:25–28, M40.3
28:26–27, L31.2
28:28, L5, L7

Rom
13:7, M76.1, L86
13:8–10, M76.3, L48.1
16:19, M28.2

1 Cor
7:10–11, M65.1, K51
9:14, M28.1
11:23–25, M81, K62, L93.2
15:12, M76.2, L87
15:20–28, M76.4, K59.7, L88
15:32, L54

Gal
5:13–15, M76.3
5:14, L48.1

Phil
4:6, L55

1 Thess
4:15–16, M78.4, K60.4
5:2, M78.5

1 Tim
5:18, M28.1

Jas
2:8, L48.1

1 Pet
4:15–16, M12.2, L25.1

Rev
1:7, M78.4, K60.4
13:9, M30.2
16:15, M78.5